HALSBURY'S
Laws of England

FIFTH EDITION
2014

Volume 41A

This is volume 41A of the Fifth Edition of Halsbury's Laws of England, containing the fourth part of the title EMPLOYMENT.

The title EMPLOYMENT replaces the EMPLOYMENT title contained in volumes 39 (2009), 40 (2009), 41 (2009).

Volumes 39 (2009), 40 (2009), 41 (2009) may now be archived.

For a full list of volumes comprised in a current set of Halsbury's Laws of England please see overleaf.

Fifth Edition volumes:

1 (2008), 2 (2008), 3 (2011), 4 (2011), 5 (2013), 6 (2011), 7 (2008), 8 (2010), 9 (2012), 10 (2012), 11 (2009), 12 (2009), 13 (2009), 14 (2009), 15 (2009), 16 (2011), 17 (2011), 18 (2009), 19 (2011), 20 (2014), 21 (2011), 22 (2012), 23 (2013), 24 (2010), 25 (2010), 26 (2010), 27 (2010), 28 (2010), 30 (2012), 31 (2012), 32 (2012), 33 (2013), 34 (2011), 35 (2011), 36 (2011), 37 (2013), 38 (2013), 38A (2013), 39 (2014), 40 (2014), 41 (2014), 41A (2014), 42 (2011), 43 (2011), 44 (2011), 45 (2010), 46 (2010), 47 (2014), 47A (2014), 48 (2008), 49 (2008), 50 (2008), 51 (2013), 52 (2014), 53 (2014), 54 (2008), 55 (2012), 56 (2011), 57 (2012), 58 (2014), 58A (2014), 59 (2014), 59A (2014), 60 (2011), 61 (2010), 62 (2012), 63 (2012), 64 (2012), 65 (2008), 66 (2009), 67 (2008), 68 (2008), 69 (2009), 70 (2012), 71 (2013), 72 (2009), 73 (2009), 74 (2011), 75 (2013), 76 (2013), 77 (2010), 78 (2010), 79 (2014), 80 (2013), 81 (2010), 82 (2010), 83 (2010), 84 (2013), 84A (2013), 85 (2012), 86 (2013), 87 (2012), 88 (2012), 88A (2013), 89 (2011), 90 (2011), 91 (2012), 92 (2010), 93 (2008), 94 (2008), 95 (2013), 96 (2012), 97 (2010), 97A (2014), 98 (2013), 99 (2012), 100 (2009), 101 (2009), 102 (2010), 103 (2010), 104 (2014)

Fourth Edition volumes (bold figures represent reissues):

12(1)

Additional Materials:

Sentencing and Disposition of Offenders (*Release and Recall of Prisoners*) containing vol **92** (2010) paras 761–820; *Tort* (*Conversion and Wrongful Interference with Goods*) containing vol **45(2)** (Reissue) paras 542–686

Fourth and Fifth Edition volumes:

2014 Consolidated Index (A–E), 2014 Consolidated Index (F–O), 2014 Consolidated Index (P–Z), 2015 Consolidated Table of Statutes, 2015 Consolidated Table of Statutory Instruments, etc, 2014 Consolidated Table of Cases (A–G), 2014 Consolidated Table of Cases (H–Q), 2014 Consolidated Table of Cases (R–Z, ECJ Cases)

Updating and ancillary materials:

2014 Annual Cumulative Supplement; Monthly Current Service; Annual Abridgments 1974–2013

November 2014

HALSBURY'S
Laws of England

Volume 41A

2014

 LexisNexis®

Members of the LexisNexis Group worldwide

United Kingdom	LexisNexis, a Division of Reed Elsevier (UK) Ltd, Lexis House, 30 Farringdon Street, LONDON, EC4A 4HH, and 9–10, St Andrew Square, EDINBURGH, EH2 2AF
Australia	LexisNexis Butterworths, Chatswood, New South Wales
Austria	LexisNexis Verlag ARD Orac GmbH & Co KG, Vienna
Benelux	LexisNexis Benelux, Amsterdam
Canada	LexisNexis Canada, Markham, Ontario
China	LexisNexis China, Beijing and Shanghai
France	LexisNexis SA, Paris
Germany	LexisNexis GmbH, Dusseldorf
Hong Kong	LexisNexis Hong Kong, Hong Kong
India	LexisNexis India, New Delhi
Italy	Giuffrè Editore, Milan
Japan	LexisNexis Japan, Tokyo
Malaysia	Malayan Law Journal Sdn Bhd, Kuala Lumpur
New Zealand	LexisNexis NZ Ltd, Wellington
Singapore	LexisNexis Singapore, Singapore
South Africa	LexisNexis Butterworths, Durban
USA	LexisNexis, Dayton, Ohio

FIRST EDITION	*Published in 31 volumes between 1907 and 1917*
SECOND EDITION	*Published in 37 volumes between 1931 and 1942*
THIRD EDITION	*Published in 43 volumes between 1952 and 1964*
FOURTH EDITION	*Published in 56 volumes between 1973 and 1987, with reissues between 1988 and 2008*
FIFTH EDITION	*Published between 2008 and 2014, with reissues from 2014*

A CIP Catalogue record for this book is available from the British Library.

ISBN 13 (complete set, standard binding): 9781405734394

ISBN 13: 9781405790277

ISBN 978-1-4057-9027-7

Typeset by Letterpart Limited, Caterham on the Hill, Surrey CR3 5XL
Printed and bound by CPI Group (UK) Ltd, Croydon, CR0 4YY
Visit LexisNexis at www.lexisnexis.co.uk

EMPLOYMENT

Consultant Editor

IAN SMITH, LLB, MA,

of Gray's Inn, Barrister;

Emeritus Professor of Employment Law,

School of Law, University of East Anglia

The law stated in this volume is in general that in force on 1 October 2014, although subsequent changes have been included wherever possible.

Any future updating material will be found in the Current Service and annual Cumulative Supplement to Halsbury's Laws of England.

TABLE OF CONTENTS

HOW TO USE HALSBURY'S LAWS OF ENGLAND

Volumes

Each text volume of Halsbury's Laws of England contains the law on the titles contained in it as at a date stated at the front of the volume (the operative date).

Information contained in Halsbury's Laws of England may be accessed in several ways.

First, by using the tables of contents.

Each volume contains both a general Table of Contents, and a specific Table of Contents for each title contained in it. From these tables you will be directed to the relevant part of the work.

Readers should note that the current arrangement of titles can be found in the Current Service.

Secondly, by using tables of statutes, statutory instruments, cases or other materials.

If you know the name of the Act, statutory instrument or case with which your research is concerned, you should consult the Consolidated Tables of statutes, cases and so on (published as separate volumes) which will direct you to the relevant volume and paragraph. The Consolidated Tables will indicate if the volume referred to is a Fifth Edition volume.

(Each individual text volume also includes tables of those materials used as authority in that volume.)

Thirdly, by using the indexes.

If you are uncertain of the general subject area of your research, you should go to the Consolidated Index (published as separate volumes) for reference to the relevant volume(s) and paragraph(s). The Consolidated Index will indicate if the volume referred to is a Fifth Edition volume.

(Each individual text volume also includes an index to the material contained therein.)

Additional Materials

The reorganisation of the title scheme of Halsbury's Laws for the Fifth Edition means that from time to time Fourth Edition volumes will be *partially* replaced by Fifth Edition volumes.

In certain instances an Additional Materials softbound book will be issued, in which will be reproduced material which has not yet been replaced by a Fifth Edition title. This will enable users to remove specific Fourth Edition volumes from the shelf and save valuable space pending the replacement of that material in the Fifth Edition. These softbound books are supplied to volumes subscribers free of charge. They continue to form part of the set of Halsbury's Laws Fourth Edition Reissue, and will be updated by the annual Cumulative Supplement and monthly Noter-Up in the usual way.

Updating publications

The text volumes of Halsbury's Laws should be used in conjunction with the annual Cumulative Supplement and the monthly Noter-Up.

The annual Cumulative Supplement

The Supplement gives details of all changes between the operative date of the text volume and the operative date of the Supplement. It is arranged in the same volume, title and paragraph order as the text volumes. Developments affecting particular points of law are noted to the relevant paragraph(s) of the text volumes. As from the commencement of the Fifth Edition, the Supplement will clearly distinguish between Fourth and Fifth Edition titles.

For narrative treatment of material noted in the Cumulative Supplement, go to the Annual Abridgment volume for the relevant year.

Destination Tables

In certain titles in the annual *Cumulative Supplement*, reference is made to Destination Tables showing the destination of consolidated legislation. Those Destination Tables are to be found either at the end of the titles within the annual *Cumulative Supplement*, or in a separate *Destination Tables* booklet provided from time to time with the *Cumulative Supplement*.

The Noter-Up

The Noter-Up is contained in the Current Service Noter-Up booklet, issued monthly and noting changes since the publication of the annual Cumulative Supplement. Also arranged in the same volume, title and paragraph order as the text volumes, the Noter-Up follows the style of the Cumulative Supplement. As from the commencement of the Fifth Edition, the Noter-Up will clearly distinguish between Fourth and Fifth Edition titles.

For narrative treatment of material noted in the Noter-Up, go to the relevant Monthly Review.

REFERENCES AND ABBREVIATIONS

ACT	Australian Capital Territory
A-G	Attorney General
Admin	Administrative Court
Admlty	Admiralty Court
Adv-Gen	Advocate General
affd	affirmed
affg	affirming
Alta	Alberta
App	Appendix
art	article
Aust	Australia
B	Baron
BC	British Columbia
C	Command Paper (of a series published before 1900)
c	chapter number of an Act
CA	Court of Appeal
CAC	Central Arbitration Committee
CA in Ch	Court of Appeal in Chancery
CB	Chief Baron
CCA	Court of Criminal Appeal
CCR	County Court Rules 1981 (as subsequently amended)
CCR	Court for Crown Cases Reserved
C-MAC	Courts-Martial Appeal Court
CO	Crown Office
COD	Crown Office Digest
CPR	Civil Procedure Rules
Can	Canada
Cd	Command Paper (of the series published 1900–18)
Cf	compare
Ch	Chancery Division
ch	chapter
cl	clause
Cm	Command Paper (of the series published 1986 to date)

Cmd	Command Paper (of the series published 1919–56)
Cmnd	Command Paper (of the series published 1956–86)
Comm	Commercial Court
Comr....................................	Commissioner
Court Forms (2nd Edn)..........	Atkin's Encyclopaedia of Court Forms in Civil Proceedings, 2nd Edn. See note 2 post.
CrimPR	Criminal Procedure Rules
DC..	Divisional Court
DPP	Director of Public Prosecutions
EAT	Employment Appeal Tribunal
EC	European Community
ECJ.......................................	Court of Justice of the European Community
EComHR...............................	European Commission of Human Rights
ECSC.....................................	European Coal and Steel Community
ECtHR Rules of Court............	Rules of Court of the European Court of Human Rights
EEC.......................................	European Economic Community
EFTA	European Free Trade Association
EWCA Civ	Official neutral citation for judgments of the Court of Appeal (Civil Division)
EWCA Crim...........................	Official neutral citation for judgments of the Court of Appeal (Criminal Division)
EWHC...................................	Official neutral citation for judgments of the High Court
Edn.......................................	Edition
Euratom	European Atomic Energy Community
Ex Ch	Court of Exchequer Chamber
ex p	ex parte
Fam	Family Division
Fed	Federal
Forms & Precedents (5th Edn)......................................	Encyclopaedia of Forms and Precedents other than Court Forms, 5th Edn. See note 2 post.
GLC	Greater London Council
HC	High Court
HC	House of Commons
HK	Hong Kong
HL..	House of Lords
IAT.......................................	Immigration Appeal Tribunal
ILM......................................	International Legal Materials
INLR	Immigration and Nationality Law Reports
IRC.......................................	Inland Revenue Commissioners
Ind.......................................	India

Int Rels	International Relations
Ir	Ireland
J	Justice
JA	Judge of Appeal
Kan	Kansas
LA	Lord Advocate
LC	Lord Chancellor
LCC	London County Council
LCJ	Lord Chief Justice
LJ	Lord Justice of Appeal
LoN	League of Nations
MR	Master of the Rolls
Man	Manitoba
n	note
NB	New Brunswick
NI	Northern Ireland
NS	Nova Scotia
NSW	New South Wales
NY	New York
NZ	New Zealand
OHIM	Office for Harmonisation in the Internal Market
OJ	The Official Journal of the European Community published by the Office for Official Publications of the European Community
Ont	Ontario
P	President
PC	Judicial Committee of the Privy Council
PEI	Prince Edward Island
Pat	Patents Court
q	question
QB	Queen's Bench Division
QBD	Queen's Bench Division of the High Court
Qld	Queensland
Que	Quebec
r	rule
RDC	Rural District Council
RPC	Restrictive Practices Court
RSC	Rules of the Supreme Court 1965 (as subsequently amended)
reg	regulation
Res	Resolution
revsd	reversed

Rly	Railway
s	section
SA	South Africa
S Aust	South Australia
SC	Supreme Court
SI	Statutory Instruments published by authority
SR & O	Statutory Rules and Orders published by authority
SR & O Rev 1904	Revised Edition comprising all Public and General Statutory Rules and Orders in force on 31 December 1903
SR & O Rev 1948	Revised Edition comprising all Public and General Statutory Rules and Orders and Statutory Instruments in force on 31 December 1948
SRNI	Statutory Rules of Northern Ireland
STI	Simon's Tax Intelligence (1973–1995); Simon's Weekly Tax Intelligence (1996-current)
Sask	Saskatchewan
Sch	Schedule
Sess	Session
Sing	Singapore
TCC	Technology and Construction Court
TS	Treaty Series
Tanz	Tanzania
Tas	Tasmania
UDC	Urban District Council
UKHL	Official neutral citation for judgments of the House of Lords
UKPC	Official neutral citation for judgments of the Privy Council
UN	United Nations
V-C	Vice-Chancellor
Vict	Victoria
W Aust	Western Australia
Zimb	Zimbabwe

NOTE 1. A general list of the abbreviations of law reports and other sources used in this work can be found at the beginning of the Consolidated Table of Cases.

NOTE 2. Where references are made to other publications, the volume number precedes and the page number follows the name of the publication; eg the reference '12 Forms & Precedents (5th Edn) 44' refers to volume 12 of the Encyclopaedia of Forms and Precedents, page 44.

NOTE 3. An English statute is cited by short title or, where there is no short title, by regnal year and chapter number together with the name by which it is commonly known or a description of its subject matter and date. In the case of a foreign statute, the mode of citation generally follows the style of citation in use in the country concerned with the addition, where necessary, of the name of the country in parentheses.

NOTE 4. A statutory instrument is cited by short title, if any, followed by the year and number, or, if unnumbered, the date.

TABLE OF STATUTES

TABLE OF STATUTORY INSTRUMENTS

N

TABLE OF CIVIL PROCEDURE

Civil Procedure Rules 1998, SI 1998/3132 (CPR)

Practice Directions

TABLE OF EUROPEAN
UNION LEGISLATION

TABLE OF
NON-STATUTORY MATERIAL

TABLE OF CASES

PARA

PARA

PARA

PARA

Z

Decisions of the European Court of Justice are listed below numerically. These decisions
are also included in the preceding alphabetical list.

PARA

PARA

PARA

EMPLOYMENT

VOLUME 39

10. INDUSTRIAL RELATIONS

(1) COLLECTIVE BARGAINING

1093. Meanings of 'collective bargaining' and 'collective agreement'.
'Collective bargaining' means[1] negotiations[2] relating to or connected with one or more of the following matters:

(1) terms and conditions of employment, or the physical conditions in which any workers[3] are required to work;

(2) engagement or non-engagement, or termination or suspension of employment or the duties of employment, of one or more workers;

(3) allocation of work or the duties of employment between workers or groups of workers;

(4) matters of discipline;

(5) a worker's membership or non-membership of a trade union[4];

(6) facilities for officials[5] of trade unions; and

(7) machinery for negotiation or consultation, and other procedures, relating to any of the above matters, including the recognition[6] by employers[7] or employers' associations[8] of the right of a trade union to represent workers in such negotiations or consultation or in the carrying out of such procedures[9].

'Collective agreement' means any agreement or arrangement made by or on behalf of one or more trade unions and one or more employers or employers' associations and relating to one or more of the matters specified above[10].

1 Ie for the purposes of the Trade Union and Labour Relations (Consolidation) Act 1992: see PARAS 891 et seq, 1094 et seq.

2 This requirement of negotiation is a key element; mere consultation or discussion may not be enough (*Lake & Elliott Founders and Engineers Ltd and the Association of Scientific, Technical and Managerial Staff* CAC Award 86/3), nor may the advising of individual members (*BP Chemicals Ltd and the Transport and General Workers' Union* CAC Award 86/1). As to information and consultation see also *Stewart v Moray Council* [2006] ICR 1253, [2006] IRLR 592, EAT. This may be particularly important in the context of recognition, which must be 'for the purposes of collective bargaining': see PARA 1094.

3 As to the meaning of 'worker' see PARA 892.

4 As to the meaning of 'trade union' see PARA 891.

5 As to the meaning of 'official', in relation to a trade union, see PARA 1018.

6 As to the meaning of 'recognition', in relation to a trade union, see PARA 1094.

7 As to the meaning of 'employer' see PARA 892; and as to Crown employment etc see PARA 893 et seq.

8 As to the meaning of 'employers' association' see PARA 1079.

9 Trade Union and Labour Relations (Consolidation) Act 1992 s 178(1), (2). As to collective agreement provisions being apt for incorporation into individual contracts of employment see PARA 116 note 16. A dispute relating to one or more of the matters listed in heads (1)–(7) in the text is a trade dispute: see s 244(1); and PARA 1361.

10 Trade Union and Labour Relations (Consolidation) Act 1992 s 178(1). See further PARAS 1175–1178.

1094. Trade union recognition. 'Recognition', in relation to a trade union[1], means[2] the recognition of the union by an employer[3], or two or more associated employers[4], to any extent, for the purpose of collective bargaining[5].

As well as being an important feature of practical industrial relations, recognition of a trade union by an employer or employers' association may be a legal requirement; thus, as well as being listed[6] and independent[7], a trade union must also be recognised if it is to exercise legal rights to disclosure of information[8], consultation on redundancies[9], consultation on transfers of undertakings[10], consultation on health and safety matters[11], consultation on pensions matters[12], and for its officials and members to have a right to time off work[13].

Certain indirect ways of seeking recognition in practice are specifically rendered illegal[14].

Where recognition has been voluntarily agreed, that is to say where the statutory recognition procedure[15] has not been used, there are no legal limitations on derecognition by an employer, which thus remains a matter of industrial practice[16].

1　As to the meaning of 'trade union' see PARA 891.
2　Ie for the purposes of the Trade Union and Labour Relations (Consolidation) Act 1992: see PARAS 891 et seq, 1095 et seq.
3　As to the meaning of 'employer' see PARA 892.
4　As to the meaning of 'associated employer' see PARA 1026 note 8.
5　Trade Union and Labour Relations (Consolidation) Act 1992 s 178(3). 'Recognised' and other related expressions are to be construed accordingly: s 178(3). As to the meaning of 'collective bargaining' see PARA 1093. The requirement that the recognition be for the purpose of collective bargaining means that lesser acceptance of the trade union by the employer, eg only for the purpose of representing members under disciplinary or grievance procedures, may not be enough: *Union of Shop, Distributive and Allied Workers v Sketchley Ltd* [1981] ICR 644, [1981] IRLR 291, EAT; *R v Central Arbitration Committee, ex p BTP Tioxide Ltd* [1981] ICR 843, [1982] IRLR 60. However, the phrase 'to any extent' denotes that, once the necessary negotiating relationship is shown, that is sufficient and it does not matter that the recognition is only partial, ie restricted to certain topics only.
　　There is no need for an express recognition agreement (*National Union of Tailors and Garment Workers v Charles Ingram & Co Ltd* [1978] 1 All ER 1271, [1977] ICR 530, EAT); but, although recognition may evolve over a period of time without any such express agreement, in such a case the evidence must be clear and point towards some form of continuing, mutual relationship and willingness to negotiate (*National Union of Gold, Silver and Allied Trades v Albury Bros Ltd* [1979] ICR 84, [1978] IRLR 504, CA; *Union of Shop, Distributive and Allied Workers v Sketchley Ltd* above). Isolated incidents of dealings with a union may not be sufficient: *Cleveland County Council v Springett* [1985] IRLR 131, EAT; *Transport and General Workers' Union v Dyer* [1977] IRLR 93, EAT; cf *Joshua Wilson & Bros Ltd v Union of Shop, Distributive and Allied Workers* [1978] 3 All ER 4, [1978] ICR 614, EAT. Recognition of a union by an employers' association to which the employer in question belongs does not per se mean that the employer must be taken to recognise the union, since recognition normally means by an individual employer: *National Union of Gold, Silver and Allied Trades v Albury Bros Ltd* above.
6　See PARA 900.
7　See PARA 904.
8　See PARA 1179 et seq.
9　See PARA 1185 et seq.
10　See PARA 1196 et seq.
11　See PARAS 1201, 1202.
12　See PARAS 1205, 1206.
13　See PARA 1065 et seq.
14　These are: (1) putting union recognition requirements into contracts for the supply of goods and services (see PARA 1183); (2) refusing to deal or tender on the grounds of union non-recognition (see PARA 1184); and (3) organising industrial action aimed at imposing a union recognition requirement (see PARA 1368).
15　As to the statutory procedure for recognition see PARA 1097 et seq.
16　This is because: (1) informal arrangements can always be resiled from by an employer; and (2) even where there has been an express recognition agreement, it will have been in a collective agreement which itself is not legally enforceable (see PARA 1175; and *National Coal Board v National Union of Mineworkers* [1986] ICR 736, [1986] IRLR 439 (where the union tried unsuccessfully to oppose partial derecognition by arguing (inter alia) that the agreement in question had legal effect)). One qualification is that, even where an employer derecognises a union, that will not affect any legal incidents of the recognition that existed prior to that date (eg an obligation to consult on redundancies declared before then: *Selfridges Ltd and the*

Manufacturing Science Finance Union CAC Award 91/1). On a broader level, the fact that an employer derecognises a union and withdraws from an existing collective agreement does not affect the continuing validity of any terms and conditions of employment of individual employees which were incorporated into their contracts from that agreement: see PARAS 117, 1176.

1095. Recognition and transfers of undertakings. Where, before a relevant transfer of an undertaking[1], an independent trade union[2] is recognised[3] to any extent[4] by the transferor in respect of employees[5] of any description who, in consequence of the transfer, became employees of the transferee, then, if after the transfer the transferred organised grouping of resources or employees maintains an identity distinct from the remainder of the transferee's undertaking:

(1)   the union is deemed to have been recognised by the transferee to the same extent in respect of employees of that description so employed; and

(2)   any agreement for recognition may be varied or rescinded accordingly[6].

1   The concept of a 'relevant transfer' of an 'undertaking' under the Transfer of Undertakings (Protection of Employment) Regulations 2006, SI 2006/246, is considered in PARA 137. See also reg 6(1).

2   As to the meaning of 'independent trade union' see PARA 904.

3   As to the meaning of 'recognised' see PARA 1094 (definition applied by the Transfer of Undertakings (Protection of Employment) Regulations 2006, SI 2006/246, reg 2(1)).

4   See PARA 1094 note 5.

5   As to the meaning of 'employee' for these purposes see PARA 137 note 8. Under this definition there must be an employment relationship of sorts; an equity partner in a partnership was held not to qualify: *Cowell v Quilter Goodison & Co Ltd and QG Management Services Ltd* [1989] IRLR 392, CA (decided under the Transfer of Undertakings (Protection of Employment) Regulations 1981, SI 1981/1794 (revoked)).

6   Transfer of Undertakings (Protection of Employment) Regulations 2006, SI 2006/246, reg 6(1), (2). The extent of the protection in practice for existing recognition given by reg 6 is uncertain and may be very little. The aim appears to be to preserve such recognition into the future with the transferee employer (an analogy with the continuation of existing contracts of employment on the same terms: see PARA 139) and so alter fundamentally the common law position under which a recognition agreement was personal to the employer and so would not survive a transfer (see *Union of Construction, Allied Trades and Technicians v Burrage* [1978] ICR 314, EAT (decided under earlier legislation). As to the position where an employee objects to becoming employed by the transferee see the Transfer of Undertakings (Protection of Employment) Regulations 2006, SI 2006/246, reg 4(7)–(11); and PARA 141.

    Although reg 6 provides for recognition to survive a transfer, it appears to do little to prevent the transferee employer from revoking it at any time thereafter, for three reasons: (1) no specific remedy is provided by reg 6 for breach of it; (2) there is unlikely to be any contractual remedy because the collective agreement containing the recognition agreement, if it is express, is not legally enforceable, and any informal agreement will have similar status (see PARA 1094 note 16); (3) reg 6(2)(b) (see head (2) in the text) states that 'any agreement for recognition may be varied or rescinded accordingly' which, if taken literally, emphasises the transferee's right of revocation. With regard to the last point, it is established that the regulations may be interpreted purposively, in order to put into effect Council Directive (EC) 2001/23 (OJ L82, 22/03/2001, p 16) on which they are based (see *Litster v Forth Dry Dock and Engineering Co Ltd (in receivership)* [1990] 1 AC 546, [1989] ICR 341, HL), but in this instance that Directive is vague, providing only, 'If the undertaking, business or part of an undertaking or business preserves its autonomy, the status and function of the representatives or of the representation of the employees affected by the transfer shall be preserved': see art 6(1).

    Where recognition has been gained under the statutory recognition procedure (see PARA 1097 et seq), presumably any statutory restrictions on derecognition (see PARA 1149 et seq) continue to apply, and are transferred to the transferee employer.

1096. Partnerships at work. The Secretary of State may spend money or provide money to other persons for the purpose of encouraging and helping employers[1], or their representatives, and employees[2], or their representatives, to improve the way they work together[3].

Money may be provided in such way as the Secretary of State thinks fit, whether as grants or otherwise, and on such terms as he thinks fit, whether as to repayment or otherwise[4].

1 There is no statutory definition of 'employer' for these purposes.
2 There is no statutory definition of 'employee' for these purposes.
3 Employment Relations Act 1999 s 30(1). As to the Secretary of State see PARA 5 note 21.
4 Employment Relations Act 1999 s 30(2).

(2) STATUTORY TRADE UNION RECOGNITION PROCEDURE

(i) Statutory Right to Trade Union Recognition

A. STATUTORY RIGHT TO RECOGNITION; IN GENERAL

1097. Statutory procedure for trade union recognition. There is a statutory procedure under which an independent trade union[1] may demand that the employer recognise it as the bargaining unit for a specific group of workers in respect of pay, hours and holidays[2].

The statutory procedure:

(1) seeks to cover every eventuality, laying down several different procedures, covering initial recognition[3], variation of recognition[4] and derecognition[5]; and, although the statutory procedure is available to an independent trade union only, an employer may voluntarily agree to recognise a non-independent trade union, but a non-independent trade union may not use any of the statutory procedures;

(2) may not be used against a small employer[6], but such an employer may voluntarily agree to recognise a union but he may not be compelled to do so;

(3) places throughout an emphasis on agreement rather than compulsion, both employers and unions being encouraged at every stage to settle their differences by agreement, if necessary with the Advisory, Conciliation and Arbitration Service[7] or the Central Arbitration Committee (the 'CAC')[8]; but, in default of agreement, the CAC has power to adjudicate.

Where an independent trade union is recognised under the statutory procedure, it has the right to negotiate about pay[9], hours and holidays only[10]; the employer may agree to negotiate with the union on other matters but cannot be compelled to do so. As a general rule the statutory procedures may be invoked once every three years ('the relevant period') only[11]. Clear time limits are set for the various stages in the statutory procedure, subject to the right to extend those limits.

An independent trade union may not normally invoke the statutory right to recognition if that would disturb settled bargaining practice. Thus, if one union is already recognised in respect of any of the workers concerned, any claim by another under the statutory procedure is ruled out, subject to certain exceptions.

In order to claim the statutory right of recognition, a union must show that at least 10 per cent of the workers in the proposed bargaining unit are members of the union[12].

Speculative and dubious claims are discouraged. A claimant union needs to show that it can probably count on the support of a majority of workers concerned; and, if it is to succeed, the union ultimately needs to be able to rely on gaining a majority of the votes in a secret ballot of the workers concerned and the support of at least 40 per cent of the workers in the bargaining unit[13].

An employer must invite the union to send representatives to a meeting for the purpose of consulting about training for workers[14]; and he must not dismiss[15] or victimise[16] an employee for advocating or opposing recognition or derecognition.

1   As to the meaning of 'independent trade union' see PARA 904.
2   Ie the Trade Union and Labour Relations (Consolidation) Act 1992 Sch A1 (see PARA 1098 et seq), which came into force on 6 June 2000 (see the Employment Relations Act 1999 (Commencement No 6 and Transitional Provisions) Order 2000, SI 2000/1338, art 2(a)). As to termination of an agreement for recognition see PARA 1128.
     Two previous attempts were made to give a statutory right of recognition. The Industrial Relations Act 1971 ss 44–60 (repealed) gave unions a right to demand recognition by an unwilling employer but the TUC unions chose not to comply with the conditions on which it was given. The Employment Protection Act 1975 ss 11–21 (repealed) subsequently renewed that right without such stringent conditions, leaving ACAS to adjudicate in the event of a dispute; but the system proved to be unsatisfactory (see ACAS Annual Report 1980).
3   See PARA 1103 et seq.
4   See PARA 1132 et seq.
5   See PARA 1149 et seq.
6   See PARA 1104.
7   As to the Advisory, Conciliation and Arbitration Service ('ACAS') see PARA 1213 et seq.
8   As to the Central Arbitration Committee see PARA 1226 et seq. As to the power of the Central Arbitration Committee to require the supply of specified information to enable or assist it to exercise any of its functions see the Trade Union and Labour Relations (Consolidation) Act 1992 Sch A1 para 170A; and PARA 1102. As to the power of the Secretary of State to prohibit employers and unions from using unfair practices in relation to an application of a specified description see the Trade Union and Labour Relations (Consolidation) Act 1992 Sch A1 para 166B; and PARA 1174.
9   For these purposes, 'pay' includes pension contributions and benefits: *UNIFI v Union Bank of Nigeria plc* [2001] IRLR 712. However see also PARA 1103 note 3.
10 See PARA 1103 note 3.
11 See PARA 1128.
12 See PARAS 1108–1109.
13 See PARA 1122.
14 See PARAS 1172–1173.
15 See PARA 1171.
16 See PARAS 1169–1170.

1098.   General duty of the Central Arbitration Committee.   In exercising functions[1] in any particular case, the Central Arbitration Committee[2] must have regard to the object[3] of encouraging and promoting fair and efficient practices and arrangements in the workplace[4].

1   Ie under the Trade Union and Labour Relations (Consolidation) Act 1992 Sch A1: see also PARA 1099 et seq.
2   As to the Central Arbitration Committee see PARA 1226 et seq. As to the power of the Central Arbitration Committee to require the supply of specified information to enable or assist it to exercise any of its functions see the Trade Union and Labour Relations (Consolidation) Act 1992 Sch A1 para 170A; and PARA 1102.
3   Ie so far as having regard to that object is consistent with applying other provisions of the Trade Union and Labour Relations (Consolidation) Act 1992 Sch A1 in the case concerned.
4   Trade Union and Labour Relations (Consolidation) Act 1992 Sch A1 paras 171, 172(1) (Sch A1 added by the Employment Relations Act 1999 Sch 1).

See *R (on the application of Cable & Wireless Services UK Ltd) v Central Arbitration Committee* [2008] EWHC 115 (Admin), [2008] ICR 693, [2008] IRLR 425 where it was said that Parliament had deliberately given the Central Arbitration Committee a wide discretion and that, although it is subject to judicial review, the court will need a lot of convincing to intervene and will not do so where a merits objection is being dressed up as a judicial review application.

1099. Directions about certain applications to the Central Arbitration Committee. The Secretary of State[1] may make to the Central Arbitration Committee[2] (the 'CAC') directions as to the order in which the CAC must consider the admissibility of the applications in relation to any case where:

(1) two or more applications are made to the CAC;

(2) each application is a relevant application[3];

(3) each application relates to the same bargaining unit; and

(4) the CAC has not accepted any of the applications[4].

The directions may include:

(a) provision to deal with a case where a relevant application is made while the CAC is still considering the admissibility of another one relating to the same bargaining unit; and

(b) other incidental provisions[5].

1 As to the Secretary of State see PARA 5 note 21.
2 As to the Central Arbitration Committee see PARA 1226 et seq. As to the power of the Central Arbitration Committee to require the supply of specified information to enable or assist it to exercise any of its functions see the Trade Union and Labour Relations (Consolidation) Act 1992 Sch A1 para 170A; and PARA 1102.
3 For these purposes, a relevant application is an application under the Trade Union and Labour Relations (Consolidation) Act 1992 Sch A1 para 101 (see PARA 1150), Sch A1 para 106 (see PARA 1153), Sch A1 para 107 (see PARA 1153), Sch A1 para 112 (see PARA 1154) or Sch A1 para 128 (see PARA 1161): Sch A1 para 169(4) (Sch A1 added by the Employment Relations Act 1999 Sch 1).
4 Trade Union and Labour Relations (Consolidation) Act 1992 Sch A1 paras 169(1), (2), 172(1) (as added: see note 3).
5 Trade Union and Labour Relations (Consolidation) Act 1992 Sch A1 paras 169(3), 172(1) (as added: see note 3).

1100. Power to make provision about effect of amalgamations etc. The Secretary of State[1] may by order make provision for any case where: (1) an application has been made, a declaration has been issued, or any other thing has been done[2] by, to or in relation to a union, or anything has been done in consequence of anything so done, and the union amalgamates or transfers all or any of its engagements[3]; (2) an application has been made, a declaration has been issued, or any other thing has been done[4] in relation to a group[5] of workers[6], or anything has been done in consequence of anything so done, and the person who was the employer[7] of the workers constituting that group at the time the thing was done is no longer the employer of all of the workers constituting that group, whether as a result of a transfer of the whole or part of an undertaking or business or otherwise[8].

1 As to the Secretary of State see PARA 5 note 21.
2 Ie done under or for the purposes of the Trade Union and Labour Relations (Consolidation) Act 1992 Sch A1.
3 Trade Union and Labour Relations (Consolidation) Act 1992 Sch A1 para 169A(1) (Sch A1 paras 169A–169C added by the Employment Relations Act 2004 s 18). An order under the Trade Union and Labour Relations (Consolidation) Act 1992 Sch A1 para 169A may, in particular, make provision for cases where an amalgamated union, or union to which engagements are transferred, does not have a certificate of independence: Sch A1 para 169A(2) (as so added). As to certificates of independence see PARA 905.

As to the power of the Central Arbitration Committee to require the supply of specified information to enable or assist it to exercise any of its functions see the Trade Union and Labour Relations (Consolidation) Act 1992 Sch A1 para 170A; and PARA 1102.

4   See note 2.

5   'Group' includes two or more groups taken together: Trade Union and Labour Relations (Consolidation) Act 1992 Sch A1 para 169B(2) (as added: see note 3).

6   As to the meaning of 'worker' see PARA 892.

7   As to the meaning of 'employer' see PARA 892.

8   Trade Union and Labour Relations (Consolidation) Act 1992 Sch A1 para 169B(1) (as added: see note 3). An order under Sch A1 para 169A or 169B may amend Sch A1, include supplementary, incidental, saving or transitional provisions, and make different provision for different cases or circumstances, and must be made by statutory instrument: Sch A1 para 169C(1), (2) (as so added). No such order may be made unless a draft of it has been laid before Parliament and approved by a resolution of each House of Parliament: Sch A1 para 169C(3) (as so added).

1101. Notice of declarations by the Central Arbitration Committee. If the Central Arbitration Committee[1] issues a declaration[2], it must notify the parties[3] of the declaration and its contents[4].

1   As to the Central Arbitration Committee see PARA 1226 et seq. As to the power of the Central Arbitration Committee to require the supply of specified information to enable or assist it to exercise any of its functions see the Trade Union and Labour Relations (Consolidation) Act 1992 Sch A1 para 170A; and PARA 1102.

2   Ie under the Trade Union and Labour Relations (Consolidation) Act 1992 Sch A1: see PARA 1103 et seq.

3   For these purposes, the reference to the parties is to: (1) the union, or unions, concerned and the employer concerned; and (2) if the declaration is issued in consequence of an application by a worker or workers, the worker or workers making it: Trade Union and Labour Relations (Consolidation) Act 1992 Sch A1 para 170(2) (Sch A1 added by the Employment Relations Act 1999 s 1(1), (3), Sch 1). As to the meaning of 'trade union' see PARA 891.

4   Trade Union and Labour Relations (Consolidation) Act 1992 Sch A1 paras 170(1), 172(1) (as added: see note 3).

1102. Supply of information to the Central Arbitration Committee. The Central Arbitration Committee[1] (the 'CAC') may, if it considers it necessary to do so to enable or assist it to exercise any of its functions[2], exercise any or all of the following powers[3]:

(1)   the power to require an employer[4] to supply the CAC case manager[5], within such period as the CAC may specify, with specified[6] information concerning either or both of (a) the workers[7] in a specified bargaining unit[8] who work for the employer[9]; and (b) the likelihood of a majority of those workers being in favour of the conduct by a specified union[10], or specified unions, of collective bargaining[11] on their behalf[12];

(2)   the power to require a union to supply the CAC case manager, within such period as the CAC may specify, with specified information concerning either or both of (a) the workers in a specified bargaining unit who are members of the union[13]; and (b) the likelihood of a majority of workers in a specified bargaining unit being in favour of the conduct by the union, or by it and other specified unions, of collective bargaining on their behalf[14];

(3)   the power to require an applicant worker[15] to supply the CAC case manager, within such period as the CAC may specify, with specified information concerning the likelihood of a majority of the workers in his bargaining unit being in favour of having bargaining arrangements ended[16].

The recipient of such a requirement must, within the specified period, supply the CAC case manager with such of the specified information as is in the recipient's possession[17].

1 As to the Central Arbitration Committee see PARA 1226 et seq.
2 Ie its functions under the Trade Union and Labour Relations (Consolidation) Act 1992 Sch A1.
3 Trade Union and Labour Relations (Consolidation) Act 1992 Sch A1 para 170A(1) (Sch A1 para 170A added by the Employment Relations Act 2004 s 19).
4 As to the meaning of 'employer' see PARA 892.
5 'CAC case manager' means the member of staff provided to the CAC by the Advisory, Conciliation and Arbitration Service ('ACAS') who is named in the requirement, but the CAC may, by notice given to the recipient of such a requirement, change the member of that staff who is to be the CAC case manager for the purposes of that requirement: Trade Union and Labour Relations (Consolidation) Act 1992 Sch A1 para 170A(9) (as added: see note 3). As to ACAS see PARA 1213 et seq.
6 'Specified' means specified in a requirement under the Trade Union and Labour Relations (Consolidation) Act 1992 Sch A1 para 170A: Sch A1 para 170A(9) (as added: see note 3).
7 As to the meaning of 'worker' see PARA 892.
8 As to the meaning of references to the bargaining unit see PARA 1103 note 3.
9 Trade Union and Labour Relations (Consolidation) Act 1992 Sch A1 para 170A(2)(a) (as added: see note 3).
10 As to the meaning of 'trade union' see PARA 891.
11 'Collective bargaining' is to be construed in accordance with the Trade Union and Labour Relations (Consolidation) Act 1992 Sch A1 para 3 (see PARA 1103 note 3): Sch A1 para 170A(9) (as added: see note 3).
12 Trade Union and Labour Relations (Consolidation) Act 1992 Sch A1 para 170A(2)(b) (as added: see note 3).
13 Trade Union and Labour Relations (Consolidation) Act 1992 Sch A1 para 170A(3)(a) (as added: see note 3).
14 Trade Union and Labour Relations (Consolidation) Act 1992 Sch A1 para 170A(3)(b) (as added: see note 3).
15 'Applicant worker' means a worker who falls within a bargaining unit and has made an application under the Trade Union and Labour Relations (Consolidation) Act 1992 Sch A1 para 112 (see PARA 1154) or Sch A1 para 137 (see PARA 1163) to have bargaining arrangements ended: Sch A1 para 170A(9) (as added: see note 3).
16 Trade Union and Labour Relations (Consolidation) Act 1992 Sch A1 para 170A(4) (as added: see note 3).
17 Trade Union and Labour Relations (Consolidation) Act 1992 Sch A1 para 170A(5) (as added: see note 3). From the information so supplied, the CAC case manager must prepare a report and submit it to the CAC: Sch A1 para 170A(6) (as so added). If an employer, a union or a worker fails to comply with Sch A1 para 170A(5), the report must mention that failure, and the CAC may draw an inference against the party concerned: Sch A1 para 170A(7) (as so added). The CAC must give a copy of the report to the employer, to the union or unions and, in the case of an application under Sch A1 para 112 or Sch A1 para 137, to the applicant worker or applicant workers: Sch A1 para 170A(8) (as so added).

B. REQUEST FOR TRADE UNION RECOGNITION

1103. Request for recognition to conduct collective bargaining. A trade union[1], or trade unions, seeking recognition[2] to be entitled to conduct collective bargaining[3] on behalf of a group or groups of workers may make a request for recognition[4] in accordance with the relevant statutory provisions[5].

1 As to the meaning of 'trade union' see PARA 891.
2 As to the meaning of 'recognition' see PARA 1094.
3 For these purposes, the meaning of collective bargaining given by the Trade Union and Labour Relations (Consolidation) Act 1992 s 178(1) (see PARA 1093) does not apply: Sch A1 para 3(1), (2) (Sch A1 added by the Employment Relations Act 1999 Sch 1). References to collective bargaining are to negotiations relating to pay, hours and holidays; but this has effect subject to the Trade Union and Labour Relations (Consolidation) Act 1992 Sch A1 para 3(4): Sch A1 para 3(1), (3) (as so added). If the parties agree matters as the subject of collective

bargaining, references to collective bargaining are to negotiations relating to the agreed matters; and this is the case whether the agreement is made before or after the time when the Central Arbitration Committee issues a declaration, or the parties agree, that the union is, or unions are, entitled to conduct collective bargaining on behalf of a bargaining unit: Sch A1 paras 3(1), (4), 172(1) (as so added). Schedule A1 para 3(4) does not apply in construing Sch A1 para 31(3) (see PARA 1123): Sch A1 para 3(1), (5) (as so added). Schedule A1 para 3(2)–(5) does not apply in construing Sch A1 para 35 (see PARA 1108) or Sch A1 para 44 (see PARA 1115): Sch A1 para 3(1), (6) (as so added). As to the Central Arbitration Committee see PARA 1226 et seq. As to the effect of Sch A1 para 3(6) see *R (on the application of Boots Management Services Ltd) v Central Arbitration Committee* [2014] EWHC 65 (Admin), [2014] IRLR 278, [2014] All ER (D) 148 (Jan); and *R (on the application of Boots Management Services Ltd) v Central Arbitration Committee (Secretary of State for Business, Innovation and Skills intervening)* [2014] EWHC 2930 (Admin) (compatibility with Convention for the Protection of Human Rights and Fundamental Freedoms (Rome, 4 November 1950; TS 71 (1953); Cmd 8969) ('European Convention on Human Rights') art 11 (see RIGHTS AND FREEDOMS vol 88A (2013) PARAS 436–460 (freedom of assembly), PARAS 461–493 (freedom of association))).

References to the parties are to the union, or unions, and the employer: Trade Union and Labour Relations (Consolidation) Act 1992 Sch A1 para 2(1), (5) (as so added). References to the bargaining unit are to the group of workers concerned, or the groups taken together: Sch A1 para 2(1), (2) (as so added). References to an appropriate bargaining unit's being decided by the CAC are to a bargaining unit's being decided by the CAC to be appropriate under Sch A1 para 19(2) or Sch A1 para 19(3) or Sch A1 para 19A(2) or (3) (see PARA 1110): Sch A1 para 2(3A) (added by the Employment Relations Act 2004 Sch 1 para 23(1), (2)). References to the employer are to the employer of the workers constituting the bargaining unit concerned: Trade Union and Labour Relations (Consolidation) Act 1992 Sch A1 para 2(1), (4) (Sch A1 added by the Employment Relations Act 1999 Sch 1). As to the meaning of 'employer' generally see PARA 892; and as to the meaning of 'worker' see PARA 892.

In Sch A1, 'pay' does not include terms relating to a person's membership of or rights under, or his employer's contributions to, an occupational pension scheme as defined by the Pension Schemes Act 1993 s 1, or a personal pension scheme as so defined (see PERSONAL AND OCCUPATIONAL PENSIONS vol 80 (2013) PARA 208): Trade Union and Labour Relations (Consolidation) Act 1992 Sch A1 para 171A(1) (Sch A1 para 171A added by the Employment Relations Act 2004 s 20). As to the meaning of 'pay' see also PARA 1097 note 9.

The Secretary of State may by order amend: (1) the Trade Union and Labour Relations (Consolidation) Act 1992 Sch A1 para 171A(1); (2) Sch A1 para 3(3), Sch A1 para 54(4) (see PARA 1131 note 16) or Sch A1 para 94(6)(b) (see PARA 1132), by adding specified matters relating to pensions to the matters there specified to which negotiations may relate; and (3) Sch A1 para 35(2)(b) (see PARA 1108) or Sch A1 para 44(2)(b) (see PARA 1115 head (1)(b) in the text), by adding specified matters relating to pensions to the core topics there specified: Sch A1 para 171A(2), (3) (as so added). As to the Secretary of State see PARA 5 note 21. Such an order may: (a) include supplementary, incidental, saving or transitional provisions including provision amending Sch A1; (b) make different provision for different cases; (c) make provision deeming the matters to which any pre-commencement declaration of recognition relates; and (d) make provision deeming the matters to which any pre-commencement declaration of recognition or method of collective bargaining could relate: Sch A1 para 171A(4), (5) (as so added). 'Pre-commencement declaration of recognition' means a declaration of recognition issued by the Central Arbitration Committee before the coming into force of the order; 'pre-commencement method of collective bargaining' means a method of collective bargaining specified by the Central Arbitration Committee before the coming into force of the order; and references to a post-commencement declaration of recognition or method of collective bargaining are to be construed accordingly: Sch A1 para 171A(6) (as so added). An order under Sch A1 para 171A must be made by statutory instrument, and no such order may be made unless a draft of it has been laid before Parliament and approved by a resolution of each House of Parliament: Sch A1 para 171A(7) (as so added).

4   Ie in accordance with the Trade Union and Labour Relations (Consolidation) Act 1992 Sch A1 Pt I (paras 1–51): see also PARA 1104 et seq.

5   Trade Union and Labour Relations (Consolidation) Act 1992 Sch A1 para 1 (as added: see note 3). See also *Netjets Management Ltd v Central Arbitration Committee* [2012] EWHC 2685 (Admin), [2013] 1 All ER 288, [2012] IRLR 986 (panel had correctly identified the most important factors leading to the conclusion that the connection of workers within the proposed bargaining unit, taken as a group, with Great Britain was sufficiently strong for the interested party to be able to seek recognition for the purposes of conducting collective bargaining on their behalf; the appropriate time to take into account individual characteristics was when

considering the bargaining unit; *R (on the application of the British Broadcasting Corpn) v Central Arbitration Committee* [2003] EWHC 1375 (Admin), [2003] ICR 1542, [2003] IRLR 460 applied).

1104. Request for trade union recognition. The union[1] or unions seeking recognition[2] must make a request for recognition to the employer[3]; and the following provisions apply to the request[4].

The request is not valid unless:

(1) it is received by the employer[5];

(2) the union, or each of the unions, has a certificate of independence[6];

(3) the employer, taken with any associated employer[7] or employers, employs:

  (a) at least 21 workers[8] on the day the employer receives the request; or

  (b) an average of at least 21 workers[9] in the 13 weeks ending with that day[10];

(4) it is:

  (a) in writing;

  (b) identifies the union or unions and the bargaining unit[11]; and

  (c) states that it is made under[12] the statutory provisions[13].

1 As to the meaning of 'trade union' see PARA 891.
2 As to the meaning of 'recognition' see PARA 1094.
3 Trade Union and Labour Relations (Consolidation) Act 1992 Sch A1 para 4(1) (Sch A1 added by the Employment Relations Act 1999 Sch 1). As to the meaning of 'employer' see PARA 1103 note 3. The Secretary of State may by order made by statutory instrument prescribe the form of requests and the procedure for making them; and, if he does so, the request is not valid unless it complies with the order: Trade Union and Labour Relations (Consolidation) Act 1992 Sch A1 para 9 (as so added). As to the Secretary of State see PARA 5 note 21. At the date at which this volume states the law no such order had been made.
4 Trade Union and Labour Relations (Consolidation) Act 1992 Sch A1 para 4(2) (as added: see note 3).
5 Trade Union and Labour Relations (Consolidation) Act 1992 Sch A1 para 5 (as added: see note 3).
6 Trade Union and Labour Relations (Consolidation) Act 1992 Sch A1 para 6 (as added (see note 3); amended by the Employment Relations Act 2004 s 50(6)). As to certificates of independence see PARA 905.
7 As to the meaning of 'associated employer' see PARA 1026 note 8.
8 As to the meaning of 'worker' see PARA 892. For these purposes, any worker employed by an associated company incorporated outside Great Britain is to be ignored unless the day the request was made fell within a period during which he ordinarily worked in Great Britain: Trade Union and Labour Relations (Consolidation) Act 1992 Sch A1 para 7(3) (as added: see note 3). For the purposes of Sch A1 para 7(3) and Sch A1 para 7(4) (see note 9), a worker who is employed on board a ship registered in the register maintained under the Merchant Shipping Act 1995 s 8 (see SHIPPING AND MARITIME LAW vol 93 (2008) PARA 254) is to be treated as ordinarily working in Great Britain unless: (1) the ship's entry in the register specifies a port outside Great Britain as the port to which the vessel is to be treated as belonging; (2) the employment is wholly outside Great Britain; or (3) the worker is not ordinarily resident in Great Britain: Trade Union and Labour Relations (Consolidation) Act 1992 Sch A1 para 7(5) (as so added). As to the meaning of 'Great Britain' see PARA 2 note 12.

   The Secretary of State may by order: (a) provide that Sch A1 para 7(1)–(5) is not to apply, or is not to apply in specified circumstances; or (b) vary the number of workers for the time being specified in Sch A1 para 7(1); and different provision may be made for different circumstances: Sch A1 para 7(6) (as so added). Such an order must be made by statutory instrument and may include supplementary, incidental, saving or transitional provisions: Sch A1 para 7(7) (as so added). No such order is to be made unless a draft of it has been laid before Parliament and approved by a resolution of each House of Parliament: Sch A1 para 7(8) (as so added). At the date at which this volume states the law no such order had been made.

   If the CAC represents to the Secretary of State that a provision of Sch A1 has an unsatisfactory effect and should be amended, the Secretary of State, with a view to rectifying the effect, may amend the provision by exercising any of the powers conferred on him by Sch A1 para 7(6), Sch A1 para 29(5) (see PARA 1122), Sch A1 para 121(6) (see PARA 1159 note 8), Sch A1 para 166A (see PARA 1111 note 14), Sch A1 para 166B (see PARA 1174), Sch A1 para 169A (see PARA 1100), Sch A1 para 169B (see PARA 1100) and Sch A1 para 171A (see PARA 1103), or may amend the provision by order in such other way as he thinks fit: Sch A1 para 166(1), (2) (Sch A1 para 166(1), (2) substituted, Sch A1 para 166(2A), (2B) added, and Sch A1 para 166(3) amended by the Employment Relations Act 2004 s 15). The Secretary of State need not proceed in a way proposed by the CAC, if it proposes one: Trade Union and Labour Relations (Consolidation) Act 1992 Sch A1 para 166(2A) (as so added). Nothing in Sch A1 para 166 prevents the Secretary of State from exercising any of the powers mentioned above in the absence of a representation from the CAC: Sch A1 para 166(2B) (as so added). Such an order must be made by statutory instrument; and no such order is to be made unless a draft of it has been laid before Parliament and approved by a resolution of each House of Parliament: Trade Union and Labour Relations (Consolidation) Act 1992 Sch A1 para 166(3), (4) (Sch A1 as added (see note 3); Sch A1 para 166(3) as so amended). At the date at which this volume states the law no such order had been made.

For the purposes of Sch A1 para 7(1)(2), an agency worker whose contract within the Agency Workers Regulations 2010, SI 2010/93, reg 3(1)(b) (contract with the temporary work agency: see PARA 97) is not a contract of employment is to be treated as having a contract of employment with the temporary work agency for the duration of the assignment with the employer (and 'assignment' has the same meaning as in those 2010 Regulations): Trade Union and Labour Relations (Consolidation) Act 1992 Sch A1 para 7(5A), (5B) (added by SI 2010/93).

9 To find the average: (1) take the number of workers employed in each of the 13 weeks, including workers not employed for the whole of the week; (2) aggregate the 13 numbers; and (3) divide the aggregate by 13: Trade Union and Labour Relations (Consolidation) Act 1992 Sch A1 para 7(2) (as added: see note 3). For these purposes, any worker employed by an associated company incorporated outside Great Britain is to be ignored in relation to a week unless the whole or any part of that week fell within a period during which he ordinarily worked in Great Britain: Sch A1 para 7(4) (as so added). See also note 8.

10 Trade Union and Labour Relations (Consolidation) Act 1992 Sch A1 para 7(1) (as added: see note 3). See also note 8.

11 As to the meaning of references to the bargaining unit see PARA 1103 note 3.

12 Ie is made under the Trade Union and Labour Relations (Consolidation) Act 1992 Sch A1 Pt I (paras 1–51).

13 Trade Union and Labour Relations (Consolidation) Act 1992 Sch A1 para 8 (as added: see note 3).

1105. Agreement between parties as to bargaining unit and recognition.

If, before the end of the first period[1], the parties[2] agree a bargaining unit[3] and that the union[4] is, or unions are, to be recognised as entitled to conduct collective bargaining[5] on behalf of the unit, no further steps[6] are to be taken[7]. If, before the end of the first period, the employer informs the union, or unions, that the employer does not accept the request for recognition but is willing to negotiate, the parties may conduct negotiations with a view to agreeing a bargaining unit and that the union is, or unions are, to be recognised as entitled to conduct collective bargaining on behalf of the unit[8].

If such an agreement is made before the end of the second period[9], no further steps[10] are to be taken[11]. The employer and the union, or unions, may request the Advisory, Conciliation and Arbitration Service[12] to assist in conducting the negotiations[13].

1 For these purposes, the first period is the period of ten working days starting with the day after that on which the employer receives the request for recognition: Trade Union and Labour Relations (Consolidation) Act 1992 Sch A1 para 10(6) (Sch A1 added by the Employment Relations Act 1999 Sch 1). For the purposes of the Trade Union and Labour Relations (Consolidation) Act 1992 Sch A1 in its application to a part of Great Britain, a working day is a day other than: (1) a Saturday or a Sunday; (2) Christmas Day or Good Friday; or (3) a day which is a bank holiday under the Banking and Financial Dealings Act 1971 (see TIME vol 97 (2010) PARA 321) in that part of Great Britain: Sch A1 para 172(2) (as so added). As to the

meaning of 'employer' see PARA 1103 note 3; and as to the meaning of 'recognition' see PARA 1094. As to the meaning of 'Great Britain' see PARA 2 note 12.

2   As to the meaning of references to the parties see PARA 1103 note 3.

3   As to the meaning of references to the bargaining unit see PARA 1103 note 3.

4   As to the meaning of 'trade union' see PARA 891.

5   As to the meaning of references to collective bargaining see PARA 1103 note 3.

6   Ie no further steps under the Trade Union and Labour Relations (Consolidation) Act 1992 Sch A1 Pt I (paras 1–51): see PARAS 1103–1104, 1106 et seq.

7   Trade Union and Labour Relations (Consolidation) Act 1992 Sch A1 para 10(1) (as added: see note 1).

8   Trade Union and Labour Relations (Consolidation) Act 1992 Sch A1 para 10(2), (3) (as added: see note 1).

9   For these purposes, the second period is: (1) the period of 20 working days starting with the day after that on which the first period ends; or (2) such longer period, so starting, as the parties may from time to time agree: Trade Union and Labour Relations (Consolidation) Act 1992 Sch A1 para 10(7) (as added: see note 1).

10 See note 6.

11 Trade Union and Labour Relations (Consolidation) Act 1992 Sch A1 para 10(4) (as added: see note 1).

12 As to the Advisory, Conciliation and Arbitration Service ('ACAS') see PARA 1213 et seq.

13 Trade Union and Labour Relations (Consolidation) Act 1992 Sch A1 para 10(5) (as added: see note 1).

1106. Procedure where employer rejects request for recognition. If:

  (1)   before the end of the first period[1], the employer[2] fails to respond to the request for recognition[3]; or

  (2)   before the end of the first period, the employer informs the union[4], or unions, that the employer does not accept the request, without indicating a willingness to negotiate,

the union, or unions, may apply to the Central Arbitration Committee[5] to decide both these questions:

  (a)   whether the proposed bargaining unit[6] is appropriate;

  (b)   whether the union has, or unions have, the support of a majority of the workers[7] constituting the appropriate bargaining unit[8].

1   As to the meaning of 'first period' see PARA 1105 note 1.

2   As to the meaning of 'employer' see PARA 1103 note 3.

3   As to the meaning of 'recognition' see PARA 1094.

4   As to the meaning of 'trade union' see PARA 891.

5   As to the Central Arbitration Committee see PARA 1226 et seq.

6   For these purposes, references to the proposed bargaining unit are to the bargaining unit proposed in the request for recognition: Trade Union and Labour Relations (Consolidation) Act 1992 Sch A1 para 2(1), (3) (Sch A1 added by the Employment Relations Act 1999 Sch 1). References to an appropriate bargaining unit's being decided by the Central Arbitration Committee are to a bargaining unit's being decided by the Central Arbitration Committee to be appropriate under the Trade Union and Labour Relations (Consolidation) Act 1992 Sch A1 para 19(2) or Sch A1 para 19(3) or Sch A1 para 19A(2) or (3) (see PARA 1110): Sch A1 para 2(3A) (added by the Employment Relations Act 2004 Sch 1 para 23(1), (2)). See also PARA 1103 note 3.

   As to provision made in relation to union communications with workers after the acceptance of an application to the Central Arbitration Committee see the Trade Union and Labour Relations (Consolidation) Act 1992 Sch A1 paras 19C–19F; and PARA 1111.

7   As to the meaning of 'worker' see PARA 892.

8   Trade Union and Labour Relations (Consolidation) Act 1992 Sch A1 paras 11(1), (2), 172(1) (Sch A1 as added (see note 6); Sch A1 para 11(2) amended by the Employment Relations Act 2004 s 1(1)).

   The term 'appropriate' in the Trade Union and Labour Relations (Consolidation) Act 1992 Sch A1 para 11(2) directs the Committee to examine whether the proposed bargaining unit is suitable enough for the purpose proposed: *R (on the application of Kwik-Fit (GB) Ltd) v Central Arbitration Committee* [2002] EWCA Civ 512, [2002] ICR 1212, [2002] IRLR 395.

1107.   Failure of negotiations on recognition.   If:

(1)   the employer[1] informs the union[2], or unions, that the employer does not accept the request for recognition but is willing to negotiate[3]; and

(2)   no agreement is made before the end of the second period[4],

the union, or unions, may apply to the Central Arbitration Committee[5] (the 'CAC') to decide both these questions:

(a)   whether the proposed bargaining unit[6] is appropriate;

(b)   whether the union has, or unions have, the support of a majority of the workers[7] constituting the appropriate bargaining unit[8].

If:

(i)   the employer informs the union, or unions, that the employer does not accept the request for recognition but is willing to negotiate[9]; and

(ii)   before the end of the second period, the parties[10] agree a bargaining unit but not that the union is, or unions are, to be recognised as entitled to conduct collective bargaining[11] on behalf of the unit,

the union, or unions, may apply to the CAC to decide the question whether the union has, or unions have, the support of a majority of the workers constituting the bargaining unit[12].

No application may, however, be made under the above provisions if, within the period of ten working days[13] starting with the day after that on which the employer so informs the union, or unions, that he does not accept the request for recognition but is willing to negotiate[14], the employer proposes that the Advisory, Conciliation and Arbitration Service[15] be requested to assist in conducting the negotiations and:

(A)   the union rejects, or unions reject, the proposal; or

(B)   the union fails, or unions fail, to accept the proposal within the period of ten working days starting with the day after that on which the employer makes the proposal[16].

1   As to the meaning of 'employer' see PARA 892.
2   As to the meaning of 'trade union' see PARA 891.
3   Ie under the Trade Union and Labour Relations (Consolidation) Act 1992 Sch A1 para 10(2): see PARA 1105.
4   As to the meaning of 'second period' see PARA 1105 note 9.
5   As to the Central Arbitration Committee see PARA 1226 et seq.
6   As to the meaning of references to the bargaining unit see PARA 1103 note 3; and as to the meaning of references to the proposed bargaining unit see PARA 1106 note 6.
7   As to the meaning of 'worker' see PARA 892.
8   Trade Union and Labour Relations (Consolidation) Act 1992 Sch A1 paras 12(1), (2), 172(1) (Sch A1 added by the Employment Relations Act 1999 Sch 1; the Trade Union and Labour Relations (Consolidation) Act 1992 Sch A1 para 11(2) amended by the Employment Relations Act 2004 s 1(2)).
        As to provision made in relation to union communications with workers after the acceptance of an application to the Central Arbitration Committee see the Trade Union and Labour Relations (Consolidation) Act 1992 Sch A1 paras 19C–19F; and PARA 1111.
9   See note 3.
10   As to the meaning of references to the parties see PARA 1103 note 3.
11   As to the meaning of references to collective bargaining see PARA 1103 note 3.
12   Trade Union and Labour Relations (Consolidation) Act 1992 Sch A1 para 12(3), (4) (as added: see note 8).
13   As to the meaning of 'working day' see PARA 1105 note 1.
14   See note 3.
15   As to the Advisory, Conciliation and Arbitration Service ('ACAS') see PARA 1213 et seq.
16   Trade Union and Labour Relations (Consolidation) Act 1992 Sch A1 para 12(5) (as added: see note 8).

C. ADMISSIBILITY AND ACCEPTANCE OF APPLICATIONS FOR RECOGNITION

1108.   Admissibility of applications for recognition.   An application is not admissible where the employer[1] rejects the request[2] or negotiations fail[3]:

(1)   unless it is made in such form, and supported by such documents, as the Central Arbitration Committee[4] (the 'CAC') specifies[5];

(2)   unless the union[6] gives, or unions give, to the employer notice of the application and a copy of the application and any documents supporting it[7];

(3)   if the CAC is satisfied that there is already in force a collective agreement[8] under which a union is, or unions are, recognised[9] as entitled to conduct collective bargaining[10] on behalf of any workers[11] falling within the relevant bargaining unit[12]; but that provision[13] does not apply to such an application if:

    (a)   the union, or unions, recognised under the collective agreement and the union, or unions, making the application are the same[14]; and

    (b)   the matters in respect of which the union is, or unions are, entitled to conduct collective bargaining do not include all of the following: pay, hours and holidays (the 'core topics')[15];

(4)   unless the CAC decides that:

    (a)   members of the union, or unions, constitute at least 10 per cent of the workers constituting the relevant bargaining unit[16]; and

    (b)   a majority of the workers constituting the relevant bargaining unit would be likely to favour recognition of the union, or unions, as entitled to conduct collective bargaining on behalf of the bargaining unit[17];

and the CAC must give reasons for the decision[18].

In the case of such an application made by more than one union, the application is not admissible unless:

(i)   the unions show that they will co-operate with each other in a manner likely to secure and maintain stable and effective collective bargaining arrangements; and

(ii)   the unions show that, if the employer wishes, they will enter into arrangements under which collective bargaining is conducted by the unions acting together on behalf of the workers constituting the relevant bargaining unit[19].

1   As to the meaning of 'employer' see PARA 892.
2   Ie under the Trade Union and Labour Relations (Consolidation) Act 1992 Sch A1 para 11: see PARA 1106.
3   Ie under the Trade Union and Labour Relations (Consolidation) Act 1992 Sch A1 para 12: see PARA 1107.
4   As to the Central Arbitration Committee see PARA 1226 et seq.
5   Trade Union and Labour Relations (Consolidation) Act 1992 Sch A1 paras 33, 172(1) (Sch A1 added by the Employment Relations Act 1999 Sch 1).
6   As to the meaning of 'trade union' see PARA 891.
7   Trade Union and Labour Relations (Consolidation) Act 1992 Sch A1 para 34 (as added: see note 5).
8   As to the meaning of 'collective agreement' see PARA 1093.
9   As to the meaning of 'recognised' see PARA 1094.
10   As to the meaning of references to collective bargaining see PARA 1103 note 3.
11   As to the meaning of 'worker' see PARA 892. The term 'on behalf of' does not specifically require the support of the workers: *R (on the application of the National Union of Journalists) v Central Arbitration Committee* [2005] EWCA Civ 1309, [2006] ICR 1, [2006] IRLR 53.

12 Trade Union and Labour Relations (Consolidation) Act 1992 Sch A1 para 35(1) (as added: see note 5). For these purposes, the relevant bargaining unit is (1) the proposed bargaining unit, where the application is under Sch A1 para 11(2) (see PARA 1106) or Sch A1 para 12(2) (see PARA 1107); (2) the agreed bargaining unit, where the application is under Sch A1 para 12(4) (see PARA 1107): Sch A1 para 35(6) (as so added). As to the meaning of references to the proposed bargaining unit see PARA 1106 note 6.

A declaration of recognition which is the subject of a declaration under Sch A1 para 83(2) (see PARA 1142) is, for the purposes of Sch A1 para 35(1) to be treated as ceasing to have effect to the extent specified in Sch A1 para 83(2) on the making of the declaration under Sch A1 para 83(2): Sch A1 para 35(3) (as so added).

In applying Sch A1 para 35(1), an agreement for recognition ('the agreement in question') must be ignored if: (a) the union does not have, or none of the unions has, a certificate of independence (see PARA 905); (b) at some time there was an agreement ('the old agreement') between the employer and the union under which the union, whether alone or with other unions, was recognised and entitled to conduct collective bargaining on behalf of a group of workers which was the same or substantially the same as the group covered by the agreement in question; and (c) the old agreement ceased to have effect in the period of three years ending with the date of the agreement in question: Sch A1 para 35(4) (as so added; amended by the Employment Relations Act 2004 s 50(6)).

There is no rule that an applicant union must be given priority over an existing one merely because it is more representative: *R (on the application of the National Union of Journalists) v Central Arbitration Committee* [2004] EWHC 2612 (Admin), [2005] ICR 493, [2005] IRLR 28.

The CAC must give effect to the Trade Union and Labour Relations (Consolidation) Act 1992 Sch A1 para 35 in accordance with its terms, even if that means that a union's right to engage in collective bargaining is violated: *R (on the application of Boots Management Services Ltd) v Central Arbitration Committee* [2014] EWHC 65 (Admin), [2014] IRLR 278, [2014] All ER (D) 148 (Jan).

13 Ie the Trade Union and Labour Relations (Consolidation) Act 1992 Sch A1 para 35(1).

14 It is for the CAC to decide whether one group of workers is the same or substantially the same as another; but, in deciding, the CAC may take account of the views of any person it believes has an interest in the matter: Trade Union and Labour Relations (Consolidation) Act 1992 Sch A1 para 35(5) (as added: see note 5). See also note 12.

15 Trade Union and Labour Relations (Consolidation) Act 1992 Sch A1 para 35(2) (as added (see note 5); amended by the Employment Relations Act 2004 s 11). See also note 12.

16 For these purposes, the relevant bargaining unit is: (1) the proposed bargaining unit, where the application is under the Trade Union and Labour Relations (Consolidation) Act 1992 Sch A1 para 11(2) (see PARA 1106) or Sch A1 para 12(2) (see PARA 1107); (2) the agreed bargaining unit, where the application is under Sch A1 para 12(4) (see PARA 1107): Sch A1 para 36(2) (as added: see note 5).

17 Trade Union and Labour Relations (Consolidation) Act 1992 Sch A1 para 36(1) (as added: see note 5).

18 Trade Union and Labour Relations (Consolidation) Act 1992 Sch A1 para 36(3) (as added: see note 5).

19 Trade Union and Labour Relations (Consolidation) Act 1992 Sch A1 para 37(1), (2) (as added: see note 5). For these purposes, the relevant bargaining unit is: (1) the proposed bargaining unit, where the application is under Sch A1 para 11(2) (see PARA 1106) or Sch A1 para 12(2) (see PARA 1107); (2) the agreed bargaining unit, where the application is under Sch A1 para 12(4) (see PARA 1107): Sch A1 para 37(3) (as so added; amended by the Employment Relations Act 2004 Sch 1 para 23(1), (8)).

1109. Acceptance of applications for recognition. The Central Arbitration Committee[1] (the 'CAC') must give notice to the parties[2] of receipt of an application made[3] by the union[4], or unions[5].

If:

(1)   two or more relevant applications[6] are made;

(2)   at least one worker[7] falling within one of the relevant bargaining units[8] also falls within the other relevant bargaining unit, or units; and

(3)   the CAC has not accepted any of the applications,

the following provisions apply[9].

Within the acceptance period[10], the CAC must decide, with regard to each relevant application, whether the 10 per cent test is satisfied[11]. The 10 per cent test is satisfied if members of the union, or unions, constitute at least 10 per cent of the workers constituting the relevant bargaining unit[12]. If the CAC decides that the 10 per cent test is satisfied with regard to:

(a)   more than one of the relevant applications, or the 10 per cent test is satisfied with regard to none of the relevant applications, the CAC must not accept any of the relevant applications[13];

(b)   one only of the relevant applications, the CAC must proceed[14] with regard to that application, and must not accept any of the other relevant applications[15].

The CAC must give notice of its decision to the parties[16]. If the CAC does not so accept an application, no further steps[17] are to be taken in relation to that application[18].

In the case of any application with regard to which no decision has to be made under the above provisions or any application with regard to which the CAC must proceed under the following provisions[19], the following provisions apply[20].

Within the acceptance period[21], the CAC must decide whether the request for recognition[22] to which the application relates is valid[23] and the application is duly made[24] and admissible[25] within the specified terms[26]. In deciding those questions, the CAC must consider any evidence which it has been given by the employer[27] or the union, or unions[28]. If the CAC decides that the request is not valid or that the application is not duly made or is not admissible:

(i)   the CAC must give notice of its decision to the parties;

(ii)   the CAC must not accept the application; and

(iii)   no further steps[29] are to be taken[30].

If the CAC decides that the request is valid and the application is duly made and is admissible, it must accept the application and give notice of the acceptance to the parties[31].

1   As to the Central Arbitration Committee see PARA 1226 et seq.
2   As to the meaning of references to the parties see PARA 1103 note 3.
3   Ie under the Trade Union and Labour Relations (Consolidation) Act 1992 Sch A1 para 11 (see PARA 1106) or Sch A1 para 12 (see PARA 1107).
4   As to the meaning of 'trade union' see PARA 891.
5   Trade Union and Labour Relations (Consolidation) Act 1992 Sch A1 paras 13, 172(1) (Sch A1 added by the Employment Relations Act 1999 Sch 1).
6   For these purposes, a relevant application is an application under the Trade Union and Labour Relations (Consolidation) Act 1992 Sch A1 para 11 or Sch A1 para 12: Sch A1 para 14(2) (as added: see note 5).
7   As to the meaning of 'worker' see PARA 892.
8   In relation to a relevant application, the relevant bargaining unit is: (1) the proposed bargaining unit, where the application is under the Trade Union and Labour Relations (Consolidation) Act 1992 Sch A1 para 11(2) (see PARA 1106) or Sch A1 para 12(2) (see PARA 1107); (2) the agreed bargaining unit, where the application is under Sch A1 para 12(4) (see PARA 1107): Sch A1 para 14(3) (as added: see note 5). As to the meaning of references to the bargaining unit see PARA 1103 note 3; and as to the meaning of references to the proposed bargaining unit see PARA 1106 note 6.
9   Trade Union and Labour Relations (Consolidation) Act 1992 Sch A1 para 14(1) (as added: see note 5).
10   For these purposes, the acceptance period is: (1) the period of ten working days starting with the day after that on which the CAC receives the last relevant application; or (2) such longer period, so starting, as the CAC may specify to the parties by notice containing reasons for the extension: Trade Union and Labour Relations (Consolidation) Act 1992 Sch A1 para 14(6) (as added: see note 5). As to the meaning of 'working day' see PARA 1105 note 1.
11   Trade Union and Labour Relations (Consolidation) Act 1992 Sch A1 para 14(4) (as added: see note 5).

12 Trade Union and Labour Relations (Consolidation) Act 1992 Sch A1 para 14(5) (as added: see note 5).
13 Trade Union and Labour Relations (Consolidation) Act 1992 Sch A1 para 14(7) (as added: see note 5).
14 Ie under the Trade Union and Labour Relations (Consolidation) Act 1992 Sch A1 para 15.
15 Trade Union and Labour Relations (Consolidation) Act 1992 Sch A1 para 14(8) (as added: see note 5).
16 Trade Union and Labour Relations (Consolidation) Act 1992 Sch A1 para 14(9) (as added: see note 5).
17 Ie no further steps under the Trade Union and Labour Relations (Consolidation) Act 1992 Sch A1 Pt I (paras 1–51): see PARAS 1103 et seq, 1110 et seq.
18 Trade Union and Labour Relations (Consolidation) Act 1992 Sch A1 para 14(10) (as added: see note 5).
19 Ie by virtue of the Trade Union and Labour Relations (Consolidation) Act 1992 Sch A1 para 14.
20 Trade Union and Labour Relations (Consolidation) Act 1992 Sch A1 para 15(1) (as added: see note 5).
21 For these purposes, the acceptance period is: (1) the period of ten working days starting with the day after that on which the CAC receives the application; or (2) such longer period, so starting, as the CAC may specify to the parties by notice containing reasons for the extension: Trade Union and Labour Relations (Consolidation) Act 1992 Sch A1 para 15(6) (as added: see note 5).
22 As to the meaning of 'recognition' see PARA 1094.
23 Ie within the terms of the Trade Union and Labour Relations (Consolidation) Act 1992 Sch A1 paras 5–9: see PARA 1104.
24 Ie in accordance with the Trade Union and Labour Relations (Consolidation) Act 1992 Sch A1 para 11 (see PARA 1106) or Sch A1 para 12 (see PARA 1107).
25 Ie admissible within the terms of the Trade Union and Labour Relations (Consolidation) Act 1992 Sch A1 paras 33–42: see PARAS 1108, 1125.
26 Trade Union and Labour Relations (Consolidation) Act 1992 Sch A1 para 15(2) (as added: see note 5).
27 As to the meaning of 'employer' see PARA 1103 note 3.
28 Trade Union and Labour Relations (Consolidation) Act 1992 Sch A1 para 15(3) (as added: see note 5).
29 See note 17.
30 Trade Union and Labour Relations (Consolidation) Act 1992 Sch A1 para 15(4) (as added: see note 5).
31 Trade Union and Labour Relations (Consolidation) Act 1992 Sch A1 para 15(5) (as added: see note 5).

1110. Appropriate bargaining unit. If the Central Arbitration Committee[1] (the 'CAC') accepts an application[2], it must try to help the parties[3] to reach, within the appropriate period[4], an agreement as to what the appropriate bargaining unit[5] is[6].

If the CAC accepts such an application[7], within five working days starting with the day after that on which the CAC gives the employer notice of acceptance of the application, the employer must supply to the union or unions, and to the CAC: (1) a list of the categories of worker in the proposed bargaining unit; (2) a list of the workplaces[8] at which the workers in the proposed bargaining unit work; and (3) the number of workers the employer reasonably believes to be in each category at each workplace[9].

If (a) the CAC accepts such an application[10]; (b) the parties have not agreed an appropriate bargaining unit at the end of the appropriate period[11]; and (c) at the end of that period either no relevant request[12] has been made or such a request has been made but the relevant condition[13] has not been met, the CAC must decide the appropriate bargaining unit within the decision period[14]. If the CAC decides that the proposed bargaining unit is not appropriate, it must also decide within the decision period a bargaining unit which is appropriate[15].

If (i) the CAC accepts such an application[16]; (ii) during the appropriate period the CAC is requested by the union or unions to make a decision; and (iii) the

CAC is, either at the time the request is made or at a later time during the appropriate period, of the opinion that the employer has failed to comply with the relevant duty[17], the CAC must decide whether the proposed bargaining unit is appropriate within the decision period[18]. If the CAC decides that the proposed bargaining unit is not appropriate, it must also decide within the decision period a bargaining unit which is appropriate[19].

If the CAC has to decide whether a bargaining unit is appropriate[20], it must take into account the need for the unit to be compatible with effective management and the following matters, so far as they do not conflict with that need:

(A) the views of the employer[21] and of the union[22], or unions;

(B) existing national and local bargaining arrangements;

(C) the desirability of avoiding small fragmented bargaining units within an undertaking[23];

(D) the characteristics of workers[24] falling within the bargaining unit under consideration and of any other employees[25] of the employer whom the CAC considers relevant;

(E) the location of workers[26].

The CAC must give notice of its decision to the parties[27].

1   As to the Central Arbitration Committee see PARA 1226 et seq.

2   Ie an application under the Trade Union and Labour Relations (Consolidation) Act 1992 Sch A1 para 11(2) (see PARA 1106) or Sch A1 para 12(2) (see PARA 1107).

3   As to the meaning of references to the parties see PARA 1103 note 3.

4   For these purposes, the appropriate period is (subject to any notice under the Trade Union and Labour Relations (Consolidation) Act 1992 Sch A1 para 18(3), (4) or (5): see below): (1) the period of 20 working days starting with the day after that on which the CAC gives notice of acceptance of the application; or (2) such longer period, so starting, as the CAC may specify to the parties by notice containing reasons for the extension: Sch A1 para 18(2) (Sch A1 added by the Employment Relations Act 1999 Sch 1; the Trade Union and Labour Relations (Consolidation) Act 1992 Sch A1 para 18(2) amended by the Employment Relations Act 2004 s 2(1), (2)). As to the meaning of 'working day' see PARA 1105 note 1.

    If, during the appropriate period, the CAC concludes that there is no reasonable prospect of the parties agreeing an appropriate bargaining unit before the time when, apart from this provision, the appropriate period would end, the CAC may, by a notice given to the parties, declare that the appropriate period ends with the date of the notice: Trade Union and Labour Relations (Consolidation) Act 1992 Sch A1 para 18(3) (Sch A1 para 18(3)–(7) added by the Employment Relations Act 2004 s 2(1), (3)). Such a notice must contain reasons for reaching the conclusion: Trade Union and Labour Relations (Consolidation) Act 1992 Sch A1 para 18(6) (as so added). If, during the appropriate period, the parties apply to the CAC for a declaration that the appropriate period is to end with a date, specified in the application, which is earlier than the date with which it would otherwise end, the CAC may, by a notice given to the parties, declare that the appropriate period ends with the specified date: Sch A1 para 18(4) (as so added). Where the CAC has made such a declaration, it may by notice given to the parties before the specified date specify a later date with which the appropriate period ends, and such notice must contain reasons for the extension of the appropriate period: Sch A1 para 18(5), (7) (as so added).

5   As to the meaning of references to the bargaining unit see PARA 1103 note 3.

6   Trade Union and Labour Relations (Consolidation) Act 1992 Sch A1 paras 18(1), 172(1) (as added: see note 4).

7   See note 2.

8   For the purposes of the Trade Union and Labour Relations (Consolidation) Act 1992 Sch A1 para 18A, the workplace at which a worker works is, if the person works at or from a single set of premises, those premises, and in any other case, the premises with which the worker's employment has the closest connection: Sch A1 para 18A(5) (Sch A1 para 18A added by the Employment Relations Act 2004 s 3).

9   Trade Union and Labour Relations (Consolidation) Act 1992 Sch A1 para 18A(1), (2) (as added: see note 8). The lists and numbers supplied must be as accurate as is reasonably practicable in the light of the information in the possession of the employer at the time he

complies with Sch A1 para 18A(2), and the lists and numbers supplied to the union or unions, and to the CAC must be the same: Sch A1 para 18A(3), (4) (as so added).

10 See note 2.

11 Ie defined by the Trade Union and Labour Relations (Consolidation) Act 1992 Sch A1 para 18: see the text and notes 1–6.

12 Ie no request under the Trade Union and Labour Relations (Consolidation) Act 1992 Sch A1 para 19A(1)(b): see head (ii) in the text.

13 Ie the condition in the Trade Union and Labour Relations (Consolidation) Act 1992 Sch A1 para 19A(1)(c): see head (iii) in the text.

14 Trade Union and Labour Relations (Consolidation) Act 1992 Sch A1 para 19(1), (2) (Sch A1 para 19 substituted, Sch A1 paras 19A, 19B added by the Employment Relations Act 2004 s 4). Here the decision period is: (1) the period of ten working days starting with the day after that on which the appropriate period ends; or (2) such longer period, so starting, as the CAC may specify to the parties by notice containing reasons for the extension: Trade Union and Labour Relations (Consolidation) Act 1992 Sch A1 para 19(4) (as so substituted).

15 Trade Union and Labour Relations (Consolidation) Act 1992 Sch A1 para 19(3) (as substituted: see note 14).

16 See note 2.

17 Ie the duty imposed by the Trade Union and Labour Relations (Consolidation) Act 1992 Sch A1 para 18A: see the text and notes 7–9.

18 Trade Union and Labour Relations (Consolidation) Act 1992 Sch A1 para 19A(1), (2) (as added: see note 14). Here the decision period is: (1) the period of ten working days starting with the day after that with on which the request is made; or (2) such longer period so starting as the CAC may specify to the parties by notice containing reasons for the extension: Sch A1 para 19A(4) (as so added).

19 Trade Union and Labour Relations (Consolidation) Act 1992 Sch A1 para 19A(3) (as added: see note 14).

20 Ie for the purposes of the Trade Union and Labour Relations (Consolidation) Act 1992 Sch A1 para 19(2) or (3) or Sch A1 para 19A(2) or (3).

21 As to the meaning of 'employer' see PARA 1103 note 3.

22 As to the meaning of 'trade union' see PARA 891.

23 As to the Trade Union and Labour Relations (Consolidation) Act 1992 Sch A1 para 19B(3)(c) (see head (C) in the text), in particular 'small fragmented bargaining units' see *R (on the application of Cable & Wireless Services UK Ltd) v Central Arbitration Committee* [2008] EWHC 115 (Admin), [2008] ICR 693, [2008] IRLR 425.

24 As to the meaning of 'worker' see PARA 892.

25 As to the meaning of 'employee' see PARA 892.

26 Trade Union and Labour Relations (Consolidation) Act 1992 Sch A1 para 19B(1)–(3) (as added: see note 14). In taking an employer's views into account for the purpose of deciding whether the proposed bargaining unit is appropriate, the CAC must take into account any view the employer has about any other bargaining unit that he considers would be appropriate: Sch A1 para 19B(4) (as so added).

27 Trade Union and Labour Relations (Consolidation) Act 1992 Sch A1 para 19B(5) (as added: see note 14).

1111. Union communications with workers after acceptance of application for recognition. If the Central Arbitration Committee[1] (the 'CAC') accepts an application[2], the union[3] or unions may apply to the CAC for the appointment of a suitable independent person[4] to handle communications during the initial period[5] between the union or unions and the relevant workers[6]. On such an application the CAC must as soon as reasonably practicable make the appointment required[7] and inform the parties of the name of the appointed person and the date of his appointment[8].

An employer[9] who is so informed by the CAC must, so far as it is reasonable to expect him to do so[10]:

(1)   give to the CAC, within the period of ten working days starting with the day after that on which the employer is informed, the names and home addresses of the relevant workers[11];

(2)   if the relevant workers change as a result of an appropriate bargaining

unit being agreed by the parties or decided by the CAC, give to the CAC, within the period of ten working days starting with the day after that on which the bargaining unit is agreed or the CAC's decision is notified to the employer, the names and home addresses of those who are now the relevant workers[12];

(3) give to the CAC, as soon as reasonably practicable, the name and home address of any worker who joins the bargaining unit after the employer has complied with head (1) or head (2) above[13]; and

(4) inform the CAC, as soon as reasonably practicable, of any worker whose name has been given to the CAC under head (1), head (2) or head (3) above and who ceases to be a relevant worker otherwise than by reason of a change mentioned in head (2) above[14].

As soon as reasonably practicable after it receives any such information, the CAC must pass it on to the appointed person[15].

During the initial period, the appointed person must, if asked to do so by the union or unions, send to any worker whose name and address have been passed on to the appointed person[16] and who is, so far as the appointed person is aware, still a relevant worker, any information supplied by the union, or unions, to the appointed person[17]. The costs of the appointed person[18] must be borne, if the application[19] was made by one union, by the union, and if the application was made by more than one union, by the unions in such proportions as they jointly indicate to the appointed person or, in the absence of such an indication, in equal shares[20]. The appointed person may send to the union, or each of the unions, a demand stating his costs and the amount of those costs to be borne by the recipient[21].

If the CAC is satisfied that the employer has failed to fulfil a duty[22] and the initial period has not yet ended, the CAC may order the employer to take such steps to remedy the failure as the CAC considers reasonable and specifies in the order[23], and to do so within such period as the CAC considers reasonable and specifies in the order[24]. If the CAC is satisfied that the employer has failed to comply with a remedial order[25] and the initial period has not yet ended, the CAC must as soon as reasonably practicable notify the employer and the union, or unions, that it is satisfied that the employer has failed to comply[26]. If:

(a) the CAC is satisfied that the employer has failed to comply with a remedial order;

(b) the parties have agreed an appropriate bargaining unit or the CAC has decided an appropriate bargaining unit;

(c) in the case of an application by the union or unions to the CAC to decide whether a proposed bargaining unit is appropriate or whether the union has, or unions have, the support of a majority of the workers constituting the bargaining unit[27], the CAC, if required to do so, has decided[28] that the application is not invalid; and

(d) the initial period has not yet ended[29],

the CAC may issue a declaration that the union is, or unions are, recognised as entitled to conduct collective bargaining on behalf of the workers constituting the bargaining unit[30].

1 As to the Central Arbitration Committee see PARA 1226 et seq.
2 Ie an application under the Trade Union and Labour Relations (Consolidation) Act 1992 Sch A1 para 11(2), 12(2) or (4): see PARAS 1106–1107.
3 As to the meaning of 'trade union' see PARA 891.
4 A person is a suitable independent person if he satisfies such conditions as may be specified for the purposes of the Trade Union and Labour Relations (Consolidation) Act 1992 Sch A1

para 25(7)(a) (see PARA 1118 note 15) by an order under that provision, or is himself specified for those purposes by such an order, and if there are no grounds for believing either that he will carry out any functions arising from his appointment otherwise than competently or that his independence in relation to those functions might reasonably be called into question: Sch A1 para 19C(6) (Sch A1 paras 19C–19F added by the Employment Relations Act 2004 s 5(1)).

5   The initial period is the period starting with the day on which the CAC informs the parties under the Trade Union and Labour Relations (Consolidation) Act 1992 Sch A1 para 19C(7)(b) (see the text and note 8) and ending with the first day on which (1) the application under Sch A1 para 11 or Sch 1A para 12 (see PARA 1107) is withdrawn; (2) the CAC gives notice to the union or unions of a decision under Sch A1 para 20 (see PARA 1114) that the application is invalid; (3) the CAC notifies the union or unions of a declaration issued under Sch A1 para 19F(5) (see the text and note 30) or 22(2) (see PARA 1117); or (4) the CAC informs the union or unions under Sch A1 para 25(9) (see PARA 1118) of the name of the person appointed to conduct a ballot: Sch A1 para 19C(5) (as added: see note 4). As to the meaning of references to the parties see PARA 1103 note 3.

6   Trade Union and Labour Relations (Consolidation) Act 1992 Sch A1 para 19C(1), (2) (as added: see note 4). In the case of an application under Sch A1 para 11(2) (see PARA 1106) or Sch A1 para 12(2) (see PARA 1107), the relevant workers are, in relation to any time before an appropriate bargaining unit is agreed by the parties or decided by the CAC, those falling within the proposed bargaining unit, and in relation to any time after an appropriate bargaining unit is so agreed or decided, those falling within the bargaining unit agreed or decided upon; and in the case of an application under Sch A1 para 12(4), the relevant workers are those falling within the bargaining unit agreed by the parties: Sch A1 para 19C(3), (4) (as so added). As to the meaning of references to the bargaining unit see PARA 1103 note 3.

7   Trade Union and Labour Relations (Consolidation) Act 1992 Sch A1 para 19C(7)(a) (as added: see note 4).

8   Trade Union and Labour Relations (Consolidation) Act 1992 Sch A1 para 19C(7)(b) (as added: see note 4).

9   As to the meaning of 'employer' see PARA 1103 note 3.

10 Trade Union and Labour Relations (Consolidation) Act 1992 Sch A1 para 19D(1) (as added: see note 4).

11 Trade Union and Labour Relations (Consolidation) Act 1992 Sch A1 para 19D(2)(a) (as added: see note 4).

12 Trade Union and Labour Relations (Consolidation) Act 1992 Sch A1 para 19D(2)(b) (as added: see note 4).

13 Trade Union and Labour Relations (Consolidation) Act 1992 Sch A1 para 19D(2)(c) (as added: see note 4).

14 Trade Union and Labour Relations (Consolidation) Act 1992 Sch A1 para 19D(2)(d) (as added: see note 4). Nothing in Sch A1 para 19D(2) requires the employer to give information to the CAC after the end of the initial period: Sch A1 para 19D(3) (as so added).

    The Secretary of State may by order provide, in relation to any provision of Sch A1 paras 19D(2), 26(4) (see also PARA 1120) or Sch A1 para 118(4) (see PARA 1157) which requires the employer to give to the CAC a worker's home address, that the employer must give to the CAC, in addition to the worker's home address, an address of a specified kind for the worker; and for these purposes, 'address' includes any address or number to which information may be sent by any means: Sch A1 para 166A(1)–(3) (Sch A1 para 166A added by the Employment Relations Act 2004 s 16). Such an order may amend the Trade Union and Labour Relations (Consolidation) Act 1992 Sch A1, include supplementary or incidental provision including, in particular, provision amending Sch A1 paras 19E(1)(a), 26(6)(a) (see also PARA 1120 head (i) in the text) or Sch A1 para 118(6)(a) (see PARA 1157), and make different provision for different cases or circumstances: Sch A1 para 166A(4) (as so added). As to the Secretary of State see PARA 5 note 21. Such an order must be made by statutory instrument, but no such order may be made unless a draft of it has been laid before Parliament and approved by a resolution of each House of Parliament: Sch A1 para 166A(5), (6) (as so added).

15 Trade Union and Labour Relations (Consolidation) Act 1992 Sch A1 para 19D(4) (as added: see note 4).

16 Ie under the Trade Union and Labour Relations (Consolidation) Act 1992 Sch A1 para 19D(4).

17 Trade Union and Labour Relations (Consolidation) Act 1992d Sch A1 para 19E(1) (as added: see note 4).

18 References to the costs of the appointed person are to (1) the costs wholly, exclusively and necessarily incurred by the appointed person in connection with handling during the initial period communications between the union or unions and the relevant workers; (2) such

reasonable amount as the appointed person charges for his services; and (3) such other costs as the union or unions agree: Trade Union and Labour Relations (Consolidation) Act 1992 Sch A1 para 19E(7) (as added: see note 4).

19 Ie the application under the Trade Union and Labour Relations (Consolidation) Act 1992 Sch A1 para 19C: see the text and notes 1–8.

20 Trade Union and Labour Relations (Consolidation) Act 1992 Sch A1 para 19E(2) (as added: see note 4).

21 Trade Union and Labour Relations (Consolidation) Act 1992 Sch A1 para 19E(3) (as added: see note 4). In such a case the recipient must pay the amount stated to the person sending the demand and must do so within 15 working days starting with the day after that on which the demand is received: Sch A1 para 19E(4) (as so added). If the amount stated is not paid accordingly it is, if the County Court so orders, recoverable under the County Courts Act 1984 s 85 (see CIVIL PROCEDURE vol 12 (2009) PARA 1283) or otherwise as if it were payable under an order of that court: Sch A1 para 19E(5) (as so added; amended by the Crime and Courts Act 2013 Sch 9 Pt 3 para 52(1)(b), (2)). Where a warrant of control is issued under the County Courts Act 1984 s 85 to recover an amount in accordance with the Trade Union and Labour Relations (Consolidation) Act 1992 Sch 1A para 19E(5), the power conferred by the warrant is exercisable to the same extent and in the same manner as if the union were a body corporate, against any property held in trust for the union other than protected property as defined in s 23(2) (see PARA 928): Sch A1 para 19E(6) (as so added; amended by the Tribunals, Courts and Enforcement Act 2007, s 62(3), Sch 13, paras 108, 109(1), (3)).

Where a demand has been made under the Trade Union and Labour Relations (Consolidation) Act 1992 Sch A1 para 19E(3), the recipient of the demand may appeal to an employment tribunal against the demand within four weeks starting with the day after receipt of the demand: Sch A1 para 165A(1)–(3) (Sch A1 para 165A added by the Employment Relations Act 2004 s 14). On an appeal against such a demand, the tribunal must dismiss the appeal unless it is shown that the amount specified in the demand as the costs of the appointed person is too great, or the amount specified in the demand as the amount of those costs to be borne by the recipient is too great: Trade Union and Labour Relations (Consolidation) Act 1992 Sch A1 para 165A(4) (as so added). If an appeal is allowed, the tribunal must rectify the demand and the demand has effect as if it had originally been made as so rectified: Sch A1 para 165A(6) (as so added). If a person has appealed against a demand and the appeal has not been withdrawn or finally determined, the demand is not enforceable until the appeal has been withdrawn or finally determined: Sch A1 para 165A(7)(a) (as so added). However, as from the withdrawal or final determination of the appeal, the demand is enforceable as if Sch A1 para 165A(7)(a) had not had effect: Sch A1 para 165A(7)(b) (as so added).

22 Ie a duty under the Trade Union and Labour Relations (Consolidation) Act 1992 Sch A1 para 19D(2): see the text and notes 11–14.

23 Trade Union and Labour Relations (Consolidation) Act 1992 Sch A1 para 19F(1)(a) (as added: see note 4).

24 Trade Union and Labour Relations (Consolidation) Act 1992 Sch A1 para 19F(1)(b) (as added: see note 4).

25 Ie an order under the Trade Union and Labour Relations (Consolidation) Act 1992 Sch A1 para 19F(1).

26 Trade Union and Labour Relations (Consolidation) Act 1992 Sch A1 para 19F(2) (as added: see note 4). A remedial order and a notice under Sch A1 para 19F(2) must draw the recipient's attention to the effect of Sch A1 para 19F(4), (5) (see the text and notes 27–30): Sch A1 para 19F(3) (as so added).

27 Ie an application under the Trade Union and Labour Relations (Consolidation) Act 1992 Sch A1 para 11(2) (see PARA 1106) or Sch A1 para 12(2) (see PARA 1107).

28 Ie under the Trade Union and Labour Relations (Consolidation) Act 1992 Sch A1 para 20: see PARA 1114.

29 Trade Union and Labour Relations (Consolidation) Act 1992 Sch A1 para 19F(4) (as added: see note 4).

30 Trade Union and Labour Relations (Consolidation) Act 1992 Sch A1 para 19F(5) (as added: see note 4).

D. WITHDRAWAL OF APPLICATION FOR RECOGNITION; NOTICE TO CEASE CONSIDERATION OF APPLICATION

1112. Withdrawal of application for recognition. If an application[1] is accepted by the Central Arbitration Committee[2] (the 'CAC'), the union[3], or unions, may not withdraw the application after:

(1) the CAC issues a declaration[4]; or

(2) the union, or the last of the unions, receives notice[5] that the CAC intends to arrange for the holding of a secret ballot[6].

If an application is withdrawn by the union, or unions, the CAC must give notice of the withdrawal to the employer[7]; and no further steps are[8] to be taken[9].

1 Ie an application under the Trade Union and Labour Relations (Consolidation) Act 1992 Sch A1 para 11(2) (see PARA 1106) or Sch A1 para 12(2) (see PARA 1107).
2 As to the Central Arbitration Committee see PARA 1226 et seq.
3 As to the meaning of 'trade union' see PARA 891.
4 Ie a declaration under the Trade Union and Labour Relations (Consolidation) Act 1992 Sch A1 para 19F(5) (see PARA 1111) or Sch A1 para 22(2) (see PARA 1117).
5 Ie under the Trade Union and Labour Relations (Consolidation) Act 1992 Sch A1 para 22(3) (see PARA 1117) or Sch A1 para 23(2) (see PARA 1118).
6 Trade Union and Labour Relations (Consolidation) Act 1992 Sch A1 paras 16(1), 172(1) (Sch A1 added by the Employment Relations Act 1999 Sch 1; and the Trade Union and Labour Relations (Consolidation) Act 1992 Sch A1 para 16(1) amended by the Employment Relations Act 2004 Sch 1 paras 23(1), (3)).
7 As to the meaning of 'employer' see PARA 1103 note 3.
8 Ie no further steps are to be taken under the Trade Union and Labour Relations (Consolidation) Act 1992 Sch A1 Pt I (paras 1–51): see PARAS 1103 et seq, 1113 et seq.
9 Trade Union and Labour Relations (Consolidation) Act 1992 Sch A1 para 16(2) (as added: see note 6).

1113. Notice to cease consideration of application for union recognition. If the Central Arbitration Committee[1] (the 'CAC') has received an application[2] and it has not decided whether the application is admissible, or it has decided that the application is admissible, no further steps are to be taken[3] if, before the final event occurs[4], the parties[5] give notice to the CAC that they want no further steps to be taken[6].

1 As to the Central Arbitration Committee see PARA 1226 et seq.
2 Ie under the Trade Union and Labour Relations (Consolidation) Act 1992 Sch A1 para 11(2) (see PARA 1106) or Sch A1 para 12(2) (see PARA 1107).
3 Ie under the Trade Union and Labour Relations (Consolidation) Act 1992 Sch A1 Pt I (paras 1–51): see PARAS 1103 et seq, 1114 et seq.
4 For these purposes, the final event occurs when the first of the following occurs: (1) the CAC issues a declaration under the Trade Union and Labour Relations (Consolidation) Act 1992 Sch A1 para 19F(5) (see PARA 1111) or Sch A1 para 22(2) (see PARA 1117) in consequence of the application; (2) the last day of the notification period ends; and the notification period is that defined by Sch A1 para 24(6) (see PARA 1118 note 10) and arising from the application: Sch A1 para 17(3) (Sch A1 added by the Employment Relations Act 1999 Sch 1; the Trade Union and Labour Relations (Consolidation) Act 1992 Sch A1 para 17(3) amended by the Employment Relations Act 2004 Sch 1 para 23(1), (4)).
5 As to the meaning of references to the parties see PARA 1103 note 3.
6 Trade Union and Labour Relations (Consolidation) Act 1992 Sch A1 paras 17(1), (2), 172(1) (as added: see note 4).

E. TRADE UNION RECOGNITION

1114. Validity of accepted application for union recognition; in general. If:

(1) the Central Arbitration Committee[1] (the 'CAC') accepts an application[2];

(2)   the parties[3] have agreed an appropriate bargaining unit[4] at the end of the appropriate period[5], or the CAC has decided an appropriate bargaining unit; and

(3)   that bargaining unit differs from the proposed bargaining unit[6],

then, within the decision period[7], the CAC must decide whether the application is[8] invalid[9].

In deciding whether the application is invalid, the CAC must consider any evidence which it has been given by the employer[10] or the union[11], or unions[12]. If the CAC decides that the application is invalid:

(a)   the CAC must give notice of its decision to the parties;

(b)   the CAC must not proceed with the application; and

(c)   no further steps[13] to be taken[14].

If the CAC decides that the application is not invalid, it must proceed with the application and give notice to the parties that it is so proceeding[15].

1   As to the Central Arbitration Committee see PARA 1226 et seq.
2   Ie under the Trade Union and Labour Relations (Consolidation) Act 1992 Sch A1 para 11(2) (see PARA 1106) or Sch A1 para 12(2) (see PARA 1107).
3   As to the meaning of references to the parties see PARA 1103 note 3.
4   As to the meaning of references to the bargaining unit see PARA 1103 note 3.
5   Ie defined by the Trade Union and Labour Relations (Consolidation) Act 1992 Sch A1 para 18: see PARA 1110.
6   As to the meaning of references to the proposed bargaining unit see PARA 1106 note 6.
7   For these purposes, the decision period is: (1) the period of ten working days starting with the day after that on which the parties agree an appropriate bargaining unit or the CAC decides an appropriate bargaining unit; or (2) such longer period, so starting, as the CAC may specify to the parties by notice containing reasons for the extension: Trade Union and Labour Relations (Consolidation) Act 1992 Sch A1 para 20(6) (Sch A1 added by the Employment Relations Act 1999 Sch 1). As to the meaning of 'working day' see PARA 1105 note 1.
8   Ie within the terms of the Trade Union and Labour Relations (Consolidation) Act 1992 Sch A1 paras 43–50: see PARA 1115.
9   Trade Union and Labour Relations (Consolidation) Act 1992 Sch A1 paras 20(1), (2), 172(1) (as added (see note 7); amended by the Employment Relations Act 2004 Sch 1 para 23(1), (5)).
10   As to the meaning of 'employer' see PARA 1103 note 3.
11   As to the meaning of 'trade union' see PARA 891.
12   Trade Union and Labour Relations (Consolidation) Act 1992 Sch A1 para 20(3) (as added: see note 7).
13   Ie no further steps under the Trade Union and Labour Relations (Consolidation) Act 1992 Sch A1 Pt I (paras 1–51): see PARAS 1103 et seq, 1115 et seq.
14   Trade Union and Labour Relations (Consolidation) Act 1992 Sch A1 para 20(4) (as added: see note 7).
15   Trade Union and Labour Relations (Consolidation) Act 1992 Sch A1 para 20(5) (as added: see note 7).

1115.   General provisions about validity of an application.   If the Central Arbitration Committee[1] (the 'CAC') has to decide[2] whether an application is valid, the following provisions[3] apply[4].

The application in question[5] is invalid:

(1)   if the CAC is satisfied that there is already in force a collective agreement[6] under which a union[7] is, or unions are, recognised[8] as entitled to conduct collective bargaining[9] on behalf of any workers[10] falling within the relevant bargaining unit[11]; but that provision does not apply to the application in question if:

(a)   the union, or unions, recognised under the collective agreement and the union, or unions, making the application in question are the same; and

(b)   the matters in respect of which the union is, or unions are, entitled to conduct collective bargaining do not include all of the following: pay, hours and holidays (the 'core topics')[12];

(2) unless the CAC decides that:

    (a) members of the union, or unions, constitute at least 10 per cent of the workers constituting the relevant bargaining unit; and

    (b) a majority of the workers constituting the relevant bargaining unit would be likely to favour recognition of the union, or unions, as entitled to conduct collective bargaining on behalf of the bargaining unit[13].

If:

(i) the CAC accepts an application[14] relating to a bargaining unit or proceeds[15] with an application relating to a bargaining unit;

(ii) the application has not been withdrawn[16];

(iii) no notice has been given that the parties want no further steps to be taken[17];

(iv) the CAC has not issued a declaration as to a union's entitlement or non-entitlement to recognition[18] in relation to that bargaining unit; and

(v) no notification has been made by a party or parties that they do not want the CAC to arrange for the holding of the ballot[19],

the application in question[20] is invalid if at least one worker falling within the relevant bargaining unit also falls within that bargaining unit and the application in question is made by a union, or unions, other than the union, or unions, which made that application[21].

If the CAC accepts an application[22] relating to a bargaining unit or proceeds[23] with an application relating to a bargaining unit, the application in question is invalid if the application is made within the period of three years starting with the day after that on which the CAC gave notice of acceptance of that application, the relevant bargaining unit is the same or substantially the same[24] as that bargaining unit and the application is made by the union, or unions, which made that application[25].

If the CAC issues a declaration[26] that a union is, or unions are, not entitled to be recognised as entitled to conduct collective bargaining on behalf of a bargaining unit[27], the application in question[28] is invalid if:

(A) the application is made within the period of three years starting with the date of the declaration;

(B) the relevant bargaining unit is the same or substantially the same[29] as the bargaining unit mentioned above; and

(C) the application is made by the union, or unions, which made the application leading to the declaration[30].

If the CAC issues a declaration[31] that bargaining arrangements are to cease to have effect, the application in question is invalid[32] if the application is made within the period of three years starting with the day after that on which the declaration was issued, the relevant bargaining unit is the same or substantially the same[33] as the bargaining unit to which the bargaining arrangements mentioned above relate and the application is made by the union which was a party, or unions which were parties, to the proceedings leading to the declaration[34].

1   As to the Central Arbitration Committee see PARA 1226 et seq.

2   Ie under the Trade Union and Labour Relations (Consolidation) Act 1992 Sch A1 para 20: see PARA 1114.

3   Ie the Trade Union and Labour Relations (Consolidation) Act 1992 Sch A1 paras 44–50: see the text and notes 4–34.

4 Trade Union and Labour Relations (Consolidation) Act 1992 Sch A1 paras 43(1), 172(1) (Sch A1 added by the Employment Relations Act 1999 Sch 1).

5 For these purposes, references to the application in question are to the application the validity of which the CAC has to decide under the Trade Union and Labour Relations (Consolidation) Act 1992 Sch A1 para 20 (see PARA 1114): Sch A1 para 43(2)(a) (as added: see note 4).

6 As to the meaning of 'collective agreement' see PARA 1093.

7 As to the meaning of 'trade union' see PARA 891.

8 As to the meaning of 'recognised' and cognate expressions see PARA 1094.

9 As to the meaning of references to collective bargaining see PARA 1103 note 3.

10 As to the meaning of 'worker' see PARA 892.

11 Trade Union and Labour Relations (Consolidation) Act 1992 Sch A1 para 44(1) (as added: see note 4). For these purposes, references to the relevant bargaining unit are to the bargaining unit agreed by the parties or decided by the CAC: Sch A1 para 43(2)(b) (as so added). As to the meanings of references to the bargaining unit and to the parties see PARA 1103 note 3.

A declaration of recognition which is the subject of a declaration under Sch A1 para 83(2) (see PARA 1142) is, for the purposes of Sch A1 para 44(1) to be treated as ceasing to have effect to the extent specified in Sch A1 para 83(2) on the making of the declaration under Sch A1 para 83(2): Sch A1 para 44(3) (as so added).

In applying Sch A1 para 44(1), an agreement for recognition ('the agreement in question') is to be ignored if: (1) the union does not have, or none of the unions has, a certificate of independence (see PARA 905); (2) at some time there was an agreement ('the old agreement') between the employer and the union under which the union, whether alone or with other unions, was recognised as entitled to conduct collective bargaining on behalf of a group of workers which was the same or substantially the same as the group covered by the agreement in question; and (3) the old agreement ceased to have effect in the period of three years ending with the date of the agreement in question: Sch A1 para 44(4) (as so added; amended by the Employment Relations Act 2004 s 50(6)). It is for the CAC to decide whether one group of workers is the same or substantially the same as another; but, in deciding, the CAC may take account of the views of any person it believes has an interest in the matter: Trade Union and Labour Relations (Consolidation) Act 1992 Sch A1 para 44(5) (as so added). As to the meaning of 'employer' see PARA 1103 note 3.

12 Trade Union and Labour Relations (Consolidation) Act 1992 Sch A1 para 44(2) (as added (see note 4); amended by the Employment Relations Act 2004 s 11). See (in a slightly different context) *R (on the application of the National Union of Journalists) v Central Arbitration Committee* [2004] EWHC 2612 (Admin), [2005] ICR 493, [2005] IRLR 28, cited in PARA 1108.

13 Trade Union and Labour Relations (Consolidation) Act 1992 Sch A1 para 45 (as added: see note 4).

14 Ie under the Trade Union and Labour Relations (Consolidation) Act 1992 Sch A1 para 11(2) (see PARA 1106) or Sch A1 para 12(2) (see PARA 1107).

15 See note 2.

16 As to the withdrawal of an application see PARA 1112.

17 Ie no notice has been given under the Trade Union and Labour Relations (Consolidation) Act 1992 Sch A1 para 17(2): see PARA 1113.

18 Ie a declaration under the Trade Union and Labour Relations (Consolidation) Act 1992 Sch A1 para 19F(5) (see PARA 1111), Sch A1 para 22(2) (see PARA 1117), Sch A1 para 27(2) (see PARA 1120), Sch A1 para 27D(3) (see PARA 1119), Sch A1 para 27D(4) (see PARA 1119), Sch A1 para 29(3) (see PARA 1122) or Sch A1 para 29(4) (see PARA 1122).

19 Ie under the Trade Union and Labour Relations (Consolidation) Act 1992 Sch A1 para 24(2): see PARA 1118.

20 See note 5.

21 Trade Union and Labour Relations (Consolidation) Act 1992 Sch A1 para 46(1), (2) (as added (see note 4); Sch A1 para 46(1) amended by the Employment Relations Act 2004 Sch 1 paras 23(1), (12)).

22 See note 14.

23 See note 2.

24 For these purposes, it is for the CAC to decide whether one bargaining unit is the same or substantially the same as another; but, in deciding, the CAC may take account of the views of any person it believes as an interest in the matter: Trade Union and Labour Relations (Consolidation) Act 1992 Sch A1 para 50(1), (2) (as added: see note 4).

25 Trade Union and Labour Relations (Consolidation) Act 1992 Sch A1 para 47(1), (2) (as added: see note 4). Schedule A1 para 47 does not apply if Sch A1 para 48 or Sch A1 para 49 (see the text and notes 31–34) applies: Sch A1 para 47(3) (as so added).

26 Ie under the Trade Union and Labour Relations (Consolidation) Act 1992 Sch A1 para 27D(4) (see PARA 1119) or Sch A1 para 29(4) (see PARA 1122).

27 Ie whether the ballot concerned is arranged under the Trade Union and Labour Relations (Consolidation) Act 1992 Sch A1 Pt I (paras 1–52) (see PARAS 1103 et seq, 1126) or Sch A1 Pt III (paras 64–95) (see PARA 1132 et seq).

28 See note 5.

29 For these purposes, it is for the CAC to decide whether one bargaining unit is the same or substantially the same as another; but, in deciding, the CAC may take account of the views of any person it believes has an interest in the matter: Trade Union and Labour Relations (Consolidation) Act 1992 Sch A1 para 50(1), (2) (as added: see note 4).

30 Trade Union and Labour Relations (Consolidation) Act 1992 Sch A1 para 48(1), (2) (as added (see note 4); Sch A1 para 48(1) amended by the Employment Relations Act 2004 Sch 1 para 23(1), (13)(a)).

31 Ie under the Trade Union and Labour Relations (Consolidation) Act 1992 Sch A1 para 119D(4), (5) (see PARA 1156) or Sch A1 para 121(3) (see PARA 1159).

32 Ie whether the ballot concerned is arranged under the Trade Union and Labour Relations (Consolidation) Act 1992 Sch A1 Pt IV (paras 96–121) (see PARA 1149 et seq) or Sch A1 Pt V (paras 122–133) (see PARA 1160 et seq).

33 See note 29.

34 Trade Union and Labour Relations (Consolidation) Act 1992 Sch A1 para 49(1), (2) (as added (see note 4); amended by the Employment Relations Act 2004 Sch 1 para 23(1), (14)(a)).

1116. Duty to proceed with accepted application for union recognition. If:

(1)   the Central Arbitration Committee[1] (the 'CAC') accepts an application[2];

(2)   the parties[3] have agreed an appropriate bargaining unit[4] at the end of the appropriate period[5], or the CAC has decided an appropriate bargaining unit; and

(3)   that bargaining unit is the same as the proposed bargaining unit,

or if the CAC accepts an application to decide the question whether the union[6] has, or unions have, the support of a majority of the workers[7] constituting the bargaining unit[8], the CAC must proceed with the application[9].

1   As to the Central Arbitration Committee see PARA 1226 et seq.

2   Ie under the Trade Union and Labour Relations (Consolidation) Act 1992 Sch A1 para 11(2) (see PARA 1106) or Sch A1 para 12(2) (see PARA 1107).

3   As to the meaning of references to the parties see PARA 1103 note 3.

4   As to the meaning of references to the bargaining unit see PARA 1103 note 3.

5   Ie defined by the Trade Union and Labour Relations (Consolidation) Act 1992 Sch A1 para 18: see PARA 1110.

6   As to the meaning of 'trade union' see PARA 891.

7   As to the meaning of 'worker' see PARA 892.

8   Ie an application under the Trade Union and Labour Relations (Consolidation) Act 1992 Sch A1 para 12(4): see PARA 1107.

9   Trade Union and Labour Relations (Consolidation) Act 1992 Sch A1 paras 21(1)–(3), 172(1) (Sch A1 added by the Employment Relations Act 1999 Sch 1; the Trade Union and Labour Relations (Consolidation) Act 1992 Sch A1 para 21(1) amended by the Employment Relations Act 2004 Sch 1 para 23(1), (5)).

1117. Issuing of declaration regarding union recognition. If:

(1)   the Central Arbitration Committee[1] (the 'CAC') proceeds with an application[2]; and

(2)   the CAC is satisfied that a majority of the workers[3] constituting the bargaining unit[4] are members of the union[5], or unions,

the CAC must issue a declaration that the union is, or unions are, recognised[6] as entitled to conduct collective bargaining[7] on behalf of the workers constituting the bargaining unit[8].

If, however, any of the three qualifying conditions specified below is fulfilled, then, instead of issuing such a declaration, the CAC must give notice to the parties[9] that it intends to arrange for the holding of a secret ballot in which the workers constituting the bargaining unit are asked whether they want the union, or unions, to conduct collective bargaining on their behalf[10]. Those three qualifying conditions are:

(a) the CAC is satisfied that a ballot should be held in the interests of good industrial relations;

(b) the CAC has evidence, which it considers to be credible, from a significant number of the union members within the bargaining unit that they do not want the union (or unions) to conduct collective bargaining on their behalf;

(c) membership evidence[11] is produced which leads the CAC to conclude that there are doubts whether a significant number of the union members within the bargaining unit want the union, or unions, to conduct collective bargaining on their behalf[12].

1 As to the Central Arbitration Committee see PARA 1226 et seq.
2 Ie proceeds with an application in accordance with the Trade Union and Labour Relations (Consolidation) Act 1992 Sch A1 para 20 (see PARA 1114) or Sch A1 para 21 (see PARA 1116) and makes no declaration under Sch A1 para 19F(5) (see PARA 1111).
3 As to the meaning of 'worker' see PARA 892.
4 As to the meaning of references to the bargaining unit see PARA 1103 note 3.
5 As to the meaning of 'trade union' see PARA 891.
6 As to the meaning of 'recognised' see PARA 1094.
7 As to the meaning of 'collective bargaining' see PARA 1103 note 3.
8 Trade Union and Labour Relations (Consolidation) Act 1992 Sch A1 paras 22(1), (2), 172(1) (Sch A1 added by the Employment Relations Act 1999 Sch 1; the Trade Union and Labour Relations (Consolidation) Act 1992 Sch A1 para 22(1) amended by the Employment Relations Act 2004 s 5(2)).
   The Secretary of State may issue guidance to the CAC on the way in which it is to exercise its functions under the Trade Union and Labour Relations (Consolidation) Act 1992 Sch A1 para 22; and the CAC must take into account any such guidance in exercising those functions: Sch A1 para 167(1), (2) (as so added). No guidance is, however, to apply with regard to an application made to the CAC before the guidance in question was issued: Sch A1 para 167(3) (as so added). The Secretary of State must lay before each House of Parliament any guidance so issued and arrange for any such guidance to be published by such means as appear to him to be most appropriate for drawing it to the attention of persons likely to be affected by it: Sch A1 para 167(4) (as so added).
9 As to the meaning of references to the parties see PARA 1103 note 3.
10 Trade Union and Labour Relations (Consolidation) Act 1992 Sch A1 para 22(3) (as added: see note 8).
11 For these purposes, membership evidence is: (1) evidence about the circumstances in which union members became members; (2) evidence about the length of time for which union members have been members, in a case where the CAC is satisfied that such evidence should be taken into account: Trade Union and Labour Relations (Consolidation) Act 1992 Sch A1 para 22(5) (as added: see note 8).
12 Trade Union and Labour Relations (Consolidation) Act 1992 Sch A1 para 22(4) (as added (see note 8); amended by the Employment Relations Act 2004 s 6(1)).

1118. Secret recognition ballot. If:

(1) the Central Arbitration Committee[1] (the 'CAC') proceeds with an application[2]; and

(2) the CAC is not satisfied that a majority of the workers constituting the bargaining unit[3] are members of the union[4], or unions,

the CAC must give notice to the parties[5] that it intends to arrange for the holding of a secret ballot in which the workers[6] constituting the bargaining unit are asked whether they want the union, or unions, to conduct collective bargaining[7] on their behalf[8].

If the CAC gives notice[9], then, within the notification period[10], the union, or unions, or the union, or unions, and the employer, may notify the CAC that the party making the notification does not, or the parties making the notification do not, want the CAC to arrange for the holding of the ballot[11]. If the CAC is so notified:

(a)   it must not arrange for the holding of the ballot;

(b)   it must inform the parties that it will not arrange for the holding of the ballot and why; and

(c)   no further steps[12] to be taken[13];

and, if the CAC is not so notified, it must arrange for the holding of the ballot[14]. If the CAC so arranges for the holding of a ballot, the ballot must:

(i)   be conducted by a qualified independent person[15] appointed by the CAC[16];

(ii) be conducted within the period of 20 working days starting with the day after that on which the qualified independent person is appointed or such longer period, so starting, as the CAC may decide[17];

(iii) be conducted at a workplace or workplaces decided by the CAC, by post or by a combination of those methods[18], depending on the CAC's preference[19].

In deciding how the ballot is to be conducted, the CAC must take into account the likelihood of the ballot being affected by unfairness or malpractice if it were conducted at a workplace or workplaces, costs and practicality and such other matters as the CAC considers appropriate[20]. As soon as is reasonably practicable after the CAC is required[21] to arrange for the holding of a ballot, it must inform the parties:

(A)   that it is so required;

(B)   of the name of the person appointed to conduct the ballot and the date of his appointment;

(C)   of the period within which the ballot must be conducted;

(D)   whether the ballot is to be conducted by post or at a workplace or workplaces;

(E)   of the workplace or workplaces concerned, if the ballot is to be conducted at a workplace or workplaces[22].

1   As to the Central Arbitration Committee see PARA 1226 et seq.

2   Ie proceeds with an application in accordance with the Trade Union and Labour Relations (Consolidation) Act 1992 Sch A1 para 20 (see PARA 1114) or Sch A1 para 21 (see PARA 1116) and makes no declaration under Sch A1 para 19F(5) (see PARA 1111).

3   As to the meaning of references to the bargaining unit see PARA 1103 note 3.

4   As to the meaning of 'trade union' see PARA 891.

5   As to the meaning of references to the parties see PARA 1103 note 3.

6   As to the meaning of 'worker' see PARA 892.

7   As to the meaning of references to collective bargaining see PARA 1103 note 3.

8   Trade Union and Labour Relations (Consolidation) Act 1992 Sch A1 paras 23(1), (2), 172(1) (Sch A1 added by the Employment Relations Act 1999 Sch 1; the Trade Union and Labour Relations (Consolidation) Act 1992 Sch A1 para 23(1) amended by the Employment Relations Act 2004 s 5(2)).

9   Ie under the Trade Union and Labour Relations (Consolidation) Act 1992 Sch A1 para 22(3) (see PARA 1117) or Sch A1 para 23(2) (see the text and notes 1–8).

10 The notification period is, in relation to notification by the union (or unions), (1) the period of ten working days starting with the day on which the union (or last of the unions) receives the CAC's notice under the Trade Union and Labour Relations (Consolidation) Act 1992 Sch A1 para 22(3) (see PARA 1117) or Sch A1 para 23(2) (see the text and notes 1–8); or (2) such longer period so starting as the CAC may specify to the parties by notice: Sch A1 para 24(5) (Sch A1 para 24(5) substituted, Sch A1 para 24(6), (7) added by the Employment Relations Act 2004 s 7). As to the meaning of 'working day' see PARA 1105 note 1; and as to the meaning of

'employer' see PARA 1103 note 3. The notification period is, in relation to notification by the union (or unions) and the employer, (a) the period of ten working days starting with the day on which the last of the parties receives the CAC's notice under the Trade Union and Labour Relations (Consolidation) Act 1992 Sch A1 para 22(3) or Sch A1 para 23(2); or (b) such longer period so starting as the CAC may specify to the parties by notice: Sch A1 para 24(6) (as so added). The CAC may give a notice under Sch A1 para 24(5)(b) (see head (2) above) or Sch A1 para 24(6)(b) (see head (b) above) only if the parties have applied jointly to it for the giving of such a notice: Sch A1 para 24(7) (as so added).

11 Trade Union and Labour Relations (Consolidation) Act 1992 Sch A1 para 24(1), (2) (as added: see note 8).

12 Ie no further steps under the Trade Union and Labour Relations (Consolidation) Act 1992 Sch A1 Pt I (paras 1–51) (see PARAS 1103 et seq, 1119 et seq).

13 Trade Union and Labour Relations (Consolidation) Act 1992 Sch A1 para 24(3) (as added: see note 8).

14 Trade Union and Labour Relations (Consolidation) Act 1992 Sch A1 para 24(4) (as added: see note 8).

15 For these purposes, a person is a qualified independent person if: (1) he satisfies such conditions as may be specified for these purposes by order of the Secretary of State or is himself so specified; and (2) there are no grounds for believing either that he will carry out any functions conferred on him in relation to the ballot otherwise than competently or that his independence in relation to the ballot might reasonably be called into question: Trade Union and Labour Relations (Consolidation) Act 1992 Sch A1 para 25(7) (as added: see note 8). An order under head (1) above must be made by statutory instrument subject to annulment in pursuance of a resolution of either House of Parliament: Sch A1 para 25(8) (as so added). In exercise of the power so conferred the Secretary of State made the Recognition and Derecognition Ballots (Qualified Persons) Order 2000, SI 2000/1306, which came into force on 6 June 2000: art 1(1).

The conditions so specified are that: (a) in relation to an individual, he has in force a practising certificate issued by the Law Society of England and Wales or the Law Society of Scotland or is eligible for appointment as a statutory auditor under the Companies Act 2006 Pt 42 (ss 1209–1264) (see COMPANIES vol 15 (2009) PARA 957 et seq); and (b) in relation to a partnership, every member of the partnership is an individual who satisfies the condition specified in head (a) above: Recognition and Derecognition Ballots (Qualified Persons) Order 2000, SI 2000/1306, arts 2, 3 (amended by SI 2010/437). The persons so specified are Association of Electoral Administrators; DRS Data Services Limited; Electoral Reform Services Limited; Involvement and Participation Association; Opt2Vote Limited; and Popularis Limited: Recognition and Derecognition Ballots (Qualified Persons) Order 2000, SI 2000/1306, art 4 (substituted by SI 2010/437).

16 Trade Union and Labour Relations (Consolidation) Act 1992 Sch A1 para 25(1), (2) (as added: see note 8).

17 Trade Union and Labour Relations (Consolidation) Act 1992 Sch A1 para 25(1), (3) (as added: see note 8).

18 The CAC may not decide that the ballot is to be so conducted unless there are special factors making such a decision appropriate; and special factors include: (1) factors arising from the location of workers or the nature of their employment; and (2) factors put to the CAC by the employer or the union, or unions: Trade Union and Labour Relations (Consolidation) Act 1992 Sch A1 para 25(1), (6) (as added: see note 8).

If the CAC decides that the ballot must, in whole or in part, be conducted at a workplace or workplaces, it may require arrangements to be made for workers who, but for the arrangements, would be prevented by the CAC's decision from voting by post, and who are unable, for reasons relating to those workers as individuals, to cast their votes in the ballot at the workplace or at any of the workplaces, to be given the opportunity to vote by post, if they request it far enough in advance of the ballot for it to be practicable: Sch A1 para 25(6A) (added by the Employment Relations Act 2004 s 8(1)). The CAC's imposition of such a requirement is not to be treated for the purposes of the Trade Union and Labour Relations (Consolidation) Act 1992 Sch A1 para 25(6) as a decision that the ballot must be conducted as mentioned in Sch A1 para 25(4)(c) (ie the combination of methods referred to in head (iii) in the text): Sch A1 para 25(6A) (as so added).

19 Trade Union and Labour Relations (Consolidation) Act 1992 Sch A1 para 25(1), (4) (as added: see Recognition and Derecognition Ballots (Qualified Persons) Order 2000, SI 2000/1306, arts 2, 3 (amended by SI 2010/437).).

20 Trade Union and Labour Relations (Consolidation) Act 1992 Sch A1 para 25(1), (5) (as added: see note 8).

21 Ie under the Trade Union and Labour Relations (Consolidation) Act 1992 Sch A1 para 24.

22 Trade Union and Labour Relations (Consolidation) Act 1992 Sch A1 para 25(1), (9) (as added: see note 8). Each of the parties so informed must refrain from using any unfair practice: see Sch A1 paras 27A–27F; and PARA 1119.

1119. Unfair practices in relation to recognition ballots. Each of the parties[1] informed by the Central Arbitration Committee[2] (the 'CAC') must refrain from using any unfair practice[3]. A party uses an unfair practice if, with a view to influencing the result of the ballot, the party:

(1) offers to pay money or give money's worth to a worker[4] entitled to vote in the ballot in return for the worker's agreement to vote in a particular way or to abstain from voting;

(2) makes an outcome-specific offer[5] to a worker entitled to vote in the ballot;

(3) coerces or attempts to coerce a worker entitled to vote in the ballot to disclose
    (a) whether he intends to vote or abstain from voting in the ballot; or
    (b) how he intends to vote, or how he has voted, in the ballot;

(4) dismisses or threatens to dismiss a worker;

(5) takes or threatens to take disciplinary action against a worker;

(6) subjects or threatens to subject a worker to any other detriment; or

(7) uses or attempts to use undue influence on a worker entitled to vote in the ballot[6].

A party may complain to the CAC that another party has failed to comply with the above provisions[7]. The CAC must decide within the decision period[8] whether the complaint is well-founded[9]. If the CAC decides that such a complaint is well-founded, it must, as soon as is reasonably practicable, issue a declaration to that effect[10]. It may also (i) order the party concerned to take any action specified in the order within such period as may be so specified[11]; and/or (ii) give notice to the employer[12] and to the union or unions that it intends to arrange for the holding of a secret ballot in which the workers constituting the bargaining unit are asked whether they want the union or unions to conduct collective bargaining on their behalf[13].

If the CAC issues a declaration that a complaint is well-founded and the declaration states that the unfair practice used consisted of or included the use of violence or the dismissal of a union official, or if the CAC has made an order under head (i) above and (A) it is satisfied that the party subject to the order has failed to comply with it; or (B) it makes another declaration in relation to a complaint against that party, then if the party concerned is the employer, the CAC may issue a declaration that the union is, or unions are, recognised as entitled to conduct collective bargaining on behalf of the bargaining unit[14]. If the party concerned is a union, the CAC may issue a declaration that the union is, or unions are, not entitled to be so recognised[15].

If the CAC issues a declaration that a complaint is well-founded and gives notice under head (ii) above or issues a declaration under head (B) above, then if the ballot in connection with which the complaint was made has not been held, the CAC must take steps to cancel it[16]. If that ballot is held, it will have no effect[17].

1 As to the meaning of references to the parties see PARA 1103 note 3.
2 Ie informed under the Trade Union and Labour Relations (Consolidation) Act 1992 Sch A1 para 25(9): see PARA 1118. As to the Central Arbitration Committee see PARA 1226 et seq.
3 Trade Union and Labour Relations (Consolidation) Act 1992 Sch A1 para 27A(1) (Sch A1 paras 27A–27F added by the Employment Relations Act 2004 s 10(1)).

4 As to the meaning of 'worker' see PARA 892.

5 For these purposes, an outcome-specific offer is an offer to pay money or give money's worth which (1) is conditional on the issuing by the CAC of a declaration that the union is, or unions are, recognised as entitled to conduct collective bargaining on behalf of the bargaining unit, or the union is, or unions are, not entitled to be so recognised; and (2) is not conditional on anything which is done or occurs as a result of the declaration in question: Trade Union and Labour Relations (Consolidation) Act 1992 Sch A1 para 27A(3) (as added: see note 3). As to the meaning of 'trade union' see PARA 891.

6 Trade Union and Labour Relations (Consolidation) Act 1992 Sch A1 para 27A(2) (as added: see note 3). The duty imposed by Sch A1 para 27A does not confer any rights on a worker, but that does not affect any other right which a worker may have: Sch A1 para 27A(4) (as so added). The power of the Advisory, Conciliation and Arbitration Service under s 199(1) (see PARA 1223) and the power of the Secretary of State under s 203(1)(a) (see PARA 1231 head (1) in the text) are to be taken to include power to issue Codes of Practice about unfair practices for the purposes of Sch A1 para 27A: Sch A1 para 27A(5) (as so added). As to the Advisory, Conciliation and Arbitration Service ('ACAS') see PARA 1213 et seq.

7 Trade Union and Labour Relations (Consolidation) Act 1992 Sch A1 para 27B(1) (as added: see note 3). A complaint must be made on or before the first working day after the date of the ballot or, if votes may be cast in the ballot on more than one day, the last of those days: Sch A1 para 27B(2) (as so added). As to the meaning of 'working day' see PARA 1105 note 1.

8 The decision period is the period of ten working days starting with the day after that on which the complaint was received by the CAC, or such longer period so starting as the CAC may specify to the parties by a notice containing reasons for the extension: Trade Union and Labour Relations (Consolidation) Act 1992 Sch A1 para 27B(5) (as added: see note 3). If, at the beginning of the decision period, the ballot has not begun, the CAC may by notice to the parties and the qualified independent person postpone the date on which it is to begin until a date which falls after the end of the decision period: Sch A1 para 27B(6) (as so added). As to the meaning of 'qualified independent person' see PARA 1118 note 15.

9 Trade Union and Labour Relations (Consolidation) Act 1992 Sch A1 para 27B(3) (as added: see note 3). A complaint is well-founded if the CAC finds that the party complained against used an unfair practice and the CAC is satisfied that the use of that practice changed or was likely to change, in the case of a worker entitled to vote in the ballot, his intention to vote or to abstain from voting, his intention to vote in a particular way or how he voted: Sch A1 para 27B(4) (as so added).

10 Trade Union and Labour Relations (Consolidation) Act 1992 Sch A1 para 27C(1), (2) (as added: see note 3).

11 Trade Union and Labour Relations (Consolidation) Act 1992 Sch A1 para 27C(1), (3)(a) (as added: see note 3). The action specified in such an order must be such as the CAC considers reasonable in order to mitigate the effect of the failure of the party concerned to comply with the duty imposed by Sch A1 para 27A (see the text and notes 1–6): Sch A1 para 27C(1), (5) (as so added). The CAC may give more than one such order: Sch A1 para 27C(1), (6) (as so added).

12 As to the meaning of 'employer' see PARA 892.

13 Trade Union and Labour Relations (Consolidation) Act 1992 Sch A1 para 27C(1), (3)(b) (as added: see note 3). The CAC may give an order or notice under Sch A1 para 27C(3) either at the same time as it issues a declaration under Sch A1 para 27C(2) or at any other time before it acts under Sch A1 para 29 (see PARA 1122): Sch A1 para 27C(4) (as so added). If the CAC gives a notice under Sch A1 para 27C(3)(b), Sch A1 paras 24–29 (see PARAS 1118–1122) apply, with modifications, as they apply in relation to a notice given under Sch A1 para 22(3) (see PARA 1117) or Sch A1 para 23(2) (see PARA 1118): see Sch A1 para 27F(1), (2) (as so added). In each of Sch A1 para 24(5)(a), (6)(a) (see PARA 1118 note 10) for 'ten working days' there is substituted 'five working days' for these purposes: Sch A1 para 27F(3) (as so added). For these purposes, an employer's duty under Sch A1 para 26(4)(a) (see PARA 1120 head (3)(a) in the text) is limited to (1) giving the CAC the names and home addresses of any workers in the bargaining unit which have not previously been given to it in accordance with that duty; (2) giving the CAC the names and home addresses of those workers who have joined the bargaining unit since he last gave the CAC information in accordance with that duty; (3) informing the CAC of any change to the name or home address of a worker whose name and home address have previously been given to the CAC in accordance with that duty; and (4) informing the CAC of any worker whose name had previously been given to it in accordance with that duty who has ceased to be within the bargaining unit: Sch A1 para 27F(4) (as so added). Any order given under Sch A1 para 27(1) or Sch A1 para 27C(3)(a) (see PARA 1119) for the purposes of the cancelled or ineffectual ballot is to have effect (to the extent that the CAC specifies in a notice to the parties) as if it were made for the purposes of the ballot to which the notice under Sch A1

para 27C(3)(b) relates: Sch A1 para 27F(5) (as so added). The gross costs of the ballot are to be borne by such of the parties and in such proportions as the CAC may determine and, accordingly, Sch A1 para 28(2), (3) (see PARA 1121) is omitted and the reference in Sch A1 para 28(4) to the employer and the union (or each of the unions) is construed as a reference to the party or parties which bear the costs in accordance with the CAC's determination: Sch A1 para 27F(6) (as so added).

14 Trade Union and Labour Relations (Consolidation) Act 1992 Sch A1 para 27D(1)–(3) (as added: see note 3).

15 Trade Union and Labour Relations (Consolidation) Act 1992 Sch A1 para 27D(1), (2), (4) (as added: see note 3). The powers conferred by Sch A1 para 27D are in addition to those conferred by Sch A1 para 27C(3): Sch A1 para 27D(5) (as so added).

16 Trade Union and Labour Relations (Consolidation) Act 1992 Sch A1 para 27E(1), (2) (as added: see note 3).

17 Trade Union and Labour Relations (Consolidation) Act 1992 Sch A1 para 27E(1), (3) (as added: see note 3).

1120.   Employer's duties with regard to recognition ballot.   An employer[1] who is informed by the Central Arbitration Committee[2] (the 'CAC') that a ballot is required and of the arrangements for the ballot[3] must comply with the following five duties[4]:

(1) the first duty is to co-operate generally, in connection with the ballot, with the union[5], or unions, and the person appointed to conduct the ballot, the second and third duties not prejudicing the generality of this[6];

(2) the second duty is to give the union, or unions, such access to the workers[7] constituting the bargaining unit[8] as is reasonable to enable the union, or unions, to inform the workers of the object of the ballot and to seek their support and their opinions on the issues involved[9];

(3) the third duty is to do the following, so far as it is reasonable to expect the employer to do so:

(a) to give to the CAC, within the period of ten working days[10] starting with the day after that on which the employer is informed that a ballot is required and of the arrangements for the ballot[11], the names and home addresses of the workers constituting the bargaining unit;

(b) to give to the CAC, as soon as is reasonably practicable, the name and home address of any worker who joins the unit after the employer has complied with head (3)(a) above;

(c) to inform the CAC, as soon as is reasonably practicable, of any worker whose name has been given to the CAC under the relevant other provision[12] or under head (3)(a) or (3)(b) above and who ceases to be within the unit[13];.

(4) the fourth duty is to refrain from making any offer to any or all of the workers constituting the bargaining unit which:

(a) has or is likely to have the effect of inducing any or all of them not to attend any relevant meeting[14] between the union, or unions, and the workers constituting the bargaining unit; and

(b) is not reasonable in the circumstances[15]; and

(5) the fifth duty is to refrain from taking or threatening to take any action against a worker solely or mainly on the grounds that he:

(a) attended or took part in any relevant meeting between the union, or unions, and the workers constituting the bargaining unit; or

(b) indicated his intention to attend or take part in such a meeting[16].

As soon as is reasonably practicable after the CAC receives any information under head (3) above, it must pass it on to the person appointed to conduct the ballot[17]. If asked to do so by the union, or unions, the person appointed to conduct the ballot must send to any worker:

(i)   whose name and home address have been passed on to him[18]; and

(ii)   who is still within the unit, so far as the person so appointed is aware, any information supplied by the union, or unions, to the person so appointed[19]; but that duty does not apply unless the union bears, or unions bear, the cost of sending the information[20].

If the CAC is satisfied that the employer has failed to fulfil any of the above duties imposed on him[21], and the ballot has not been held, the CAC may order the employer:

(A)   to take such steps to remedy the failure as the CAC considers reasonable and specifies in the order; and

(B)   to do so within such period as the CAC considers reasonable and specifies in the order[22].

If the CAC is satisfied that the employer has failed to comply with such an order, and the ballot has not been held, the CAC may issue a declaration that the union is, or unions are, recognised as entitled to conduct collective bargaining on behalf of the bargaining unit[23]. If the CAC issues such a declaration, it must take steps to cancel the holding of the ballot; and, if the ballot is held, it has no effect[24].

1   As to the meaning of 'employer' see PARA 892.
2   As to the Central Arbitration Committee see PARA 1226 et seq.
3   Ie under the Trade Union and Labour Relations (Consolidation) Act 1992 Sch A1 para 25(9): see PARA 1118.
4   Trade Union and Labour Relations (Consolidation) Act 1992 Sch A1 paras 26(1), 172(1) (Sch A1 added by the Employment Relations Act 1999 Sch 1; the Trade Union and Labour Relations (Consolidation) Act 1992 Sch A1 para 26(1) amended by the Employment Relations Act 2004 s 9(1), (2)).
5   As to the meaning of 'trade union' see PARA 891.
6   Trade Union and Labour Relations (Consolidation) Act 1992 Sch A1 para 26(2) (as added: see note 4).
7   As to the meaning of 'worker' see PARA 892.
8   As to the meaning of references to the bargaining unit see PARA 1103 note 3.
9   Trade Union and Labour Relations (Consolidation) Act 1992 Sch A1 para 26(3) (as added: see note 4).
     Without prejudice to the generality of the second duty, an employer is to be taken to have failed to comply with that duty if: (1) he refuses a request for a meeting between the union or unions and any or all of the workers constituting the bargaining unit to be held in the absence of the employer or any representative of his, other than one who has been invited to attend the meeting, and it is not reasonable in the circumstances for him to do so; (2) he or a representative of his attends such a meeting without having been invited to do so; (3) he seeks to record or otherwise be informed of the proceedings at any such meeting and it is not reasonable in the circumstances for him to do so; or (4) he refuses to give an undertaking that he will not seek to record or otherwise be informed of the proceedings at any such meeting unless it is reasonable in the circumstances for him to do either of those things: Sch A1 para 26(4D) (Sch A1 para 26(4A)–(4E) added by the Employment Relations Act 2004 s 9(1), (3)).
     Each of the following powers is to be taken to include power to issue Codes of Practice about reasonable access for the purposes of the Trade Union and Labour Relations (Consolidation) Act 1992 Sch A1 para 26(3), and about the fourth duty (see head (4) in the text): (a) the power of the Advisory, Conciliation and Arbitration Service under s 199(1) (see PARA 1223); (b) the power of the Secretary of State under s 203(1)(a) (see PARA 1231 head (1) in the text): Sch A1 para 26(8), (9) (Sch A1 para 26(8) substituted, Sch A1 para 26(9) added by the Employment Relations Act 2004 s 9(1), (4)). See also PARA 1174. As to the Advisory, Conciliation and Arbitration Service ('ACAS') see PARA 1213 et seq.
10   As to the meaning of 'working day' see PARA 1105 note 1.

11 Ie under the Trade Union and Labour Relations (Consolidation) Act 1992 Sch A1 para 25(9): see PARA 1118.

12 Ie under the Trade Union and Labour Relations (Consolidation) Act 1992 Sch A1 para 19D: see PARA 1111.

13 Trade Union and Labour Relations (Consolidation) Act 1992 Sch A1 para 26(4) (as added (see note 4); and amended by the Employment Relations Act 2004 s 5(3)).
    Head (3)(a) in the text does not apply to names and addresses that the employer has already given to the CAC under Sch A1 para 19D (see PARA 1111): Sch A1 para 26(4F) (Sch A1 para 26(4F)–(4H) added by the Employment Relations Act 2004 s 5(4)). Where, because of the Trade Union and Labour Relations (Consolidation) Act 1992 Sch A1 para 26(4F), the employer does not have to comply with head (3)(a) in the text, the reference in head (3)(b) in the text to the time when the employer complied with head (3)(a) in the text is to be read as a reference to the time when the employer is informed under Sch A1 para 25(9) (see PARA 1118): Sch A1 para 26(4G) (as so added). If a person was appointed on an application under Sch A1 para 19C (see PARA 1111), and the person appointed to conduct the ballot is not that person, the CAC must, as soon as is reasonably practicable, pass on to the person appointed to conduct the ballot the names and addresses given to it under Sch A1 para 19D (see PARA 1111): Sch A1 para 26(4H) (as so added).
    As to the type of order which the Secretary of State may make in relation to any provision of Sch A1 para 26(4) which requires the employer to give to the CAC a worker's home address, see Sch A1 para 166A; and PARA 1111 note 14.

14 A meeting is a relevant meeting in relation to a worker for the purposes of the Trade Union and Labour Relations (Consolidation) Act 1992 Sch A1 para 26(4A), (4B) if it is organised in accordance with any agreement reached concerning the second duty (see head (2) in the text) or as a result of a step ordered to be taken under Sch A1 para 27 (see the text and notes 21–24) to remedy a failure to comply with that duty and it is one which the employer is, by such an agreement or order, required to permit the worker to attend: Sch A1 para 26(4C) (as added: see note 9).

15 Trade Union and Labour Relations (Consolidation) Act 1992 Sch A1 para 26(4A) (as added: see note 9). The fourth and fifth duties do not confer any rights on a worker, but that does not affect any other right which a worker may have: Sch A1 para 26(4E) (as so added).

16 Trade Union and Labour Relations (Consolidation) Act 1992 Sch A1 para 26(4B) (as added: see note 9). See also Sch A1 para 26(4E); and note 15.

17 Trade Union and Labour Relations (Consolidation) Act 1992 Sch A1 para 26(5) (as added: see note 4).

18 Ie under the Trade Union and Labour Relations (Consolidation) Act 1992 Sch A1 para 19D: see PARA 1111.

19 Trade Union and Labour Relations (Consolidation) Act 1992 Sch A1 para 26(6) (as added (see note 4); amended by the Employment Relations Act 2004 s 5(5)).

20 Trade Union and Labour Relations (Consolidation) Act 1992 Sch A1 para 26(7) (as added: see note 4).

21 Ie by the Trade Union and Labour Relations (Consolidation) Act 1992 Sch A1 para 26.

22 Trade Union and Labour Relations (Consolidation) Act 1992 Sch A1 para 27(1) (as added (see note 4); amended by the Employment Relations Act 2004 s 9(1), (5)).

23 Trade Union and Labour Relations (Consolidation) Act 1992 Sch A1 para 27(2) (as added: see note 4).

24 Trade Union and Labour Relations (Consolidation) Act 1992 Sch A1 para 27(3) (as added: see note 4).

1121. Costs of recognition ballot. If the holding of a ballot has been arranged[1], and whether or not it has been cancelled, the following provisions apply[2].

The gross costs of the ballot[3] must be borne as to half, by the employer, and as to half, by the union, or unions[4]. If there is more than one union, they must bear their half of the gross costs in such proportions as they jointly indicate to the person appointed to conduct the ballot or, in the absence of such an indication, in equal shares[5]. The person appointed to conduct the ballot may send to the employer and the union, or each of the unions, a demand stating the gross costs of the ballot and the amount of the gross costs to be borne by the recipient[6]. In such a case, the recipient must pay the amount stated to the person sending the demand, and must do so within the period of 15 working days[7] starting with the day after that on which the demand is received[8].

1   Ie under the Trade Union and Labour Relations (Consolidation) Act 1992 Sch A1 para 24: see PARA 1118.

2   Trade Union and Labour Relations (Consolidation) Act 1992 Sch A1 para 28(1) (Sch A1 added by the Employment Relations Act 1999 Sch 1).

3   For these purposes, references to the costs of the ballot are to: (1) the costs wholly, exclusively and necessarily incurred in connection with the ballot by the person appointed to conduct it; (2) such reasonable amount as the person appointed to conduct the ballot charges for his services; and (3) such other costs as the employer and the union, or unions, agree: Trade Union and Labour Relations (Consolidation) Act 1992 Sch A1 para 28(7) (as added: see note 2). As to the meaning of 'employer' see PARA 1103 note 3; and as to the meaning of 'trade union' see PARA 891.

4   Trade Union and Labour Relations (Consolidation) Act 1992 Sch A1 para 28(2) (as added: see note 2).

5   Trade Union and Labour Relations (Consolidation) Act 1992 Sch A1 para 28(3) (as added: see note 2).

6   Trade Union and Labour Relations (Consolidation) Act 1992 Sch A1 para 28(4) (as added: see note 2). Where a demand has been made under Sch A1 para 28(4) or Sch A1 para 120(4) (see PARA 1158), the recipient of the demand may appeal to an employment tribunal against the demand within four weeks starting with the day after receipt of the demand: Sch A1 para 165A(1)–(3) (Sch A1 para 165A added by the Employment Relations Act 2004 s 14). On an appeal against such a demand, the tribunal must dismiss the appeal unless it is shown that the amount specified in the demand as the gross costs of the ballot is too great, or the amount specified in the demand as the amount of the gross costs to be borne by the recipient is too great: Trade Union and Labour Relations (Consolidation) Act 1992 Sch A1 para 165A(5) (as so added). If an appeal is allowed, the tribunal must rectify the demand and the demand has effect as if it had originally been made as so rectified: Sch A1 para 165A(6) (as so added). If a person has appealed against a demand and the appeal has not been withdrawn or finally determined, the demand is not enforceable until the appeal has been withdrawn or finally determined: Sch A1 para 165A(7)(a) (as so added). However, as from the withdrawal or final determination of the appeal, the demand is enforceable as if Sch A1 para 165A(7)(a) had not had effect: Sch A1 para 165A(7)(b) (as so added). As to employment tribunals see PARA 1399 et seq.

7   As to the meaning of 'working day' see PARA 1105 note 1.

8   Trade Union and Labour Relations (Consolidation) Act 1992 Sch A1 para 28(5) (as added: see note 2). In England and Wales, if the amount stated is not so paid it is, if the County Court so orders, recoverable under the County Courts Act 1984 s 85 (see CIVIL PROCEDURE vol 12 (2009) PARA 1283) or otherwise as if it were payable under an order of that court: Trade Union and Labour Relations (Consolidation) Act 1992 Sch A1 para 28(6) (as added (see note 2); amended by the Tribunals, Courts and Enforcement Act 2007 Sch 13 paras 108, 110(1), (2); the Crime and Courts Act 2013 Sch 9 Pt 3 para 52(1)(b), (2)). Where a warrant of control is issued under the County Courts Act 1984 s 85 to recover an amount in accordance with the Trade Union and Labour Relations (Consolidation) Act 1992 Sch A1 para 28(6), the power conferred by the warrant is exercisable to the same extent and in the same manner as if the union were a body corporate, against any property held in trust for the union other than protected property as defined in s 23(2) (see PARA 928): Sch A1 para 28(6A) (added by the Employment Relations Act 2004 Sch 1 para 23(1), (6); amended by the Tribunals, Courts and Enforcement Act 2007 Sch 13, paras 108, 110(1), (3)).

1122.   Procedure following recognition ballot. As soon as is reasonably practicable after the Central Arbitration Committee[1] (the 'CAC') is informed of the result of a ballot by the person conducting it, the CAC must act under the following provisions[2].

The CAC must inform the employer[3] and the union[4], or unions, of the result of the ballot[5]. If the result is that the union is, or unions are, supported by a majority of the workers[6] voting, and at least 40 per cent of the workers constituting the bargaining unit[7], the CAC must issue a declaration that the union is, or unions are, recognised as entitled to conduct collective bargaining[8] on behalf of the bargaining unit[9]. If the result is otherwise, the CAC must issue a declaration that the union is, or unions are, not entitled to be so recognised[10].

1   As to the Central Arbitration Committee see PARA 1226 et seq.
2   Trade Union and Labour Relations (Consolidation) Act 1992 Sch A1 paras 29(1), 172(1) (Sch A1 added by the Employment Relations Act 1999 Sch 1). The duty to act does not apply if the CAC gives a notice under the Trade Union and Labour Relations (Consolidation) Act 1992 Sch A1 para 27C(3)(b) (see PARA 1119): Sch A1 para 29(1A) (added by the Employment Relations Act 2004 s 10(2)).
    The CAC has jurisdiction to investigate the circumstances of a ballot and, if appropriate, to order a ballot to be rerun to remedy a defect in the previous ballot: *R (on the application of Ultraframe (UK) Ltd) v Central Arbitration Committee* [2005] EWCA Civ 560, [2005] ICR 1194, [2005] IRLR 641.
3   As to the meaning of 'employer' see PARA 1103 note 3.
4   As to the meaning of 'trade union' see PARA 891.
5   Trade Union and Labour Relations (Consolidation) Act 1992 Sch A1 para 29(2) (as added: see note 2).
6   As to the meaning of 'worker' see PARA 892.
7   As to the meaning of references to the bargaining unit see PARA 1103 note 3.
8   As to the meaning of references to collective bargaining see PARA 1103 note 3.
9   Trade Union and Labour Relations (Consolidation) Act 1992 Sch A1 para 29(3) (as added: see note 2). The Secretary of State may by order amend Sch A1 para 29(3) so as to specify a different degree of support; and different provision may be made for different circumstances: Sch A1 para 29(5) (as so added). Such an order must be made by statutory instrument; but no such order is to be made unless a draft of it has been laid before Parliament and approved by a resolution of each House of Parliament: Sch A1 para 29(6), (7) (as so added). At the date at which this volume states the law no such order had been made.
10 Trade Union and Labour Relations (Consolidation) Act 1992 Sch A1 para 29(4) (as added: see note 2).

F. CONSEQUENCES OF RECOGNITION

1123. Consequences of trade union recognition. If the Central Arbitration Committee[1] (the 'CAC') issues a declaration[2] that the union[3] is, or unions are, recognised[4] as entitled to conduct collective bargaining[5] on behalf of a bargaining unit[6], the parties[7] may in the negotiation period[8] conduct negotiations with a view to agreeing a method by which they will conduct collective bargaining[9]; and, if no agreement is made in the negotiation period, the employer[10] or the union, or unions, may apply to the CAC for assistance[11].

If an application for assistance is so made to the CAC, the following provisions apply[12]. The CAC must try to help the parties to reach in the agreement period[13] an agreement on a method by which they will conduct collective bargaining[14]. If, at the end of the agreement period, the parties have not made such an agreement, the CAC must specify to the parties the method by which they are to conduct collective bargaining[15]. Any method so specified has effect as if it were contained in a legally enforceable contract made by the parties[16]; but, if the parties agree in writing that that provision is not to apply, or is not to apply to particular parts of the method specified by the CAC, or to vary or replace the method specified by the CAC, the written agreement has effect as a legally enforceable contract made by the parties[17]. Specific performance is the only remedy available for breach of anything which is such a legally enforceable contract[18]. If, at any time before a specification is made[19], the parties jointly apply to the CAC requesting it to stop taking steps under the above provisions[20], the CAC must comply with the request[21].

1   As to the Central Arbitration Committee see PARA 1226 et seq.

2 Ie under the Trade Union and Labour Relations (Consolidation) Act 1992 Sch A1 Pt I (paras 1–51): see PARAS 1103 et seq, 1124 et seq.
3 As to the meaning of 'trade union' see PARA 891.
4 As to the meaning of 'recognised' see PARA 1094.
5 As to the meaning of references to collective bargaining see PARA 1103 note 3.
6 As to the meaning of references to the bargaining unit see PARA 1103 note 3.
7 As to the meaning of references to the parties see PARA 1103 note 3.
8 For these purposes, the negotiation period is: (1) the period of 30 working days starting with the start day; or (2) such longer period, so starting, as the parties may from time to time agree: Trade Union and Labour Relations (Consolidation) Act 1992 Sch A1 para 30(4) (Sch A1 added by the Employment Relations Act 1999 Sch 1). As to the meaning of 'working day' see PARA 1105 note 1. The start day is the day after that on which the parties are notified of the declaration: Trade Union and Labour Relations (Consolidation) Act 1992 Sch A1 para 30(5) (as so added).
9 Trade Union and Labour Relations (Consolidation) Act 1992 Sch A1 paras 30(1), (2), 172(1) (as added: see note 8). As to the position where the agreed method is not carried out see PARA 1124.
10 As to the meaning of 'employer' see PARA 1103 note 3.
11 Trade Union and Labour Relations (Consolidation) Act 1992 Sch A1 para 30(3) (as added: see note 8).
12 Trade Union and Labour Relations (Consolidation) Act 1992 Sch A1 para 31(1) (as added: see note 8).
13 For these purposes, the agreement period is: (1) the period of 20 working days starting with the day after that on which the CAC receives the application under the Trade Union and Labour Relations (Consolidation) Act 1992 Sch A1 para 30; or (2) such longer period, so starting, as the CAC may decide with the consent of the parties: Sch A1 para 31(8) (as added: see note 8).
14 Trade Union and Labour Relations (Consolidation) Act 1992 Sch A1 para 31(2) (as added: see note 8).
15 Trade Union and Labour Relations (Consolidation) Act 1992 Sch A1 para 31(3) (as added: see note 8). After consulting the Advisory, Conciliation and Arbitration Service, the Secretary of State may by order specify a method by which collective bargaining might be conducted: Sch A1 para 168(1) (as so added). If such an order is made, the CAC must take it into account under Sch A1 para 31(3), but may depart from the method specified by the order to such extent as the CAC thinks it is appropriate to do so in the circumstances: Sch A1 para 168(2) (as so added). Such an order must be made by statutory instrument subject to annulment in pursuance of a resolution of either House of Parliament: Sch A1 para 168(3) (as so added). In exercise of the power so conferred the Secretary of State made the Trade Union Recognition (Method of Collective Bargaining) Order 2000, SI 2000/1300, which came into force on 6 June 2000: art 1. The method specified for the purposes of the Trade Union and Labour Relations (Consolidation) Act 1992 Sch A1 para 31(3) is the method set out under the heading 'the specified method' in the Trade Union Recognition (Method of Collective Bargaining) Order 2000, SI 2000/1300, art 2, Schedule: art 2. As to the Advisory, Conciliation and Arbitration Service ('ACAS') see PARA 1213 et seq.
16 Trade Union and Labour Relations (Consolidation) Act 1992 Sch A1 para 31(4) (as added: see note 8).
17 Trade Union and Labour Relations (Consolidation) Act 1992 Sch A1 para 31(5) (as added: see note 8).
18 Trade Union and Labour Relations (Consolidation) Act 1992 Sch A1 para 31(6) (as added: see note 8).
19 Ie under the Trade Union and Labour Relations (Consolidation) Act 1992 Sch A1 para 31(3).
20 Ie under the Trade Union and Labour Relations (Consolidation) Act 1992 Sch A1 para 31.
21 Trade Union and Labour Relations (Consolidation) Act 1992 Sch A1 para 31(7) (as added: see note 8).

1124. Failure to carry out agreed method of conducting collective bargaining.
If:

(1) the Central Arbitration Committee[1] (the 'CAC') issues a declaration[2] that the union[3] is, or unions are, recognised[4] as entitled to conduct collective bargaining[5] on behalf of a bargaining unit[6];

(2) the parties[7] agree a method by which they will conduct collective bargaining; and

(3) one or more of the parties fails to carry out the agreement,

the employer[8] or the union, or unions, may apply to the CAC for assistance[9].

1 As to the Central Arbitration Committee see PARA 1226 et seq.
2 Ie under the Trade Union and Labour Relations (Consolidation) Act 1992 Sch A1 Pt I (paras 1–51): see PARAS 1103 et seq, 1125 et seq.
3 As to the meaning of 'trade union' see PARA 891.
4 As to the meaning of 'recognised' see PARA 1094.
5 As to the meaning of references to collective bargaining see PARA 1103 note 3.
6 As to the meaning of references to the bargaining unit see PARA 1103 note 3.
7 As to the meaning of references to the parties see PARA 1103 note 3.
8 As to the meaning of 'employer' see PARA 1103 note 3.
9 Trade Union and Labour Relations (Consolidation) Act 1992 Sch A1 paras 32(1), (2), 172(1) (Sch A1 added by the Employment Relations Act 1999 Sch 1; and the Trade Union and Labour Relations (Consolidation) Act 1992 Sch A1 para 32(2) amended by the Employment Relations Act 2004 Sch 1 para 23(1), (7)). The Trade Union and Labour Relations (Consolidation) Act 1992 Sch A1 para 31 (see PARA 1123) applies as if 'para 30' (in each place) read 'para 30 or para 32': Sch A1 para 32(3) (as so added).

G. ADMISSIBILITY OF FURTHER APPLICATIONS RELATING TO A BARGAINING UNIT

1125. Admissibility of further applications relating to a bargaining unit. If:

(1) the Central Arbitration Committee[1] (the 'CAC') accepts a relevant application[2] relating to a bargaining unit[3] or proceeds[4] with an application relating to a bargaining unit;

(2) the application has not been withdrawn[5];

(3) no notice has been given[6];

(4) the CAC has not issued a declaration[7] in relation to that bargaining unit; and

(5) no notification has been made[8],

another relevant application is not admissible if at least one worker[9] falling within the relevant bargaining unit[10] also falls within that bargaining unit and the application is made by a union[11], or unions, other than the union, or unions, which made that application[12].

If the CAC accepts a relevant application[13] relating to a bargaining unit or proceeds[14] with an application relating to a bargaining unit, another relevant application is not admissible if:

(a) the application is made within the period of three years starting with the day after that on which the CAC gave notice of acceptance of that application;

(b) the relevant bargaining unit[15] is the same or substantially the same[16] as that bargaining unit; and

(c) the application is made by the union, or unions, which made that application[17].

If the CAC issues a declaration[18] that a union is, or unions are, not entitled to be recognised[19] as entitled to conduct collective bargaining[20] on behalf of a bargaining unit[21], an application where an employer[22] rejects a request[23] or where negotiations fail[24] is not admissible if:

(i) the application is made within the period of three years starting with the day after that on which the declaration was issued;

(ii) the relevant bargaining unit[25] is the same or substantially the same as that bargaining unit; and

(iii) the application is made by the union, or unions, which made the application leading to the declaration[26].

If the CAC issues a declaration[27] that bargaining arrangements are to cease to have effect[28], an application where an employer rejects a request[29] or where negotiations fail[30] is not admissible if:

(A)   the application is made within the period of three years starting with the day after that on which the declaration was issued;

(B)   the relevant bargaining unit[31] is the same or substantially the same[32] as that bargaining unit to which those bargaining arrangements relate; and

(C)   the application is made by the union which was a party, or unions which were parties, to the proceedings leading to the declaration[33].

1   As to the Central Arbitration Committee see PARA 1226 et seq.
2   For these purposes, a relevant application is an application under the Trade Union and Labour Relations (Consolidation) Act 1992 Sch A1 para 11(2) (see PARA 1106) or Sch A1 para 12(2) (see PARA 1107): Sch A1 para 38(3) (Sch A1 added by the Employment Relations Act 1999 Sch 1).
3   As to the meaning of references to the bargaining unit see PARA 1103 note 3.
4   Ie proceeds under the Trade Union and Labour Relations (Consolidation) Act 1992 Sch A1 para 20: see PARA 1114.
5   As to withdrawal of an application see PARA 1112.
6   Ie under the Trade Union and Labour Relations (Consolidation) Act 1992 Sch A1 para 17(2): see PARA 1113.
7   Ie under the Trade Union and Labour Relations (Consolidation) Act 1992 Sch A1 para 19F(5) (see PARA 1111), Sch A1 para 22(2) (see PARA 1117), Sch A1 para 27(2) (see PARA 1120), Sch A1 para 27D(3), (4) (see PARA 1119), Sch A1 para 29(3) (see PARA 1122) or Sch A1 para 29(4) (see PARA 1122).
8   Ie under the Trade Union and Labour Relations (Consolidation) Act 1992 Sch A1 para 24(2): see PARA 1118.
9   As to the meaning of 'worker' see PARA 892.
10 For these purposes, the relevant bargaining unit is: (1) the proposed bargaining unit, where the application is under the Trade Union and Labour Relations (Consolidation) Act 1992 Sch A1 para 11(2) (see PARA 1106) or Sch A1 para 12(2) (see PARA 1107); and (2) the agreed bargaining unit, where the application is under Sch A1 para 12(4) (see PARA 1107): Sch A1 para 38(4) (as added: see note 2).
11 As to the meaning of 'trade union' see PARA 891.
12 Trade Union and Labour Relations (Consolidation) Act 1992 Sch A1 para 38(1), (2) (as added (see note 2); amended by the Employment Relations Act 2004 Sch 1 para 23(1), (9)).
13 For these purposes, a relevant application is an application under the Trade Union and Labour Relations (Consolidation) Act 1992 Sch A1 para 11(2) (see PARA 1106) or Sch A1 para 12(2) (see PARA 1107): Sch A1 para 39(3) (as added: see note 2).
14 Ie under the Trade Union and Labour Relations (Consolidation) Act 1992 Sch A1 para 20: see PARA 1114.
15 For these purposes, the relevant bargaining unit is: (1) the proposed bargaining unit, where the application is under the Trade Union and Labour Relations (Consolidation) Act 1992 Sch A1 para 11(2) (see PARA 1106) or Sch A1 para 12(2) (see PARA 1107); and (2) the agreed bargaining unit, where the application is under Sch A1 para 12(4) (see PARA 1107): Sch A1 para 39(4) (as added: see note 2).
16 For these purposes, it is for the CAC to decide whether one bargaining unit is the same or substantially the same as another; but, in deciding, the CAC may take account of the views of any person it believes has an interest in the matter: Trade Union and Labour Relations (Consolidation) Act 1992 Sch A1 para 42(1), (2) (as added: see note 2).
17 Trade Union and Labour Relations (Consolidation) Act 1992 Sch A1 para 39(1), (2) (as added: see note 2). Schedule A1 para 39 does not apply if Sch A1 para 40 or Sch A1 para 41 applies: Sch A1 para 39(5) (as so added).
18 Ie under the Trade Union and Labour Relations (Consolidation) Act 1992 Sch A1 para 27D(4) (see PARA 1119) or Sch A1 para 29(4) (see PARA 1122).
19 As to the meaning of 'recognised' see PARA 1094.
20 As to the meaning of 'collective bargaining' see PARA 1103 note 3.
21 Ie whether the ballot concerned is arranged under the Trade Union and Labour Relations (Consolidation) Act 1992 Sch A1 Pt I (paras 1–51) (see PARAS 1103 et seq, 1126) or Sch A1 Pt III (paras 64–95) (see PARA 1132 et seq).
22 As to the meaning of 'employer' see PARA 1103 note 3.

23 Ie an application under the Trade Union and Labour Relations (Consolidation) Act 1992 Sch A1 para 11: see PARA 1106.
24 Ie an application under the Trade Union and Labour Relations (Consolidation) Act 1992 Sch A1 para 12: see PARA 1107.
25 For these purposes, the relevant bargaining unit is: (1) the proposed bargaining unit, where the application is under the Trade Union and Labour Relations (Consolidation) Act 1992 Sch A1 para 11(2) (see PARA 1106) or Sch A1 para 12(2) (see PARA 1107); and (2) the agreed bargaining unit, where the application is under Sch A1 para 12(4) (see PARA 1107): Sch A1 para 40(3) (as added: see note 2).
26 Trade Union and Labour Relations (Consolidation) Act 1992 Sch A1 para 40(1), (2) (as added (see note 2); Sch A1 para 40(1) amended by the Employment Relations Act 2004 Sch 1 para 23(1), (10)).
27 Ie under the Trade Union and Labour Relations (Consolidation) Act 1992 Sch A1 para 119D(4) (see PARA 1156), Sch A1 para 119H(5) (see PARA 1156 note 16) or Sch A1 para 121(3) (see PARA 1159).
28 Ie whether the ballot concerned is arranged under the Trade Union and Labour Relations (Consolidation) Act 1992 Sch A1 Pt IV (paras 96–121) (see PARA 1149 et seq) or Sch A1 Pt V (paras 122–133) (see PARA 1160 et seq).
29 See note 23.
30 See note 24.
31 For these purposes, the relevant bargaining unit is: (1) the proposed bargaining unit, where the application is under the Trade Union and Labour Relations (Consolidation) Act 1992 Sch A1 para 11(2) (see PARA 1106) or Sch A1 para 12(2) (see PARA 1107); and (2) the agreed bargaining unit, where the application is under Sch A1 para 12(4) (see PARA 1107): Sch A1 para 41(3) (as added: see note 2).
32 See note 16.
33 Trade Union and Labour Relations (Consolidation) Act 1992 Sch A1 para 41(1), (2) (as added (see note 2); Sch A1 para 41(1) amended by the Employment Relations Act 2004 Sch 1 para 23(1), (11)).

H. COMPETING APPLICATIONS FOR UNION RECOGNITION

1126. Competing applications for union recognition. If:

(1) the Central Arbitration Committee[1] (the 'CAC') decides that the competing application[2] is not admissible[3] or is invalid[4];

(2) at the time the decision is made the parties[5] to the original application[6] have not agreed the appropriate bargaining unit[7] and the CAC has not decided the appropriate bargaining unit[8], in relation to the application; and

(3) the 10 per cent test[9] is satisfied with regard to the competing application,

then, in such a case:

(a) the CAC must cancel the original application;
(b) the CAC must give notice to the parties to the application that it has been cancelled;
(c) no further steps are to be taken[10] in relation to the application; and
(d) the application is to be treated as if it had never been admissible[11].

1 As to the Central Arbitration Committee see PARA 1226 et seq.
2 For these purposes, the competing application is the other application referred to in the Trade Union and Labour Relations (Consolidation) Act 1992 Sch A1 para 38(2) (see PARA 1125) or the application in question referred to in Sch A1 para 46(2) (see PARA 1115): Sch A1 para 51(1)(b) (Sch A1 added by the Employment Relations Act 1999 Sch 1).
3 Ie by reason of the Trade Union and Labour Relations (Consolidation) Act 1992 Sch A1 para 38: see PARA 1125.
4 Ie by reason of the Trade Union and Labour Relations (Consolidation) Act 1992 Sch A1 para 46: see PARA 1115.
5 As to the meaning of references to the parties see PARA 1103 note 3.

6   For these purposes, the original application is the application referred to in the Trade Union and Labour Relations (Consolidation) Act 1992 Sch A1 para 38(1) (see PARA 1125) or Sch A1 para 46(1) (see PARA 1115); but an application cannot be an original application unless it was made under Sch A1 para 11(2) (see PARA 1106) or Sch A1 para 12(2) (see PARA 1107): Sch A1 para 51(1)(a) (as added: see note 2).

7   Ie under the Trade Union and Labour Relations (Consolidation) Act 1992 Sch A1 para 18: see PARA 1110.

8   Ie under the Trade Union and Labour Relations (Consolidation) Act 1992 Sch A1 para 19 or Sch A1 para 19A: see PARA 1110.

9   Ie within the meaning given by the Trade Union and Labour Relations (Consolidation) Act 1992 Sch A1 para 14: see PARA 1109.

10   Ie under the Trade Union and Labour Relations (Consolidation) Act 1992 Sch A1 Pt I (paras 1–51): see PARA 1103 et seq.

11   Trade Union and Labour Relations (Consolidation) Act 1992 Sch A1 para 51(2), (3) (as added (see note 2); Sch A1 para 51(2) amended by the Employment Relations Act 2004 Sch 1 para 23(1), (15)).

(ii)   Voluntary Trade Union Recognition

A.   DETERMINATION OF TYPE OF AGREEMENT

1127.   Determination as to whether agreement if one for trade union recognition. If one or more of the parties[1] to an agreement apply to the Central Arbitration Committee[2] (the 'CAC') for a decision whether or not the agreement is an agreement for recognition[3], the CAC must:

(1)   give notice of receipt of such an application to any parties to the agreement who are not parties to the application[4];

(2)   within the decision period[5] decide whether the agreement is an agreement for recognition[6].

If the CAC decides that the agreement:

(a)   is an agreement for recognition, it must issue a declaration to that effect[7];

(b)   is not an agreement for recognition, it must issue a declaration to that effect[8].

1   In relation to an agreement for recognition, references to the parties are to the union, or unions, and the employer who are parties to the agreement: Trade Union and Labour Relations (Consolidation) Act 1992 Sch A1 para 53(1), (3) (Sch A1 added by the Employment Relations Act 1999 Sch 1). An agreement is an agreement for recognition if the following conditions are fulfilled in relation to it: (1) the agreement is made in the permitted period between a union, or unions, and an employer in consequence of a request made under the Trade Union and Labour Relations (Consolidation) Act 1992 Sch A1 para 4 (see PARA 1104) and valid within the terms of Sch A1 paras 5–9 (see PARA 1104); (2) under the agreement the union is, or unions are, recognised as entitled to conduct collective bargaining on behalf of a group or groups of workers employed by the employer; (3) if Sch A1 para 52(5) (see below) applies to the agreement, it is satisfied: Sch A1 para 52(1), (2) (as so added). As to the meaning of 'trade union' see PARA 891; and as to the meaning of recognised' see PARA 1094. As to the meanings of 'employer' and 'worker' see PARA 892.

     The permitted period is the period which begins with the day on which the employer receives the request and ends when the first of the following occurs (Sch A1 para 52(1), (3) (as so added; Sch A1 para 52(3) amended by the Employment Relations Act 2004 Sch 1 para 23(1), (16))), ie:

     (a)   the union withdraws, or unions withdraw, the request;

     (b)   the union withdraws, or unions withdraw, any application under Sch A1 para 11(2) (see PARA 1106) or Sch A1 para 12(2) (see PARA 1107) made in consequence of the request;

     (c)   the CAC gives notice of a decision under Sch A1 para 14(7) (see PARA 1109) which precludes it from accepting such an application under Sch A1 para 11 or Sch A1 para 12;

     (d)   the CAC gives notice under Sch A1 para 15(4)(a) (see PARA 1109 head (i) in the text) or

Sch A1 para 20(4)(a) (see PARA 1114 head (a) in the text) in relation to such an application under Sch A1 para 11 or Sch A1 para 12;

(e)   the parties give notice to the CAC under Sch A1 para 17(2) (see PARA 1113) in relation to such an application under Sch A1 para 11 or Sch A1 para 12;

(f)   the CAC issues a declaration under Sch A1 para 19F(5) (see PARA 1111) or Sch A1 para 22(2) (see PARA 1117) in consequence of such an application under Sch A1 para 11 or Sch A1 para 12;

(g)   the CAC is notified under Sch A1 para 24(2) (see PARA 1118) in relation to such an application under Sch A1 para 11 or Sch A1 para 12;

(h)   the last day of the notification period ends, the notification period being that defined by Sch A1 para 24(6) (see PARA 1118 note 10) and arising from such an application under Sch A1 para 11 or Sch A1 para 12;

(i)   the CAC is required under Sch A1 para 51(3) (see PARA 1126) to cancel such an application under Sch A1 para 11 or Sch A1 para 12.

The meaning of collective bargaining given by the Trade Union and Labour Relations (Consolidation) Act 1992 s 178(1) (see PARA 1093) does not apply: Sch A1 para 54(1), (2) (as so added). Except in Sch A1 para 63(2) (see PARA 1131), in relation to an agreement for recognition, references to collective bargaining are to negotiations relating to the matters in respect of which the union is, or unions are, recognised as entitled to conduct negotiations under the agreement for recognition: Sch A1 para 54(1), (3) (as so added).

Schedule Sch A1 para 52(5) applies to an agreement if: (i) at the time it is made, the CAC has received an application under Sch A1 para 11 or Sch A1 para 12 in consequence of the request mentioned in Sch A1 para 52(2); and (ii) the CAC has not decided whether the application is admissible or it has decided that it is admissible: Sch A1 para 52(1), (4) (as so added). Schedule A1 para 52(5) is satisfied if, in relation to the application under Sch A1 para 11 or Sch A1 para 12, the parties give notice to the CAC under Sch A1 para 17 (see PARA 1113) before the final event (as defined in Sch A1 para 17) (see PARA 1113 note 4) occurs: Sch A1 para 52(1), (5) (as so added).

2   As to the Central Arbitration Committee see PARA 1226 et seq.

3   Trade Union and Labour Relations (Consolidation) Act 1992 Sch A1 para 55(1) (as added: see note 1).

4   Trade Union and Labour Relations (Consolidation) Act 1992 Sch A1 para 55(2) (as added: see note 1).

5   For these purposes, the decision period is: (1) the period of ten working days starting with the day after that on which the CAC receives the application under the Trade Union and Labour Relations (Consolidation) Act 1992 Sch A1 para 55(1); or (2) such longer period, so starting, as the CAC may specify to the parties to the agreement by notice containing reasons for the extension: Sch A1 para 55(6) (as added: see note 1). As to the meaning of 'working day' see PARA 1105 note 1.

6   Trade Union and Labour Relations (Consolidation) Act 1992 Sch A1 para 55(3) (as added: see note 1).

7   Trade Union and Labour Relations (Consolidation) Act 1992 Sch A1 para 55(4) (as added: see note 1).

8   Trade Union and Labour Relations (Consolidation) Act 1992 Sch A1 para 55(5) (as added: see note 1).

B. TERMINATION OF AGREEMENT FOR RECOGNITION

1128. Termination of agreement for recognition. The employer[1] may not terminate an agreement for recognition[2] before the relevant period[3] ends[4]. After that period ends, the employer may terminate the agreement, with or without the consent of the union[5], or unions[6]. The union, or unions, may terminate an agreement for recognition at any time, with or without the consent of the employer[7]. If an agreement for recognition is terminated, as from the termination the agreement and any provisions relating to the collective bargaining method[8] cease to have effect[9].

1   As to the meaning of 'employer' see PARA 892.
2   As to the meaning of 'agreement for recognition' see PARA 1127 note 1.

3 For these purposes, the relevant period is the period of three years starting with the day after the date of the agreement: Trade Union and Labour Relations (Consolidation) Act 1992 Sch A1 para 56(5) (Sch A1 added by the Employment Relations Act 1999 Sch 1).

4 Trade Union and Labour Relations (Consolidation) Act 1992 Sch A1 para 56(1) (as added: see note 3). Schedule A1 para 56(1)–(3) has effect subject to the terms of the agreement or any other agreement of the parties: Sch A1 para 56(4) (as so added). As to the meaning of references to the parties see PARA 1127 note 1.

5 As to the meaning of 'trade union' see PARA 891.

6 Trade Union and Labour Relations (Consolidation) Act 1992 Sch A1 para 56(2) (as added: see note 3). See also note 4.

7 Trade Union and Labour Relations (Consolidation) Act 1992 Sch A1 para 56(3) (as added: see note 3). See also note 4.

8 For these purposes, provisions relating to the collective bargaining method are: (1) any agreement between the parties as to the method by which collective bargaining is to be conducted with regard to the bargaining unit; or (2) anything effective as, or as if contained in, a legally enforceable contract and relating to the method by which collective bargaining is to be conducted with regard to the bargaining unit: Trade Union and Labour Relations (Consolidation) Act 1992 Sch A1 para 57(2) (as added: see note 3). In relation to an agreement for recognition, references to the bargaining unit are to the group of workers, or the groups taken together, to which the agreement for recognition relates: Sch A1 para 53(1), (2) (as so added). As to the meaning of 'collective bargaining' see PARA 1127 note 1; and as to the meaning of 'worker' see PARA 892.

9 Trade Union and Labour Relations (Consolidation) Act 1992 Sch A1 para 57(1) (as added: see note 3).

C. APPLICATION TO CENTRAL ARBITRATION COMMITTEE TO SPECIFY METHOD FOR COLLECTIVE BARGAINING

1129. Agreement of method by which parties will conduct collective bargaining. If the parties[1] make an agreement for recognition[2], the parties may in the negotiation period[3] conduct negotiations with a view to agreeing a method by which they will conduct collective bargaining[4]. If no agreement is made in the negotiation period, the employer[5] or the union[6], or unions, may apply to the Central Arbitration Committee[7] (the 'CAC') for assistance[8].

If the parties to an agreement for recognition agree a method by which they will conduct collective bargaining and one or more of the parties fails to carry out the agreement as to a method, the employer or the union, or unions, may apply to the CAC for assistance[9].

1 As to the meaning of references to the parties see PARA 1127 note 1.

2 As to the meaning of 'agreement for recognition' see PARA 1127 note 1.

3 For these purposes, the negotiation period is: (1) the period of 30 working days starting with the start day; or (2) such longer period, so starting, as the parties may from time to time agree: Trade Union and Labour Relations (Consolidation) Act 1992 Sch A1 para 58(1), (4) (Sch A1 added by the Employment Relations Act 1999 Sch 1). The start day is the day after that on which the agreement is made: Trade Union and Labour Relations (Consolidation) Act 1992 Sch A1 para 58(1), (5) (as so added). As to the meaning of 'working day' see PARA 1105 note 1.

4 Trade Union and Labour Relations (Consolidation) Act 1992 Sch A1 para 58(1), (2) (as added: see note 3). As to the meaning of references to collective bargaining see PARA 1127 note 1. As to the procedure on an application see PARA 1130.

5 As to the meaning of 'employer' see PARA 892.

6 As to the meaning of 'trade union' see PARA 891.

7 As to the Central Arbitration Committee see PARA 1226 et seq.

8 Trade Union and Labour Relations (Consolidation) Act 1992 Sch A1 paras 58(1), (3), 172(1) (as added: see note 3).

9 Trade Union and Labour Relations (Consolidation) Act 1992 Sch A1 para 59(1), (2) (as added: see note 3).

1130. Procedure where application for Central Arbitration Committee's assistance is made. If an application for assistance is made[1] to the Central Arbitration Committee[2] (the 'CAC'), the application is not admissible unless the conditions in heads (1) and (2) below are satisfied[3]. Those conditions are:

    (1)   that the employer[4], taken with any associated employer[5] or employers, must:

        (a)   employ at least 21 workers[6] on the day the application is made; or

        (b)   employ an average[7] of at least 21 workers[8] in the 13 weeks ending with that day[9];

    (2)   that the union[10], or every union, has a certificate of independence[11] that it is independent[12].

An application to the CAC:

    (i)   is not admissible unless it is made in such form as the CAC specifies and it is supported by such documents as the CAC specifies[13];

    (ii)   which is made by a union, or unions, is not admissible unless the union gives, or unions give, to the employer notice of the application and a copy of the application and any documents supporting it[14];

    (iii)   which is made by an employer is not admissible unless the employer gives to the union, or each of the unions, notice of the application and a copy of the application and any documents supporting it[15].

1   Ie under the Trade Union and Labour Relations (Consolidation) Act 1992 Sch A1 para 58 or Sch A1 para 59: see PARA 1129.
2   As to the Central Arbitration Committee see PARA 1226 et seq.
3   Trade Union and Labour Relations (Consolidation) Act 1992 Sch A1 para 60(1), (2) (Sch A1 added by the Employment Relations Act 1999 Sch 1). An order made under the Trade Union and Labour Relations (Consolidation) Act 1992 Sch A1 para 7(6) (see PARA 1104) may also: (1) provide that Sch A1 para 60(2) and Sch A1 para 60(3), (5)–(8) (see the text and notes 4–9) are not to apply, or are not to apply in specified circumstances; or (2) vary the number of workers for the time being specified in Sch A1 para 60(3) (see the text and notes 4–9): Sch A1 para 60(9) (as so added).
4   As to the meaning of 'employer' see PARA 892.
5   As to the meaning of 'associated employer' see PARA 1026 note 8.
6   As to the meaning of 'worker' see PARA 892. For these purposes, any worker employed by an associated company incorporated outside Great Britain is to be ignored unless the day the application was made fell within a period during which he ordinarily worked in Great Britain: Trade Union and Labour Relations (Consolidation) Act 1992 Sch A1 para 60(1), (6) (as added: see note 3). As to the meaning of 'Great Britain' see PARA 2 note 12. See also note 3.
        For the purposes of Sch A1 para 60(6) and Sch A1 para 60(7) (see note 8), a worker who is employed on board a ship registered in the register maintained under the Merchant Shipping Act 1995 s 8 (see SHIPPING AND MARITIME LAW vol 93 (2008) PARA 254) is to be treated as ordinarily working in Great Britain unless: (1) the ship's entry in the register specifies a port outside Great Britain as the port to which the vessel is to be treated as belonging; (2) the employment is wholly outside Great Britain; or (3) the worker is not ordinarily resident in Great Britain: Trade Union and Labour Relations (Consolidation) Act 1992 Sch A1 para 60(1), (8) (as so added). See also note 3.
7   To find the average for these purposes: (1) take the number of workers employed in each of the 13 weeks, including workers not employed for the whole of the week; (2) aggregate the 13 numbers; (3) divide the aggregate by 13: Trade Union and Labour Relations (Consolidation) Act 1992 Sch A1 para 60(1), (5) (as added: see note 3). See also note 3.
8   For these purposes, any worker employed by an associated company incorporated outside Great Britain is to be ignored in relation to a week unless the whole or any part of that week fell within a period during which he ordinarily worked in Great Britain: Trade Union and Labour Relations (Consolidation) Act 1992 Sch A1 para 60(1), (7) (as added: see note 3). See also notes 3, 6.
9   Trade Union and Labour Relations (Consolidation) Act 1992 Sch A1 para 60(3) (as added: see note 3). See also note 3.
10   As to the meaning of 'trade union' see PARA 891.
11   As to the meaning of 'certificate of independence' see PARA 1008 note 6.

12 Trade Union and Labour Relations (Consolidation) Act 1992 Sch A1 para 60(4) (as added (see note 3); amended by the Employment Relations Act 2004 s 50(6)).
13 Trade Union and Labour Relations (Consolidation) Act 1992 Sch A1 para 61(1) (as added: see note 3).
14 Trade Union and Labour Relations (Consolidation) Act 1992 Sch A1 para 61(2) (as added: see note 3).
15 Trade Union and Labour Relations (Consolidation) Act 1992 Sch A1 para 61(3) (as added: see note 3).

1131.   Central Arbitration Committee's response to application to specify method for collective bargaining. The Central Arbitration Committee[1] (the 'CAC') must give notice to the parties[2] of receipt of an application[3] to specify a method by which they will conduct collective bargaining[4].

Within the acceptance period[5], the CAC must decide whether the application is[6] admissible[7]. In deciding whether an application is admissible, the CAC must consider any evidence which it has been given by the employer[8] or the union[9], or unions[10]. If the CAC decides that the application is not admissible:

(1)   the CAC must give notice of its decision to the parties;
(2)   the CAC must not accept the application; and
(3)   no further steps[11] are to be taken[12].

If the CAC decides that the application is admissible, it must accept the application and give notice of the acceptance to the parties[13]. If the CAC accepts an application, it must try to help the parties to reach in the agreement period[14] an agreement[15] on a method by which they will conduct collective bargaining[15]. If, at the end of the agreement period, the parties have not made such an agreement, the CAC must specify to the parties the method by which they are to conduct collective bargaining[16]. Any method so specified has effect as if it were contained in a legally enforceable contract made by the parties[17]; but, if the parties agree in writing that that provision is not to apply, or is not to apply to particular parts of the method specified by the CAC, or to vary or replace the method specified by the CAC, the written agreement has effect as a legally enforceable contract made by the parties[18]. Specific performance is the only remedy available for breach of anything which is such a legally enforceable contract[19].

If the CAC accepts an application, the applicant may not withdraw it after the end of the agreement period[20]. If, at any time before a specification is made[21], the parties jointly apply to the CAC requesting it to stop taking steps under the above provisions, the CAC must comply with the request[22].

1   As to the Central Arbitration Committee see PARA 1226 et seq.
2   As to the meaning of references to the parties see PARA 1127 note 1.
3   Ie an application under the Trade Union and Labour Relations (Consolidation) Act 1992 Sch A1 para 58 or Sch A1 para 59: see PARA 1129.
4   See the Trade Union and Labour Relations (Consolidation) Act 1992 Sch A1 para 62(1) (Sch A1 added by the Employment Relations Act 1999 Sch 1).
5   For these purposes, the acceptance period is: (1) the period of ten working days starting with the day after that on which the CAC receives the application; or (2) such longer period, so starting, as the CAC may specify to the parties by notice containing reasons for the extension: Trade Union and Labour Relations (Consolidation) Act 1992 Sch A1 para 62(6) (as added: see note 4). As to the meaning of 'working day' see PARA 1105 note 1.
6   Ie within the terms of the Trade Union and Labour Relations (Consolidation) Act 1992 Sch A1 paras 60, 61: see PARA 1130.
7   Trade Union and Labour Relations (Consolidation) Act 1992 Sch A1 para 62(2) (as added: see note 4).
8   As to the meaning of 'employer' see PARA 892.
9   As to the meaning of 'trade union' see PARA 891.
10 Trade Union and Labour Relations (Consolidation) Act 1992 Sch A1 para 62(3) (as added: see note 4).

11 Ie no further steps are to be taken under the Trade Union and Labour Relations (Consolidation) Act 1992 Sch A1 Pt II (paras 52–63): see PARA 1127 et seq.

12 Trade Union and Labour Relations (Consolidation) Act 1992 Sch A1 para 62(4) (as added: see note 4).

13 Trade Union and Labour Relations (Consolidation) Act 1992 Sch A1 para 62(5) (as added: see note 4).

14 For these purposes, the agreement period is: (1) the period of 20 working days starting with the day after that on which the CAC gives notice of acceptance of the application; or (2) such longer period, so starting, as the parties may from time to time agree: Trade Union and Labour Relations (Consolidation) Act 1992 Sch A1 para 63(8) (as added: see note 4).

15 Trade Union and Labour Relations (Consolidation) Act 1992 Sch A1 para 63(1) (as added: see note 4). As to the meaning of 'collective bargaining' see PARA 1127 note 1.

16 Trade Union and Labour Relations (Consolidation) Act 1992 Sch A1 para 63(2) (as added: see note 4). For these purposes only, the reference to collective bargaining is to negotiations relating to pay, hours and holidays: Sch A1 para 54(1), (4) (as so added). After consulting the Advisory, Conciliation and Arbitration Service, the Secretary of State may by order specify for these purposes a method by which collective bargaining might be conducted: Sch A1 para 168(1) (as so added). If such an order is made, the CAC must take it into account under Sch A1 para 63(2), but may depart from the method specified by the order to such extent as the CAC thinks it is appropriate to do so in the circumstances: Sch A1 para 168(2) (as so added). Such an order must be made by statutory instrument subject to annulment in pursuance of a resolution of either House of Parliament: Sch A1 para 168(3) (as so added). In exercise of the power so conferred the Secretary of State made the Trade Union Recognition (Method of Collective Bargaining) Order 2000, SI 2000/1300, which came into force on 6 June 2000: art 1. The method specified for the purposes of the Trade Union and Labour Relations (Consolidation) Act 1992 Sch A1 para 63(2) is the method set out under the heading 'the specified method' in the Trade Union Recognition (Method of Collective Bargaining) Order 2000, SI 2000/1300, art 2, Schedule: art 2. As to the Advisory, Conciliation and Arbitration Service ('ACAS') see PARA 1213 et seq.

17 Trade Union and Labour Relations (Consolidation) Act 1992 Sch A1 para 63(3) (as added: see note 4).

18 Trade Union and Labour Relations (Consolidation) Act 1992 Sch A1 para 63(4) (as added: see note 4).

19 Trade Union and Labour Relations (Consolidation) Act 1992 Sch A1 para 63(5) (as added: see note 4).

20 Trade Union and Labour Relations (Consolidation) Act 1992 Sch A1 para 63(6) (as added: see note 4).

21 Ie under the Trade Union and Labour Relations (Consolidation) Act 1992 Sch A1 para 63(2).

22 Trade Union and Labour Relations (Consolidation) Act 1992 Sch A1 para 63(7) (as added: see note 4).

(iii) Changes affecting Bargaining Unit

A. APPLICATION OF PROVISIONS REGARDING CHANGES AFFECTING THE BARGAINING UNIT

1132. Changes affecting the bargaining unit; in general. The following provisions[1] apply if:

    (1)   the Central Arbitration Committee[2] (the 'CAC') has issued a declaration that a union[3] is, or unions are, recognised[4] as entitled to conduct collective bargaining[5] on behalf of a bargaining unit; and

    (2)   provisions relating to the collective bargaining method[6] apply in relation to the unit[7].

1 Ie the Trade Union and Labour Relations (Consolidation) Act 1992 Sch A1 Pt III (paras 64–95): see also PARA 1133 et seq.

2 As to the Central Arbitration Committee see PARA 1226 et seq.

3 As to the meaning of 'trade union' see PARA 891.

4 As to the meaning of 'recognised' see PARA 1094.

5 Except in relation to the Trade Union and Labour Relations (Consolidation) Act 1992 Sch A1 para 69(5) (see PARA 1134 note 6), Sch A1 para 78(5) (see PARA 1140), Sch A1 para 83(6) (see

PARA 1142), the meaning of collective bargaining given by s 178(1) (see PARA 1093) does not apply: Sch A1 para 94(1), (2) (Sch A1 added by the Employment Relations Act 1999 Sch 1).

In relation to a new unit, references to collective bargaining are to negotiations relating to the matters which were the subject of collective bargaining in relation to the corresponding original unit; and the corresponding original unit is the unit which was the subject of an application under the Trade Union and Labour Relations (Consolidation) Act 1992 Sch A1 para 66 (see PARA 1133) or Sch A1 para 75 (see PARA 1138) in consequence of which the new unit was agreed by the parties or decided by the CAC: Sch A1 para 94(1), (3) (as so added). References to the original unit are to the bargaining unit on whose behalf the union is, or unions are, recognised as entitled to conduct collective bargaining: Sch A1 para 64(2)(a) (as so added). References to the parties are to the employer and the union, or unions, concerned: Sch A1 para 65 (as so added). As to the meaning of 'employer' see PARA 892.

If, however, the parties agree matters as the subject of collective bargaining in relation to the new unit, references to collective bargaining in relation to that unit are to negotiations relating to the agreed matters; and this is the case whether the agreement is made before or after the time when the CAC issues a declaration that the union is, or unions are, recognised as entitled to conduct collective bargaining on behalf of the new unit: Sch A1 para 94(1), (4) (as so added).

In relation to a residual unit in relation to which a declaration is issued under Sch A1 para 91 (see PARA 1145), references to collective bargaining are to negotiations relating to the matters which were the subject of collective bargaining in relation to the corresponding parent unit: Sch A1 para 94(1), (5) (as so added).

In construing Sch A1 para 69(3)(c) (see PARA 1134 head (c) in the text), Sch A1 para 78(3)(c) (see PARA 1140 head (3) in the text), Sch A1 para 85(2)(c) (see PARA 1144 head (3) in the text), Sch A1 para 87(6)(b) (see PARA 1144) and Sch A1 para 89(6)(b) (see PARA 1144), Sch A1 para 94(3), (4) does not apply; and references to collective bargaining are to negotiations relating to pay, hours and holidays: Sch A1 para 94(1), (6) (as so added).

6   For these purposes, provisions relating to the collective bargaining method are: (1) the parties' agreement as to the method by which collective bargaining is to be conducted with regard to the original unit; (2) anything effective as, or as if contained in, a legally enforceable contract and relating to the method by which collective bargaining is to be conducted with regard to the original unit; or (3) any provision of the Trade Union and Labour Relations (Consolidation) Act 1992 Sch A1 Pt III (paras 64–95) that a method of collective bargaining is to have effect with regard to the original unit: Sch A1 para 64(3) (as added: see note 5).

7   Trade Union and Labour Relations (Consolidation) Act 1992 Sch A1 para 64(1) (as added: see note 5).

B. EITHER PARTY BELIEVES BARGAINING UNIT NO LONGER APPROPRIATE

1133. Application for decision as to what is an appropriate bargaining unit.
If the employer[1] believes or the union[2] believes, or unions believe, that the original unit[3] is no longer an appropriate bargaining unit, the employer or union, or unions, may apply to the Central Arbitration Committee[4] (the 'CAC') to make a decision as to what is an appropriate bargaining unit[5]. Such an application is not admissible unless the CAC decides that it is likely that the original unit is no longer appropriate by reason of any of the matters specified in heads (1) to (3) below[6]. Those matters are:

(1)   a change in the organisation or structure of the business carried on by the employer;

(2)   a change in the activities pursued by the employer in the course of the business carried on by him;

(3)   a substantial change in the number of workers[7] employed in the original unit[8].

The CAC must give notice to the parties[9] of receipt of such an application[10].

Within the acceptance period[11], the CAC must decide whether the application is[12] admissible[13]. In deciding whether the application is admissible, the CAC must consider any evidence which it has been given by the employer or the union, or unions[14]. If the CAC decides that the application is not admissible:

(a)   the CAC must give notice of its decision to the parties;

  (b)   the CAC must not accept the application; and

  (c)   no further steps[15] are to be taken[16].

If the CAC decides that the application is admissible, it must accept the application and give notice of the acceptance to the parties[17].

1   As to the meaning of 'employer' see PARA 892.

2   As to the meaning of 'trade union' see PARA 891.

3   As to the meaning of references to the original unit see PARA 1132 note 5.

4   As to the Central Arbitration Committee see PARA 1226 et seq.

5   Trade Union and Labour Relations (Consolidation) Act 1992 Sch A1 para 66(1), (2) (Sch A1 added by the Employment Relations Act 1999 Sch 1). As to the application of Sch A1 paras 66–68 see PARA 1132.

6   Trade Union and Labour Relations (Consolidation) Act 1992 Sch A1 para 67(1) (as added: see note 5). As to the admissibility of applications see further PARA 1146; and as to the withdrawal of applications see PARA 1147.

7   As to the meaning of 'worker' see PARA 892.

8   Trade Union and Labour Relations (Consolidation) Act 1992 Sch A1 para 67(2) (as added: see note 5). See also note 5.

9   As to the meaning of references to the parties see PARA 1132 note 5.

10 Trade Union and Labour Relations (Consolidation) Act 1992 Sch A1 para 68(1) (as added: see note 5). See also note 5.

11 For these purposes, the acceptance period is: (1) the period of ten working days starting with the day after that on which the Central Arbitration Committee receives the application; or (2) such longer period, so starting, as the CAC may specify to the parties by notice containing reasons for the extension: Trade Union and Labour Relations (Consolidation) Act 1992 Sch A1 para 68(6) (as added: see note 5). As to the meaning of 'working day' see PARA 1105 note 1.

12 Ie within the terms of the Trade Union and Labour Relations (Consolidation) Act 1992 Sch A1 para 67 (see the text and notes 6–8) and Sch A1 para 92 (see PARA 1146).

13 Trade Union and Labour Relations (Consolidation) Act 1992 Sch A1 para 68(2) (as added: see note 5). As to the application of the Trade Union and Labour Relations (Consolidation) Act 1992 Sch A1 para 68 see PARA 1132.

14 Trade Union and Labour Relations (Consolidation) Act 1992 Sch A1 para 68(3) (as added: see note 5). See also note 13.

15 Ie no further steps are to be taken under the Trade Union and Labour Relations (Consolidation) Act 1992 Sch A1 Pt III (paras 64–95): see also PARAS 1132, 1134 et seq.

16 Trade Union and Labour Relations (Consolidation) Act 1992 Sch A1 para 68(4) (as added: see note 5). See also note 13.

17 Trade Union and Labour Relations (Consolidation) Act 1992 Sch A1 para 68(5) (as added: see note 5). See also note 13.

1134. Parties agree a new bargaining unit or units. If:

  (1)   the Central Arbitration Committee[1] (the 'CAC') gives notice of acceptance of the application for a decision as to what is an appropriate bargaining unit[2]; and

  (2)   before the end of the first period[3] the parties agree a bargaining unit or units ('the new unit or units') differing from the original unit[4] and inform the CAC of their agreement,

then, if in the CAC's opinion the new unit, or any of the new units, contains at least one worker[5] falling within an outside bargaining unit[6], no further steps[7] are to be taken[8]. If the above provisions do not apply:

  (a)   the CAC must issue a declaration that the union is, or unions are, recognised as entitled to conduct collective bargaining on behalf of the new unit or units;

  (b)   so far as it affects workers in the new unit, or units, who fall within the original unit, the declaration has effect in place of any declaration that the union is, or unions are, recognised as entitled to conduct collective bargaining on behalf of the original unit;

  (c)   the method of collective bargaining relating to the original unit has effect in relation to the new unit or units, with any modifications which the CAC considers necessary to take account of the change of bargaining unit and specifies in the declaration[9].

1   As to the Central Arbitration Committee see PARA 1226 et seq.
2   Ie an application under the Trade Union and Labour Relations (Consolidation) Act 1992 Sch A1 para 66: see PARA 1133.
3   For these purposes, the first period is: (1) the period of ten working days starting with the day after that on which the CAC gives notice of acceptance of the application; or (2) such longer period, so starting, as the parties may from time to time agree and notify to the CAC: Trade Union and Labour Relations (Consolidation) Act 1992 Sch A1 para 69(4) (Sch A1 added by the Employment Relations Act 1999 Sch 1). As to the meaning of 'working day' see PARA 1105 note 1; and as to the meaning of references to the parties see PARA 1132 note 5.
4   As to the meaning of references to the original unit see PARA 1132 note 5.
5   As to the meaning of 'worker' see PARA 892.
6   For these purposes, an outside bargaining unit is a bargaining unit which fulfils these conditions: (1) it is not the original unit; (2) a union is, or unions are, recognised as entitled to conduct collective bargaining on its behalf; (3) the union, or at least one of the unions, is not a party referred to in the Trade Union and Labour Relations (Consolidation) Act 1992 Sch A1 para 64 (see PARA 1132): Sch A1 para 69(5) (as added: see note 3). As to the meaning of 'trade union' see PARA 891; as to the meaning of 'recognised' see PARA 1094; and as to the meaning of references to collective bargaining see PARA 1132 note 5.
7   Ie no further steps are to be taken under the Trade Union and Labour Relations (Consolidation) Act 1992 Sch A1 Pt III (paras 64–95): see also PARAS 1132–1133, 1135 et seq.
8   See the Trade Union and Labour Relations (Consolidation) Act 1992 Sch A1 para 69(1), (2) (as added: see note 3). As to the application of Sch A1 para 69 see PARA 1132.
9   Trade Union and Labour Relations (Consolidation) Act 1992 Sch A1 para 69(3) (as added: see note 3). See also note 8.

1135. Parties do not agree a new bargaining unit or units. If:
(1)   the Central Arbitration Committee[1] (the 'CAC') gives notice of acceptance of the application for a decision as to what is an appropriate bargaining unit[2]; and
(2)   the parties[3] do not inform the CAC before the end of the first period[4] that they have agreed a bargaining unit or units differing from the original unit[5],
then, during the second period[6]:
(a)   the CAC must decide whether or not the original unit continues to be an appropriate bargaining unit;
(b)   if the CAC decides that the original unit does not so continue, it must decide what other bargaining unit is, or units are, appropriate; and
(c)   the CAC must give notice to the parties of its decision or decisions under heads (a) and (b) above[7].
In deciding whether or not the original unit continues to be an appropriate bargaining unit, the CAC must take into account only these matters:
(i)   any change in the organisation or structure of the business carried on by the employer[8];
(ii)   any change in the activities pursued by the employer in the course of the business carried on by him;
(iii) any substantial change in the number of workers[9] employed in the original unit[10].
In deciding what other bargaining unit is, or units are, appropriate, the CAC must take into account the need for the unit, or units, to be compatible with effective management and the following matters, so far as they do not conflict with that need:
(A)   the views of the employer and of the union[11], or unions;

(B)   existing national and local bargaining arrangements[12];

(C)   the desirability of avoiding small fragmented bargaining units within an undertaking;

(D)   the characteristics of workers falling within the original unit and of any other employees[13] of the employer whom the CAC considers relevant;

(E)   the location of workers[14].

If the CAC decides that two or more bargaining units are appropriate, its decision must be such that no worker falls within more than one of them[15].

If the CAC gives notice under the above provisions of a decision that the original unit continues to be an appropriate bargaining unit, no further steps are[16] to be taken[17].

1   As to the Central Arbitration Committee see PARA 1226 et seq.

2   Ie an application under the Trade Union and Labour Relations (Consolidation) Act 1992 Sch A1 para 66: see PARA 1133.

3   As to the meaning of references to the parties see PARA 1132 note 5.

4   As to the meaning of 'first period' see PARA 1134 note 3.

5   As to the meaning of references to the original unit see PARA 1132 note 5.

6   For these purposes, the second period is: (1) the period of ten working days starting with the day after that on which the first period ends; or (2) such longer period, so starting, as the CAC may specify to the parties by notice containing reasons for the extension: Trade Union and Labour Relations (Consolidation) Act 1992 Sch A1 para 70(7) (Sch A1 added by the Employment Relations Act 1999 Sch 1). As to the meaning of 'working day' see PARA 1105 note 1.

7   Trade Union and Labour Relations (Consolidation) Act 1992 Sch A1 para 70(1), (2) (as added: see note 6). As to the application of Sch A1 paras 70, 71 see PARA 1132.

8   As to the meaning of 'employer' see PARA 892.

9   As to the meaning of 'worker' see PARA 892.

10   Trade Union and Labour Relations (Consolidation) Act 1992 Sch A1 para 70(3) (as added: see note 6).

11   As to the meaning of 'trade union' see PARA 891.

12   For these purposes, references to the bargaining arrangements are to the declaration and to the provisions relating to the collective bargaining method which apply in relation to the original unit: Trade Union and Labour Relations (Consolidation) Act 1992 Sch A1 para 64(2)(b) (as added: see note 6). As to the meaning of 'provisions relating to the collective bargaining method' see PARA 1132 note 6.

13   As to the meaning of 'employee' see PARA 892.

14   Trade Union and Labour Relations (Consolidation) Act 1992 Sch A1 para 70(4), (5) (as added: see note 6). See also note 7.

15   Trade Union and Labour Relations (Consolidation) Act 1992 Sch A1 para 70(6) (as added: see note 6). See also note 7. Schedule A1 para 82 (see PARA 1141) applies if the CAC gives notice under Sch A1 para 70 of: (1) a decision that the original unit is no longer an appropriate bargaining unit; and (2) a decision as to the bargaining unit which is, or units which are, appropriate: Sch A1 para 72 (as so added).

16   Ie no further steps are to be taken under the Trade Union and Labour Relations (Consolidation) Act 1992 Sch A1 Pt III (paras 64–95): see also PARAS 1132 et seq, 1136 et seq.

17   Trade Union and Labour Relations (Consolidation) Act 1992 Sch A1 para 71 (as added: see note 6). See also note 7.

1136. Bargaining arrangements ceasing to apply. If:

(1)   the parties[1] agree[2] a bargaining unit or units differing from the original unit[3];

(2)   the relevant provision[4] does not apply; and

(3)   at least one worker[5] falling within the original unit does not fall within the new unit, or any of the new units,

then, in such a case, the Central Arbitration Committee[6] (the 'CAC') must issue a declaration that the bargaining arrangements[7], so far as relating to the worker or workers mentioned in head (3) above, are to cease to have effect on a date specified by the CAC in the declaration; and the bargaining arrangements cease to have effect accordingly[8].

1 As to the meaning of references to the parties see PARA 1132 note 5.
2 Ie under the Trade Union and Labour Relations (Consolidation) Act 1992 Sch A1 para 69: see PARA 1134.
3 As to the meaning of references to the original unit see PARA 1132 note 5.
4 Ie the Trade Union and Labour Relations (Consolidation) Act 1992 Sch A1 para 69(2): see PARA 1134.
5 As to the meaning of 'worker' see PARA 892.
6 As to the Central Arbitration Committee see PARA 1226 et seq.
7 As to the meaning of references to the bargaining arrangements see PARA 1135 note 12.
8 Trade Union and Labour Relations (Consolidation) Act 1992 Sch A1 para 73(1), (2) (Sch A1 added by the Employment Relations Act 1999 Sch 1). As to the application of the Trade Union and Labour Relations (Consolidation) Act 1992 Sch A1 para 73 see PARA 1132.

C. EMPLOYER BELIEVES BARGAINING UNIT HAS CEASED TO EXIST

1137. Notice where employer believes bargaining unit has ceased to exist. If the employer[1] believes that the original unit[2] has ceased to exist, and wishes the bargaining arrangements[3] to cease to have effect, he must give the union[4], or each of the unions, a notice complying with the following provisions and must give a copy of the notice to the Central Arbitration Committee (the 'CAC')[5]. A notice so complies if it:

(1)   identifies the unit and the bargaining arrangements;
(2)   states the date on which the notice is given;
(3)   states that the unit has ceased to exist; and
(4)   states that the bargaining arrangements are to cease to have effect on a date which is specified in the notice and which falls after the end of the period of 35 working days[6] starting with the day after that on which the notice is given[7].

Within the validation period[8], the CAC must decide whether the notice complies with the above provisions[9]. If the CAC decides that the notice does not so comply, the CAC must give the parties notice of its decision; and the employer's notice is to be treated as not having been given[10]. If the CAC decides that the notice so complies, it must give the parties notice of the decision[11].

1   As to the meaning of 'employer' see PARA 892.
2   As to the meaning of references to the original unit see PARA 1132 note 5.
3   As to the meaning of references to the bargaining arrangements see PARA 1135 note 12.
4   As to the meaning of 'trade union' see PARA 891.
5   Trade Union and Labour Relations (Consolidation) Act 1992 Sch A1 paras 74(1), 172(1) (Sch A1 added by the Employment Relations Act 1999 Sch 1). As to the application of the Trade Union and Labour Relations (Consolidation) Act 1992 Sch A1 para 74 see PARA 1132. As to the Central Arbitration Committee see PARA 1226 et seq.
6   As to the meaning of 'working day' see PARA 1105 note 1.
7   Trade Union and Labour Relations (Consolidation) Act 1992 Sch A1 para 74(2) (as added: see note 5). See also note 5.
8   For these purposes, the validation period is: (1) the period of ten working days starting with the day after that on which the CAC receives the copy of the notice; or (2) such longer period, so starting, as the CAC may specify to the parties by notice containing reasons for the extension: Trade Union and Labour Relations (Consolidation) Act 1992 Sch A1 para 74(7) (as added: see note 5). As to the meaning of references to the parties see PARA 1132 note 5.
9   Trade Union and Labour Relations (Consolidation) Act 1992 Sch A1 para 74(3) (as added: see note 5).
10 Trade Union and Labour Relations (Consolidation) Act 1992 Sch A1 para 74(4) (as added: see note 5).

11 Trade Union and Labour Relations (Consolidation) Act 1992 Sch A1 para 74(5) (as added: see note 5). The bargaining arrangements cease to have effect on the date specified under Sch A1 para 74(2)(d) (see head (4) in the text) if: (1) the CAC gives notice under Sch A1 para 74(5); and (2) the union does not, or unions do not, apply to the CAC under Sch A1 para 75 (see PARA 1138): Sch A1 para 74(6) (as so added).

1138. Application for certain questions as to the original bargaining unit to be decided. If the Central Arbitration Committee[1] (the 'CAC') gives notice[2] and, within the period of ten working days[3] starting with the day after that on which the notice is given, the union[4] makes, or unions make, an application to the CAC for a decision on the questions specified in heads (1) and (2) below, the CAC must give notice to the parties of receipt of such an application[5]. The questions are:

(1) whether the original unit[6] has ceased to exist; and
(2) whether the original unit is no longer appropriate by reason of any of the following matters:
  (a) a change in the organisation or structure of the business carried on by the employer[7];
  (b) a change in the activities pursued by the employer in the course of the business carried on by him;
  (c) a substantial change in the number of workers[8] employed in the original unit[9].

Within the acceptance period[10], the Central Arbitration Committee (the 'CAC') must decide whether the application is[11] admissible[12].

In deciding whether the application is admissible, the CAC must consider any evidence which it has been given by the employer or the union, or unions[13]. If the CAC decides that the application is not admissible:

(i) the CAC must give notice of its decision to the parties;
(ii) the CAC must not accept the application; and
(iii) no further steps[14] are to be taken[15].

If the CAC decides that the application is admissible, it must accept the application and give notice of the acceptance to the parties[16].

1 As to the Central Arbitration Committee see PARA 1226 et seq.
2 Ie under the Trade Union and Labour Relations (Consolidation) Act 1992 Sch A1 para 74(5): see PARA 1137.
3 As to the meaning of 'working day' see PARA 1105 note 1.
4 As to the meaning of 'trade union' see PARA 891.
5 Trade Union and Labour Relations (Consolidation) Act 1992 Sch A1 paras 75(1), 76(1), 172(1) (Sch A1 added by the Employment Relations Act 1999 Sch 1). As to the application of the Trade Union and Labour Relations (Consolidation) Act 1992 Sch A1 paras 75–76 see PARA 1132.
6 As to the meaning of references to the original unit see PARA 1132 note 5.
7 As to the meaning of 'employer' see PARA 892.
8 As to the meaning of 'worker' see PARA 892.
9 Trade Union and Labour Relations (Consolidation) Act 1992 Sch A1 para 75(2), (3) (as added: see note 5). See also note 5.
10 For these purposes, the acceptance period is: (1) the period of ten working days starting with the day after that on which the CAC receives the application; or (2) such longer period, so starting, as the CAC may specify to the parties by notice containing reasons for the extension: Trade Union and Labour Relations (Consolidation) Act 1992 Sch A1 para 76(6) (as added: see note 5). As to the meaning of references to the parties see PARA 1132 note 5.
11 Ie admissible within the terms of the Trade Union and Labour Relations (Consolidation) Act 1992 Sch A1 para 92: see PARA 1146.
12 Trade Union and Labour Relations (Consolidation) Act 1992 Sch A1 para 76(2) (as added: see note 5). As to the withdrawal of applications see PARA 1147.
13 Trade Union and Labour Relations (Consolidation) Act 1992 Sch A1 para 76(3) (as added: see note 5).

14 Ie no further steps under the Trade Union and Labour Relations (Consolidation) Act 1992 Sch A1 Pt III (paras 64–95): see also PARAS 1132 et seq, 1139 et seq.

15 Trade Union and Labour Relations (Consolidation) Act 1992 Sch A1 para 76(4) (as added: see note 5).

16 Trade Union and Labour Relations (Consolidation) Act 1992 Sch A1 para 76(5) (as added: see note 5).

1139. Procedure following acceptance of application for certain questions as to the original bargaining unit to be decided. If the Central Arbitration Committee[1] (the 'CAC') accepts an application for certain questions as to the original bargaining unit to be decided[2]:

(1) it must give the employer[3] and the union[4], or unions, an opportunity to put their views on the questions in relation to which the application was made; and

(2) it must decide the questions before the end of the decision period[5].

If the CAC decides that the original unit[6] has ceased to exist, the CAC must give the parties notice of its decision; and the bargaining arrangements[7] cease to have effect on the termination date[8]. If the CAC decides that the original unit has not ceased to exist, and that it is not the case that the original unit is no longer appropriate[9], the CAC must give the parties notice of its decision; and the employer's notice is to be treated as not having been given[10]. If the CAC decides that the original unit has not ceased to exist, and that the original unit is no longer appropriate[11], the CAC must give the parties notice of its decision[12].

1 As to the Central Arbitration Committee see PARA 1226 et seq.

2 Ie an application under the Trade Union and Labour Relations (Consolidation) Act 1992 Sch A1 para 75: see PARA 1138.

3 As to the meaning of 'employer' see PARA 892.

4 As to the meaning of 'trade union' see PARA 891.

5 See the Trade Union and Labour Relations (Consolidation) Act 1992 Sch A1 paras 77(1), 172(1) (Sch A1 added by the Employment Relations Act 1999 Sch 1). For these purposes, the decision period is: (1) the period of ten working days starting with the day after that on which the CAC gives notice of acceptance of the application; or (2) such longer period, so starting, as the CAC may specify to the parties by notice containing reasons for the extension: Sch A1 para 77(5) (as so added). As to the application of Sch A1 para 77 see PARA 1132. As to the meaning of 'working day' see PARA 1105 note 1; and as to the meaning of references to the parties see PARA 1132 note 5.

6 As to the meaning of references to the original unit see PARA 1132 note 5.

7 As to the meaning of references to the bargaining arrangements see PARA 1135 note 12.

8 Trade Union and Labour Relations (Consolidation) Act 1992 Sch A1 para 77(2) (as added: see note 5). See also note 5. For these purposes, the termination date is the later of the dates specified under Sch A1 para 74(2)(d) (see PARA 1137 head (4) in the text) and the day after the last day of the decision period: Sch A1 para 77(6) (as so added).

9 Ie by reason of any of the matters specified in the Trade Union and Labour Relations (Consolidation) Act 1992 Sch A1 para 75(3): see PARA 1138 heads (2)(a)–(c) in the text.

10 Trade Union and Labour Relations (Consolidation) Act 1992 Sch A1 para 77(3) (as added: see note 5). See also note 5.

11 See note 9.

12 Trade Union and Labour Relations (Consolidation) Act 1992 Sch A1 para 77(4) (as added: see note 5). See also note 5.

1140. Parties agree different bargaining unit or units. If the Central Arbitration Committee[1] (the 'CAC') gives notice[2] and, before the end of the first period[3], the parties agree a bargaining unit or units ('the new unit or units') differing from the original unit[4] and inform the CAC of their agreement, then, if, in the CAC's opinion, the new unit, or any of the new units, contains at least one worker[5] falling within an outside bargaining unit[6], no further steps[7] are to be taken[8].

If the above provisions do not apply:

(1)   the CAC must issue a declaration that the union is, or unions are, recognised as entitled to conduct collective bargaining on behalf of the new unit or units;

(2)   so far as it affects workers in the new unit, or units, who fall within the original unit, the declaration has effect in place of any declaration that the union is, or unions are, recognised as entitled to conduct collective bargaining on behalf of the original unit;

(3)   the method of collective bargaining relating to the original unit has effect in relation to the new unit or units, with any modifications which the CAC considers necessary to take account of the change of bargaining unit and specifies in the declaration[9].

If the CAC gives notice[10] and the parties do not inform the CAC before the end of the first period that they have agreed a bargaining unit or units differing from the original unit, then, during the second period[11], the CAC must decide what other bargaining unit is, or units are, appropriate and give notice of its decision to the parties[12]. In deciding what other bargaining unit is, or units are, appropriate, the CAC must take into account:

(a)   the need for the unit or units to be compatible with effective management;

(b)   the following matters, so far as they do not conflict with that need:
       (i)   the views of the employer and of the union, or unions;
       (ii)   existing national and local bargaining arrangements;
       (iii)   the desirability of avoiding small fragmented bargaining units within an undertaking;
       (iv)   the characteristics of workers falling within the original unit and of any other employees[13] of the employer whom the CAC considers relevant;
       (v)   the location of workers[14].

If the CAC decides that two or more bargaining units are appropriate, its decision must be such that no worker falls within more than one of them[15].

If:

(A)   the parties agree[16] a bargaining unit or units differing from the original unit;

(B)   certain of the above provisions[17] do not apply; and

(C)   at least one worker falling within the original unit does not fall within the new unit, or any of the new units,

then, in such a case, the CAC must issue a declaration that the bargaining arrangements, so far as relating to the worker or workers mentioned in head (C) above, are to cease to have effect on a date specified by the CAC in the declaration; and the bargaining arrangements cease to have effect accordingly[18].

1   As to the Central Arbitration Committee see PARA 1226 et seq.
2   Ie under the Trade Union and Labour Relations (Consolidation) Act 1992 Sch A1 para 77(4): see PARA 1139.
3   For these purposes, the first period is: (1) the period of ten working days starting with the day after that on which the CAC gives notice under the Trade Union and Labour Relations (Consolidation) Act 1992 Sch A1 para 77(4); or (2) such longer period, so starting, as the parties may from time to time agree and notify to the CAC: Sch A1 para 78(4) (Sch A1 added by the Employment Relations Act 1999 Sch 1). As to the meaning of 'working day' see PARA 1105 note 1; and as to the meaning of references to the parties see PARA 1132 note 5.
4   As to the meaning of references to the original unit see PARA 1132 note 5.
5   As to the meaning of 'worker' see PARA 892.

6   For these purposes, an outside bargaining unit is a bargaining unit which fulfils these conditions: (1) it is not the original unit; (2) a union is, or unions are, recognised as entitled to conduct collective bargaining on its behalf; (3) the union, or at least one of the unions, is not a party referred to in the Trade Union and Labour Relations (Consolidation) Act 1992 Sch A1 para 64 (see PARA 1132): Sch A1 para 78(5) (as added: see note 3). As to the meaning of 'trade union' see PARA 891; as to the meaning of 'recognised' see PARA 1094; and as to the meaning of references to collective bargaining see PARA 1132 note 5.

7   Ie no further steps are to be taken under the Trade Union and Labour Relations (Consolidation) Act 1992 Sch A1 Pt III (paras 64–95): see also PARAS 1132 et seq, 1141 et seq.

8   Trade Union and Labour Relations (Consolidation) Act 1992 Sch A1 para 78(1), (2) (as added: see note 3). As to the application of Sch A1 paras 78–81 see PARA 1132.

9   Trade Union and Labour Relations (Consolidation) Act 1992 Sch A1 para 78(3) (as added: see note 3). See also note 8.

10 See note 2.

11 For these purposes, the second period is: (1) the period of ten working days starting with the day after that on which the first period ends; or (2) such longer period, so starting, as the CAC may specify to the parties by notice containing reasons for the extension: Trade Union and Labour Relations (Consolidation) Act 1992 Sch A1 para 79(6) (as added: see note 3).

12 Trade Union and Labour Relations (Consolidation) Act 1992 Sch A1 para 79(1), (2) (as added: see note 3). Schedule Sch A1 para 82 (see PARA 1141) applies if the CAC gives notice under Sch A1 para 79 of a decision as to the bargaining unit which is, or units which are, appropriate: Sch A1 para 80 (as so added). See also note 8.

13 As to the meaning of 'employee' see PARA 892.

14 Trade Union and Labour Relations (Consolidation) Act 1992 Sch A1 para 79(3), (4) (as added: see note 3). See also note 8.

15 Trade Union and Labour Relations (Consolidation) Act 1992 Sch A1 para 79(5) (as added: see note 3). See also note 8.

16 Ie under the Trade Union and Labour Relations (Consolidation) Act 1992 Sch A1 para 78.

17 Ie the Trade Union and Labour Relations (Consolidation) Act 1992 Sch A1 para 78(2).

18 Trade Union and Labour Relations (Consolidation) Act 1992 Sch A1 para 81(1), (2) (as added: see note 3). See also note 8.

D. POSITION WHERE CENTRAL ARBITRATION COMMITTEE DECIDES NEW BARGAINING UNIT

1141. Procedure where Central Arbitration Committee decides new bargaining unit; in general. If:

(1)   the Central Arbitration Committee[1] (the 'CAC') gives notice[2] of a decision that the original unit[3] is no longer an appropriate bargaining unit and a decision as to the bargaining unit which is, or units which are, appropriate[4]; or

(2)   the CAC gives notice[5] of a decision as to the bargaining unit which is, or units which are, appropriate[6],

the CAC must proceed in the manner set out by statute[7] with regard to the appropriate unit, if there is one only, or must proceed in that manner with regard to each appropriate unit separately, if there are two or more[8].

1   As to the Central Arbitration Committee see PARA 1226 et seq.

2   Ie under the Trade Union and Labour Relations (Consolidation) Act 1992 Sch A1 para 70: see PARA 1135.

3   As to the meaning of references to the original unit see PARA 1132 note 5.

4   Trade Union and Labour Relations (Consolidation) Act 1992 Sch A1 para 82(1) (Sch A1 added by the Employment Relations Act 1999 Sch 1). As to the application of Sch A1 para 82 see PARA 1132.

5   Ie under the Trade Union and Labour Relations (Consolidation) Act 1992 Sch A1 para 79: see PARA 1140.

6   Trade Union and Labour Relations (Consolidation) Act 1992 Sch A1 para 82(2) (as added: see note 4). See also note 4.

7   Ie in the manner stated in the Trade Union and Labour Relations (Consolidation) Act 1992 Sch A1 paras 83–89: see PARA 1142 et seq. For the purposes of Sch A1 paras 83–89, references to the new unit are to the appropriate unit under consideration: Sch A1 para 82(4) (as added: see note 4).

8   Trade Union and Labour Relations (Consolidation) Act 1992 Sch A1 para 82(3) (as added: see note 4). See also note 4.

1142.   Procedure where new unit contains at least one worker falling within a statutory outside bargaining unit. If, in the opinion of the Central Arbitration Committee[1] (the 'CAC'), the new unit[2] contains at least one worker[3] falling within a statutory outside bargaining unit[4], the CAC must issue a declaration that the relevant bargaining arrangements[5], so far as relating to workers falling within the new unit, are to cease to have effect on a date specified[6] by the CAC in the declaration; and the relevant bargaining arrangements cease to have effect accordingly[7].

1   As to the Central Arbitration Committee see PARA 1226 et seq.
2   As to the meaning of references to the new unit see PARA 1141 note 7.
3   As to the meaning of 'worker' see PARA 892.
4   For these purposes, a statutory outside bargaining unit is a bargaining unit which fulfils these conditions: (1) it is not the original unit; (2) a union is, or unions are, recognised as entitled to conduct collective bargaining on its behalf by virtue of a declaration of the CAC; (3) the union, or at least one of the unions, is not a party referred to in the Trade Union and Labour Relations (Consolidation) Act 1992 Sch A1 para 64 (see PARA 1132): Sch A1 para 83(7) (Sch A1 added by the Employment Relations Act 1999 Sch 1). As to the meaning of references to the original unit see PARA 1132 note 5; as to the meaning of 'trade union' see PARA 891; as to the meaning of 'recognised' see PARA 1094; and as to the meaning of references to collective bargaining see PARA 1132 note 5.
5   For these purposes, the relevant bargaining arrangements are: (1) the bargaining arrangements relating to the original unit; and (2) the bargaining arrangements relating to each statutory outside bargaining unit containing workers who fall within the new unit: Trade Union and Labour Relations (Consolidation) Act 1992 Sch A1 para 83(3) (as added: see note 4). The bargaining arrangements relating to the original unit are the bargaining arrangements as defined in Sch A1 para 64 (see PARA 1135 note 12): Sch A1 para 83(4) (as so added). The bargaining arrangements relating to an outside unit are: (a) the declaration recognising a union, or unions, as entitled to conduct collective bargaining on behalf of the workers constituting the outside unit; and (b) the provisions relating to the collective bargaining method: Sch A1 para 83(5) (as so added).
     The provisions relating to the collective bargaining method are: (i) any agreement by the employer and the union, or unions, as to the method by which collective bargaining is to be conducted with regard to the outside unit; (ii) anything effective as, or as if contained in, a legally enforceable contract and relating to the method by which collective bargaining is to be conducted with regard to the outside unit; or (iii) any provision of Sch A1 Pt III (paras 64–95) (see also PARAS 1132 et seq, 1143 et seq) that a method of collective bargaining is to have effect with regard to the outside unit: Sch A1 para 83(6) (as so added). As to the meaning of 'employer' see PARA 892.
6   The date so specified must be: (1) the date on which the relevant period expires; or (2) if the CAC believes that to maintain the relevant bargaining arrangements would be impracticable or contrary to the interests of good industrial relations, the date after the date on which the declaration is issued; and the relevant period is the period of 65 working days starting with the day after that on which the declaration is issued: Trade Union and Labour Relations (Consolidation) Act 1992 Sch A1 para 83(8) (as added (see note 4); amended by the Employment Relations Act 2004 Sch 1 para 23(1), (17)). As to the meaning of 'working day' see PARA 1105 note 1.
7   Trade Union and Labour Relations (Consolidation) Act 1992 Sch A1 para 83(1), (2) (as added: see note 4). As to the application of Sch A1 para 83 see PARA 1132.

1143.   Procedure where new unit contains at least one worker falling within a voluntary outside bargaining unit. If, in the opinion of the Central Arbitration Committee[1] (the 'CAC'), the new unit[2] contains at least one worker[3] falling within a voluntary outside bargaining unit[4], but no worker falling within a statutory outside bargaining unit[5], the CAC must issue a declaration that the original bargaining arrangements[6], so far as relating to workers falling within the new unit, are to cease to have effect on a date specified[7] by the CAC in the declaration; and the original bargaining arrangements cease to have effect accordingly[8].

1   As to the Central Arbitration Committee see PARA 1226 et seq.
2   As to the meaning of references to the new unit see PARA 1141 note 7.
3   As to the meaning of 'worker' see PARA 892.
4   For these purposes, a voluntary outside bargaining unit is a bargaining unit which fulfils these conditions: (1) it is not the original unit; (2) a union is, or unions are, recognised as entitled to conduct collective bargaining on its behalf by virtue of an agreement with the employer; (3) the union, or at least one of the unions, is not a party referred to in the Trade Union and Labour Relations (Consolidation) Act 1992 Sch A1 para 64 (see PARA 1132): Sch A1 para 84(4) (Sch A1 added by the Employment Relations Act 1999 Sch 1). As to the meaning of 'trade union' see PARA 891; as to the meaning of 'recognised' see PARA 1094; and as to the meaning of references to collective bargaining and to the original unit see PARA 1132 note 5.
5   As to the meaning of 'statutory outside bargaining unit' see PARA 1142 note 4.
6   For these purposes, the original bargaining arrangements are the bargaining arrangements as defined in the Trade Union and Labour Relations (Consolidation) Act 1992 Sch A1 para 64 (see PARA 1135 note 12): Sch A1 para 84(3) (as added: see note 4).
7   The date so specified must be: (1) the date on which the relevant period expires; or (2) if the CAC believes that to maintain the original bargaining arrangements would be impracticable or contrary to the interests of good industrial relations, the date after the date on which the declaration is issued; and the relevant period is the period of 65 working days starting with the day after that on which the declaration is issued: Trade Union and Labour Relations (Consolidation) Act 1992 Sch A1 para 84(5) (as added: see note 4). As to the meaning of 'working day' see PARA 1105 note 1.
8   Trade Union and Labour Relations (Consolidation) Act 1992 Sch A1 para 84(1), (2) (as added: see note 4). As to the application of Sch A1 para 84 see PARA 1132.

1144.   Procedure where new unit does not contain at least one worker falling within either a statutory or a voluntary outside bargaining unit. If the opinion of the Central Arbitration Committee[1] (the 'CAC') is not that the new unit[2] contains at least one worker[3] falling within either a statutory or a voluntary outside bargaining unit[4], it must decide whether the difference between the original unit[5] and the new unit is such that the support of the union[6], or unions, within the new unit needs to be assessed and inform the parties[7] of its decision[8].

If the CAC's decision is that such support does not need to be assessed:

(1)   the CAC must issue a declaration that the union is, or unions are, recognised[9] as entitled to conduct collective bargaining[10] on behalf of the new unit;

(2)   so far as it affects workers in the new unit who fall within the original unit, the declaration has effect in place of any declaration that the union is, or unions are, recognised as entitled to conduct collective bargaining on behalf of the original unit;

(3)   the method of collective bargaining relating to the original unit has effect in relation to the new unit, with any modifications which the CAC considers necessary to take account of the change of bargaining unit and specifies in the declaration[11].

If the CAC decides[12] that the support of the union, or unions, within the new unit needs to be assessed, the following provisions apply[13]. The CAC must decide these questions:

(a)   whether members of the union, or unions, constitute at least 10 per cent of the workers constituting the new unit;

(b)   whether a majority of the workers constituting the new unit would be likely to favour recognition of the union, or unions, as entitled to conduct collective bargaining on behalf of the new unit[14].

If the CAC decides one or both of the questions in the negative, the CAC must issue a declaration that the bargaining arrangements[15], so far as relating to workers falling within the new unit, are to cease to have effect on a date specified by the CAC in the declaration; and the bargaining arrangements cease to have effect accordingly[16].

If the CAC decides both the question in heads (a) and (b) above in the affirmative and the CAC is satisfied that a majority of the workers constituting the new unit are members of the union, or unions, the CAC must issue a declaration that the union is, or unions are, recognised as entitled to conduct collective bargaining on behalf of the workers constituting the new unit[17]. If, however, any of the following three qualifying conditions is fulfilled:

(i)   the CAC is satisfied that a ballot should be held in the interests of good industrial relations;

(ii)   the CAC has evidence, which it considers to be credible, from a significant number of the union members within the bargaining unit that they do not want the union, or unions, to conduct collective bargaining on their behalf;

(iii)   membership evidence[18] is produced which leads the CAC to conclude that there are doubts whether a significant number of the union members within the new unit want the union, or unions, to conduct collective bargaining on their behalf,

then, instead of issuing such a declaration[19], the CAC must give notice to the parties that it intends to arrange for the holding of a secret ballot in which the workers constituting the new unit are asked whether they want the union, or unions, to conduct collective bargaining on their behalf[20].

If the CAC issues such a declaration[21], so far as it affects workers in the new unit who fall within the original unit, the declaration has effect in place of any declaration that the union is, or unions are, recognised as entitled to conduct collective bargaining on behalf of the original unit[22]. The method of collective bargaining relating to the original unit has effect in relation to the new unit, with any modifications which the CAC considers necessary to take account of the change of bargaining unit and specifies in the declaration[23].

If the CAC decides both the questions in heads (a) and (b) above in the affirmative and the CAC is not satisfied that a majority of the workers constituting the new unit are members of the union, or unions, the CAC must give notice to the parties that it intends to arrange for the holding of a secret ballot in which the workers constituting the new units are asked whether they want the union, or unions, to conduct collective bargaining on their behalf[24].

If the CAC gives notice that it intends to arrange for the holding of a secret ballot[25], the union, or unions, may within the notification period[26] notify the CAC that the union does not, or unions do not, want the CAC to arrange for the holding of the ballot[27]. If the CAC is so notified:

(A)   it must not arrange for the holding of the ballot;

(B)   it must inform the parties[28] that it will not arrange for the holding of the ballot, and why;

(C)   it must issue a declaration that the bargaining arrangements, so far as relating to workers falling within the new unit[29], are to cease to have effect on a date specified by it in the declaration; and

(D)   the bargaining arrangements cease to have effect accordingly[30].

If the CAC is not so notified, it must arrange for the holding of the ballot[31].

If, as a result of the ballot, the CAC issues a declaration that the union is, or unions are, recognised as entitled to conduct collective bargaining on behalf of the new unit, so far as it affects workers in the new unit who fall within the original unit, the declaration has effect in place of any declaration that the union is, or unions are, recognised as entitled to conduct collective bargaining on behalf of the original unit[32]. The method of collective bargaining relating to the original unit has effect in relation to the new unit, with any modifications which the CAC considers necessary to take account of the change of bargaining unit and specifies in the declaration[33].

If, as a result of the ballot, the CAC issues a declaration that the union is, or unions are, not entitled to be recognised as entitled to conduct collective bargaining on behalf of the new unit, the CAC must state in the declaration the date on which the bargaining arrangements, so far as relating to workers falling within the new unit, are to cease to have effect; and the bargaining arrangements cease to have effect accordingly[34].

1   As to the Central Arbitration Committee see PARA 1226 et seq.
2   As to the meaning of references to the new unit see PARA 1141 note 7.
3   As to the meaning of 'worker' see PARA 892.
4   Ie if the CAC's opinion is not that mentioned in the Trade Union and Labour Relations (Consolidation) Act 1992 Sch A1 para 83(1) (see PARA 1142) or Sch A1 para 84(1) (see PARA 1143).
5   As to the meaning of references to the original unit see PARA 1132 note 5.
6   As to the meaning of 'trade union' see PARA 891.
7   As to the meaning of references to the parties see PARA 1132 note 5.
8   Trade Union and Labour Relations (Consolidation) Act 1992 Sch A1 para 85(1) (Sch A1 added by the Employment Relations Act 1999 Sch 1). As to the application of Sch A1 para 85 see PARA 1132.
9   As to the meaning of 'recognised' see PARA 1094.
10   As to the meaning of references to collective bargaining see PARA 1132 note 5.
11   Trade Union and Labour Relations (Consolidation) Act 1992 Sch A1 para 85(2) (as added: see note 8). See also note 8.
12   Ie under the Trade Union and Labour Relations (Consolidation) Act 1992 Sch A1 para 85(1): see PARA 1144.
13   Trade Union and Labour Relations (Consolidation) Act 1992 Sch A1 para 86(1) (Sch A1 added by the Employment Relations Act 1999 Sch 1). As to the application of the Trade Union and Labour Relations (Consolidation) Act 1992 Sch A1 paras 86–87 see PARA 1132.
14   Trade Union and Labour Relations (Consolidation) Act 1992 Sch A1 para 86(2) (as added: see note 8). See also note 13.
15   As to the meaning of references to the bargaining arrangements see PARA 1135 note 12.
16   Trade Union and Labour Relations (Consolidation) Act 1992 Sch A1 para 86(3) (as added: see note 8). See also note 13.
17   Trade Union and Labour Relations (Consolidation) Act 1992 Sch A1 para 87(1), (2) (as added: see note 8). See also note 13.
      The Secretary of State may issue guidance to the CAC on the way in which it is to exercise its functions under the Trade Union and Labour Relations (Consolidation) Act 1992 Sch A1 para 87; and the CAC must take into account any such guidance in exercising those functions: Trade Union and Labour Relations (Consolidation) Act 1992 Sch A1 para 167(1), (2) (as so added). No guidance is, however, to apply with regard to an application made to the CAC before the guidance in question was issued: Sch A1 para 167(3) (as so added). The Secretary of State must lay before each House of Parliament any guidance so issued and arrange for any such guidance to be published by such means as appear to him to be most appropriate for drawing it to the attention of persons likely to be affected by it: Sch A1 para 167(4) (as so added).
18   For these purposes, membership evidence is: (1) evidence about the circumstances in which union members became members; (2) evidence about the length of time for which union

members have been members, in a case where the CAC is satisfied that such evidence should be taken into account: Trade Union and Labour Relations (Consolidation) Act 1992 Sch A1 para 87(5) (as added: see note 8).

19 Ie under the Trade Union and Labour Relations (Consolidation) Act 1992 Sch A1 para 87(2).

20 Trade Union and Labour Relations (Consolidation) Act 1992 Sch A1 para 87(3), (4) (as added (see note 8); Sch A1 para 87(4) amended by the Employment Relations Act 2004 s 6(2)).

21 See note 19.

22 Trade Union and Labour Relations (Consolidation) Act 1992 Sch A1 para 87(6)(a) (as added: see note 8).

23 Trade Union and Labour Relations (Consolidation) Act 1992 Sch A1 para 87(6)(b) (as added: see note 8).

24 Trade Union and Labour Relations (Consolidation) Act 1992 Sch A1 para 88(1), (2) (as added: see note 8).

25 Ie under the Trade Union and Labour Relations (Consolidation) Act 1992 Sch A1 para 87(3) or Sch A1 para 88(2): see the text and notes 19–20, 24.

26 For these purposes, the notification period is the period of ten working days starting with the day after that on which the union, or last of the unions, receives the CAC's notice: Trade Union and Labour Relations (Consolidation) Act 1992 Sch A1 para 89(1) (as added: see note 8). (As to the meaning of 'working day' see PARA 1105 note 1.

27 Trade Union and Labour Relations (Consolidation) Act 1992 Sch A1 para 89(1) (as added: see note 8). As to the application of Sch A1 para 89 see PARA 1132.

28 As to the meaning of references to the parties see note 7.

29 As to the meaning of references to the new unit see note 2.

30 Trade Union and Labour Relations (Consolidation) Act 1992 Sch A1 para 89(2) (as added: see note 8).

31 Trade Union and Labour Relations (Consolidation) Act 1992 Sch A1 para 89(3) (as added: see note 8). Schedule A1 para 25 (see PARA 1118) applies if the CAC arranges under Sch A1 para 89 for the holding of a ballot, as well as if the CAC arranges under Sch A1 para 24 (see PARA 1118) for the holding of a ballot: Sch A1 para 89(4) (as so added). Schedule A1 paras 26–29 (see PARAS 1120–1122) apply accordingly, but as if references to the bargaining unit were references to the new unit, and Sch A1 para 26(4F)–(4H) and the references in Sch A1 para 26(4), (6) to Sch A1 para 19D were omitted: Sch A1 para 89(5) (as so added; amended by the Employment Relations Act 2004 Sch 1 para 23(1), (18)).

32 Trade Union and Labour Relations (Consolidation) Act 1992 Sch A1 para 89(6)(a) (as added: see note 8). Schedule A1 para 89(6)(a), (b) (also applies if the CAC issues a declaration under Sch A1 para 27(2) or Sch A1 para 27D(3) (see PARA 1119): Sch A1 para 89(8) (as so added; amended by the Employment Relations Act 2004 Sch 1 para 23(1), (19)).

33 Trade Union and Labour Relations (Consolidation) Act 1992 Sch A1 para 89(6)(b) (as added: see note 8).

34 Trade Union and Labour Relations (Consolidation) Act 1992 Sch A1 para 89(7)(a), (b) (as added: see note 8). Schedule Sch A1 para 89(7)(a), (b) also applies if the CAC issues a declaration under Sch A1 para 27D(4) (see PARA 1119): Sch A1 para 89(9) (added by the Employment Relations Act 2004 Sch 1 para 23(1), (20)).

1145. Residual workers. If:

(1) the Central Arbitration Committee[1] (the 'CAC') decides an appropriate bargaining unit or units[2]; and

(2) at least one worker[3] falling within the original unit[4] does not fall within the new unit, or any of the new units,

then, in such a case the CAC must issue a declaration that the bargaining arrangements[5], so far as relating to the worker or workers mentioned in head (2) above, are to cease to have effect on a date specified by the CAC in the declaration; and the bargaining arrangements cease to have effect accordingly[6].

If:

(a) the CAC has followed the statutory procedure[7] with regard to the new unit, if there is one only, or with regard to each new unit, if there are two or more; and

(b) in so doing, the CAC has issued one or more declarations[8], the CAC must consider each declaration so issued, and, in relation to each declaration, identify each statutory outside bargaining unit[9] which contains at least one worker who also falls within the new unit to which the declaration relates, each such statutory outside bargaining unit so identified being referred to as a 'parent unit'[10].

The CAC must then consider each parent unit, and, in relation to each parent unit, identify any workers who fall within the parent unit but who do not fall within the new unit, or any of the new units, the workers so identified in relation to a parent unit being referred to as a 'residual unit'[11]. In relation to each residual unit, the CAC must issue a declaration that the outside union[12] is, or outside unions are, recognised as entitled to conduct collective bargaining on its behalf[13]. If the CAC issues such a declaration:

(i) the declaration has effect in place of the existing declaration that the outside union is, or outside unions are, recognised as entitled to conduct collective bargaining on behalf of the parent unit, so far as the existing declaration relates to the residual unit;

(ii) if there is a method of collective bargaining relating to the parent unit, it has effect in relation to the residual unit with any modifications which the CAC considers necessary to take account of the change of bargaining unit and specifies in the declaration[14].

1 As to the Central Arbitration Committee see PARA 1226 et seq.
2 Ie under the Trade Union and Labour Relations (Consolidation) Act 1992 Sch A1 para 70 (see PARA 1135) or Sch 1 para 79 (see PARA 1140).
3 As to the meaning of 'worker' see PARA 892.
4 As to the meaning of references to the original unit see PARA 1132 note 5.
5 As to the meaning of references to the bargaining arrangements see PARA 1135 note 12.
6 Trade Union and Labour Relations (Consolidation) Act 1992 Sch A1 para 90(1), (2) (Sch A1 added by the Employment Relations Act 1999 Sch 1). As to the application of the Trade Union and Labour Relations (Consolidation) Act 1992 Sch A1 paras 90–91 see PARA 1132.
7 Ie as stated in the Trade Union and Labour Relations (Consolidation) Act 1992 Sch A1 paras 83–89: see PARA 1142 et seq.
8 Ie under the Trade Union and Labour Relations (Consolidation) Act 1992 Sch A1 para 83: see PARA 1142.
9 As to the meaning of 'statutory outside bargaining unit' see PARA 1142 note 4.
10 Trade Union and Labour Relations (Consolidation) Act 1992 Sch A1 para 91(1), (2) (as added: see note 6).
11 Trade Union and Labour Relations (Consolidation) Act 1992 Sch A1 para 91(3) (as added: see note 6).
12 For these purposes, references to the outside union, or to outside unions, in relation to a residual unit, are to the union which is, or unions which are, recognised as entitled to conduct collective bargaining on behalf of its parent unit: Trade Union and Labour Relations (Consolidation) Act 1992 Sch A1 para 91(6) (as added: see note 6). As to the meaning of 'trade union' see PARA 891; as to the meaning of 'recognised' see PARA 1094; and as to the meaning of references to collective bargaining see PARA 1132 note 5.
13 Trade Union and Labour Relations (Consolidation) Act 1992 Sch A1 para 91(4) (as added: see note 6). No such declaration must, however, be issued in relation to a residual unit if the CAC has received an application under Sch A1 para 66 (see PARA 1133) or Sch A1 para 75 (see PARA 1138) in relation to its parent unit: Sch A1 para 91(5) (as so added).
14 Trade Union and Labour Relations (Consolidation) Act 1992 Sch A1 para 91(7) (as added: see note 6).

E. ADMISSIBILITY AND WITHDRAWAL OF APPLICATIONS RELATING TO CHANGES IN A BARGAINING UNIT

1146. Admissibility of applications relating to changes in a bargaining unit.
An application relating to changes in a bargaining unit[1] to the Central Arbitration Committee[2] (the 'CAC'):

(1)   is not admissible unless it is made in such form as the CAC specifies and it is supported by such documents as the CAC specifies[3];

(2)   which is made by a union[4], or unions, to the CAC is not admissible unless the union gives, or unions give, to the employer[5] notice of the application and a copy of the application and any documents supporting it[6];

(3)   which is made by an employer to the CAC is not admissible unless the employer gives to the union, or each of the unions, notice of the application and a copy of the application and any documents supporting it[7].

1   Ie an application under the Trade Union and Labour Relations (Consolidation) Act 1992 Sch A1 Pt III (paras 64–95): see also PARA 1132 et seq.
2   As to the Central Arbitration Committee see PARA 1226 et seq.
3   Trade Union and Labour Relations (Consolidation) Act 1992 Sch A1 para 92(1) (Sch A1 added by the Employment Relations Act 1999 Sch 1). As to the application of Sch A1 para 92 see PARA 1132.
4   As to the meaning of 'trade union' see PARA 891.
5   As to the meaning of 'employer' see PARA 892.
6   Trade Union and Labour Relations (Consolidation) Act 1992 Sch A1 para 92(2) (as added: see note 3).
7   Trade Union and Labour Relations (Consolidation) Act 1992 Sch A1 para 92(3) (as added: see note 3).

1147.   Withdrawal of applications relating to changes in a bargaining unit.   If an application on the grounds that either party believes that the bargaining unit is no longer appropriate[1] or that the employer believes that the bargaining unit has ceased to exist[2] is accepted by the Central Arbitration Committee[3] (the 'CAC'), the applicant, or applicants, may not withdraw the application:

(1)   after the CAC issues a declaration[4];

(2)   after the CAC makes a decision[5];

(3)   after the CAC issues a declaration[6] in relation to the new unit, where there is only one, or a declaration[7] in relation to any of the new units, where there is more than one;

(4)   after the union[8] has, or unions have, notified the CAC[9] in relation to the new unit, where there is only one, or any of the new units, where there is more than one; or

(5)   after the end of the notification period[10] and relating to the new unit, where there is only one, or any of the new units, where there is more than one[11].

If an application is withdrawn by the applicant, or applicants, the CAC must give notice of the withdrawal to the other party, or parties[12]; and no further steps are[13] to be taken[14].

1   Ie an application under the Trade Union and Labour Relations (Consolidation) Act 1992 Sch A1 para 66: see PARA 1133.
2   Ie an application under the Trade Union and Labour Relations (Consolidation) Act 1992 Sch A1 para 75: see PARA 1138.
3   As to the Central Arbitration Committee see PARA 1226 et seq.
4   Ie under the Trade Union and Labour Relations (Consolidation) Act 1992 Sch A1 para 69(3) (see PARA 1134) or, as the case may be, Sch A1 para 78(3) (see PARA 1140).
5   Ie decides under the Trade Union and Labour Relations (Consolidation) Act 1992 Sch A1 para 77(2) (see PARA 1139) or Sch A1 para 77(3) (see PARA 1139).
6   Ie under the Trade Union and Labour Relations (Consolidation) Act 1992 Sch A1 para 83(2) (see PARA 1142) or Sch A1 para 85(2), Sch A1 para 86(3) or Sch A1 para 87(2) (see PARA 1144).
7   See note 6.
8   As to the meaning of 'trade union' see PARA 891.

9 Ie under the Trade Union and Labour Relations (Consolidation) Act 1992 Sch A1 para 89(1): see PARA 1144.
10 Ie the notification period referred to in the Trade Union and Labour Relations (Consolidation) Act 1992 Sch A1 para 89(1): see PARA 1144.
11 Trade Union and Labour Relations (Consolidation) Act 1992 Sch A1 para 93(1) (Sch A1 added by the Employment Relations Act 1999 Sch 1; the Trade Union and Labour Relations (Consolidation) Act 1992 Sch A1 para 93(1) amended by the Employment Relations Act 2004 Sch 1 para 23(1), (21)). As to the application of the Trade Union and Labour Relations (Consolidation) Act 1992 Sch A1 para 93 see PARA 1132.
12 As to the meaning of references to the parties see PARA 1132 note 5.
13 Ie no further steps are to be taken under the Trade Union and Labour Relations (Consolidation) Act 1992 Sch A1 Pt III (paras 64–95): see also PARA 1132 et seq.
14 Trade Union and Labour Relations (Consolidation) Act 1992 Sch A1 para 93(2) (as added: see note 11).

F. METHOD OF COLLECTIVE BARGAINING IN RELATION TO NEW UNIT

1148.   Method of collective bargaining in relation to a new unit. Where a method of collective bargaining[1] has effect in relation to a new unit, that method has effect as if it were contained in a legally enforceable contract made by the parties[2]; but, if the parties agree in writing that that provision is not to apply, or is not to apply to particular parts of the method, or to vary or replace the method, the written agreement has effect as a legally enforceable contract made by the parties[3].

Specific performance is the only remedy available for breach of anything which is a legally enforceable contract by virtue of the above provisions[4].

1 As to the meaning of references to collective bargaining see PARA 1132 note 5.
2 Trade Union and Labour Relations (Consolidation) Act 1992 Sch A1 para 95(1), (2) (Sch A1 added by the Employment Relations Act 1999 Sch 1). As to the application of the Trade Union and Labour Relations (Consolidation) Act 1992 Sch A1 para 95 see PARA 1132. As to the meaning of references to the parties see PARA 1132 note 5.
3 Trade Union and Labour Relations (Consolidation) Act 1992 Sch A1 para 95(1), (3) (as added: see note 2).
4 Trade Union and Labour Relations (Consolidation) Act 1992 Sch A1 para 95(1), (4) (as added: see note 2).

(iv) Trade Union Derecognition; in general

A. APPLICATION OF GENERAL PROVISIONS RELATING TO DERECOGNITION

1149.   Application of general provisions relating to derecognition. Part IV of the relevant schedule to the Trade Union and Labour Relations (Consolidation) Act 1992, which sets out general statutory provisions relating to derecognition,[1] applies if the Central Arbitration Committee[2] has issued a declaration that a union[3] is, or unions are, recognised[4] as entitled to conduct collective bargaining[5] on behalf of a bargaining unit[6].

1 Ie the Trade Union and Labour Relations (Consolidation) Act 1992 Sch A1 Pt IV (paras 96–121): see PARA 1150 et seq.
2 As to the Central Arbitration Committee see PARA 1226 et seq.
3 As to the meaning of 'trade union' see PARA 891.
4 As to the meaning of 'recognised' see PARA 1094.
5 As to the meaning of 'collective bargaining' see PARA 1093.
6 See the Trade Union and Labour Relations (Consolidation) Act 1992 Sch A1 para 96(1) (Sch A1 added by the Employment Relations Act 1999 Sch 1). In such a case references in the Trade Union and Labour Relations (Consolidation) Act 1992 Sch A1 Pt IV (paras 96–121) to the bargaining arrangements are to the declaration and to the provisions relating to the collective

bargaining method: Trade Union and Labour Relations (Consolidation) Act 1992 Sch A1 para 96(2) (as so added). For these purposes, the provisions relating to the collective bargaining method are: (1) the parties' agreement as to the method by which collective bargaining is to be conducted; (2) anything effective as, or as if contained in, a legally enforceable contract and relating to the method by which collective bargaining is to be conducted; or (3) any provision of Sch A1 Pt III (paras 64–95) (see PARA 1132 et seq) that a method of collective bargaining is to have effect: Sch A1 para 96(3) (as so added). References to the parties are to the employer and the union, or unions, concerned: Sch A1 para 98 (as so added). As to the meaning of 'employer' see PARA 892.

B. EMPLOYER EMPLOYS FEWER THAN 21 WORKERS

1150. Notice for bargaining arrangements to cease and related applications to the Central Arbitration Committee. If:

(1) the employer[1] believes that he, taken with any associated employer[2] or employers, employed an average of fewer than 21 workers[3] in any period of 13 weeks[4]; and

(2) that period ends on or after the relevant date[5],

then, if the employer wishes the bargaining arrangements[6] to cease to have effect, he must give the union[7], or each of the unions, a notice complying with the following provisions and must give a copy of the notice to the Central Arbitration Committee[8].

A notice complies with those provisions if:

(a) it is not invalidated[9];

(b) it identifies the bargaining arrangements;

(c) it specifies the period of 13 weeks in question;

(d) it states the date on which the notice is given;

(e) it is given within the period of five working days[10] starting with the day after the last day of the specified period of 13 weeks;

(f) it states that the employer, taken with any associated employer or employers, employed an average of fewer than 21 workers in the specified period of 13 weeks[11]; and

(g) it states that the bargaining arrangements are to cease to have effect on a date which is specified in the notice and which falls after the end of the period of 35 working days starting with the day after that on which the notice is given[12].

If an employer gives the relevant notice[13], within the validation period[14] the CAC must decide whether the notice complies with heads (a) to (g) above[15].

If the CAC decides that the notice does not so comply, the CAC must give the parties notice of its decision; and the employer's notice is to be treated as not having been given[16].

If the CAC decides that the notice so complies, it must give the parties notice of the decision[17]. If the CAC gives such notice, and, within the period of ten working days starting with the day after that on which the notice is given, the union makes, or unions make, an application to the CAC for a decision whether the period of 13 weeks specified in head (c) above ends on or after the relevant date[18] and whether the statement made under head (f) above is correct, an application is not admissible:

(i) unless it is made in such form as the CAC specifies and it is supported by such documents as the CAC specifies[19];

(ii) unless the union gives, or unions give, to the employer notice of the application and a copy of the application and any documents supporting it[20];

and the CAC must give notice to the parties of receipt of such an application[21].

Within the acceptance period[22], the CAC must decide whether the application is[23] admissible[24]. In deciding whether an application is admissible, the CAC must consider any evidence which it has been given by the employer or the union, or unions[25]. If the CAC decides that the application is not admissible:

(A) the CAC must give notice of its decision to the parties[26];
(B) the CAC must not accept the application;
(C) no further steps are to be taken[27]; and
(D) the bargaining arrangements cease to have effect on the specified date[28].

If the CAC decides that the application is admissible, it must accept the application and give notice of the acceptance to the parties[29].

If the CAC accepts an application, it must give the employer and the union, or unions, an opportunity to put their views on the questions whether the period of 13 weeks specified in head (c) above ends on or after the relevant date[30] and whether the statement made under head (f) above is correct[31]. It must decide the questions within the decision period[32] and give reasons for the decision[33].

If the CAC decides that the period of 13 weeks specified in head (c) above ends on or after the relevant date and that the statement made under head (f) above is correct, the bargaining arrangements cease to have effect on the termination date[34]. If, however, the CAC decides that the period of 13 weeks specified in head (c) above does not end on or after the relevant date or that the statement made under head (f) above is not correct, the employer's notice[35] is to be treated as not having been given[36].

1   As to the meaning of 'employer' see PARA 892.
2   As to the meaning of 'associated employer' see PARA 1026 note 8.
3   As to the meaning of 'worker' see PARA 892.
4   For these purposes, any worker employed by an associated company incorporated outside Great Britain is to be ignored in relation to a week unless the whole or any part of that week fell within a period during which he ordinarily worked in Great Britain: Trade Union and Labour Relations (Consolidation) Act 1992 Sch A1 para 99(5) (Sch A1 added by the Employment Relations Act 1999 Sch 1). A worker who is employed on board a ship registered in the register maintained under the Merchant Shipping Act 1995 s 8 (see **SHIPPING AND MARITIME LAW** vol 93 (2008) PARA 254) is to be treated as ordinarily working in Great Britain unless: (1) the ship's entry in the register specifies a port outside Great Britain as the port to which the vessel is to be treated as belonging; (2) the employment is wholly outside Great Britain; or (3) the worker is not ordinarily resident in Great Britain: Trade Union and Labour Relations (Consolidation) Act 1992 Sch A1 para 99(6) (as so added). As to the meaning of 'Great Britain' see PARA 2 note 12.

  An order made under the Trade Union and Labour Relations (Consolidation) Act 1992 Sch A1 para 7(6) (see PARA 1104) may also: (a) provide that Sch A1 para 99(1)–(6) and Sch A1 paras 99A–103 are not to apply, or are not to apply in specified circumstances; or (b) vary the number of workers for the time being specified in Sch A1 para 99(1)(a) (see head (1) in the text) and Sch A1 para 99(3)(e) (see text head (f) in the text): Sch A1 para 99(7) (as so added; amended by the Employment Relations Act 2004 s 12(1), (3)).

  For the purposes of Sch A1 para 99(1), (4), an agency worker whose contract within the Agency Workers Regulations 2010, SI 2010/93, reg 3(1)(b) (contract with the temporary work agency: see PARA 97) is not a contract of employment is to be treated as having a contract of employment with the temporary work agency for the duration of the assignment with the employer (and 'assignment' has the same meaning as in those 2010 Regulations): Trade Union and Labour Relations (Consolidation) Act 1992 Sch A1 para 99(5A), (5B) (added by SI 2010/93).

5   For these purposes, the relevant date is the date of the expiry of the period of three years starting with the date of the Central Arbitration Committee's declaration: Trade Union and Labour Relations (Consolidation) Act 1992 Sch A1 para 97 (as added: see note 4). As to the Central Arbitration Committee see PARA 1226 et seq.
6   As to the meaning of references to the bargaining arrangements see PARA 1149 note 6.
7   As to the meaning of 'trade union' see PARA 891.

8   Trade Union and Labour Relations (Consolidation) Act 1992 Sch A1 para 99(1), (2) (as added:
    see note 4). As to the application of Sch A1 para 99 see PARA 1149. As to the treatment of
    certain agency workers for these purposes see note 4.
        A notice given for the purposes of Sch A1 para 99(2) ('the notice in question') is invalidated
    if (1) a relevant application was made, or an earlier notice under Sch A1 para 99(2) was given,
    within the period of three years prior to the date when the notice in question was given; (2) the
    relevant application, or that earlier notice, and the notice in question relate to the same
    bargaining unit; and (3) the Central Arbitration Committee (the 'CAC') accepted the relevant
    application or, as the case may be, decided under Sch A1 para 100 (see the text and notes 12–16)
    that the earlier notice under Sch A1 para 99(2) complied with Sch A1 para 99(3): Sch A1
    para 99A(1) (Sch A1 para 99A added by the Employment Relations Act 2004 s 12(1), (4)). A
    'relevant application' is an application made to the CAC by the employer under the Trade Union
    and Labour Relations (Consolidation) Act 1992 Sch A1 para 106 (see PARA 1153), Sch A1
    para 107 (see PARA 1153) or Sch A1 para 128 (see PARA 1161), or by a worker, or workers,
    under Sch A1 para 112 (see PARA 1154): Sch A1 para 99A(2) (as so added).
9   Ie invalidated by the Trade Union and Labour Relations (Consolidation) Act 1992 Sch A1
    para 99A: see note 8.
10 As to the meaning of 'working day' see PARA 1105 note 1.
11 To find the average number of workers employed by the employer, taken with any associated
    employer or employers, in the specified period of 13 weeks: (1) take the number of workers
    employed in each of the 13 weeks, including workers not employed for the whole of the week;
    (2) aggregate the 13 numbers; (3) divide the aggregate by 13: Trade Union and Labour Relations
    (Consolidation) Act 1992 Sch A1 para 99(4) (as added: see note 4). As to the treatment of
    certain agency workers for these purposes see note 4.
12 Trade Union and Labour Relations (Consolidation) Act 1992 Sch A1 para 99(3) (as added (see
    note 4); amended by the Employment Relations Act 2004 s 12(1), (2)).
13 Ie notice for the purposes of the Trade Union and Labour Relations (Consolidation) Act 1992
    Sch A1 para 99(2): see the text and notes 1–8.
14 For these purposes, the validation period is: (1) the period of ten working days starting with the
    day after that on which the Central Arbitration Committee receives the copy of the notice; or (2)
    such longer period, so starting, as the CAC may specify to the parties by notice containing
    reasons for the extension: Trade Union and Labour Relations (Consolidation) Act 1992 Sch A1
    para 100(5) (as added: see note 4).
15 Trade Union and Labour Relations (Consolidation) Act 1992 Sch A1 para 100(1) (as added (see
    note 4); amended by the Employment Relations Act 2004 s 12(5)). As to the application of the
    Trade Union and Labour Relations (Consolidation) Act 1992 Sch A1 para 100 see PARA 1149;
    and as to the Secretary of State's power to amend the provisions of Sch A1 para 100 see note 4.
16 Trade Union and Labour Relations (Consolidation) Act 1992 Sch A1 para 100(2) (as added: see
    note 4).
17 Trade Union and Labour Relations (Consolidation) Act 1992 Sch A1 para 100(3) (as added: see
    note 4). The bargaining arrangements cease to have effect on the date specified in Sch A1
    para 99(3)(f) (see head (g) in the text) if: (1) the CAC gives notice under Sch A1 para 100(3);
    and (2) the union does not, or unions do not, apply to the CAC under Sch A1 para 101 (see the
    text and notes 17–19): Sch A1 para 100(4) (as so added).
18 As to the meaning of 'relevant date' see note 5.
19 Trade Union and Labour Relations (Consolidation) Act 1992 Sch A1 para 101(1), (2) (as added:
    see note 4). As to the application of Sch A1 para 101 see PARA 1149; and as to the Secretary of
    State's power to amend the provisions of Sch A1 para 101 see note 4.
20 Trade Union and Labour Relations (Consolidation) Act 1992 Sch A1 para 101(1), (3) (as added:
    see note 4).
21 Trade Union and Labour Relations (Consolidation) Act 1992 Sch A1 para 102(1) (as added: see
    note 4). As to the application of Sch A1 para 102 see PARA 1149; and as to the Secretary of
    State's power to amend the provisions of Sch A1 para 102 see note 4.
22 For these purposes, the acceptance period is: (1) the period of ten working days starting with the
    day after that on which the Central Arbitration Committee receives the application; or (2) such
    longer period, so starting, as the CAC may specify to the parties by notice containing reasons for
    the extension: Trade Union and Labour Relations (Consolidation) Act 1992 Sch A1 para 102(6)
    (as added: see note 4).
23 Ie within the terms of the Trade Union and Labour Relations (Consolidation) Act 1992 Sch A1
    para 101: see the text and notes 18–20.
24 Trade Union and Labour Relations (Consolidation) Act 1992 Sch A1 para 102(2) (as added: see
    note 4). As to the application of Sch A1 para 102 see PARA 1149; and as to the Secretary of
    State's power to amend the provisions of Sch A1 para 102 see note 4.

25 Trade Union and Labour Relations (Consolidation) Act 1992 Sch A1 para 102(3) (as added: see note 4).

26 As to the meaning of references to the parties see PARA 1149 note 6.

27 Ie under the Trade Union and Labour Relations (Consolidation) Act 1992 Sch A1 Pt IV (paras 96–121): see also PARAS 1149, 1151 et seq.

28 Trade Union and Labour Relations (Consolidation) Act 1992 Sch A1 para 102(4) (as added: see note 4). For these purposes, 'specified date' means the date specified under Sch A1 para 99(3)(f) (see head (g) in the text): Sch A1 para 102(4) (as so added).

29 Trade Union and Labour Relations (Consolidation) Act 1992 Sch A1 para 102(5) (as added: see note 4).

30 As to the meaning of 'relevant date' see note 5.

31 Trade Union and Labour Relations (Consolidation) Act 1992 Sch A1 para 103(1)(a) (as added: see note 4). As to the application of Sch A1 para 103 see PARA 1149; and as to the Secretary of State's power to amend the provisions of Sch A1 para 103 see note 4.

32 For these purposes, the decision period is: (1) the period of ten working days starting with the day after that on which the CAC gives notice of acceptance of the application; or (2) such longer period, so starting, as the CAC may specify to the parties by notice containing reasons for the extension: Trade Union and Labour Relations (Consolidation) Act 1992 Sch A1 para 103(4) (as added: see note 4).

33 Trade Union and Labour Relations (Consolidation) Act 1992 Sch A1 para 103(1)(b) (as added: see note 4).

34 Trade Union and Labour Relations (Consolidation) Act 1992 Sch A1 para 103(2) (as added: see note 4). For these purposes, the termination date is the later of: (1) the date specified under Sch A1 para 99(3)(f) (see head (g) in the text); and (2) the day after the last day of the decision period: Sch A1 para 103(5) (as so added).

35 Ie the notice under the Trade Union and Labour Relations (Consolidation) Act 1992 Sch A1 para 99: see the text and notes 1–12.

36 See the Trade Union and Labour Relations (Consolidation) Act 1992 Sch A1 para 103(3) (as added: see note 4). Schedule A1 para 103(3) does not prevent the notice from being treated as having been given for the purposes of Sch A1 para 109(1) (see PARA 1153), Sch A1 para 113(1) (see PARA 1154), Sch A1 para 130(1) (see PARA 1161) and, in its application to a later notice given for the purposes of Sch A1 para 99(2), Sch A1 para 99A(1) (see note 4): Sch A1 para 103(3A), (3B) (added by the Employment Relations Act 2004 s 12(7)).

C. EMPLOYER'S REQUEST TO END BARGAINING ARRANGEMENTS

1151. Employer's request to end bargaining arrangements; in general. The following provisions[1] apply if after the relevant date[2] the employer[3] requests the union[4], or each of the unions, to agree to end the bargaining arrangements[5]. The request is not valid unless:

   (1)   it is in writing;

   (2)   it is received by the union, or each of the unions;

   (3)   it identifies the bargaining arrangements; and

   (4)   it states that it is made under the statutory provisions[6] relating to recognition for the purposes of collective bargaining[7].

1 Ie the Trade Union and Labour Relations (Consolidation) Act 1992 Sch A1 paras 105–111: see PARAS 1152–1153.

2 As to the meaning of 'relevant date' see PARA 1150 note 5.

3 As to the meaning of 'employer' see PARA 892.

4 As to the meaning of 'trade union' see PARA 891.

5 Trade Union and Labour Relations (Consolidation) Act 1992 Sch A1 para 104(1) (Sch A1 added by the Employment Relations Act 1999 Sch 1). As to the meaning of references to the bargaining arrangements see PARA 1149 note 6.

6 Ie the Trade Union and Labour Relations (Consolidation) Act 1992 Sch A1: see also PARAS 1103 et seq, 1152 et seq.

7 Trade Union and Labour Relations (Consolidation) Act 1992 Sch A1 para 104(2) (as added: see note 5).

1152. Agreement to end bargaining arrangements. If, before the end of the first period[1], the parties[2] agree to end the bargaining arrangements[3], no further steps[4] are to be taken[5].

If, before the end of the first period:

(1)   the union informs the employer[6] that the union does not accept the request but is willing to negotiate; or

(2)   the unions inform the employer that the unions do not accept the request but are willing to negotiate,

the parties may conduct negotiations with a view to agreeing to end the bargaining arrangements[7].

If such an agreement is made before the end of the second period[8], no further steps[9] are to be taken[10]. The employer and the union, or unions, may request the Advisory, Conciliation and Arbitration Service[11] to assist in conducting the negotiations[12].

1   For these purposes, the first period is the period of ten working days starting with the day after: (1) the day on which the union receives the request; or (2) the last day on which any of the unions receives the request: Trade Union and Labour Relations (Consolidation) Act 1992 Sch A1 para 105(6) (Sch A1 added by the Employment Relations Act 1999 Sch 1). As to the meaning of 'working day' see PARA 1105 note 1; and as to the meaning of 'trade union' see PARA 891.

2   As to the meaning of references to the parties see PARA 1149 note 6.

3   As to the meaning of references to the bargaining arrangements see PARA 1149 note 6.

4   Ie no further steps under the Trade Union and Labour Relations (Consolidation) Act 1992 Sch A1 Pt IV (paras 96–121): see also PARAS 1149 et seq, 1153 et seq.

5   Trade Union and Labour Relations (Consolidation) Act 1992 Sch A1 para 105(1) (as added: see note 1). As to the application of Sch A1 para 105 see PARAS 1149, 1151.

6   As to the meaning of 'employer' see PARA 892.

7   Trade Union and Labour Relations (Consolidation) Act 1992 Sch A1 para 105(2), (3) (as added: see note 1).

8   For these purposes, the second period is: (1) the period of 20 working days starting with the day after that on which the first period ends; or (2) such longer period, so starting, as the parties may from time to time agree: Trade Union and Labour Relations (Consolidation) Act 1992 Sch A1 para 105(7) (as added: see note 1).

9   See note 4.

10 Trade Union and Labour Relations (Consolidation) Act 1992 Sch A1 para 105(4) (as added: see note 1).

11 As to the Advisory, Conciliation and Arbitration Service ('ACAS') see PARA 1213 et seq.

12 Trade Union and Labour Relations (Consolidation) Act 1992 Sch A1 para 105(5) (as added: see note 1).

1153. Application for holding of secret ballot to decide whether the bargaining arrangements should be ended. If:

(1)   before the end of the first period[1] the union[2] fails, or unions fail, to respond to the request; or

(2)   before the end of the first period the union informs the employer[3] that it does not, or unions inform the employer that they do not, accept the request, without indicating a willingness to negotiate,

the employer may apply to the Central Arbitration Committee[4] (the 'CAC') for the holding of a secret ballot to decide whether the bargaining arrangements[5] should be ended[6].

If:

(a)   the union informs, or unions inform, the employer that the union, or unions, does not, or do not, accept the request but is, or are, willing to negotiate[7]; and

(b)   no agreement is made before the end of the second period[8], the employer may apply to the CAC for the holding of a secret ballot to decide whether the bargaining arrangements should be ended[9]; but no application may be made if, within the period of ten working days[10] starting with the day after that on which the union so informs, or unions so inform, the employer, the union proposes, or unions propose, that the Advisory, Conciliation and Arbitration Service[11] be requested to assist in conducting the negotiations and:

(i)   the employer rejects the proposal; or

(ii)   the employer fails to accept the proposal within the period of ten working days starting with the day after that on which the union makes, or unions make the proposal[12].

The CAC must give notice to the parties of receipt of an application under the above provisions[13].

An application for the holding of a secret ballot under the above provisions is not admissible:

(A)   unless it is made in such form as the CAC specifies and it is supported by such documents as the CAC specifies[14];

(B)   unless the employer gives to the union, or each of the unions, notice of the application and a copy of the application and any documents supporting it[15];

(C)   if a relevant application[16] was made, or a notice[17] was given, within the period of three years prior to the date of the application, the relevant application, or the notice, and the application relate to the same bargaining unit and the CAC accepted the relevant application or, as the case may be, decided[18] that the notice was in compliance[19];

(D)   unless the CAC decides that at least 10 per cent of the workers constituting the bargaining unit favour an end of the bargaining arrangements and a majority of the workers constituting the bargaining unit would be likely to favour an end of the bargaining arrangements[20];

and the CAC must give reasons for the decision under head (4) above[21].

Within the acceptance period[22], the CAC must decide whether the request is valid[23] and the application is duly made[24] and duly[25] admissible[26]. In deciding those questions, the CAC must consider any evidence which it has been given by the employer or the union, or unions[27]. If the CAC decides that the request is not valid or the application is not duly made[28] or is not admissible, the CAC must give notice of its decision to the parties[29], it must not accept the application and no further steps[30] are to be taken[31]. If the CAC decides that the request is valid and the application is duly made[32] and is admissible, it must accept the application and give notice of the acceptance to the parties[14].

1   As to the meaning of 'first period' see PARA 1152 note 1.
2   As to the meaning of 'trade union' see PARA 891.
3   As to the meaning of 'employer' see PARA 892.
4   As to the Central Arbitration Committee see PARA 1226 et seq.
5   As to the meaning of references to the bargaining arrangements see PARA 1149 note 6.
6   Trade Union and Labour Relations (Consolidation) Act 1992 Sch A1 paras 106(1), (2), 172(1) (Sch A1 added by the Employment Relations Act 1999 Sch 1). As to the admissibility and validity of the application see PARA 1150.
7   Ie under the Trade Union and Labour Relations (Consolidation) Act 1992 Sch A1 para 105(2): see PARA 1152.
8   As to the meaning of 'second period' see PARA 1152 note 8.
9   Trade Union and Labour Relations (Consolidation) Act 1992 Sch A1 para 107(1), (2) (as added: see note 6).
10 As to the meaning of 'working day' see PARA 1105 note 1.
11 As to the Advisory, Conciliation and Arbitration Service ('ACAS') see PARA 1213 et seq.

12 Trade Union and Labour Relations (Consolidation) Act 1992 Sch A1 para 107(3) (as added: see note 6).
13 Trade Union and Labour Relations (Consolidation) Act 1992 Sch A1 para 111(1) (as added: see note 6).
14 Trade Union and Labour Relations (Consolidation) Act 1992 Sch A1 para 108(1) (as added: see note 6).
15 Trade Union and Labour Relations (Consolidation) Act 1992 Sch A1 para 108(2) (as added: see note 6).
16 For these purposes, a relevant application is an application made to the CAC: (1) by the employer under the Trade Union and Labour Relations (Consolidation) Act 1992 Sch A1 para 106, Sch A1 para 107 or Sch A1 para 128 (see PARA 1161); or (2) by a worker, or workers, under Sch A1 para 112 (see PARA 1154): Sch A1 para 109(2) (as added (see note 6); amended by the Employment Relations Act 2004 s 12(9), Sch 2). As to the meaning of 'worker' see PARA 892.
17 Ie a notice under the Trade Union and Labour Relations (Consolidation) Act 1992 Sch A1 para 99(2): see PARA 1150.
18 Ie decided under the Trade Union and Labour Relations (Consolidation) Act 1992 Sch A1 para 100: see PARA 1150.
19 Trade Union and Labour Relations (Consolidation) Act 1992 Sch A1 para 109(1) (as added (see note 6); amended by the Employment Relations Act 2004 s 12(8)). The reference to compliance is to compliance with the Trade Union and Labour Relations (Consolidation) Act 1992 Sch A1 para 99(3); see PARA 1150.
20 Trade Union and Labour Relations (Consolidation) Act 1992 Sch A1 para 110(1) (as added: see note 6).
21 Trade Union and Labour Relations (Consolidation) Act 1992 Sch A1 para 110(2) (as added: see note 6).
22 For these purposes, the acceptance period is: (1) the period of ten working days starting with the day after that on which the Central Arbitration Committee receives the application; or (2) such longer period, so starting, as the CAC may specify to the parties by notice containing reasons for the extension: Trade Union and Labour Relations (Consolidation) Act 1992 Sch A1 para 111(6) (as added: see note 6).
23 Ie within the terms of the Trade Union and Labour Relations (Consolidation) Act 1992 Sch A1 para 104: see PARA 1151.
24 Ie made in accordance with the Trade Union and Labour Relations (Consolidation) Act 1992 Sch A1 para 106 or Sch A1 para 107: see the text and notes 1–12.
25 Ie admissible within the terms of the Trade Union and Labour Relations (Consolidation) Act 1992 Sch A1 paras 108–110: see the text and notes 14–21.
26 Trade Union and Labour Relations (Consolidation) Act 1992 Sch A1 para 111(2) (as added: see note 6).
27 Trade Union and Labour Relations (Consolidation) Act 1992 Sch A1 para 111(3) (as added: see note 6).
28 See note 24.
29 As to the meaning of references to the parties see PARA 1149 note 6.
30 Ie under the Trade Union and Labour Relations (Consolidation) Act 1992 Sch A1 Pt IV (paras 96–121): see also PARAS 1149 et seq, 1154 et seq.
31 Trade Union and Labour Relations (Consolidation) Act 1992 Sch A1 para 111(4) (as added: see note 6).
32 See note 24.
14 Trade Union and Labour Relations (Consolidation) Act 1992 Sch A1 para 111(5) (as added: see note 6).

D. WORKERS' APPLICATION TO END BARGAINING ARRANGEMENTS

1154. Workers' application to end bargaining arrangements. A worker[1] or workers falling within the bargaining unit may after the relevant date[2] apply to the Central Arbitration Committee[3] (the 'CAC') to have the bargaining arrangements[4] ended[5]. An application is not admissible:

(1)   unless it is made in such form as the CAC specifies and it is supported by such documents as the CAC specifies[6];

(2)   unless the worker gives, or workers give, to the employer[7] and to the

union[8], or each of the unions, notice of the application and a copy of the application and any documents supporting it[9];

(3) if:

    (a) a relevant application[10] was made, or a notice[11] was given, within the period of three years prior to the date of the application under the above provisions[12];

    (b) the relevant application, or the notice, and the application relate to the same bargaining unit; and

    (c) the CAC accepted the relevant application or, as the case may be, decided[13] that the notice was in compliance[14];

(4) unless the CAC decides that at least ten per cent of the workers constituting the bargaining unit favour an end of the bargaining arrangements and a majority of the workers constituting the bargaining unit would be likely to favour an end of the bargaining arrangements[15];

and the CAC must give reasons for the decision under head (4) above[16].

The CAC must give notice to the worker, or workers, the employer and the union, or unions, of receipt of such an application[17]. Within the acceptance period[18], the CAC must decide whether the application is[19] admissible[20]. In deciding whether the application is admissible, the CAC must consider any evidence which it has been given by the employer, the union, or unions, or any of the workers falling within the bargaining unit[21]. If the CAC decides that the application is not admissible:

    (i) the CAC must give notice of its decision to the worker, or workers, the employer and the union, or unions;

    (ii) the CAC must not accept the application; and

    (iii) no further steps[22] are to be taken[23].

If the CAC decides that the application is admissible, it must accept the application and give notice of the acceptance to the worker, or workers, the employer and the union, or unions[24].

If the CAC accepts the application, in the negotiation period[25] the CAC must help the employer, the union, or unions, and the worker, or workers, with a view to the employer and the union, or unions, agreeing to end the bargaining arrangements or the worker, or workers, withdrawing the application[26].

1 As to the meaning of 'worker' see PARA 892.
2 As to the meaning of 'relevant date' see PARA 1150 note 5.
3 As to the Central Arbitration Committee see PARA 1226 et seq.
4 As to the meaning of references to the bargaining arrangements see PARA 1149 note 6.
5 Trade Union and Labour Relations (Consolidation) Act 1992 Sch A1 para 112(1) (Sch A1 added by the Employment Relations Act 1999 Sch 1).
6 Trade Union and Labour Relations (Consolidation) Act 1992 Sch A1 para 112(2) (as added: see note 5).
7 As to the meaning of 'employer' see PARA 892.
8 As to the meaning of 'trade union' see PARA 891.
9 Trade Union and Labour Relations (Consolidation) Act 1992 Sch A1 para 112(3) (as added: see note 5).
10 For these purposes, a relevant application is an application made to the CAC: (1) by the employer under the Trade Union and Labour Relations (Consolidation) Act 1992 Sch A1 para 106 or Sch A1 para 107 (see PARA 1153), or Sch A1 para 128 (see PARA 1161); or (2) by a worker, or workers, under Sch A1 para 112: Sch A1 para 113(2) (as added (see note 5); amended by the Employment Relations Act 2004 s 12(9), Sch 2).
11 Ie a notice under the Trade Union and Labour Relations (Consolidation) Act 1992 Sch A1 para 99(2): see PARA 1150.
12 Ie under the Trade Union and Labour Relations (Consolidation) Act 1992 Sch A1 para 112.
13 Ie decided under the Trade Union and Labour Relations (Consolidation) Act 1992 Sch A1 para 100: see PARA 1150.

14 Trade Union and Labour Relations (Consolidation) Act 1992 Sch A1 para 113(1) (as added (see note 5); amended by the Employment Relations Act 2004 s 12(8)). The reference to compliance is to compliance with the Trade Union and Labour Relations (Consolidation) Act 1992 Sch A1 para 99(3); see PARA 1150.
15 Trade Union and Labour Relations (Consolidation) Act 1992 Sch A1 para 114(1) (as added: see note 5).
16 Trade Union and Labour Relations (Consolidation) Act 1992 Sch A1 para 114(2) (as added: see note 5).
17 Trade Union and Labour Relations (Consolidation) Act 1992 Sch A1 para 115(1) (as added: see note 5).
18 For these purposes, the acceptance period is: (1) the period of ten working days starting with the day after that on which the CAC receives the application; or (2) such longer period, so starting, as the CAC may specify to the worker, or workers, the employer and the union, or unions, by notice containing reasons for the extension: Trade Union and Labour Relations (Consolidation) Act 1992 Sch A1 para 115(6) (as added: see note 5). As to the meaning of 'working day' see PARA 1105 note 1.
19 Ie is admissible within the terms of the Trade Union and Labour Relations (Consolidation) Act 1992 Sch A1 paras 112–114: see the text and notes 1–16.
20 Trade Union and Labour Relations (Consolidation) Act 1992 Sch A1 para 115(2) (as added: see note 5).
21 Trade Union and Labour Relations (Consolidation) Act 1992 Sch A1 para 115(3) (as added: see note 5).
22 Ie no further steps under the Trade Union and Labour Relations (Consolidation) Act 1992 Sch A1 Pt IV (paras 96–121): see also PARAS 1149 et seq, 1155 et seq.
23 Trade Union and Labour Relations (Consolidation) Act 1992 Sch A1 para 115(4) (as added: see note 5).
24 Trade Union and Labour Relations (Consolidation) Act 1992 Sch A1 para 115(5) (as added: see note 5).
25 For these purposes, the negotiation period is: (1) the period of 20 working days starting with the day after that on which the CAC gives notice of acceptance of the application; or (2) such longer period, so starting, as the CAC may decide with the consent of the worker, or workers, the employer and the union, or unions: Trade Union and Labour Relations (Consolidation) Act 1992 Sch A1 para 116(2) (as added: see note 5).
26 Trade Union and Labour Relations (Consolidation) Act 1992 Sch A1 para 116(1) (as added: see note 5).

E. BALLOT ON TRADE UNION DERECOGNITION

1155. Ballot on derecognition; general requirements. If:
  (1)   the Central Arbitration Committee[1] (the 'CAC') accepts an application for the holding of a secret ballot[2]; or
  (2)   the CAC accepts an application to end bargaining arrangements[3] and in the prescribed period[4] there is no agreement or withdrawal[5],
the following provisions apply[6].

The CAC must arrange for the holding of a secret ballot in which the workers[7] constituting the bargaining unit are asked whether the bargaining arrangements[8] should be ended[9].

The ballot must:
  (a)   be conducted by a qualified independent person[10] appointed by the CAC[11];
  (b)   be conducted within the period of 20 working days[12] starting with the day after that on which the qualified independent person is appointed or such longer period, so starting, as the CAC may decide[13];
  (c)   be conducted at a workplace or workplaces decided by the CAC, by post, or by a combination of those methods, depending on the CAC's preference[14].

In deciding how the ballot is to be conducted, the CAC must take into account:

(i)   the likelihood of the ballot being affected by unfairness or malpractice if it were conducted at a workplace or workplaces;

(ii)   costs and practicality; and

(iii) such other matters as the CAC considers appropriate[15].

As soon as is reasonably practicable after the CAC is required[16] to arrange for the holding of a ballot, it must inform the employer and the union, or unions:

(A)   that it is so required;

(B)   of the name of the person appointed to conduct the ballot and the date of his appointment;

(C)   of the period within which the ballot must be conducted;

(D)   whether the ballot is to be conducted by post or at a workplace or workplaces;

(E)   of the workplace or workplaces concerned, if the ballot is to be conducted at a workplace or workplaces[17].

1   As to the Central Arbitration Committee see PARA 1226 et seq.

2   Ie an application under the Trade Union and Labour Relations (Consolidation) Act 1992 Sch A1 para 106 or Sch A1 para 107 (see PARA 1153).

3   Ie an application under the Trade Union and Labour Relations (Consolidation) Act 1992 Sch A1 para 112: see PARA 1154.

4   Ie the period mentioned in the Trade Union and Labour Relations (Consolidation) Act 1992 Sch A1 para 116(1): see PARA 1154.

5   Ie as described in the Trade Union and Labour Relations (Consolidation) Act 1992 Sch A1 para 116(1): see PARA 1154.

6   Trade Union and Labour Relations (Consolidation) Act 1992 Sch A1 paras 117(1), (2), 172(1) (Sch A1 added by the Employment Relations Act 1999 Sch 1).

7   As to the meaning of 'worker' see PARA 892.

8   As to the meaning of references to the bargaining arrangements see PARA 1149 note 6.

9   Trade Union and Labour Relations (Consolidation) Act 1992 Sch A1 para 117(3) (as added: see note 6).

10   For these purposes, a person is a qualified independent person if: (1) he satisfies such conditions as may be specified for the purposes of the Trade Union and Labour Relations (Consolidation) Act 1992 Sch A1 para 117 by order of the Secretary of State or is himself so specified; and (2) there are no grounds for believing either that he will carry out any functions conferred on him in relation to the ballot otherwise than competently or that his independence in relation to the ballot might reasonably be called into question: Sch A1 para 117(9) (as added: see note 6). An order under head (1) above must be made by statutory instrument subject to annulment in pursuance of a resolution of either House of Parliament: Sch A1 para 117(10) (as so added). In exercise of the power so conferred the Secretary of State made the Recognition and Derecognition Ballots (Qualified Persons) Order 2000, SI 2000/1306, which came into force on 6 June 2000: art 1(1). As to the Secretary of State see PARA 5 note 21.

     The conditions so specified are that: (a) in relation to an individual, he has in force a practising certificate issued by the Law Society of England and Wales or the Law Society of Scotland or is eligible for appointment as a statutory auditor under the Companies Act 2006 Pt 42 (ss 1209–1264) (see COMPANIES vol 15 (2009) PARA 957 et seq); and (b) in relation to a partnership, every member of the partnership is an individual who satisfies the condition specified in head (a) above: Recognition and Derecognition Ballots (Qualified Persons) Order 2000, SI 2000/1306, arts 2, 3 (amended by SI 2010/437). The persons so specified are Association of Electoral Administrators; DRS Data Services Limited; Electoral Reform Services Limited; Involvement and Participation Association; Opt2Vote Limited; and Popularis Limited: Recognition and Derecognition Ballots (Qualified Persons) Order 2000, SI 2000/1306, art 4 (substituted by SI 2010/437).

11   Trade Union and Labour Relations (Consolidation) Act 1992 Sch A1 para 117(4) (as added: see note 6).

12   As to the meaning of 'working day' see PARA 1105 note 1.

13   Trade Union and Labour Relations (Consolidation) Act 1992 Sch A1 para 117(5) (as added: see note 6).

14   Trade Union and Labour Relations (Consolidation) Act 1992 Sch A1 para 117(6) (as added: see note 6). The CAC may not decide that the ballot is to be conducted as mentioned in Sch A1 para 117(6)(c) (ie by a combination of methods as mentioned in head (c) in the text) unless there

are special factors making such a decision appropriate; and special factors include: (1) factors arising from the location of workers or the nature of their employment; (2) factors put to the CAC by the employer or the union, or unions: Sch A1 para 117(8) (as so added). If the CAC decides that the ballot must, in whole or in part, be conducted at a workplace, or workplaces, it may require arrangements to be made for workers who, but for the arrangements, would be prevented by the CAC's decision from voting by post, and who are unable, for reasons relating to those workers as individuals, to cast their votes in the ballot at the workplace, or at any of the workplaces, to be given the opportunity to vote by post, if they request it far enough in advance of the ballot for it to be practicable; and the CAC's imposition of such a requirement is not to be treated for the purposes of Sch A1 para 117(8) as a decision that the ballot must be conducted as mentioned in Sch A1 para 117(6)(c): Sch A1 para 117(8A) (added by the Employment Relations Act 2004 s 8(2)). As to the meaning of 'employer' see PARA 892; and as to the meaning of 'trade union' see PARA 891.

15 Trade Union and Labour Relations (Consolidation) Act 1992 Sch A1 para 117(7) (as added: see note 6).

16 Ie under the Trade Union and Labour Relations (Consolidation) Act 1992 Sch A1 para 117(3).

17 Trade Union and Labour Relations (Consolidation) Act 1992 Sch A1 para 117(11) (as added: see note 6). Each of the parties so informed must refrain from using any unfair practice: see Sch A1 paras 119A–119I; and PARA 1156.

1156. Unfair practices in relation to derecognition ballots. Each of the parties[1] informed by the Central Arbitration Committee (the 'CAC') of arrangements for a derecognition ballot[2] must refrain from using any unfair practice[3]. A party uses an unfair practice if, with a view to influencing the result of the ballot, the party:

(1) offers to pay money or give money's worth to a worker[4] entitled to vote in the ballot in return for the worker's agreement to vote in a particular way or to abstain from voting;

(2) makes an outcome-specific offer[5] to a worker entitled to vote in the ballot;

(3) coerces or attempts to coerce a worker entitled to vote in the ballot to disclose whether he intends to vote or abstain from voting in the ballot; or how he intends to vote, or how he has voted, in the ballot;

(4) dismisses or threatens to dismiss a worker;

(5) takes or threatens to take disciplinary action against a worker;

(6) subjects or threatens to subject a worker to any other detriment; or

(7) uses or attempts to use undue influence on a worker entitled to vote in the ballot[6].

A party may complain to the CAC that another party has failed to comply with the above provisions[7]. The CAC must decide within the decision period[8] whether the complaint is well-founded[9]. If the CAC decides that such a complaint is well-founded, it must, as soon as is reasonably practicable, issue a declaration to that effect[10]. It may also (a) order the party concerned to take any action specified in the order within such period as may be so specified[11]; and/or (b) make arrangements for the holding of a secret ballot in which the workers constituting the bargaining unit are asked whether the bargaining arrangements should be ended[12].

If the CAC issues a declaration that a complaint is well-founded and the declaration states that the unfair practice used consisted of or included the use of violence or the dismissal of a union[13] official, or if the CAC has made an order under head (a) above and (i) it is satisfied that the party subject to the order has failed to comply with it; or (ii) it makes another declaration in relation to a complaint against that party, then if the party concerned is the employer[14], the CAC may refuse the employer's application[15] for the holding of a secret ballot[16].

If the party concerned is a union, the CAC may issue a declaration that the bargaining arrangements are to cease to have effect on a date specified by the CAC in the declaration[17].

If the CAC issues a declaration that a complaint is well-founded, and:

(A) makes arrangements under head (b) above;

(B) refuses[18] an application for the holding of a secret ballot[19] or for the ending of bargaining arrangements[20]; or

(C) issues a declaration[21] that bargaining arrangements are to cease to have effect,

then if the ballot in connection with which the complaint was made has not been held, the CAC must take steps to cancel it[22]. If that ballot is held, it will have no effect[23].

Where:

(*aa*) a ballot has been arranged in consequence of an application to end bargaining arrangements[24];

(*bb*) the CAC has given the employer a specified order[25]; and

(*cc*) the ballot for the purposes of which the order was made, or any other ballot for the purposes of which it has effect, has not been held,

the applicant worker, or each of the applicant workers, and the union, or each of the unions, is entitled to enforce obedience to the order[26]. The order may be enforced in the same way as an order of the County Court[26].

1 As to the meaning of references to the parties see PARA 1149 note 6.

2 Ie informed under the Trade Union and Labour Relations (Consolidation) Act 1992 Sch A1 para 117(11) (see PARA 1155). As to the Central Arbitration Committee see PARA 1226 et seq.

3 Trade Union and Labour Relations (Consolidation) Act 1992 Sch A1 para 119A(1) (Sch A1 paras 119A–119I added by the Employment Relations Act 2004 s 13(1)).

4 As to the meaning of 'worker' see PARA 892.

5 For these purposes, an outcome-specific offer is an offer to pay money or give money's worth which (1) is conditional on (a) the issuing by the CAC of a declaration that the bargaining arrangements are to cease to have effect; or (b) the refusal by the CAC of an application under the Trade Union and Labour Relations (Consolidation) Act 1992 Sch A1 para 106 or Sch A1 para 107 (see PARA 1153) or Sch A1 para 112 (see PARA 1154); and (2) is not conditional on anything which is done or occurs as a result of that declaration or, as the case may be, of that refusal: Sch A1 para 119A(3) (as added: see note 3).

6 Trade Union and Labour Relations (Consolidation) Act 1992 Sch A1 para 119A(2) (as added: see note 3). The duty imposed by Sch A1 para 119A does not confer any rights on a worker, but that does not affect any other right which a worker may have: Sch A1 para 119A(4) (as so added). The power of the Advisory, Conciliation and Arbitration Service under s 199(1) (see PARA 1223) and the power of the Secretary of State under s 203(1)(a) (see PARA 1231 head (1) in the text) are to be taken to include power to issue Codes of Practice about unfair practices for the purposes of Sch A1 para 119A: Sch A1 para 119A(5) (as so added).

7 Trade Union and Labour Relations (Consolidation) Act 1992 Sch A1 para 119B(1) (as added: see note 3). Such a complaint must be made on or before the first working day after the date of the ballot or, if votes may be cast in the ballot on more than one day, the last of those days: Sch A1 para 119B(2) (as so added).

8 The decision period is the period of ten working days starting with the day after that on which the complaint was received by the CAC, or such longer period so starting as the CAC may specify to the parties by a notice containing reasons for the extension: Trade Union and Labour Relations (Consolidation) Act 1992 Sch A1 para 119B(5) (as added: see note 3). If, at the beginning of the decision period, the ballot has not begun, the CAC may by notice to the parties and the qualified independent person postpone the date on which it is to begin until a date which falls after the end of the decision period: Sch A1 para 119B(6) (as so added). As to the meaning of 'qualified independent person' see PARA 1155 note 10.

9 Trade Union and Labour Relations (Consolidation) Act 1992 Sch A1 para 119B(3) (as added: see note 3). A complaint is well-founded if the CAC finds that the party complained against used an unfair practice and the CAC is satisfied that the use of that practice changed or was likely to

change, in the case of a worker entitled to vote in the ballot, his intention to vote or to abstain from voting, his intention to vote in a particular way or how he voted: Sch A1 para 119B(4) (as so added).

10   Trade Union and Labour Relations (Consolidation) Act 1992 Sch A1 para 119C(1), (2) (as added: see note 3).

11   Trade Union and Labour Relations (Consolidation) Act 1992 Sch A1 para 119C(1), (3)(a) (as added: see note 3). The action specified in such an order must be such as the CAC considers reasonable in order to mitigate the effect of the failure of the party complained against to comply with the duty imposed by Sch A1 para 119A (see the text and notes 1–6): Sch A1 para 119C(1), (5) (as so added). The CAC may give more than one such order: Sch A1 para 119C(1), (6) (as so added).

12   Trade Union and Labour Relations (Consolidation) Act 1992 Sch A1 para 119C(1), (3)(b) (as added: see note 3). The CAC may give an order or make arrangements under Sch A1 para 119C(3) either at the same time as it issues a declaration under Sch A1 para 119C(2) or at any other time before it acts under Sch A1 para 121 (see PARA 1159): Sch A1 para 119C(4) (as so added). If the CAC makes arrangements under Sch A1 para 119C(3)(b):

    (1)   Sch A1 paras 117(4)–(11) (see PARA 1155), Sch A1 paras 118–121 (see PARAS 1157–1159) apply, with modifications (see below), as they apply in relation to arrangements made under Sch A1 para 117(3) (see PARA 1155) (see Sch A1 para 119F(1), (2) (as so added));

    (2)   an employer's duty under Sch A1 para 118(4)(a) (see PARA 1157) is limited to: (a) giving the CAC the names and home addresses of any workers in the bargaining unit which have not previously been given to it in accordance with that duty; (b) giving the CAC the names and home addresses of those workers who have joined the bargaining unit since he last gave the CAC information in accordance with that duty; (c) informing the CAC of any change to the name or home address of a worker whose name and home address have previously been given to the CAC in accordance with that duty; and (d) informing the CAC of any worker whose name had previously been given to it in accordance with that duty who has ceased to be within the bargaining unit (Sch A1 para 119F(3) (as so added));

    (3)   any order given under Sch A1 para 119(1) (see PARA 1157) or Sch A1 para 119C(3)(a) (see the text and note 11) for the purposes of the cancelled or ineffectual ballot has effect (to the extent that the CAC specifies in a notice to the parties) as if it were made for the purposes of the ballot for which arrangements are made under Sch A1 para 119C(3)(b) (Sch A1 para 119F(4) (as so added));

    (4)   the gross costs of the ballot are borne by such of the parties and in such proportions as the CAC may determine and, accordingly, Sch A1 para 120(2), (3) (see PARA 1158) is omitted and the reference in Sch A1 para 120(4) to the employer and the union, or each of the unions, is construed as a reference to the party or parties which bear the costs in accordance with the CAC's determination (Sch A1 para 119F(5) (as so added)).

Schedule A1 paras 119A–119C, 119E, 119F apply, with modifications (see below), in relation to an application under Sch A1 para 112 (see PARA 1154) as they apply in relation to an application under Sch A1 para 106 or 107 (see PARA 1153): see Sch A1 para 119G(1) (as so added). References in those paragraphs (and, accordingly, in Sch A1 para 119H(3)) to a party are read as including references to the applicant worker or workers; but this is subject to Sch A1 para 119G(3): Sch A1 para 119G(2) (as so added). The reference in Sch A1 para 119A(1) to a party informed under Sch A1 para 117(11) (see PARA 1155) are read as including a reference to the applicant worker or workers: Sch A1 para 119G(3) (as so added).

13   As to the meaning of 'trade union' see PARA 891.

14   As to the meaning of 'employer' see PARA 892.

15   Ie an application under the Trade Union and Labour Relations (Consolidation) Act 1992 Sch A1 para 106 or Sch A1 para 107 (see PARA 1153).

16   Trade Union and Labour Relations (Consolidation) Act 1992 Sch A1 para 119D(1)–(3) (as added: see note 3).

If, in relation to an application under Sch A1 para 112 (see PARA 1154) for the ending of bargaining arrangements, the CAC issues a declaration that a complaint is well-founded and the declaration states that the unfair practice used consisted of or included the use of violence or the dismissal of a union official, or the CAC has made an order under Sch A1 para 119C(3)(a) (see head (a) in the text) and (1) it is satisfied that the party subject to the order has failed to comply with it; or (2) it makes another declaration under Sch A1 para 119C(2) in relation to a complaint against that party, then if the party concerned is the employer, the CAC may order him to refrain from further campaigning in relation to the ballot: Sch A1 para 119H(1)–(4) (as so added). If the party concerned is a union, the CAC may issue a declaration that the bargaining arrangements are to cease to have effect on a date specified by the CAC in the declaration, and if such a declaration is issued the bargaining arrangements will cease to have effect accordingly: Sch A1 para 119H(5), (7) (as so added). If the party concerned is the applicant worker, or any of the applicant workers, the CAC may refuse the application under Sch A1 para 112: Sch A1 para 119H(6) (as so added). The powers conferred by Sch A1 para 119H are in addition to those conferred by Sch A1 para 119C(3): Sch A1 para 119H(8) (as so added).

17 Trade Union and Labour Relations (Consolidation) Act 1992 Sch A1 para 119D(1), (2), (4) (as added: see note 3). If such a declaration is issued, the bargaining arrangements will cease to have effect accordingly: Sch A1 para 119D(5) (as so added). The powers conferred by Sch A1 para 119D are in addition to those conferred by Sch A1 para 119C(3): Sch A1 para 119D(6) (as so added).

18 Ie refuses under the Trade Union and Labour Relations (Consolidation) Act 1992 Sch A1 para 119D(3) or Sch A1 para 119H(6).

19 Ie an application under the Trade Union and Labour Relations (Consolidation) Act 1992 Sch A1 para 106 or Sch A1 107: see PARA 1153.

20 Ie an application under the Trade Union and Labour Relations (Consolidation) Act 1992 Sch A1 para 112: see Sch A1 PARA 1154.

21 Ie a declaration under the Trade Union and Labour Relations (Consolidation) Act 1992 Sch A1 para 119D(4) or Sch A1 para 119H(5).

22 Trade Union and Labour Relations (Consolidation) Act 1992 Sch A1 para 119E(1), (2) (as added: see note 3).

23 Trade Union and Labour Relations (Consolidation) Act 1992 Sch A1 para 119E(1), (3) (as added: see note 3).

24 Ie under the Trade Union and Labour Relations (Consolidation) Act 1992 Sch A1 para 112: see PARA 1154.

25 Ie an order under the Trade Union and Labour Relations (Consolidation) Act 1992 Sch A1 para 119(1) (see PARA 1157), Sch A1 para 119C(3) or Sch A1 para 119H(4).

26 Trade Union and Labour Relations (Consolidation) Act 1992 Sch A1 para 119I(1), (2) (as added: see note 3).

26 Trade Union and Labour Relations (Consolidation) Act 1992 Sch A1 para 119I(1), (3)(a) (as added: see note 3).

1157. Employer's duties in connection with derecognition ballot. An employer[1] who is informed by the Central Arbitration Committee[2] (the 'CAC') of the holding of a derecognition ballot[3] must comply with the following five duties[4]:

(1) the first duty is to co-operate generally, in connection with the ballot, with the union[5], or unions, and the person appointed to conduct the ballot, the second and third duties not prejudicing the generality of this[6];

(2) the second duty is to give to the union, or unions, such access to the workers[7] constituting the bargaining unit as is reasonable to enable the union, or unions, to inform the workers of the object of the ballot and to seek their support and their opinions on the issues involved[8];

(3) the third duty is to do the following, so far as it is reasonable to expect the employer to do so:

(a) to give to the CAC, within the period of ten working days[9] starting with the day after that on which the employer is so informed of the holding of a ballot[10], the names and home addresses of the workers constituting the bargaining unit;

(b) to give to the CAC, as soon as is reasonably practicable, the name and home address of any worker who joins the unit after the employer has complied with head (a) above;

(c) to inform the CAC, as soon as is reasonably practicable, of any worker whose name has been given to the CAC under head (a) or head (b) above but who ceases to be within the unit[11];

(4)   the fourth duty is to refrain from making any offer to any or all of the workers constituting the bargaining unit which has or is likely to have the effect of inducing any or all of them not to attend any relevant meeting[12] between the union or unions and the workers constituting the bargaining unit, and which is not reasonable in the circumstances[13]; and

(5)   the fifth duty is to refrain from taking or threatening to take any action against a worker solely or mainly on the grounds that he attended or took part in any relevant meeting between the union or unions and the workers constituting the bargaining unit, or indicated his intention to attend or take part in such a meeting[14].

As soon as is reasonably practicable after the CAC receives any information under head (3) above, it must pass it on to the person appointed to conduct the ballot[15]. If asked to do so by the union, or unions, the person appointed to conduct the ballot must send to any worker whose name and home address have been so given, and who is still within the unit, so far as the person so appointed is aware, any information supplied by the union, or unions, to the person so appointed[16]; but that duty does not apply unless the union bears, or unions bear, the cost of sending the information[17].

If the CAC is satisfied that the employer has failed to fulfil any of the duties imposed on him by heads (1) to (5) above, and the ballot has not been held, the CAC may order the employer:

(i)   to take such steps to remedy the failure as the CAC considers reasonable and specifies in the order; and

(ii)   to do so within such period as the CAC considers reasonable and specifies in the order[18].

1   As to the meaning of 'employer' see PARA 892.

2   As to the Central Arbitration Committee see PARA 1226 et seq.

3   Ie under the Trade Union and Labour Relations (Consolidation) Act 1992 Sch A1 para 117(11): see PARA 1155.

4   See the Trade Union and Labour Relations (Consolidation) Act 1992 Sch A1 paras 118(1), 172(1) (Sch A1 added by the Employment Relations Act 1999 Sch 1; the Trade Union and Labour Relations (Consolidation) Act 1992 Sch A1 para 118(1) amended by the Employment Relations Act 2004 s 9(6), (7)).

5   As to the meaning of 'trade union' see PARA 891.

6   Trade Union and Labour Relations (Consolidation) Act 1992 Sch A1 para 118(2) (as added: see note 4).

7   As to the meaning of 'worker' see PARA 892.

8   Trade Union and Labour Relations (Consolidation) Act 1992 Sch A1 para 118(3) (as added: see note 4).

Each of the following powers is to be taken to include power to issue Codes of Practice about reasonable access for the purposes of Sch A1 para 118(3), and about the fourth duty (see head (4) in the text): (1) the power of the Advisory, Conciliation and Arbitration Service under s 199(1) (see PARA 1223); (2) the power of the Secretary of State under s 203(1)(a) (see PARA 1231 head (1) in the text): Sch A1 para 118(8), (9) (Sch A1 para 118(8) substituted and Sch A1 para 118(9) added by the Employment Relations Act 2004 s 9(6), (9)). See the Code of Practice on Access and Unfair Practices during Recognition and Derecognition Ballots; and PARA 1174. As to the Advisory, Conciliation and Arbitration Service ('ACAS') see PARA 1213 et seq.

Without prejudice to the generality of the second duty (see head (2) in the text), an employer is to be taken to have failed to comply with that duty if: (a) he refuses a request for a meeting between the union or unions and any or all of the workers constituting the bargaining unit to be held in the absence of the employer or any representative of his, other than one who has been invited to attend the meeting, and it is not reasonable in the circumstances for him to do so; (b) he or a representative of his attends such a meeting without having been invited to do so; (c) he seeks to record or otherwise be informed of the proceedings at any such meeting and it is not reasonable in the circumstances for him to do so; or (d) he refuses to give an undertaking that he will not seek to record or otherwise be informed of the proceedings at any such meeting unless it is reasonable in the circumstances for him to do either of those things: Trade Union and Labour Relations (Consolidation) Act 1992 Sch A1 para 118(4D) (Sch A1 para 118(4A)–(4E) added by the Employment Relations Act 2004 s 9(6), (8)).

9   As to the meaning of 'working day' see PARA 1105 note 1.

10 See note 3.

11 See the Trade Union and Labour Relations (Consolidation) Act 1992 Sch A1 para 118(4) (as added: see note 4). As to the type of order which the Secretary of State may make in relation to any provision of Sch A1 para 118(4) which requires the employer to give to the CAC a worker's home address, see Sch A1 para 166A; and PARA 1111 note 14.

12 A meeting is a relevant meeting in relation to a worker for the purposes of the Trade Union and Labour Relations (Consolidation) Act 1992 Sch A1 para 118(4A), (4B) if it is organised in accordance with any agreement reached concerning the second duty or as a result of a step ordered to be taken under Sch A1 para 119 (see the text and note 18) to remedy a failure to comply with that duty and it is one which the employer is, by such an agreement or order, required to permit the worker to attend: Sch A1 para 118(4C) (as added: see note 8).

13 Trade Union and Labour Relations (Consolidation) Act 1992 Sch A1 para 118(4A) (as added: see note 8). The fourth and fifth duties do not confer any rights on a worker, but that does not affect any other right which a worker may have: Sch A1 para 118(4E) (as so added).

14 Trade Union and Labour Relations (Consolidation) Act 1992 Sch A1 para 118(4B) (as added: see note 8). See also note 13.

15 Trade Union and Labour Relations (Consolidation) Act 1992 Sch A1 para 118(5) (as added: see note 4).

16 Trade Union and Labour Relations (Consolidation) Act 1992 Sch A1 para 118(6) (as added: see note 4).

17 Trade Union and Labour Relations (Consolidation) Act 1992 Sch A1 para 118(7) (as added: see note 4).

18 Trade Union and Labour Relations (Consolidation) Act 1992 Sch A1 para 119(1) (as added (see note 4); amended by the Employment Relations Act 2004 s 9(6), (10)). Further, if the ballot has been arranged in consequence of an application under the Trade Union and Labour Relations (Consolidation) Act 1992 Sch A1 para 106 or Sch A1 para 107 (see PARA 1153), the CAC is satisfied that the employer has failed to comply with an order under Sch A1 para 119(1), and the ballot has not been held, the CAC may refuse the application: Sch A1 para 119(2) (as so added). If the CAC refuses an application under Sch A1 para 119(2), it must take steps to cancel the holding of the ballot; and, if the ballot is held, it has no effect: Sch A1 para 119(4) (as so added).

1158.   Costs of the derecognition ballot.   If the holding of a derecognition ballot has been arranged[1], whether or not it has been cancelled, the following provisions apply[2].

The gross costs of the ballot[3] must be borne, as to half, by the employer and, as to half, by the union, or unions[4]. If there is more than one union, they must bear their half of the gross costs in such proportions as they jointly indicate to the person appointed to conduct the ballot or, in the absence of such an indication, in equal shares[5]. The person appointed to conduct the ballot may send to the employer and the union, or each of the unions, a demand stating the gross costs of the ballot and the amount of the gross costs to be borne by the recipient[6]. In such a case the recipient must pay the amount stated to the person sending the demand, and must do so within the period of 15 working days[7] starting with the day after that on which the demand is received[8]. In England and Wales, if the amount stated is not so paid, it is, if the County Court orders, recoverable[9] as if it were payable under an order of that court[10].

1   Ie under the Trade Union and Labour Relations (Consolidation) Act 1992 Sch A1 para 117(3): see PARA 1155.

2   See the Trade Union and Labour Relations (Consolidation) Act 1992 Sch A1 para 120(1) (Sch A1 added by the Employment Relations Act 1999 Sch 1).

3   For these purposes, references to the costs of the ballot are to: (1) the costs wholly, exclusively and necessarily incurred in connection with the ballot by the person appointed to conduct it; (2) such reasonable amount as the person appointed to conduct the ballot charges for his services;

and (3) such other costs as the employer and the union, or unions, agree: Trade Union and Labour Relations (Consolidation) Act 1992 Sch A1 para 120(7) (as added: see note 2). As to the meaning of 'employer' see PARA 892; and as to the meaning of 'trade union' see PARA 891.

4   Trade Union and Labour Relations (Consolidation) Act 1992 Sch A1 para 120(2) (as added: see note 2).

5   Trade Union and Labour Relations (Consolidation) Act 1992 Sch A1 para 120(3) (as added: see note 2).

6   Trade Union and Labour Relations (Consolidation) Act 1992 Sch A1 para 120(4) (as added: see note 2). Where a demand has been made under Sch A1 para 120(4), the recipient of the demand may appeal against it: see Sch A1 para 165A; and PARA 1121 note 6.

7   As to the meaning of 'working day' see PARA 1105 note 1.

8   Trade Union and Labour Relations (Consolidation) Act 1992 Sch A1 para 120(5) (as added: see note 2).

9   Ie under the County Courts Act 1984 s 85 (see CIVIL PROCEDURE vol 12 (2009) PARA 1283) or otherwise.

10   Trade Union and Labour Relations (Consolidation) Act 1992 Sch A1 para 120(6) (as added (see note 2); amended by the Tribunals, Courts and Enforcement Act 2007 Sch 13 paras 108, 111(1), (2); the Crime and Courts Act 2013 Sch 9 Pt 3 para 52(1)(b), (2)). Where a warrant of control is issued under the County Courts Act 1984 s 85 to recover an amount in accordance with the Trade Union and Labour Relations (Consolidation) Act 1992 Sch A1 para 120(6), the power conferred by the warrant is exercisable, to the same extent and in the same manner as if the union were a body corporate, against any property held in trust for the union other than protected property as defined in s 23(2) (see PARA 928): Sch A1 para 120(6A) (added by the Employment Relations Act 2004 Sch 1 para 23(1), (23); amended by the Tribunals, Courts and Enforcement Act 2007 Sch 13 paras 108, 111(1), (3)).

1159.   Procedure following the derecognition ballot.   As soon as is reasonably practicable after the Central Arbitration Committee[1] (the 'CAC') is informed of the result of a ballot by the person conducting it, the CAC must act under the following provisions[2].

The CAC must inform the employer[3] and the union[4], or unions, of the result of the ballot[5]. If the result is that the proposition that the bargaining arrangements[6] should be ended is supported by:

(1)   a majority of the workers[7] voting; and

(2)   at least 40 per cent of the workers constituting the bargaining unit,

the CAC must issue a declaration that the bargaining arrangements are to cease to have effect on a date specified by the CAC in the declaration[8]. If the result is otherwise, the CAC must refuse the application[9] which has been made[10]. If such a declaration is issued[11], the bargaining arrangements cease to have effect accordingly[12].

1   As to the Central Arbitration Committee see PARA 1226 et seq.

2   Trade Union and Labour Relations (Consolidation) Act 1992 Sch A1 para 121(1) (Sch A1 added by the Employment Relations Act 1999 Sch 1). The duty to act does not apply if the CAC makes arrangements under the Trade Union and Labour Relations (Consolidation) Act 1992 Sch A1 para 119C(3)(b) (see PARA 1156): Sch A1 para 121(1A) (added by the Employment Relations Act 2004 s 13(2)).

3   As to the meaning of 'employer' see PARA 892.

4   As to the meaning of 'trade union' see PARA 891.

5   Trade Union and Labour Relations (Consolidation) Act 1992 Sch A1 para 121(2) (as added: see note 2).

6   As to the meaning of references to the bargaining arrangements see PARA 1149 note 6.

7   As to the meaning of 'worker' see PARA 892.

8   Trade Union and Labour Relations (Consolidation) Act 1992 Sch A1 para 121(3) (as added: see note 2). The Secretary of State may by order amend Sch A1 para 121(3) so as to specify a different degree of support; and different provision may be made for different circumstances: Sch A1 para 121(6) (as so added). As to the Secretary of State see PARA 5 note 21. Such an order must be made by statutory instrument; and no such order is to be made unless a draft of it has

been laid before Parliament and approved by a resolution of each House of Parliament: Sch A1 para 121(7), (8) (as so added). At the date at which this volume states the law, no such order had been made.

9 Ie under the Trade Union and Labour Relations (Consolidation) Act 1992 Sch A1 para 106 or Sch A1 para 107 (see PARA 1153) or Sch A1 para 112 (see PARA 1154).

10 Trade Union and Labour Relations (Consolidation) Act 1992 Sch A1 para 121(4) (as added: see note 2).

11 Ie under the Trade Union and Labour Relations (Consolidation) Act 1992 Sch A1 para 121(3).

12 Trade Union and Labour Relations (Consolidation) Act 1992 Sch A1 para 121(5) (as added: see note 2).

(v) Trade Union Derecognition where Recognition Automatic

1160. Application of provisions relating to derecognition where recognition automatic. Part V of the relevant schedule to the Trade Union and Labour Relations (Consolidation) Act 1992[1] applies if:

(1) the Central Arbitration Committee[2] (the 'CAC') has issued a declaration[3] that a union[4] is, or unions are, recognised[5] as entitled to conduct collective bargaining[6] on behalf of a bargaining unit and the parties[7] have agreed[8] a method by which they will conduct collective bargaining[9]; or

(2) the CAC has issued a declaration[10] that a union is, or unions are, recognised as entitled to conduct collective bargaining on behalf of a bargaining unit and the CAC has specified to the parties[11] the method by which they are to conduct collective bargaining[12]; or

(3) the CAC has issued a declaration[13] that a union is, or unions are, recognised as entitled to conduct collective bargaining on behalf of a bargaining unit[14].

1 Ie the Trade Union and Labour Relations (Consolidation) Act 1992 Sch A1 Pt V (paras 122–133): see also PARA 1161.

2 As to the Central Arbitration Committee see PARA 1226 et seq.

3 Ie under the Trade Union and Labour Relations (Consolidation) Act 1992 Sch A1 para 19F(5) (see PARA 1111), Sch A1 para 22(2) (see PARA 1117), Sch A1 para 27(2) (see PARA 1120) and Sch A1 para 27D(3) (see PARA 1119).

4 As to the meaning of 'trade union' see PARA 891.

5 As to the meaning of 'recognised' see PARA 1094.

6 As to the meaning of 'collective bargaining' see PARA 1093.

7 For these purposes, references to the parties are to the employer and the union, or unions, concerned: Trade Union and Labour Relations (Consolidation) Act 1992 Sch A1 para 126 (Sch A1 added by the Employment Relations Act 1999 Sch 1). As to the meaning of 'employer' see PARA 892.

8 Ie under the Trade Union and Labour Relations (Consolidation) Act 1992 Sch A1 para 30 (see PARA 1123) or Sch A1 para 31 (see PARA 1123).

9 Trade Union and Labour Relations (Consolidation) Act 1992 Sch A1 para 122(1) (as added (see note 7); amended by the Employment Relations Act 2004 Sch 1 para 23(1), (24)). In such a case references in the Trade Union and Labour Relations (Consolidation) Act 1992 Sch A1 Pt V (paras 122–133) to the bargaining arrangements are to the declaration and the parties' agreement: Sch A1 para 122(2) (as so added).

10 See note 3.

11 Ie under the Trade Union and Labour Relations (Consolidation) Act 1992 Sch A1 para 31(3): see PARA 1123.

12 Trade Union and Labour Relations (Consolidation) Act 1992 Sch A1 para 123(1) (as added (see note 7); amended by the Employment Relations Act 2004 Sch 1 para 23(1), (25)). In such a case references in the Trade Union and Labour Relations (Consolidation) Act 1992 Sch A1 Pt V (paras 122–133) to the bargaining arrangements are to the declaration and anything effective as, or as if contained in, a legally enforceable contract: Sch A1 para 123(2) (as so added).

13 Ie under the Trade Union and Labour Relations (Consolidation) Act 1992 Sch A1 para 87(2): see PARA 1144.

14 Trade Union and Labour Relations (Consolidation) Act 1992 Sch A1 para 124(1) (as added: see note 7). In such a case references in Sch A1 Pt V (paras 122–133) to the bargaining arrangements are to the declaration and Sch A1 para 87(6)(b) (see PARA 1144): Sch A1 para 124(2) (as so added).

1161. Employer's request to end bargaining arrangements. The employer[1] may after the relevant date[2] request the union[3], or each of the unions, to agree to end the bargaining arrangements[4]. The request is not valid unless it:

(1)   is in writing;

(2)   is received by the union, or each of the unions;

(3)   identifies the bargaining arrangements;

(4)   states that it is made under the relevant statutory provisions[5]; and

(5)   states that fewer than half of the workers[6] constituting the bargaining unit are members of the union, or unions[7].

If, before the end of the negotiation period[8], the parties[9] agree to end the bargaining arrangements, no further steps are[10] to be taken[11]. If no such agreement is made before the end of the negotiation period, the employer may apply to the Central Arbitration Committee (the 'CAC') for the holding of a secret ballot to decide whether the bargaining arrangements should be ended[12]. Such an application is not admissible:

(a)   unless it is made in such form as the CAC specifies and it is supported by such documents as the CAC specifies[13];

(b)   unless the employer gives to the union, or each of the unions, notice of the application and a copy of the application and any documents supporting it[14];

(c)   if:

    (i)   a relevant application[15] was made, or a notice[16] was given, within the period of three years prior to the date of the application under the above provisions;

    (ii)   the relevant application, or notice[17], and the application relate to the same bargaining unit; and

    (iii)   the CAC accepted the relevant application or (as the case may be) decided[18] that the notice was in compliance[19];

(d)   unless the CAC is satisfied that fewer than half of the workers constituting the bargaining unit are members of the union, or unions[20];

and the CAC must give reasons for the decision under head (d) above[21].

The CAC must give notice to the parties of receipt of such an application[22].

Within the acceptance period[23], the CAC must decide whether the request is valid[24] and the application is[25] admissible[26]. In deciding those questions, the CAC must consider any evidence which it has been given by the parties[27]. If the CAC decides that the request is not valid or the application is not admissible:

(A)   the CAC must give notice of its decision to the parties;

(B)   the CAC must not accept the application; and

(C)   no further steps[28] are to be taken[29].

If the CAC decides that the request is valid and the application is admissible, it must accept the application and give notice of the acceptance to the parties[30].

1 As to the meaning of 'employer' see PARA 892.

2 For these purposes, the relevant date is the date of the expiry of the period of three years starting with the date of the Central Arbitration Committee's declaration: Trade Union and Labour Relations (Consolidation) Act 1992 Sch A1 para 125 (Sch A1 added by the Employment Relations Act 1999 Sch 1). As to the Central Arbitration Committee see PARA 1226 et seq.

3 As to the meaning of 'trade union' see PARA 891.

4 Trade Union and Labour Relations (Consolidation) Act 1992 Sch A1 para 127(1) (as added: see note 2). As to the application of Sch A1 paras 127, 128, 133 see PARA 1160. As to the meaning of references to the bargaining arrangements see PARA 1160 notes 9, 12, 14.

5 Ie under the Trade Union and Labour Relations (Consolidation) Act 1992 Sch A1 Pt V (paras 122–133): see the text and notes 1–4, 6–30; and PARA 1160.

6 As to the meaning of 'worker' see PARA 892.

7 Trade Union and Labour Relations (Consolidation) Act 1992 Sch A1 para 127(2) (as added: see note 2).

8 For these purposes, the negotiation period is the period of ten working days starting with the day after: (1) the day on which the union receives the request; or (2) the last day on which any of the unions receives the request, or such longer period, so starting, as the parties may from time to time agree: Trade Union and Labour Relations (Consolidation) Act 1992 Sch A1 para 128(3) (as added: see note 2). As to the meaning of 'working day' see PARA 1105 note 1.

9 As to the meaning of references to the parties see PARA 1160 note 7.

10 Ie no further steps are to be taken under the Trade Union and Labour Relations (Consolidation) Act 1992 Sch A1 Pt V (paras 122–133).

11 Trade Union and Labour Relations (Consolidation) Act 1992 Sch A1 para 128(1) (as added: see note 2). Schedule A1 para 117 (ballot on derecognition: see PARA 1155) applies if the CAC accepts an application under Sch A1 para 128, as well as in the cases mentioned in Sch A1 para 117(1), (2): Sch A1 para 133(1) (as so added). Schedule A1 paras 118–121 (see PARA 1157) apply accordingly, but as if: (1) the references in Sch A1 para 119(2)(a) and Sch A1 para 119D(3) (see PARA 1156) to Sch A1 para 106 or Sch A1 para 107 (see PARA 1153) were to Sch A1 para 106, Sch A1 para 107 or Sch A1 para 128; (2) the references in Sch A1 para 119A(3)(a)(ii) (see PARA 1156 note 5 head (1)(a)), Sch A1 para 119E(1)(b) (see PARA 1156 head (B) in the text) and Sch A1 para 121(4) (see PARA 1159) to Sch A1 para 106, Sch A1 para 107 or Sch A1 para 112 (see PARA 1154) were to Sch A1 para 106, Sch A1 para 107, Sch A1 para 112 or Sch A1 para 128: Sch A1 para 133(2) (as so added; amended by the Employment Relations Act 2004 Sch 1 para 23(1), (6)).

12 Trade Union and Labour Relations (Consolidation) Act 1992 Sch A1 para 128(2) (as added: see note 2).

13 Trade Union and Labour Relations (Consolidation) Act 1992 Sch A1 para 129(1) (as added: see note 2). As to the application of the Trade Union and Labour Relations (Consolidation) Act 1992 Sch A1 paras 129–132 see PARA 1160.

14 Trade Union and Labour Relations (Consolidation) Act 1992 Sch A1 para 129(2) (as added: see note 2).

15 For these purposes, a relevant application is an application made to the CAC: (1) by the employer under Sch A1 para 106 or Sch A1 para 107 (see PARA 1153) or Sch A1 para 128 (see the text and notes 8–12); or (2) by a worker, or workers, under Sch A1 para 112 (see PARA 1154): Sch A1 para 130(2) (as added (see note 2); amended by the Employment Relations Act 2004 s 12(9), Sch 2).

16 Ie a notice under the Trade Union and Labour Relations (Consolidation) Act 1992 Sch A1 para 99(2): see PARA 1150.

17 See note 16.

18 Ie decided under the Trade Union and Labour Relations (Consolidation) Act 1992 Sch A1 para 100: see PARA 1150.

19 Trade Union and Labour Relations (Consolidation) Act 1992 Sch A1 para 130(1) (as added (see note 2); amended by the Employment Relations Act 2004 s 12(8)). The reference to compliance is to compliance with the Trade Union and Labour Relations (Consolidation) Act 1992 Sch A1 para 99(3); see PARA 1150.

20 Trade Union and Labour Relations (Consolidation) Act 1992 Sch A1 para 131(1) (as added: see note 2).

21 Trade Union and Labour Relations (Consolidation) Act 1992 Sch A1 para 131(2) (as added: see note 2).

22 Trade Union and Labour Relations (Consolidation) Act 1992 Sch A1 para 132(1) (as added: see note 2).

23 For these purposes, the acceptance period is: (1) the period of ten working days starting with the day after that on which the Central Arbitration Committee receives the application; or (2) such longer period, so starting, as the CAC may specify to the parties by notice containing reasons for the extension: Trade Union and Labour Relations (Consolidation) Act 1992 Sch A1 para 132(6) (as added: see note 2).

24 Ie within the terms of the Trade Union and Labour Relations (Consolidation) Act 1992 Sch A1 para 127: see the text and notes 1–7.

25 Ie within the terms of the Trade Union and Labour Relations (Consolidation) Act 1992 Sch A1 paras 129–131: see the text and notes 13–21.

26 Trade Union and Labour Relations (Consolidation) Act 1992 Sch A1 para 132(2) (as added: see note 2).

27 Trade Union and Labour Relations (Consolidation) Act 1992 Sch A1 para 132(3) (as added: see note 2).

28 Ie no further steps under the Trade Union and Labour Relations (Consolidation) Act 1992 Sch A1 Pt V (paras 122–133): see the text and notes 1–27, 29–30; and PARA 1160.

29 Trade Union and Labour Relations (Consolidation) Act 1992 Sch A1 para 132(4) (as added: see note 2).

30 Trade Union and Labour Relations (Consolidation) Act 1992 Sch A1 para 132(5) (as added: see note 2).

(vi) Trade Union Derecognition where Union not Independent

1162. Application of provisions relating to derecognition where union not independent. Part VI of the relevant schedule to the Trade Union and Labour Relations (Consolidation) Act 1992[1] applies if:

(1) an employer[2] and a union[3], or unions, have agreed that the union is, or unions are, recognised[4] as entitled to conduct collective bargaining[5] on behalf of a group or groups of workers[6]; and

(2) the union does not have, or none of the unions has, a certificate of independence[7].

1 Ie the Trade Union and Labour Relations (Consolidation) Act 1992 Sch A1 Pt VI (paras 134–148): see also PARA 1163 et seq.

2 As to the meaning of 'employer' see PARA 892.

3 As to the meaning of 'trade union' see PARA 891.

4 As to the meaning of 'recognised' see PARA 1094.

5 For these purposes, the meaning of collective bargaining given by the Trade Union and Labour Relations (Consolidation) Act 1992 s 178(1) (see PARA 1093) does not apply: Sch A1 para 136 (Sch A1 added by the Employment Relations Act 1999 Sch 1). Although no alternative meaning for the phrase 'collective bargaining' is offered by the Trade Union and Labour Relations (Consolidation) Act 1992 Sch A1 para 136, applying the ordinary principles of statutory interpretation allows the phrase to be interpreted for the purposes of Sch A1 para 134 as meaning negotiations over any matters which the parties have agreed should be the subject of collective bargaining: *R (on the application of Boots Management Services Ltd) v Central Arbitration Committee (Secretary of State for Business, Innovation and Skills intervening)* [2014] EWHC 2930 (Admin). See also the Trade Union and Labour Relations (Consolidation) Act 1992 Sch A1 para 3; and PARA 1103 note 3.

6 As to the meaning of 'worker' see PARA 892.

7 Trade Union and Labour Relations (Consolidation) Act 1992 Sch A1 para 134(1) (as added (see note 5); amended by the Employment Relations Act 2004 s 50(6)). As to certificates of independence see PARA 905. In such a case references to the bargaining arrangements are to: (1) the parties' agreement mentioned in the Trade Union and Labour Relations (Consolidation) Act 1992 Sch A1 para 134(1)(a) (see head (1) in the text); and (2) any agreement between the parties as to the method by which they will conduct collective bargaining: Sch A1 para 134(2) (as so added). For these purposes, references to the parties are to the employer and the union, or unions: Sch A1 para 135(a) (as so added).

1163. Workers' application to have bargaining arrangements ended. A worker[1] or workers falling within the bargaining unit[2] may apply to the Central Arbitration Committee[3] (the 'CAC') to have the bargaining arrangements[4] ended[5]. An application is not admissible:

(1) unless it is made in such form as the CAC specifies and it is supported by such documents as the CAC specifies[6];

(2) unless the worker gives, or workers give, to the employer[7] and to the union[8], or each of the unions, notice of the application and a copy of the application and any documents supporting it[9];

(3)   if the CAC is satisfied that any of the unions has a certificate of independence[10];

(4)   unless the CAC decides that at least 10 per cent of the workers constituting the bargaining unit favour an end of the bargaining arrangements and a majority of the workers constituting the bargaining unit would be likely to favour an end of the bargaining arrangements[11];

(5)   if the CAC is satisfied that the union, or any of the unions, has made an application to the certification officer[12] for a certificate that it is independent and the certification officer has not come to a decision on the application, or each of the applications[13];

and the CAC must give reasons for the decision under head (4) above[14].

The CAC must give notice to the worker, or workers, the employer and the union, or unions, of receipt of an application under the above provisions[15]. Within the acceptance period[16], the CAC must decide whether the application is[17] admissible[18]. In deciding whether the application is admissible, the CAC must consider any evidence which it has been given by the employer, the union, or unions, or any of the workers falling within the bargaining unit[19]. If the CAC decides that the application is not admissible:

(a)   the CAC must give notice of its decision to the worker, or workers, the employer and the union, or unions;

(b)   the CAC must not accept the application; and

(c)   no further steps[20] are to be taken[21].

If the CAC decides that the application is admissible, it must accept the application and give notice of the acceptance to the worker, or workers, the employer and the union, or unions[22].

If the CAC accepts the application, in the negotiation period[23] the CAC must help the employer, the union, or unions, and the worker, or workers, with a view to the employer and the union, or unions, agreeing to end the bargaining arrangements or the worker, or workers, withdrawing the application[24].

If:

(i)   the CAC accepts an application;

(ii)   during the relevant period[25] the CAC is satisfied that the union, or each of the unions, has made an application to the certification officer[26] for a certificate that it is independent, that the application, or each of the applications, to the certification officer was made before the application to have the bargaining arrangements ended and that the certification officer has not come to a decision on the application, or each of the applications;

(iii) at the time the CAC is so satisfied, there has been no agreement or withdrawal of the application[27],

then, in such a case, the relevant statutory provisions[28] cease to apply from the time when the CAC is satisfied as mentioned in head (ii) above[29].

If the CAC is subsequently satisfied that the certification officer has come to a decision on the application, or each of the applications mentioned in head (ii) above, and his decision is that the union, or any of the unions, which made an application to him[30] is independent, then, in such a case, the CAC must give the worker, or workers, the employer and the union, or unions, notice that it is so satisfied; and the application to have the bargaining arrangements ended is to be treated as not having been made[31].

If the CAC is subsequently satisfied that the certification officer has come to a decision on the application, or each of the applications mentioned in head (ii) above, and his decision is that the union, or each of the unions, which made an application to him[32] is not independent, the CAC must give the worker, or workers, the employer and the union, or unions, notice that it is so satisfied[33]. In the new negotiation period[34] the CAC must help the employer, the union, or unions, and the worker, or workers, with a view to the employer and the union, or unions, agreeing to end the bargaining arrangements or the worker, or workers, withdrawing the application[35].

If:

(A)   the CAC accepts an application to have the bargaining arrangements ended, the above provision[36] does not apply and during the relevant period[37] the CAC is satisfied that a certificate of independence has been issued[38] to the union, or any of the unions[39]; or

(B)   the CAC gives notice[40], and during the relevant period[41] the CAC is satisfied that a certificate of independence has been issued[42] to the union, or any of the unions[43],

the CAC must give the worker, or workers, the employer and the union, or unions, notice that it is satisfied that a certificate of independence has been issued to the union, or any of the unions[44]; and the application to have the bargaining arrangements ended is to be treated as not having been made[45].

1   As to the meaning of 'worker' see PARA 892.
2   For these purposes, references to the bargaining unit are to the group of workers referred to in the Trade Union and Labour Relations (Consolidation) Act 1992 Sch A1 para 134(1)(a) (see PARA 1162 head (1) in the text), or the groups taken together: Sch A1 para 135(b) (Sch A1 added by the Employment Relations Act 1999 Sch 1).
3   As to the Central Arbitration Committee see PARA 1226 et seq.
4   As to the meaning of references to the bargaining arrangements see PARA 1162 note 7.
5   Trade Union and Labour Relations (Consolidation) Act 1992 Sch A1 para 137(1) (as added: see note 2). As to the application of Sch A1 paras 137–141 see PARA 1162.
6   Trade Union and Labour Relations (Consolidation) Act 1992 Sch A1 para 137(2) (as added: see note 2).
7   As to the meaning of 'employer' see PARA 892.
8   As to the meaning of 'trade union' see PARA 891.
9   Trade Union and Labour Relations (Consolidation) Act 1992 Sch A1 para 137(3) (as added: see note 2).
10   Trade Union and Labour Relations (Consolidation) Act 1992 Sch A1 para 138 (as added (see note 2); amended by the Employment Relations Act 2004 s 50(6)). As to certificates of independence see PARA 905.
11   Trade Union and Labour Relations (Consolidation) Act 1992 Sch A1 para 139(1) (as added: see note 2).
12   Ie under the Trade Union and Labour Relations (Consolidation) Act 1992 s 6: see PARA 905. As to the certification officer see PARA 1443.
13   Trade Union and Labour Relations (Consolidation) Act 1992 Sch A1 para 140 (as added: see note 2).
14   Trade Union and Labour Relations (Consolidation) Act 1992 Sch A1 para 139(2) (as added: see note 2).
15   Trade Union and Labour Relations (Consolidation) Act 1992 Sch A1 para 141(1) (as added: see note 2).
16   For these purposes, the acceptance period is: (1) the period of ten working days starting with the day after that on which the Central Arbitration Committee receives the application; or (2) such longer period, so starting, as the CAC may specify to the worker, or workers, the employer and the union, or unions, by notice containing reasons for the extension: Trade Union and Labour Relations (Consolidation) Act 1992 Sch A1 para 141(6) (as added: see note 2). As to the meaning of 'working day' see PARA 1105 note 1.
17   Ie is acceptable within the terms of the Trade Union and Labour Relations (Consolidation) Act 1992 Sch A1 paras 137–140: see the text and notes 1–14.
18   Trade Union and Labour Relations (Consolidation) Act 1992 Sch A1 para 141(2) (as added: see note 2).

19 Trade Union and Labour Relations (Consolidation) Act 1992 Sch A1 para 141(3) (as added: see note 2).
20 Ie no further steps under the Trade Union and Labour Relations (Consolidation) Act 1992 Sch A1 Pt V (paras 134–148): see the text and notes 1–19, 21–45; and PARAS 1162, 1164–1165.
21 Trade Union and Labour Relations (Consolidation) Act 1992 Sch A1 para 141(4) (as added: see note 2).
22 Trade Union and Labour Relations (Consolidation) Act 1992 Sch A1 para 141(5) (as added: see note 2).
23 For these purposes, the negotiation period is: (1) the period of 20 working days starting with the day after that on which the CAC gives notice of acceptance of the application; or (2) such longer period, so starting, as the CAC may decide with the consent of the worker, or workers, the employer and the union, or unions: Trade Union and Labour Relations (Consolidation) Act 1992 Sch A1 para 142(2) (as added: see note 2).
24 Trade Union and Labour Relations (Consolidation) Act 1992 Sch A1 para 142(1) (as added: see note 2). As to the application of Sch A1 paras 142–146 see PARA 1162.
25 Ie the period mentioned in the Trade Union and Labour Relations (Consolidation) Act 1992 Sch A1 para 142(1) or Sch A1 para 145(3) see the text and notes 23–24, 34–35.
26 See note 12.
27 Ie as described in the Trade Union and Labour Relations (Consolidation) Act 1992 Sch A1 para 142(1) or Sch A1 para 145(3).
28 Ie the Trade Union and Labour Relations (Consolidation) Act 1992 Sch A1 para 142(1) or Sch A1 para 145(3): see the text and notes 23–24, 34–35.
29 Trade Union and Labour Relations (Consolidation) Act 1992 Sch A1 para 143(1), (2) (as added: see note 2).
30 See note 12.
31 See the Trade Union and Labour Relations (Consolidation) Act 1992 Sch A1 para 144(1), (2) (as added: see note 2).
32 See note 12.
33 Trade Union and Labour Relations (Consolidation) Act 1992 Sch A1 para 145(1), (2) (as added: see note 2).
34 For these purposes, the new negotiation period is: (1) the period of 20 working days starting with the day after that on which the CAC gives notice under the Trade Union and Labour Relations (Consolidation) Act 1992 Sch A1 para 145(2); or (2) such longer period, so starting, as the CAC may decide with the consent of the worker, or workers, the employer and the union, or unions: Sch A1 para 145(4) (as added: see note 2).
35 Trade Union and Labour Relations (Consolidation) Act 1992 Sch A1 para 145(3) (as added: see note 2).
36 Ie the Trade Union and Labour Relations (Consolidation) Act 1992 Sch A1 para 143: see the text and notes 25–29.
37 In such a case, the relevant period is the period starting with the first day of the negotiation period, as defined in the Trade Union and Labour Relations (Consolidation) Act 1992 Sch A1 para 142(2) (see note 23), and ending with the first of the following to occur: (1) any agreement by the employer and the union, or unions, to end the bargaining arrangements; (2) any withdrawal of the application by the worker, or workers; (3) the CAC being informed of the result of a ballot held by virtue of Sch A1 Pt V (paras 134–148) by the person conducting it: Sch A1 para 146(2) (as added: see note 2).
38 See note 12.
39 Trade Union and Labour Relations (Consolidation) Act 1992 Sch A1 para 146(1) (as added: see note 2).
40 Ie under the Trade Union and Labour Relations (Consolidation) Act 1992 Sch A1 para 145(2): see the text and notes 32–33.
41 In such a case, the relevant period is the period starting with the first day of the new negotiation period as defined in the Trade Union and Labour Relations (Consolidation) Act 1992 Sch A1 para 142(2) (see note 23), and ending with the first of the following to occur: (1) any agreement by the employer and the union, or unions, to end the bargaining arrangements; (2) any withdrawal of the application by the worker, or workers; (3) the CAC being informed of the result of a ballot held by virtue of Sch A1 Pt V (paras 134–148) by the person conducting it: Sch A1 para 146(4) (as added: see note 2).
42 See note 12.
43 Trade Union and Labour Relations (Consolidation) Act 1992 Sch A1 para 146(3) (as added: see note 2).
44 Ie as mentioned in the Trade Union and Labour Relations (Consolidation) Act 1992 Sch A1 para 146(1)(c) (see head (A) in the text) or Sch A1 para 146(3)(b) (see head (B) in the text).

45 Trade Union and Labour Relations (Consolidation) Act 1992 Sch A1 para 146(5) (as added: see note 2).

1164.   Ballot on derecognition where workers' application to have bargaining arrangements ended is accepted. The statutory provisions relating to ballots on derecognition[1] apply[2] if:

(1)   the Central Arbitration Committee[3] accepts a worker's application to have the bargaining arrangements ended[4]; and

(2)   in the relevant period[5] there is no agreement or withdrawal[6] of the application[7].

1 Ie the Trade Union and Labour Relations (Consolidation) Act 1992 Sch A1 para 117 (see PARA 1155) and Sch A1 paras 118–121 (see PARAS 1157–1159). However Sch A1 paras 118–121 apply as if:
    (1)   the references in Sch A1 para 119H(1) (see PARA 1156 note 16) and Sch A1 para 119I(1)(a) (see PARA 1156 head (*aa*) in the text) to Sch A1 para 112 (see PARA 1154) were to Sch A1 para 112 or Sch A1 para 137 (see PARA 1163) (Sch A1 para 147(2)(a) (Sch A1 added by the Employment Relations Act 1999 Sch 1; the Trade Union and Labour Relations (Consolidation) Act 1992 Sch A1 para 147(2)(a), (b) amended by the Employment Relations Act 2004 Sch 1 para 23(1), (27)));
    (2)   the references in Sch A1 para 119A(3)(a)(ii) (see PARA 1156 note 5 head (1)(b)), Sch A1 para 119E(1)(b) (see PARA 1156 head (B) in the text) and Sch A1 para 121(4) (see PARA 1159) to Sch A1 para 106 or Sch A1 para 107 (see PARA 1153), or Sch A1 para 112 (see PARA 1154) were to Sch A1 para 106, Sch A1 para 107, Sch A1 para 112 or Sch A1 para 137 (Sch A1 para 147(2)(b) (as so added and amended));
    (3)   the reference in Sch A1 para 119(4) (see PARA 1157) to the CAC's refusing an application under Sch A1 para 119(2) (see PARA 1157) included a reference to its being required to give notice under Sch A1 para 146(5) (see PARA 1163) (Sch A1 para 147(2)(c) (as so added).
2 Ie as well as in the cases mentioned in the Trade Union and Labour Relations (Consolidation) Act 1992 Sch A1 para 117(1), (2): see PARA 1155.
3 As to the Central Arbitration Committee see PARA 1226 et seq.
4 Ie an application under the Trade Union and Labour Relations (Consolidation) Act 1992 Sch A1 para 137: see PARA 1163.
5 Ie the period mentioned in the Trade Union and Labour Relations (Consolidation) Act 1992 Sch A1 para 142(1) or Sch A1 para 145(3) (see PARA 1163).
6 Ie as described in the Trade Union and Labour Relations (Consolidation) Act 1992 Sch A1 para 142(1) or Sch A1 para 145(3) (see PARA 1163).
7 Trade Union and Labour Relations (Consolidation) Act 1992 Sch A1 para 147(1), (2) (as added: see note 1).

1165.   Trade union derecognition; other cases. If, as a result of a declaration by the Central Arbitration Committee[1] (the 'CAC'), another union[2] is, or other unions are, recognised as entitled to conduct collective bargaining[3] on behalf of a group of workers[4] at least one of whom falls within the bargaining unit[5], the CAC must issue a declaration that the bargaining arrangements[6] are to cease to have effect on a date specified by the CAC in the declaration[7]. If a declaration is so issued, the bargaining arrangements cease to have effect accordingly[8]. It is for the CAC to decide whether the above provisions[9] are fulfilled; but, in deciding, the CAC may take account of the views of any person it believes has an interest in the matter[10].

1 As to the Central Arbitration Committee see PARA 1226 et seq.
2 As to the meaning of 'trade union' see PARA 891.
3 As to the meaning of 'collective bargaining' see PARA 1162 note 5.
4 As to the meaning of 'worker' see PARA 892.
5 As to the meaning of references to the bargaining unit see PARA 1163 note 2.
6 As to the meaning of references to the bargaining arrangements see PARA 1162 note 7.

7   Trade Union and Labour Relations (Consolidation) Act 1992 Sch A1 paras 148(1), (2), 172(1)
    (Sch A1 added by the Employment Relations Act 1999 Sch 1).
8   Trade Union and Labour Relations (Consolidation) Act 1992 Sch A1 para 148(3) (as added: see
    note 7).
9   Ie the Trade Union and Labour Relations (Consolidation) Act 1992 Sch A1 para 148(1).
10 Trade Union and Labour Relations (Consolidation) Act 1992 Sch A1 para 148(4) (as added: see
    note 7).

(vii) Trade Union's Loss of Independence

1166.   Application of provisions relating to loss of independence.   Part VII of
the relevant schedule to the Trade Union and Labour Relations (Consolidation)
Act 1992[1] applies:

(1)   if the Central Arbitration Committee[2] (the 'CAC') has issued a
      declaration that a union[3] is, or unions are, recognised[4] as entitled to
      conduct collective bargaining[5] on behalf of a bargaining unit[6]; or

(2)   if:
      (a)   the parties[7] have agreed that a union is, or unions are, recognised
            as entitled to conduct collective bargaining on behalf of a
            bargaining unit;
      (b)   the CAC has specified to the parties[8] the method by which they
            are to conduct collective bargaining; and
      (c)   the parties have not agreed in writing to replace the method or
            that the CAC's obligation, when deciding whether an application
            to specify the method is admissible, to consider any evidence
            which it has been given by the employer or the union, or unions[9],
            is not to apply[10].

1   Ie the Trade Union and Labour Relations (Consolidation) Act 1992 Sch A1 Pt VII
    (paras 149–155): see also PARAS 1167–1168.
2   As to the Central Arbitration Committee see PARA 1226 et seq.
3   As to the meaning of 'trade union' see PARA 891.
4   As to the meaning of 'recognised' see PARA 1094.
5   As to the meaning of 'collective bargaining' see PARA 1093.
6   Trade Union and Labour Relations (Consolidation) Act 1992 Sch A1 paras 149(1), 172(1)
    (Sch A1 added by the Employment Relations Act 1999 Sch 1).
      In such a case references in Sch A1 Pt VII (paras 149–155) to the bargaining arrangements
    are to the declaration and to the provisions relating to the collective bargaining method: Sch A1
    para 149(2) (as so added). For these purposes, the provisions relating to the collective
    bargaining method are: (1) the parties' agreement as to the method by which collective
    bargaining is to be conducted; (2) anything effective as, or as if contained in, a legally
    enforceable contract and relating to the method by which collective bargaining is to be
    conducted; or (3) any provision of Sch A1 Pt III (paras 64–95) (see PARA 1132 et seq) that a
    method of collective bargaining is to have effect: Sch A1 para 149(3) (as so added).
7   For these purposes, references to the parties are to the employer and the union, or unions,
    concerned: Trade Union and Labour Relations (Consolidation) Act 1992 Sch A1 para 151 (as
    added: see note 6). As to the meaning of 'employer' see PARA 892.
8   Ie under the Trade Union and Labour Relations (Consolidation) Act 1992 Sch A1 para 63(2):
    see PARA 1131.
9   Ie the Trade Union and Labour Relations (Consolidation) Act 1992 Sch A1 para 63(3): see PARA
    1131.
10 Trade Union and Labour Relations (Consolidation) Act 1992 Sch A1 para 150(1) (as added: see
    note 6).
      In such a case references in Sch A1 Pt VII (paras 149–155) to the bargaining arrangements
    are to: (1) the parties' agreement mentioned in Sch A1 para 150(1)(a) (see head (2)(a) in the
    text); and (2) anything effective as, or as if contained in, a legally enforceable contract by virtue
    of Sch A1 para 63 (see PARA 1131): Sch A1 para 150(2) (as so added).

1167.   Effect of withdrawal of union's certificate of independence.   If:

(1)   only one union[1] is a party and the certification officer[2] withdraws[3] the union's certificate of independence; or

(2)   more than one union is a party and the certification officer withdraws the certificate of independence of each union, whether different certificates are withdrawn on the same or on different days,

then, on the day after:

(a)   the day on which the certification officer informs the union, or unions, of the withdrawal, or withdrawals; or

(b)   if there is more than one union, and he informs them on different days, the last of those days,

the bargaining arrangements[4] cease to have effect[5]; and the parties[6] are to be taken to agree that the union is, or unions are, recognised[7] as entitled to conduct collective bargaining[8] on behalf of the bargaining unit concerned[9].

1   As to the meaning of 'trade union' see PARA 891.
2   As to the certification officer see PARA 1443.
3   Ie under the Trade Union and Labour Relations (Consolidation) Act 1992 s 7: see PARA 906.
4   As to the meaning of references to the bargaining arrangements see PARA 1166 notes 6, 10.
5   The Trade Union and Labour Relations (Consolidation) Act 1992 Sch A1 Pts III–VI (paras 64–148) (see PARA 1132 et seq) do not apply in the case of the parties at any time when, by virtue of Sch A1 Pt VIII (paras 149–155) (see also PARAS 1166, 1168), the bargaining arrangements do not have effect: Sch A1 para 154 (Sch A1 added by the Employment Relations Act 1999 Sch 1). As to the application of the Trade Union and Labour Relations (Consolidation) Act 1992 Sch A1 para 154 see PARA 1166.
6   As to the meaning of references to the parties see PARA 1166 note 7.
7   As to the meaning of 'recognised' see PARA 1094.
8   As to the meaning of 'collective bargaining' see PARA 1093.
9   Trade Union and Labour Relations (Consolidation) Act 1992 Sch A1 para 152(1)–(4) (as added: see note 5). As to the application of Sch A1 para 152 see PARA 1166.

1168. Reissue of union's certificate of independence. If:

(1)   only one union[1] is a party, the provisions relating to the withdrawal of the union's certificate of independence[2] apply and, as a result of an appeal[3] against the decision to withdraw the certificate, the certificate officer[4] issues a certificate that the union is independent; or

(2)   more than one union is a party, the provisions relating to the withdrawal of the union's certificate of independence[5] apply and, as a result of an appeal[6] against a decision to withdraw a certificate, the certification officer issues a certificate that any of the unions concerned is independent,

then, beginning with the day after the day on which the certification officer issues the certificate or, if there is more than one union, the day on which he issues the first or only certificate, the bargaining arrangements[7] have effect again[8]; and the provisions relating to the withdrawal of the union's certificate of independence[9] cease to apply[10].

1   As to the meaning of 'trade union' see PARA 891.
2   Ie the Trade Union and Labour Relations (Consolidation) Act 1992 Sch A1 para 152: see PARA 1167.
3   Ie under the Trade Union and Labour Relations (Consolidation) Act 1992 s 9: see PARA 906.
4   As to the certification officer see PARA 1443.
5   See note 2.
6   See note 3.
7   As to the meaning of references to the bargaining arrangements see PARA 1166 notes 6, 10.
8   If: (1) by virtue of the Trade Union and Labour Relations (Consolidation) Act 1992 Sch A1 para 153, the bargaining arrangements have effect again beginning with a particular day; and (2) in consequence s 70B (see PARA 1172) applies in relation to the bargaining unit concerned,

then, for the purposes of s 70B(3), that day is to be taken to be the day on which s 70B first applies in relation to the unit: Sch A1 para 155 (Sch A1 added by the Employment Relations Act 1999 Sch 1). As to the application of the Trade Union and Labour Relations (Consolidation) Act 1992 Sch A1 para 155 see PARA 1166.

9 See note 2.
10 Trade Union and Labour Relations (Consolidation) Act 1992 Sch A1 para 153(1)–(4) (as added: see note 8). As to the application of Sch A1 para 153 see PARA 1166.

(viii) Worker's Right Not to be Subjected to Detriment on Grounds related to Trade Union Recognition

1169. Right not to be subjected to any detriment. A worker[1] has a right not to be subjected to any detriment by any act, or any deliberate failure to act, by his employer[2] if the act or failure takes place on any of the following grounds[3]. Those grounds are that:

(1) the worker acted with a view to obtaining or preventing recognition[4] of a union[5], or unions, by the employer[6];

(2) the worker indicated that he supported or did not support recognition of a union, or unions, by the employer[7];

(3) the worker acted with a view to securing or preventing the ending[8] of bargaining arrangements[9];

(4) the worker indicated that he supported or did not support the ending[10] of bargaining arrangements;

(5) the worker influenced or sought to influence the way in which votes were to be cast by other workers in a ballot[11];

(6) the worker influenced or sought to influence other workers to vote or to abstain from voting in such a ballot;

(7) the worker voted in such a ballot;

(8) the worker proposed to do, failed to do, or proposed to decline to do, any of the things referred to in heads (1) to (7) above[12];

but a ground does not fall within heads (1) to (8) above if it constitutes an unreasonable act or omission by the worker[13].

The above provisions do not apply if the worker is an employee[14] and the detriment amounts to dismissal[15].

1 As to the meaning of 'worker' see PARA 892.
2 As to the meaning of 'employer' see PARA 892.
3 Trade Union and Labour Relations (Consolidation) Act 1992 Sch A1 para 156(1) (Sch A1 added by the Employment Relations Act 1999 Sch 1).
4 As to the meaning of 'recognition' see PARA 1094.
5 As to the meaning of 'trade union' see PARA 891.
6 Ie under the Trade Union and Labour Relations (Consolidation) Act 1992 Sch A1: see PARA 1103 et seq.
7 See note 6.
8 See note 6.
9 As to the meaning of references to the bargaining arrangements see PARAS 1135 note 12, 1149 note 6, 1160 notes 9, 12, 14, 1162 note 7, 1166 notes 6, 10.
10 See note 6.
11 See note 6.
12 Trade Union and Labour Relations (Consolidation) Act 1992 Sch A1 para 156(2) (as added: see note 3). As to the right to make a complaint to an employment tribunal see PARA 1170.
13 Trade Union and Labour Relations (Consolidation) Act 1992 Sch A1 para 156(3) (as added: see note 3).
14 As to the meaning of 'employee' see PARA 892.
15 Trade Union and Labour Relations (Consolidation) Act 1992 Sch A1 para 156(4) (as added: see note 3). For these purposes, 'dismissal' has the same meaning as in the Employment Rights

Act 1996 Pt X (ss 94–134A) (see PARA 757 et seq): Trade Union and Labour Relations (Consolidation) Act 1992 Sch A1 para 156(4) (as so added).

1170. Complaint to employment tribunal that worker has been subjected to detriment. A worker[1] may present a complaint to an employment tribunal[2] on the ground that he has been subjected to a detriment in contravention[3] of his statutory rights[4]. Apart from that remedy by way of complaint, a worker has no remedy for infringement of his statutory right not to be subjected to any such detriment[5].

An employment tribunal must not consider such a complaint unless it is presented[6]:

(1)		before the end of the period of three months starting with the date of the act[7] or failure[8] to which the complaint relates or, if that act or failure is part of a series of similar acts or failures, or both, the last of them[9], subject to an extension to facilitate conciliation before the institution of proceedings[10]; or

(2)		where the tribunal is satisfied that it was not reasonably practicable for the complaint to be presented before the end of that period, within such further period as it considers reasonable[11].

On such a complaint it is for the employer to show the ground on which he acted or failed to act[12].

If the employment tribunal finds that such a complaint is well-founded, it must make a declaration to that effect and may make an award of compensation to be paid by the employer to the complainant in respect of the act or failure complained of[13]. The amount of the compensation awarded must be such as the tribunal considers just and equitable in all the circumstances, having regard to the infringement complained of and to any loss sustained by the complainant which is attributable to the act or failure which infringed his right[14]. The loss is to be taken to include any expenses reasonably incurred by the complainant in consequence of the act or failure complained of and loss of any benefit which he might reasonably be expected to have had but for that act or failure[15]. In ascertaining the loss, the tribunal must apply the same rule concerning the duty of a person to mitigate his loss as applies to damages recoverable under the common law of England and Wales[16]. If the tribunal finds that the act or failure complained of was to any extent caused or contributed to by action of the complainant, it must reduce the amount of the compensation by such proportion as it considers just and equitable, having regard to that finding[17].

If the employment tribunal finds that such a complaint is well-founded and the detriment of which the worker has complained is the termination of his worker's contract[18] but the contract was not a contract of employment[19], any compensation so awarded must not exceed the specified limit[18].

1		As to the meaning of 'worker' see PARA 892.
2		As to employment tribunals see PARA 1399 et seq.
3		Ie in contravention of the Trade Union and Labour (Consolidation) Act 1992 Sch A1 para 156: see PARA 1169. As to the meaning of 'contravention' and cognate expressions see PARA 915 note 6.
4		Trade Union and Labour Relations (Consolidation) Act 1992 Sch A1 para 156(5) (Sch A1 added by the Employment Relations Act 1999 Sch 1). The provisions of the Employment Tribunals Act 1996 ss 18A–18B (conciliation) (see PARAS 152–153) apply in the case of matters which could be the subject of employment tribunal proceedings under the Trade Union and Labour Relations (Consolidation) Act 1992 Sch A1 para 156, and the Employment Tribunals Act 1996 s 18C applies in the case of such proceedings themselves: see s 18(1)(a), (1A) (s 18(1)(a) substituted by SI 2014/431; the Employment Tribunals Act 1996 s 18(1A) added by the Enterprise and Regulatory Reform Act 2013 Sch 1 paras 2, 5(1), (7)).

An appeal lies to the Employment Appeal Tribunal on any question of law arising from any decision of, or arising in any proceedings before, an employment tribunal under or by virtue of the Trade Union and Labour Relations (Consolidation) Act 1992: see the Employment Tribunals Act 1996 s 21(1)(d); and PARA 1428. As to the Employment Appeal Tribunal see PARA 1422 et seq.

5 Trade Union and Labour (Consolidation) Act 1992 Sch A1 para 156(6) (as added: see note 4).

6 As to when a complaint is presented see PARAS 990 note 4, 1461.

7 For these purposes, where an act extends over a period, the reference to the date of the act is a reference to the last day of that period: Trade Union and Labour (Consolidation) Act 1992 Sch A1 para 157(2)(a) (as added: see note 4).

8 For these purposes, a failure to act is to be treated as done when it was decided on: Trade Union and Labour (Consolidation) Act 1992 Sch A1 para 157(2)(b) (as added: see note 4). In the absence of evidence establishing the contrary, an employer is to be taken to decide on a failure to act: (1) when he does an act inconsistent with doing the failed act; or (2) if he has done no such inconsistent act, when the period expires within which he might reasonably have been expected to do the failed act if it was to be done: Sch A1 para 157(3) (as so added). As to the meaning of 'employer' see PARA 892.

9 Trade Union and Labour Relations (Consolidation) Act 1992 Sch A1 para 157(1)(a) (as added: see note 4). For the case law on the extension of time limits, especially in the context of the law of unfair dismissal, see PARA 1453. See also note 10.

10 The Trade Union and Labour Relations (Consolidation) Act 1992 s 292A (extension of time limits to facilitate conciliation before institution of proceedings: see PARA 1455) applies for the purposes of Sch A1 para 157(1)(a): Sch A1 para 157(4) (added by the Enterprise and Regulatory Reform Act 2013 Sch 2 paras 1, 14).

11 Trade Union and Labour Relations (Consolidation) Act 1992 Sch A1 para 157(1)(b) (as added: see note 4).

12 Trade Union and Labour Relations (Consolidation) Act 1992 Sch A1 para 158 (as added: see note 4).

13 Trade Union and Labour Relations (Consolidation) Act 1992 Sch A1 para 159(1) (as added: see note 4).

14 Trade Union and Labour Relations (Consolidation) Act 1992 Sch A1 para 159(2) (as added: see note 4).

15 Trade Union and Labour Relations (Consolidation) Act 1992 Sch A1 para 159(3) (as added: see note 4).

16 Trade Union and Labour Relations (Consolidation) Act 1992 Sch A1 para 159(4) (as added: see note 4). As to the duty to mitigate in the context of unfair dismissal law see PARA 822.

17 Trade Union and Labour Relations (Consolidation) Act 1992 Sch A1 para 159(5) (as added: see note 4).

18 For these purposes, references to a worker's contract are to the contract mentioned in the Trade Union and Labour Relations (Consolidation) Act 1992 s 296(1)(a) or (b) (see PARA 892 heads (1)–(2) in the text) or the arrangements for the employment mentioned in s 296(1)(c) (see PARA 892 head (3) in the text): Sch A1 para 165 (as added: see note 4).

19 As to the meaning of 'contract of employment' see PARA 892.

20 Trade Union and Labour Relations (Consolidation) Act 1992 Sch A1 para 160(1) (as added: see note 4). The limit so specified is the total of: (1) the sum which would be the basic award for unfair dismissal, calculated in accordance with the Employment Rights Act 1996 s 119 (see PARA 815) if the worker had been an employee and the contract terminated had been a contract of employment; and (2) the sum for the time being specified in s 124(1) (see PARA 823) which is the limit for a compensatory award to a person calculated in accordance with s 123 (see PARAS 818–819): Trade Union and Labour Relations (Consolidation) Act 1992 Sch A1 para 160(2) (as so added).

1171.   Unfair dismissal on grounds related to trade union recognition. The dismissal[1] of an employee[2] is to be regarded as unfair[3] if the dismissal was made for a reason set out in heads (1) to (8) below, or for reasons the main one of which is one of those so set out[4]. Those reasons are that:

(1) the employee acted with a view to obtaining or preventing recognition[5] of a union[6], or unions, by the employer[7];

(2) the employee indicated that he supported or did not support recognition of a union, or unions, by the employer[8];

(3)   the employee acted with a view to securing or preventing the ending[9] of bargaining arrangements[10];

(4)   the employee indicated that he supported or did not support the ending[11] of bargaining arrangements;

(5)   the employee influenced, or sought to influence, the way in which votes were to be cast by other workers[12] in a ballot[13];

(6)   the employee influenced or sought to influence other workers to vote or to abstain from voting in such a ballot;

(7)   the employee voted in such a ballot;

(8)   the employee proposed to do, failed to do, or proposed to decline to do, any of the things referred to in heads (1) to (7) above[14].

A reason does not fall within heads (1) to (8) above if it constitutes an unreasonable act or omission by the employee[15].

The dismissal of an employee is also to be regarded as unfair[16] if the reason or principal reason[17] for the dismissal was that he was redundant but it is shown: (a) that the circumstances constituting the redundancy applied equally to one or more other employees in the same undertaking who held positions similar to that held by him and who have not been dismissed by the employer; and (b) that the reason (or, if more than one, the principal reason) why he was selected for dismissal was one falling within heads (1) to (8) above[18].

1   As to the meaning of 'dismissal' see PARA 1056 note 1.
2   As to the meaning of 'employee' see PARA 892.
3   Ie for the purposes of the Employment Rights Act 1996 Pt X (ss 94–134A): see PARA 757 et seq.
4   Trade Union and Labour Relations (Consolidation) Act 1992 Sch A1 para 161(1) (Sch A1 added by the Employment Relations Act 1999 Sch 1). The Employment Rights Act 1996 s 108 (qualifying period for unfair dismissal protection) (see PARA 758) does not apply to a dismissal which, by virtue of the Trade Union and Labour Relations (Consolidation) Act 1992 Sch A1 para 161 or Sch A1 para 162 is regarded as unfair for the purposes of the Employment Rights Act 1996 Pt X: see the Trade Union and Labour Relations (Consolidation) Act 1992 Sch A1 para 164 (as so added).
5   As to the meaning of 'recognition' see PARA 1094.
6   As to the meaning of 'trade union' see PARA 891.
7   Ie under the Trade Union and Labour Relations (Consolidation) Act 1992 Sch A1: see PARA 1103 et seq. As to the meaning of 'employer' see PARA 892.
8   See note 7.
9   See note 7.
10   As to the meaning of references to the bargaining arrangements see PARAS 1135 note 12, 1149 note 6, 1160 notes 9, 12, 14, 1162 note 7, 1166 notes 6, 10.
11   See note 7.
12   As to the meaning of 'worker' see PARA 892.
13   Ie a ballot arranged under the Trade Union and Labour Relations (Consolidation) Act 1992 Sch A1.
14   Trade Union and Labour Relations (Consolidation) Act 1992 Sch A1 para 161(2) (as added: see note 4).
15   Trade Union and Labour Relations (Consolidation) Act 1992 Sch A1 para 161(3) (as added: see note 4).
16   See note 3.
17   As to the meaning of 'reason or principal reason' see PARA 769.
18   Trade Union and Labour Relations (Consolidation) Act 1992 Sch A1 para 162 (as added: see note 4).

(ix) Training for Workers within Bargaining Unit

1172. Consultation on training for workers within a bargaining unit. Where:

(1)   a trade union[1] is recognised[2] as entitled to conduct collective bargaining on behalf of a bargaining unit[3]; and

(2)   a method for the conduct of collective bargaining is specified by the Central Arbitration Committee[4], and is not the subject of an agreement[5],

the employer[6] must from time to time invite the trade union to send representatives to a meeting[7] for the purpose of:

(a)   consulting about the employer's policy on training for workers[8] within the bargaining unit;

(b)   consulting about his plans for training for those workers during the period of six months starting with the day of the meeting[9]; and

(c)   reporting about training provided for those workers since the previous meeting[10].

The employer must, before the period of two weeks ending with the date of a meeting, provide to the trade union any information without which the union's representatives would be to a material extent impeded in participating in the meeting, and which it would be in accordance with good industrial relations practice to disclose for the purposes of the meeting[11]. If that information includes information relating to the employment situation the employer must, so far as not so required, also provide at the same time to the trade union the following information:

(i)   the number of agency workers[12] working temporarily for and under the supervision and direction of the employer;

(ii)   the parts of the employer's undertaking in which those agency workers are working; and

(iii)   the type of work those agency workers are carrying out[13].

The employer must take account of any written representations about matters raised at a meeting which he receives from the trade union within the period of four weeks starting with the date of the meeting[14].

1   As to the meaning of 'trade union' see PARA 891. Where more than one trade union is recognised as entitled to conduct collective bargaining on behalf of a bargaining unit, a reference in the Trade Union and Labour Relations (Consolidation) Act 1992 s 70B to 'the trade union' is a reference to each trade union: s 70B(7) (s 70B added by the Employment Relations Act 1999 s 5). As to the meaning of 'recognised' see PARA 1094; and as to the meaning of 'collective bargaining' see PARA 1103 note 3.

2   Ie in accordance with the Trade Union and Labour Relations (Consolidation) Act 1992 Sch A1 (paras 1–172): see PARA 1103 et seq.

3   Ie within the meaning of the Trade Union and Labour Relations (Consolidation) Act 1992 Sch A1 Pt I (paras 1–51): see PARA 1103 note 3.

4   Ie under the Trade Union and Labour Relations (Consolidation) Act 1992 Sch A1 para 31(3): see PARA 1123.

5   Ie under the Trade Union and Labour Relations (Consolidation) Act 1992 Sch A1 para 31(5)(a) or (b): see PARA 1123.

6   As to the meaning of 'employer' see PARA 892.

7   The date set for such a meeting must not be later than: (1) in the case of a first meeting, the end of the period of six months starting with the day on which the Trade Union and Labour Relations (Consolidation) Act 1992 s 70B first applies in relation to a bargaining unit; and (2) in the case of each subsequent meeting, the end of the period of six months starting with the day of the previous meeting: s 70B(3) (as added: see note 1). The Secretary of State may by order made by statutory instrument amend any of s 70B(2)–(6): s 70B(9) (as so added). No such order is to be made unless a draft has been laid before, and approved by resolution of, each House of Parliament: s 70B(10) (as so added). At the date at which this volume states the law, no such order had been made. As to the Secretary of State see PARA 5 note 21.

8   As to the meaning of 'worker' see PARA 892.

9   Where, at a meeting under the Trade Union and Labour Relations (Consolidation) Act 1992 s 70B ('meeting 1'), an employer indicates his intention to convene a subsequent meeting ('meeting 2') before the expiry of the period of six months beginning with the date of meeting 1,

then, for the reference to a period of six months in s 70B(2)(b) (see head (b) in the text), there is to be substituted a reference to the expected period between meeting 1 and meeting 2: s 70B(8) (as added: see note 1).

10 Trade Union and Labour Relations (Consolidation) Act 1992 s 70B(1), (2) (as added: see note 1). As to the right to make a complaint to an employment tribunal see PARA 1173. See also note 7.

11 Trade Union and Labour Relations (Consolidation) Act 1992 s 70B(4) (as added: see note 1). Section s 182(1) (restrictions on disclosure of information) (see PARA 1181) applies in relation to the provision of information under s 70B(4), (4A) as it applies in relation to the disclosure of information under s 181 (see PARA 1179): s 70B(5) (as so added; amended by SI 2010/93). See also note 7.

12 As to the meaning of 'agency worker' see PARA 1104 note 8.

13 Trade Union and Labour Relations (Consolidation) Act 1992 s 70B(4A) (added by SI 2010/93). See also notes 7, 11.

14 Trade Union and Labour Relations (Consolidation) Act 1992 s 70B(6) (as added: see note 1). See also note 7.

1173. Employer's failure to consult on training for workers within a bargaining unit. A trade union[1] may present a complaint to an employment tribunal[2] that an employer[3] has failed to comply with his obligations as to consultation on training[4] for workers within a bargaining unit[5].

An employment tribunal must not consider such a complaint unless it is presented[6]:

(1) before the end of the period of three months beginning with the date of the alleged failure[7], subject to an extension to facilitate conciliation before the institution of proceedings[8]; or

(2) within such further period as the tribunal considers reasonable in a case where it is satisfied that it was not reasonably practicable for the complaint to be presented before the end of that period of three months[9].

Where an employment tribunal finds such a complaint well-founded, it must make a declaration to that effect and may make an award of compensation to be paid by the employer to each person who was, at the time when the failure occurred, a member of the bargaining unit[10]. The amount of the award must not, in relation to each person, exceed two weeks' pay[11]. Proceedings for enforcement of an award of such compensation may, in relation to each person to whom compensation is payable, be commenced by that person and may not be commenced by a trade union[12].

1 As to the meaning of 'trade union' see PARA 891.

2 As to employment tribunals see PARA 1399 et seq.

3 As to the meaning of 'employer' see PARA 892.

4 Ie under the Trade Union and Labour Relations (Consolidation) Act 1992 s 70B: see PARA 1172.

5 See the Trade Union and Labour Relations (Consolidation) Act 1992 s 70C(1) (s 70C added by the Employment Relations Act 1999 s 5). The provisions of the Employment Tribunals Act 1996 ss 18A–18B (conciliation) (see PARAS 152–153) apply in the case of matters which could be the subject of employment tribunal proceedings under the Trade Union and Labour Relations (Consolidation) Act 1992 s 70C, and the Employment Tribunals Act 1996 s 18C applies in the case of such proceedings themselves: see s 18(1)(a), (1A) (s 18(1)(a) substituted by SI 2014/431; the Employment Tribunals Act 1996 s 18(1A) added by the Enterprise and Regulatory Reform Act 2013 Sch 1 paras 2, 5(1), (7)). An appeal lies to the Employment Appeal Tribunal on any question of law arising from any decision of, or arising in any proceedings before, an employment tribunal under or by virtue of the Trade Union and Labour Relations (Consolidation) Act 1992: see the Employment Tribunals Act 1996 s 21(1)(d); and PARA 1428. As to the Employment Appeal Tribunal see PARA 1422 et seq.

6 As to when a complaint is presented see PARAS 990 note 4, 1461.

7 Trade Union and Labour Relations (Consolidation) Act 1992 s 70C(2)(a) (as added: see note 5). For the case law on the extension of time limits, especially in the context of the law of unfair dismissal, see PARA 1453. See also note 8.

8 The Trade Union and Labour Relations (Consolidation) Act 1992 s 292A (extension of time limits to facilitate conciliation before institution of proceedings: see PARA 1455) applies for the purposes of s 70C(2)(a): s 70C(2A) (added by the Enterprise and Regulatory Reform Act 2013 Sch 2 paras 1, 4).

9 Trade Union and Labour Relations (Consolidation) Act 1992 s 70C(2)(b) (as added: see note 5).

10 Trade Union and Labour Relations (Consolidation) Act 1992 s 70C(3) (as added: see note 5).

11 Trade Union and Labour Relations (Consolidation) Act 1992 s 70C(4) (as added: see note 5). For these purposes, a week's pay: (1) is to be calculated in accordance with the Employment Rights Act 1996 Pt XIV Ch II (ss 220–229) (see PARA 143 et seq), taking the date of the employer's failure as the calculation date; and (2) is subject to the limit in s 227(1) (see PARA 147): Trade Union and Labour Relations (Consolidation) Act 1992 s 70C(5) (as so added).

12 Trade Union and Labour Relations (Consolidation) Act 1992 s 70C(6) (as added: see note 5).

(x) Secretary of State's Power to Prohibit Unfair Practices with regard to Trade Union Recognition and Derecognition

1174. Secretary of State's power to make order prohibiting use of unfair practices. The Secretary of State[1] may by order[2] provide that, during any period beginning and ending with the occurrence of specified[3] events, employers[4] and unions[5] to which the order applies are prohibited from using such practices as are specified as unfair practices in relation to an application[6] of a specified description[7].

Such an order may (1) make provision about the consequences of a contravention of any prohibition imposed by the order[8]; (2) confer functions on the Central Arbitration Committee[9]; (3) contain provision extending for the purposes of the order either or both of the power of the Advisory, Conciliation and Arbitration Service[10] and the power of the Secretary of State[11] to issue Codes of Practice[12]; and (4) include supplementary or incidental provisions[13] and make different provision for different cases or circumstances[14].

1 As to the Secretary of State see PARA 5 note 21.

2 Such an order must be made by statutory instrument, and no such order may be made unless a draft of it has been laid before and approved by a resolution of each House of Parliament: Trade Union and Labour Relations (Consolidation) Act 1992 Sch A1 para 166B(6), (7) (Sch A1 para 166B added by the Employment Relations Act 2004 s 17).

   The Secretary of State has issued also in exercise of the power conferred on him by the Trade Union and Labour Relations (Consolidation) Act 1992 s 203 (see PARA 1231) the Code of Practice on Access and Unfair Practices during Recognition and Derecognition Ballots, which was brought into force on 1 October 2005 by the Employment Code of Practice (Access and Unfair Practices during Recognition and Derecognition Ballots) Order 2005, SI 2005/2421: see art 2.

3 'Specified' means specified in an order under the Trade Union and Labour Relations (Consolidation) Act 1992 Sch A1 para 166B: Sch A1 para 166B(8) (as added: see note 2).

4 As to the meaning of 'employer' see PARA 892.

5 As to the meaning of 'trade union' see PARA 891.

6 Ie an application under the Trade Union and Labour Relations (Consolidation) Act 1992 Sch A1: see PARA 1099 et seq.

7 Trade Union and Labour Relations (Consolidation) Act 1992 Sch A1 para 166B(1) (as added: see note 2).

8 Trade Union and Labour Relations (Consolidation) Act 1992 Sch A1 para 166B(2) (as added: see note 2). Such an order may also make provision modifying the effect of any provision of Sch A1 in the event of such a contravention: Sch A1 para 166B(2) (as so added).

9 Trade Union and Labour Relations (Consolidation) Act 1992 Sch A1 para 166B(3) (as added: see note 2). As to the Central Arbitration Committee see PARA 1226 et seq.

10 Ie under the Trade Union and Labour Relations (Consolidation) Act 1992 s 199(1): see PARA 1223. As to the Advisory, Conciliation and Arbitration Service ('ACAS') see PARA 1213 et seq.

11 Ie under the Trade Union and Labour Relations (Consolidation) Act 1992 s 203(1)(a): see PARA 1231 head (1) in the text.

12 Trade Union and Labour Relations (Consolidation) Act 1992 Sch A1 para 166B(4) (as added: see note 2).
13 Ie including provision amending the Trade Union and Labour Relations (Consolidation) Act 1992 Sch A1.
14 Trade Union and Labour Relations (Consolidation) Act 1992 Sch A1 para 166B(5) (as added: see note 2).

(3) COLLECTIVE AGREEMENTS

1175. Collective agreements unenforceable unless certain conditions are satisfied. At common law a collective agreement was not legally enforceable, owing to a lack of intention to create legal relations[1].

The common law is now superseded by statute which provides that a collective agreement[2] is conclusively presumed not to have been intended by the parties to be a legally enforceable contract unless the agreement:

(1)   is in writing; and
(2)   contains a provision which, however expressed, states that the parties intend that the agreement is to be a legally enforceable contract[3].

A collective agreement which does satisfy those conditions is conclusively presumed to have been intended by the parties to be a legally enforceable contract[4].

If a collective agreement is in writing and contains a provision which, however expressed, states that the parties intend that one or more parts of the agreement specified in that provision, but not the whole of the agreement, is or are to be a legally enforceable contract, then:

(a)   the specified part or parts is or are conclusively presumed to have been intended by the parties to be a legally enforceable contract; and
(b)   the remainder of the agreement is conclusively presumed not to have been so intended to be such a contract[5].

The effect of the transfer of an undertaking on a collective agreement made by or on behalf of the transferor with a trade union recognised by the transferor in respect of any employee whose contract of employment is preserved[6] is discussed in an earlier part of this title[7].

1   *Ford Motor Co Ltd v Amalgamated Union of Engineering and Foundry Workers* [1969] 2 QB 303, [1969] 2 All ER 481.
2   As to the meaning of 'collective agreement' see PARA 1093.
3   Trade Union and Labour Relations (Consolidation) Act 1992 s 179(1). The presumptions contained in s 179 are matters of substance (affecting the very existence or otherwise of a contract), not merely matters of procedure or procedural bars to enforcement: *Monterosso Shipping Co Ltd v International Transport Workers' Federation, The Rosso* [1982] 3 All ER 841, [1982] ICR 675, CA. Although the Trade Union and Labour Relations (Consolidation) Act 1992 s 179 provides that a written contrary indication may be effective 'however expressed', that written indication must be clear if it is to rebut the presumption; use of the word 'binding' may not be enough, because that will be consistent with the parties intending the agreement to be 'binding in honour only', a well-known industrial relations phrase: *National Coal Board v National Union of Mineworkers* [1986] ICR 736, [1986] IRLR 439.
4   Trade Union and Labour Relations (Consolidation) Act 1992 s 179(2).
5   Trade Union and Labour Relations (Consolidation) Act 1992 s 179(3). A part of a collective agreement which, by virtue of s 179(3)(b) (see head (b) in the text), is not a legally enforceable contract may, however, be referred to for the purpose of interpreting a part of the agreement which is such a contract: s 179(4).
     Section 179 does not apply to a collective agreement made on or after 1 December 1971 and before 16 September 1974: Sch 3 para 5.
6   Ie by virtue of the Transfer of Undertakings (Protection of Employment) Regulations 2006, SI 2006/246, reg 4: see PARA 139.

7   See the Transfer of Undertakings (Protection of Employment) Regulations 2006, SI 2006/246, reg 5; and PARA 139 note 24.

1176. Incorporation of collective agreements into contracts of employment. Although a collective agreement is not itself legally binding[1], individual provisions may obtain independent contractual effect if they are incorporated into the contracts of employment of particular employees, either expressly or impliedly[2]. Where such a provision is so incorporated, the fact that it has independent contractual effect means that it can continue in force even if the employer resiles from the collective agreement, unless and until varied or revoked in some contractually acceptable way[3].

1   See PARA 1175.
2   See PARA 116.
3   See PARA 117.

1177. No-strike clauses in collective agreements. Any terms of a collective agreement[1] which prohibit or restrict the right of workers[2] to engage in a strike or other industrial action[3], or have the effect of prohibiting or restricting that right, are not to form part of any contract between a worker and the person for whom he works unless the following conditions are met[4]. The conditions are that the collective agreement:

(1)   is in writing;

(2)   contains a provision expressly stating that those terms are to be or may be incorporated in such a contract;

(3)   is reasonably accessible at his place of work to the worker to whom it applies and is available for him to consult during working hours; and

(4)   is one where each trade union[5] which is a party to the agreement is an independent trade union[6],

and that the contract with the worker expressly or impliedly incorporates those terms in the contract[7].

The effect of the transfer of an undertaking on a collective agreement made by or on behalf of the transferor with a trade union recognised by the transferor in respect of any employee whose contract of employment is preserved[8] is discussed in an earlier part of this title[9].

1   As to the meaning of 'collective agreement' see PARA 1093.
2   As to the meaning of 'worker' see PARA 892.
3   There is no statutory definition of 'strike' or 'other industrial action' for these purposes. For the case law on these terms as they apply in the context of unfair dismissal law etc see PARA 1340.
4   Trade Union and Labour Relations (Consolidation) Act 1992 s 180(1).
5   As to the meaning of 'trade union' see PARA 891.
6   As to the meaning of 'independent trade union' see PARA 904.
7   Trade Union and Labour Relations (Consolidation) Act 1992 s 180(2). These provisions have effect notwithstanding anything in s 179 (see PARA 1175) and notwithstanding any provision to the contrary in any agreement, including a collective agreement or a contract with any worker: s 180(3).
    This provision was introduced after the decision in *Rookes v Barnard* [1964] AC 1129, [1964] 1 All ER 367, HL (no-strike clause incorporated into contracts of employment, forming the basis for the tort of intimidation: see TORT vol 97 (2010) PARA 622) and limits the circumstances in which that decision would apply. See also *Camden Exhibition and Display Ltd v Lynott* [1966] 1 QB 555, [1965] 3 All ER 28, CA.
8   Ie by virtue of the Transfer of Undertakings (Protection of Employment) Regulations 2006, SI 2006/246, reg 4: see PARA 139.
9   See the Transfer of Undertakings (Protection of Employment) Regulations 2006, SI 2006/246, reg 5; and PARA 139 note 24.

1178. Discriminatory collective agreements. A term of a collective agreement[1] is void in so far as it constitutes, promotes or provides for treatment of a description prohibited by the Equality Act 2010[2].

1   As to the meaning of 'collective agreement' see PARA 1093 (definition applied by the Equality Act 2010 s 148(4)).
2   Equality Act 2010 s 145(1). See further DISCRIMINATION vol 33 (2013) PARA 5.

(4) DISCLOSURE OF INFORMATION FOR COLLECTIVE BARGAINING

1179. Employer's duty to disclose information for purposes of collective bargaining. An employer[1] who recognises[2] an independent trade union[3] must, for the purposes of all stages of collective bargaining[4] about matters, and in relation to descriptions of workers[5], in respect of which the union is recognised by him[6], disclose to representatives[7] of the union, on request[8], all information relating to the employer's undertaking, including information relating to use of agency workers[9] in that undertaking, which is in his possession, or that of an associated employer[10], and is information:

(1)   without which the trade union representatives would be to a material extent impeded in carrying on collective bargaining with him; and

(2)   which it would be in accordance with good industrial relations practice that he should disclose to them for the purposes of collective bargaining[11].

In determining what would be in accordance with good industrial relations practice, regard is to be had to the relevant provisions of any Code of Practice issued by the Advisory, Conciliation and Arbitration Service[12], but not so as to exclude any other evidence of what that practice is[13].

1   As to the meaning of 'employer' see PARA 892.
2   As to the meaning of 'recognition' and cognate expressions see PARA 1094.
3   As to the meaning of 'independent trade union' see PARA 904.
4   As to the meaning of 'collective bargaining' see PARA 1093.
5   As to the meaning of 'worker' see PARA 892.
6   It is this requirement that imposes one of the principal restrictions on the statutory right, namely that, if the recognition is only partial, the obligation to disclose only applies to information relating to those matters in respect of which the union is recognised: *R v Central Arbitration Committee, ex p BTP Tioxide Ltd* [1981] ICR 843, [1982] IRLR 60.
7   For these purposes, 'representative', in relation to a trade union, means an official or other person authorised by the union to carry on such collective bargaining: Trade Union and Labour Relations (Consolidation) Act 1992 s 181(1). As to the meaning of 'official', in relation to a trade union, see PARA 1018.
8   The request must, if the employer so requests, be in writing or be confirmed in writing: Trade Union and Labour Relations (Consolidation) Act 1992 s 181(3). Information which an employer is required to disclose to trade union representatives must, if they so request, be disclosed or confirmed in writing: s 181(5).
9   As to the meaning of 'agency worker' see PARA 1104 note 8.
10 As to the meaning of 'associated employer' see PARA 1026 note 8.
11 Trade Union and Labour Relations (Consolidation) Act 1992 s 181(1), (2) (amended by SI 2010/93). For the many awards issued by the Central Arbitration Committee (see PARA 1182) under these provisions see Harvey on Industrial Relations and Employment Law, Division NI [2501] et seq.
12 As to the Code of Practice see PARA 1180; and as to the constitution and powers of the Advisory, Conciliation and Arbitration Service ('ACAS') see PARA 1213 et seq.
13 Trade Union and Labour Relations (Consolidation) Act 1992 s 181(4).

1180. **The Code of Practice on Disclosure of Information to Trade Unions for Collective Bargaining Purposes.** Pursuant to its statutory powers to issue Codes of Practice[1], the Advisory, Conciliation and Arbitration Service[2] has issued the Code of Practice on Disclosure of Information to Trade Unions for Collective Bargaining Purposes[3]. The provisions of the Code are admissible in evidence and may be taken into account in determining any question relating to disclosure of information before the Central Arbitration Committee; but failure to observe any provisions of the Code does not of itself render a person liable to any proceedings[4].

The Code makes the following general points about the putting into practice of the statutory obligations:

(1) trade unions should identify and request the information they require for collective bargaining in advance of negotiations wherever practicable; requests should state as precisely as possible all information required and should conform to an agreed procedure, allowing a reasonable period for consideration and reply[5]; they should keep employers informed of the names of their authorised representatives[6], co-ordinate requests if other unions are involved[7], and ensure that their negotiators are properly trained[8];

(2) employers should aim to be as open and helpful as possible in meeting union requests for information, giving reasons for any refusal[9]; agreed information should be given as soon as possible, and should be presented in a readily understandable form and style[10];

(3) both parties should endeavour to reach agreement on implementing the statutory obligations, including agreement for the provision of information on a regular basis[11]; and they should establish voluntary procedures to resolve any disputes[12].

The Code further states that, in determining what information will be relevant, negotiators should take account of the subject matter of the negotiations and the issues raised during them; the level at which negotiations take place (department, plant, division or company level); the size of the company; and the type of business the company is engaged in[13]. It then gives the following examples of information that could be relevant in certain collective bargaining situations:

(a) pay and benefits: principles and structure of payment systems; job evaluation systems and grading criteria; earnings and hours analysed according to work-group, grade, plant, sex, out-workers and home-workers, department or division, giving, where appropriate, distributions and make-up of pay showing any additions to basic rate or salary; total pay bill; details of fringe benefits and non-wage labour costs;

(b) conditions of service: policies on recruitment, redeployment, redundancy, training, equal opportunity and promotion; appraisal systems; health, welfare and safety matters;

(c) manpower: numbers employed analysed according to grade, department, location, age and sex; labour turnover; absenteeism; overtime and short-time; manning standards; planned changes in work methods, materials, equipment or organisation; available manpower plans; investment plans;

(d)   performance: productivity and efficiency data; savings from increased productivity and output; return on capital invested; sales and state of order book; and

(e)   financial: cost structures; gross and net profits; sources of earnings; assets; liabilities; allocation of profits; details of government financial assistance; transfer prices; loans to parent or subsidiary companies and interest charged[14].

1   Ie under the Trade Union and Labour Relations (Consolidation) Act 1992 ss 199–202: see PARA 1223.
2   As to the constitution and powers of the Advisory, Conciliation and Arbitration Service ('ACAS') see PARA 1213 et seq.
3   The current Code was brought into force on 5 February 1998 by the Employment Protection Code of Practice (Disclosure of Information) Order 1998, SI 1998/45, art 2. In formulating the provisions of any Code of Practice relating to the disclosure of information, ACAS must have regard to the provisions of the Trade Union and Labour Relations (Consolidation) Act 1992 s 182(1) (restrictions on the duty to disclose) (see PARA 1181): s 182(1).
4   See the Trade Union and Labour Relations (Consolidation) Act 1992 s 207; and PARA 1224.
5   See the Code of Practice on Disclosure of Information to Trade Unions for Collective Bargaining Purposes para 16.
6   See the Code of Practice on Disclosure of Information to Trade Unions for Collective Bargaining Purposes para 17.
7   See the Code of Practice on Disclosure of Information to Trade Unions for Collective Bargaining Purposes para 18.
8   See the Code of Practice on Disclosure of Information to Trade Unions for Collective Bargaining Purposes para 19.
9   See the Code of Practice on Disclosure of Information to Trade Unions for Collective Bargaining Purposes para 20.
10   See the Code of Practice on Disclosure of Information to Trade Unions for Collective Bargaining Purposes para 21.
11   See the Code of Practice on Disclosure of Information to Trade Unions for Collective Bargaining Purposes para 22.
12   See the Code of Practice on Disclosure of Information to Trade Unions for Collective Bargaining Purposes para 23.
13   See the Code of Practice on Disclosure of Information to Trade Unions for Collective Bargaining Purposes para 10.
14   See the Code of Practice on Disclosure of Information to Trade Unions for Collective Bargaining Purposes para 11. These examples are not intended to represent a check list of information that should be provided for all negotiations; nor are they meant to be an exhaustive list of types of information as other items may be relevant in particular negotiations: para 12.

1181.   Restrictions on the duty to disclose information for purposes of collective bargaining.   An employer[1] is not required[2] to disclose information:

(1)   the disclosure of which would be against the interests of national security; or

(2)   which he could not disclose without contravening a prohibition imposed by or under any enactment; or

(3)   which has been communicated to him in confidence, or which he has otherwise obtained in consequence of the confidence reposed in him by another person; or

(4)   which relates specifically to an individual, unless that individual has consented to its being disclosed; or

(5)   the disclosure of which would cause substantial injury to his undertaking[3] for reasons other than its effect on collective bargaining[4]; or

(6)   obtained by him for the purpose of bringing, prosecuting or defending any legal proceedings[5].

In the performance of his duty to disclose information, an employer is not required:

(a) to produce, or allow inspection of, any document, other than a document prepared for the purpose of conveying or confirming the information, or to make a copy of or extracts from any document; or

(b) to compile or assemble any information where the compilation or assembly would involve an amount of work or expenditure out of reasonable proportion to the value of the information in the conduct of collective bargaining[6].

1 As to the meaning of 'employer' see PARA 892.
2 Ie by the Trade Union and Labour Relations (Consolidation) Act 1992 s 181: see PARA 1179.
3 As to the construction of this reference to the employer's undertaking in relation to Crown employment or employment as a relevant member of the House of Lords or House of Commons staff see PARAS 893 note 3, 894 note 4, 895 note 4.
4 The Code of Practice on Disclosure of Information to Trade Unions for Collective Bargaining Purposes (see PARA 1180) gives the following guidance on this particular head:
   (1) some examples of information which, if disclosed in particular circumstances, might cause substantial injury are: cost information on individual products; detailed analysis of proposed investment, marketing or pricing policies; price quotas or the make-up of tender prices; but information which has to be made available publicly, e g under the Companies Acts, would not fall into this category (Code of Practice on Disclosure of Information to Trade Unions for Collective Bargaining Purposes para 14);
   (2) substantial injury may occur if e g certain customers would be lost to competitors, or suppliers would refuse to supply necessary materials, or the ability to raise funds to finance the company would be seriously impaired as a result of disclosing certain information; the burden of establishing a claim that disclosure of certain information would cause substantial injury lies with the employer (Code of Practice on Disclosure of Information to Trade Unions for Collective Bargaining Purposes para 15).
   In formulating the provisions of any Code of Practice relating to the disclosure of information, ACAS must have regard to the provisions of the Trade Union and Labour Relations (Consolidation) Act 1992 s 182(1) (see heads (1)–(6) in the text): s 182(1). As to the meaning of 'collective bargaining' see PARA 1093. As to the Advisory, Conciliation and Arbitration Service ('ACAS') see PARA 1213 et seq.
5 Trade Union and Labour Relations (Consolidation) Act 1992 s 182(1).
6 Trade Union and Labour Relations (Consolidation) Act 1992 s 182(2). For the awards of the Central Arbitration Committee concerning the restrictions under s 182 see Harvey on Industrial Relations and Employment Law, Division NI [2634] et seq.

1182. Employer's failure to disclose information for purposes of collective bargaining. A trade union[1] may present a complaint to the Central Arbitration Committee[2] (the 'CAC') that an employer[3] has failed to disclose to representatives[4] of the union information which he was required to disclose to them[5], or to confirm such information in writing in accordance with the statutory requirements[6].

If, on receipt of a complaint, the CAC is of the opinion that it is reasonably likely to be settled by conciliation, it must refer the complaint to the Advisory, Conciliation and Arbitration Service[7] ('ACAS') and must notify the trade union and employer accordingly, whereupon ACAS must seek to promote a settlement of the matter[8]. If a complaint is not referred to ACAS, or if it is so referred and ACAS informs the CAC that further attempts at conciliation are unlikely to result in a settlement, the CAC must proceed to hear and determine the complaint and must make a declaration stating whether it finds the complaint well-founded, wholly or in part, and stating the reasons for its findings[9].

If the CAC finds the complaint wholly or partly well-founded, the declaration must specify:

(1) the information in respect of which the CAC finds that the complaint is well-founded;

(2) the date, or, if more than one, the earliest date, on which the employer refused or failed to disclose or, as the case may be, to confirm in writing, any of the information in question; and

(3) a period, not being less than one week from the date of the declaration, within which the employer ought to disclose that information, or, as the case may be, to confirm it in writing[10].

After the expiration of the period specified in head (3) above, the trade union may present a further complaint to the CAC that the employer has failed to disclose or, as the case may be, to confirm in writing to representatives of the union information specified in the declaration[11]. On receipt of a further complaint, the CAC must proceed to hear and determine the complaint and must make a declaration stating whether it finds the complaint well-founded, wholly or in part, and stating the reasons for its finding[12]. If the CAC finds the further complaint wholly or partly well-founded, the declaration must specify the information in respect of which it finds that that complaint is well-founded[13].

On or after presenting a further complaint of failure to disclose or confirm information[14], the trade union may present to the CAC a claim, in writing, in respect of one or more descriptions of employees[15] specified in the claim that their contracts should include the terms and conditions specified in the claim[16].

If the CAC finds, or has found, the further complaint wholly or partly well-founded, it may, after hearing the parties, make an award that, in respect of any description of employees specified in the claim, the employer must from a specified date[17] observe either:

(a) the terms and conditions specified in the claim; or

(b) other terms and conditions which the CAC considers appropriate[18].

Terms and conditions which an employer is required by such an award to observe in respect of an employee have effect as part of the employee's contract of employment[19] as from the date specified in the award, except in so far as superseded or varied:

(i) by a subsequent such award;

(ii) by a collective agreement[20] between the employer and the union for the time being representing that employee; or

(iii) by express or implied agreement between the employee and the employer so far as that agreement effects an improvement in terms and conditions having effect by virtue of the award[21].

The statutory restriction on contracting out[22] does not apply to such an agreement as is referred to in head (ii) or head (iii) above to the extent that it varies or supersedes an award under the above provisions[23].

1   In order to qualify for the right to receive bargaining information in the first place, the trade union must be both independent and recognised: see PARA 1179. As to the meaning of 'trade union' see PARA 891.

2   As to the Central Arbitration Committee see PARA 1226 et seq.

3   As to the meaning of 'employer' see PARA 892.

4   As to the meaning of 'representative' for these purposes see PARA 1179 note 7.

5   Ie by the Trade Union and Labour Relations (Consolidation) Act 1992 s 181: see PARA 1179.

6   Trade Union and Labour Relations (Consolidation) Act 1992 s 183(1). Such a complaint must be in writing and in such form as the CAC may require: s 183(1).

7   As to the Advisory, Conciliation and Arbitration Service ('ACAS') see PARA 1213 et seq.

8 Trade Union and Labour Relations (Consolidation) Act 1992 s 183(2). If a complaint so referred is not settled or withdrawn and ACAS is of the opinion that further attempts at conciliation are unlikely to result in a settlement, it must inform the CAC of its opinion: s 183(2).

9 Trade Union and Labour Relations (Consolidation) Act 1992 s 183(3). On the hearing of a complaint, any person who the CAC considers has a proper interest in the complaint is entitled to be heard by the CAC, but a failure to accord a hearing to a person other than the trade union or employer directly concerned does not affect the validity of any decision of the CAC in those proceedings: s 183(4).

On a hearing of a complaint, a certificate signed by or on behalf of a Minister of the Crown and certifying that a particular request for information could not be complied with except by disclosing information the disclosure of which would have been against the interests of national security is conclusive evidence of that fact; and a document which purports to be such a certificate is to be taken to be such a certificate unless the contrary is proved: s 183(6). As to the exemption from the requirement of disclosure on the grounds of national security see s 182(1)(a); and PARA 1181 head (1) in the text.

10 Trade Union and Labour Relations (Consolidation) Act 1992 s 183(5). For the awards issued by the Central Arbitration Committee concerning complaints under s 183 see Harvey on Industrial Relations and Employment Law, Division NI [2682] et seq. In making a declaration, the CAC has no power to declare what should be disclosed in the future: *R v Central Arbitration Committee, ex p BTP Tioxide Ltd* [1981] ICR 843, [1982] IRLR 60.

11 Trade Union and Labour Relations (Consolidation) Act 1992 s 184(1). The complaint must be in writing and in such form as the CAC may require: s 184(1).

12 Trade Union and Labour Relations (Consolidation) Act 1992 s 184(2). On the hearing of a further complaint, any person who the CAC considers has a proper interest in that complaint is entitled to be heard by the CAC, but a failure to accord a hearing to a person other than the trade union and employer directly concerned does not affect the validity of any decision of the CAC in those proceedings: s 184(3).

13 Trade Union and Labour Relations (Consolidation) Act 1992 s 184(4). The provisions of s 184 do not apply to Crown employment or employment as a relevant member of the House of Lords or House of Commons staff: see PARAS 893 note 2, 894 note 2, 895 note 2.

14 Ie under the Trade Union and Labour Relations (Consolidation) Act 1992 s 184: see the text and notes 11–13.

15 This is expressed not to apply to 'workers who are not employees'; this is because the remedy lies in the insertion of improved terms and conditions into contracts of employment, whereas the term 'worker' (used generally in this context) is wider than just a person under such a contract: see PARA 892.

16 Trade Union and Labour Relations (Consolidation) Act 1992 s 185(1). The right to present a claim expires if the employer discloses or, as the case may be, confirms in writing to representatives of the trade union the information specified in the declaration under s 183(5) (see the text and note 10) or s 184(4) (see the text and note 13); and a claim presented is to be treated as withdrawn if the employer does so before the CAC makes an award on the claim: s 185(2). The provisions of s 185 do not apply to Crown employment or employment as a relevant member of the House of Lords or House of Commons staff: see PARAS 893 note 2, 894 note 2, 895 note 2.

17 The date specified may be earlier than that on which the award is made but not earlier than the date specified in accordance with the Trade Union and Labour Relations (Consolidation) Act 1992 s 183(5)(b) (see head (2) in the text) in the declaration made by the CAC on the original complaint: s 185(3).

18 Trade Union and Labour Relations (Consolidation) Act 1992 s 185(3). An award may be made only in respect of a description of employees, and must comprise only terms and conditions relating to matters in respect of which the trade union making the claim is recognised by the employer: s 185(4). No award may be made under s 185 in respect of terms and conditions of employment which are fixed by virtue of any enactment: s 185(7). As to the meaning of 'recognised' see PARA 1094.

19 As to the meaning of 'contract of employment' see PARA 892.

20 As to the meaning of 'collective agreement' see PARA 1093.

21 Trade Union and Labour Relations (Consolidation) Act 1992 s 185(5). Where: (1) by virtue of any enactment, other than one contained in s 185, providing for minimum remuneration or terms and conditions, a contract of employment is to have effect as modified by an award, order or other instrument under that enactment; and (2) by virtue of an award under s 185, any terms and conditions are to have effect as part of that contract, that contract has effect in accordance

with that award, order or other instrument or in accordance with the award under s 185, whichever is the more favourable, in respect of any terms and conditions of that contract, to the employee: s 185(6).

22 Ie the Trade Union and Labour Relations (Consolidation) Act 1992 s 288(1): see PARA 150.

23 Trade Union and Labour Relations (Consolidation) Act 1992 s 288(3)(a).

(5) AVOIDANCE OF, AND PROHIBITION ON, TRADE UNION RECOGNITION REQUIREMENTS

1183.   Trade union recognition requirement in contract is void. A term or condition of a contract for the supply of goods or services is void in so far as it purports to require a party to the contract to recognise[1] one or more trade unions[2], whether or not named in the contract, for the purpose of negotiating on behalf of workers[3], or any class of worker, employed by him, or to negotiate or consult with, or with an official[4] of, one or more trade unions, whether or not so named[5].

The above provisions bind the Crown[6].

1   As to the meaning of 'recognition' and cognate expressions see PARA 1094.
2   As to the meaning of 'trade union' see PARA 891.
3   As to the meaning of 'worker' see PARA 892.
4   As to the meaning of 'official', in relation to a trade union, see PARA 1018.

5   Trade Union and Labour Relations (Consolidation) Act 1992 s 186. There are equivalent provisions (attacking the practice of 'contract compliance') in relation to union membership requirements in s 144: see PARA 1069. It is unlawful to refuse to deal with a supplier on grounds of lack of trade union recognition: see s 187; and PARA 1184. Any industrial action to induce a person to incorporate into a contract a term which is void under s 186 is not protected by the statutory immunities: see s 225(1)(a); and PARA 1368 head (1) in the text.

6   Trade Union and Labour Relations (Consolidation) Act 1992 s 276(2).

1184.   Refusal to deal on grounds of trade union exclusion prohibited. A person may not refuse to deal with a supplier or prospective supplier of goods or services if the ground, or one of the grounds, for his action is that the person against whom it is taken does not, or is not likely to, recognise[1] one or more trade unions[2] for the purpose of negotiating on behalf of workers[3], or any class of worker, employed by him, or negotiate or consult with, or with an official[4] of, one or more trade unions[5].

A person refuses to deal with a person if:

(1)   where he maintains, in whatever form, a list of approved suppliers of goods or services, or of persons from whom tenders for the supply of goods or services may be invited, he fails to include the name of that person in that list; or

(2)   in relation to a proposed contract for the supply of goods or services:

   (a)   he excludes that person from the group of persons from whom tenders for the supply of the goods or services are invited; or

   (b)   he fails to permit that person to submit such a tender; or

   (c)   he otherwise determines not to enter into a contract with that person for the supply of the goods or services; or

(3)   he terminates a contract with that person for the supply of goods or services[6].

The obligation to comply with the above provisions is a duty owed to the person with whom there is a refusal to deal and to any other person who may be adversely affected by its contravention[7]; and a breach of the duty is actionable accordingly, subject to the defences and other incidents applying to actions for breach of statutory duty[8].

The above provisions bind the Crown[9].

1 As to the meaning of 'recognition' and cognate expressions see PARA 1094.
2 As to the meaning of 'trade union' see PARA 891.
3 As to the meaning of 'worker' see PARA 892.
4 As to the meaning of 'official', in relation to a trade union, see PARA 1018.
5 Trade Union and Labour Relations (Consolidation) Act 1992 s 187(1). There are equivalent provisions on refusal to deal on grounds of union membership: see s 145; and PARA 1070.
6 Trade Union and Labour Relations (Consolidation) Act 1992 s 187(2) (amended by the Trade Union Reform and Employment Rights Act 1993 Sch 7 para 23).
7 As to the meaning of 'contravention' and cognate expressions see PARA 915 note 6.
8 Trade Union and Labour Relations (Consolidation) Act 1992 s 187(3). As to breach of statutory duty see TORT vol 97 (2010) PARA 495 et seq. The statutory immunities are withdrawn from any act which constitutes an inducement or attempted inducement of a person to contravene s 187: see s 225(1)(b); and PARA 1368 head (2) in the text.
9 Trade Union and Labour Relations (Consolidation) Act 1992 s 276(2).

(6) PROCEDURE FOR HANDLING REDUNDANCIES

(i) Consultation with Employees' Representatives

1185. Employer's duty to consult about proposed redundancies. Where an employer[1] is proposing[2] to dismiss[3] as redundant[4] 20 or more employees[5] at one establishment[6] within a period of 90 days or less[7], the employer must consult[8] about the dismissals all the persons who are appropriate representatives[9] of any of the employees who may be affected by the proposed dismissals or may be affected by measures taken in connection with those dismissals[10].

The consultation must begin in good time[11], and in any event:

(1) where the employer is proposing to dismiss 100 or more employees, at least 45 days before the first of the dismissals takes effect; and

(2) otherwise, at least 30 days before the first of the dismissals takes effect[12].

Where the employer has invited any of the affected employees to elect employee representatives[13] and the invitation was issued long enough before the time when consultation is so required to begin to allow them to elect representatives by that time, the employer is to be treated as complying with these requirements in relation to those employees if he complies with them as soon as is reasonably practicable after the election of the representatives[14].

The consultation must include consultation about ways of avoiding the dismissals, reducing the numbers of employees to be dismissed and mitigating the consequences of the dismissals; and it is to be undertaken by the employer with a view to reaching agreement with the appropriate representatives[15].

For the purposes of the consultation, the employer must disclose in writing[16] to the appropriate representatives:

(a) the reasons for his proposals;

(b) the numbers and descriptions of employees whom it is proposed to dismiss as redundant;

(c) the total number of employees of any such description employed by the employer at the establishment in question;

(d) the proposed method of selecting[17] the employees who may be dismissed;

(e)   the proposed method of carrying out the dismissals, with due regard to
       any agreed procedure, including the period over which the dismissals
       are to take effect;

(f)   the proposed method of calculating the amount of any redundancy
       payments to be made, otherwise than in compliance with an obligation
       imposed by or by virtue of any enactment, to employees who may be
       dismissed;

(g)   the number of agency workers[18] working temporarily for and under the
       supervision and direction of the employer;

(h)   the parts of the employer's undertaking in which those agency workers
       are working; and

(i)   the type of work those agency workers are carrying out[19].

1   As to the meaning of 'employer' see PARA 892. Irrespective of whether collective redundancies
     are contemplated or projected as a result of a decision of the undertaking which employs the
     workers concerned or a decision of its parent company, it is always the former which is obliged,
     as the employer, to start consultations with the representatives of its workers: Case C-44/08
     Akavan Erityisalojen Keskusliitto AEK ry v Fujitsu Siemens Computers Oy [2009] ECR
     I-08163, [2010] 1 CMLR 309, [2010] ICR 444, ECJ (in the context of a group of undertakings,
     a decision by the parent company which had the direct effect of compelling one of its
     subsidiaries to terminate the contracts of employees affected by the collective redundancies
     could be taken only on the conclusion of the consultation procedure within that subsidiary,
     failing which the subsidiary, as the employer, was liable for the consequences of failure to
     comply with that procedure).

2   The requirement that the employer be 'proposing' redundancies means that there must be
     something more definite than the mere contemplation of possible redundancies: *Association of
     Patternmakers and Allied Craftsmen v Kirvin Ltd* [1978] IRLR 318, EAT; *Hough v Leyland
     DAF Ltd* [1991] ICR 696, [1991] IRLR 194, EAT. This means that the primary consideration of
     policy (whether redundancies are necessary) remains a managerial matter, with consultation
     effectively being limited to questions as to how that policy is to be carried out: *National and
     Local Government Officers' Association v National Travel (Midlands) Ltd* [1978] ICR
     598, EAT; *Union of Shop, Distributive and Allied Workers v Leancut Bacon Ltd (in liquidation)*
     [1981] IRLR 295, EAT.
        This clearly established approach of domestic law may, however, be in conflict with Council
     Directive (EC) 98/59 (OJ L225, 12.8.98, p 16), on the predecessor of which these provisions are
     based (see note 10). Article 2(1) requires consultation to begin 'where an employer is
     contemplating collective redundancies', which apparently refers to an earlier stage than that of
     'proposing' them (see Case 284/83 *Dansk Metalarbejderforbund v H Nielsen & Søn,
     Maskinfabrik A/S (in liquidation)* [1985] ECR 553, [1986] 1 CMLR 91, ECJ), with the result
     that domestic law does not enact what is now Council Directive (EC) 98/59 (OJ L225, 12.8.98,
     p 16) properly: *R v British Coal Corpn, ex p Vardy* [1993] ICR 720 at 753, sub nom *R v British
     Coal Corpn and Secretary of State for Trade and Industry, ex p Vardy* [1993] IRLR 104 at
     116, DC obiter per Glidewell LJ (but see the doubts subsequently expressed as to this by
     Blackburne J in *Griffin v South West Water Services Ltd* [1995] IRLR 15). The amendments
     made by the Trade Union Reform and Employment Rights Act 1993 (see note 10) did not
     address this point, save possibly that the required consultation must now include consultation
     over ways of avoiding the dismissals; but this is still likely to occur after the employer has taken
     the initial decision and 'proposed' the redundancies. There can be a 'proposal' where an
     employer decides on two possible courses of action, only one of which would result in
     redundancies: *Scotch Premier Meat Ltd v Burns* [2000] IRLR 639, EAT. See also *MSF v Refuge
     Assurance plc* [2002] ICR 1365, [2002] IRLR 324, EAT (and see note 6); *Hardy v Tourism
     South East* [2005] IRLR 242, [2005] All ER (D) 201 (Jan), EAT.
        See also European Parliament and Council Directive (EC) 2002/14 (OJ L80, 23.3.2002,
     p 29), which establishes a general framework for informing and consulting employees in the
     European Union. See PARA 1288 note 13.

3   As to the meaning of 'dismiss' see PARA 1056 note 1. 'Dismiss' includes accepting volunteers for
     redundancy if their volunteering was against the background of impending dismissals
     (ie volunteers count towards the 20 or 100 necessary to trigger the statutory obligations):
     Optare Group Ltd v TGWU [2007] IRLR 931, [2007] All ER (D) 135 (Jul), EAT.

4   For these purposes, references to dismissal as redundant are references to dismissal for a reason not related to the individual concerned or for a number of reasons all of which are not so related; and, for the purposes of any proceedings under the Trade Union and Labour Relations (Consolidation) Act 1992 Pt IV Ch II (ss 188–198B) (see also PARA 1188 et seq), where an employee is or is proposed to be dismissed, it is to be presumed, unless the contrary is proved, that he is or is proposed to be dismissed as redundant: s 195(1), (2) (substituted by the Trade Union Reform and Employment Rights Act 1993 s 34(1), (5)). One consequence of this wider definition of redundancy for these purposes is that the consultation requirements can apply where the employer collectively dismisses the staff in order to re-engage them on new (imposed) terms and conditions of employment, even though there are ultimately no job losses: *GMB v Man Truck & Bus UK Ltd* [2000] ICR 1101, [2000] IRLR 636, EAT. As to dismissals at the expiry of fixed-term contracts see the Trade Union and Labour Relations (Consolidation) Act 1992 s 282(2) (substituted by SI 2013/763); and PARA 1194; see also *University of Stirling v University and College Union* [2014] CSIH 5, [2014] IRLR 287 (decided under that provision prior to its substitution) (dismissals at the expiry of fixed term contracts not necessarily dismissals for redundancy subject to the statutory requirement to consult).

5   As to the meaning of 'employee' see PARA 892. As to excluded classes of employment see PARA 1194.
    Council Directive (EC) 98/59 (OJ L225, 12.8.98, p 16) (see note 10) and European Parliament and Council Directive (EC) 2002/14 (OJ L80, 23.3.2002, p 29) (see note 2) preclude legislation that excludes a specific category of employees from the calculation of staff numbers, even if the exclusion is only temporary or in pursuit of a legitimate aim of social policy to encourage recruitment: Case C-385/05 *Confederation Generale du Travail (CGT) v Premier Ministre* [2007] ECR I-611, [2007] 2 CMLR 163, ECJ.
    See also Case C-323/08 *Rodríguez Mayor v Herencia yacente de Rafael de las Heras Dávila* [2009] ECR I-11621, [2010] All ER (EC) 489, [2010] 2 CMLR 590, ECJ (termination of employment contracts connected to the death of an employer who was a natural person did not fall within the scope of the concept of collective redundancies within the meaning of Council Directive (EC) 98/59); Case C-583/10 *United States of America v Nolan* [2013] 1 CMLR 961, [2013] ICR 193, [2012] IRLR 1020, ECJ (on a reference of the question as to whether an employer's obligation to consult about collective redundancies pursuant to Council Directive (EC) 98/59 arose when the employer was proposing, but had not yet made, a strategic business or operational decision that would foreseeably or inevitably lead to collective redundancies, or only when that decision had been made and it was then proposing consequential redundancies; dismissal of employees at a US Army base in England exempted from the provisions of Council Directive (EC) 98/59 by art 1(2)(b) (exclusion of workers employed by public administrative bodies or by establishments governed by public law or by equivalent bodies), irrespective of whether the base belonged to a non-member state, and so the Court of Justice of the European Union ('CJEU') did not have jurisdiction to give an interpretation of the provisions of the Directive, even though it had been implemented in domestic law, because the relevant provisions of that had not been so made applicable in a direct and unconditional way: see also note 10); and see *United States of America v Nolan* [2014] EWCA Civ 71, [2014] ICR 685, [2014] IRLR 302 (it had made perfectly good sense for Parliament to have settled for a touchstone for exclusion which had used common law concepts and would be comparatively easy to apply domestically while recognising that it might be narrower in its effect than the exclusion provided for in the Directive; accordingly, the decision of the Court of Justice of the European Union had not meant that the instant appeal would be allowed; and a further hearing would be required to determine the issue that had originally led to the reference to the CJEU).

6   'Establishment' is not defined for these purposes. In *Barley v Amey Roadstone Corpn Ltd (No 2)* [1978] ICR 190, EAT, previous case law on the term as it appeared in the (repealed) legislation on selective employment tax was applied. Difficulties can arise in the case of multiple work sites: see *Barratt Developments (Bradford) Ltd v Union of Construction, Allied Trades and Technicians* [1978] ICR 319, [1977] IRLR 403, EAT (14 building sites connected by telephone to headquarters held to be one establishment); *Bakers' Union v Clarks of Hove Ltd* [1977] IRLR 167 (revsd on a different point sub nom *Clarks of Hove Ltd v Bakers' Union* [1978] 2 All ER 15, [1977] ICR 838, EAT, and that decision subsequently revsd [1979] 1 All ER 152, [1978] ICR 1076, CA (bakery and 28 retail outlets held to be one establishment)).
    In the Employment Appeal Tribunal's view, Council Directive (EC) 98/59 should apply where an employer proposes 20 or more redundancies across the whole of the undertaking within 90 days, whether or not the undertaking consists of several establishments: see *MSF v Refuge Assurance plc* [2002] ICR 1365, [2002] IRLR 324, EAT (the Directive looks for 20 dismissals across all the establishments collectively and in consequence the Trade Union and Labour Relations (Consolidation) Act 1992 s 188 imperfectly transposed the Directive in that

respect but as a matter of interpretation, nothing could be done about it); *Renfrewshire Council v Educational Institute of Scotland* [2013] ICR 172, [2013] IRLR 76, EAT (it was inappropriate to depart from *MSF v Refuge Assurance plc*; 'establishment' likely in many if not most circumstances to be less than whole undertaking of employer concerned); cf *Usdaw v Ethel Austin Ltd (in administration), Usdaw v Unite the Union* [2014] 1 CMLR 633, [2013] ICR 1300, [2013] IRLR 686, EAT (court was entitled to construe the Trade Union and Labour Relations (Consolidation) Act 1992 s 188(1) so that it complied with the obligation under Council Directive (EC) 98/59 so that the words 'at one establishment' ought to be deleted from the Trade Union and Labour Relations (Consolidation) Act 1992 s 188(1) as a matter of construction pursuant to the court's obligations to apply the purpose of that Directive, applying *Coleman v EBR Attridge Law LLP* [2010] ICR 242, [2010] IRLR 10, EAT; on appeal a reference has been made to the Court of Justice of the European Union as to the compatibility of the Trade Union and Labour Relations (Consolidation) Act 1992 s 188 with the Directive: see *USDAW v Ethel Austin Ltd (in administration)* [2014] EWCA Civ 142, [2014] 2 CMLR 1364). See also Case C-449/93 *Rockfon A/S v Specialarbejderforbundet i Danmark* [1995] ECR I-4291, [1996] ICR 673, [1996] IRLR 168, ECJ (concept of 'establishment' in Council Directive (EC) 98/59, in particular in art 1(1)(a), designates, depending on the circumstances, the unit to which the workers made redundant are assigned to carry out their duties; it is not essential that the power to effect the redundancies must lie within that unit); Case C-270/05 *Athinaiki Chartopoiia AE v Panagiotidis* [2007] ECR I-1499, [2007] IRLR 284, ECJ which allows the 'establishment' to be small with little independent development, thus potentially allowing the employer to split up a redundancy over several sites and minimising (or potentially even extinguishing) the statutory consultation requirement.

7 In determining how many employees an employer is proposing to dismiss as redundant, no account is to be taken of employees in respect of whose proposed dismissal consultation has already begun: Trade Union and Labour Relations (Consolidation) Act 1992 s 188(3).

8 There is no statutory definition of 'consultation', although the Trade Union and Labour Relations (Consolidation) Act 1992 s 188(4) (see heads (a)–(i) in the text) lists information that is to be given for the purposes of the consultation. Consultation must be real, not just a sham or pretence, and the union must be given a proper opportunity to consider the employer's proposals: *Transport and General Workers' Union v Ledbury Preserves (1928) Ltd* [1985] IRLR 412, EAT. In addition, the union must be given adequate information and time, and the employer must give conscientious consideration to any response: *R v British Coal Corpn and Secretary of State for Trade and Industry, ex p Price* [1994] IRLR 72, DC. See Case C-12/08 *Mono Car Styling SA v Dervis Odemis* [2009] ECR I-6653, [2009] 3 CMLR 1589, [2009] All ER (D) 114 (Aug), ECJ (Council Directive (EC) 98/59 art 2 interpreted as precluding national rules which reduced the obligations of an employer who intended to proceed with collective redundancies below those laid down in art 2).

In a case of complete closure of the establishment, the obligation to consult over avoiding proposed redundancies inevitably involves engaging with the reasons for the dismissal and in turn, requires consultation over the reasons for the closure, thus where closure and dismissals are inextricably linked, the duty to consult over the reasons arises: *UK Coal Mining Ltd v National Union of Mineworkers (Northumberland Area)* [2008] ICR 163, [2008] IRLR 4, EAT.

9 As to the meaning of 'appropriate representatives' see PARA 1187.

10 Trade Union and Labour Relations (Consolidation) Act 1992 s 188(1) (substituted by SI 1995/2587; amended by SI 1999/1925). The previous provisions (ie the Employment Protection Act 1975 ss 99–107 (repealed)) were passed to give effect to Council Directive (EC) 75/129 (OJ L48, 22/02/1975, p 29) on collective redundancies. Amendments to the Trade Union and Labour Relations (Consolidation) Act 1992 ss 188–192 were made by the Trade Union Reform and Employment Rights Act 1993 s 34 in order to comply with Council Directive (EC) 92/56 (OJ L348, 28.11.92, p 1). Council Directive (EC) 75/129 and Council Directive (EC) 92/56 have now been repealed and consolidated in Council Directive (EC) 98/59 (OJ L225, 12.8.98, p 16).

As to the obligation to consult where the redundancy decision is of a sovereign nature see United States of America v Nolan *United States of America v Nolan* [2014] EWCA Civ 71, [2014] ICR 685, [2014] IRLR 302, cited in note 5. The obligation to consult applies where the employer's activities are terminated by a judicial decision ordering its dissolution and winding up on the grounds of insolvency, even where national legislation provides for the termination of employment contracts with immediate effect: Cases C-235/10–C-239/10 *Claes v Landsbanki Luxembourg SA (in liquidation)* [2011] ECR I-1113, [2011] ICR 1364, ECJ.

The Trade Union and Labour Relations (Consolidation) Act 1992 s 188 does not confer any rights on a trade union, a representative or an employee except as provided by ss 189–192 (see PARAS 1188–1191): s 188(8) (amended by SI 1995/2587). As to the Secretary of State's power by order to adapt, modify or exclude these provisions where he is satisfied that a collective agreement provides alternative procedures at least as favourable to employees see the Trade Union and Labour Relations (Consolidation) Act 1992 s 198; and PARA 1195.

The obligation under s 188 is subject to the 'special circumstances' defence in s 188(7) (see PARA 1188), the method of enforcement being the device of the 'protective award' (see PARAS 1189–1190).

11 The wording used in the Trade Union and Labour Relations (Consolidation) Act 1992 s 188(2) (as originally enacted) was 'at the earliest opportunity'. Under that wording, it was held that consultation should normally precede the issue of any notices of dismissal: *National Union of Teachers v Avon County Council* [1978] ICR 626, [1978] IRLR 55, EAT. Whether this is so or not, the requirement is not met if the time permitted is so short as to make the whole exercise a sham: *Transport and General Workers' Union v Ledbury Preserves (1928) Ltd* [1985] IRLR 412, EAT. One further change of substance made to the Trade Union and Labour Relations (Consolidation) Act 1992 s 188(1), (2) (as originally enacted) is that the consultation requirement now only applies if 20 or more employees are to be made redundant; thus, earlier case authority that timely consultation is required even if only one employee is threatened is no longer authoritative.

There is no general rule that consultation cannot begin until full information (required by statute: see note 16) has been given to the representatives: *MSF v GEC Ferranti (Defence Systems) Ltd (No 2)* [1994] IRLR 113, EAT.

Whether consultation takes place in good time is a matter of fact and degree: *Unison v Leicestershire County Council* [2006] EWCA Civ 825, [2006] IRLR 810.

See also Case C-188/03 *Junk v Kuhnel* [2005] ECR I-885, [2005] IRLR 310, ECJ on when consultation must begin (and end) in order to be meaningful (ie before any notice of dismissal is given, not just before any notice ends, contrary to previous United Kingdom practice and contrary to what had been said in *Middlesborough Borough Council v Transport and General Workers' Union* [2002] IRLR 332, [2001] All ER (D) 79 (May), EAT (see note 15)).

12 Trade Union and Labour Relations (Consolidation) Act 1992 s 188(1A) (added by SI 1995/2587; amended by SI 2013/763). This refers to the proposed date of the first dismissal, not the actual date (which could be expedited, eg by agreement with the union for mutual benefit), otherwise the statutory provisions would be unworkable: *E Green & Son (Castings) Ltd v Association of Scientific, Technical and Managerial Staffs* [1984] ICR 352, [1984] IRLR 135, EAT, partly distinguishing *GKN Sankey Ltd v National Society of Motor Mechanics* [1980] ICR 148, [1980] IRLR 8, EAT, and disapproving dicta in *National Union of Teachers v Avon County Council* [1978] ICR 626, [1978] IRLR 55, EAT. One limitation on the Trade Union and Labour Relations (Consolidation) Act 1992 s 188 is that the concept of 'associated employers' (see PARA 1026 note 8) does not apply for these purposes, so the number proposed by one company ('the employer') cannot be aggregated with any others being made redundant by another company, even if the two companies are in common ownership, and even if they operate from the same establishment: *E Green & Son (Castings) Ltd v Association of Scientific, Technical and Managerial Staffs* [1984] ICR 352, [1984] IRLR 135, EAT.

13 See PARA 1187.

14 Trade Union and Labour Relations (Consolidation) Act 1992 s 188(7A) (added by SI 1995/2587; substituted by SI 1999/1925). If, after the employer has invited affected employees to elect representatives, the affected employer fails to do so within a reasonable time, the only obligation on the employer becomes one to give the required information (see note 16) to each affected employee: Trade Union and Labour Relations (Consolidation) Act 1992 s 188(7B) (added by SI 1999/1925). See also note 11.

15 Trade Union and Labour Relations (Consolidation) Act 1992 s 188(2) (substituted by SI 1995/2587).

The employer's duty to consult on the matters contained in the Trade Union and Labour Relations (Consolidation) Act 1992 s 188(2) is mandatory and it is not open to an employer to argue that consultation, as to whether to declare redundancies at all, would be futile: *Middlesborough Borough Council v Transport and General Workers' Union* [2002] IRLR 332, [2001] All ER (D) 79 (May), EAT. See also Case C-188/03 *Junk v Kuhnel* [2005] ECR I-885, [2005] IRLR 310, ECJ; and note 11. 'Consultation [...] with a view to reaching agreement' in the Trade Union and Labour Relations (Consolidation) Act 1992 s 188(2) is not to be equated merely to the passive receipt of information about an employer's plans; it is more akin to negotiation and it is the employer's duty to ensure that the consultation takes the form required by the legislation. It is not enough to provide an opportunity for consultation on the particular topics: if the matters set out in s 188(2) are not raised by the employees, it is for the employer to raise them: *Kelly v Hesley Group Ltd* [2013] IRLR 514, EAT.

16 That information must be given to each of the appropriate representatives by being delivered to
    them or sent by post to an address notified by them to the employer, or, in the case of
    representatives of a trade union, sent by post to the union at the address of its head or main
    office: Trade Union and Labour Relations (Consolidation) Act 1992 s 188(5) (amended by
    SI 1995/2587). As to the construction of references to requiring or authorising a document or
    other thing to be sent by post see PARA 962 note 10. If information is given but not in writing,
    that may be viewed as a technical breach, and the tribunal may decline to make a protective
    award: see *Amalgamated Society of Boilermakers, Shipwrights, Blacksmiths and Structural
    Workers v George Wimpey ME and C Ltd* [1977] IRLR 95, EAT; and PARA 1189 note 19. The
    employer must allow the appropriate representatives access to the affected employees, and
    afford to those representatives such accommodation and other facilities as may be appropriate:
    Trade Union and Labour Relations (Consolidation) Act 1992 s 188(5A) (added by
    SI 1995/2587; amended by SI 1999/1925). Where the Trade Union and Labour Relations
    (Consolidation) Act 1992 s 198A (see PARA 1186) applies and the transferee elects to carry out
    pre-transfer consultation (and has not cancelled the election), the application under s 198A(4)(a)
    of s 188(5), (5A) is (both before and after the transfer) subject to the following modifications:
    (1) in s 188(5), for 'the employer' there is substituted 'the transferor or transferee'; (2) in
    s 188(5A) for '[must] allow the appropriate representatives access to the affected employees and
    [must] afford to those representatives such accommodation and other facilities as may be
    appropriate' there is substituted '[must] ensure that the appropriate representatives are allowed
    access to the affected transferring individuals and that such accommodation and other facilities
    as may be appropriate are afforded to those representatives' s 198B(1)(b), (c) (added by
    SI 2014/16). As to the meanings of 'pre-transfer consultation' and 'transferring individual' see
    PARA 1186; and as to the meaning of 'affected transferring individual' see PARA 1186 note 8.
17 As to the importance of a fair selection procedure in the law of unfair dismissal see PARA 782.
18 As to the meaning of 'agency worker' see PARA 1104 note 8.
19 Trade Union and Labour Relations (Consolidation) Act 1992 s 188(4) (amended by the Trade
    Union Reform and Employment Rights Act 1993 s 34(1), (2)(a), Sch 10; and by SI 1995/2587;
    SI 2010/93). Information must also be given to the Department for Work and Pensions (see PARA
    1192), but simply to copy that to the trade union may not be sufficient to satisfy the statutory
    requirements, depending on the facts: see *GEC Ferranti Defence Systems Ltd v MSF* [1993]
    IRLR 101, EAT. There is no rule that full information must be given; whether sufficient
    information has been given to discharge the statutory obligation is a question of fact: *MSF v
    GEC Ferranti (Defence Systems) Ltd (No 2)* [1994] IRLR 113, EAT.

**1186.   Pre-transfer consultation where affected employees being transferred to
the employer from another undertaking.**   Where the following conditions are
met:

(1)   there is to be, or is likely to be, a relevant transfer[1];

(2)   the transferee is proposing to dismiss[2] as redundant[3] 20 or more
       employees[4] at one establishment[5] within a period of 90 days or less; and

(3)   the individuals who work for the transferor and who are to be (or are
       likely to be) transferred to the transferee's employment under the
       transfer ('transferring individuals') include one or more individuals who
       may be affected by the proposed dismissals or by measures taken in
       connection with the proposed dismissals,

the transferee may elect to consult[6], or to start to consult, representatives[7] of
affected transferring individuals[8] about the proposed dismissals before the
transfer takes place ('pre-transfer consultation')[9]. Any such election may be made
only if the transferor agrees to it, and must be made by way of written notice to
the transferor[10].

If the transferee elects to carry out pre-transfer consultation:

(a)   the statutory provisions setting out the procedure for handling collective
       redundancies[11] apply from the time of the election, and continues to
       apply after the transfer, as if the transferee were already the transferring
       individuals' employer and as if any transferring individuals who may be

affected by the proposed dismissals were already employed at the establishment mentioned in head (2) above[12], but subject to certain modifications[13]; and

(b) the transferor may provide information or other assistance to the transferee to help the transferee meet the statutory requirements[14].

A transferee who elects to carry out pre-transfer consultation may cancel that election at any time by written notice to the transferor[15]. If the transferee cancels an election to carry out pre-transfer consultation:

(i) the statutory provisions setting out the procedure for handling collective redundancies[16] no longer apply as mentioned in head (a) above;

(ii) anything done under those provisions has no effect so far as it was done in reliance on the election;

(iii) if the transferee notified an appropriate representative, a transferring individual or the Secretary of State[17] of the election or the proposed dismissals, the transferee must notify him of the cancellation as soon as reasonably practicable; and

(iv) the transferee may not make another election to undertake pre-transfer consultation[18] in relation to the proposed dismissals[19].

1 For the purposes of the Trade Union and Labour Relations (Consolidation) Act 1992 ss 198A, 198B (see the text and notes 2–19; and PARAS 1185 note 16, 1187 notes 11–13, 1188, 1190 notes 4, 8, 1191 note 2, 1192 notes 15–16), 'relevant transfer' means (1) a relevant transfer under the Transfer of Undertakings (Protection of Employment) Regulations 2006, SI 2006/246 (see PARA 137 et seq); (2) anything else regarded, by virtue of an enactment, as a relevant transfer for the purposes of those 2006 Regulations; or (3) where an enactment provides a power to make provision which is the same as or similar to those Regulations, any other novation of a contract of employment effected in the exercise of that power, and 'transferor' and 'transferee' are to be construed accordingly: Trade Union and Labour Relations (Consolidation) Act 1992 s 198A(7) (ss 198A, 198B added by SI 2014/16). As to the novation of contracts generally see CONTRACT vol 22 (2012) PARA 598 et seq.
2 As to the meaning of 'dismiss' see PARA 1056 note 1. See also PARA 1185 note 3.
3 See PARA 1185 note 4.
4 As to the meaning of 'employee' see PARA 892. As to excluded classes of employment see PARA 1194. See also PARA 1185 note 5.
5 See PARA 1185 note 6.
6 See PARA 1185 note 8.
7 As to the meaning of 'appropriate representatives' see PARA 1187.
8 For the purposes of the Trade Union and Labour Relations (Consolidation) Act 1992 ss 198A, 198B, 'affected transferring individual' means a transferring individual who may be affected by the proposed dismissals or who may be affected by measures taken in connection with the proposed dismissals: s 198A(7) (as added: see note 1).
9 Trade Union and Labour Relations (Consolidation) Act 1992 s 198A(1), (2) (as added: see note 1).
10 Trade Union and Labour Relations (Consolidation) Act 1992 s 198A(3) (as added: see note 1).
11 Ie the Trade Union and Labour Relations (Consolidation) Act 1992 ss 188–198B: see PARAS 1185, 1187 et seq.
12 Trade Union and Labour Relations (Consolidation) Act 1992 s 198A(4)(a) (as added: see note 1).
13 Ie subject to the Trade Union and Labour Relations (Consolidation) Act 1992 s 198B: s 198A(4)(a) (as added: see note 1).
14 Trade Union and Labour Relations (Consolidation) Act 1992 s 198A(4)(b) (as added: see note 1). The statutory requirements referred to are the requirements of Pt IV Ch II (ss 188–198B).
15 Trade Union and Labour Relations (Consolidation) Act 1992 s 198A(5) (as added: see note 1).
16 See note 11.
17 As to the Secretary of State see PARA 5 note 21.
18 Ie another election under the Trade Union and Labour Relations (Consolidation) Act 1992 s 198A(2): see the text and notes 6–9.
19 Trade Union and Labour Relations (Consolidation) Act 1992 s 198A(6) (as added: see note 1).

1187. Appropriate representatives of employees affected by proposed collective redundancies. As originally enacted[1], the consultation requirements[2] operated only where there was a recognised trade union[3]. There was no challenge to this in times of high union membership, when that requirement was for most purposes the appropriate one; but, when union membership declined, it meant that the requirement itself applied less frequently. The original enactment was essentially challenged by the European Commission on the basis of failure to transpose the relevant Council Directive[4] properly, given that that Directive requires consultation with 'workers' representatives' more generally; and this challenge was upheld by the European Court of Justice[5]. As a result, the consultation requirement was widened, to cover 'appropriate representatives'[6], thus including cases where no trade union is recognised.

For these purposes, the appropriate representatives of any affected employees[7] are:

(1) if the employees are of a description in respect of which an independent trade union[8] is recognised[9] by their employer[10], representatives of the trade union[11]; or

(2) in any other case, whichever of the following employee representatives[12] the employer chooses:

    (a) employee representatives appointed or elected by the affected employees otherwise than for these purposes, who, having regard to the purposes for and the method by which they were appointed or elected, have authority from those employees to receive information and to be consulted about the proposed dismissals on their behalf;

    (b) employee representatives elected by the affected employees for these purposes in an election satisfying the specified requirements[13].

The requirements so specified under head (2)(b) above are that:

(i) the employer must make such arrangements as are reasonably practical to ensure that the election is fair;

(ii) the employer must determine the number of representatives to be elected so that there are sufficient representatives to represent the interests of all the affected employees, having regard to the number and classes of those employees:

(iii) the employer must determine whether the affected employees should be represented either by representatives of all the affected employees or by representatives of particular classes of those employees;

(iv) before the election the employer must determine the term of office as employee representatives so that it is of sufficient length to enable information to be given and the required consultations to be completed;

(v) the candidates for election as employee representatives are affected employees on the date of the election;

(vi) no affected employee is unreasonably excluded from standing for election;

(vii) all affected employees on the date of the election are entitled to vote for employee representatives;

(viii) the employees entitled to vote may vote for as many candidates as there are representatives to be elected to represent them or, if there are to be representatives for particular classes of employees, may vote for as many candidates as there are representatives to be elected to represent their particular class of employee;

(ix) the election is conducted so as to secure that, so far as is reasonably practicable, those voting do so in secret, and the votes given at the election are accurately counted[14].

1 See PARA 1185 note 10.
2 Ie the requirement in the Trade Union and Labour Relations (Consolidation) Act 1992 s 188: see PARA 1185.
3 As to the meaning of 'recognised trade union' see PARA 1094.
4 Ie Council Directive (EC) 75/129 (OJ L39, 14.2.76, p 40) (now repealed and replaced by Council Directive (EC) 98/59 (OJ L225, 12.8.98, p 16). See also PARA 1185 note 10.
5 Case C-383/92 *EC Commission v United Kingdom* [1994] ECR I-2479, [1994] ICR 664, ECJ.
6 Ie by the Collective Redundancies and Transfer of Undertakings (Protection of Employment) (Amendment) Regulations 1995, SI 1995/2587.
7 For these purposes, references to affected employees are references to employees who may be affected by the proposed dismissals or who may be affected by measures taken in connection with such dismissals: Trade Union and Labour Relations (Consolidation) Act 1992 s 196(3) (added by SI 1999/1925). As to the meaning of 'employee' see PARA 892.
8 As to the meaning of 'independent trade union' see PARA 904.
9 There may be an obligation to consult if there is recognition in respect of that description of employees, even if, in the case of a recognition agreement covering several different establishments owned by the employer, there are no actual union members at the particular establishment where the redundancies are being proposed: *Northern Ireland Hotel and Catering College and North Eastern Education and Library Board Governing Body v National Association of Teachers in Further and Higher Education* [1995] IRLR 83, NI CA.
10 As to the meaning of 'employer' see PARA 892.
11 For these purposes, references to representatives of a trade union, in relation to an employer, are to officials or other persons authorised by the trade union to carry on collective bargaining with the employer: Trade Union and Labour Relations (Consolidation) Act 1992 s 196(2) (s 196 substituted by SI 1995/2587). As to the meaning of 'official', in relation to a trade union, see PARA 1018; and as to the meaning of 'collective bargaining' see PARA 1093.
   Where the Trade Union and Labour Relations (Consolidation) Act 1992 s 198A (see PARA 1186) applies and the transferee elects to carry out pre-transfer consultation (and has not cancelled the election), references in Pt IV Ch II (ss 188–198B) to representatives of a trade union are to officials or other persons authorised by the trade union to carry on collective bargaining with the transferee: s 196(2) (substituted for these purposes by s 198B(1)(k), itself added by SI 2014/16). As to the meaning of 'pre-transfer consultation' see PARA 1186; and as to the meanings of 'transferee' and 'relevant transfer' see PARA 1186 note 1.
12 For these purposes, persons are employee representatives if: (1) they have been elected by employees for the specific purpose of being consulted by their employer about dismissals proposed by him; or (2) having been elected or appointed by employees, whether before or after dismissals have been proposed by their employer, otherwise than for that specific purpose, it is appropriate, having regard to the purposes for which they were elected, for the employer to consult them about dismissals proposed by him, and, in either case, they are employed by the employer at the time when they are elected or appointed: Trade Union and Labour Relations (Consolidation) Act 1992 s 196(1) (as substituted (see note 11; amended by SI 1999/1925). Where the Trade Union and Labour Relations (Consolidation) Act 1992 s 198A (see PARA 1186) applies and the transferee elects to carry out pre-transfer consultation (and has not cancelled the election), s 196(1) is modified so that in the closing words, for 'employed by the employer' there is substituted 'employed by the transferor or transferee': s 198B(1)(j) (added by SI 2014/16).
   Employee representatives have a right to reasonable time off work to perform their functions or undergo relevant training: see the Employment Rights Act 1996 ss 61–63; and PARA 1209. They are also protected from suffering detriment in dismissal (see s 47; and PARA 1208) and from being dismissed or made redundant (see ss 103, 105(1), (6); and PARAS 781, 791) on such grounds.
13 Trade Union and Labour Relations (Consolidation) Act 1992 s 188(1B) (added by SI 1995/2587; substituted by SI 1999/1925). Where s 198A (see PARA 1186) applies and the transferee elects to carry out pre-transfer consultation (and has not cancelled the election), the application under s 198A(4)(a) of s 188 is (both before and after the transfer) subject to the modification that for s 188(1B)(a) (see head (a) in the text) there is substituted '(a) for

transferring individuals of a description in respect of which an independent trade union is recognised by the transferor, representatives of that trade union; (aa) for employees, other than transferring individuals, of a description in respect of which an independent trade union is recognised by the transferee, representatives of that trade union, or': s 198B(1)(a) (added by SI 2014/16). As to the meaning of 'transferring individual' see PARA 1186.

14 Trade Union and Labour Relations (Consolidation) Act 1992 s 188A(1) (s 188A added by SI 1999/1925). An 'election' takes place for the purposes of the Trade Union and Labour Relations (Consolidation) Act 1992 s 188A(1) when, pursuant to and on completion of fair arrangements (or a free selection), the number of employee nominees or candidates matches the number of representatives to be elected and no further candidates are proposed. Those persons are properly to be described as the 'elected' representatives. In such circumstances, no ballot or vote is required; Parliament must be taken to have appreciated that it would not be uncommon that the number of candidates from a given workforce may fall short of, or precisely tally with, the number of representatives to be elected): *Phillips v Xtera Communications Ltd* [2012] ICR 171, [2011] IRLR 724, EAT.

Where, after an election of employee representatives satisfying the requirements of the Trade Union and Labour Relations (Consolidation) Act 1992 s 188A(1) has been held, one of those elected ceases to act as an employee representative and any of those employees are no longer represented, they are to elect another representative by an election satisfying the requirements of s 188A(1)(a), (e), (f), (i) (see heads (i), (v), (vi), (ix) in the text): s 188A(2) (as so added).

1188. The special circumstances defence.
If in any case there are special circumstances which render it not reasonably practicable for an employer[1] to comply with a requirement of consultation or information regarding proposed redundancies[2], he must take all such steps towards compliance with that requirement as are reasonably practicable in those circumstances[3]. Where the decision leading to the proposed dismissals[4] is that of a person controlling the employer, directly or indirectly, a failure on the part of that person to provide information to the employer does not, however, constitute special circumstances rendering it not reasonably practicable for the employer to comply with such a requirement[5].

Where the affected employees are being transferred to the employer from another undertaking[6] and the transferee[7] elects to carry out pre-transfer consultation[8] and has not cancelled the election, a failure on the part of the transferor[9] to provide information or other assistance to the transferee does not constitute special circumstances rendering it not reasonably practicable for the transferee to comply with such a requirement as is mentioned above[10].

1 As to the meaning of 'employer' see PARA 892.

2 Ie under the Trade Union and Labour Relations (Consolidation) Act 1992 s 188(1A), (2) or (4): see PARA 1185.

3 Trade Union and Labour Relations (Consolidation) Act 1992 s 188(7) (amended by SI 1995/2587). The special circumstances must relate to the facts of the case; there are no general rules relating to special types of employer or special categories of circumstances. Insolvency and the appointment of a receiver are not per se special circumstances (*Clarks of Hove Ltd v Bakers' Union* [1979] 1 All ER 152, [1978] ICR 1076, CA; *Association of Patternmakers and Allied Craftsmen v Kirvin Ltd* [1978] IRLR 318, EAT); it normally requires something more in the nature of a sudden disaster (*GMB v Rankin and Harrison (as joint administrative receivers of Lawtex plc and Lawtex Babywear Ltd)* [1992] IRLR 514, EAT). Collapse of negotiations for further finance or the sale of the business may constitute special circumstances (*Hamish Armour (receiver of Barry Staines Ltd) v Association of Scientific, Technical and Managerial Staffs* [1979] IRLR 24, EAT; *Union of Shop, Distributive and Allied Workers v Leancut Bacon Ltd (in liquidation)* [1981] IRLR 295, EAT), as may the difficulty of predicting the end of a contract *(Amalgamated Society of Boilermakers, Shipwrights, Blacksmiths and Structural Workers v George Wimpey ME and C Ltd* [1977] IRLR 95, EAT). It is, however, not enough for the employer to show simply that he was not at fault: *Union of Construction, Allied Trades and Technicians v H Rooke & Son Ltd* [1978] ICR 818, [1978] IRLR 204, EAT.

See also *Shanahan Engineering Ltd v Unite the Union* [2010] All ER (D) 108 (Mar), EAT (even if the special circumstances defence means that it was not reasonably practicable to consult for the full 30 or 45 days in question (see PARA 1185), there may still be liability if the employer did not consult for whatever period would have been possible, short of that).

4   As to the requirement that redundancies must be 'proposed' see PARA 1185 note 2; and as to the meaning of 'dismissal' see PARA 1056 note 1.

5   Trade Union and Labour Relations (Consolidation) Act 1992 s 188(7) (amended by the Trade Union Reform and Employment Rights Act 1993 s 34(1), (2)(c)). See *GMB v Amicus, Amicus v Beloit Walmsley Ltd* [2003] ICR 1396, [2004] IRLR 18, EAT.

6   Ie where the Trade Union and Labour Relations (Consolidation) Act 1992 s 198A applies: see PARA 1186.

7   As to the meaning of 'transferee' see PARA 1186 note 1.

8   As to the meaning of 'pre-transfer consultation' see PARA 1186.

9   As to the meaning of 'transferor' see PARA 1186 note 1.

10 See the Trade Union and Labour Relations (Consolidation) Act 1992 s 198B(1)(d) (added by SI 2014/16), which modifies the Trade Union and Labour Relations (Consolidation) Act 1992 s 188(7) for these purposes.

1189.   Employer's failure to comply with consultation etc requirements; complaint and protective award.   Where an employer[1] has failed to comply with a requirement of consultation or information[2], or the election of employee representatives[3], a complaint may be presented to an employment tribunal on that ground:

(1)   in the case of a failure relating to the election of employee representatives, by any of the affected employees[4] or by any of the employees who have been dismissed as redundant[5];

(2)   in the case of any other failure relating to employee representatives, by any of the employee representatives to whom the failure related[6];

(3)   in the case of failure relating to representatives of a trade union[7], by the trade union[8]; and

(4)   in any other case, by any of the affected employees or by any of the employees who have been dismissed as redundant[9].

An employment tribunal must not consider such a complaint unless it is presented[10] to the tribunal:

(a)   before the date on which the last of the dismissals to which the complaint relates takes effect[11]; or

(b)   during the period of three months beginning with that date[12], subject to an extension to facilitate conciliation before the institution of proceedings[13]; or

(c)   where the tribunal is satisfied that it was not reasonably practicable for the complaint to be presented during the period of three months, within such further period as it considers reasonable[14].

If the tribunal finds the complaint well-founded, it must make a declaration to that effect and may also make a protective award[15].

A protective award is an award in respect of one or more descriptions of employees who have been dismissed as redundant, or whom it is proposed to dismiss as redundant, and in respect of whose dismissal or proposed dismissal the employer has failed to comply with a requirement of consultation or information, ordering the employer to pay remuneration[16] for the protected period[17]. The protected period begins with the date on which the first of the dismissals to which the complaint relates takes effect[18] or the date of the award, whichever is the earlier, and is to be of such length as the tribunal determines to be just and equitable in all the circumstances, having regard to the seriousness of the employer's default in complying with any of the consultation and information requirements, but is not to exceed 90 days[19].

1   As to the meaning of 'employer' see PARA 892.
2   Ie the requirements of the Trade Union and Labour Relations (Consolidation) Act 1992 s 188: see PARA 1185.
3   Ie the requirements of the Trade Union and Labour Relations (Consolidation) Act 1992 s 188A: see PARA 1187. As to the meaning of 'employee representatives' see PARA 1187 note 12.
4   As to the meaning of references to affected employees see PARA 1187 note 7.
5   As to the meaning of references to dismissed as redundant see PARA 1185 note 4.
6   Only the employee representatives have standing to present a complaint under head (2) in the text: *Mercy v Northgate HR Ltd* [2007] EWCA Civ 1304, [2008] ICR 410, [2008] IRLR 222.
7   As to the meaning of references to the representatives of a trade union see PARA 1187 note 11.
8   Any protective award made under head (3) in the text is applicable only to those employees in respect of whom the trade union is recognised by the employer: *Transport & General Workers Union v Brauer Coley Ltd* [2007] ICR 226, [2007] IRLR 207, EAT.
9   Trade Union and Labour Relations (Consolidation) Act 1992 s 189(1) (substituted by SI 1999/1925). If, on such a complaint, a question arises as to whether or not an employee representative was an appropriate representative for the purposes of the Trade Union and Labour Relations (Consolidation) Act 1992 s 188, it is for the employer to show that the employee representative had the authority to represent the affected employees: s 189(1A) (s 189(1A), (1B) added by SI 1999/1925); and see *Kelly v Hesley Group Ltd* [2013] IRLR 514, [2013] All ER (D) 350 (May), EAT. On a complaint under the Trade Union and Labour Relations (Consolidation) Act 1992 s 189(1)(a) (see head (1) in the text), it is for the employer to show that the election requirements of s 188A (see PARA 1187) have been satisfied: s 189(1B) (as so added).
      If, on such a complaint, a question arises: (1) whether there were special circumstances which rendered it not reasonably practicable for the employer to comply with any requirement of s 188; or (2) whether he took all such steps towards compliance with that requirement as were reasonably practicable in those circumstances, it is for the employer to show that they were and that he did: s 189(6). As to the 'special circumstance' defence see PARA 1188.
      Where s 198A (see PARA 1186) applies and the transferee elects to carry out pre-transfer consultation (and has not cancelled the election), then if on a complaint under s 189 a question arises whether the transferor agreed to an election or the transferee gave notice of an election as required under s 198A(3), it is for the transferee to show that the agreement or notice was given as required: s 189(7) (added for these purposes by s 198B(1)(f), itself added by SI 2014/16).
10 As to when a complaint is presented see PARAS 990 note 4, 1461.
11 Trade Union and Labour Relations (Consolidation) Act 1992 s 189(5)(a) (s 189(5) amended by the Employment Rights (Dispute Resolution) Act 1998 s 1(2)(a); and by SI 1995/2587). For the case law on the extension of time limits, especially in the context of the law of unfair dismissal, see PARA 1453.
      The provisions of the Employment Tribunals Act 1996 ss 18A–18B (conciliation) (see PARAS 152–153) apply in the case of matters which could be the subject of employment tribunal proceedings under the Trade Union and Labour Relations (Consolidation) Act 1992 s 189, and the Employment Tribunals Act 1996 s 18C applies in the case of such proceedings themselves: see s 18(1)(a), (1A) (s 18(1)(a) substituted by SI 2014/431; the Employment Tribunals Act 1996 s 18(1A) added by the Enterprise and Regulatory Reform Act 2013 Sch 1 paras 2, 5(1), (7)).As to employment tribunals see PARA 1399 et seq. An appeal lies to the Employment Appeal Tribunal on any question of law arising from any decision of, or arising in any proceedings before, an employment tribunal under or by virtue of the Trade Union and Labour Relations (Consolidation) Act 1992: see the Employment Tribunals Act 1996 s 21(1)(d); and PARA 1428. As to the Employment Appeal Tribunal see PARA 1422 et seq.
12 Trade Union and Labour Relations (Consolidation) Act 1992 s 189(5)(b) (as amended: see note 11). As to conciliation see notes 11–12.
13 Where the complaint concerns a failure to comply with a requirement of the Trade Union and Labour Relations (Consolidation) Act 1992 s 188 or s 188A, s 292A (extension of time limits to facilitate conciliation before institution of proceedings: see PARA 1455) applies for the purposes of s 189(5)(b): s 189(5A) (added by the Enterprise and Regulatory Reform Act 2013 Sch 2 paras 1, 11; amended by SI 2014/431).
14 Trade Union and Labour Relations (Consolidation) Act 1992 s 189(5)(c) (as amended: see note 11). As to conciliation see note 11.
15 Trade Union and Labour Relations (Consolidation) Act 1992 s 189(2). As to guidelines for employment tribunals deciding whether to make a protective award, see *GMB v Susie Radin Ltd*

[2004] EWCA Civ 180, [2004] 2 All ER 279, [2004] ICR 893 (applied in *Day v Haine* [2008] EWCA Civ 626, [2008] ICR 1102, [2008] IRLR 642); *Amicus v GBS Tooling Ltd* (in administration) [2005] IRLR 683, EAT; and note 19. See also *Lancaster University v University and College Union* [2011] IRLR 4, [2010] All ER (D) 270 (Dec), EAT.

Where, on a complaint under the Trade Union and Labour Relations (Consolidation) Act 1992 s 189, an employment tribunal at the hearing announces to the parties the effect of a decision to make a protective award, or (where it has made no such announcement) sends a decision to make such an award to the parties, the Secretary of the Tribunals must forthwith notify the Secretary of State of specified particulars relating to the award: Employment Protection (Recoupment of Jobseeker's Allowance and Income Support) Regulations 1996, SI 1996/2349, reg 5(1) (amended by the Employment Rights (Dispute Resolution) Act 1998 s 1(2)(a)). Where an employment tribunal makes such an announcement in the presence of the employer or his representative it must advise him of his duties under the Employment Protection (Recoupment of Jobseeker's Allowance and Income Support) Regulations 1996, SI 1996/2349, reg 6, and explain the effect of reg 7 (see PARA 1478) and reg 8 (see PARA 1478) in relation to remuneration under the protective award: reg 5(2)(a) (amended by the Employment Rights (Dispute Resolution) Act 1998 s 1(2)(a)). Without prejudice to this, any decision of an employment tribunal to make a protective award under the Trade Union and Labour Relations (Consolidation) Act 1992 s 189 must contain a statement advising the employer of his duties under the Employment Protection (Recoupment of Jobseeker's Allowance and Income Support) Regulations 1996, SI 1996/2349, reg 6 and an explanation of the effect of reg 7 and reg 8 in relation to remuneration under the protective award: reg 5(2)(b) (amended by the Employment Rights (Dispute Resolution) Act 1998 s 1(2)(a)). Where an employment tribunal makes a protective award under the Trade Union and Labour Relations (Consolidation) Act 1992 s 189 against an employer, the employer must give to the Secretary of State in writing the name, address and national insurance number of every employee to whom the award relates, and the date of termination (or proposed termination) of the employment of each such employee: Employment Protection (Recoupment of Jobseeker's Allowance and Income Support) Regulations 1996, SI 1996/2349, reg 6(1) (amended by the Employment Rights (Dispute Resolution) Act 1998 s 1(2)(a)). The employer must comply with this requirement within the period of ten days commencing on the day on which the employment tribunal at the hearing announces to the parties the effect of a decision to make a protective award or (in the case where no such announcement is made) on the day on which the relevant decision is sent to the parties: Employment Protection (Recoupment of Jobseeker's Allowance and Income Support) Regulations 1996, SI 1996/2349, reg 6(2) (amended by the Employment Rights (Dispute Resolution) Act 1998 s 1(2)(a)). However, where, in any case, it is not reasonably practicable for the employer to comply with this requirement within the period of ten days that is so applicable he must comply as soon as reasonably practicable after the expiration of that period: Employment Protection (Recoupment of Jobseeker's Allowance and Income Support) Regulations 1996, SI 1996/2349, reg 6(3).

16 As to the rate of remuneration payable see PARA 1190.

17 Trade Union and Labour Relations (Consolidation) Act 1992 s 189(3). On a purely literal construction, s 189(3) might be read as giving any claimant the right to seek a protective award covering every employee in respect of whom the employer had failed to consult, but that provision has to be read in its context: the award a personal claimant obtains may not be stretched to cover those outside the bargaining unit whether the members were members of the union or not, and whether the outsiders were represented by some other person or union or not: *Independent Insurance Co Ltd (in provisional liquidation) v Aspinall* [2011] ICR 1234, [2011] IRLR 716, EAT (nothing to suggest that an individual applicant could be considered to represent all other applicants in similar circumstances unless he had been elected; and legislative history suggests that it was intended that the right should be limited to those persons who had been represented by a trade union or employer only, or to claim in their own right only).

18 The phrase 'date on which the first of the dismissals ... takes effect' means the original proposed date, not necessarily the actual date: *E Green & Son (Castings) Ltd v Association of Scientific, Technical and Managerial Staffs* [1984] ICR 352, [1984] IRLR 135, EAT; *Transport and General Workers' Union v Ledbury Preserves (1928) Ltd* [1986] ICR 855, [1986] IRLR 492, EAT.

19 Trade Union and Labour Relations (Consolidation) Act 1992 s 189(4) (amended by SI 1999/1925). As to the Secretary of State's power by order to vary this maximum period see the Trade Union and Labour Relations (Consolidation) Act 1992 s 197(1)(b); and PARA 1195.

Departing from previous authority (*Talke Fashions Ltd v Amalgamated Society of Textile Workers and Kindred Trades* [1978] 2 All ER 649, [1977] ICR 833, EAT) it is now established that the purpose of a protective award is not merely compensatory, but is meant to be penal and to act as a deterrent to breach by an employer; thus a tribunal should start at the maximum award and only reduce it if the employer proves factors in mitigation: *GMB v Susie Radin Ltd* [2004] EWCA Civ 180, [2004] 2 All ER 279, [2004] ICR 893. For applications of this approach see *Amicus v GBS Tooling Ltd (in administration)* [2005] IRLR 683, EAT; and *UNISON v Leicestershire City Council* [2006] EWCA Civ 825, [2006] IRLR 810, [2007] LGR 208; and it can also be seen in some of the other earlier case law, under which for example it was held that actual loss to the employee is not necessary and so an award may be made in full, even if the employee found other work immediately: *Spillers-French (Holdings) Ltd v Union of Shop, Distributive and Allied Workers* [1980] 1 All ER 231, [1980] ICR 31, EAT. A tribunal may decline to make an award if the employer's breach is only technical (*Amalgamated Society of Boilermakers, Shipwrights, Blacksmiths and Structural Workers v George Wimpey ME and C Ltd* [1977] IRLR 95, EAT); but a breach should not be viewed as technical and overlooked on the basis that to have given the correct amount of consultation time would have made no difference (*Transport and General Workers' Union v Gainsborough Distributors (UK) Ltd* [1978] IRLR 460, EAT; *Sovereign Distribution Services Ltd v Transport and General Workers' Union* [1990] ICR 31, [1989] IRLR 334, EAT). Where a winding-up order is made in respect of the employer, that does not mean that any protected period must cease on the date of the order: *AEEU and GMB v Clydesdale Group plc (in receivership)* [1995] IRLR 527, EAT. Similarly, the fact that the employer has already gone into liquidation is not a reason to decline to make a protective award: *Smith v Cherry Lewis Ltd (in receivership)* [2005] IRLR 86, EAT. However, the rule in *GMB v Susie Radin Ltd* [2004] EWCA Civ 180, [2004] 2 All ER 279, [2004] ICR 893 only applies where there has been no consultation; where there has been some, but inadequate, consultation, the tribunal is not bound to start at the maximum award: see *Barnet London Borough v Unison* (2013) UKEAT/0191/13/RN.

The 90-day maximum applies, whether the consultation requirement was for 30 or 90 days: *Hutchins v Permacell Finesse Ltd* [2008] All ER (D) 112 (Jan), EAT.

1190. Entitlement under a protective award. Where an employment tribunal has made a protective award[1], every employee[2] of a description to which the award relates is entitled[3] to be paid remuneration by his employer[4] for the protected period[5]. The rate of remuneration payable is a week's pay[6] for each week of the period; and remuneration in respect of a period less than one week is to be calculated by reducing proportionately the amount of a week's pay[7].

An employee may present a complaint to an employment tribunal on the ground that he is an employee of a description to which a protective award relates and that the employer has failed, wholly or in part, to pay him remuneration under the award[8]. The tribunal must not entertain such a complaint unless it is presented[9] to the tribunal:

(1) before the end of the period of three months beginning with the day (or, if the complaint relates to more than one day, the last of the days) in respect of which the complaint is made of failure to pay remuneration[10], subject to an extension to facilitate conciliation before the institution of proceedings[11]; or

(2) where the tribunal is satisfied that it was not reasonably practicable for the complaint to be presented within the period of three months, within such further period as it may consider reasonable[12].

Where the tribunal finds such a complaint well-founded, it must order the employer to pay the complainant the amount of remuneration which it finds is due to him[13].

1 See PARA 1189.
2 As to the meaning of 'employee' see PARA 892.
3 Ie subject to the Trade Union and Labour Relations (Consolidation) Act 1992 s 190(2), (4)–(6) (see the text and notes 4–11) and s 191 (see PARA 1191).
4 As to the meaning of 'employer' see PARA 892. Where the Trade Union and Labour Relations (Consolidation) Act 1992 s 198A (see PARA 1186) applies and the transferee elects to carry out pre-transfer consultation (and has not cancelled the election), then where an employment tribunal makes a protective award under s 189 (see PARA 1189) ordering the transferee to pay

remuneration for a protected period in respect of a transferring individual, so far as the protected period falls before the relevant transfer, the individual's employer before the transfer is to be treated as the employer for the purpose of determining under ss 190(2)–(6) (see the text and notes 5–7) the period (if any) in respect of which, and the rate at which, the individual is entitled to be paid remuneration by the transferee under s 190(1): s 198B(1)(e) (added by SI 2014/16). As to the meaning of 'pre-transfer consultation' see PARA 1186; and as to the meanings of 'transferee' and 'relevant transfer' see PARA 1186 note 1.

5   Trade Union and Labour Relations (Consolidation) Act 1992 s 190(1) (amended by the Employment Rights (Dispute Resolution) Act 1998 s 1(2)(a)). As to the protected period see PARA 1189. An employee is not entitled to remuneration under a protective award in respect of a period during which he is employed by the employer unless he would be entitled to be paid by the employer in respect of that period by virtue of his contract of employment or by virtue of the Employment Rights Act 1996 ss 87–91 (rights of employee in period of notice) (see PARA 737 et seq) if that period fell within the period of notice required to be given by s 86(1) (see PARA 736): Trade Union and Labour Relations (Consolidation) Act 1992 s 190(4) (amended by the Employment Rights Act 1996 Sch 1 para 56(1), (14)(a)). If the employee dies during the protected period, the award has effect in his case as if the protected period ended on his death: Trade Union and Labour Relations (Consolidation) Act 1992 s 190(6). As to the meaning of 'contract of employment' see PARA 892.

Any jobseeker's allowance or income support already paid to the employee may be recouped from any amount ordered to be paid by a tribunal either under the original award or in the case of default by an employer: see the Employment Protection (Recoupment of Jobseeker's Allowance and Income Support) Regulations 1996, SI 1996/2349, reg 3(1)(b), Schedule, Table relating to Monetary Awards, item 16.

An employee who remains employed during a protected period and who is not under notice is not precluded from receiving a protective award: *Beall v Cranswick Country Foods plc* [2007] ICR 691, [2006] All ER (D) 315 (Dec), EAT.

6   The Employment Rights Act 1996 Pt XIV Ch II (ss 220–229) (see PARA 143 et seq) applies with respect to the calculation of a week's pay for these purposes, the calculation date for these purposes being the date on which the protective award was made or, in the case of an employee who was dismissed before that date, the date which, by virtue of s 226(5), is the calculation date for the purpose of computing the amount of a redundancy payment in relation to that dismissal, whether or not the employee concerned is entitled to any such payment: Trade Union and Labour Relations (Consolidation) Act 1992 s 190(5) (amended by the Employment Rights Act 1996 Sch 1 para 56(1), (14)(b)). As to the meaning of 'dismissal' see PARA 1056 note 1.

7   Trade Union and Labour Relations (Consolidation) Act 1992 s 190(2).

8   Trade Union and Labour Relations (Consolidation) Act 1992 s 192(1). The remedy of an employee for infringement of his right to remuneration under a protective award is by way of such a complaint, and not otherwise: s 192(4). Where s 198A (see PARA 1186) applies and the transferee elects to carry out pre-transfer consultation (and has not cancelled the election), then If on a complaint under s 192 a question arises whether the transferor agreed to an election or the transferee gave notice of an election as required under s 198A(3), it is for the transferee to show that the agreement or notice was given as required: s 192(5) (added by s 198B(1)(g), itself added by SI 2014/16).

The provisions of the Employment Tribunals Act 1996 ss 18A–18B (conciliation) (see PARAS 152–153) apply in the case of matters which could be the subject of employment tribunal proceedings under the Trade Union and Labour Relations (Consolidation) Act 1992 s 192, and the Employment Tribunals Act 1996 s 18C applies in the case of such proceedings themselves: see s 18(1)(a), (1A) (s 18(1)(a) substituted by SI 2014/431; the Employment Tribunals Act 1996 s 18(1A) added by the Enterprise and Regulatory Reform Act 2013 Sch 1 paras 2, 5(1), (7)). As to employment tribunals see PARA 1399 et seq. An appeal lies to the Employment Appeal Tribunal on any question of law arising from any decision of, or arising in any proceedings before, an employment tribunal under the Trade Union and Labour Relations (Consolidation) Act 1992: see the Employment Tribunals Act 1996 s 21(1)(d); ; and PARA 1428. As to the Employment Appeal Tribunal see PARA 1422 et seq.

9   As to when a complaint is presented see PARAS 990 note 4, 1461.

10 Trade Union and Labour Relations (Consolidation) Act 1992 s 192(2)(a).

11 The Trade Union and Labour Relations (Consolidation) Act 1992 s 292A (extension of time limits to facilitate conciliation before institution of proceedings: see PARA 1455) applies for the purposes of s 192(2)(a) (see head (1) in the text): s 192(2A) (added by the Enterprise and Regulatory Reform Act 2013 Sch 2 paras 1, 12).

12 Trade Union and Labour Relations (Consolidation) Act 1992 s 192(2)(b). Where the protective award has not been made by the tribunal until after the period of three months from the end of

the protected period, it will always be 'not reasonably practicable' for the complaint to be presented in time, and a complaint will be acceptable under s 192(2)(b) (see head (2) in the text) as long as whatever delay does occur was reasonable in all the circumstances: *Howlett Marine Services Ltd v Bowlam* [2001] ICR 595, [2001] IRLR 201, EAT. For the case law on the extension of time limits, especially in the context of the law of unfair dismissal, see PARA 1453.
13 Trade Union and Labour Relations (Consolidation) Act 1992 s 192(3).

1191. Termination of employment during the protected period. Where the employee[1] is employed by the employer[2] during the protected period[3] and he is fairly dismissed[4] by his employer otherwise than as redundant[5], or he unreasonably terminates the contract of employment[6], then he is not entitled to remuneration under the protective award[7] in respect of any period during which, but for that dismissal or termination, he would have been employed[8].

If an employer makes an employee an offer, whether in writing or not and whether before or after the ending of his employment under the previous contract, to renew his contract of employment, or to re-engage him under a new contract, so that the renewal or re-engagement would take effect before or during the protected period and either:

(1)   the provisions of the contract as renewed, or of the new contract, as to the capacity and place in which he would be employed, and as to the other terms and conditions of his employment, would not differ from the corresponding provisions of the previous contract; or

(2)   the offer constitutes an offer of suitable employment[9] in relation to the employee,

the following provisions have effect[10].

If the employee unreasonably refuses the offer, he is not entitled to remuneration under the protective award in respect of a period during which, but for that refusal, he would have been employed[11]. If the employee's contract of employment is renewed, or he is re-engaged under a new contract of employment in pursuance of an offer of suitable employment, there is to be a trial period in relation to the contract as renewed or the new contract, whether or not there has been a previous trial period[12]. If during the trial period:

(a)   the employee, for whatever reason, terminates the contract or gives notice to terminate it and the contract is thereafter in consequence terminated; or

(b)   the employer, for a reason connected with or arising out of the change to the renewed, or new, employment, terminates the contract, or gives notice to terminate it and the contract is thereafter in consequence terminated,

the employee remains entitled under the protective award unless, in a case falling within head (a) above, he acted unreasonably in terminating or giving notice to terminate the contract[13].

1 As to the meaning of 'employee' see PARA 892.
2 As to the meaning of 'employer' see PARA 892. Where the Trade Union and Labour Relations (Consolidation) Act 1992 s 198A (see PARA 1186) applies and the transferee elects to carry out pre-transfer consultation (and has not cancelled the election), then where an employment tribunal makes a protective award under s 189 (see PARA 1189) ordering the transferee to pay remuneration for a protected period in respect of a transferring individual, so far as the protected period falls before the relevant transfer, the individual's employer before the transfer is to be treated as the employer for the purpose of determining under s 191 (see the text and notes 3–13) the period (if any) in respect of which, and the rate at which, the individual is entitled to be paid remuneration by the transferee under s 190(1) (see PARA 1190): s 198B(1)(e) (added by SI 2014/16). As to the meaning of 'pre-transfer consultation' see PARA 1186; and as to the meanings of 'transferee' and 'relevant transfer' see PARA 1186 note 1.

3   As to the protected period see PARA 1189.
4   As to the meaning of 'dismiss' see PARA 1056 note 1.
5   As to the meaning of references to dismissal as redundant see PARA 1185 note 4.
6   As to the meaning of 'contract of employment' see PARA 892.
7   As to the protective award see PARA 1189; and as to entitlement under a protective award to remuneration see PARA 1190.
8   Trade Union and Labour Relations (Consolidation) Act 1992 s 191(1) (amended by the Trade Union Reform and Employment Rights Act 1993 Sch 8 para 70). The Trade Union and Labour Relations (Consolidation) Act 1992 s 191(1) is subject to s 191(2)–(7): s 191(1) (as so amended).
9   As to the interpretation of 'suitable employment' in the context of the corresponding provisions relating to individual redundancy law see PARA 874 note 13.
10 Trade Union and Labour Relations (Consolidation) Act 1992 s 191(2).
11 Trade Union and Labour Relations (Consolidation) Act 1992 s 191(3).
12 Trade Union and Labour Relations (Consolidation) Act 1992 s 191(4). The trial period begins with the ending of the employee's employment under the previous contract and ends with the expiration of the period of four weeks beginning with the date on which he starts work under the contract as renewed, or the new contract, or such longer period as may be agreed in accordance with s 191(6) for the purpose of retraining the employee for employment under that contract: s 191(5). Any such agreement: (1) must be made between the employer and the employee or his representative before the employee starts work under the contract as renewed, or, as the case may be, the new contract; (2) must be in writing; (3) must specify the date of the end of the trial period; and (4) must specify the terms and conditions of employment which will apply in the employee's case after the end of that period: s 191(6). As to trial periods in the context of individual redundancy law see PARA 865 note 13.
13 Trade Union and Labour Relations (Consolidation) Act 1992 s 191(7).

(ii) Notification of Redundancies to the Secretary of State

1192.   Employer's duty to notify the Secretary of State of certain redundancies. An employer[1] proposing[2] to dismiss[3] as redundant[4] 100 or more employees[5] at one establishment[6] within a period of 90 days or less must notify the Secretary of State[7] in writing of his proposal before giving notice to terminate an employee's contract of employment in respect of any of those dismissals, and at least 45 days before the first of those dismissals takes effect[8]; and, where he so proposes to dismiss 20 or more employees at one establishment within such a period, the employer must so notify the Secretary of State in writing before giving notice to terminate an employee's contract of employment in respect of any of those dismissals, and at least 30 days before the first of those dismissals takes effect[9]. After receiving a notice from the employer, the Secretary of State may by written notice require the employer to give him such further information as may be specified in the notice[10].

A notice given under these provisions must:

(1)   be given to the Secretary of State by delivery to him or by sending it by post[11] to him, at such address as the Secretary of State may direct in relation to the establishment where the employees proposed to be dismissed are employed;

(2)   where there are representatives to be consulted[12], identify them and state the date when consultation with them began;

(3)   be in such form and contain such additional particulars as the Secretary of State may direct[13].

Where there are representatives to be consulted[14], the employer must give to each of them a copy of any notice so given[15].

If in any case there are special circumstances rendering it not reasonably practicable for the employer to comply with any of the above requirements, he must take all such steps towards compliance with that requirement as are reasonably practicable in the circumstances[16].

1   As to the meaning of 'employer' see PARA 892.
2   As to the requirement that the employer must be proposing redundancies see PARA 1185 note 2.
3   As to the meaning of 'dismiss' see PARA 1056 note 1.
4   As to the meaning of references to dismissal as redundant see PARA 1185 note 4.
5   As to the meaning of 'employee' see PARA 892.
6   There is no statutory definition of 'establishment' for these purposes; but c f PARA 1185 note 6.
7   As to the Secretary of State see PARA 5 note 21.
8   Trade Union and Labour Relations (Consolidation) Act 1992 s 193(1) (amended by SI 2006/2387; SI 2013/763). As to failure to notify see PARA 1193; and as to the Secretary of State's power by order to vary the provisions of the Trade Union and Labour Relations (Consolidation) Act 1992 s 193(1) see s 197(1)(a); and PARA 1195.
9   Trade Union and Labour Relations (Consolidation) Act 1992 s 193(2) (amended by SI 1995/2587; SI 2006/2387). In determining how many employees an employer is proposing to dismiss as redundant within these periods, no account is to be taken of employees in respect of whose proposed dismissal notice has already been given to the Secretary of State: Trade Union and Labour Relations (Consolidation) Act 1992 s 193(3). The concept of 'associated employers' (see PARA 1026 note 8) does not apply for these purposes: see PARA 1185 note 12.
10   Trade Union and Labour Relations (Consolidation) Act 1992 s 193(5).
11   As to the construction of references to requiring or authorising a document or other thing to be sent by post see PARA 962 note 10.
12   Ie under the Trade Union and Labour Relations (Consolidation) Act 1992 s 188: see PARA 1185.
13   Trade Union and Labour Relations (Consolidation) Act 1992 s 193(4) (amended by SI 1995/2587).
14   See note 12.
15   Trade Union and Labour Relations (Consolidation) Act 1992 s 193(6) (amended by SI 1995/2587). The copy must be delivered to them or sent by post to an address notified by them to the employer, or, in the case of representatives of a trade union, sent by post to the union at the address of its head or main office: Trade Union and Labour Relations (Consolidation) Act 1992 s 193(6) (as so amended). Section 193(6) is modified where s 198A (see PARA 1186) applies and the transferee elects to carry out pre-transfer consultation (and has not cancelled the election), so that for 'the employer' the second time it appears there is substituted 'the transferor or transferee': see s 198B(1)(h) (added by SI 2014/16). As to the meaning of 'pre-transfer consultation' see PARA 1186; and as to the meanings of 'transferee' and 'relevant transfer' see PARA 1186 note 1.
     If all that the employer does is to copy the notice to the Secretary of State to the union, that may not on the facts be enough to satisfy the requirement to inform the recognised union under s 188(4) (see PARA 1185): see *GEC Ferranti Defence Systems Ltd v MSF* [1993] IRLR 101, EAT.
16   Trade Union and Labour Relations (Consolidation) Act 1992 s 193(7). Where the decision leading to the proposed dismissals is that of a person controlling the employer, directly or indirectly, a failure on the part of that person to provide information to the employer does not constitute special circumstances rendering it not reasonably practicable for the employer to comply with any of those requirements: s 193(7) (amended by the Trade Union Reform and Employment Rights Act 1993 s 34(1), (4)). Where the Trade Union and Labour Relations (Consolidation) Act 1992 s 198A (see PARA 1186) applies and the transferee elects to carry out pre-transfer consultation (and has not cancelled the election), a failure on the part of the transferor to provide information or other assistance to the transferee does not constitute special circumstances rendering it not reasonably practicable for the transferee to comply with any of those requirements: s 193(7) (modified for these purposes by s 198B(1)(i), itself added by SI 2014/16).
     There is a similar 'special circumstances' defence in the Trade Union and Labour Relations (Consolidation) Act 1992 s 188: see PARA 1188. It is not enough, to come within this defence, that the employer was unaware of the obligation to notify: *Secretary of State for Employment v Helitron Ltd* [1980] ICR 523, EAT.

1193.   Failure to notify the Secretary of State of proposed redundancies.   An employer[1] who fails to give the required notice as to proposed redundancies[2] to the Secretary of State commits an offence and is liable on summary conviction to a fine not exceeding level 5 on the standard scale[3].

Where such an offence committed by a body corporate is proved to have been committed with the consent or connivance of, or to be attributable to neglect on the part of, any director, manager, secretary or other similar officer of the body corporate, or any person purporting to act in any such capacity, he, as well as the body corporate, is guilty of the offence and liable to be proceeded against and punished accordingly[4].

1   As to the meaning of 'employer' see PARA 892.
2   Ie in accordance with the Trade Union and Labour Relations (Consolidation) Act 1992 s 193: see PARA 1192.
3   Trade Union and Labour Relations (Consolidation) Act 1992 s 194(1). Proceedings in England and Wales for such an offence may be instituted only by or with the consent of the Secretary of State or by an officer authorised for that purpose by special or general directions of the Secretary of State; and an officer so authorised may prosecute or conduct proceedings for such an offence before a magistrates' court: s 194(2) (amended by the Legal Services Act 2007 Sch 21 paras 104, 105, Sch 23).
4   Trade Union and Labour Relations (Consolidation) Act 1992 s 194(3). Where the affairs of a body corporate are managed by its members, s 194(3) applies in relation to the acts and defaults of a member in connection with his functions of management as if he were a director of the body corporate: s 194(4).

(iii) Exclusion and Modification of Statutory Procedure for Handling Redundancies

1194. Classes of employment excluded from statutory procedure for handling redundancies. The statutory procedure for handling redundancies[1] does not apply to employment under a fixed term contract[2] unless the employer[3] is proposing to dismiss the employee as redundant[4] and the dismissal will take effect before the expiry of the specific term, the completion of the particular task or the occurrence or non-occurrence of the specific event whereby the contract will terminate in the normal course, as the case may be[5]. Nor does it apply to Crown employment[6], employment as a relevant member of the House of Lords staff[7] or as a relevant member of the House of Commons staff[8], or employment as master or as member of the crew of a fishing vessel where the employee is remunerated only by a share in the profits or gross earnings of the vessel[9].

The statutory provisions relating to the duty to notify the Secretary of State of certain redundancies[10] do not apply to employment where under his contract of employment an employee works outside Great Britain[11].

The Secretary of State may by order made by statutory instrument provide that any of the statutory provisions relating to that procedure are not to apply to persons or to employment of such classes as may be prescribed by the order, or are to apply to persons or employments of such classes as may be prescribed by the order subject to such exceptions and modifications as may be so prescribed[12].

1   Ie the Trade Union and Labour Relations (Consolidation) Act 1992 Pt IV Ch II (ss 188–198B): see PARA 1185 et seq.
2   For these purposes, 'fixed term contract' means a contract of employment that, under its provisions determining how it will terminate in the normal course, will terminate (1) on the expiry of a specific term; (2) on the completion of a particular task; or (3) on the occurrence or non-occurrence of any other specific event other than the attainment by the employee of any normal and bona fide retiring age in the establishment for an employee holding the position held by him: Trade Union and Labour Relations (Consolidation) Act 1992 s 282(1) (s 282 substituted by SI 2013/763). As to the meaning of 'employee' see PARA 892.
3   As to the meaning of 'employer' see PARA 892.
4   As to the meaning of 'dismiss' see PARA 1056 note 1.
5   See the Trade Union and Labour Relations (Consolidation) Act 1992 s 282(1), (2) (as substituted: see note 2). See also *University of Stirling v University and College Union* [2014]

CSIH 5, [2014] IRLR 287 (decided under the Trade Union and Labour Relations (Consolidation) Act 1992 s 282 as originally enacted); and PARA 1185.
6   See the Trade Union and Labour Relations (Consolidation) Act 1992 s 273(2); and PARA 893 note 2. In the case of public employment there might, however, be alternative remedies in public law by way of judicial review if lack of consultation breaches legitimate expectations or is irrational: *Re NUPE and COHSE's Application* [1989] IRLR 202; *R v British Coal Corpn, ex p Vardy* [1993] ICR 720, sub nom *R v British Coal Corpn and Secretary of State for Trade and Industry, ex p Vardy* [1993] IRLR 104, DC; and see *R v British Coal Corpn and Secretary of State for Trade and Industry, ex p Price* [1994] IRLR 72, DC. See further JUDICIAL REVIEW vol 61 (2010) PARA 601 et seq.
7   See the Trade Union and Labour Relations (Consolidation) Act 1992 s 277(1A); and PARA 894 note 2. As to the meaning of 'relevant member of the House of Lords staff' see PARA 894 note 3.
8   See the Trade Union and Labour Relations (Consolidation) Act 1992 s 278(2); and PARA 895 note 2. As to the meaning of 'relevant member of the House of Commons staff' see PARA 895 note 3.
9   Trade Union and Labour Relations (Consolidation) Act 1992 s 284. See also PARA 1071.
10 Ie the Trade Union and Labour Relations (Consolidation) Act 1992 ss 193–194: see PARAS 1192–1193.
11 Trade Union and Labour Relations (Consolidation) Act 1992 s 285(1) (amended by the Employment Relations Act 1999 s 32(1)). As to the meaning of 'Great Britain' see PARA 2 note 12. As to the treatment for these purposes of employment on board a ship registered in the United Kingdom see the Trade Union and Labour Relations (Consolidation) Act 1992 s 285(2); and PARA 1071 note 8.
12 See the Trade Union and Labour Relations (Consolidation) Act 1992 s 286; and PARA 1072.

1195.   Powers to vary and adapt statutory procedure for handling redundancies. The Secretary of State[1] may, by order made by statutory instrument[2], vary the statutory requirements as to consultation[3] and notification[4] and the maximum protected period[5], but no such order is to be made which has the effect of reducing to less than 30 days the periods[6] which must elapse before the first of the dismissals[7] takes effect[8].

Where there is a collective agreement[9] in force which establishes arrangements:

(1)   for providing alternative employment for employees[10] to whom the agreement relates if they are dismissed as redundant[11] by an employer[12] to whom it relates; or

(2)   for handling the dismissal of employees as redundant,

then, on the application of all the parties to the agreement and if the Secretary of State is satisfied, having regard to the provisions of the agreement, that the arrangements are on the whole at least as favourable to those employees as the statutory procedure for handling redundancies[13], he may, by order made by statutory instrument, adapt, modify or exclude any of the statutory provisions both in their application to all or any of those employees and in their application to any other employees of any such employer[14]. The Secretary of State may not, however, make such an order unless the agreement:

(a)   provides for procedures to be followed, whether by arbitration or otherwise, in cases where an employee to whom the agreement relates claims that any employer or other person to whom the agreement relates has not complied with the provisions of the agreement; and

(b)   provides that those procedures include a right to arbitration or adjudication by an independent referee or body in cases where, by reason of an equality of votes or otherwise, a decision cannot otherwise be reached,

or indicates that any such employee may present a complaint to an employment tribunal that any such employer or other person has not complied with those provisions[15]. Such an order may confer on an employment tribunal to which a complaint is so presented such powers and duties as the Secretary of State considers appropriate[16].

The statutory restriction on contracting out[17] does not apply to any provision in a collective agreement excluding rights under the statutory procedure for handling redundancies if an order under the above provisions[18] is in force in respect of it[19].

1 As to the Secretary of State see PARA 5 note 21.
2 No such order may be made unless a draft of the order has been laid before Parliament and approved by a resolution of each House of Parliament: Trade Union and Labour Relations (Consolidation) Act 1992 s 197(2).
3 Ie the provisions of the Trade Union and Labour Relations (Consolidation) Act 1992 s 188(2) (sic): see PARA 1185. It is submitted that this is a drafting error and that the reference to s 188(2) is to be read as a reference to s 188(1A): see PARA 1185. See also the Trade Union and Labour Relations (Consolidation) Act 1992 (Amendment) Order 2013, SI 2013/763, art 3(2), cited in note 8.
4 Ie the provisions of the Trade Union and Labour Relations (Consolidation) Act 1992 s 193(1): see PARA 1192.
5 Ie the period referred to at the end of the Trade Union and Labour Relations (Consolidation) Act 1992 s 189(4): see PARA 1189.
6 Ie the periods referred to in the Trade Union and Labour Relations (Consolidation) Act 1992 s 188(2) (sic) and s 193(1). See also note 3.
7 As to the meaning of 'dismissal' see PARA 1056 note 1.
8 Trade Union and Labour Relations (Consolidation) Act 1992 s 197(1). Partly in the exercise of this power, the Secretary of State has made the Trade Union and Labour Relations (Consolidation) Act 1992 (Amendment) Order 2013, SI 2013/763, which came into force on 6 April 2013 (art 1) and which amends the Trade Union and Labour Relations (Consolidation) Act 1992 ss 188(1A), 193(1) (see the Trade Union and Labour Relations (Consolidation) Act 1992 (Amendment) Order 2013, SI 2013/763, art 3(1)–(3)).
9 As to the meaning of 'collective agreement' see PARA 1093.
10 As to the meaning of 'employee' see PARA 892.
11 As to the meaning of references to dismissal as redundant see PARA 1185 note 4.
12 As to the meaning of 'employer' see PARA 892.
13 Ie the provisions of the Trade Union and Labour Relations (Consolidation) Act 1992 Pt IV Ch II (ss 188–198B): see PARA 1185 et seq.
14 Trade Union and Labour Relations (Consolidation) Act 1992 s 198(1), (2) (s 198(1) amended by the Trade Union Reform and Employment Rights Act 1993 Sch 8 para 71).
15 Trade Union and Labour Relations (Consolidation) Act 1992 s 198(3) (amended by the Employment Rights (Dispute Resolution) Act 1998 s 1(2)(a)).
16 Trade Union and Labour Relations (Consolidation) Act 1992 s 198(4) (amended by the Employment Rights (Dispute Resolution) Act 1998 s 1(2)(a)). An order under the Trade Union and Labour Relations (Consolidation) Act 1992 s 198 may be varied or revoked by a subsequent order thereunder either in pursuance of an application made by all or any of the parties to the agreement in question or without any such application: s 198(5).
17 Ie the Trade Union and Labour Relations (Consolidation) Act 1992 s 288(1): see PARA 150.
18 Ie an order under the Trade Union and Labour Relations (Consolidation) Act 1992 s 198.
19 Trade Union and Labour Relations (Consolidation) Act 1992 s 288(3)(b).

(7) OTHER DUTIES OF INFORMATION AND CONSULTATION

(i) Information and Consultation on Transfer of Undertaking

1196. Appropriate representatives in the case of a transfer of an undertaking. For the purposes of the statutory rules on information[1] and consultation[2] in the case of a transfer of undertaking[3], the appropriate representatives of any employees[4] are:

(1)   if the employees are of a description in respect of which an independent trade union[5] is recognised[6] by their employer[7], representatives of the trade union; or

(2)   in any other case, whichever of the following employee representatives the employer chooses:

   (a)   employee representatives appointed or elected by the affected employees[8] otherwise than for these purposes, who, having regard to the purpose for, and the method by, which they were appointed or elected, have authority from those employees to receive information and to be consulted about the transfer on their behalf;

   (b)   employee representatives elected[9] by them for these purposes[10].

Where the latter option is chosen, the election must comply with the following requirements, namely that:

(i)   the employer must make such arrangements as are reasonably practical to ensure that the election is fair;

(ii)   the employer must determine the number of representatives to be elected so that there are sufficient representatives to represent the interests of all the affected employees having regard to the number and classes of those employees;

(iii)   the employer must determine whether the affected employees should be represented either by representatives of all the affected employees or by representatives of particular classes of those employees;

(iv)   before the election the employer must determine the term of office as employee representatives so that it is of sufficient length to enable information to be given and consultations to be completed;

(v)   the candidates for election as employee representatives are affected employees on the date of the election;

(vi)   no affected employee is unreasonably excluded from standing for election;

(vii)   all affected employees on the date of the election are entitled to vote for employee representatives;

(viii)   the employees entitled to vote may vote for as many candidates as there are representatives to be elected to represent them or, if there are to be representatives for particular classes of employees, may vote for as many candidates as there are representatives to be elected to represent their particular class of employee;

(ix)   the election is conducted so as to secure that, so far as is reasonably practicable, those voting do so in secret, and the votes given at the election are accurately counted[11].

There are restrictions on contracting out of the above provisions[12].

1   See PARA 1197.
2   See PARA 1198.
3   As to such transfers generally see PARA 137 et seq.
4   As to the meaning of 'employee' see PARA 137 note 8. For the purposes of the Transfer of Undertakings (Protection of Employment) Regulations 2006, SI 2006/246, the representative of a trade union recognised by an employer is an official or other person authorised to carry on collective bargaining with that employer by that trade union: see reg 2(2), cited in PARA 138 note 13.
     There may be either existing representatives or new ones specially elected for the purpose. It is the employer's responsibility to ensure that consultation is offered to appropriate representatives (see PARA 1198). If they are to be existing representatives, their remit and method of election or appointment must give them suitable authority from the employees

concerned: see *Employment Rights on the Transfer of an Undertaking: A Guide to the 2006 TUPE Regulations (as amended by the Collective Redundancies and Transfer of Undertakings (Protection of Employment) (Amendment) Regulations 2014) for Employees, Employers and Representatives* (Jan 2014) p 36; and see *Smith v Jackson Lloyd Ltd* [2014] All ER (D) 157 (Apr), EAT (a purposive application of the Regulations is required, but their clear purpose is to ensure that employees give meaningful consent to those who are nominated to represent them collectively; following a relevant transfer under the Transfer of Undertakings Protection of Employment Regulations 2006, SI 2006/246, reg 3(1)(a) (see PARA 137), the mandates of the first employer's employee representatives had expired, there was no TUPE consultation in this case, and no evidence that consent to the representatives continuing to act after expiry of their terms of office was sought or obtained; the relevant employees had *locus standi* (correctly applying the statutory test contained in the Transfer of Undertakings (Protection of Employment) Regulations 2006, SI 2006/246, regs 13(3)(b)(i), 15(3)) and had been entitled to pursue their claims for protective awards in their own names).

5   As to the meaning of 'independent trade union' see PARA 904.
6   As to the meaning of 'recognised' for these purposes see PARA 1095 note 3.
7   As to the meaning of 'employer' for these purposes see PARA 137 note 8; but see note 8.
8   For the purposes of the Transfer of Undertakings (Protection of Employment) Regulations 2006, SI 2006/246, regs 13, 13A, 14, 15 (see PARAS 1197–1200), references to affected employees, in relation to a relevant transfer, are to any employees of the transferor or the transferee, whether or not assigned to the organised grouping of resources or employees that is the subject of the relevant transfer, who may be affected by the transfer or may be affected by measures taken in connection with it; and references to the employer are to be construed accordingly: reg 13(1) (amended by SI 2014/16). As to the meaning of 'assigned' see PARA 138 note 13; and as to the meaning of 'relevant transfer' see PARA 137. 'Measures' is in general to be given a wide construction: *Institute of Professional Civil Servants v Secretary of State for Defence* [1987] 3 CMLR 35, [1987] IRLR 373; and see PARA 1197 note 6.
   The duties imposed on an employer by the Transfer of Undertakings (Protection of Employment) Regulations 2006, SI 2006/246, reg 13 apply irrespective of whether the decision resulting in the relevant transfer is taken by the employer or a person controlling the employer: reg 13(12).
9   Ie in an election satisfying the requirements of the Transfer of Undertakings (Protection of Employment) Regulations 2006, SI 2006/246, reg 14(1).
10 Transfer of Undertakings (Protection of Employment) Regulations 2006, SI 2006/246, reg 13(3).
11 Transfer of Undertakings (Protection of Employment) Regulations 2006, SI 2006/246, reg 14(1). Where, after an election of employee representatives satisfying the requirements of reg 14(1) has been held, one of those elected ceases to act as an employee representative and any of those employees are no longer represented, those employees must elect another representative by an election satisfying the requirements of reg 14(1)(a), (e), (f), (i) (see heads (i), (v), (vi), (ix) in the text): reg 14(2).
12 See the Transfer of Undertakings (Protection of Employment) Regulations 2006, SI 2006/246, reg 18, cited in PARA 137.

1197. Employer's duty to inform appropriate representatives of affected employees. Long enough before a relevant transfer[1] to enable the employer[2] of any affected employees[3] to consult the appropriate representatives[4] of any affected employees, the employer must inform those representatives of:

(1)   the fact that the relevant transfer is to take place, when, approximately, it is to take place and the reasons for it; and

(2)   the legal, economic and social implications of the transfer for the affected employees[5]; and

(3)   the measures[6] which he envisages he will, in connection with the transfer, take in relation to those employees or, if he envisages that no measures will be so taken, that fact; and

(4)   if the employer is the transferor, the measures which the transferee envisages he will, in connection with the transfer, take in relation to such of those employees as become[7] employees of the transferee after the transfer or, if he envisages that no measures will be so taken, that fact[8].

Where information is to be so supplied by an employer, this must include suitable information relating to the use of agency workers[9] (if any) by that employer[10].

The transferee must give the transferor such information at such a time as will enable the transferor to perform the duty imposed on him by virtue of head (4) above[11].

If, at the time when the employer is required to give information under heads (1) to (4) above, the employer employs fewer than ten employees, there are no appropriate representatives[12] and the employer has not invited any of the affected employees to elect employee representatives, he may comply with the duty to inform set out above by performing any duty which relates to appropriate representatives as if each of the affected employees were an appropriate representative[13].

There are restrictions on contracting out of the above provisions[14].

1 As to the meaning of 'relevant transfer' see PARA 137.

2 As to the meaning of 'employer' for these purposes see PARAS 137 note 8, 1196 note 8. As to the position where the employer is a micro-business see the text and notes 12–13.

3 As to the meaning of references to affected employees see PARA 1196 note 8.

4 As to the meaning of 'appropriate representatives' see PARA 1196.

5 An employer is obliged to describe what he genuinely believes to be the legal, social and economic implications of transfer of undertaking but does not have to warrant the legal accuracy of that opinion: *Communication Workers Union v Royal Mail Group Ltd* [2009] EWCA Civ 1045, [2010] 2 All ER 823, [2010] ICR 83 (employer had got the law at least partly wrong, because some employees had been still in their posts right up to the transfer and so they were automatically transferred, in spite of the relocation clause, so there was an obligation to consult but, as a matter of statutory interpretation, the language of Transfer of Undertakings (Protection of Employment) Regulations 2006, SI 2006/246, reg 13(2) (see heads (1)–(4) in the text) (when read as a whole) is not that of warranty and/or strict liability).

6 'Measures' is to be construed widely; but it cannot cover matters such as manpower projections (though it could cover intended steps to meet such projections) or measures taken which would have been inevitable anyway and are causally unconnected with the transfer: *Institution of Professional Civil Servants v Secretary of State for Defence* [1987] 3 CMLR 35, [1987] IRLR 373 (a case under the Dockyard Services Act 1986 which applied the Transfer of Undertakings (Protection of Employment) Regulations 1981, SI 1981/1794 (the predecessor of the Transfer of Undertakings (Protection of Employment) Regulations 2006, SI 2006/246) to a transfer of dockyard undertakings).

7 Ie by virtue of the Transfer of Undertakings (Protection of Employment) Regulations 2006, SI 2006/246, reg 4: see PARA 139. As to the situation where an employee objects to becoming employed by the transferee see PARAS 139, 141.

8 Transfer of Undertakings (Protection of Employment) Regulations 2006, SI 2006/246, reg 13(2). See also note 5. The information which is to be given to the appropriate representatives must be given to each of them by being delivered to them, or sent by post to an address notified by them to the employer, or, in the case of representatives of a trade union, sent by post to the union at the address of its head or main office: reg 13(5). Where information to be divulged is not factual, but based on appraisal or judgment, the obligation is only to divulge the results of the employer's deliberations, not the information, calculation or assumptions used or made by the employer: *Institution of Professional Civil Servants v Secretary of State for Defence* [1987] 3 CMLR 35, [1987] IRLR 373 (cited in note 6). See also *Todd v Strain* [2011] IRLR 11, [2010] All ER (D) 108 (Oct), EAT; and see *Marcroft v Heartland (Midlands) Ltd* [2011] EWCA Civ 438, [2011] IRLR 599 (compliance with the Transfer of Undertakings (Protection of Employment) Regulations 2006, SI 2006/246, reg 13 not a condition precedent to an effective transfer of a contract of employment). As to the construction of references to requiring or authorising a document or other thing to be sent by post see PARA 962 note 10.

The duties imposed on an employer by the Transfer of Undertakings (Protection of Employment) Regulations 2006, SI 2006/246, reg 13 apply irrespective of whether the decision resulting in the relevant transfer is taken by the employer or a person controlling the employer: reg 13(12).

9 'Suitable information relating to the use of agency workers' means (1) the number of agency workers working temporarily for and under the supervision and direction of the employer; (2) the parts of the employer's undertaking in which those agency workers are working; and (3) the

type of work those agency workers are carrying out: Transfer of Undertakings (Protection of Employment) Regulations 2006, SI 2006/246, reg 13(2A)(b) (reg 13(2A) added by SI 2010/93). 'Agency worker' is not defined for these purposes; but see PARAS 11, 95 et seq.

10 Transfer of Undertakings (Protection of Employment) Regulations 2006, SI 2006/246, reg 13(2A)(a) (as added: see note 9). See also note 8.

11 Transfer of Undertakings (Protection of Employment) Regulations 2006, SI 2006/246, reg 13(4). Regulation 13(4) does not impose an obligation on a transferee to provide information to employees of the transferor: *Allen v Morrisons Facilities Services Ltd* [2014] ICR 792, [2014] IRLR 514, EAT. The only route for employees of the transferor to obtain compensation from the transferee for breach of his obligations to a transferor under the Transfer of Undertakings (Protection of Employment) Regulations 2006, SI 2006/246, reg 13(4) is to pursue a claim against the transferor for breach of reg 13(2)(d) (see head (4) in the text) and for the transferor to give notice to and join the transferee as a party to the proceedings under reg 15(5) (see PARA 1200 note 5): *Allen v Morrisons Facilities Services Ltd.*

12 Ie within the meaning of the Transfer of Undertakings (Protection of Employment) Regulations 2006, SI 2006/246, reg 13(3): see PARA 1196.

13 Transfer of Undertakings (Protection of Employment) Regulations 2006, SI 2006/246, reg 13(A)(1), (2) (added by SI 2014/16).

14 See the Transfer of Undertakings (Protection of Employment) Regulations 2006, SI 2006/246, reg 18, cited in PARA 137.

1198. The duty to consult appropriate representatives of affected employees.
Where an employer[1] of an affected employee[2] envisages that he will, in connection with the transfer[3], be taking measures[4] in relation to any such employee, he must consult the appropriate representatives[5] of that employee, with a view to seeking their agreement to the intended measures[6]. In the course of those consultations the employer must:

(1) consider any representations made by the appropriate representatives; and

(2) reply to those representations and, if he rejects any of those representations, state his reasons[7].

The employer must allow the appropriate representatives access to any affected employees and must afford to those representatives such accommodation and other facilities as may be appropriate[8].

If, at the time when the employer is required to give information about a relevant transfer[9], the employer employs fewer than ten employees, there are no appropriate representatives[10] and the employer has not invited any of the affected employees to elect employee representatives, he may comply with the duty to consult set out above by performing any duty which relates to appropriate representatives as if each of the affected employees were an appropriate representative[11].

There are restrictions on contracting out of the above provisions[12].

1 As to the meaning of 'employer' for these purposes see PARAS 137 note 8, 1196 note 8. As to the position where the employer is a micro-business see the text and notes 9–11.

2 As to the meaning of references to affected employees see PARA 1196 note 8.

3 As to the meaning of 'relevant transfer' see PARA 137.

4 As to the meaning of 'measures' see PARA 1197 note 6.

5 As to the meaning of 'appropriate representatives' see PARA 1196.

6 Transfer of Undertakings (Protection of Employment) Regulations 2006, SI 2006/246, reg 13(6). The obligation is to consult on the facts as the employer believes them to be; the employer does not warrant the correctness of these facts: *Royal Mail Group Ltd v Communication Workers Union* [2009] ICR 357, [2009] IRLR 108, EAT; affd [2009] EWCA Civ 1045, [2010] 2 All ER 823, [2010] ICR 83, [2009] IRLR 1046. Once there has been any necessary consultation by the transferor with its affected employees and by the transferee with its affected employees before the transfer, there is no further obligation on the transferee employer to consult with transferred

employees after the transfer: *Amicus v City Building (Glasgow) LLP* [2009] IRLR 253, EAT. For the case law on the meaning of 'consult' in the context of collective redundancies see PARA 1185 note 8.

The duties imposed on an employer by the Transfer of Undertakings (Protection of Employment) Regulations 2006, SI 2006/246, reg 13 apply irrespective of whether the decision resulting in the relevant transfer is taken by the employer or a person controlling the employer: reg 13(12).

7   Transfer of Undertakings (Protection of Employment) Regulations 2006, SI 2006/246, reg 13(7).
8   Transfer of Undertakings (Protection of Employment) Regulations 2006, SI 2006/246, reg 13(8).
9   Ie under the Transfer of Undertakings (Protection of Employment) Regulations 2006, SI 2006/246, reg 13(2): see PARA 1197.
10 Ie within the meaning of the Transfer of Undertakings (Protection of Employment) Regulations 2006, SI 2006/246, reg 13(3): see PARA 1196.
11 Transfer of Undertakings (Protection of Employment) Regulations 2006, SI 2006/246, reg 13(A)(1), (2) (added by SI 2014/16).
12 See the Transfer of Undertakings (Protection of Employment) Regulations 2006, SI 2006/246, reg 18, cited in PARA 137.

1199.   The special circumstances defence and default provisions in relation to elected representatives.   If in any case there are special circumstances which render it not reasonably practicable for an employer[1] to perform a duty imposed on him to consult or inform[2], he must take all such steps towards performing that duty as are reasonably practicable in the circumstances[3].

Where:

(1)   the employer has invited any of the affected employees[4] to elect employee representatives[5]; and

(2)   the invitation was issued long enough before the time when the employer is required[6] to give information to allow them to elect representatives by that time,

the employer is to be treated as complying with the statutory requirements[7] in relation to those employees if he complies with those requirements as soon as is reasonably practicable after the election of the representatives[8].

If, after the employer has invited affected employees to elect representatives, they fail to do so within a reasonable time, he must give to each affected employee the required[9] information[10].

There are restrictions on contracting out of the above provisions[11].

1   As to the meaning of 'employer' for these purposes see PARAS 137 note 8, 1196 note 8. As to the position where the employer is a micro-business see PARAS 1197, 1198.
2   Ie a duty imposed on him by any of the provisions of the Transfer of Undertakings (Protection of Employment) Regulations 2006, SI 2006/246, reg 13(2)–(7): see PARAS 1196–1198.
3   Transfer of Undertakings (Protection of Employment) Regulations 2006, SI 2006/246, reg 13(9). There is a similarly drafted defence in relation to consultation on collective redundancies; for the case law under that defence see PARA 1188.
    The duties imposed on an employer by reg 13 apply irrespective of whether the decision resulting in the relevant transfer is taken by the employer or a person controlling the employer: reg 13(12).
4   As to the meaning of references to affected employees see PARA 1196 note 8.
5   As to the election of employee representatives see PARA 1196.
6   Ie under the Transfer of Undertakings (Protection of Employment) Regulations 2006, SI 2006/246, reg 13(2): see PARA 1197.
7   Ie the requirements of the Transfer of Undertakings (Protection of Employment) Regulations 2006, SI 2006/246, reg 13.
8   Transfer of Undertakings (Protection of Employment) Regulations 2006, SI 2006/246, reg 13(10).
9   Ie the information required by the Transfer of Undertakings (Protection of Employment) Regulations 2006, SI 2006/246, reg 13(2): see PARA 1197.
10 Transfer of Undertakings (Protection of Employment) Regulations 2006, SI 2006/246, reg 13(11).

11 See the Transfer of Undertakings (Protection of Employment) Regulations 2006, SI 2006/246, reg 18, cited in PARA 137.

1200. Remedies for employer's failure to inform or consult. Where an employer[1] has failed to comply with a requirement to inform or consult[2], a complaint may be presented to an employment tribunal on that ground:

(1) in the case of a failure relating to the election of employee representatives[3], by any of his employees who are affected employees[4];

(2) in the case of any other failure relating to employee representatives, by any of the employee representatives to whom the failure related;

(3) in the case of failure relating to representatives of a trade union, by the trade union; and

(4) in any other case, by any of his employees who are affected employees[5].

Where the tribunal finds such a complaint against a transferee[6] well-founded, it must make a declaration to that effect, and may order the transferee to pay appropriate compensation[7] to such descriptions of affected employees as may be specified in the award[8].

Where the tribunal finds such a complaint against a transferor[9] well-founded it must make a declaration to that effect and may (a) order the transferor to pay appropriate compensation to such descriptions of affected employees as may be specified in the award[10]; or (b) if the complaint is that the transferor did not perform the relevant duty in regard to affected employees[11] and the transferor (after giving due notice) shows the facts so mentioned, order the transferee to pay appropriate compensation to such descriptions of affected employees as may be specified in the award[12].

An employee may present a complaint to an employment tribunal on the ground that he is an employee of a description to which an order for compensation[13] relates and that the transferor or transferee has failed, wholly or in part, to pay him compensation in pursuance of the order[14]. Where the tribunal finds such a further complaint[15] well-founded, it must order the employer to pay the complainant the amount of compensation which it finds is due to him[16].

An employment tribunal must not consider such a complaint or further complaint unless it is presented[17] to the tribunal before the end of the period of three months beginning with, in respect of a complaint[18], the date on which the relevant transfer is completed, in respect of a further complaint[19], the date of the tribunal's order[20], or within such further period as the tribunal considers reasonable in a case where it is satisfied that it was not reasonably practicable for the complaint to be presented before the end of the period of three months[21]. Provision is made for the extension of these time limits in order to facilitate conciliation before the institution of proceedings[22].

1 As to the meaning of 'employer' for these purposes see PARAS 137 note 8, 1196 note 8. As to the position where the employer is a micro-business see PARAS 1197, 1198.

2 Ie within the Transfer of Undertakings (Protection of Employment) Regulations 2006, SI 2006/246, reg 13 or reg 14: see PARAS 1196–1198.

3 As to the election of employee representatives see PARA 1196.

4 As to the meaning of references to affected employees see PARA 1196 note 8.

5 Transfer of Undertakings (Protection of Employment) Regulations 2006, SI 2006/246, reg 15(1). If necessary, the complaint may be presented before the transfer is effected: *Banking Insurance and Finance Union v Barclays Bank plc* [1987] ICR 495, EAT. If, on such a complaint, a question arises whether or not it was reasonably practicable for an employer to perform a particular duty or what steps he took towards performing it, it is for him to show: (1) that there were special circumstances which rendered it not reasonably practicable for him to perform the duty; and (2) that he took all such steps towards its performance as were reasonably practicable in those circumstances: Transfer of Undertakings (Protection of Employment) Regulations 2006,

SI 2006/246, reg 15(2). If, on such a complaint, a question arises as to whether or not any employee representative was an appropriate representative for the purposes of reg 13, it is for the employer to show that the employee representative had the necessary authority to represent the affected employees, except where the question is whether or not reg 13A (micro-businesses: see PARAS 1197, 1198) applied: reg 15(3) (amended by SI 2014/16). If, on such a complaint, a question arises as to whether or not the Transfer of Undertakings (Protection of Employment) Regulations 2006, SI 2006/246, reg 13A applied, it is for the employer to show that the conditions in reg 13A(1)(a), (b) applied at the time referred to in reg 13A(1): reg 15(3A) (added by SI 2014/16).

In relation to any complaint under the Transfer of Undertakings (Protection of Employment) Regulations 2006, SI 2006/246, reg 15(1), a failure on the part of a person controlling (directly or indirectly) the employer to provide information to the employer does not constitute special circumstances rendering it not reasonably practicable for the employer to comply with such a requirement: reg 15(6).

On a complaint under reg 15(1)(a) (see head (1) in the text), it is for the employer to show that the requirements of reg 14 (election of employee representatives) (see PARA 1196) have been satisfied: reg 15(4). As to the special circumstances defence see PARA 1199.

On any such complaint against a transferor that he has failed to perform the duty imposed on him by virtue of reg 13(2)(d) (see PARA 1197 head (4) in the text) or reg 13(9) (see PARA 1199), he may not show that it was not reasonably practicable for him to perform the duty in question for the reason that the transferee had failed to give him the requisite information at the requisite time in accordance with reg 13(4) (see PARA 1196), unless he gives the transferee notice of his intention to show that fact; and the giving of such notice makes the transferee a party to the proceedings: reg 15(5).

6   As to the meaning of 'transferee' see PARA 137.
7   For these purposes, 'appropriate compensation' means such sum, not exceeding 13 weeks' pay for the employee in question as the tribunal considers just and equitable having regard to the seriousness of the failure of the employer to comply with his duty: Transfer of Undertakings (Protection of Employment) Regulations 2006, SI 2006/246, reg 16(3). The Employment Rights Act 1996 ss 220–228 (see PARA 143 et seq) apply for calculating the amount of a week's pay for an employee for these purposes; and the calculation date for the purposes of that calculation is: (1) in the case of an employee who is dismissed by reason of redundancy, within the meaning of s 139 (see PARAS 870, 871) and s 155 (see PARAS 836, 855, 870), the date which is the calculation date for the purposes of any entitlement of his to a redundancy payment within the meaning of those provisions or which would be that calculation date if he were so entitled; (2) in the case of an employee who is dismissed for any other reason, the effective date of termination, within the meaning of ss 95(1), (2), 97 (see PARA 764), of his contract of employment; and (3) in any other case, the date of the transfer in question: Transfer of Undertakings (Protection of Employment) Regulations 2006, SI 2006/246, reg 16(4). As to the meaning of 'relevant transfer' see PARA 137.

    When assessing compensation for failure to consult, the tribunal should adopt the same approach as that adopted when assessing compensation for failure to consult under the Trade Union and Labour Relations (Consolidation) Act 1992 s 188 (see PARA 1185 et seq): *Sweetin v Coral Racing* [2006] IRLR 252, [2006] All ER (D) 74 (Mar), EAT (a case decided under the Transfer of Undertakings (Protection of Employment) Regulations 1981, SI 1981/1794 (revoked and replaced)); and see *GMB Northern v Cable Realisations Ltd* [2010] IRLR 42, EAT. It is, however, wrong in principle to award maximum compensation in circumstances where some (although inadequate) information had been given and the measures requiring consultation were of very limited significance: see *Todd v Strain* [2011] IRLR 11, EAT.

8   Transfer of Undertakings (Protection of Employment) Regulations 2006, SI 2006/246, reg 15(7).
9   As to the meaning of 'transferor' see PARA 137.
10 This is subject to the Transfer of Undertakings (Protection of Employment) Regulations 2006, SI 2006/246, reg 15(9). The transferee is jointly and severally liable with the transferor in respect of compensation payable under reg 15(8)(a) (see head (a) in the text) or reg 15(11) (see the text and note 16): reg 15(9).
11 Ie the duty mentioned in the Transfer of Undertakings (Protection of Employment) Regulations 2006, SI 2006/246, reg 15(5): see note 5.
12 Transfer of Undertakings (Protection of Employment) Regulations 2006, SI 2006/246, reg 15(8).
13 Ie under the Transfer of Undertakings (Protection of Employment) Regulations 2006, SI 2006/246, reg 15(7) or (8).
14 See the Transfer of Undertakings (Protection of Employment) Regulations 2006, SI 2006/246, reg 15(10).

15 Ie a complaint under the Transfer of Undertakings (Protection of Employment) Regulations 2006, SI 2006/246, reg 15(10).
16 Transfer of Undertakings (Protection of Employment) Regulations 2006, SI 2006/246, reg 15(11). See also reg 15(9); and note 10.
17 As to when a complaint is presented see PARAS 990 note 4, 1461.
18 Ie a complaint under the Transfer of Undertakings (Protection of Employment) Regulations 2006, SI 2006/246, reg 15(1).
19 Ie a complaint under the Transfer of Undertakings (Protection of Employment) Regulations 2006, SI 2006/246, reg 15(10).
20 Ie order under the Transfer of Undertakings (Protection of Employment) Regulations 2006, SI 2006/246, reg 15(7) or (8).
21 Transfer of Undertakings (Protection of Employment) Regulations 2006, SI 2006/246, reg 15(12). For the case law on the extension of time limits, especially in the context of the law of unfair dismissal, see PARA 1453. The existence of this time limit after the transfer does not preclude a complaint being made before the transfer is effected: *South Durham Health Authority v UNISON* [1995] ICR 495, [1995] IRLR 407, EAT. The Employment Rights Act 1996 s 205(1) (complaint to be sole remedy for breach of relevant rights) (see PARA 1406) and the Employment Tribunals Act 1996 ss 18A–18C (conciliation) (see PARAS 152–153) apply to the rights conferred by the Transfer of Undertakings (Protection of Employment) Regulations 2006, SI 2006/246, reg 15 and to proceedings under reg 16 as they apply to the rights conferred by those Acts and the employment tribunals proceedings mentioned in those Acts: Transfer of Undertakings (Protection of Employment) Regulations 2006, SI 2006/246, reg 16(1) (amended by SI 2014/386). As to employment tribunals see PARA 1399 et seq. An appeal lies, and lies only, to the Employment Appeal Tribunal on a question of law arising from any decision of, or arising in any proceedings before, an employment tribunal under or by virtue of the Transfer of Undertakings (Protection of Employment) Regulations 2006, SI 2006/246; and the Tribunals and Inquiries Act 1992 s 11(1) (appeal from certain tribunals to the High Court) does not apply in relation to any such proceedings: Transfer of Undertakings (Protection of Employment) Regulations 2006, SI 2006/246, reg 16(2). As to the Employment Appeal Tribunal see PARA 1422 et seq.
22 The Transfer of Undertakings (Protection of Employment) Regulations 2006, SI 2006/246, reg 16A (see PARA 140) applies for the purposes of reg 15(12): reg 15(13) (regs 12(2A), 16A added by SI 2014/853).

(ii) Information and Consultation on Health and Safety

1201. The duty to consult trade union appointed safety representatives. It is the duty of every employer to consult any safety representatives appointed by recognised trade unions[1] from amongst the employees[2] in accordance with regulations[3], with a view to the making and maintenance of arrangements which will enable him and his employees to co-operate effectively in promoting and developing measures to ensure the health and safety at work of the employees, and in checking the effectiveness of such measures[4].

In particular, every employer[5] must consult such safety representatives in good time with regard to:

(1)   the introduction of any measure at the workplace[6] which may substantially affect the health and safety of the employees the safety representatives concerned represent;

(2)   his arrangements for appointing or, as the case may be, nominating competent persons[7];

(3)   any health and safety information he is required to provide to the employees the safety representatives concerned represent by or under the relevant statutory provisions[8];

(4)   the planning and organisation of any health and safety training he is required by or under the relevant statutory provisions to provide to those employees; and

(5) the health and safety consequences for those employees of the introduction, including the planning thereof, of new technologies into the workplace[9].

1 As to the meaning of 'recognised trade union' for these purposes see PARA 1073 note 1.
2 As to the meaning of 'employee' for these purposes see HEALTH AND SAFETY AT WORK vol 52 (2014) PARA 302. A non-employee may not be a safety representative under these provisions; the fact of union appointment cannot affect the person's employment status: *Costain Building & Civil Engineering Ltd v Smith* [2000] ICR 215, EAT (agency-supplied worker's appointment held invalid).
3 Ie under the Safety Representatives and Safety Committees Regulations 1977, SI 1977/500, reg 3: see PARA 1073.
4 Health and Safety at Work etc Act 1974 s 2(6).
5 As to the meaning of 'employer' for these purposes see PARA 1073 note 20.
6 As to the meaning of 'workplace' see PARA 1073 note 9.
7 Ie in accordance with the Management of Health and Safety at Work Regulations 1999, SI 1999/3242, regs 7(1), 8(1)(b) (see HEALTH AND SAFETY AT WORK vol 52 (2014) PARAS 400–401) or the Regulatory Reform (Fire Safety) Order 2005, SI 2005/1541, art 13(3)(b) (see FIRE AND RESCUE SERVICES vol 51 (2013) PARA 78; HEALTH AND SAFETY AT WORK vol 53 (2014) PARA 627).
8 Ie the 'relevant statutory provisions' within the meaning of the Health and Safety at Work etc Act 1974 s 53(1): see HEALTH AND SAFETY AT WORK vol 52 (2014) PARA 302.
9 Safety Representatives and Safety Committees Regulations 1977, SI 1977/500, reg 4A(1) (added by SI 1992/2051; amended by SI 1999/3242; SI 2005/1541). As to exemption from this requirement see the Safety Representatives and Safety Committees Regulations 1977, SI 1977/500, reg 10; and PARA 1073.

1202. The duty to disclose information to trade union appointed safety representatives. As well as there being duties on employers to give information to employees, by way of formal safety statements[1] or otherwise[2], there is a duty to inform safety representatives appointed by recognised trade unions[3]. If they have given the employer[4] reasonable notice, such safety representatives are entitled[5] to inspect and take copies of any document relevant to the workplace[6] or to the employees the safety representatives represent which the employer is required to keep by virtue of any relevant statutory provision[7], except a document consisting of or relating to any health record of an identifiable individual[8]. In addition, an employer must make available to safety representatives the information, within the employer's knowledge, necessary to enable them to fulfil their functions, except:

(1) any information the disclosure of which would be against the interests of national security[9]; or
(2) any information which he could not disclose without contravening a prohibition imposed by or under an enactment; or
(3) any information relating specifically to an individual, unless he has consented to its being disclosed; or
(4) any information the disclosure of which would, for reasons other than its effect on health, safety or welfare at work[10], cause substantial injury to the employer's undertaking or, where the information was supplied to him by some other person, to the undertaking of that other person; or
(5) any information obtained by the employer for the purpose of bringing, prosecuting or defending any legal proceedings[11].

The above provisions do not, however, require an employer to produce or allow inspection of any document or part of a document which is not related to health, safety or welfare[12].

1 See the Health and Safety at Work etc Act 1974 s 2(3); and HEALTH AND SAFETY AT WORK vol 52 (2014) PARA 358.

2　See eg the Management of Health and Safety at Work Regulations 1999, SI 1999/3242, reg 10; and HEALTH AND SAFETY AT WORK vol 52 (2014) PARAS 394, 404.

3　As to the appointment and functions of such safety representatives see PARA 1073.

4　As to the meaning of 'employer' for these purposes see PARA 1073 note 20.

5　Ie for the performance of their functions under the Health and Safety at Work etc Act 1974 s 2(4) and under the Safety Representatives and Safety Committees Regulations 1977, SI 1977/500: see PARA 1073.

6　As to the meaning of 'workplace' see PARA 1073 note 9.

7　Ie within the meaning of the Health and Safety at Work etc Act 1974 s 53(1): see HEALTH AND SAFETY AT WORK vol 52 (2014) PARA 302.

8　Safety Representatives and Safety Committees Regulations 1977, SI 1977/500, reg 7(1).

9　As to restrictions on the rights of inspection on grounds of national security see also the Safety Representatives and Safety Committees Regulations 1977, SI 1977/500, reg 2(3); and PARA 1073.

10　As to the meaning of 'welfare at work' see PARA 1073 note 10.

11　Safety Representatives and Safety Committees Regulations 1977, SI 1977/500, reg 7(2). As to the equivalent exceptions to the duty to disclose in relation to bargaining information see PARA 1181.

12　Safety Representatives and Safety Committees Regulations 1977, SI 1977/500, reg 7(3). As to exemption from the requirement to disclose see reg 10; and PARA 1073.

1203.　The duty to consult on health and safety matters where no trade union is recognised. The obligation to consult employees on health and safety matters was originally cast only in terms of consulting safety representatives appointed by recognised trade unions[1]. However, the relevant EC Council Directive[2] required more general consultation, which was not satisfied by the existing law, in times of lower levels of recognition of trade unions. New obligations were, therefore, introduced, requiring consultation with the workforce itself or elected workforce representatives, in any case where there is no recognised trade union[3].

Where there are employees[4] who are not represented by trade union appointed safety representatives[5], the employer must consult those employees in good time on matters relating to health and safety at work and, in particular, with regard to:

(1)　the introduction of any measure at the workplace[6] which may substantially affect the health and safety of those employees;

(2)　his arrangements for appointing or, as the case may be, nominating persons[7];

(3)　any health and safety information he is required to provide to those employees by or under the relevant statutory provisions[8];

(4)　the planning and organisation of any health and safety training he is required to provide to those employees by or under the relevant statutory provisions; and

(5)　the health and safety consequences for those employees of the introduction, including the planning thereof, of new technologies in the workplace[9].

The required consultation is to be with either:

(a)　the employees directly; or

(b)　in respect of any group of employees, one or more persons in that group who was or were elected, by the employees in that group at the time of the election, to represent that group for the purposes of such consultation ('representatives of employee safety')[10].

Where an employer chooses the latter option and consults representatives of employee safety, each of those representatives has, for the period for which they are consulted, the following functions:

(i)　to make representations to the employer on potential hazards and dangerous occurrences at the workplace which affect, or could affect, the group of employees he represents;

(ii) to make representations to the employer on general matters affecting the health and safety at work of the group of employees he represents and, in particular, on such matters as he is consulted about[11];

(iii) to represent the group of employees he represents in consultations at the workplace[12] with health and safety inspectors[13].

1 See PARA 1201.

2 Ie Council Directive (EC) 89/391 (OJ L 183, 29.6.89, p 1) arts 10, 11: see HEALTH AND SAFETY AT WORK vol 52 (2014) PARA 311.

3 Ie by the Health and Safety (Consultation with Employees) Regulations 1996, SI 1996/1513: see the text and notes 4–13; and PARA 1204. For the corresponding extensions of consultation and information requirements to non-unionised workforces in the contexts of collective redundancies and transfers of undertakings see PARAS 1187, 1196. Breach of the Health and Safety (Consultation with Employees) Regulations 1996, SI 1996/1513, does not confer any right of action in civil proceedings, except where they specifically give such a right: see reg 9.

4 For these purposes, 'employee' has the meaning assigned to it by the Health and Safety at Work etc Act 1974 s 53(1) (see HEALTH AND SAFETY AT WORK vol 52 (2014) PARA 302) but does not include a person employed as a domestic servant in a private household; and 'employer' is to be construed accordingly: Health and Safety (Consultation with Employees) Regulations 1996, SI 1996/1513, reg 2(1).

5 Ie under the Safety Representatives and Safety Committees Regulations 1977, SI 1977/50: see PARA 1201.

6 For these purposes, 'workplace' means, in relation to an employee, any place or places where that employee is likely to work or which he is likely to frequent in the course of his employment or incidentally to it and, in relation to a representative of employee safety, any place or places where the employees he represents are likely so to work or frequent: Health and Safety (Consultation with Employees) Regulations 1996, SI 1996/1513, reg 2(1).

7 Ie in accordance with the Management of Health and Safety at Work Regulations 1999, SI 1999/3242, regs 7(1), 8(1)(b) (see HEALTH AND SAFETY AT WORK vol 52 (2014) PARAS 400–401) or the Regulatory Reform (Fire Safety) Order 2005, SI 2005/1541, art 13(3)(b) (see FIRE AND RESCUE SERVICES vol 51 (2013) PARA 78; HEALTH AND SAFETY AT WORK vol 53 (2014) PARA 627).

8 For these purposes, 'relevant statutory provisions' has the meaning assigned to it by the Health and Safety at Work etc Act 1974 s 53(1) (see HEALTH AND SAFETY AT WORK vol 52 (2014) PARA 302): Health and Safety (Consultation with Employees) Regulations 1996, SI 1996/1513, reg 2(1).

9 Health and Safety (Consultation with Employees) Regulations 1996, SI 1996/1513, reg 3 (amended by SI 1999/3242; SI 2005/1541).

10 Health and Safety (Consultation with Employees) Regulations 1996, SI 1996/1513, regs 2(1), 4(1). Where an employer consults representatives of employee safety, he must inform the employees represented by those representatives of: (1) the names of those representatives; and (2) the group of employees represented by those representatives: reg 4(2). Where an employer who has been consulting representatives of employee safety decides to consult employees directly, he must inform the employees and the representatives of that fact: reg 4(4). As to the rights of representatives of employee safety to training, time off, facilities and protection from victimisation and dismissal see PARAS 1073 et seq, 1207–1210.

11 Ie under the Health and Safety (Consultation with Employees) Regulations 1996, SI 1996/1513, reg 3.

12 Ie consultations with inspectors appointed under the Health and Safety at Work etc Act 1974 s 19(1): see HEALTH AND SAFETY AT WORK vol 52 (2014) PARA 338.

13 Health and Safety (Consultation with Employees) Regulations 1996, SI 1996/1513, reg 6. An employer must not consult a person as a representative of employee safety if: (1) that person has notified the employer that he does not intend to represent the group of employees for the purposes of such consultation; (2) that person has ceased to be employed in the group of employees which he represents; (3) the period for which that person was elected has expired without that person being re-elected; or (4) that person has become incapacitated from carrying out his functions under the Health and Safety (Consultation with Employees) Regulations 1996, SI 1996/1513; and, where an employer thus discontinues consultation with that person, he must inform the employees in the group concerned of that fact: reg 4(3).

1204. Duty to provide information where no trade union is recognised.
Where an employer[1] consults employees[2] directly[3], he must[4] make available to those employees such information, within the employer's knowledge, as is necessary to enable them to participate fully and effectively in the consultation[5].

Where an employer consults representatives of employee safety[6], he must[7] make available to those representatives such information, within the employer's knowledge, as is:

(1)   necessary to enable them to participate fully and effectively in the consultation and in the carrying out of their functions[8];

(2)   contained in any record which he is required to keep under the reporting requirements[9] and which relates to the workplace[10] or the group of employees represented by those representatives[11].

Nothing in the above provisions requires an employer to make available any information:

(a)   the disclosure of which would be against the interests of national security;

(b)   which he could not disclose without contravening a prohibition imposed by or under any enactment;

(c)   relating specifically to an individual, unless he has consented to its being disclosed;

(d)   the disclosure of which would, for reasons other than its effect on health or safety, cause substantial injury to the employer's undertaking or, where the information was supplied to him by some other person, to the undertaking of that other person; or

(e)   obtained by the employer for the purpose of bringing, prosecuting or defending any legal proceedings,

or to provide or allow the inspection of any document or part of a document which is not related to health or safety[12].

1   As to the meaning of 'employer' see PARA 1203 note 4.
2   As to the meaning of 'employee' see PARA 1203 note 4.
3   Ie under the Health and Safety (Consultation with Employees) Regulations 1996, SI 1996/1513, reg 4(1)(a): see PARA 1203 head (a) in the text.
4   Ie subject to the Health and Safety (Consultation with Employees) Regulations 1996, SI 1996/1513, reg 5(3): see the text and note 12.
5   Health and Safety (Consultation with Employees) Regulations 1996, SI 1996/1513, reg 5(1).
6   Ie under the Health and Safety (Consultation with Employees) Regulations 1996, SI 1996/1513, reg 4(1)(b): see PARA 1203 head (b) in the text.
7   See note 4.
8   As to the functions of representatives of employee safety see the Health and Safety (Consultation with Employees) Regulations 1996, SI 1996/1513, reg 6; and PARA 1203.
9   Ie under the Reporting of Injuries, Diseases and Dangerous Occurrences Regulations 2013, SI 2013/1471, reg 12: see HEALTH AND SAFETY AT WORK vol 52 (2014) PARA 375.
10 As to the meaning of 'workplace' see PARA 1203 note 6.
11 Health and Safety (Consultation with Employees) Regulations 1996, SI 1996/1513, reg 5(2) (amended by SI 2013/1471).
12 Health and Safety (Consultation with Employees) Regulations 1996, SI 1996/1513, reg 5(3).

(iii) Information and Consultation on Pensions

1205. The duty to consult about pensions. A notice of intention to make an election with a view to the issue of a contracted-out certificate[1] in relation to an occupational pension scheme must be given to, among others, all independent trade unions[2] recognised in relation to the earners[3] concerned[4]. An employer[5] who has given such a notice must undertake consultations, if he has not already done so, about the matters covered by the notice with all independent trade unions so recognised[6]. Any question:

(1) whether an organisation is an independent trade union so recognised; or

(2) whether an employer has complied with the requirements as to consultation,

may be referred to an employment tribunal, in the case of head (1) above, by the employer or the organisation concerned, and, in the case of head (2) above, by the employer or an independent trade union so recognised[7].

1 Ie under the Occupational Pension Schemes (Contracting-out) Regulations 1996, SI 1996/1172, reg 2: see PERSONAL AND OCCUPATIONAL PENSIONS vol 80 (2013) PARA 400.

2 For these purposes, 'independent trade union' means an independent trade union recognised to any extent for the purpose of collective bargaining: Occupational Pension Schemes (Contracting-out) Regulations 1996, SI 1996/1172, reg 1(2). As to the meaning of 'recognised' see PARA 1094; and as to the meaning of 'collective bargaining' for the purposes of the Trade Union and Labour Relations (Consolidation) Act 1992 see PARA 1093.

3 For these purposes, 'earner' and 'earnings' are to be construed in accordance with the Social Security Contributions and Benefits Act 1992 ss 3, 4, 112 (whereby 'earnings' include any remuneration or profit derived from an employment and 'earner' is to be construed accordingly) (see WELFARE BENEFITS AND STATE PENSIONS vol 104 (2014) PARA 382): Pension Schemes Act 1993 s 181(1).

4 See the Occupational Pension Schemes (Contracting-out) Regulations 1996, SI 1996/1172, reg 3(1)(d); and PERSONAL AND OCCUPATIONAL PENSIONS vol 80 (2013) PARA 400.

5 For these purposes, 'employer' includes a person who is treated as an employer by virtue of the Occupational Pension Schemes (Contracting-out) Regulations 1996, SI 1996/1172, reg 1(4), (5) or regs 12–14 (special provisions for certain public employees, holding companies and subsidiaries, public service pension schemes and holders of full-time judicial office) (see PERSONAL AND OCCUPATIONAL PENSIONS vol 80 (2013) PARA 400): reg 1(2).

6 Occupational Pension Schemes (Contracting-out) Regulations 1996, SI 1996/1172, reg 4(1). There is an equivalent requirement of consultation if the employer elects to vary or surrender a contracted-out certificate: see reg 9(6); and PERSONAL AND OCCUPATIONAL PENSIONS vol 80 (2013) PARA 418.

7 Occupational Pension Schemes (Contracting-out) Regulations 1996, SI 1996/1172, reg 4(2), (3) (amended by the Employment Rights (Dispute Resolution) Act 1998 s 1(2)(a)). There is an equivalent right to refer any question whether an employer has complied with the requirement to consult under the Occupational Pension Schemes (Contracting-out) Regulations 1996, SI 1996/1172, reg 9 to an employment tribunal: see reg 9(6); and note 6.

1206. The duty to disclose specified pensions information. A recognised trade union[1] is a 'relevant person' for the purposes of the Occupational and Personal Pension Schemes (Disclosure of Information) Regulations 2013[2]. Those regulations require the trustees or managers of an occupational pension scheme[3] or a personal pension scheme[4] to give specified information[5] to such a relevant person[6]. There is no such requirement, however, if no person who employs a member or prospective member in relation to whom the trade union is a recognised trade union has informed the trustees or managers of the scheme that the trade union is a recognised trade union[7].

Where in relation to an occupational pension scheme a person fails without reasonable excuse to comply with any requirement so imposed, the Pensions Regulator[8] may, by notice in writing, require that person to pay, within 28 days, a penalty that must not, in the case of an individual, exceed £5,000, and in any other case exceed £50,000[8].

1 'Recognised trade union' means an independent trade union (within the meaning given in the Employment Rights Act 1996 s 235(1) (see PARA 150 note 9) that is recognised to any extent for the purposes of collective bargaining in relation to members and prospective members of a scheme: Occupational and Personal Pension Schemes (Disclosure of Information)

Regulations 2013, SI 2013/2734, reg 2. Where there is a question about whether an organisation is a recognised trade union, that question must be referred to an employment tribunal: reg 3. 'Member' (1) in relation to an occupational pension scheme, has the meaning given in the Pensions Act 1995 s 124(1) (see PERSONAL AND OCCUPATIONAL PENSIONS vol 80 (2013) PARA 491 note 16); and (2) in relation to a personal pension scheme, means a member of the scheme; and 'prospective member' means a person who, under the terms of his contract of service, the scheme rules or both (a) can choose to become a member of the scheme; (b) will be able to choose to become a member of the scheme if he continues in the same employment for a certain period of time; (c) will become a member of the scheme automatically unless he chooses not to become a member of the scheme; or (d) can become a member of the scheme if his employer consents: Occupational and Personal Pension Schemes (Disclosure of Information) Regulations 2013, SI 2013/2734, reg 2.

2   See the Occupational and Personal Pension Schemes (Disclosure of Information) Regulations 2013, SI 2013/2734, reg 2.

3   Ie an occupational pension scheme that falls within the Occupational and Personal Pension Schemes (Disclosure of Information) Regulations 2013, SI 2013/2734, Sch 1 para 1: see PERSONAL AND OCCUPATIONAL PENSIONS.

4   Ie a personal pension scheme that falls within the Occupational and Personal Pension Schemes (Disclosure of Information) Regulations 2013, SI 2013/2734, Sch 1 para 2: see PERSONAL AND OCCUPATIONAL PENSIONS.

5   In the case of an occupational pension scheme, the trustees or managers must give information in accordance with the Occupational and Personal Pension Schemes (Disclosure of Information) Regulations 2013, SI 2013/2734, reg 6 (basic scheme information), regs 8–22 (changes to information, information to be given on request, funding statements, benefit statements and illustrations, lifestyling and accessing benefits, and changes to benefits), and regs 24–25 (information about winding up); and in the case of a personal pension scheme they must give information in accordance with reg 10 (information in relation to former stakeholder pension schemes), regs 17–18 (statements of benefits (money purchase benefits) and lifestyling), regs 19, 21 (accessing benefits) and reg 23 (information about winding up): see reg 4(1), (5).

6   See the Occupational and Personal Pension Schemes (Disclosure of Information) Regulations 2013, SI 2013/2734, reg 4(1), (5). For exceptions see reg 4(2), (3), (6). Subject to reg 4(6), the trustees or managers of a pension scheme that is (1) an occupational pension scheme that does not fall within Sch 1 para 1; or (2) established under the Salvation Army Act 1963, must give information in accordance with the Occupational and Personal Pension Schemes (Disclosure of Information) Regulations 2013, SI 2013/2734, reg 7 (basic scheme information): reg 4(4).

7   See the Occupational and Personal Pension Schemes (Disclosure of Information) Regulations 2013, SI 2013/2734, reg 4(6)(b).

8   As to the Pensions Regulator see PERSONAL AND OCCUPATIONAL PENSIONS vol 80 (2013) PARA 479 et seq.

9   Occupational and Personal Pension Schemes (Disclosure of Information) Regulations 2013, SI 2013/2734, reg 5.

(8) RIGHTS OF EMPLOYEE REPRESENTATIVES

1207. Employee representatives; in general. When it was necessary to extend obligations to consult on impending collective redundancies[1] or transfers of undertaking[2] to include workplaces where there is no recognised trade union, this was done by adopting the use of directly elected employee representatives[3]. Such representatives did not qualify for the existing employment protection measures given to trade union representatives[4], and so special provision had to be made in relation to protection from detriment[5] and from unfair dismissal[6] and the right to time off work to fulfil the representative's obligations[7].

Similarly, when the obligations to consult on health and safety matters were extended to workplaces with no recognised trade union[8], protection was given to representatives of employee safety from detriment[9] and unfair dismissal[10] and rights specifically enacted in relation to training, time off work and provision of facilities[11].

1   See PARA 1185 et seq.
2   See PARA 1196 et seq.
3   See PARA 1187.
4   As to the provisions relating to victimisation for trade union reasons see PARA 1048 et seq; as to the provisions relating to dismissal for trade union reasons see PARA 1056 et seq; and as to the provisions relating to time off for trade union duties and activities see PARA 1065 et seq. Trade union appointed safety representatives are given similar protection and rights separately: see PARAS 1074, 1076, 1077.
5   See PARA 1208.
6   See the Employment Rights Act 1996 s 103 and PARA 791; and, in relation to selection for redundancy on such grounds, s 105 and PARA 782.
7   See PARA 1209.
8   See PARAS 1203, 1204.
9   See the Employment Rights Act 1996 s 44; and PARA 614.
10 See the Employment Rights Act 1996 s 100 and PARA 786; and, in relation to selection for redundancy on such grounds, s 105 and PARA 781.
11 See PARA 1210.

1208.   Protection from suffering detriment as an employee representative.   An employee[1] has the right not to be subjected to any detriment[2] by any act, or any deliberate failure to act, by his employer[3] done on the ground that, being:

(1)   an employee representative[4] for the purposes of the law relating to collective redundancies[5] or transfers of undertaking[6]; or

(2)   a candidate in an election in which any person elected will, on being elected, be such an employee representative,

he performed, or proposed to perform, any functions or activities as such an employee representative or candidate[7].

The above provisions do not apply where the detriment in question amounts to dismissal[8].

1   As to the meaning of 'employee' for the purposes of the Employment Rights Act 1996 see PARA 2.
2   As to the meaning of 'detriment' see PARAS 614 note 2, 1048 note 2.
3   As to the meaning of 'employer' for the purposes of the Employment Rights Act 1996 see PARA 2.
4   See PARA 1187.
5   Ie for the purposes of the Trade Union and Labour Relations (Consolidation) Act 1992 Pt IV Ch II (ss 188–198B): see PARA 1185 et seq.
6   Ie for the purposes of the Transfer of Undertakings (Protection of Employment) Regulations 2006, SI 2006/246, regs 9, 13, 15: see PARAS 138, 1196 et seq.
7   Employment Rights Act 1996 s 47(1) (amended by SI 2006/246). An employee also has the right not to be subjected to any detriment by any act, or by any deliberate failure to act, by his employer done on the ground of his participation in an election of employee representatives for the purposes of the Trade Union and Labour Relations (Consolidation) Act 1992 Pt IV Ch II (see PARA 1185 et seq) or the Transfer of Undertakings (Protection of Employment) Regulations 2006, SI 2006/246, regs 9, 13, 15 (see PARAS 138, 1196 et seq): Employment Rights Act 1996 s 47(1A) (added by SI 1999/1925; amended by SI 2006/246).
      As to the right to make a complaint to an employment tribunal see the Employment Rights Act 1996 s 48; and PARA 625; and as to remedies see s 49; and PARA 626. The provisions of the Employment Tribunals Act 1996 ss 18A–18B (conciliation) (see PARAS 152–153) apply in the case of matters which could be the subject of employment tribunal proceedings under the Employment Rights Act 1996 Pt V (ss 43M–49A), and the Employment Tribunals Act 1996 s 18C applies in the case of such proceedings themselves: see s 18(1)(b), (1A) (s 18(1)(b) substituted by SI 2014/431; the Employment Tribunals Act 1996 s 18(1A) added by the Enterprise and Regulatory Reform Act 2013 Sch 1 paras 2, 5(1), (7)).
8   Employment Rights Act 1996 s 47(2) (amended by the Employment Relations Act 1999 Sch 9). For these purposes, 'dismissal' has the meaning given in the Employment Rights Act 1996 Pt X (ss 94–134A) (see PARA 757 et seq): s 47(2) (as so amended). Dismissal on these grounds is covered by ss 103, 105: see PARAS 781, 791.

1209. Time off work for employee representatives. An employee[1] who is:

(1)   an employee representative[2] for the purposes of the law relating to collective redundancies[3] or transfers of undertaking[4]; or

(2)   a candidate in an election in which any person elected will, on being elected, be such an employee representative,

is entitled to be permitted by his employer[5] to take reasonable time off during the employee's working hours[6] in order to perform his functions as such an employee representative or candidate, or in order to undergo training to perform such functions[7].

An employee who is so permitted to take time off is entitled to be paid remuneration by his employer for that time at the appropriate hourly rate[8].

An employee may present a claim to an employment tribunal that his employer has either unreasonably refused to permit him to take such time off or has failed to pay the whole or any part of any amount to which the employee is so entitled[9]. An employment tribunal must not consider such a complaint unless it is presented[10]:

(a)   before the end of the period of three months beginning with the day on which the time off was taken or on which it is alleged the time off should have been permitted[11], subject to an extension because of mediation in certain European cross-border disputes[12] or to facilitate conciliation before the institution of proceedings[13]; or

(b)   within such further period as the tribunal considers reasonable in a case where it is satisfied that it was not reasonably practicable for the complaint to be presented before the end of that period of three months[14].

Where an employment tribunal finds that such a complaint is well-founded, it must make a declaration to that effect[15]. If the complaint is that the employer has unreasonably refused to permit the employee to take time off, the tribunal must also order the employer to pay to the employee an amount equal to the remuneration to which he would otherwise have been entitled if the employer had not refused[16]. If the complaint is that the employer has failed to pay the employee the whole or part of any amount to which he is entitled, the tribunal must also order the employer to pay to the employee the amount which it finds due to him[17].

1   As to the meaning of 'employee' for the purposes of the Employment Rights Act 1996 see PARA 2.

2   See PARA 1187.

3   Ie for the purposes of the Trade Union and Labour Relations (Consolidation) Act 1992 Pt IV Ch II (ss 188–198B): see PARA 1185 et seq.

4   Ie for the purposes of the Transfer of Undertakings (Protection of Employment) Regulations 2006, SI 2006/246, regs 9, 13, 15: see PARAS 138, 1196 et seq.

5   As to the meaning of 'employer' for the purposes of the Employment Rights Act 1996 see PARA 2.

6   For these purposes, the working hours of an employee are to be taken to be any time when, in accordance with his contract of employment, the employee is required to be at work: Employment Rights Act 1996 s 61(2). As to the meaning of 'contract of employment' for the purposes of the Employment Rights Act 1996 see PARA 2.

7   Employment Rights Act 1996 s 61(1) (amended by SI 1999/1925; SI 2006/246).

8   Employment Rights Act 1996 s 62(1). For these purposes, the appropriate hourly rate, in relation to an employee, is the amount of one week's pay divided by the number of normal working hours in a week for the employee when employed under the contract of employment in force on the day when the time off is taken: s 62(2). As to the calculation of a week's pay, and as to the determination of normal working hours, see PARA 142 et seq.

Where, however, the number of normal working hours differs from week to week or over a longer period, the amount of one week's pay must be divided instead by: (1) the average number of normal working hours calculated by dividing by 12 the total number of the employee's normal working hours during the period of 12 weeks ending with the last complete week before the day on which the time off is taken; or (2) where the employee has not been employed for a sufficient period to enable the calculation to be made under head (1) above, a number which fairly represents the number of normal working hours in a week, having regard to such of the following considerations as are appropriate in the circumstances: (a) the average number of normal working hours in a week which the employee could expect in accordance with the terms of his contract; and (b) the average number of normal working hours of other employees engaged in relevant comparable employment with the same employer: s 62(3), (4).

A right to any amount under s 62(1) does not affect any right of an employee in relation to remuneration under his contract of employment ('contractual remuneration'): s 62(5). However, any contractual remuneration paid to an employee in respect of a period of time off under s 61 goes towards discharging any liability of the employer to pay remuneration under s 62(1) in respect of that period; and, conversely, any payment of remuneration under s 62(1) in respect of a period goes towards discharging any liability of the employer to pay contractual remuneration in respect of that period: s 62(6).

9 Employment Rights Act 1996 s 63(1) (s 63(1), (2), (3) amended by the Employment Rights (Dispute Resolution) Act 1998 s 1(2)(a)).

10 As to when a complaint is presented see PARAS 990 note 4, 1461.

11 Employment Rights Act 1996 s 63(2)(a) (as amended: see note 9). For the case law on the extension of time limits, especially in the context of the law of unfair dismissal, see PARA 1453. See also the text and notes 12–13.
The provisions of the Employment Tribunals Act 1996 ss 18A–18B (conciliation) (see PARAS 152–153) apply in the case of matters which could be the subject of employment tribunal proceedings under the Employment Rights Act 1996 Pt VI (ss 50–63C), and the Employment Tribunals Act 1996 s 18C applies in the case of such proceedings themselves: see s 18(1)(b), (1A) (s 18(1)(b) substituted by SI 2014/431; the Employment Tribunals Act 1996 s 18(1A) added by the Enterprise and Regulatory Reform Act 2013 Sch 1 paras 2, 5(1), (7)).

12 The Employment Rights Act 1996 s 207A(3) (extension because of mediation in certain European cross-border disputes: see PARA 1454) applies for the purposes of head (a) in the text: s 63(2A) (added by SI 2011/1133).

13 The Employment Rights Act 1996 s 207B (extension of time limits to facilitate conciliation before institution of proceedings: see PARA 1455) applies for the purposes of head (a) in the text: s 63(2A) (as added (see note 12); amended by the Enterprise and Regulatory Reform Act 2013 Sch 2 paras 15, 26).

14 Employment Rights Act 1996 s 63(2)(b) (as amended: see note 9). See also note 11.

15 Employment Rights Act 1996 s 63(3) (as amended: see note 9).

16 Employment Rights Act 1996 s 63(4).

17 Employment Rights Act 1996 s 63(5).

1210. Rights of representatives of employee safety. Where an employer, in a workplace without a recognised trade union, consults on health and safety matters with directly elected representatives of employee safety[1], those representatives have statutory protection from detriment and unfair dismissal[2]. Further, where an employer[3] consults such representatives, he must:

(1)   ensure that each of those representatives is provided with such training in respect of that representative's functions[4] as is reasonable in all the circumstances and meet any reasonable costs associated with such training, including travel and subsistence costs[5];

(2)   permit each of those representatives to take such time off with pay[6] during that representative's working hours as is necessary for the purpose of that representative performing those functions or undertaking any such training[7]; and

(3)   provide such other facilities and assistance as such a representative may reasonably require for the purpose of carrying out those functions[8].

A person (the 'complainant') may present a complaint to an employment tribunal that his employer has failed:

(a)   to permit him to take time off[9]; or

(b)   to pay him[10] for such time off[11].

An employment tribunal must not consider such a complaint unless it is presented[12] within three months of the date when the failure occurred or within such further period as the tribunal considers reasonable in a case where it is satisfied that it was not reasonably practicable for the complaint to be presented within the period of three months[13]; but this is subject to an extension to facilitate conciliation before the institution of proceedings[14].

Where an employment tribunal finds a complaint under head (a) above well-founded, it must make a declaration to that effect and may make an award of compensation to be paid by the employer to the complainant, which must be such amount as the tribunal considers just and equitable in all the circumstances, having regard to the employer's default in failing to permit time off to be taken and to any loss sustained by the complainant which is attributable to the matters complained of[15]. Where, on a complaint under head (b) above, an employment tribunal finds that the employer has failed to pay the complainant the whole or part of the amount required to be paid, it must order the employer to pay the complainant the amount which it finds due to him[16].

1   See PARA 1203.
2   See PARAS 1207, 1208.
3   As to the meaning of 'employer' for these purposes see PARA 1203 note 4.
4   Ie under the Health and Safety (Consultation with Employees) Regulations 1996, SI 1996/1513: see PARA 1203.
5   Health and Safety (Consultation with Employees) Regulations 1996, SI 1996/1513, reg 7(1)(a).
6   Where a person is so permitted to take time off, his employer must pay him: (1) where the person's remuneration for the work he would ordinarily have been doing during that time does not vary with the amount of work done, as if he had worked at that work for the whole of that time; (2) where the person's remuneration for that work varies with the amount of work done, an amount calculated by reference to the average hourly earnings for that work: Health and Safety (Consultation with Employees) Regulations 1996, SI 1996/1513, Sch 1 para 1. The average hourly earnings referred to in head (2) above are the average hourly earnings of the person concerned or, if no fair estimate can be made of those earnings, the average hourly earnings for work of that description of persons in comparable employment with the same employer or, if there are no such persons, a figure of average hourly earnings which is reasonable in all the circumstances: Sch 1 para 2.

     Any payment to a person by an employer in respect of a period of time off: (a) if it is a payment which discharges any liability which the employer may have under the Trade Union and Labour Relations (Consolidation) Act 1992 s 168 or 169 (time off for carrying out trade union duties) (see PARA 1020), in respect of that period, also discharges his liability in respect of the same period under the Health and Safety (Consultation with Employees) Regulations 1996, SI 1996/1513, reg 7(1)(b) or 7(2); (b) if it is a payment under any contractual obligation, goes towards discharging the employer's liability in respect of the same period under reg 7(1)(b) or 7(2); (c) if it is a payment under reg 7(1)(b) or 7(2), goes towards discharging any liability of the employer to pay contractual remuneration in respect of the same period: Sch 1 para 3.
7   Health and Safety (Consultation with Employees) Regulations 1996, SI 1996/1513, reg 7(1)(b). In addition, an employer must permit a candidate standing for election as a representative of employee safety reasonable time off with pay during that person's working hours in order to perform his duties as such a candidate: reg 7(2).
8   Health and Safety (Consultation with Employees) Regulations 1996, SI 1996/1513, reg 7(4).
9   Ie in accordance with the Health and Safety (Consultation with Employees) Regulations 1996, SI 1996/1513, reg 7(1)(b) or 7(2).
10   Ie in accordance with the Health and Safety (Consultation with Employees) Regulations 1996, SI 1996/1513, reg 7(1)(b) or reg 7(2), Sch 1.
11   Health and Safety (Consultation with Employees) Regulations 1996, SI 1996/1513, Sch 2 paras 1, 2 (amended by the Employment Rights (Dispute Resolution) Act 1998 s 1(2)(a)).
12   As to when a complaint is presented see PARAS 990 note 4, 1461.

13 Health and Safety (Consultation with Employees) Regulations 1996, SI 1996/1513, Sch 2 para 3. For the case law on the extension of time limits, especially in the context of the law of unfair dismissal, see PARA 1453.

14 The Health and Safety (Consultation with Employees) Regulations 1996, SI 1996/1513, Sch 2 para 3 is subject to Sch 2 para 3A: Sch 2 para 3 (amended by SI 2014/431). In working out when the three month time limit set by the Health and Safety (Consultation with Employees) Regulations 1996, SI 1996/1513, expires the period beginning with the day after Day A and ending with Day B is not to be counted: Sch 2 para 3A(2) (Sch 2 para 3A added by SI 2014/431). If the three month time limit set by the Health and Safety (Consultation with Employees) Regulations 1996, SI 1996/1513, Sch 2 para 3 would (if not extended by Sch 2 para 3A) expire during the period beginning with Day A and ending one month after Day B, the time limit expires instead at the end of that period: Sch 2 para 3A(3) (as so added). Day A is the day on which the worker concerned complies with the requirement in the Employment Tribunals Act 1996 s 18A(1) (see PARA 152) (requirement to contact ACAS before instituting proceedings) in relation to the matter in respect of which the proceedings are brought; and Day B is the day on which the worker concerned receives or, if earlier, is treated as receiving (by virtue of regulations made under s 18A(11)) the certificate issued under s 18A(4): Health and Safety (Consultation with Employees) Regulations 1996, SI 1996/1513, Sch 2 para 3A(1) (as so added). The power conferred on the employment tribunal by Sch 2 para 3 to extend the three month time limit set by Sch 2 para 3 is exercisable in relation to that time limit as extended by Sch 2 para 3A: Sch 2 para 3A(4) (as so added).

15 Health and Safety (Consultation with Employees) Regulations 1996, SI 1996/1513, Sch 2 para 4 (amended by the Employment Rights (Dispute Resolution) Act 1998 s 1(2)(a)).

16 Health and Safety (Consultation with Employees) Regulations 1996, SI 1996/1513, Sch 2 para 5 (amended by the Employment Rights (Dispute Resolution) Act 1998 s 1(2)(a)).

(9) SETTLEMENT OF INDUSTRIAL DISPUTES

(i) Industrial Disputes; in general

1211. Voluntary procedures for settlement of industrial disputes preferable. A basic principle of long standing in industrial relations is that voluntary resolution of a dispute is preferable to external adjudication. Voluntary procedures for such resolution are common where trade unions are recognised[1] but, being usually contained in collective agreements or arrangements, they are not normally legally binding[2] or entered into pursuant to any legal requirement or machinery. The law provides, where appropriate, that, in deciding whether to offer external conciliation, mediation or arbitration, the Advisory, Conciliation and Arbitration Service[3] should consider first the desirability of the parties using internal agreed procedures for settling the dispute[4].

1 See PARA 1094.
2 See PARA 1175.
3 As to the Advisory, Conciliation and Arbitration Service ('ACAS') see PARA 1213 et seq.
4 See PARAS 1218, 1220.

1212. Meaning of 'trade dispute'. When, as part of the reform of the law of industrial disputes, the definition of 'trade dispute' was narrowed by the Employment Act 1982[1], the existing, broader definition was retained for the purposes of establishing the jurisdiction of the Advisory, Conciliation and Arbitration Service[2] and courts of inquiry[3]. Thus, there are currently two statutory definitions of 'trade dispute' in the Trade Union and Labour Relations (Consolidation) Act 1992[4]. For the purposes of that jurisdiction, 'trade dispute' means a dispute[5] between employers and workers[6], or between workers and workers, which is connected with[7] one or more of the following matters:

(1) terms and conditions of employment[8], or the physical conditions in which any workers are required to work;

(2)   engagement or non-engagement, or termination or suspension of employment or the duties of employment, of one or more workers;

(3)   allocation of work or the duties of employment as between workers or groups of workers;

(4)   matters of discipline;

(5)   the membership or non-membership of a trade union[9] on the part of a worker;

(6)   facilities for officials[10] of trade unions; and

(7)   machinery for negotiation or consultation, and other procedures, relating to any of the above matters, including the recognition by employers or employers' associations[11] of the right of a trade union to represent workers in any such negotiation or consultation or in the carrying out of such procedures[12].

For these purposes, there is a trade dispute even though it relates to matters occurring outside Great Britain[13]. A dispute to which a trade union or employers' association is a party is to be treated for these purposes as a dispute to which workers or, as the case may be, employers are parties[14]; and a dispute between a Minister of the Crown and any workers is to be treated as a dispute between an employer and those workers, notwithstanding that he is not the employer of those workers, if the dispute relates to matters which:

(a)   have been referred for consideration by a joint body on which, by virtue of any provisions made by or under any enactment, that Minister is represented; or

(b)   cannot be settled without that Minister exercising a power conferred on him by or under an enactment[15].

1   The amended definition, applicable generally in the law relating to industrial disputes, now appears in the Trade Union and Labour Relations (Consolidation) Act 1992 s 244: see PARAS 1359–1361. The principal limitations enacted by the Employment Act 1982 (repealed) were: (1) the restriction to disputes between workers and their own employer; (2) the requirement that the dispute must 'relate wholly or mainly to' the enumerated topics; (3) the narrowing of the territorial requirement; and (4) the repeal of the provision deeming there to be a trade dispute if either a trade union or employers' association was involved. The actual subject matter of a dispute (see heads (1)–(7) in the text) was not, however, amended.

2   As to the Advisory, Conciliation and Arbitration Service ('ACAS') see PARA 1213 et seq.

3   Ie for the purposes of the Trade Union and Labour Relations (Consolidation) Act 1992 Pt IV (ss 178–218): see PARA 1217 et seq. The text and notes 5–15 below only consider aspects of this broader definition which differ from the narrower definition (considered in PARAS 1360–1361).

4   A further statutory definition applies for the purposes of social security and welfare benefits law: see the Jobseekers Act 1995 s 35(1), which defines a trade dispute as 'any dispute between employers and employees, or between employees and employees, which is connected with the employment or non-employment or the terms of employment or the conditions of employment of any persons, whether employees in the employment of the employer with whom the dispute arises, or not'. That definition is of historical interest because it is taken from the original formulation in the Trade Disputes Act 1906 (repealed). As to the effect of a trade dispute on social security and welfare benefits see PARA 1355 et seq.

5   The test whether there is a dispute is objective: *NWL Ltd v Woods, NWL Ltd v Nelson* [1979] 3 All ER 614, [1979] ICR 867, HL. Steps must have been taken towards raising the dispute (*Conway v Wade* [1909] AC 506, HL); but there is no need for the parties to have adopted rigid positions or to have entered into discussions (*Beetham v Trinidad Cement Ltd* [1960] AC 132, [1960] 1 All ER 274, PC; *Health Computing Ltd v Meek* [1981] ICR 24, [1980] IRLR 437).

6   For these purposes, 'worker', in relation to a dispute to which an employer is a party, includes any worker even if not employed by that employer: Trade Union and Labour Relations (Consolidation) Act 1992 s 218(5). As to the meaning of 'worker' generally see PARA 892. There can thus be a dispute between an employer and workers of a different employer: *Hadmor Productions Ltd v Hamilton* [1983] 1 AC 191, [1982] ICR 114, HL. The one matter which is not covered is a dispute between two employers: *Larkin v Long* [1915] AC 814, HL. As to the meaning of 'employer' see PARA 892.

7	This relatively loose causal requirement means that, provided that there is a connection with one of the enumerated matters, it is irrelevant if the predominant object of the dispute is political or personal: *NWL Ltd v Woods, NWL Ltd v Nelson* [1979] 3 All ER 614, [1979] ICR 867, HL; *Duport Steels Ltd v Sirs* [1980] 1 All ER 529, [1980] ICR 161, HL. It is only if there is no such causal connection at all that there is no trade dispute, eg where the action is purely personal or political: *JT Stratford & Son Ltd v Lindley* [1965] AC 269, [1964] 3 All ER 102, HL; *Torquay Hotels Co Ltd v Cousins* [1969] 2 Ch 106, [1969] 1 All ER 522, CA; *BBC v Hearn* [1978] 1 All ER 111, [1977] ICR 685, CA; *Express Newspapers Ltd v Keys* [1980] IRLR 247.

8	For these purposes, 'employment' includes any relationship whereby one person personally does work or performs services for another: Trade Union and Labour Relations (Consolidation) Act 1992 s 218(5). As to the meaning of 'employment' generally see PARA 892.

9	As to the meaning of 'trade union' see PARA 891.

10	As to the meaning of 'official', in relation to a trade union, see PARA 1018.

11	As to the meaning of 'employers' association' see PARA 1079.

12	Trade Union and Labour Relations (Consolidation) Act 1992 s 218(1). As to a consideration of heads (1)–(7) in the text see PARA 1361.

13	Trade Union and Labour Relations (Consolidation) Act 1992 s 218(3).

14	Trade Union and Labour Relations (Consolidation) Act 1992 s 218(4). This means that there can be a trade dispute, for these purposes, purely between representative organisations, without the need for direct involvement of individual workers: *Camellia Tanker Ltd SA v International Transport Workers' Federation* [1976] ICR 274, [1976] IRLR 190, CA; *NWL Ltd v Woods, NWL Ltd v Nelson* [1979] 3 All ER 614, [1979] ICR 867, HL.

15	Trade Union and Labour Relations (Consolidation) Act 1992 s 218(2).

(ii) Advisory, Conciliation and Arbitration Service ('ACAS')

1213. Constitution of ACAS; proceedings of the Council. The Advisory, Conciliation and Arbitration Service ('ACAS') is a body corporate of which the corporators are the members of its Council[1], which is to consist of a chairman and nine[2] ordinary members appointed by the Secretary of State after consultation (as to three of the members) with such organisations representing employers[3] as he considers appropriate and (as to a further three of the members) with such organisations representing workers[4] as he considers appropriate[5]. ACAS is directed by its Council[6].

The Secretary of State may appoint up to three deputy chairmen, who may be appointed from the ordinary members or in addition to them[7]. The members of the Council hold and must vacate office in accordance with their terms of appointment, subject to the following provisions[8]. Appointment as chairman, deputy chairman or ordinary member may be a full-time or part-time appointment; and the Secretary of State may, with the consent of the member concerned, vary the terms of his appointment as to whether his appointment is full-time or part-time[9]. A person may not be appointed to the Council for a term exceeding five years, but previous membership does not affect eligibility for reappointment[10]. ACAS must pay to the members of its Council such remuneration and travelling and other allowances as may be determined by the Secretary of State[11].

A member may at any time resign his membership, and the chairman or a deputy chairman may at any time resign his office as such, by notice in writing to the Secretary of State[12]. If the Secretary of State is satisfied that a member:

(1)	has been absent from meetings of the Council for a period longer than six consecutive months without the permission of the Council; or

(2)	has become bankrupt or has had a debt relief order[13] made in respect of him or has made an arrangement with his creditors; or

(3)	is incapacitated by physical or mental illness; or

(4)	is otherwise unable or unfit to discharge the functions of a member, the Secretary of State may declare his office as a member to be vacant and must notify the declaration in such manner as he thinks fit, whereupon the office becomes vacant[14].

The Council is to determine its own procedure, including the quorum necessary for its meetings[15]. If the Secretary of State has not appointed a deputy chairman, the Council may choose a member to act as chairman in the absence or incapacity of the chairman[16]. The validity of proceedings of the Council is not affected by any vacancy among the members of the Council or by any defect in the appointment of any of them[17].

The fixing of the common seal of ACAS must be authenticated by the signature of the secretary of ACAS[18] or some other person authorised by ACAS to act for that purpose; and a document purporting to be duly executed under that seal is to be received in evidence and is deemed to be so executed unless the contrary is proved[19].

1 Trade Union and Labour Relations (Consolidation) Act 1992 s 247(1), (2). The functions of ACAS, and those of its officers and servants (see PARA 1214), are exercised on behalf of the Crown, but not so as to make it subject to directions of any kind from any Minister of the Crown as to the manner in which it is to exercise its functions under any enactment: s 247(3). For the purposes of civil proceedings arising out of those functions, the Crown Proceedings Act 1947 (see CROWN PROCEEDINGS AND CROWN PRACTICE) applies to ACAS as if it were a government department: Trade Union and Labour Relations (Consolidation) Act 1992 s 247(4). Nothing in the Statistics of Trade Act 1947 s 9 (restriction on disclosure of information obtained under that Act) (see TRADE AND INDUSTRY vol 97 (2010) PARA 1017) prevents or penalises the disclosure to ACAS, for the purpose of the exercise of any of its functions, of information obtained under that Act by a government department: Trade Union and Labour Relations (Consolidation) Act 1992 s 247(5). As to the functions of ACAS see PARA 1217 et seq. ACAS is subject to investigation by the Parliamentary Commissioner for Administration: see the Parliamentary Commissioner Act 1967 Sch 2 (substituted by SI 2011/2986). As to such investigations see CONSTITUTIONAL AND ADMINISTRATIVE LAW vol 20 (2014) PARAS 634–637.

2 The Secretary of State may, if he thinks fit, appoint a further two ordinary members who are to be appointed so as to take office at the same time: Trade Union and Labour Relations (Consolidation) Act 1992 s 248(3). As to the Secretary of State see PARA 5 note 21.

3 As to the meaning of 'employer' see PARA 892. As to employers' associations see PARA 1079 et seq.

4 As to the meaning of 'worker' see PARA 892.

5 Trade Union and Labour Relations (Consolidation) Act 1992 s 248(1), (2). Where further members are appointed under s 248(3) (see note 2), similar consultation must take place before those appointments are made: see s 248(3). All members of the Council of ACAS are disqualified for membership of the House of Commons: see the House of Commons Disqualification Act 1975 s 1(1), Sch 1 Pt II; and PARLIAMENT vol 78 (2010) PARA 908.

6 Trade Union and Labour Relations (Consolidation) Act 1992 s 248(1).

7 Trade Union and Labour Relations (Consolidation) Act 1992 s 248(4).

8 Trade Union and Labour Relations (Consolidation) Act 1992 s 249(1).

9 Trade Union and Labour Relations (Consolidation) Act 1992 s 249(2) (amended by the Trade Union Reform and Employment Rights Act 1993 Sch 10).

10 Trade Union and Labour Relations (Consolidation) Act 1992 s 249(3).

11 Trade Union and Labour Relations (Consolidation) Act 1992 s 250(1). The Secretary of State may pay, or make provision for payment, to or in respect of a member of the Council such pension, allowance or gratuity on death or retirement as he may determine with the approval of the Treasury: s 250(2), (4). As to the Treasury see CONSTITUTIONAL AND ADMINISTRATIVE LAW vol 20 (2014) PARA 262 et seq.

12 Trade Union and Labour Relations (Consolidation) Act 1992 s 249(4). A deputy chairman appointed in addition to the ordinary members of the Council ceases, on resigning his office as deputy chairman, to be a member of the Council: s 249(4).

13 Ie under the Insolvency Act 1986 Pt VIIA (ss 251A–251X): see BANKRUPTCY AND INDIVIDUAL INSOLVENCY vol 5 (2013) PARA 91 et seq.

14 Trade Union and Labour Relations (Consolidation) Act 1992 s 249(5) (amended by SI 2012/2404). If the chairman or a deputy chairman ceases to be a member of the Council, he also ceases to be chairman or, as the case may be, a deputy chairman: Trade Union and Labour

Relations (Consolidation) Act 1992 s 249(5). Where a person ceases to be a member of the Council otherwise than on the expiry of his term of office and it appears to the Secretary of State that there are special circumstances which make it right for him to receive compensation, the Secretary of State may make him a payment of such amount as he may determine with the approval of the Treasury: s 250(3), (4). Section 250(3) refers to 'the holder of the Council' but it is submitted that this is a drafting error and should read 'a member of the Council': see the Employment Protection Act 1975 s 10(3), Sch 1 paras 28(a), 31 (repealed), from which the Trade Union and Labour Relations (Consolidation) Act 1992 s 250(3) is derived. Cf s 262(3) (cited in PARA 1226 note 15), where a similar drafting error occurs.

14 Trade Union and Labour Relations (Consolidation) Act 1992 s 248(5).
15 Trade Union and Labour Relations (Consolidation) Act 1992 s 248(6).
16 Trade Union and Labour Relations (Consolidation) Act 1992 s 248(7).
17 As to the power to appoint a secretary see PARA 1214.
18 Trade Union and Labour Relations (Consolidation) Act 1992 s 251(5).

1214. ACAS offices, secretary, officers and staff. The Advisory, Conciliation and Arbitration Service[1] ('ACAS') may, with the approval of the Secretary of State, appoint a secretary[2] and such other officers and staff as it may determine[3]. The consent of the Secretary of State, which may not be given without the approval of the Treasury[4], is required as to their terms and conditions of service and as to the numbers and manners of appointment of the officers and staff[5].

ACAS must maintain offices in such of the major centres of employment in Great Britain as it thinks fit for the purposes of discharging its functions under any enactment[6].

ACAS must designate some of its officers to perform the functions of conciliation officers under any enactment, whenever passed, relating to matters which are or could be the subject of proceedings before an employment tribunal[7].

The Secretary of State must pay to ACAS such sums as are approved by the Treasury and as he considers appropriate for the purpose of enabling ACAS to perform its functions[8]; and ACAS must pay to the Treasury, at such times in each accounting year as may be determined by the Treasury, sums of such amounts as may be so determined as being equivalent to the increase in that year of such liabilities of the Secretary of State as are attributable to the provision of pensions, allowances or gratuities to or in respect of persons who are or have been in the service of ACAS in so far as that increase results from the service of those persons during that accounting year and to the expense to be incurred in administering those pensions, allowances or gratuities[9].

1 As to the constitution of ACAS see PARA 1213; and as to the functions of ACAS see PARA 1217 et seq.
2 Trade Union and Labour Relations (Consolidation) Act 1992 s 251(1).
3 Trade Union and Labour Relations (Consolidation) Act 1992 s 251(2).
4 Trade Union and Labour Relations (Consolidation) Act 1992 s 251(3).
5 See the Trade Union and Labour Relations (Consolidation) Act 1992 s 251(1), (2).
6 Trade Union and Labour Relations (Consolidation) Act 1992 s 247(6). As to the prohibition of disclosure of information held by ACAS relating to a worker, an employer of a worker or a trade union see PARA 1215.
7 Trade Union and Labour Relations (Consolidation) Act 1992 s 211(1) (amended by the Employment Rights (Dispute Resolution) Act 1998 s 1(2)(a)). References in any such enactment to a conciliation officer are to an officer designated under the Trade Union and Labour Relations (Consolidation) Act 1992 s 211: s 211(2). These functions are usually referred to as 'individual conciliation' to distinguish such conciliation from collective conciliation in trade disputes (see PARA 1218); as to their exercise in the context of unfair dismissal law see PARA 809 et seq. Similar rules apply elsewhere, wherever such functions are given to ACAS: see the Employment Tribunals Act 1996 s 18; and see PARAS 152–153.
8 Trade Union and Labour Relations (Consolidation) Act 1992 s 252(1). ACAS may pay to: (1) persons appointed under s 210(2) (conciliation) (see PARA 1218) who are not officers or servants

of ACAS; and (2) arbitrators appointed by ACAS under any enactment, such fees and travelling and other allowances as may be determined by the Secretary of State with the approval of the Treasury: s 252(2). As to the Treasury see CONSTITUTIONAL AND ADMINISTRATIVE LAW vol 20 (2014) PARA 262 et seq.

9   Trade Union and Labour Relations (Consolidation) Act 1992 s 251(4).

1215. Prohibition on disclosure of information held by ACAS. Information held by the Advisory, Conciliation and Arbitration Service[1] ('ACAS') must not be disclosed if the information relates to a worker[2], an employer[3] of a worker or a trade union[4] (a 'relevant person'), and is held by ACAS in connection with the provision of a service by ACAS[5] or its officers[6]. This does not prohibit the disclosure of information if:

(1)   the disclosure is made for the purpose of enabling or assisting ACAS to carry out any of its functions under the Trade Union and Labour Relations (Consolidation) Act 1992;

(2)   the disclosure is made for the purpose of enabling or assisting an officer of ACAS to carry out the functions of a conciliation officer[7] under any enactment;

(3)   the disclosure is made for the purpose of enabling or assisting a person appointed by ACAS[8] or an arbitrator or arbiter appointed by ACAS under any enactment to carry out functions specified in the appointment;

(4)   the disclosure is made for the purposes of a criminal investigation or criminal proceedings, whether or not within the United Kingdom[9];

(5)   the disclosure is made in order to comply with a court order;

(6)   the disclosure is made in a manner that ensures that no relevant person to whom the information relates can be identified; or

(7)   the disclosure is made with the consent of each relevant person to whom the information relates[10].

Heads (1) to (7) above do not, however, authorise the making of a disclosure which contravenes the Data Protection Act 1998[11].

A person who discloses information in contravention of these provisions commits an offence and is liable on summary conviction to a fine not exceeding level 5 on the standard scale[12]. Proceedings in England and Wales for such an offence under this section may be instituted only with the consent of the Director of Public Prosecutions[13].

1   As to the constitution of ACAS see PARA 1213; and as to the functions of ACAS see PARA 1217 et seq.
2   As to the meaning of 'worker' see PARA 892.
3   As to the meaning of 'employer' see PARA 892.
4   As to the meaning of 'trade union' see PARA 891.
5   For these purposes, information held by a person appointed by ACAS under the Trade Union and Labour Relations (Consolidation) Act 1992 s 210(2) (conciliation: see PARA 1218) in connection with functions specified in the appointment, or an arbitrator or arbiter appointed by ACAS under any enactment in connection with functions specified in the appointment, is information that is held by ACAS in connection with the provision of a service by ACAS: s 251B(6) (s 251B added by the Enterprise and Regulatory Reform Act 2013 s 10).
6   Trade Union and Labour Relations (Consolidation) Act 1992 s 251B(1) (as added: see note 5). As to the officers of ACAS see PARA 1214.
7   As to conciliation officers see PARA 1214.
8   Ie under the Trade Union and Labour Relations (Consolidation) Act 1992 210(2): see PARA 1218.
9   As to the meaning of 'United Kingdom' see PARA 2 note 12.
10   Trade Union and Labour Relations (Consolidation) Act 1992 s 251B(2) (as added: see note 5).

11 Trade Union and Labour Relations (Consolidation) Act 1992 s 251B(3) (as added: see note 5). As to the Data Protection Act 1998 see CONFIDENCE AND INFORMATIONAL PRIVACY vol 19 (2011) PARA 95 et seq.

12 Trade Union and Labour Relations (Consolidation) Act 1992 s 251B(4) (as added: see note 5). As to the standard scale see SENTENCING AND DISPOSITION OF OFFENDERS vol 92 (2010) PARA 142.

13 Trade Union and Labour Relations (Consolidation) Act 1992 s 251B(5) (as added: see note 5).

1216. ACAS annual report and accounts. As soon as practicable after the end of each financial year[1], the Advisory, Conciliation and Arbitration Service[2] ('ACAS') must make a report to the Secretary of State on its activities during that year. The Secretary of State must lay a copy of the report before each House of Parliament and arrange for it to be published[3].

ACAS must keep proper accounts and proper records in relation to the accounts and must prepare in respect of each financial year a statement of accounts, in such form as the Secretary of State, with the approval of the Treasury, may direct[4]. Not later than 30 November following the end of the financial year to which the statement relates, ACAS must send copies of the statement to the Secretary of State and to the Comptroller and Auditor General[5]; and the Comptroller and Auditor General must examine, certify and report on each such statement and must lay a copy of the statement and of his report before each House of Parliament[6].

1 For these purposes, 'financial year' means the 12 months ending with 31 March: Trade Union and Labour Relations (Consolidation) Act 1992 s 272.

2 As to the constitution of ACAS see PARA 1213; as to ACAS officers and staff see PARA 1214; and as to the duties and functions of ACAS see PARA 1217 et seq.

3 Trade Union and Labour Relations (Consolidation) Act 1992 s 253(1) (amended by the Employment Relations Act 1999 s 27(1)).

4 Trade Union and Labour Relations (Consolidation) Act 1992 s 253(2).

5 Trade Union and Labour Relations (Consolidation) Act 1992 s 253(3). As to the Comptroller and Auditor General see CONSTITUTIONAL AND ADMINISTRATIVE LAW vol 20 (2014) PARAS 494–496.

6 Trade Union and Labour Relations (Consolidation) Act 1992 s 253(4).

1217. General duty of ACAS. It is the general duty of the Advisory, Conciliation and Arbitration Service[1] ('ACAS') to promote the improvement of industrial relations[2].

1 As to the constitution of ACAS see PARA 1213; and as to its specific powers and duties see PARA 1218 et seq.

2 Trade Union and Labour Relations (Consolidation) Act 1992 s 209 (amended by the Employment Relations Act 1999 ss 26, 44, Sch 9 Table 5). The original formulation of this duty had included the duty to encourage the extension of collective bargaining and the development and reform of collective bargaining; that element was repealed by the Trade Union Reform and Employment Rights Act 1993 s 43(1), which substituted the wording 'in particular by exercising its functions in relation to the settlement of trade disputes by means of conciliation and arbitration'. This wording was then repealed by the Employment Relations Act 1999 s 26, on the basis that it was too restrictive and undervalued the functions of ACAS in relation to advice (as to which see PARA 1221).

1218. ACAS's power to assist with the settlement of disputes. Where a trade dispute[1] exists or is apprehended, the Advisory, Conciliation and Arbitration Service[2] ('ACAS') may, at the request of one or more parties to the dispute or otherwise, offer the parties to the dispute its assistance with a view to bringing about a settlement[3]. The assistance may be by way of conciliation or by other means, and may include the appointment of a person other than an officer or servant of ACAS[4] to offer assistance to the parties to the dispute with a view to bringing about a settlement[5]. In exercising such functions, ACAS must have regard to the desirability of encouraging the parties to the dispute to use any appropriate agreed procedures for negotiation or the settlement of disputes[6].

1   As to the meaning of 'trade dispute' see PARA 1212.
2   As to the constitution and general duty of ACAS see PARAS 1213, 1217.
3   Trade Union and Labour Relations (Consolidation) Act 1992 s 210(1). As to individual conciliation see PARAS 152–153. As to the information required by ACAS for the purposes of settling recognition disputes see s 210A; and PARA 1219.
4   As to ACAS officers and staff see PARA 1214.
5   Trade Union and Labour Relations (Consolidation) Act 1992 s 210(2). As to the power to pay fees and allowances to persons so appointed see PARA 1214 note 8. Section 210(2) is the basis of the practice of mediation, ie the appointment of an independent person to make recommendations; this is more formal than conciliation, but falls short of an arbitration by which the parties expect to be bound. As to ACAS's power to arrange arbitration see PARA 1220.
6   Trade Union and Labour Relations (Consolidation) Act 1992 s 210(3).

1219.   Information required by ACAS for purposes of settling recognition disputes.   Where the Advisory, Conciliation and Arbitration Service[1] ('ACAS') is exercising its functions[2] with a view to bringing about a settlement of a recognition dispute[3], the parties[4] to the recognition dispute may jointly request ACAS or a person nominated by ACAS to (1) hold a ballot of the workers involved in the dispute; (2) ascertain the union membership of the workers involved in the dispute[5].

At any time after ACAS has received such a request it may require any party to the recognition dispute to supply ACAS with specified[6] information concerning the workers involved in the dispute, and to do so within such period as it may specify[7]. The recipient of such a requirement must, within the specified period, supply ACAS with such of the specified information as is in the recipient's possession[8].

1   As to the constitution and general duty of ACAS see PARAS 1213, 1217 respectively. For these purposes, references to ACAS include references to a person nominated by ACAS, and anything done by such a person is to be regarded as done in the exercise of the functions of ACAS mentioned in the Trade Union and Labour Relations (Consolidation) Act 1992 s 210A(1): s 210A(3) (s 210A added by the Employment Relations Act 2004 s 21).
2   Ie its functions under the Trade Union and Labour Relations (Consolidation) Act 1992 s 210: see PARA 1218.
3   'Recognition dispute' means a trade dispute between employers and workers which is connected wholly or partly with the recognition by employers or employers' associations of the right of a trade union to represent workers in negotiations, consultations or other procedures relating to any of the matters mentioned in the Trade Union and Labour Relations (Consolidation) Act 1992 s 218(1)(a)–(f) (see PARA 1212): s 210A(10) (as added: see note 1). As to the meaning of 'employer' see PARA 892; as to the meaning of 'employers' association' see PARA 1079; and as to the meaning of 'trade union' see PARA 891. 'Workers' has the meaning given in s 218(5) (see PARA 1212 note 6): s 210A(10) (as so added).
4   'Party', in relation to a recognition dispute, means each of the employers, employers' associations and trade unions involved in the dispute: Trade Union and Labour Relations (Consolidation) Act 1992 s 210A(10) (as added: see note 1).
5   Trade Union and Labour Relations (Consolidation) Act 1992 s 210A(1), (2) (as added: see note 1). Such a request may be withdrawn by any party to the recognition dispute at any time and, if it is withdrawn, ACAS must take no further steps to hold the ballot or to ascertain the union membership of the workers involved in the dispute: s 210A(7) (as so added). Nothing in s 210A requires ACAS to comply with such a request: s 210A(9) (as so added).
6   'Specified' means specified in a requirement under the Trade Union and Labour Relations (Consolidation) Act 1992 s 210A: s 210A(10) (as added: see note 1).
7   Trade Union and Labour Relations (Consolidation) Act 1992 s 210A(3) (as added: see note 1). ACAS may impose such a requirement only if it considers that it is necessary to do so for the exercise of the functions mentioned in s 210A(1) and in order to enable or assist it to comply with the request: s 210A(5) (as so added).

8   Trade Union and Labour Relations (Consolidation) Act 1992 s 210A(6) (as added: see note 1). If a party to a recognition dispute fails to comply with s 210A(6), ACAS must take no further steps to hold the ballot or to ascertain the union membership of the workers involved in the dispute: s 210A(8) (as so added).

1220. ACAS's power to arrange arbitration. Where a trade dispute[1] exists or is apprehended, the Advisory, Conciliation and Arbitration Service[2] ('ACAS') may, at the request of one or more of the parties and with the consent of all the parties to the dispute[3], refer all or any of the matters to which the dispute relates for settlement to the arbitration of one or more persons appointed by ACAS for that purpose, not being officers or employees of ACAS[4], or the Central Arbitration Committee (the 'CAC')[5].

In exercising these functions, ACAS must consider the likelihood of the dispute being settled by conciliation[6]. Where there exist appropriate agreed procedures for negotiation or the settlement of disputes, ACAS must not refer a matter for settlement to arbitration unless either:

(1)   those procedures have been used and have failed to result in a settlement; or

(2)   there is, in the opinion of ACAS, a special reason which justifies arbitration as an alternative to those procedures[7].

In addition to its general arbitral powers, ACAS is specifically empowered to prepare a scheme for the use of arbitration in flexible working and unfair dismissal cases (and any other type of case specified by the Secretary of State by order), as an alternative to a formal complaint to an employment tribunal[8].

1   As to the meaning of 'trade dispute' see PARA 1212.
2   As to the constitution and general duty of ACAS see PARAS 1213, 1217; as to ACAS officers and staff see PARA 1214; and as to the power to pay fees and allowances to arbitrators so appointed see PARA 1214 note 8.
3   This consent is important in practice because, although the arbitration award is not legally binding (not being under the Arbitration Act 1996: see note 5), ACAS will not arrange arbitration unless both parties agree to be bound in honour to accept the award.
4   Where a matter is so referred to arbitration, if more than one arbitrator is appointed, ACAS must appoint one of them to act as chairman, and the award may be published if ACAS so decides and all the parties consent: Trade Union and Labour Relations (Consolidation) Act 1992 s 212(4).
5   Trade Union and Labour Relations (Consolidation) Act 1992 s 212(1). The Arbitration Act 1996 Pt I (ss 1–84) (see **ARBITRATION**) does not apply to such an arbitration: Trade Union and Labour Relations (Consolidation) Act 1992 s 212(5) (amended by the Arbitration Act 1996 Sch 3 para 56).

     As to the Central Arbitration Committee see PARA 1226 et seq. By virtue of the Trade Union and Labour Relations (Consolidation) Act 1992 s 264(3), decisions of the CAC in the exercise of any of its functions must be published: see PARA 1230. In practice, however, this is not construed by the CAC as applying to purely consensual arbitrations under s 212, which are only published with the consent of the parties.

     ACAS may also, in accordance with any dismissal procedures agreement (within the meaning of the Employment Rights Act 1996: see PARA 150 note 9), refer any matter to the arbitration of a person appointed by ACAS for the purpose, not being an officer or employee of ACAS: Trade Union and Labour Relations (Consolidation) Act 1992 s 212B (added by the Employment Rights (Dispute Resolution) Act 1998 Sch 1 para 7).
6   Trade Union and Labour Relations (Consolidation) Act 1992 s 212(2). As to conciliation see s 210; and PARA 1218.
7   Trade Union and Labour Relations (Consolidation) Act 1992 s 212(3).
8   See the Trade Union and Labour Relations (Consolidation) Act 1992 s 212A; and PARA 824. As to arbitration schemes prepared under s 212A see the ACAS Arbitration Scheme (Great Britain) Order 2004, SI 2004/753; and the ACAS (Flexible Working) Arbitration Scheme (Great Britain) Order 2004, SI 2004/2333 (see PARA 109 note 4).

1221. ACAS's power to give advice. The Advisory, Conciliation and Arbitration Service[1] ('ACAS') may, on request or otherwise, give employers[2], employers' associations[3], workers[4] and trade unions[5] such advice as it thinks appropriate on matters concerned with or affecting or likely to affect industrial relations[6]. It may also publish general advice on matters concerned with or affecting or likely to affect industrial relations[7].

1 As to the constitution and general duty of ACAS see PARAS 1213, 1217.
2 As to the meaning of 'employer' see PARA 892.
3 As to the meaning of 'employers' association' see PARA 1079.
4 As to the meaning of 'worker' see PARA 892.
5 As to the meaning of 'trade union' see PARA 891.
6 Trade Union and Labour Relations (Consolidation) Act 1992 s 213(1) (s 213 substituted by the Trade Union Reform and Employment Rights Act 1993 s 43(2)).
7 Trade Union and Labour Relations (Consolidation) Act 1992 s 213(2) (as substituted: see note 6). ACAS also has power to publish Codes of Practice, in relation to which a special procedure applies: see PARA 1223.

1222. ACAS's power to conduct inquiries. The Advisory, Conciliation and Arbitration Service[1] ('ACAS') may, if it thinks fit, inquire into any question relating to industrial relations generally or into industrial relations in any particular industry or in any particular undertaking or part of an undertaking[2].

The findings of such an inquiry, together with any advice given by ACAS in connection with those findings, may be published by ACAS if it appears to ACAS that publication is desirable for the improvement of industrial relations, either generally or in relation to the specific question inquired into, and if, after sending a draft of the findings to all parties appearing to be concerned and taking account of their views, it thinks fit[3].

1 As to the constitution and general duty of ACAS see PARAS 1213, 1217.
2 Trade Union and Labour Relations (Consolidation) Act 1992 s 214(1).
3 Trade Union and Labour Relations (Consolidation) Act 1992 s 214(2).

1223. ACAS's power to issue and revise Codes of Practice. The Advisory, Conciliation and Arbitration Service[1] ('ACAS') may issue Codes of Practice containing such practical guidance as it thinks fit for the purpose of promoting the improvement of industrial relations or for purposes connected with trade union learning representatives[2]; and it must, in particular, provide practical guidance, in one or more Codes of Practice, on the following matters:

(1) the time off to be permitted by an employer[3] to a trade union official[4] in accordance with the statutory right to time off for carrying out trade union duties[5];

(2) the time off to be permitted by an employer to a trade union member in accordance with the statutory right to time off for trade union activities[6]; and

(3) the information to be disclosed by employers to trade union representatives in accordance with the statutory rights[7] to disclosure of information for the purposes of collective bargaining[8].

ACAS may from time to time revise the whole or any part of a Code of Practice issued by it and issue that revised Code[9].

Where ACAS proposes to issue a Code of Practice, or a revised Code, it must prepare and publish a draft of the Code, must consider any representations made to it about the draft and may modify the draft accordingly[10]. If ACAS determines to proceed with the draft, it must transmit it to the Secretary of State who, if he approves of it, must lay it before both Houses of Parliament and, if he does not approve of it, must publish details of his reasons for withholding approval[11]. If, within the period of 40 days[12] beginning with the day on which the draft is laid before Parliament, either House so resolves, no further proceedings may be taken on the draft (but without prejudice to the laying before Parliament of a new draft), but, if no such resolution is passed, ACAS must issue the Code in the form of the draft[13]. In the case, however, of a Code containing certain practical guidance[14] the Code must not be issued unless the draft has been approved by a resolution of each House of Parliament; and, if it is so approved, ACAS must issue the Code in the form of the draft[15].

A Code of Practice issued by ACAS may be revised by it in accordance with the following provisions for the purpose of bringing it into conformity with subsequent statutory provisions[16] by the making of consequential amendments and the omission of obsolete passages[17]. Where ACAS proposes so to revise a Code, it must transmit a draft of the revised Code to the Secretary of State, who must lay the draft before each House of Parliament, if he approves of it, and must publish details of his reasons for withholding approval, if he does not approve of it[18]. If, within the period of 40 days[19] beginning with the day on which the draft is laid before Parliament either House so resolves, no further proceedings may be taken on the draft (but without prejudice to the laying before Parliament of a new draft), but, if no such resolution is passed, ACAS must issue the Code in the form of the draft[20].

A Code of Practice, or a revised Code, so issued comes into effect on such day as the Secretary of State may appoint by order made by statutory instrument[21]. A Code of Practice issued by ACAS may, at its request, be revoked by the Secretary of State by such an order[22]. If ACAS requests the Secretary of State to revoke a Code and he decides not to do so, he must publish details of his reasons for his decision[23].

If ACAS is of the opinion that the provisions of a Code of Practice to be issued by it will supersede the whole or part of a Code previously issued by it or by the Secretary of State[24], it must state in the new Code that, on the day on which the new Code comes into effect, the old Code or a specified part of it ceases to have effect[25].

1 As to the constitution and general duty of ACAS see PARAS 1213, 1217.
2 Trade Union and Labour Relations (Consolidation) Act 1992 s 199(1) (amended by the Employment Act 2002 s 43(1), (7)). As to trade union learning representatives see PARA 1065. As to the effect of failure to comply with a Code of Practice see PARA 1224; and see also PARAS 1232–1234. As to the revised ACAS Code of Practice on Disciplinary and Grievance Procedures see PARAS 698, 700 et seq.
3 As to the meaning of 'employer' see PARA 892.
4 As to the meaning of 'official', in relation to a trade union, see PARA 1018; and as to the meaning of 'trade union' see PARA 891.
5 Ie in accordance with the Trade Union and Labour Relations (Consolidation) Act 1992 s 168: see PARAS 1065, 1068. The guidance must include guidance on the circumstances in which a trade union official is to be permitted to take time off under s 168 in respect of duties connected with industrial action: s 199(3). See the Code of Practice on Time Off for Trade Union Duties and Activities: and PARA 1067.
6 Ie in accordance with the Trade Union and Labour Relations (Consolidation) Act 1992 s 170: see PARA 1066. The guidance must include guidance on the question whether, and the circumstances in which, a trade union member is to be permitted to take time off under s 170 for trade union activities connected with industrial action: s 199(3).
7 Ie in accordance with the Trade Union and Labour Relations (Consolidation) Act 1992 ss 181, 182: see PARA 1179 et seq.
8 Trade Union and Labour Relations (Consolidation) Act 1992 s 199(2). As to the meaning of 'collective bargaining' see PARA 1093.

9 Trade Union and Labour Relations (Consolidation) Act 1992 s 199(4). See also the text and notes 16–21.
10 Trade Union and Labour Relations (Consolidation) Act 1992 s 200(1). See note 21.
11 Trade Union and Labour Relations (Consolidation) Act 1992 s 200(2). See note 21. As to the Secretary of State see PARA 5 note 21.
12 In reckoning the period of 40 days, no account is to be taken of any period during which Parliament is dissolved or prorogued or during which both Houses are adjourned for more than four days: Trade Union and Labour Relations (Consolidation) Act 1992 s 200(4). If copies of the draft are laid before the two Houses of Parliament on different days, the period begins with the later of the two days: s 200(4)(a). See note 21.
13 Trade Union and Labour Relations (Consolidation) Act 1992 s 200(4). See note 21.
14 Ie practice advice (1) on the time off to be permitted to a trade union learning representative in accordance with the Trade Union and Labour Relations (Consolidation) Act 1992 s 168A (time off for training and carrying out functions as a learning representative) (see PARA 1065); (2) on the training that is sufficient to enable a trade union learning representative to carry on the activities mentioned in s 168A(2) (activities for which time off is to be permitted) (see PARA 1065); or (3) on any of the matters referred to in s 199(2) (see heads (1)–(3) in the text).
15 Trade Union and Labour Relations (Consolidation) Act 1992 s 200(3) (amended by the Employment Act 2002 s 43(1), (8)). This procedure does not, however, apply where a revised Code is issued under the Trade Union and Labour Relations (Consolidation) Act 1992 s 201: see the text and notes 16–21.
16 For these purposes, 'subsequent statutory provisions' means provisions made by or under an Act of Parliament and coming into force after the Code was issued, whether before or after the commencement of the Trade Union and Labour Relations (Consolidation) Act 1992: s 201(1).
17 Trade Union and Labour Relations (Consolidation) Act 1992 s 201(1).
18 Trade Union and Labour Relations (Consolidation) Act 1992 s 201(2).
19 In reckoning the period of 40 days, no account is to be taken of any period during which Parliament is dissolved or prorogued or during which both Houses are adjourned for more than four days: Trade Union and Labour Relations (Consolidation) Act 1992 s 201(3). If copies of the draft are laid before the two Houses of Parliament on different days, the period begins with the later of the two days: s 201(3).
20 Trade Union and Labour Relations (Consolidation) Act 1992 s 201(3), (4).
21 Trade Union and Labour Relations (Consolidation) Act 1992 ss 200(5), 201(4). The order may contain such transitional provisions and savings as appear to the Secretary of State to be appropriate: ss 200(5), 201(4). The following orders have been made under ss 199, 200: (1) the Employment Protection Code of Practice (Disclosure of Information) Order 1998, SI 1998/45 (see PARA 1180 et seq); (2) the Employment Protection Code of Practice (Time Off for Trade Union Duties and Activities) Order 2009, SI 2009/3223 (see PARA 1067); (3) the Employment Code of Practice (Disciplinary and Grievance Procedures) Order 2009, SI 2009/771 (see PARA 701 et seq); (4) the Employment Code of Practice (Settlement Agreements) Order 2013, SI 2013/1665 (see PARA 804 note 4). The power in the Trade Union and Labour Relations (Consolidation) Act 1992 s 199(1) (see the text and notes 1–2) is expressly extended to cover questions of access during recognition or derecognition ballots: see Sch A1 para 26(8), (9) and PARA 1120; Sch A1 para 118(8), (9) and PARA 1157.
22 Trade Union and Labour Relations (Consolidation) Act 1992 s 202(1). The order may contain such transitional provisions and savings as appear to the Secretary of State to be appropriate: s 202(1). Such an order must not be made unless a draft of it has been laid before and approved by resolution of each House of Parliament: s 202(3). At the date at which this volume states the law no such order had been made but, by virtue of Sch 3 para 1(2) (see PARA 891 note 1) and the Interpretation Act 1978 s 17(2)(b), the Employment Codes of Practice (Revocation) Order 1991, SI 1991/1264 (revoking Codes of Practice relating to industrial relations and closed shop agreements and arrangements) has effect as if so made.
23 Trade Union and Labour Relations (Consolidation) Act 1992 s 202(2).
24 As to the Secretary of State's power to issue Codes of Practice see PARA 1231.
25 Trade Union and Labour Relations (Consolidation) Act 1992 s 208(1). This provision does not affect any transitional provisions or savings made by the order bringing the new Code into effect: s 208(3).

1224. Effect of failure to comply with a Code of Practice issued by ACAS. A failure on the part of any person to observe any provision of a Code of Practice issued by the Advisory, Conciliation and Arbitration Service ('ACAS')[1] does not of itself render him liable to any proceedings[2]. Any such Code is, however, admissible in evidence in any proceedings before an employment tribunal[3] or before the Central Arbitration Committee (the 'CAC')[4]; and any provision of the Code which appears to the tribunal or the CAC to be relevant to any question arising in the proceedings must be taken into account in determining that question[5].

An unreasonable failure by the employer or employee to comply with a relevant Code of Practice may result in the adjustment of an employment tribunal award[6].

1   Ie a Code of Practice issued under the Trade Union and Labour Relations (Consolidation) Act 1992 Pt IV Ch III (ss 199–208): see PARA 1223. As to the constitution and general duty of ACAS see PARAS 1213, 1217. As to the revised ACAS Code of Practice on Disciplinary and Grievance Procedures see PARA 701 et seq.
2   Trade Union and Labour Relations (Consolidation) Act 1992 s 207(1). See also PARAS 1232–1234.
3   As to employment tribunals see PARA 1399 et seq.
4   As to the Central Arbitration Committee see PARA 1226 et seq.
5   Trade Union and Labour Relations (Consolidation) Act 1992 s 207(2) (amended by the Employment Rights (Dispute Resolution) Act 1998 s 1(2)(a)).
6   See the Trade Union and Labour Relations (Consolidation) Act 1992 s 207A; and PARA 1234.

1225. Fees for the exercise of functions by ACAS. The Advisory, Conciliation and Arbitration Service[1] ('ACAS') may, in any case in which it thinks it appropriate to do so, charge a fee for exercising a function in relation to[2] any person[3].

The Secretary of State may direct ACAS to charge fees, in accordance with the direction, for exercising any function specified in the direction, but he must not give such a direction without consulting ACAS[4]. A direction must specify whether fees are to be charged, in respect of the exercise of any specified function, at the full economic cost level[5] or at a level less than the full economic cost[6] but not less than a specified proportion or percentage of that cost[7].

No liability to pay a fee so charged arises on the part of any person unless ACAS has notified that person that a fee may or will be charged[8].

1   As to the constitution and general duty of ACAS see PARAS 1213, 1217; and as to the functions of ACAS see PARA 1218 et seq.
2   For these purposes, a function is exercised 'in relation to' a person who avails himself of the benefit of its exercise, whether or not he requested its exercise and whether the function is such as to be exercisable in relation to a particular person only or in relation to persons generally; and, where a function is exercised in relation to two or more persons, the fee chargeable for its exercise is to be apportioned among them as ACAS thinks appropriate: Trade Union and Labour Relations (Consolidation) Act 1992 s 251A(8) (s 251A added by the Trade Union Reform and Employment Rights Act 1993 s 44).
3   Trade Union and Labour Relations (Consolidation) Act 1992 s 251A(1) (as added: see note 2).
4   Trade Union and Labour Relations (Consolidation) Act 1992 s 251A(2) (as added: see note 2). Such a direction may require ACAS to charge fees in respect of the exercise of a function only in specified descriptions of case: s 251A(3) (as so added).
5   Where a direction requires fees to be charged at the full economic cost level, ACAS must fix the fee for the case at an amount estimated to be sufficient to cover the administrative costs of ACAS of exercising the function, including an appropriate sum in respect of general staff costs and overheads: Trade Union and Labour Relations (Consolidation) Act 1992 s 251A(5) (as added: see note 2).
6   Where a direction requires fees to be charged at a level less than the full economic cost, ACAS must fix the fee for the case at such amount, not being less than the proportion or percentage specified in the direction, as it thinks appropriate, computing the cost in the same way as under the Trade Union and Labour Relations (Consolidation) Act 1992 s 251A(5) (see note 5): s 251A(6) (as added: see note 2).
7   Trade Union and Labour Relations (Consolidation) Act 1992 s 251A(4) (as added: see note 2).
8   Trade Union and Labour Relations (Consolidation) Act 1992 s 251A(7) (as added: see note 2)

(iii) Central Arbitration Committee ('CAC')

1226. Constitution of the CAC. The Central Arbitration Committee (the 'CAC') was established by the Employment Protection Act 1975[1] and continues in existence under the Trade Union and Labour Relations (Consolidation) Act 1992[2]. The CAC is to consist of members appointed by the Secretary of State, who is to appoint a member as chairman, and may appoint a member as deputy chairman or members as deputy chairmen[3]. The Secretary of State may appoint as members only persons experienced in industrial relations, and they are to include some persons whose experience is as representatives of employers and some whose experience is as representatives of workers[4]. Before making an appointment, the Secretary of State must consult the Advisory, Conciliation and Arbitration Service ('ACAS')[5] and may consult other persons[6].

The members of the CAC hold and must vacate office in accordance with their terms of appointment[7]; and the Secretary of State may, with the consent of the member concerned, vary the terms of his appointment as to whether he is a full-time or part-time member[8]. A person may not be appointed to the CAC for a period exceeding five years, but previous membership does not affect eligibility for reappointment[9].

A member may at any time resign his membership, and the chairman or a deputy chairman may at any time resign his office as such, by notice in writing to the Secretary of State[10]. If the Secretary of State is satisfied that a member:

(1) has become bankrupt, has had a debt relief order[11] made in respect of him or has or made an arrangement with his creditors; or

(2) is incapacitated by physical or mental illness; or

(3) is otherwise unable or unfit to discharge the functions of a member,

the Secretary of State may declare his office as a member to be vacant and must notify the declaration in such manner as he thinks fit, whereupon the office becomes vacant[12]. The validity of any proceedings of the CAC is not affected by any vacancy among the members of the CAC or by any defect in the appointment of a member of the CAC[13].

ACAS must pay to the members of the CAC such remuneration and travelling and other allowances as may be determined by the Secretary of State with the approval of the Treasury[14] and the Secretary of State may, with the like approval, pay, or make provision for payment, to or in respect of a member of the CAC such pension, allowance or gratuity on death or retirement as he may determine[15].

ACAS must provide for the CAC the requisite staff from among the officers and servants of ACAS[16] and the requisite accommodation, equipment and other facilities[17].

1 Ie by the Employment Protection Act 1975 s 10 (repealed).

2 Trade Union and Labour Relations (Consolidation) Act 1992 s 259(1). As to the functions of the CAC see PARA 1227. Any reference to the former Industrial Arbitration Board in relation to which the Employment Protection Act 1975 s 10(2) (repealed) applied immediately before 16 October 1992 is to continue to be construed as a reference to the Central Arbitration Committee: Trade Union and Labour Relations (Consolidation) Act 1992 s 302, Sch 3 para 7.

3 Trade Union and Labour Relations (Consolidation) Act 1992 s 260(1), (2) (s 260(1)–(3) substituted and s 260(3A) added by the Employment Relations Act 1999 s 24). At any time when the chairman of the CAC is absent or otherwise incapable of acting, or there is a vacancy in the office of chairman, and the CAC has a deputy chairman or deputy chairmen: (1) the deputy chairman, if there is only one; or (2) if there is more than one, such of the deputy chairmen as they may agree or as the Secretary of State may direct, in default of agreement, may perform any of the functions of chairman of the CAC: Trade Union and Labour Relations

(Consolidation) Act 1992 s 260(4). At any time when every person who is chairman or deputy chairman is absent or otherwise incapable of acting, or there is no such person present, such member of the CAC as the Secretary of State may direct may perform any of the functions of the chairman of the CAC: s 260(5).

4   Trade Union and Labour Relations (Consolidation) Act 1992 s 260(3) (as substituted: see note 3).
5   As to the Advisory, Conciliation and Arbitration Service ('ACAS') see PARA 1213 et seq.
6   Trade Union and Labour Relations (Consolidation) Act 1992 s 260(3A) (as added: see note 3).
7   Trade Union and Labour Relations (Consolidation) Act 1992 s 261(1).
8   Trade Union and Labour Relations (Consolidation) Act 1992 s 261(3). All members of the CAC are disqualified for membership of the House of Commons: see the House of Commons Disqualification Act 1975 s 1(1), Sch 1 Pt II; and PARLIAMENT vol 78 (2010) PARA 908.
9   Trade Union and Labour Relations (Consolidation) Act 1992 s 261(2).
10 Trade Union and Labour Relations (Consolidation) Act 1992 s 261(4). If the chairman or a deputy chairman ceases to be a member of the CAC, he also ceases to be chairman or, as the case may be, a deputy chairman: s 261(6).
11 Ie under the Insolvency Act 1986 Pt VIIA (ss 251A–251X): see BANKRUPTCY AND INDIVIDUAL INSOLVENCY vol 5 (2013) PARA 91 et seq.
12 Trade Union and Labour Relations (Consolidation) Act 1992 s 261(5) (amended by SI 2012/2404).
13 Trade Union and Labour Relations (Consolidation) Act 1992 s 260(6).
14 Trade Union and Labour Relations (Consolidation) Act 1992 s 262(1), (4). As to the Treasury see CONSTITUTIONAL AND ADMINISTRATIVE LAW vol 20 (2014) PARA 262 et seq.
15 Trade Union and Labour Relations (Consolidation) Act 1992 s 262(2), (4). Where a person ceases to be a member of the CAC otherwise than on the expiry of his term of office and it appears to the Secretary of State that there are special circumstances which make it right for him to receive compensation, the Secretary of State may make him a payment of such amount as he may determine with the approval of the Treasury: s 262(3), (4). Section 262(3) refers to 'the holder of the Committee' but it is submitted that this is a drafting error and should read 'a member of the Committee': see the Employment Protection Act 1975 s 10(3), Sch 1 paras 28(b), 31 (repealed), from which the Trade Union and Labour Relations (Consolidation) Act 1992 s 262(3) is derived. Cf s 250(3) (cited in PARA 1213 note 14), where a similar drafting error occurs.
16 As to ACAS officers and staff see PARA 1214.
17 Trade Union and Labour Relations (Consolidation) Act 1992 s 259(3).

1227.   CAC's functions and annual report.   When originally established[1], the Central Arbitration Committee (the 'CAC') had an extensive jurisdiction in relation to then existing statutory schemes for the extension of collectively bargained terms and conditions throughout an industry[2] and the enforcement of fair wages in government contracts[3]. These examples of legislative intervention in the labour market no longer exist[4] and the case load of the CAC declined significantly. This left as its remaining functions the enforcement of the provisions requiring employers to release bargaining information to recognised trade unions[5] and arbitration on matters voluntarily submitted to it by the parties through the Advisory, Conciliation and Arbitration Service ('ACAS')[6]. To these were added certain enforcement functions in relation to European Works Councils[7]. When, however, a new statutory procedure for obtaining the recognition of a trade union was enacted[8], jurisdiction to enforce this procedure was given to the CAC[9]; at the same time, reforms were made to its constitution to reflect its renewed importance and the necessary expansion of its membership[10].

These functions are performed on behalf of the Crown, but not so as to make the CAC subject to directions of any kind from any Minister of the Crown as to the manner in which it is to exercise them[11].

Any provision in an agreement, whether a contract of employment[12] or not, is void in so far as it purports to preclude a person from bringing proceedings before the CAC under any provision of the Trade Union and Labour Relations (Consolidation) Act 1992[13] or under certain of the provisions relating to European Works Councils[14].

As soon as practicable after the end of each financial year[15], ACAS must make a report to the Secretary of State on the activities of the CAC during that year; and, for that purpose, the CAC must, as soon as practicable after the end of each calendar year, transmit to ACAS an account of its activities during that year[16]. The accounts prepared by ACAS in respect of any financial year must show separately any sums disbursed[17] to or on behalf of the CAC[18].

1   Ie under the Employment Protection Act 1975 s 10 (repealed): see PARA 1226.
2   Ie under the Employment Protection Act 1975 s 98, Sch 11 (repealed).
3   Ie under the House of Commons Fair Wages Resolution (1946) (rescinded).
4   'Schedule 11 claims' were abolished by the Employment Act 1980; and the Fair Wages Resolution was rescinded at the end of 1982. The CAC also had a role in the original statutory procedure under the Employment Protection Act 1975 (repealed) for obtaining recognition of a trade union, but this too was abolished by the Employment Act 1980.
5   See PARAS 1179–1182.
6   See PARA 1220. As to the constitution and general duty of ACAS see PARAS 1213, 1217.
7   Ie under the Transnational Information and Consultation of Employment Regulations 1999, SI 1999/3323: see PARA 1237 et seq.
8   See PARA 1097 et seq.
9   See the Trade Union and Labour Relations (Consolidation) Act 1992 Sch A1 para 11; and PARA 1106. As to the general duty of the Central Arbitration Committee in relation to the statutory recognition procedure see PARA 1098.
10 See the Trade Union and Labour Relations (Consolidation) Act 1992 ss 260(1)–(3A); and PARA 1226. When the CAC is discharging its functions under the statutory recognition procedure, special rules apply to its proceedings: see PARA 1229.
11 Trade Union and Labour Relations (Consolidation) Act 1992 s 259(2).
12 As to the meaning of 'contract of employment' see PARA 892.
13 Trade Union and Labour Relations (Consolidation) Act 1992 s 288(1)(b)(i) (amended by the Employment Rights (Dispute Resolution) Act 1998 s 1(2)(a)). Similar restrictions on contracting out apply in relation to proceedings before an employment tribunal: see PARA 150.
14 See the Transnational Information and Consultation of Employees Regulations 1999, SI 1999/3323, reg 40(1)(b); and PARA 1238 head (2) in the text.
15 As to the meaning of 'financial year' see PARA 1216 note 1.
16 Trade Union and Labour Relations (Consolidation) Act 1992 s 265(1) (amended by the Employment Relations Act 1999 s 27(2)).
17 Ie in consequence of the provisions of the Trade Union and Labour Relations (Consolidation) Act 1992 Pt VI (ss 247–272): see PARAS 1213 et seq, 1228 et seq.
18 Trade Union and Labour Relations (Consolidation) Act 1992 s 265(2).

1228. General procedure of the CAC. For the purpose of discharging its functions in any particular case, the Central Arbitration Committee[1] (the 'CAC') is to consist of the chairman and such other members as the chairman may direct[2]. It may, however, sit in two or more divisions constituted of such members as the chairman may direct; and, in a division in which the chairman does not sit, his functions must be performed by a deputy chairman[3]. At the discretion of the chairman and where it appears expedient to do so, the CAC may:

(1)   call in the aid of one or more assessors and may settle the matter wholly or partly with their assistance[4]; and

(2)   sit in private[5].

If in any case the CAC cannot reach a unanimous decision on its award, the chairman must decide the matter acting with the full powers of an umpire[6].

Subject to the above provisions, the CAC is to determine its own procedure[7].

1 As to the constitution and functions of the Central Arbitration Committee see PARAS 1226–1227; and as to the special rules relating to proceedings under the statutory recognition procedure see PARA 1229.
2 Trade Union and Labour Relations (Consolidation) Act 1992 s 263(1).
3 Trade Union and Labour Relations (Consolidation) Act 1992 s 263(1) proviso. As to the appointment and duties of deputy chairmen see PARA 1226.
4 Trade Union and Labour Relations (Consolidation) Act 1992 s 263(2).
5 Trade Union and Labour Relations (Consolidation) Act 1992 s 263(3).
6 Trade Union and Labour Relations (Consolidation) Act 1992 s 263(4).
7 Trade Union and Labour Relations (Consolidation) Act 1992 s 263(5). The Arbitration Act 1996 Pt I (ss 1–84) (see **ARBITRATION**) does not apply to proceedings before the CAC: Trade Union and Labour Relations (Consolidation) Act 1992 s 263(6) (amended by the Arbitration Act 1996 Sch 3 para 56). In relation to the discharge of the CAC's functions under the Trade Union and Labour Relations (Consolidation) Act 1992 Sch A1 (see PARA 1097 et seq), s 263A (see PARA 1229) and s 263(6) apply but s 263(1)–(5) does not apply: s 263(7) (added by the Employment Relations Act 1999 s 25(1), (2)).

1229. CAC's procedure in statutory recognition cases. For the purpose of discharging its functions under the statutory recognition procedure[1], the Central Arbitration Committee[2] (the 'CAC') is to consist of a panel established under the following provisions[3].

The chairman of the CAC must establish a panel or panels; and a panel must consist of these three persons appointed by him:

(1) the chairman or a deputy chairman of the CAC, who is to be chairman of the panel;

(2) a member of the CAC whose experience is as a representative of employers[4];

(3) a member of the CAC whose experience is as a representative of workers[5].

The chairman of the CAC is to decide which panel is to deal with a particular case[6]. A panel may at the discretion of its chairman sit in private where it appears expedient to do so[7].

If a panel cannot reach a unanimous decision on a question arising before it and a majority of the panel have the same opinion, the question must be decided according to that opinion[8].

If a panel cannot reach a unanimous decision on a question arising before it and a majority of the panel do not have the same opinion, the chairman of the panel must decide the question acting with the full powers of an umpire[9].

Subject to the above provisions, a panel is to determine its own procedure[10].

1 Ie under the Trade Union and Labour Relations (Consolidation) Act 1992 Sch A1: see PARA 1097 et seq. See also note 3.
2 As to the constitution and functions of the Central Arbitration Committee see PARAS 1226–1227.
3 Trade Union and Labour Relations (Consolidation) Act 1992 s 263A(1) (s 263A added by the Employment Relations Act 1999 s 25(1), (3)). In such a case the Trade Union and Labour Relations (Consolidation) Act 1992 s 263A(6) (see PARA 1228 note 7) apply but s 263(1)–(5) (see PARA 1228) does not apply: s 263(7) (added by the Employment Relations Act 1999 s 25(1), (2)). The reference in the Trade Union and Labour Relations (Consolidation) Act 1992 s 163A(1) to the CAC's functions under Sch A1 does not include a reference to its functions under Sch A1 para 166 (see PARA 1104 note 8): s 263A(8) (added by the Employment Relations Act 2004 Sch 1 para 15).
4 As to the meaning of 'employer' see PARA 892.
5 Trade Union and Labour Relations (Consolidation) Act 1992 s 263A(2) (as added: see note 3). As to the meaning of 'worker' see PARA 892. As to the appointment of chairman, deputy chairmen and members see PARA 1226.
6 Trade Union and Labour Relations (Consolidation) Act 1992 s 263A(3) (as added: see note 3).
7 Trade Union and Labour Relations (Consolidation) Act 1992 s 263A(4) (as added: see note 3).

8   Trade Union and Labour Relations (Consolidation) Act 1992 s 263A(5) (as added: see note 3).
9   Trade Union and Labour Relations (Consolidation) Act 1992 s 263A(6) (as added: see note 3).
10 Trade Union and Labour Relations (Consolidation) Act 1992 s 263A(7) (as added: see note 3).

1230. CAC awards. The Central Arbitration Committee[1] (the 'CAC') may correct in any award, or in any decision or declaration of the CAC under the statutory recognition procedure[2], any clerical mistake or error arising from an accidental slip or omission[3].

If a question arises as to the interpretation of an award of the CAC or of such a decision or declaration of the CAC, any party may apply to the CAC for a decision; and the CAC must decide the question after hearing the parties or, if the parties consent, without a hearing, and must notify the parties[4].

Decisions of the CAC in the exercise of any of its functions must be published[5].

1   As to the constitution and functions of the Central Arbitration Committee see PARAS 1226–1227.
2   Ie under the Trade Union and Labour Relations (Consolidation) Act 1992 Sch A1: see PARA 1097 et seq.
3   Trade Union and Labour Relations (Consolidation) Act 1992 s 264(1) (amended by the Employment Relations Act 1999 s 25(1), (4)(a)).
4   Trade Union and Labour Relations (Consolidation) Act 1992 s 264(2) (amended by the Employment Relations Act 1999 s 25(1), (4)(b)).
5   Trade Union and Labour Relations (Consolidation) Act 1992 s 264(3). In practice in the past this has been interpreted as applying to awards under statutory powers of decision-making (in particular in relation to disclosure of bargaining information) but not to awards in consensual arbitrations: see PARA 1220 note 5.

(iv) The Secretary of State

1231. Power of the Secretary of State to issue and revise Codes of Practice. The Secretary of State[1] may issue Codes of Practice containing such practical guidance as he thinks fit for the purpose:

(1)   of promoting the improvement of industrial relations; or

(2)   of promoting what appear to him to be desirable practices in relation to the conduct by trade unions[2] of ballots and elections or for purposes connected with trade union learning representatives[3].

He may from time to time revise the whole or any part of a Code of Practice issued by him, and issue that revised Code[4].

When the Secretary of State proposes to issue a Code of Practice, or a revised Code, he must, after consultation with the Advisory, Conciliation and Arbitration Service ('ACAS')[5], prepare and publish a draft of the Code and consider any representations made to him about the draft; and he may modify the draft accordingly[6]. If he determines to proceed with the draft, he must lay it before both Houses of Parliament and, if it is approved by resolution of each House, he must issue the Code in the form of the draft[7]. A Code so issued comes into effect on such day as the Secretary of State may by order made by statutory instrument appoint[8].

A Code of Practice issued by the Secretary of State may be revised by him in accordance with the following procedure for the purpose of bringing it into conformity with subsequent statutory provisions[9] by the making of consequential amendments and the omission of obsolete passages[10]. Where he proposes so to revise a Code, he must lay a draft of the revised Code before each House of Parliament[11]; and, if within the period of 40 days[12] beginning with the day on which the draft is laid before Parliament either House so resolves, no further proceedings may be taken thereon, but without prejudice to the laying before Parliament of a new draft[13]. If no such resolution is passed, the Secretary of State must issue the Code in the form of the draft and it comes into effect on such day as he may by order made by statutory instrument appoint[14].

A Code of Practice issued by the Secretary of State may be revoked by him by order made by statutory instrument[15]; but no such order may be made unless a draft of it has been laid before and approved by resolution of each House of Parliament[16].

If the Secretary of State is of the opinion that the provisions of a Code of Practice to be issued by him will supersede the whole or part of a Code previously issued by him or by ACAS, he must state in the new Code that, on the day on which the new Code comes into effect, the old Code or a specified part of it ceases to have effect[17].

1   As to the Secretary of State see PARA 5 note 21.
2   As to the meaning of 'trade union' see PARA 891.
3   Trade Union and Labour Relations (Consolidation) Act 1992 s 203(1) (amended by the Employment Act 2002 s 43(1), (7)). As to trade union learning representatives see PARA 1065.
4   Trade Union and Labour Relations (Consolidation) Act 1992 s 203(2). As to the effect of failure to comply with a Code of Practice see PARA 1232.
5   As to the constitution and general duty of the Advisory, Conciliation and Arbitration Service ('ACAS') see PARAS 1213, 1217; and as to the power of ACAS to issue and revise Codes of Practice see PARA 1223.
6   Trade Union and Labour Relations (Consolidation) Act 1992 s 204(1).
7   Trade Union and Labour Relations (Consolidation) Act 1992 s 204(2).
8   Trade Union and Labour Relations (Consolidation) Act 1992 s 204(3). Such a statutory instrument is subject to annulment in pursuance of a resolution of either House of Parliament, and may contain such transitional provisions or savings as appear to the Secretary of State to be necessary or expedient: s 204(3), (4). In exercise of the power so conferred the Secretary of State made the Employment Code of Practice (Industrial Action Ballots and Notice to Employers) Order 2005, SI 2005/2420 (see PARA 1371) and the Employment Code of Practice (Access and Unfair Practices during Recognition and Derecognition Ballots) Order 2005, SI 2005/2421 (see PARA 1174) and, by virtue of the Trade Union and Labour Relations (Consolidation) Act 1992 Sch 3 para 1(2) (see PARA 891 note 1) and the Interpretation Act 1978 s 17(2)(b), the Employment Code of Practice (Picketing) Order 1992, SI 1992/476 (see PARA 1386) has effect as if so made.
      The power in the Trade Union and Labour Relations (Consolidation) Act 1992 s 203(1) (see the text and notes 2–3) is expressly extended to cover questions of access during recognition or derecognition ballots: see Sch A1 para 26(8), (9) and PARA 1120; Sch A1 para 118(8), (9) and PARA 1157.
9   For these purposes, 'subsequent statutory provisions' means provisions made by or under an Act of Parliament and coming into force after the Code was issued, whether before or after the commencement of the Trade Union and Labour Relations (Consolidation) Act 1992: s 205(1).
10 Trade Union and Labour Relations (Consolidation) Act 1992 s 205(1).
11 Trade Union and Labour Relations (Consolidation) Act 1992 s 205(2).
12 In reckoning the period of 40 days, no account is to be taken of any period during which Parliament is dissolved or prorogued or during which both Houses are adjourned for more than four days: Trade Union and Labour Relations (Consolidation) Act 1992 s 205(3). If copies of the draft are laid before the two Houses of Parliament on different days, the period is counted from the later of the two days: s 205(3).
13 Trade Union and Labour Relations (Consolidation) Act 1992 s 205(3).
14 Trade Union and Labour Relations (Consolidation) Act 1992 s 205(4). The order may contain such transitional provisions and savings as appear to the Secretary of State to be appropriate: s 205(4).
15 Trade Union and Labour Relations (Consolidation) Act 1992 s 206(1).
16 Trade Union and Labour Relations (Consolidation) Act 1992 s 206(2). The order may contain such transitional provisions and savings as appear to the Secretary of State to be appropriate: s 206(1).

17 Trade Union and Labour Relations (Consolidation) Act 1992 s 208(2). This provision does not affect any transitional provisions or savings made by the order bringing the new Code into effect: s 208(3).

1232. Effect of failure to comply with a Code of Practice issued by the Secretary of State. A failure on the part of any person to observe any provision of a Code of Practice issued by the Secretary of State[1] does not of itself render him liable to any proceedings[2]. Any such Code is, however, admissible in evidence in any proceedings before a court or employment tribunal[3] or before the Central Arbitration Committee (the 'CAC')[4]; and any provision of the Code which appears to the court, tribunal or CAC to be relevant to any question arising in those proceedings must be taken into account in determining that question[5].

An unreasonable failure by the employer or employee to comply with a relevant Code of Practice may result in the adjustment of an employment tribunal award[6].

1 Ie a Code of Practice issued under the Trade Union and Labour Relations (Consolidation) Act 1992 Pt IV Ch III (ss 199–208): see PARA 1231.
2 Trade Union and Labour Relations (Consolidation) Act 1992 s 207(1). See also PARA 1224 (effect of failure to comply with Code of Practice issued by ACAS).
3 As to employment tribunals see PARA 1399 et seq.
4 As to the Central Arbitration Committee see PARA 1226 et seq.
5 Trade Union and Labour Relations (Consolidation) Act 1992 s 207(3) (amended by the Employment Rights (Dispute Resolution) Act 1998 s 1(2)(a)).
6 See the Trade Union and Labour Relations (Consolidation) Act 1992 s 207A; and PARA 1234.

1233. Courts of inquiry. Where a trade dispute[1] exists or is apprehended, the Secretary of State may inquire into the causes and circumstances of the dispute and, if he thinks fit, appoint a court of inquiry and refer to it any matters appearing to him to be connected with or relevant to the dispute[2].

A court of inquiry is to consist of either a chairman and such other persons as the Secretary of State thinks fit to appoint or one person appointed by the Secretary of State, as the Secretary of State thinks fit[3]. A court may conduct its inquiry in public or in private, at its discretion[4]. The Secretary of State may make rules regulating its procedure, including rules as to summoning of witnesses, quorum[5] and the appointment of committees, and enabling the court to call for such documents as it may determine to be relevant to the subject matter of the inquiry[6]. If, and to the extent that, it is so authorised by such rules, a court of inquiry may by order require any person who appears to it to have knowledge of the subject matter of the inquiry:

(1) to supply, in writing or otherwise, such particulars in relation thereto as the court may require; and

(2) where necessary, to attend before the court and give evidence on oath; and the court may administer, or authorise any person to administer, an oath for that purpose[7].

The court of inquiry must inquire into the matters referred to it and report on them to the Secretary of State and may make interim reports, if it thinks fit[8]. Any report of the court, and any minority report, must be laid before both Houses of Parliament as soon as possible[9]. The Secretary of State may, before or after the report has been laid before Parliament, publish or cause to be published from time to time, in such manner as he thinks fit, any information obtained or conclusions arrived at by the court as the result or in the course of its inquiry[10].

He must also, from time to time, present to Parliament a report of his proceedings under the above provisions[11].

1   As to the meaning of 'trade dispute' see PARA 1212.
2   Trade Union and Labour Relations (Consolidation) Act 1992 s 215(1). As to the Secretary of State see PARA 5 note 21.
3   Trade Union and Labour Relations (Consolidation) Act 1992 s 216(1).
4   Trade Union and Labour Relations (Consolidation) Act 1992 s 216(3).
5   A court may act notwithstanding any vacancy in its number: Trade Union and Labour Relations (Consolidation) Act 1992 s 216(2).
6   Trade Union and Labour Relations (Consolidation) Act 1992 s 216(4). Provision must be made by such rules with respect to the cases in which persons may appear by a relevant lawyer in proceedings before a court of inquiry; and, except as so provided, no person is entitled to appear in such proceedings by a relevant lawyer: s 216(6) (amended by the Legal Services Act 2007 Sch 21 paras 104, 106(a). At the date at which this volume states the law no such rules had been made and none had effect as if so made. 'Relevant lawyer' means a person who, for the purposes of the Legal Services Act 2007, is an authorised person in relation to an activity which constitutes the exercise of a right of audience or the conduct of litigation within the meaning of that Act: Trade Union and Labour Relations (Consolidation) Act 1992 s 216(7)(a) (added by the Legal Services Act 2007 Sch 21 paras 104, 106(b)).
7   Trade Union and Labour Relations (Consolidation) Act 1992 s 216(5).
8   Trade Union and Labour Relations (Consolidation) Act 1992 s 215(2).
9   Trade Union and Labour Relations (Consolidation) Act 1992 s 215(3).
10   Trade Union and Labour Relations (Consolidation) Act 1992 s 215(4). However, no report or publication made or authorised by the court or the Secretary of State is to include any information obtained by the court in the course of its inquiry as to any trade union or as to any individual business, whether carried on by a person, firm or company, which is not available otherwise than through evidence given at the inquiry, except with the consent of the secretary of the trade union or of the person, firm or company in question; nor is any individual member of the court or any person concerned in the inquiry to disclose such information without such consent: s 215(5). As to the meaning of 'trade union' see PARA 891.
11   Trade Union and Labour Relations (Consolidation) Act 1992 s 215(6).

(v) Adjustment of Employment Tribunal Awards

1234. Effect of failure to comply with a Code of Practice: adjustment of awards. If, in the case of relevant proceedings[1], it appears to the employment tribunal that (1) the claim to which the proceedings relate concerns a matter to which a relevant Code of Practice[2] applies; (2) the employer[3] has failed to comply with that Code in relation to that matter; and (3) that failure was unreasonable, the employment tribunal may, if it considers it just and equitable in all the circumstances to do so, increase any award it makes to the employee by no more than 25 per cent[4].

If, in the case of such proceedings[5], it appears to the employment tribunal that (a) the claim to which the proceedings relate concerns a matter to which a relevant Code of Practice applies; (b) the employee has failed to comply with that Code in relation to that matter; and (c) that failure was unreasonable, the employment tribunal may, if it considers it just and equitable in all the circumstances to do so, reduce any award it makes to the employee by no more than 25 per cent[6].

Where an award falls to be adjusted under the above provisions[7] and under the relevant provisions of the Employment Act 2002[8], the adjustment under the above provisions must be made before the adjustment under the provisions of the 2002 Act[9].

1   Ie proceedings to which the Trade Union and Labour Relations (Consolidation) Act 1992 s 207A applies. Section 207A applies to proceedings before an employment tribunal relating to a claim by an employee under any of the jurisdictions listed in Sch A2 (see below): s 207A(1)

(s 207A, Sch A2 added by the Employment Act 2008 s 3(1)–(3)). As to employment tribunals see PARA 1399 et seq. As to the meaning of 'employee' see PARA 892.

The tribunal jurisdictions are as follows (Trade Union and Labour Relations (Consolidation) Act 1992 Sch A2 (as so added; amended by the Equality Act 2010 Sch 26 Pt 1 para 24(1)–(3), Sch 27 Pt 1; and by SI 2010/493), ie:

(1) the Trade Union and Labour Relations (Consolidation) Act 1992 s 145A (inducements relating to union membership or activities) (see PARA 1051); s 145B (inducements relating to collective bargaining) (see PARA 1052); s 146 (detriment in relation to union membership and activities) (see PARA 1048); Sch A1 para 156 (detriment in relation to union recognition rights) (see PARA 1169);

(2) the Employment Rights Act 1996 s 23 (unauthorised deductions and payments) (see PARA 259); s 48 (detriment in employment) (see PARA 625); s 111 (unfair dismissal) (see PARA 804); s 163 (redundancy payments) (see PARA 886);

(3) the National Minimum Wage Act 1998 s 24 (detriment in relation to national minimum wage) (see PARA 249);

(4) the Equality Act 2010 ss 120, 127 (discrimination etc in work cases: see DISCRIMINATION vol 33 (2013) PARAS 344, 347)

(5) the Employment Tribunal Extension of Jurisdiction (England and Wales) Order 1994, SI 1994/1623 (breach of employment contract and termination) (see PARA 1408) and corresponding provisions for Scotland;

(6) the Working Time Regulations 1998, SI 1998/1833, reg 30 (breach of regulations) (see PARA 319);

(7) the Transnational Information and Consultation of Employees Regulations 1999, SI 1999/3323, reg 32 (detriment relating to European Works Councils) (see PARA 1278);

(8) the European Public Limited-Liability Company Regulations 2004, SI 2004/2326, reg 45 (detriment in employment) (revoked; see now the European Public Limited-Liability Company (Employee Involvement) (Great Britain) Regulations 2009, SI 2009/2401, regs 31, 32; and PARA 1334);

(9) the Information and Consultation of Employees Regulations 2004, SI 2004/3426, reg 33 (detriment in employment) (see PARA 1313);

(10) the Occupational and Personal Pension Schemes (Consultation by Employers and Miscellaneous Amendment) Regulations 2006, SI 2006/349, Schedule para 8 (detriment in employment) (see PERSONAL AND OCCUPATIONAL PENSIONS vol 80 (2013) PARA 486);

(11) the European Cooperative Society (Involvement of Employees) Regulations 2006, SI 2006/2059, reg 34 (detriment in relation to involvement in a European Cooperative Society) (see PARA 1338);

(12) the Cross-border Railway Services (Working Time) Regulations 2008, SI 2008/1660, reg 17 (breach of regulations; as to those regulations see RAILWAYS AND TRAMWAYS vol 86 (2013) PARA 328 note 7); and

(13) the Employment Relations Act 1999 (Blacklists) Regulations 2010, SI 2010/493, reg 9 (detriment connected with prohibited list: see PARA 1040).

The Secretary of State may by order amend the Trade Union and Labour Relations (Consolidation) Act 1992 Sch A2 for the purpose of adding a jurisdiction to the list in that Schedule or removing a jurisdiction from that list: s 207A(6) (as so added). The power of the Secretary of State to make an order under s 207A(6) includes power to make such incidental, supplementary, consequential or transitional provision as the Secretary of State thinks fit: s 207A(7) (as so added). An order under s 207A(6) must be made by statutory instrument: s 207A(8) (as so added). No order must be made under s 207A(6) unless a draft of the statutory instrument containing it has been laid before Parliament and approved by a resolution of each House: s 207A(9) (as so added). As to the Secretary of State see PARA 5 note 21.

2 In the Trade Union and Labour Relations (Consolidation) Act 1992 s 207A(2), (3) 'relevant Code of Practice' means a Code of Practice issued under Pt IV Ch III (ss 199–208) (see also PARAS 1223, 1231) which relates exclusively or primarily to procedure for the resolution of disputes: s 207A(4) (as added: see note 1). As to resolution of disputes see PARA 698 et seq. See also note 1.

3 As to the meaning of 'employer' see PARA 892.

4 Trade Union and Labour Relations (Consolidation) Act 1992 s 207A(2) (as added: see note 1).

5 Ie proceedings to which the Trade Union and Labour Relations (Consolidation) Act 1992 s 207A applies: see note 1.

6 Trade Union and Labour Relations (Consolidation) Act 1992 s 207A(3) (as added: see note 1).

7 Ie the Trade Union and Labour Relations (Consolidation) Act 1992 s 207A.

8 Ie the Employment Act 2002 s 38: see PARA 127.

9 Trade Union and Labour Relations (Consolidation) Act 1992 s 207A(5) (as added: see note 1).

(10) INDUSTRIAL DEMOCRACY AND WORKER PARTICIPATION

(i) Company Directors' Duties with regard to Employee Involvement

1235. Duties of company directors; matters to be included in directors' report. The matters to which the directors[1] of a company are to have regard in the performance of their functions[2] include the interests of the company's employees in general, as well as the interests of its members[3].

Where a company employs an average number of persons in each week in the United Kingdom which exceeds 250, the directors' annual report must contain a statement describing the action that has been taken to introduce, maintain and develop arrangements aimed at:

(1)   providing employees systematically with information on matters of concern to them as employees;

(2)   consulting employees or their representatives on a regular basis so that the views of employees can be taken into account in making decisions which are likely to affect their interests;

(3)   encouraging the involvement of employees in the company's performance through an employees' share scheme or by some other means; and

(4)   achieving a common awareness on the part of all employees of the financial and economic factors affecting the performance of the company[4].

1   As to the meanings of 'director' and 'shadow director' see COMPANIES vol 14 (2009) PARA 478.
2   As to the powers and duties of directors generally see COMPANIES vol 14 (2009) PARA 540 et seq.
3   See the Companies Act 2006 s 172; and COMPANIES vol 14 (2009) PARAS 544–545. The possible clash between the interests of members and of employees was shown by the decision in *Parke v Daily News Ltd* [1962] Ch 927, [1962] 2 All ER 929 (in the context of earlier provisions), that it was improper for a company ceasing to carry on business to give ex gratia payments to employees, and that an individual member could restrain such actions. The Companies Act 2006 s 247 empowers a company to make provision for the benefit of employees or former employees on the cessation or transfer of the undertaking, even if such provision is not in the best interests of the company: see COMPANIES vol 14 (2009) PARA 546.
4   See the Large and Medium-sized Companies and Groups (Accounts and Reports) Regulations 2008, SI 2008/410, Sch 7 Pt 4 (para 11); and COMPANIES. vol 15 (2009) PARA 828. There is also a statutory requirement relating to a statement in the report on the company's policy on disabled employees: see COMPANIES vol 15 (2009) PARA 823.

(ii) European Works Councils etc

A.   EU REQUIREMENTS AS TO EUROPEAN WORKS COUNCILS ETC

1236. European Union requirements for transnational information and consultation. A European Parliament and Council Directive (the Transnational Information and Consultation Directive)[1], whose purpose is to improve the right to information[2] and to consultation[3] of employees in:

(1)   EU-scale undertakings, that is undertakings with at least 1,000 employees within the member states and at least 150 employees in each of at least two member states[4]; and

(2)   EU-scale groups of undertakings (controlling undertakings and their controlled undertakings) with the following characteristics:

(a)   at least 1,000 employees within the member states;

(b)   at least two group undertakings in different member states; and

(c)   at least one group undertaking with at least 150 employees in one member state and at least one other group undertaking with at least 150 employees in another member state[5],

requires that a European Works Council[6] or a procedure for informing and consulting employees must be established in every such undertaking or group of undertakings, where requested in the prescribed manner[7], with the purpose of informing and consulting employees. The arrangements for informing and consulting employees are to be defined and implemented in such a way as to ensure their effectiveness and to enable the undertaking or group of undertakings to take decisions effectively[8]. Information and consultation of employees must occur at the relevant level of management and representation, according to the subject under discussion. To achieve that, the competence of the European Works Council and the scope of the information and consultation procedure for employees governed by the Directive are limited to transnational issues[9].

Unless a wider scope is provided for[10], the powers and competence of European Works Councils and the scope of information and consultation procedures established to achieve the purpose specified above must, in the case of an EU-scale undertaking, cover all the establishments located within the member states and, in the case of an EU-scale group of undertakings, all group undertakings located within the member states[11].

Member states may provide that the Directive is not to apply to merchant navy crews[12].

The Directive makes provision with regard to:

(i)   central management's responsibility for the establishment of a European Works Council or an employee information and consultation procedure[13];

(ii)   the establishment of a special negotiating body to achieve the objective of the Directive[14];

(iii)   the content of the agreement effected in writing between the central management and the special negotiating body[15];

(iv)   subsidiary requirements to be laid down by the legislation of the member state in which the central management is situated[16];

(v)   the treatment of confidential information[17];

(vi)   the operation of the European Works Council and the information and consultation procedure for workers[18];

(vii)   the role of employees' representatives and their protection[19];

(viii) the relationship of the Directive with other EU and national provisions[20]; and

(ix)   procedures where the structure of the EU-scale undertaking or EU-scale group of undertakings changes significantly[21].

Each member state must ensure that the management of establishments of an EU-scale undertaking and the management of undertakings which form part of an EU-scale group of undertakings which are situated within its territory and their employees' representatives or, as the case may be, employees abide by the obligations laid down by the Directive, regardless of whether or not the central management is situated within its territory[22]. Member states must provide for appropriate measures in the event of failure to comply with the Directive; in particular, they must ensure that adequate administrative or judicial procedures are available to enable the obligations deriving from the Directive to be enforced[23]. Where, however, an agreement or agreements covering the entire workforce, providing for the transnational information and consultation of employees has or have been concluded under the predecessor EU legislation[24], or where such agreements are adjusted because of changes in the structure of the undertakings or groups of undertakings, or an agreement concluded pursuant to that legislation was signed or revised during the transitional period[25], the national law applicable when the agreement was signed or revised continues to apply[26].

Member States were to bring into force the laws, regulations and administrative provisions necessary to comply with certain provisions of the Directive[27] no later than 5 June 2011 or to ensure that management and labour introduce on that date the required provisions by way of agreement, the member states being obliged to take all necessary steps enabling them at all times to guarantee the results imposed by the Directive[28].

1   Ie European Parliament and Council Directive (EC) 2009/38 (OJ L122, 16/05/2009, p 28). That Directive replaces Council Directive (EC) 94/45 (OJ L254, 30.9.94, p 64), as extended by Council Directive (EC) 97/74 (OJ L10, 16.1.1998, p 22) (both now repealed).

2   'Information' means transmission of data by the employer to the employees' representatives in order to enable them to acquaint themselves with the subject matter and to examine it; information must be given at such time, in such fashion and with such content as are appropriate to enable employees' representatives to undertake an in-depth assessment of the possible impact and, where appropriate, prepare for consultations with the competent organ of the EU-scale undertaking or group of undertakings: see European Parliament and Council Directive (EC) 2009/38 (OJ L122, 16/05/2009, p 28) art 2(1)(f). 'Employees' representatives' means the employees' representatives provided for by national law and/or practice: art 2(1)(d).

3   'Consultation' means the establishment of dialogue and exchange of views between employees' representatives and central management or any more appropriate level of management, at such time, in such fashion and with such content as enables employees' representatives to express an opinion on the basis of the information provided about the proposed measures to which the consultation is related, without prejudice to the responsibilities of the management, and within a reasonable time, which may be taken into account within the EU-scale undertaking or EU-scale group of undertakings: see art 2(1)(g). 'Central management' means the central management of the EU-scale undertaking or, in the case of an EU-scale group of undertakings, of the controlling undertaking: see art 2(1)(e). As to the meaning of 'controlling undertaking' see art 3.

4   Such undertakings are described in European Parliament and Council Directive (EC) 2009/38 (OJ L122, 16/05/2009, p 28) as 'EU-scale undertakings' and defined in art 2(1)(a); but the European Community has now been replaced by the European Union: see EUROPEAN UNION vol 47A (2014) PARA 7. The prescribed thresholds for the size of the workforce are to be based on the average number of employees, including part-time employees, employed during the previous two years calculated according to national legislation and/or practice: art 2(2).

5   Such undertakings are described in European Parliament and Council Directive (EC) 2009/38 (OJ L122, 16/05/2009, p 28) as 'EU-scale groups of undertakings' and defined in art 2(1)(b), (c); but the European Community has now been replaced by the European Union: see EUROPEAN UNION vol 47A (2014) PARA 7.

6   'European Works Council' means a council established in accordance with European Parliament and Council Directive (EC) 2009/38 (OJ L122, 16/05/2009, p 28) art 1(2) or the provisions of Annex I, with the purpose of informing and consulting employees: art 2(1)(h).

7   Ie the manner laid down in European Parliament and Council Directive (EC) 2009/38 (OJ L122, 16/05/2009, p 28) art 5(1).

8   See European Parliament and Council Directive (EC) 2009/38 (OJ L122, 16/05/2009, p 28) art 1(1), (2). Notwithstanding art 1(2), where an EU-scale group of undertakings within the meaning of art 2(1)(c) comprises one or more undertakings or groups of undertakings which are EU-scale undertakings or EU-scale groups of undertakings within the meaning of art 2(1)(a) or (c), a European Works Council must be established at the level of the group unless the agreements referred to in art 6 (see the text and note 15) provide otherwise: see art 1(5).

9   European Parliament and Council Directive (EC) 2009/38 (OJ L122, 16/05/2009, p 28) art 1(3). Matters are to be considered to be transnational where they concern the EU-scale undertaking or EU-scale group of undertakings as a whole, or at least two undertakings or establishments of the undertaking or group situated in two different member states: see art 1(4).

10 Ie in the agreements referred to in European Parliament and Council Directive (EC) 2009/38 (OJ L122, 16/05/2009, p 28) art 6.

11 See European Parliament and Council Directive (EC) 2009/38 (OJ L122, 16/05/2009, p 28) art 1(6).

12 European Parliament and Council Directive (EC) 2009/38 (OJ L122, 16/05/2009, p 28) art 1(7).

13 See European Parliament and Council Directive (EC) 2009/38 (OJ L122, 16/05/2009, p 28) art 4. See also Case C-440/00 *Gesamtbetriebsrat der Kühne & Nagel AG & Co KG v Kühne & Nagel AG & Co KG* [2004] ECR I-787, [2004] 2 CMLR 1242, [2004] IRLR 332, ECJ (decided under previous legislation).

14 See European Parliament and Council Directive (EC) 2009/38 (OJ L122, 16/05/2009, p 28) art 5.

15 See European Parliament and Council Directive (EC) 2009/38 (OJ L122, 16/05/2009, p 28) art 6.

16 See European Parliament and Council Directive (EC) 2009/38 (OJ L122, 16/05/2009, p 28) art 7, Annex I.

17 See European Parliament and Council Directive (EC) 2009/38 (OJ L122, 16/05/2009, p 28) art 8.

18 See European Parliament and Council Directive (EC) 2009/38 (OJ L122, 16/05/2009, p 28) art 9.

19 See European Parliament and Council Directive (EC) 2009/38 (OJ L122, 16/05/2009, p 28) art 10.

20 See European Parliament and Council Directive (EC) 2009/38 (OJ L122, 16/05/2009, p 28) art 12.

21 See European Parliament and Council Directive (EC) 2009/38 (OJ L122, 16/05/2009, p 28) art 13.

22 See European Parliament and Council Directive (EC) 2009/38 (OJ L122, 16/05/2009, p 28) art 11(1).

23 See European Parliament and Council Directive (EC) 2009/38 (OJ L122, 16/05/2009, p 28) art 11(2).

24 Ie under Council Directive (EC) 94/45 (OJ L254, 30.9.94, p 64) art 6 (repealed).

25 Ie between 5 June 2009 and 5 June 2011.

26 See European Parliament and Council Directive (EC) 2009/38 (OJ L122, 16/05/2009, p 28) art 14(1). Upon expiry of the agreements referred to in art 14(1), the parties to those agreements may decide jointly to renew or revise them. Where this is not the case, the provisions of European Parliament and Council Directive (EC) 2009/38 (OJ L122, 16/05/2009, p 28) apply: art 14(2).

27 Ie European Parliament and Council Directive (EC) 2009/38 (OJ L122, 16/05/2009, p 28) arts 1(2)–(4), 2(1)(f)–(g), 3(4), 4(4), 5(2)(b), (c), (4), 6(2)(b), (c), (e), (g), 10, 12–14, Annex I point 1(a), (c) and (d), points 2–3.

28 European Parliament and Council Directive (EC) 2009/38 (OJ L122, 16/05/2009, p 28) art 16(1).

1237. Implementation of the Transnational Information and Consultation Directive. For the purpose of implementing in the United Kingdom the EU requirements on the establishment of a European Works Council or a procedure in EU-scale undertakings and EU-scale groups of undertakings for the purpose of informing and consulting employees[1] the Transnational Information and Consultation of Employees Regulations 1999[2] were made. They contain provisions relating to:

(1) employee numbers and requests to negotiate the establishment of a European Works Council or an information and consultation procedure[3];

(2) the special negotiating body[4];

(3) European Works Councils and the information and consultation procedures[5];

(4) compliance and enforcement[6];

(5) confidential information[7];

(6) protections for members of a European Works Council etc[8];

(7) administration[9]; and

(8)   exceptions[10].

To the extent that the establishment of more than one European Works Council in an EU-scale undertaking[11] or EU-scale group of undertakings[12] is permitted[13], the Transnational Information and Consultation of Employees Regulations 1999 are to be construed accordingly[14].

1   Ie Council Directive (EC) 94/45 (OJ L254, 30.9.94, p 64), as extended by Council Directive (EC) 97/74 (OJ L10, 16.1.1998, p 22) (both now repealed and replaced by European Parliament and Council Directive (EC) 2009/38 (OJ L122, 16/05/2009, p 28): see PARA 1236). References to the repealed Directive are to be construed as references to European Parliament and Council Directive (EC) 2009/38 (OJ L122, 16/05/2009, p 28) and are to be read in accordance with the correlation table in Annex III: art 17.

2   Ie the Transnational Information and Consultation of Employees Regulations 1999, SI 1999/3323: see the text and notes 3–14; and PARA 1238 et seq. The provisions of regs 7–41 (see PARA 1242 et seq) and of reg 46 (see PARA 1287) apply in relation to an EU-scale undertaking or EU-scale group of undertakings only where, in accordance with reg 5 (see PARA 1240), the central management is situated in the United Kingdom: see reg 4(1). However, the following provisions apply in relation to an EU-scale undertaking or EU-scale group of undertakings, whether or not the central management is situated in the United Kingdom: (1) regs 7, 8(1), (2), (4) (the provision of information on employee numbers) (see PARAS 1242–1243); (2) regs 13–15 (UK members of the special negotiating body) (see PARAS 1248–1250); (3) reg 18, to the extent that it applies reg 18(1), Schedule paras 3–5 (UK members of the European Works Council) (see PARAS 1255–1257); (4) reg 23(1)–(5) (breach of statutory duty) (see PARA 1273); (5) regs 25–33 (protections for members of a European Works Council etc) (see PARA 1275 et seq); (6) regs 34–39 (enforcement bodies) (see PARA 1279 et seq), to the extent that they relate to applications made or complaints presented under any of the other provisions referred to in heads (1)–(5) above or head (7) below; and (7) regs 40, 41 (restrictions on contracting out) (see PARA 1238): reg 4(2) (amended by virtue of SI 2011/1043). As to the meaning of 'EU-scale undertaking' see note 11; and as to the meaning of 'EU-scale group of undertakings' see note 12.

    The Transnational Information and Consultation of Employees Regulations 1999, SI 1999/3323, do not apply to a company established in accordance with the European Public Limited-Liability Company Regulations 2004, SI 2004/2326, that is an EU-scale undertaking, or a controlling undertaking of an EU-scale group of undertakings, except where the special negotiating body has taken the decision referred to in the European Public Limited-Liability Company (Employee Involvement) (Great Britain) Regulations 2009, SI 2009/2401, reg 17 (decision not to open, or to terminate, negotiations: see PARA 1326) or the corresponding Northern Ireland legislation: see the Transnational Information and Consultation of Employees Regulations 1999, SI 1999/3323, reg 46A (added by SI 2004/2326; substituted by SI 2009/2401). Nor do they apply to a European Co-operative Society that is an EU-scale undertaking or a controlling undertaking of an EU-scale group of undertakings, except where a decision has been taken not to open, or to terminate, negotiations in accordance with the European Cooperative Society (Involvement of Employees) Regulations 2006, SI 2006/2059, reg 19, Sch 1 para 13 (see PARA 1338): see the Transnational Information and Consultation of Employees Regulations 1999, SI 1999/3323, reg 46B (added by SI 2006/2059).

3   See the Transnational Information and Consultation of Employees Regulations 1999, SI 1999/3323, Pt II (regs 6–10); and PARA 1241 et seq. For these purposes, 'European Works Council' means the council, established under and in accordance with: (1) reg 17 (see PARA 1252), or reg 18 (see PARA 1253) and the provisions of reg 18(1), Schedule (see PARA 1254 et seq); or (2) where appropriate, the provisions of the law or practice of a member state other than the United Kingdom which are designed to give effect to European Parliament and Council Directive (EC) 2009/38 (OJ L122, 16/05/2009, p 28) art 6 or 7, Annex, with the purpose of informing and consulting employees: Transnational Information and Consultation of Employees Regulations 1999, SI 1999/3323, reg 2(1); and as to references to the Directive see note 1.

    For these purposes, 'member state' means a state which is a Contracting Party to the Agreement on the European Economic Area (Oporto, 2 May 1992 (Cm 2073; OJ L1, 3.1.94, p 3)); adjusted by the Protocol (Brussels, 17 March 1993 (OJ L1, 3.1.94, p 572)), as it has effect for the time being: Transnational Information and Consultation of Employees Regulations 1999, SI 1999/3323, reg 2(1).

4   See the Transnational Information and Consultation of Employees Regulations 1999, SI 1999/3323, Pt III (regs 11–15); and PARA 1246 et seq.

5 See the Transnational Information and Consultation of Employees Regulations 1999, SI 1999/3323, Pt IV (regs 16–19F), Schedule; and PARA 1251 et seq.
6 See the Transnational Information and Consultation of Employees Regulations 1999, SI 1999/3323, Pt V (regs 20–22); and PARAS 1269–1272.
7 See the Transnational Information and Consultation of Employees Regulations 1999, SI 1999/3323, Pt VI (regs 23–24); and PARA 1273–1274.
8 See the Transnational Information and Consultation of Employees Regulations 1999, SI 1999/3323, Pt VII (regs 25–33); and PARA 1275 et seq.
9 See the Transnational Information and Consultation of Employees Regulations 1999, SI 1999/3323, Pt VIII (regs 34–39); and PARA 1279 et seq.
10 See the Transnational Information and Consultation of Employees Regulations 1999, SI 1999/3323, Pt IX (regs 42–46B); note 2; and PARA 1282 et seq.
11 For these purposes, 'EU-scale undertaking' means an undertaking with at least 1,000 employees within the member states and at least 150 employees in each of at least two member states: see the Transnational Information and Consultation of Employees Regulations 1999, SI 1999/3323, reg 2(1) (amended by virtue of SI 2011/1043). An agency worker who has a contract within the Agency Workers Regulations 2010, SI 2010/93, reg 3(1)(b) (contract with the temporary work agency: see PARA 97) with a temporary work agency which is an EU-scale undertaking or EU-scale group of undertakings at the relevant date, which is not a contract of employment, is be treated as being employed by that agency for the duration of his assignment with a hirer for the purposes of (1) calculating the number of employees within the definitions of EU-scale undertaking' and 'EU-scale group of undertakings' in the Transnational Information and Consultation of Employees Regulations 1999, SI 1999/3323, reg 2; and (2) the means of calculating the number of employees in reg 6 (see PARA 1241): reg 2(4C) (added by SI 2010/1088; amended by virtue of SI 2011/1043). As to the meaning of 'employee' see PARA 1238 note 1. 'Agency worker' has the meaning provided for in the Agency Workers Regulations 2010, SI 2010/93, reg 3 (see PARA 97); 'hirer' has the meaning provided for in reg 2 (see PARA 97 note 3) and 'temporary work agency' has the meaning provided for in reg 4 (see PARA 97): Transnational Information and Consultation of Employees Regulations 1999, SI 1999/3323, reg 2(1) (definitions added by SI 2010/1088).
12 For these purposes, 'EU-scale group of undertakings' means a group of undertakings which has: (1) at least 1,000 employees within the member states; (2) at least two group undertakings in different member states; and (3) at least one group undertaking with at least 150 employees in one member state and at least one other group undertaking with at least 150 employees in another member state: see the Transnational Information and Consultation of Employees Regulations 1999, SI 1999/3323, reg 2(1) (as amended: see note 11). 'Group of undertakings' means a controlling undertaking and its controlled undertakings (reg 2(1)); and 'group undertaking' means an undertaking which is part of an EU-scale group of undertakings (reg 2(1)). As to the meanings of 'controlling undertaking' and 'controlled undertaking' see PARA 1239. See also note 11.
13 Ie by European Parliament and Council Directive (EC) 2009/38 (OJ L122, 16/05/2009, p 28.
14 Transnational Information and Consultation of Employees Regulations 1999, SI 1999/3323, reg 2(2); and see note 1.

1238. Restrictions on contracting out of transnational information and consultation requirements. Any provision in any agreement, whether an employee's[1] contract or not, is void in so far as it purports:

(1) to exclude or limit the operation of any of the provisions relating to European Works Councils[2], other than a provision relating to the protection for members of a European Works Council etc[3]; or

(2) to preclude a person from bringing any proceedings before the Employment Appeal Tribunal[4] or the Central Arbitration Committee[5] under any of the provisions relating to European Works Councils[6], other than a provision[7] relating to the protection for members of a European Works Council etc[8];

but the above provisions[9] do not apply to any agreement to refrain from continuing any proceedings referred to in head (2) above made after the proceedings have been instituted[10].

Any provision in any agreement, whether an employee's contract or not, is void in so far as it purports:

(a)   to exclude or limit the operation of any provision relating to the protection for members of a European Works Council etc[11]; or

(b)   to preclude a person from bringing any proceedings before an employment tribunal[12] relating to the protection for members of a European Works Council etc[13];

but the above provisions[14] do not apply to any agreement to refrain from instituting or continuing proceedings before an employment tribunal:

(i)   where a conciliation officer has taken action[15] under the Employment Tribunals Act 1996[16];

(ii) where conciliation is available[17], if the conditions regulating settlement agreements[18] are satisfied in relation to the agreement[19].

For the purposes of head (ii) above, the conditions regulating settlement agreements are that:

(A)   the agreement must be in writing;

(B)   the agreement must relate to the particular proceedings;

(C)   the employee must have received advice from a relevant independent adviser[20] as to the terms and effect of the proposed agreement and, in particular, its effect on his ability to pursue his rights before an employment tribunal;

(D)   there must be in force, when the adviser gives the advice, a contract of insurance, or an indemnity provided for members of a profession or professional body, covering the risk of a claim by the employee in respect of loss arising in consequence of the advice;

(E)   the agreement must identify the adviser; and

(F)   the agreement must state that the conditions in heads (A) to (E) above are satisfied[21].

1   For these purposes, 'employee' means an individual who has entered into or works under a contract of employment and in the Transnational Information and Consultation of Employees Regulations 1999, SI 1999/3323, Pt VII (regs 25–33) (see PARA 1275 et seq) and reg 41 (see the text and notes 11–21) includes, where the employment has ceased, an individual who worked under a contract of employment: reg 2(1). 'Contract of employment' means a contract of service or apprenticeship, whether express or implied, and (if it is express) whether oral or in writing: reg 2(1).

2   Ie any provision of the Transnational Information and Consultation of Employees Regulations 1999, SI 1999/3323: see PARAS 1237, 1239 et seq.

3   Ie other than a provision of the Transnational Information and Consultation of Employees Regulations 1999, SI 1999/3323, Pt VII: see PARA 1275 et seq.

4   As to the Employment Appeal Tribunal see PARA 1422 et seq.

5   As to the Central Arbitration Committee see PARA 1226 et seq.

6   See note 2.

7   See note 3.

8   Transnational Information and Consultation of Employees Regulations 1999, SI 1999/3323, reg 40(1). As to the application of the Transnational Information and Consultation of Employees Regulations 1999, SI 1999/3323, generally see PARA 1237 note 2. See also PARA 1282 et seq.

9   Ie the Transnational Information and Consultation of Employees Regulations 1999, SI 1999/3323, reg 40(1).

10 Transnational Information and Consultation of Employees Regulations 1999, SI 1999/3323, reg 40(2).

11 Ie a provision of the Transnational Information and Consultation of Employees Regulations 1999, SI 1999/3323, Pt VII: see PARA 1275 et seq.

12 Ie under the Transnational Information and Consultation of Employees Regulations 1999, SI 1999/3323, Pt VII. As to employment tribunals see PARA 1399 et seq.

13 Transnational Information and Consultation of Employees Regulations 1999, SI 1999/3323, reg 41(1).

14 Ie the Transnational Information and Consultation of Employees Regulations 1999, SI 1999/3323, reg 41(1).

15 Ie under any of the Employment Tribunals Act 1996 ss 18–18C (conciliation) (see PARAS 152–153).

16 Transnational Information and Consultation of Employees Regulations 1999, SI 1999/3323, reg 41(2)(a) (amended by SI 2014/386).

17 Ie in proceedings within the Employment Tribunals Act 1996 s 18(1)(k): see PARA 152 note 1.

18 Ie under the Transnational Information and Consultation of Employees Regulations 1999, SI 1999/3323.

19 Transnational Information and Consultation of Employees Regulations 1999, SI 1999/3323, reg 41(3)(a) (amended by SI 2013/1956).

20 For these purposes, a person is a relevant independent adviser: (1) if he is a qualified lawyer; (2) if he is an officer, official, employee or member of an independent trade union who has been certified in writing by the trade union as competent to give advice and as authorised to do so on behalf of the trade union; (3) if he works at an advice centre, whether as an employee or a volunteer, and has been certified in writing by the centre as competent to give advice and as authorised to do so on behalf of the centre: Transnational Information and Consultation of Employees Regulations 1999, SI 1999/3323, reg 41(5). A person is, however, not a relevant independent adviser for these purposes: (a) if he is employed by, or is acting in the matter for, the employer or an associated employer; (b) in the case of a person within reg 41(5)(b) or (c) (see heads (2)–(3) above), if the trade union or advice centre is the employer or an associated employer; (c) in the case of a person within reg 41(5)(c) (see head (3) above), if the employee makes a payment for the advice received from him: reg 41(6). 'Qualified lawyer' means, as respects England and Wales, a person who, for the purposes of the Legal Services Act 2007, is an authorised person in relation to an activity which constitutes the exercise of a right of audience or the conduct of litigation (within the meaning of that Act): Transnational Information and Consultation of Employees Regulations 1999, SI 1999/3323, reg 41(7) (amended by SI 2009/3348). A person will be treated as being a qualified lawyer if he is a Fellow of the Institute of Legal Executives practising in a solicitor's practice (including a body recognised under section 9 of the Administration of Justice Act 1985 s 9): Transnational Information and Consultation of Employees Regulations 1999, SI 1999/3323, reg 41(7A) (added by SI 2004/2518; amended by SI 2009/3348). Any two employers are to be treated as associated if: (i) one is a company of which the other, directly or indirectly, has control; or (ii) both are companies of which a third person, directly or indirectly, has control; and 'associated employer' is to be construed accordingly: Transnational Information and Consultation of Employees Regulations 1999, SI 1999/3323, reg 41(8). 'Independent trade union' has the same meaning as in the Trade Union and Labour Relations (Consolidation) Act 1992 (see PARA 904): Transnational Information and Consultation of Employees Regulations 1999, SI 1999/3323, reg 2(1).

21 Transnational Information and Consultation of Employees Regulations 1999, SI 1999/3323, reg 41(4) (amended by SI 2013/1956).

B. CONTROLLED AND CONTROLLING UNDERTAKINGS

1239. Meanings of 'controlling undertaking' and 'controlled undertaking'. 'Controlling undertaking' means an undertaking which can exercise a dominant influence over another undertaking by virtue, for example, of ownership, financial participation or the rules which govern it; and 'controlled undertaking' means an undertaking over which such a dominant influence can be exercised[1].

The ability of an undertaking to exercise a dominant influence over another undertaking is to be presumed, unless the contrary is proved, when, in relation to another undertaking, it directly or indirectly:

(1)   can appoint more than half of the members of that undertaking's administrative, management or supervisory body;

(2)   controls a majority of the votes attached to that undertaking's issued share capital; or

(3)   holds a majority of that undertaking's subscribed capital[2].

In applying the criteria in heads (1) to (3) above, a controlling undertaking's rights as regards voting and appointment include:

(a)   the rights of its other controlled undertakings; and

(b)   the rights of any person or body acting in his or its own name but on behalf of the controlling undertaking or of any other of the controlling undertaking's controlled undertakings[3].

An undertaking is not[4] a controlling undertaking of another undertaking in which it has holdings where the first undertaking is a company referred to in the relevant Council Regulation[5] on the control of concentrations between undertakings[6].

A dominant influence is not to be presumed to be exercised solely by virtue of the fact that an office holder is exercising functions, according to the law of a member state[7], relating to liquidation, winding up, insolvency, cessation of payments, compositions of creditors or analogous proceedings[8].

Where the law governing an undertaking is the law of a member state, the law applicable in order to determine whether an undertaking is a controlling undertaking is the law of that member state[9]; and, where the law governing an undertaking is not that of a member state, the law applicable is the law of the member state within whose territory:

(i)   the representative of the undertaking is situated; or

(ii)   in the absence of such a representative, the management of the group undertaking which employs the greatest number of employees is situated[10].

If two or more undertakings, whether situated in the same or in different member states, meet one or more of the criteria in heads (1) to (3) above in relation to another undertaking, the criteria are to be applied in the order listed in relation to each of the first-mentioned undertakings and that which meets the criterion that is highest in the order listed is to be presumed, unless the contrary is proved, to exercise a dominant influence over the undertaking in question[11].

1   Transnational Information and Consultation of Employees Regulations 1999, SI 1999/3323, regs 2(1), 3(1). As to the application of the Transnational Information and Consultation of Employees Regulations 1999, SI 1999/3323, generally see PARA 1237 note 2. See also PARA 1282 et seq.

2   Transnational Information and Consultation of Employees Regulations 1999, SI 1999/3323, reg 3(2).

3   Transnational Information and Consultation of Employees Regulations 1999, SI 1999/3323, reg 3(3).

4   Ie notwithstanding the Transnational Information and Consultation of Employees Regulations 1999, SI 1999/3323, reg 3(1), (2).

5   Ie a company referred to in Council Regulation (EC) 139/2004 (OJ L24, 29.1.2004, p 1) art 3(5)(a) (credit institutions, financial institutions, insurance companies) or art 3(5)(c) (financial holding companies).

6   Transnational Information and Consultation of Employees Regulations 1999, SI 1999/3323, reg 3(4) (amended by SI 2004/1079).

7   As to the meaning of 'member state' see PARA 1237 note 3.

8   Transnational Information and Consultation of Employees Regulations 1999, SI 1999/3323, reg 3(5).

9   Transnational Information and Consultation of Employees Regulations 1999, SI 1999/3323, reg 3(6).

10   Transnational Information and Consultation of Employees Regulations 1999, SI 1999/3323, reg 3(7).

11   Transnational Information and Consultation of Employees Regulations 1999, SI 1999/3323, reg 3(8).

1240.   The central management.   The central management[1] is responsible for creating the conditions and means necessary for the setting up of a European Works Council[2] or an information and consultation procedure[3] in an EU-scale undertaking or EU-scale group of undertakings where:

(1)   the central management is situated in the United Kingdom;

(2)   the central management is not situated in a member state[4] and the representative agent of the central management, to be designated if necessary, is situated in the United Kingdom; or

(3)   neither the central management nor the representative agent, whether or not as a result of being designated, is situated in a member state and:

    (a)   in the case of an EU-scale undertaking, there are employed in an establishment, which is situated in the United Kingdom, more employees than are employed in any other establishment which is situated in a member state; or

    (b)   in the case of an EU-scale group of undertakings, there are employed in a group undertaking, which is situated in the United Kingdom, more employees than are employed in any other group undertaking which is situated in a member state,

and the central management initiates, or is required[5] to initiate, negotiations for a European Works Council or information and consultation procedure[6].

Where the circumstances described in head (2) or head (3) above apply, the central management is to be treated[7] as being situated in the United Kingdom and the representative agent referred to in head (2) above, or the management of the establishment referred to in head (3)(a) above or of the group undertaking referred to in head (3)(b) above, is to be treated, respectively, as being the central management[8].

1   For these purposes, 'central management' means: (1) the central management of an EU-scale undertaking; or (2) in the case of an EU-scale group of undertakings, the central management of the controlling undertaking, or, where appropriate, the central management of an undertaking or group of undertakings that could be or is claimed to be an EU-scale undertaking or EU-scale group of undertakings: Transnational Information and Consultation of Employees Regulations 1999, SI 1999/3323, reg 2(1) (amended by virtue of SI 2011/1043). As to the meanings of 'EU-scale undertaking' and 'EU-scale group of undertakings' see PARA 1237 notes 11–12.

2   As to the meaning of 'European Works Council' see PARA 1237 note 3.

3   For these purposes, 'information and consultation procedure' means one or more information and consultation procedures agreed under: (1) the Transnational Information and Consultation of Employees Regulations 1999, SI 1999/3323, reg 17 (see PARA 1252); or (2) where appropriate, the provisions of the law or practice of a member state other than the United Kingdom which are designed to give effect to European Parliament and Council Directive (EC) 2009/38 (OJ L122, 16/05/2009, p 28) art 6(3) (see PARA 1236): Transnational Information and Consultation of Employees Regulations 1999, SI 1999/3323, reg 2(1); and see PARA 1237 note 1. 'Consultation' means the exchange of views and establishment of dialogue between members of a European Works Council in the context of a European Works Council, or information and consultation representatives in the context of an information and consultation procedure, and central management or any more appropriate level of management (reg 2(1)); and 'information and consultation representative' means a person who represents employees in the context of an information and consultation procedure (reg 2(1)). As to the meaning of 'employee' see PARA 1238 note 1.

4   As to the meaning of 'member state' see PARA 1237 note 3.

5   Ie by the Transnational Information and Consultation of Employees Regulations 1999, SI 1999/3323, reg 7(1): see PARA 1242.

6   Transnational Information and Consultation of Employees Regulations 1999, SI 1999/3323, reg 5(1). As to the application of the Transnational Information and Consultation of Employees Regulations 1999, SI 1999/3323, generally see PARA 1237 note 2. See also PARA 1282 et seq.

7   Ie for the purposes of the Transnational Information and Consultation of Employees Regulations 1999, SI 1999/3323: see PARAS 1237 et seq, 1241 et seq.

8   Transnational Information and Consultation of Employees Regulations 1999, SI 1999/3323, reg 5(2).

C. EMPLOYEE NUMBERS AND REQUEST TO NEGOTIATE ESTABLISHMENT OF A EUROPEAN WORKS COUNCIL OR INFORMATION AND CONSULTATION PROCEDURE

1241. Calculation of numbers of employees. For the purposes of determining whether an undertaking is an EU-scale undertaking[1] or a group of undertakings[2] is an EU-scale group of undertakings[3], the number of employees[4] employed by the undertaking, or group of undertakings, is to be determined, in the case of UK employees[5], by ascertaining the average number of employees employed during a two-year period, calculated as follows[6]. The average number of UK employees is to be ascertained by:

(1)   determining the number of UK employees in each month in the two-year period preceding the relevant date[7], whether they were employed throughout the month or not;

(2)   adding together all of the monthly numbers; and

dividing the number so determined by 24[8].

For the purposes of the calculation in head (1) above, if for the whole of a month within the two-year period an employee works under a contract by virtue of which he would have worked for 75 hours or less in that month:

(a)   were the month to have contained 21 working days;

(b)   were the employee to have had no absences from work; and

(c)   were the employee to have worked no overtime,

the employee may be counted as half a person for the month in question, if the UK management[9] so decides[10].

For the purposes of determining whether an undertaking is an EU-scale undertaking or a group of undertakings is an EU-scale group of undertakings, the number of employees employed by the undertaking, or group of undertakings, is to be determined, in the case of employees in another member state, by ascertaining the average number of employees employed during a two-year period, calculated in accordance with the provisions of the law or practice of that member state which is designed to give effect to the Transnational Information and Consultation Directive[11].

1   As to the meaning of 'EU-scale undertaking' see PARA 1237 note 11.
2   As to the meaning of 'group of undertakings' see PARA 1237 note 12.
3   As to the meaning of 'EU-scale group of undertakings' see PARA 1237 note 12.
4   As to the meaning of 'employee' see PARA 1238 note 1.
5   For these purposes, references to 'UK employees' are references to employees who are employed in the United Kingdom by an EU-scale undertaking or EU-scale group of undertakings: Transnational Information and Consultation of Employees Regulations 1999, SI 1999/3323, reg 2(3) (amended by virtue of SI 2011/1043).
6   Transnational Information and Consultation of Employees Regulations 1999, SI 1999/3323, reg 6(1)(a). As to the application of the Transnational Information and Consultation of Employees Regulations 1999, SI 1999/3323, generally see PARA 1237 note 2; and as to the treatment of agency workers see reg 2(4C), cited in PARA 1237 note 11. See also PARA 1282 et seq.
7   For these purposes, and for the purposes of Transnational Information and Consultation of Employees Regulations 1999, SI 1999/3323, reg 2(4C) (see PARA 1237 note 11), reg 7 (see PARA 1242), reg 8 (see PARA 1243), reg 9 (see PARA 1244), reg 10 (see PARA 1245), reg 19F (see PARA 1268) and reg 20 (see PARA 1269), 'relevant date' means: (1) where a request under reg 7 is made and no valid request under reg 9 has been made, the last day of the month preceding the month in which the request under reg 7 is made; and (2) where a valid request under reg 9 is made, whether or not a request under reg 7 has been made, the last day of the month preceding the month in which the request under reg 9 is made: reg 6(4) (amended by SI 2010/1088).

Where appropriate, the references in the Transnational Information and Consultation of Employees Regulations 1999, SI 1999/3323, reg 6(4) to regs 7, 9 are to be read, instead, as references to the provisions of the law or practice of a member state other than the United Kingdom which are designed to give effect to what is now European Parliament and Council Directive (EC) 2009/38 (OJ L122, 16/05/2009, p 28) arts 4(1), 5(1) (see PARA 1236): Transnational Information and Consultation of Employees Regulations 1999, SI 1999/3323, reg 6(5); and see PARA 1237 note 1. As to the meaning of 'member state' see PARA 1237 note 3.

8   Transnational Information and Consultation of Employees Regulations 1999, SI 1999/3323, reg 6(2).

9   For these purposes, 'UK management' means the management which is, or would be, subject to the obligation in the Transnational Information and Consultation of Employees Regulations 1999, SI 1999/3323, reg 13(2) (see PARA 1248) or reg 18(1), Schedule para 4(1) (see PARA 1256), being either the central management in the United Kingdom or the local management in the United Kingdom: reg 2(1). 'Local management' means the management of one or more establishments in an EU-scale undertaking or of one or more undertakings in an EU-scale group of undertakings which is not the central management: reg 2(1). As to the meaning of 'central management' see PARA 1240 note 1.

10 Transnational Information and Consultation of Employees Regulations 1999, SI 1999/3323, reg 6(3).

11 Transnational Information and Consultation of Employees Regulations 1999, SI 1999/3323, reg 6(1)(b).

1242. Entitlement to information from management. An employee[1] or an employees' representative[2] may request information from the management of an establishment, or of an undertaking, in the United Kingdom (the 'recipient') for the purpose of determining whether, in the case of an establishment, it is part of an EU-scale undertaking[3] or EU-scale group of undertakings[4] or, in the case of an undertaking, it is an EU-scale undertaking or is part of an EU-scale group of undertakings[5].

The recipient must obtain and provide the employee or employees' representative who has made the request with information:

(1)   on the average number of employees[6] employed by the undertaking, or as the case may be the group of undertakings, in the United Kingdom and in each of the other member states[7] in the last two years; and

(2)   relating to the structure of the undertaking, or as the case may be the group of undertakings, and of its workforce, in the United Kingdom and in each of the other member states in the last two years[8].

Where information disclosed under heads (1) and (2) above includes information as to the employment situation in the undertaking, or as the case may be the group of undertakings, this must include suitable information relating to the use of agency workers[9], if any[10].

1   As to the meaning of 'employee' see PARA 1238 note 1.

2   For these purposes, 'employees' representatives' means: (1) if the employees are of a description in respect of which an independent trade union is recognised by their employer for the purpose of collective bargaining, representatives of the trade union who normally take part as negotiators in the collective bargaining process; and (2) any other employee representatives elected or appointed by employees to positions in which they are expected to receive, on behalf of the employees, information: (a) which is relevant to the terms and conditions of employment of the employees; or (b) about the activities of the undertaking which may significantly affect the interests of the employees, but excluding representatives who are expected to receive information relevant only to a specific aspect of the terms and conditions or interests of the employees, such as health and safety or collective redundancies: Transnational Information and Consultation of Employees Regulations 1999, SI 1999/3323, reg 2(1). As to the meaning of 'independent trade union' see PARA 1238 note 20.

3   As to the meaning of 'EU-scale undertaking' see PARA 1237 note 11.

4   As to the meaning of 'EU-scale group of undertakings' see PARA 1237 note 12.

5   Transnational Information and Consultation of Employees Regulations 1999, SI 1999/3323, reg 7(1), (2) (amended by virtue of SI 2011/1043). As to the application of the Transnational Information and Consultation of Employees Regulations 1999, SI 1999/3323, generally see PARA 1237 note 2. See also PARA 1282 et seq.
6   As to the calculation of the number of employees see PARA 1241.
7   As to the meaning of 'member state' see PARA 1237 note 3.
8   Transnational Information and Consultation of Employees Regulations 1999, SI 1999/3323, reg 7(3) (substituted by SI 2010/1088).
9   'Suitable information relating to the use of agency workers' means (1) the number of agency workers working temporarily for and under the supervision and direction of the undertaking; (2) the parts of the undertaking in which those agency workers are working; and (3) the type of work those agency workers are carrying out: Transnational Information and Consultation of Employees Regulations 1999, SI 1999/3323, reg 2(1) (definition added by SI 2010/1088). As to the meaning of 'agency worker' see PARA 1237 note 11.
10 Transnational Information and Consultation of Employees Regulations 1999, SI 1999/3323, reg 7(4) (added by SI 2010/1088).

1243.   Complaint of management's failure to provide information. An employee[1] or employees' representative[2] who has requested information[3] may present a complaint to the Central Arbitration Committee[4] (the 'CAC') that:

(1)   the recipient[5] has failed to provide, or as the case may be to obtain and provide, the relevant information[6]; or

(2)   the information which has been provided by the recipient is false or incomplete in a material particular[7].

The CAC must not consider a complaint so presented unless it is made after the expiry of a period of one month beginning on the date on which the complainant made his request[8] for information[9].

Where the CAC finds the complaint well-founded it must make an order requiring the recipient to disclose information to the complainant; the order must specify:

(a)   the information in respect of which the CAC finds that the complaint is well-founded and which is to be disclosed, or as the case may be obtained and disclosed, to the complainant;

(b)   the date (or if more than one, the earliest date) on which the recipient refused or failed to disclose, or as the case may be obtain and disclose, information, or disclosed false or incomplete information; and

(c)   a date (not less than one week from the date of the order) by which the recipient must disclose, or as the case may be obtain and disclose, the information specified in the order[10].

If the CAC considers that, from the information it has obtained in considering the complaint, it is beyond doubt that the undertaking is, or that the establishment is part of, an EU-scale undertaking[11] or that the establishment or undertaking is part of an EU-scale group of undertakings[12], it may make a declaration to that effect[13].

1   As to the meaning of 'employee' see PARA 1238 note 1.
2   As to the meaning of 'employees' representatives' see PARA 1242 note 2.
3   Ie under the Transnational Information and Consultation of Employees Regulations 1999, SI 1999/3323, reg 7: see PARA 1242.
4   As to the Central Arbitration Committee see PARA 1226 et seq.
5   As to the meaning of 'recipient' see PARA 1242.
6   Ie the information referred to in the Transnational Information and Consultation of Employees Regulations 1999, SI 1999/3323, reg 7(3): see PARA 1242.
7   Transnational Information and Consultation of Employees Regulations 1999, SI 1999/3323, reg 8(1) (amended by SI 2010/1088). As to proceedings before the Central Arbitration Committee see PARA 1280; and as to ACAS conciliation see PARA 1281. As to the application of

the Transnational Information and Consultation of Employees Regulations 1999, SI 1999/3323, generally see PARA 1237 note 2. See also PARA 1282 et seq.
8 See note 3.
9 Transnational Information and Consultation of Employees Regulations 1999, SI 1999/3323, reg 8(4).
10 Transnational Information and Consultation of Employees Regulations 1999, SI 1999/3323, reg 8(2) (substituted by SI 2010/1088).
11 As to the meaning of 'EU-scale undertaking' see PARA 1237 note 11.
12 As to the meaning of 'EU-scale group of undertakings' see PARA 1237 note 12.
13 Transnational Information and Consultation of Employees Regulations 1999, SI 1999/3323, reg 8(3) (amended by virtue of SI 2011/1043).

1244. Request to negotiate an agreement for a European Works Council or information and consultation procedure. The central management[1] must initiate negotiations for the establishment of a European Works Council[2] or an information and consultation procedure[3] where a valid request has been made by employees[4] or employees' representatives[5], and on the relevant date[6] the undertaking is an EU-scale undertaking[7] or the group of undertakings is an EU-scale group of undertakings[8].

A valid request may consist of:
(1) a single request made by at least 100 employees, or employees' representatives who represent at least that number, in at least two undertakings or establishments in at least two different member states[9]; or
(2) a number of separate requests made on the same or different days by employees, or by employees' representatives, which, when taken together, mean that at least 100 employees, or employees' representatives who represent at least that number, in at least two undertakings or establishments in at least two different member states have made requests[10].

To amount to a valid request, the single request referred to in head (1) above, or each separate request referred to in head (2) above, must:
(a) be in writing;
(b) be sent to the central management or the local management[11];
(c) specify the date on which it was sent; and
(d) where appropriate, be made after the expiry of a period of two years, commencing on the date of the relevant decision[12], unless the special negotiating body[13] and central management have otherwise agreed[14].

The date on which a valid request is made is:
(i) where it consists of a single request satisfying head (1) above or of separate requests made on the same day satisfying head (2) above, the date on which the request is, or requests are, sent; and
(ii) where it consists of separate requests made on different days satisfying head (2) above, the date of the sending of the request which resulted in the requirements of head (2) above being satisfied[15].

The central management may, however, initiate the negotiations for the establishment of a European Works Council or an information and consultation procedure[16] on its own initiative[17].

1 As to the meaning of 'central management' see PARA 1240 note 1.
2 As to the meaning of 'European Works Council' see PARA 1237 note 3.
3 As to the meaning of 'information and consultation procedure' see PARA 1240 note 3.
4 As to the meaning of 'employee' see PARA 1238 note 1.
5 As to the meaning of 'employees' representatives' see PARA 1242 note 2.
6 As to the meaning of 'relevant date' see PARA 1241 note 7.

7   As to the meaning of 'EU-scale undertaking' see PARA 1237 note 11.
8   Transnational Information and Consultation of Employees Regulations 1999, SI 1999/3323, reg 9(1) (amended by virtue of SI 2011/1043). As to the meaning of 'EU-scale group of undertakings' see PARA 1237 note 12. As to the application of the Transnational Information and Consultation of Employees Regulations 1999, SI 1999/3323, generally see PARA 1237 note 2. See also PARA 1282 et seq.
9   As to the meaning of 'member state' see PARA 1237 note 3.
10 Transnational Information and Consultation of Employees Regulations 1999, SI 1999/3323, reg 9(2).
11 As to the meaning of 'local management' see PARA 1241 note 9.
12 Ie under the Transnational Information and Consultation of Employees Regulations 1999, SI 1999/3323, reg 16(3): see PARA 1251.
13 For these purposes, 'special negotiating body' means the body established for the purposes of negotiating with central management an agreement for a European Works Council or an information and consultation procedure: Transnational Information and Consultation of Employees Regulations 1999, SI 1999/3323, reg 2(1). As to the functions of the special negotiating body see PARA 1246; and as to the composition of the special negotiating body see PARA 1247.
14 Transnational Information and Consultation of Employees Regulations 1999, SI 1999/3323, reg 9(3).
15 Transnational Information and Consultation of Employees Regulations 1999, SI 1999/3323, reg 9(4).
16 Ie the negotiations referred to in the Transnational Information and Consultation of Employees Regulations 1999, SI 1999/3323, reg 9(1).
17 Transnational Information and Consultation of Employees Regulations 1999, SI 1999/3323, reg 9(5).

1245.   Dispute as to whether valid request made or whether relevant obligation applies.   If the central management[1] considers that a request, or separate request, for the establishment of a European Works Council[2] or an information and consultation procedure[3] did not satisfy any of the relevant requirements[4], it may apply to the Central Arbitration Committee[5] (the 'CAC') for a declaration as to whether the request satisfied the requirement[6].

The CAC must only consider an application for a declaration so made if:

(1)   the application is made within a three-month period beginning on the date when a request, or, if more than one, the first request, was duly made[7], whether or not that request satisfied the relevant requirements[8];

(2)   the application is made before the central management takes any step to initiate negotiations for the establishment of a European Works Council or an information and consultation procedure; and

(3)   at the time when the application is made, there has been no application[9] by the central management for a declaration[10].

If the central management considers for any reason that the obligation to initiate negotiations for the establishment of a European Works Council or an information and consultation procedure[11] did not apply to it on the relevant date[12], it may, within a period of three months commencing on the date on which the valid request was made, apply to the CAC for a declaration as to whether that obligation applied to it on the relevant date[13].

Where the date on which the valid request was made is a date falling before the date of any declaration made pursuant to an application made under these provisions, the operation of the relevant periods of time[14] is to be suspended for a period of time commencing on the date of the application and ending on the date of the declaration[15]; but, if, on an application for a declaration under the above provisions, the CAC does not make any declaration in favour of the central management and considers that the central management has, in making the application or conducting the proceedings, acted frivolously, vexatiously, or otherwise unreasonably, the CAC must make a declaration to the effect that that provision[16] does not apply[17].

1　As to the meaning of 'central management' see PARA 1240 note 1.
2　As to the meaning of 'European Works Council' see PARA 1237 note 3.
3　As to the meaning of 'information and consultation procedure' see PARA 1240 note 3.
4　Ie any requirement of the Transnational Information and Consultation of Employees Regulations 1999, SI 1999/3323, reg 9(2) or (3): see PARA 1244.
5　As to the Central Arbitration Committee see PARA 1226 et seq.
6　Transnational Information and Consultation of Employees Regulations 1999, SI 1999/3323, reg 10(1). As to proceedings before the Central Arbitration Committee see PARA 1280; and as to ACAS conciliation see PARA 1281. As to the application of the Transnational Information and Consultation of Employees Regulations 1999, SI 1999/3323, generally see PARA 1237 note 2. See also PARA 1282 et seq.
7　Ie for the purposes of the Transnational Information and Consultation of Employees Regulations 1999, SI 1999/3323, reg 9: see PARA 1244.
8　See note 4.
9　Ie under the Transnational Information and Consultation of Employees Regulations 1999, SI 1999/3323, reg 10(3): see the text and notes 11–13.
10　Transnational Information and Consultation of Employees Regulations 1999, SI 1999/3323, reg 10(2).
11　Ie the obligation under the Transnational Information and Consultation of Employees Regulations 1999, SI 1999/3323, reg 9(1).
12　As to the meaning of 'relevant date' see PARA 1241 note 7.
13　Transnational Information and Consultation of Employees Regulations 1999, SI 1999/3323, reg 10(3).
14　Ie the operation of the periods of time specified in the Transnational Information and Consultation of Employees Regulations 1999, SI 1999/3323, reg 18(1)(b), (c): see PARA 1253 heads (2), (3) in the text.
15　Transnational Information and Consultation of Employees Regulations 1999, SI 1999/3323, reg 10(4).
16　Ie the Transnational Information and Consultation of Employees Regulations 1999, SI 1999/3323, reg 10(4).
17　Transnational Information and Consultation of Employees Regulations 1999, SI 1999/3323, reg 10(5).

D.　SPECIAL NEGOTIATING BODY

1246.　Functions of the special negotiating body. The special negotiating body[1] has the task of determining, with the central management[2], by written agreement, the scope, composition, functions and term of office of a European Works Council[3] or the arrangements for implementing an information and consultation procedure[4].

1　As to the meaning of 'special negotiating body' see PARA 1244 note 13.
2　As to the meaning of 'central management' see PARA 1240 note 1.
3　As to the meaning of 'European Works Council' see PARA 1237 note 3.
4　Transnational Information and Consultation of Employees Regulations 1999, SI 1999/3323, reg 11. As to the meaning of 'information and consultation procedure' see PARA 1240 note 3. As to the application of the Transnational Information and Consultation of Employees Regulations 1999, SI 1999/3323, generally see PARA 1237 note 2. See also PARA 1282 et seq.

1247.　Composition of the special negotiating body. The special negotiating body[1] is to be constituted in accordance with the following provisions[2]. In each member state[3] in which employees[4] of an EU-scale undertaking[5] or EU-scale group of undertakings[6] are employed to work, those employees must elect or appoint one member of the special negotiating body for each 10 per cent (or fraction of 10 per cent) which those employees represent of the total number of employees of the EU-scale undertaking or EU-scale group of undertakings employed in those member states[7].

The special negotiating body must inform the central management[8], local managements[9] and the European social partner organisations of the composition of the special negotiating body and of the date it proposes to start the negotiations[10].

1 As to the meaning of 'special negotiating body' see PARA 1244 note 13.

2 Transnational Information and Consultation of Employees Regulations 1999, SI 1999/3323, reg 12(1) (reg 12 substituted by SI 2010/1088). This provision does not apply to a special negotiating body constituted before 5 June 2011: Transnational Information and Consultation of Employees Regulations 1999, SI 1999/3323, reg 12(3) (as so substituted). As to the application of the Transnational Information and Consultation of Employees Regulations 1999, SI 1999/3323, generally see PARA 1237 note 2. See also PARA 1282 et seq.

Where immediately before 15 January 2000: (1) a special negotiating body has been validly requested or established under the provisions of the law or practice of a member state, other than the United Kingdom, which was designed to give effect to Council Directive (EC) 94/45 (OJ L254, 30.9.94, p 64) (now repealed and replaced: see PARA 1237 note 1); (2) no article 6 agreement (see PARA 1282) is in force; and (3) no article 7 European Works Council (see PARA 1283) has been established, the Transnational Information and Consultation of Employees Regulations 1999, SI 1999/3323, reg 47(2), (3) applies: reg 47(1). Where the central management is situated in the United Kingdom, the Transnational Information and Consultation of Employees Regulations 1999, SI 1999/3323, apply, with the modifications specified in reg 47(4)–(6), as if a valid request had been made under reg 9 (see PARA 1244) and, where appropriate, as if the special negotiating body had been established under the Transnational Information and Consultation of Employees Regulations 1999, SI 1999/3323: reg 47(2). Where the central management is not situated in the United Kingdom, the provisions referred to in reg 4(2) (see PARA 1237 note 2) apply with the modifications specified in reg 47(5), (6): reg 47(3).

Regulation 12 applies in respect of the composition of the special negotiating body only to the extent that it determines the number of UK members on the special negotiating body but does not affect in any way the number of non-UK members on the special negotiating body: reg 47(4).

Where, as a result of the implementation of Council Directive (EC) 97/74 (OJ L10, 16.1.1998, p 22) (revoked and replaced: see PARA 1236) by a member state, including the United Kingdom, there are required to be UK members on the special negotiating body and, immediately before 15 January 2000: (a) no person has been designated to attend meetings of the special negotiating body as a representative of employees in the United Kingdom; or (b) one or more persons has or have been designated to attend meetings of the special negotiating body as a representative of employees in the United Kingdom, then, in the case mentioned in head (a) above, the UK members of the special negotiating body must be elected or appointed in accordance with the Transnational Information and Consultation of Employees Regulations 1999, SI 1999/3323, regs 13–15 (see PARAS 1248–1250), and, in the case mentioned in head (b) above, the person or persons is or are to be treated as from 15 January 2000 as a UK member of the special negotiating body who has been elected or appointed in accordance with regs 13–15: reg 47(5). 'UK member of the special negotiating body' means a member of the special negotiating body who represents UK employees for the purposes of negotiating with central management an agreement for a European Works Council or an information and consultation procedure: reg 2(1).

Where the number of persons referred to in head (b) above is: (i) in a case where reg 12 applies, less than the number of UK members of the special negotiating body required by reg 12; or (ii) in a case where reg 12 does not apply, less than the number of UK members of the special negotiating body required by the provisions of the law or practice of the member state under which the special negotiating body was established, the additional number of UK members of the special negotiating body needed to secure compliance with reg 12 or, as the case may be, the law or practice of the member state referred to in head (ii) above must be elected or appointed in accordance with regs 13–15: reg 47(6).

3 As to the meaning of 'member state' see PARA 1237 note 3.
4 As to the meaning of 'employee' see PARA 1238 note 1.
5 As to the meaning of 'EU-scale undertaking' see PARA 1237 note 11.

6   As to the meaning of 'EU-scale group of undertakings' see PARA 1237 note 12.
7   Transnational Information and Consultation of Employees Regulations 1999, SI 1999/3323, reg 12(2) (as substituted: see note 2).
8   As to the meaning of 'central management' see PARA 1240 note 1.
9   As to the meaning of 'local management' see PARA 1241 note 9.
10 Transnational Information and Consultation of Employees Regulations 1999, SI 1999/3323, reg 12(4) (as substituted: see note 2).

1248. Ballot arrangements for election of UK members of special negotiating body. The UK members of the special negotiating body[1] must be elected[2] by a ballot of the UK employees[3]. The UK management[4] must arrange for the holding of such a ballot of employees which satisfies the following requirements[5]. Those requirements are that:

(1)   the ballot of the UK employees must comprise a single ballot but may instead, if the UK management so decides, comprise separate ballots of employees in such constituencies as the UK management may determine where:

    (a)   the number of UK members of the special negotiating body to be elected is more than one; and

    (b)   the UK management considers that, if separate ballots were held for those constituencies, the UK members of the special negotiating body to be elected would better reflect the interests of the UK employees as a whole than if a single ballot were held;

(2)   a UK employee who is an employee of the EU-scale undertaking[6] or the EU-scale group of undertakings[7] on the day on which votes may be cast in the ballot, or if the votes may be cast on more than one day, on the first day of those days, is entitled to vote in the ballot of the UK employees;

(3)   any UK employee, or UK employees' representative[8], who is an employee of, or an employees' representative[9] in, the EU-scale undertaking or EU-scale group of undertakings immediately before the latest time at which a person may become a candidate in the ballot, is entitled to stand in the ballot of the UK employees as a candidate for election as a UK member of the special negotiating body;

(4)   the UK management must appoint an independent ballot supervisor[10] to supervise the conduct of the ballot of the UK employees but may instead, where there are to be separate ballots, appoint more than one independent ballot supervisor, each of whom is to supervise such of the separate ballots as the UK management may determine, provided that each separate ballot is supervised by a supervisor;

(5)   after the UK management has formulated proposals as to the arrangements for the ballot of the UK employees and before it has published the final arrangements under head (6) below, it must, so far as reasonably practicable, consult with the UK employees' representatives on the proposed arrangements for the ballot of the UK employees;

(6)   the UK management must publish the final arrangements for the ballot of the UK employees in such manner as to bring them to the attention of, so far as reasonably practicable, the UK employees and the UK employees' representatives[11].

Any UK employee or UK employees' representative who believes that the arrangements for the ballot of the UK employees are defective[12] may, within a period of 21 days beginning on the date on which the UK management published the final arrangements under head (6) above, present a complaint to the Central Arbitration Committee (the 'CAC')[13].

Where the CAC finds the complaint well-founded, it must make a declaration to that effect and may make an order requiring the UK management to modify the arrangements it has made for the ballot of the UK employees or to satisfy the requirements in head (5) or head (6) above[14]; and such an order must specify the modifications to the arrangements which the UK management is required to make and the requirements which it must satisfy[15].

1   As to the meaning of 'UK members of the special negotiating body' see PARA 1247 note 2.
2   Ie subject to the Transnational Information and Consultation of Employees Regulations 1999, SI 1999/3323, reg 15: see PARA 1250.
3   Transnational Information and Consultation of Employees Regulations 1999, SI 1999/3323, reg 13(1). As to the meaning of references to UK employees see PARA 1241 note 5. As to the application of the Transnational Information and Consultation of Employees Regulations 1999, SI 1999/3323, generally see PARA 1237 note 2. See also PARA 1282 et seq.
4   As to the meaning of 'UK management' see PARA 1241 note 9.
5   Transnational Information and Consultation of Employees Regulations 1999, SI 1999/3323, reg 13(2).
6   As to the meaning of 'EU-scale undertaking' see PARA 1237 note 11.
7   As to the meaning of 'EU-scale group of undertakings' see PARA 1237 note 12.
8   For these purposes, references to UK employees' representatives are references to employees' representatives who represent UK employees: Transnational Information and Consultation of Employees Regulations 1999, SI 1999/3323, reg 2(4).
9   As to the meaning of 'employees' representatives' see PARA 1242 note 2.
10   For these purposes, a person is an independent ballot supervisor if the UK management reasonably believes that he will carry out any functions conferred on him in relation to the ballot competently and has no reasonable grounds for believing that his independence in relation to the ballot might reasonably be called into question: Transnational Information and Consultation of Employees Regulations 1999, SI 1999/3323, reg 13(7).
11   Transnational Information and Consultation of Employees Regulations 1999, SI 1999/3323, reg 13(3) (amended by virtue of SI 2011/1043)
12   For these purposes, the arrangements for the ballot of the UK employees are defective if: (1) any of the requirements specified in the Transnational Information and Consultation of Employees Regulations 1999, SI 1999/3323, reg 13(3)(b)-(f) (see heads (2)-(6) in the text) is not satisfied; or (2) in a case where the ballot is to comprise separate ballots, the constituencies determined by the UK management do not reflect adequately the interests of the UK employees as a whole: reg 13(8).
13   Transnational Information and Consultation of Employees Regulations 1999, SI 1999/3323, reg 13(4). As to the Central Arbitration Committee see PARA 1226 et seq; as to proceedings before the Central Arbitration Committee see PARA 1280; and as to ACAS conciliation see PARA 1281.
14   Transnational Information and Consultation of Employees Regulations 1999, SI 1999/3323, reg 13(5).
15   Transnational Information and Consultation of Employees Regulations 1999, SI 1999/3323, reg 13(6).

1249.   Conduct of ballot for election of UK members of special negotiating body.   The UK management[1] must ensure that a duly appointed ballot supervisor[2] carries out his functions under the following provisions and that there is no interference with his carrying out of those functions from the UK management, or the central management[3], where it is not also the UK management and must comply with all reasonable requests made by a ballot supervisor for the purposes of, or in connection with, the carrying out of those functions[4].

A ballot supervisor's appointment must require that he:

(1)   supervises the conduct of the ballot, or the separate ballots he is being

appointed to supervise, in accordance with the arrangements for the ballot of the UK employees[5] published by the UK management[6] or, where appropriate, in accordance with the arrangements as required to be modified by an order made as a result of a complaint being presented on the grounds that the ballot arrangements are defective[7];

(2)   does not conduct the ballot or any of the separate ballots before the UK management has satisfied the relevant requirement[8] and:

    (a)   where no complaint has been presented on the grounds that the ballot arrangements are defective[9], before the expiry of a period of 21 days beginning on the date on which the UK management published its arrangements[10]; or

    (b)   where a complaint has been presented on the grounds that the ballot arrangements are defective[11], before the complaint has been determined and, where appropriate, the arrangements have been modified as required by an order made as a result of the complaint;

(3)   conducts the ballot, or each separate ballot, so as to secure that:

    (a)   so far as reasonably practicable, those entitled to vote are given the opportunity to vote;

    (b)   so far as reasonably practicable, those entitled to stand as candidates are given the opportunity to stand;

    (c)   so far as is reasonably practicable, those voting are able to do so in secret; and

    (d)   the votes given in the ballot are fairly and accurately counted[12].

As soon as reasonably practicable after the holding of the ballot, the ballot supervisor must publish the results of the ballot in such manner as to make them available to the UK management and, so far as reasonably practicable, the UK employees entitled to vote in the ballot and the persons who stood as candidates in the ballot[13].

A ballot supervisor must publish a report (an 'ineffective ballot report') where he considers, whether or not on the basis of representations made to him by another person, that:

(i)   any of the requirements referred to in heads (1) to (3) above was not satisfied with the result that the outcome of the ballot would have been different; or

(ii)   there was interference with the carrying out of his functions or a failure by management to comply with all reasonable requests made by him with the result that he was unable to form a proper judgment as to whether each of the requirements referred to in heads (1) to (3) above was satisfied in relation to the ballot[14];

and, where a ballot supervisor publishes an ineffective ballot report, the report must be published within a period of one month commencing on the date on which the ballot supervisor publishes[15] the results of the ballot[16].

A ballot supervisor must publish an ineffective ballot report in such manner as to make it available to the UK management and, so far as reasonably practicable, the UK employees entitled to vote in the ballot and the persons who stood as candidates in the ballot[17]. Where a ballot supervisor publishes an ineffective ballot report, then:

(A)   if there has been a single ballot or an ineffective ballot report has been published in respect of every separate ballot, the outcome of the ballot or ballots has no effect and the UK management is again under the obligation to arrange for the holding of a ballot of employees[18];

(B)   if there have been separate ballots and head (A) above does not apply, the UK management must arrange for the separate ballot or ballots in respect of which an ineffective ballot report was issued to be reheld[19], no such ballot having effect until it has been reheld and no ineffective ballot report has been published in respect of it[20].

All costs relating to the holding of a ballot, including payments made to a ballot supervisor for supervising the conduct of the ballot, must be borne by the central management, whether or not an ineffective ballot report has been made[21].

1   As to the meaning of 'UK management' see PARA 1241 note 9.
2   Ie the ballot supervisor appointed under the Transnational Information and Consultation of Employees Regulations 1999, SI 1999/3323, reg 13(3)(d): see PARA 1248 head (4) in the text.
3   As to the meaning of 'central management' see PARA 1240 note 1.
4   Transnational Information and Consultation of Employees Regulations 1999, SI 1999/3323, reg 14(1). As to the application of the Transnational Information and Consultation of Employees Regulations 1999, SI 1999/3323, generally see PARA 1237 note 2. See also PARA 1282 et seq.
5   As to the meaning of references to UK employees see PARA 1241 note 5.
6   Ie under the Transnational Information and Consultation of Employees Regulations 1999, SI 1999/3323, reg 13(3)(f): see PARA 1248 head (6) in the text.
7   Ie under the Transnational Information and Consultation of Employees Regulations 1999, SI 1999/3323, reg 13(4): see PARA 1248.
8   Ie the requirement specified in the Transnational Information and Consultation of Employees Regulations 1999, SI 1999/3323, reg 13(3)(e): see PARA 1248 head (5) in the text.
9   See note 7.
10 See note 6.
11 See note 7.
12 Transnational Information and Consultation of Employees Regulations 1999, SI 1999/3323, reg 14(2).
13 Transnational Information and Consultation of Employees Regulations 1999, SI 1999/3323, reg 14(3).
14 Transnational Information and Consultation of Employees Regulations 1999, SI 1999/3323, reg 14(4).
15 Ie under the Transnational Information and Consultation of Employees Regulations 1999, SI 1999/3323, reg 14(3).
16 Transnational Information and Consultation of Employees Regulations 1999, SI 1999/3323, reg 14(5).
17 Transnational Information and Consultation of Employees Regulations 1999, SI 1999/3323, reg 14(6).
18 Ie the obligation in the Transnational Information and Consultation of Employees Regulations 1999, SI 1999/3323, reg 13(2): see PARA 1248.
19 Ie in accordance with the Transnational Information and Consultation of Employees Regulations 1999, SI 1999/3323, reg 13: see PARA 1248.
20 Transnational Information and Consultation of Employees Regulations 1999, SI 1999/3323, reg 14(7).
21 Transnational Information and Consultation of Employees Regulations 1999, SI 1999/3323, reg 14(8).

1250.   Membership of special negotiating body where consultative committee exists. Where a consultative committee[1] exists:

(1)   no UK member of the special negotiating body[2] is to be elected by a ballot of the UK employees, except in the circumstances specified below[3]; and

(2)   the committee is entitled to nominate from its number the UK members of the special negotiating body[4].

Where the consultative committee fails to nominate any UK members of the special negotiating body, all the UK members of the special negotiating body must be elected by a ballot[5] of the UK employees[6].

Where the consultative committee nominates such number of persons to be a UK member, or UK members, of the special negotiating body, which number is less or more than the number of UK members of the special negotiating body required, the consultative committee is to be treated as having failed to nominate any UK members of the special negotiating body[7].

The consultative committee must publish the names of the persons whom it has nominated to be UK members of the special negotiating body in such manner as to bring them to the attention of the UK management and, so far as reasonably practicable, the UK employees and UK employees' representatives[8].

Where the UK management, a UK employee or a UK employees' representative believes that:

(a) the consultative committee does not satisfy the relevant requirements[9]; or

(b) any of the persons nominated by the consultative committee is not entitled to be nominated,

it, or, as the case may be, he, may, within a period of 21 days beginning on the date on which the consultative committee published[10] the names of persons nominated, present a complaint to the Central Arbitration Committee (the 'CAC')[11].

Where the CAC finds the complaint well-founded, it must make a declaration to that effect[12]; and, where the CAC has made such a declaration:

(i) no nomination made by the consultative committee has effect; and

(ii) all the UK members of the special negotiating body must be elected by a ballot[13] of the UK employees[14].

Where the consultative committee nominates any person to be a UK member of the special negotiating body, that nomination has effect after:

(A) where no complaint has been so presented[15], the expiry of a period of 21 days beginning on the date on which the consultative committee published[16] the names of persons nominated; or

(B) where a complaint has been so presented[17], the complaint has been determined without a declaration[18] having been made[19].

1 For these purposes, 'consultative committee' means a body of persons: (1) whose normal functions include or comprise the carrying out of an information and consultation function; (2) which is able to carry out its information and consultation function without interference from the UK management, or from the central management, where it is not also the UK management; (3) which, in carrying out its information and consultation function, represents all the UK employees; and (4) which consists wholly of persons who were elected by a ballot, which may have consisted of a number of separate ballots, in which all the employees who, at the time, were UK employees were entitled to vote: Transnational Information and Consultation of Employees Regulations 1999, SI 1999/3323, reg 15(4). 'Information and consultation function' means the function of: (a) receiving, on behalf of all the UK employees, information which may significantly affect the interests of the UK employees, but excluding information which is relevant only to a specific aspect of the interests of the employees, such as health and safety or collective redundancies; and (b) being consulted by the UK management or the central management, where it is not also the UK management, on the information referred to in head (a) above: reg 15(5). As to the meaning of 'UK management' see PARA 1241 note 9; as to the meaning of 'central management' see PARA 1240 note 1; as to the meaning of references to UK employees see PARA 1241 note 5; and as to the meaning of 'employee' see PARA 1238 note 1.

2 As to the meaning of 'UK member of the special negotiating body' see PARA 1247 note 2.

3 Ie except in the circumstances specified in the Transnational Information and Consultation of Employees Regulations 1999, SI 1999/3323, reg 15(2), (3) or (9).

4   Transnational Information and Consultation of Employees Regulations 1999, SI 1999/3323, reg 15(1).
5   Ie in accordance with the Transnational Information and Consultation of Employees Regulations 1999, SI 1999/3323, regs 13–14: see PARAS 1248–1249.
6   Transnational Information and Consultation of Employees Regulations 1999, SI 1999/3323, reg 15(2). As to the application of the Transnational Information and Consultation of Employees Regulations 1999, SI 1999/3323, generally see PARA 1237 note 2. See also PARA 1282 et seq.
7   Transnational Information and Consultation of Employees Regulations 1999, SI 1999/3323, reg 15(3).
8   Transnational Information and Consultation of Employees Regulations 1999, SI 1999/3323, reg 15(6). As to the meaning of references to UK employees' representatives see PARA 1248 note 8.
9   Ie the requirements in Transnational Information and Consultation of Employees Regulations 1999, SI 1999/3323, reg 15(4): see note 1.
10 Ie under the Transnational Information and Consultation of Employees Regulations 1999, SI 1999/3323, reg 15(6).
11 Transnational Information and Consultation of Employees Regulations 1999, SI 1999/3323, reg 15(7). As to the Central Arbitration Committee see PARA 1226 et seq; as to proceedings before the Central Arbitration Committee see PARA 1280; and as to ACAS conciliation see PARA 1281.
12 Transnational Information and Consultation of Employees Regulations 1999, SI 1999/3323, reg 15(8).
13 See note 5.
14 Transnational Information and Consultation of Employees Regulations 1999, SI 1999/3323, reg 15(9).
15 Ie under the Transnational Information and Consultation of Employees Regulations 1999, SI 1999/3323, reg 15(7).
16 See note 10.
17 See note 15.
18 Ie a declaration under the Transnational Information and Consultation of Employees Regulations 1999, SI 1999/3323, reg 15(8): see the text and note 12.
19 Transnational Information and Consultation of Employees Regulations 1999, SI 1999/3323, reg 15(10).

E. EUROPEAN WORKS COUNCIL AND INFORMATION AND CONSULTATION PROCEDURE

(A) European Works Council and Information and Consultation Procedure;
in general

1251. Negotiation procedure. With a view to concluding an agreement[1], the central management[2] must convene a meeting with the special negotiating body[3] and must inform local managements[4] accordingly[5]. Within a reasonable time both before and after any meeting with the central management, the members of the special negotiating body are entitled to meet without the central management or its representatives being present, using any means necessary for communication at those meetings[6].

The special negotiating body must[7] take decisions by a majority of the votes cast by its members and each member of the special negotiating body is to have one vote[8].

The special negotiating body may decide not to open negotiations with central management or to terminate negotiations; and any such decision must be taken by at least two-thirds of the votes cast by its members[9]. Any decision so made has the following effects:

(1)   the procedure to negotiate and conclude the agreement[10] ceases from the date of the decision; and

(2)   a purported request made[11] less than two years after the date of the

decision is not to be treated as such a request, unless the special negotiating body and the central management otherwise agree[12].

For the purpose of the negotiations, the special negotiating body may be assisted by experts[13] of its choice who may, at its request, attend in an advisory capacity any meeting with central management convened[14] in accordance with the above provisions[15].

The central management must pay for any reasonable expenses relating to the negotiations that are necessary to enable the special negotiating body to carry out its functions in an appropriate manner; but, where the special negotiating body is assisted by more than one expert, the central management is not required to pay such expenses in respect of more than one of them[16].

1 Ie an agreement referred to in the Transnational Information and Consultation of Employees Regulations 1999, SI 1999/3323, reg 17: see PARA 1252.
2 As to the meaning of 'central management' see PARA 1240 note 1.
3 As to the meaning of 'special negotiating body' see PARA 1244 note 13.
4 As to the meaning of 'local management' see PARA 1241 note 9.
5 Transnational Information and Consultation of Employees Regulations 1999, SI 1999/3323, reg 16(1). As to the application of the Transnational Information and Consultation of Employees Regulations 1999, SI 1999/3323, generally see PARA 1237 note 2. See also PARA 1282 et seq.
6 Transnational Information and Consultation of Employees Regulations 1999, SI 1999/3323, reg 16(1A) (added by SI 2010/1088). A complaint may be made to the Central Arbitration Committee by a relevant applicant who considers that, because of the failure of a defaulter, the members of the special negotiating body have been unable to meet in accordance with the Transnational Information and Consultation of Employees Regulations 1999, SI 1999/3323, reg 16(1A): see reg 21A(1)(a); and PARA 1271.
7 Ie subject to the Transnational Information and Consultation of Employees Regulations 1999, SI 1999/3323, reg 16(3): see the text and note 9.
8 Transnational Information and Consultation of Employees Regulations 1999, SI 1999/3323, reg 16(2).
9 Transnational Information and Consultation of Employees Regulations 1999, SI 1999/3323, reg 16(3).
10 See note 1.
11 Ie under the Transnational Information and Consultation of Employees Regulations 1999, SI 1999/3323, reg 9: see PARA 1244.
12 Transnational Information and Consultation of Employees Regulations 1999, SI 1999/3323, reg 16(4).
13 These may include representatives of European trade union organisations: Transnational Information and Consultation of Employees Regulations 1999, SI 1999/3323, reg 16(5) (amended by SI 2010/1088).
14 Ie any meeting convened in accordance with the Transnational Information and Consultation of Employees Regulations 1999, SI 1999/3323, reg 16(1) (see the text and notes 1–5).
15 Transnational Information and Consultation of Employees Regulations 1999, SI 1999/3323, reg 16(5) (as amended: see note 13).
16 Transnational Information and Consultation of Employees Regulations 1999, SI 1999/3323, reg 16(6).

1252.   Content and scope of a European Works Council agreement and information and consultation procedure. The central management[1] and the special negotiating body[2] (the 'parties') are under a duty to negotiate in a spirit of co-operation with a view to reaching a written agreement on the detailed arrangements for the information and consultation of employees[3] in an EU-scale undertaking[4] or EU-scale group of undertakings[5].

The parties may decide in writing to establish an information and consultation procedure[6] instead of a European Works Council[7].

Without prejudice to the autonomy of the parties, where the parties decide to proceed with the establishment of a European Works Council, the agreement establishing it must determine:

(1)   the undertakings of the EU-scale group of undertakings or the establishments of the EU-scale undertaking which are covered by the agreement;

(2)   the composition of the European Works Council, the number of members, the allocation of seats and the term of office of the members[8];

(3)   the functions and the procedure for information and consultation of the European Works Council and arrangements to link information and consultation of the European Works Council with information and consultation of national employee representation bodies[9];

(4)   the venue, frequency and duration of meetings of the European Works Council;

(5)   where the parties decide that it is necessary to establish a select committee, the composition of the select committee, the procedure for appointing its members, the functions and the procedural rules;

(6)   the financial and material resources to be allocated to the European Works Council;

(7)   the duration of the agreement and the procedure for its renegotiation; and

(8)   the date of entry into force of the agreement and its duration, the arrangements for amending or terminating the agreement, the circumstances in which the agreement is to be renegotiated including where the structure of the EU-scale undertaking or EU-scale group of undertakings changes and the procedure for renegotiation of the agreement[10].

If the parties decide to establish an information and consultation procedure instead of a European Works Council, the agreement establishing the procedure must specify a method by which the information and consultation representatives[11] are to enjoy the right to meet to discuss the information conveyed to them[12].

Where an EU-scale group of undertakings comprises one or more undertakings or groups of undertakings which are themselves EU-scale undertakings or EU-scale groups of undertakings, the European Works Council must be established at the level of the first-mentioned EU-scale group of undertakings, unless an agreement[13] provides otherwise[14].

Unless a wider scope is provided for in an agreement[15], the powers and competence of a European Works Council and the scope of an information and consultation procedure, in the case of an EU-scale undertaking, cover all the establishments located within the member states[16] and, in the case of an EU-scale group of undertakings, all group undertakings located within the member states[17].

Where information disclosed under a European Works Council agreement or an information and consultation procedure includes information as to the employment situation in the EU-scale undertaking or, as the case may be, the EU-scale group of undertakings, this must include suitable information relating to the use of agency workers[18], if any[19].

Where a European Works Council or information and consultation procedure has been established under the above provisions[20], or a European Works Council has been established by virtue of the subsidiary requirements[21], the central management, or any more appropriate level of management, must give information[22] to members of a European Works Council, or information and consultation representatives, as the case may be, in accordance with the following provision[23]. The content of the information, the time when, and manner in which it is given, must be such as to enable the recipients to acquaint themselves with and examine its subject matter, undertake a detailed assessment of its possible impact and, where appropriate, prepare for consultation[24].

The central management, or any more appropriate level of management, must consult with members of a European Works Council, or information and consultation representatives, as the case may be, in accordance with the following provision[25]. The content of the consultation, the time when, and manner in which it takes place, must be such as to enable a European Works Council or information and consultation representatives to express an opinion on the basis of the information provided to them[26]. That opinion must be provided within a reasonable time after the information is provided to the European Works Council or the information and consultation representatives and, having regard to the responsibilities of management to take decisions effectively, may be taken into account by the central management or any more appropriate level of management[27].

Both the information provided to the members of a European Works Council or information and consultation representatives, and the consultation of the members of a European Works Council or information and consultation representatives, is to be limited to transnational matters[28].

1   As to the meaning of 'central management' see PARA 1240 note 1.
2   As to the meaning of 'special negotiating body' see PARA 1244 note 13.
3   As to the meaning of 'employee' see PARA 1238 note 1.
4   As to the meaning of 'EU-scale undertaking' see PARA 1237 note 11.
5   Transnational Information and Consultation of Employees Regulations 1999, SI 1999/3323, reg 17(1), (2) (amended by virtue of SI 2011/1043). As to the meaning of 'EU-scale group of undertakings' see PARA 1237 note 12. As to the application of the Transnational Information and Consultation of Employees Regulations 1999, SI 1999/3323, generally see PARA 1237 note 2. See also PARA 1282 et seq.
6   As to the meaning of 'information and consultation procedure' see PARA 1240 note 3.
7   Transnational Information and Consultation of Employees Regulations 1999, SI 1999/3323, reg 17(3). As to the meaning of 'European Works Council' see PARA 1237 note 3.
8   In determining the allocation of seats under head (2) in the text, an agreement must, so far as reasonably practicable, take into account the need for balanced representation of employees with regard to their role and gender and the sector in which they work: Transnational Information and Consultation of Employees Regulations 1999, SI 1999/3323, reg 17(4A) (added by SI 2010/1088).
9   'National employee representation body' means (1) where the employees are of a description in respect of which an independent trade union is recognised by their employer for the purpose of collective bargaining, that trade union, and (2) a body which has not been established with information and consultation on transnational matters as its main purpose, to which any employee representatives are elected or appointed by employees, as a result of which they hold positions in which they are expected to receive, on behalf of the employees, information (a) which is relevant to the terms and conditions of employment of the employees; or (b) about the activities of the undertaking which may significantly affect the interests of the employees (including information relevant only to a specific aspect of the terms and conditions or interests of the employees, such as health and safety or collective redundancies): Transnational Information and Consultation of Employees Regulations 1999, SI 1999/3323, reg 2(1) (definition added by SI 2010/1088). For these purposes, and the purposes of the Transnational Information and Consultation of Employees Regulations 1999, SI 1999/3323, reg 18A (see the text and notes 20–28), matters are transnational where they concern (i) the EU-scale undertaking or EU-scale group of undertakings as a whole; or (ii) at least two undertakings or establishments of the EU-scale undertaking or EU-scale group of undertakings situated in two different member states: reg 2(4A) (added by SI 2010/1088; (amended by virtue of

SI 2011/1043). As to the meaning of 'independent trade union' see PARA 1238 note 20; and as to the meaning of 'employees' representatives' see PARA 1242 note 2.

The arrangements to link information and consultation of a European Works Council with information and consultation of the national employee representation bodies (A) in the Transnational Information and Consultation of Employees Regulations 1999, SI 1999/3323, reg 17(4)(c) (see head (3) in the text) may relate to any matters including, as the case may be, the content of the information, the time when, or manner in which it is given, or the content of the consultation, the time when, or manner in which it takes place; (B) in reg 17(4)(c) and in reg 19E (see PARA 1267) are subject to the limitation in reg 18A(7) (see the text and note 28); and (C) in regs 17(4)(c), 19E are not to affect the main purpose for which a national employee representation body was established: reg 2(4B) (as so added).

10 Transnational Information and Consultation of Employees Regulations 1999, SI 1999/3323, reg 17(4) (amended by SI 2010/1088; and by virtue of SI 2011/1043). Any such agreement is not to be subject to the provisions of the Transnational Information and Consultation of Employees Regulations 1999, SI 1999/3323, Schedule (see PARA 1254 et seq), except to the extent that the parties provide in the agreement that any of those requirements are to apply: reg 17(6).

11 As to the meaning of 'information and consultation representative' see PARA 1240 note 3.

12 Transnational Information and Consultation of Employees Regulations 1999, SI 1999/3323, reg 17(5) (substituted by SI 2010/1088). Any such agreement is not to be subject to the provisions of the Transnational Information and Consultation of Employees Regulations 1999, SI 1999/3323, Schedule (see PARA 1254 et seq), except to the extent that the parties provide in the agreement that any of those requirements are to apply: reg 17(6).

13 Ie an agreement referred to in the Transnational Information and Consultation of Employees Regulations 1999, SI 1999/3323, reg 17(4).

14 Transnational Information and Consultation of Employees Regulations 1999, SI 1999/3323, reg 17(7).

15 Ie an agreement under the Transnational Information and Consultation of Employees Regulations 1999, SI 1999/3323, reg 17(1).

16 As to the meaning of 'member state' see PARA 1237 note 3.

17 Transnational Information and Consultation of Employees Regulations 1999, SI 1999/3323, reg 17(8) (amended by virtue of SI 2011/1043).

18 As to the meaning of 'suitable information relating to the use of agency workers', and as to the meaning of 'agency worker', see PARA 1237 note 11.

19 Transnational Information and Consultation of Employees Regulations 1999, SI 1999/3323, reg 17(9) (added by SI 2010/1088; amended by virtue of SI 2011/1043).

20 Ie under the Transnational Information and Consultation of Employees Regulations 1999, SI 1999/3323, reg 17: see the text and notes 1–19.

21 Ie by virtue of the Transnational Information and Consultation of Employees Regulations 1999, SI 1999/3323, reg 18: see PARA 1253.

22 Where information as to the employment situation in the EU-scale undertaking or, as the case may be, the EU-scale group of undertakings, is disclosed by the central management or any more appropriate level of management, this must include suitable information relating to the use of agency workers (if any): Transnational Information and Consultation of Employees Regulations 1999, SI 1999/3323, reg 18A(8) (reg 18A added by SI 2010/1088; amended by virtue of SI 2011/1043).

23 Transnational Information and Consultation of Employees Regulations 1999, SI 1999/3323, reg 18A(1), (2) (as added: see note 22).

24 Transnational Information and Consultation of Employees Regulations 1999, SI 1999/3323, reg 18A(3) (as added: see note 22).

25 Transnational Information and Consultation of Employees Regulations 1999, SI 1999/3323, reg 18A(1), (4) (as added: see note 22).

26 Transnational Information and Consultation of Employees Regulations 1999, SI 1999/3323, reg 18A(5) (as added: see note 22).

27 Transnational Information and Consultation of Employees Regulations 1999, SI 1999/3323, reg 18A(6) (as added: see note 22).

28 Transnational Information and Consultation of Employees Regulations 1999, SI 1999/3323, reg 18A(7) (as added: see note 22).

(B) European Works Councils; Subsidiary Requirements

1253. Application of the subsidiary requirements relating to European Works Councils. The subsidiary requirements[1] apply if:

(1) the parties[2] so agree;

(2) within the period of six months beginning on the date on which a valid request[3] was made, the central management[4] refuses to commence negotiations; or

(3) after the expiry of a period of three years beginning on the date on which a valid request[5] was made, the parties have failed to conclude an agreement[6] and the special negotiating body[7] has not taken the decision[8] not to open negotiations with central management or to terminate negotiations[9].

1 Ie the provisions of the Transnational Information and Consultation of Employees Regulations 1999, SI 1999/3323, reg 18(1), Schedule: see PARA 1254 et seq.
2 As to the meaning of 'parties' see PARA 1252.
3 Ie referred to in the Transnational Information and Consultation of Employees Regulations 1999, SI 1999/3323, reg 9: see PARA 1244.
4 As to the meaning of 'central management' see PARA 1240 note 1.
5 See note 3.
6 Ie under the Transnational Information and Consultation of Employees Regulations 1999, SI 1999/3323, reg 17: see PARA 1252.
7 As to the meaning of 'special negotiating body' see PARA 1244 note 13.
8 Ie under the Transnational Information and Consultation of Employees Regulations 1999, SI 1999/3323, reg 16(3): see PARA 1251.
9 Transnational Information and Consultation of Employees Regulations 1999, SI 1999/3323, reg 18(1). As to the application of the Transnational Information and Consultation of Employees Regulations 1999, SI 1999/3323, generally see PARA 1237 note 2. See also PARA 1282 et seq.

1254. Establishment and composition of European Works Council in accordance with the subsidiary requirements. Where the subsidiary requirements apply[1],a European Works Council[2] must be established in accordance with them in the EU-scale undertaking[3] or EU-scale group of undertakings[4].

The European Works Council must be constituted as follows[5]. In each member state[6] in which employees[7] of an EU-scale undertaking or EU-scale group of undertakings are employed to work, those employees must elect or appoint one member of the European Works Council for each 10 percent (or fraction of 10 per cent) which those employees represent of the total number of employees of the EU-scale undertaking or EU-scale group of undertakings employed in those member states[8]. The European Works Council must inform the central management[9] and any more appropriate level of management of the composition of the European Works Council[10]. To ensure that it can co-ordinate its activities, the European Works Council must elect from among its members a select committee comprising no more than five members who are to act on behalf of the European Works Council[11].

1 Ie where the provisions of the Transnational Information and Consultation of Employees Regulations 1999, SI 1999/3323, reg 18(1), Schedule apply. As to the application of reg 18(1), Schedule see PARA 1253; and as to the application of the Transnational Information and Consultation of Employees Regulations 1999, SI 1999/3323, generally see PARA 1237 note 2. See also PARA 1282 et seq.
2 As to the meaning of 'European Works Council' see PARA 1237 note 3.
3 As to the meaning of 'EU-scale undertaking' see PARA 1237 note 11.
4 Transnational Information and Consultation of Employees Regulations 1999, SI 1999/3323, Schedule para 1 (amended by virtue of SI 2011/1043). As to the meaning of 'EU-scale group of undertakings' see PARA 1237 note 12. The Transnational Information and Consultation of Employees Regulations 1999, SI 1999/3323, reg 18A (information and consultation) applies to a European Works Council so constituted: see PARA 1252.

5 Transnational Information and Consultation of Employees Regulations 1999, SI 1999/3323, Schedule para 2(1) (Schedule para 2 substituted by SI 2010/1088).
6 As to the meaning of 'member state' see PARA 1237 note 3.
7 As to the meaning of 'employee' see PARA 1238 note 1.
8 Transnational Information and Consultation of Employees Regulations 1999, SI 1999/3323, Schedule para 2(2) (as substituted (see note 5); (amended by virtue of SI 2011/1043).
9 As to the meaning of 'central management' see PARA 1240 note 1.
10 Transnational Information and Consultation of Employees Regulations 1999, SI 1999/3323, Schedule para 2(3) (as substituted: see note 5).
11 Transnational Information and Consultation of Employees Regulations 1999, SI 1999/3323, Schedule para 2(4) (as substituted: see note 5).

1255. Appointment or election of UK members of European Works Council established in accordance with the subsidiary requirements. Where the subsidiary requirements apply[1], the UK members of the European Works Council[2] must be UK employees[3] and:

(1) in a case where all of those employees are represented by UK employees' representatives[4], must be elected or appointed by such employees' representatives;

(2) in a case where not all of those employees are represented by UK employees' representatives, must be elected by ballot[5].

For these purposes, all the UK employees are represented by UK employees' representatives if each of the employees referred to in head (1) above is a UK employee:

(a) in respect of which an independent trade union[6] is recognised by his employer for the purpose of collective bargaining; or

(b) who has elected or appointed an employees' representative for the purpose of receiving, on the employee's behalf, information:

(i)   which is relevant to the employee's terms and conditions of employment; or

(ii) about the activities of the undertaking which may significantly affect the employee's interests,

but excluding representatives who are expected to receive information relevant only to a specific aspect of the terms and conditions or interests of the employee, such as health and safety or collective redundancies[7].

Where head (1) above applies, the election or appointment of members of the European Works Council must be carried out by whatever method the UK employees' representatives decide[8]; and, where head (2) above applies, the UK members of the European Works Council are to be elected[9] by a ballot of the UK employees[10].

1 Ie where the provisions of the Transnational Information and Consultation of Employees Regulations 1999, SI 1999/3323, reg 18(1), Schedule apply. As to the application of reg 18(1), Schedule see PARA 1253; and as to the application of the Transnational Information and Consultation of Employees Regulations 1999, SI 1999/3323, generally see PARA 1237 note 2. See also PARA 1282 et seq.
2 As to the meaning of 'European Works Council' see PARA 1237 note 3.
3 As to the meaning of references to UK employees see PARA 1241 note 5; and as to the meaning of 'employee' see PARA 1238 note 1.
4 As to the meaning of references to UK employees' representatives see PARA 1248 note 8.
5 Transnational Information and Consultation of Employees Regulations 1999, SI 1999/3323, Schedule para 3(1).
6 As to the meaning of 'independent trade union' see PARA 1238 note 20.
7 Transnational Information and Consultation of Employees Regulations 1999, SI 1999/3323, Schedule para 3(2).
8 Transnational Information and Consultation of Employees Regulations 1999, SI 1999/3323, Schedule para 3(3).

9 Ie in accordance with the Transnational Information and Consultation of Employees Regulations 1999, SI 1999/3323, Schedule paras 4–5: see PARAS 1256–1257.
10 Transnational Information and Consultation of Employees Regulations 1999, SI 1999/3323, Schedule para 3(4).

1256. Ballot arrangements for election of UK members of European Works Council established in accordance with the subsidiary requirements. Where the subsidiary requirements apply[1], the UK management[2] must arrange for the holding of a ballot of employees[3] which satisfies the following requirements[4]. Those requirements are that:

(1) the ballot of the UK employees[5] must comprise a single ballot, but may instead, if the UK management so decides, comprise separate ballots of employees in such constituencies as the UK management may determine where:

    (a) the number of UK members of the European Works Council[6] to be elected is more than one; and

    (b) the UK management considers that, if separate ballots were held for those constituencies, the UK members of the European Works Council to be elected would better reflect the interests of the UK employees as a whole than if a single ballot were held;

(2) a UK employee who is an employee of the EU-scale undertaking[7] or the EU-scale group of undertakings[8] on the day on which votes may be cast in the ballot or, if the votes may be cast on more than one day, on the first day of those days is entitled to vote in a ballot of the UK employees;

(3) any UK employee who is an employee of the EU-scale undertaking or EU-scale group of undertakings immediately before the latest time at which a person may become a candidate in the ballot is entitled to stand in the ballot of the UK employees as a candidate for election as a UK member of the European Works Council;

(4) the UK management must appoint an independent ballot supervisor[9] to supervise the conduct of the ballot of the UK employees but may instead, where there are to be separate ballots, appoint more than one independent ballot supervisor, each of whom is to supervise such of the separate ballots as the UK management may determine, provided that each separate ballot is supervised by a supervisor;

(5) after the UK management has formulated proposals as to the arrangements for the ballot of the UK employees and before it has published the final arrangements under head (6) below, it must, so far as reasonably practicable, consult with the UK employees' representatives[10] on the proposed arrangements for the ballot of the UK employees;

(6) the UK management must publish the final arrangements for the ballot of the UK employees in such manner as to bring them to the attention of, so far as reasonably practicable, the UK employees and the UK employees' representatives[11].

Any UK employee or UK employees' representative who believes that the arrangements for the ballot of the UK employees are defective[12] may, within a period of 21 days beginning on the date the UK management published the final arrangements under head (6) above, present a complaint to the Central Arbitration Committee (the 'CAC')[13]. Where the CAC finds the complaint well-founded, it must make a declaration to that effect and may make an order requiring the UK management to modify the arrangements it has made for the ballot of the UK employees or to satisfy the requirements in head (5) or head (6) above[14]; and such an order must specify the modifications to the arrangements which the UK management is required to make and the requirements which it must satisfy[15].

1   Ie where the provisions of the Transnational Information and Consultation of Employees Regulations 1999, SI 1999/3323, reg 18(1), Schedule apply. As to the application of reg 18(1), Schedule see PARA 1253; and as to the application of the Transnational Information and Consultation of Employees Regulations 1999, SI 1999/3323, generally see PARA 1237 note 2. See also PARA 1282 et seq.
2   As to the meaning of 'UK management' see PARA 1241 note 9.
3   Ie a ballot of employees referred to in the Transnational Information and Consultation of Employees Regulations 1999, SI 1999/3323, Schedule para 3(4): see PARA 1255. As to the meaning of 'employee' see PARA 1238 note 1.
4   Transnational Information and Consultation of Employees Regulations 1999, SI 1999/3323, Schedule para 4(1).
5   As to the meaning of references to UK employees see PARA 1241 note 5.
6   As to the meaning of 'European Works Council' see PARA 1237 note 3.
7   As to the meaning of 'EU-scale undertaking' see PARA 1237 note 11.
8   As to the meaning of 'EU-scale group of undertakings' see PARA 1237 note 12.
9   For these purposes, a person is an independent ballot supervisor if the UK management reasonably believes that he will carry out any functions conferred on him in relation to the ballot competently and has no reasonable grounds for believing that his independence in relation to the ballot might reasonably be called into question: Transnational Information and Consultation of Employees Regulations 1999, SI 1999/3323, Schedule para 4(6).
10 As to the meaning of references to UK employees' representatives see PARA 1248 note 8.
11 Transnational Information and Consultation of Employees Regulations 1999, SI 1999/3323, Schedule para 4(2) (amended by virtue of SI 2011/1043).
12 For these purposes, the arrangements for the ballot of the UK employees are defective if: (1) any of the requirements specified in the Transnational Information and Consultation of Employees Regulations 1999, SI 1999/3323, Schedule para 4(2)(b)–(f) (see heads (2)–(6) in the text) is not satisfied; or (2) in a case where the ballot is to comprise separate ballots, the constituencies determined by the UK management do not reflect adequately the interests of the UK employees as a whole: Schedule para 4(7).
13 Transnational Information and Consultation of Employees Regulations 1999, SI 1999/3323, Schedule para 4(3). As to the Central Arbitration Committee see PARA 1226 et seq; as to proceedings before the Central Arbitration Committee see PARA 1280; and as to ACAS conciliation see PARA 1281.
14 Transnational Information and Consultation of Employees Regulations 1999, SI 1999/3323, Schedule para 4(4).
15 Transnational Information and Consultation of Employees Regulations 1999, SI 1999/3323, Schedule para 4(5).

1257.   Conduct of ballot for election of UK members of European Works Council established in accordance with the subsidiary requirements.   Where the subsidiary requirements apply[1], the UK management[2] must ensure that a duly appointed ballot supervisor[3] carries out his functions under these provisions and that there is no interference with his carrying out of those functions from the UK management, or the central management[4], where it is not also the UK management, and must comply with all reasonable requests made by a ballot supervisor for the purposes of, or in connection with, the carrying out of those functions[5].

A ballot supervisor's appointment must require that he:

(1)   supervises the conduct of the ballot, or the separate ballots he is being appointed to supervise, in accordance with the arrangements for the ballot of the UK employees[6] published by the UK management[7] or, where appropriate, in accordance with the arrangements as required to

be modified by an order made as a result of a complaint which has been presented on the grounds that the ballot arrangements are defective[8];

(2)   does not conduct the ballot or any of the separate ballots before the UK management has satisfied the relevant procedural requirement[9] and:

   (a)   where no complaint has been presented on the grounds that the ballot arrangements are defective[10], before the expiry of a period of 21 days beginning on the date on which the UK management published its arrangements[11]; or

   (b)   where a complaint has been presented on the grounds that the ballot arrangements are defective[12], before the complaint has been determined and, where appropriate, the arrangements have been modified as required by an order made as a result of the complaint;

(3)   conducts the ballot, or each separate ballot, so as to secure that:

   (a)   so far as reasonably practicable, those entitled to vote are given the opportunity to vote;

   (b)   so far as reasonably practicable, those entitled to stand as candidates are given the opportunity to stand;

   (c)   so far as is reasonably practicable, those voting are able to do so in secret; and

   (d)   the votes given in the ballot are fairly and accurately counted[13].

As soon as reasonably practicable after the holding of the ballot, or each separate ballot, the ballot supervisor must publish the results of the ballot in such manner as to make them available to the UK management and, so far as reasonably practicable, the UK employees entitled to vote in the ballot or who stood as candidates in the ballot[14].

A ballot supervisor must publish an ineffective ballot report where he considers, whether or not on the basis of representations made to him by another person, that:

   (i)   any of the requirements referred to in heads (1) to (3) above was not satisfied with the result that the outcome of the ballot would have been different; or

   (ii)   there was interference with the carrying out of his functions or a failure by management to comply with all reasonable requests made by him with the result that he was unable to form a proper judgment as to whether each of the requirements referred to in heads (1) to (3) above was satisfied in relation to the ballot[15].

Where a ballot supervisor publishes an ineffective ballot report, the report must be published within a period of one month commencing on the date on which the ballot supervisor publishes the results[16] of the ballot[17]. A ballot supervisor must publish an ineffective ballot report in such manner as to make it available to the UK management and, so far as reasonably practicable, the UK employees entitled to vote in the ballot or who stood as candidates in the ballot[18].

Where a ballot supervisor publishes an ineffective ballot report, then:

   (A)   if there has been a single ballot or an ineffective ballot report has been published in respect of every separate ballot, the outcome of the ballot or ballots has no effect and the UK management is again under the obligation to arrange for the holding of a ballot of employees[19];

   (B)   if there have been separate ballots and head (A) above does not apply, the UK management must arrange for the separate ballot or ballots in respect of which an ineffective ballot report was issued to be reheld[20] and no such ballot has effect until it has been so reheld and no ineffective ballot report has been published in respect of it[21].

All costs relating to the holding of a ballot, including payments made to a ballot supervisor for supervising the conduct of the ballot, must be borne by the central management, whether or not an ineffective ballot report has been made[22].

1 Ie where the provisions of the Transnational Information and Consultation of Employees Regulations 1999, SI 1999/3323, reg 18(1), Schedule apply. As to the application of reg 18(1), Schedule see PARA 1253; and as to the application of the Transnational Information and Consultation of Employees Regulations 1999, SI 1999/3323, generally see PARA 1237 note 2. See also PARA 1282 et seq.

2 As to the meaning of 'UK management' see PARA 1241 note 9.

3 Ie a ballot supervisor appointed under the Transnational Information and Consultation of Employees Regulations 1999, SI 1999/3323, Schedule para 4(2)(d): see PARA 1256 head (4) in the text.

4 As to the meaning of 'central management' see PARA 1240 note 1.

5 Transnational Information and Consultation of Employees Regulations 1999, SI 1999/3323, Schedule para 5(1).

6 As to the meaning of references to UK employees see PARA 1241 note 5.

7 Ie under the Transnational Information and Consultation of Employees Regulations 1999, SI 1999/3323, Schedule para 4(2)(f): see PARA 1256 head (6) in the text.

8 Ie under the Transnational Information and Consultation of Employees Regulations 1999, SI 1999/3323, Schedule para 4(3): see PARA 1256.

9 Ie the requirement specified in the Transnational Information and Consultation of Employees Regulations 1999, SI 1999/3323, Schedule para 4(2)(e): see PARA 1256 head (5) in the text.

10 See note 8.

11 See note 7.

12 See note 8.

13 Transnational Information and Consultation of Employees Regulations 1999, SI 1999/3323, Schedule para 5(2).

14 Transnational Information and Consultation of Employees Regulations 1999, SI 1999/3323, Schedule para 5(3).

15 Transnational Information and Consultation of Employees Regulations 1999, SI 1999/3323, Schedule para 5(4).

16 Ie the results of a ballot under the Transnational Information and Consultation of Employees Regulations 1999, SI 1999/3323, Schedule para 5(3).

17 Transnational Information and Consultation of Employees Regulations 1999, SI 1999/3323, Schedule para 5(5).

18 Transnational Information and Consultation of Employees Regulations 1999, SI 1999/3323, Schedule para 5(6).

19 Ie the obligation under the Transnational Information and Consultation of Employees Regulations 1999, SI 1999/3323, Schedule para 4(1): see PARA 1256.

20 Ie in accordance with the Transnational Information and Consultation of Employees Regulations 1999, SI 1999/3323, Schedule para 4 (see PARA 1256) and Schedule para 5.

21 Transnational Information and Consultation of Employees Regulations 1999, SI 1999/3323, Schedule para 5(7).

22 Transnational Information and Consultation of Employees Regulations 1999, SI 1999/3323, Schedule para 5(8).

1258. Competence of European Works Council established in accordance with the subsidiary requirements. Where the subsidiary requirements apply[1], the competence of the European Works Council[2] is limited to information and consultation on the matters which concern the EU-scale undertaking[3] or EU-scale group of undertakings[4] as a whole or at least two of its establishments or group undertakings[5] situated in different member states[6] or, as the case may be[7], to those matters concerning all of its establishments or group undertakings situated within the member states or concerning at least two of its establishments or group undertakings situated in different member states[8].

Information and consultation of employees[9] must take place between members of a European Works Council and the most appropriate level of management according to the matters under discussion[10].

1   Ie where the provisions of the Transnational Information and Consultation of Employees Regulations 1999, SI 1999/3323, reg 18(1), Schedule apply. As to the application of reg 18(1), Schedule see PARA 1253; and as to the application of the Transnational Information and Consultation of Employees Regulations 1999, SI 1999/3323, generally see PARA 1237 note 2. See also PARA 1282 et seq.
2   As to the meaning of 'European Works Council' see PARA 1237 note 3.
3   As to the meaning of 'EU-scale undertaking' see PARA 1237 note 11.
4   As to the meaning of 'EU-scale group of undertakings' see PARA 1237 note 12.
5   As to the meaning of 'group undertaking' see PARA 1237 note 12.
6   Transnational Information and Consultation of Employees Regulations 1999, SI 1999/3323, Schedule para 6(1) (amended by virtue of SI 2011/1043). As to the meaning of 'member state' see PARA 1237 note 3.
7   Ie in the case of an EU-scale undertaking or EU-scale group of undertakings falling within the Transnational Information and Consultation of Employees Regulations 1999, SI 1999/3323, reg 5(1)(b) or (c): see PARA 1240 heads (2), (3) in the text.
8   Transnational Information and Consultation of Employees Regulations 1999, SI 1999/3323, Schedule para 6(2).
9   As to the meaning of 'employee' see PARA 1238 note 1.
10 Transnational Information and Consultation of Employees Regulations 1999, SI 1999/3323, Schedule para 6(3) (added by SI 2010/1088).

1259.   Information and consultation meetings where the subsidiary requirements apply. Where the subsidiary requirements apply[1], the European Works Council[2] has the right[3] to meet with the central management[4] once a year in an information and consultation meeting, to be informed and consulted, on the basis of a report drawn up by the central management, on the progress of the business of the EU-scale undertaking[5] or EU-scale group of undertakings[6] and its prospects[7]. The central management must inform the local managements[8] accordingly[9].

The information provided to the European Works Council must relate in particular to the structure, economic and financial situation, the probable development of the business and of production and sales of the EU-scale undertaking or EU-scale group of undertakings[10]. Where information is to be disclosed under these provisions which includes information as to the employment situation in the EU-scale undertaking or, as the case may be, the EU-scale group of undertakings, this must include suitable information relating to the use of agency workers[11] (if any)[12].

The information and consultation meeting must relate in particular to the situation and probable trend of employment, investments, and substantial changes concerning organisation, introduction of new working methods or production processes, transfers of production, mergers, cut-backs or closures of undertakings, establishments or important parts of such undertakings or establishments, and collective redundancies[13].

1   Ie where the provisions of the Transnational Information and Consultation of Employees Regulations 1999, SI 1999/3323, reg 18(1), Schedule apply. As to the application of reg 18(1), Schedule see PARA 1253; and as to the application of the Transnational Information and Consultation of Employees Regulations 1999, SI 1999/3323, generally see PARA 1237 note 2. See also PARA 1282 et seq.
2   As to the meaning of 'European Works Council' see PARA 1237 note 3.
3   Ie subject to the Transnational Information and Consultation of Employees Regulations 1999, SI 1999/3323, Schedule para 8: see PARA 1260.
4   As to the meaning of 'central management' see PARA 1240 note 1.
5   As to the meaning of 'EU-scale undertaking' see PARA 1237 note 11.

6   As to the meaning of 'EU-scale group of undertakings' see PARA 1237 note 12.

7   Transnational Information and Consultation of Employees Regulations 1999, SI 1999/3323, Schedule para 7(1) (amended by virtue of SI 2011/1043). The employer must ensure that the consultation referred to in the Transnational Information and Consultation of Employees Regulations 1999, SI 1999/3323, Schedule para 7(1) is conducted in such a way that the members of the European Works Council can, if they so request, meet with the central management and obtain a reasoned response from the central management to any opinion expressed by those representatives on the report referred to in Schedule para 7(1): Schedule para 9(7) (added by SI 2010/1088). Information and consultation carried out in accordance with the Transnational Information and Consultation of Employees Regulations 1999, SI 1999/3323, Schedule must be carried out subject to reg 23 (see PARA 1273): Schedule para 9(8) (as so added).

8   As to the meaning of 'local management' see PARA 1241 note 9.

9   Transnational Information and Consultation of Employees Regulations 1999, SI 1999/3323, Schedule para 7(2).

10   Transnational Information and Consultation of Employees Regulations 1999, SI 1999/3323, Schedule para 7(3) (substituted by SI 2010/1088).

11   As to the meaning of 'suitable information relating to the use of agency workers' see PARA 1242 note 9; and as to the meaning of 'agency worker' see PARA 1237 note 11.

12   Transnational Information and Consultation of Employees Regulations 1999, SI 1999/3323, Schedule para 8A (added by SI 2010/1088).

13   Transnational Information and Consultation of Employees Regulations 1999, SI 1999/3323, Schedule para 7(4) (added by SI 2010/1088).

1260. Exceptional information and consultation meetings where the subsidiary requirements apply. Where the subsidiary requirements apply[1], and there are exceptional circumstances affecting the interests of employees[2] to a considerable extent, particularly in the event of relocations, the closure of establishments or undertakings or collective redundancies, the select committee or, where no such committee exists, the European Works Council[3] has the right to be informed[4]. It has the right to meet in an exceptional information and consultation meeting, at its request, the central management[5], or any other more appropriate level of management within the EU-scale undertaking[6] or group of undertakings[7] having its own powers of decision, so as to be informed and consulted[8].

Those members of the European Works Council who have been elected or appointed by the establishments or undertakings which are directly concerned by the circumstances in question also have the right to participate in an exceptional information and consultation meeting[9] organised with the select committee which has been duly[10] elected[11].

The exceptional information and consultation meeting[12] must take place as soon as possible on the basis of a report drawn up by the central management or any other appropriate level of management of the EU-scale undertaking or EU-scale group of undertakings, on which an opinion may be delivered at the end of the meeting or within a reasonable time[13]. It does not affect the prerogatives of the central management[14].

1   Ie where the provisions of the Transnational Information and Consultation of Employees Regulations 1999, SI 1999/3323, reg 18(1), Schedule apply. As to the application of reg 18(1), Schedule see PARA 1253; and as to the application of the Transnational Information and Consultation of Employees Regulations 1999, SI 1999/3323, generally see PARA 1237 note 2. See also PARA 1282 et seq.

2   As to the meaning of 'employee' see PARA 1238 note 1.

3   As to the meaning of 'European Works Council' see PARA 1237 note 3.

4   Transnational Information and Consultation of Employees Regulations 1999, SI 1999/3323, Schedule para 8(1).

     Where information is to be disclosed under Schedule para 8 which includes information as to the employment situation in the EU-scale undertaking or, as the case may be, the EU-scale group of undertakings, this must include suitable information relating to the use of agency workers (if any): Transnational Information and Consultation of Employees Regulations 1999, SI 1999/3323, Schedule para 8A (added by SI 2010/1088). As to the meaning of 'suitable information relating to the use of agency workers' see PARA 1242 note 9; and as to the meaning of 'agency worker' see PARA 1237 note 11.

5 As to the meaning of 'central management' see PARA 1240 note 1.

6 As to the meaning of 'EU-scale undertaking' see PARA 1237 note 11.

7 As to the meaning of 'EU-scale group of undertakings' see PARA 1237 note 12.

8 Transnational Information and Consultation of Employees Regulations 1999, SI 1999/3323, Schedule para 8(1) (amended by SI 2010/1088; and by virtue of SI 2011/1043). The employer must ensure that the consultation referred to in the Transnational Information and Consultation of Employees Regulations 1999, SI 1999/3323, Schedule para 8(1) is conducted in such a way that the members of the European Works Council can, if they so request, meet with the central management and obtain a reasoned response from the central management to any opinion expressed by those representatives on the report referred to in Schedule para 8(3) (see the text and notes 12–13): Schedule para 9(7) (added by SI 2010/1088). Information and consultation carried out in accordance with the Transnational Information and Consultation of Employees Regulations 1999, SI 1999/3323, Schedule must be carried out subject to reg 23 (see PARA 1273): Schedule para 9(8) (as so added).

9 Ie the exceptional information and consultation meeting referred to in the Transnational Information and Consultation of Employees Regulations 1999, SI 1999/3323, Schedule para 8(1).

10 Ie duly elected under the Transnational Information and Consultation of Employees Regulations 1999, SI 1999/3323, Schedule para 2(4): see PARA 1254.

11 Transnational Information and Consultation of Employees Regulations 1999, SI 1999/3323, Schedule para 8(2) (amended by SI 2010/1088); Interpretation Act 1978 s 17(2).

12 See note 9.

13 Transnational Information and Consultation of Employees Regulations 1999, SI 1999/3323, Schedule para 8(3) (amended by virtue of SI 2011/1043). The employer must ensure that the consultation referred to in the Transnational Information and Consultation of Employees Regulations 1999, SI 1999/3323, Schedule para 7(1) is conducted in such a way that the members of the European Works Council can, if they so request, meet with the central management and obtain a reasoned response from the central management to any opinion expressed by those representatives on the report referred to in Schedule para 7(1): Schedule para 9(7) (added by SI 2010/1088). Information and consultation carried out in accordance with the Transnational Information and Consultation of Employees Regulations 1999, SI 1999/3323, Schedule must be carried out subject to reg 23 (see PARA 1273): Schedule para 9(8) (as so added).

14 Transnational Information and Consultation of Employees Regulations 1999, SI 1999/3323, Schedule para 8(4).

1261. Procedures for meetings and financial arrangements where the subsidiary requirements apply. Where the subsidiary requirements apply[1], before an information and consultation meeting[2] or exceptional information and consultation meeting[3] with the central management[4], the European Works Council[5] or the select committee, enlarged[6] where necessary, is entitled to meet without the management concerned being present[7].

The members of the European Works Council must[8] inform:

(1) the employees' representatives[9] of the employees[10] in the establishments of an EU-scale undertaking[11] or in the undertakings of an EU-scale group of undertakings[12]; or

(2) to the extent that any employees are not represented by employees' representatives, the employees themselves,

of the content and outcome of the information and consultation procedure which has been duly[13] carried out[14].

The European Works Council must adopt its own rules of procedure[15]; and the European Works Council or the select committee may be assisted by experts of its choice, in so far as this is necessary for it to carry out its tasks[16].

The operating expenses of the European Works Council must be borne by the central management; but, where the European Works Council is assisted by more than one expert, the central management is not required to pay such expenses in respect of more than one of them[17].

The central management must provide the members of the European Works Council and its select committee with such financial and material resources as enable them to perform their duties in an appropriate manner. In particular, the cost of organising meetings and arranging for interpretation facilities and the accommodation and travelling expenses of members of the European Works Council and its select committee must be met by the central management unless the central management and European Works Council, or select committee, otherwise agree[18].

1 Ie where the provisions of the Transnational Information and Consultation of Employees Regulations 1999, SI 1999/3323, reg 18(1), Schedule apply. As to the application of reg 18(1), Schedule see PARA 1253; and as to the application of the Transnational Information and Consultation of Employees Regulations 1999, SI 1999/3323, generally see PARA 1237 note 2. See also PARA 1282 et seq.
2 As to the information and consultation meeting see PARA 1259.
3 As to the exceptional information and consultation meeting see PARA 1260.
4 As to the meaning of 'central management' see PARA 1240 note 1.
5 As to the meaning of 'European Works Council' see PARA 1237 note 3.
6 Ie in accordance with the Transnational Information and Consultation of Employees Regulations 1999, SI 1999/3323, Schedule para 8(2): see PARA 1260.
7 Transnational Information and Consultation of Employees Regulations 1999, SI 1999/3323, Schedule para 9(1).
8 Ie subject to the Transnational Information and Consultation of Employees Regulations 1999, SI 1999/3323, reg 23: see PARA 1273.
9 As to the meaning of 'employees' representatives' see PARA 1242 note 2.
10 As to the meaning of 'employee' see PARA 1238 note 1.
11 As to the meaning of 'EU-scale undertaking' see PARA 1237 note 11.
12 As to the meaning of 'EU-scale group of undertakings' see PARA 1237 note 12.
13 Ie duly carried out in accordance with the Transnational Information and Consultation of Employees Regulations 1999, SI 1999/3323, Schedule: see PARA 1254 et seq.
14 Transnational Information and Consultation of Employees Regulations 1999, SI 1999/3323, Schedule para 9(2) (amended by virtue of SI 2011/1043).
15 Transnational Information and Consultation of Employees Regulations 1999, SI 1999/3323, Schedule para 9(3).
16 Transnational Information and Consultation of Employees Regulations 1999, SI 1999/3323, Schedule para 9(4).
17 Transnational Information and Consultation of Employees Regulations 1999, SI 1999/3323, Schedule para 9(5).
18 Transnational Information and Consultation of Employees Regulations 1999, SI 1999/3323, Schedule para 9(6) (amended by SI 2010/1088).

1262. Continuing application of the subsidiary requirements. Where the subsidiary requirements apply[1], four years after the European Works Council[2] is established, it must examine whether to open negotiations for the conclusion of an agreement[3] or to continue to apply the subsidiary requirements which have been duly[4] adopted[5].

If the European Works Council decides to negotiate an agreement[6], it must notify the central management[7] in writing to that effect; and:

(1) such notification is to be treated as a valid request to negotiate an agreement for a European Works Council or information and consultation procedure[8]; and

(2) the provisions relating to negotiation procedure[9], the content and scope of a European Works Council agreement and information and

consultation procedure[10] and the subsidiary requirements[11] apply in respect of the negotiations for an agreement as if references[12] to the special negotiating body[13] were references to the European Works Council[14].

1 Ie where the provisions of the Transnational Information and Consultation of Employees Regulations 1999, SI 1999/3323, reg 18(1), Schedule apply. As to the application of reg 18(1), Schedule see PARA 1253; and as to the application of the Transnational Information and Consultation of Employees Regulations 1999, SI 1999/3323, generally see PARA 1237 note 2. See also PARA 1282 et seq.
2 As to the meaning of 'European Works Council' see PARA 1237 note 3.
3 Ie an agreement referred to in the Transnational Information and Consultation of Employees Regulations 1999, SI 1999/3323, reg 17: see PARA 1252.
4 Ie adopted in accordance with the Transnational Information and Consultation of Employees Regulations 1999, SI 1999/3323, reg 18(1), Schedule: see PARA 1254 et seq.
5 Transnational Information and Consultation of Employees Regulations 1999, SI 1999/3323, Schedule para 10(1).
6 Ie in accordance with the Transnational Information and Consultation of Employees Regulations 1999, SI 1999/3323, reg 17.
7 As to the meaning of 'central management' see PARA 1240 note 1.
8 Ie a valid request made under the Transnational Information and Consultation of Employees Regulations 1999, SI 1999/3323, reg 9: see PARA 1244.
9 Ie the Transnational Information and Consultation of Employees Regulations 1999, SI 1999/3323, reg 16: see PARA 1251.
10 Ie the Transnational Information and Consultation of Employees Regulations 1999, SI 1999/3323, reg 17: see PARA 1252.
11 Ie the Transnational Information and Consultation of Employees Regulations 1999, SI 1999/3323, reg 18: see PARA 1253.
12 Ie in the Transnational Information and Consultation of Employees Regulations 1999, SI 1999/3323: see PARAS 1237 et seq, 1263 et seq.
13 As to the meaning of 'special negotiating body' see PARA 1244 note 13.
14 Transnational Information and Consultation of Employees Regulations 1999, SI 1999/3323, Schedule para 10(2).

(C) Further Provisions regarding Co-operation, Information and Consultation

1263. Co-operation between central management and European Works Council. The central management[1] and the European Works Council[2] are under a duty to work in a spirit of co-operation with due regard to their reciprocal rights and obligations[3]; and that duty applies also to the central management and information and consultation representatives[4].

1 As to the meaning of 'central management' see PARA 1240 note 1.
2 As to the meaning of 'European Works Council' see PARA 1237 note 3.
3 Transnational Information and Consultation of Employees Regulations 1999, SI 1999/3323, reg 19(1). As to the application of the Transnational Information and Consultation of Employees Regulations 1999, SI 1999/3323, generally see PARA 1237 note 2. See also PARA 1282 et seq.
4 Transnational Information and Consultation of Employees Regulations 1999, SI 1999/3323, reg 19(2). As to the meaning of 'information and consultation representative' see PARA 1240 note 3.

1264. Central management's obligation to provide means required. The central management[1] must provide the members of a European Works Council[2] with the means required to fulfil their duty to represent collectively the interests of the employees[3] of the EU-scale undertaking[4] or EU-scale group of undertakings[5] under the Transnational Information and Consultation of Employees Regulations 1999[6].

1 As to the meaning of 'central management' see PARA 1240 note 1.

2   As to the meaning of 'European Works Council' see PARA 1237 note 3.
3   As to the meaning of 'employee' see PARA 1238 note 1.
4   As to the meaning of 'EU-scale undertaking' see PARA 1237 note 11.
5   As to the meaning of 'EU-scale group of undertakings' see PARA 1237 note 12.
6   Transnational Information and Consultation of Employees Regulations 1999, SI 1999/3323, reg 19A(1) (reg 19A added by SI 2010/1088; amended by virtue of SI 2011/1043). The obligation on central management in the Transnational Information and Consultation of Employees Regulations 1999, SI 1999/3323, reg 19A(1) does not, however, include an obligation to provide a member of a European Works Council with (1) time off during working hours to perform functions as such a member, or remuneration for such time off (as required by regs 25, 26: see PARA 1275); (2) the means required to undertake training (as required by reg 19B: see PARA 1265); or (3) time off during working hours to undertake training, or remuneration for such time off (as required by regs 25, 26): reg 19A(2) (as so added).
    A complaint may be made to the Central Arbitration Committee by a relevant applicant who considers that, because of the failure of a defaulter, the members of the European Works Council have not been provided with the means required to fulfil their duty to represent collectively the interests of the employees of the EU-scale undertaking or EU-scale group of undertakings in accordance with reg 19A: see reg 21A(1)(b); and PARA 1271.

1265.   Right to training for members of special negotiating body or European Works Council.   The central management[1] must provide an employee[2] who is a member of a special negotiating body[3] or a member of a European Works Council[4] with the means required to undertaking training to the extent necessary for the exercise of the employee's representative duties[5].

1   As to the meaning of 'central management' see PARA 1240 note 1.
2   As to the meaning of 'employee' see PARA 1238 note 1.
3   As to the meaning of 'special negotiating body' see PARA 1244 note 13.
4   As to the meaning of 'European Works Council' see PARA 1237 note 3.
5   Transnational Information and Consultation of Employees Regulations 1999, SI 1999/3323, reg 19B(1) (reg 19B added by SI 2010/1088). The obligation on central management referred to in the Transnational Information and Consultation of Employees Regulations 1999, SI 1999/3323, reg 19B(1) does not, however, include an obligation to provide time off during working hours to undertaking training, or remuneration for such time off (as required by regs 25, 26: see PARA 1275): reg 19B(2) (as so added).
    A complaint may be made to the Central Arbitration Committee by a relevant applicant who considers that, because of the failure of a defaulter, a member of a special negotiating body or a member of the European Works Council has not been provided with the means required to undertake the training referred to in reg 19B: see reg 21A(1)(c); and PARA 1271.

1266.   European Works Council's duty to inform of content and outcome of information and consultation procedure.   A European Works Council[1] must[2] inform:

(1)   the employees' representatives[3] in the establishments of an EU-scale undertaking[4] or in the undertakings of an EU-scale group of undertakings[5]; or

(2)   to the extent that any employees[6] are not represented by employees' representatives, the employees themselves,

of the content and outcome of the information and consultation procedure[7] carried out in accordance with the Transnational Information and Consultation of Employees Regulations 1999[8].

An employee or employees' representative may present a complaint to the Central Arbitration Committee (the 'CAC')[9] that:

(a)   the European Works Council has failed to inform them under the above provisions of the content or outcome of the information and consultation procedure; or

(b)   the information which has been provided by the European Works Council is false or incomplete in a material particular[10].

A complaint brought under head (a) or head (b) above must be brought within a period of six months beginning with the date of the alleged failure to inform, or the provision of false or incomplete information[11].

Where the CAC finds the complaint well-founded it must make an order requiring the European Works Council to disclose information to the complainant; and the order must specify:

(i)   the information in respect of which the CAC finds that the complaint is well-founded and which is to be disclosed to the complainant;

(ii)   the date (or if more than one, the earliest date) on which the European Works Council refused or failed to disclose information, or disclosed false or incomplete information; and

(iii)   a date (not less than one week from the date of the order) by which the European Works Council must disclose the information specified in the order[12].

The CAC must not find such a complaint well-founded where it considers that the failure to inform, or the provision of false or incomplete information, resulted from a failure by the central management[13] to provide the members of the European Works Council with the means required to fulfil their duty[14] to represent collectively the interests of the employees of the EU-scale undertaking or EU-scale group of undertakings[15].

1   As to the meaning of 'European Works Council' see PARA 1237 note 3.
2   Ie subject to the Transnational Information and Consultation of Employees Regulations 1999, SI 1999/3323, reg 23: see PARA 1273.
3   As to the meaning of 'employees' representatives' see PARA 1242 note 2.
4   As to the meaning of 'EU-scale undertaking' see PARA 1237 note 11.
5   As to the meaning of 'EU-scale group of undertakings' see PARA 1237 note 12.
6   As to the meaning of 'employee' see PARA 1238 note 1.
7   As to the meaning of 'information and consultation procedure' see PARA 1240 note 3.
8   Transnational Information and Consultation of Employees Regulations 1999, SI 1999/3323, reg 19C (added by SI 2010/1088; amended by virtue of SI 2011/1043).
9   As to the Central Arbitration Committee see PARA 1226 et seq.
10 Transnational Information and Consultation of Employees Regulations 1999, SI 1999/3323, reg 19D(1) (reg 19D added by SI 2010/1088). As to proceedings before the Central Arbitration Committee see PARA 1280; and as to ACAS conciliation see PARA 1281.
11 Transnational Information and Consultation of Employees Regulations 1999, SI 1999/3323, reg 19D(4) (as added: see note 10).
12 Transnational Information and Consultation of Employees Regulations 1999, SI 1999/3323, reg 19D(2) (as added: see note 10).
13 As to the meaning of 'central management' see PARA 1240 note 1.
14 Ie as required by the Transnational Information and Consultation of Employees Regulations 1999, SI 1999/3323, reg 19A: see PARA 1264.
15 Transnational Information and Consultation of Employees Regulations 1999, SI 1999/3323, reg 19D(3) (as added (see note 10); amended by virtue of SI 2011/1043).

1267.   Links between European Works Council and national employee representation bodies.   Where:

(1)   no arrangements to link information and consultation of a European Works Council[1] with information and consultation of national employee representation bodies have been made[2]; and

(2)   there are circumstances likely to lead to substantial changes in work organisation or contractual relations,

the management of every undertaking belonging to the EU-scale group of undertakings[3], the central management[4], or the representative agent or the management treated as the central management of the EU-scale undertaking[5] or EU-scale group of undertakings[6], as the case may be, must ensure that the procedures for informing and consulting the European Works Council and the national employee representation bodies[7] in relation to the substantial changes in work organisation or contractual relations referred to in head (2) above are linked so as to begin within a reasonable time of each other[8].

1   As to the meaning of 'European Works Council' see PARA 1237 note 3.
2   Ie under the Transnational Information and Consultation of Employees Regulations 1999, SI 1999/3323, reg 17(4)(c): see PARA 1252.
3   As to the meaning of 'EU-scale group of undertakings' see PARA 1237 note 12.
4   As to the meaning of 'central management' see PARA 1240 note 1.
5   As to the meaning of 'EU-scale undertaking' see PARA 1237 note 11.
6   Ie within the meaning of the Transnational Information and Consultation of Employees Regulations 1999, SI 1999/3323, reg 5(2): see PARA 1240.
7   The national employee representation bodies referred to in the text are those bodies which are entitled, whether by law, agreement or custom and practice, to be informed and consulted on the substantial changes in work organisation or contractual relations referred to in the Transnational Information and Consultation of Employees Regulations 1999, SI 1999/3323, reg 19E(1)(b) (see head (2) in the text): reg 19E(3) (reg 19E added by SI 2010/1088).
8   Transnational Information and Consultation of Employees Regulations 1999, SI 1999/3323, reg 19E(1), (2) (as added (see note 7); amended by virtue of SI 2011/1043). This is subject to the Transnational Information and Consultation of Employees Regulations 1999, SI 1999/3323, reg 2(4B) (see PARA 1252 note 9): reg 19E(1) (as so added).
     A complaint may be made to the Central Arbitration Committee by a relevant applicant who considers that reg 19E(2) applies, and that because of the failure of a defaulter, the European Works Council and the national employee representation bodies have not been informed and consulted in accordance with reg 19E: see reg 21A(1)(d); and PARA 1271.

1268.   Adaptation where the structure of a EU-scale undertaking or EU-scale group of undertakings changes significantly.   The central management[1] must initiate negotiations for the establishment of a European Works Council[2] or an information and consultation procedure[3] where the structure of an EU-scale undertaking[4] or EU-scale group of undertakings[5] changes significantly[6] and:

(1)   there is in force:
   (a)   one European Works Council agreement, or one agreement for an information and consultation procedure;
   (b)   more than one European Works Council agreement;
   (c)   more than one agreement for an information and consultation procedure;
   (d)   at least one European Works Council agreement and at least one agreement for an information and consultation procedure,
   and there are no provisions for the continuance of the European Works Council or information and consultation procedure, as the case may be, where there are significant changes in the structure of the EU-scale undertaking or EU-scale group of undertakings, or there are such provisions but there is a conflict between them[7];

(2)   a valid request[8] has been made by employees[9] or employees' representatives[10] and on the relevant date[11] the undertaking is an EU-scale undertaking or the group of undertakings is an EU-scale group of undertakings[12].

Notwithstanding the above requirement[13], the central management may initiate the negotiations referred to above[14] on its own initiative[15].

Where the central management has initiated negotiations[16], there must be on the special negotiating body[17] at least three members of every existing European Works Council in addition to the members elected or appointed in accordance[18] with the statutory requirement[19].

Before the establishment of a European Works Council or an information and consultation procedure under the above provisions[20], any agreement establishing an existing European Works Council or information and consultation procedure is to continue to operate in accordance with its terms, and may be adapted by agreement between the members of the European Works Council and the central management, or the information and consultation representatives[21] and the central management, as the case may be, as a result of the change in structure[22] referred to above[23].

Where information is to be disclosed under a European Works Council agreement or an information and consultation procedure which includes information as to the employment situation in the EU-scale undertaking or, as the case may be, the EU-scale group of undertakings, this must include suitable information relating to the use of agency workers[24] (if any)[25].

1   As to the meaning of 'central management' see PARA 1240 note 1.
2   As to the meaning of 'European Works Council' see PARA 1237 note 3.
3   As to the meaning of 'information and consultation procedure' see PARA 1240 note 3.
4   As to the meaning of 'EU-scale undertaking' see PARA 1237 note 11.
5   As to the meaning of 'EU-scale group of undertakings' see PARA 1237 note 12.

6   Transnational Information and Consultation of Employees Regulations 1999, SI 1999/3323, reg 19F(1) (reg 19F added by SI 2010/1088; amended by virtue of SI 2011/1043).

7   Transnational Information and Consultation of Employees Regulations 1999, SI 1999/3323, reg 19F(2) (as added and amended: see note 6).

8   Ie within the meaning of the Transnational Information and Consultation of Employees Regulations 1999, SI 1999/3323, reg 9(2), (3): see PARA 1244.

9   As to the meaning of 'employee' see PARA 1238 note 1.

10 As to the meaning of 'employees' representatives' see PARA 1242 note 2.

11 As to the meaning of 'relevant date' see PARA 1241 note 7.

12 Transnational Information and Consultation of Employees Regulations 1999, SI 1999/3323, reg 19F(3) (as added and amended: see note 6).

13 Ie notwithstanding the Transnational Information and Consultation of Employees Regulations 1999, SI 1999/3323, reg 19F(1) (see the text and notes 1–6).

14 Ie the negotiations referred to in the Transnational Information and Consultation of Employees Regulations 1999, SI 1999/3323, reg 19F(1) (see the text and notes 1–6).

15 Transnational Information and Consultation of Employees Regulations 1999, SI 1999/3323, reg 19F(4) (as added: see note 6).

16 Ie under the Transnational Information and Consultation of Employees Regulations 1999, SI 1999/3323, reg 19F(1) (see the text and notes 1–6) or reg 19F(4) (see the text and notes 13–15).

17 As to the meaning of 'special negotiating body' see PARA 1244 note 13.

18 Ie in accordance with the Transnational Information and Consultation of Employees Regulations 1999, SI 1999/3323, reg 12(2): see PARA 1247.

19 Transnational Information and Consultation of Employees Regulations 1999, SI 1999/3323, reg 19F(5) (as added: see note 6).

20 See note 16.

21 As to the meaning of 'information and consultation representative' see PARA 1240 note 3.

22 Ie the change in structured referred to in the Transnational Information and Consultation of Employees Regulations 1999, SI 1999/3323, reg 19F(1) (see the text and notes 1–6).

23 Transnational Information and Consultation of Employees Regulations 1999, SI 1999/3323, reg 19F(6) (as added: see note 6).

24 As to the meaning of 'suitable information relating to the use of agency workers' see PARA 1242 note 9; and as to the meaning of 'agency worker' see PARA 1237 note 11.

25 Transnational Information and Consultation of Employees Regulations 1999, SI 1999/3323, reg 19F(6) (as added and amended: see note 6).

F.   COMPLIANCE WITH AND ENFORCEMENT OF TRANSNATIONAL INFORMATION AND CONSULTATION REGULATIONS

1269. Failure to establish European Works Council or information and consultation procedure. A complaint may be presented to the Central Arbitration Committee (the 'CAC')[1] by a relevant applicant[2] who considers:

(1)   that the parties[3] have reached agreement on the establishment of a European Works Council[4] or an information and consultation procedure[5], or that the subsidiary requirements[6] apply; and

(2)   that, because of a failure[7] of the central management, the European Works Council or information and consultation procedure has not been established at all, or has not been established fully in accordance with the terms of the agreement[8] or, as the case may be, in accordance with the subsidiary requirements[9].

Where the CAC finds the complaint well-founded, it must make a decision to that effect and may make an order requiring the central management to take such steps as are necessary to establish the European Works Council or information and consultation procedure in accordance with the terms of the agreement[10] or, as the case may be, to establish a European Works Council in accordance with the subsidiary requirements[11]. Such an order must specify:

(a)   the steps which the central management is required to take;

(b)   the date of the failure of the central management; and

(c)   the period within which the order must be complied with[12].

No order of the CAC under the above provisions has the effect of suspending or altering the effect of any act done or of any agreement made by the central management or the local management[13].

The CAC must not find such a complaint to be well-founded where:

(i)   the central management made no application in relation to the request[14], or, where the request consisted of separate requests, was unable by reason of the time limit imposed[15] to make an application[16] in relation to a particular request, and shows that the request was not a valid request because a relevant requirement[17] was not satisfied; or

(ii)   the central management made no application[18] but shows that the relevant obligation[19] did not, for any reason, apply to it on the relevant date[20].

If the CAC makes a decision that it finds the complaint well-founded[21], the relevant applicant may, within the period of three months beginning with the date on which the decision is made, make an application to the Employment Appeal Tribunal ('the appeal tribunal') for a penalty notice to be issued[22]. Where such an application is made, the appeal tribunal must issue a written penalty notice to the central management requiring it to pay a penalty to the Secretary of State in respect of the failure[23]; but this does not apply if the appeal tribunal is satisfied, on hearing the representations of the central management, that the failure resulted from a reason beyond the central management's control or that it has some other reasonable excuse for its failure[24].

1   As to the Central Arbitration Committee see PARA 1226 et seq.

2   For these purposes, 'relevant applicant' means: (1) in a case where a special negotiating body exists, the special negotiating body; or (2) in a case where a special negotiating body does not exist, an employee, employees' representative, or person who was a member of the special negotiating body, if that body existed previously: Transnational Information and Consultation of Employees Regulations 1999, SI 1999/3323, reg 20(3). As to the meaning of 'special negotiating body' see PARA 1244 note 13; as to the meaning of 'employee' see PARA 1238 note 1; and as to the meaning of 'employees' representatives' see PARA 1242 note 2.

3 As to the meaning of 'parties' see PARA 1252.
4 As to the meaning of 'European Works Council' see PARA 1237 note 3.
5 As to the meaning of 'information and consultation procedure' see PARA 1240 note 3.
6 Ie the Transnational Information and Consultation of Employees Regulations 1999, SI 1999/3323, reg 18: see PARA 1253.
7 For these purposes, 'failure' means an act or omission; and a failure by the local management is to be treated as a failure by the central management: Transnational Information and Consultation of Employees Regulations 1999, SI 1999/3323, reg 20(2). As to the meaning of 'local management' see PARA 1241 note 9; and as to the meaning of 'central management' see PARA 1240 note 1.
8 Ie the agreement under the Transnational Information and Consultation of Employees Regulations 1999, SI 1999/3323, reg 17: see PARA 1252.
9 Transnational Information and Consultation of Employees Regulations 1999, SI 1999/3323, reg 20(1) (amended by SI 2010/1088). As to the subsidiary requirements see the Transnational Information and Consultation of Employees Regulations 1999, SI 1999/3323, reg 18(1), Schedule; and PARA 1253 et seq. As to proceedings before the Central Arbitration Committee see PARA 1280; and as to ACAS conciliation see PARA 1281. As to the application of the Transnational Information and Consultation of Employees Regulations 1999, SI 1999/3323, generally see PARA 1237 note 2. See also PARA 1282 et seq.
10 See note 8.
11 Transnational Information and Consultation of Employees Regulations 1999, SI 1999/3323, reg 20(4) (amended by SI 2010/1088).
12 Transnational Information and Consultation of Employees Regulations 1999, SI 1999/3323, reg 20(6).
13 Transnational Information and Consultation of Employees Regulations 1999, SI 1999/3323, reg 20(10) (amended by SI 2010/1088).
14 Ie under the Transnational Information and Consultation of Employees Regulations 1999, SI 1999/3323, reg 10(1): see PARA 1245.
15 Ie the time limit in the Transnational Information and Consultation of Employees Regulations 1999, SI 1999/3323, reg 10(2)(a): see PARA 1245 head (1).
16 Ie under the Transnational Information and Consultation of Employees Regulations 1999, SI 1999/3323, reg 10.
17 Ie a requirement of the Transnational Information and Consultation of Employees Regulations 1999, SI 1999/3323, reg 9(2) or (3): see PARA 1244.
18 Ie under the Transnational Information and Consultation of Employees Regulations 1999, SI 1999/3323, reg 10(3): see PARA 1245.
19 Ie the obligation in the Transnational Information and Consultation of Employees Regulations 1999, SI 1999/3323, reg 9(1): see PARA 1244.
20 Transnational Information and Consultation of Employees Regulations 1999, SI 1999/3323, reg 20(5) (amended by SI 2010/1088). As to the meaning of 'relevant date' see PARA 1241 note 7.
21 Ie a decision under the Transnational Information and Consultation of Employees Regulations 1999, SI 1999/3323, reg 20(4): see the text and notes 10–11.
22 Transnational Information and Consultation of Employees Regulations 1999, SI 1999/3323, reg 20(7) (substituted by SI 2010/1088). This provision refers to the Appeal Tribunal, rather than the CAC, having made the decision that it finds the complaint well-founded, but it is thought that this is an error and that the intended wording is that set out in the text to note 21. The Transnational Information and Consultation of Employees Regulations 1999, SI 1999/3323, reg 22 (see PARA 1272) applies in respect of a penalty notice issued under reg 20: reg 20(9). Every application under reg 20(7) must be made by way of application in writing in, or substantially in, accordance with the Employment Appeal Tribunal Rules 1993, SI 1993/2854, Schedule Form 4B and must be served on the Appeal Tribunal together with a copy of the declaration referred to in the Transnational Information and Consultation of Employees Regulations 1999, SI 1999/3323, reg 20(4) (see the text and notes 10–11), or an explanation as to why none is included: Employment Appeal Tribunal Rules 1993, SI 1993/2854, r 16AA (added by SI 2004/2526; amended by SI 2004/3426; SI 2007/2974; SI 2010/1088). As to applications made under the Employment Appeal Tribunal Rules 1993, SI 1993/2854, r 16AA see further r 16B (substituted by SI 2010/1088); the Employment Appeal Tribunal Rules 1993, SI 1993/2854, r 16C (added by SI 2001/1128; amended by SI 2004/2526; SI 2010/1088); the Employment Appeal Tribunal Rules 1993, SI 1993/2854, r 16D (added by SI 2001/1128); and the Employment Appeal Tribunal Rules 1993, SI 1993/2854, Schedule Form 5A (added by SI 2001/1128; amended by SI 2010/1088). As to the Employment Appeal Tribunal see PARA 1422 et seq.

23 Transnational Information and Consultation of Employees Regulations 1999, SI 1999/3323, reg 20(7A) (added by SI 2010/1088). As to the Secretary of State see PARA 5 note 21.
24 Transnational Information and Consultation of Employees Regulations 1999, SI 1999/3323, reg 20(8) (amended by SI 2010/1088).

1270. Disputes about operation of European Works Council or information and consultation procedure. Where:

(1) a European Works Council[1] or information and consultation procedure[2] has been established[3]; or

(2) a European Works Council has been established by virtue of the subsidiary requirements[4],

a complaint may be presented to the Central Arbitration Committee (the 'CAC')[5] by a relevant applicant[6] who considers that, because of the failure[7] of a defaulter:

(a) the terms of the agreement[8] or, as the case may be, the subsidiary requirements[9], have not been complied with; or

(b) the information and consultation requirements[10] have not been complied with, or the information which has been provided by the management under those requirements is false or incomplete in a material particular[11].

A complaint brought under the above provisions must be brought within a period of six months beginning with the date of the alleged failure or non-compliance[12].

Where the CAC finds the complaint well-founded, it must make a decision to that effect and may make an order requiring the defaulter to take such steps as are necessary to comply with the terms of the agreement[13] or, as the case may be, the subsidiary requirements[14]. Such an order must specify:

(i) the steps which the defaulter is required to take;

(ii) the date of the failure; and

(iii) the period within which the order must be complied with[15].

If the CAC makes such a decision and the defaulter in question is the central management, the relevant applicant may, within the period of three months beginning with the date on which the decision is made, make an application to the Employment Appeal Tribunal ('the appeal tribunal') for a penalty notice to be issued[16]. Where such an application is made, the appeal tribunal must issue a written penalty notice to the central management requiring it to pay a penalty to the Secretary of State in respect of the failure[17]; but that does not apply if the appeal tribunal is satisfied, on hearing the representations of the central management, that the failure resulted from a reason beyond the central management's control or that it has some other reasonable excuse for its failure[18].

No order of the CAC under the above provisions has the effect of suspending or altering the effect of any act done or of any agreement made by the central management or the local management[19].

1 As to the meaning of 'European Works Council' see PARA 1237 note 3.
2 As to the meaning of 'information and consultation procedure' see PARA 1240 note 3.
3 Ie under the Transnational Information and Consultation of Employees Regulations 1999, SI 1999/3323, reg 17: see PARA 1252.
4 Ie by virtue of the Transnational Information and Consultation of Employees Regulations 1999, SI 1999/3323, reg 18: see PARA 1253.
5 As to the Central Arbitration Committee see PARA 1226 et seq.
6 For these purposes, 'relevant applicant' means: (1) in the case of a failure concerning a European Works Council, either the central management or the European Works Council; or (2) in the case of a failure concerning an information and consultation procedure, either the central

management or any one or more of the information and consultation representatives; and 'defaulter' means the persons mentioned in head (1) or head (2) above against whom the complaint is presented: Transnational Information and Consultation of Employees Regulations 1999, SI 1999/3323, reg 21(3). As to the meaning of 'central management' see PARA 1240 note 1; and as to the meaning of 'information and consultation representative' see PARA 1240 note 3.

7   For these purposes, 'failure' means an act or omission; and a failure by the local management is to be treated as a failure by the central management: Transnational Information and Consultation of Employees Regulations 1999, SI 1999/3323, reg 21(2). As to the meaning of 'local management' see PARA 1241 note 9.

8   See note 3.

9   Ie the provisions of the Transnational Information and Consultation of Employees Regulations 1999, SI 1999/3323, reg 18(1), Schedule: see PARA 1254 et seq.

10 Ie the Transnational Information and Consultation of Employees Regulations 1999, SI 1999/3323, reg 18A: see PARA 1252.

11 Transnational Information and Consultation of Employees Regulations 1999, SI 1999/3323, reg 21(1), (1A) (respectively substituted and added by SI 2010/1088). As to proceedings before the Central Arbitration Committee see PARA 1280; and as to ACAS conciliation see PARA 1281. As to the application of the Transnational Information and Consultation of Employees Regulations 1999, SI 1999/3323, generally see PARA 1237 note 2. See also PARA 1282 et seq.

12 Transnational Information and Consultation of Employees Regulations 1999, SI 1999/3323, reg 21(1B) (added by SI 2010/1088).

13 See note 3.

14 Transnational Information and Consultation of Employees Regulations 1999, SI 1999/3323, reg 21(4) (amended by SI 2010/1088).

15 Transnational Information and Consultation of Employees Regulations 1999, SI 1999/3323, reg 21(5).

16 Transnational Information and Consultation of Employees Regulations 1999, SI 1999/3323, reg 21(6) (amended by SI 2010/1088). The Transnational Information and Consultation of Employees Regulations 1999, SI 1999/3323, reg 22 (see PARA 1272) applies in respect of a penalty notice issued under reg 21: reg 21(8). Every application under reg 21(6) must be made by way of application in writing in, or substantially in, accordance with the Employment Appeal Tribunal Rules 1993, SI 1993/2854, Schedule Form 4B and must be served on the Appeal Tribunal together with a copy of the declaration referred to in the Transnational Information and Consultation of Employees Regulations 1999, SI 1999/3323, reg 21(4) (see the text and notes 13–14), or an explanation as to why none is included: Employment Appeal Tribunal Rules 1993, SI 1993/2854, r 16AA (added by SI 2004/2526; amended by SI 2004/3426; SI 2007/2974; SI 2010/1088). As to applications made under the Employment Appeal Tribunal Rules 1993, SI 1993/2854, r 16AA see further r 16B (substituted by SI 2010/1088); the Employment Appeal Tribunal Rules 1993, SI 1993/2854, r 16C (added by SI 2001/1128; amended by SI 2004/2526; SI 2010/1088); the Employment Appeal Tribunal Rules 1993, SI 1993/2854, r 16D (added by SI 2001/1128); and the Employment Appeal Tribunal Rules 1993, SI 1993/2854, Schedule Form 5A (added by SI 2001/1128; amended by SI 2010/1088). As to the Employment Appeal Tribunal see PARA 1422 et seq.

17 Transnational Information and Consultation of Employees Regulations 1999, SI 1999/3323, reg 21(6A) (added by SI 2010/1088). As to the Secretary of State see PARA 5 note 21.

18 Transnational Information and Consultation of Employees Regulations 1999, SI 1999/3323, reg 21(7) (amended by SI 2010/1088).

19 Transnational Information and Consultation of Employees Regulations 1999, SI 1999/3323, reg 21(9) (amended by SI 2010/1088).

1271. Disputes about failures of management. A complaint may be presented to the Central Arbitration Committee (the 'CAC')[1] by a relevant applicant[2] who considers that:

(1)   because of the failure of a defaulter[3], the members of the special negotiating body have been unable to meet without the central management or its representatives being present[4];

(2)   because of the failure of a defaulter, the members of the European Works Council have not been provided with the means required to fulfil

their duty to represent collectively the interests of the employees of the
EU-scale undertaking or EU-scale group of undertakings[5];

(3)　　because of the failure of a defaulter, a member of a special negotiating
body or a member of the European Works Council has not been
provided with the means required to undertake the specified training[6];
or

(4)　　the obligation to ensure that the procedures for informing and
consulting the European Works Council and the national employee
representation bodies in relation to substantial changes in work
organisation or contractual relations are linked[7] applies and that,
because of the failure of a defaulter, the European Works Council and
the national employee representation bodies have not been informed
and consulted[8] in accordance with the relevant statutory requirement[9].

A complaint brought under the above provisions must be brought within a
period of six months beginning with the date of the alleged failure[10].

Where the CAC finds the complaint well-founded it must make a decision to
that effect and may make an order requiring the defaulter to take such steps as
are necessary to comply with the relevant[11] statutory requirements[12]. An order so
made must specify:

(a)　　the steps which the defaulter is required to take;

(b)　　the date of the failure; and

(c)　　the period within which the order must be complied with[13].

No order of the CAC under these provisions is to have the effect of suspending
or altering the effect of any act done or of any agreement made by the central
management or the local management[14].

If the CAC makes a that the complaint is well-founded[15], the relevant
applicant may, within the period of three months beginning with the date on
which the decision is made, make an application to the Employment Appeal
Tribunal ('the appeal tribunal') for a penalty notice to be issued[16]. Where such an
application is made, the appeal tribunal must issue a written penalty notice to the
defaulter requiring it to pay a penalty to the Secretary of State in respect of the
failure[17]; but this does not apply if the appeal tribunal is satisfied, on hearing the
representations of the defaulter, that the failure resulted from a reason beyond
the defaulter's control or that it has some other reasonable excuse for its
failure[18].

1　　As to the Central Arbitration Committee see PARA 1226 et seq.

2　　For these purposes, 'relevant applicant' means: (1) for a complaint in relation to the
Transnational Information and Consultation of Employees Regulations 1999, SI 1999/3323,
reg 16(1A) (see PARA 1251), a member of the special negotiating body; (2) for a complaint in
relation to reg 19A (see PARA 1264), a member of the European Works Council; (3) for a
complaint in relation to reg 19B (see PARA 1265), a member of the special negotiating body or a
member of the European Works Council; (4) for a complaint in relation to reg 19E(2) (see PARA
1267), a member of the European Works Council, a national employee representation body, an
employee, or an employees' representative: reg 21A(10)(c) (reg 21A added by SI 2010/1088). As
to the meaning of 'special negotiating body' see PARA 1244 note 13; as to the meaning of
'European Works Council' see PARA 1237 note 3; as to the meaning of 'national employee
representation body' see PARA 1252 note 9; as to the meaning of 'employee' see PARA 1238 note
1; and as to the meaning of 'employees' representatives' see PARA 1242 note 2.

3　　For these purposes, 'failure' means an act or omission and a failure by the local management is
to be treated as a failure by the central management: Transnational Information and
Consultation of Employees Regulations 1999, SI 1999/3323, reg 21A(10)(b) (as added: see note
2). 'Defaulter' means, as the case may be (1) the management of any undertaking belonging to
the EU-scale group of undertakings; (2) the central management; or (3) the representative agent
or the management treated as the central management of the EU-scale undertaking or EU-scale

group of undertakings within the meaning of reg 5(2) (see PARA 1240): reg 21A(1)(a) (as so added; amended by virtue of SI 2011/1043). As to the meaning of 'local management' see PARA 1241 note 9; as to the meaning of 'central management' see PARA 1240 note 1; as to the meaning of 'EU-scale undertaking' see PARA 1237 note 11; and as to the meaning of 'EU-scale group of undertakings' see PARA 1237 note 12.

4 Ie in accordance with the Transnational Information and Consultation of Employees Regulations 1999, SI 1999/3323, reg 16(1A): see PARA 1251.

5 Ie in accordance with the Transnational Information and Consultation of Employees Regulations 1999, SI 1999/3323, reg 19A: see PARA 1264.

6 Ie the training referred to in the Transnational Information and Consultation of Employees Regulations 1999, SI 1999/3323, reg 19B: see PARA 1265.

7 Ie the Transnational Information and Consultation of Employees Regulations 1999, SI 1999/3323, reg 19E(2): see PARA 1267.

8 Ie in accordance with the Transnational Information and Consultation of Employees Regulations 1999, SI 1999/3323, reg 19E: see PARA 1267.

9 Transnational Information and Consultation of Employees Regulations 1999, SI 1999/3323, reg 21A(1) (as added (see note 2); amended by virtue of SI 2011/1043). As to proceedings before the Central Arbitration Committee see PARA 1280; and as to ACAS conciliation see PARA 1281. As to the application of the Transnational Information and Consultation of Employees Regulations 1999, SI 1999/3323, generally see PARA 1237 note 2. See also PARA 1282 et seq.

10 Transnational Information and Consultation of Employees Regulations 1999, SI 1999/3323, reg 21A(2) (as added: see note 2).

11 Ie steps to comply with the Transnational Information and Consultation of Employees Regulations 1999, SI 1999/3323, reg 16(1A), reg 19A, reg 19B or reg 19E(2), as the case may be.

12 Transnational Information and Consultation of Employees Regulations 1999, SI 1999/3323, reg 21A(3) (as added: see note 2).

13 Transnational Information and Consultation of Employees Regulations 1999, SI 1999/3323, reg 21A(4) (as added: see note 2).

14 Transnational Information and Consultation of Employees Regulations 1999, SI 1999/3323, reg 21A(9) (as added: see note 2).

15 Ie a decision under the Transnational Information and Consultation of Employees Regulations 1999, SI 1999/3323, reg 21A(3): see the text and notes 11–12.

16 Transnational Information and Consultation of Employees Regulations 1999, SI 1999/3323, reg 21A(5) (as added: see note 2). Every application under reg 21A(5) must be made by way of application in writing in, or substantially in, accordance with the Employment Appeal Tribunal Rules 1993, SI 1993/2854, Schedule Form 4B and must be served on the Appeal Tribunal together with a copy of the declaration referred to in the Transnational Information and Consultation of Employees Regulations 1999, SI 1999/3323, reg 21A(3) (see the text and notes 11–12), or an explanation as to why none is included: Employment Appeal Tribunal Rules 1993, SI 1993/2854, r 16AA (added by SI 2004/2526; amended by SI 2004/3426; SI 2007/2974; SI 2010/1088). As to applications made under the Employment Appeal Tribunal Rules 1993, SI 1993/2854, r 16AA see further r 16B (substituted by SI 2010/1088); the Employment Appeal Tribunal Rules 1993, SI 1993/2854, r 16C (added by SI 2001/1128; amended by SI 2004/2526; SI 2010/1088); the Employment Appeal Tribunal Rules 1993, SI 1993/2854, r 16D (added by SI 2001/1128); and the Employment Appeal Tribunal Rules 1993, SI 1993/2854, Schedule Form 5A (added by SI 2001/1128; amended by SI 2010/1088). As to the Employment Appeal Tribunal see PARA 1422 et seq.

17 Transnational Information and Consultation of Employees Regulations 1999, SI 1999/3323, reg 21A(6) (as added: see note 2). Regulation 22 (see PARA 1272) applies to a penalty notice issued under reg 21A: reg 21A(8) (as so added). As to the Secretary of State see PARA 5 note 21.

18 Transnational Information and Consultation of Employees Regulations 1999, SI 1999/3323, reg 21A(7) (as added: see note 2).

1272. Penalties set by the Employment Appeal Tribunal. A penalty notice issued[1] by the Employment Appeal Tribunal[2] must specify:

(1) the amount of the penalty which is payable;

(2) the date before which the penalty must be paid[3]; and

(3) the failure and period to which the penalty relates[4];

but no penalty so set by the Employment Appeal Tribunal may exceed £100,000[5].

When setting the amount of the penalty, the Employment Appeal Tribunal must take into account:

(a) the gravity of the failure;

(b) the period of time over which the failure occurred;

(c) the reason for the failure;

(d) the number of employees[6] affected by the failure; and

(e) the number of employees of the EU-scale undertaking[7] or EU-scale group of undertakings[8] in the member states[9].

If the specified date in a penalty notice has passed and:

(i) the period during which an appeal may be made has expired without an appeal having been made; or

(ii) such an appeal has been made and determined,

the Secretary of State may recover from the central management[10], as a civil debt due to him, any amount payable under the penalty notice which remains outstanding[11]; but the making of an appeal suspends the effect of a penalty notice[12].

Any sums received[13] by the Secretary of State or in Northern Ireland the Department for Employment and Learning, must be paid into, respectively, the Consolidated Fund or the Consolidated Fund of Northern Ireland[14].

1   Ie under the Transnational Information and Consultation of Employees Regulations 1999, SI 1999/3323, reg 20 (see PARA 1269), reg 21 (see PARA 1270) or reg 21A (see PARA 1271).

2   As to the Employment Appeal Tribunal see PARA 1422 et seq.

3   The date so specified must not be earlier than the end of the period within which an appeal against a decision or order made by the Central Arbitration Committee (the 'CAC') under the Transnational Information and Consultation of Employees Regulations 1999, SI 1999/3323, reg 20 (see PARA 1269), reg 21 (see PARA 1270) or reg 21A (see PARA 1271) may be made: reg 22(4) (amended by SI 2010/1088).

4   Transnational Information and Consultation of Employees Regulations 1999, SI 1999/3323, reg 22(1) (amended by SI 2010/1088). As to the application of the Transnational Information and Consultation of Employees Regulations 1999, SI 1999/3323, generally see PARA 1237 note 2. See also PARA 1282 et seq.

5   Transnational Information and Consultation of Employees Regulations 1999, SI 1999/3323, reg 22(2) (amended by SI 2010/1088).

6   As to the meaning of 'employee' see PARA 1238 note 1.

7   As to the meaning of 'EU-scale undertaking' see PARA 1237 note 11.

8   As to the meaning of 'EU-scale group of undertakings' see PARA 1237 note 12.

9   Transnational Information and Consultation of Employees Regulations 1999, SI 1999/3323, reg 22(3) (amended by virtue of SI 2011/1043). As to the meaning of 'member state' see PARA 1237 note 3.

10 As to the meaning of 'central management' see PARA 1240 note 1. As to the Secretary of State see PARA 5 note 21.

11 Transnational Information and Consultation of Employees Regulations 1999, SI 1999/3323, reg 22(5).

12 Transnational Information and Consultation of Employees Regulations 1999, SI 1999/3323, reg 22(6).

13 Ie under the Transnational Information and Consultation of Employees Regulations 1999, SI 1999/3323, reg 20 (see PARA 1269), reg 21 (see PARA 1270), reg 21A (see PARA 1271) or reg 22 (see the text and notes 1–12).

14 Transnational Information and Consultation of Employees Regulations 1999, SI 1999/3323, reg 22(7) (substituted by SI 2010/1088). As to the Consolidated Fund see CONSTITUTIONAL AND ADMINISTRATIVE LAW vol 20 (2014) PARA 480 et seq; PARLIAMENT vol 78 (2010) PARA 1028 et seq.

G. CONFIDENTIAL INFORMATION

1273. Breach of statutory duty not to disclose confidential information. A person who is or at any time was:

(1) a member of a special negotiating body[1] or a European Works Council[2];

(2) an information and consultation representative[3]; or

(3) an expert assisting a special negotiating body, a European Works Council or its select committee, or information and consultation representatives,

(a 'recipient') must not disclose any information or document which is or has been in his possession by virtue of his position as described in head (1), head (2) or head (3) above, which the central management[4] has entrusted to him on terms requiring it to be held in confidence[5].

The obligation to comply with that requirement is a duty owed to the central management, and a breach of the duty is actionable accordingly, subject to the defences and other incidents applying to claims for breach of statutory duty[6]; but no claim so lies where the recipient reasonably believed the disclosure to be a protected disclosure[7].

A recipient whom the central management, which is situated in the United Kingdom, has entrusted with any information or document on terms requiring it to be held in confidence may apply to the Central Arbitration Committee[8] (the 'CAC') for a declaration as to whether it was reasonable for the central management to impose such a requirement[9]. If the CAC considers that the disclosure of the information or document by the recipient would not, or would not be likely to, prejudice or cause serious harm to the undertaking, it must make a declaration that it was not reasonable for the central management to require the recipient to hold the information or document in confidence[10]. If a declaration is so made, the information or document is not at any time thereafter to be regarded as having been entrusted to the recipient who made the application[11], or to any other recipient, on terms requiring it to be held in confidence[12].

1 As to the meaning of 'special negotiating body' see PARA 1244 note 13.

2 As to the meaning of 'European Works Council' see PARA 1237 note 3.

3 As to the meaning of 'information and consultation representative' see PARA 1240 note 3.

4 As to the meaning of 'central management' see PARA 1240 note 1.

5 Transnational Information and Consultation of Employees Regulations 1999, SI 1999/3323, reg 23(1), (2). As to the application of the Transnational Information and Consultation of Employees Regulations 1999, SI 1999/3323, generally see PARA 1237 note 2. See also PARA 1282 et seq.

6 Transnational Information and Consultation of Employees Regulations 1999, SI 1999/3323, reg 23(3). Regulation 23(3) does not affect the liability which any person may incur, nor affect any right which any person may have, apart from reg 23(3): reg 23(4). As to breach of statutory duty see TORT vol 97 (2010) PARA 495 et seq.

7 Transnational Information and Consultation of Employees Regulations 1999, SI 1999/3323, reg 23(5). For these purposes, 'protected disclosure' has the meaning given to that expression by the Employment Rights Act 1996 s 43A (see PARA 69) or the corresponding Northern Ireland legislation: see the Transnational Information and Consultation of Employees Regulations 1999, SI 1999/3323, reg 23(5).

8 As to the Central Arbitration Committee see PARA 1226 et seq.

9 Transnational Information and Consultation of Employees Regulations 1999, SI 1999/3323, reg 23(6). As to proceedings before the Central Arbitration Committee see PARA 1280; and as to ACAS conciliation see PARA 1281.

10 Transnational Information and Consultation of Employees Regulations 1999, SI 1999/3323, reg 23(7).

11 Ie under the Transnational Information and Consultation of Employees Regulations 1999, SI 1999/3323, reg 23(6).

12 Transnational Information and Consultation of Employees Regulations 1999, SI 1999/3323, reg 23(8).

1274. Withholding of information by central management. The central management[1] is not required to disclose any information or document to a recipient[2] when the nature of the information or document is such that, according to objective criteria, the disclosure of the information or document would seriously harm the functioning of, or would be prejudicial to, the undertaking or group of undertakings[3] concerned[4].

Where there is a dispute between the central management and a recipient as to whether the nature of the information or document which the central management has failed to provide is such as is described above[5], the central management or a recipient may apply to the Central Arbitration Committee[6] (the 'CAC') for a declaration as to whether the information or document is of such a nature[7]. If the CAC makes a declaration that the disclosure of the information or document in question would not, according to objective criteria, seriously harm the functioning of, or be prejudicial to, the undertaking or group of undertakings concerned, the CAC must order the central management to disclose the information or document[8]. Such an order must specify:

(1) the information or document to be disclosed;

(2) the recipient or recipients to whom the information or document is to be disclosed;

(3) any terms on which the information or document is to be disclosed; and

(4) the date before which the information or document is to be disclosed[9].

1 As to the meaning of 'central management' see PARA 1240 note 1.
2 As to the meaning of 'recipient' see PARA 1273.
3 As to the meaning of 'group of undertakings' see PARA 1237 note 12.

4 Transnational Information and Consultation of Employees Regulations 1999, SI 1999/3323, reg 24(1). As to the application of the Transnational Information and Consultation of Employees Regulations 1999, SI 1999/3323, generally see PARA 1237 note 2. See also PARA 1282 et seq.

5 Ie such as is described in the Transnational Information and Consultation of Employees Regulations 1999, SI 1999/3323, reg 24(1).

6 As to the Central Arbitration Committee see PARA 1226 et seq.

7 Transnational Information and Consultation of Employees Regulations 1999, SI 1999/3323, reg 24(2). As to proceedings before the Central Arbitration Committee see PARA 1280; and as to ACAS conciliation see PARA 1281.

8 Transnational Information and Consultation of Employees Regulations 1999, SI 1999/3323, reg 24(3).

9 Transnational Information and Consultation of Employees Regulations 1999, SI 1999/3323, reg 24(4).

H. PROTECTIONS FOR MEMBERS OF A EUROPEAN WORKS COUNCIL ETC

1275. Right to time off for members of a European Works Council etc. An employee[1] who is:

(1) a member of a special negotiating body[2];

(2) a member of a European Works Council[3];

(3) an information and consultation representative[4]; or

(4) a candidate in an election in which any person elected will, on being elected, be such a member or representative,

is entitled to be permitted by his employer to take reasonable time off during the employee's working hours[5] in order to perform his functions as such a member, representative or candidate[6].

An employer must permit an employee who is a member of a special negotiating body or a member of a European Works Council to take reasonable time off during the employee's working hours in order to undertake the specified[7] training[8].

An employee who is so permitted to take time off is entitled to be paid remuneration by his employer for the time taken off at the appropriate hourly rate[9]; but a right to be paid such an amount does not affect any right of an employee in relation to remuneration under his contract of employment ('contractual remuneration')[10].

1 As to the meaning of 'employee' see PARA 1238 note 1.
2 As to the meaning of 'special negotiating body' see PARA 1244 note 13.
3 As to the meaning of 'European Works Council' see PARA 1237 note 3.
4 As to the meaning of 'information and consultation representative' see PARA 1240 note 3.
5 For these purposes, the working hours of an employee are to be taken to be any time when, in accordance with his contract of employment, the employee is required to be at work: Transnational Information and Consultation of Employees Regulations 1999, SI 1999/3323, reg 25(2). As to the meaning of 'contract of employment' see PARA 1238 note 1.
6 Transnational Information and Consultation of Employees Regulations 1999, SI 1999/3323, reg 25(1). As to the application of the Transnational Information and Consultation of Employees Regulations 1999, SI 1999/3323, generally see PARA 1237 note 2. See also PARA 1282 et seq.
7 Ie the training referred to in the Transnational Information and Consultation of Employees Regulations 1999, SI 1999/3323, reg 19B: see PARA 1265.
8 Transnational Information and Consultation of Employees Regulations 1999, SI 1999/3323, reg 25(1A) (added by SI 2010/1088).
9 Transnational Information and Consultation of Employees Regulations 1999, SI 1999/3323, reg 26(1). For these purposes, the appropriate hourly rate, in relation to an employee, is the amount of one week's pay divided by the number of normal working hours in a week for that employee when employed under the contract of employment in force on the day when the time off is taken: reg 26(3). Where, however, the number of normal working hours differs from week to week or over a longer period, the amount of one week's pay must be divided instead by: (1) the average number of normal working hours calculated by dividing by 12 the total number of the employee's normal working hours during the period of 12 weeks ending with the last complete week before the day on which the time off is taken; or (2) where the employee has not been employed for a sufficient period to enable the calculation to be made under head (1) above, a number which fairly represents the number of normal working hours in a week having regard to such of the following considerations as are appropriate in the circumstances: (a) the average number of normal working hours in a week which the employee could expect in accordance with the terms of his contract; and (b) the average number of normal working hours of other employees engaged in relevant comparable employment with the same employer: reg 26(4), (5). For these purposes, the Employment Rights Act 1996 Pt XIV Ch II (ss 220–229) (calculation of a week's pay) (see PARA 143 et seq) applies as it applies in relation to s 62 (see PARA 1209): Transnational Information and Consultation of Employees Regulations 1999, SI 1999/3323, reg 26(2). As to the right of complaint to an employment tribunal see PARA 1276.
8 Transnational Information and Consultation of Employees Regulations 1999, SI 1999/3323, reg 26(6). However, any contractual remuneration paid to an employee in respect of a period of time off under reg 26 goes towards discharging any liability of the employer under reg 26(1) in respect of that period; and, conversely, any payment under reg 26(1) in respect of a period goes towards discharging any liability of the employer to pay contractual remuneration in respect of that period: reg 26(7). As to the right of complaint to an employment tribunal see PARA 1276.

1276. Right to time off; complaint to employment tribunal. An employee[1] may present a complaint to an employment tribunal[2] that his employer:

(1) has unreasonably refused to permit him to take time off to perform his functions as a member of a European Works Council etc[3]; or

(2) has failed to pay the whole or any part of any amount to which the employee is entitled[4] for such time off[5].

Subject to an extension of the time limit to facilitate conciliation before the institution of proceedings[6], a tribunal must not consider such a complaint unless it is presented[7]:

(a)   before the end of the period of three months beginning with the day on which the time off was taken or on which it is alleged the time off should have been permitted[8]; or

(b)   within such further period as the tribunal considers reasonable in a case where it is satisfied that it was not reasonably practicable for the complaint to be presented before the end of that period of three months[9].

Where a tribunal finds such a complaint well-founded, it must make a declaration to that effect[10].

If the complaint is that the employer has unreasonably refused to permit the employee to take time off, the tribunal must also order the employer to pay to the employee an amount equal to the remuneration to which he would have been entitled[11] if the employer had not refused[12].

If the complaint is that the employer has failed to pay the employee the whole or part of any amount to which he is entitled[13], the tribunal must also order the employer to pay to the employee the amount which it finds due to him[14].

1   As to the meaning of 'employee' see PARA 1238 note 1.
2   As to employment tribunals see PARA 1399 et seq.
3   Ie as required by the Transnational Information and Consultation of Employees Regulations 1999, SI 1999/3323, reg 25: see PARA 1275.
4   Ie under the Transnational Information and Consultation of Employees Regulations 1999, SI 1999/3323, reg 26: see PARA 1275.
5   Transnational Information and Consultation of Employees Regulations 1999, SI 1999/3323, reg 27(1). As to the application of the Transnational Information and Consultation of Employees Regulations 1999, SI 1999/3323, generally see PARA 1237 note 2. See also PARA 1282 et seq.
         The provisions of the Employment Tribunals Act 1996 ss 18A–18B (conciliation) (see PARAS 152–153) apply in the case of matters which could be the subject of employment tribunal proceedings under the Transnational Information and Consultation of Employees Regulations 1999, SI 1999/3323, reg 27, and the Employment Tribunals Act 1996 s 18C applies in the case of such proceedings themselves: see s 18(1)(k), (1A) (s 18(1)(k) substituted by SI 2014/431; the Employment Tribunals Act 1996 s 18(1A) added by the Enterprise and Regulatory Reform Act 2013 Sch 1 paras 2, 5(1), (7)).
6   The Transnational Information and Consultation of Employees Regulations 1999, SI 1999/3323, reg 27A (extension of time limits to facilitate conciliation before institution of proceedings: see notes 8–9) applies for these purposes: reg 27(2A) (added by SI 2014/386).
7   As to when a complaint is presented see PARAS 990 note 4, 1461.
8   Transnational Information and Consultation of Employees Regulations 1999, SI 1999/3323, reg 27(2)(a). For the case law on the extension of time limits, especially in the context of the law of unfair dismissal, see PARA 1453.
         In working out when the time limit set by reg 27(2)(a) expires the period beginning with the day after Day A and ending with Day B is not to be counted: reg 27A(2) (reg 27A added by SI 2014/386). If the time limit set by the Transnational Information and Consultation of Employees Regulations 1999, SI 1999/3323, reg 27(2)(a) would (if not extended by this provision) expire during the period beginning with Day A and ending one month after Day B, the time limit expires instead at the end of that period: reg 27A(3) (as so added). For these purposes, Day A is the day on which the worker concerned complies with the requirement in the Employment Tribunals Act 1996 s 18A(1) (requirement to contact ACAS before instituting proceedings: see PARA 152) in relation to the matter in respect of which the proceedings are brought, and Day B is the day on which the worker concerned receives or, if earlier, is treated as receiving (by virtue of regulations made under s 18A(11)) the certificate issued under s 18A(4): Transnational Information and Consultation of Employees Regulations 1999, SI 1999/3323, reg 27A(1) (as so added).
9   Transnational Information and Consultation of Employees Regulations 1999, SI 1999/3323, reg 27(2)(b). The power conferred on the employment tribunal by reg 27(2)(b) to extend the

time limit set by reg 27(2)(a) (see head (a) in the text) is exercisable in relation to that time limit as extended by reg 27A (see note 8): reg 27A(4) (added by SI 2014/386).
10 Transnational Information and Consultation of Employees Regulations 1999, SI 1999/3323, reg 27(3).
11 See note 4.
12 Transnational Information and Consultation of Employees Regulations 1999, SI 1999/3323, reg 27(4).
13 See note 4.
14 Transnational Information and Consultation of Employees Regulations 1999, SI 1999/3323, reg 27(5).

1277. Unfair dismissal of member of European Works Council etc. An employee[1] who is:
- (1) a member of a special negotiating body[2];
- (2) a member of a European Works Council[3];
- (3) an information and consultation representative[4];
- (4) a candidate in an election in which any person elected will, on being elected, be such a member or representative,

and is dismissed is to be regarded as unfairly dismissed[5], if the reason (or, if more than one, the principal reason[6]) for the dismissal is that:
- (a) the employee performed any functions or activities as such a member, representative or candidate; or
- (b) the employee, or a person acting on his behalf, made a request to exercise an entitlement conferred on the employee to time off[7] or, as the case may be, remuneration for time off[8],

or proposed to do so[9].

Any employee, whether or not he is an employee falling within heads (1) to (4) above, who is dismissed is to be regarded as unfairly dismissed[10], if the reason (or, if more than one, the principal reason) for the dismissal is that the employee:
- (i) took, or proposed to take, any proceedings before an employment tribunal[11] to enforce a right or secure an entitlement conferred on him[12];
- (ii) exercised, or proposed to exercise, any entitlement to apply or complain to the Employment Appeal Tribunal[13] or the Central Arbitration Committee[14] conferred on him[15];
- (iii) requested, or proposed to request, information[16];
- (iv) acted with a view to securing that a special negotiating body, a European Works Council or an information and consultation procedure[17] did or did not come into existence;
- (v) indicated that he supported, or did not support, the coming into existence of a special negotiating body, a European Works Council or an information and consultation procedure;
- (vi) stood as a candidate in an election in which any person elected would, on being elected, be a member of a special negotiating body or of a European Works Council or an information and consultation representative;
- (vii) influenced or sought to influence the way in which votes were to be cast by other employees in a ballot which had been arranged[18];
- (viii) voted in such a ballot;
- (ix) expressed doubts, whether to a ballot supervisor or otherwise, as to whether such a ballot had been properly conducted; or
- (x) proposed to do, failed to do, or proposed to decline to do, any of the things mentioned in heads (iv) to (ix) above[19].

1   As to the meaning of 'employee' see PARA 1238 note 1.
2   As to the meaning of 'special negotiating body' see PARA 1244 note 13.
3   As to the meaning of 'European Works Council' see PARA 1237 note 3.
4   As to the meaning of 'information and consultation representative' see PARA 1240 note 3.
5   Ie unfairly dismissed for the purposes of the Employment Rights Act 1996 Pt X (ss 94–134A):
    see PARA 757 et seq.
6   As to the meaning of 'reason or principal reason' see PARA 769.
7   Ie under the Transnational Information and Consultation of Employees Regulations 1999,
    SI 1999/3323, reg 25: see PARA 1275.
8   Ie under the Transnational Information and Consultation of Employees Regulations 1999,
    SI 1999/3323, reg 26: see PARA 1275.
9   Transnational Information and Consultation of Employees Regulations 1999, SI 1999/3323,
    reg 28(1)–(3). As to the application of the Transnational Information and Consultation of
    Employees Regulations 1999, SI 1999/3323, generally see PARA 1237 note 2. See also PARA 1282
    et seq.
        The reason in reg 28(3)(a) (see head (a) in the text) does not apply where the reason, or
    principal reason, for the dismissal is that, in the performance, or purported performance, of the
    employee's functions or activities, he has disclosed any information or document in breach of
    the duty in reg 23(1) (see PARA 1273), unless the employee reasonably believed the disclosure to
    be a protected disclosure within the meaning given to that expression by the Employment Rights
    Act 1996 s 43A (see PARA 69): Transnational Information and Consultation of Employees
    Regulations 1999, SI 1999/3323, reg 28(4).
        The two-year qualifying period (see the Employment Rights Act 1996 s 108(1); and PARA
    758) normally applying to unfair dismissal claims applies to a dismissal, or selection for
    redundancy, on the grounds in the Transnational Information and Consultation of Employees
    Regulations 1999, SI 1999/3323, reg 28(3) or reg 28(6) (see heads (i)–(x) in the text), read with
    reg 28(4), (7): see the Employment Rights Act 1996 s 108(3)(hh); and PARA 758 note 9.
10 See note 5.
11 As to employment tribunals see PARA 1399 et seq.
12 Ie by the Transnational Information and Consultation of Employees Regulations 1999,
    SI 1999/3323: see PARA 1237 et seq.
13 As to the Employment Appeal Tribunal see PARA 1422 et seq.
14 As to the Central Arbitration Committee see PARA 1226 et seq.
15 See note 12.
16 Ie in accordance with the Transnational Information and Consultation of Employees
    Regulations 1999, SI 1999/3323, reg 7: see PARA 1242.
17 As to the meaning of 'information and consultation procedure' see PARA 1240 note 3.
18 Ie under the Transnational Information and Consultation of Employees Regulations 1999,
    SI 1999/3323.
19 Transnational Information and Consultation of Employees Regulations 1999, SI 1999/3323,
    reg 28(1), (5), (6). See also note 9. It is immaterial for the purposes of reg 28(6)(a) (see head (i)
    in the text): (1) whether or not the employee has the right; or (2) whether or not the right has
    been infringed; but, for reg 28(6)(a) to apply, the claim to the right and, if applicable, the claim
    that it has been infringed must be made in good faith: reg 28(7).

**1278.   Right not to be subjected to any detriment on grounds relating to
membership of European Works Council etc.**   An employee[1] who is:

(1)   a member of a special negotiating body[2];

(2)   a member of a European Works Council[3];

(3)   an information and consultation representative[4];

(4)   a candidate in an election in which any person elected will, on being
      elected, be such a member or representative,

has the right not to be subjected to any detriment by any act, or failure to act, by
his employer, done on the ground that:

(a)   the employee performed any functions or activities as such a member,
      representative or candidate; or

(b)   the employee, or a person acting on his behalf, made a request to
      exercise an entitlement conferred on the employee to time off[5] or, as the
      case may be, remuneration for time off[6],

or proposed to do so[7].

Any employee, whether or not he is an employee falling within heads (1) to (4) above, has the right not to be subjected to any detriment by any act, or failure to act, by his employer, done on the ground that the employee:

(i)   took, or proposed to take, any proceedings before an employment tribunal[8] to enforce a right or secure an entitlement conferred on him[9];

(ii)   exercised, or proposed to exercise, any entitlement to apply or complain to the Employment Appeal Tribunal[10] or the Central Arbitration Committee[11] conferred on him[12];

(iii)   requested, or proposed to request, information[13];

(iv)   acted with a view to securing that a special negotiating body, a European Works Council or an information and consultation procedure[14] did or did not come into existence;

(v)   indicated that he supported, or did not support, the coming into existence of a special negotiating body, a European Works Council or an information and consultation procedure;

(vi)   stood as a candidate in an election in which any person elected would, on being elected, be a member of a special negotiating body or of a European Works Council or an information and consultation representative;

(vii)   influenced or sought to influence the way in which votes were to be cast by other employees in a ballot which had been arranged[15];

(viii) voted in such a ballot;

(ix)   expressed doubts, whether to a ballot supervisor or otherwise, as to whether such a ballot had been properly conducted; or

(x)   proposed to do, failed to do, or proposed to decline to do, any of the things mentioned in heads (iv) to (ix) above[16].

The above provisions do not apply where the detriment in question amounts to dismissal[17].

An employee may present a complaint to an employment tribunal that he has been subjected to a detriment in contravention of the above provisions[18].

1   As to the meaning of 'employee' see PARA 1238 note 1.
2   As to the meaning of 'special negotiating body' see PARA 1244 note 13.
3   As to the meaning of 'European Works Council' see PARA 1237 note 3.
4   As to the meaning of 'information and consultation representative' see PARA 1240 note 3.
5   Ie under the Transnational Information and Consultation of Employees Regulations 1999, SI 1999/3323, reg 25: see PARA 1275.
6   Ie under the Transnational Information and Consultation of Employees Regulations 1999, SI 1999/3323, reg 26: see PARA 1275.
7   Transnational Information and Consultation of Employees Regulations 1999, SI 1999/3323, reg 31(1)–(3). As to the application of the Transnational Information and Consultation of Employees Regulations 1999, SI 1999/3323, generally see PARA 1237 note 2. See also PARA 1282 et seq.
        The ground in reg 31(3)(a) (see head (a) in the text) does not apply where the ground for subjection to detriment is that, in the performance, or purported performance, of the employee's functions or activities, he has disclosed any information or document in breach of the duty in reg 23(1) (see PARA 1273), unless the employee reasonably believed the disclosure to be a protected disclosure within the meaning given to that expression by the Employment Rights Act 1996 s 43A (see PARA 69): Transnational Information and Consultation of Employees Regulations 1999, SI 1999/3323, reg 31(4).
8   As to employment tribunals see PARA 1399 et seq.
9   Ie by the Transnational Information and Consultation of Employees Regulations 1999, SI 1999/3323: see PARA 1237 et seq.
10   As to the Employment Appeal Tribunal see PARA 1422 et seq.
11   As to the Central Arbitration Committee see PARA 1226 et seq.

12 See note 9.
13 Ie in accordance with the Transnational Information and Consultation of Employees Regulations 1999, SI 1999/3323, reg 7: see PARA 1242.
14 As to the meaning of 'information and consultation procedure' see PARA 1240 note 3.
15 Ie under the Transnational Information and Consultation of Employees Regulations 1999, SI 1999/3323.
16 Transnational Information and Consultation of Employees Regulations 1999, SI 1999/3323, reg 31(1), (5), (6). It is immaterial for the purposes of reg 31(6)(a) (see head (i) in the text): (1) whether or not the employee has the right; or (2) whether or not the right has been infringed; but, for reg 31(6)(a) to apply, the claim to the right and, if applicable, the claim that it has been infringed must be made in good faith: reg 31(7).
17 Transnational Information and Consultation of Employees Regulations 1999, SI 1999/3323, reg 32(3).
18 Transnational Information and Consultation of Employees Regulations 1999, SI 1999/3323, reg 32(1). The provisions of the Employment Rights Act 1996 s 48(2)–(4) (complaint to employment tribunal) (see PARA 625) and s 49 (remedies on a complaint) (see PARA 626) apply in relation to a complaint under the Transnational Information and Consultation of Employees Regulations 1999, SI 1999/3323, reg 32 as they apply in relation to a complaint under the Employment Rights Act 1996 s 48, but taking references in those provisions to the employer as references to the employer within the meaning of the Transnational Information and Consultation of Employees Regulations 1999, SI 1999/3323, reg 31(1): reg 32(2).
    The provisions of the Employment Tribunals Act 1996 ss 18A–18B (conciliation) (see PARAS 152–153) apply in the case of matters which could be the subject of employment tribunal proceedings under the Transnational Information and Consultation of Employees Regulations 1999, SI 1999/3323, reg 32, and the Employment Tribunals Act 1996 s 18C applies in the case of such proceedings themselves: see s 18(1)(k), (1A) (s 18(1)(k) substituted by SI 2014/431; the Employment Tribunals Act 1996 s 18(1A) added by the Enterprise and Regulatory Reform Act 2013 Sch 1 paras 2, 5(1), (7)).

I. JURISDICTION AND PROCEDURAL REQUIREMENTS; CONCILIATION

1279.   Jurisdiction of the Employment Appeal Tribunal under the Transnational Information and Consultation of Employees Regulations 1999. Any proceedings before the Employment Appeal Tribunal[1] must:
  (1)   where the central management[2] is situated in England and Wales, be in England and Wales;
  (2)   where the central management is situated in Scotland, be in Scotland[3].

1 Ie any proceedings under the Transnational Information and Consultation of Employees Regulations 1999, SI 1999/3323 (see PARA 1237 et seq) other than proceedings before the Employment Appeal Tribunal under the Employment Tribunals Act 1996 s 21(1)(i): see PARA 1428. As to the Employment Appeal Tribunal see PARA 1422 et seq.
2 As to the meaning of 'central management' see PARA 1240 note 1.
3 Transnational Information and Consultation of Employees Regulations 1999, SI 1999/3323, reg 34(1). Regulation 34(1) applies: (1) to proceedings before the Employment Appeal Tribunal arising under reg 8 (see PARA 1243) as if for the words 'central management' there were substituted the words 'recipient (within the meaning given to that term by reg 7)' (reg 34(2)); and (2) to proceedings before the Employment Appeal Tribunal arising under reg 13 (see PARA 1248) or reg 15 (see PARA 1250) or reg 18(1), Schedule para 4 (see PARA 1256) as if for the words 'central management' there were substituted the words 'UK management' (reg 34(3)). As to the application of the Transnational Information and Consultation of Employees Regulations 1999, SI 1999/3323, generally see PARA 1237 note 2. See also PARA 1282 et seq.

1280.   Proceedings before the Central Arbitration Committee under the Transnational Information and Consultation of Employees Regulations 1999. Where[1] a person presents a complaint or makes an application to the Central Arbitration Committee[2] (the 'CAC'), the complaint or application must be in writing and in such form as the CAC may require[3].

In its consideration of such an application or complaint, the CAC must make such inquiries as it sees fit and give any person who it considers has a proper interest in the application or complaint an opportunity to be heard[4].

Where the central management[5] is situated in England and Wales:

(1)   a declaration or order made by the CAC[6] may be relied on as if it were a declaration or order made by the High Court; and

(2)   an order made by the CAC[7] may be enforced in the same way as an order of the High Court[8].

A declaration or order made by the CAC[9] must be in writing and state the reasons for the CAC's findings[10].

An appeal lies to the Employment Appeal Tribunal[11] on any question of law arising from any declaration or order of, or arising in any proceedings[12] before, the CAC[13].

1   Ie under the Transnational Information and Consultation of Employees Regulations 1999, SI 1999/3323: see PARA 1237 et seq.
2   As to the Central Arbitration Committee see PARA 1226 et seq.
3   Transnational Information and Consultation of Employees Regulations 1999, SI 1999/3323, reg 38(1). As to the application of the Transnational Information and Consultation of Employees Regulations 1999, SI 1999/3323, generally see PARA 1237 note 2. See also PARA 1282 et seq.
4   Transnational Information and Consultation of Employees Regulations 1999, SI 1999/3323, reg 38(2).
5   As to the meaning of 'central management' see PARA 1240 note 1.
6   See note 1.
7   See note 1.
8   Transnational Information and Consultation of Employees Regulations 1999, SI 1999/3323, reg 38(3). Regulation 38(3), (4) (see heads (a)–(b) below): (1) applies to an order made under reg 8 (see PARA 1243) as if for the words 'central management' there were substituted the words 'recipient' (reg 38(5)); and (2) applies, as appropriate, to a declaration or order made under reg 13 (see PARA 1248) or reg 15 (see PARA 1250) or Schedule para 4 (see PARA 1256) as if for the words 'central management' there were substituted the words 'UK management' (reg 38(6)).
     Where the central management is situated in Scotland: (a) a declaration or order made by the CAC under the Transnational Information and Consultation of Employees Regulations 1999, SI 1999/3323, may be relied on as if it were a declaration or order made by the Court of Session; and (b) an order made by the CAC may be enforced in the same way as an order of the Court of Session: reg 38(4).
9   See note 1.
10   Transnational Information and Consultation of Employees Regulations 1999, SI 1999/3323, reg 38(7).
11   As to the Employment Appeal Tribunal see PARA 1422 et seq; and as to the jurisdiction of the Employment Appeal Tribunal see PARA 1279.
12   See note 1.
13   Transnational Information and Consultation of Employees Regulations 1999, SI 1999/3323, reg 38(8).

1281.   References to the Advisory, Conciliation and Arbitration Service. If, on receipt of an application or complaint[1], the Central Arbitration Committee[2] (the 'CAC') is of the opinion that it is reasonably likely to be settled by conciliation, it must refer the application or complaint to the Advisory, Conciliation and Arbitration Service[3] ('ACAS') and must notify the applicant or complainant and any persons whom it considers have a proper interest in the application or complaint accordingly, whereupon ACAS must seek to promote a settlement of the matter[4].

If an application or complaint so referred is not settled or withdrawn and ACAS is of the opinion that further attempts at conciliation are unlikely to result in a settlement, it must inform the CAC of its opinion[5].

If the application or complaint is not referred to ACAS, or if it is so referred, then, on ACAS informing the CAC of its opinion that further attempts at conciliation are unlikely to result in a settlement, the CAC must proceed to hear and determine the application or complaint[6].

1   Ie under the Transnational Information and Consultation of Employees Regulations 1999, SI 1999/3323: see PARA 1237 et seq.

2   As to the Central Arbitration Committee see PARA 1226 et seq.

3   As to the Advisory, Conciliation and Arbitration Service ('ACAS') see PARA 1213 et seq.

4   Transnational Information and Consultation of Employees Regulations 1999, SI 1999/3323, reg 39(1) (amended by SI 2010/1088). As to the application of the Transnational Information and Consultation of Employees Regulations 1999, SI 1999/3323, generally see PARA 1237 note 2. See also PARA 1282 et seq.

5   Transnational Information and Consultation of Employees Regulations 1999, SI 1999/3323, reg 39(2) (amended by SI 2010/1088).

7   Transnational Information and Consultation of Employees Regulations 1999, SI 1999/3323, reg 39(3) (amended by SI 2010/1088).

J. EXCEPTIONS TO PROVISIONS RELATING TO EUROPEAN WORKS COUNCILS ETC

1282. Article 6 agreements. Where[1] the central management[2] is situated in the United Kingdom and, immediately before 15 January 2000[3], an agreement for the establishment of a European Works Council[4] or information and consultation procedure[5] made under the provisions of the law or practice of a member state[6], other than the United Kingdom, which are designed to give effect to the relevant provisions of the Transnational Information and Consultation Directive[7] (an 'article 6 agreement') is in force, the provisions which apply only where the central management is situated in the United Kingdom[8] only apply if:

(1)   the parties to the article 6 agreement agree or have agreed, whether before, on or after 15 January 2000, to the effect that the provisions relating to European Works Councils[9] which would have applied in respect of the agreement had it been made under the statutory provisions relating to European Works Councils[10] should apply in respect of the article 6 agreement; or

(2)   the article 6 agreement ceases to have effect[11].

1   Ie in accordance with the Transnational Information and Consultation of Employees Regulations 1999, SI 1999/3323, reg 5: see PARA 1240.

2   As to the meaning of 'central management' see PARA 1240 note 1.

3   Ie the date on which the Transnational Information and Consultation of Employees Regulations 1999, SI 1999/3323, came into force.

4   As to the meaning of 'European Works Council' see PARA 1237 note 3.

5   As to the meaning of 'information and consultation procedure' see PARA 1240 note 3.

6   As to the meaning of 'member state' see PARA 1237 note 3.

7   Ie the provisions of European Parliament and Council Directive (EC) 2009/38 (OJ L122, 16/05/2009, p 28) art 6: see PARA 1236. That Directive replaces Council Directive (EC) 94/45 (OJ L254, 30.9.94, p 64), as extended by Council Directive (EC) 97/74 (OJ L10, 16.1.1998, p 22) (now repealed and replaced: see PARA 1237 note 1). For a correlation table between the provisions of the former and the current Directives see European Parliament and Council Directive (EC) 2009/38 (OJ L122, 16/05/2009, p 28) Annex III.

8   Ie the provisions referred to in the Transnational Information and Consultation of Employees Regulations 1999, SI 1999/3323, reg 4(1): see PARA 1237.

9   Ie the provisions of the Transnational Information and Consultation of Employees Regulations 1999, SI 1999/3323.

10 Ie under the Transnational Information and Consultation of Employees Regulations 1999, SI 1999/3323, reg 17: see PARA 1252.

11 Transnational Information and Consultation of Employees Regulations 1999, SI 1999/3323, regs 1(1), 42(1), (2). Where reg 42(1)(a) (see head (1) in the text) applies, the Transnational

Information and Consultation of Employees Regulations 1999, SI 1999/3323, apply as if the article 6 agreement had been made under the Transnational Information and Consultation of Employees Regulations 1999, SI 1999/3323, reg 17: reg 42(3). As to other exceptions and the application of the Transnational Information and Consultation of Employees Regulations 1999, SI 1999/3323, generally see PARA 1237 note 2.

1283. Article 7 European Works Councils. Where[1] the central management[2] is situated in the United Kingdom, and, immediately before 15 January 2000[3], a European Works Council[4] established under the provisions of the law or practice of a member state[5], other than the United Kingdom, which are designed to give effect to the provisions of the Transnational Information and Consultation Directive[6] (an 'article 7 European Works Council') exists, the provisions which apply only where the central management is situated in the United Kingdom[7] only apply if:

(1) the central management and European Works Council agree or have agreed, whether before, on or after 15 January 2000, to the effect that the statutory provisions relating to European Works Councils which would have applied in respect of the European Works Council, had it been made[8] under the statutory provisions relating to European Works Councils, should apply in respect of the article 7 European Works Council; or

(2) the European Works Council decides, under the provisions of the law or practice of a member state, other than the United Kingdom, which are designed to give effect to the provisions of the relevant Council Directive[9], to negotiate an agreement for a European Works Council or an information and consultation procedure[10].

1 Ie in accordance with the Transnational Information and Consultation of Employees Regulations 1999, SI 1999/3323, reg 5: see PARA 1240.
2 As to the meaning of 'central management' see PARA 1240 note 1.
3 Ie the date on which the Transnational Information and Consultation of Employees Regulations 1999, SI 1999/3323, came into force.
4 As to the meaning of 'European Works Council' see PARA 1237 note 3.
5 As to the meaning of 'member state' see PARA 1237 note 3.
6 Ie the provisions of European Parliament and Council Directive (EC) 2009/38 (OJ L122, 16/05/2009, p 28), art 7: see PARA 1236. That Directive replaces Council Directive (EC) 94/45 (OJ L254, 30.9.94, p 64), as extended by Council Directive (EC) 97/74 (OJ L10, 16.1.1998, p 22) (now repealed and replaced: see PARA 1237 note 1). For a correlation table between the provisions of the former and the current Directives see European Parliament and Council Directive (EC) 2009/38 (OJ L122, 16/05/2009, p 28) Annex III.
7 Ie the provisions referred to in the Transnational Information and Consultation of Employees Regulations 1999, SI 1999/3323, reg 4(1): see PARA 1237.
8 Ie by virtue of the Transnational Information and Consultation of Employees Regulations 1999, SI 1999/3323, reg 18: see PARA 1253.
9 Ie the provisions of what is now European Parliament and Council Directive (EC) 2009/38 (OJ L122, 16/05/2009, p 28) Annex I para 1(f).
10 Transnational Information and Consultation of Employees Regulations 1999, SI 1999/3323, regs 1(1), 43(1), (2). Where reg 43(1) (a) or (b) (see heads (1), (2) in the text) applies, the Transnational Information and Consultation of Employees Regulations 1999, SI 1999/3323, apply, subject to the modifications referred to in reg 48(4)–(6) (see below), as if the article 7 European Works Council had been established, by virtue of the Transnational Information and Consultation of Employees Regulations 1999, SI 1999/3323, reg 18 (see PARA 1253), under the Transnational Information and Consultation of Employees Regulations 1999, SI 1999/3323, and, in a case where reg 43(1)(b) (see head (2) in the text) applies, as if a decision had been taken under Schedule para 10(2) (see PARA 1262): reg 43(3).

Where, immediately before 15 January 2000, a European Works Council has been established under the provisions of the law or practice of a member state other than the United Kingdom, which are designed to give effect to what is now European Parliament and Council

Directive (EC) 2009/38 (OJ L122, 16/05/2009, p 28), art 7, Annex I, the Transnational Information and Consultation of Employees Regulations 1999, SI 1999/3323, reg 48(2), (3) applies: regs 1(1), 48(1).

Where the central management is situated in the United Kingdom and reg 43(1)(a) or (b) (see heads (1), (2) in the text) applies, the Transnational Information and Consultation of Employees Regulations 1999, SI 1999/3323, apply with the modifications specified in reg 48(4)–(6) (see below) as if the European Works Council had been established under the Transnational Information and Consultation of Employees Regulations 1999, SI 1999/3323: reg 48(2).

Where the central management is not situated in the United Kingdom, or is situated in the United Kingdom but neither reg 43(1)(a) nor reg 43(1)(b) applies, the provisions referred to in reg 4(2) (see PARA 1237) apply with the modifications specified in reg 48(5), (6) (see below): reg 48(3).

Regulation 18(1), Schedule para 2 (see PARA 1254) applies in respect of the composition of the European Works Council only to the extent that it determines the number of UK members on the European Works Council but does not affect in any way the number of non-UK members on the European Works Council: reg 48(4).

Where, as a result of the implementation of what is now European Parliament and Council Directive (EC) 2009/38 (OJ L122, 16/05/2009, p 28) (see PARA 1236) by a member state, including the United Kingdom, there are required to be UK members on the European Works Council and, immediately before 15 January 2000: (1) no person has been designated to attend meetings of the European Works Council as a representative of employees in the United Kingdom; or (2) one or more persons has or have been designated to attend meetings of the European Works Council as a representative of employees in the United Kingdom, then, in the case mentioned in head (1) above, the UK members of the European Works Council must be appointed or elected in accordance with the Transnational Information and Consultation of Employees Regulations 1999, SI 1999/3323, Schedule paras 3–5 (see PARAS 1255–1257), and, in the case mentioned in head (2) above, the person or persons is or are to be treated as from 15 January 2000 as a UK member of the European Works Council who has been elected or appointed in accordance with Schedule paras 3–5: reg 48(5).

Where the number of persons referred to in head (2) above is: (a) in a case where Schedule para 2 (see PARA 1254) applies, less than the number of UK members of the European Works Council required by Schedule para 2; or (b) in a case where Schedule para 2 does not apply, less than the number of UK members of the European Works Council required by the law or practice of the member state under which the European Works Council was established, the additional number of UK members needed to secure compliance with Schedule para 2 or, as the case may be, the law or practice of the member state referred to in head (b) above must be elected or appointed in accordance with Schedule paras 3–5: reg 48(6).

As to other exceptions and the application of the Transnational Information and Consultation of Employees Regulations 1999, SI 1999/3323, generally see PARA 1237 note 2.

1284.   Article 3 agreements. None of the obligations in the Transnational Information and Consultation of Employees Regulations 1999[1], except those with regard to adaptation[2], applies[3] to an EU-scale undertaking[4] or EU-scale group of undertakings[5] where specified conditions[6] are satisfied[7]. Those conditions are that:

(1)   an agreement is in force which was in force immediately before 16 December 1999, covers the entire workforce in the member states[8] and provides for the transnational information and consultation of employees[9]; and

(2)   the obligation (whether arising under those 1999 Regulations or under the national law or practice of any other member state) to initiate negotiations for the establishment of a European Works Council[10] or information and consultation procedure[11] would otherwise have applied to the EU-scale undertaking or EU-scale group of undertakings solely as a result of the Extension Directive[12].

Certain provisions of the 1999 Regulations[13], however, apply where the structure of a EU-scale undertaking or EU-scale group of undertakings changes significantly and there is:

(a)		one European Works Council agreement, or one agreement for an information and consultation procedure;
(b)		more than one European Works Council agreement;
(c)		more than one agreement for an information and consultation procedure; or
(d)		at least one European Works Council agreement and at least one agreement for an information and consultation procedure,

in force and there are no provisions for the continuance of the European Works Council or information and consultation procedure, as the case may be, where there are significant changes in the structure of the EU-scale undertaking or EU-scale group of undertakings or there are such provisions, but there is a conflict between them[14].

Certain other provisions of those Regulations[15] apply to an employee who is a member of a special negotiating body[16] or a candidate in an election in which any person elected will, on being elected, be such a member, where the structure of a EU-scale undertaking or EU-scale group of undertakings changes significantly and heads (i) and (ii) below apply[17], namely where:

(i)		there is:
  (A)		one European Works Council agreement, or one agreement for an information and consultation procedure;
  (B)		more than one European Works Council agreement;
  (C)		more than one agreement for an information and consultation procedure; or
  (D)		at least one European Works Council agreement and at least one agreement for an information and consultation procedure,

  in force and there are no provisions for the continuance of the European Works Council or information and consultation procedure, as the case may be, where there are significant changes in the structure of the EU-scale undertaking or EU-scale group of undertakings or there are such provisions, but there is a conflict between them[18];

(ii)		the central management[19] has initiated negotiations[20] for the establishment of a European Works Council or an information and consultation procedure[21].

1		Ie none of the obligations in the Transnational Information and Consultation of Employees Regulations 1999, SI 1999/3323: see PARA 1237 et seq.
2		Ie except those in the Transnational Information and Consultation of Employees Regulations 1999, SI 1999/3323, reg 19F: see PARA 1268.
3		Ie subject to the Transnational Information and Consultation of Employees Regulations 1999, SI 1999/3323, reg 44(4), (5): see the text and notes 13–17.
4		As to the meaning of 'EU-scale undertaking' see PARA 1237 note 11.
5		As to the meaning of 'EU-scale group of undertakings' see PARA 1237 note 12.
6		Ie the conditions specified in Council Directive (EC) 97/74 (OJ L10, 16.1.1998, p 22) ('the Extension Directive') art 3 (now repealed).
7		Transnational Information and Consultation of Employees Regulations 1999, SI 1999/3323, reg 44(1) (reg 44 substituted by SI 2010/1088; amended by virtue of SI 2011/1043).
8		As to the meaning of 'member state' see PARA 1237 note 3.
9		Transnational Information and Consultation of Employees Regulations 1999, SI 1999/3323, reg 44(2)(a) (as substituted: see note 7). As to the meaning of 'employee' see PARA 1238 note 1. If an agreement when taken together with one or more other agreements satisfies the requirements specified in reg 44(2)(a), that agreement, when taken together with such other agreements, is to be treated as an agreement for the purposes of reg 44(2): reg 44(3) (as so substituted).
10		As to the meaning of 'European Works Council' see PARA 1237 note 3.
11		As to the meaning of 'information and consultation procedure' see PARA 1240 note 3.

12 Transnational Information and Consultation of Employees Regulations 1999, SI 1999/3323, reg 44(2)(b) (as substituted and amended: see note 7).
13 Ie the Transnational Information and Consultation of Employees Regulations 1999, SI 1999/3323, regs 9–18: see PARA 1244 et seq.
14 Transnational Information and Consultation of Employees Regulations 1999, SI 1999/3323, reg 44(4) (as substituted and amended: see note 7).
15 Ie the Transnational Information and Consultation of Employees Regulations 1999, SI 1999/3323, regs 25(1), (2), 26–28, 31, 32: see PARA 1275 et seq.
16 As to the meaning of 'special negotiating body' see PARA 1244 note 13.
17 Transnational Information and Consultation of Employees Regulations 1999, SI 1999/3323, reg 44(5) (as substituted and amended: see note 7).
18 Transnational Information and Consultation of Employees Regulations 1999, SI 1999/3323, reg 44(6) (as substituted and amended: see note 7).
19 As to the meaning of 'central management' see PARA 1240 note 1.
20 Ie under the Transnational Information and Consultation of Employees Regulations 1999, SI 1999/3323, reg 19F(1) or (3): see PARA 1268.
21 Transnational Information and Consultation of Employees Regulations 1999, SI 1999/3323, reg 44(7) (as substituted: see note 7).

1285.   'Article 13 agreements'.   None of the obligations in the Transnational Information and Consultation of Employees Regulations 1999[1], except those with regard to adaptation[2], applies[3] to an EU-scale undertaking[4] or EU-scale group of undertakings[5] where the specified conditions[6] are satisfied[7]. Those conditions are that an agreement is in force which:

(1)   was in force immediately before whichever is the earlier of 23 September 1996 and the day after the date on which the national law or practice giving effect to the Transnational Information and Consultation Directive[8] came into force in the member state[9] (other than the United Kingdom) whose national law governs the agreement;

(2)   covers the entire workforce in the member states; and

(3)   provides for the transnational information and consultation of employees[10].

If an agreement when taken together with one or more other agreements satisfies the requirements specified in heads (1) to (3) above, that agreement, when taken together with such other agreements, is to be treated as an agreement for the purposes of those heads[11].

Certain provisions of the 1999 Regulations[12], however, apply where the structure of a EU-scale undertaking or EU-scale group of undertakings changes significantly and there is:

(a)   one European Works Council[13] agreement or one agreement for an information and consultation procedure[14];

(b)   more than one European Works Council agreement;

(c)   more than one agreement for an information and consultation procedure; or

(d)   at least one European Works Council agreement and at least one agreement for an information and consultation procedure,

in force and there are no provisions for the continuance of the European Works Council or information and consultation procedure, as the case may be, where there are significant changes in the structure of the EU-scale undertaking or EU-scale group of undertakings or there are such provisions, but there is a conflict between them[15].

Certain other provisions of those Regulations[16] apply to an employee who is a member of a special negotiating body[17] or a candidate in an election in which any person elected will, on being elected, be such a member, where the structure of a EU-scale undertaking or EU-scale group of undertakings changes significantly and heads (i) and (ii) below apply[18], namely where:

(i)   there is:

    (A)   one European Works Council agreement, or one agreement for an information and consultation procedure;

    (B)   more than one European Works Council agreement;

    (C)   more than one agreement for an information and consultation procedure; or

    (D)   at least one European Works Council agreement and at least one agreement for an information and consultation procedure,

    in force and there are no provisions for the continuance of the European Works Council or information and consultation procedure, as the case may be, where there are significant changes in the structure of the EU-scale undertaking or EU-scale group of undertakings or there are such provisions, but there is a conflict between them[19];

(ii)   the central management[20] has initiated negotiations[21] for the establishment of a European Works Council or an information and consultation procedure[22].

1 Ie none of the obligations in the Transnational Information and Consultation of Employees Regulations 1999, SI 1999/3323: see PARA 1237 et seq.

2 Ie except those in the Transnational Information and Consultation of Employees Regulations 1999, SI 1999/3323, reg 19F: see PARA 1268.

3 Ie subject to the Transnational Information and Consultation of Employees Regulations 1999, SI 1999/3323, reg 45(4), (5): see the text and notes 12–18.

4 As to the meaning of 'EU-scale undertaking' see PARA 1237 note 11.

5 As to the meaning of 'EU-scale group of undertakings' see PARA 1237 note 12.

6 Ie the conditions specified in Council Directive (EC) 94/45 (OJ L254, 30.9.94, p 64) art 13 (now repealed and replaced: see PARA 1236 note 1). For a correlation table between the provisions of the former and the current Directives see European Parliament and Council Directive (EC) 2009/38 (OJ L122, 16/05/2009, p 28) Annex III. However, it is submitted that in this instance the reference in the text is intended to be to the former, rather than the current, Directive.

7 Transnational Information and Consultation of Employees Regulations 1999, SI 1999/3323, reg 45(1) (reg 45 substituted by SI 2010/1088; amended by virtue of SI 2011/1043). As to other exceptions and the application of the Transnational Information and Consultation of Employees Regulations 1999, SI 1999/3323, generally see PARA 1237 note 2.

8 Ie Council Directive (EC) 94/45 (OJ L254, 30.9.94, p 64) (now repealed and replaced: see PARA 1237 note 1).

9 As to the meaning of 'member state' see PARA 1237 note 3.

10 Transnational Information and Consultation of Employees Regulations 1999, SI 1999/3323, reg 45(2) (as substituted: see note 7). As to the meaning of 'employee' see PARA 1238 note 1.

11 Transnational Information and Consultation of Employees Regulations 1999, SI 1999/3323, reg 45(3) (as substituted: see note 7).

12 Ie the Transnational Information and Consultation of Employees Regulations 1999, SI 1999/3323, regs 9–18: see PARA 1244 et seq.

13 As to the meaning of 'European Works Council' see PARA 1237 note 3.

14 As to the meaning of 'information and consultation procedure' see PARA 1240 note 3.

15 Transnational Information and Consultation of Employees Regulations 1999, SI 1999/3323, reg 45(4) (as substituted and amended: see note 7).

16 Ie the Transnational Information and Consultation of Employees Regulations 1999, SI 1999/3323, regs 25(1), (2), 26–28, 31–32: see PARA 1275 et seq.

17 As to the meaning of 'special negotiating body' see PARA 1244 note 13.

18 Transnational Information and Consultation of Employees Regulations 1999, SI 1999/3323, reg 45(5) (as substituted and amended: see note 7).

19 Transnational Information and Consultation of Employees Regulations 1999, SI 1999/3323, reg 45(6) (as substituted and amended: see note 7).

20 As to the meaning of 'central management' see PARA 1240 note 1.

21 Ie under the Transnational Information and Consultation of Employees Regulations 1999, SI 1999/3323, reg 19F(1) or (3): see PARA 1268.

22 Transnational Information and Consultation of Employees Regulations 1999, SI 1999/3323, reg 45(7) (as substituted: see note 7).

1286. Agreements signed or revised on or after 5 June 2009 and before 5 June 2011. Where an agreement is in force which establishes[1] a European Works Council[2] or information and consultation procedure[3] and it was signed or revised on or after 5 June 2009 and before 5 June 2011, the Transnational Information and Consultation of Employees Regulations 1999[4] apply to an EU-scale undertaking[5] or EU-scale group of undertakings[6] as if the specified statutory amendments to those Regulations[7] had not been made[8].

Certain provisions of the 1999 Regulations[9] apply where the structure of an EU-scale undertaking or EU-scale group of undertakings changes significantly and there is:

(1) one European Works Council[10] agreement, or one agreement for an information and consultation procedure[11];

(2) more than one European Works Council agreement;

(3) more than one agreement for an information and consultation procedure; or

(4) at least one European Works Council agreement and at least one agreement for an information and consultation procedure,

in force and there are no provisions for the continuance of the European Works Council or information and consultation procedure, as the case may be, where there are significant changes in the structure of the EU-scale undertaking or EU-scale group of undertakings or there are such provisions, but there is a conflict between them[12].

1 Ie under the Transnational Information and Consultation of Employees Regulations 1999, SI 1999/3323, reg 17: see PARA 1252.

2 As to the meaning of 'European Works Council' see PARA 1237 note 3.

3 As to the meaning of 'information and consultation procedure' see PARA 1240 note 3.

4 Ie the Transnational Information and Consultation of Employees Regulations 1999, SI 1999/3323: see PARA 1237 et seq.

5 As to the meaning of 'EU-scale undertaking' see PARA 1237 note 11.

6 As to the meaning of 'EU-scale group of undertakings' see PARA 1237 note 12.

7 Ie the amendments made by the provisions of the Transnational Information and Consultation of Employees (Amendment) Regulations 2010, SI 2010/1088, specified in the Transnational Information and Consultation of Employees Regulations 1999, SI 1999/3323, reg 45A(3) (reg 45A added by SI 2010/1088)), ie:

    (1) the Transnational Information and Consultation of Employees (Amendment) Regulations 2010, SI 2010/1088, reg 3, in so far as it inserts the definition of 'national employee representation bodies' into the Transnational Information and Consultation of Employees Regulations 1999, SI 1999/3323, reg 2 and adds reg 2(4A), (4B);

    (2) the Transnational Information and Consultation of Employees (Amendment) Regulations 2010, SI 2010/1088, regs 5–10;

    (3) reg 11, in so far as it adds the Transnational Information and Consultation of Employees Regulations 1999, SI 1999/3323, regs 19A–19E;

    (4) the Transnational Information and Consultation of Employees (Amendment) Regulations 2010, SI 2010/1088, reg 13, in so far as it adds the Transnational Information and Consultation of Employees Regulations 1999, SI 1999/3323, reg 21(1A)(b);

    (5) the Transnational Information and Consultation of Employees (Amendment) Regulations 2010, SI 2010/1088, reg 14, in so far as it adds the Transnational Information and Consultation of Employees Regulations 1999, SI 1999/3323, reg 21A(1)(b)–(d) and makes provision for the resolution of complaints in relation to regs 19A, 19B, 19E(2);

    (6) the Transnational Information and Consultation of Employees (Amendment) Regulations 2010, SI 2010/1088, reg 16;

(7)   reg 23, in so far as it amends the Transnational Information and Consultation of Employees Regulations 1999, SI 1999/3323, regs 44, 45; and

(8)   the Transnational Information and Consultation of Employees (Amendment) Regulations 2010, SI 2010/1088, regs 24–29.

8   Transnational Information and Consultation of Employees Regulations 1999, SI 1999/3323, reg 45A(1), (2), (5) (as added (see note 7); amended by virtue of SI 2011/1043). This is subject to the Transnational Information and Consultation of Employees Regulations 1999, SI 1999/3323, reg 45A(4) (see the text and notes 9–12): reg 45A(1) (as so added). As to other exceptions and the application of the Transnational Information and Consultation of Employees Regulations 1999, SI 1999/3323, generally see PARA 1237 note 2.

9   Ie the Transnational Information and Consultation of Employees Regulations 1999, SI 1999/3323, regs 9–18: see PARA 1244 et seq.

10   As to the meaning of 'European Works Council' see PARA 1237 note 3.

11   As to the meaning of 'information and consultation procedure' see PARA 1240 note 3.

12   Transnational Information and Consultation of Employees Regulations 1999, SI 1999/3323, reg 45A(4) (as added and amended: see notes 7–8).

1287.   Members of the merchant navy.   No long haul crew member[1] is to be:

(1)   a member of a special negotiating body[2];

(2)   a member of a European Works Council[3]; or

(3)   an information and consultation representative[4];

but the above provisions[5] do not apply where the central management[6] decides that the long haul crew member in question is to be permitted to be, as the case may be, a member of a special negotiating body or of a European Works Council, or an information and consultation representative[7].

Where the above provisions[8] apply, no long haul crew member is:

(a)   to stand as a candidate for election as a member of a special negotiating body or of a European Works Council, or as an information and consultation representative; or

(b)   to be appointed or nominated to be a member of a special negotiating body or of a European Works Council, or an information and consultation representative[9].

1   For these purposes, a 'long haul crew member' means a person who is a member of a merchant navy crew other than: (1) a ferry worker; or (2) a person who normally works on voyages the duration of which is less than 48 hours: Transnational Information and Consultation of Employees Regulations 1999, SI 1999/3323, reg 46(2).

2   As to the meaning of 'special negotiating body' see PARA 1244 note 13.

3   As to the meaning of 'European Works Council' see PARA 1237 note 3.

4   Transnational Information and Consultation of Employees Regulations 1999, SI 1999/3323, reg 46(1). As to the meaning of 'information and consultation representative' see PARA 1240 note 3. As to other exceptions and the application of the Transnational Information and Consultation of Employees Regulations 1999, SI 1999/3323, generally see PARA 1237 note 2.

5   Ie the Transnational Information and Consultation of Employees Regulations 1999, SI 1999/3323, reg 46(1).

6   As to the meaning of 'central management' see PARA 1240 note 1.

7   Transnational Information and Consultation of Employees Regulations 1999, SI 1999/3323, reg 46(3).

8   See note 5.

9   Transnational Information and Consultation of Employees Regulations 1999, SI 1999/3323, reg 46(4).

(iii)   Information and Consultation of Employees

A. REGULATIONS AS TO INFORMATION AND CONSULTATION; INTRODUCTION

1288.   Information and consultation powers of Secretary of State.   The Secretary of State[1] may, by statutory instrument[2], make regulations for the purpose of conferring on employees of an employer to whom the regulations apply, or on representatives of those employees, rights to be informed by the employer about prescribed[3] matters, and to be consulted by the employer about prescribed matters[4].

Such regulations must make provision as to the employers to whom the regulations apply which may include provision (1) applying the regulations by reference to factors including the number of employees in the United Kingdom in the employer's undertaking; (2) as to the method by which the number of employees in an employer's undertaking is to be calculated; and (3) applying the regulations to different descriptions of employer with effect from different dates[5].

Further, any such regulations may make provision (a) as to the circumstances in which the rights to be informed about prescribed matters[6] arise and the extent of those rights; (b) for and about the initiation and conduct of negotiations between employers to whom the regulations apply and their employees for the purposes of reaching an agreement satisfying prescribed conditions about the provision of information to the employees, and consultation of them, whether that provision or consultation is to be direct or through representatives; (c) about the representatives the employees may have for the purposes of the regulations and the method by which those representatives are to be selected; or (d) as to the resolution of disputes and the enforcement of obligations imposed by the regulations or by an agreement of the kind mentioned in head (b) above[7].

Any regulations made may confer jurisdiction, including exclusive jurisdiction, on employment tribunals and on the Employment Appeal Tribunal[8]; confer functions on the Central Arbitration Committee[9]; require or authorise the holding of ballots[10]; amend, apply with or without modifications, or make provision similar to any provision of the specified enactments[11]; include supplemental, incidental, consequential and transitional provision, including provision amending any enactment[12]; and make different provision for different cases or circumstances[13].

1   As to the Secretary of State see PARA 5 note 21.
2   Employment Relations Act 2004 s 42(7). No such regulations may be made unless a draft of the regulations has been laid before Parliament and approved by a resolution of each House: s 42(8). See the Information and Consultation of Employees Regulations 2004, SI 2004/3426; and PARA 1289 et seq.
3   Ie prescribed by regulations under the Employment Relations Act 2004 s 42: s 42(9). See note 2.
4   Employment Relations Act 2004 s 42(1).
5   Employment Relations Act 2004 s 42(2).
6   Ie the rights mentioned in the Employment Relations Act 2004 s 42(1).
7   Employment Relations Act 2004 s 42(3).
8   Employment Relations Act 2004 s 42(4)(a). As to the Employment Appeal Tribunal see PARA 1422 et seq.
9   Employment Relations Act 2004 s 42(4)(b). As to the Central Arbitration Committee see PARA 1226 et seq.
10   Employment Relations Act 2004 s 42(4)(c).
11   Ie the Employment Rights Act 1996 including, in particular, Pt V (ss 43M–49A) (protection from suffering detriment in employment: see PARA 612 et seq), Pt X (ss 94–134A) (unfair dismissal: see PARA 757 et seq) and Pt XIII (ss 191–209) (miscellaneous provisions); the Employment Tribunals Act 1996; or the Trade Union and Labour Relations (Consolidation) Act 1992: Employment Relations Act 2004 s 42(4)(d).
12   Employment Relations Act 2004 s 42(4)(e).
13   Employment Relations Act 2004 s 42(4)(f). Regulations made under s 42(1) may also make any provision which appears to the Secretary of State to be necessary or expedient for the purpose of implementing European Parliament and Council Directive (EC) 2002/14 (OJ L80, 23.3.2002, p 29) establishing a general framework for informing and consulting employees in the European

Community (see COMPANIES vol 14 (2009) PARA 23), or for the purpose of dealing with any matter arising out of or related to the United Kingdom's obligations under that Directive: Employment Relations Act 2004 s 42(5). Nothing in s 42(2)–(5) prejudices the generality of s 42: s 42(6). See also note 2.

1289. Application of the Information and Consultation of Employees Regulations 2004. The Information and Consultation of Employees Regulations 2004[1] apply to undertakings[2] (1) employing in the United Kingdom[3], in accordance with the relevant calculation[4], at least 50 employees; and (2) whose registered office, head office or principal place of business is situated in Great Britain[5]. However, where the registered office is situated in Great Britain and the head office or principal place of business is situated in Northern Ireland or vice versa, the Regulations only apply where the majority of employees are employed to work in Great Britain[6].

1 Ie the Information and Consultation of Employees Regulations 2004, SI 2004/3426. The Regulations have been made under the Employment Relations Act 2004 s 42 (see PARA 1288) for the purpose of implementing in Great Britain European Parliament and Council Directive (EC) 2002/14 (OJ L80, 23.2.2002, p 29) establishing a general framework for informing and consulting employees in the European Community (the 'Information and Consultation Directive'). The Advisory, Conciliation and Arbitration Service ('ACAS') issues guidance on good practice in establishing and operating information and consultation procedures, accessible at the date at which this volume states the law at www.acas.org.uk. As to ACAS see PARA 1213 et seq. The Central Arbitration Committee (the 'CAC') has issued a Guide for Employers and Employees (revised 2012) explaining its role under the Regulations, accessible at the date at which this volume states the law at www.cac.gov.uk. As to the CAC see PARA 1226 et seq.
2 'Undertaking' means a public or private undertaking carrying out an economic activity, whether or not operating for gain: Information and Consultation of Employees Regulations 2004, SI 2004/3426, reg 2. In the 2004 Regulations, an undertaking to which the Regulations apply is referred to, in relation to its employees, as 'the employer': reg 3(3).
3 As to the meaning of 'United Kingdom' see PARA 2 note 12.
4 Ie the calculation in the Information and Consultation of Employees Regulations 2004, SI 2004/3426, reg 4. Subject to reg 4(4), the number of employees for the purposes of reg 3(1) is determined by ascertaining the average number of employees employed in the previous 12 months, calculated in accordance with reg 4(2): reg 4(1). Subject to reg 4(3), the average number of employees is to be ascertained by determining the number of employees employed in each month in the previous 12 months (whether they were employed throughout the month or not), adding together those monthly figures and dividing the number by 12: reg 4(2). For the purposes of the calculation in reg 4(2) if, for the whole of a month within the 12 month period, an employee works under a contract by virtue of which he would have worked for 75 hours or less in that month (1) were the month to have contained 21 working days; (2) were the employee to have had no absences from work; and (3) were the employee to have worked no overtime, the employee may be counted as representing half of a full-time employee for the month in question, if the employer so decides: reg 4(3). If the undertaking has been in existence for less than 12 months, the references to 12 months in reg 4(1), (2) and (3), and the divisor of 12 referred to in reg 4(2), are replaced by the number of months the undertaking has been in existence: reg 4(4).
　　'Employee' means an individual who has entered into or works under a contract of employment and in Pt VIII (regs 27–34) (see PARA 1311 et seq) and reg 40 (see PARA 1291) includes, where the employment has ceased, an individual who worked under a contract of employment; and 'contract of employment' means a contract of service or apprenticeship, whether express or implied, and (if it is express) whether oral or in writing: reg 2. As to the meaning of 'writing' see PARA 2 note 8.
　　The following provisions apply to an agency worker whose contract within the Agency Workers Regulations 2010, SI 2010/93, reg 3(1)(b) (contract with the temporary work agency: see PARA 97) is not a contract of employment: Information and Consultation of Employees Regulations 2004, SI 2004/3426, reg 3A(1) (reg 3A added by SI 2010/93). For the purposes of the Information and Consultation of Employees Regulations 2004, SI 2004/3426, reg 3, 4, Sch 1 (see the text and notes 1–6), any agency worker who has a contract with a temporary work agency is to be treated as being employed by that temporary work agency for the duration of that agency worker's assignment with the employer: reg 3A(2) (as so added). 'Agency worker' has the same meaning as in the Agency Workers Regulations 2010, SI 2010/93, reg 3 (see PARA

97); 'assignment' has the same meaning as in reg 2 (see PARA 99 note 4) and 'temporary work agency' has the same meaning as in reg 4 (see PARA 97): Information and Consultation of Employees Regulations 2004, SI 2004/3426, regs 2, 3A(3) (definition in reg 2, and reg 3A(3), added by SI 2010/93).

5 Information and Consultation of Employees Regulations 2004, SI 2004/3426, reg 3(1), Sch 1. Regulation 4(1)(b) (see head (2) in the text) is subject to reg 4(2). As to the meaning of 'Great Britain' see PARA 2 note 12.

 The application of the Regulations was phased in, so that they applied from 6 April 2005 to undertakings employing in the United Kingdom, in accordance with the relevant calculation, at least 150 employees; from 6 April 2007 to undertakings employing at least 100 employees and from 6 April 2008 to undertakings employing at least 50 employees, as stated in the text.

6 Information and Consultation of Employees Regulations 2004, SI 2004/3426, reg 3(2).

1290. Entitlement to data for the purpose of determining the number of employees. An employee[1] or an employees' representative may request data from the employer[2] for the purpose of determining the number of people employed by the employer's undertaking[3] in the United Kingdom[4]. Any such request for data[5] must be in writing[6] and be dated[7].

The employer must provide the employee or the employees' representative who made the request with data to enable him to (1) make the relevant calculation of the numbers of employees[8], and (2) determine[9] what number of employees constitutes 10 per cent of the employees in the undertaking[10].

An employee or an employees' representative who has requested data under the above provisions may present a complaint to the Central Arbitration Committee (the 'CAC')[11] that (a) the employer has failed to provide the data referred to in heads (1) and (2) above; or (b) the data which has been provided by the employer is false or incomplete in a material particular[12]. Where the CAC finds the complaint to be well-founded it must make an order requiring the employer to disclose data to the complainant; and the order must specify (i) the data in respect of which the CAC finds that the complaint is well-founded and which is to be disclosed to the complainant; (ii) the date (or if more than one, the earliest date) on which the employer refused or failed to disclose data, or disclosed false or incomplete information; (iii) a date, not being less than one week from the date of the order, by which the employer must disclose the data specified in the order[13].

The CAC must not consider a complaint[14] unless it is made after the expiry of a period of one month beginning on the date on which the complainant made his request for data[15].

1 As to the meaning of 'employee' see PARA 1289 note 4.
2 As to the meaning of 'employer' see PARA 1289 note 2.
3 As to the meaning of 'undertaking' see PARA 1289 note 2.
4 Information and Consultation of Employees Regulations 2004, SI 2004/3426, reg 5(1). As to the meaning of 'United Kingdom' see PARA 2 note 12.
5 Ie made under the Information and Consultation of Employees Regulations 2004, SI 2004/3426, reg 5(1).
6 As to the meaning of 'writing' see PARA 2 note 8.
7 Information and Consultation of Employees Regulations 2004, SI 2004/3426, reg 5(2).
8 Ie the calculation referred to in the Information and Consultation of Employees Regulations 2004, SI 2004/3426, reg 4: see PARA 1289 note 4.
9 Ie for the purposes of the Information and Consultation of Employees Regulations 2004, SI 2004/3426, reg 7(2): see PARA 1294.
10 Information and Consultation of Employees Regulations 2004, SI 2004/3426, reg 5(3).
11 As to the Central Arbitration Committee see PARA 1226 et seq.
12 Information and Consultation of Employees Regulations 2004, SI 2004/3426, reg 6(1).
13 Information and Consultation of Employees Regulations 2004, SI 2004/3426, reg 6(2).

14 Ie presented under the Information and Consultation of Employees Regulations 2004, SI 2004/3426, reg 6.
15 Information and Consultation of Employees Regulations 2004, SI 2004/3426, reg 6(3).

1291. Restrictions on contracting out of the Information and Consultation of Employees Regulations 2004. Any provision in any agreement (whether an employee's[1] contract or not) is void in so far as it purports (1) to exclude or limit the operation of any provision of the Information and Consultation of Employees Regulations 2004[2] other than a provision of Part VIII[3]; or (2) to preclude a person from bringing any proceedings before the Central Arbitration Committee (the 'CAC')[4] or the Employment Appeal Tribunal[5] under any provision of the Regulations other than a provision of Part VIII[6].

Any provision in any agreement (whether an employee's contract or not) is void in so far as it purports (a) to exclude or limit the operation of any provision of Part VIII of the Information and Consultation of Employees Regulations 2004; or (b) to preclude a person from bringing any proceedings before an employment tribunal[7] under Part VIII[8].

1 As to the meaning of 'employee' see PARA 1289 note 4.
2 Ie the Information and Consultation of Employees Regulations 2004, SI 2004/3426: see also PARAS 1289–1290, 1292 et seq.
3 Ie the Information and Consultation of Employees Regulations 2004, SI 2004/3426, Pt VIII (regs 27–34): see PARA 1311 et seq.
4 As to the Central Arbitration Committee see PARA 1226 et seq.
5 As to the Employment Appeal Tribunal see PARA 1422 et seq.
6 Information and Consultation of Employees Regulations 2004, SI 2004/3426, reg 39(1). Regulation 39(1) does not apply to any agreement to refrain from continuing any proceedings referred to in reg 39(1)(b) (see head (2) in the text) made after the proceedings have been instituted: reg 39(2).
7 As to employment tribunals see PARA 1399 et seq.
8 Information and Consultation of Employees Regulations 2004, SI 2004/3426, reg 40(1).
    Regulation 40(1) does not apply to any agreement to refrain from instituting or continuing proceedings before an employment tribunal where a conciliation officer has taken action under any of the Employment Tribunals Act 1996 ss 18A–18C (conciliation: see PARAS 152–153): Information and Consultation of Employees Regulations 2004, SI 2004/3426, reg 40(2) (amended by SI 2014/386). Neither does it apply to any agreement to refrain from instituting or continuing before an employment tribunal proceedings within the Employment Tribunals Act 1996 s 18(1) (proceedings under the Information and Consultation of Employees Regulations 2004, SI 2004/3426, where conciliation is available) (see PARA 152 note 1) if the conditions regulating settlement agreements under the 2004 Regulations are satisfied in relation to the agreement: reg 40(3) (amended by SI 2013/1956). For these purposes the conditions regulating settlement agreements are that (1) the agreement must be in writing; (2) the agreement must relate to the particular proceedings; (3) the employee must have received advice from a relevant independent adviser as to the terms and effect of the proposed agreement and, in particular, its effect on his ability to pursue his rights before an employment tribunal; (4) there must be in force, when the adviser gives the advice, a contract of insurance, or an indemnity provided for members of a profession or a professional body, covering the risk of a claim by the employee in respect of loss arising in consequence of the advice; (5) the agreement must identify the adviser; and (6) the agreement must state that the conditions in heads (1)–(5) above are satisfied: Information and Consultation of Employees Regulations 2004, SI 2004/3426, reg 40(4) (amended by SI 2013/1956). A person is a relevant independent adviser for the purposes of head (3) above (a) if he is a qualified lawyer; (b) if he is an officer, official, employee or member of an independent trade union who has been certified in writing by the trade union as competent to give advice and as authorised to do so on behalf of the trade union; or (c) if he works at an advice centre (whether as an employee or as a volunteer) and has been certified in writing by the centre as competent to give advice and as authorised to do so on behalf of the centre: Information and Consultation of Employees Regulations 2004, SI 2004/3426, reg 40(5). However a person is not a relevant independent adviser for the purposes of head (3) above (i) if he is, is employed by or is acting in the matter for the employer or an associated employer; (ii) in the case of a person within head (b) or head (c) above, if the trade union or advice centre is the

employer or an associated employer; or (iii) in the case of a person within head (c) above, if the employee makes a payment for the advice received from him: reg 40(6). For the purposes of reg 40(6) any two employers are treated as associated if one is a company of which the other (directly or indirectly) has control; or both are companies of which a third person (directly or indirectly) has control; and 'associated employer' is construed accordingly: reg 40(9).

In head (a) above, 'qualified lawyer' means (A) as respects England and Wales, a person who, for the purposes of the Legal Services Act 2007 is an authorised person in relation to an activity which constitutes the exercise of a right of audience or the conduct of litigation (within the meaning of that Act); and (B) as respects Scotland, an advocate (whether in practice as such or employed to give legal advice) or a solicitor who holds a practising certificate: Information and Consultation of Employees Regulations 2004, SI 2004/3426, reg 40(7) (amended by SI 2009/3348). A person is treated as being a qualified lawyer within the meaning of head (A) above if he is a Fellow of the Institute of Legal Executives practising in a solicitor's practice (including a body recognised under the Administration of Justice Act 1985 s 9: see LEGAL PROFESSIONS vol 65 (2008) PARA 515): Information and Consultation of Employees Regulations 2004, SI 2004/3426, reg 40(8) (amended by SI 2009/3348).

1292. Application of the Information and Consultation of Employees Regulations 2004 to Crown employment. The Information and Consultation of Employees Regulations 2004[1] have effect in relation to Crown employment[2] and persons in Crown employment as they have effect in relation to other employment and other employees[3].

For the purposes of the application of the Regulations in relation to Crown employment in accordance with the above provision[4] (1) references to an employee are construed as references to a person in Crown employment; and (2) references to a contract of employment[5] are construed as references to the terms of employment of a person in Crown employment[6].

1 Ie the Information and Consultation of Employees Regulations 2004, SI 2004/3426: see also PARAS 1289–1291, 1293 et seq.
2 In the Information and Consultation of Employees Regulations 2004, SI 2004/3426, 'Crown employment' means employment in an undertaking to which the Regulations apply and which is under or for the purposes of a government department or any officer or body exercising on behalf of the Crown functions conferred by a statutory provision: reg 42(2). As to the meaning of 'undertaking' see PARA 1289 note 2.
3 Information and Consultation of Employees Regulations 2004, SI 2004/3426, reg 42(1). As to the meaning of 'employee' see PARA 1289 note 4.
4 Ie the Information and Consultation of Employees Regulations 2004, SI 2004/3426, reg 42(1): see the text and notes 1–3.
5 As to the meaning of 'contract of employment' see PARA 1289 note 4.
6 Information and Consultation of Employees Regulations 2004, SI 2004/3426, reg 42(3).

1293. Exception for merchant navy. No long haul crew member[1] must be (1) a negotiating representative[2]; or (2) an information and consultation representative[3]. This does not, however, apply where the employer[4] decides that the long haul crew member in question is permitted to be, as the case may be, a negotiating representative or an information and consultation representative[5].

Where the provision[6] applies, no long haul crew member must (a) stand as a candidate for election as a negotiating representative or an information and consultation representative; or (b) be appointed or elected to be a negotiating representative or an information and consultation representative[7].

1 For these purposes, a 'long haul crew member' means a person who is a member of a merchant navy crew other than (1) a ferry worker; or (2) a person who normally works on voyages the duration of which is less than 48 hours: Information and Consultation of Employees Regulations 2004, SI 2004/3426, reg 43(2).
2 As to the meaning of 'negotiating representative' see PARA 1295 note 3.

3 Information and Consultation of Employees Regulations 2004, SI 2004/3426, reg 43(1). As to the meaning of 'information and consultation representative' see PARA 1295 note 3. Regulation 43(1) is subject to reg 43(3) (see the text and notes 5–6): reg 43(1).

4 As to the meaning of 'employer' see PARA 1289 note 2.

5 Information and Consultation of Employees Regulations 2004, SI 2004/3426, reg 43(3).

6 Ie the Information and Consultation of Employees Regulations 2004, SI 2004/3426, reg 43(1): see the text and notes 1–3.

7 Information and Consultation of Employees Regulations 2004, SI 2004/3426, reg 43(4).

B. NEGOTIATED AGREEMENTS

1294. Employee request to negotiate agreement in respect of information and consultation. On receipt of a valid employee request[1], the employer must[2] initiate negotiations by taking certain steps[3].

An employee request is not a valid employee request unless it consists of (1) a single request made by at least ten per cent[4] of the employees in the undertaking[5]; or (2) a number of separate requests made on the same or different days by employees which when taken together mean that at least ten per cent of the employees in that undertaking have made requests, provided that the requests are made within a period of six months[6].

An employee request is not a valid employee request unless the single request referred to in head (1) above or each separate request referred to in head (2) above (a) is in writing[7]; (b) is sent to the registered office, head office or principal place of business of the employer or to the Central Arbitration Committee (the 'CAC')[8]; and (c) specifies the names of the employees making it and the date on which it is sent[9].

If the employer decides to hold a ballot[10], the employer must not be required to initiate negotiations unless and until the outcome of the ballot is[11] that the employees endorse the employee request[12].

If an application is made to the CAC in the context of a dispute[13], the employer must not be required to initiate negotiations unless and until the CAC declares that there was a valid employee request or that the employer's notification was valid[14].

1 'Employee request' means a request by employees under the Information and Consultation of Employees Regulations 2004, SI 2004/3426, reg 7 for the employer to initiate negotiations to reach an agreement under the Regulations: reg 2. As to the meanings of 'employer' and 'employee' see PARA 1289 notes 2, 4.

2 Ie subject to the Information and Consultation of Employees Regulations 2004, SI 2004/3426, reg 7(8), (9): see the text and notes 10–14.

3 Information and Consultation of Employees Regulations 2004, SI 2004/3426, reg 7(1). The steps are set out in reg 14(1): see PARA 1300.

4 Where the figure of 10% in the Information and Consultation of Employees Regulations 2004, SI 2004/3426, reg 7(2) would result in less than 15 or more than 2,500 employees being required in order for a valid employee request to be made, reg 7(2) has effect as if, for the figure of 10%, there were substituted the figure of 15, or as the case may be, 2,500: reg 7(3).

5 As to the meaning of 'undertaking' see PARA 1289 note 2.

6 Information and Consultation of Employees Regulations 2004, SI 2004/3426, reg 7(2). Regulation 7(2) is subject to reg 7(3): see note 4.

7 As to the meaning of 'writing' see PARA 2 note 8.

8 As to the Central Arbitration Committee see PARA 1226 et seq. Where a request is sent to the CAC under head (b) in the text), the CAC must (1) notify the employer that the request has been made as soon as reasonably practicable; (2) request from the employer such information as it needs to verify the number and names of the employees who have made the request; and (3) inform the employer and the employees who have made the request how many employees have made the request on the basis of the information provided by the employees and the employer:

reg 7(5). Where the CAC requests information from the employer under reg 7(5)(b) (see head (2) above), the employer must provide the information requested as soon as reasonably practicable: reg 7(6).

9   Information and Consultation of Employees Regulations 2004, SI 2004/3426, reg 7(4). The date on which an employee request is made is (1) where the request consists of a single request satisfying reg 7(2)(a) (see head (1) in the text) or of separate requests made on the same day satisfying reg 7(2)(b) (see head (2) in the text), the date on which the request is or requests are sent to the employer by the employees or the date on which the CAC informs the employer and the employees in accordance with reg 7(5)(c) (see note 8 head (3)) of how many employees have made the request; and (2) where the request consists of separate requests made on different days, the date on which the request which results in reg 7(2)(b) being satisfied is sent to the employer by the employees, or the CAC informs the employer and the employees in accordance with reg 7(5)(c) of how many employees have made the request where that request results in reg 7(2)(b) being satisfied: reg 7(7).

10 Ie under the Information and Consultation of Employees Regulations 2004, SI 2004/3426, reg 8 or reg 9 (see PARA 1295).

11 Ie the outcome of the ballot is that in the Information and Consultation of Employees Regulations 2004, SI 2004/3426,reg 8(5)(b): see PARA 1295.

12 Information and Consultation of Employees Regulations 2004, SI 2004/3426, reg 7(8).

13 Ie an application is made under the Information and Consultation of Employees Regulations 2004, SI 2004/3426, reg 13: see PARA 1299.

14 Information and Consultation of Employees Regulations 2004, SI 2004/3426, reg 7(9).

1295.   Pre-existing agreements: ballot for endorsement of employee request.
Where a valid employee request[1] has been made[2] by fewer than 40 per cent of employees employed in the undertaking on the date that request was made and where there exists one or more than one pre-existing agreements[3] which:

(1)   are in writing[4];
(2)   cover all the employees of the undertaking;
(3)   have been approved by the employees; and
(4)   set out how the employer is to give information[5] to the employees or their representatives and seek their views on such information[6],

the employer may, instead of initiating negotiations[7], hold a ballot to seek the endorsement of the employees of the undertaking for the employee request in accordance with heads (a) and (b) below and heads (i) to (iii) below[8].

The employer must (a) inform the employees in writing within one month of the date of the employee request that he intends to hold a ballot[9]; and (b) arrange for the ballot to be held as soon as reasonably practicable thereafter, provided that the ballot does not take place before a period of 21 days has passed since the employer informed the employees under head (a) above[10].

A ballot must satisfy the following requirements:

(i)   the employer must make such arrangements as are reasonably practicable to ensure that the ballot is fair;
(ii)   all employees of the undertaking on the day on which the votes may be cast in the ballot, or if the votes may be cast on more than one day, on the first day of those days, must be given an entitlement to vote in the ballot;
(iii) the ballot must be conducted so as to secure that so far as is reasonably practicable, those voting do so in secret; and the votes given in the ballot are accurately counted[11].

Where the employer holds a ballot under the above provisions he must, as soon as reasonably practicable after the date of the ballot[12], inform the employees of the result[13]. If the employees endorse[14] the employee request, the employer is under the obligation[15] to initiate negotiations[16]. If the employees do not endorse the employee request, the employer is no longer under the obligation to initiate negotiations[17].

An employee or an employees' representative who believes that an employer has not, pursuant to head (a) above, informed his employees that he intends to hold a ballot within the period specified may apply to the Central Arbitration Committee (the 'CAC')[18] for a declaration that the employer is under the duty to initiate negotiations[19].

Where an employer, acting pursuant to head (a) above, has informed the employees that he intends to hold a ballot, any employee or employees' representative who believes that the employer has not complied with head (b) above may present a complaint to the CAC[20]. Where the CAC finds such a complaint well-founded it must make an order requiring the employer to hold the ballot within such period as the order may specify[21].

Where:

(A)   in relation to an undertaking a valid employee request such as is mentioned above has been made and there exists one or more pre-existing agreements which satisfy the requirements in heads (1) to (4) above[22];

(B)   the pre-existing agreement or one of the pre-existing agreements covers employees in one or more undertakings other than the undertaking mentioned in head (A) above; and

(C)   the other undertaking or each of the other undertakings mentioned in head (B) above is one in respect of which there is an agreement that satisfied, or are agreements that taken together satisfied, the requirements in heads (1) to (4) above on the date on which the valid employee request was made in respect of the undertaking mentioned in head (A) above; and

(D)   the valid employee request in relation to the undertaking mentioned in head (A) above either alone, or aggregated with any requests made by employees in the undertakings mentioned in head (B) above within the period of six months preceding the date of the valid employee request[23], is made by fewer than 40 per cent of the employees in the undertakings mentioned in heads (A) and (B) above[24],

the employers may hold a combined ballot for endorsement of the employee request[25] and in that event the general provision on ballots for endorsement of employee requests[26] applies to the ballot with the modification that references to employees are treated as referring to the employees employed in all of the undertakings referred to in heads (A) and (B) above[27].

1   'Valid employee request' means an employee request made to their employer by the employees of an undertaking to which the Information and Consultation of Employees Regulations 2004, SI 2004/3426, apply (under reg 3) (see PARA 1289) that satisfies the requirements of reg 7 (see PARA 1294) and is not prevented from being valid by reg 12 (see PARA 1298): reg 2. As to the meaning of 'employee request' see PARA 1294 note 1; as to the meaning of 'employee' see PARA 1289 note 4; and as to the meanings of 'employer' and 'undertaking' see PARA 1289 note 2.

2   Ie made under the Information and Consultation of Employees Regulations 2004, SI 2004/3426, reg 7: see PARA 1294.

3   'Pre-existing agreement' means an agreement between an employer and his employees or their representatives which (1) is made prior to the making of an employee request; and (2) satisfies the conditions set out in the Information and Consultation of Employees Regulations 2004, SI 2004/3426, reg 8(1)(a)–(d) (see heads (1)–(4) in the text), but does not include an agreement concluded in accordance the Transnational Information and Consultation of Employees

Regulations 1999, SI 1999/3323, reg 17 (see PARA 1252) or regs 42–45 (see PARA 1282 et seq) or a negotiated agreement: Information and Consultation of Employees Regulations 2004, SI 2004/3426, reg 2.

'Negotiated agreement' means (a) an agreement between the employer and the negotiating representatives reached through negotiations as provided for in reg 14 (see PARA 1300) which satisfies the requirements of reg 16(1) (see PARA 1301); or (b) an agreement between the employer and the information and consultation representatives referred to in reg 18(2) (see PARA 1303); and 'negotiating representative' means a person elected or appointed pursuant to reg 14(1)(a) (see PARA 1300 head (1) in the text): reg 2. 'Information and consultation representative' means (i) in the case of a negotiated agreement which provides as mentioned in reg 16(1)(f)(i) (see PARA 1301 head (6)(a) in the text), a person appointed or elected in accordance with that agreement; or (ii) a person elected in accordance with reg 19(1) (see PARA 1304): reg 2.

4   As to the meaning of 'writing' see PARA 2 note 8.
5   'Information' means data transmitted by the employer (1) to the information and consultation representatives; or (2) in the case of a negotiated agreement which provides as mentioned in the Information and Consultation of Employees Regulations 2004, SI 2004/3426, reg 16(1)(f)(ii) (see PARA 1301 head (6)(b) in the text in the text), directly to the employees, in order to enable those representatives or those employees to examine and to acquaint themselves with the subject matter of the data: reg 2.

Where information about the employment situation is to be provided under a pre-existing agreement by an employer, such information must include suitable information relating to the use of agency workers (if any) in that undertaking: reg 8A (added by SI 2010/93). As to the meaning of 'agency worker' see PARA 1289 note 4. 'Suitable information relating to the use of agency workers' means information as to (1) the number of agency workers working temporarily for and under the supervision and direction of the employer; (2) the parts of the employer's undertaking in which those agency workers are working; and (3) the type of work those agency workers are carrying out: Information and Consultation of Employees Regulations 2004, SI 2004/3426, reg 2 (definition added by SI 2010/93).

6   Information and Consultation of Employees Regulations 2004, SI 2004/3426, reg 8(1). Regulation 8(1) is subject to reg 9: see the text and notes 22–27. See generally *Stewart v Moray Council* [2006] ICR 1253, [2006] IRLR 592, EAT, both as to the decision and obiter. The Employment Appeal Tribunal upheld the Central Arbitration Committee's holding that the employer's pre-existing agreement defence was not made out because one of the three agreements in the case did not meet the requirement of the Information and Consultation of Employees Regulations 2004, SI 2004/3426, reg 8(1)(d) (see head (4) in the text), also stating that in the case of multiple agreements, while reg 8(1)(b) (see head (2) in the text) on coverage had to be met by those agreements together, the other requirements have to be met by each individual agreement. Although this determined the appeal the tribunal also went on to give useful guidance on the question of union involvement, stating that the three agreements did meet the requirement of reg 8(1)(b) (see head (2) in the text) even though they only required consultation with trade unions. In respect of reg 8(1)(c) (see head (3) in the text) the tribunal said that the requirement that the agreements be 'approved by the employees' was met by approval by the trade unions collectively (even though non-unionists could take no part in that process) provided that the majority of employees were union members.

7   Ie in accordance with the Information and Consultation of Employees Regulations 2004, SI 2004/3426, reg 7(1): see PARA 1294.
8   Information and Consultation of Employees Regulations 2004, SI 2004/3426, reg 8(2).
9   Ie under the Information and Consultation of Employees Regulations 2004, SI 2004/3426, reg 8.
10 Information and Consultation of Employees Regulations 2004, SI 2004/3426, reg 8(3).
11 Information and Consultation of Employees Regulations 2004, SI 2004/3426, reg 8(4).
12 'Date of the ballot' means the day or last day on which voting may take place and, where voting in different parts of the ballot is arranged to take place on different days or during periods ending on different days, the last of those days: Information and Consultation of Employees Regulations 2004, SI 2004/3426, reg 2.
13 Information and Consultation of Employees Regulations 2004, SI 2004/3426, reg 8(5)(a).
14 For the purposes of the Information and Consultation of Employees Regulations 2004, SI 2004/3426, reg 8(5), the employees are to be regarded as having endorsed the employee request if (1) at least 40% of the employees employed in the undertaking; and (2) the majority of the employees who vote in the ballot, have voted in favour of endorsing the request: reg 8(6).
15 Ie in the Information and Consultation of Employees Regulations 2004, SI 2004/3426, reg 7(1): see PARA 1294.

16 Information and Consultation of Employees Regulations 2004, SI 2004/3426, reg 8(5)(b).
17 Information and Consultation of Employees Regulations 2004, SI 2004/3426, reg 8(5)(c).
18 As to the Central Arbitration Committee see PARA 1226 et seq.
19 Information and Consultation of Employees Regulations 2004, SI 2004/3426, reg 8(7).
20 Information and Consultation of Employees Regulations 2004, SI 2004/3426, reg 8(8).
21 Information and Consultation of Employees Regulations 2004, SI 2004/3426, reg 8(9).
22 Ie the requirements of the Information and Consultation of Employees Regulations 2004, SI 2004/3426, reg 8(1) (see the text and notes 1–6) are satisfied.
23 Ie the valid employee request mentioned in the Information and Consultation of Employees Regulations 2004, SI 2004/3426, reg 8(1): see the text and notes 1–6.
24 See the Information and Consultation of Employees Regulations 2004, SI 2004/3426, reg 9(1).
25 Ie in accordance with the Information and Consultation of Employees Regulations 2004, SI 2004/3426, reg 9.
26 Ie the Information and Consultation of Employees Regulations 2004, SI 2004/3426, reg 8: see the text and notes 1–21.
27 Information and Consultation of Employees Regulations 2004, SI 2004/3426, reg 9(2). Notwithstanding reg 9(2), the undertaking mentioned in head (A) in the text may choose to hold the ballot for endorsement of the employee request in accordance with reg 8 rather than under reg 9: reg 9(3).

1296. Complaint about ballot for endorsement of employee request. Any employee[1] in the specified undertaking[2] or one of the specified undertakings[3] or representative of such employees who believes that a requirement has not been satisfied that has to be satisfied in order to entitle either the employer[4] to hold a ballot[5], or the employers to hold a combined ballot[6] may, within 21 days of the employer informing the employees of the relevant undertaking[7], present a complaint to the Central Arbitration Committee (the 'CAC')[8].

Any employee or employees' representative who believes that the arrangements for a ballot held[9] did not satisfy one or more of certain requirements[10] may, within 21 days of the date of the ballot, present a complaint to the CAC[11].

Where the CAC finds a complaint under the above provisions[12] well-founded it must:

(1) in the case of a finding on a complaint under the first above category[13] that any of certain requirements[14] was not satisfied in relation to the undertaking[15], make an order requiring the relevant employer[16] to initiate negotiations[17];

(2) in the case of a finding on a complaint under the first above category that any of certain requirements[18] has not been satisfied, make an order that no combined ballot take place and requiring the relevant employer[19], according to the preference he has expressed, to initiate negotiations[20] or, within such period as the order may specify, to conduct a ballot[21]; and

(3) in the case of a complaint under the second above category[22]:

(a) where prior to the order being made, the relevant employer[23] makes representations to the CAC that he would prefer to initiate negotiations[24], make an order requiring that employer to do so; or

(b) in the absence of such representations, order the employer or employers to hold the ballot[25], again within such period as the order may specify[26].

1 As to the meaning of 'employee' see PARA 1289 note 4.
2 Ie any employee in the undertaking referred to in the Information and Consultation of Employees Regulations 2004, SI 2004/3426, reg 8(1): see PARA 1295. As to the meaning of 'undertaking' see PARA 1289 note 2.
3 Ie one of the undertakings referred to in the Information and Consultation of Employees Regulations 2004, SI 2004/3426, reg 9(1): see PARA 1295.

4   As to the meaning of 'employer' see PARA 1289 note 2.
5   Ie in accordance with the Information and Consultation of Employees Regulations 2004, SI 2004/3426, reg 8(2): see PARA 1295.
6   Ie in accordance with the Information and Consultation of Employees Regulations 2004, SI 2004/3426, reg 9(2): see PARA 1295.
7   Ie under the Information and Consultation of Employees Regulations 2004, SI 2004/3426, reg 8(3)(a): see PARA 1295 head (a) in the text.
8   Information and Consultation of Employees Regulations 2004, SI 2004/3426, reg 10(1). As to the Central Arbitration Committee see PARA 1226 et seq.
9   Ie held under the Information and Consultation of Employees Regulations 2004, SI 2004/3426, reg 8 or reg 9 as the case may be.
10 Ie the requirements of the Information and Consultation of Employees Regulations 2004, SI 2004/3426, reg 8(4): see PARA 1295 heads (i)–(iii) in the text.
11 Information and Consultation of Employees Regulations 2004, SI 2004/3426, reg 10(2).
12 Ie a complaint under the Information and Consultation of Employees Regulations 2004, SI 2004/3426, reg 10(1) or reg 10(2).
13 Ie a complaint under the Information and Consultation of Employees Regulations 2004, SI 2004/3426, reg 10(1).
14 Ie any requirement set out in the Information and Consultation of Employees Regulations 2004, SI 2004/3426, reg 8(1)(a)–(d): see PARA 1295 heads (1)–(4) in the text.
15 Ie the undertaking referred to in the Information and Consultation of Employees Regulations 2004, SI 2004/3426, reg 8(1) (see PARA 1295) or reg 9(1)(a) (see PARA 1295 head (A) in the text).
16 Ie the employer to whom the Information and Consultation of Employees Regulations 2004, SI 2004/3426, reg 8(1) (see PARA 1295) or reg 9(1)(a) (see PARA 1295 head (A) in the text) relates.
17 Information and Consultation of Employees Regulations 2004, SI 2004/3426, reg 10(3)(a). The reference is to initiating negotiations in accordance with reg 7(1): see PARA 1294.
18 Ie any requirement set out in the Information and Consultation of Employees Regulations 2004, SI 2004/3426, reg 9(1)(b)–(d): see PARA 1295 heads (B)–(D) in the text.
19 Ie the employer to whom the Information and Consultation of Employees Regulations 2004, SI 2004/3426, reg 9(1)(a) (see PARA 1295 head (A) in the text) relates.
20 Ie initiate negotiations in accordance with the Information and Consultation of Employees Regulations 2004, SI 2004/3426, reg 7(1): see PARA 1294.
21 Information and Consultation of Employees Regulations 2004, SI 2004/3426, reg 10(3)(b). The reference is to a ballot under reg 8: see PARA 1295.
22 Ie under the Information and Consultation of Employees Regulations 2004, SI 2004/3426, reg 10(2).
23 Ie the employer referred to in the Information and Consultation of Employees Regulations 2004, SI 2004/3426, reg 8(1) (see PARA 1295) or reg 9(1)(a) (see PARA 1295 head (A) in the text).
24 Ie initiate negotiations under the Information and Consultation of Employees Regulations 2004, SI 2004/3426, reg 7(1): see PARA 1294.
25 Ie under the Information and Consultation of Employees Regulations 2004, SI 2004/3426, reg 8 or reg 9, as the case may be.
26 Information and Consultation of Employees Regulations 2004, SI 2004/3426, reg 10(3)(c).

1297.   Employer notification of decision to initiate negotiations. The employer[1] may start the negotiation process[2] on his own initiative by issuing a written notification satisfying the requirements below[3].

The notification must: (1) state that the employer intends to start the negotiating process and that the notification is given for the purpose of the Information and Consultation of Employees Regulations 2004[4]; (2) state the date on which it is issued; and (3) be published in such a manner as to bring it to the attention of, so far as reasonably practicable, all the employees[5] of the undertaking[6].

1   As to the meaning of 'employer' see PARA 1289 note 2.
2   Ie the negotiation process set out in the Information and Consultation of Employees Regulations 2004, SI 2004/3426, reg 14(1): see PARA 1300.
3   Information and Consultation of Employees Regulations 2004, SI 2004/3426, reg 11(1). The requirements are those of reg 11(2). Where the employer issues such a notification regs 14–17

(see PARA 1300 et seq) apply: see reg 11(1). 'Employer notification' means a notification by the employer under reg 11 that he wishes to initiate negotiations to reach an agreement under the Regulations: reg 2.
4 Ie the Information and Consultation of Employees Regulations 2004, SI 2004/3426.
5 As to the meaning of 'employee' see PARA 1289 note 4.
6 Information and Consultation of Employees Regulations 2004, SI 2004/3426, reg 11(2). As to the meaning of 'undertaking' see PARA 1289 note 2.

1298. Restrictions on employee request and employer notification. No employee request[1] or employer notification[2] is valid if it is made or issued, as the case may be, (1) where a negotiated agreement[3] applies, within a period of three years from the date of the agreement or, where the agreement is terminated within that period, before the date on which the termination takes effect; (2) where the standard information and consultation provisions[4] apply within a period of three years from the date on which they started to apply; and (3) where the employer[5] has held a ballot[6], or was one of the employers who held a ballot[7] and the result was that the employees[8] did not endorse the valid employee request[9], within a period of three years from the date of that request[10].

The above provision does not, however, apply where there are material changes in the undertaking[11] during the applicable period having the result (a) where a ballot[12] had the result that the employees did not endorse the valid employee request, that there is no longer a pre-existing agreement[13] which satisfies the relevant requirements[14]; or (b) where a negotiated agreement exists, that the agreement no longer complies with the requirement[15] that it must cover all the employees of the undertaking[16].

1 As to the meaning of 'employee request' see PARA 1294 note 1.
2 As to the meaning of 'employer notification' see PARA 1297 note 3.
3 As to the meaning of 'negotiated agreement' see PARA 1295 note 3.
4 'Standard information and consultation provisions' means the provisions set out in the Information and Consultation of Employees Regulations 2004, SI 2004/3426, reg 20 (see PARA 1305): reg 2.
5 As to the meaning of 'employer' see PARA 1289 note 2.
6 Ie under the Information and Consultation of Employees Regulations 2004, SI 2004/3426, reg 8: see PARA 1295.
7 Ie under the Information and Consultation of Employees Regulations 2004, SI 2004/3426, reg 9: see PARA 1295.
8 As to the meaning of 'employee' see PARA 1289 note 4.
9 Ie referred to in the Information and Consultation of Employees Regulations 2004, SI 2004/3426, reg 8(1). See also PARA 1295 note 1.
10 Information and Consultation of Employees Regulations 2004, SI 2004/3426, reg 12(1). Regulation 12(1) is subject to reg 12(2): see heads (a)–(b) in the text.
11 As to the meaning of 'undertaking' see PARA 1289 note 2.
12 Ie held under the Information and Consultation of Employees Regulations 2004, SI 2004/3426, reg 8 or reg 9: see PARA 1295.
13 As to the meaning of 'pre-existing agreement' see PARA 1295 note 3.
14 Ie the requirements of the Information and Consultation of Employees Regulations 2004, SI 2004/3426, reg 8(1)(b), (c) (see PARA 1295 heads (2)–(3) in the text) or in the case of reg 9, that there is no longer an agreement satisfying reg 9(1)(b) (see PARA 1295 head (B) in the text).
15 Ie in the Information and Consultation of Employees Regulations 2004, SI 2004/3426, reg 16(1): see PARA 1301.
16 Information and Consultation of Employees Regulations 2004, SI 2004/3426, reg 12(2).

1299. Dispute about employee request, employer notification, etc. If the employer[1] considers that there was no valid employee request[2] (1) because the employee request[3] did not satisfy any of the relevant requirements[4] or was prevented from being valid[5]; or (2) because the undertaking[6] was not one to which the Information and Consultation of Employees Regulations 2004 applied[7] on the date on which the employee request was made, the employer may apply to the Central Arbitration Committee (the 'CAC')[8] for a declaration as to whether there was a valid employee request[9].

If an employee[10] or an employees' representative considers that an employer notification[11] was not valid because it did not comply with one or more of the relevant requirements[12] or was prevented from being valid[13], he may apply to the CAC for a declaration as to whether the notification was valid[14].

The CAC must only consider such an application for a declaration[15] if the application is made within a one month period beginning on the date of the employee request or the date on which the employer notification is made[16].

1   As to the meaning of 'employer' see PARA 1289 note 2.
2   As to the meaning of 'valid employee request' see PARA 1295 note 1.
3   As to the meaning of 'employee request' see PARA 1294 note 1.
4   Ie any requirement of the Information and Consultation of Employees Regulations 2004, SI 2004/3426, reg 7(2)–(4): see PARA 1294.
5   Ie by the Information and Consultation of Employees Regulations 2004, SI 2004/3426, reg 12: see PARA 1298.
6   As to the meaning of 'undertaking' see PARA 1289 note 2.
7   Ie to which the Information and Consultation of Employees Regulations 2004, SI 2004/3426, applied (under reg 3) (see PARA 1289).
8   As to the Central Arbitration Committee see PARA 1226 et seq.
9   Information and Consultation of Employees Regulations 2004, SI 2004/3426, reg 13(1).
10 As to the meaning of 'employee' see PARA 1289 note 4.
11 As to the meaning of 'employer notification' see PARA 1297 note 3.
12 Ie the requirements in the Information and Consultation of Employees Regulations 2004, SI 2004/3426, reg 11(2): see PARA 1297.
13 See note 5.
14 Information and Consultation of Employees Regulations 2004, SI 2004/3426, reg 13(2).
15 Ie an application under the Information and Consultation of Employees Regulations 2004, SI 2004/3426, reg 13(1) or reg 13(2).
16 Information and Consultation of Employees Regulations 2004, SI 2004/3426, reg 13(3).

1300.   Negotiations to reach an agreement.   In order to initiate negotiations to reach an agreement under the Information and Consultation of Employees Regulations 2004[1] the employer[2] must as soon as reasonably practicable (1) make arrangements[3] for the employees of the undertaking to elect or appoint negotiating representatives; and thereafter (2) inform the employees in writing[4] of the identity of the negotiating representatives; and (3) invite the negotiating representatives to enter into negotiations to reach a negotiated agreement[5].

The negotiations referred to in head (3) above must last for a period not exceeding six months commencing at the end of the period of three months beginning with the date on which the valid employee request[6] was made or the valid employer notification[7] was issued; but the following periods do not count towards the three month period:
(a)   where the employer holds a ballot[8], the period between the employer notifying the employees of his decision to hold such a ballot and whichever of the following dates is applicable:
    (i)   where there is no complaint to the Central Arbitration Committee (the 'CAC')[9], the date of the ballot;
    (ii) where there is a complaint to the CAC[10] and the complaint is dismissed by the CAC or on appeal, the date on which it is finally dismissed;
    (iii) where there is a complaint to the CAC and the outcome, whether of the complaint or of any appeal from it, is an order to hold the ballot[11] again, the date of the ballot that most recently took place;

(iv) where there is a complaint to the CAC[12] and the outcome, whether of the complaint or of any appeal from it, is an order requiring the employer to initiate negotiations[13], the date on which the order is made[14];

(b) where an application for a declaration is made to the CAC[15], the period between the date of that application and the final decision of the CAC or any appeal from that decision[16]; and

(c) where a complaint about the election or appointment of negotiating representatives is presented[17], the time between the date of the complaint and the determination of the complaint, including any appeal and, where the complaint is upheld, the further period until the negotiating representatives are re-elected or re-appointed[18].

Where a complaint about the ballot for employee approval of a negotiated agreement is presented[19], the time between the date the complaint is presented to the CAC and the determination of the complaint (including any appeal and, where the complaint is upheld, the further period until the re-holding of the ballot) does not count towards the above six month period[20].

If, before the end of the six month period[21], the employer and a majority of the negotiating representatives agree that that period should be extended, it may be extended by such period as the parties agree and thereafter may be further extended by such period or periods as the parties agree[22].

Where one or more employers wish to initiate negotiations to reach an agreement to cover employees in more than one undertaking, any employer whose employees have not made a valid employee request and who has not issued a valid employer notification, must issue such a notification[23].

1 Ie the Information and Consultation of Employees Regulations 2004, SI 2004/3426.
2 As to the meaning of 'employer' see PARA 1289 note 2.
3 Ie arrangements satisfying the Information and Consultation of Employees Regulations 2004, SI 2004/3426, reg 14(2). The requirements for the election or appointment of negotiating representatives under reg 14(1)(a) (see head (1) in the text) are that (1) the election or appointment of the representatives must be arranged in such a way that, following their election or appointment, all employees of the undertaking are represented by one or more representatives; and (2) all employees of the undertaking must be entitled to take part in the election or appointment of the representatives and, where there is an election, all employees of the undertaking on the day on which the votes may be cast in the ballot, or if the votes may be cast on more than one day, on the first day of those days, must be given an entitlement to vote in the ballot: reg 14(2). As to the meanings of 'undertaking' and 'employee' see PARA 1289 notes 2, 4. As to the meaning of 'negotiating representative' see PARA 1295 note 3.
   If an employee or an employees' representative considers that one or both of the requirements for the appointment or election of negotiating representatives set out in reg 14(2) (see heads (1)–(2) above) have not been complied with, he may, within 21 days of the election or appointment, present a complaint to the CAC: reg 15(1). Where the CAC finds the complaint well-founded it must make an order requiring the employer to arrange for the process of election or appointment of negotiating representatives referred to in reg 14 to take place again within such period as the order must specify: reg 15(2).
4 As to the meaning of 'writing' see PARA 2 note 8.
5 Information and Consultation of Employees Regulations 2004, SI 2004/3426, reg 14(1). As to the meaning of 'negotiated agreement' see PARA 1295 note 3. The requirement is that this stage should be completed 'as soon as reasonably practicable'; this does not mean that negotiations have to be entered into (under head (3) in the text) within the initial three-month period specified in reg 14(3): *Darnton v Bournemouth University* [2009] IRLR 4, CAC.
6 As to the meaning of 'valid employee request' see PARA 1295 note 1; and as to the meaning of 'employee request' see PARA 1294 note 1.
7 As to the meaning of 'employer notification' see PARA 1297 note 3.
8 Ie pursuant to the Information and Consultation of Employees Regulations 2004, SI 2004/3426, reg 8 or reg 9: see PARA 1295.

9 Ie under the Information and Consultation of Employees Regulations 2004, SI 2004/3426,
   reg 10: see PARA 1296. As to the Central Arbitration Committee see PARA 1226 et seq.
10 See note 9.
11 Ie under the Information and Consultation of Employees Regulations 2004, SI 2004/3426, reg 8
   or reg 9: see PARA 1295.
12 See note 9.
13 Ie in accordance with the Information and Consultation of Employees Regulations 2004,
   SI 2004/3426, reg 7(1): see PARA 1294.
14 Information and Consultation of Employees Regulations 2004, SI 2004/3426, reg 14(3)(a).
15 Ie pursuant to the Information and Consultation of Employees Regulations 2004, SI 2004/3426,
   reg 13: see PARA 1299.
16 Information and Consultation of Employees Regulations 2004, SI 2004/3426, reg 14(3)(b).
17 Ie pursuant to the Information and Consultation of Employees Regulations 2004, SI 2004/3426,
   reg 15: see note 3.
18 Information and Consultation of Employees Regulations 2004, SI 2004/3426, reg 14(3)(c).
19 Ie pursuant to the Information and Consultation of Employees Regulations 2004, SI 2004/3426,
   reg 17: see PARA 1301.
20 Information and Consultation of Employees Regulations 2004, SI 2004/3426, reg 14(4). The
   reference is to the six month period mentioned in reg 14(3).
21 Ie the six-month period referred to in the Information and Consultation of Employees
   Regulations 2004, SI 2004/3426, reg 14(3).
22 Information and Consultation of Employees Regulations 2004, SI 2004/3426, reg 14(5).
23 Information and Consultation of Employees Regulations 2004, SI 2004/3426, reg 14(6). Where
   reg 14(6) applies, the provisions of reg 14(1)–(5) and reg 15 (see note 3) and reg 16 (see PARA
   1301) apply with the following modifications: (1) the references to the employees of the
   undertaking refer to the employees of all the undertakings to be covered by any agreement
   negotiated; and (2) references to employees refer to employees of all the undertakings to be
   covered by any agreement negotiated: reg 14(7).

1301. Negotiated agreements. A negotiated agreement[1] must cover all
employees[2] of the undertaking[3] and may consist either of a single agreement or
of different parts (each being approved as required[4]) which, taken together, cover
all the employees of the undertaking[5]. The single agreement or each part must:

(1)   set out the circumstances in which the employer[6] must inform and
       consult the employees to which it relates;
(2)   be in writing[7];
(3)   be dated;
(4)   be approved as required[8];
(5)   be signed by or on behalf of the employer;
(6)   either:
       (a)   provide for the appointment or election of information and
              consultation representatives[9] to whom the employer must provide
              the information[10] and whom the employer must consult in the
              circumstances referred to in head (1) above; or
       (b)   provide that the employer must provide information directly to
              the employees to which it relates and consult those employees
              directly in the circumstances referred to in head (1) above; and
(7)   provide that where an employer is to provide information about the
       employment situation, under that agreement or under any part, such
       information must include suitable information relating to the use of
       agency workers[11] (if any) in that undertaking[12].

Where a negotiated agreement consist of different parts they may provide
differently in relation to the matters referred to in heads (1) and (6) above[13].

Where the employer holds a ballot to secure approval of the agreement[14] he
must, as soon as reasonably practicable after the date of the ballot, inform the
employees entitled to vote of the result[15]. Any negotiating representative who

believes that the arrangements for such a ballot did not satisfy one or more of the relevant requirements[16] may, within 21 days of the date of the ballot, present a complaint to the Central Arbitration Committee (the 'CAC')[17]. Where the CAC finds the complaint well-founded it must make an order requiring the employer to hold the ballot again within such period as the order may specify[18].

1 As to the meaning of 'negotiated agreement' see PARA 1295 note 3.
2 As to the meaning of 'employee' see PARA 1289 note 4.
3 As to the meaning of 'undertaking' see PARA 1289 note 2.
4 Ie in accordance with the Information and Consultation of Employees Regulations 2004, SI 2004/3426, reg 16(4): see note 8.
5 Information and Consultation of Employees Regulations 2004, SI 2004/3426, reg 16(1).
6 As to the meaning of 'employer' see PARA 1289 note 2.
7 As to the meaning of 'writing' see PARA 2 note 8.
8 Ie in accordance with the Information and Consultation of Employees Regulations 2004, SI 2004/3426, reg 16(3)–(5). A negotiated agreement consisting of a single agreement must be treated as being approved for the purpose of reg 16(1)(d) (see head (4) in the text) if (1) it has been signed by all the negotiating representatives; or (2) it has been signed by a majority of negotiating representatives and either (a) approved in writing by at least 50% of employees employed in the undertaking; or (b) approved by a ballot of those employees, the arrangements for which satisfied the requirements set out in reg 16(5) (see below), in which at least 50% of the employees voting, voted in favour of approval: reg 16(3). As to the meaning of 'negotiating representative' see PARA 1295 note 3.
   A part must be treated as being approved for the purpose of reg 16(1)(d) (see head (4) in the text) if the part (i) has been signed by all the negotiating representatives involved in negotiating the part; or (ii) has been signed by a majority of those negotiating representatives and either (A) approved in writing by at least 50% of employees (employed in the undertaking) to which the part relates; or (B) approved by a ballot of those employees, the arrangements for which satisfied the requirements set out in reg 16(5) (see below), in which at least 50% of the employees voting, voted in favour of approving the part: reg 16(4).
   The ballots referred to in reg 16(3), (4) must satisfy the following requirements: (*aa*) the employer must make such arrangements as are reasonably practicable to ensure that the ballot is fair; (*bb*) all employees of the undertaking or, as the case may be, to whom the part of the agreement relates, on the day on which the votes may be cast in the ballot, or if the votes may be cast on more than one day, on the first day of those days, must be given an entitlement to vote in the ballot; and (*cc*) the ballot must be conducted so as to secure that so far as is reasonably practicable, those voting do so in secret; and the votes given in the ballot are accurately counted: reg 16(5).
9 As to the meaning of 'information and consultation representative' see PARA 1295 note 3.
10 As to the meaning of 'information' see PARA 1295 note 5.
11 As to the meaning of 'suitable information relating to the use of agency workers' see PARA 1295 note 5; and as to the meaning of 'agency worker' see PARA 1289 note 4.
12 Information and Consultation of Employees Regulations 2004, SI 2004/3426, reg 16(1)(a)–(g) (amended by SI 2010/93).
13 Information and Consultation of Employees Regulations 2004, SI 2004/3426, reg 16(2).
14 Ie under the Information and Consultation of Employees Regulations 2004, SI 2004/3426, reg 16: see note 8.
15 See the Information and Consultation of Employees Regulations 2004, SI 2004/3426, reg 16(6).
16 Ie the requirements set out in the Information and Consultation of Employees Regulations 2004, SI 2004/3426, reg 16(5): see note 8.
17 Information and Consultation of Employees Regulations 2004, SI 2004/3426, reg 17(1). As to the Central Arbitration Committee see PARA 1226 et seq.
18 Information and Consultation of Employees Regulations 2004, SI 2004/3426, reg 17(2).

1302. Negotiated agreements and listed changes to pension schemes. A requirement in any negotiated agreement[1] or any part of such an agreement made before 6 April 2006 to inform and consult employees[2] or their representatives about a listed change[3] ceases to apply once (1) the employer[4] is under a duty under specified provisions of the Occupational and Personal Pension Schemes (Consultation by Employers and Miscellaneous Amendment)

Regulations 2006[5]; and (2) he has notified the information and consultation representatives[6] or, where he must consult employees directly, the employees in writing[7] that he will be complying with his duty under the provisions of those 2006 Regulations, instead of his obligations under the negotiated agreement, provided that the notification is given on each occasion on which the employer has become or is about to become subject to the duty[8].

1   As to the meaning of 'employer' see PARA 1289 note 2.
2   As to the meaning of 'employee' see PARA 1289 note 4.
3   For these purposes, 'listed change' has the meaning given by the Occupational and Personal Pension Schemes (Consultation by Employers and Miscellaneous Amendment) Regulations 2006, SI 2006/349, reg 6(2) (see PERSONAL AND OCCUPATIONAL PENSIONS vol 80 (2013) PARA 486): Information and Consultation of Employees Regulations 2004, SI 2004/3426, reg 17A(2) (reg 17A added by SI 2006/514).
4   As to the meaning of 'employer' see PARA 1289 note 2.
5   Ie the Occupational and Personal Pension Schemes (Consultation by Employers and Miscellaneous Amendment) Regulations 2006, SI 2006/349, regs 7(3), 11–13: see PERSONAL AND OCCUPATIONAL PENSIONS vol 80 (2013) PARA 486.
6   As to the meaning of 'information and consultation representative' see PARA 1295 note 3.
7   As to the meaning of 'writing' see PARA 2 note 8.
8   Information and Consultation of Employees Regulations 2004, SI 2004/3426, reg 17A(1) (as added: see note 3).

C. STANDARD INFORMATION AND CONSULTATION PROVISIONS

1303.   Application of standard information and consultation provisions. Where the employer[1] is under a duty, following the making of a valid employee request[2] or issue of a valid employer notification[3], to initiate negotiations[4] but does not do so, the standard information and consultation provisions[5] apply from the date (1) which is six months from the date on which the valid employee request was made or the valid employer notification was issued; or (2) information and consultation representatives are elected[6], whichever is the sooner[7]. In addition if the parties do not reach a negotiated agreement[8] within the relevant time limit[9] the standard information and consultation provisions apply from the date (a) which is six months from the date on which that time limit expires; or (b) information and consultation representatives are elected[10], whichever is the sooner[11].

However, where the standard information and consultation provisions apply, the employer and the information and consultation representatives elected[12] may, at any time, reach an agreement that provisions other than the standard information and consultation provisions shall apply[13].

1   As to the meaning of 'employer' see PARA 1289 note 2.
2   As to the meaning of 'valid employee request' see PARA 1295 note 1.
3   As to the meaning of 'employer notification' see PARA 1297 note 3.
4   Ie in accordance with the Information and Consultation of Employees Regulations 2004, SI 2004/3426, reg 14: see PARA 1300.
5   As to the meaning of 'standard information and consultation provisions' see PARA 1298 note 4.
6   Ie elected under the Information and Consultation of Employees Regulations 2004, SI 2004/3426, reg 19: see PARA 1304.
7   Information and Consultation of Employees Regulations 2004, SI 2004/3426, reg 18(1)(a). Regulation 18(1) is subject to reg 18(2).
8   As to the meaning of 'negotiated agreement' see PARA 1295 note 3.
9   Ie the time limit referred to in the Information and Consultation of Employees Regulations 2004, SI 2004/3426, reg 14(3), or that period extended by agreement under reg 14(5): see PARA 1300.
10   Ie under the Information and Consultation of Employees Regulations 2004, SI 2004/3426, reg 19: see PARA 1304.

11 Information and Consultation of Employees Regulations 2004, SI 2004/3426, reg 18(1)(b). Regulation 18(1) is subject to reg 18(2).

12 Ie pursuant to Information and Consultation of Employees Regulations 2004, SI 2004/3426, reg 19: see PARA 1304.

13 Information and Consultation of Employees Regulations 2004, SI 2004/3426, reg 18(2). An agreement referred to in reg 18(2) only has effect if it covers all the employees of the undertaking, complies with the requirements listed in reg 16(1)(a)–(c), (e), (f) (see PARA 1301 heads (1)–(3), (5)–(6) in the text), and is signed by a majority of the information and consultation representatives: reg 18(3). As to the meanings of 'undertaking' and 'employee' see PARA 1289 notes 2, 4.

1304. Election of information and consultation representatives. Where the standard information and consultation provisions[1] are to apply, the employer[2] must, before the standard information and consultation provisions start to apply, arrange for the holding of a ballot of its employees[3] to elect the relevant number of information and consultation representatives[4].

An employee or an employee's representative may complain to the Central Arbitration Committee (the 'CAC')[5] that the employer has not arranged for the holding of a ballot in accordance with the above provision[6]. Where the CAC finds the complaint well-founded, it must make an order requiring the employer to arrange, or re-arrange, and hold the ballot[7]. Where the CAC finds such a complaint[8] well-founded, the employee or the employee's representative may make an application to the Employment Appeal Tribunal[9].

1 As to the meaning of 'standard information and consultation provisions' see PARA 1298 note 4.
2 As to the meaning of 'employer' see PARA 1289 note 2.
3 As to the meaning of 'employee' see PARA 1289 note 4.
4 Information and Consultation of Employees Regulations 2004, SI 2004/3426, reg 19(1). For these purposes, the 'relevant number of information and consultation representatives' means one representative per 50 employees or part thereof, provided that that number is at least two and does not exceed 25: reg 19(3). As to the meaning of 'information and consultation representative' see PARA 1295 note 3. The provisions in Sch 2 apply in relation to the arrangements for and conduct of any such ballot: reg 19(2). As to ballot arrangements see Sch 2 paras 1–7; and as to conduct of the ballot see Sch 2 paras 8–15.
5 As to the Central Arbitration Committee see PARA 1226 et seq.
6 Information and Consultation of Employees Regulations 2004, SI 2004/3426, reg 19(4). The provision referred to is reg 19(1).
7 Information and Consultation of Employees Regulations 2004, SI 2004/3426, reg 19(5).
8 Ie under the Information and Consultation of Employees Regulations 2004, SI 2004/3426, reg 19(4).
9 Information and Consultation of Employees Regulations 2004, SI 2004/3426, reg 19(6). Such an application is under reg 22(6), and reg 22(7), (8) (see PARA 1307) applies to any such application: see reg 19(6). As to the Employment Appeal Tribunal see PARA 1422 et seq.

1305. Standard information and consultation provisions. Where the standard information and consultation provisions[1] apply[2], the employer[3] must provide the information and consultation representatives[4] with information[5] on:

(1) the recent and probable development of the undertaking's[6] activities and economic situation;

(2) the situation, structure and probable development of employment within the undertaking[7] and on any anticipatory measures envisaged, in particular, where there is a threat to employment within the undertaking; and

(3) decisions likely to lead to substantial changes in work organisation or in contractual relations[8].

The employer must consult the information and consultation representatives on the matters referred to in heads (2) and (3) above[9]. The employer must ensure that such consultation[10] is conducted:

(a)   in such a way as to ensure that the timing, method and content of the consultation are appropriate;

(b)   on the basis of the information supplied by the employer to the information and consultation representatives and of any opinion which those representatives express to the employer;

(c)   in such a way as to enable the information and consultation representatives to meet the employer at the relevant level of management depending on the subject under discussion and to obtain a reasoned response from the employer to any such opinion; and

(d)   in relation to matters falling within head (3) above, with a view to reaching agreement on decisions within the scope of the employer's powers[11].

Where there is an obligation in the Information and Consultation of Employees Regulations 2004[12] on the employer to inform and consult his employees, a failure on the part of a person who controls the employer (either directly or indirectly) to provide information to the employer does not constitute a valid reason for the employer failing to inform and consult[13].

1   As to the meaning of 'standard information and consultation provisions' see PARA 1298 note 4.
2   Ie pursuant to the Information and Consultation of Employees Regulations 2004, SI 2004/3426, reg 18: see PARA 1303.
3   As to the meaning of 'employer' see PARA 1289 note 2.
4   As to the meaning of 'information and consultation representative' see PARA 1295 note 3.
5   The information referred to in the Information and Consultation of Employees Regulations 2004, SI 2004/3426, reg 20(1) must be given at such time, in such fashion and with such content as is appropriate to enable, in particular, the information and consultation representatives to conduct an adequate study and, where necessary, to prepare for consultation: reg 20(2). As to the meaning generally of 'information' see also PARA 1295 note 5.
6   As to the meaning of 'undertaking' see PARA 1289 note 2.
7   Such information must include suitable information relating to the use of agency workers (if any) in that undertaking: Information and Consultation of Employees Regulations 2004, SI 2004/3426, reg 20(1)(b) (amended by SI 2010/93). As to the meaning of 'suitable information relating to the use of agency workers' see PARA 1295 note 5; and as to the meaning of 'agency worker' see PARA 1289 note 4.
8   Information and Consultation of Employees Regulations 2004, SI 2004/3426, reg 20(1) (amended by SI 2006/2405; SI 2010/93). Included in the decisions referred to in the Information and Consultation of Employees Regulations 2004, SI 2004/3426, reg 20(1)(c) (see head (3) in the text) are those referred to in (1) the Trade Union and Labour Relations (Consolidation) Act 1992 ss 188–192 (see PARA 1185 et seq); and (2) the Transfer of Undertakings (Protection of Employment) Regulations 2006, SI 2006/246, regs 13–16 (see PARA 1196 et seq).

The Information and Consultation of Employees Regulations 2004, SI 2004/3426, reg 20(1)(c) (see head (3) in the text) is subject to reg 20(5): see reg 20(1)(c). The duties in reg 20 to inform and consult the information and consultation representatives on decisions falling within reg 20(1)(c) cease to apply once the employer is under a duty under (a) the Trade Union and Labour Relations (Consolidation) Act 1992 s 188 (duty of employer to consult representatives) (see PARAS 1185–1188); (b) the Transfer of Undertakings (Protection of Employment) Regulations 2006, SI 2006/246, reg 13 (duty to inform and consult representatives) (see PARAS 1196–1199); or (c) any of the Occupational and Personal Pension Schemes (Consultation by Employers and Miscellaneous Amendment) Regulations 2006, SI 2006/349, reg 11–13 (see PERSONAL AND OCCUPATIONAL PENSIONS vol 80 (2013) PARA 486), and he has notified the information and consultation representatives in writing that he will be complying with his duty under the legislation referred to in head (a), head (b) or head (c) above, as the case may be, instead of under the Information and Consultation of Employees Regulations 2004, SI 2004/3426, provided that the notification is given on each occasion on which the employer has become or is about to become subject to the duty: reg 20(5) (amended by SI 2006/514; SI 2006/2405). As to the meaning of 'writing' see PARA 2 note 8.

9 Information and Consultation of Employees Regulations 2004, SI 2004/3426, reg 20(3).

10 Information and Consultation of Employees Regulations 2004, SI 2004/3426, reg 20(4).

11 'Consultation' means the exchange of views and establishment of a dialogue between (1) information and consultation representatives and the employer; or (2) in the case of a negotiated agreement which provides as mentioned in the Information and Consultation of Employees Regulations 2004, SI 2004/3426, reg 16(1)(f)(ii) (see PARA 1301 head (6)(b) in the text), the employees and the employer: reg 2. As to the meaning of 'employee' see PARA 1289 note 4.

12 Ie the Information and Consultation of Employees Regulations 2004, SI 2004/3426: see also PARAS 1289 et seq, 1306 et seq.

13 Information and Consultation of Employees Regulations 2004, SI 2004/3426, reg 20(6).

D. CO-OPERATION, COMPLIANCE AND ENFORCEMENT

1306. Parties' duty of co-operation. The parties[1] are under a duty, when negotiating or implementing a negotiated agreement[2] or when implementing the standard information and consultation provisions[3], to work in a spirit of co-operation and with due regard for their reciprocal rights and obligations, taking into account the interests of both the undertaking[4] and the employees[5].

1 'Parties' means the employer and the negotiating representatives or the information and consultation representatives, as the case may be: Information and Consultation of Employees Regulations 2004, SI 2004/3426, reg 2. As to the meaning of 'employer' see PARA 1289 note 2; as to the meanings of 'information and consultation representative' and 'negotiating representative' see PARA 1295 note 3.

2 As to the meaning of 'negotiated agreement' see PARA 1295 note 3.

3 As to the meaning of 'standard information and consultation provisions' see PARA 1298 note 4.

4 As to the meaning of 'undertaking' see PARA 1289 note 2.

5 Information and Consultation of Employees Regulations 2004, SI 2004/3426, reg 21. As to the meaning of 'employee' see PARA 1289 note 4.

1307. Disputes about operation of a negotiated agreement or the standard information and consultation provisions. Where a negotiated agreement[1] has been agreed or the standard information and consultation provisions[2] apply, a complaint may be presented to the Central Arbitration Committee (the 'CAC')[3] by a relevant applicant[4] who considers that the employer[5] has failed to comply with the terms of the negotiated agreement or, as the case may be, one or more of the standard information and consultation provisions[6].

Such a complaint[7] must be brought within a period of three months commencing with the date of the alleged failure[8]. Where the CAC finds the complaint well-founded it must make a declaration to that effect and may make an order requiring the employer to take such steps as are necessary to comply with the terms of the negotiated agreement or, as the case may be, the standard information and consultation provisions[9]. Such an order must specify (1) the steps which the employer is required to take; and (2) the period within which the order must be complied with[10].

If the CAC makes such a declaration[11] the relevant applicant may, within the period of three months beginning with the date on which the declaration is made, make an application to the Employment Appeal Tribunal[12] for a penalty notice[13] to be issued[14].

Where such an application is made, the Employment Appeal Tribunal must issue a written penalty notice to the employer requiring him to pay a penalty to the Secretary of State[15] in respect of the failure unless satisfied, on hearing representations from the employer, that the failure resulted from a reason beyond the employer's control or that he has some other reasonable excuse for his failure[16].

No such order of the CAC under the above provisions[17] has the effect of suspending or altering the effect of any act done or of any agreement made by the employer or of preventing or delaying any act or agreement which the employer proposes to do or to make[18].

1   As to the meaning of 'negotiated agreement' see PARA 1295 note 3.
2   As to the meaning of 'standard information and consultation provisions' see PARA 1298 note 4.
3   As to the Central Arbitration Committee see PARA 1226 et seq.
4   For these purposes, 'relevant applicant' means (1) in a case where information and consultation representatives have been elected or appointed, an information and consultation representative; or (2) in a case where no information and consultation representatives have been elected or appointed, an employee or an employees' representative: Information and Consultation of Employees Regulations 2004, SI 2004/3426, reg 22(3). As to the meaning of 'information and consultation representative' see PARA 1295 note 3.
5   As to the meaning of 'employer' see PARA 1289 note 2.
6   Information and Consultation of Employees Regulations 2004, SI 2004/3426, reg 22(1). The remedy for infringement of the rights conferred by Pts I–VI (regs 1–24) is by way of complaint to the CAC, and not otherwise: reg 24.
7   Ie under the Information and Consultation of Employees Regulations 2004, SI 2004/3426, reg 22(1).
8   Information and Consultation of Employees Regulations 2004, SI 2004/3426, reg 22(2). For these purposes, 'failure' means an act or omission: reg 22(3).
9   Information and Consultation of Employees Regulations 2004, SI 2004/3426, reg 22(4).
10 Information and Consultation of Employees Regulations 2004, SI 2004/3426, reg 22(5).
11 Ie a declaration under the Information and Consultation of Employees Regulations 2004, SI 2004/3426, reg 22(4).
12 As to the Employment Appeal Tribunal see PARA 1422 et seq. See also note 14.
13 The Information and Consultation of Employees Regulations 2004, SI 2004/3426, reg 23 (see PARA 1308) applies in respect of a penalty notice issued under reg 22: reg 22(8).
14 Information and Consultation of Employees Regulations 2004, SI 2004/3426, reg 22(6). Every application under reg 22(6) must be made by way of application in writing in, or substantially in, accordance with the Employment Appeal Tribunal Rules 1993, SI 1993/2854, Schedule Form 4B and must be served on the Appeal Tribunal together with a copy of the declaration referred to in the Information and Consultation of Employees Regulations 2004, SI 2004/3426, reg 22(4) (see the text and note 9), or an explanation as to why none is included: Employment Appeal Tribunal Rules 1993, SI 1993/2854, r 16AA (added by SI 2004/2526; amended by SI 2004/3426; SI 2007/2974; SI 2010/1088). As to applications made under the Employment Appeal Tribunal Rules 1993, SI 1993/2854, r 16AA see further r 16B (substituted by SI 2010/1088); the Employment Appeal Tribunal Rules 1993, SI 1993/2854, r 16C (added by SI 2001/1128; amended by SI 2004/2526; SI 2010/1088); the Employment Appeal Tribunal Rules 1993, SI 1993/2854, r 16D (added by SI 2001/1128); and the Employment Appeal Tribunal Rules 1993, SI 1993/2854, Schedule Form 5A (added by SI 2001/1128; amended by SI 2010/1088).
15 As to the Secretary of State see PARA 5 note 21.
16 Information and Consultation of Employees Regulations 2004, SI 2004/3426, reg 22(7). As to the level of fine (in this case said to be sufficiently high to deter others from ignoring the relevant provisions in the same way) see *Amicus v Macmillan Publishers Ltd* [2007] IRLR 885, [2007] All ER (D) 121 (Aug), EAT.
17 Ie order under the Information and Consultation of Employees Regulations 2004, SI 2004/3426, reg 22.
18 Information and Consultation of Employees Regulations 2004, SI 2004/3426, reg 22(9).

1308.   Penalties under the Information and Consultation of Employees Regulations 2004.   A penalty notice[1] must specify (1) the amount of the penalty which is payable; (2) the date before which the penalty must be paid[2]; and (3) the failure and period to which the penalty relates[3]. No penalty set by the Employment Appeal Tribunal[4] may exceed £75,000[5].

Matters to be taken into account by the Employment Appeal Tribunal when setting the amount of the penalty must include: (a) the gravity of the failure; (b) the period of time over which the failure occurred; (c) the reason for the failure;

(d) the number of employees[6] affected by the failure; and (e) the number of employees employed by the undertaking[7] or, where a negotiated agreement[8] covers employees in more than one undertaking, the number of employees employed by both or all of the undertakings[9].

If the specified date in a penalty notice has passed and (i) the period during which an appeal may be made has expired without an appeal having been made; or (ii) such an appeal has been made and determined, the Secretary of State[10] may recover from the employer[11], as a civil debt due to him, any amount payable under the penalty notice which remains outstanding[12].

The making of an appeal suspends the effect of a penalty notice[13].

1 Ie a penalty notice issued under the Information and Consultation of Employees Regulations 2004, SI 2004/3426, reg 22: see PARA 1307.
2 The date specified under the Information and Consultation of Employees Regulations 2004, SI 2004/3426, reg 23(1)(b) (see head (2) in the text) must not be earlier than the end of the period within which an appeal against a declaration or order made by the Central Arbitration Committee (the 'CAC') under reg 22 (see PARA 1307) may be made: reg 23(4). As to the Central Arbitration Committee see PARA 1226 et seq.
3 Information and Consultation of Employees Regulations 2004, SI 2004/3426, reg 23(1).
4 Ie by the Information and Consultation of Employees Regulations 2004, SI 2004/3426, reg 23. As to the Employment Appeal Tribunal see PARA 1422 et seq.
5 Information and Consultation of Employees Regulations 2004, SI 2004/3426, reg 23(2).
6 As to the meaning of 'employee' see PARA 1289 note 4.
7 As to the meaning of 'undertaking' see PARA 1289 note 2.
8 As to the meaning of 'negotiated agreement' see PARA 1295 note 3.
9 Information and Consultation of Employees Regulations 2004, SI 2004/3426, reg 23(3). The matters listed in reg 23(3) (see heads (a)–(e) in the text) are not exhaustive and additional factors may also be taken into account; the number of employees affected by the failure is not, taken alone, particularly relevant in determining the gravity of the breach: *Brown v G4 Security (Cheltenham)* [2010] All ER (D) 84 (Aug), EAT.
10 As to the Secretary of State see PARA 5 note 21.
11 As to the meaning of 'employer' see PARA 1289 note 2.
12 Information and Consultation of Employees Regulations 2004, SI 2004/3426, reg 23(5). Any sums received by the Secretary of State under reg 22 (see PARA 1307) or reg 23 must be paid into the Consolidated Fund: reg 23(7). As to the Consolidated Fund see CONSTITUTIONAL AND ADMINISTRATIVE LAW vol 20 (2014) PARA 480 et seq; PARLIAMENT vol 78 (2010) PARA 1028 et seq.
13 Information and Consultation of Employees Regulations 2004, SI 2004/3426, reg 23(6).

E. CONFIDENTIAL INFORMATION

1309. Breach of statutory duty not to disclose confidential information. A person to whom the employer[1], pursuant to his obligations under the Information and Consultation of Employees Regulations 2004[2], entrusts any information[3] or document on terms requiring it to be held in confidence must not disclose that information or document except, where the terms permit him to do so, in accordance with those terms[4]. The obligation to comply with the above provision is a duty owed to the employer, and a breach of the duty is actionable accordingly (subject to the defences and other incidents applying to claims for breaches of statutory duty)[5]. This does not affect any legal liability which any person may incur by disclosing the information or document, or any right which any person may otherwise have in relation to such disclosure[6]; and no such claim lies where the recipient reasonably believed the disclosure to be a 'protected disclosure'[7].

A recipient to whom the employer has entrusted any information or document on terms requiring it to be held in confidence may apply to the Central Arbitration Committee (the 'CAC')[8] for a declaration as to whether it was reasonable for the employer to require the recipient to hold the information or document in confidence[9]. On such an application, if the CAC considers that the disclosure of the information or document by the recipient would not, or would not be likely to, harm the legitimate interests of the undertaking[10], it must make a declaration that it was not reasonable for the employer to require the recipient to hold the information or document in confidence[11]. If such a declaration is made, the information or document must not at any time thereafter be regarded as having been entrusted to the recipient who made the application[12], or to any other recipient, on terms requiring it to be held in confidence[13].

1   As to the meaning of 'employer' see PARA 1289 note 2.
2   Ie the Information and Consultation of Employees Regulations 2004, SI 2004/3426.
3   As to the meaning of 'information' see PARA 1295 note 5.
4   Information and Consultation of Employees Regulations 2004, SI 2004/3426, reg 25(1). In reg 25 a person referred to in reg 25(1) to whom information or a document is entrusted is referred to as a 'recipient': reg 25(2).
5   See the Information and Consultation of Employees Regulations 2004, SI 2004/3426, reg 25(3).
6   Information and Consultation of Employees Regulations 2004, SI 2004/3426, reg 25(4).
7   Information and Consultation of Employees Regulations 2004, SI 2004/3426, reg 25(5). The reference in the text to a 'protected disclosure' is to a 'protected disclosure' within the meaning given to that expression by the Employment Rights Act 1996 s 43A: see PARA 69.
8   As to the Central Arbitration Committee see PARA 1226 et seq.
9   Information and Consultation of Employees Regulations 2004, SI 2004/3426, reg 25(6).
10 As to the meaning of 'undertaking' see PARA 1289 note 2.
11 Information and Consultation of Employees Regulations 2004, SI 2004/3426, reg 25(7).
12 Ie under the Information and Consultation of Employees Regulations 2004, SI 2004/3426, reg 25(6): see the text and notes 8–9.
13 Information and Consultation of Employees Regulations 2004, SI 2004/3426, reg 25(8).

1310.   Withholding of information by the employer. The employer[1] is not required to disclose any information[2] or document to a person for the purposes of the Information and Consultation of Employees Regulations 2004[3] where the nature of the information or document is such that, according to objective criteria, the disclosure of the information or document would seriously harm the functioning of, or would be prejudicial to, the undertaking[4].

If there is a dispute between the employer and:

(1)   where information and consultation representatives[5] have been elected or appointed, such a representative; or

(2)   where no information and consultation representatives have been elected or appointed, an employee[6] or an employees' representative,

as to whether the nature of the information or document which the employer has failed to provide is such as is described above[7], the employer or a person referred to in head (1) or head (2) above may apply to the Central Arbitration Committee (the 'CAC')[8] for a declaration as to whether the information or document is of such a nature[9].

If the CAC makes a declaration that the disclosure of the information or document in question would not, according to objective criteria, be seriously harmful or prejudicial as mentioned above[10], the CAC must order the employer to disclose the information or document[11]. Such an order[12] must specify (a) the information or document to be disclosed; (b) the person or persons to whom the information or document is to be disclosed; (c) any terms on which the information or document is to be disclosed; and (d) the date before which the information or document is to be disclosed[13].

1   As to the meaning of 'employer' see PARA 1289 note 2.
2   As to the meaning of 'information' see PARA 1295 note 5.

3   Ie the Information and Consultation of Employees Regulations 2004, SI 2004/3426.
4   Information and Consultation of Employees Regulations 2004, SI 2004/3426, reg 26(1). As to
    the meaning of 'undertaking' see PARA 1289 note 2.
5   As to the meaning of 'information and consultation representative' see PARA 1295 note 3.
6   As to the meaning of 'employee' see PARA 1289 note 4.
7   Ie in the Information and Consultation of Employees Regulations 2004, SI 2004/3426,
    reg 26(1).
8   As to the Central Arbitration Committee see PARA 1226 et seq.
9   Information and Consultation of Employees Regulations 2004, SI 2004/3426, reg 26(2).
10 See note 7.
11 Information and Consultation of Employees Regulations 2004, SI 2004/3426, reg 26(3).
12 Ie under the Information and Consultation of Employees Regulations 2004, SI 2004/3426,
    reg 26(3).
13 Information and Consultation of Employees Regulations 2004, SI 2004/3426, reg 26(4).

F. PROTECTIONS FOR INFORMATION AND CONSULTATION REPRESENTATIVES ETC

1311.   Right to time off for negotiating representatives and information and consultation representatives.   An employee[1] who is a negotiating representative[2] or an information and consultation representative[3], is entitled to be permitted by his employer[4] to take reasonable time off during the employee's working hours[5] in order to perform his functions as such a representative[6].

An employee who is permitted to take time off[7] is entitled to be paid remuneration by his employer for the time taken off at the appropriate hourly rate[8]. A right to any amount under this provision does not affect any right of an employee in relation to remuneration under his contract of employment ('contractual remuneration')[9]. Any contractual remuneration paid to an employee in respect of a period of time off[10] goes towards discharging any liability of the employer to pay remuneration under the above provision[11] in respect of that period, and, conversely, any payment of remuneration under that provision in respect of a period goes towards discharging any liability of the employer to pay contractual remuneration in respect of that period[12].

An employee may present a complaint to an employment tribunal[13] that his employer (a) has unreasonably refused to permit him to take time off as required[14]; or (b) has failed to pay the whole or part of any amount to which the employee is entitled[15]. Subject to an extension to facilitate conciliation before the institution of proceedings[16], a tribunal must not consider such a complaint unless it is presented (i) before the end of the period of three months beginning with the day on which the time off was taken or on which it is alleged the time off should have been permitted[17]; or (ii) within such further period as the tribunal considers reasonable in a case where it is satisfied that it was not reasonably practicable for the complaint to be presented before the end of that period of three months[18].

Where a tribunal finds such a complaint well-founded, the tribunal must make a declaration to that effect[19]. If the complaint is that the employer has unreasonably refused to permit the employee to take time off, the tribunal must also order the employer to pay to the employee an amount equal to the remuneration to which he would have been entitled[20] if the employer had not refused[21]. If the complaint is that the employer has failed to pay the employee the whole or part of any amount to which he is entitled[22], the tribunal must also order the employer to pay to the employee the amount it finds due to him[23].

1   As to the meaning of 'employee' see PARA 1289 note 4.
2   As to the meaning of 'negotiating representative' see PARA 1295 note 3.
3   As to the meaning of 'information and consultation representative' see PARA 1295 note 3.
4   As to the meaning of 'employer' see PARA 1289 note 2.

5   For the purposes of the Information and Consultation of Employees Regulations 2004, SI 2004/3426, reg 27, the working hours of an employee are be taken to be any time when, in accordance with his contract of employment, the employee is required to be at work: reg 27(2). As to the meaning of 'contract of employment' see PARA 1289 note 4.

6   Information and Consultation of Employees Regulations 2004, SI 2004/3426, reg 27(1).

7   Ie under the Information and Consultation of Employees Regulations 2004, SI 2004/3426, reg 27: see the text and notes 1–6.

8   Information and Consultation of Employees Regulations 2004, SI 2004/3426, reg 28(1). The appropriate hourly rate, in relation to an employee, is the amount of one week's pay divided by the number of normal working hours in a week for that employee when employed under the contract of employment in force on the day when time is taken: reg 28(3). However where the number of normal working hours differs from week to week or over a longer period, the amount of one week's pay must be divided instead by (1) the average number of normal working hours calculated by dividing by 12 the total number of the employee's normal working hours during the period of 12 weeks ending with the last complete week before the day on which the time is taken off; or (2) where the employee has not been employed for a sufficient period to enable the calculations to be made under head (1) above, a number which fairly represents the number of normal working hours in a week having regard to such of certain specified considerations specified in reg 28(5) as are appropriate in the circumstances: reg 28(4). These considerations are: (1) the average number of normal working hours in a week which the employee could expect in accordance with the terms of his contract; and (2) the average number of normal working hours of other employees engaged in relevant comparable employment with the same employer: reg 28(5).

     The Employment Rights Act 1996 Pt XIV Ch II (ss 220–229) (a week's pay) (see PARA 143 et seq) applies in relation to the Information and Consultation of Employees Regulations 2004, SI 2004/3426, reg 28 as it applies in relation to the Employment Rights Act 1996 s 62 (see PARA 1209): Information and Consultation of Employees Regulations 2004, SI 2004/3426, reg 28(2).

9   Information and Consultation of Employees Regulations 2004, SI 2004/3426, reg 28(6).

10   See note 7.

11   Ie under the Information and Consultation of Employees Regulations 2004, SI 2004/3426, reg 28(1).

12   Information and Consultation of Employees Regulations 2004, SI 2004/3426, reg 28(7).

13   As to employment tribunals see PARA 1399 et seq.

14   Ie as required by the Information and Consultation of Employees Regulations 2004, SI 2004/3426, reg 27.

15   Information and Consultation of Employees Regulations 2004, SI 2004/3426, reg 29(1). The entitlement referred to in the text is entitlement under reg 28.

     The provisions of the Employment Tribunals Act 1996 ss 18A–18B (conciliation) (see PARAS 152–153) apply in the case of matters which could be the subject of employment tribunal proceedings under the Information and Consultation of Employees Regulations 2004, SI 2004/3426, reg 29, and the Employment Tribunals Act 1996 s 18C applies in the case of such proceedings themselves: see s 18(1)(s), (1A) (s 18(1)(b) substituted by SI 2014/431; the Employment Tribunals Act 1996 s 18(1A) added by the Enterprise and Regulatory Reform Act 2013 Sch 1 paras 2, 5(1), (7)).

16   The Information and Consultation of Employees Regulations 2004, SI 2004/3426, reg 29A (extension of time limits to facilitate conciliation before institution of proceedings: see notes 17–18) applies for these purposes: reg 29(2A) (added by SI 2014/386).

17   Information and Consultation of Employees Regulations 2004, SI 2004/3426, reg 29(2)(a). In working out when the time limit set by reg 29(2)(a) (see head (i) in the text) expires the period beginning with the day after Day A and ending with Day B is not to be counted: reg 29A(2) (reg 29A added by SI 2014/386). For these purposes, Day A is the day on which the worker concerned complies with the requirement in the Employment Tribunals Act 1996 s 18A(1) (requirement to contact ACAS before instituting proceedings: see PARA 152) in relation to the matter in respect of which the proceedings are brought; and Day B is the day on which the worker concerned receives or, if earlier, is treated as receiving (by virtue of regulations made under s 18A(11) the certificate issued under s 18A(4): Information and Consultation of Employees Regulations 2004, SI 2004/3426, reg 29A(1) (as so added). If the time limit set by reg 29(2)(a) would (if not extended by reg 29A(3)) expire during the period beginning with Day A and ending one month after Day B, the time limit expires instead at the end of that period: reg 29A(3) (as so added).

18   Information and Consultation of Employees Regulations 2004, SI 2004/3426, reg 29(2)(b). The power conferred on the employment tribunal by reg 29(2)(b) (see head (ii) in the text) to extend

the time limit set by reg 29(2)(a) (see head (i) in the text) is exercisable in relation to that time limit as extended by reg 29A: reg 29A(4) (as added: see note 17).

19 Information and Consultation of Employees Regulations 2004, SI 2004/3426, reg 29(3).
20 Ie under the Information and Consultation of Employees Regulations 2004, SI 2004/3426, reg 28.
21 Information and Consultation of Employees Regulations 2004, SI 2004/3426, reg 29(4).
22 See note 20.
23 Information and Consultation of Employees Regulations 2004, SI 2004/3426, reg 29(5).

1312. Protection of information and consultation representative etc against unfair dismissal. An employee[1] who is dismissed and who is:

(1) an employees' representative;
(2) a negotiating representative[2];
(3) an information and consultation representative[3]; or
(4) a candidate in an election in which any person elected will, on being elected, be such a representative[4],

is regarded as unfairly dismissed[5] if the reason (or, if more than one, the principal reason) for the dismissal is that:

(a) the employee performed or proposed to perform any functions or activities as such a representative or candidate[6];
(b) the employee exercised or proposed to exercise an entitlement conferred[7] on the employee; or
(c) the employee (or a person acting on his behalf) made or proposed to make a request to exercise such an entitlement[8].

An employee who is dismissed and is any employee, whether or not he is an employee to whom heads (1) to (4) above apply[9] is regarded as unfairly dismissed[10] if the reason (or, if more than one, the principal reason) for the dismissal is that the employee:

(i) took, or proposed to take, any proceedings before an employment tribunal to enforce a right or secure an entitlement conferred on him by the Information and Consultation of Employees Regulations 2004[11];
(ii) exercised, or proposed to exercise, any entitlement to apply or complain to the Central Arbitration Committee (the 'CAC')[12] or the Employment Appeal Tribunal[13] conferred by the Information and Consultation of Employees Regulations 2004 or to exercise the right to appeal in connection with any rights conferred by those Regulations;
(iii) requested, or proposed to request, data[14];
(iv) acted with a view to securing that an agreement was or was not negotiated or that the standard information and consultation provisions[15] did or did not become applicable;
(v) indicated that he supported or did not support the coming into existence of a negotiated agreement[16] or the application of the standard information and consultation provisions;
(vi) stood as a candidate in an election in which any person elected would, on being elected, be a negotiating representative or an information and consultation representative;
(vii) influenced or sought to influence by lawful means the way in which votes were to be cast by other employees in a ballot arranged under the Information and Consultation of Employees Regulations 2004;
(viii) voted in such a ballot;
(ix) expressed doubts, whether to a ballot supervisor or otherwise, as to whether such a ballot had been properly conducted; or

(x)   proposed to do, failed to do, or proposed to decline to do, any of the things mentioned in heads (iv) to (ix) above[17].

1   As to the meaning of 'employee' see PARA 1289 note 4.
2   As to the meaning of 'negotiating representative' see PARA 1295 note 3.
3   As to the meaning of 'information and consultation representative' see PARA 1295 note 3.
4   Information and Consultation of Employees Regulations 2004, SI 2004/3426, reg 30(2).
5   Ie for the purposes of the Employment Rights Act 1996 Pt X (ss 94–134A): see PARA 757 et seq.
6   The Information and Consultation of Employees Regulations 2004, SI 2004/3426, reg 30(1) does not apply in the circumstances set out in reg 30(3)(a) (see head (a) in the text) where the reason (or principal reason) for the dismissal is that in the performance, or purported performance, of the employee's functions or activities he has disclosed any information or document in breach of the duty in reg 25 (see PARA 1309), unless the employee reasonably believed the disclosure to be a 'protected disclosure' within the meaning given to that expression by the Employment Rights Act 1996 s 43A (see PARA 69): Information and Consultation of Employees Regulations 2004, SI 2004/3426, reg 30(4). As to the meaning of 'information' see PARA 1295 note 5.
7   Ie by the Information and Consultation of Employees Regulations 2004, SI 2004/3426, reg 27 or reg 28: see PARA 1311.
8   Information and Consultation of Employees Regulations 2004, SI 2004/3426, reg 30(1), (3). Where a dismissal is unfair under reg 30(3), read with reg 30(4) (see note 6), the qualifying period for unfair dismissal does not apply: see the Employment Rights Act 1996 s 108(3)(l); and PARA 758 note 9.
9   Information and Consultation of Employees Regulations 2004, SI 2004/3426, reg 30(1), (5).
10   See note 5.
11   Ie conferred on him by the Information and Consultation of Employees Regulations 2004, SI 2004/3426.
     It is immaterial for the purpose of reg 30(6)(a) (see head (i) in the text) (1) whether or not the employee has the right or entitlement; or (2) whether or not the right has been infringed; but for that provision to apply, the claim to the right and, if applicable, the claim that it has been infringed must be made in good faith: reg 30(7).
12   As to the Central Arbitration Committee see PARA 1226 et seq.
13   As to the Employment Appeal Tribunal see PARA 1422 et seq.
14   Ie in accordance with the Information and Consultation of Employees Regulations 2004, SI 2004/3426, reg 5: see PARA 1290.
15   As to the meaning of 'standard information and consultation provisions' see PARA 1298 note 4.
16   As to the meaning of 'negotiated agreement' see PARA 1295 note 3.
17   Information and Consultation of Employees Regulations 2004, SI 2004/3426, reg 30(1), (6). Where a dismissal is unfair under reg 30(6), read with reg 30(7) (see note 11), the qualifying period for unfair dismissal does not apply: see the Employment Rights Act 1996 s 108(3)(l); and PARA 758 note 9.

1313. Right of information and consultation representative etc not to be subjected to any detriment. An employee[1] who is:

(1)   an employees' representative;

(2)   a negotiating representative[2];

(3)   an information and consultation representative[3]; or

(4)   a candidate in an election in which any person elected will, on being elected, be such a representative[4],

has the right not to be subjected to any detriment[5] by any act, or deliberate failure to act, by his employer[6], done on the ground that:

(a)   the employee performed or proposed to perform any functions or activities as such a representative or candidate[7];

(b)   the employee exercised or proposed to exercise an entitlement conferred[8] on the employee; or

(c)   the employee (or a person acting on his behalf) made or proposed to make a request to exercise such an entitlement[9].

An employee who is any employee, whether or not he is an employee to whom heads (1) to (4) apply,[10] has the right not to be subjected to any detriment by any act, or deliberate failure to act, by his employer, done on the ground that the employee:

(i) took, or proposed to take, any proceedings before an employment tribunal[11] to enforce a right or secure an entitlement conferred on him by the Information and Consultation of Employees Regulations 2004[12];

(ii) exercised, or proposed to exercise, any entitlement to apply or complain to the Central Arbitration Committee (the 'CAC')[13] or the Employment Appeal Tribunal[14] conferred by the Information and Consultation of Employees Regulations 2004 or to exercise the right to appeal in connection with any rights conferred by those Regulations;

(iii) requested, or proposed to request, data[15];

(iv) acted with a view to securing that an agreement was or was not negotiated or that the standard information and consultation provisions[16] did or did not become applicable;

(v) indicated that he supported or did not support the coming into existence of a negotiated agreement[17] or the application of the standard information and consultation provisions;

(vi) stood as a candidate in an election in which any person elected would, on being elected, be a negotiating representative or an information and consultation representative;

(vii) influenced or sought to influence by lawful means the way in which votes were to be cast by other employees in a ballot arranged under the Information and Consultation of Employees Regulations 2004;

(viii) voted in such a ballot;

(ix) expressed doubts, whether to a ballot supervisor or otherwise, as to whether such a ballot had been properly conducted; or

(x) proposed to do, failed to do, or proposed to decline to do, any of the things mentioned in heads (iv) to (ix) above[18].

An employee may present a complaint to an employment tribunal that he has been subjected to a detriment in contravention of the above provisions[19].

1   As to the meaning of 'employee' see PARA 1289 note 4.
2   As to the meaning of 'negotiating representative' see PARA 1295 note 3.
3   As to the meaning of 'information and consultation representative' see PARA 1295 note 3.
4   Information and Consultation of Employees Regulations 2004, SI 2004/3426, reg 32(1), (2).
5   The Information and Consultation of Employees Regulations 2004, SI 2004/3426, reg 32 does not apply where the detriment in question amounts to dismissal: reg 32(8). As to dismissal see reg 30; and PARA 1312.
6   As to the meaning of 'employer' see PARA 1289 note 2.
7   The Information and Consultation of Employees Regulations 2004, SI 2004/3426, reg 32(1) does not apply in the circumstances set out in reg 32(3)(a) (see head (a) in the text) where the ground (or principal ground) for the subjection to detriment is that in the performance, or purported performance, of the employee's functions or activities he has disclosed any information or document in breach of the duty in reg 25 (see PARA 1309), unless the employee reasonably believed the disclosure to be a 'protected disclosure' within the meaning given to that expression by the Employment Rights Act 1996 s 43A (see PARA 69): Information and Consultation of Employees Regulations 2004, SI 2004/3426, reg 32(4). As to the meaning of 'information' see PARA 1295 note 5.
8   Ie by the Information and Consultation of Employees Regulations 2004, SI 2004/3426, reg 27 or reg 28: see PARA 1311.
9   Information and Consultation of Employees Regulations 2004, SI 2004/3426, reg 32(1), (3).
10 Information and Consultation of Employees Regulations 2004, SI 2004/3426, reg 32(1), (5).
11 As to employment tribunals see PARA 1399 et seq.
12 Ie the Information and Consultation of Employees Regulations 2004, SI 2004/3426.

It is immaterial for the purpose of reg 32(6)(a) (see head (i) in the text) (1) whether or not the employee has the right or entitlement; or (2) whether or not the right has been infringed, but for that provision to apply, the claim to the right and, if applicable, the claim that it has been infringed must be made in good faith: reg 32(7).

13 As to the Central Arbitration Committee see PARA 1226 et seq.
14 As to the Employment Appeal Tribunal see PARA 1422 et seq.
15 Ie in accordance with the Information and Consultation of Employees Regulations 2004, SI 2004/3426, reg 5: see PARA 1290.
16 As to the meaning of 'standard information and consultation provisions' see PARA 1298 note 4.
17 As to the meaning of 'negotiated agreement' see PARA 1295 note 3.
18 Information and Consultation of Employees Regulations 2004, SI 2004/3426, reg 32(1), (6).
19 Information and Consultation of Employees Regulations 2004, SI 2004/3426, reg 33(1). The provisions of the Employment Rights Act 1996 ss 48(2)–(4), 49(1)–(5) (complaints to employment tribunals and remedies) (see PARAS 625, 626, 1076) apply in relation to a complaint under the Information and Consultation of Employees Regulations 2004, SI 2004/3426, reg 33 as they apply in relation to a complaint under the Employment Rights Act 1996 s 48 but taking references to the employer as references to the employer within the meaning of the Information and Consultation of Employees Regulations 2004, SI 2004/3426, reg 32(1): reg 33(2).
   The provisions of the Employment Tribunals Act 1996 ss 18A–18B (conciliation) (see PARAS 152–153) apply in the case of matters which could be the subject of employment tribunal proceedings under the Information and Consultation of Employees Regulations 2004, SI 2004/3426, reg 33, and the Employment Tribunals Act 1996 s 18C applies in the case of such proceedings themselves: see s 18(1)(s), (1A) (s 18(1)(s) substituted by SI 2014/431; the Employment Tribunals Act 1996 s 18(1A) added by the Enterprise and Regulatory Reform Act 2013 Sch 1 paras 2, 5(1), (7)).

G. JURISDICTION AND PROCEDURAL REQUIREMENTS; CONCILIATION

1314. CAC proceedings under the Information and Consultation of Employees Regulations 2004. Where under the Information and Consultation of Employees Regulations 2004[1] a person presents a complaint or makes an application to the Central Arbitration Committee (the 'CAC')[2] the complaint or application must be in writing and in such form as the CAC may require[3]. In its consideration of a complaint or application under those Regulations, the CAC must make such inquiries as it sees fit and so far as reasonably practicable give any person whom it considers has a proper interest in the complaint or application an opportunity to be heard[4].

The CAC may draw an adverse inference from a party's failure to comply with any reasonable request to provide information[5] or documents relevant to a complaint presented to it or an application made to it[6].

A declaration or order made by the CAC under the 2004 Regulations may be relied on in relation to an employer[7] whose registered office, head office or principal place of business is in England or Wales, as if it were a declaration or order made by the High Court[8].

A declaration or order made by the CAC under the 2004 Regulations must be in writing and state the reasons for the CAC's findings[9].

An appeal lies to the Employment Appeal Tribunal[10] on any question of law arising from any declaration or order of, or arising in any proceedings before, the CAC under the 2004 Regulations[11].

1 Ie the Information and Consultation of Employees Regulations 2004, SI 2004/3426: see PARA 1289 et seq.
2 As to the Central Arbitration Committee see PARA 1226 et seq.
3 Information and Consultation of Employees Regulations 2004, SI 2004/3426, reg 35(1).
4 Information and Consultation of Employees Regulations 2004, SI 2004/3426, reg 35(2).
5 As to the meaning of 'information' see PARA 1295 note 5.
6 Information and Consultation of Employees Regulations 2004, SI 2004/3426, reg 35(3).
7 As to the meaning of 'employer' see PARA 1289 note 2.

8 Information and Consultation of Employees Regulations 2004, SI 2004/3426, reg 35(4)(a). Such a declaration or order may be relied on in relation to an employer whose registered office, head office or principal place of business is in Scotland as if it were a declaration or order made by the Court of Session: reg 35(4)(b).
9 Information and Consultation of Employees Regulations 2004, SI 2004/3426, reg 35(5).
10 As to the Employment Appeal Tribunal see PARA 1422 et seq.
11 Information and Consultation of Employees Regulations 2004, SI 2004/3426, reg 35(6).

1315. Employment Appeal Tribunal proceedings under the Information and Consultation of Employees Regulations 2004. Subject to an exception[1], any proceedings before the Employment Appeal Tribunal[2] arising under the Information and Consultation of Employees Regulations 2004[3] must, where the registered office or, where there is no registered office, the head office or principal place of business is situated in England and Wales[4], be held in England and Wales[5].

1 Proceedings under the Employment Tribunals Act 1996 s 21(1)(q) (appeals from employment tribunals on questions of law: see PARA 1428 head (16) in the text) are excluded from the provision set out in the text and notes 2–5. The Information and Consultation of Employees Regulations 2004, SI 2004/3426, reg 36(1)(a) refers to proceedings under the Employment Tribunals Act 1996 s 21(1)(n) but it is submitted that this is a drafting error and that the proper reference is to s 21(1)(q).
2 As to the Employment Appeal Tribunal see PARA 1422 et seq.
3 Ie the Information and Consultation of Employees Regulations 2004, SI 2004/3426: see PARA 1289 et seq.
4 As to the meanings of 'England' and 'Wales' see PARA 2 note 12.
5 Information and Consultation of Employees Regulations 2004, SI 2004/3426, reg 36(1)(a). Where the registered office or, where there is no registered office, the head office or principal place of business is situated in Scotland, the proceedings must be held in Scotland: reg 36(1)(b).

1316. Advisory, Conciliation and Arbitration Service assistance under the Information and Consultation of Employees Regulations 2004. If on receipt of an application or complaint under the Information and Consultation of Employees Regulations 2004[1] the Central Arbitration Committee (the 'CAC')[2] is of the opinion that it is reasonably likely to be settled by conciliation or other assistance provided by the Advisory, Conciliation and Arbitration Service ('ACAS')[3] in accordance with the provision below[4], it must refer the application or complaint to ACAS and must notify the applicant or complainant and any persons whom it considers have a proper interest in the application or complaint accordingly[5].

Where the CAC so refers[6] an application or complaint to ACAS certain relevant provisions of the Trade Union and Labour Relations (Consolidation) Act 1992[7] apply, and ACAS may offer the parties to the application or complaint its assistance under those provisions with a view to bringing about a settlement[8].

If ACAS does not consider it appropriate to offer its assistance[9] it must inform the CAC[10]. If ACAS has offered the parties its assistance[11], the application or complaint referred has not thereafter been settled or withdrawn, and ACAS is of the opinion that no provision or further provision of its assistance is likely to result in a settlement or withdrawal, it must inform the CAC of its opinion[12].

If (1) an application or complaint is not referred to ACAS; or (2) it is so referred, but ACAS informs the CAC as above[13], the CAC must proceed to hear and determine the application or complaint[14].

1 Ie the Information and Consultation of Employees Regulations 2004, SI 2004/3426: see PARA 1289 et seq.
2 As to the Central Arbitration Committee see PARA 1226 et seq.
3 As to the Advisory, Conciliation and Arbitration Service ('ACAS') see PARA 1213 et seq.

4 Ie in accordance with the Information and Consultation of Employees Regulations 2004, SI 2004/3426, reg 38(2): see the text and notes 7–8.
5 Information and Consultation of Employees Regulations 2004, SI 2004/3426, reg 38(1).
6 Ie under the Information and Consultation of Employees Regulations 2004, SI 2004/3426, reg 38(1).
7 Ie the Trade Union and Labour Relations (Consolidation) Act 1992 s 210 (power of ACAS to offer assistance to settle disputes): see PARA 1218.
8 Information and Consultation of Employees Regulations 2004, SI 2004/3426, reg 38(2). Such assistance is offered as if (1) the dispute or difference between the parties amounted to a trade dispute as defined in the Trade Union and Labour Relations (Consolidation) Act 1992 s 218 (see PARA 1212); and (2) the parties to the application or complaint had requested the assistance of ACAS under s 210 (see PARA 1218): see the Information and Consultation of Employees Regulations 2004, SI 2004/3426, reg 38(2).
9 Ie in accordance with the Information and Consultation of Employees Regulations 2004, SI 2004/3426, reg 38(2).
10 Information and Consultation of Employees Regulations 2004, SI 2004/3426, reg 38(3).
11 See note 9.
12 Information and Consultation of Employees Regulations 2004, SI 2004/3426, reg 38(4).
13 Ie as mentioned in the Information and Consultation of Employees Regulations 2004, SI 2004/3426, reg 38(3) or (4).
14 Information and Consultation of Employees Regulations 2004, SI 2004/3426, reg 38(5).

(iv) Employee Involvement in European Companies

A. EMPLOYEE INVOLVEMENT IN EUROPEAN COMPANIES; INTRODUCTION

1317. Application of the European Public Limited-Liability Company (Employee Involvement) (Great Britain) Regulations 2009. The European Public Limited-Liability Company (Employee Involvement) (Great Britain) Regulations 2009[1], which came into force on 1 October 2009[2], continue the implementation in Great Britain of the Council Directive[3] supplementing the Council Regulation on the Statute for a European Company[4] with regard to the involvement of employees in the form of public limited-liability company, Societas Europaea, known as the 'SE'[5].

The 2009 Regulations apply where a participating company[6] intends to establish an SE whose registered office is to be in Great Britain, or where an SE has its registered office in Great Britain[7].

Where there are UK employees[8], Part 3 of those Regulations[9] also applies (regardless of where the registered office is to be situated) in relation to the election or appointment of UK members of the special negotiating body[10], unless the majority of those employees is employed to work in Northern Ireland[11].

Parts 6 to 9 of the 2009 Regulations[12] also apply (regardless of where the registered office of the SE is, or is intended to be situated) if any of the following is registered or, as the case may be, situated in Great Britain:
(1) a participating company, its concerned subsidiaries or establishments[13];
(2) a subsidiary of an SE;
(3) an establishment of an SE;
(4) an employee or an employees' representative[14].

Nothing in the 2009 Regulations affects involvement rights of employees of an SE, its subsidiaries or establishments provided for by law or practice in the EEA state[15] in which they were employed immediately prior to the registration of the SE[16]; but this does not apply to rights to participation[17].

1 Ie the European Public Limited-Liability Company (Employee Involvement) (Great Britain) Regulations 2009, SI 2009/2401: see PARA 1319 et seq.

2 European Public Limited-Liability Company (Employee Involvement) (Great Britain) Regulations 2009, SI 2009/2401, reg 1(2). The 2009 Regulations are made by the Secretary of State as the designated minister under the European Communities Act 1972 s 2(2) (see CONSTITUTIONAL AND ADMINISTRATIVE LAW vol 20 (2014) PARA 156). See further EUROPEAN UNION.

3 Ie Council Directive (EC) 2001/86 (OJ L294, 10.11.2001, p 22) supplementing the Statute for a European Company with regard to the involvement of employees.

4 Ie Council Regulation (EC) 2157/2001 (OJ L294, 10.11.2001, p 1) on the Statute for a European Company: see COMPANIES vol 15 (2009) PARA 1633 et seq.

5 'SE' means a European Public Limited-Liability Company (or Societas Europaea) within the meaning of Council Regulation (EC) 2157/2001 (OJ L294, 10.11.2001, p 1): European Public Limited-Liability Company (Employee Involvement) (Great Britain) Regulations 2009, SI 2009/2401, reg 3(1). Except as otherwise provided, references in the 2009 Regulations to an SE are to an SE that is to be, or is, registered in Great Britain: reg 3(4).

6 'Participating companies' means the companies directly participating in the establishing of an SE: Council Directive (EC) 2001/86 (OJ L294, 10.11.2001, p 22) art 2(b) (definition applied by the European Public Limited-Liability Company (Employee Involvement) (Great Britain) Regulations 2009, SI 2009/2401, reg 2(2)).

7 European Public Limited-Liability Company (Employee Involvement) (Great Britain) Regulations 2009, SI 2009/2401, reg 4(1). As to the meaning of 'Great Britain' see PARA 2 note 12.

8 'UK employee' means an employee employed to work in the United Kingdom; and 'employee' means an individual who has entered into or works under a contract of employment and includes, where the employment has ceased, an individual who worked under a contract of employment: European Public Limited-Liability Company (Employee Involvement) (Great Britain) Regulations 2009, SI 2009/2401, reg 3(1). As to the meaning of 'United Kingdom' see PARA 2 note 12.

9 Ie the European Public Limited-Liability Company (Employee Involvement) (Great Britain) Regulations 2009, SI 2009/2401, Pt 3 (regs 10–13): see PARAS 1321–1324.

10 'UK members of the special negotiating body' means members of the special negotiating body elected or appointed by UK employees: European Public Limited-Liability Company (Employee Involvement) (Great Britain) Regulations 2009, SI 2009/2401, reg 3(1). 'Special negotiating body' means the body established in accordance with Council Directive (EC) 2001/86 (OJ L294, 10.11.2001, p 22) art 3 to negotiate with the competent body of the participating companies regarding the establishment of arrangements for the involvement of employees within the SE: art 2(g) (definition applied by the European Public Limited-Liability Company (Employee Involvement) (Great Britain) Regulations 2009, SI 2009/2401, reg 2(2)). 'Involvement of employees' means any mechanism, including information, consultation and participation, through which employees' representatives may exercise an influence on decisions to be taken within the company: Council Directive (EC) 2001/86 (OJ L294, 10.11.2001, p 22) art 2(h) (definition as so applied). 'Information' means the informing of the body representative of the employees and/or employees' representatives by the competent organ of the SE on questions which concern the SE itself and any of its subsidiaries or establishments situated in another member state or which exceed the powers of the decision-making organs in a single member state at a time, in a manner and with a content which allows the employees' representatives to undertake an in-depth assessment of the possible impact and, where appropriate, prepare consultations with the competent organ of the SE: art 2(i) (definition as so applied). 'Consultation' means the establishment of dialogue and exchange of views between the body representative of the employees and/or the employees' representatives and the competent organ of the SE, at a time, in a manner and with a content which allows the employees' representatives, on the basis of information provided, to express an opinion on measures envisaged by the competent organ which may be taken into account in the decision-making process within the SE: art 2(j) (definition as so applied).

11 European Public Limited-Liability Company (Employee Involvement) (Great Britain) Regulations 2009, SI 2009/2401, reg 4(2).

12 Ie the European Public Limited-Liability Company (Employee Involvement) (Great Britain) Regulations 2009, SI 2009/2401, Pts 6–9 (regs 20–41): see PARA 1328 et seq.

13 'Concerned subsidiary or establishment' means a subsidiary or establishment of a participating company which is proposed to become a subsidiary or establishment of the SE upon its formation: Council Directive (EC) 2001/86 (OJ L294, 10.11.2001, p 22) art 2(d) (definition applied by the European Public Limited-Liability Company (Employee Involvement) (Great Britain) Regulations 2009, SI 2009/2401, reg 2(2)). 'Subsidiary' of a company means an undertaking over which that company exercises a dominant influence defined in accordance

with what is now European Parliament and Council Directive (EC) 2009/38 (OJ L122, 16/05/2009, p 28) art 3(2)–(7): Council Directive (EC) 2001/86 (OJ L294, 10.11.2001, p 22) art 2(c) (amended by virtue of European Parliament and Council Directive (EC) 2009/38 (OJ L122, 16/05/2009, p 28) art 17, Annex III; definition as so applied).
14 European Public Limited-Liability Company (Employee Involvement) (Great Britain) Regulations 2009, SI 2009/2401, reg 4(3).
15 'EEA state' is not defined for these purposes, but is taken to mean a state which is a contracting party to the Agreement on the European Economic Area (Oporto, 2 May 1992; OJ L1, 3.1.94, p 3; Cm 2073) as adjusted by the Protocol (Brussels, 17 March 1993; OJ L1, 3.1.94, p 571; Cm 2183).
16 European Public Limited-Liability Company (Employee Involvement) (Great Britain) Regulations 2009, SI 2009/2401, reg 41(1).
17 European Public Limited-Liability Company (Employee Involvement) (Great Britain) Regulations 2009, SI 2009/2401, reg 41(2). As to the meaning of 'participation' see PARA 1325 note 9.

1318. Restrictions on contracting out of the European Public Limited-Liability Company (Employee Involvement) (Great Britain) Regulations 2009. Any provision in any agreement, whether an employee's[1] contract or not, is void in so far as it purports to exclude or limit the operation of any provision of the European Public Limited-Liability Company (Employee Involvement) (Great Britain) Regulations 2009[2], other than a provision of Part 8[3] of those Regulations, or to preclude a person from bringing any proceedings before the Central Arbitration Committee (the 'CAC')[4] under any provision of those Regulations other than a provision of that Part[5]; but this does not apply to any agreement to refrain from continuing any such proceedings made after the proceedings have been instituted[6].

Any provision in any agreement, whether an employee's contract or not, is also void in so far as it purports to exclude or limit the operation of any provision of Part 8 of the 2009 Regulations, or to preclude a person from bringing any proceedings before an employment tribunal[7] under that Part[8]; but this does not apply to any agreement to refrain from instituting or continuing proceedings before an employment tribunal where a conciliation officer has taken action[9] under the Employment Tribunals Act 1996[10]. Nor does it apply to any agreement to refrain from instituting or continuing certain proceedings[11] before an employment tribunal if the conditions regulating settlement agreements[12] are satisfied in relation to the agreement[13]. For these purposes, the conditions regulating settlement agreements are as follows:

(1)   the agreement must be in writing;
(2)   the agreement must relate to the particular proceedings;
(3)   the employee must have received advice from a relevant independent adviser[14] as to the terms and effect of the proposed agreement and, in particular, its effect on the ability of the employee to pursue the employee's rights before an employment tribunal;
(4)   there must be in force, when the adviser gives the advice, a contract of insurance, or an indemnity provided for members of a profession or professional body, covering the risk of a claim by the employee in respect of loss arising in consequence of the advice;
(5)   the agreement must identify the adviser;
(6)   the agreement must state that the conditions in heads (1) to (5) above are satisfied[15].

1   As to the meaning of 'employee' see PARA 1317 note 8.
2   Ie the European Public Limited-Liability Company (Employee Involvement) (Great Britain) Regulations 2009, SI 2009/2401: see also PARAS 1317, 1319 et seq.

3 Ie a provision of the European Public Limited-Liability Company (Employee Involvement) (Great Britain) Regulations 2009, SI 2009/2401, Pt 8 (protection for members of special negotiating body etc): see PARAS 1332–1334.

4 As to the Central Arbitration Committee see PARA 1226 et seq. As to proceedings before the Central Arbitration Committee see PARA 1335; and as to ACAS conciliation see PARA 1337.

5 European Public Limited-Liability Company (Employee Involvement) (Great Britain) Regulations 2009, SI 2009/2401, reg 38(1).

6 European Public Limited-Liability Company (Employee Involvement) (Great Britain) Regulations 2009, SI 2009/2401, reg 38(2).

7 As to employment tribunals see PARA 1399 et seq.

8 European Public Limited-Liability Company (Employee Involvement) (Great Britain) Regulations 2009, SI 2009/2401, reg 39(1).

9 Ie action under any of the Employment Tribunals Act 1996 ss 18A–18C: see PARAS 152–153.

10 European Public Limited-Liability Company (Employee Involvement) (Great Britain) Regulations 2009, SI 2009/2401, reg 39(2) (amended by SI 2014/386).

11 Ie proceedings within the Employment Tribunals Act 1996 s 18(1)(y) (proceedings under the European Public Limited-Liability Company (Employee Involvement) (Great Britain) Regulations 2009, SI 2009/2401, where conciliation is available: see PARA 152 note 1).

12 Ie settlement agreements under the European Public Limited-Liability Company (Employee Involvement) (Great Britain) Regulations 2009, SI 2009/2401.

13 European Public Limited-Liability Company (Employee Involvement) (Great Britain) Regulations 2009, SI 2009/2401, reg 39(3) (amended by SI 2013/1956; SI 2014/431).

14 For these purposes, a 'relevant independent adviser' is a person who is any of the following: (1) a qualified lawyer; (2) an officer, official, employee or member of an independent trade union who has been certified in writing by the trade union as competent to give advice and authorised to do so on behalf of the trade union; (3) a person who works at an advice centre (whether as an employee or as a volunteer) and has been certified in writing by the centre as competent to give advice and authorised to do so on behalf of the centre; but a person is not a relevant independent adviser for the purposes of head (3) above in relation to the employee in any of the following cases: (a) if the person is, is employed by, or is acting in the matter for, the employer or an associated employer; (b) in the case of a person within head (2) or head (3) above, if the trade union or advice centre is the employer or an associated employer; (c) in the case of a person within head (3) above, if the employee makes a payment for the advice received: European Public Limited-Liability Company (Employee Involvement) (Great Britain) Regulations 2009, SI 2009/2401, reg 39(5), (6).

For the purposes of head (1) above, 'qualified lawyer' means any of the following: (i) as respects England and Wales, a barrister (whether in practice as such or employed to give legal advice), a solicitor who holds a practising certificate or a person, other than a barrister or solicitor, who is an authorised advocate or authorised litigator (within the meaning of the Courts and Legal Services Act 1990); (ii) as respects Scotland, an advocate (whether in practice as such or employed to give legal advice) or a solicitor who holds a practising certificate: see the European Public Limited-Liability Company (Employee Involvement) (Great Britain) Regulations 2009, SI 2009/2401, reg 39(7). Cf 'qualified lawyer' as it is defined for other purposes in PARAS 1238 note 20, 1291 note 8.

For the purposes of reg 39(6) (see heads (a)–(c) above), any two employers are 'associated' if one is a company of which the other (directly or indirectly) has control, or both are companies of which a third person (directly or indirectly) has control, and 'associated employer' is to be construed accordingly: reg 39(8).

15 European Public Limited-Liability Company (Employee Involvement) (Great Britain) Regulations 2009, SI 2009/2401, reg 39(4) (amended by SI 2013/1956).

B. PARTICIPATING COMPANIES AND SPECIAL NEGOTIATING BODY

1319. Duty on the participating company to provide information. When the competent organ of a participating company[1] decides to form an SE[2], that organ must, as soon as possible after publishing the draft terms of merger, creating a holding company, or agreeing a plan to form a subsidiary[3] or to transform into an SE, provide information[4] to the employees' representatives[5] of the participating company, its concerned subsidiaries and establishments[6] or, if no such representatives exist, the employees themselves[7]. That information must include, as a minimum, information:

(1) identifying the participating companies, concerned subsidiaries and establishments,

(2) giving the number of employees employed by each participating company and concerned subsidiary and at each concerned establishment;

(3) giving the number of employees employed to work in each EEA state[8];

(4) giving the number of agency workers[9] working temporarily for and under the supervision and direction of the undertaking;

(5) as to the parts of the undertaking in which those agency workers are working; and

(6) as to the type of work those agency workers are carrying out[10].

When a special negotiating body[11] has been formed[12] the competent organs of each participating company must provide that body with such information as is necessary to keep it informed of the plan and progress of establishing the SE up to the time the SE has been registered[13].

An employees' representative, or an employee for whom there is no such representative, may present a complaint to the Central Arbitration Committee (the 'CAC')[14] that:

(a) the competent organ of a participating company has failed to provide the information referred to in the above provisions[15]; or

(b) the information provided by the competent organ of a participating company for the purpose of complying with those provisions is false or incomplete in a material particular[16].

If the CAC finds the complaint well-founded, it must make an order requiring the competent organ to disclose information to the complainant[17]. The order must specify the information in respect of which the CAC finds that the complaint is well-founded and which is to be disclosed to the complainant, and a date (not less than one week after the date of the order) by which the competent organ must disclose the information specified in the order[18].

1 As to the meaning of 'participating company' see PARA 1317 note 6.
2 As to the meaning of 'SE' see PARA 1317 note 5.
3 As to the meaning of 'subsidiary' see PARA 1317 note 13.
4 As to the meaning of 'information' see PARA 1317 note 10.
5 'Employees' representatives' means (1) if the employees are of a description in respect of which an independent trade union is recognised by their employer for the purpose of collective bargaining, representatives of the trade union who normally take part as negotiators in the collective bargaining process, and (2) any other employees of their employer who are elected or appointed as employee representatives to positions in which they are expected to receive, on behalf of the employees, information (a) which is relevant to the terms and conditions of employment of the employees, or (b) about the activities of the undertaking which may significantly affect the interests of the employees, but excluding representatives who are expected to receive information relevant only to a specific aspect of the terms and conditions or interests of the employees, such as health and safety or collective redundancies: European Public Limited-Liability Company (Employee Involvement) (Great Britain) Regulations 2009, SI 2009/2401, reg 3(1). As to the meaning of 'employee' see PARA 1317 note 8.
6 As to the meanings of 'concerned subsidiary' and 'concerned establishment' see PARA 1317 note 13.
7 European Public Limited-Liability Company (Employee Involvement) (Great Britain) Regulations 2009, SI 2009/2401, reg 5(1).
8 'EEA state' is not defined for these purposes, but see PARA 1317 note 15.

9 'Agency worker' has the same meaning as in the Agency Workers Regulations 2010, SI 2010/93, reg 3 (see PARA 97): European Public Limited-Liability Company (Employee Involvement) (Great Britain) Regulations 2009, SI 2009/2401, reg 3(1).

10 See the European Public Limited-Liability Company (Employee Involvement) (Great Britain) Regulations 2009, SI 2009/2401, reg 5(2) (amended by SI 2010/93).

11 As to the meaning of 'special negotiating body' see PARA 1317 note 10.

12 Ie in accordance with the European Public Limited-Liability Company (Employee Involvement) (Great Britain) Regulations 2009, SI 2009/2401, reg 8: see PARA 1320.

13 European Public Limited-Liability Company (Employee Involvement) (Great Britain) Regulations 2009, SI 2009/2401, reg 5(3).

14 As to the Central Arbitration Committee see PARA 1226 et seq. As to proceedings before the Central Arbitration Committee see PARA 1335; and as to ACAS conciliation see PARA 1337.

15 Ie the information referred to in the European Public Limited-Liability Company (Employee Involvement) (Great Britain) Regulations 2009, SI 2009/2401, reg 5: see the text and notes 1–13.

16 European Public Limited-Liability Company (Employee Involvement) (Great Britain) Regulations 2009, SI 2009/2401, reg 6(1).

17 European Public Limited-Liability Company (Employee Involvement) (Great Britain) Regulations 2009, SI 2009/2401, reg 6(2).

18 European Public Limited-Liability Company (Employee Involvement) (Great Britain) Regulations 2009, SI 2009/2401, reg 6(3).

1320. Function and composition of special negotiating body. The special negotiating body[1] and the competent organs of the participating companies[2] have the task of reaching an employee involvement agreement[3].

The competent organs of the participating companies must make arrangements for the establishment of a special negotiating body[4] constituted in accordance with the following provisions[5]. In each EEA state[6] in which employees of a participating company or concerned subsidiary[7] are employed to work, those employees must be given an entitlement to elect or appoint one member of the special negotiating body for each 10 per cent, or fraction of 10 per cent, which those employees represent of the total workforce[8]. These members are the 'ordinary members'[9]. If, in the case of an SE to be established by merger[10], following such an election or appointment the members elected or appointed to the special negotiating body do not include at least one eligible member[11] in respect of each relevant company, the employees of any relevant company in respect of which there is no eligible member must be given an entitlement[12] to elect or appoint an additional member to the special negotiating body[13]; but the number of additional members which the employees are so entitled to elect or appoint must not exceed 20 per cent of the number of ordinary members elected or appointed[14]. If the number of additional members would exceed that percentage, the employees who are entitled to appoint or elect the additional members are:

(1) if one additional member is to be appointed or elected, those employed by the company not represented[15] having the highest number of employees;

(2) if more than one additional member is to be appointed or elected, those employed by the companies in each EEA state that are not represented[16] having the highest number of employees in descending order, starting with the company with the highest number, followed by those employed by the companies in each EEA state that are not so represented having the second highest number of employees in descending order, starting with the company (among those companies) with the highest number[17].

The competent organs of the participating companies must, as soon as reasonably practicable and in any event no later than one month after the establishment of the special negotiating body, inform their employees and those of their concerned subsidiaries of the identity of the members of the special negotiating body[18].

If, following the appointment or election of members to the special negotiating body in accordance with these provisions, changes to the participating companies, concerned subsidiaries or concerned establishments[19] result in the number of ordinary or additional members which employees would be entitled to elect or appoint under these provisions either increasing or decreasing, the original appointment or election of members of the special negotiating body ceases to have effect, and those employees are entitled[20] to elect or appoint the new number of members[21].

If a member of the special negotiating body is no longer willing or able to continue serving as such a member, the employees whom the member represents are entitled to elect or appoint a new member in place of that member[22].

An application may be presented to the Central Arbitration Committee (the 'CAC')[23] for a declaration that the special negotiating body has not been established at all or has not been established properly in accordance with the provisions set out above[24]. Such an application may be presented by any of the following:

(a) a person elected or appointed to be a member of the special negotiating body;

(b) an employees' representative[25];

(c) where there is no employees' representative in respect of a participating company or concerned subsidiary, an employee of that participating company or concerned subsidiary;

(d) the competent organ of a participating company or concerned subsidiary[26].

The CAC may only consider such an application if it is made within a period of one month following the date or, if more than one, the last date on which the participating companies complied or should have complied with the obligation to inform their employees[27] of the identity of the members of the special negotiating body[28]. If the CAC finds the application well-founded it must make a declaration that the special negotiating body has not been established at all or has not been established properly, and the competent organs of the participating companies continue to be under the obligation[29] to make arrangements for the establishment of a special negotiating body[30].

1　As to the meaning of 'special negotiating body' see PARA 1317 note 10.

2　As to the meaning of 'participating company' see PARA 1317 note 6.

3　European Public Limited-Liability Company (Employee Involvement) (Great Britain) Regulations 2009, SI 2009/2401, reg 7. 'Employee involvement agreement' means an agreement reached between the special negotiating body and the competent organs of the participating companies governing the arrangements for the involvement of employees within the SE: European Public Limited-Liability Company (Employee Involvement) (Great Britain) Regulations 2009, SI 2009/2401, reg 3(1). As to the meaning of 'SE' see PARA 1317 note 5; and as to the meaning of 'involvement of employees' see PARA 1317 note 10. As to the meaning of 'employee' see PARA 1317 note 8. As to the negotiation of that agreement see PARAS 1325–1326.

4　As to the meaning of 'special negotiating body' see PARA 1317 note 10.

5　European Public Limited-Liability Company (Employee Involvement) (Great Britain) Regulations 2009, SI 2009/2401, reg 8(1).

6　'EEA state' is not defined for these purposes, but see PARA 1317 note 15.

7　As to the meaning of 'concerned subsidiary' see PARA 1317 note 13.

8 European Public Limited-Liability Company (Employee Involvement) (Great Britain) Regulations 2009, SI 2009/2401, reg 8(2). For these purposes, 'the total workforce' means the total number of employees employed by all participating companies and concerned subsidiaries throughout all EEA states: reg 8(8).

9 European Public Limited-Liability Company (Employee Involvement) (Great Britain) Regulations 2009, SI 2009/2401, reg 8(2).

10 'SE established by merger' means an SE established in accordance with Council Regulation (EC) 2157/2001 (OJ L294, 10.11.2001, p 1) art 2(1) (see COMPANIES vol 15 (2009) PARA 1633): European Public Limited-Liability Company (Employee Involvement) (Great Britain) Regulations 2009, SI 2009/2401, reg 3(1).

11 For these purposes, 'eligible member' means a person who is (1) in the case of a relevant company registered in an EEA state whose legislation allows representatives of trade unions who are not employees to be elected to the special negotiating body, an employee of the relevant company or a trade union representative; (2) in the case of a relevant company not registered in such an EEA state, an employee of the relevant company; and 'relevant company' means a participating company which has employees in the EEA state in which it is registered and which it is proposed will cease to exist on or following the registration of the SE: European Public Limited-Liability Company (Employee Involvement) (Great Britain) Regulations 2009, SI 2009/2401, reg 8(8).

12 Ie subject to the European Public Limited-Liability Company (Employee Involvement) (Great Britain) Regulations 2009, SI 2009/2401, reg 8(4): see the text and notes 13–17.

13 European Public Limited-Liability Company (Employee Involvement) (Great Britain) Regulations 2009, SI 2009/2401, reg 8(3).

14 Ie elected or appointed under the European Public Limited-Liability Company (Employee Involvement) (Great Britain) Regulations 2009, SI 2009/2401, reg 8(2) (see the text and notes 6–9): see reg 8(4).

15 Ie not represented under the European Public Limited-Liability Company (Employee Involvement) (Great Britain) Regulations 2009, SI 2009/2401, reg 8(3): see the text and notes 10–13.

16 See note 15.

17 European Public Limited-Liability Company (Employee Involvement) (Great Britain) Regulations 2009, SI 2009/2401, reg 8(4).

18 European Public Limited-Liability Company (Employee Involvement) (Great Britain) Regulations 2009, SI 2009/2401, reg 8(5).

19 As to the meaning of 'concerned establishment' see PARA 1317 note 13.

20 Ie in accordance with the provisions of the European Public Limited-Liability Company (Employee Involvement) (Great Britain) Regulations 2009, SI 2009/2401.

21 European Public Limited-Liability Company (Employee Involvement) (Great Britain) Regulations 2009, SI 2009/2401, reg 8(6).

22 European Public Limited-Liability Company (Employee Involvement) (Great Britain) Regulations 2009, SI 2009/2401, reg 8(7).

23 As to the Central Arbitration Committee see PARA 1226 et seq. As to proceedings before the Central Arbitration Committee see PARA 1335; and as to ACAS conciliation see PARA 1337.

24 European Public Limited-Liability Company (Employee Involvement) (Great Britain) Regulations 2009, SI 2009/2401, reg 9(1).

25 As to the meaning of 'employee's representative' see PARA 1319 note 5.

26 European Public Limited-Liability Company (Employee Involvement) (Great Britain) Regulations 2009, SI 2009/2401, reg 9(2).

27 Ie the obligation under the European Public Limited-Liability Company (Employee Involvement) (Great Britain) Regulations 2009, SI 2009/2401, reg 8(5): see the text and note 18.

28 See the European Public Limited-Liability Company (Employee Involvement) (Great Britain) Regulations 2009, SI 2009/2401, reg 9(3).

29 Ie the obligation under the European Public Limited-Liability Company (Employee Involvement) (Great Britain) Regulations 2009, SI 2009/2401, reg 8(1): see the text and notes 4–5.

30 See the European Public Limited-Liability Company (Employee Involvement) (Great Britain) Regulations 2009, SI 2009/2401, reg 9(4).

1321. Election of UK members of the special negotiating body: ballot arrangements. The UK members of the special negotiating body[1] must be elected[2] by balloting the UK employees[3]. The management of the participating companies[4] that employ UK employees ('the management') must arrange for the holding of a ballot or ballots of those employees in accordance with the specified requirements[5]. Those requirements are:

(1)   in relation to the election of ordinary members[6], that:

      (a)   if the number of members which UK employees are entitled to elect to the special negotiating body is equal to the number of participating companies which have UK employees, there must be separate ballots of the UK employees in each participating company;

      (b)   if the number of members which the UK employees are entitled to elect to the special negotiating body is greater than the number of participating companies which have UK employees, there must be separate ballots of the UK employees in each participating company and the management must ensure, as far as practicable, that at least one member representing each such participating company is elected to the special negotiating body and that the number of members representing each company is proportionate to the number of employees in that company;

      (c)   if the number of members which the UK employees are entitled to elect to the special negotiating body is smaller than the number of participating companies which have employees in the United Kingdom, the number of ballots held must be equivalent to the number of members to be elected, a separate ballot must be held in respect of each of the participating companies with the higher or highest number of employees, and it must be ensured that any employees of a participating company in respect of which a ballot does not have to be held are entitled to vote in a ballot held in respect of one of the other participating companies;

      (d)   if there are any UK employees employed by a concerned subsidiary or establishment[7] of non-UK participating companies, the management must ensure that those employees are entitled to vote in a ballot held pursuant to these provisions[8];

(2)   that in relation to the ballot of additional members[9] the management must hold a separate ballot in respect of each participating company entitled to elect an additional member[10];

(3)   that, in a ballot in respect of a particular participating company, all UK employees employed by that participating company or by its concerned subsidiaries or at its concerned establishments are entitled to vote[11];

(4)   that a person is entitled to stand as a candidate for election as a member of the special negotiating body in a ballot in respect of a particular participating company if, immediately before the latest time at which a person may become a candidate, the person is:

(a)   a UK employee employed by that participating company, by any of its concerned subsidiaries or at any of its concerned establishments; or

(b)   if the management of that participating company so permits, a representative of a trade union who is not an employee of that participating company or any of its concerned subsidiaries[12];

(5)   that the management must appoint[13] a person (a 'ballot supervisor') to supervise the conduct of the ballot of UK employees, or, where there is to be more than one ballot, to supervise the conduct of each of the separate ballots, and, in a case where there is to be more than one

ballot, may appoint different persons to supervise the conduct of such different separate ballots as the management may determine[14];

(6) that after the management has formulated proposals as to the arrangements for the ballot of UK employees and before it has published the final arrangements under head (7) below it must, so far as reasonably practicable, consult the UK employees' representatives[15] on the proposed arrangements for the ballot of UK employees[16]; and

(7) that the management must publish the final arrangements for the ballot of UK employees in such manner as to bring them to the attention of, so far as reasonably practicable, all UK employees and the UK employees' representatives[17].

Any UK employee or UK employees' representative who believes that the arrangements for the ballot of the UK employees do not comply with the requirements of heads (1) to (7) above may, within a period of 21 days beginning on the date on which the management published the final arrangements under head (7) above, present a complaint to the Central Arbitration Committee (the 'CAC')[18]. If the CAC finds the complaint well-founded, it must make a declaration to that effect and may make an order requiring the management to modify the arrangements it has made for the ballot of UK employees or to satisfy the requirements in head (6) or head (7) above[19]. Such an order must specify the modifications to the arrangements which the management is required to make, and the requirements it must satisfy[20].

1 As to the meanings of 'special negotiating body' and 'UK members of the special negotiating body' see PARA 1317 note 10.

2 Ie subject to the European Public Limited-Liability Company (Employee Involvement) (Great Britain) Regulations 2009, SI 2009/2401, reg 11: see PARA 1322.

3 European Public Limited-Liability Company (Employee Involvement) (Great Britain) Regulations 2009, SI 2009/2401, reg 10(1). As to the meaning of 'UK employee' see PARA 1317 note 8.

4 As to the meaning of 'participating company' see PARA 1317 note 6.

5 European Public Limited-Liability Company (Employee Involvement) (Great Britain) Regulations 2009, SI 2009/2401, reg 10(2).

6 Ie under the European Public Limited-Liability Company (Employee Involvement) (Great Britain) Regulations 2009, SI 2009/2401, reg 8(2): see PARA 1320.

7 As to the meanings of 'concerned subsidiary' and 'concerned establishment' see PARA 1317 note 13.

8 European Public Limited-Liability Company (Employee Involvement) (Great Britain) Regulations 2009, SI 2009/2401, reg 10(3)(a).

9 Ie under the European Public Limited-Liability Company (Employee Involvement) (Great Britain) Regulations 2009, SI 2009/2401, reg 8(3): see PARA 1320.

10 European Public Limited-Liability Company (Employee Involvement) (Great Britain) Regulations 2009, SI 2009/2401, reg 10(3)(b).

11 European Public Limited-Liability Company (Employee Involvement) (Great Britain) Regulations 2009, SI 2009/2401, reg 10(3)(c).

12 European Public Limited-Liability Company (Employee Involvement) (Great Britain) Regulations 2009, SI 2009/2401, reg 10(3)(d).

13 Ie in accordance with the European Public Limited-Liability Company (Employee Involvement) (Great Britain) Regulations 2009, SI 2009/2401, reg 8(7): see note 14.

14 European Public Limited-Liability Company (Employee Involvement) (Great Britain) Regulations 2009, SI 2009/2401, reg 10(3)(e). The management may appoint a person to be a ballot supervisor for these purposes only if the management reasonably believes that the person will carry out competently any functions conferred on the person in relation to the ballot, and has no reasonable grounds for believing that the person's independence in relation to the ballot might reasonably be called into question: reg 10(7).

15 As to the meaning of 'employee's representatives' see PARA 1319 note 5.

16 European Public Limited-Liability Company (Employee Involvement) (Great Britain) Regulations 2009, SI 2009/2401, reg 10(3)(f).

17 European Public Limited-Liability Company (Employee Involvement) (Great Britain) Regulations 2009, SI 2009/2401, reg 10(3)(g).
18 European Public Limited-Liability Company (Employee Involvement) (Great Britain) Regulations 2009, SI 2009/2401, reg 10(4). As to the Central Arbitration Committee see PARA 1226 et seq. As to proceedings before the Central Arbitration Committee see PARA 1335; and as to ACAS conciliation see PARA 1337.
19 European Public Limited-Liability Company (Employee Involvement) (Great Britain) Regulations 2009, SI 2009/2401, reg 10(5).
20 European Public Limited-Liability Company (Employee Involvement) (Great Britain) Regulations 2009, SI 2009/2401, reg 10(6).

1322.   Election of UK members of the special negotiating body: conduct of the ballot.   The management[1] must:

(1)   ensure that a ballot supervisor appointed under the relevant regulation[2] carries out the functions conferred or imposed on the ballot supervisor under the following provisions[3];

(2)   ensure that there is no interference from the management with the ballot supervisor's carrying out of those functions[4];

(3)   comply with all reasonable requests made by a ballot supervisor for the purposes of, or in connection with, the carrying out of those functions[5].

A ballot supervisor's appointment must require that the ballot supervisor:

(a)   supervises the conduct of the ballot, or the separate ballots, that the ballot supervisor is being appointed to supervise, in accordance with the arrangements for the ballot of UK employees[6] published by the management[7] or, where appropriate, in accordance with the arrangements as required to be modified by an order made as a result of a complaint presented[8] to the Central Arbitration Committee (the 'CAC')[9];

(b)   does not conduct the ballot or any of the separate ballots before the management has satisfied the specified requirement as to publication[10] and either

(i)   where no complaint has been presented[11] to the CAC, before the expiry of a period of 21 days beginning on the date on which the management published[12] its arrangements; or

(ii)   where a complaint has been presented[13], before the complaint has been determined and, where appropriate, the arrangements have been modified as required by an order made as a result of that complaint[14];

(c)   conducts the ballot, or each separate ballot, so as to secure that:

(i)   so far as reasonably practicable, those entitled to vote are given the opportunity to vote;

(ii)   so far as reasonably practicable, those entitled to stand as candidates are given the opportunity to stand;

(iii)   so far as reasonably practicable, those voting are able to do so in secret; and

(iv)   the votes given in the ballot are fairly and accurately counted[15].

As soon as reasonably practicable after the holding of the ballot, the ballot supervisor must publish the results of the ballot in such manner as to make them available to the management and, so far as reasonably practicable, to the UK employees entitled to vote in the ballot and the persons who stood as candidates[16].

If a ballot supervisor considers, whether on the basis of representations made to him by another person or otherwise:

(A) that any of the requirements referred to in heads (a) to (c) above was not satisfied, with the result that the outcome of the ballot would have been different; or

(B) that there was interference with the carrying out of the ballot supervisor's functions, or a failure by the management to comply with all reasonable requests made by the ballot supervisor, with the result that the ballot supervisor was unable to form a proper judgement as to whether each of the requirements referred to in heads (a) to (c) above was satisfied in the ballot,

the ballot supervisor must publish a report ('an ineffective ballot report')[17]. Where a ballot supervisor publishes an ineffective ballot report, the report must be published within a period of one month commencing on the date on which the ballot supervisor publishes[18] the results of the ballot[19]. A ballot supervisor must publish an ineffective ballot report in such manner as to make it available to the management and, so far as reasonably practicable, to the UK employees entitled to vote in the ballot and the persons who stood as candidates in the ballot[20]. Where a ballot supervisor publishes an ineffective ballot report, then:

(*aa*) if there has been a single ballot, or if an ineffective ballot report has been published in respect of every separate ballot, the outcome of the ballot or ballots has no effect and the management is again under the obligation[21] arrange for the holding of a ballot or ballots;

(*bb*) if there have been separate ballots and head (*aa*) above does not apply, the management must arrange for the separate ballot or ballots in respect of which an ineffective ballot report was published to be re-held[22] and no such ballot has effect until it has been re-held and no ineffective ballot report has been published in respect of it[23].

All costs relating to the holding of a ballot, including payments made to a ballot supervisor for supervising the conduct of the ballot, must be borne by the management, whether or not an ineffective ballot report has been published[24].

1 As to the meaning of the 'management' see PARA 1321.
2 Ie under the European Public Limited-Liability Company (Employee Involvement) (Great Britain) Regulations 2009, SI 2009/2401, reg 10(3)(e): see PARA 1321.
3 European Public Limited-Liability Company (Employee Involvement) (Great Britain) Regulations 2009, SI 2009/2401, reg 11(1)(a).
4 European Public Limited-Liability Company (Employee Involvement) (Great Britain) Regulations 2009, SI 2009/2401, reg 11(1)(b).
5 European Public Limited-Liability Company (Employee Involvement) (Great Britain) Regulations 2009, SI 2009/2401, reg 11(1)(c).
6 As to the meaning of 'UK employee' see PARA 1317 note 8.
7 Ie under the European Public Limited-Liability Company (Employee Involvement) (Great Britain) Regulations 2009, SI 2009/2401, reg 10(3)(g): see PARA 1321.
8 Ie under the European Public Limited-Liability Company (Employee Involvement) (Great Britain) Regulations 2009, SI 2009/2401, reg 10(4): see PARA 1321.
9 See the European Public Limited-Liability Company (Employee Involvement) (Great Britain) Regulations 2009, SI 2009/2401, reg 11(2)(a). As to the Central Arbitration Committee see PARA 1226 et seq. As to proceedings before the Central Arbitration Committee see PARA 1335; and as to ACAS conciliation see PARA 1337.
10 Ie the requirement specified in the European Public Limited-Liability Company (Employee Involvement) (Great Britain) Regulations 2009, SI 2009/2401, reg 10(3)(g): see PARA 1321.
11 See note 8.
12 See note 7.
13 See note 8.
14 See the European Public Limited-Liability Company (Employee Involvement) (Great Britain) Regulations 2009, SI 2009/2401, reg 11(2)(b).
15 European Public Limited-Liability Company (Employee Involvement) (Great Britain) Regulations 2009, SI 2009/2401, reg 11(2)(c).

16 European Public Limited-Liability Company (Employee Involvement) (Great Britain) Regulations 2009, SI 2009/2401, reg 11(3).

17 European Public Limited-Liability Company (Employee Involvement) (Great Britain) Regulations 2009, SI 2009/2401, reg 11(4).

18 Ie under the European Public Limited-Liability Company (Employee Involvement) (Great Britain) Regulations 2009, SI 2009/2401, reg 11(3): see the text and note 16.

19 European Public Limited-Liability Company (Employee Involvement) (Great Britain) Regulations 2009, SI 2009/2401, reg 11(5).

20 European Public Limited-Liability Company (Employee Involvement) (Great Britain) Regulations 2009, SI 2009/2401, reg 11(6).

21 Ie the obligation in the European Public Limited-Liability Company (Employee Involvement) (Great Britain) Regulations 2009, SI 2009/2401, reg 10(2): see PARA 1321.

22 Ie in accordance with the European Public Limited-Liability Company (Employee Involvement) (Great Britain) Regulations 2009, SI 2009/2401, regs 10, 11: see the text and notes 1–21; and PARA 1321.

23 European Public Limited-Liability Company (Employee Involvement) (Great Britain) Regulations 2009, SI 2009/2401, reg 11(7).

24 European Public Limited-Liability Company (Employee Involvement) (Great Britain) Regulations 2009, SI 2009/2401, reg 11(8).

1323. Appointment of UK members by a consultative committee. Where certain statutory provisions[1] would otherwise require a ballot to be held, but there exists in the participating company[2] in respect of which a ballot would be held[3] a consultative committee[4], then the election provided for[5] must not take place and the consultative committee is entitled to appoint the UK member or members of the special negotiating body[6] who would otherwise be elected[7]. Any such appointment by the consultative committee must comply with the following provision[8], namely that the committee may appoint as a member of the special negotiating body either one of its number, or, if the management[9] of the participating company in respect of which the consultative committee exists so permits, a trade union representative who is not an employee of that company[10].

The consultative committee must publish the names of the persons whom it has appointed to be members of the special negotiating body in such a manner as to bring them to the attention of the management of the participating company and, so far as reasonably practicable, the employees and the employees' representatives[11] of that company and its concerned subsidiaries[12].

Where the management of the participating company, or an employee or an employees' representative, believes either that the consultative committee does not satisfy the statutory requirements[13], or that any of the persons appointed by the consultative committee is not entitled to be appointed, the management of the participating company or, as the case may be, the employee or the employees' representative may present a complaint to the Central Arbitration Committee (the 'CAC')[14] within a period of 21 days beginning on the date on which the consultative committee published[15] the names of the persons appointed[16]. If the CAC finds the complaint well-founded it must make a declaration to that effect[17]. Where the CAC has made such a declaration, any appointment made by the consultative committee is ineffective, and the members of the special negotiating body must be elected by a ballot[18] of the employees[19].

Where the consultative committee appoints any person to be a member of the special negotiating body, that appointment has effect:

(1) where no complaint has been presented to the CAC[20], after the expiry of a period of 21 days beginning on the date on which the consultative committee published[21] the names of the persons appointed;

(2)   where such a complaint has been presented, as from the day on which the complaint has been determined without a declaration[22] being made[23].

1   Ie the European Public Limited-Liability Company (Employee Involvement) (Great Britain) Regulations 2009, SI 2009/2401, reg 10(3)(a)(i) or (ii) or (b): see PARA 1321.
2   As to the meaning of 'participating company' see PARA 1317 note 6.
3   Ie under European Public Limited-Liability Company (Employee Involvement) (Great Britain) Regulations 2009, SI 2009/2401, reg 10: see PARA 1321.
4   For these purposes, a 'consultative committee' means a body of persons (1) whose normal functions include or comprise the carrying out of an information and consultation function; (2) which is able to carry out its information and consultation function without interference from the management of the participating company; (3) which, in carrying out its information and consultation function, represents all the employees of the participating company; and (4) which consists wholly of persons who are employees of the participating company or its concerned subsidiaries: European Public Limited-Liability Company (Employee Involvement) (Great Britain) Regulations 2009, SI 2009/2401, reg 12(4). 'Information and consultation function' means the function of (a) receiving, on behalf of all the employees of the participating company, information which may significantly affect the interests of the employees of that company, but excluding information which is relevant only to a specific aspect of the interests of the employees, such as health and safety or collective redundancies; and (b) being consulted by the management of the participating company on the information referred to in head (a) above: reg 12(5). As to the meaning of 'employee' see PARA 1317 note 8; as to the meaning of 'information' see PARA 1317 note 10; and as to the meaning of 'concerned subsidiary' see PARA 1317 note 13.
5   Ie provided for in the European Public Limited-Liability Company (Employee Involvement) (Great Britain) Regulations 2009, SI 2009/2401, reg 10: see PARA 1321.
6   As to the meanings of 'UK members of the special negotiating body' and 'special negotiating body' see PARA 1317 note 10.
7   European Public Limited-Liability Company (Employee Involvement) (Great Britain) Regulations 2009, SI 2009/2401, reg 12(1), (2)(a), (b).
8   European Public Limited-Liability Company (Employee Involvement) (Great Britain) Regulations 2009, SI 2009/2401, reg 12(2)(c).
9   As to the meaning of the 'management' see PARA 1321.
10 See the European Public Limited-Liability Company (Employee Involvement) (Great Britain) Regulations 2009, SI 2009/2401, reg 12(3).
11 As to the meaning of 'employees' representatives' see PARA 1319 note 5.
12 European Public Limited-Liability Company (Employee Involvement) (Great Britain) Regulations 2009, SI 2009/2401, reg 12(6).
13 Ie the requirements of the European Public Limited-Liability Company (Employee Involvement) (Great Britain) Regulations 2009, SI 2009/2401, reg 12(4): see note 4.
14 As to the Central Arbitration Committee see PARA 1226 et seq. As to proceedings before the Central Arbitration Committee see PARA 1335; and as to ACAS conciliation see PARA 1337.
15 Ie under the European Public Limited-Liability Company (Employee Involvement) (Great Britain) Regulations 2009, SI 2009/2401, reg 12(6): see the text and notes 11–12.
16 European Public Limited-Liability Company (Employee Involvement) (Great Britain) Regulations 2009, SI 2009/2401, reg 12(7).
17 European Public Limited-Liability Company (Employee Involvement) (Great Britain) Regulations 2009, SI 2009/2401, reg 12(8).
18 Ie in accordance with the European Public Limited-Liability Company (Employee Involvement) (Great Britain) Regulations 2009, SI 2009/2401, reg 10: see PARA 1321.
19 European Public Limited-Liability Company (Employee Involvement) (Great Britain) Regulations 2009, SI 2009/2401, reg 12(9).
20 Ie under European Public Limited-Liability Company (Employee Involvement) (Great Britain) Regulations 2009, SI 2009/2401, reg 12(7): see the text and notes 13–16.
21 See note 15.
22 Ie a declaration European Public Limited-Liability Company (Employee Involvement) (Great Britain) Regulations 2009, SI 2009/2401, reg 12(8): see the text and note 17.
23 European Public Limited-Liability Company (Employee Involvement) (Great Britain) Regulations 2009, SI 2009/2401, reg 12(10).

1324. Representation of employees. A member of the special negotiating body[1] elected in a ballot[2] is treated as representing the employees[3] for the time being of the participating company[4] and of any concerned subsidiary or establishment[5] whose employees were entitled to vote in the ballot in which the member was elected[6]. If an additional member is elected[7], that additional member, and not any member elected as previously mentioned[8], is treated as representing the employees for the time being of the participating company and of any concerned subsidiary or establishment whose employees were entitled to vote in the ballot in which the additional member was elected[9].

When a member of the special negotiating body is appointed by a consultative committee[10], the employees whom the consultative committee represents and the employees of any concerned subsidiary are treated as being represented by the member so appointed[11].

1   As to the meaning of 'special negotiating body' see PARA 1317 note 10.
2   Ie in accordance with the European Public Limited-Liability Company (Employee Involvement) (Great Britain) Regulations 2009, SI 2009/2401, reg 8(2): see PARA 1320.
3   As to the meaning of 'employee' see PARA 1317 note 8.
4   As to the meaning of 'participating company' see PARA 1317 note 6.
5   As to the meanings of 'concerned subsidiary' and 'concerned establishment' see PARA 1317 note 13.
6   See the European Public Limited-Liability Company (Employee Involvement) (Great Britain) Regulations 2009, SI 2009/2401, reg 13(1).
7   Ie in accordance with the European Public Limited-Liability Company (Employee Involvement) (Great Britain) Regulations 2009, SI 2009/2401, reg 8(3) and (4): see PARA 1320.
8   Ie any member elected in accordance with the European Public Limited-Liability Company (Employee Involvement) (Great Britain) Regulations 2009, SI 2009/2401, reg 8(2): see PARA 1320.
9   European Public Limited-Liability Company (Employee Involvement) (Great Britain) Regulations 2009, SI 2009/2401, reg 13(2).
10   Ie in accordance with the European Public Limited-Liability Company (Employee Involvement) (Great Britain) Regulations 2009, SI 2009/2401, reg 12: see PARA 1323.
11   European Public Limited-Liability Company (Employee Involvement) (Great Britain) Regulations 2009, SI 2009/2401, reg 13(3).

C. NEGOTIATION OF EMPLOYEE INVOLVEMENT AGREEMENT

1325. Employee involvement agreement. The competent organs of the participating companies[1] and the special negotiating body[2] ('the parties')[3] are under a duty to negotiate in a spirit of cooperation with a view to reaching an employee involvement agreement[4]. That duty commences one month after the date or, if more than one, the last date on which the members of the special negotiating body were elected or appointed and applies:

(1)   for the period of six months starting with the day on which the duty commenced or, where an employee involvement agreement is successfully negotiated within that period, until the completion of the negotiations;

(2)   where the parties agree before the end of that six month period that it is to be extended, for the period of twelve months starting with the day on which the duty commenced or, where an employee involvement agreement is successfully negotiated within the twelve month period, until the completion of the negotiations[5].

The employee involvement agreement must be in writing[6] and must specify each of the following:

(a)   the scope of the agreement;

(b) the composition, number of members and allocation of seats on the representative body[7];

(c) the functions and the procedure for the information and consultation of the representative body;

(d) the frequency of meetings of the representative body;

(e) the financial and material resources to be allocated to the representative body;

(f) if, during negotiations, the parties decide to establish one or more information and consultation[8] procedures instead of a representative body, the arrangements for implementing those procedures;

(g) if, during negotiations, the parties decide to establish arrangements for participation[9], the substance of those arrangements including, if applicable, the number of members in the SE's[10] administrative or supervisory body which the employees will be entitled to elect, appoint, recommend or oppose, the procedures as to how these members may be elected, appointed, recommended or opposed by the employees, and their rights;

(h) the date of entry into force of the agreement and its duration, the circumstances, if any, in which the agreement is required to be re-negotiated and the procedure for its re-negotiation[11].

Heads (a) to (h) above are without prejudice to the autonomy of the parties and are subject to the following provision[12], namely that in relation to an SE to be established by way of transformation[13], the employee involvement agreement must provide for the elements of employee involvement at all levels to be at least as favourable as those which exist in the company to be transformed into an SE[14].

The employee involvement agreement is not subject to the standard rules on employee involvement[15], unless it contains a provision to the contrary[16].

Where under the employee involvement agreement the competent organ of the SE is to provide information on the employment situation in that company, such information must include suitable information relating to the use of agency workers[17], if any, in that company[18].

If the parties decide, in accordance with head (f) above, to establish one or more information and consultation procedures instead of a representative body, and those procedures include a provision for representatives to be elected or appointed to act in relation to information and consultation, those representatives are 'information and consultation representatives'[19].

1 As to the meaning of 'participating company' see PARA 1317 note 6.

2 As to the meaning of 'special negotiating body' see PARA 1317 note 10.

3 European Public Limited-Liability Company (Employee Involvement) (Great Britain) Regulations 2009, SI 2009/2401, reg 14(1).

4 European Public Limited-Liability Company (Employee Involvement) (Great Britain) Regulations 2009, SI 2009/2401, reg 14(2). As to the meaning of 'employee involvement agreement' see PARA 1320 note 3.

5 European Public Limited-Liability Company (Employee Involvement) (Great Britain) Regulations 2009, SI 2009/2401, reg 14(3).

6 European Public Limited-Liability Company (Employee Involvement) (Great Britain) Regulations 2009, SI 2009/2401, reg 15(1).

7 'Representative body' means the persons elected or appointed under the employee involvement agreement or under the standard rules on employee involvement (as to which see note 15): European Public Limited-Liability Company (Employee Involvement) (Great Britain) Regulations 2009, SI 2009/2401, reg 3(1).

8 As to the meanings of 'information' and 'consultation' see PARA 1317 note 10.

9 'Participation' means the influence of the representative body and the employees' representatives in the SE or a participating company by way of the right to (1) elect or appoint some of the members of the SE's or the participating company's supervisory or administrative organ; or (2) recommend or oppose the appointment of some or all of the members of the SE's or the participating company's supervisory or administrative organ: European Public Limited-Liability Company (Employee Involvement) (Great Britain) Regulations 2009, SI 2009/2401, reg 3(1). See also note 10.

10 As to the meaning of 'SE' see PARA 1317 note 5.

11 European Public Limited-Liability Company (Employee Involvement) (Great Britain) Regulations 2009, SI 2009/2401, reg 15(2).

12 See note 11.

13 'SE established by transformation' means an SE established in accordance with Council Regulation (EC) 2157/2001 (OJ L294, 10.11.2001, p 1) art 2(4) (see COMPANIES vol 15 (2009) PARA 1633): European Public Limited-Liability Company (Employee Involvement) (Great Britain) Regulations 2009, SI 2009/2401, reg 3(1).

14 European Public Limited-Liability Company (Employee Involvement) (Great Britain) Regulations 2009, SI 2009/2401, reg 15(4).

15 'Standard rules on employee involvement' means the rules in the European Public Limited-Liability Company (Employee Involvement) (Great Britain) Regulations 2009, SI 2009/2401, Schedule: reg 2(1). Those rules cover (1) composition of the representative body (see Schedule Pt 1 (paras 1–5)); (2) standard rules for information and consultation (see Schedule Pt 2 (paras 6–11) (amended by SI 2010/93)); and (3) standard rules for participation (see the European Public Limited-Liability Company (Employee Involvement) (Great Britain) Regulations 2009, SI 2009/2401, Schedule Pt 3 (paras 12–14)). As to the application of the standard rules see also PARA 1327.

16 European Public Limited-Liability Company (Employee Involvement) (Great Britain) Regulations 2009, SI 2009/2401, reg 15(3).

17 'Suitable information relating to the use of agency workers' means (1) the number of agency workers working temporarily for and under the supervision and direction of the undertaking; (2) the parts of the undertaking in which those agency workers are working; and (3) the type of work those agency workers are carrying out: European Public Limited-Liability Company (Employee Involvement) (Great Britain) Regulations 2009, SI 2009/2401, reg 3(1) (definition added by SI 2010/93). As to the meaning of 'agency worker' see PARA 1319 note 9.

18 European Public Limited-Liability Company (Employee Involvement) (Great Britain) Regulations 2009, SI 2009/2401, reg 15(3A) (added by SI 2010/93).

19 European Public Limited-Liability Company (Employee Involvement) (Great Britain) Regulations 2009, SI 2009/2401, regs 2(1), 15(5).

1326. Decisions of special negotiating body. Each member of the special negotiating body[1] has one vote[2]. Subject to the prescribed exceptions[3], the special negotiating body must take decisions by an absolute majority vote[4]. In the following circumstances, however, any decision which would result in a reduction of participation rights[5] must be taken by a two thirds majority vote[6]:

(1)   where an SE is to be established by merger[7] and at least 25 per cent of the employees employed to work in the EEA states by the participating companies which are due to merge have participation rights;

(2)   where an SE is to be established by formation of a holding company or of a subsidiary company[8] and at least 50 per cent of the total number of employees employed to work in the EEA states by the participating companies have participation rights[9].

Where the special negotiating body takes a decision[10] it must publish the details of the decision in such a manner as to bring the decision, so far as reasonably practicable, to the attention of the employees whom it represents, and such publication must take place as soon as reasonably practicable and, in any event, no later than 14 days after the decision has been taken[11].

For the purpose of negotiations, the special negotiating body may be assisted by experts of its choice[12].

The participating company or companies must pay for any reasonable expenses of the functioning of the special negotiating body, and any reasonable expenses relating to the negotiations that are necessary to enable the special negotiating body to carry out its functions in an appropriate manner, but where the special negotiating body is assisted by more than one expert the participating company is not required to pay such expenses in respect of more than one of them[13].

The special negotiating body may decide, by a two thirds majority vote, not to open negotiations with the competent organs of the participating companies, or to terminate any such negotiations[14]; but it cannot take that decision in relation to an SE to be established by transformation[15] if any employees of the company to be transformed have participation rights[16]. Any decision so made has the following effects:

(a)   the duty[17] to negotiate with a view to reaching an employee involvement agreement[18] ceases as from the date of the decision;

(b)   any rules relating to the information and consultation[19] of employees in an EEA state in which employees of the SE are employed apply to the employees of the SE in that EEA state;

(c)   the special negotiating body is to be reconvened only if a request that meets the prescribed conditions[20] is made by employees or employees' representatives[21].

If a person who is a member of the special negotiating body, or who is an employees' representative or an employee for whom there is no such representative, believes that the special negotiating body has taken a decision referred to above and:

(i)   that the decision was not taken by the required majority[22]; or

(ii)   that the special negotiating body failed to publish the decision[23],

the person may present a complaint to the Central Arbitration Committee (the 'CAC')[24] within 21 days after the date on which the special negotiating body published its decision[25] or, if it has not done so, the date by which it should have so published its decision[26]. Where the CAC finds the complaint well-founded, it must make a declaration that the decision was not taken properly and that it is of no effect[27].

1   As to the meaning of 'special negotiating body' see PARA 1317 note 10.
2   European Public Limited-Liability Company (Employee Involvement) (Great Britain) Regulations 2009, SI 2009/2401, reg 16(1).
3   Ie except in those cases where the European Public Limited-Liability Company (Employee Involvement) (Great Britain) Regulations 2009, SI 2009/2401, reg 16(3) (see the text and notes 5–9) or reg 17 (see the text and notes 14–21) provides otherwise.
4   European Public Limited-Liability Company (Employee Involvement) (Great Britain) Regulations 2009, SI 2009/2401, reg 16(2). 'Absolute majority vote' means a vote passed by a majority of the total membership of the special negotiating body where the members voting with that majority represent the majority of the employees of the participating companies and their concerned subsidiaries and establishments employed in the EEA states: reg 2(1). As to the meaning of 'employee' see PARA 1317 note 8; as to the meaning of 'participating company' see PARA 1317 note 6; and as to the meanings of 'concerned subsidiary' and 'concerned establishment' see PARA 1317 note 13. 'EEA state' is not defined for these purposes, but see PARA 1317 note 15.
5   For these purposes, 'reduction of participation rights' means that the body representative of the employees has participation rights in relation to a smaller proportion of members of the supervisory or administrative organs of the SE than the employees' representatives had in the participating company which gave participation rights in relation to the highest proportion of such members in that company: European Public Limited-Liability Company (Employee Involvement) (Great Britain) Regulations 2009, SI 2009/2401, reg 16(3). As to the meaning of 'participation' see PARA 1325 note 9; and as to the meaning of 'SE' see PARA 1317 note 5.

6 'Two thirds majority vote' means a vote passed by a majority of at least two thirds of the total membership of the special negotiating body where the members voting with that majority (1) represent at least two thirds of the employees of the participating companies and their concerned subsidiaries and establishments employed in the EEA states; and (2) include members representing employees employed in at least two EEA states: European Public Limited-Liability Company (Employee Involvement) (Great Britain) Regulations 2009, SI 2009/2401, reg 3(1).

7 As to the meaning of 'SE established by merger' see PARA 1320 note 10.

8 'SE established by formation of a holding company or subsidiary company' means an SE established in accordance with Council Regulation (EC) 2157/2001 (OJ L294, 10.11.2001, p 1) art 2(2) or art 2(3), as the case may be (see COMPANIES vol 15 (2009) PARA 1633): European Public Limited-Liability Company (Employee Involvement) (Great Britain) Regulations 2009, SI 2009/2401, reg 3(1).

9 European Public Limited-Liability Company (Employee Involvement) (Great Britain) Regulations 2009, SI 2009/2401, reg 16(3).

10 Ie under the European Public Limited-Liability Company (Employee Involvement) (Great Britain) Regulations 2009, SI 2009/2401, reg 16 (see the text and notes 1–9) or under reg 17 (see the text and notes 14–21).

11 European Public Limited-Liability Company (Employee Involvement) (Great Britain) Regulations 2009, SI 2009/2401, reg 16(4).

12 European Public Limited-Liability Company (Employee Involvement) (Great Britain) Regulations 2009, SI 2009/2401, reg 16(5).

13 European Public Limited-Liability Company (Employee Involvement) (Great Britain) Regulations 2009, SI 2009/2401, reg 16(6).

14 European Public Limited-Liability Company (Employee Involvement) (Great Britain) Regulations 2009, SI 2009/2401, reg 17(1).

15 As to the meaning of 'SE established by transformation' see PARA 1325 note 13.

16 European Public Limited-Liability Company (Employee Involvement) (Great Britain) Regulations 2009, SI 2009/2401, reg 17(2).

17 Ie the duty in the European Public Limited-Liability Company (Employee Involvement) (Great Britain) Regulations 2009, SI 2009/2401, reg 14(2): see PARA 1325.

18 As to the meaning of 'employee involvement agreement' see PARA 1320 note 3.

19 As to the meanings of 'information' and 'consultation' see PARA 1317 note 10.

20 Ie the conditions in the European Public Limited-Liability Company (Employee Involvement) (Great Britain) Regulations 2009, SI 2009/2401, reg 17(4). Those conditions are that the request is made (1) in writing; (2) by at least 10% of the employees of (a) the participating companies and their concerned subsidiaries; or (b) where the SE has been registered, the SE and its subsidiaries, or by employees' representatives representing at least that percentage of those employees; (3) no earlier than two years after the decision made under reg 17(1) was or should have been published in accordance with reg 16(4) unless (i) the special negotiating body; and (ii) the competent organs of every participating company or, where the SE has been registered, the SE, agree to the special negotiating body being reconvened earlier: reg 17(4). As to the meaning of 'employees' representatives' see PARA 1319 note 5.

21 European Public Limited-Liability Company (Employee Involvement) (Great Britain) Regulations 2009, SI 2009/2401, reg 17(3).

22 Ie the majority required by the European Public Limited-Liability Company (Employee Involvement) (Great Britain) Regulations 2009, SI 2009/2401, reg 16 or reg 17, as the case may be.

23 Ie in accordance with the European Public Limited-Liability Company (Employee Involvement) (Great Britain) Regulations 2009, SI 2009/2401, reg 16(4).

24 As to the Central Arbitration Committee see PARA 1226 et seq. As to proceedings before the Central Arbitration Committee see PARA 1335; and as to ACAS conciliation see PARA 1337.

25 See note 23.

26 European Public Limited-Liability Company (Employee Involvement) (Great Britain) Regulations 2009, SI 2009/2401, reg 18(1).

27 European Public Limited-Liability Company (Employee Involvement) (Great Britain) Regulations 2009, SI 2009/2401, reg 18(2).

D. STANDARD RULES ON EMPLOYEE INVOLVEMENT

1327. Application of the standard rules on employee involvement. Where the parties[1] agree that the standard rules on employee involvement[2] are to apply, or where the specified period[3] has expired without the parties reaching an employee involvement agreement[4], and where:

(1)   the competent organs of each of the participating companies[5] agree that the standard rules on employee involvement are to apply and so continue with the registration of the SE[6]; and

(2)   the special negotiating body[7] has not taken any decision[8] either not to open, or to terminate, the negotiations[9],

the competent organ of the SE and its subsidiaries[10] and establishments must make arrangements for the involvement of employees[11] of the SE and its subsidiaries and establishments in accordance with the standard rules on employee involvement[12].

The standard rules on participation[13], however, apply only in the following circumstances:

(a)   in the case of an SE established by merger[14] if, before registration of the SE, one or more forms of participation existed in at least one of the participating companies and either that participation applied to at least 25 per cent of the total number of employees[15] of the participating companies employed in the EEA states[16], or that participation applied to less than 25 per cent of the total number of employees of the participating companies employed in the EEA states but the special negotiating body has decided that the standard rules on participation will apply to the employees of the SE; or

(b)   in the case of an SE established by formation of a holding company or subsidiary company[17] if, before registration of the SE, one or more forms of employee participation existed in at least one of the participating companies and either that participation applied to at least 50 per cent of the total number of employees of the participating companies employed in the EEA states, or that participation applied to less than 50 per cent of the total number of employees of the participating companies employed in the EEA states but the special negotiating body has decided that the standard rules on participation will apply to the employees of the SE[18].

Where the standard rules on participation apply, and more than one form of employee participation exists in the participating companies, the special negotiating body must decide which of the existing forms of participation is to exist in the SE and must inform the competent organs of the participating companies accordingly[19].

1   As to the meaning of 'the parties' see PARA 1325.
2   As to the meaning of 'standard rules on employee involvement' see PARA 1325 note 15.
3   Ie the period specified in the European Public Limited-Liability Company (Employee Involvement) (Great Britain) Regulations 2009, SI 2009/2401, reg 14(3)(a) or, where applicable, reg 14(3)(b): see PARA 1325.
4   As to the meaning of 'employee involvement agreement' see PARA 1320 note 3.
5   As to the meaning of 'participating company' see PARA 1317 note 6.
6   As to the meaning of 'SE' see PARA 1317 note 5.
7   As to the meaning of 'special negotiating body' see PARA 1317 note 10.
8   Ie under the European Public Limited-Liability Company (Employee Involvement) (Great Britain) Regulations 2009, SI 2009/2401, reg 17(1): see PARA 1326.

9   Ie the negotiations referred to in the European Public Limited-Liability Company (Employee Involvement) (Great Britain) Regulations 2009, SI 2009/2401, reg 17: see PARA 1326.

10   As to the meaning of 'subsidiary' see PARA 1317 note 13.

11   As to the meaning of 'employee' see PARA 1317 note 8.

12   European Public Limited-Liability Company (Employee Involvement) (Great Britain) Regulations 2009, SI 2009/2401, reg 19(1), (2).

13   Ie the rules set out in the European Public Limited-Liability Company (Employee Involvement) (Great Britain) Regulations 2009, SI 2009/2401, Schedule Pt 3 (paras 12–14).

14   As to the meaning of 'SE established by merger' see PARA 1320 note 10.

15   The following provisions apply to an agency worker whose contract within the Agency Workers Regulations 2010, SI 2010/93, reg 3(1)(b) (contract with the temporary work agency: see PARA 97) is not a contract of employment: (1) for the purposes of the European Public Limited-Liability Company (Employee Involvement) (Great Britain) Regulations 2009, SI 2009/2401, reg 19(3)(a), (b) (see heads (a)–(b) in the text), any agency worker who has a contract with a temporary work agency, which was at the relevant time a participating company, is to be treated as having been employed by that temporary work agency for the duration of his assignment with a hirer; and (2) 'assignment' and 'hirer' have the same meanings as in the Agency Workers Regulations 2010, SI 2010/93, reg 2 (see PARA 97 note 3), and 'temporary work agency' has the same meaning as in reg 4 (see PARA 97): European Public Limited-Liability Company (Employee Involvement) (Great Britain) Regulations 2009, SI 2009/2401, reg 19(3A) (added by SI 2010/93). As to the meaning of 'agency worker' see PARA 1319 note 9.

16   'EEA state' is not defined for these purposes, but see PARA 1317 note 15.

17   As to the meaning of 'SE established by formation of a holding company or subsidiary company' see PARA 1326 note 8.

18   European Public Limited-Liability Company (Employee Involvement) (Great Britain) Regulations 2009, SI 2009/2401, reg 19(3). See also note 15.

19   European Public Limited-Liability Company (Employee Involvement) (Great Britain) Regulations 2009, SI 2009/2401, reg 19(4).

E. COMPLIANCE WITH AND ENFORCEMENT OF REQUIREMENTS FOR EMPLOYEE INVOLVEMENT

1328. Disputes about operation of employee involvement agreement or standard rules on employee involvement. Where either an employee involvement agreement[1] has been agreed, or the standard rules on employee involvement[2] apply[3], a complaint may be presented to the Central Arbitration Committee (the 'CAC')[4] by a relevant applicant[5] who considers that the competent organ of a participating company[6] or of the SE has failed to comply with the terms of the employee involvement agreement or, as the case may be, one or more of the standard information and consultation provisions[7]. Such a complaint must be brought within the period of three months commencing with the date of the alleged failure[8], or, where the failure takes place over a period, the last day of that period[9].

Where it finds the complaint well-founded, the CAC must make a declaration to that effect, and may make an order requiring the SE to take such steps as are necessary to comply with the terms of the employee involvement agreement or, as the case may be, the standard rules on employee involvement[10]. An order so made must specify the steps which the SE is required to take, the date of the failure and the period within which the order must be complied with[11]. No such order of the CAC has the effect of suspending or altering the effect of any act done or of any agreement made by the participating company or the SE[12].

If the CAC makes a declaration under the above provision[13], the relevant applicant may, within the period of three months beginning with the day on which the decision is made, make an application to the Employment Appeal Tribunal[14] for a penalty notice to be issued[15]. Where such an application is made, the Appeal Tribunal must issue a written penalty notice to the SE requiring it to pay a penalty to the Secretary of State[16] in respect of the failure, unless the Appeal Tribunal is satisfied, on hearing representations from the SE, either that the failure resulted from a reason beyond its control, or that it has some other reasonable excuse for its failure[17]. A penalty notice so issued must specify the amount of the penalty which is payable, the date before which the penalty must be paid[18] and the failure and period to which the penalty relates[19]. No penalty set by the Appeal Tribunal under this provision may exceed £75,000[20]. When setting the amount of the penalty, the Appeal Tribunal must take into account:

(1)   the gravity of the failure;
(2)   the period of time over which the failure occurred;
(3)   the reason for the failure;
(4)   the number of employees affected by the failure;
(5)   the number of employees employed by the undertaking[21].

The making of an appeal suspends the effect of the penalty notice[22]. If the specified date in a penalty notice has passed and either the period during which an appeal may be made has expired without an appeal having been made, or such an appeal has been made and determined, the Secretary of State may recover from the SE, as a civil debt due to him, any amount payable under the penalty notice which remains outstanding[23].

Any sums received by the Secretary of State under the above provisions[24] must be paid into the Consolidated Fund[25].

1   As to the meaning of 'employee involvement agreement' see PARA 1320 note 3.
2   As to the meaning of 'standard rules on employee involvement' see PARA 1325 note 15.
3   As to the application of the standard rules on employee involvement see PARA 1327.
4   As to the Central Arbitration Committee see PARA 1226 et seq. As to proceedings before the Central Arbitration Committee see PARA 1335; and as to ACAS conciliation see PARA 1337.
5   For these purposes, 'relevant applicant' means (1) in a case where a representative body has been appointed or elected, a member of that body; (2) in a case where no representative body has been elected or appointed, an information and consultation representative or an employee of the SE: European Public Limited-Liability Company (Employee Involvement) (Great Britain) Regulations 2009, SI 2009/2401, reg 20(3). As to the meaning of 'employee' see PARA 1317 note 8; and as to the meaning of 'SE' see PARA 1317 note 5. As to the meaning of 'information and consultation representative' see PARA 1325; and as to the meaning of 'representative body' see PARA 1325 note 7.
6   As to the meaning of 'participating company' see PARA 1317 note 6.
7   European Public Limited-Liability Company (Employee Involvement) (Great Britain) Regulations 2009, SI 2009/2401, reg 20(1). The standard information and consultation provisions are contained in Schedule Pt 2 (paras 6–11) (amended by SI 2010/93). The remedy for infringement of the rights conferred by the 2009 Regulations is by way of complaint to the CAC in accordance with those Regulations and not otherwise: European Public Limited-Liability Company (Employee Involvement) (Great Britain) Regulations 2009, SI 2009/2401, reg 23.
8   For these purposes, 'failure' means an act or omission: European Public Limited-Liability Company (Employee Involvement) (Great Britain) Regulations 2009, SI 2009/2401, reg 20(3).
9   European Public Limited-Liability Company (Employee Involvement) (Great Britain) Regulations 2009, SI 2009/2401, reg 20(2).
10   European Public Limited-Liability Company (Employee Involvement) (Great Britain) Regulations 2009, SI 2009/2401, reg 20(4).
11   European Public Limited-Liability Company (Employee Involvement) (Great Britain) Regulations 2009, SI 2009/2401, reg 20(5).
12   European Public Limited-Liability Company (Employee Involvement) (Great Britain) Regulations 2009, SI 2009/2401, reg 20(9).
13   Ie under the European Public Limited-Liability Company (Employee Involvement) (Great Britain) Regulations 2009, SI 2009/2401, reg 20(4): see the text and note 10.
14   As to the Employment Appeal Tribunal see PARA 1422 et seq.
15   European Public Limited-Liability Company (Employee Involvement) (Great Britain) Regulations 2009, SI 2009/2401, reg 20(6). Regulation 21 (see the text and notes 18–25) applies

in respect of a penalty notice issued under reg 20: reg 20(8). Every application under reg 20(6) must be made by way of application in writing in, or substantially in, accordance with the Employment Appeal Tribunal Rules 1993, SI 1993/2854, Schedule Form 4B and must be served on the Appeal Tribunal together with a copy of the declaration referred to in the European Public Limited-Liability Company (Employee Involvement) (Great Britain) Regulations 2009, SI 2009/2401, reg 20(4) (see the text and note 10), or an explanation as to why none is included: Employment Appeal Tribunal Rules 1993, SI 1993/2854, r 16AA (added by SI 2004/2526; amended by SI 2004/3426; SI 2007/2974; SI 2010/1088). As to applications made under the Employment Appeal Tribunal Rules 1993, SI 1993/2854, r 16AA see further r 16B (substituted by SI 2010/1088); the Employment Appeal Tribunal Rules 1993, SI 1993/2854, r 16C (added by SI 2001/1128; amended by SI 2004/2526; SI 2010/1088); the Employment Appeal Tribunal Rules 1993, SI 1993/2854, r 16D (added by SI 2001/1128); and the Employment Appeal Tribunal Rules 1993, SI 1993/2854, Schedule Form 5A (added by SI 2001/1128; amended by SI 2010/1088).

16 As to the Secretary of State see PARA 5 note 21.
17 European Public Limited-Liability Company (Employee Involvement) (Great Britain) Regulations 2009, SI 2009/2401, reg 20(7).
18 The date so specified must not be earlier than the end of the period within which an appeal against a decision or order made by the CAC under reg 20 may be made: European Public Limited-Liability Company (Employee Involvement) (Great Britain) Regulations 2009, SI 2009/2401, reg 21(4).
19 European Public Limited-Liability Company (Employee Involvement) (Great Britain) Regulations 2009, SI 2009/2401, reg 21(1).
20 European Public Limited-Liability Company (Employee Involvement) (Great Britain) Regulations 2009, SI 2009/2401, reg 21(2).
21 European Public Limited-Liability Company (Employee Involvement) (Great Britain) Regulations 2009, SI 2009/2401, reg 21(3).
22 European Public Limited-Liability Company (Employee Involvement) (Great Britain) Regulations 2009, SI 2009/2401, reg 21(6).
23 European Public Limited-Liability Company (Employee Involvement) (Great Britain) Regulations 2009, SI 2009/2401, reg 21(5).
24 Ie under the European Public Limited-Liability Company (Employee Involvement) (Great Britain) Regulations 2009, SI 2009/2401, reg 20 or reg 21: see the text and notes 1–23.
25 European Public Limited-Liability Company (Employee Involvement) (Great Britain) Regulations 2009, SI 2009/2401, reg 21(7). As to the Consolidated Fund see CONSTITUTIONAL AND ADMINISTRATIVE LAW vol 20 (2014) PARA 480 et seq; PARLIAMENT vol 78 (2010) PARA 1028 et seq.

1329. Misuse of procedures under the European Public Limited-Liability Company (Employee Involvement) (Great Britain) Regulations 2009. If an employees' representative[1], or an employee[2] for whom there is no such representative, believes that a participating company[3] or an SE[4] is misusing or intending to misuse the SE or the powers in the European Public Limited-Liability Company (Employee Involvement) (Great Britain) Regulations 2009[5] for the purpose of:

(1) depriving the employees of that participating company or of any of its concerned subsidiaries[6] or, as the case may be, of the SE or of any of its subsidiaries of their rights to employee involvement; or

(2) withholding rights from any of those employees,

the representative or, as the case may be, the employee may make a complaint to the Central Arbitration Committee (the 'CAC')[7]. Where a complaint is so made to the CAC before registration of the SE, or within the period of 12 months following the date of its registration, the CAC must uphold the complaint unless the respondent proves that it did not misuse or intend to misuse the SE or the powers in the 2009 Regulations for a purpose specified in head (1) or head (2) above[8].

If it finds the complaint to be well founded, the CAC must make a declaration to that effect, and may make an order requiring the participating company or the

SE, as the case may be, to take such action as is specified in the order to ensure that the employees referred to in head (1) above are not deprived of their rights to employee involvement or that such rights are not withheld from them[9].

No such order of the CAC has the effect of suspending or altering the effect of any act done or of any agreement made by the participating company or the SE[10].

If the CAC makes a declaration under the above provision, the relevant applicant may, within the period of three months beginning with the day on which the decision is made, make an application to the Employment Appeal Tribunal[11] for a penalty notice to be issued[12]. Where such an application is made, the Appeal Tribunal must issue a written penalty notice to the SE requiring it to pay a penalty to the Secretary of State[13] in respect of the failure, unless the Appeal Tribunal is satisfied, on hearing representations from the SE, either that the failure resulted from a reason beyond its control, or that it has some other reasonable excuse for its failure[14]. A penalty notice so issued must specify the amount of the penalty which is payable, the date before which the penalty must be paid[15] and the failure and period to which the penalty relates[16]. No penalty set by the Appeal Tribunal under this provision may exceed £75,000[17]. When setting the amount of the penalty, the Appeal Tribunal must take into account:

(a)   the gravity of the failure;
(b)   the period of time over which the failure occurred;
(c)   the reason for the failure;
(d)   the number of employees affected by the failure;
(e)   the number of employees employed by the undertaking[18].

The making of an appeal suspends the effect of the penalty notice[19]. If the specified date in a penalty notice has passed and either the period during which an appeal may be made has expired without an appeal having been made, or such an appeal has been made and determined, the Secretary of State may recover from the SE, as a civil debt due to him, any amount payable under the penalty notice which remains outstanding[20].

Any sums received by the Secretary of State under the above provisions must be paid into the Consolidated Fund[21].

1   As to the meaning of 'employees' representatives' see PARA 1319 note 5.
2   As to the meaning of 'employee' see PARA 1317 note 8.
3   As to the meaning of 'participating company' see PARA 1317 note 6.
4   As to the meaning of 'SE' see PARA 1317 note 5.
5   Ie the European Public Limited-Liability Company (Employee Involvement) (Great Britain) Regulations 2009, SI 2009/2401: see also PARAS 1317 et seq, 1330 et seq.
6   As to the meaning of 'concerned subsidiary' see PARA 1317 note 13.
7   European Public Limited-Liability Company (Employee Involvement) (Great Britain) Regulations 2009, SI 2009/2401, reg 22(1). The remedy for infringement of the rights conferred by the 2009 Regulations is by way of complaint to the CAC in accordance with those Regulations and not otherwise: European Public Limited-Liability Company (Employee Involvement) (Great Britain) Regulations 2009, SI 2009/2401, reg 23.
8   European Public Limited-Liability Company (Employee Involvement) (Great Britain) Regulations 2009, SI 2009/2401, reg 22(2).
9   European Public Limited-Liability Company (Employee Involvement) (Great Britain) Regulations 2009, SI 2009/2401, reg 22(3). The provisions of regs 20(6)–(9), 21 apply where the CAC makes a declaration or order reg 22(3) as they apply where it makes a declaration or order under reg 20(4) (see PARA 1328): reg 22(3).
10 European Public Limited-Liability Company (Employee Involvement) (Great Britain) Regulations 2009, SI 2009/2401, reg 20(9) (applied for these purposes: see note 9).
11 As to the Employment Appeal Tribunal see PARA 1422 et seq.

12 European Public Limited-Liability Company (Employee Involvement) (Great Britain) Regulations 2009, SI 2009/2401, reg 20(6) (applied for these purposes: see note 9).
13 As to the Secretary of State see PARA 5 note 21.
14 European Public Limited-Liability Company (Employee Involvement) (Great Britain) Regulations 2009, SI 2009/2401, reg 20(7) (applied for these purposes: see note 9).
15 The date so specified must not be earlier than the end of the period within which an appeal against a decision or order made by the CAC may be made: European Public Limited-Liability Company (Employee Involvement) (Great Britain) Regulations 2009, SI 2009/2401, reg 21(4) (applied for these purposes: see note 9).
16 European Public Limited-Liability Company (Employee Involvement) (Great Britain) Regulations 2009, SI 2009/2401, reg 21(1) (applied for these purposes: see note 9).
17 European Public Limited-Liability Company (Employee Involvement) (Great Britain) Regulations 2009, SI 2009/2401, reg 21(2) (applied for these purposes: see note 9).
18 European Public Limited-Liability Company (Employee Involvement) (Great Britain) Regulations 2009, SI 2009/2401, reg 21(3) (applied for these purposes: see note 9).
19 European Public Limited-Liability Company (Employee Involvement) (Great Britain) Regulations 2009, SI 2009/2401, reg 21(6) (applied for these purposes: see note 9).
20 European Public Limited-Liability Company (Employee Involvement) (Great Britain) Regulations 2009, SI 2009/2401, reg 21(5) (applied for these purposes: see note 9).
21 European Public Limited-Liability Company (Employee Involvement) (Great Britain) Regulations 2009, SI 2009/2401, reg 21(7) (applied for these purposes: see note 9). As to the Consolidated Fund see CONSTITUTIONAL AND ADMINISTRATIVE LAW vol 20 (2014) PARA 480 et seq; PARLIAMENT vol 78 (2010) PARA 1028 et seq.

F. CONFIDENTIAL INFORMATION RELATING TO EMPLOYEE INVOLVEMENT

1330. Breach of statutory duty with regard to confidential information.
Where a body which is (1) an SE[1]; (2) a subsidiary[2] of an SE; (3) a participating company[3]; or (4) a concerned subsidiary[4] entrusts a person (a 'recipient'), pursuant to the provisions of the European Public Limited-Liability Company (Employee Involvement) (Great Britain) Regulations 2009[5], with any information[6] or document on terms requiring it to be held in confidence, the person must not disclose that information or document except in accordance with the terms on which it was disclosed to him[7]. Where the above provision applies, the obligation to comply with it is a duty owed to the body that disclosed the information or document to the recipient, and a breach of the duty is actionable accordingly, subject to the defences and other incidents applying to claims for breach of statutory duty[8]; but this does not affect:

(a) any legal liability which any person may otherwise incur by disclosing the information or document; or

(b) any right which any person may otherwise have in relation to such disclosure[9].

No claim lies[10], however, where the recipient reasonably believed the disclosure to be a 'protected disclosure'[11].

A recipient to whom a body mentioned in heads (1) to (4) above has, pursuant to the provisions of the 2009 Regulations, entrusted any information or document on terms requiring it to be held in confidence may apply to the Central Arbitration Committee (the 'CAC')[12] for a declaration as to whether it was reasonable for the body to require the recipient to hold the information or document in confidence[13]. If the CAC considers that the disclosure of the information or the document by the recipient would not, or would not be likely to, harm the legitimate interests of the undertaking, it must make a declaration that it was not reasonable for the body to require the recipient to hold the information or document in confidence[14]. If such a declaration is made, the information or document is not at any time after the making of the declaration to be regarded as having been entrusted to the recipient who made the application[15], or to any other recipient, on terms requiring it to be held in confidence[16].

1 As to the meaning of 'SE' see PARA 1317 note 5.
2 As to the meaning of 'subsidiary' see PARA 1317 note 13.
3 As to the meaning of 'participating company' see PARA 1317 note 6.
4 As to the meaning of 'concerned subsidiary' and 'see PARA 1317 note 13.
5 Ie the European Public Limited-Liability Company (Employee Involvement) (Great Britain) Regulations 2009, SI 2009/2401: see also PARAS 1317 et seq, 1331 et seq.
6 As to the meaning of 'information' see PARA 1317 note 10.
7 European Public Limited-Liability Company (Employee Involvement) (Great Britain) Regulations 2009, SI 2009/2401, reg 24(1), (2).
8 See the European Public Limited-Liability Company (Employee Involvement) (Great Britain) Regulations 2009, SI 2009/2401, reg 24(3). As to breach of statutory duty see further TORT vol 97 (2010) PARA 495 et seq.
9 European Public Limited-Liability Company (Employee Involvement) (Great Britain) Regulations 2009, SI 2009/2401, reg 24(4).
10 Ie under the European Public Limited-Liability Company (Employee Involvement) (Great Britain) Regulations 2009, SI 2009/2401, reg 24(3).
11 See the European Public Limited-Liability Company (Employee Involvement) (Great Britain) Regulations 2009, SI 2009/2401, reg 24(5). The reference in the text to a 'protected disclosure' is to a protected disclosure within the meaning given by the Employment Rights Act 1996 s 43A (see PARA 69): see the European Public Limited-Liability Company (Employee Involvement) (Great Britain) Regulations 2009, SI 2009/2401, reg 24(5).
12 As to the Central Arbitration Committee see PARA 1226 et seq. As to proceedings before the Central Arbitration Committee see PARA 1335; and as to ACAS conciliation see PARA 1337.
13 European Public Limited-Liability Company (Employee Involvement) (Great Britain) Regulations 2009, SI 2009/2401, reg 24(6).
14 European Public Limited-Liability Company (Employee Involvement) (Great Britain) Regulations 2009, SI 2009/2401, reg 24(7).
15 Ie the application under the European Public Limited-Liability Company (Employee Involvement) (Great Britain) Regulations 2009, SI 2009/2401, reg 24(5): see the text and notes 10–11.
16 European Public Limited-Liability Company (Employee Involvement) (Great Britain) Regulations 2009, SI 2009/2401, reg 24(8).

1331. Withholding of information by SE or participating company. Neither an SE[1] nor a participating company[2] is required to disclose any information[3] or document to a person for the purposes of the European Public Limited-Liability Company (Employee Involvement) (Great Britain) Regulations 2009[4] where the nature of the information or document is such that, according to objective criteria, the disclosure of the information or document would seriously harm the functioning of, or would be prejudicial to, the SE or any subsidiary[5] or establishment of the SE, or the participating company or any subsidiary or establishment of the participating company[6].

Where there is a dispute between the SE or a participating company, and where:

(1)   a representative body[7] has been appointed or elected, a member of that body; or

(2)   a representative body has not been appointed or elected, an information and consultation representative[8] or an employee[9],

and where the dispute is as to whether the nature of the information or document which the SE or the participating company has failed to provide is such as is described above[10], the SE or participating company, or a person referred to in head (1) or head (2) above, may apply to the Central Arbitration Committee (the 'CAC')[11] for a declaration as to whether the information or document is of such a nature[12]. If the CAC makes a declaration that the disclosure of the information or document in question would not, according to objective criteria, be seriously harmful or prejudicial as mentioned above[13], the CAC must order the company to disclose the information or document[14]. Such an order must specify:

(a)   the information or document to be disclosed;

(b)   the person or persons to whom the information or document is to be disclosed;

(c)   any terms on which the information or document is to be disclosed;

(d)   the date before which the information or document is to be disclosed[15].

1   As to the meaning of 'SE' see PARA 1317 note 5.
2   As to the meaning of 'participating company' see PARA 1317 note 6.
3   As to the meaning of 'information' see PARA 1317 note 10.
4   Ie the European Public Limited-Liability Company (Employee Involvement) (Great Britain) Regulations 2009, SI 2009/2401: see also PARAS 1317 et seq, 1332 et seq.
5   As to the meaning of 'subsidiary' see PARA 1317 note 13.
6   European Public Limited-Liability Company (Employee Involvement) (Great Britain) Regulations 2009, SI 2009/2401, reg 25(1).
7   As to the meaning of 'representative body' see PARA 1325 note 7.
8   As to the meaning of 'information and consultation representative' see PARA 1325.
9   As to the meaning of 'employee' see PARA 1317 note 8.
10   Ie such as is described in the European Public Limited-Liability Company (Employee Involvement) (Great Britain) Regulations 2009, SI 2009/2401, reg 25(1): see the text and notes 1–6.
11   As to the Central Arbitration Committee see PARA 1226 et seq. As to proceedings before the Central Arbitration Committee see PARA 1335; and as to ACAS conciliation see PARA 1337.
12   European Public Limited-Liability Company (Employee Involvement) (Great Britain) Regulations 2009, SI 2009/2401, reg 25(2).
13   Ie as mentioned in the European Public Limited-Liability Company (Employee Involvement) (Great Britain) Regulations 2009, SI 2009/2401, reg 25(1): see the text and notes 1–6.
14   European Public Limited-Liability Company (Employee Involvement) (Great Britain) Regulations 2009, SI 2009/2401, reg 25(3).
15   European Public Limited-Liability Company (Employee Involvement) (Great Britain) Regulations 2009, SI 2009/2401, reg 25(4).

G. PROTECTION FOR MEMBERS OF SPECIAL NEGOTIATING BODY ETC

1332.   Right to time off for members of special negotiating body etc.   Where an employee[1] is any of the following:

(1)   a member of a special negotiating body[2];

(2)   a member of a representative body[3];

(3)   an information and consultation representative[4];

(4)   an employee member on a supervisory or administrative organ[5],

(5)   a candidate in an election in which any person elected will, on being elected, be such a member or a representative,

the employee is entitled to be permitted by the employer to take reasonable time off during working hours[6] in order to perform functions as such a member, representative or candidate[7].

An employee who is permitted to take time off under the above provision is entitled to be paid remuneration by the employer for the time taken off at the appropriate hourly rate[8]. A right to any amount under this provision does not affect any right of an employee in relation to remuneration under his contract of employment[9]; but any contractual remuneration paid to an employee in respect of a period of time off under the right to take reasonable time off during working hours[10] goes towards discharging any liability of the employer to pay remuneration[11] in respect of that period, and conversely, any payment of remuneration[12] in respect of a period goes towards discharging any liability of the employer to pay contractual remuneration in respect of that period[13].

An employee may present a complaint to an employment tribunal[14] that the employer has unreasonably refused to permit the employee to take time off as required[15] or has failed to pay the whole or any part of any amount to which the employee is entitled[16] under the above provision[17]. Subject to an extension to facilitate conciliation before the institution of proceedings[18], a tribunal must not consider such a complaint under this regulation unless it is presented:

(a) before the end of the period of three months beginning with the day on which the time off was taken or on which it is alleged the time off should have been permitted[19]; or

(b) within such further period as the tribunal considers reasonable in a case where it is satisfied that it was not reasonably practicable for the complaint to be presented before the end of that period of three months[20].

Where a tribunal finds such a complaint well-founded, the tribunal must make a declaration to that effect[21]. If the complaint is that the employer has unreasonably refused to permit the employee to take time off, the tribunal must also order the employer to pay to the employee an amount equal to the remuneration to which the employee would have been entitled[22] if the employer had not refused[23]. If the complaint is that the employer has failed to pay the employee the whole or part of any amount to which the employee is entitled[24], the tribunal must also order the employer to pay to the employee the amount which it finds is due to the employee[25].

1 As to the meaning of 'employee' see PARA 1317 note 8.
2 As to the meaning of 'special negotiating body' see PARA 1317 note 10.
3 As to the meaning of 'representative body' see PARA 1325 note 7.
4 As to the meaning of 'information and consultation representative' see PARA 1325.
5 An SE comprises (1) a general meeting of shareholders and (2) either a supervisory organ and a management organ (two-tier system) or an administrative organ (one-tier system) depending on the form adopted in the statutes: see Council Regulation (EC) 2157/2001 (OJ L294, 10.11.2001, p 1) on the Statute for a European Company art 38; and COMPANIES vol 15 (2009) PARA 1652. As to the meaning of 'SE' see PARA 1317 note 5.
6 For these purposes, 'working hours' means any time when, in accordance with the employee's contract of employment, the employee is required to be at work: European Public Limited-Liability Company (Employee Involvement) (Great Britain) Regulations 2009, SI 2009/2401, reg 26(2).
7 European Public Limited-Liability Company (Employee Involvement) (Great Britain) Regulations 2009, SI 2009/2401, reg 26(1).
8 European Public Limited-Liability Company (Employee Involvement) (Great Britain) Regulations 2009, SI 2009/2401, reg 27(1). The appropriate hourly rate, in relation to an employee, is the amount of one week's pay divided by the number of normal working hours in a week for that employee when employed under the contract of employment in force on the day when the time is taken: reg 27(3). But where the number of normal working hours differs from week to week or over a longer period, the amount of one week's pay is to be divided instead by (1) the average number of normal working hours calculated by dividing by 12 the total number of the employee's normal working hours during the period of 12 weeks ending with the last complete week before the day on which the time off is taken; or (2) where the employee has not been employed for a sufficient period to enable the calculation to be made under head (1) above, a number which fairly represents the number of normal working hours in a week having regard to such of the considerations specified in reg 27(5) as are appropriate in the circumstances: reg 27(4). The considerations are (a) the average number of normal working hours in a week which the employee could expect in accordance with the terms of the contract; (b) the average number of normal working hours of other employees engaged in relevant comparable employment with the same employer: reg 27(5). The Employment Rights Act 1996 Pt XIV Ch II (ss 220–229) (a week's pay) (see PARA 143 et seq) applies in relation to this provision as it

applies in relation to s 62 (see PARA 1209): European Public Limited-Liability Company (Employee Involvement) (Great Britain) Regulations 2009, SI 2009/2401, reg 27(2).

9   European Public Limited-Liability Company (Employee Involvement) (Great Britain) Regulations 2009, SI 2009/2401, reg 27(6).

10 Ie under the European Public Limited-Liability Company (Employee Involvement) (Great Britain) Regulations 2009, SI 2009/2401, reg 26: see the text and notes 1–7.

11 Ie under the European Public Limited-Liability Company (Employee Involvement) (Great Britain) Regulations 2009, SI 2009/2401, reg 27(1): see the text and note 8.

12 See note 11.

13 European Public Limited-Liability Company (Employee Involvement) (Great Britain) Regulations 2009, SI 2009/2401, reg 27(7).

14 As to employment tribunals see PARA 1399 et seq.

15 Ie under the European Public Limited-Liability Company (Employee Involvement) (Great Britain) Regulations 2009, SI 2009/2401, reg 26: see the text and notes 1–7.

16 Ie under the European Public Limited-Liability Company (Employee Involvement) (Great Britain) Regulations 2009, SI 2009/2401, reg 27: see the text and notes 8–13.

17 European Public Limited-Liability Company (Employee Involvement) (Great Britain) Regulations 2009, SI 2009/2401, reg 28(1).

18 The European Public Limited-Liability Company (Employee Involvement) (Great Britain) Regulations 2009, SI 2009/2401, reg 28A (extension of time limits to facilitate conciliation before institution of proceedings: see notes 19–20) applies for these purposes: reg 28(2A) (added by SI 2014/386).

19 European Public Limited-Liability Company (Employee Involvement) (Great Britain) Regulations 2009, SI 2009/2401, reg 28(2)(a). In working out when the time limit set by reg 28(2)(a) expires the period beginning with the day after Day A and ending with Day B is not to be counted: reg 28A(2) (reg 28A added by SI 2014/386). If the time limit set by the European Public Limited-Liability Company (Employee Involvement) (Great Britain) Regulations 2009, SI 2009/2401, reg 28(2)(a) would (if not extended by this provision) expire during the period beginning with Day A and ending one month after Day B, the time limit expires instead at the end of that period: reg 28A(3) (as so added). For these purposes, Day A is the day on which the worker concerned complies with the requirement in the Employment Tribunals Act 1996 s 18A(1) (requirement to contact ACAS before instituting proceedings: see PARA 152) in relation to the matter in respect of which the proceedings are brought; and Day B is the day on which the worker concerned receives or, if earlier, is treated as receiving (by virtue of regulations made under s 18A(11)) the certificate issued under s 18A(4): European Public Limited-Liability Company (Employee Involvement) (Great Britain) Regulations 2009, SI 2009/2401, reg 28A(1) (as so added).

The provisions of the Employment Tribunals Act 1996 ss 18A–18B (conciliation) (see PARAS 152–153) apply in the case of matters which could be the subject of employment tribunal proceedings under the European Public Limited-Liability Company (Employee Involvement) (Great Britain) Regulations 2009, SI 2009/2401, reg 28, and the Employment Tribunals Act 1996 s 18C applies in the case of such proceedings themselves: see s 18(1)(y), (1A) (s 18(1)(y) substituted by SI 2014/431; the Employment Tribunals Act 1996 s 18(1A) added by the Enterprise and Regulatory Reform Act 2013 Sch 1 paras 2, 5(1), (7)).

20 European Public Limited-Liability Company (Employee Involvement) (Great Britain) Regulations 2009, SI 2009/2401, reg 28(2)(b). The power conferred on the employment tribunal by reg 28(2)(b) (see head (a) in the text) to extend the time limit set by reg 28(2)(a) (see head (b) in the text) is exercisable in relation to that time limit as extended by reg 28A (see note 19): reg 28A(4) (as added: see note 19). See also note 20.

21 European Public Limited-Liability Company (Employee Involvement) (Great Britain) Regulations 2009, SI 2009/2401, reg 28(3).

22 See note 16.

23 European Public Limited-Liability Company (Employee Involvement) (Great Britain) Regulations 2009, SI 2009/2401, reg 28(4).

24 See note 16.

25 European Public Limited-Liability Company (Employee Involvement) (Great Britain) Regulations 2009, SI 2009/2401, reg 28(5).

1333.   Unfair dismissal on grounds relating to employee involvement.   An employee[1] who is dismissed[2] is to be regarded as unfairly dismissed[3] if:

(1)   he is any of the following, namely:

(a)   a member of a special negotiating body[4];

(b)   a member of a representative body[5];

(c)   an information and consultation representative[6];

(d)   an employee member in a supervisory or administrative organ[7];

(e)   a candidate in an election in which any person elected will, on being elected, be such a member or a representative,

and the reason, or, if more than one, the principal reason, for the dismissal is a reason specified in heads (i) and (ii) below[8]; or

(2)   he is any employee, whether or not heads (a) to (e) above also apply, and the reason, or, if more than one, the principal reason, for the dismissal is a reason specified in heads (A) to (I) below[9].

The reasons mentioned in head (1) above are:

(i)   that the employee performed, or proposed to perform, any functions or activities as such a member, representative or candidate[10]; but this does not apply if the reason, or principal reason, for the dismissal is that, in the performance or purported performance of the employee's functions or activities, the employee has disclosed any information or document in breach of the statutory duty of confidentiality[11] and the case is not one where the employee reasonably believed the disclosure to be a 'protected disclosure'[12] within the meaning given by the Employment Rights Act 1996[13];

(ii)   that the employee, or a person acting on behalf of the employee, made or proposed to make a request to exercise an entitlement to time off work or remuneration for such time conferred[14] on the employee[15].

The reasons mentioned in head (2) above are that the employee did any of the following:

(A)   took, or proposed to take, any proceedings before an employment tribunal[16] to enforce any right conferred on him by the European Public Limited-Liability Company (Employee Involvement) (Great Britain) Regulations 2009[17];

(B)   exercised, or proposed to exercise, any entitlement to apply or complain to the Central Arbitration Committee (the 'CAC')[18] or the Employment Appeal Tribunal[19] conferred by those 2009 Regulations or exercised, or proposed to exercise, the right to appeal in connection with any rights conferred by those Regulations;

(C)   acted with a view to securing that a special negotiating body, a representative body or an information and consultation procedure did or did not come into existence;

(D)   indicated that the employee did or did not support the coming into existence of a special negotiating body, a representative body or an information and consultation procedure;

(E)   stood as a candidate in an election in which any person elected would, on being elected, be a member of a special negotiating body or a representative body, an employee member on a supervisory or administrative organ, or an information and consultation representative;

(F)   influenced, or sought to influence, by lawful means the way in which votes were to be cast by other employees in a ballot arranged under the 2009 Regulations;

(G)   voted in such a ballot;

(H)   expressed doubts, whether to a ballot supervisor or otherwise, as to whether such a ballot had been properly conducted;

(I) proposed to do, failed to do, or proposed to decline to do, any of the things mentioned in heads (D) to (H) above[20].

1 As to the meaning of 'employee' see PARA 1317 note 8.
2 'Dismissed' and 'dismissal', in relation to an employee, have the same meaning as in the Employment Rights Act 1996 Pt X (ss 94–134A) (see PARA 757 et seq): European Public Limited-Liability Company (Employee Involvement) (Great Britain) Regulations 2009, SI 2009/2401, reg 3(1). See also notes 10, 20.
3 Ie for the purposes of the Employment Rights Act 1996 Pt X.
4 As to the meaning of 'special negotiating body' see PARA 1317 note 10.
5 As to the meaning of 'representative body' see PARA 1325 note 7.
6 As to the meaning of 'information and consultation representative' see PARA 1325.
7 As to the structure of an SE, and supervisory or administrative organs, see PARA 1332 note 5; and as to the meaning of 'SE' see PARA 1317 note 5.
8 European Public Limited-Liability Company (Employee Involvement) (Great Britain) Regulations 2009, SI 2009/2401, reg 29(1)(a), (2).
9 European Public Limited-Liability Company (Employee Involvement) (Great Britain) Regulations 2009, SI 2009/2401, reg 29(1)(b), (5).
10 European Public Limited-Liability Company (Employee Involvement) (Great Britain) Regulations 2009, SI 2009/2401, reg 29(3)(a). Where a dismissal is unfair under reg 29(3), the qualifying period for unfair dismissal does not apply: see s 108(3)(k); and PARA 758 note 9.
11 Ie the duty in the European Public Limited-Liability Company (Employee Involvement) (Great Britain) Regulations 2009, SI 2009/2401, reg 24: see PARA 1330.
12 Ie a protected disclosure within the meaning given by the Employment Rights Act 1996 s 43A: see PARA 69.
13 European Public Limited-Liability Company (Employee Involvement) (Great Britain) Regulations 2009, SI 2009/2401, reg 29(4).
14 Ie conferred by the European Public Limited-Liability Company (Employee Involvement) (Great Britain) Regulations 2009, SI 2009/2401, reg 26 or reg 27: see PARA 1332.
15 See the European Public Limited-Liability Company (Employee Involvement) (Great Britain) Regulations 2009, SI 2009/2401, reg 29(3)(b). See note 10.
16 As to employment tribunals see PARA 1399 et seq.
17 Ie by the European Public Limited-Liability Company (Employee Involvement) (Great Britain) Regulations 2009, SI 2009/2401: see also PARAS 1317 et seq, 1334 et seq. It is immaterial for the purposes of reg 29(6)(a) (see head (A) in the text) whether or not the employee has the right, or whether or not the right has been infringed, but for reg 29(6)(a) to apply, the claim to the right and, if applicable, the claim that it has been infringed must be made in good faith: reg 29(7).
18 As to the Central Arbitration Committee see PARA 1226 et seq. As to proceedings before the Central Arbitration Committee see PARA 1335; and as to ACAS conciliation see PARA 1337.
19 As to the Employment Appeal Tribunal see PARA 1422 et seq.
20 European Public Limited-Liability Company (Employee Involvement) (Great Britain) Regulations 2009, SI 2009/2401, reg 29(6). Where a dismissal is unfair under reg 29(6), the qualifying period for unfair dismissal does not apply: see s 108(3)(k); and PARA 758 note 9.

1334. Right not to be subjected to detriment on grounds relating to employee involvement. An employee[1] who is any of the following:
(1) a member of a special negotiating body[2];
(2) a member of a representative body[3];
(3) an information and consultation representative[4];
(4) an employee member on a supervisory or administrative organ[5];
(5) a candidate in an election in which any person elected will, on being elected, be such a member or representative,
has the right not to be subjected to any detriment[6] by any act, or deliberate failure to act, by the employer, done on a ground specified in heads (a) to (b) below[7]. Those grounds are:
(a) that the employee performed or proposed to perform any functions or activities as such a member, representative or candidate[8]; but this does not apply if the ground for the subjection to detriment is that in the performance, or purported performance, of the employee's functions or

activities the employee has disclosed any information or document in breach of the statutory duty of confidentiality[9] and the case is not one where the employee reasonably believed the disclosure to be a 'protected disclosure'[10] within the meaning given by the Employment Rights Act 1996[11];

(b)   that the employee, or a person acting on behalf of the employee, made or proposed to make a request to exercise an entitlement to time off work or remuneration for such time conferred[12] on the employee[13].

Any employee, whether or not heads (1) to (5) above also apply, has the right not to be subjected to any detriment by any act, or deliberate failure to act, by the employer, done on a ground specified in heads (i) to (ix) below[14]. Those grounds are that the employee did any of the following:

(i)   took, or proposed to take, any proceedings before an employment tribunal[15] to enforce any right conferred on him by the European Public Limited-Liability Company (Employee Involvement) (Great Britain) Regulations 2009[16];

(ii)   exercised, or proposed to exercise, any entitlement to apply or complain to the central Arbitration Committee (the 'CAC')[17] or the Employment Appeal Tribunal[18] conferred by those Regulations or exercised, or proposed to exercise, the right to appeal in connection with any rights conferred by those Regulations;

(iii)   acted with a view to securing that a special negotiating body, a representative body or an information and consultation procedure did or did not come into existence;

(iv)   indicated that the employee did or did not support the coming into existence of a special negotiating body, a representative body or an information and consultation procedure;

(v)   stood as a candidate in an election in which any person elected would, on being elected, be a member of a special negotiating body or a representative body, an employee member on a supervisory or administrative organ, or an information and consultation representative;

(vi)   influenced, or sought to influence, by lawful means the way in which votes were to be cast by other employees in a ballot arranged under the 2009 Regulations;

(vii)   voted in such a ballot;

(viii) expressed doubts, whether to a ballot supervisor or otherwise, as to whether such a ballot had been properly conducted;

(ix)   proposed to do, failed to do, or proposed to decline to do, any of the things mentioned in heads (iv) to (viii) above[19].

An employee may present a complaint to an employment tribunal that he has been subjected to a detriment in contravention of the above provisions[20].

1   As to the meaning of 'employee' see PARA 1317 note 8.
2   As to the meaning of 'special negotiating body' see PARA 1317 note 10.
3   As to the meaning of 'representative body' see PARA 1325 note 7.
4   As to the meaning of 'information and consultation representative' see PARA 1325.
5   As to the structure of an SE, and supervisory or administrative organs, see PARA 1332 note 5; and as to the meaning of 'SE' see PARA 1317 note 5.
6   The European Public Limited-Liability Company (Employee Involvement) (Great Britain) Regulations 2009, SI 2009/2401, reg 31 (see the text and notes 1–5, 7–19) does not apply where the detriment in question amounts to dismissal: reg 31(8). As to the meaning of 'dismissal' see PARA 1333 note 2; and as to protection against unfair dismissal see PARA 1333.

7   European Public Limited-Liability Company (Employee Involvement) (Great Britain) Regulations 2009, SI 2009/2401, reg 31(1), (2).
8   European Public Limited-Liability Company (Employee Involvement) (Great Britain) Regulations 2009, SI 2009/2401, reg 31(3)(a).
9   Ie the duty in the European Public Limited-Liability Company (Employee Involvement) (Great Britain) Regulations 2009, SI 2009/2401, reg 24: see PARA 1330.
10   Ie a protected disclosure within the meaning given by the Employment Rights Act 1996 s 43A: see PARA 69.
11   European Public Limited-Liability Company (Employee Involvement) (Great Britain) Regulations 2009, SI 2009/2401, reg 31(4).
12   Ie conferred by the European Public Limited-Liability Company (Employee Involvement) (Great Britain) Regulations 2009, SI 2009/2401, reg 26 or reg 27: see PARA 1332.
13   European Public Limited-Liability Company (Employee Involvement) (Great Britain) Regulations 2009, SI 2009/2401, reg 31(3)(b).
14   European Public Limited-Liability Company (Employee Involvement) (Great Britain) Regulations 2009, SI 2009/2401, reg 31(1), (5).
15   As to employment tribunals see PARA 1399 et seq.
16   Ie by the European Public Limited-Liability Company (Employee Involvement) (Great Britain) Regulations 2009, SI 2009/2401: see also PARAS 1317 et seq, 1335 et seq. It is immaterial for the purposes of reg 31(6)(a) (see head (i) in the text), whether or not the employee has the right, or whether or not the right has been infringed, but for reg 31(6)(a) to apply, the claim to the right and, if applicable, the claim that it has been infringed must be made in good faith: reg 31(7).
17   As to the Central Arbitration Committee see PARA 1226 et seq. As to proceedings before the Central Arbitration Committee see PARA 1335; and as to ACAS conciliation see PARA 1337.
18   As to the Employment Appeal Tribunal see PARA 1422 et seq.
19   European Public Limited-Liability Company (Employee Involvement) (Great Britain) Regulations 2009, SI 2009/2401, reg 31(6).
20   European Public Limited-Liability Company (Employee Involvement) (Great Britain) Regulations 2009, SI 2009/2401, reg 32(1). The provisions of the Employment Rights Act 1996 s 48(2)–(4) (complaints to employment tribunals: see PARA 625) apply in relation to a complaint under the European Public Limited-Liability Company (Employee Involvement) (Great Britain) Regulations 2009, SI 2009/2401, reg 32 as they apply in relation to a complaint under the Employment Rights Act 1996 s 48 of that Act but taking references in those provisions to the employer as references to the employer within the meaning of the European Public Limited-Liability Company (Employee Involvement) (Great Britain) Regulations 2009, SI 2009/2401, reg 31(1): reg 32(2). The provisions of the Employment Rights Act 1996 s 49(1)–(5) (remedies: see PARA 626) apply in relation to a complaint under the European Public Limited-Liability Company (Employee Involvement) (Great Britain) Regulations 2009, SI 2009/2401, reg 32: reg 32(3).

     The provisions of the Employment Tribunals Act 1996 ss 18A–18B (conciliation) (see PARAS 152–153) apply in the case of matters which could be the subject of employment tribunal proceedings under the European Public Limited-Liability Company (Employee Involvement) (Great Britain) Regulations 2009, SI 2009/2401, reg 32, and the Employment Tribunals Act 1996 s 18C applies in the case of such proceedings themselves: see s 18(1)(y), (1A) (s 18(1)(y) substituted by SI 2014/431; the Employment Tribunals Act 1996 s 18(1A) added by the Enterprise and Regulatory Reform Act 2013 Sch 1 paras 2, 5(1), (7)).

H. JURISDICTION AND PROCEDURAL REQUIREMENTS; CONCILIATION

1335. CAC proceedings under the European Public Limited-Liability Company (Employee Involvement) (Great Britain) Regulations 2009. Where under the European Public Limited-Liability Company (Employee Involvement) (Great Britain) Regulations 2009[1] a person presents a complaint or makes an application to the Central Arbitration Committee (the 'CAC')[2], the complaint or application must be in writing and in such form as the CAC may require[3]. In its consideration of a complaint or application under those Regulations, the CAC must make such inquiries as it sees fit, and give any person whom it considers has a proper interest in the complaint or application an opportunity to be heard[4].

     Where the participating company[5], concerned subsidiary or establishment[6] or the SE[7] has its registered office in England and Wales, a declaration made by the

CAC under the 2009 Regulations may be relied on as if it were a declaration or order made by the High Court in England and Wales, and an order made by the CAC under those Regulations may be enforced in the same way as an order of the High Court in England and Wales[8].

A declaration or order made by the CAC under the 2009 Regulations must be in writing and state the reasons for the CAC's findings[9]. An appeal lies to the Employment Appeal Tribunal[10] on any question of law arising from any declaration or order of, or arising in any proceedings before, the CAC under the 2009 Regulations[11].

1 Ie the European Public Limited-Liability Company (Employee Involvement) (Great Britain) Regulations 2009, SI 2009/2401: see PARA 1317 et seq.
2 As to the Central Arbitration Committee see PARA 1226 et seq.
3 European Public Limited-Liability Company (Employee Involvement) (Great Britain) Regulations 2009, SI 2009/2401, reg 34(1).
4 European Public Limited-Liability Company (Employee Involvement) (Great Britain) Regulations 2009, SI 2009/2401, reg 34(2).
5 As to the meaning of 'participating company' see PARA 1317 note 6.
6 As to the meanings of 'concerned subsidiary' and 'concerned establishment' see PARA 1317 note 13.
7 As to the meaning of 'SE' see PARA 1317 note 5.
8 European Public Limited-Liability Company (Employee Involvement) (Great Britain) Regulations 2009, SI 2009/2401, reg 34(3). Where a participating company or concerned subsidiary or an SE has its registered office in Scotland a declaration or order made by the CAC under the 2009 Regulations may be relied on as if it were a declaration or order made by the Court of Session, and an order made by the CAC under those Regulations may be enforced in the same way as an order of the Court of Session: reg 34(4).
9 European Public Limited-Liability Company (Employee Involvement) (Great Britain) Regulations 2009, SI 2009/2401, reg 34(5).
10 As to the Employment Appeal Tribunal see PARA 1422 et seq. See also PARA 1336.
11 European Public Limited-Liability Company (Employee Involvement) (Great Britain) Regulations 2009, SI 2009/2401, reg 34(6).

1336. Employment Appeal Tribunal proceedings under the European Public Limited-Liability Company (Employee Involvement) (Great Britain) Regulations 2009. Except for certain appeals on questions of law[1], any proceedings before the Employment Appeal Tribunal[2] under the European Public Limited-Liability Company (Employee Involvement) (Great Britain) Regulations 2009[3] must, where the registered office of the participating company[4], concerned subsidiary[5] or the SE[6] is situated in England and Wales, be held in England and Wales[7].

1 Ie other than appeals under the Employment Tribunals Act 1996 s 21(1)(w) (appeals from employment tribunals on questions of law: see PARA 1428).
2 As to the Employment Appeal Tribunal see PARA 1422 et seq.
3 Ie the European Public Limited-Liability Company (Employee Involvement) (Great Britain) Regulations 2009, SI 2009/2401: see PARA 1317 et seq.
4 As to the meaning of 'participating company' see PARA 1317 note 6.
5 As to the meaning of 'concerned subsidiary' see PARA 1317 note 13.
6 As to the meaning of 'SE' see PARA 1317 note 5.
7 European Public Limited-Liability Company (Employee Involvement) (Great Britain) Regulations 2009, SI 2009/2401, reg 35(1)(a). Where the registered office of the participating company, concerned subsidiary or the SE is situated in Scotland, such proceedings must be held in Scotland: reg 35(1)(b).

1337. Advisory, Conciliation and Arbitration Service assistance under the European Public Limited-Liability Company (Employee Involvement) (Great Britain) Regulations 2009. If, on receipt of an application or complaint under the European Public Limited-Liability Company (Employee Involvement) (Great

Britain) Regulations 2009[1], the Central Arbitration Committee (the 'CAC')[2] is of the opinion that it is reasonably likely to be settled by conciliation, it must refer the application or complaint to the Advisory, Conciliation and Arbitration Service ('ACAS')[3], and notify the applicant or complainant and any persons whom it considers have a proper interest in the application or complaint accordingly[4]. ACAS must seek to promote a settlement of the matter[5].

If an application or complaint so referred is not settled or withdrawn, and ACAS is of the opinion that further attempts at conciliation are unlikely to result in a settlement, ACAS must inform the CAC of that opinion[6].

If the application or complaint is not referred to ACAS, or it is so referred, but ACAS informs the CAC of its opinion that further attempts at conciliation are unlikely to result in a settlement, the CAC must proceed to hear and determine the application or complaint[7].

1 Ie the European Public Limited-Liability Company (Employee Involvement) (Great Britain) Regulations 2009, SI 2009/2401: see PARA 1317 et seq.
2 As to the Central Arbitration Committee see PARA 1226 et seq; and as to proceedings before the Central Arbitration Committee see PARA 1335.
3 As to ACAS see PARA 1213 et seq.
4 European Public Limited-Liability Company (Employee Involvement) (Great Britain) Regulations 2009, SI 2009/2401, reg 37(1).
5 European Public Limited-Liability Company (Employee Involvement) (Great Britain) Regulations 2009, SI 2009/2401, reg 37(1).
6 European Public Limited-Liability Company (Employee Involvement) (Great Britain) Regulations 2009, SI 2009/2401, reg 37(2).
7 European Public Limited-Liability Company (Employee Involvement) (Great Britain) Regulations 2009, SI 2009/2401, reg 37(3).

(v) Employee Involvement in the European Co-operative Society

1338. Involvement of employees in the European Co-operative Society. The European Co-operative Society (Involvement of Employees) Regulations 2006[1], which came into force on 18 August 2006[2], have been made for the purposes of implementing a Council Directive[3] supplementing the Statute for a European Co-operative Society ('SCE')[4] with regard to the involvement of employees[5]. The SCE is a less significant entity so far as England and Wales are concerned than the SE[6] so the 2006 Regulations are not set out in full in this work.

Part 2 of the 2006 Regulations[7] sets out details of the participating individuals and legal entities and the special negotiating body which should negotiate the employee involvement agreement. It makes provision for the circumstances in which the Regulations apply[8] and the exemption of certain formations below a de minimis threshold from the provisions of the Regulations[9]. There is also provision for the Regulations to apply if a formerly exempt SCE increases in size to fall above the threshold or a request is made by a sufficient proportion of the workforce[10]. A duty is imposed on participating individuals or legal entities involved in forming an SCE to provide information to the employees or their representatives, who may complain to the Central Arbitration Committee (the 'CAC')[11] if such information is not provided correctly[12]. The function of the special negotiating body is defined as is its composition[13], and there is provision for a right of complaint[14] if the special negotiating body is not established in accordance with the prescribed requirements[15].

Part 3 of the 2006 Regulations[16] addresses the election or appointment of UK members of the special negotiating body. It sets out details of the arrangements for and conduct of the ballot by which members of the body should be elected[17] and provides that in certain circumstances members be appointed by a consultative committee instead of being elected by a ballot[18]. There is a right of complaint to the CAC on the grounds that the consultative committee is not correctly constituted[19]. Part 3 also sets out when an individual is to be treated as an employee representative after being elected or appointed[20].

Part 4 of the 2006 Regulations[21] deals with negotiation of the employee involvement agreement. It includes the timing of the requirement to negotiate the agreement[22] and the content and scope of the agreement[23]. Provision is made for the decision-making procedure of the special negotiating body[24] and the consequences of a decision not to open or to terminate negotiations with the participating individuals or legal entities[25]. Decisions of the special negotiating body may be subject to complaint to the CAC[26].

Part 5 of the 2006 Regulations[27] sets out standard rules on employee involvement which apply either if the parties so agree or have reached the end of the negotiation period without an agreement being reached and certain other criteria apply. Standard rules on participation will apply in certain circumstances[28].

Part 6 of the 2006 Regulations[29] deals with compliance and enforcement. Complaints may be brought before the CAC where the terms of the employee involvement agreement or the information and consultation provisions have not been complied with and if the complaint is well founded a penalty notice may be issued by the Employment Appeal Tribunal[30]. A complaint may also be brought over the misuse of procedures[31].

Part 7 of the 2006 Regulations[32] deals with confidential information and provides that it is a breach of statutory duty for a recipient of such information to disclose it except in accordance with the terms on which it was disclosed to him[33]. There is also provision for the withholding of information in certain circumstances[34].

Part 8 of the 2006 Regulations[35] covers protection for members of the special negotiating body and other representatives. Provision is made for rights to time off and remuneration for that time[36], protection from unfair dismissal[37] and protection from detriment[38] and for recourse to an employment tribunal[39] for breach of such rights.

Part 9 of the 2006 Regulations[40] deals with miscellaneous provisions and covers matters relating to CAC proceedings[41], the Employment Appeal Tribunal[42] and the Advisory, Conciliation and Arbitration Service ('ACAS')[43].There are also restrictions on contracting out of the provisions of the Regulations[44] and provision is also made for the interaction with other existing rights[45].

1 Ie the European Co-operative Society (Involvement of Employees) Regulations 2006, SI 2006/2059: see the text and notes 2–45.

2 European Co-operative Society (Involvement of Employees) Regulations 2006, SI 2006/2059, reg 1(2).

3 Ie Council Directive (EC) 2003/72 (OJ L207, 18.8.2003, p 25).

4 Ie Council Regulation (EC) 1435/2003 (OJ L207, 18.8.2003, p 1) on the Statute for a European Cooperative Society ('SCE') (corrected in OJ L49, 17.2.2007 p 35), for the purposes of which the European Co-operative Society Regulations 2006, SI 2006/2078, have been made: see COMPANIES vol 14 (2009) PARA 22.

5 The European Co-operative Society (Involvement of Employees) Regulations 2006, SI 2006/2059, were made by the Secretary of State as a Minister designated for the purposes of the European Communities Act 1972 s 2(2) in respect of measures relating to employment rights and duties: see CONSTITUTIONAL AND ADMINISTRATIVE LAW vol 20 (2014) PARA 156. See further EUROPEAN UNION.

6 As to the meaning of 'SE' see PARA 1317 note 5; and as to employee involvement in SEs see the European Public Limited-Liability Company (Employee Involvement) (Great Britain) Regulations 2009, SI 2009/2401; and PARA 1317 et seq.

7 Ie the European Co-operative Society (Involvement of Employees) Regulations 2006, SI 2006/2059, Pt 2 (regs 4–11, Sch 1) (amended by SI 2010/93).

8 See the European Co-operative Society (Involvement of Employees) Regulations 2006, SI 2006/2059, reg 4.

9 See the European Co-operative Society (Involvement of Employees) Regulations 2006, SI 2006/2059, reg 5.

10 See the European Co-operative Society (Involvement of Employees) Regulations 2006, SI 2006/2059, reg 6.

11 As to the Central Arbitration Committee see PARA 1226 et seq.

12 See the European Co-operative Society (Involvement of Employees) Regulations 2006, SI 2006/2059, regs 7, 8 (amended by SI 2010/93).

13 See the European Co-operative Society (Involvement of Employees) Regulations 2006, SI 2006/2059, regs 9, 10.

14 See the European Co-operative Society (Involvement of Employees) Regulations 2006, SI 2006/2059, reg 11.

15 As to the prescribed requirements see the European Co-operative Society (Involvement of Employees) Regulations 2006, SI 2006/2059, reg 10.

16 Ie the European Co-operative Society (Involvement of Employees) Regulations 2006, SI 2006/2059, Pt 3 (regs 12–15).

17 See the European Co-operative Society (Involvement of Employees) Regulations 2006, SI 2006/2059, regs 12, 13.

18 See the European Co-operative Society (Involvement of Employees) Regulations 2006, SI 2006/2059, reg 14.

19 See the European Co-operative Society (Involvement of Employees) Regulations 2006, SI 2006/2059, reg 14.

20 See the European Co-operative Society (Involvement of Employees) Regulations 2006, SI 2006/2059, reg 15.

21 Ie the European Co-operative Society (Involvement of Employees) Regulations 2006, SI 2006/2059, Pt 4 (regs 16–20) (amended by SI 2010/93).

22 See the European Co-operative Society (Involvement of Employees) Regulations 2006, SI 2006/2059, reg 16.

23 See the European Co-operative Society (Involvement of Employees) Regulations 2006, SI 2006/2059, reg 17 (amended by SI 2010/93).

24 See the European Co-operative Society (Involvement of Employees) Regulations 2006, SI 2006/2059, reg 18.

25 See the European Co-operative Society (Involvement of Employees) Regulations 2006, SI 2006/2059, reg 19.

26 See the European Co-operative Society (Involvement of Employees) Regulations 2006, SI 2006/2059, reg 20.

27 Ie the European Co-operative Society (Involvement of Employees) Regulations 2006, SI 2006/2059, Pt 5 (reg 21, Sch 2 (amended by SI 2010/93)).

28 See the European Co-operative Society (Involvement of Employees) Regulations 2006, SI 2006/2059, Sch 2 Pt 3 (para 7).

29 Ie the European Co-operative Society (Involvement of Employees) Regulations 2006, SI 2006/2059, Pt 6 (regs 22–25).

30 See the European Co-operative Society (Involvement of Employees) Regulations 2006, SI 2006/2059, regs 22, 23. As to the Employment Appeal Tribunal see PARA 1422 et seq.

31 See the European Co-operative Society (Involvement of Employees) Regulations 2006, SI 2006/2059, reg 24.

32 Ie the European Co-operative Society (Involvement of Employees) Regulations 2006, SI 2006/2059, Pt 7 (regs 26, 27).

33 See the European Co-operative Society (Involvement of Employees) Regulations 2006, SI 2006/2059, reg 26.

34 See the European Co-operative Society (Involvement of Employees) Regulations 2006, SI 2006/2059, reg 27.

35 Ie the European Co-operative Society (Involvement of Employees) Regulations 2006, SI 2006/2059, Pt 8 (regs 28–35 (amended by SI 2014/386)). See also the Employment Tribunals Act 1996 s 18(1)(u), (1A) (s 18(1)(u) substituted by SI 2014/431; the Employment Tribunals Act 1996 s 18(1A) added by the Enterprise and Regulatory Reform Act 2013 Sch 1 paras 2, 5(1), (7)).

36 See the European Co-operative Society (Involvement of Employees) Regulations 2006, SI 2006/2059, regs 28, 29.
37 See the European Co-operative Society (Involvement of Employees) Regulations 2006, SI 2006/2059, reg 31. Where a dismissal is unfair under reg 31(3) or 31(6), the qualifying period for unfair dismissal does not apply: see s 108(3)(o); and PARA 758 note 9.
38 See the European Co-operative Society (Involvement of Employees) Regulations 2006, SI 2006/2059, reg 33.
39 As to employment tribunals see PARA 1399 et seq.
40 Ie the European Co-operative Society (Involvement of Employees) Regulations 2006, SI 2006/2059, Pt 9 (regs 36–43 (amended by SI 2009/3348; SI 2013/1956; SI 2014/386; SI 2014/431)).
41 See the European Co-operative Society (Involvement of Employees) Regulations 2006, SI 2006/2059, reg 36.
42 See the European Co-operative Society (Involvement of Employees) Regulations 2006, SI 2006/2059, regs 37, 38.
43 See the European Co-operative Society (Involvement of Employees) Regulations 2006, SI 2006/2059, reg 39. As to ACAS see PARA 1213 et seq.
44 See the European Co-operative Society (Involvement of Employees) Regulations 2006, SI 2006/2059, regs 40, 41 (as amended: see note 40).
45 See the European Co-operative Society (Involvement of Employees) Regulations 2006, SI 2006/2059, reg 43.

11. INDUSTRIAL ACTION

(1) THE RIGHT TO TAKE INDUSTRIAL ACTION

1339. The right to strike or take part in other industrial action. There is no unqualified right to strike as such in English law[1], nor to take part in other industrial action[2] short of a strike. Industrial action may involve the commission of criminal offences[3], and participation in industrial action is likely to constitute a breach of contract on the part of the individual workers involved[4], and may lead to summary dismissal, damages, the withholding of wages, and the loss of statutory employment rights and welfare benefits[5]. In certain circumstances, however, the dismissal of an employee for taking part in official industrial action will be automatically unfair[6]. A lockout[7] is likely to constitute a breach of contract on the part of the employer, unless the employer first gives due notice to terminate the contracts of the workers concerned[8].

Industrial action also potentially involves the commission of several torts[9], although acts in contemplation or furtherance of a trade dispute[10] enjoy statutory immunity against liability for certain economic torts[11]. The protection of the statutory immunities is, however, excluded in certain circumstances[12].

1 Under the Human Rights Act 1998 Sch 1 Pt I art 11(1), everyone has the right to freedom of peaceful assembly and to freedom of association with others, including the right to form and to join trade unions for the protection of his interests (see **RIGHTS AND FREEDOMS** vol 88A (2013) PARA 461) but this does not explicitly confer a right to strike (*Ministry of Justice v Prison Officers Association* [2008] EWHC 239 (QB), [2008] ICR 702, [2008] IRLR 380). Further, lawful restrictions may be imposed on the exercise of the rights in the Human Rights Act 1998 Sch 1 Pt I art 11(1) by members of the armed forces, of the police or of the administration of the state: see art 11(2); and **RIGHTS AND FREEDOMS** vol 88A (2013) PARA 461. As to the meaning of 'strike' see PARA 1340. As to art 11 see also Application 31045/10 *National Union of Rail, Maritime and Transport Workers v United Kingdom* [2014] IRLR 467, ECtHR, cited in PARAS 1367 note 13, 1372 note 11.
2 As to the meaning of 'other industrial action' see PARA 1340.
3 See PARA 1341.
4 See PARA 1342.
5 See PARAS 1345–1358.
6 See PARA 1352.
7 As to the meaning of 'lockout' see PARA 1340.
8 See PARA 1342.
9 See PARA 1343.
10 See PARA 1359 et seq.
11 See PARA 1363.
12 See PARAS 1365–1382.

1340. Meanings of 'strike', 'lockout' and 'other industrial action'. There is no single statutory definition of the terms 'strike', 'lockout' and 'other industrial action', applicable in all circumstances. For the purposes of certain statutory provisions concerning industrial action[1], 'strike' means any concerted stoppage of work[2]. 'Strike' and 'lockout' are defined for the purposes of the statutory provisions relating to continuity of employment and redundancy[3], but, while those definitions may afford guidance, they are not applicable per se in other contexts[4]. There is no statutory definition of 'other industrial action'[5]. The terms are to be given their natural meaning, and this is essentially a question of fact, not of law[6].

'Strike' has been defined as a concerted stoppage of work done with a view to improving wages or conditions or giving vent to a grievance or making a protest about something or other or supporting or sympathising with other workers in such endeavour and is distinct from a stoppage which is brought about by an external event such as a bomb scare or by apprehension of danger[7]; and such concerted action may also be central to other industrial action, especially where the action is such that an individual could have undertaken it without breach of contract[8]. 'Strike' encompasses any refusal by employees to work for periods of time for which they are employed to work, provided that it is concerted, that is to say, mutually planned; and it is not restricted to stoppages of all work but covers stoppages of particular days and particular hours[9].

Whether the employees, or, in the case of a lockout, the employer, are or is acting in breach of contract may be relevant, but is not a legal requirement[10]; this point is of particular significance in relation to 'other industrial action' which, being undefined and not tied to a definable breach of employment contracts, is potentially open-ended, and has been held to cover such activities as a refusal to work voluntary overtime, even though under no contractual obligation to work it[11], a go-slow[12], a work-to-rule[13] and a refusal to operate new machinery[14]. 'Other industrial action' does not, however, include activities more properly defined as 'trade union activities' as opposed to industrial action[15].

1 Ie for the purposes of the Trade Union and Labour Relations (Consolidation) Act 1992 Pt V (ss 219–246), except for the purposes of s 229(2) (see note 2): see PARA 1348 et seq.

2 Trade Union and Labour Relations (Consolidation) Act 1992 s 246 (definition amended by the Employment Relations Act 1999 Sch 3 paras 1, 6(1), (4)). For the purposes of the Trade Union and Labour Relations (Consolidation) Act 1992 s 229(2) (voting paper) (see PARA 1376) an overtime ban and a call-out ban constitute industrial action short of a strike: s 229(2A) (added by the Employment Relations Act 1999 Sch 3 paras 1, 6(1), (2)). In *Connex South Eastern Ltd v National Union of Rail, Maritime and Transport Workers* [1999] IRLR 249, CA, a ban on overtime working and on rest-day working was held to constitute a concerted stoppage of work and, therefore, a 'strike' for the purposes of the provisions on industrial action ballots (see PARA 1370 et seq); but see now the Trade Union and Labour Relations (Consolidation) Act 1992 s 229(2A); and also PARA 1376 note 8. See also *British Telecommunications plc v Communication Workers Union* [2003] EWHC 937 (QB), [2004] IRLR 58 (trade union's mistaken belief that 'strike action' included all forms of withdrawal of labour unlikely to render strike invalid).

3 See the Employment Rights Act 1996 s 235(4), (5); and PARA 134 notes 4, 7.

4 *Express & Star Ltd v Bunday* [1988] ICR 379, [1987] IRLR 422, CA; *McCormick v Horsepower Ltd* [1980] ICR 278, [1980] IRLR 182, EAT (affd on other grounds [1981] 2 All ER 746, [1981] ICR 535, CA); *Rasool v Hepworth Pipe Co Ltd* [1980] ICR 494, sub nom *Rasool v Hepworth Pipe Co Ltd (No 2)* [1980] IRLR 137, EAT. *Fisher v York Trailer Co Ltd* [1979] ICR 834, [1979] IRLR 385, EAT is no longer good law on this point.

5 As to the meaning of 'other industrial action' in the context of the statutory right to a ballot before such action see the Trade Union and Labour Relations (Consolidation) Act 1992 s 62(6); and PARA 1025 note 5.

6 *Coates v Modern Methods and Materials Ltd* [1983] QB 192, [1982] ICR 763, CA; *Power Packing Casemakers Ltd v Faust* [1983] QB 471, [1983] ICR 292, CA; *Express & Star Ltd v Bunday* [1988] ICR 379, [1987] IRLR 422, CA. Cf the criticism of this approach in *Naylor v Orton & Smith Ltd* [1983] ICR 665 at 673, [1983] IRLR 233 at 237, EAT per Browne-Wilkinson P. Cf *Knowles v Fire Brigades Union* [1996] 4 All ER 653, [1997] ICR 595, CA (the question of what constitutes industrial action for the purposes of the Trade Union and Labour Relations (Consolidation) Act 1992 s 65(2)(a) is a mixed question of fact and law, to be judged in the context of the 1992 Act, and requires an examination of all the circumstances, including the contracts of employment of the employees and whether any breach of, or departure from, the terms of the contract is involved, the effect on the employer of what is done or omitted and the object which the union or the employees seek to achieve: see PARA 1030).

7 *Tramp Shipping Corpn v Greenwich Marine Inc* [1975] 2 All ER 989 at 991, 992, [1975] ICR 261 at 266, CA per Lord Denning MR. See also *Coates v Modern Methods and Materials Ltd* [1983] QB 192, [1982] ICR 763, CA obiter per Eveleigh LJ.

8 *Power Packing Casemakers Ltd v Faust* [1983] QB 471, [1983] ICR 292, CA.

9 *Connex South Eastern Ltd v National Union of Rail, Maritime and Transport Workers* [1999] IRLR 249, CA; but see note 2.

10 *Power Packing Casemakers Ltd v Faust* [1983] QB 471, [1983] ICR 292, CA; *Bolton Roadways Ltd v Edwards* [1987] IRLR 392, EAT; *Express & Star Ltd v Bunday* [1988] ICR 379, [1987] IRLR 422, CA.
11 *Power Packing Casemakers Ltd v Faust* [1983] QB 471, [1983] ICR 292, CA.
12 *Drew v St Edmundsbury Borough Council* [1980] ICR 513, [1980] IRLR 459, EAT.
13 *Secretary of State for Employment v Associated Society of Locomotive Engineers and Firemen (No 2)* [1972] 2 QB 455, [1972] ICR 19, CA.
14 *Thompson v Eaton Ltd* [1976] ICR 336, [1976] IRLR 308, EAT.
15 *Rasool v Hepworth Pipe Co Ltd* [1980] ICR 494, sub nom *Rasool v Hepworth Pipe Co Ltd (No 2)* [1980] IRLR 137, EAT (unauthorised union meeting in working hours not, on the facts, industrial action).

(2) POTENTIAL LIABILITIES FOR INDUSTRIAL ACTION

1341. Criminal liability for industrial action. Industrial action may constitute a criminal conspiracy[1]. Criminal offences may also be committed where industrial action involves the armed forces[2], the police[3], merchant seamen[4], postal or telecommunications workers[5] or aliens[6]. It is also an offence for any person wilfully and maliciously to break a contract of service or hiring, knowing or having reasonable cause to believe that the probable consequence of his doing so, either alone or in combination with others, will be to endanger human life or cause serious bodily injury, or to expose valuable property, whether real or personal, to destruction or serious injury[7]. Picketing may also involve the commission of a criminal offence[8].

1 Conspiracy to commit a crime is a statutory offence (see the Criminal Law Act 1977 s 1(1); and CRIMINAL LAW vol 25 (2010) PARA 74 et seq), but the statutory offence is not committed where the act in question is done in contemplation or furtherance of a trade dispute and constitutes no more than a summary offence not punishable with imprisonment: see the Trade Union and Labour Relations (Consolidation) Act 1992 s 242; and PARA 1364. As to the offence of conspiracy generally see CRIMINAL LAW vol 25 (2010) PARA 73 et seq.
2 See PARA 1391.
3 See PARA 1392.
4 See PARA 1393.
5 See PARA 1394.
6 See PARA 1395.
7 See PARA 1396.
8 See PARA 1383.

1342. Liability for industrial action in contract. Industrial action does not necessarily involve a breach of contract on the part of the workers concerned; it is a question to be decided by considering the terms of the particular contract[1] and the form which the industrial action takes. A worker may lawfully strike[2] by first giving due notice[3] to terminate his contract[4]. If he does not do so, the strike is likely to be[5] in breach of his contract[6] and hence unlawful[7]. An overtime ban is likely to be a breach of contract if the overtime is compulsory[8]; a refusal to handle goods will also usually involve breaches of contract[9]; and a withdrawal of co-operation[10], a work-to-rule[11] or a go-slow[12] may be a breach of contract. In such cases it is irrelevant that due notice is given of the intention to take industrial action[13].

A lockout[14] will not involve a breach of contract if the employer first gives due notice[15] to terminate the contracts of the workers concerned. Otherwise a lockout is likely to be[16] a breach of contract and hence unlawful[17].

1 Ie including the implied terms: *British Telecommunications plc v Ticehurst* [1992] ICR 383, sub nom *Ticehurst and Thompson v British Telecommunications plc* [1992] IRLR 219, CA (implied duty of faithful service).

2   As to the meaning of 'strike' see PARA 1340.

3   The length of notice required is that specified by the contract, subject, where relevant, to a
statutory minimum notice period: see the Employment Rights Act 1996 s 86; and PARA 735 et
seq. Where due notice is given, but the notice is not expressly notice to terminate (eg 'there will
be a withdrawal of labour'), the older authorities apparently treat the notice as implied notice of
termination and the strike as lawful: *Allen v Flood* [1898] AC 1, HL; *Smithies v National
Association of Operative Plasterers* [1909] 1 KB 310, CA; *Santen v Busnach* (1913) 29 TLR
214, CA; *White v Riley* [1921] 1 Ch 1, CA. Subsequent authorities have tended to treat a strike
in such circumstances as a breach of contract, and the notice as a notice of breach: *Rookes v
Barnard* [1963] 1 QB 623, [1962] 2 All ER 579, CA per Donovan LJ (on appeal [1964] AC
1129 at 1204, [1964] 1 All ER 367 at 396, HL per Lord Devlin); *JT Stratford & Son Ltd v
Lindley* [1965] AC 269 at 285, [1964] 2 All ER 209 at 217, CA per Lord Denning MR (revsd
[1965] AC 307, [1964] 3 All ER 102, HL); *Simmons v Hoover Ltd* [1977] QB 284, [1977] ICR
61, EAT; *Wilkins v Cantrell and Cochrane (GB) Ltd* [1978] IRLR 483, EAT; *Haddow v Inner
London Education Authority* [1979] ICR 202, EAT. More recently it has been suggested that
whether an ambiguous strike notice is to be treated as notice of breach or as implied notice to
terminate is a question of construction: *Boxfoldia Ltd v National Graphical Association (1982)*
[1988] ICR 752, [1988] IRLR 383 per Saville J. As to the suggestion that strike notice suspends
a contract of employment (*Morgan v Fry* [1968] 2 QB 710 at 728, [1968] 3 All ER 452 at
458, CA per Lord Denning MR) see *Simmons v Hoover Ltd* [1977] QB 284, [1977] ICR
61, EAT.

4   *Gaskell v Lancashire and Cheshire Miners' Federation* (1912) 28 TLR 518, CA; *Russell v
Amalgamated Society of Carpenters and Joiners* [1912] AC 421, HL.

5   Whether a strike is in breach of contract depends on the terms of the contract and the
circumstances. A strike without notice or on short notice will be a breach of contract (*Denaby
and Cadeby Main Collieries Ltd v Yorkshire Miners' Association* [1906] AC 384, HL; *Smithies
v National Association of Operative Plasterers* [1909] 1 KB 310, CA) unless, presumably, the
workers have a right to quit without notice by reason of the employer's prior breach of contract
(perhaps if he has locked them out). A stoppage limited in time or extent is a breach of contract:
South Wales Miners' Federation v Glamorgan Coal Co Ltd [1905] AC 239, HL (one-day strike);
Bowes & Partners v Press [1894] 1 QB 202, CA (refusal to work alongside non-unionist).

6   A strike in breach of contract does not of itself terminate the contract, but entitles the employer
to dismiss without notice: *Simmons v Hoover Ltd* [1977] QB 284, [1977] ICR 61, EAT. As to
the effect of industrial action on the contract of employment see PARAS 1345–1348.

7   As to the effect of industrial action on statutory employment rights and on welfare benefits see
PARAS 1349–1358.

8   *Camden Exhibition and Display Ltd v Lynott* [1966] 1 QB 555, [1965] 3 All ER 28, CA; *Gorse
v Durham County Council* [1971] 2 All ER 666, [1971] 1 WLR 775; *Solihull Metropolitan
Borough v National Union of Teachers* [1985] IRLR 211. Quaere whether a refusal to work
voluntary (ie non-contractual) overtime might constitute a breach of the implied duty of faithful
service if done with a disruptive purpose: see *British Telecommunications plc v Ticehurst* [1992]
ICR 383, sub nom *Ticehurst and Thompson v British Telecommunications plc* [1992] IRLR
219, CA.

9   *JT Stratford & Son Ltd v Lindley* [1965] AC 269, [1964] 3 All ER 102, HL; *Torquay
Hotel Co Ltd v Cousins* [1969] 2 Ch 106, [1969] 1 All ER 522, CA; *Heatons Transport
(St Helens) Ltd v Transport and General Workers' Union* [1973] AC 15, [1972] ICR 308, HL;
Express Newspapers Ltd v McShane [1980] AC 672, [1980] ICR 42, HL; *Marina Shipping Ltd
v Laughton* [1982] QB 1127, [1982] ICR 215, CA; *Merkur Island Shipping Corpn v Laughton*
[1983] 2 AC 570, [1983] ICR 490, HL. There is no breach if the workers are never in fact asked
to handle the 'black' goods: *DC Thompson & Co Ltd v Deakin* [1952] Ch 646, [1952] 2 All ER
361, CA. It seems that there would be no breach if there were a term in the contract of
employment that the workers be not required to handle 'black' items: *Hadmor Productions Ltd
v Hamilton* [1983] 1 AC 191, [1982] ICR 114, HL. As to the restriction of the statutory
immunities in cases of secondary action see PARA 1367.

10   *British Telecommunications plc v Ticehurst* [1992] ICR 383, sub nom *Ticehurst and Thompson
v British Telecommunications plc* [1992] IRLR 219, CA (cited in note 8); *Secretary of State for
Employment v Associated Society of Locomotive Engineers and Firemen (No 2)* [1972] 2 QB
455, [1972] 2 All ER 949, CA; *Sim v Rotherham Metropolitan Borough Council* [1987]
Ch 216, [1986] ICR 897.

11   *Secretary of State for Employment v Associated Society of Locomotive Engineers and Firemen
(No 2)* [1972] 2 QB 455, [1972] 2 All ER 949, CA; cf *British Telecommunications plc v
Ticehurst* [1992] ICR 383, sub nom *Ticehurst and Thompson v British Telecommunications plc*
[1992] IRLR 219, CA (cited in note 8).

12 *Secretary of State for Employment v Associated Society of Locomotive Engineers and Firemen (No 2)* [1972] 2 QB 455, [1972] 2 All ER 949, CA; *Chappell v Times Newspapers Ltd* [1975] 2 All ER 233, [1975] ICR 145, CA; *Drew v St Edmundsbury Borough Council* [1980] ICR 513, [1980] IRLR 459, EAT; *Miles v Wakefield Metropolitan District Council* [1987] AC 539, [1987] ICR 368, HL; *General Engineering Services Ltd v Kingston and St Andrew Corpn* [1988] 3 All ER 867, [1989] ICR 88, PC (cf *British Telecommunications plc v Ticehurst* [1992] ICR 383, sub nom *Ticehurst and Thompson v British Telecommunications plc* [1992] IRLR 219, CA (cited in note 8)).

13 See notes 3, 5.

14 As to the meaning of 'lockout' see PARA 1340.

15 See note 3. The employer may lawfully dismiss workers without notice if they have repudiated their contracts, e g by going on strike: see PARA 1345.

16 Whether a lockout is a breach of contract will depend on the terms of the contract and the circumstances: *Express & Star Ltd v Bunday* [1988] ICR 379, [1987] IRLR 422, CA. A right to lock out will not be implied into the contract: *Cummings v Charles Connell & Co (Shipbuilders) Ltd* 1969 SLT 25, Ct of Sess; cf *Hanley v Pease & Partners Ltd* [1915] 1 KB 698, DC; *Marshall v English Electric Co Ltd* [1945] 1 All ER 653, CA; *Waine v R Oliver (Plant Hire) Ltd* [1977] IRLR 434, EAT. A lockout in breach of contract does not of itself terminate the contract, but it may entitle the workers to quit without notice: *E & J Davis Transport Ltd v Chattaway* [1972] ICR 267, NIRC.

17 As to the effect of a lockout on statutory employment rights and on welfare benefits see PARAS 1349–1358.

1343. Liability for industrial action in tort. Industrial action potentially[1] involves the commission of a number of torts. Of particular relevance are the economic torts of inducing a breach of contract[2], causing loss by unlawful means, interfering with the trade or business of another by unlawful means, intimidation and conspiracy[3]. Torts connected with picketing[4] are considered below[5].

1 As to the statutory immunity from suit in tort for acts done in contemplation or furtherance of a trade dispute see PARA 1359 et seq. For the purposes of the torts referred to in the Trade Union and Labour Relations (Consolidation) Act 1992 s 219(1) (see PARA 1363), where a person holds any office or employment under the Crown on terms which do not constitute a contract of employment between that person and the Crown, those terms are nevertheless deemed to constitute such a contract: see s 245; and PARA 1363 note 8.

2 The tort of inducing breach of contract has been extended to cover inducing breach of fiduciary duty (*Prudential Assurance Co Ltd v Lorenz* (1971) 11 KIR 78) and inducing breach of statutory duty (*Meade v Haringey London Borough Council* [1979] 2 All ER 1016, [1979] ICR 494, CA; *Barretts & Baird (Wholesale) Ltd v Institution of Professional Civil Servants* [1987] IRLR 3; and see *Associated British Ports v Transport and General Workers' Union* [1989] IRLR 291; affd on other grounds [1989] 3 All ER 822, [1989] ICR 557 at 590, HL (revsng [1989] 3 All ER 796, [1989] ICR 557, CA)).

3 As to the economic torts generally see TORT vol 97 (2010) PARA 612 et seq. They were subject to major re-evaluation and categorisation in the (non-employment) decision of the House of Lords in *OBG Ltd v Allen, Douglas v Hello! Ltd (No 3), Mainstream Properties Ltd v Young* [2007] UKHL 21, [2008] 1 AC 1, [2007] IRLR 608.

4 Eg public and private nuisance, harassment and trespass to the highway: see TORT vol 97 (2010) PARA 401 et seq.

5 See PARA 1384.

1344. Other possible liabilities for industrial action. Industrial action may constitute a breach of fiduciary duty[1], or a breach of statutory duty[2], by those taking part. Further, there is now also the possibility that industrial action (in particular to protect local pay rates for competitors using labour from elsewhere within the EU) could be illegal because it constitutes a breach of fundamental rights under EU law[3]. A transaction entered into under threat of industrial action is liable to be set aside on the ground of unlawful economic duress, and money paid in such circumstances may be recoverable in an action for restitution[4].

1 *Prudential Assurance Co Ltd v Lorenz* (1971) 11 KIR 78. As to the tort of inducing breach of fiduciary duty see PARA 1343.

2 *Associated British Ports v Transport and General Workers' Union* [1989] IRLR 291; affd on other grounds [1989] 3 All ER 822, [1989] ICR 557 at 590, HL (revsng [1989] 3 All ER 796, [1989] ICR 557, CA).

3 In particular, such action could breach what is now the Treaty on the Functioning of the European Union (Rome, 25 March 1957; TS 1 (1973); Cmnd 5179) ('TFEU') art 49 (freedom of establishment) (see Case C-438/05 *International Transport Workers' Federation v Viking Line ABP* [2008] All ER (EC) 127, [2008] IRLR 143, ECJ); or what is now the TFEU art 56 (freedom to provide services) (see Case C-341/05 *Laval un Partneri Ltd v Svenska Byggnadsarbetareforbundet* [2008] All ER (EC) 166, [2008] IRLR 160, ECJ). One problem here is that the issue of use of labour from another member state was addressed by the Posted Worker Directive (ie European Parliament and Council Directive (EC) 96/71 concerning the posting of workers in the framework of the provision of services (OJ L18, 21.1.97, p 1)), but that only obliges the foreign contractor to respect the host state's minimum wage requirements (see art 3(1)(c)); it does not protect the going rate for that work within the host state. A member state cannot not rely on the public policy exception referred to in art 3(10) in order to apply to undertakings posting staff on its territory the requirement relating to the automatic adjustment of wages other than minimum wages to reflect changes in the cost of living: Case C-19/06 *European Commission v Luxembourg* [2008] ECR I-4323, [2009] All ER (EC) 1049, ECJ. See also Case E-12/10 *EFTA Surveillance Authority v Iceland*, EFTA Ct. If industrial action by a trade union breaches the TFEU art 49 or art 56, it may be restrainable by injunction unless the union can objectively justify it (ie as a legitimate aim, pursued by proportionate means). In *International Transport Workers' Federation v Viking Line ABP* [2008] All ER (EC) 127, [2008] IRLR 143, ECJ the issue of justification was remitted to the national court but in *Laval un Partneri Ltd v Svenska Byggnadsarbetareforbundet* [2008] All ER (EC) 166, [2008] IRLR 160, ECJ the European Court of Justice went further and held that there was no justification (for action by a Swedish trade union to stop a Latvian company using its own national labour on a Swedish site at lower rates than those negotiated with the Swedish employers). An attempt to protect local labour rates by a local authority in Germany (rather than a trade union) was also held to be unlawful and not justified: Case C-346/06 *Rüffert v Land Niedersachsen* [2008] All ER (EC) 902, [2008] IRLR 467, ECJ. The exercise of the fundamental right to bargain collectively has to be reconciled with the requirements that stem from the freedoms protected by the Treaty on the Functioning of the European Union and has to be in accordance with the principle of proportionality: Case C-271/08 *EC Commission v Germany* [2010] ECR I-7091, [2011] All ER (EC) 912, ECJ.

4 *Universe Tankships Inc of Monrovia v International Transport Workers' Federation* [1983] 1 AC 366, [1982] ICR 262, HL; cf *B and S Contracts and Design Ltd v Victor Green Publications Ltd* [1984] ICR 419, CA; *Dimskal Shipping Co SA v International Transport Workers' Federation, The Evia Luck (No 2)* [1992] 2 AC 152, [1992] ICR 37, HL. As to the significance of the statutory immunity against liability for the economic torts in such cases see PARA 1363 note 5.

(3) EFFECT OF INDUSTRIAL ACTION ON THE INDIVIDUAL

(i) Effect on the Contract of Employment

1345. Summary dismissal as a result of industrial action. Industrial action by employees normally means that they are in breach of contract[1]; if such breach is sufficiently serious to be repudiatory, as is usually the case with a strike or other industrial action, the employer may lawfully dismiss the employees summarily[2]. This does not, however, mean that such dismissals will necessarily be fair or unfair, because the statutory action for unfair dismissal operates on entirely separate principles[3].

1 There is a long-standing problem as to the effect of any strike notice given by a union: see the cases cited in PARA 1342 note 3.

2 *Simmons v Hoover Ltd* [1977] QB 284, [1977] ICR 61, EAT; *Wilkins v Cantrell and Cochrane (GB) Ltd* [1978] IRLR 483, EAT; *Haddow v Inner London Education Authority* [1979] ICR

202, EAT. As to summary dismissal generally see PARA 743. *Simmons v Hoover Ltd* [1977] QB 284, [1977] ICR 61, EAT, is still good law: at common law an employer is entitled summarily to dismiss an employee who refuses to work. Legislative developments since 1976 do not affect that proposition; nor does the case law of the ECHR or the ECJ. The issue is still relevant to the applicability of the modified dismissal procedure, which only applies where the employee has committed misconduct justifying summary dismissal: *Sehmi v Gate Gourmet London Ltd, Sandhu v Gate Gourmet London Ltd* [2009] IRLR 807, [2009] All ER (D) 46 (Aug), EAT.

3 See PARA 1350. Similarly, questions of continuity of employment through strikes or other industrial action are dealt with by the legislation, not as a matter of common law or contract: see PARA 134.

1346. Liability for damages as a result of industrial action. When an employee is in breach of contract by taking part in industrial action[1], he may be sued for damages by the employer[2]. In such a claim the measure of damages will prima facie be the cost of a replacement for the employee, minus the amount that the employee would have been paid[3]. If, however, a causal connection can be shown between the employee's failure to work and loss of output by the employer, the latter may seek damages for the value of that output, minus what would have been the costs of obtaining it[4], which could be considerably more than the cost of replacing the employee[5].

1 See PARA 1345 note 1.

2 *National Coal Board v Galley* [1958] 1 All ER 91, [1958] 1 WLR 16, CA. In practice this course of action is rarely undertaken. Where there is collective action by many employees, it would be unrealistically cumbersome to sue each individually; hence the importance of any right an employer may have simply to withhold amounts from wages in respect of time spent on industrial action: see PARA 1347. It is significant that in *Sim v Rotherham Metropolitan Borough Council* [1987] Ch 216, [1986] ICR 897, the union argued (unsuccessfully) that there was no such right of set-off against wages due, and that the only action open to the employers was to sue employees for damages individually, on the assumption that that would be impracticable.

3 *National Coal Board v Galley* [1958] 1 All ER 91, [1958] 1 WLR 16, CA; and see *Richards v Hayward* (1841) 2 Man & G 574.

4 *Ebbw Vale Steel, Iron & Coal Co v Tew* (1935) 79 Sol Jo 593, CA. In *National Coal Board v Galley* [1958] 1 All ER 91, [1958] 1 WLR 16, CA, the employers had sued for such consequential loss amounting to £100, but on the facts (the pit deputy in question would only have been doing safety work on the shift he missed, not working at the coal face) the causal connection was not established and so the employers were restricted to the net cost of replacement of approximately £4. Another possible form of consequential loss would be the amount of any wasted expenditure, including pre-contractual expenses, if the employee's actions meant the cancellation of the work in question: *Anglia Television Ltd v Reed* [1972] 1 QB 60, [1971] 3 All ER 690, CA.

   Where recoverable consequential loss has been incurred because of two or more employees acting in concert, it is prima facie correct to divide the loss between the number of employees: *National Coal Board v Galley* [1958] 1 All ER 91 at 102, [1958] 1 WLR 16 at 27, CA. If, however, the necessary causal link cannot be shown between the employee's act and the employer's loss, the employee cannot be liable for loss resulting from others staying away from work (even where he has acted in concert with them), unless the action is brought not just for breach of contract but in tort for conspiracy or inducing fellow employees to break their contracts: *National Coal Board v Galley* [1958] 1 All ER 91 at 103,, [1958] 1 WLR 16 at 28, CA.

5 Faced with the employee's breach of contract, the employer will be subject to the usual common law requirement to mitigate the loss: see *British Westinghouse Electric and Manufacturing Co Ltd v Underground Electric Rlys Co of London Ltd* [1912] AC 673 at 689, HL per Lord Haldane; and DAMAGES vol 12(1) (Reissue) PARA 859. Thus, if it is feasible to replace the employee, the employer will be expected to do so (even though that may decrease the potential damages significantly), and, if he does not do so, the employee should be able to argue failure to mitigate.

   A contract of employment could include an express term specifying a sum to be paid in the event of breach by the employee; such a term would be enforceable if it is a genuine pre-estimate of the loss likely to be sustained by the employer, but not if it is in the nature of a penalty. As to liquidated damages and penalties see DAMAGES vol 12(1) (Reissue) PARAS 808, 1065 et seq.

1347.   Withholding of wages as a result of industrial action.   Where an employee, as part of industrial action, refuses to work, his employer is entitled to withhold pay; this is most clearly the case with a total refusal to work, but also applies to a partial refusal, in which case the employer may either:

(1)   withhold a pro rata amount reflecting the work not done; or

(2)   make it clear that he will not accept defective performance and on that basis refuse to pay wages at all, even for any work actually done by the employee[1].

An employee may be liable to such withholding of wages, partial or total, even if what he does is not contrary to the strict wording of his contract (such as in the case of a 'work-to-rule' or 'work-to-contract' or refusal to work voluntary overtime) if he is thereby in breach of an implied term in the contract to serve the employer faithfully within the requirements of the contract[2]. If, however, the employer accepts the defective performance without objection, the employee may argue that the employer has in fact waived the breach of contract and so has lost the right to make deductions[3].

A deduction from wages on the basis of the employee's participation in a strike or other industrial action is not subject to the normal statutory requirements relating to the making of deductions[4].

1   See PARA 29.
2   *British Telecommunications plc v Ticehurst* [1992] ICR 383, sub nom *Ticehurst and Thompson v British Telecommunications plc* [1992] IRLR 219, CA.
3   *Bond v CAV Ltd, Neads v CAV Ltd* [1983] IRLR 360.
4   Ie the requirements of the Employment Rights Act 1996 Pt II (ss 13–27): see PARA 254 et seq. The normal requirement in s 13(1) is that such a deduction must be authorised either by statute or by prior written agreement: see PARA 255. However, s 14(5) exempts a deduction made by the employer on account of the worker's having taken part in a strike or other industrial action: see PARA 256. Once a deduction is made on those grounds, the exemption applies and no complaint may be made to an employment tribunal; a tribunal may not look behind the deduction to determine whether any deduction was lawful in the first place, any such question being a matter, therefore, for consideration by the ordinary courts in a common law action: *Sunderland Polytechnic v Evans* [1993] ICR 392, [1993] IRLR 196, EAT, disapproving the reasoning (under a different, but analogous, head of what is now the Employment Rights Act 1996 s 14) in *Home Office v Ayres* [1992] ICR 175, [1992] IRLR 59, EAT.

1348.   No compulsion to work.   No court may, whether by way of an order for specific performance of a contract of employment or an injunction restraining the breach or threatened breach of such a contract, compel an employee[1] to do any work or attend at any place for the doing of any work[2].

1   As to the meaning of 'employee' see PARA 892.
2   Trade Union and Labour Relations (Consolidation) Act 1992 s 236. As to the normal rule against enforcement of a contract of employment see PARA 826.

(ii) Effect on Statutory Employment Rights

1349.   Effect of industrial action on continuity of employment.   The continuity of an employee's employment for statutory purposes is not broken by the employee's participation in a strike, but the time so spent does not count towards computing that employee's period of continuous employment with the employer[1].

1   See the Employment Rights Act 1996 s 216; and PARA 134.

1350. Dismissal of those taking part in unofficial industrial action. An employee[1] has no right to complain of unfair dismissal if at the time of dismissal[2] he was taking part[3] in an unofficial strike[4] or other unofficial industrial action[5].

For these purposes, a strike or other industrial action is unofficial in relation to an employee unless:

(1) he is a member of a trade union[6] and the action is authorised or indorsed by that union[7]; or

(2) he is not a member of a trade union but there are among those taking part in the industrial action members of a trade union by which the action has been authorised or indorsed,

provided that a strike or other industrial action is not to be regarded as unofficial if none of those taking part in it is a member of a trade union[8].

The above provisions do not apply to the dismissal of an employee if it is shown that the reason (or, if more than one, the principal reason[9]) for the dismissal or, in a redundancy case[10], for selecting the employee for dismissal was a specified reason[11] relating to jury service[12], family matters[13], health and safety[14], working time[15], employee representatives[16], protected disclosure[17], flexible working[18], pension scheme membership[19], study and training[20] or time off[21] for dependants[22].

1 As to the meaning of 'employee' see PARA 892.
2 For these purposes, the 'time of dismissal' means: (1) where the employee's contract of employment is terminated by notice, when the notice is given; (2) where the employee's contract of employment is terminated without notice, when the termination takes effect; and (3) where the employee is employed under a contract for a fixed term which expires without being renewed under the same contract, when that term expires: Trade Union and Labour Relations (Consolidation) Act 1992 s 237(5). As to the meaning of 'dismissal' see PARA 1056 note 1; and as to the meaning of 'contract of employment' see PARA 892. In a case of dismissal by letter without notice, 'time of dismissal' for the purposes of s 237(5) refers to the date that the letter is actually received and the employee has had a reasonable opportunity of reading it: see e g *Brown v Southall and Knight* [1980] ICR 617, [1980] IRLR 130, EAT; *GISDA Cyf v Barratt* [2010] UKSC 41, [2010] 4 All ER 851, [2010] ICR 1475, [2010] IRLR 1073; and PARA 764.
3 As to when an employee takes part in industrial action for these purposes see PARA 1351 note 7.
4 As to the meaning of 'strike' see PARA 1340.
5 Trade Union and Labour Relations (Consolidation) Act 1992 s 237(1). As to the meaning of 'other industrial action' see PARA 1340. Nothing in s 237 affects the question who are relevant employees for the purposes of s 238: see s 238(3); and PARA 1351. Industrial action taken because an employer has dismissed one or more employees for taking unofficial action is not protected from liability in tort by the statutory immunities in s 219: see s 223; and PARA 1366.

Section 237 is to be construed as one with the Employment Rights Act 1996 Pt X (ss 94–134A) (see PARA 757 et seq): Trade Union and Labour Relations (Consolidation) Act 1992 s 239(1) (amended by the Employment Rights Act 1996 Sch 1 para 56(1), (16)(a); and the Employment Relations Act 1999 Sch 5 paras 1, 4(1), (2)). See, however, PARA 1352 note 4. The Secretary of State may by order provide for the provisions of the Trade Union and Labour Relations (Consolidation) Act 1992 s 237 not to apply, or to apply with prescribed amendments and modifications, to persons or employment of such classes as may be prescribed in the order: see s 286(1), (2); and PARA 1072.

Where an employment tribunal finds that an employee was participating in unofficial industrial action within the meaning of Trade Union and Labour Relations (Consolidation) Act 1992 s 237 at the moment that he received his letter of dismissal it has no jurisdiction to decide his claim for unfair dismissal, notwithstanding that he had not been so participating when the letter was sent, because the essential issue is not one of contract (i e whether there was a fundamental breach of contract justifying summary dismissal), but whether dismissal was within the range of reasonable responses: *Sehmi v Gate Gourmet London Ltd, Sandhu v Gate Gourmet London Ltd* [2009] IRLR 807, [2009] All ER (D) 46 (Aug), EAT (unauthorised and unexplained absence from work at a time when industrial action is in progress will constitute participation; in a case where large numbers of employees deliberately absent themselves from work in unofficial strike action, in a manner which is plainly liable to do serious damage to the employer's business, it will be within the range of reasonable responses for the employer to dismiss, even where the absence is not very prolonged, and, indeed, there is no universal rule that in the case of an employee returning to work after alleged participation in unofficial industrial action it is unfair to dismiss without any form of hearing or any examination of the circumstances).

6 As to the meaning of 'trade union' see PARA 891.

7 The provisions of the Trade Union and Labour Relations (Consolidation) Act 1992 s 20(2) (see PARA 1388) apply for the purpose of determining whether industrial action is to be taken to have been authorised or indorsed by a trade union: s 237(3). The question whether industrial action is to be so taken in any case is to be determined by reference to the facts as at the time of dismissal, provided that, where an act is repudiated as mentioned in s 21 (see PARA 1389), industrial action is not thereby to be treated as unofficial before the end of the next working day after the day on which the repudiation takes place: s 237(4). For these purposes, 'working day' means any day which is not a Saturday or Sunday, Christmas Day, Good Friday or a bank holiday under the Banking and Financial Dealings Act 1971 (see TIME vol 97 (2010) PARA 321): Trade Union and Labour Relations (Consolidation) Act 1992 s 237(5).

8 Trade Union and Labour Relations (Consolidation) Act 1992 s 237(2). Membership of a trade union for purposes unconnected with the employment in question is to be disregarded; but an employee who was a member of a trade union when he began to take part in industrial action is to continue to be treated as a member for the purpose of determining whether that action is unofficial in relation to him or another, notwithstanding that he may in fact have ceased to be a member: s 237(6).

9 As to the meaning of 'reason or principal reason' see PARA 769.

10 For these purposes, 'redundancy case' has the meaning given in the Employment Rights Act 1996 s 105(9) (see PARA 781 note 4): Trade Union and Labour Relations (Consolidation) Act 1992 s 237(1A) (added by the Trade Union Reform and Employment Rights Act 1993 Sch 8 para 76; amended for this purpose by the Employment Rights Act 1996 Sch 1 para 56(1), (15)(b)).

11 Ie a reason for dismissal specified in or under one of the provisions set out in the Trade Union and Labour Relations (Consolidation) Act 1992 s 237(1A). For these purposes, a reference to a specified reason for dismissal includes a reference to specified circumstances of dismissal: s 237(1A) (as added (see note 10); amended for this purpose by the Employment Relations Act 1999 Sch 4 Pt III paras 1, 2(b)).

12 Ie under the Employment Rights Act 1996 s 98B: see PARA 785.

13 Ie under the Employment Rights Act 1996 s 99: see PARA 784.

14 Ie under the Employment Rights Act 1996 s 100: see PARA 786.

15 Ie under the Employment Rights Act 1996 s 101A(1)(d): see PARA 788.

16 Ie under the Employment Rights Act 1996 s 103: see PARA 791.

17 Ie under the Employment Rights Act 1996 s 103A: see PARA 792.

18 Ie under the Employment Rights Act 1996 s 104C: see PARA 796.

19 Ie under the Employment Rights Act 1996 s 104D: see PARA 797.

20 Ie under the Employment Rights Act 1996 s 104E: see PARA 798.

21 Ie under the Employment Rights Act 1996 s 104 (see PARA 793) in its application in relation to time off under s 57A (see PARA 347).

22 Trade Union and Labour Relations (Consolidation) Act 1992 s 237(1A) (as added (see note 10); and amended (see notes 10–11); also amended by the Employment Relations Act 1999 Sch 4 Pt III paras 1, 2(a); the Employment Relations Act 2004 ss 40(8), 41(1); the Pensions Act 2008 s 57(1), (6); the Apprenticeships, Skills, Children and Learning Act 2009 Sch 1 paras 12, 14).

1351. Dismissals in connection with other industrial action. Except where an employee[1] is to be regarded as unfairly dismissed for taking protected industrial action[2], where an employee (the 'complainant') has a right to complain of unfair dismissal and claims to have been unfairly dismissed[3], and at the date of the dismissal[4] the employer[5] was conducting or instituting a lockout[6] or the complainant was taking part[7] in a strike or other industrial action[8], an employment tribunal is not to determine whether the dismissal was fair or unfair unless it is shown:

(1) that one or more relevant employees of the same employer has or have not been dismissed[9]; or

(2) that a relevant employee has, before the expiry of the period of three

months beginning with that employee's date of dismissal, been offered re-engagement[10] and that the complainant has not been offered re-engagement[11].

For these purposes, 'relevant employees' means:

(a)   in relation to a lockout, employees who were directly interested[12] in the dispute in contemplation or furtherance of which the lockout occurred; and

(b)   in relation to a strike or other industrial action, those employees at the establishment[13] who were taking part in the action at the complainant's date of dismissal[14].

The above provisions[15] do not apply:

(i)   to the dismissal of an employee if it is shown that the reason (or, if more than one, the principal reason[16]) for the dismissal or, in a redundancy case[17], for selecting the employee for dismissal, was a specified reason[18] relating to jury service[19], family matters[20], health and safety[21], working time[22], employee representatives[23], flexible working[24], pension scheme membership[25], study and training[26] or time off[27] for dependants[28]; or

(ii)   in relation to an employee who is regarded as unfairly dismissed by virtue of having taken[29] protected industrial action[30].

1   As to the meaning of 'employee' see PARA 892.
2   See PARA 1352.
3   As to the meaning of 'dismissal' see PARA 1056 note 1.
4   For these purposes, 'date of dismissal' means: (1) where the employee's contract of employment was terminated by notice, the date on which the employer's notice was given; and (2) in any other case, the effective date of termination: Trade Union and Labour Relations (Consolidation) Act 1992 s 238(5). As to the meaning of 'effective date of termination', in relation to an employee, see PARA 1058 note 3; and as to the meaning of 'contract of employment' see PARA 892. A letter warning of possible dismissal if work is not resumed is not 'notice': *Bolton Roadways Ltd v Edwards* [1987] IRLR 392, EAT. The employee must be taking part in the action at the time of dismissal; and the Trade Union and Labour Relations (Consolidation) Act 1992 s 238 does not apply if the employees are dismissed on the same day but after the industrial action has ended: *Heath v JF Longman (Meat Salesmen) Ltd* [1973] 2 All ER 1228, [1973] ICR 407, NIRC.
5   As to the meaning of 'employer' see PARA 892.
6   As to the meaning of 'lockout' see PARA 1340.
7   Whether a particular employee was taking part in a strike or other industrial action is a question of fact: *Coates v Modern Methods and Materials Ltd* [1983] QB 192, [1982] ICR 763, CA. The test is objective and thus not dependent on the employee's motive for taking part (eg through fear of crossing a picket line): *Coates v Modern Methods and Materials Ltd, Naylor v Orton & Smith Ltd* [1983] ICR 665, [1983] IRLR 233, EAT. As the test is objective, the question whether the employer knew that the employee in question was taking part is not determinative: *Manifold Industries Ltd v Sims* [1991] ICR 504, [1991] IRLR 242, EAT, following *Bolton Roadways Ltd v Edwards* [1987] IRLR 392, EAT, but not following *McKenzie v Crosville Motor Services Ltd* [1990] ICR 172, [1989] IRLR 516, EAT; *Jenkins v P & O European Ferries (Dover) Ltd* [1991] ICR 652, EAT; cf *Hindle Gears Ltd v McGinty* [1985] ICR 111, [1984] IRLR 477, EAT. An employee may still be participating in the action if sick or on holiday, provided that he is in fact associating himself with the action in some way: *Williams v Western Mail and Echo Ltd* [1980] ICR 366, [1980] IRLR 222, EAT; *Bolton Roadways Ltd v Edwards*[1987] IRLR 392, EAT; cf *Hindle Gears Ltd v McGinty* [1985] ICR 111, [1984] IRLR 477, EAT; *Rogers v Chloride Systems Ltd* [1992] ICR 198, EAT. An employee may be participating by declaring that he will not attend for work when next due to do so, eg in the case of a shift worker (*Winnett v Seamarks Bros Ltd* [1978] ICR 1240, [1978] IRLR 387, EAT) but this must be made clear (*Dixon v Wilson Walton Engineering Ltd* [1979] ICR 438) and continues until the action ceases or he states his intention of ceasing (see *Williams v Western Mail and Echo Ltd* [1980] ICR 366, [1980] IRLR 222, EAT). A threat to take industrial action will not constitute taking part in such action (*Midland Plastics v Till* [1983] ICR 118, [1983] IRLR 9, EAT) unless the threat is sufficiently definite and imminent (*Winnett v Seamarks Bros Ltd* [1978] ICR 1240, [1978] IRLR 387, EAT; *Lewis and Britton v E Mason & Sons* [1994] IRLR 4, EAT).

8 As to the meaning of 'strike' and 'other industrial action' see PARA 1340.

9 The time for deciding whether all relevant employees have been dismissed is, at the latest, the conclusion of the tribunal hearing: *P & O European Ferries (Dover) Ltd v Byrne* [1989] ICR 779, [1989] IRLR 254, EAT (not applying dicta pointing to the beginning of the hearing in *McCormick v Horsepower Ltd* [1981] 2 All ER 746, [1981] ICR 535, CA); *Manifold Industries Ltd v Sims* [1991] ICR 504, [1991] IRLR 242, EAT. Employees who have voluntarily resigned are not 'relevant employees' for these purposes: *Manifold Industries Ltd v Sims* [1991] ICR 504, [1991] IRLR 242, EAT. As the Trade Union and Labour Relations (Consolidation) Act 1992 s 238 applies where the employees are dismissed while taking part in the industrial action (*Heath v JF Longman (Meat Salesmen) Ltd* [1973] 2 All ER 1228, [1973] ICR 407, NIRC; *Midland Plastics v Till* [1983] ICR 118, [1983] IRLR 9, EAT), but not necessarily because they are taking part in it, it is not possible to argue that its exclusion of unfair dismissal actions should not apply where it is alleged that the employer has 'engineered' or provoked the strike in order to be able to dismiss the employees (*Marsden v Fairey Stainless Ltd* [1979] IRLR 103, EAT; and see *Power Packing Casemakers Ltd v Faust* [1983] QB 471, [1983] ICR 292, CA). *Thompson v Eaton Ltd* [1976] 3 All ER 384, [1976] ICR 336, EAT is no longer good law on this point. Cf PARA 1352.

10 For these purposes, an offer of re-engagement means an offer, made either by the original employer or by a successor of that employer or an associated employer, to re-engage an employee, either in the job which he held immediately before the date of dismissal or in a different job which would be reasonably suitable in his case: Trade Union and Labour Relations (Consolidation) Act 1992 s 238(4). As to the meaning of 'associated employer' see PARA 1026 note 8. 'Job' and 'successor' have the meanings given in the Employment Rights Act 1996 s 235 (see PARAS 119, 133): see the Trade Union and Labour Relations (Consolidation) Act 1992 s 239(1) (amended by the Employment Rights Act 1996 Sch 1 para 56(1), (16)(a); the Employment Relations Act 1999 Sch 5 paras 1, 41(1), (2)), which applies these definitions.

An offer of re-engagement may satisfy this statutory definition even if subject to conditions: *Williams v National Theatre Board Ltd* [1982] ICR 715, [1982] IRLR 377, CA. An offer of re-engagement can take the form of a tacit acceptance of continuance of the contract, without the need for an identifiable offer: *Bolton Roadways Ltd v Edwards* [1987] IRLR 392, EAT. If, however, an identifiable offer is made, it must be effectively communicated: *Tomczynski v JK Millar Ltd* (1976) 11 ITR 127, EAT. Where a dismissed employee is re-engaged by mistake, that will only be an effective offer of re-engagement if the employer knew, or had constructive knowledge, of the true facts; a re-engagement resulting from fraud on the part of the employee does not affect the employer's protection: *Bigham v GKN Kwikform Ltd* [1992] ICR 113, sub nom *Bigham and Keogh v GKN Kwikform Ltd* [1992] IRLR 4, EAT. A general advertising campaign offering employment to those who apply does not in itself amount to an offer of employment to any particular individual: *Crosville Wales Ltd v Tracey* [1993] IRLR 60, EAT.

11 Trade Union and Labour Relations (Consolidation) Act 1992 s 238(1), (2) (s 238(2) amended by the Employment Rights (Dispute Resolution) Act 1998 s 1(2)(a)). The Trade Union and Labour Relations (Consolidation) Act 1992 s 238 is to be construed as one with the Employment Rights Act 1996 Pt X (ss 94–134A) (see PARA 757 et seq): Trade Union and Labour Relations (Consolidation) Act 1992 s 239(1) (as amended: see note 10).

Where it is shown that the condition referred to in s 238(2)(b) (see head (2) in the text) is fulfilled, the references in the Employment Rights Act 1996 ss 98–106 (see PARA 765 et seq) and the Trade Union and Labour Relations (Consolidation) Act 1992 ss 152, 153 (see PARA 1056) to the reason or principal reason for which the complainant was dismissed are to be read as references to the reason or principal reason he has not been offered re-engagement: s 239(3) (amended by the Employment Rights Act 1996 Sch 1 para 56(1), (16)(c)).

In relation to a complaint to which the Trade Union and Labour Relations (Consolidation) Act 1992 s 238 applies, the Employment Rights Act 1996 s 111(2) (time limit for complaint) (see PARA 804) does not apply, but an employment tribunal must not consider the complaint unless it is presented to the tribunal: (1) before the end of the period of six months beginning with the date of the complainant's dismissal, as defined by the Trade Union and Labour Relations (Consolidation) Act 1992 s 238(5) (see note 4); or (2) where the tribunal is satisfied that it was not reasonably practicable for the complaint to be presented before the end of that period, within such further period as the tribunal considers reasonable: s 239(2) (amended by the Employment Rights Act 1996 Sch 1 para 56(1), (16)(b); the Employment Rights (Dispute Resolution) Act 1998 s 1(2)(a); the Employment Relations Act 1999 Sch 5 paras 1, 4(1),(4)).

12 A wide range of employees can be directly interested in a dispute: *Fisher v York Trailer Co Ltd* [1979] ICR 834, [1979] IRLR 385, EAT. The reforms in the Employment Act 1982 (now repealed) which made selective dismissal easier for employers only apply to industrial action by

employees, not to lockouts by employers, so that an employee who was locked out but has returned to work by the date of the dismissal may still be a relevant employee: *H Campey & Sons Ltd v Bellwood* [1987] ICR 311, EAT.

13 'Establishment' is not defined for these purposes. As to the meaning of 'establishment' in the context of redundancy consultation see PARA 1185 note 6.

14 Trade Union and Labour Relations (Consolidation) Act 1992 s 238(3). Nothing in s 237 (see PARA 1350) affects the question who are relevant employees for the purposes of s 238: s 238(3).

15 Ie the provisions in the Trade Union and Labour Relations (Consolidation) Act 1992 s 238(2).

16 As to the meaning of 'reason or principal reason' see PARA 769.

17 For these purposes, 'redundancy case' has the meaning given in the Employment Rights Act 1996 s 105(9) (see PARA 781 note 4): Trade Union and Labour Relations (Consolidation) Act 1992 s 238(2A) (added by the Trade Union Reform and Employment Rights Act 1993 Sch 8 para 77; amended for this purpose by the Employment Rights Act 1996 Sch 1 para 56(1), (15)(b)).

18 Ie a reason for dismissal specified in or under one of the provisions set out in the Trade Union and Labour Relations (Consolidation) Act 1992 s 238(2A). For these purposes, a reference to a specified reason for dismissal includes a reference to specified circumstances of dismissal: s 238(2A) (as added (see note 17); amended for this purpose by the Employment Relations Act 1999 Sch 4 Pt III paras 1, 3(b)).

19 Ie under the Employment Rights Act 1996 s 98B: see PARA 785.

20 Ie under the Employment Rights Act 1996 s 99: see PARA 784.

21 Ie under the Employment Rights Act 1996 s 100: see PARA 786.

22 Ie under the Employment Rights Act 1996 s 101A(1)(d): see PARA 788.

23 Ie under the Employment Rights Act 1996 s 103: see PARA 791.

24 Ie under the Employment Rights Act 1996 s 104C: see PARA 796.

25 Ie under the Employment Rights Act 1996 s 104D: see PARA 797.

26 Ie under the Employment Rights Act 1996 s 104E: see PARA 798.

27 Ie under the Employment Rights Act 1996 s 104 (see PARA 793) in its application in relation to time off under s 57A (see PARA 347).

28 Trade Union and Labour Relations (Consolidation) Act 1992 s 238(2A) (as added (see note 17); and amended (see notes 17–18); also amended by the Employment Relations Act 1999 Sch 4 Pt III paras 1, 3(a); the Employment Relations Act 2004 ss 40(9), 41(2); the Pensions Act 2008 s 57(1), (7); the Apprenticeships, Skills, Children and Learning Act 2009 Sch 1 paras 12, 15).

29 Ie by virtue of the Trade Union and Labour Relations (Consolidation) Act 1992 s 238A: see PARA 1352.

30 Trade Union and Labour Relations (Consolidation) Act 1992 s 238(2B) (added by the Employment Relations Act 1999 Sch 5 paras 1, 2).

1352. Participation in official industrial action. An employee[1] who is dismissed is to be regarded[2] as unfairly dismissed if the reason (or, if more than one, the principal reason[3]) for the dismissal is that the employee took protected industrial action[4], and any of the following circumstances applies to the dismissal[5]:

(1) the date of the dismissal is within the protected period[6]; or

(2) the date of the dismissal is after the end of that period, and the employee had stopped taking protected industrial action before the end of that period[7]; or

(3) the date of the dismissal is after the end of that period, the employee had not stopped taking protected industrial action before the end of that period, and the employer[8] had not taken such procedural steps as would have been reasonable for the purposes of resolving the dispute to which the protected industrial action relates[9].

In determining whether an employer has taken those steps, regard is to be had, in particular, to:

(a) whether the employer or a union had complied with procedures established by any applicable collective or other agreement[10];

(b) whether the employer or a union offered or agreed to commence or resume negotiations after the start of the protected industrial action;

(c)   whether the employer or a union unreasonably refused, after the start of the protected industrial action, a request that conciliation services be used;

(d)   whether the employer or a union unreasonably refused, after the start of the protected industrial action, a request that mediation services be used in relation to procedures to be adopted for the purposes of resolving the dispute;

(e)   where there was agreement to use either of the services mentioned in heads (c) and (d) above, certain specified matters[11];

but, in determining whether an employer has taken those steps, no regard is to be had to the merits of the dispute[12].

1   As to the meaning of 'employee' see PARA 892.
2   Ie for the purposes of the Employment Rights Act 1996 Pt X (ss 94–134A): see PARA 757 et seq.
3   As to the meaning of 'reason or principal reason' see PARA 769.
4   Trade Union and Labour Relations (Consolidation) Act 1992 s 238A(2)(a) (s 238A added by the Employment Relations Act 1999 Sch 5 paras 1, 3). For these purposes, an employee takes protected industrial action if he commits an act which, or a series of acts each of which, he is induced to commit by an act which by virtue of the Trade Union and Labour Relations (Consolidation) Act 1992 s 219 (see PARA 1363) is not actionable in tort: s 238A(1) (as so added). For the purposes of s 238A, no account is to be taken of the repudiation of any act by a trade union as mentioned in s 21 (see PARA 1389) in relation to anything which occurs before the end of the next working day (within the meaning of s 237: see PARA 1350 note 7) after the day on which the repudiation takes place: s 238A(8) (as so added). As to the meaning of 'trade union' see PARA 891.
    Section s 238A is to be construed as one with the Employment Rights Act 1996 Pt X (ss 94–134A) (see PARA 757 et seq); but s 108 (qualifying period) (see PARA 758) does not apply in relation to the Trade Union and Labour Relations (Consolidation) Act 1992 s 238A: see s 239(1) (amended by the Employment Rights Act 1996 Sch 1 para 56(1), (16)(a); the Employment Relations Act 1999 Sch 5 paras 1, 4(1)–(3)).
    In relation to a complaint to which the Trade Union and Labour Relations (Consolidation) Act 1992 s 238A applies, the Employment Rights Act 1996 s 111(2) (time limit for complaint) (see PARA 804) does not apply, but an employment tribunal must not consider the complaint unless it is presented to the tribunal: (1) before the end of the period of six months beginning with the date of the complainant's dismissal, as defined by the Trade Union and Labour Relations (Consolidation) Act 1992 s 238(5) (see PARA 1351 note 4); or (2) where the tribunal is satisfied that it was not reasonably practicable for the complaint to be presented before the end of that period, within such further period as the tribunal considers reasonable: s 239(2) (amended by the Employment Rights Act 1996 Sch 1 para 56(1), (16)(b); the Employment Rights (Dispute Resolution) Act 1998 s 1(2)(a); the Employment Relations Act 1999 Sch 5 paras 1, 4(1),(4)).
    In relation to a complaint under the Employment Rights Act 1996 s 111 (unfair dismissal; complaint to employment tribunal) (see PARA 804) that a dismissal was unfair by virtue of the Trade Union and Labour Relations (Consolidation) Act 1992 s 238A: (a) no order is to be made under the Employment Rights Act 1996 s 113 (reinstatement or re-engagement) (see PARA 811) until after the conclusion of protected industrial action by any employee in relation to the relevant dispute; (b) regulations under the Employment Tribunals Act 1996 s 7 (see PARA 1410) may make provision about the adjournment and renewal of applications, including provision requiring adjournment in specified circumstances; and (c) regulations under s 9 (see PARA 1414) may require a pre-hearing review to be carried out in specified circumstances: Trade Union and Labour Relations (Consolidation) Act 1992 s 239(4) (added by the Employment Relations Act 1999 Sch 5 paras 1, 4(1), (5)).
5   Trade Union and Labour Relations (Consolidation) Act 1992 s 238A(2)(b) (as added: see note 4).
6   Trade Union and Labour Relations (Consolidation) Act 1992 s 238A(3) (as added (see note 4); amended by the Employment Relations Act 2004 ss 26(1), (2), 27(1), (2)). 'Date of dismissal' has the meaning given by the Trade Union and Labour Relations (Consolidation) Act 1992 s 238(5) (see PARA 1351 note 4): s 238A(9) (added by the Employment Relations Act 2004 s 27(1), (5)). For the purposes of the Trade Union and Labour Relations (Consolidation) Act 1992 s 238A, the 'protected period', in relation to the dismissal of an employee, is the sum of the basic period and any extension period in relation to that employee: s 238A(7A)

(s 238(7A)–(7D) added by the Employment Relations Act 2004 s 26(1), (3)). The basic period is 12 weeks beginning with the first day of protected industrial action: Trade Union and Labour Relations (Consolidation) Act 1992 s 238A(7B) (as so added). An extension period in relation to an employee is a period equal to the number of days falling on or after the first day of protected industrial action, but before the protected period ends, during the whole or any part of which the employee is locked out by his employer: s 238A(7C) (as so added). The 'first day of protected industrial action' means the day on which the employee starts to take protected industrial action, even if on that day he is locked out by his employer: s 238A(7D) (as so added).

7   Trade Union and Labour Relations (Consolidation) Act 1992 s 238A(4) (as added (see note 4); amended by the Employment Relations Act 2004 s 27(1), (3)).

8   As to the meaning of 'employer' see PARA 892.

9   Trade Union and Labour Relations (Consolidation) Act 1992 s 238A(5) (as added (see note 4); amended by the Employment Relations Act 2004 s 27(1), (4)).

10 As to the meaning of 'collective agreement' see PARA 1093.

11 Trade Union and Labour Relations (Consolidation) Act 1992 s 238A(6) (added (see note 4); amended by the Employment Relations Act 2004 s 28(1)). The specified matters referred to are those specified in the Trade Union and Labour Relations (Consolidation) Act 1992 s 238B. The matters so specified are (1) whether, at meetings arranged by the service provider, the employer or, as the case may be, a union, was represented by an appropriate person; (2) whether the employer or a union, so far as requested to do so, co-operated in the making of arrangements for meetings to be held with the service provider; (3) whether the employer or a union fulfilled any commitment given by it during the provision of the service to take particular action; and (4) whether, at meetings arranged by the service provider between the parties making use of the service, the representatives of the employer or a union answered any reasonable question put to them concerning the matter subject to conciliation or mediation: s 238B(1)–(5) (s 238B added by the Employment Relations Act 2004 s 28(2)). An 'appropriate person' is (a) in relation to the employer, a person with the authority to settle the matter subject to conciliation or mediation on behalf of the employer, or a person authorised by a person of that type to make recommendations to him with regard to the settlement of that matter; and (b) in relation to a union, a person who is responsible for handling on the union's behalf the matter subject to conciliation or mediation: Trade Union and Labour Relations (Consolidation) Act 1992 s 238B(6) (as so added). References to the 'service provider' are to any person who provided a service mentioned in s 238A(6)(c) or (d) (see heads (c)–(d) in the text): s 238B(1) (as so added). For the purposes of head (3) above, regard may be had to any timetable which was agreed for the taking of the action in question or, if no timetable was agreed, to how long it was before the action was taken: s 238B(7) (as so added).

In any proceedings in which regard must be had to the matters referred to in head (e) in the text (see heads (1)–(4) above), (i) notes taken by or on behalf of the service provider are not admissible in evidence; (ii) the service provider must refuse to give evidence as to anything communicated to him in connection with the performance of his functions as a conciliator or mediator if, in his opinion, to give the evidence would involve his making a damaging disclosure; and (iii) the service provider may refuse to give evidence as to whether, for the purposes of head (4) above, a particular question was or was not a reasonable one: s 238B(8) (as so added). For these purposes, a 'damaging disclosure' is a disclosure of information which is commercially sensitive, or a disclosure of information that has not previously been disclosed which relates to a position taken by a party using the conciliation or mediation service on the settlement of the matter subject to conciliation or mediation, to which the person who communicated the information to the service provider has not consented: s 238B(9) (as so added).

12 Trade Union and Labour Relations (Consolidation) Act 1992 s 238A(7) (as added: see note 4).

1353.   Participation in industrial action; effect on redundancy payments. The normal exclusion from the right to a redundancy payment of an employee dismissed for misconduct[1] does not apply in the case of an employee under notice of termination of employment who takes part in a strike and is dismissed by the employer for that reason[2].

1   See PARA 872.
2   See the Employment Rights Act 1996 s 140(2); and PARA 873.

1354. Effect of industrial action on guarantee payments. An employee is not entitled to a guarantee payment[1] in respect of a workless day[2] if the failure to provide him with work occurs in consequence of a strike, lockout or other industrial action involving any employee of his employer or of an associated employer[3].

1 As to guarantee payments generally see PARA 261 et seq.
2 As to the meaning of 'workless day' see PARA 261 note 3.
3 See the Employment Rights Act 1996 s 29(3); and PARA 262.

(iii) Effect on Welfare Benefits

1355. Effect of trade disputes on jobseeker's allowance. Where there is a stoppage of work which causes a person not to be employed on any day, and the stoppage of work is due to a trade dispute[1] at his place of work[2], that person is not entitled to a jobseeker's allowance for the week which includes that day unless he proves that he is not directly interested in the dispute[3]. If a person who is thus prevented from being entitled to a jobseeker's allowance proves that during the stoppage:

(1) he became bona fide employed elsewhere;
(2) his employment was terminated by reason of redundancy[4]; or
(3) he bona fide resumed employment with his employer but subsequently left for a reason other than the trade dispute,

the above provisions[5] are to be taken to have ceased to apply to him on the occurrence of the event referred to in head (1) or head (2) above or, as the case may be, the first event referred to in head (3) above[6].

A person who withdraws his labour on any day in furtherance of a trade dispute, but to whom the above provisions[7] do not apply, is not entitled to a jobseeker's allowance for the week which includes that day[8].

1 As to the meaning of 'trade dispute' for these purposes see PARA 1212 note 4.
2 For these purposes, 'place of work', in relation to any person, means the premises or place at which he was employed, but, where separate branches of work which are commonly carried on as separate businesses in separate premises or at separate places are in any case carried on in separate departments on the same premises or at the same place, each of those departments is deemed for these purposes to be separate premises or a separate place, as the case may be: Jobseekers Act 1995 s 14(4), (5).
3 Jobseekers Act 1995 s 14(1). As to the meaning of 'directly interested' see *Presho v Insurance Officer* [1984] AC 310, [1984] ICR 463, HL (under the (repealed) provisions on unemployment benefit, which applied the same phrase). See further WELFARE BENEFITS AND STATE PENSIONS vol 104 (2014) PARA 438.
4 Ie within the meaning of the Employment Rights Act 1996 s 139(1): see PARA 870.
5 Ie the Jobseekers Act 1995 s 14(1).
6 See the Jobseekers Act 1995 s 14(3); and WELFARE BENEFITS AND STATE PENSIONS vol 104 (2014) PARA 438.
7 See note 5.
8 See the Jobseekers Act 1995 s 14(2); and WELFARE BENEFITS AND STATE PENSIONS vol 104 (2014) PARA 438. This provision fills a potential lacuna in s 14(1) where the employee withdraws his labour but this does not cause a stoppage of work.

1356. Effect of trade dispute on income support. Where a person is prevented from being entitled to a jobseeker's allowance owing to a trade dispute[1], or would be so prevented if otherwise entitled to that benefit, then, except during any period of incapacity for work or within the maternity period, that person is ineligible for income support, although a claim may be made in respect of that person's partner and children[2]. Further, from this entitlement must be deducted any payments received by reason of being without employment, including any repayment of income tax[3] and also the relevant sum which is subject to annual uprating[4].

Income support may continue to be paid for a period of 15 days after a return to work after a trade dispute[5], but the amounts so paid are recoverable, if necessary by the service of a deduction notice on the person's employer requiring the deduction of stipulated amounts from that person's pay[6].

1   Ie by the Jobseekers Act 1995 s 14: see PARA 1355.
2   See the Social Security Contributions and Benefits Act 1992 s 126(1)–(4) (s 126 repealed by the Welfare Reform Act 2012 Sch 14 Pt 1, partly as from a day to be appointed); and WELFARE BENEFITS AND STATE PENSIONS vol 104 (2014) PARA 295. As to the prospective abolition of income support see WELFARE BENEFITS AND STATE PENSIONS vol 104 (2014) PARA 292.
3   See the Social Security Contributions and Benefits Act 1992 s 126(5)(a) (repealed, partly as from a day to be appointed: see note 2); and WELFARE BENEFITS AND STATE PENSIONS vol 104 (2014) PARA 295. See also note 2.
4   See the Social Security Contributions and Benefits Act 1992 s 126(5)(b), (8) (repealed, partly as from a day to be appointed: see note 2); and WELFARE BENEFITS AND STATE PENSIONS vol 104 (2014) PARA 295. For these purposes, the relevant sum is £40 per week: see s 126(7) (repealed, partly as from a day to be appointed (see note 2); amended by SI 2014/516). See also note 2.
5   See the Social Security Contributions and Benefits Act 1992 s 127 (s 127 repealed by the Welfare Reform Act 2012 Sch 14 Pt 1, partly as from a day to be appointed); and WELFARE BENEFITS AND STATE PENSIONS vol 104 (2014) PARA 295. See also note 2.
6   See the Social Security (Payments on Account, Overpayments and Recovery) Regulations 1988, SI 1988/664, Pt VIII (regs 18–29) (revoked as far as relating to child benefit or guardian allowance by SI 2003/492); and WELFARE BENEFITS AND STATE PENSIONS vol 104 (2014) PARA 295.

1357. Effect of trade dispute on universal credit. When calculating a person's earned income for the purposes of an award of universal credit[1], a person who has had employed earnings and has withdrawn his labour in furtherance of a trade dispute[2] is, unless his contract of service has been terminated, to be assumed to have employed earnings at the same level as he would have had were it not for the trade dispute[3].

No reduction of a claimant's benefit is to be made[4] for a sanctionable failure where:

(1)   the sanctionable failure is failure to apply for a particular vacancy for paid work, or failure to take up an offer of paid work, and the vacancy is because of a strike arising from a trade dispute[5];

(2)   the sanctionable failure is that the claimant voluntarily ceases paid work, or loses pay, because of a strike arising from a trade dispute[6].

1   As to entitlement to universal credit see WELFARE BENEFITS AND STATE PENSIONS vol 104 (2014) PARA 45 et seq.
2   As to the meaning of 'trade dispute' see PARA 1360 (definition applied by the Universal Credit Regulations 2013, SI 2013/376, reg 2).
3   See the Universal Credit Regulations 2013, SI 2013/376, reg 56; and WELFARE BENEFITS AND STATE PENSIONS vol 104 (2014) PARA 58.
4   Ie under the Welfare Reform Act 2012 s 26 (higher level sanctions) or s 27 (other sanctions): see WELFARE BENEFITS AND STATE PENSIONS vol 104 (2014) PARAS 108–109.
5   See the Universal Credit Regulations 2013, SI 2013/376, reg 113(1)(a); and WELFARE BENEFITS AND STATE PENSIONS vol 104 (2014) PARA 115.
6   See the Universal Credit Regulations 2013, SI 2013/376, reg 113(1)(a); and WELFARE BENEFITS AND STATE PENSIONS vol 104 (2014) PARA 115.

1358. Effect of trade dispute on statutory sick pay. An employee is not entitled to statutory sick pay[1] if on the date on which he would otherwise have become eligible there is a stoppage of work due to a trade dispute[2] at the employee's place of employment[3], unless the employee proves that at no time on or before that date did he have a direct interest[4] in the trade dispute in question[5].

1 As to statutory sick pay generally see PARA 558 et seq.
2 'Trade dispute' is not defined for these purposes; but c f PARA 1212 note 4.
3 'Place of employment' is not defined for these purposes; but c f the meaning of 'place of work' in PARA 1355 note 2.
4 As to the meaning of 'directly interested' see PARA 1355 note 3.
5 See the Social Security Contributions and Benefits Act 1992 s 153(3), Sch 11 paras 1, 2(g), 7; and PARA 574.

(4) TRADE DISPUTE IMMUNITY

1359. Trade dispute immunity; in general. An act[1] done by a person in contemplation or furtherance[2] of a trade dispute[3] is protected[4] by certain statutory immunities against liability for certain economic torts[5]. Such an act is also to be disregarded for the purposes of the statutory offence of conspiracy where the act constitutes no more than a summary offence not punishable with imprisonment[6]. Further, it is lawful for a person in contemplation or furtherance of a trade dispute to attend at or near his own place of work or, in the case of a trade union official, at or near the place of work of a member of the union whom he is accompanying and whom he represents, for the purpose only of peaceful picketing[7].

1 As to the meaning of 'act' see PARA 1028 note 11.
2 As to the meaning of 'in contemplation or furtherance' see PARA 1362.
3 As to the meaning of 'trade dispute' for these purposes see PARAS 1360–1361.
4 Ie is not actionable: see the Trade Union and Labour Relations (Consolidation) Act 1992 s 219(1); and PARA 1363.
5 See the Trade Union and Labour Relations (Consolidation) Act 1992 s 219; and PARA 1363.
6 See PARA 1364.
7 See PARA 1385.

1360. The parties to a trade dispute. For the purposes of the statutory provisions relating to industrial action[1], 'trade dispute' means a dispute between workers[2] and their own employer[3] which relates wholly or mainly[4] to one or more of a number of specified matters[5].

1 Ie for the purposes of the Trade Union and Labour Relations (Consolidation) Act 1992 Pt V (ss 219–246): see the text and notes 2–5; and PARA 1361 et seq. A wider definition of 'trade dispute' is used for the purposes of Pt IV (ss 178–218): see PARA 1212. Cf also the Jobseekers Act 1995 s 35(1); and PARA 1212 note 4.
2 In relation to a dispute with an employer, 'worker' means a worker employed by that employer, or a person who has ceased to be so employed if his employment was terminated in connection with the dispute or if the termination of his employment was one of the circumstances giving rise to the dispute: Trade Union and Labour Relations (Consolidation) Act 1992 s 244(5). For these purposes, 'employment' includes any relationship whereby one person personally does work or performs services for another: s 244(5). As to the meanings of 'worker' and 'employment' generally see PARA 892. The workers may be represented by a trade union: *National Association of Local Government Officers v Bolton Corpn* [1943] AC 166, [1942] 2 All ER 425, HL; *Bird v O'Neal* [1960] AC 907, [1960] 3 All ER 254, PC; *Beetham v Trinidad Cement Ltd* [1960] AC 132, [1960] 1 All ER 274, PC. However, a dispute in which a union acts on its own behalf as distinct from on behalf of workers is not a trade dispute: *JT Stratford & Son Ltd v Lindley* [1965] AC 269, [1964] 3 All ER 102, HL; *Torquay Hotel Co Ltd v Cousins* [1969] 2 Ch 106, [1969] 1 All ER 522, CA. A union may not now raise a dispute on behalf of workers who are not themselves in dispute with their employer: c f *Camellia Tanker Ltd SA v International Transport Workers' Federation* [1976] ICR 274, [1976] IRLR 190, CA; *NWL Ltd v Woods, NWL Ltd v Nelson* [1979] 3 All ER 614, [1979] ICR 867, HL (both decided under the pre-1982 law).

3   As to the meaning of 'employer' see PARA 892. A dispute between a Minister of the Crown and any workers is to be treated as a dispute between those workers and their employer, notwithstanding that he is not the employer of those workers, if the dispute relates to matters which: (1) have been referred for consideration by a joint body on which, by virtue of provision made by or under any enactment, the Minister is represented; or (2) cannot be settled without his exercising a power conferred on him by or under an enactment: Trade Union and Labour Relations (Consolidation) Act 1992 s 244(2). As to Crown employees and contracts see PARA 1363 note 8.

     An employer cannot evade being a party to a trade dispute simply by changing his legal identity: *Examite Ltd v Whittaker* [1977] IRLR 312, CA (where a firm became incorporated); *Porr v Shaw, Johnson and Holden, The Marabu Porr* [1979] 2 Lloyd's Rep 331, CA (where a company used its subsidiary as a device). Cf, however, *Dimbleby & Sons Ltd v National Union of Journalists* [1984] 1 All ER 751, [1984] ICR 386, HL (where the court refused to lift the veil of incorporation). There is no trade dispute where the dispute is essentially between two groups of employers (*Larkin v Long* [1915] AC 814, HL), or two groups of workers (*Cory Lighterage Ltd v Transport and General Workers' Union* [1973] 2 All ER 558, [1973] ICR 339, CA). A dispute relating to terms and conditions of employment between an unidentified future employer and future employees is not a trade dispute: *University College London Hospital NHS Trust v UNISON* [1999] ICR 204, [1999] IRLR 31, CA, approved in Application 53574/99 *UNISON v United Kingdom* [2002] IRLR 497, ECtHR.

4   See PARA 1361 note 1.

5   Trade Union and Labour Relations (Consolidation) Act 1992 s 244(1). The specified matters are those listed in s 244(1)(a)–(g): see PARA 1361 heads (1)–(7). A dispute between staff employed to work at a school having a delegated budget and the school's governing body which relates wholly or mainly to one or more of the matters set out in s 244(1) is a trade dispute within the meaning of the Trade Union and Labour Relations (Consolidation) Act 1992, save that, in any case where there is a trade dispute only by virtue of the operation of this provision, nothing in s 219 (see PARA 1363) prevents an act from being actionable in tort where the inducement, interference or threat mentioned in s 219 relates to a contract the performance of which does not affect directly or indirectly the school over which the governing body in question exercises its functions: Education (Modification of Enactments Relating to Employment) (England) Order 2003, SI 2003/1964, art 5(1), (2); Education (Modification of Enactments Relating to Employment) (Wales) Order 2006, SI 2006/1073, art 5(1), (2).

1361. The subject matter of a trade dispute. A trade dispute must relate wholly or mainly[1] to one or more of the following:

(1)   terms and conditions of employment[2], or the physical conditions in which workers[3] are required to work[4];

(2)   the engagement or non-engagement of one or more workers, or the termination[5] or suspension of employment or the duties of employment of one or more workers[6];

(3)   the allocation of work or the duties of employment between workers or groups of workers[7];

(4)   matters of discipline[8];

(5)   a worker's membership or non-membership of a trade union[9];

(6)   facilities for officials of a trade union[10]; and

(7)   machinery for negotiation or consultation or other procedures relating to any of the above matters, including the recognition by employers[11] or employers' associations[12] of the right of a trade union to represent workers in such negotiation or consultation or in the carrying out of such procedures[13].

There is a trade dispute even though it relates to matters occurring outside the United Kingdom, so long as the person or persons whose actions[14] in the United Kingdom are said to be in contemplation or furtherance[15] of a trade dispute relating to matters occurring outside the United Kingdom are likely to be affected in respect of one or more of the matters specified in heads (1) to (7) above by the outcome of the dispute[16].

1 Trade Union and Labour Relations (Consolidation) Act 1992 s 244(1). See *Mercury Communications Ltd v Scott-Gamer* [1984] Ch 37, [1984] ICR 74, CA; *Associated British Ports v Transport and General Workers' Union* [1989] IRLR 291 at 301 per Millett J (affd on other grounds [1989] 3 All ER 822, [1989] ICR 557 at 590, HL (revsng [1989] 3 All ER 796, [1989] ICR 557, CA)); *Wandsworth London Borough Council v National Association of Schoolmasters/Union of Women Teachers* [1994] ICR 81, [1993] IRLR 344, CA; *University College London Hospital NHS Trust v UNISON* [1999] ICR 204, [1999] IRLR 31, CA; *Westminster City Council v UNISON* [2001] EWCA Civ 443, [2001] ICR 1046, [2001] IRLR 524. The definition of 'trade dispute' was amended by the Employment Act 1982 s 18 (repealed); before then the dispute merely had to be 'connected with' one or more of the listed matters. The change was intended to emphasise that there is no trade dispute where the motive is predominantly political (see *National Sailors' and Firemen's Union of Great Britain and Ireland v Reed* [1926] Ch 536; *Associated Newspapers Group Ltd v Flynn* (1970) 10 KIR 17; *Sherard v Amalgamated Union of Engineering Workers* [1973] ICR 421, CA; *General Aviation Services (UK) Ltd v Transport and General Workers' Union* [1985] ICR 615, [1976] IRLR 224, HL; *Express Newspapers Ltd v Keys* [1980] IRLR 247; *Duport Steels Ltd v Sirs* [1980] 1 All ER 529, [1980] ICR 161, HL; *Mercury Communications Ltd v Scott-Gamer* above; *University College London Hospital NHS Trust v UNISON* above; *Westminster City Council v UNISON*[2001] EWCA Civ 443, [2001] ICR 1046, [2001] IRLR 524) or personal (see *Conway v Wade* [1909] AC 506, HL; *Dallimore v Williams and Jesson* (1912) 29 TLR 67, CA; *Huntley v Thornton* [1957] 1 All ER 234, [1957] 1 WLR 321) or vindictive (see *JT Stratford & Son Ltd v Lindley* [1965] AC 269, [1964] 3 All ER 102, HL; *Torquay Hotel Co Ltd v Cousins* [1969] 2 Ch 106, [1969] 1 All ER 522, CA; *Universe Tankships Inc of Monrovia v International Transport Workers' Federation* [1983] 1 AC 366, [1982] ICR 262, HL), or is otherwise not a 'trade' objective (see *BBC v Hearn* [1978] 1 All ER 111, [1977] ICR 685, CA (anti-apartheid); *NWL Ltd v Woods, NWL Ltd v Nelson* [1979] 3 All ER 614, [1979] ICR 867, HL (flags of convenience)). Strike action by teachers relating to their refusal to teach a disruptive pupil constitutes a trade dispute over terms and conditions for the purposes of the Trade Union and Labour Relations (Consolidation) Act 1992 s 244(1): *P v National Association of Schoolmasters/Union of Women Teachers* [2003] UKHL 8, [2003] 2 AC 663, [2003] 1 All ER 993. The pre-1982 definition of 'trade dispute' whereby the dispute needed only to be 'connected with' one or more of the specified matters still applies for the purposes of the Trade Union and Labour Relations (Consolidation) Act 1992 Pt IV (ss 178–218): see s 218(1); and PARA 1212.

2 This may include terms understood and applied by the parties in practice, or habitually, or by common consent, without ever being incorporated into the contract (*BBC v Hearn* [1978] 1 All ER 111, [1977] ICR 685, CA; *Hadmor Productions Ltd v Hamilton* [1983] 1 AC 191, [1982] ICR 114, HL); but not everything that is in a contract of employment is necessarily a term or condition of employment (*Universe Tankships Inc of Monrovia v International Transport Workers' Federation* [1983] 1 AC 366, [1982] ICR 262, HL). A dispute over the proper interpretation of a term in the contract and the legality of an instruction by the employer is capable of being a dispute related to terms and conditions of employment: *P v National Association of School Masters/Union of Women Teachers* [2001] EWCA Civ 652, [2001] ICR 1241, [2001] IRLR 532. The terms and conditions do not have to be those of the striking workers: *British Telecommunications plc v Communication Workers Union* [2003] EWHC 937 (QB), [2004] IRLR 58. As to the meaning of 'employment' for these purposes see PARA 1360 note 2.

3 As to the meaning of 'worker' for these purposes see PARA 1360 note 2.

4 Trade Union and Labour Relations (Consolidation) Act 1992 s 244(1)(a).

5 This head may include genuine fears of redundancy: *General Aviation Services (UK) Ltd v Transport and General Workers' Union* [1985] ICR 615, [1976] IRLR 224, HL; *Health Computing Ltd v Meek* [1981] ICR 24, [1980] IRLR 437; *Hadmor Productions Ltd v Hamilton* [1983] 1 AC 191, [1982] ICR 114, HL; cf *Mercury Communications Ltd v Scott-Gamer* [1984] Ch 37, [1984] ICR 74, CA.

6 Trade Union and Labour Relations (Consolidation) Act 1992 s 244(1)(b).

7 Trade Union and Labour Relations (Consolidation) Act 1992 s 244(1)(c). By virtue of the meaning of 'worker' for these purposes, in order to qualify as a trade dispute, the dispute must relate to the allocation of duties between workers employed by the same employer: *Dimbleby & Sons Ltd v National Union of Journalists* [1984] 1 All ER 751, [1984] ICR 386, HL.

8 Trade Union and Labour Relations (Consolidation) Act 1992 s 244(1)(d).

9 Trade Union and Labour Relations (Consolidation) Act 1992 s 244(1)(e). Industrial action to enforce trade union membership will, however, be unprotected by the statutory immunities: see PARA 1365. As to the meaning of 'trade union' see PARA 891.

10   Trade Union and Labour Relations (Consolidation) Act 1992 s 244(1)(f). As to the meaning of
     'official', in relation to a trade union, see PARA 1018.
11   As to the meaning of 'employer' see PARA 892; but c f PARA 1360 notes 2–3.
12   As to the meaning of 'employers' association' see PARA 1079.
13   Trade Union and Labour Relations (Consolidation) Act 1992 s 244(1)(g).
14   As to the meaning of 'action' see PARA 1028 note 11.
15   As to the meaning of 'in contemplation or furtherance' see PARA 1362.
16   Trade Union and Labour Relations (Consolidation) Act 1992 s 244(3).

1362.   Meaning of 'in contemplation or furtherance of a trade dispute'.   An act
may be done in contemplation of an impending dispute[1], or in furtherance[2] of an
existing dispute[3], if it is done with the object of promoting the interests of one of
the parties to the dispute[4]. The issue is whether the person acting in
contemplation or furtherance of the dispute honestly believes that his act may
advance the interests of one of them[5]. An act[6], threat or demand done or made
by one person or organisation against another which, if resisted, would have led
to a trade dispute[7] with that other is to be treated as being done or made in
contemplation of a trade dispute with that other, notwithstanding that no
dispute arises because the other person or organisation submits to the act or
threat or accedes to the demand[8].

1   A dispute means something fairly definite, more than a mere grumble (*Conway v Wade* [1909]
    AC 506, HL), but the parties need not have adopted inflexible attitudes (*Beetham v Trinidad
    Cement Ltd* [1960] AC 132, [1960] 1 All ER 274, PC); indeed they can be in dispute without
    ever having had direct contact with each other (*Health Computing Ltd v Meek* [1981] ICR 24,
    [1980] IRLR 437).
2   The statutory protection does not extend to acts done in consequence of a dispute that has been
    settled: *JT Stratford & Son Ltd v Lindley* [1965] AC 269, [1964] 3 All ER 102, HL; *Stewart v
    Amalgamated Union of Engineering Workers (Engineering Section)* [1973] ICR 128, [1973]
    IRLR 57, NIRC.
3   The question whether a trade dispute exists or is apprehended is an objective one: *Bents
    Brewery Co Ltd v Hogan* [1945] 2 All ER 570; *NWL Ltd v Woods, NWL Ltd v Nelson* [1979]
    3 All ER 614, [1979] ICR 867, HL; *Express Newspapers Ltd v McShane* [1980] AC 672, [1980]
    ICR 42, HL.
4   *Conway v Wade* [1909] AC 506, HL; *Express Newspapers Ltd v McShane* [1980] AC 672,
    [1980] ICR 42, HL. Cf the test of whether an act is done in contemplation or furtherance of a
    dispute: see the text and note 5.
5   *NWL Ltd v Woods, NWL Ltd v Nelson* [1979] 3 All ER 614, [1979] ICR 867, HL; *Express
    Newspapers Ltd v McShane* [1980] AC 672, [1980] ICR 42, HL; *Duport Steels Ltd v Sirs*
    [1980] 1 All ER 529, [1980] ICR 161, HL, overruling earlier cases which had said that the test
    was objective, i e whether the act done was reasonably likely to achieve the actor's purpose. As
    to the relevance of motive see *Norbrook Laboratories Ltd v King, Norbrook Laboratories Ltd v
    Sands* [1984] IRLR 200, NI CA; *Associated British Ports v Transport and General Workers'
    Union* [1989] IRLR 291; affd on other grounds [1989] 3 All ER 822, [1989] ICR 557 at
    590, HL (revsing [1989] 3 All ER 796, [1989] ICR 557, CA).
6   As to the meaning of 'act' see PARA 1028 note 11.
7   As to the meaning of 'trade dispute' see PARAS 1360–1361.
8   Trade Union and Labour Relations (Consolidation) Act 1992 s 244(4), reversing the decision in
    Cory Lighterage Ltd v Transport and General Workers' Union [1973] 2 All ER 558, [1973] ICR
    339, CA. See also *Hadmor Productions Ltd v Hamilton* [1983] 1 AC 191, [1982] ICR 114, HL.

1363.   Immunity against liability for the economic torts.   An act[1] done by a
person in contemplation or furtherance[2] of a trade dispute[3] is not actionable[4] in
tort[5] on the ground only[6]:

(1)   that it induces another person to break a contract[7] or interferes with its
      performance or induces any other person to interfere with its
      performance; or

(2)   that it consists in his threatening that a contract, whether one to which

he is a party or not, will be broken or its performance interfered with, or that he will induce another person to break a contract or to interfere with its performance[8].

Furthermore, an agreement or combination by two or more persons to do or procure the doing of any act in contemplation or furtherance of a trade dispute is not actionable in tort if the act is one which, if done without any such agreement or combination, would not be actionable in tort[9].

The above statutory immunities have effect subject to certain statutory provisions[10] which exclude their protection in certain circumstances and to the statutory requirements of a ballot[11] and notice to the employer[12] before industrial action[13]. Accordingly, liability in tort for an act in contemplation or furtherance of a trade dispute is to be considered in three stages[14]:

(a)   the existence of any common law liability[15];

(b)   the availability of a statutory immunity[16]; and

(c)   the statutory exclusion of that immunity with the result that liability is restored[17].

1   As to the meaning of 'act' see PARA 1028 note 11.
2   As to the meaning of 'in contemplation or furtherance' see PARA 1362.
3   As to the meaning of 'trade dispute' see PARAS 1360–1361.
4   Ie not actionable by anyone, and thus for practical purposes lawful. In particular, such an act cannot constitute 'unlawful means' for the purpose of establishing an indirect tort: *Hadmor Productions Ltd v Hamilton* [1983] 1 AC 191, [1982] ICR 114, HL (where it was held that the provision provided a defence to an alleged interference with the business expectations of persons between whom there was no contract).
5   The Trade Union and Labour Relations (Consolidation) Act 1992 s 219(1) strictly does not afford a defence to any other liability, eg criminal, contractual or equitable; but see *Universe Tankships Inc of Monrovia v International Transport Workers' Federation* [1983] 1 AC 366, [1982] ICR 262, HL (where this provision was taken as a guide to public policy in distinguishing between permissible commercial pressure and unlawful economic duress in an action for restitution of money paid under duress); and see *Dimskal Shipping Co SA v International Transport Workers' Federation, The Evia Luck* (No 2) [1992] 2 AC 152, [1992] ICR 37, HL.
6   The Trade Union and Labour Relations (Consolidation) Act 1992 s 219(1) affords a defence to liability for the specified torts only; there is no defence to liability for other non-specified torts, eg nuisance, trespass, defamation, deceit or torts based on breach of statutory duty.
7   The Trade Union and Labour Relations (Consolidation) Act 1992 s 219(1) protects against interference with contractual obligations only: *Prudential Assurance Co Ltd v Lorenz* (1971) 11 KIR 78 (no defence to inducing a breach of the equitable duty to account); *Meade v Haringey London Borough Council* [1979] 2 All ER 1016, [1979] ICR 494, CA (no defence to inducing a breach of statutory duty); and see *Barretts & Baird (Wholesale) Ltd v Institution of Professional Civil Servants* [1987] IRLR 3; *Associated British Ports v Transport and General Workers' Union* [1989] IRLR 291; affd on other grounds [1989] 3 All ER 822, [1989] ICR 557 at 590, HL (revsing [1989] 3 All ER 796, [1989] ICR 557, CA). The Trade Union and Labour Relations (Consolidation) Act 1992 s 219(1) affords an indirect defence to the torts of interfering with contract or business by unlawful means or conspiracy to use unlawful means, where the unlawful means alleged are acts which are themselves rendered not actionable by s 219: see *Hadmor Productions Ltd v Hamilton* [1983] 1 AC 191, [1982] ICR 114, HL (cited in note 4).
8   Trade Union and Labour Relations (Consolidation) Act 1992 s 219(1). Where a person holds any office or employment under the Crown on terms which do not constitute a contract of employment between that person and the Crown, those terms are nevertheless deemed to constitute such a contract for the purposes of: (1) the law relating to liability in tort of a person who commits an act which: (a) induces another person to break a contract, interferes with the performance of a contract or induces another person to interfere with its performance; or (b) consists in a threat that a contract will be broken or its performance interfered with, or that any person will be induced to break a contract or interfere with its performance; and (2) the provisions of the Trade Union and Labour Relations (Consolidation) Act 1992 or any other Act which refer, whether in relation to contracts generally or only in relation to contracts of employment, to such an act: s 245. As to Crown employment generally see PARA 893.

9   Trade Union and Labour Relations (Consolidation) Act 1992 s 219(2). This provision is
    primarily intended to defend against the tort of conspiracy to injure as opposed to conspiracy to
    use unlawful means (see *Rookes v Barnard* [1964] AC 1129, [1964] 1 All ER 367, HL), but
    arguably its terms are wide enough to defend against the latter too where the means used are not
    tortious. As to the position if the means used are tortious see note 7.
10 Ie the Trade Union and Labour Relations (Consolidation) Act 1992 ss 222–225 (action excluded
    from protection): see PARA 1365 et seq.
11 Ie the Trade Union and Labour Relations (Consolidation) Act 1992 s 226: see PARA 1370.
12 Ie the Trade Union and Labour Relations (Consolidation) Act 1992 s 234A: see PARA 1382.
13 Trade Union and Labour Relations (Consolidation) Act 1992 s 219(4) (amended by the Trade
    Union Reform and Employment Rights Act 1993 Sch 8 para 72).
14 As to the adoption of this approach see *Marina Shipping Ltd v Laughton* [1982] QB 1127,
    [1982] ICR 215, CA; *Hadmor Productions Ltd v Hamilton* [1983] 1 AC 191, [1982] ICR
    114, HL; *Merkur Island Shipping Corpn v Laughton* [1983] 2 AC 570, [1983] ICR 490, HL;
    Dimbleby & Sons Ltd v National Union of Journalists [1984] 1 All ER 751, [1984] ICR
    386, HL.
15 As to liability in tort at common law see PARA 1343.
16 Ie under the Trade Union and Labour Relations (Consolidation) Act 1992 s 219.
17 See the text and notes 10–13. See also the Trade Union and Labour Relations (Consolidation)
    Act 1992 s 219(3) (liability for unlawful picketing); and PARA 1369. As to further liabilities for
    picketing see PARA 1383 et seq.

1364.   Immunity from criminal conspiracy.   Where, in pursuance of any
agreement which could constitute the statutory offence of conspiracy[1], the acts in
question in relation to an offence are to be done in contemplation or
furtherance[2] of a trade dispute[3], that offence is to be disregarded[4] if it is a
summary offence which is not punishable with imprisonment[5].

1   Ie any such agreement as is mentioned in the Criminal Law Act 1977 s 1(1): see CRIMINAL LAW
    vol 25 (2010) PARA 74.
2   As to the meaning of 'in contemplation or furtherance' see PARA 1362.
3   As to the meaning of 'trade dispute' see PARAS 1360–1361.
4   Ie for the purposes of the Criminal Law Act 1977 s 1(1).
5   Trade Union and Labour Relations (Consolidation) Act 1992 s 242(1). Section 242 extends to
    England and Wales only: s 242(2). As to the immunity for peaceful picketing see s 220; and PARA
    1385.

(5) RESTRICTIONS ON THE TRADE DISPUTE IMMUNITY

(i) Action Excluded from Protection

1365.   Action to enforce trade union membership.   An act[1] is not protected[2] by
the statutory immunity[3] against liability for certain economic torts[4] if the reason,
or one of the reasons[5], for which the act is done is the fact or belief that a
particular employer[6]:

(1)   is employing[7], has employed or might employ a person who is not a
        member of a trade union[8]; or
(2)   is failing, has failed or might fail to discriminate[9] against such a
        person[10].

Nor is an act so protected if it constitutes, or is one of a number of acts which
together constitute, an inducement or attempted inducement of a person either:

(a)   to incorporate in a contract to which he is a party, or a proposed
        contract to which he intends to be a party, a term or condition relating
        to union membership which would be void[11] by statute; or
(b)   to contravene the statutory restrictions[12] concerning a refusal to deal
        with a supplier of goods or services on grounds relating to union
        membership[13].

1   As to the meaning of 'act' see PARA 1028 note 11.

2   For these purposes, 'not protected' means excluded from the protection afforded by the Trade Union and Labour Relations (Consolidation) Act 1992 s 219 (see PARA 1363), or, where the expression is used with reference to a particular person, excluded from that protection as respects that person: s 219(4) (amended by the Trade Union Reform and Employment Rights Act 1993 Sch 8 para 72).

3   Ie under the Trade Union and Labour Relations (Consolidation) Act 1992 s 219. As to the trade dispute immunity see PARA 1359 et seq.

4   Ie those referred to in the Trade Union and Labour Relations (Consolidation) Act 1992 s 219(1), (2): see PARA 1363.

5   Where there is more than one reason for the tortious act, it seems that the prohibited reason need not be the predominant reason in order for the statutory immunities to be excluded: see the Trade Union and Labour Relations (Consolidation) Act 1992 s 222(1).

6   As to the meaning of 'employer' see PARA 892; but c f note 7.

7   For these purposes, references to an employer employing a person are to a person acting in the capacity of the person for whom a worker works or normally works: Trade Union and Labour Relations (Consolidation) Act 1992 s 222(4). As to the meaning of 'worker' see PARA 892.

8   As to the meaning of 'trade union' see PARA 891. For these purposes, references to not being a member of a trade union are to not being a member of any trade union, or of a particular trade union, or of one of a number of particular trade unions; and any such reference includes a reference to not being a member of a particular branch or section of a trade union or of one of a number of particular branches or sections of a trade union: Trade Union and Labour Relations (Consolidation) Act 1992 s 222(5). As to the meaning of 'branch or section', in relation to a trade union, see PARA 898 note 5.

9   For these purposes, an employer discriminates against a person if, but only if, he ensures that his conduct in relation to: (1) persons, or persons of any description, employed by him, or who apply to him to be considered, or are considered by him, for employment; or (2) the provision of employment for such persons, is different in some or all cases according to whether or not they are members of a trade union, and is more favourable to those who are: Trade Union and Labour Relations (Consolidation) Act 1992 s 222(2).

10 Trade Union and Labour Relations (Consolidation) Act 1992 s 222(1).

11 Ie under the Trade Union and Labour Relations (Consolidation) Act 1992 s 144: see PARA 1069.

12 Ie those contained in the Trade Union and Labour Relations (Consolidation) Act 1992 s 145: see PARA 1070.

13 Trade Union and Labour Relations (Consolidation) Act 1992 s 222(3). As to the meanings of 'refuse to deal' and 'union membership grounds' see PARA 1070.

1366. Action taken because of dismissal for taking unofficial action. An act[1] is not protected[2] by the statutory immunity[3] against liability for certain economic torts[4] if the reason, or one of the reasons[5], for doing it is the fact or belief that an employer[6] has dismissed[7] one or more employees[8] in circumstances such that, by virtue of the statutory provisions relating to dismissal in connection with unofficial action[9], they have no right to complain of unfair dismissal[10].

1   As to the meaning of 'act' see PARA 1028 note 11.

2   As to the meaning of 'not protected' see PARA 1365 note 2.

3   Ie under the Trade Union and Labour Relations (Consolidation) Act 1992 s 219: see PARA 1363.

4   Ie those referred to in the Trade Union and Labour Relations (Consolidation) Act 1992 s 219(1), (2): see PARA 1363.

5   Where there is more than one reason for the tortious act, it seems that the prohibited reason need not be the predominant reason in order for the statutory immunities to be excluded: see the Trade Union and Labour Relations (Consolidation) Act 1992 s 223.

6   As to the meaning of 'employer' see PARA 892.

7   As to the meaning of 'dismiss' see PARA 1056 note 1.

8   As to the meaning of 'employee' see PARA 892.

9   Ie by virtue of the Trade Union and Labour Relations (Consolidation) Act 1992 s 237: see PARA 1350.

10 Trade Union and Labour Relations (Consolidation) Act 1992 s 223.

1367. Secondary action. An act[1] is not protected[2] by the statutory immunity[3] against liability for certain economic torts[4] if one of the facts relied on for the purpose of establishing liability is that there has been secondary action which is not lawful picketing[5].

There is secondary action in relation to a trade dispute[6] when, and only when, a person:

(1)   induces another to break a contract of employment[7] or interferes or induces another to interfere with its performance; or

(2)   threatens that a contract of employment under which he or another is employed will be broken or its performance interfered with, or that he will induce another to break a contract of employment or to interfere with its performance,

and the employer under the contract of employment is not the employer party to the dispute[8].

An act in contemplation or furtherance[9] of a trade dispute which is primary action[10] in relation to that dispute may not be relied on as secondary action in relation to another trade dispute[11].

The European Court of Human Rights has held that this statutory prohibition on secondary industrial action is not a breach of the right to freedom of association guaranteed[12] by the European Convention on Human Rights[13].

1   As to the meaning of 'act' see PARA 1028 note 11.
2   As to the meaning of 'not protected' see PARA 1365 note 2.
3   Ie under the Trade Union and Labour Relations (Consolidation) Act 1992 s 219: see PARA 1363.
4   Ie those referred to in the Trade Union and Labour Relations (Consolidation) Act 1992 s 219(1), (2): see PARA 1363.
5   Trade Union and Labour Relations (Consolidation) Act 1992 s 224(1). For these purposes, 'lawful picketing' means acts done in the course of such attendance as is declared lawful by s 220 (see PARA 1385): (1) by a worker employed, or, in the case of a worker not in employment, last employed, by the employer party to the dispute; or (2) by a trade union official whose attendance is lawful by virtue of s 220(1)(b) (see PARA 1385 head (2)): s 224(3). An employer is not to be treated as party to a dispute between another employer and workers of that employer; and, where more than one employer is in dispute with his workers, the dispute between each employer and his workers is to be treated as a separate dispute: s 224(4). The court will not lift the veil of incorporation: *Dimbleby & Sons Ltd v National Union of Journalists* [1984] 1 All ER 751, [1984] ICR 386, HL. For the purposes of the Trade Union and Labour Relations (Consolidation) Act 1992 s 224(4), 'worker' has the same meaning as in s 244 (meaning of 'trade dispute') (see PARA 1360 note 2): s 224(4). As to the meanings of 'worker' generally, and of 'employer', see PARA 892; as to the meaning of 'trade union' see PARA 891; and as to the meaning of 'official', in relation to a trade union, see PARA 1018.
6   As to the meaning of 'trade dispute' see PARAS 1360–1361.
7   For these purposes, 'contract of employment' includes any contract under which one person personally does work or performs services for another; and related expressions are to be construed accordingly: Trade Union and Labour Relations (Consolidation) Act 1992 s 224(6). As to the meaning of 'contract of employment' generally see PARA 892.
8   Trade Union and Labour Relations (Consolidation) Act 1992 s 224(2).
9   As to the meaning of 'in contemplation or furtherance' see PARA 1362.
10   For these purposes, 'primary action' means such action as is mentioned in the Trade Union and Labour Relations (Consolidation) Act 1992 s 224(2)(a) or (b) (see heads (1)–(2) in the text) where the employer under the contract of employment is the employer party to the dispute: s 224(5).
11   Trade Union and Labour Relations (Consolidation) Act 1992 s 224(5).
12   Ie guaranteed by the Convention for the Protection of Human Rights and Fundamental Freedoms (Rome, 4 November 1950; TS 71 (1953); Cmd 8969) (the 'European Convention on Human Rights') art 11 (now incorporated into domestic law by the Human Rights Act 1998 Sch 1 Pt I art 11: see RIGHTS AND FREEDOMS vol 88A (2013) PARA 461 et seq).
13   See Application 31045/10 *National Union of Rail, Maritime and Transport Workers v United Kingdom* [2014] IRLR 467, ECtHR (where the union claimed that UK strike law is unduly

restrictive of its freedom of association under the European Convention on Human Rights art 11 on two grounds: (1) the inordinate complexity of the law relating to strike notices (see the Trade Union and Labour Relations (Consolidation) Act 1992 ss 226, 226A; and PARA 1372); and (2) the total ban on sympathetic industrial action under ss 224, 244).

1368. Pressure to impose trade union recognition requirement. An act[1] is not protected[2] by the statutory immunity[3] against liability for certain economic torts[4] if it constitutes, or is one of a number of acts which together constitute, an inducement or attempted inducement of a person either:

(1)   to incorporate in a contract to which he is a party, or a proposed contract to which he intends to be a party, a term or condition relating to trade union recognition[5] which is or would be void[6] by statute; or

(2)   to contravene the statutory restrictions[7] concerning a refusal to deal with a supplier of goods or services on grounds of union exclusion[8].

Nor is an act protected if the following conditions are satisfied:

(a)   it interferes with the supply, whether or not under a contract, of goods or services, or can reasonably be expected to have that effect; and

(b)   one of the facts relied on for the purpose of establishing liability is that a person has:

   (i)   induced another to break a contract of employment[9] or interfered or induced another to interfere with its performance; or

   (ii)   threatened that a contract of employment under which he or another is employed will be broken or its performance interfered with, or that he will induce another to break a contract of employment or to interfere with its performance; and

(c)   the reason, or one of the reasons, for doing the act is the fact or belief that the supplier, not being the employer[10] under the contract of employment mentioned in head (b) above, does not or might not recognise one or more trade unions for the purposes of negotiating on behalf of workers[11], or any class of worker, employed by him, or negotiate or consult with, or with an official[12] of, one or more trade unions[13].

1   As to the meaning of 'act' see PARA 1028 note 11.
2   As to the meaning of 'not protected' see PARA 1365 note 2.
3   Ie under the Trade Union and Labour Relations (Consolidation) Act 1992 s 219: see PARA 1363.
4   Ie those referred to in the Trade Union and Labour Relations (Consolidation) Act 1992 s 219(1), (2): see PARA 1363.
5   As to the meaning of 'trade union' see PARA 891; and as to the meaning of 'recognition' see PARA 1094.
6   Ie under the Trade Union and Labour Relations (Consolidation) Act 1992 s 186: see PARA 1183.
7   Ie those contained in the Trade Union and Labour Relations (Consolidation) Act 1992 s 187: see PARA 1184.
8   Trade Union and Labour Relations (Consolidation) Act 1992 s 225(1).
9   As to the meaning of 'contract of employment' see PARA 892.
10   As to the meaning of 'employer' see PARA 892.
11   As to the meaning of 'worker' see PARA 892.
12   As to the meaning of 'official', in relation to a trade union, see PARA 1018.
13   Trade Union and Labour Relations (Consolidation) Act 1992 s 225(2).

1369. Unlawful picketing. Nothing in the provisions conferring statutory immunity[1] from liability for certain economic torts[2] prevents an act[3] done in the course of picketing from being actionable in tort unless it is done in the course of attendance declared lawful by the statutory provisions[4] relating to peaceful picketing[5].

1   Ie the Trade Union and Labour Relations (Consolidation) Act 1992 s 219(1), (2): see PARA 1363.
2   Ie those referred to in the Trade Union and Labour Relations (Consolidation) Act 1992
    s 219(1), (2).
3   As to the meaning of 'act' see PARA 1028 note 11.
4   Ie by the Trade Union and Labour Relations (Consolidation) Act 1992 s 220: see PARA 1385.
5   Trade Union and Labour Relations (Consolidation) Act 1992 s 219(3).

(ii) Industrial Action Ballots

1370.   Requirement of a ballot before industrial action.   An act[1] done by a
trade union[2] to induce[3] a person[4] to take part, or continue to take part, in
industrial action[5] is not protected[6] by the statutory immunity[7] against liability
for certain economic torts[8] unless the industrial action has the support of a
ballot[9].

Industrial action is to be regarded as having the support of a ballot[10] only if:

(1)   the union has held a ballot in respect of the action in relation to which
       the statutory requirements with regard to the appointment of a
       scrutineer[11] and entitlement to vote and voting procedure[12] were
       satisfied, and in which the majority[13] voting in the ballot answered 'Yes'
       to the question applicable[14] to industrial action of the kind to which the
       act of inducement relates[15];

(2)   such of the statutory requirements relating to the scrutineer's report[16] as
       have fallen to be satisfied at the relevant time[17] have been satisfied[18];

(3)   the statutory requirements[19] concerning the inducement of a member
       denied entitlement to vote do not prevent the industrial action from
       being regarded as having the support of the ballot[20]; and

(4)   the statutory requirements[21] concerning the calling of industrial action
       are satisfied[22].

If the statutory requirements[23] concerning the informing of employers of the
result of a ballot fall to be satisfied in relation to an employer, as respects that
employer industrial action is not to be regarded as having the support of a ballot
unless those requirements are satisfied in relation to that employer[24].

1   As to the meaning of 'act' see PARA 1028 note 11.
2   An act is taken to have been done by a trade union if it was authorised or indorsed by the union
    in accordance with the Trade Union and Labour Relations (Consolidation) Act 1992 s 20
    (statutory provisions concerning the liability of a union for the economic torts) (see PARA 1388):
    see s 20(1). As to the meaning of 'trade union' see PARA 891. As to the application of the
    balloting requirements to federated trade unions see *Shipping Co Uniform Inc v International
    Transport Workers' Federation* [1985] ICR 245, [1985] IRLR 71.
3   For these purposes, an inducement, in relation to a person, includes an inducement which is or
    would be ineffective, whether because of his unwillingness to be influenced by it or for any other
    reason: Trade Union and Labour Relations (Consolidation) Act 1992 s 226(4).
4   For these purposes, and for the purposes of the Trade Union and Labour Relations
    (Consolidation) Act 1992 ss 226A–234A (see PARA 1372 et seq), references to a contract of
    employment include any contract under which one person personally does work or performs
    services for another; and 'employer' and related expressions are to be construed accordingly:
    s 235 (amended by the Trade Union Reform and Employment Rights Act 1993 Sch 8 para 75).
    The statutory balloting requirements thus apply both to employees and to those who personally
    do work or perform services for another. As to the meaning of 'employee' see PARA 892.
5   There is no statutory definition of 'industrial action' for these purposes. For its meaning in the
    context of the statutory right to a ballot before such action see the Trade Union and Labour
    Relations (Consolidation) Act 1992 s 62(6); and PARA 1025 note 5; and as to the interpretation
    of the phrase 'other industrial action' in the context of the law of unfair dismissal etc see PARA
    1340.
6   As to the meaning of 'not protected' see PARA 1365 note 2.
7   Ie under the Trade Union and Labour Relations (Consolidation) Act 1992 s 219: see PARA 1363.

8 Ie those referred to in the Trade Union and Labour Relations (Consolidation) Act 1992 s 219(1), (2): see PARA 1363.

9 Trade Union and Labour Relations (Consolidation) Act 1992 s 226(1)(a) (substituted by the Trade Union Reform and Employment Rights Act 1993 s 18(1)). The immunities are also excluded as respects an employer if the union has failed to comply with the statutory requirements concerning notice of the ballot and sample voting papers in relation to that employer: see the Trade Union and Labour Relations (Consolidation) Act 1992 s 226(1)(b); and PARA 1372. Industrial action retains the support of a ballot even if newly recruited union members take part in the industrial action, having joined the union after the ballot has taken place: *London Underground Ltd v National Union of Railwaymen, Maritime and Transport Staff* [1996] ICR 170, sub nom *London Underground Ltd v National Union of Rail, Maritime and Transport Workers* [1995] IRLR 636, CA; and see PARA 1374.

10 Where separate workplace ballots are held by virtue of the Trade Union and Labour Relations (Consolidation) Act 1992 s 228(1) (see PARA 1375): (1) industrial action is to be regarded as having the support of a ballot if the conditions specified in s 226(2) (see heads (1)–(4) in the text) are satisfied; and (2) the trade union is to be taken to have complied with the requirements relating to a ballot imposed by s 226A (see PARA 1372) if those requirements are complied with, in relation to the ballot for the place of work of the person induced to take part, or continue to take part, in the industrial action: s 226(3) (amended by the Trade Union Reform and Employment Rights Act 1993 Sch 8 para 73(c)).

11 Ie the requirements of the Trade Union and Labour Relations (Consolidation) Act 1992 s 226B (see PARA 1373), so far as applicable before and during the holding of the ballot.

12 Ie the requirements of the Trade Union and Labour Relations (Consolidation) Act 1992 ss 227–231: see PARA 1374 et seq.

13 Industrial action has the support of a ballot if a simple majority of union members vote in favour of it, not necessarily a majority of all those taking part in the ballot: *West Midlands Travel Ltd v Transport and General Workers' Union* [1994] ICR 978, [1994] IRLR 578, CA.

14 Ie in accordance with the Trade Union and Labour Relations (Consolidation) Act 1992 s 229(2): see PARA 1376.

15 Trade Union and Labour Relations (Consolidation) Act 1992 s 226(2)(a) (substituted by the Trade Union Reform and Employment Rights Act 1993 Sch 8 para 73(b); amended by the Employment Relations Act 1999 Sch 3 paras 1, 2(1), (2)). Cf *Post Office v Union of Communication Workers* [1990] 3 All ER 199, [1990] ICR 258, CA; and see PARA 1376. Where there are several questions on a ballot paper which relate to different kinds of industrial action, 'ballot' within the meaning of the Trade Union and Labour Relations (Consolidation) Act 1992 s 226(2)(a) does not refer to the entire voting process but to each individual question, which must be considered separately: *West Midlands Travel Ltd v Transport and General Workers' Union* [1994] ICR 978, [1994] IRLR 578, CA. An industrial action ballot must also be conducted in accordance with the Code of Practice on Industrial Action Ballots and Notice to Employers: see PARA 1371.

16 Ie the requirements of the Trade Union and Labour Relations (Consolidation) Act 1992 s 226B, so far as applicable after the holding of the ballot, and of s 231B: see PARA 1373.

17 For these purposes, 'relevant time', in relation to an act by a trade union to induce a person to take part, or continue to take part, in industrial action, means the time at which proceedings are commenced in respect of the act: Trade Union and Labour Relations (Consolidation) Act 1992 s 226(1) (amended by the Trade Union Reform and Employment Rights Act 1993 Sch 8 para 73(a)).

18 Trade Union and Labour Relations (Consolidation) Act 1992 s 226(2)(b) (substituted by the Trade Union Reform and Employment Rights Act 1993 Sch 8 para 73(b); and amended by the Employment Relations Act 1999 Sch 9).

19 Ie the requirements of the Trade Union and Labour Relations (Consolidation) Act 1992 s 232A: see PARA 1374.

20 Trade Union and Labour Relations (Consolidation) Act 1992 s 226(2)(bb) (added by the Employment Relations Act 1999 Sch 3 paras 1, 2(1), (2)).

21 Ie the requirements of the Trade Union and Labour Relations (Consolidation) Act 1992 s 233: see PARA 1380.

22 Trade Union and Labour Relations (Consolidation) Act 1992 s 226(2)(c) (substituted by the Trade Union Reform and Employment Rights Act 1993 Sch 8 para 73(b)). Failure to comply with the statutory requirements as to balloting also entitles a member of the union induced to take part in the industrial action to apply to the court for an order requiring the union to ensure: (1) that there is no further inducement of members to take part in the action; and (2) that no member engages in conduct after the making of the order as a result of the prior inducement: see the Trade Union and Labour Relations (Consolidation) Act 1992 s 62(3); and PARA 1025.

23 Ie the requirements of the Trade Union and Labour Relations (Consolidation) Act 1992 s 231A: see PARA 1378.
24 Trade Union and Labour Relations (Consolidation) Act 1992 s 226(3A) (added by the Employment Relations Act 1999 Sch 3 paras 1, 2(1), (3)).

1371. Code of Practice on Industrial Action Ballots and Notice to Employers. Pursuant to his statutory powers to issue Codes of Practice[1], the Secretary of State has issued the Code of Practice on Industrial Action Ballots and Notice to Employers[2]. The provisions of the Code are admissible in evidence and are to be taken into account, whenever relevant, by any court, tribunal or the Central Arbitration Committee; but failure to observe any provisions of the Code does not of itself render a person liable to any proceedings[3].

Section A of the Code set out its general purposes[4]; and Section B concerns whether a ballot is appropriate and deals with observing procedural agreements[5] and balloting by more than one union[6].

Section C concerns preparing for an industrial action ballot and deals with arranging for the independent scrutiny of the ballot[7], providing a ballot notice to employers[8], providing a sample voting paper or sample voting papers to employers[9], establishing the entitlement to vote (the 'balloting constituency')[10], balloting members at more than one workplace[11], the balloting method[12], voting papers generally[13], the printing and distribution of the voting papers[14] and communication with members[15].

Section D concerns the holding of an industrial action ballot and deals with entitlement to vote[16], checks on the number of voting papers for return[17] and ensuring secrecy of voting[18].

Section E concerns the procedure following an industrial action ballot and deals with the counting of votes[19], announcing details of the result of a ballot[20], obtaining and providing copies of the scrutineer's report[21], a union's decision to authorise or indorse industrial action[22] and seeking members' views after a union has authorised or indorsed industrial action[23].

1 Ie in exercise of the power conferred on him by the Trade Union and Labour Relations (Consolidation) Act 1992 ss 203, 204: see PARA 1231. As to the Secretary of State see PARA 5 note 21.
2 The current revised Code was brought into force on 1 October 2005 by the Employment Code of Practice (Industrial Action Ballots and Notice to Employers) Order 2005, SI 2005/2420, art 2.
3 See the Trade Union and Labour Relations (Consolidation) Act 1992 s 207(1), (3); and PARA 1232.
4 See the Code of Practice on Industrial Action Ballots and Notice to Employers paras 1–5. As to trade union liability see Annex 1.
5 See the Code of Practice on Industrial Action Ballots and Notice to Employers para 6.
6 See the Code of Practice on Industrial Action Ballots and Notice to Employers para 7.
7 See the Code of Practice on Industrial Action Ballots and Notice to Employers paras 8–13.
8 See the Code of Practice on Industrial Action Ballots and Notice to Employers paras 14–18.
9 See the Code of Practice on Industrial Action Ballots and Notice to Employers paras 19, 20. For an example of a voting paper see Annex 2.
10 See the Code of Practice on Industrial Action Ballots and Notice to Employers paras 21–23.
11 See the Code of Practice on Industrial Action Ballots and Notice to Employers paras 24, 25.
12 See the Code of Practice on Industrial Action Ballots and Notice to Employers paras 26–28.
13 See the Code of Practice on Industrial Action Ballots and Notice to Employers paras 29–33.
14 See the Code of Practice on Industrial Action Ballots and Notice to Employers paras 34, 35.
15 See the Code of Practice on Industrial Action Ballots and Notice to Employers para 36.
16 See the Code of Practice on Industrial Action Ballots and Notice to Employers para 37.
17 See the Code of Practice on Industrial Action Ballots and Notice to Employers para 38.
18 See the Code of Practice on Industrial Action Ballots and Notice to Employers paras 39, 40.
19 See the Code of Practice on Industrial Action Ballots and Notice to Employers paras 41, 42.

20 See the Code of Practice on Industrial Action Ballots and Notice to Employers paras 43–46.
21 See the Code of Practice on Industrial Action Ballots and Notice to Employers paras 47–49.
22 See the Code of Practice on Industrial Action Ballots and Notice to Employers paras 50–52.
23 See the Code of Practice on Industrial Action Ballots and Notice to Employers para 53.

1372. Notice of the industrial action ballot and sample voting paper for employers. A trade union[1] proposing to hold a ballot on industrial action must take such steps as are reasonably necessary to ensure that:

(1) not later than the seventh day before the opening day[2] of the ballot, the specified notice[3]; and

(2) not later than the third day before the opening day of the ballot, the specified sample voting paper[4],

are received by every person who it is reasonable for the union to believe (at the latest time when steps could be taken to comply with head (1) above) will be the employer[5] of persons who will be entitled to vote in the ballot[6].

The notice referred to in head (1) above is a notice in writing:

(a) stating that the union intends to hold the ballot;

(b) specifying the date which the union reasonably believes will be the opening day of the ballot; and

(c) containing:

(i) a list of the categories of employee[7] to which the employees concerned[8] belong and a list of the workplaces at which the employees concerned work[9], with the total number of employees concerned, the number of the employees concerned in each of the categories of employee mentioned, and the number of the employees concerned who work at each workplace in the list of workplaces mentioned, together with an explanation of how those figures were arrived at[10]; or

(ii) where some or all of the employees concerned are employees from whose wages the employer makes deductions representing payments to the union, either those lists and figures and that explanation or such information as will enable the employer readily to deduce the total number of employees concerned, the categories of employee to which the employees concerned belong and the number of employees concerned in each of those categories, and the workplaces at which the employees concerned work and the number of them who work at each of those workplaces[11].

The sample voting paper referred to in head (2) above is a sample of the form of voting paper which is to be sent to the employees concerned, or, where the employees concerned are not all to be sent the same form of voting paper, a sample of each form of voting paper which is to be sent to any of them[12].

Where the above requirements fall to be complied with in relation to a person's employer, an act[13] done by a trade union[14] to induce[15] that person to take part, or continue to take part, in industrial action[16] is not protected[17] by the statutory immunity[18] against liability for certain economic torts[19] as respects that employer[20] unless the union has complied with those requirements in relation to him[21].

1 As to the meaning of 'trade union' see PARA 891.
2 For these purposes, references to the opening day of the ballot are references to the first day when a voting paper is sent to any person entitled to vote in the ballot: Trade Union and Labour

Relations (Consolidation) Act 1992 s 226A(4) (s 262A added by the Trade Union Reform and Employment Rights Act 1993 s 18(2)). As to entitlement to vote see PARA 1374.

3   Ie the notice specified in the Trade Union and Labour Relations (Consolidation) Act 1992 s 226A(2): see heads (a)–(c) in the text.

4   Ie the sample voting paper specified in the Trade Union and Labour Relations (Consolidation) Act 1992 s 226A(2F): see the text and note 12.

5   As to the meaning of 'employer' see PARAS 892, 1370 note 4.

6   Trade Union and Labour Relations (Consolidation) Act 1992 s 226A(1) (as added (see note 2); amended by the Employment Relations Act 2004 s 22(1), (2)).

7   As to the meaning of 'employee' see PARAS 892, 1370 note 4.

8   References in the Trade Union and Labour Relations (Consolidation) Act 1992 s 226A to the employees concerned are references to those employees of the employer in question who the union reasonably believes will be entitled to vote in the ballot: s 226A(2H) (s 226A(2A)–(2I) added by the Employment Relations Act 2004 s 22(1), (4)). Nothing in s 226A requires a union to supply an employer with the names of the employees concerned: s 226A(2G) (as so added).

9   For the purposes of the Trade Union and Labour Relations (Consolidation) Act 1992 s 226A, the workplace at which an employee works is, in relation to an employee who works at or from a single set of premises, those premises, and in relation to any other employee, the premises with which his employment has the closest connection: s 226A(2I) (as added: see note 8).

10 Trade Union and Labour Relations (Consolidation) Act 1992 s 226A(2)(a), (b) (c)(i) (as added (see note 2); amended by the Employment Relations Act 2004 s 22(1), (3)); Trade Union and Labour Relations (Consolidation) Act 1992 s 226A(2A), (2B) (as added: see note 8). See *Metroline Travel Ltd v Unite* [2012] EWHC 1778 (QB), [2012] IRLR 749, [2012] All ER (D) 185 (Jun) (bus companies were entitled to interim injunctions; the likelihood was that the union would have failed to establish at trial that it had defined the ballot constituency in the Trade Union and Labour Relations (Consolidation) Act 1992 s 226A ballot notices or identified the relevant employees in the s 234A strike notices (see PARA 1382); the legislative purpose of both sets of notice provisions is to enable an employer to know which part or parts of its workforce are being invited to take industrial action so that it can best prepare for such action if it takes place).

The lists and figures supplied under the Trade Union and Labour Relations (Consolidation) Act 1992 s 226A must be as accurate as is reasonably practicable in the light of the information in the possession of the union at the time when it complies with s 226A(1)(a) (see head (1) in the text): s 226A(2D) (as so added). See also note 11.

11 Trade Union and Labour Relations (Consolidation) Act 1992 s 226A(2)(c)(ii) (as added and amended: see notes 2, 8); Trade Union and Labour Relations (Consolidation) Act 1992 s 226A(2C) (as added: see note 8). See also note 10.

The information mentioned in s 226A(2C) that is supplied under s 226A must be as accurate as is reasonably practicable in the light of the information in the possession of the union at the time when it complies with s 226A(1)(a) (see head (1) in the text): s 226A(2D) (as so added). For these purposes information is in the possession of the union if it is held, for union purposes, in a document, whether in electronic form or any other form, and in the possession or under control of an officer or employee of the union: s 226A(2E) (as so added). Information possessed by union officials, including branch secretaries, may be regarded as being in the union's possession: see *London Underground Ltd v National Union of Rail, Maritime and Transport Workers* [2001] EWCA Civ 211, [2001] ICR 647, sub nom *National Union of Rail, Maritime and Transport Workers v London Underground Ltd* [2001] IRLR 228.

See *Serco Ltd (t/a Serco Docklands) v National Union of Rail, Maritime and Transport Workers; London and Birmingham Railway Ltd (t/a London Midland) v Associated Society of Locomotive Engineers and Firemen* [2011] EWCA Civ 226, [2011] 3 All ER 913, [2011] ICR 848, (duty to provide information that was 'reasonably practicable' was limited by information actually possessed by the union at the time when it complied with its obligation; union was not under an obligation by virtue of the notification duty under the Trade Union and Labour Relations (Consolidation) Act 1992 s 226A to obtain further information or alternatively to set up systems to improve its record keeping; applying *Metrobus Ltd v Unite the Union* [2009] EWCA Civ 829, [2010] ICR 173, [2009] IRLR 851).

Some earlier decisions ascribed a much wider meaning to the expression, 'in the possession of the union', but they must now be regarded as wrongly decided on that point: see e g *EDF Energy Powerlink Ltd v National Union of Rail, Maritime and Transport Workers* [2009] EWHC 2852 (QB), [2010] IRLR 114 (duty on the union was to do its reasonable best to address the essential criteria and to explain as far as it could how it got to the information that it supplied; employer would be entitled to know who was being balloted in respect of those trades and who might be called out pursuant to the ballot in an industrial dispute).

See also *London Underground Ltd v National Union of Rail, Maritime and Transport Workers* [2001] EWCA Civ 211, [2001] ICR 647, sub nom *National Union of Rail, Maritime and Transport Workers v London Underground Ltd* [2001] IRLR 228; *Westminster City Council v UNISON* [2001] EWCA Civ 443, [2001] ICR 1046, [2001] IRLR 524; Application 31045/10 *National Union of Rail, Maritime and Transport Workers v United Kingdom* [2014] IRLR 467, (2014) Times, 30 April, ECtHR (where the union claimed that UK strike law is unduly restrictive of its freedom of association under the European Convention on Human Rights art 11 on two grounds: (1) the inordinate complexity of the law relating to strike notices; and (2) the total ban on sympathetic industrial action under ss 224, 244 (see PARA 1367); the ECtHR ruled against the latter argument and did not find it necessary to rule on the former).

12 Trade Union and Labour Relations (Consolidation) Act 1992 s 226A(2F) (as added: see note 8). As to the content of the voting paper see PARA 1376.

  In its application to a ballot in which merchant seamen to whom the Trade Union and Labour Relations (Consolidation) Act 1992 s 230(2A) (see PARA 1377) applies are entitled to vote, s 226A has effect with the substitution in s 226A(2F), for references to the voting paper which is to be sent to the employees, of references to the voting paper which is to be sent or otherwise provided to them: s 226A(5) (as added (see note 2); amended by the Employment Relations Act 2004 s 22(1), (6)).

13 As to the meaning of 'act' see PARA 1028 note 11.

14 See PARA 1370 note 2.

15 As to the meaning of 'inducement', in relation to a person, see PARA 1370 note 3.

16 As to the meaning of 'industrial action' see PARA 1370 note 5.

17 As to the meaning of 'not protected' see PARA 1365 note 2.

18 Ie under the Trade Union and Labour Relations (Consolidation) Act 1992 s 219: see PARA 1363.

19 Ie those referred to in the Trade Union and Labour Relations (Consolidation) Act 1992 s 219(1), (2): see PARA 1363.

20 While the statutory immunities are excluded only as respects the employer in relation to whom the requirements apply, such an act may nevertheless constitute an unlawful act for the purposes of an application under the Trade Union and Labour Relations (Consolidation) Act 1992 s 235A (applications by individuals where industrial action affects the supply of goods and services) (see PARA 1441): see s 235A(2)(a); and PARA 1441 note 2 head (1).

21 Trade Union and Labour Relations (Consolidation) Act 1992 s 226(1)(b) (substituted by the Trade Union Reform and Employment Rights Act 1993 s 18(1)).

1373. Independent scrutiny of industrial action ballot. Before the ballot in respect of the industrial action[1] is held, the trade union[2] must appoint a qualified person (the 'scrutineer') whose terms of appointment must require him to take such steps in relation to the ballot as appear to him to be appropriate for the purpose of enabling him to make a report[3] to the trade union on the ballot[4]; but that requirement does not apply unless the number of members entitled to vote in the ballot, or, where separate workplace ballots are held[5], the aggregate of the number of members entitled to vote in each of them, exceeds 50[6].

A person is a qualified person in relation to a ballot if he satisfies such conditions as may be specified for these purposes by order of the Secretary of State[7] or is himself so specified[8], and the trade union has no grounds for believing either that he will carry out his functions[9] otherwise than competently or that his independence in relation to the union, or in relation to the ballot, might reasonably be called into question[10].

The trade union must ensure that the scrutineer duly carries out his functions and that there is no interference with his carrying out of those functions from the union or any of its members, officials[11] or employees[12]. The union must also comply with all reasonable requests made by the scrutineer for the purposes of, or in connection with, the carrying out of his functions[13].

The scrutineer's terms of appointment must also require him to make his report as soon as reasonably practicable after the date of the ballot[14], and, in any event, not later than the end of the period of four weeks beginning with that date[15]. The report must state whether the scrutineer is satisfied:

(1)   that there are no reasonable grounds for believing that there was any contravention[16] of a requirement imposed by or under any enactment in relation to the ballot;

(2)   that the arrangements made with respect to the production, storage, distribution, return or other handling of the voting papers used in the ballot, and the arrangements for the counting of the votes, included all such security arrangements as were reasonably practicable for the purpose of minimising the risk that any unfairness or malpractice might occur; and

(3)   that he has been able to carry out his functions without any interference from the trade union or any of its members, officials or employees;

and, if he is not satisfied as to any of these matters, the report must give particulars of his reason for not being satisfied as to that matter[17].

If, at any time within six months from the date of the ballot, any person entitled to vote in the ballot, or the employer[18] of any such person, requests a copy of the scrutineer's report, the trade union must provide him with one as soon as practicable, either free of charge or on payment of such reasonable fee as may be specified by the trade union[19].

1   As to the requirement to hold a ballot before industrial action see PARA 1370; and as to the meaning of 'industrial action' see PARA 1370 note 5.

2   As to the meaning of 'trade union' see PARA 891.

3   Ie in accordance with the Trade Union and Labour Relations (Consolidation) Act 1992 s 231B: see the text and notes 16–19.

4   See the Trade Union and Labour Relations (Consolidation) Act 1992 s 226B(1)(a) (s 226B added by the Trade Union Reform and Employment Rights Act 1993 s 20(1)). The name of the independent scrutineer must be stated on each voting paper: see the Trade Union and Labour Relations (Consolidation) Act 1992 s 229(1A)(a); and PARA 1376 head (1).

5   Ie in accordance with the Trade Union and Labour Relations (Consolidation) Act 1992 s 228(1): see PARA 1375. As to entitlement to vote see PARA 1374.

6   Trade Union and Labour Relations (Consolidation) Act 1992 s 226C (added by the Trade Union Reform and Employment Rights Act 1993 s 20(4)).

7   Any such order must be made by statutory instrument which is subject to annulment in pursuance of a resolution of either House of Parliament: Trade Union and Labour Relations (Consolidation) Act 1992 s 226B(2) (as added: see note 4). Partly in exercise of the power so conferred the Secretary of State made the Trade Union Ballots and Elections (Independent Scrutineer Qualifications) Order 1993, SI 1993/1909, which came into force on 30 August 1993: art 1(1). As to the conditions to be satisfied by individuals and partnerships see arts 1(2), 3–6; and PARA 966 note 5.

8   As to the persons so specified see the Trade Union Ballots and Elections (Independent Scrutineer Qualifications) Order 1993, SI 1993/1909, art 7; and PARA 966 note 6.

9   Ie the functions conferred on him under the Trade Union and Labour Relations (Consolidation) Act 1992 s 226B(1).

10   Trade Union and Labour Relations (Consolidation) Act 1992 s 226B(2) (as added: see note 4).

11   As to the meaning of 'official', in relation to a trade union, see PARA 1018.

12   Trade Union and Labour Relations (Consolidation) Act 1992 s 226B(3) (as added: see note 4). As to the meaning of 'employee' see PARAS 892, 1370 note 4.

13   Trade Union and Labour Relations (Consolidation) Act 1992 s 226B(4) (as added: see note 4).

14   For these purposes, 'date of the ballot' means, in the case of a ballot in which votes may be cast on more than one day, the last of those days: Trade Union and Labour Relations (Consolidation) Act 1992 s 246.

15   See the Trade Union and Labour Relations (Consolidation) Act 1992 s 226B(1)(b) (as added: see note 4).

16   As to the meaning of 'contravention' and cognate expressions see PARA 915 note 6.

17   Trade Union and Labour Relations (Consolidation) Act 1992 s 231B(1) (s 231B added by the Trade Union Reform and Employment Rights Act 1993 s 20(3)). Nothing in the Trade Union and Labour Relations (Consolidation) Act 1992 s 231B imposes a requirement on a trade union unless the number of members entitled to vote in the ballot or, where separate workplace ballots

are held in accordance with s 228(1), the aggregate of the number of members entitled to vote in each of them, exceeds 50: s 226C (as added: see note 6).

18 As to the meaning of 'employer' see PARAS 892, 1370 note 4.

19 Trade Union and Labour Relations (Consolidation) Act 1992 s 231B(2) (as added: see note 17).

1374. Entitlement to vote in industrial action ballot. Entitlement to vote in a ballot on industrial action must be accorded equally to all[1] the members[2] of the trade union[3] who it is reasonable at the time of the ballot[4] for the union to believe will be induced by the union to take part or, as the case may be, to continue to take part in the industrial action in question[5], and to no others[6].

Industrial action is not to be regarded as having the support of a ballot if the following conditions apply in the case of any person:

(1) he was a member of the trade union at the time when the ballot was held;

(2) it was reasonable at that time[7] for the trade union to believe that he would be induced to take part or, as the case may be, to continue to take part in the industrial action;

(3) he was not accorded entitlement to vote in the ballot[8]; and

(4) he was induced by the trade union to take part or, as the case may be, to continue to take part in the industrial action[9].

1 A trade union which has overseas members may choose whether or not to accord any of those members entitlement to vote in a ballot on industrial action: see PARA 1379. As to the right to a ballot before industrial action see also the Trade Union and Labour Relations (Consolidation) Act 1992 s 62; and PARA 1025.

2 As to the application of the balloting requirements to federated trade unions see *Shipping Co Uniform Inc v International Transport Workers' Federation* [1985] ICR 245, [1985] IRLR 71.

3 As to the meaning of 'trade union' see PARA 891.

4 For these purposes, 'at the time of the ballot' means the time when the ballot papers were sent out: *P v National Association of School Masters/Union of Women Teachers* [2001] EWCA Civ 652, [2001] ICR 1241, [2001] IRLR 532.

5 Industrial action has the support of a ballot if newly recruited union members take part in the industrial action having joined the union after the ballot has taken place: *London Underground Ltd v National Union of Railwaymen, Maritime and Transport Staff* [2001] EWCA Civ 211, [1996] ICR 170, sub nom *London Underground Ltd v National Union of Rail, Maritime and Transport Workers* [1995] IRLR 636, disapproving the earlier suggestion that, de minimis apart, any call for industrial action following a ballot should expressly be limited to those who were employed by the employer, and given an opportunity of voting, at the time of the ballot: *Post Office v Union of Communication Workers* [1990] 3 All ER 199 at 205, [1990] ICR 258 at 268, CA obiter per Lord Donaldson of Lymington MR. See also *London Underground Ltd v Associated Society of Locomotive Engineers & Firemen* [2011] EWHC 3506 (QB), [2012] IRLR 196 (ballot properly held: fact that the ballot had included persons who would not themselves go on strike had not rendered the ballot in breach of Trade Union and Labour Relations (Consolidation) Act 1992 s 227; ballot constituency under s 227 is not limited to those who will be on strike, i e actually withdrawing their labour in breach of contract on a particular day). As to the meaning of 'industrial action' for these purposes see PARA 1370 note 5.

6 Trade Union and Labour Relations (Consolidation) Act 1992 s 227(1) (amended by the Employment Relations Act 2004 s 23). If, in relation to a ballot, there is a failure to comply with the Trade Union and Labour Relations (Consolidation) Act 1992 ss 227(1), 230(2), 230(2B) and the failure is accidental and on a scale which is unlikely to affect the result of the ballot, the failure is to be disregarded for all purposes, including, in particular, those of s 232A(c) (see head (3) in the text): s 232B(1), (2) (s 232B added by the Employment Relations Act 1999 Sch 3 paras 1, 9; amended by the Employment Relations Act 2004 s 24(1)); and see also PARA 1377. Cf *National Union of Rail, Maritime and Transport Workers v Midland Mainline Ltd* [2001] EWCA Civ 1206, [2001] IRLR 813, [2001] 38 LS Gaz R 37.

7 See note 4.

8 The failure to accord entitlement to vote is to be disregarded where the failure is accidental and would not have affected the ballot: *P v National Association of School Masters/Union of*

Women Teachers [2001] EWCA Civ 652, [2001] ICR 1241, [2001] IRLR 532. The predecessor of this provision, ie the Trade Union and Labour Relations (Consolidation) Act 1992 s 227(2) (repealed), referred to a person who was 'denied entitlement to vote in the ballot'. Under that repealed provision, denial of a person's entitlement to vote in the ballot was held to imply something more than an inadvertent failure to give him an opportunity to vote: *British Railways Board v National Union of Railwaymen* [1989] ICR 678 at 683, [1989] IRLR 349 at 351, CA per Lord Donaldson of Lymington MR.

9   Trade Union and Labour Relations (Consolidation) Act 1992 s 232A (added by the Employment Relations Act 1999 Sch 3 paras 1, 8).

1375.   Separate workplace industrial action ballots.   If the members entitled to vote in a ballot on industrial action[1] do not all have the same workplace[2], a separate ballot must be held for each workplace; and entitlement to vote in each ballot must be accorded equally to, and restricted to, members of the union who are entitled to vote[3] and have that workplace[4]; but those provisions do not apply if the union reasonably believes that all those members have the same workplace[5].

Where, however, separate ballots would be required[6] to be held for each workplace, a ballot may be held in place of some or all of the separate ballots if one of the provisions in heads (1) to (3) below is satisfied in relation to the ballot[7]:

(1)   if the workplace of each member entitled to vote in the ballot is the workplace of at least one member of the union who is affected by the dispute[8];

(2)   if entitlement to vote is accorded to, and limited to, all the members of the union who:

(a)   according to the union's reasonable belief have an occupation of a particular kind or have any of a number of particular kinds of occupation; and

(b)   are employed by a particular employer, or by any of a number of particular employers, with whom the union is in dispute[9];

(3)   if entitlement to vote is accorded to, and limited to, all the members of the union who are employed by a particular employer, or by any of a number of particular employers, with whom the union is in dispute[10].

1   Ie by virtue of the Trade Union and Labour Relations (Consolidation) Act 1992 s 227: see PARA 1374.

2   For these purposes, 'workplace', in relation to a person who is employed, means: (1) if the person works at or from a single set of premises, those premises; and (2) in any other case, the premises with which the person's employment has the closest connection: Trade Union and Labour Relations (Consolidation) Act 1992 s 228(4) (s 228 substituted, and s 228A added, by Employment Relations Act 1999 Sch 3 paras 1, 5). In the Trade Union and Labour Relations (Consolidation) Act 1992 s 228(4) (as originally enacted), 'place of work' was defined, in relation to such a person, as 'the premises occupied by his employer at or from which that person works'; and it was held that those words were to be considered in the context of legislation dealing with industrial relations and the conduct of trade unions, and, in particular, with the way in which ballots are to be conducted prior to industrial action, and it was not relevant that the word 'occupation' might be construed more narrowly in some other area of the law: *Intercity West Coast Ltd v National Union of Rail, Maritime and Transport Workers* [1996] IRLR 583, CA.

3   See note 1.

4   Trade Union and Labour Relations (Consolidation) Act 1992 s 228(1), (3) (as substituted: see note 2).

5   Trade Union and Labour Relations (Consolidation) Act 1992 s 228(2) (as substituted: see note 2).

6   Ie by the Trade Union and Labour Relations (Consolidation) Act 1992 s 228(3).

7   Trade Union and Labour Relations (Consolidation) Act 1992 s 228A(1) (as added: see note 2).

8 Trade Union and Labour Relations (Consolidation) Act 1992 s 228A(2) (as added: see note 2). For these purposes, the following are members of the union affected by a dispute: (1) if the dispute relates, wholly or partly, to a decision which the union reasonably believes the employer has made or will make concerning a matter specified in s 244(1)(a), (b) or (c) (meaning of 'trade dispute') (see PARA 1361 heads (1)–(3)), members whom the decision directly affects; (2) if the dispute relates, wholly or partly, to a matter specified in s 244(1)(d) (see PARA 1361 head (4)), members whom the matter directly affects; (3) if the dispute relates, wholly or partly, to a matter specified in s 244(1)(e) (see PARA 1361 head (5)), persons whose membership or non-membership is in dispute; (4) if the dispute relates, wholly or partly, to a matter specified in s 244(1)(f) (see PARA 1361 head (6)), officials of the union who have used or would use the facilities concerned in the dispute: s 228A(5) (as so added). As to the meaning of 'employer' see PARA 892; and as to the meaning of 'official', in relation to a trade union, see PARA 1018.
9 Trade Union and Labour Relations (Consolidation) Act 1992 s 228A(3) (as added: see note 2).
10 Trade Union and Labour Relations (Consolidation) Act 1992 s 228A(4) (as added: see note 2).

1376. Voting paper in industrial action ballot. The method of voting in a ballot on industrial action must be by the marking of a voting paper by the person voting[1]. Each voting paper must:

(1) state the name of the independent scrutineer[2];
(2) clearly specify the address[3] to which, and the date by which, it is to be returned[4];
(3) be given one of a series of consecutive whole numbers, every one of which must be used in giving a different number in that series to each voting paper printed or otherwise produced for the purposes of the ballot[5];
(4) be marked with its number[6];
(5) contain at least one of the two questions required by statute[7] in relation to willingness to participate in industrial action[8];
(6) specify who is authorised[9] to call on members to take part, or to continue to take part, in the industrial action in the event of a vote in favour of such action[10]; and
(7) contain the required statement[11] explaining the consequences of participation in industrial action[12].

1 Trade Union and Labour Relations (Consolidation) Act 1992 s 229(1).
2 Trade Union and Labour Relations (Consolidation) Act 1992 s 229(1A)(a) (s 229(1A) added by the Trade Union Reform and Employment Rights Act 1993 s 20(2)). As to independent scrutiny of industrial action ballots see PARA 1373. Nothing in the Trade Union and Labour Relations (Consolidation) Act 1992 s 229(1A)(a) imposes a requirement on a trade union unless the number of members entitled to vote in the ballot or, where separate workplace ballots are held in accordance with s 228(1) (see PARA 1375), the aggregate of the number of members entitled to vote in each of them, exceeds 50: s 226C (added by the Trade Union Reform and Employment Rights Act 1993 s 20(4)). As to entitlement to vote see PARA 1374.
3 In its application to a ballot in which merchant seamen to whom the Trade Union and Labour Relations (Consolidation) Act 1992 s 230(2A) (see PARA 1377) applies are entitled to vote, s 229(1A) has effect with the substitution, for the reference to the address to which the voting paper is to be returned, of a reference to the ship to which the seamen belong: s 229(1A) (as added: see note 2). 'Merchant seaman' is not defined for these purposes; but cf PARAS 1377 note 6, 1379 note 6.
4 Trade Union and Labour Relations (Consolidation) Act 1992 s 229(1A)(b) (as added: see note 2).
5 Trade Union and Labour Relations (Consolidation) Act 1992 s 229(1A)(c) (as added: see note 2).
6 Trade Union and Labour Relations (Consolidation) Act 1992 s 229(1A)(d) (as added: see note 2).
7 Those questions are: (1) a question, however framed, which requires the person answering it to say, by answering 'Yes' or 'No', whether he is prepared to take part or, as the case may be, to continue to take part, in a strike; (2) a question, however framed, which requires the person answering it to say, by answering 'Yes' or 'No', whether he is prepared to take part or, as the

case may be, to continue to take part, in industrial action short of a strike: Trade Union and Labour Relations (Consolidation) Act 1992 s 229(2).

8   Trade Union and Labour Relations (Consolidation) Act 1992 s 229(2). For these purposes, an overtime ban and a call-out ban constitute industrial action short of a strike: s 229(2A) (added by the Employment Relations Act 1999 Sch 3 paras 1, 6(1), (2)). Cf *Connex South Eastern Ltd v National Union of Rail, Maritime and Transport Workers* [1999] IRLR 249, CA; and see PARA 1340. The definition of 'strike' in the Trade Union and Labour Relations (Consolidation) Act 1992 s 246 (see PARA 1340 text and note 2) does not apply for the purposes of s 229(2): s 246 (amended by the Employment Relations Act 1999 Sch 3 paras 1, 6(1), (4)). As to the meaning of 'industrial action' see PARA 1370 note 5.

A single 'rolled-up' question covering both a strike and industrial action short of a strike will not be valid: *Post Office v Union of Communication Workers* [1990] 3 All ER 199, [1990] ICR 258, CA. Where there are several questions on a ballot paper which relate to different kinds of industrial action, 'ballot' within the meaning of the Trade Union and Labour Relations (Consolidation) Act 1992 s 226(2)(a) (see PARA 1370 head (1)) does not refer to the entire voting process but to each individual question, which must be considered separately: *West Midlands Travel Ltd v Transport and General Workers' Union* [1994] ICR 978, [1994] IRLR 578, CA. As to the position where a ballot paper poses a question which, either wholly or in part, asks whether the member is prepared to participate in a strike by reference to issues other than trade disputes see *London Underground Ltd v National Union of Railwaymen* [1989] IRLR 341. Cf *Associated British Ports v Transport and General Workers' Union* [1989] IRLR 291 at 301 per Millett J (affd on other grounds [1989] 3 All ER 822, [1989] ICR 557 at 590, HL (revsing [1989] 3 All ER 796, [1989] ICR 557, CA)).

9   Ie for the purposes of the Trade Union and Labour Relations (Consolidation) Act 1992 s 233: see PARA 1380. The person or description of persons so specified need not be authorised under the rules of the union, but must be one of those for whose acts the union is taken to be responsible under s 20(2) (see PARA 1388): s 229(3) (amended by the Trade Union Reform and Employment Rights Act 1993 Sch 7 para 25). As to the meaning of 'rules', in relation to a trade union, see PARA 898 note 5.

10   Trade Union and Labour Relations (Consolidation) Act 1992 s 229(3) (as amended: see note 9).

11   The required statement is: 'If you take part in a strike or other industrial action, you may be in breach of your contract of employment. However, if you are dismissed for taking part in strike or other industrial action which is called officially and is otherwise lawful, the dismissal will be unfair if it takes place fewer than 12 weeks after you started taking part in the action, and depending on the circumstances may be unfair if it takes place later': Trade Union and Labour Relations (Consolidation) Act 1992 s 229(4) (amended by the Employment Relations Act 1999 Sch 3 para 6(1), (3); the Employment Relations Act 2004 Sch 1 para 13). This statement must appear on every voting paper without being qualified or commented on by anything else on the voting paper: Trade Union and Labour Relations (Consolidation) Act 1992 s 229(4) (as so amended). As to the meaning of 'contract of employment' see PARAS 892, 1370 note 4.

12   Trade Union and Labour Relations (Consolidation) Act 1992 s 229(4) (as amended: see note 11).

1377.   Conduct of industrial action ballot. Every person who is entitled to vote[1] in a ballot on industrial action must be allowed to do so without interference from, or constraint imposed by, the union or any of its members, officials[2] or employees[3], and, so far as is reasonably practicable, must be enabled to do so without incurring any direct cost to himself[4]. So far as is reasonably practicable[5], every person[6] who is entitled to vote in the ballot must have a voting paper sent to him by post[7] at his home address or another address which he has requested the union in writing to treat as his postal address, and must be given a convenient opportunity to vote by post[8]. The ballot must be conducted so as to secure that, so far as is reasonably practicable, those voting do so in secret, and the votes given in the ballot are fairly and accurately counted[9].

If, in relation to a ballot, there is a failure, or there are failures, to comply with certain statutory provisions[10], and the failure is accidental and on a scale which is unlikely to affect the result of the ballot or, as the case may be, the failures are accidental and taken together are on a scale which is unlikely to affect the result of the ballot, the failure, or failures, is or are to be disregarded for all purposes[11].

1   As to entitlement to vote in an industrial action ballot see PARA 1374.
2   As to the meaning of 'official', in relation to a trade union, see PARA 1018; and as to the meaning of 'trade union' see PARA 891.
3   As to the interpretation of 'interference' in the equivalent provisions relating to elections for union office see PARA 962 note 6; and as to the meaning of 'employee' see PARA 892.
4   Trade Union and Labour Relations (Consolidation) Act 1992 s 230(1). As to the interpretation of 'cost' in the equivalent provisions relating to elections for union office see PARA 962 note 9.
5   An inadvertent failure to supply voting papers to some of those entitled to vote will not invalidate the ballot if the union has done what is reasonably practicable in the circumstances: *British Railways Board v National Union of Railwaymen* [1989] ICR 678, [1989] IRLR 349, CA; cf *National Union of Rail, Maritime and Transport Workers v Midland Mainline Ltd* [2001] EWCA Civ 1206, [2001] IRLR 813, [2001] 38 LS Gaz R 37. While the phrase 'reasonably practical' indicates an objective test, it gives union officers discretion to exercise their own judgment about what are appropriate steps in a given situation: *Balfour Beatty Engineering Services Ltd v Unite the Union* [2012] EWHC 267 (QB), [2012] ICR 822, [2012] IRLR 452. It is now expressly provided that small, accidental failures to comply with this provision are to be disregarded: see the text and notes 10–11.
6   Ie other than an overseas member (see PARA 1379) or a person falling within the Trade Union and Labour Relations (Consolidation) Act 1992 s 230(2A). If, in the case of a merchant seaman, the trade union reasonably believes that: (1) he will be employed in a ship either at sea or at a place outside Great Britain at some time in the period during which votes may be cast; and (2) it will be convenient for him to receive a voting paper and to vote while on the ship or while at a place where the ship is rather than in accordance with s 230(2), he must, if it is reasonably practicable: (a) have a voting paper made available to him while on the ship or while at a place where the ship is; and (b) be given an opportunity to vote while on the ship or while at a place where the ship is: s 230(2A), (2B) (substituted by the Employment Relations Act 1999 Sch 3 paras 1, 7). Small, accidental failures are to be disregarded: see the text and notes 10–11. For these purposes, 'merchant seaman' means a person whose employment, or the greater part of it, is carried out on board sea-going ships: Trade Union and Labour Relations (Consolidation) Act 1992 s 230(2C) (added by the Trade Union Reform and Employment Rights Act 1993 s 17).
7   As to the construction of references to requiring or authorising a document or other thing to be sent by post see PARA 962 note 10.
8   Trade Union and Labour Relations (Consolidation) Act 1992 s 230(2) (substituted by the Trade Union Reform and Employment Rights Act 1993 s 17).
9   Trade Union and Labour Relations (Consolidation) Act 1992 s 230(4). An inaccuracy in counting is to be disregarded if it is accidental and on a scale which could not affect the result of the ballot: s 230(4).
10 Ie the provisions in the Trade Union and Labour Relations (Consolidation) Act 1992 s 227(1) (entitlement to vote: see PARA 1374), s 230(2) (see the text and notes 5–8) and s 230(2B) (see note 6). The requirement to disregard small accidental failures has been held also to apply to a failure to accord entitlement to vote under the Trade Union and Labour Relations (Consolidation) Act 1992 s 232A (see PARA 1374): *P v National Association of School Masters/Union of Women Teachers* [2001] EWCA Civ 652, [2001] ICR 1241, [2001] IRLR 532.
11 Trade Union and Labour Relations (Consolidation) Act 1992 s 232B(1), (2) (added by Employment Relations Act 1999 Sch 3 paras 1, 9; amended by the Employment Relations Act 2004 s 24(1)). The failure or failures are to be disregarded for all purposes, including, in particular, those of the Trade Union and Labour Relations (Consolidation) Act 1992 s 232A(c) (see PARA 1374 head (3)): see s 232B(1) (as so added and amended). See, however, See *British Airways plc v Unite the Union* [2009] EWHC 3541 (QB), [2010] IRLR 423, [2010] All ER (D) 112 (Jan) (ballot and strike notification erroneously included members not entitled to vote; unintentional failure could not be regarded as accidental failure even allowing for a purposive interpretation of the Trade Union and Labour Relations (Consolidation) Act 1992 s 232B).

1378.   Information as to result of industrial action ballot.   As soon as is reasonably practicable after the holding of a ballot on industrial action, the trade union[1] must take such steps as are reasonably necessary to ensure that all persons[2] entitled to vote[3] in the ballot, and every relevant employer[4], are informed of the following matters:

(1)   the number of votes cast in the ballot;

(2)   the number of individuals answering 'Yes' to the question asked in the ballot, or, where more than one question was asked, to each question[5];

(3)   the number of individuals answering 'No' to the question asked in the ballot, or, where more than one question was asked, to each question; and

(4)   the number of spoiled voting papers[6].

Where overseas members have voted, the information provided must distinguish between them and other members[7].

1   As to the meaning of 'trade union' see PARA 891.
2   Ie other than overseas members: see PARA 1379.
3   As to entitlement to vote in an industrial action ballot see PARA 1374.
4   For these purposes, 'relevant employer' means an employer who it is reasonable for the trade union to believe, at the time when the steps are taken, was at the time of the ballot the employer of any persons entitled to vote: Trade Union and Labour Relations (Consolidation) Act 1992 s 231A(2) (s 231A added by the Trade Union Reform and Employment Rights Act 1993 s 19). As to the meaning of 'employer' see PARAS 892, 1370 note 4.
5   As to the questions required by statute see PARA 1376.
6   Trade Union and Labour Relations (Consolidation) Act 1992 ss 231, 231A(1) (s 231A as added: see note 4). For a case where the union was deemed not to have informed the employer as soon as reasonably practicable see *Metrobus Ltd v Unite the Union* [2009] EWCA Civ 829, [2010] ICR 173, [2009] IRLR 851, (a union which used a scrutineer to conduct its ballot should, as part of its agreement with the scrutineer for the purpose, require a report to be provided promptly after the closure of the ballot, and should be entitled, if it was not forthcoming within the anticipated time, to inquire of the scrutineer as to the position). The dissemination of results to union members should not undermine the entire ballot process, however: *British Airways plc v Unite the Union (No 2)* [2010] EWCA Civ 669, [2010] ICR 1316, [2010] IRLR 809 (ballot had been carried out impeccably and the ballot results had been provided on the defendant's website, which represented a practical approach to dissemination of results and had been sufficient to comply with the Trade Union and Labour Relations (Consolidation) Act 1992 s 231; it would be unrealistic to expect the defendant to prove that every eligible member had been sent an individual report of the ballot results).
7   See the Trade Union and Labour Relations (Consolidation) Act 1992 s 232(2); and PARA 1379 note 4.

1379.   Balloting of overseas members. A trade union[1] which has overseas members may choose whether or not to accord any of those members entitlement to vote[2] in a ballot on industrial action[3]. Nothing in the statutory requirements[4] concerning ballots on industrial action applies in relation to an overseas member or a vote cast by such a member[5].

An 'overseas member' of a trade union is a member of the union, other than a merchant seaman[6] or offshore worker[7], who is outside Great Britain throughout the period during which votes may be cast[8], save that, for these purposes, a member who is in Northern Ireland[9] throughout that period is not to be treated as an overseas member:

(1)   where the ballot is a workplace ballot[10] and his place of work is in Great Britain[11]; or

(2)   where the ballot is a general ballot[12] and relates to industrial action involving members both in Great Britain and in Northern Ireland[13].

1   As to the meaning of 'trade union' see PARA 891.
2   As to entitlement to vote in a ballot on industrial action see PARA 1374.

3   Trade Union and Labour Relations (Consolidation) Act 1992 s 232(1) (amended by the Trade Union Reform and Employment Rights Act 1993 Sch 8 para 74(a)).
4   Ie the requirements contained in the Trade Union and Labour Relations (Consolidation) Act 1992 ss 226B–230 (see PARA 1373 et seq) and s 231B (see PARA 1373). Where overseas members have voted in the ballot: (1) the references to persons entitled to vote in s 231 and in s 231A (see PARA 1378) do not include overseas members; and (2) ss 231, 231A are to be read as requiring the information mentioned in s 231 to distinguish between overseas members and other members: s 232(2) (substituted by the Trade Union Reform and Employment Rights Act 1993 Sch 8 para 74(b)).
5   Trade Union and Labour Relations (Consolidation) Act 1992 s 232(1) (as amended: see note 3).
6   For these purposes, 'merchant seaman' means a person whose employment, or the greater part of it, is carried out on board sea-going ships: Trade Union and Labour Relations (Consolidation) Act 1992 s 232(3).
7   For these purposes, 'offshore worker' means a person in offshore employment, other than one who is in such employment in an area where the law of Northern Ireland applies: Trade Union and Labour Relations (Consolidation) Act 1992 s 232(3). As to the meaning of 'offshore employment' see PARA 970 note 5.
8   Trade Union and Labour Relations (Consolidation) Act 1992 s 232(3).
9   In relation to offshore employment, the references to Northern Ireland include any area where the law of Northern Ireland applies: Trade Union and Labour Relations (Consolidation) Act 1992 s 232(5).
10 Ie a ballot to which the Trade Union and Labour Relations (Consolidation) Act 1992 s 228(1) or (2) applies: see PARA 1375.
11 In relation to offshore employment, the references to Great Britain include any area where the law of England and Wales or Scotland applies: Trade Union and Labour Relations (Consolidation) Act 1992 s 232(5).
12 Ie a ballot to which the Trade Union and Labour Relations (Consolidation) Act 1992 s 228(3) applies: see PARA 1375.
13 Trade Union and Labour Relations (Consolidation) Act 1992 s 232(4).

1380. Calling of industrial action with support of a ballot.

Industrial action[1] is not to be regarded as having the support of a ballot unless it is called by a specified person[2], and the following conditions are satisfied[3]:

(1)   there must have been no call by the trade union[4] to take part, or continue to take part, in industrial action to which the ballot relates, or any authorisation or indorsement by the union of any such industrial action, before[5] the date of the ballot[6];

(2)   there must be a call for industrial action by a specified person[7], and industrial action to which it relates must begin before the ballot ceases[8] to be effective[9].

1   As to the meaning of 'industrial action' see PARA 1370 note 5.
2   For these purposes, a 'specified person' means a person specified, or of a description specified, in the voting paper for the ballot in accordance with the Trade Union and Labour Relations (Consolidation) Act 1992 s 229(3) (see PARA 1376), as authorised to call on members to take part or to continue to take part in the industrial action in the event of a vote in favour: s 233(2).
3   Trade Union and Labour Relations (Consolidation) Act 1992 s 233(1).
4   For these purposes, a call is to be taken to have been made by a trade union if it was authorised or indorsed by the union; and the provisions of the Trade Union and Labour Relations (Consolidation) Act 1992 s 20(2)–(4) (see PARA 1388) apply for the purpose of determining whether a call, or industrial action, is to be taken to have been so authorised or indorsed: s 233(4). As to the meaning of 'trade union' see PARA 891.
5   The prohibition on calling for industrial action before the date of the ballot does not preclude a union from recommending its members to vote in favour of industrial action: *Newham London Borough Council v National and Local Government Officers' Association* [1993] ICR 189, [1993] IRLR 83, CA.
6   Trade Union and Labour Relations (Consolidation) Act 1992 s 233(3)(a). As to the meaning of 'date of the ballot' see PARA 1373 note 14. A union does not contravene this requirement by including members who are already on strike following a previous ballot in a ballot to widen the existing industrial action: *Newham London Borough Council v National and Local Government Officers' Association* [1993] ICR 189, CA.

7   Whether industrial action is called by a specified person within the meaning of the Trade Union
    and Labour Relations (Consolidation) Act 1992 s 233(3)(a) (see head (1) in the text) is a
    question of fact and degree in each case, but s 233(3)(a) does not require an unequivocal call by
    the specified person which is free from any conditions, so that a limited degree of delegation
    may be permissible: *Tanks and Drums Ltd v Transport and General Workers' Union* [1992]
    ICR 1 at 17, 18, [1991] IRLR 372 at 375, 376, CA per Neill LJ.
8   Ie in accordance with the Trade Union and Labour Relations (Consolidation) Act 1992 s 234:
    see PARA 1381.
9   Trade Union and Labour Relations (Consolidation) Act 1992 s 233(3)(b) (amended by the
    Employment Relations Act 2004 Sch 1 para 14).

1381.   Period after which an industrial action ballot ceases to be effective.
Subject to the following provisions, a ballot on industrial action ceases to be
effective[1] in relation to industrial action[2] by members of a trade union[3] at the
end of the period, beginning with the date of the ballot[4], of four weeks[5] or of
such longer duration not exceeding eight weeks as is agreed between the union
and the members' employer[6], save that, where for the whole or part of that
period the calling or organising of industrial action is prohibited:

(1)   by virtue of a court order which subsequently lapses or is discharged,
      recalled or set aside; or

(2)   by virtue of an undertaking given to a court by any person from which
      he is subsequently released or by which he ceases to be bound,

the trade union may apply to the court for an order that the period during which
the prohibition had effect is not to count[7] towards the four-week period referred
to above[8]. The application must be made forthwith on the prohibition ceasing to
have effect:

(a)   to the court by virtue of whose decision the prohibition ceases to have
      effect; or

(b)   where an order lapses or an undertaking ceases to bind without any
      such decision, to the court by which the order was made or to which the
      undertaking was given;

and no application may be made after the end of the period of eight weeks
beginning with the date of the ballot[9].

The court must not make an order if it appears to it:

(i)   that the result of the ballot no longer represents the views of the union
      members concerned; or

(ii) that an event is likely to occur as a result of which those members
      would vote against industrial action if another ballot were to be held[10].

No appeal lies from the decision of the court to make or refuse an order under
the above provisions[11].

1   Ie for the purposes of the Trade Union and Labour Relations (Consolidation) Act 1992
    s 233(3)(b): see PARA 1380 head (2). Industrial action which commences within the statutory
    time limit may continue beyond that time, even if suspended pending negotiations, provided that
    the subsequent action is covered by the terms of the original ballot and can be considered part of
    the same dispute: *Monsanto plc v Transport and General Workers' Union* [1987] 1 All ER 358,
    [1987] ICR 269, CA. Once begun, industrial action must continue without substantial
    interruption if continued reliance is to be placed on the original ballot: *Post Office v Union of
    Communication Workers* [1990] 3 All ER 199 at 204, [1990] ICR 258 at 267, CA obiter per
    Lord Donaldson of Lymington MR.
2   As to the meaning of 'industrial action' see PARA 1370 note 5.
3   As to the meaning of 'trade union' see PARA 891.
4   As to the meaning of 'date of the ballot' see PARA 1373 note 14.
5   The ballot ceases to be effective at midnight on the final day, irrespective of the way any
    particular shift falls: *RJB Mining (UK) Ltd v National Union of Mineworkers* [1995] IRLR
    556, CA.

6   Trade Union and Labour Relations (Consolidation) Act 1992 s 234(1) (substituted by the
     Employment Relations Act 1999 Sch 3 paras 1, 10).
7   The period between the making of an application under the Trade Union and Labour Relations
     (Consolidation) Act 1992 s 234 and its determination does not count towards the period
     referred to in s 234(1); but a ballot is not to be regarded, by virtue of this provision, together
     with any order of the court, as effective for the purposes of s 233(3)(b) (see PARA 1380 head (2))
     after the end of the period of 12 weeks beginning with the date of the ballot: s 234(6).
8   Trade Union and Labour Relations (Consolidation) Act 1992 s 234(2).
9   Trade Union and Labour Relations (Consolidation) Act 1992 s 234(3).
10   Trade Union and Labour Relations (Consolidation) Act 1992 s 234(4).
11   Trade Union and Labour Relations (Consolidation) Act 1992 s 234(5).

(iii) Requirement to Give Notice to Employers of Industrial Action

1382. Notice to employers of industrial action. An act[1] done by a trade
union[2] to induce[3] a person to take part, or continue to take part, in industrial
action[4] is not protected[5] by the statutory immunity[6] against liability for certain
economic torts[7] as respects that person's employer[8] unless the union[9] has taken
or takes such steps as are reasonably necessary to ensure that the employer[10]
receives within the appropriate period[11] a relevant notice covering[12] the act[13].
    For these purposes, a 'relevant notice' is a notice in writing which:
    (1)   contains:
           (a)   a list of the categories of employee to which the affected
                  employees belong and a list of the workplaces at which the
                  affected employees work, with the total number of affected
                  employees, the number of the affected employees in each of the
                  categories of employee mentioned, and the number of the affected
                  employees who work at each workplace in the list of workplaces
                  mentioned, together with an explanation of how those figures
                  were arrived at; or
           (b)   where some or all of the affected employees are employees from
                  whose wages the employer makes deductions representing
                  payments to the union, either those lists and figures and that
                  explanation or such information as will enable the employer
                  readily to deduce the total number of affected employees, the
                  categories of employee to which the affected employees belong
                  and the number of affected employees in each of those categories,
                  and the workplaces at which the affected employees work and the
                  number of them who work at each of those workplaces[14];
    (2)   states whether industrial action is intended to be continuous or
           discontinuous[15] and specifies, where it is to be continuous, the intended
           date for any of the affected employees to begin to take part in the
           action, and, where it is to be discontinuous, the intended dates for any
           of the affected employees to take part in the action[16].
Where continuous industrial action which has been authorised or indorsed[17]
by a trade union ceases to be so authorised or indorsed, and the industrial action
has at a later date again been authorised or indorsed by the union, whether as
continuous or discontinuous action, no relevant notice covering acts done to
induce persons to take part in the earlier action operates[18] to cover acts done to
induce persons to take part in the action authorised or indorsed at the later
date[19]. In such a case, the union must give fresh notice to the employer before
inducing employees of that employer to take part in industrial action after that
date[20].

The above provisions[21] do not apply:

(i)   where industrial action ceases to be authorised or indorsed in order to enable the union to comply with a court order or an undertaking given to a court[22]; or

(ii)   where:

(A)   a union agrees with an employer, before industrial action ceases to be authorised or indorsed, that it will cease to be authorised or indorsed with effect from a date specified in the agreement (the 'suspension date') and that it may again be authorised or indorsed with effect from a date not earlier than a date specified in the agreement (the 'resumption date');

(B)   the action ceases to be authorised or indorsed with effect from the suspension date; and

(C)   the action is again authorised or indorsed with effect from a date which is not earlier than the resumption date or such later date as may be agreed between the union and the employer[23].

1   As to the meaning of 'act' see PARA 1028 note 11.
2   The provisions of the Trade Union and Labour Relations (Consolidation) Act 1992 s 20(2)–(4) (see PARA 1388) apply for the purpose of determining for the purposes of s 234A(1) who are relevant persons or committees and whether the trade union is to be taken to have authorised or indorsed the steps the person or committee took and for the purposes of s 234A(7)–(7B) (see the text and notes 21–23) whether the trade union is to be taken to have authorised or indorsed the industrial action: s 234A(9) (s 234A added by the Trade Union Reform and Employment Rights Act 1993 s 21; the Trade Union and Labour Relations (Consolidation) Act 1992 s 234A(9) amended by the Employment Relations Act 1999 Sch 3 paras 1, 11(1), (6)). See also note 9. As to the meaning of 'trade union' see PARA 891.
3   As to the meaning of 'inducement' see PARA 1370 note 3.
4   As to the meaning of 'industrial action' see PARA 1370 note 5.
5   As to the meaning of 'not protected' see PARA 1365 note 2.
6   Ie under the Trade Union and Labour Relations (Consolidation) Act 1992 s 219: see PARA 1363.
7   Ie those referred to in the Trade Union and Labour Relations (Consolidation) Act 1992 s 219(1), (2): see PARA 1363.
8   While the statutory immunities are excluded only as respects the employer in relation to whom the requirements apply, such an act may nevertheless constitute an unlawful act for the purposes of an application under the Trade Union and Labour Relations (Consolidation) Act 1992 s 235A (industrial action affecting supplies to individual): see s 235A(2)(a); and PARA 1441 note 2 head (1). As to the meaning of 'employer' see PARAS 892, 1370 note 4.
9   This requirement is to be treated as complied with if the steps were taken by other relevant persons or committees whose acts were authorised or indorsed by the union; and references to the belief or intention of the union in the Trade Union and Labour Relations (Consolidation) Act 1992 s 234A(2) or, as the case may be, s 234A(3), (5), (5C), (6) are to be construed as references to the belief or intention of the person or committee taking the steps: s 234A(8) (as added (see note 2); amended by the Employment Relations Act 2004 s 25(1), (6)).
10   The Trade Union and Labour Relations (Consolidation) Act 1992 s 234A(1) imposes a requirement in the case of an employer only if it is reasonable for the union to believe, at the latest time when steps could be taken to ensure that he receives the required notice, that he is the employer of persons who will be or have been induced to take part, or continue to take part, in the industrial action: s 234A(2) (as added: see note 2).
11   For these purposes, the appropriate period is the period: (1) beginning with the day when the union satisfies the requirement of the Trade Union and Labour Relations (Consolidation) Act 1992 s 231A (see PARA 1378) in relation to the ballot in respect of the industrial action; and (2) ending with the seventh day before the day, or before the first of the days, specified in the relevant notice: s 234A(4) (as added: see note 2).
12   For these purposes, a relevant notice covers an act done by the union if the person induced falls within a notified category of employee and the work place at which he works is a notified workplace and: (1) where he is induced to take part, or continue to take part, in industrial action which the union intends to be continuous, if the notice so states, and there is no participation by him in the industrial action before the date specified in the notice in consequence of any inducement by the union not covered by a relevant notice; and (2) where he

is induced to take part, or continue to take part, in industrial action which the union intends to be discontinuous, if there is no participation by him in the industrial action on a day not specified in the notice in consequence of any inducement by the union not covered by a relevant notice: Trade Union and Labour Relations (Consolidation) Act 1992 s 234A(5) (as added (see note 2); amended by the Employment Relations Act 2004 s 25(1), (4)). 'Notified category of employee' means a category of employee that is listed in the notice or, where the notice contains the information mentioned in the Trade Union and Labour Relations (Consolidation) Act 1992 s 234A(3C) (see the text and note 14), a category of employee that the employer, at the time he receives the notice, can readily deduce from the notice is a category of employee to which some or all of the affected employees belong: s 234A(5B)(a) (s 234A(5B)–(5D) added by the Employment Relations Act 2004 s 25(1), (5)). 'Notified workplace' means a workplace that is listed in the notice or, where the notice contains the information mentioned in the Trade Union and Labour Relations (Consolidation) Act 1992 s 234A(3C), a workplace that the employer, at the time he receives the notice, can readily deduce from the notice is the workplace at which some or all of the affected employees work: s 234A(5B)(b) (as so added). As to when action is intended to be continuous or discontinuous see note 15. As to the meaning of 'employee' see PARAS 892, 1370 note 4. See also note 14.

13 Trade Union and Labour Relations (Consolidation) Act 1992 s 234A(1) (as added: see note 2).

14 Trade Union and Labour Relations (Consolidation) Act 1992 s 234A(3)(a), (3A)–(3C) (s 234A(3)(a) substituted, s 234A(3A)–(3F) added by the Employment Relations Act 2004 s 25(1), (2)(a), (3)). See also *British Telecommunications plc v Communication Workers Union* [2003] EWHC 937 (QB), [2004] IRLR 58, cited in PARAS 1340 note 2, 1361 note 2.

The lists and figures supplied under the Trade Union and Labour Relations (Consolidation) Act 1992 s 234A, or the information mentioned that is so supplied, must be as accurate as is reasonably practicable in the light of the information in the possession of the union at the time when it complies with s 234A(1), and for these purposes information is in the possession of the union if it is held, for union purposes, in a document, whether in electronic form or any other form, and in the possession or under the control of an officer or employee of the union: s 234A(3D), (3E) (as so added).

References in s 234A to the affected employees are references to those employees of the employer who the union reasonably believes will be induced by the union, or have been so induced, to take part or continue to take part in the industrial action: s 234A(5C) (as added: see note 12). For the purposes of s 234A, the workplace at which an employee works is, in relation to an employee who works at or from a single set of premises, those premises, and in relation to any other employee, the premises with which his employment has the closest connection: s 234A(5D) (as so added). Nothing in s 234A requires a union to supply an employer with the names of the affected employees: s 234A(3F) (as so added).

15 For these purposes, a union intends industrial action to be discontinuous if it intends it to take place only on some days on which there is an opportunity to take the action and intends it to be continuous if it intends it to be not so restricted: Trade Union and Labour Relations (Consolidation) Act 1992 s 234A(6) (as added: see note 2).

16 Trade Union and Labour Relations (Consolidation) Act 1992 s 234A(3)(b) (as added: see note 2).

17 The provisions of the Trade Union and Labour Relations (Consolidation) Act 1992 s 20(2)–(4) (see PARA 1388) apply for the purpose of determining for the purposes of s 234A(7)–(7B) whether the trade union is to be taken to have authorised or indorsed the industrial action: s 234A(9) (as added and amended: see note 2).

18 Ie subject to the Trade Union and Labour Relations (Consolidation) Act 1992 s 234A(7A), (7B): see the text and notes 21–23.

19 Trade Union and Labour Relations (Consolidation) Act 1992 s 234A(7) (as added (see note 2); amended by the Employment Relations Act 1999 Sch 3 paras 1, 11(1), (4), Sch 9).

20 Ie the Trade Union and Labour Relations (Consolidation) Act 1992 s 234A applies in relation to an act to induce a person to take part, or continue to take part, in the industrial action after that date as if the references in s 234A(3)(b)(i) (see head (2) in the text) to the industrial action were to the industrial action taking place after that date: s 234A(7) (as added and amended: see note 19).

21 Ie the Trade Union and Labour Relations (Consolidation) Act 1992 s 234A(7).

22 Trade Union and Labour Relations (Consolidation) Act 1992 s 234A(7A) (s 234A(7A), (7B) added by the Employment Relations Act 1999 Sch 3 paras 1, 11(1), (5)). See also note 17.

23 Trade Union and Labour Relations (Consolidation) Act 1992 s 234A(7B) (as added: see note 22). See also note 17.

(6) POTENTIAL LIABILITIES FOR PICKETING

1383. Criminal liability for picketing. A person commits an offence who, with a view to compelling[1] another person to abstain from doing or to do any act which that person has a legal right to do or abstain from doing, wrongfully[2] and without legal authority:

(1)   uses violence to or intimidates[3] that person or his spouse or civil partner or children, or injures his property;

(2)   persistently follows[4] that person about from place to place;

(3)   hides any tools, clothes or other property owned or used by that person, or deprives him of or hinders him in the use thereof[5];

(4)   watches or besets[6] the house or other place where that person resides, works, carries on business or happens to be, or the approach to any such house or place; or

(5)   follows[7] that person with two or more persons in a disorderly manner in or through any street or road[8];

and a person guilty of such an offence is liable on summary conviction to imprisonment for a term not exceeding six months or a fine not exceeding level 5 on the standard scale, or to both[9].

In addition to these offences relating specifically to the activities of pickets, the general criminal law applies and so there may be liability for offences such as obstruction of the highway[10], obstruction of the police[11], assault[12], criminal damage[13], harassment[14] and the various offences under the Public Order Act 1986[15].

Of particular importance to the policing of pickets is the concept of breach of the peace[16]. If a police officer reasonably apprehends such a breach of the peace, it is his duty to take such steps as are necessary to prevent it (which may mean controlling the numbers and locations of the pickets)[17]; and any refusal by a picket to comply with those steps may constitute the offence of obstruction of a police officer in the course of his duty[18].

1   Compulsion is a necessary element; a purpose of dissuasion is not enough: *DPP v Fidler* [1992] 1 WLR 91, 94 Cr App Rep 286, DC; *R v McKenzie* [1892] 2 QB 519, DC; *Elsey v Smith* [1983] IRLR 292. The offence is complete even if the compulsion is ineffective: *Agnew v Munro* (1891) 28 SLR 335.

2   The conduct complained of must, by virtue of this wording, already be criminal or tortious in order for the Trade Union and Labour Relations (Consolidation) Act 1992 s 241 to apply. Thus, s 241 does not independently make conduct unlawful, but only provides specific offences or renders criminal that which was already tortious: *Ward, Lock & Co Ltd v Operative Printers' Assistants' Society* (1906) 22 TLR 327, CA; *Fowler v Kibble* [1922] 1 Ch 487, CA; *Thomas v National Union of Mineworkers (South Wales Area)* [1986] Ch 20, [1985] ICR 886. The contrary approach in *J Lyons & Sons v Wilkins* [1896] 1 Ch 811, CA (that the provisions of what is now the Trade Union and Labour Relations (Consolidation) Act 1992 s 241 act independently to render these activities unlawful per se) has not been followed. Moreover, it cannot be argued that, because an act comes within s 241, it must, therefore, be tortious, because that would 'put the cart before the horse': *Thomas v National Union of Mineworkers (South Wales Area)* [1986] Ch 20, [1985] ICR 886. However, once an act is tortious, that is enough to activate the Trade Union and Labour Relations (Consolidation) Act 1992 s 241, even if the act is then rendered immune from civil action by legislation: *Galt (Procurator Fiscal) v Philp* [1984] IRLR 156.

3   There must be some element of putting the person in fear by force or violence to the person or to property: *R v Jones* [1974] ICR 310, [1974] IRLR 117, CA; *Connor v Kent, Gibson v Lawson, Curran v Treleaven* [1891] 2 QB 545, CCR; cf *Judge v Bennett* (1887) 52 JP 247. Mass picketing is likely to constitute intimidation: *Thomas v National Union of Mineworkers (South Wales Area)* [1986] Ch 20, [1985] ICR 886.

4   See *Smith v Thomasson* (1891) 62 LT 68, 16 Cox CC 740; *R v Wall* (1907) 21 Cox CC 401; *R v Hulme* (1913) 9 Cr App Rep 77, CCA; *Elsey v Smith* [1983] IRLR 292.

5 In line with the principle in note 2, the acts in question must themselves already be unlawful in order to constitute this offence: *Fowler v Kibble* [1922] 1 Ch 487, CA.

6 This limb is particularly appropriate to picketing, especially industrial premises: *R v Bonsall* [1985] Crim LR 150. Once again, the conduct must be independently unlawful if this offence is to be committed: *Hubbard v Pitt* [1976] QB 142, [1975] ICR 308, CA. A person may 'watch and beset' from inside the property, eg during an occupation of premises: *Galt (Procurator Fiscal) v Philp* [1984] IRLR 156.

7 See *R v McKenzie* [1892] 2 QB 519, DC; *Elsey v Smith* [1983] IRLR 292.

8 Trade Union and Labour Relations (Consolidation) Act 1992 s 241(1) (amended by the Civil Partnership Act 2004 Sch 27 para 145). These offences are old, having originally been enacted as the Conspiracy and Protection of Property Act 1875 s 7 (now repealed); indeed, what is now the general immunity for certain picketing (see PARA 1385) was originally a proviso to s 7, deeming mere attendance (for the stated purposes) not to constitute 'watching and besetting'. The Public Order Act 1986 upgraded these old offences, increasing the penalties and adding the power of arrest.

9 Trade Union and Labour Relations (Consolidation) Act 1992 s 241(2). As to the standard scale see SENTENCING AND DISPOSITION OF OFFENDERS vol 92 (2010) PARA 142. As to powers of arrest without warrant generally see now the Police and Criminal Evidence Act 1984 s 24; and POLICE AND INVESTIGATORY POWERS vol 84A (2013) PARA 487.

10 See the Highways Act 1980 s 137(1); and HIGHWAYS, STREETS AND BRIDGES vol 55 (2012) PARA 351.

11 See the Police Act 1996 s 89(2); and POLICE AND INVESTIGATORY POWERS vol 84 (2013) PARA 44.

12 See CRIMINAL LAW vol 25 (2010) PARA 157 et seq.

13 See CRIMINAL LAW vol 25 (2010) PARA 326 et seq.

14 See the Protection from Harassment Act 1997; and CRIMINAL LAW vol 25 (2010) PARAS 163–164.

15 See CRIMINAL LAW vol 26 (2010) PARA 487 et seq; cf *DPP v Jones* [1999] 2 AC 240, [1999] 2 All ER 257, HL (where it was held that there is a public right of peaceful assembly on the highway for any reasonable purpose, provided that the activity does not obstruct the highway by unreasonably impeding the rights of others to pass and repass, and does not amount to a public or private nuisance).

16 The common law offence of breach of the peace was specifically retained by the Public Order Act 1986 s 40(4): see POLICE AND INVESTIGATORY POWERS vol 84A (2013) PARA 493.

17 *Piddington v Bates* [1960] 3 All ER 660, [1961] 1 WLR 162, DC (limiting numbers); *Kavanagh v Hiscock* [1974] QB 600, [1974] ICR 282, DC (keeping pickets away from factory gate); *Moss v McLachlan* [1985] IRLR 76, DC (preventing pickets reaching pit premises at all, in the light of earlier violence). During the miners' strike of 1984 to 1985 use was also made of bail conditions on arrested pickets in order to restrain them from returning to the picketed premises (especially where those were other than their own place of work): see eg *R v Mansfield Justices, ex p Sharkey* [1985] QB 613, [1985] 1 All ER 193, DC.

18 See text and note 11. If there is a breach of the peace (actual or apprehended), that may supply a common law power of arrest: *R v Howell* [1982] QB 416, 73 Cr App Rep 31, CA; and see *Wershof v Metropolitan Police Comr* [1978] 3 All ER 540, 68 Cr App Rep 82.

1384. Liability in tort for picketing. Picketing may constitute tortious action, and be restrainable as such, on ordinary principles, especially in relation to the torts of public or private nuisance[1] and trespass[2]. Such remedies are normally available, subject to the statutory immunity for peaceful picketing[3], only to the owner of the premises picketed; but it has been held that employees not on strike and seeking to attend work at the picketed premises may have a cause of action against pickets trying to prevent them from doing so, for a common law tort of harassment[4]. It is possible that picketing could also involve the commission of the statutory tort of harassment[5].

Picketing could also be the means of committing one of the economic torts[6], as, for example where pickets turn away a delivery to the picketed premises, constituting the inducement of breaches of contract[7]. Such action could constitute secondary action which is not protected by the statutory immunities[8].

To prevent that happening, it is declared that lawful picketing is not to constitute secondary action within the statutory meaning, even if it has such effect[9].

1   See NUISANCE vol 78 (2010) PARA 101 et seq; *Hubbard v Pitt* [1976] QB 142, [1975] ICR 308, CA.
2   See *Tynan v Balmer* [1967] 1 QB 91, [1966] 2 All ER 133, DC; TORT vol 97 (2010) PARA 562 et seq.
3   See PARA 1385.
4   *Thomas v National Union of Mineworkers (South Wales Area)* [1986] Ch 20, [1985] ICR 886. Doubt was expressed about this development in *News Group Newspapers Ltd v SOGAT '82 (No 2)* [1987] ICR 181 at 206, [1986] IRLR 337 at 348 per Stuart-Smith J. The existence of a common law tort of harassment as a form of private nuisance available to a person without an interest in land was accepted in *Khorasandjian v Bush* [1993] QB 727, [1993] 3 All ER 669, CA, albeit in a non-industrial context, but that case was overruled on that point in *Hunter v Canary Wharf Ltd* [1997] AC 655, [1997] 2 All ER 426, HL.
5   Ie under the Protection from Harassment Act 1997 s 3(1): see TORT vol 97 (2010) PARA 557. In *Tuppen v Microsoft Corpn* (2000) Times, 15 November it was held that the Protection from Harassment Act 1997 has a narrow ambit and breaches of it which give rise to a civil remedy are confined to cases of stalking, behaviour of an anti-social nature by neighbours and racial harassment. However, the House of Lords subsequently held that it could apply broadly, in particular to harassment at work by an employer: *Majrowski v Guy's and St Thomas's NHS Trust* [2006] UKHL 34, [2007] 1 AC 224, [2006] 4 All ER 395.
6   See PARA 1343.
7   The mere presence of pickets may constitute an inducement: *Union Traffic Ltd v Transport and General Workers' Union* [1989] ICR 98, [1989] IRLR 127, CA. The application of the civil law to picketing must, however, be kept within reasonable constraints, and it has been held that trying to influence possible customers of outlets of the employer in dispute does not constitute direct inducement or, in the absence of unlawful means, indirect inducement: *Middlebrook Mushrooms Ltd v Transport and General Workers' Union* [1993] ICR 612, [1993] IRLR 232, CA.
8   Ie since the categories of lawful secondary action in the Employment Act 1980 s 17 (repealed) were removed by the Employment Act 1990 (repealed): see now the Trade Union and Labour Relations (Consolidation) Act 1992 s 224; and PARA 1367.
9   See the Trade Union and Labour Relations (Consolidation) Act 1992 s 224; and PARA 1367. Cf, however, s 219(3); and PARA 1369.

1385.   The statutory immunity for peaceful picketing.   It is lawful[1] for a person in contemplation or furtherance of a trade dispute[2] to attend[3]:

(1)   at or near his own place of work[4]; or

(2)   if he is an official[5] of a trade union[6], at or near the place of work of a member of the union whom he is accompanying and whom he represents[7],

for the purpose only[8] of peacefully obtaining or communicating information, or peacefully persuading any person to work or abstain from working[9].

If a person works or normally works otherwise than at any one place or at a place the location of which is such that attendance there for such a purpose is impracticable, his place of work for these purposes is any premises of his employer from which he works or from which his work is administered[10].

In the case of a worker[11] not in employment where his last employment was terminated in connection with a trade dispute, or the termination of his employment was one of the circumstances giving rise to a trade dispute, in relation to that dispute his former place of work is to be treated for these purposes as his place of work[12].

At the date at which this volume states the law, a constable in uniform may not give a dispersal direction, a direction requiring any persons whose place of residence is not within the relevant locality to leave the relevant locality or any part of it, or a direction prohibiting any persons whose place of residence is not within the relevant locality from returning to the relevant locality or any part of it for a specified period[13] in respect of a group of persons who are engaged in conduct which is lawful under the above provisions[14]. However, with effect from 20 October 2014[15], this restriction is replaced by a similar restriction on the use of the dispersal powers[16] contained in the Anti-social Behaviour, Crime and Policing Act 2014[17].

1   These provisions have been said to confer a 'narrow but nevertheless real immunity' from both criminal and civil liability which could arise (see PARAS 1383–1384) from mere attendance: *Broome v DPP* [1974] AC 587 at 603, [1974] ICR 84 at 96, HL per Lord Salmon. There is no positive right to picket or stop vehicles: *Broome v DPP* [1974] AC 587, [1974] ICR 84, HL; *Kavanagh v Hiscock* [1974] QB 600, [1974] ICR 282, DC. Pickets thus remain subject to the normal law on breach of the peace: see PARA 1383.
       The immunity does not legitimise any independently criminal or tortious acts by pickets; in particular, it does not legitimise the infringement of private property rights: *Larkin v Belfast Harbour Comrs* [1908] 2 IR 214; *British Airports Authority v Ashton* [1983] 3 All ER 6, [1983] ICR 696, DC (no authority for picket line on private property).

2   As to the meaning of 'trade dispute' see PARAS 1360–1361.

3   It is only the attending that is covered by the immunity, not necessarily any further acts: see the cases cited in note 1. There is no direct limit on the numbers who may attend, but: (1) mass picketing may more easily be inferred to be for a purpose other than peaceful communication or persuasion (*Broome v DPP* [1974] AC 587, [1974] ICR 84, HL; *Thomas v National Union of Mineworkers (South Wales Area)* [1986] Ch 20, [1985] ICR 886); and (2) the Code of Practice on Picketing para 51 (see PARA 1386) suggests a limit of six pickets per entrance. Although the latter is not directly binding (see PARA 1232), it could be taken into account by a court when deciding whether the aim was peaceful, and could be indirectly enforced by a court injunction limiting picketing to that which is lawful, as in *Thomas v National Union of Mineworkers (South Wales Area)* [1986] Ch 20, [1985] ICR 886.

4   The restriction to the picket's own place of work was one of the principal limitations introduced to the predecessor of this provision by the Employment Act 1980 (repealed); pickets not at their own place of work may, therefore, be restrained by injunction: *Mersey Dock and Harbour Co v Verrinder* [1982] IRLR 152. 'At or near' is to be construed realistically, e g covering the entrance to a private industrial estate on which the employer's premises are situated: *Rayware Ltd v Transport and General Workers' Union* [1989] 3 All ER 583, [1989] ICR 457, CA. There is no statutory definition of 'place of work' for these purposes; but as to the meaning of the term 'workplace', in the context of workplace ballots, see PARA 1375 note 2.

5   As to the meaning of 'official', in relation to a trade union, see PARA 1018.

6   As to the meaning of 'trade union' see PARA 891.

7   A person who is an official of a trade union by virtue only of having been elected or appointed to be a representative of some of the members of the union is to be regarded for these purposes as representing only those members; but otherwise an official of a union is to be regarded for these purposes as representing all its members: Trade Union and Labour Relations (Consolidation) Act 1992 s 220(4).

8   The marginal note to the Trade Union and Labour Relations (Consolidation) Act 1992 s 220 refers to 'peaceful' picketing, but in this context 'peaceful' simply means picketing for this stated purpose. If a purpose other than that is inferred from the conduct of the pickets, this immunity does not apply: *Tynan v Balmer* [1967] 1 QB 91, [1966] 2 All ER 133, DC (intent to obstruct and blockade). Such an ulterior purpose may be easier to infer as numbers involved increase: *Broome v DPP* [1974] AC 587, [1974] ICR 84, HL.

9   Trade Union and Labour Relations (Consolidation) Act 1992 s 220(1). As to the further immunity in relation to any secondary effects of picketing see PARA 1384 text and note 9.

10   Trade Union and Labour Relations (Consolidation) Act 1992 s 220(2).

11   As to the meaning of 'worker' see PARA 892.

12   Trade Union and Labour Relations (Consolidation) Act 1992 s 220(3). Although this provision prima facie helps a dismissed employee in a dispute, it cannot apply to picketing premises where the ex-employee in fact never worked; thus, if the employee is dismissed and his workplace closed down, as part of the employer's move to new premises, the ex-employee may only picket the old, closed workplace, not the new premises: *News Group Newspapers Ltd v SOGAT '82 (No 2)* [1987] ICR 181, [1986] IRLR 337; *Union Traffic Ltd v Transport and General Workers' Union* [1989] ICR 98, [1989] IRLR 127, CA.

13   Ie a direction under the Anti-social Behaviour Act 2003 s 30(4) (prospectively repealed): see SENTENCING AND DISPOSITION OF OFFENDERS vol 92 (2010) PARA 504.

14 See the Anti-social Behaviour Act 2003 s 30(5)(a) (prospectively repealed by the Anti-social Behaviour, Crime and Policing Act 2014 Sch 11 para 41(c), as from a day to be appointed under s 185(1), (3)(c)); and SENTENCING AND DISPOSITION OF OFFENDERS vol 92 (2010) PARA 504.

15 Ie as from the day specified in the Anti-social Behaviour, Crime and Policing Act 2014 (Commencement No 7, Saving and Transitional Provisions) Order 2014, SI 2014/2590, art 3(b), made under the Anti-social Behaviour, Crime and Policing Act 2014 s 185(1), (3)(c).

16 Ie the power to give directions under the Anti-social Behaviour, Crime and Policing Act 2014 s 35.

17 See the Anti-social Behaviour, Crime and Policing Act 2014 s 36(4)(a).

1386.   Code of Practice on Picketing.   Pursuant to his statutory powers to issue Codes of Practice[1], the Secretary of State has issued the Code of Practice on Picketing[2]. The provisions of the Code are admissible in evidence and are to be taken into account, whenever relevant, by any court, tribunal or the Central Arbitration Committee; but failure to observe any provisions of the Code does not of itself render a person liable to any proceedings[3].

Sections A, B and C of the Code set out the relevant law relating to criminal and civil liability of pickets[4]. Section D concerns the role of the police and, as well as setting out the relevant police powers, makes the following points:

(1)   the function of the police is to uphold the law and keep the peace, not to take a view as to the merits of an industrial dispute[5];

(2)   the police have no responsibility for enforcing the civil law; in particular, it is not part of their function to help an employer to identify pickets, or to enforce the terms of an order[6].

Section E concerns limits on the numbers of pickets. After warning that mass picketing can easily become intimidatory, and pointing out that the Public Order Act 1986 gives power to the police to impose conditions on public assemblies of 20 or more persons, it goes on to state that 'pickets and their organisers should ensure that in general the number of pickets does not exceed six at any entrance to, or exit from, a workplace; frequently a smaller number will be appropriate'[7].

Section F concerns the organisation of picketing and makes the following points:

(a)   whenever picketing is official, an experienced person (preferably a trade union official) should be in charge of the picket line, with a letter of authority from the union to that effect, to show to the police or those trying to cross the picket line[8];

(b)   a picket should not be designated as an official picket unless it is actually organised by a trade union[9];

(c)   the organiser should maintain close contact with the police and seek in advance police directions as to numbers and locations[10];

(d)   other functions of organisers are to ensure that pickets know the law and act peacefully, to distribute badges or armbands to authorised pickets, to discourage picketing by outsiders, to restrict numbers, to maintain contact with union offices and to observe special arrangements for essential supplies, services or operations[11].

Section G concerns essential supplies, services and operations[12], stating that great care should be taken to ensure that picketing does not cause distress, hardship or inconvenience to members of the public, especially in relation to essential services, goods and supplies, and maintenance of plant and equipment[13]. Arrangements to safeguard these should be agreed in advance between those organising the picketing and the employers concerned[14].

1   Ie in exercise of the power conferred on him by the Trade Union and Labour Relations (Consolidation) Act 1992 s 203: see PARA 1231.

2 The current revised Code was brought into force on 1 May 1992 by the Employment Code of Practice (Picketing) Order 1992, SI 1992/476, art 2. As to the Secretary of State see PARA 5 note 21.

3 See the Trade Union and Labour Relations (Consolidation) Act 1992 s 207(1), (3); and PARA 1232.

4 See the Code of Practice on Picketing paras 1–44. See PARAS 1383–1384.

5 See the Code of Practice on Picketing para 45.

6 See the Code of Practice on Picketing para 46.

7 Code of Practice on Picketing para 51. Unlike other provisions of the Code (see the text and notes 4–6, 8–14), this provision could have definite legal effect, albeit indirectly, by being taken into account by a court when considering: (1) whether the picketing in question in the numbers present was only for the purpose of peaceful persuasion or communication (see PARA 1385); or (2) how to frame an injunction to restrict picketing to that which is lawful, as in *Thomas v National Union of Mineworkers (South Wales Area)* [1986] Ch 20, [1985] ICR 886 (injunction granted restraining the organisation of pickets at colliery in question in numbers greater than six, for any purpose other than peaceful persuasion or communication).

8 See the Code of Practice on Picketing para 54.

9 See the Code of Practice on Picketing para 55.

10 See the Code of Practice on Picketing para 56.

11 See the Code of Practice on Picketing para 57.

12 A non-exhaustive list is given in the Code of Practice on Picketing para 63 of what may constitute 'essential supplies, services and operations', as follows:

    (1)   the production, packaging, marketing and/or distribution of medical and pharmaceutical products;

    (2)   the provision of supplies and services essential to health and welfare institutions, eg hospitals and old peoples' homes;

    (3)   the provision of heating fuel for schools, residential institutions, medical institutions and private residential accommodation;

    (4)   the production and provision of other supplies for which there is a crucial need during a crisis in the interests of public health and safety (eg chlorine, lime and other agents for water purification; industrial and medical gases; sand and salt for road-gritting purposes);

    (5)   activities necessary to the maintenance of plant and machinery;

    (6)   the proper care of livestock;

    (7)   necessary safety procedures (including such procedures as are necessary to maintain plant and machinery);

    (8)   the production, packaging, marketing and/or distribution of food and animal feeding stuffs;

    (9)   the operation of essential services, such as police, fire, ambulance, medical and nursing services, air safety, coastguard and air sea rescue services, and services provided by voluntary bodies (eg Red Cross and St John's ambulances, meals on wheels, hospital car service), and mortuaries, burial and cremation services.

13 See the Code of Practice on Picketing para 62. Of all the provisions of the Code which go beyond the law as laid down in statute (see PARA 1385), this is the most difficult to see as having any legal effect, direct or indirect. Picketing which adversely affected an essential service would presumably not lose its character as 'peaceful', provided that it remained for the purpose of peaceful persuasion or communication; these provisions in the Code, therefore, seem to be merely exhortatory.

14 See the Code of Practice on Picketing para 64.

(7) LIABILITY OF TRADE UNION FOR INDUSTRIAL ACTION

1387. Trade union's vicarious liability at common law. A trade union[1] may be vicariously liable[2] at common law for torts committed by its servants or agents[3]. However, where a trade union is sued for one of the economic torts[4], the union may be liable for the act in question if, but only if, that act is taken to have been authorised or indorsed by the union in accordance with the relevant statutory provisions[5].

1   As to the meaning of 'trade union' see PARA 891.
2   *Heatons Transport (St Helens) Ltd v Transport and General Workers' Union* [1973] AC 15,
    [1972] ICR 308, HL; *General Aviation Services (UK) Ltd v Transport and General Workers'
    Union* [1985] ICR 615, [1976] IRLR 224, HL; *Thomas v National Union of Mineworkers
    (South Wales Area)* [1986] Ch 20, [1985] ICR 886; cf *News Group Newspapers Ltd v SOGAT
    '82 (No 2)* [1987] ICR 181, [1986] IRLR 337.
3   See the Trade Union and Labour Relations (Consolidation) Act 1992 s 10(1)(b); and PARA 897
    head (2).
4   Ie the torts of inducing a breach of contract or interfering with the performance of a contract,
    intimidation and conspiracy, as referred to in the Trade Union and Labour Relations
    (Consolidation) Act 1992 s 20(1): see PARA 1388.
5   Ie in accordance with the Trade Union and Labour Relations (Consolidation) Act 1992
    s 20(2)–(4): see PARA 1388.

1388.   Trade union's liability under statute for the economic torts.   Where
proceedings in tort are brought against a trade union[1]:

   (1)   on the ground that an act[2]:
        (a)   constitutes one of the economic torts of inducing a breach of
              contract or interfering with the performance of a contract[3]; or
        (b)   constitutes intimidation[4]; or
   (2)   in respect of an agreement or combination which constitutes a
        conspiracy[5],

then, for the purpose of determining in those proceedings whether the union is
liable[6] in respect of the act in question, that act is to be taken to have been done
by the union if, but only if, it is taken to have been authorised or indorsed by the
trade union in accordance with the following provisions[7].

An act is taken to have been authorised or indorsed by a trade union if it was
done, or was authorised or indorsed:

   (i)   by any person empowered by the rules[8] to do, authorise or indorse acts
        of the kind in question[9]; or
   (ii)   by the union's principal executive[10] committee or its president[11] or
        general secretary[12]; or
   (iii) by any other committee[13] of the union or any other official[14] of the
        union, whether employed by it or not[15].

In proceedings arising out of an act which is taken, by virtue of these
provisions, to have been done by a trade union, the power of the court to grant
an injunction[16] includes power to require the union to take such steps as the
court considers appropriate for ensuring that there is no, or no further,
inducement of persons to take part, or to continue to take part, in industrial
action, and that no person engages in any conduct after the granting of the
injunction by virtue of having been induced before it was granted to take part, or
to continue to take part, in industrial action[17].

1   As to the meaning of 'trade union' see PARA 891.
2   As to the meaning of 'act' see PARA 1028 note 11.
3   Ie on the ground that an act induces another person to break a contract or interferes or induces
    another person to interfere with its performance. See also PARA 1343.
4   Ie on the ground that an act consists in threatening that a contract, whether one to which the
    union is a party or not, will be broken or its performance interfered with, or that the union will
    induce another person to break a contract or interfere with its performance. See also PARA 1343.
5   Ie in respect of an agreement or combination by two or more persons to do or procure the doing
    of an act which, if it were done without any such agreement or combination, would be
    actionable in tort on a ground specified in notes 3–4. See also PARA 1343.
6   Where, for the purposes of any proceedings, an act is taken, by virtue of the Trade Union and
    Labour Relations (Consolidation) Act 1992 s 20, to have been done by a trade union, nothing in
    s 20 affects the liability of any other person, in those or any other proceedings, in respect of that

act: s 20(5). See *Gate Gourmet London Ltd v Transport and General Workers Union* [2005] EWHC 1889 (QB), [2005] IRLR 881 (injunction against trade union which indorsed unlawful activities of its picketing members).

7   Trade Union and Labour Relations (Consolidation) Act 1992 s 20(1).
8   For these purposes, 'rules', in relation to a trade union, means the written rules of the union and any other written provision forming part of the contract between a member and the other members: Trade Union and Labour Relations (Consolidation) Act 1992 s 20(7). As to the meaning of 'rules' generally see PARA 898 note 5.
9   Trade Union and Labour Relations (Consolidation) Act 1992 s 20(2)(a). The provisions of s 20(2) and s 20(3), (4) apply in relation to proceedings for failure to comply with any injunction granted by the High Court as they apply in relation to the original proceedings: s 20(6), 121.
10 As to the meaning of 'executive', in relation to a trade union, see PARA 943 note 9.
11 As to the meaning of 'president', in relation to a trade union, see PARA 921 note 3.
12 Trade Union and Labour Relations (Consolidation) Act 1992 s 20(2)(b). The provisions of s 20(2)(b) and s 20(2)(c) apply notwithstanding anything in the rules of the union, or in any contract or rule of law, but subject to the provisions of s 21 (see PARA 1389): s 20(4). See also note 9. As to the meaning of 'general secretary', in relation to a trade union, see PARA 921 note 3.
13 For these purposes, any group of persons constituted in accordance with the rules of the union is a committee of the union: Trade Union and Labour Relations (Consolidation) Act 1992 s 20(3)(a). See also note 9.
14 For these purposes, an act is taken to have been done, authorised or indorsed by an official if it was done, authorised or indorsed by, or by any member of, a group of persons of which he was a member at the material time, the purposes of which included organising or co-ordinating industrial action: Trade Union and Labour Relations (Consolidation) Act 1992 s 20(3)(b). As to the meaning of 'official', in relation to a trade union, see PARA 1018; and as to the meaning of 'industrial action' see PARA 1370 note 5. See also note 9.
15 Trade Union and Labour Relations (Consolidation) Act 1992 s 20(2)(c). See also notes 9, 12.
16 As to injunctions see PARA 1437 et seq.
17 Trade Union and Labour Relations (Consolidation) Act 1992 s 20(6). See also note 9.

1389. Repudiation by trade union of certain acts. An act[1] by a committee[2] or official[3] of a trade union[4] is not to be taken to have been authorised or indorsed[5] by the union if it was repudiated by the executive, president or general secretary as soon as reasonably practicable after coming to the knowledge of any of them[6]. The repudiation is to be treated as ineffective, however, unless the following conditions are complied with[7]:

(1)   written notice of the repudiation[8] must be given to the committee or official in question without delay; and

(2)   the union must do its best to give individual written notice of the fact and date of the repudiation, without delay, to every member of the union who it has reason to believe is taking part, or might otherwise take part, in industrial action[9] as a result of the act, and to the employer[10] of every such member[11].

An act is not to be treated as repudiated if, at any time after the union purported to repudiate it, the executive, president or general secretary has behaved in a manner which is inconsistent[12] with the purported repudiation[13].

1   As to the meaning of 'act' see PARA 1028 note 11.
2   As to the meaning of 'committee' for these purposes see PARA 1388 note 13. Such a committee does not include the executive of the union: see the Trade Union and Labour Relations (Consolidation) Act 1992 s 20(2)(b), (c); and PARA 1388. As to the meaning of 'executive', in relation to a trade union, see PARA 943 note 9.
3   As to the meaning of 'official' for these purposes see PARA 1388 note 14. Such an official does not include the president or general secretary of the union: see the Trade Union and Labour Relations (Consolidation) Act 1992 s 20(2)(b), (c); and PARA 1388. As to the meaning of 'president', in relation to a trade union, see PARA 921 note 3; and as to the meaning of 'general secretary', in relation to a trade union, see PARA 921 note 3.

4   As to the meaning of 'trade union' see PARA 891.
5   Ie by virtue only of the Trade Union and Labour Relations (Consolidation) Act 1992 s 20(2)(c):
    see PARA 1388 head (iii).
6   Trade Union and Labour Relations (Consolidation) Act 1992 s 21(1).
7   Trade Union and Labour Relations (Consolidation) Act 1992 s 21(4).
8   The notice must contain the following statement: 'Your union has repudiated the call (or calls)
    for industrial action to which this notice relates and will give no support to unofficial industrial
    action taken in response to it (or them). If you are dismissed while taking unofficial industrial
    action, you will have no right to complain of unfair dismissal': Trade Union and Labour
    Relations (Consolidation) Act 1992 s 21(3). As to the meaning of 'dismiss' see PARA 1056
    note 1; and as to the loss of unfair dismissal protection on taking part in unofficial industrial
    action see PARA 1350.
9   As to the meaning of 'industrial action' see PARA 1370 note 5.
10 As to the meaning of 'employer' see PARA 892.
11 Trade Union and Labour Relations (Consolidation) Act 1992 s 21(2).
12 The executive, president or general secretary is to be treated as so behaving if, on a request made
    to any of them within three months of the purported repudiation by a person who: (1) is a party
    to a commercial contract whose performance has been or may be interfered with as a result of
    the act in question; and (2) has not been given written notice by the union of the repudiation, it
    is not forthwith confirmed in writing that the act has been repudiated: Trade Union and Labour
    Relations (Consolidation) Act 1992 s 21(6) (amended by the Trade Union Reform and
    Employment Rights Act 1993 Sch 7 para 17). For these purposes, 'commercial contract' means
    any contract other than a contract of employment or any other contract under which a person
    agrees personally to do work or perform services for another: Trade Union and Labour
    Relations (Consolidation) Act 1992 s 21(7). As to the meaning of 'contract of employment' see
    PARA 892.
13 Trade Union and Labour Relations (Consolidation) Act 1992 s 21(5). See *Express & Star Ltd v
    National Graphical Association (1982)* [1985] IRLR 455 per Skinner J; affd [1986] ICR 589,
    [1986] IRLR 222, CA.

1390.   Statutory limit on damages in action in tort.   A statutory limit on
damages applies in any proceedings in tort brought against a trade union[1],
except proceedings:

   (1)   for personal injury[2] as a result of negligence, nuisance or breach of
         duty[3];
   (2)   for breach of duty in connection with the ownership, occupation,
         possession, control or use of property[4]; or
   (3)   brought by virtue of the statutory provisions[5] relating to product
         liability[6].

In any proceedings in tort to which the statutory limit applies, the amount
which may be awarded against the union by way of damages[7] is not to exceed:

   (a)   £10,000 if the union has fewer than 5,000 members;
   (b)   £50,000 if the union has 5,000 or more members but fewer than 25,000
         members;
   (c)   £125,000 if the union has 25,000 or more members but fewer than
         100,000 members; and
   (d)   £250,000 if the union has 100,000 or more members[8].

The Secretary of State may by order[9] amend heads (a) to (d) above so as to
vary any of the sums there specified[10].

No award of damages, costs or expenses may be enforced against protected
property[11].

1   As to the meaning of 'trade union' see PARA 891.
2   For these purposes, 'personal injury' includes any disease and any impairment of a person's
    physical or mental condition: Trade Union and Labour Relations (Consolidation) Act 1992
    s 22(5).
3   For these purposes, 'breach of duty' means breach of a duty imposed by any rule of law or by or
    under any enactment: Trade Union and Labour Relations (Consolidation) Act 1992 s 22(5).

4   For these purposes, 'property' means any property, whether real or personal: Trade Union and Labour Relations (Consolidation) Act 1992 s 22(5).
5   Ie by virtue of the Consumer Protection Act 1987 Pt I (ss 1–9): see CONSUMER PROTECTION vol 21 (2011) PARA 642 et seq.
6   Trade Union and Labour Relations (Consolidation) Act 1992 s 22(1).
7   The limit on damages does not include any costs awarded against a union (*Messenger Newspapers Group Ltd v National Graphical Association* [1984] IRLR 397; and see subsequent contempt proceedings [1984] 1 All ER 293, [1984] ICR 345, CA); nor does it include any interest awarded on damages (*Boxfoldia Ltd v National Graphical Association (1982)* [1988] ICR 752, [1988] IRLR 383). Cf the Trade Union and Labour Relations (Consolidation) Act 1992 s 23: see the text and note 11; and PARA 928.
8   Trade Union and Labour Relations (Consolidation) Act 1992 s 22(2). As to the treatment of members of a federated trade union for these purposes see s 118(3); and PARA 891 note 9 head (1).
9   Any such order must be made by statutory instrument which is subject to annulment in pursuance of a resolution of either House of Parliament: Trade Union and Labour Relations (Consolidation) Act 1992 s 22(4).
10 Trade Union and Labour Relations (Consolidation) Act 1992 s 22(3). The order may make such transitional provision as the Secretary of State considers appropriate: s 22(3). At the date at which this volume states the law no such order had been made and none has effect as if so made. As to the Secretary of State see PARA 5 note 21.
11 See the Trade Union and Labour Relations (Consolidation) Act 1992 s 23; and PARA 928. As to the meaning of 'protected property' see PARA 928 heads (a)–(e).

(8) STATUTORY RESTRICTIONS ON INDUSTRIAL ACTION

1391.   Industrial action by members of the armed forces.   A person subject to service law[1] commits an offence if he disobeys a lawful command[2] or if, without reasonable excuse, he fails to attend for any duty[3].

It is an offence if any person maliciously and advisedly endeavours to seduce any member of Her Majesty's forces from his duty or allegiance to Her Majesty[4].

1   As to persons subject to service law see ARMED FORCES vol 3 (2011) PARA 510.
2   See the Armed Forces Act 2006 s 12(1)(a); and ARMED FORCES vol 3 (2011) PARA 573.
3   See the Armed Forces Act 2006 s 15(1)(a); and ARMED FORCES vol 3 (2011) PARA 574.
4   See the Incitement to Disaffection Act 1934 s 1; and CRIMINAL LAW vol 25 (2010) PARA 363.

1392.   Industrial action by police etc and prison officers.   A police officer who participates in industrial action is likely to infringe the statutory regulations concerning the standard of conduct of police officers[1]. Furthermore, it is an offence to cause, or to attempt to cause, or to do any act calculated to cause, disaffection amongst the members of any police force, or to induce, or to attempt to induce, or to do any act calculated to induce, any member of a police force to withhold his services[2].

It is a breach of statutory duty for a person to induce the Director General of the National Crime Agency (the 'NCA') or any designated NCA officer[3] to withhold (or to continue to withhold) services as an NCA officer[4]. The Secretary of State may bring civil proceedings in respect of any apprehended contravention of this duty[5] and breach of the duty which causes the Secretary of State to sustain loss or damage is actionable, at his suit or instance, against the person in breach[6].

It is also a breach of statutory duty to induce prison officers to take or continue to take industrial action or to commit breaches of discipline[7].

1   See the Police (Conduct) Regulations 2012, SI 2012/2632; and POLICE AND INVESTIGATORY POWERS vol 84 (2013) PARA 206 et seq.
2   See the Police Act 1996 s 91(1); and POLICE AND INVESTIGATORY POWERS vol 84 (2013) PARA 44.

3   Ie designated under the Crime and Courts Act 2013 s 10: see POLICE AND INVESTIGATORY POWERS.
4   See the Crime and Courts Act 2013 s 13(1), (2); and POLICE AND INVESTIGATORY POWERS.
5   See the Crime and Courts Act 2013 s 13(4); and POLICE AND INVESTIGATORY POWERS.
6   See the Crime and Courts Act 2013 s 13(3); and POLICE AND INVESTIGATORY POWERS.
7   See the Criminal Justice and Public Order Act 1994 s 127; and PRISONS AND PRISONERS vol 85 (2012) PARA 423. This provision cannot be circumvented by reliance on the Convention for the Protection of Human Rights and Fundamental Freedoms (Rome, 4 November 1950; TS 71 (1953); Cmd 8969) (the 'European Convention on Human Rights') art 11(1) (now incorporated into domestic law by the Human Rights Act 1998 Sch 1 Pt I art 11(1): see RIGHTS AND FREEDOMS vol 88A (2013) PARA 461 et seq), since that confers no express right to strike and, moreover, the Human Rights Act 1998 Sch 1 Pt I art 11(2) affords considerable latitude to a contracting state to regulate the circumstances in which the right may be removed: *Ministry of Justice v Prison Officers Association* [2008] EWHC 239 (QB), [2008] ICR 702, [2008] IRLR 380.

1393. Industrial action by merchant seamen. It is an offence[1] for a seaman employed in a United Kingdom ship[2], at a time when the ship is at sea[3], to combine with other seamen employed in that ship:

    (1)   to disobey lawful commands;

    (2)   to neglect any duty; or

    (3)   to impede the progress of a voyage or the navigation of the ship[4].

1   The Merchant Shipping Act 1995 s 59(1)(a), (b) (see heads (1)–(2) in the text) does not apply to persons serving in fishing vessels (within the meaning of s 313(1), (3)) (see SHIPPING AND MARITIME LAW vol 93 (2008) PARA 230): see s 119(1); and SHIPPING AND MARITIME LAW vol 94 (2008) PARA 1160.
2   Ie a ship registered in the United Kingdom within the meaning of the Merchant Shipping Act 1995 Pt II (ss 8–23): see SHIPPING AND MARITIME LAW vol 93 (2008) PARA 245 et seq.
3   As to when the ship is at sea see the Merchant Shipping Act 1995 s 59(2); and SHIPPING AND MARITIME LAW vol 94 (2008) PARA 1160.
4   See the Merchant Shipping Act 1995 s 59(1); and SHIPPING AND MARITIME LAW vol 94 (2008) PARA 1160.

1394. Industrial action by postal and telecommunications workers. It is an offence for a person:

    (1)   who is engaged in the business of a postal operator, contrary to his duty and without reasonable excuse, intentionally to delay a postal packet in the course of its transmission by post[1], but that provision does not apply to the delaying of a postal packet as a result of industrial action[2] in contemplation or furtherance of a trade dispute[3];

    (2)   intentionally and without lawful authority, to intercept, at any place in the United Kingdom, any communication in the course of its transmission by means of a public postal service or a public telecommunications system[4];

    (3)   intentionally and without lawful authority, to intercept, at any place in the United Kingdom, any communication in the course of its transmission by means of a private telecommunications system, otherwise than in circumstances in which his conduct is excluded by certain statutory provisions[5] from criminal liability[6].

1   See the Postal Services Act 2000 s 83(1)(a); and POSTAL SERVICES vol 85 (2012) PARA 280.
2   For these purposes, the reference to industrial action is to be construed in accordance with the Trade Union and Labour Relations (Consolidation) Act 1992 (see PARA 1340): Postal Services Act 2000 s 83(5).
3   See the Postal Services Act 2000 s 83(4); and POSTAL SERVICES vol 85 (2012) PARA 280. For these purposes, 'trade dispute' has the meaning given by the Trade Union and Labour Relations Act 1992 s 244 (see PARA 1361): see the Postal Services Act 2000 s 83(5). Under the Post Office

Act 1953 s 58 (repealed) there was no statutory dispensation where the delay resulted from a trade dispute: see *Gouriet v Union of Post Office Workers* [1978] AC 435, [1977] 3 All ER 70, HL.

4   See the Regulation of Investigatory Powers Act 2000 s 1(1); and POLICE AND INVESTIGATORY POWERS vol 84A (2013) PARA 655; TELECOMMUNICATIONS vol 97 (2010) PARA 205. The Interception of Communications Commissioner has power to serve monetary penalty notices in relation to certain unlawful interceptions of communications: see the Regulation of Investigatory Powers Act 2000 s 1(1A), Sch A1; and POLICE AND INVESTIGATORY POWERS vol 84A (2013) PARA 655.

5   Ie by the Regulation of Investigatory Powers Act 2000 s 1(6): see POLICE AND INVESTIGATORY POWERS vol 84A (2013) PARA 655; TELECOMMUNICATIONS vol 97 (2010) PARA 205.

6   See the Regulation of Investigatory Powers Act 2000 s 1(2); and POLICE AND INVESTIGATORY POWERS vol 84A (2013) PARA 655; TELECOMMUNICATIONS vol 97 (2010) PARA 205.

1395. Promotion of industrial action by aliens. It is an offence for an alien[1] to promote or to attempt to promote industrial unrest unless he has been engaged bona fide in the industry in the United Kingdom for at least two years[2].

1   As to the meaning of 'alien' see BRITISH NATIONALITY vol 4 (2011) PARA 411.
2   See the Aliens Restriction (Amendment) Act 1919 s 3(2); and BRITISH NATIONALITY vol 4 (2011) PARA 411.

1396. Breach of contract of service or hiring involving injury to persons or property. A person[1] who wilfully and maliciously[2] breaks a contract of service or hiring, knowing or having reasonable cause to believe that the probable consequence of his doing so, either alone or in combination with others, will be to endanger human life or cause serious bodily injury, or to expose valuable property, whether real or personal, to destruction or serious injury[3], commits an offence and is liable on summary conviction to imprisonment for a term not exceeding three months or a fine not exceeding level 2 on the standard scale, or to both[4].

1   This provision does not apply to seamen: Trade Union and Labour Relations (Consolidation) Act 1992 s 240(4).
2   The Trade Union and Labour Relations (Consolidation) Act 1992 s 240(1) applies equally whether the offence is committed from malice conceived against the person endangered or injured, or, as the case may be, against the owner of the property destroyed or injured, or otherwise: s 240(2).
3   Trade Union and Labour Relations (Consolidation) Act 1992 s 240(1).
4   Trade Union and Labour Relations (Consolidation) Act 1992 s 240(1), (3). As to the standard scale see SENTENCING AND DISPOSITION OF OFFENDERS vol 92 (2010) PARA 142. As from a day to be appointed, the reference to the term of imprisonment and to both penalties is removed (ie leaving only the fine): s 240(3) (prospectively amended by the Criminal Justice Act 2003 Sch 37 Pt 9). At the date at which this volume states the law no such day had been appointed. As to the availability of an injunction to restrain a crime see *Gouriet v Union of Post Office Workers* [1978] AC 435, [1977] 3 All ER 70, HL.

(9) EMERGENCY POWERS

1397. States of emergency. Her Majesty may by Order in Council make emergency[1] regulations if satisfied that (1) an emergency has occurred, is occurring or is about to occur; (2) it is necessary to make provision for the purposes of preventing, controlling or mitigating an aspect or effect of the emergency; and (3) the need for provision referred to in head (2) above is urgent[2]. However, such regulations may not prohibit or enable the prohibition of participation in, or any activity in connection with, a strike or other industrial action[3].

1   In the Civil Contingencies Act 2004 Pt 2 (ss 19–31) 'emergency' means (1) an event or situation
    which threatens serious damage to human welfare in the United Kingdom or in a Part or region;
    (2) an event or situation which threatens serious damage to the environment of the United
    Kingdom or of a Part or region; or (3) war, or terrorism, which threatens serious damage to the
    security of the United Kingdom: see s 19(1); and see further s 19(2)–(6); and ARMED CONFLICT
    AND EMERGENCY vol 3 (2011) PARA 186.
2   See the Civil Contingencies Act 2004 ss 20(1), 21. A senior Minister of the Crown may also
    make emergency regulations if satisfied that the conditions set out in heads (1)–(3) in the text are
    satisfied, and that it would not be possible, without serious delay, to arrange for an Order in
    Council under s 20(1): see s 20(2); and see further s 20(3)–(5); and ARMED CONFLICT AND
    EMERGENCY vol 3 (2011) PARA 187 et seq. As to emergency powers generally see Pt 2
    (ss 19–31); and ARMED CONFLICT AND EMERGENCY vol 3 (2011) PARA 186 et seq. At the date at
    which this volume states the law, no such regulations were in force.
3   See the Civil Contingencies Act 2004 s 23(3)(b); and ARMED CONFLICT AND EMERGENCY vol 3
    (2011) PARA 190.

1398.   Use of the armed forces as substitute labour.   The Crown may authorise
officers and men of Her Majesty's naval, military or air forces to be temporarily
employed in urgent civilian work of national importance[1].

1   See the Emergency Powers Act 1964 s 2; and ARMED CONFLICT AND EMERGENCY vol 3 (2011)
    PARA 118.

12. LEGAL PROCEEDINGS

(1) CONSTITUTION AND JURISDICTION OF TRIBUNALS ETC

(i) Employment Tribunals

A. ESTABLISHMENT AND CONSTITUTION OF EMPLOYMENT TRIBUNALS

1399. Establishment of employment tribunals. The Secretary of State[1] may by regulations[2] make provision for the establishment of tribunals to be known as employment tribunals[3], to exercise the jurisdiction conferred on them by or by virtue of the Employment Tribunals Act 1996 or any other Act, whether passed before or after that Act[4].

The Lord Chancellor is under a general duty to ensure that there is an efficient and effective system to support the carrying on of the business of the First-tier Tribunal, the Upper Tribunal, employment tribunals and the Employment Appeal Tribunal, and that appropriate services are provided for those tribunals[5].

In relation to England and Wales[6], the President of Employment Tribunals[7] must use the resources available to:

(1) secure, so far as practicable, the speedy and efficient disposal of proceedings;

(2) determine the allocation of proceedings between tribunals[8]; and

(3) determine where and when tribunals shall sit[9].

Part I of the Arbitration Act 1996[10] does not apply to any proceedings before an employment tribunal[11].

1 As to the Secretary of State see PARA 5 note 21.
2 As to the regulations made see the Employment Tribunals (Constitution and Rules of Procedure) Regulations 2013, SI 2013/1237; and see also PARA 1400 et seq. As to the making of regulations under the Employment Tribunals Act 1996 generally see PARA 162. As to where there is possible overlap between tribunal and High Court proceedings see *GFI Holdings Ltd v Camm* [2008] All ER (D) 74 (Sep), EAT.
    Proceedings before employment tribunals must be instituted in accordance with employment tribunal procedure regulations: Employment Tribunals Act 1996 s 7(2) (amended by the Employment Rights (Dispute Resolution) Act 1998 s 1(2)(a), (b)). As to the meaning of 'employment tribunal procedure regulations' see PARA 1410.
3 Employment Tribunals Act 1996 s 1(1) (amended by the Employment Rights (Dispute Resolution) Act 1998 s 1(2)(b)). See the Employment Tribunals (Constitution and Rules of Procedure) Regulations 2013, SI 2013/1237, reg 4.
    Originally known as industrial tribunals, employment tribunals were established to exercise jurisdiction given by statute only; but they do have power to apply directly applicable EU law directly, even where the claimant is seeking to rely on that law alone, and not as an adjunct to a claim under domestic law: *Secretary of State for Scotland and Greater Glasgow Health Board v Wright and Hannah* [1993] 2 CMLR 257, [1991] IRLR 187, EAT; *McKechnie v UBM Building Supplies (Southern) Ltd* [1991] ICR 710, [1991] IRLR 283, EAT. Industrial tribunals were renamed employment tribunals by the Employment Rights (Dispute Resolution) Act 1998 s 1(1).
    Employment tribunals have no inherent power to hear common law claims, in particular those relating to the interpretation of, or granting remedies in relation to, contracts of employment. They may, however: (1) determine particulars which ought to have been included in an employee's written statement of particulars (see PARA 126), though they may not then interpret or enforce those terms (see PARA 126 note 5); and (2) hear and determine contract claims arising or outstanding on termination of the employee's employment, up to a statutory maximum amount (see the Employment Tribunals Extension of Jurisdiction (England and Wales) Order 1994, SI 1994/1623; and PARA 1408). In addition, it may be necessary for a tribunal to interpret an employment contract to the extent necessary in order to enforce a statutory right: *Kinzley v Minories Finance Ltd* [1988] ICR 113, [1987] IRLR 490, EAT.

4   See the Employment Tribunals Act 1996 s 2 (amended by the Employment Rights (Dispute Resolution) Act 1998 s 1(2)(b)).

5   See the Tribunals, Courts and Enforcement Act 2007 s 39(1), (2); and COURTS AND TRIBUNALS vol 24 (2010) PARA 868. In exercise of the powers conferred by ss 40(4), 145(1), by which the Lord Chancellor may appoint such staff as appear to him appropriate for the purpose of discharging his general duty in relation to the tribunals, the Lord Chancellor has made the Contracting Out (Administrative Work of Tribunals) Order 2009, SI 2009/121, which enables the Lord Chancellor to enter into contracts with other persons for the provision of staff for carrying out the administrative work of the tribunals listed in art 2, namely: (1) the First-tier Tribunal; (2) the Upper Tribunal; (3) employment tribunals; and (4) the Employment Appeal Tribunal: see COURTS AND TRIBUNALS vol 24 (2010) PARA 869. As to the provision of accommodation see the Tribunals, Courts and Enforcement Act 2007 s 41; and COURTS AND TRIBUNALS vol 24 (2010) PARA 870.

6   As to the meanings of 'England' and 'Wales' see PARA 2 note 12.

7   'President', in relation to England and Wales, means the President appointed from time to time in accordance with the Employment Tribunals (Constitution and Rules of Procedure) Regulations 2013, SI 2013/1237, reg 5(1) (see PARA 1400): see reg 3, Sch 1 r 1(1). As to the President see PARA 1400.

8   For these purposes, 'tribunal' means an employment tribunal established in accordance with the Employment Tribunals (Constitution and Rules of Procedure) Regulations 2013, SI 2013/1237, reg 4 (see note 3) and, in relation to any proceedings, means the tribunal responsible for the proceedings in question, whether performing administrative or judicial functions: reg 3.

9   Employment Tribunals (Constitution and Rules of Procedure) Regulations 2013, SI 2013/1237, reg 7(1). The President (England and Wales) may direct regional employment judges to take action in relation to the fulfilment of the responsibilities in reg 7(1) and the regional employment judges must follow such directions: reg 7(2). 'Regional employment judge' means a person appointed or nominated in accordance with reg 6(1) or (2) (see PARA 1401): reg 3, Sch 1 r 1(1). As to regional employment judges see PARA 1401.

10   Ie the Arbitration Act 1996 Pt I (ss 1–84): see ARBITRATION.

11   Employment Tribunals Act 1996 s 6(2) (amended by the Arbitration Act 1996 Sch 3 para 62; the Employment Rights (Dispute Resolution) Act 1998 s 1(2)(a)).

1400. President of the Employment Tribunals. There is a President[1] of Employment Tribunals, responsible for tribunals[2] in England and Wales, appointed by the Lord Chancellor[3]. He must be:

(1)   a person who satisfies the judicial-appointment eligibility condition[4] on a five-year basis;

(2)   an advocate or solicitor admitted in Scotland of at least five years standing; or

(3)   a member of the Bar of Northern Ireland or solicitor of the Supreme Court of Northern Ireland of at least five years standing[5].

The President may at any time resign from office by giving the Lord Chancellor notice in writing to that effect[6]; and the Lord Chancellor may remove him from office on the ground of inability or misbehaviour, or if the President is adjudged to be bankrupt or makes a composition or arrangement with his creditors[7].

Where the President is unable to carry out his statutory functions[8], those functions may be discharged by a person nominated by the Lord Chief Justice[9] following consultation with the Senior President of Tribunals[10].

Any power by which the President of the Employment Tribunals (England and Wales) may be removed from that office may be exercised only with the concurrence of the Lord Chief Justice of England and Wales[11].

Any person (the 'appointee') who is appointed as President of the Employment Tribunals (England and Wales) and who has not previously taken the required oaths[12] after accepting another office, must take the required oaths before the Senior President of Tribunals, or an eligible person who is nominated by the Senior President of Tribunals for the purpose of taking the oaths from the appointee[13].

1   As to the meaning of 'President' see PARA 1399 note 7.
2   As to the meaning of 'tribunal' see PARA 1399 note 8; and as to the establishment of tribunals see PARA 1399.
3   See the Employment Tribunals (Constitution and Rules of Procedure) Regulations 2013, SI 2013/1237, regs 3, 5(1). There is also a President of Employment Tribunals responsible for tribunals in Scotland who is appointed by the Lord President of the Court of Session: see regs 3, 5(1).
4   Ie the judicial-appointment eligibility condition within the meaning of the Tribunals, Courts and Enforcement Act 2007 s 50: see COURTS AND TRIBUNALS vol 24 (2010) PARA 645 note 4.
5   Employment Tribunals (Constitution and Rules of Procedure) Regulations 2013, SI 2013/1237, reg 5(2).
6   See the Employment Tribunals (Constitution and Rules of Procedure) Regulations 2013, SI 2013/1237, regs 3, 5(3).
7   See the Employment Tribunals (Constitution and Rules of Procedure) Regulations 2013, SI 2013/1237, regs 3, 5(4).
8   Ie the functions of the President set out in the Employment Tribunals (Constitution and Rules of Procedure) Regulations 2013, SI 2013/1237: see PARAS 1399, 1402 et seq.
9   The Lord Chief Justice may nominate a judicial office holder (as defined in the Constitutional Reform Act 2005 s 109(4): see COURTS AND TRIBUNALS vol 24 (2010) PARA 961 note 7) to exercise his functions under the Employment Tribunals (Constitution and Rules of Procedure) Regulations 2013, SI 2013/1237, reg 5: reg 5(6).
10   See the Employment Tribunals (Constitution and Rules of Procedure) Regulations 2013, SI 2013/1237, reg 5(5). 'Senior President of Tribunals' means the person appointed in accordance with the Tribunals, Courts and Enforcement Act 2007 s 2 (see COURTS AND TRIBUNALS vol 24 (2010) PARA 867): Employment Tribunals (Constitution and Rules of Procedure) Regulations 2013, SI 2013/1237, reg 3.
11   Employment Tribunals Act 1996 s 5B(1) (s 5B added by the Tribunals, Courts and Enforcement Act 2007 Sch 8 paras 35, 40). As to the Lord Chief Justice see COURTS AND TRIBUNALS vol 24 (2010) PARA 842. The Lord Chief Justice of England and Wales may nominate a judicial office holder (as defined in the Constitutional Reform Act 2005 s 109(4): see COURTS AND TRIBUNALS vol 24 (2010) PARA 961 note 7) to exercise his functions under the Employment Tribunals Act 1996 s 5B: s 5B(5) (as so added).
12   For these purposes, 'required oaths' means the oath of allegiance, and the judicial oath as set out in the Promissory Oaths Act 1868 (see CONSTITUTIONAL AND ADMINISTRATIVE LAW vol 20 (2014) PARAS 597–598): Employment Tribunals Act 1996 s 5C(5) (s 5C added by the Tribunals, Courts and Enforcement Act 2007 Sch 8 paras 35, 40).
13   Employment Tribunals Act 1996 s 5C(1), (2) (as added: see note 12). A person is eligible for these purposes if one or more of the following apply to him: (1) he holds high judicial office (as defined in the Constitutional Reform Act 2005 s 60(2)) (see COURTS AND TRIBUNALS vol 24 (2010) PARA 867; (2) he holds judicial office (as defined in s 109(4) (see COURTS AND TRIBUNALS vol 24 (2010) PARA 961 note 7)); (3) he holds (in Scotland) the office of sheriff: Employment Tribunals Act 1996 s 5C(4) (as so added).
     If the appointee is a President appointed before the coming into force of s 5C, the requirement in s 5C(2) applies in relation to the appointee from the coming into force of s 5C: s 5C(3) (as so added).

1401.   Panels of members for tribunals; regional employment judges.   There are three panels of members for the employment tribunals in England and Wales[1] which are:

(1)   a panel of employment judges who satisfy the statutory criteria[2] and are appointed by the Lord Chancellor[3];

(2)   a panel of persons appointed by the Lord Chancellor after consultation with organisations or associations representative of employees[4]; and

(3)   a panel of persons appointed by the Lord Chancellor after consultation with organisations or associations representative of employers[5].

Members of the panels hold and vacate office in accordance with the terms of their appointment, but may resign from office by written notice to the Lord Chancellor[6]. Any member who ceases to hold office is eligible for reappointment[7].

The President[8] may establish further specialist panels of members and may select persons from those panels to deal with proceedings in which particular specialist knowledge would be beneficial[9].

The Lord Chancellor may appoint regional employment judges[10] from the salaried employment judges on the panel referred to in head (1) above[11].

The President or the regional employment judge for an area may nominate an employment judge from the salaried employment judges on the panel referred to in head (1) above to discharge the functions of the regional employment judge for that area[12].

The Senior President of Tribunals is responsible, within the resources made available by the Lord Chancellor, for the maintenance of appropriate arrangements for the training, guidance and welfare of members of panels of members of employment tribunals (in their capacities as members of such panels, whether or not panels of employment judges)[13].

Any power by which a member of a panel[14] may be removed from membership of the panel may be exercised only with the concurrence of the Lord Chief Justice[15].

Any person (the 'appointee') who is appointed as a member of a panel[16], and who has not previously taken the required oaths[17] after accepting another office, must take the required oaths before the Senior President of Tribunals, or an eligible person who is nominated by the Senior President of Tribunals for the purpose of taking the oaths from the appointee[18].

1   Employment Tribunals (Constitution and Rules of Procedure) Regulations 2013, SI 2013/1237, reg 8(1).
2   Ie the criteria set out in the Employment Tribunals (Constitution and Rules of Procedure) Regulations 2013, SI 2013/1237, reg 5(2): see PARA 1400.
3   See the Employment Tribunals (Constitution and Rules of Procedure) Regulations 2013, SI 2013/1237, regs 3, 8(2)(a) (reg 8(2)(a) amended by SI 2014/271 (corrected by SI 2014/787)). A person who is a member of a panel of employment judges (formerly a panel of chairmen) which is appointed in accordance with regulations under the Employment Tribunals Act 1996 s 1(1) (see PARA 1399) may be referred to as an employment judge: s 3A (added by the Tribunals, Courts and Enforcement Act 2007 Sch 8 paras 35, 36; amended by the Crime and Courts Act 2013 Sch 14 Pt 7 para 13(1)); and see the Interpretation Act 1978 s 17(2)(a).
4   Employment Tribunals (Constitution and Rules of Procedure) Regulations 2013, SI 2013/1237, reg 8(2)(b).
5   Employment Tribunals (Constitution and Rules of Procedure) Regulations 2013, SI 2013/1237, reg 8(2)(c).
6   See the Employment Tribunals (Constitution and Rules of Procedure) Regulations 2013, SI 2013/1237, reg 8(3).
7   Employment Tribunals (Constitution and Rules of Procedure) Regulations 2013, SI 2013/1237, reg 8(3).
8   As to the meaning of 'the President' see PARA 1399 note 7.
9   Employment Tribunals (Constitution and Rules of Procedure) Regulations 2013, SI 2013/1237, reg 8(4).
10 Employment Tribunals (Constitution and Rules of Procedure) Regulations 2013, SI 2013/1237, reg 6(1). As to the meaning of 'regional employment judge' see PARA 1399 note 9.
11 See the Employment Tribunals (Constitution and Rules of Procedure) Regulations 2013, SI 2013/1237, reg 6(5) (amended by SI 2014/271 (corrected by SI 2014/787)).
12 See the Employment Tribunals (Constitution and Rules of Procedure) Regulations 2013, SI 2013/1237, reg 6(2), (5) (reg 6(5) as amended: see note 11). As to the functions of regional employment judges see PARA 1399 note 9.

13 Employment Tribunals Act 1996 s 5A (added by the Tribunals, Courts and Enforcement Act 2007 Sch 8 paras 35, 40; amended by the Crime and Courts Act 2013 Sch 14 Pt 7 para 13(1)). As to the Senior President of Tribunals see COURTS AND TRIBUNALS vol 24 (2010) PARA 867.

The Lord Chancellor's functions under the Employment Tribunals Act 1996 s 5A are protected functions under the Constitutional Reform Act 2005: see Sch 7 para 4 Pt A (prospectively amended for these purposes by the Tribunals, Courts and Enforcement Act 2007 s 144(1), (8)). As to the protected functions of the Lord Chancellor see CONSTITUTIONAL AND ADMINISTRATIVE LAW vol 20 (2014) PARA 261.

14 For these purposes, 'panel' means (1) a panel of employment judges of employment tribunals; or (2) any other panel of members of employment tribunals, which is appointed in accordance with regulations made under the Employment Tribunals Act 1996 s 1(1) (see PARA 1399): s 5B(4) (s 5B added by the Tribunals, Courts and Enforcement Act 2007 Sch 8 paras 35, 40; the Employment Tribunals Act 1996 s 5B(4) amended by the Crime and Courts Act 2013 Sch 14 Pt 7 para 13(1)).

15 Employment Tribunals Act 1996 s 5B(3)(b) (as added: see note 14). The Lord Chief Justice of England and Wales may nominate a judicial office holder (as defined in the Constitutional Reform Act 2005 s 109(4): see COURTS AND TRIBUNALS vol 24 (2010) PARA 961 note 7) to exercise his functions under the Employment Tribunals Act 1996 s 5B: s 5B(5) (as so added).

16 Ie as defined in the Employment Tribunals Act 1996 s 5B(4): see note 14.

17 For these purposes, 'required oaths' means the oath of allegiance, and the judicial oath as set out in the Promissory Oaths Act 1868 (see CONSTITUTIONAL AND ADMINISTRATIVE LAW vol 20 (2014) PARAS 597–598): Employment Tribunals Act 1996 s 5C(5) (s 5C added by the Tribunals, Courts and Enforcement Act 2007 Sch 8 paras 35, 40).

18 Employment Tribunals Act 1996 s 5C(1), (2) (as added: see note 17). As to the persons who are eligible for these purposes see s 5C(4), cited in PARA 1400 note 13. If the appointee is a panel member appointed before the coming into force of s 5C, the requirement in s 5C(2) applies in relation to the appointee from the coming into force of s 5C: s 5C(3) (as so added).

1402. Composition of tribunals. Subject now to major exceptions which significantly extend the incidence of proceedings heard by an employment judge sitting alone[1], the Employment Tribunals Act 1996 provides for proceedings before an employment tribunal to be heard[2] by the employment judge[3] and two other members[4], but such proceedings may, with the consent of the parties, be heard and determined in the absence of any one of those members other than the employment judge[5].

Except in relation to national security proceedings[6], where proceedings are to be determined by a tribunal comprising an employment judge and two other members, the President[7] or the regional employment judge[8] must select an employment judge[9] (who may be himself)[10] and two other members, each from one of panels of lay persons[11] appointed by the Lord Chancellor[12]. For all other proceedings, and with the same exception[13], the President or the regional employment judge must select an employment judge[14] (who may be himself)[15]. The President or a regional employment judge may select from the appropriate panel a substitute for a member previously selected to hear any proceedings[16].

Where regulations[17] make provision for a relevant tribunal judge[18], or a relevant judge[19], to be able by virtue of his office to act as a member of a panel of members of employment tribunals[21]:

(1) the persons in relation to whom this provision operates have to be persons nominated for the purposes of the provision by the Senior President of Tribunals;

(2) its operation in relation to a panel established for England and Wales in any particular case requires the consent of the President of Employment Tribunals (England and Wales);

(3) its operation as respects a particular relevant judge requires the consent

of the relevant judge and the appropriate consent[22], except where the relevant judge is the Lord Chief Justice of England and Wales; and

(4)   it operates as respects a relevant tribunal judge or a relevant judge only for the purpose of enabling him to act as a member of a panel of employment judges[23].

1   As to which see PARA 1403.

2   Ie subject to the provisions of the Employment Tribunals Act 1996 s 4(2)–(6C) (see note 3; and PARA 1403) and s 7(3A) (see PARA 1410). As to the establishment of tribunals see PARA 1399.

3   Ie the person who, in accordance with regulations made under the Employment Tribunals Act 1996 s 1(1) (see PARA 1399), is the chairman: s 4(1)(a); Interpretation Act 1978 s 17(2)(a). As to the regulations so made see the Employment Tribunals (Constitution and Rules of Procedure) Regulations 2013, SI 2013/11237, reg 9(1); and the text and notes 7–14. Where, in accordance with the Employment Tribunals Act 1996 ss 5–19 (see PARA 1405 et seq), the Secretary of State makes employment tribunal procedure regulations, the regulations may provide that any act which is required or authorised by the regulations to be done by an employment tribunal, and is of a description specified by the regulations for these purposes, may be done by the person mentioned in s 4(1)(a) alone or alone by any employment judge who, in accordance with regulations made under s 1(1) (see PARA 1399), is a member of the tribunal: s 4(6) (amended by the Employment Rights (Dispute Resolution) Act 1998 s 1(2)(a), Sch 1 para 12(1), (4); the Tribunals, Courts and Enforcement Act 2007 Sch 8 paras 35, 37). As to the Secretary of State see PARA 5 note 21. As to the meaning of 'employment judge' see PARA 1401 note 3.The Employment Tribunals Act 1996 s 4(6) in particular enables employment tribunal procedure regulations to provide that: (1) the determination of proceedings in accordance with regulations under s 7(3A), s 7(3B) or (3C)(a) (see PARA 1410 heads (iv), (v), (vi)(A)); (2) the carrying out of pre-hearing reviews in accordance with regulations under s 9(1) (see PARA 1414), including the exercise of powers in connection with such reviews in accordance with regulations under s 9(1)(b) (see PARA 1414 head (2)); or (3) the hearing and determination of a preliminary issue in accordance with regulations under s 9(4) (see PARA 1414), where it involves hearing witnesses other than the parties or their representatives as well as where, in accordance with regulations under s 7(3C)(b) (see PARA 1410 head (vi)(B)), it does not, may be done by the person mentioned in s 4(1)(a) alone or alone by any employment judge who, in accordance with regulations under s 1(1) (see PARA 1399), is a member of the tribunal: s 4(6A) (added by the Employment Rights (Dispute Resolution) Act 1998 s 3(6); amended by the Tribunals, Courts and Enforcement Act 2007 Sch 8 paras 35, 37). As to the meaning of 'employment tribunal procedure regulations' see PARA 1410.

4   The other members of the tribunal must be selected in accordance with the regulations made under the Employment Tribunals Act 1996 s 1(1) (see PARA 1399): s 4(1)(b). As to the regulations so made see the Employment Tribunals (Constitution and Rules of Procedure) Regulations 2013, SI 2013/1237, reg 9(2); and the text and note 10. The Employment Tribunals Act 1996 s 4(1)(b) is prospectively substituted by the Employment Rights (Dispute Resolution) Act 1998 s 4 but at the date at which this volume states the law this substitution was still not in force.

5   See the Employment Tribunals Act 1996 s 4(1) (amended by the Employment Rights (Dispute Resolution) Act 1998 s 1(2)(a), Sch 1 para 12(1), (2)); Interpretation Act 1978 s 17(2)(a). In such a case, before consenting, a party has the right to know whether the remaining member is representative of employers or employees: *Rabahallah v British Telecommunications plc* [2005] ICR 440, sub nom *Rabahallah v BT Group plc* [2005] IRLR 184, EAT. See also *McKenzie v Monfort International plc* [2007] All ER (D) 147 (Apr), EAT.

6   Employment Tribunals (Constitution and Rules of Procedure) Regulations 2013, SI 2013/1237, reg 9(4). As to the composition of a tribunal for the purposes of national security proceedings see PARA 1447.

7   As to the meaning of 'President' see PARA 1399 note 7.

8   As to the meaning of 'regional employment judge' see PARA 1399 note 9.

9   Employment Tribunals (Constitution and Rules of Procedure) Regulations 2013, SI 2013/1237, reg 9(1)(a).

10   See the Employment Tribunals (Constitution and Rules of Procedure) Regulations 2013, SI 2013/1237, reg 9(2).

11   Ie one member from each of the panels referred to in the Employment Tribunals (Constitution and Rules of Procedure) Regulations 2013, SI 2013/1237, reg 8(2)(b), (c): see PARA 1401 heads (2)–(3).

12 See the Employment Tribunals (Constitution and Rules of Procedure) Regulations 2013, SI 2013/1237, reg 9(1)(b). There is in general no requirement of any special knowledge or experience of the lay members chosen (eg in a race discrimination case): *Habib v Elkington & Co Ltd* [1981] ICR 435, [1981] IRLR 344, EAT; *Halford v Sharples* [1992] ICR 146, EAT.

13 See note 6.

14 Employment Tribunals (Constitution and Rules of Procedure) Regulations 2013, SI 2013/1237, reg 9(1).

15 See note 10.

16 Employment Tribunals (Constitution and Rules of Procedure) Regulations 2013, SI 2013/1237, reg 9(3). See *McKenzie v Monfort International plc* [2007] All ER (D) 147 (Apr), EAT.

17 Ie regulations under the Employment Tribunals Act 1996 s 1(1): see PARA 1399.

18 For these purposes, 'relevant tribunal judge' means: (1) a person who is a judge of the First-tier Tribunal by virtue of appointment under the Tribunals, Courts and Enforcement Act 2007 Sch 2 para 1(1) (see COURTS AND TRIBUNALS); (2) a transferred-in judge of the First-tier Tribunal; (3) a person who is a judge of the Upper Tribunal by virtue of appointment under Sch 3 para 1(1) (see COURTS AND TRIBUNALS); (4) a transferred-in judge of the Upper Tribunal; (5) a deputy judge of the Upper Tribunal; or (6) a person who is the Chamber President of a chamber of the First-tier Tribunal, or of a chamber of the Upper Tribunal, and does not fall within any of heads (1)–(5) above; or (7) the Senior President of Tribunals: Employment Tribunals Act 1996 s 5D(4)(a) (s 5D added by the Tribunals, Courts and Enforcement Act 2007 Sch 8 paras 35, 40; the Employment Tribunals Act 1996 s 5D(4)(a) amended by the Crime and Courts Act 2013 Sch 14 Pt 6 para 12(1), (4)).

19 For these purposes, 'relevant judge' means a person who: (1) is the Lord Chief Justice of England and Wales, the Master of the Rolls or an ordinary judge of the Court of Appeal in England and Wales (including the vice-president, if any, of either division of that Court); (2) is the President of the Queen's Bench Division or Family Division, or the Chancellor, of the High Court in England and Wales; (3) is a Lord Justice of Appeal in Northern Ireland; (4) is a judge of the Court of Session; (5) is a puisne judge of the High Court in England and Wales or Northern Ireland; (6) is a circuit judge; (7) is a sheriff in Scotland; (8) is a County Court judge in Northern Ireland; (9) is a district judge in England and Wales or Northern Ireland; (10) is a District Judge (Magistrates' Courts); (11) is a deputy judge of the High Court in England and Wales; (12) is a recorder; (13) is a Deputy District Judge (Magistrates' Courts); (14) is a deputy district judge appointed under the County Courts Act 1984 s 8 (see COURTS AND TRIBUNALS vol 24 (2010) PARA 785) or the Senior Courts Act 1981 s 102 (see COURTS AND TRIBUNALS vol 24 (2010) PARA 750); (15) holds an office listed in the Senior Courts Act 1981 s 89(3C), Table col 1 (senior High Court Masters etc: see COURTS AND TRIBUNALS vol 24 (2010) PARA 736, 742 et seq); (16) holds an office listed in the Senior Courts Act 1981 Sch 2 Pt 2 col 1 (High Court Masters etc: see COURTS AND TRIBUNALS vol 24 (2010) PARA 737 et seq); or (17) is the Judge Advocate General or a person appointed under the Courts-Martial (Appeals) Act 1951 s 30(1)(a) or (b) (assistants to the Judge Advocate General: see ARMED FORCES vol 3 (2011) PARA 567): Employment Tribunals Act 1996 s 5D(4)(b) (as added (see note 17); amended by the Crime and Courts Act 2013 Sch 14 Pt 6 para 12(1), (6), (7)). References in heads (4)–(10) above to office-holders do not include deputies or temporary office-holders: Employment Tribunals Act 1996 s 5D(5) (as so added).

21 Employment Tribunals Act 1996 s 5D(1) (as added: see note 17).

22 For these purposes, 'appropriate consent' means the consent of the Lord Chief Justice of England and Wales where the relevant judge is (1) an ordinary judge of the Court of Appeal in England and Wales; (2) within the Employment Tribunals Act 1996 s 5D(4)(b)(ia) (see note 20 head (2)); (3) a puisne judge of the High Court in England and Wales; (4) a circuit judge; (5) a district judge in England and Wales; (6) a District Judge (Magistrates' Courts); or (7) within s 5D(4)(b)(x)–(xvi) (see note 20 heads (11)–(17): s 5D(3)(a) (as added (see note 17); amended by the Crime and Courts Act 2013 Sch 14 Pt 6 para 12(1), (3)).

23 Employment Tribunals Act 1996 s 5D(2)(a), (b), (d), (e) (as added (see note 18); amended by the Crime and Courts Act 2013 Sch 14 Pt 6 para 12(1), (2), Pt 7 para 13(1)).

1403. Hearings by employment judge alone. Certain proceedings[1] before an employment tribunal[2] must generally[3] be heard by the employment judge alone[4]. Those proceedings are:

(1) complaints relating to unauthorised deductions of union subscriptions[5] or remuneration under a protective award[6] or applications relating to interim relief[7] for dismissal on trade union grounds[8];

(2)   complaints[9] under the Pension Schemes Act 1993[10];

(3)   references relating to written statements of particulars of employment or itemised pay statements[11] or redundancy payments[12], or complaints relating to unauthorised deductions from wages[13], guarantee payments[14], unfair dismissal[15], employer's payments upon insolvency[16] or suspension on medical grounds[17], or certain applications for interim relief[18], or the appointment of persons to act[19] on behalf of the estate of a deceased employee[20];

(4)   complaints[21] relating to failure to consult on a transfer of undertakings[22];

(5)   complaints relating to failure to allow access to records[23], and proceedings on appeals in relation to notices of underpayment[24] under the national minimum wage legislation[25];

(6)   certain complaints relating to amounts due for leave under the Working Time Regulations 1998, the Merchant Shipping (Working Time: Inland Waterways) Regulations 2003, the Civil Aviation (Working Time) Regulations 2004 and Fishing Vessels (Working Time: Sea-fishermen) Regulations 2004[26];

(7)   claims for damages[27] for breach of contract[28];

(8)   proceedings in which the parties have given their written consent to the proceedings being so heard, whether or not they have subsequently withdrawn it[29];

(9)   proceedings in which the person (or, where more than one, each of the persons) against whom the proceedings are brought does not, or has ceased to, contest the case[30].

However, such proceedings must be heard by a full tribunal[31] if an employment judge[32] so decides at any stage of the proceedings, having regard to:

(a)   whether there is a likelihood of a dispute arising on the facts which makes it desirable for the proceedings to be heard by a full tribunal;

(b)   whether there is a likelihood of an issue of law arising which would make it desirable for the proceedings to be heard by an employment judge alone;

(c)   any views of any of the parties as to whether or not the proceedings ought to be heard either by a full tribunal or by an employment judge alone; and

(d)   whether there are other proceedings which might be heard concurrently but which are not proceedings specified in heads (1) to (9) above[33].

1   Ie the proceedings specified in the Employment Tribunals Act 1996 s 4(3). The Secretary of State and the Lord Chancellor, acting jointly, may by order amend the provisions of s 4(3): s 4(4) (amended by the Tribunals, Courts and Enforcement Act 2007 Sch 8 paras 35, 38). No order may be so made unless a draft of the order has been laid before Parliament and approved by resolution of each House of Parliament: Employment Tribunals Act 1996 s 41(2). As to the exercise of this power see the Employment Tribunals Act 1996 (Tribunal Composition) Order 2009, SI 2009/789; the Employment Tribunals Act 1996 (Tribunal Composition) Order 2012, SI 2012/988. As to the Secretary of State see PARA 5 note 21. As to the Lord Chancellor see CONSTITUTIONAL AND ADMINISTRATIVE LAW vol 20 (2014) PARA 255 et seq.

2   As to the establishment of tribunals see PARA 1399.

3   Ie subject to the Employment Tribunals Act 1996 s 4(5): see the text and notes 31–33.

4   Employment Tribunals Act 1996 s 4(2) (amended by the Tribunals, Courts and Enforcement Act 2007 Sch 8 paras 35, 38). The reference is actually to the person mentioned in the Employment Tribunals Act 1996 s 4(1)(a) (see PARA 1402 note 3) alone or alone by any employment judge who in accordance with regulations made under s 1(1) (see PARA 1399), is a member of the tribunal: see s 4(2) (as so amended). As to the meaning of 'employment judge' see

PARA 1401 note 3. In claims before the employment tribunal listed for hearing by an employment judge sitting alone, there is a continuing duty before the employment judge to review the decision to list the hearing in that manner: see *Clarke v Arriva Kent Thameside Ltd* [2001] All ER (D) 485 (Jul), EAT (if parties called a number of witnesses, that was a clear indication that the case should be heard by a full tribunal).

5 Ie proceedings on a complaint under the Trade Union and Labour Relations (Consolidation) Act 1992 s 68A (employer's deduction of unauthorised subscriptions) (see PARA 1035) or s 87 (employer's failure to make deductions) (see PARA 990).

6 Ie under the Trade Union and Labour Relations (Consolidation) Act 1992 s 192: see PARA 1190.

7 Ie on an application under the Trade Union and Labour Relations (Consolidation) Act 1992 s 161 (complaint of unfair dismissal on grounds related to union membership or activities) (see PARA 1058), s 165 (application for variation or revocation of order for reinstatement or re-engagement) (see PARA 1060) or s 166 (consequences of failure to comply with order for reinstatement or re-engagement) (see PARA 1061).

8 Employment Tribunals Act 1996 s 4(3)(a) (amended by the Employment Rights (Dispute Resolution) Act 1998 s 3(1), (2), Sch 1 para 12(1), (3)). See also note 1.

9 Ie under the Pension Schemes Act 1993 s 126: see PERSONAL AND OCCUPATIONAL PENSIONS vol 80 (2013) PARA 278.

10 Employment Tribunals Act 1996 s 4(3)(b). See also note 1.

11 Ie proceedings on a reference under the Employment Rights Act 1996 s 11: see PARA 125.

12 Ie proceedings on a reference under the Employment Rights Act 1996 s 163 (failure to pay a redundancy payment) (see PARA 886) or s 170 (references regarding liability to pay a redundancy payment) (see PARA 887).

13 Ie proceedings on a complaint under the Employment Rights Act 1996 s 23: see PARA 259.

14 Ie proceedings on a complaint under the Employment Rights Act 1996 s 34: see PARA 265.

15 Ie proceedings on a complaint under the Employment Rights Act 1996 s 111: see PARA 804.

16 Ie proceedings on a complaint under the Employment Rights Act 1996 s 188: see PARA 629.

17 Ie proceedings on a complaint under the Employment Rights Act 1996 s 70(1) (see PARA 606) relating to s 64 (see PARA 596).

18 Ie proceedings on applications under the Employment Rights Act 1996 s 128 (interim relief pending determination of complaint) (see PARA 805), s 131 (application for variation or revocation of order for reinstatement or re-engagement) (see PARA 808) or s 132 (consequences of failure to comply with order for reinstatement or re-engagement) (see PARA 808).

19 Ie an appointment under the Employment Rights Act 1996 s 206(4): see PARA 1456.

20 Employment Tribunals Act 1996 s 4(3)(c) (amended by the Employment Rights (Dispute Resolution) Act 1998 s 3(1), (3); and by SI 2012/988). See also note 1.

21 Ie proceedings on a complaint under the Transfer of Undertakings (Protection of Employment) Regulations 2006, SI 2006/246, reg 15(10): see PARA 1200.

22 Employment Tribunals Act 1996 s 4(3)(ca) (added by the Employment Rights (Dispute Resolution) Act 1998 s 3(1), (4); amended by SI 2006/246). See also note 1.

23 Ie proceedings on a complaint under the National Minimum Wage Act 1998 s 11: see PARA 228.

24 Ie on an appeal under the National Minimum Wage Act 1998 s 19C: see PARA 245.

25 Employment Tribunals Act 1996 s 4(3)(cc), (cd) (added by the National Minimum Wage Act 1998 s 27(1); the Employment Tribunals Act 1996 s 4(3)(cd) amended by the Employment Act 2008 s 9(4)). See also note 1.

26 Employment Tribunals Act 1996 s 4(3)(ce), (cf), (cg), (ch) (added by SI 2009/789). See also note 1. Head (6) in the text refers to (1) proceedings on a complaint under the Working Time Regulations 1998, SI 1998/1833, reg 30 (see PARA 319) relating to an amount due under reg 14(2) (see PARA 293) or reg 16(1) (see PARA 295); (2) proceedings on a complaint under the Merchant Shipping (Working Time: Inland Waterways) Regulations 2003, SI 2003/3049, reg 18 relating to an amount due under reg 11 (see SHIPPING AND MARITIME LAW vol 94 (2008) PARA 625); (3) proceedings on a complaint under the Civil Aviation (Working Time) Regulations 2004, SI 2004/756, reg 18 relating to an amount due under reg 4 (see AIR LAW vol 2 (2008) PARAS 468, 471); (4) proceedings on a complaint under the Fishing Vessels (Working Time: Sea-fishermen) Regulations 2004, SI 2004/1713, reg 19 relating to an amount due under reg 11 (see SHIPPING AND MARITIME LAW vol 94 (2008) PARA 626).

26 Ie proceedings in respect of which an employment tribunal has jurisdiction by virtue of the Employment Tribunals Act 1996 s 3: see PARA 1407.

28 Employment Tribunals Act 1996 s 4(3)(d) (amended by the Employment Rights (Dispute Resolution) Act 1998 s 1(2)(a)). See also note 1.

29 Employment Tribunals Act 1996 s 4(3)(e). See also note 1.

30 Employment Tribunals Act 1996 s 4(3)(g). See also note 1. As to the meaning of non-contested proceedings for the purposes of s 4(3)(g) see *Parfett v John Lamb Partnership Ltd* [2008] All ER

(D) 22 (Jul), EAT ('proceedings' means the particular proceedings before the tribunal and an employer may choose not to contest liability but to contest the remedy, thus a judge could lawfully hear the liability hearing even if a full panel would be necessary to hear the remedy).

31 Ie in accordance with the Employment Tribunals Act 1996 s 4(1): see PARA 1402.

32 Ie the person who, in accordance with regulations made under the Employment Tribunals Act 1996 s 4(1) (see PARA 1402) may be the employment judge (formerly the chairman) of an employment tribunal.

33 Employment Tribunals Act 1996 s 4(5) (amended by the Employment Rights (Dispute Resolution) Act 1996 s 1(2)(a)); Interpretation Act 1978 s 17(2)(a). Quaere how the provisions of the Employment Tribunals Act 1996 s 4(2) (see the text and notes 1–5) and of s 4(5) fit together. In *Sogbetun v Hackney London Borough Council* [1998] ICR 1264, [1998] IRLR 676, EAT, the tribunal under Morison P held that a chairman (now an employment judge) cannot validly sit alone under the Employment Tribunals Act 1996 s 4(2) unless he has first exercised his discretion under s 4(5), so that a failure so to exercise it makes the eventual decision by chairmen (now employment judges) alone invalid. However, in *Post Office v Howell* [2000] ICR 913, [2000] IRLR 224, EAT, the tribunal under Charles J disagreed, holding that there was no automatic invalidity, and that failure to exercise the discretion in the Employment Tribunals Act 1996 s 4(5) was merely an 'irregularity' which may or may not have further consequences. See *Morgan v Brith Gof Cyf* [2001] ICR 978, EAT (although it was desirable for chairman (now employment judge) to consider the factors specified in the Employment Tribunals Act 1996 s 4(5), it is not an error of law if he does not do so where the issue was not raised). See also *Sterling Developments (London) Ltd v Pagano* [2007] IRLR 471, [2007] All ER (D) 01 (May), EAT (not an error of law for chairman (now employment judge) not to deal with composition issue in absence of a challenge).

1404.   Acts, determinations and decisions by legal officers. Employment tribunal procedure regulations[1] may provide that any act which may be done by an employment judge[2] and is of a description specified by the regulations for these purposes, may be done by a person appointed as a legal officer[3] and any act so done is to be treated as done by an employment tribunal[4]. Regulations under the above provision[5] may not, however, specify:

(1)   the determination of any proceedings, other than proceedings in which the parties have agreed the terms of the determination or in which the person bringing the proceedings has given notice of the withdrawal of the case; or

(2)   the carrying out[6] of pre-hearing reviews[7].

Partly as from a day to be appointed[8], the following provision has effect. A person appointed as a legal officer[9] may determine proceedings in respect of which an employment tribunal has jurisdiction, or make a decision falling to be made in the course of such proceedings, if:

(a)   the proceedings are of a description specified in an order under this subsection made by the Secretary of State and the Lord Chancellor acting jointly, and

(b)   all the parties to the proceedings consent in writing;

and any determination or decision so made is to be treated as made by an employment tribunal[10].

1 As to the meaning of 'employment tribunal procedure regulations' see PARA 1410.

2 Ie any act which by virtue of the Employment Tribunals Act 1996 s 4(6) (see PARA 1402) may be done by the person mentioned in s 4(1)(a) (see PARA 1402) alone or alone by any employment judge who, in accordance with regulations made under s 1(1) (see PARA 1399), is a member of the tribunal. As to the meaning of 'employment judge' see PARA 1401 note 3.

3 Ie appointed in accordance with regulations under the Employment Tribunals Act 1996 s 1(1) (see PARA 1399). At the date at which this volume states the law, the Employment Tribunals (Constitution and Rules of Procedure) Regulations 2013, SI 2013/1237, make no provision for the appointment of legal officers. Legal officers may, however, presumably be appointed by the Lord Chancellor under the Tribunals, Courts and Enforcement Act 2007 ss 39(1)(c), (d), 40. See further COURTS AND TRIBUNALS vol 24 (2010) PARAS 868–869.

4 Employment Tribunals Act 1996 s 4(6B) (added by the Employment Rights (Dispute Resolution) Act 1998 s 5; amended by the Tribunals, Courts and Enforcement Act 2007 Sch 8 paras 35, 37).

5 Ie under the Employment Tribunals Act 1996 s 4(6B): see the text and notes 1–4.

6 Ie in accordance with regulations under the Employment Tribunals Act 1996 s 9(1): see PARA 1414.

7 Employment Tribunals Act 1996 s 4(6C) (added by the Employment Rights (Dispute Resolution) Act 1998 s 5).

8 Ie partly as from a day to be appointed under the Enterprise and Regulatory Reform Act 2013 s 103(3). At the date at which this volume states the law, the Employment Tribunals Act 1996 s 4(6D) (see the text and notes 9–10) was in force only for the purposes of enabling the exercise of any power to make provision by regulations, rules or order made by statutory instrument: see the Enterprise and Regulatory Reform Act 2013 s 103(1)(i).

9 See note 3.

10 Employment Tribunals Act 1996 s 4(6D) (added by the Enterprise and Regulatory Reform Act 2013 s 11(1), partly as from a day to be appointed (see note 8); not yet fully in force). As to the Secretary of State see PARA 5 note 21; and as to the Lord Chancellor see CONSTITUTIONAL AND ADMINISTRATIVE LAW vol 20 (2014) PARA 255 et seq.

1405. Remuneration, fees and allowances for employment tribunal officers, members etc. The Secretary of State[1] may pay to:

(1) the President of the Employment Tribunals (England and Wales)[2];

(2) any person who is an employment judge[3] on a full-time basis; and

(4) any person who is duly appointed[4] a legal officer,

such remuneration as he may, with the consent of the Treasury[5], determine[6].

The Secretary of State may also pay to:

(a) members of employment tribunals[7];

(b) any assessors[8] appointed for the purposes of proceedings before employment tribunals; and

(c) any persons required for certain purposes of the Equality Act 2010[9] to prepare reports,

such fees and allowances as he may, with the consent of the Treasury, determine[10].

The Secretary of State may pay to any other persons such allowances as he may, with the consent of the Treasury, determine for the purposes of, or in connection with, their attendance at employment tribunals[11].

1 As to the Secretary of State see PARA 5 note 21.

2 As to the President of the Employment Tribunals (England and Wales) see PARA 1400.

3 As to the meaning of 'employment judge' see PARA 1401 note 3.

4 Ie appointed in accordance with regulations under the Employment Tribunals Act 1996 s 1(1): see PARA 1399.

5 As to the Treasury see CONSTITUTIONAL AND ADMINISTRATIVE LAW vol 20 (2014) PARA 262 et seq.

6 Employment Tribunals Act 1996 s 5(1) (amended by the Employment Rights (Dispute Resolution) Act 1998 s 1(2)(d), (e), Sch 1 para 13, Sch 2; the Tribunals, Courts and Enforcement Act 2007 Sch 8 paras 35, 39).

7 As to membership of employment tribunals see PARA 1402.

8 As to the power under the Employment Tribunals Act 1996 to provide for the appointment of one or more assessors for the purposes of any proceedings before an employment tribunal see PARA 1410 head (7).

9 Ie for the purposes of the Equality Act 2010 s 131(2): see DISCRIMINATION vol 33 (2013) PARA 349.

10 Employment Tribunals Act 1996 s 5(2) (amended by the Employment Rights (Dispute Resolution) Act 1998 s 1(2)(b); the Equality Act 2010 s 211(1), Sch 26 Pt 1 paras 27, 28 (as added by SI 2010/2279)).

11 Employment Tribunals Act 1996 s 5(3) (amended by the Employment Rights (Dispute Resolution) Act 1998 s 1(2)(b)).

B. JURISDICTION OF EMPLOYMENT TRIBUNALS

1406. Jurisdiction of employment tribunals; in general. Employment tribunals[1] are to exercise the jurisdiction conferred on them by or by virtue of the Employment Tribunals Act 1996 or any other Act, whether passed before or after that Act[2].

The remedy of an employee[3] for infringement of any of the rights conferred on him by the provisions of the 1996 Act relating to:

(1) itemised pay statements[4];
(2) guarantee payments[5];
(3) detriment in employment[6];
(4) time off work[7];
(5) suspension from work[8];
(6) maternity leave and parental leave[9];
(7) written statements of reasons for dismissal[10];
(8) unfair dismissal[11]; and
(9) an employer's insolvency[12],

is, where provision is made for a complaint or the reference of a question to an employment tribunal, by way of such a complaint or reference and not otherwise[13].

The remedy of a worker[14] in respect of unlawful deductions from wages[15] is by way of a complaint[16] and not otherwise[17].

A part-time worker[18] or a fixed-term employee[19] may present a complaint to an employment tribunal that his employer has infringed his right not to be treated less favourably or not to be subjected to a detriment[20]. An agency worker[21] may also present a complaint to an employment tribunal that a temporary work agency or the hirer has infringed a right conferred[22] on the agency worker[23].

An employee[24] who makes an application for a contract variation[25] may present a complaint to an employment tribunal that his employer has failed to comply with his statutory duties[26] in relation to such an application, or that a decision by his employer to reject the application was based on incorrect facts[27].

A worker[28] may present a complaint to an employment tribunal that his employer has refused to permit him to exercise certain of his statutory rights relating to working time; or has failed to pay him the whole or any part of any amount due to him in respect of leave to which he is entitled[29].

A worker[30] may present a complaint to an employment tribunal that he has been subjected to a detriment in contravention of the national minimum wage provisions[31].

In addition an employment tribunal has jurisdiction to hear complaints of alleged contraventions of the following provisions of the Trade Union and Labour Relations (Consolidation) Act 1992:

(a) the statutory right of trade union members not to be unjustifiably disciplined[32];
(b) the statutory right not to suffer deduction of unauthorised or excessive union subscriptions[33];
(c) the statutory right to training where a trade union is recognised as entitled to conduct collective bargaining and a method of collective bargaining has been specified[34];
(d) wrongful deduction of contributions to the political fund[35];
(e) the provisions regarding access to employment[36];

(f) the provisions relating to detriment on grounds of union membership or activities[37];

(g) unfair dismissal for trade union reasons and the granting of interim relief[38];

(h) the statutory right to time off for trade union duties and activities[39];

(i) the statutory right not to be excluded or expelled from a trade union[40];

(j) the employer's statutory duty to consult trade union representatives or employee representatives on proposed redundancies[41];

(k) the entitlement under a protective award[42]; and

(l) the right not to suffer detriment in cases concerning trade union recognition, bargaining arrangements and balloting[43].

An employment tribunal's general power to hear a complaint of unfair dismissal[44] is qualified as follows:

(i) a dismissal on grounds related to union membership is automatically unfair and subject to special remedies[45];

(ii) a dismissal for asserting a relevant statutory right[46] is also automatically unfair[47]; and

(iii) there are significant limitations on the tribunal's jurisdiction to hear a complaint if the employee was dismissed while taking part in industrial action[48].

An employment tribunal also has jurisdiction:

(A) to hear certain complaints in health and safety cases[49];

(B) to hear complaints relating to the rights of employee representatives to time off and remuneration for time off[50];

(C) to hear a complaint of an employer's failure to consult trade union representatives on the transfer of an undertaking[51];

(D) to determine certain questions relating to the employer's duty to give pensions information to trade unions[52];

(E) in relation to other employment-related matters[53] including certain contract claims[54]; and

(F) to hear complaints that a person has been refused employment or employment agency services, or has been victimised, for a reason relating to a prohibited blacklist of trade union members[55].

Public funding is not available for such proceedings[56].

1 As to the establishment of tribunals see PARA 1399.

2 Employment Tribunals Act 1996 s 2 (amended by the Employment Rights (Dispute Resolution) Act 1998 s 1(2)(b)). As to the rules of procedure see PARA 1421. The jurisdiction conferred on employment tribunals does not extend to matters concerning electoral issues: *Secretary of State for Scotland v Mann* [2001] ICR 1005, EAT.

3 As to the meaning of 'employee' see PARA 2. In relation to the rights conferred by the Employment Rights Act 1996 s 45A (see PARA 616) and s 47B (see PARA 619), the reference to an employee has effect as a reference to a worker (see note 14): s 205(1ZA) (added by SI 1998/1833); Employment Rights Act 1996 s 205(1A) (added by the Public Interest Disclosure Act 1998 ss 14, 18(2)).

As to the new employment status of employee shareholder, under which an employee shareholder agrees to have different employment rights to employees, see the Employment Rights Act 1996 s 205A; and PARA 154.

4 Ie the Employment Rights Act 1996 s 8: see PARA 124.

5 Ie the Employment Rights Act 1996 Pt III (ss 28–35): see PARA 261 et seq.

6 Ie the Employment Rights Act 1996 Pt V (ss 43M–49A): see PARA 613 et seq.

7 Ie the Employment Rights Act 1996 Pt VI (ss 50–63C): see PARA 350 et seq.

8 Ie the Employment Rights Act 1996 Pt VII (ss 64–70A): see PARA 596 et seq.

9 Ie the Employment Rights Act 1996 Pt VIII (ss 71–80E): see PARA 355 et seq.

10 Ie the Employment Rights Act 1996 s 92: see PARA 755.

11 Ie the Employment Rights Act 1996 Pt X (ss 94–134A): see PARA 757 et seq.

12 Ie the Employment Rights Act 1996 Pt XII (ss 182–190): see PARA 628 et seq.

13 Employment Rights Act 1996 s 205(1) (amended by the Employment Rights (Dispute Resolution) Act 1998 s 1(2)(a)).

14 As to the meaning of 'worker' for these purposes see PARA 5.

15 Ie under the Employment Rights Act 1996 s 13 (see PARA 255), s 15 (see PARA 255), s 18(1) (see PARA 257) or s 21(1) (see PARA 258).

16 Ie under the Employment Rights Act 1996 s 23: see PARA 259.

17 Employment Rights Act 1996 s 205(2).

18 As to the meaning of 'worker' for these purposes see PARA 75 note 2.

19 As to the meaning of 'fixed-term employee' see PARA 86 note 2.

20 See the Part-time Workers (Prevention of Less Favourable Treatment) Regulations 2000, SI 2000/1551, reg 8; and PARA 80; the Fixed-term Employees (Prevention of Less Favourable Treatment) Regulations 2002, SI 2002/2034, reg 7; and PARA 91.

21 As to the meaning of 'agency worker' see PARA 97.

22 Ie a right conferred by the Agency Workers Regulations 2010, SI 2010/93, reg 5, reg 12, reg 13 or reg 17: see PARAS 98, 101, 103, 104.

23 See the Agency Workers Regulations 2010, SI 2010/93, reg 18; and PARA 105.

24 As to the meaning of 'employee' for these purposes see PARA 2.

25 Ie an employee who makes an application under the Employment Rights Act 1996 s 80F: see PARA 108. As to the meaning of 'contract variation' see PARA 108.

26 Ie under the Employment Rights Act 1996 s 80G: see PARA 109.

27 See the Employment Rights Act 1996 s 80H(1); and PARA 111. The ACAS (Flexible Working) Arbitration Scheme (Great Britain) Order 2004, SI 2004/2333, provides for arbitration as an alternative method of resolving disputes or claims which could be the subject of proceedings before an employment tribunal arising out of a contravention or alleged contravention of the Employment Rights Act 1996 s 80H(1)(b): see PARA 111.

28 As to the meaning of 'worker' for these purposes see PARA 271.

29 See the Working Time Regulations 1998, SI 1998/1833, reg 30(1); and PARA 319. ACAS conciliation is available on such a complaint: see the Employment Tribunals Act 1996 s 18(1)(j); and PARA 152 note 1 head (9). As to the constitution and powers of ACAS see PARA 1213 et seq.

30 As to the meaning of 'worker' for these purposes see PARA 171.

31 See the National Minimum Wage Act 1998 s 24(1); and PARA 249. ACAS conciliation is available on a complaint under or by virtue of the National Minimum Wage Act 1998 s 24: see the Employment Tribunals Act 1996 s 18(1)(c); and PARA 152 note 1 head (3).

32 Ie the Trade Union and Labour Relations (Consolidation) Act 1992 s 64: see PARA 1029 et seq.

33 Ie the Trade Union and Labour Relations (Consolidation) Act 1992 s 68: see PARAS 1034–1035.

34 Ie the Trade Union and Labour Relations (Consolidation) Act 1992 s 70B; see PARAS 1172–1173.

35 Ie the Trade Union and Labour Relations (Consolidation) Act 1992 s 86: see PARAS 989–990.

36 Ie the Trade Union and Labour Relations (Consolidation) Act 1992 ss 137, 138: see PARA 1042 et seq.

37 Ie the Trade Union and Labour Relations (Consolidation) Act 1992 s 146: see PARA 1048 et seq.

38 Ie the Trade Union and Labour Relations (Consolidation) Act 1992 s 161: see PARA 1056 et seq.

39 Ie the Trade Union and Labour Relations (Consolidation) Act 1992 ss 168–170: see PARA 1065 et seq.

40 Ie the Trade Union and Labour Relations (Consolidation) Act 1992 s 174: see PARA 1026 et seq.

41 Ie the Trade Union and Labour Relations (Consolidation) Act 1992 s 188: see PARA 1185 et seq.

42 Ie the Trade Union and Labour Relations (Consolidation) Act 1992 s 190: see PARA 1190.

43 Ie the Trade Union and Labour Relations (Consolidation) Act 1992 s 70A, Sch A1 para 156: see PARAS 1169, 1170.

44 See the Employment Rights Act 1996 s 111; and PARA 804.

45 See PARA 1056 et seq. Proceedings on a complaint under the Trade Union and Labour Relations (Consolidation) Act 1992 s 68A (deduction of unauthorised subscriptions) (see PARA 1035), s 87 (unlawful deduction of political fund contributions) (see PARA 990), s 192 (payment under a protective award) (see PARA 1190) or on an application under s 161, s 165 or s 166 (interim relief) (see PARA 1056 et seq) must be heard by the employment judge of the tribunal alone, unless he decides that they should be heard by the full tribunal, having regard to the likelihood of a dispute arising on the facts, an issue of law arising, any views of the parties and whether there are other proceedings which might be heard concurrently: see the Employment Tribunals Act 1996 s 4(2)–(5); and PARA 1403.

46 Ie the rights conferred by the Trade Union and Labour Relations (Consolidation) Act 1992 s 68 (see PARA 1034), s 86 (see PARA 989), s 146 (see PARA 1048) or ss 168–170 (see PARA 1065 et seq).
47 See PARAS 1063, 1064.
48 See PARA 1350.
49 See PARAS 1076, 1077.
50 See PARAS 1209, 1210.
51 See PARA 1200.
52 See PARAS 1205, 1206.
53 See PARA 1406 et seq.
54 See the Employment Tribunals Extension of Jurisdiction (England and Wales) Order 1994, SI 1994/1623; and PARA 1408.
55 See PARA 1038 et seq.
55 See LEGAL AID vol 65 (2008) PARA 1 et seq.

1407. Power to confer jurisdiction for breach of contract of employment. The appropriate minister[1] may by order[2] provide that proceedings in respect of any specified claim[3] or any such claim which is of a description specified in the order, except a claim for damages, or for a sum due, in respect of personal injuries[4], may, subject to such exceptions, if any, as may be so specified, be brought before an employment tribunal[5]. Any such order may:

(1) provide that an employment tribunal is not in proceedings in respect of a claim, or a number of claims relating to the same contract, to order the payment of an amount exceeding such sum as may be specified in the order as the maximum amount which an employment tribunal may order to be paid in relation to a claim or in relation to a contract[6];

(2) include provisions as to the manner in which and the time within which proceedings are to be brought and modifying any other enactment[7];

(3) make different provision in relation to proceedings in respect of different descriptions of claims[8].

Where in proceedings so brought an employment tribunal finds that the whole or part of a sum claimed in the proceedings is due, the tribunal must order the respondent to the proceedings to pay the amount which it finds due[9].

Any jurisdiction conferred on an employment tribunal by virtue of these provisions in respect of any claim is exercisable concurrently with any court in England and Wales which has jurisdiction to hear and determine any proceedings in respect of the claim[10].

1 For these purposes, 'appropriate minister', as respects a claim in respect of which proceedings could be heard and determined by a court in England and Wales, means the Lord Chancellor: Employment Tribunals Act 1996 s 3(5). As to the meanings of 'England' and 'Wales' see PARA 2 note 12. As to the Lord Chancellor see CONSTITUTIONAL AND ADMINISTRATIVE LAW vol 20 (2014) PARA 255 et seq. The Lord Chancellor's functions under s 3 are protected functions under the Constitutional Reform Act 2005: see Sch 7 para 4 Pt A. As to the protected functions of the Lord Chancellor see CONSTITUTIONAL AND ADMINISTRATIVE LAW vol 20 (2014) PARA 261.

2 No such order may be so made unless a draft of the order has been laid before Parliament and approved by resolution of each House of Parliament: Employment Tribunals Act 1996 s 41(2). At the date at which this volume states the law no such order had been made but, by virtue of s 44, Sch 2 para 2 (see PARA 162), the Employment Tribunals Extension of Jurisdiction (England and Wales) Order 1994, SI 1994/1623 (see PARAS 1408, 1409) has effect as if so made.

3 The claims specified are: (1) a claim for damages for breach of a contract of employment or any other contract connected with employment; (2) a claim for a sum due under such a contract; (3) a claim for the recovery of a sum in pursuance of any enactment relating to the terms or performance of such a contract, if the claim is such that a court in England and Wales or Scotland would under the law for the time being in force have jurisdiction to hear and determine proceedings in respect of the claim: Employment Tribunals Act 1996 s 3(2). As to the meaning of 'contract of employment' see PARA 2; and as to the meaning of 'employment' see PARA 2.

For these purposes, a reference to a breach of contract includes a reference to breach of: (a) a term implied in a contract by or under any enactment or otherwise; (b) a term of a contract as modified by or under any enactment or otherwise; and (c) a term which, although not contained in a contract, is incorporated in the contract by another term of the contract: s 3(6).

4   For these purposes, 'personal injuries' includes any disease and any impairment of a person's physical or mental condition: Employment Tribunals Act 1996 s 3(5).

5   Employment Tribunals Act 1996 s 3(1), (3) (s 3(1) amended by the Employment Rights (Dispute Resolution) Act 1998 s 1(2)(a)). As to the establishment of tribunals see PARA 1399. The Secretary of State and the Lord Chancellor, acting jointly, may by order: (1) provide that the Employment Tribunals Act 1996 s 3 and s 8 (see the text and notes 6–9), if specified in the order, are not to apply to persons, or to employments, of such classes as may be prescribed in the order; or (2) provide that ss 3, 8 are to apply to persons or employments of such classes as may be prescribed in the order subject to such exceptions and modifications as may be so prescribed (s 40(1), (2) (s 40(1) amended by the Tribunals, Courts and Enforcement Act 2007 Sch 8 paras 35, 38)); but no order may be so made unless a draft of the order has been laid before Parliament and approved by resolution of each House of Parliament (Employment Tribunals Act 1996 s 41(2)). As to the making of orders under the Employment Tribunals Act 1996 generally see PARA 162. At the date at which this volume states the law, no such order had been made.

6   Employment Tribunals Act 1996 s 8(2) (amended by the Employment Rights (Dispute Resolution) Act 1998 s 1(2)(a)). See also note 5. As to the sum specified see PARA 1408.

7   Employment Tribunals Act 1996 s 8(3). See also note 5.

8   Employment Tribunals Act 1996 s 8(4). See also note 5.

9   Employment Tribunals Act 1996 s 8(1) (amended by the Employment Rights (Dispute Resolution) Act 1998 s 1(2)(a)). See also note 5.

10   Employment Tribunals Act 1996 s 3(4) (amended by the Employment Rights (Dispute Resolution) Act 1998 s 1(2)(a)). See also note 5.

1408. Contract claims on termination of employment. Proceedings may be brought[1] before an employment tribunal in respect of a claim of an employee[2] for the recovery of damages or any other sum, other than a claim for damages or for a sum due in respect of personal injuries[3], if[4]:

(1)   the claim is one permitted by statute[5] and one which a court in England and Wales[6] would under the law for the time being in force have jurisdiction to hear and determine[7];

(2)   the claim is not an excluded claim[8]; and

(3)   the claim arises or is outstanding on the termination of the employee's employment[9].

Proceedings may be brought before an employment tribunal in respect of a claim of an employer[10] for the recovery of damages or any other sum, other than a claim for damages or for a sum due in respect of personal injuries, if the conditions in heads (1) to (3) above are satisfied and if proceedings in respect of a claim of that employee have been brought before an employment tribunal by virtue of these provisions[11].

An employment tribunal must not in proceedings in respect of a contract claim, or in respect of a number of contract claims relating to the same contract, order the payment of an amount exceeding the prescribed amount[12].

1   Proceedings on a contract claim may be brought before an employment tribunal by presenting a complaint to an employment tribunal: Employment Tribunals Extension of Jurisdiction (England and Wales) Order 1994, SI 1994/1623, art 6 (amended by the Employment Rights (Dispute Resolution) Act 1998 s 1(2)(a)). For these purposes, 'contract claim' means a claim in respect of which proceedings may be brought before an employment tribunal by virtue of the Employment Tribunals Extension of Jurisdiction (England and Wales) Order 1994, SI 1994/1623, art 3 or art 4 (see the text and notes 10–11): art 1(2). As to the presentation of a complaint to an employment tribunal see PARA 1453 et seq. As to the establishment of tribunals see PARA 1399.

2   As to the meaning of 'employee' see PARA 2.

3   As to the meaning of 'personal injuries' for these purposes see PARA 1407 note 4. A claim may
    be brought for (inter alia) damages for personal injuries under provisions of the discrimination
    legislation, which is unaffected by this provision: *Sheriff v Klyne Tugs (Lowestoft) Ltd* [1999]
    ICR 1170, [1999] IRLR 481, CA; and see DISCRIMINATION vol 33 (2013) PARA 1 et seq.

4   Employment Tribunals Extension of Jurisdiction (England and Wales) Order 1994,
    SI 1994/1623, art 3 (amended by the Employment Rights (Dispute Resolution) Act 1998
    s 1(2)(a)).

5   Ie by the Employment Tribunals Act 1996 s 3(2): see PARA 1407.

6   As to the meanings of 'England' and 'Wales' see PARA 2 note 12.

7   Employment Tribunals Extension of Jurisdiction (England and Wales) Order 1994,
    SI 1994/1623, art 3(a).

8   Employment Tribunals Extension of Jurisdiction (England and Wales) Order 1994,
    SI 1994/1623, art 3(b). The claims so excluded are claims for breach of a contractual term of
    any of the following descriptions: (1) a term requiring the employer to provide living
    accommodation for the employee; (2) a term imposing an obligation on the employer or the
    employee in connection with the provision of living accommodation; (3) a term relating to
    intellectual property (which includes copyright, rights in performance, moral rights, design right,
    registered designs, patents and trade marks); (4) a term imposing an obligation of confidence;
    (5) a term which is a covenant in restraint of trade: art 5.

9   Employment Tribunals Extension of Jurisdiction (England and Wales) Order 1994,
    SI 1994/1623, art 3(c). The word 'on' in the phrase 'the claim arises or is outstanding on the
    termination of the employee's employment' must be read in a temporal rather than a causative
    sense, ie a tribunal has jurisdiction to determine a claim which is either outstanding on the date
    of the termination of an employee's employment or arises on the date of termination in a
    temporal sense, but not a claim arising (in a causative sense) from an agreement concluded after
    the date of termination of employment: *Miller Bros and FP Butler Ltd v Johnston* [2002] ICR
    744, [2002] IRLR 386, EAT; *Peninsula Business Services Ltd v Sweeney* [2004] IRLR 49, EAT.
    The phrase 'the termination of the employee's employment' must be construed by reference to
    the termination of the contract of employment, an approach which is consistent with the
    purpose of the provisions giving tribunals jurisdiction to deal with both a claim for unfair
    dismissal and a claim for damages for breach of the same contract of employment, thus avoiding
    two sets of proceedings: *Sarker v South Tees Acute Hospitals NHS Trust* [1997] ICR 673,
    [1997] IRLR 328, EAT. As to the time limits for such claims see PARA 1409. By a combination of
    the Employment Tribunals Extension of Jurisdiction (England and Wales) Order 1994,
    SI 1994/1623, art 3 and the Employment Tribunals Act 1996 s 3(2) (see PARA 1407), a tribunal
    has jurisdiction to enforce a compromise agreement which has been reneged on by an employer:
    Rock-It Cargo Ltd v Green [1997] IRLR 581, EAT.

10 As to the meaning of 'employer' see PARA 2.

11 Employment Tribunals Extension of Jurisdiction (England and Wales) Order 1994,
    SI 1994/1623, art 4 (amended by the Employment Rights (Dispute Resolution) Act 1998
    s 1(2)(a)). A counterclaim under the Employment Tribunals Extension of Jurisdiction (England
    and Wales) Order 1994, SI 1994/1623, art 4, once commenced, is an independent cause of
    action and so can survive, even if the original claim by the employee ceases: *Patel v RCMS Ltd*
    [1999] IRLR 161, EAT (original claim by employee held to be out of time, but counterclaim
    brought within its own time limit could proceed).

12 Employment Tribunals Extension of Jurisdiction (England and Wales) Order 1994,
    SI 1994/1623, art 10 (amended by the Employment Rights (Dispute Resolution) Act 1998
    s 1(2)(a)). The prescribed amount is £25,000. As to issue estoppel or cause of action estoppel see
    Fraser v HLMAD Ltd [2006] EWCA Civ 738, [2007] 1 All ER 383, [2006] ICR 1395, [2006]
    IRLR 687 (an employee cannot now take the first £25,000 from the employment tribunal and
    sue for the rest in a contract claim in the civil courts).

1409.   Time limits for claims; death and bankruptcy. Subject to the provision
made for extension of time (1) for mediation in the case of certain cross-border
disputes[1]; or (2) to facilitate conciliation before the institution of proceedings[2],
an employment tribunal must not entertain a complaint in respect of an
employee's contract claim[3] unless it is presented[4]:

(a)   within the period of three months beginning with the effective date of
      termination[5] of the contract giving rise to the claim[6]; or

(b)   where there is no effective date of termination, within the period of three months beginning with the last day on which the employee worked in the employment which has terminated[7];

(c) where the period within which a complaint must be presented in accordance with head (a) or head (b) above is extended by the statutory provisions relating to disciplinary, dismissal and grievance procedures[8], within the extended period rather than the period in head (a) or head (b) above[9]; or

(d) where the tribunal is satisfied that it was not reasonably practicable for the complaint to be presented within whichever of those periods is applicable, within such further period as the tribunal considers reasonable[10].

Subject to the provision referred to in heads (1) and (2) above[11], an employment tribunal must not entertain a complaint in respect of an employer's contract claim unless[12]:

(i) it is presented at a time when there is before the tribunal a complaint in respect of a contract claim of a particular employee which has not been settled or withdrawn[13];

(ii) it arises out of a contract with that employee[14]; and

(iii) it is presented:

(A) within the period of six weeks beginning with the day or, if more than one, the last of the days on which the employer, or other person who is the respondent party to the employee's contract claim, received from the tribunal a copy of a claim form in respect of a contract claim of that employee; or

(B) where the tribunal is satisfied that it was not reasonably practicable for the complaint to be presented within that period, within such further period as the tribunal considers reasonable[15].

Where proceedings in respect of a contract claim have been brought before an employment tribunal and an employee or employer party to them dies before their conclusion, the proceedings do not abate by reason of the death and the tribunal may, if it thinks it necessary in order to ensure that all matters in dispute may be effectually and completely determined and adjudicated on, order the personal representatives of the deceased party, or other persons whom the tribunal considers appropriate, to be made parties and the proceedings to be carried on as if they had been substituted for the deceased party[16].

Where proceedings in respect of a contract claim have been brought before an employment tribunal and the employee or employer who is the applicant party becomes bankrupt before their conclusion, the proceedings do not abate by reason of the bankruptcy and the tribunal may, if it thinks it necessary in order to ensure that all matters in dispute may be effectually and completely adjudicated on, order the person in whom the interest of the bankrupt party has vested to be made a party and the proceedings to be carried on as if he had been substituted for the bankrupt party[17].

1 Ie subject to the Employment Tribunals Extension of Jurisdiction (England and Wales) Order 1994, SI 1994/1623, art 8A. Where (1) a time limit is set by art 7(a) or (b) (see heads (a)–(b) in the text) in relation to the whole or part of a relevant dispute; (2) a mediation in relation to the relevant dispute starts before the time limit expires; and (3) if not extended by art 8A, the time limit would expire before the mediation ends or less than four weeks after it ends, the time limit expires instead at the end of four weeks after the mediation ends (subject to art 8A(4)): art 8A(2), (3) (art 8A added by SI 2011/1133). If a time limit mentioned in head (1) above has been so extended, the Employment Tribunals Extension of Jurisdiction (England and Wales) Order 1994, SI 1994/1623, art 8A(2), (3) applies to the extended time limit as it applies to a time limit mentioned in head (1) above: art 8A(4) (as so added). Where more than one time

limit applies in relation to a relevant dispute, the extension by art 8A(3) or art 8A(6) (see note 15) of one of those time limits does not affect the others: art 8A(8) (as so added).

For the purposes of art 8A, a mediation starts on the date of the agreement to mediate that is entered into by the parties and the mediator and ends on the date of the first of these to occur: (a) the parties reach an agreement in resolution of the relevant dispute; (b) a party completes the notification of the other parties that it has withdrawn from the mediation; (c) a party to whom a qualifying request is made fails to give a response reaching the other parties within 14 days of the request; (d) the parties, after being notified that the mediator's appointment has ended (by death, resignation or otherwise), fail to agree within 14 days to seek to appoint a replacement mediator; or (e) the mediation otherwise comes to an end pursuant to the terms of the agreement to mediate: art 8A(9), (10) (as so added). For these purposes, a qualifying request is a request by a party that another ('A') confirm to all parties that A is continuing with the mediation: art 8A(11) (as so added). In the case of any relevant dispute, references in art 8A to a mediation are references to the mediation so far as it relates to that dispute, and references to a party are to be read accordingly: art 8A(12) (as so added).

'Relevant dispute' means a dispute to which European Parliament and Council Directive (EC) 2008/52 (OJ L136, 24.5.2008, p 3) art 8(1) applies (certain cross-border disputes); and 'mediation' and 'mediator' have the meanings given by art 3(a), (b): Employment Tribunals Extension of Jurisdiction (England and Wales) Order 1994, SI 1994/1623, art 8A(1) (as so added).

2   Ie subject to the Employment Tribunals Extension of Jurisdiction (England and Wales) Order 1994, SI 1994/1623, art 8B. Article 8B applies where the 1994 Order provides for it to apply for the purposes of a provision of that Order ('a relevant provision'): art 8B(1) (art 8B added by SI 2014/431). In working out when the time limit set by a relevant provision expires the period beginning with the day after Day A and ending with Day B is not to be counted: Employment Tribunals Extension of Jurisdiction (England and Wales) Order 1994, SI 1994/1623, art 8B(3) (as so added). If the time limit set by a relevant provision would (if not extended by this provision) expire during the period beginning with Day A and ending one month after Day B, the time limit expires instead at the end of that period: Employment Tribunals Extension of Jurisdiction (England and Wales) Order 1994, SI 1994/1623, art 8B(4) (as so added). For these purposes, Day A is the day on which the worker concerned complies with the requirement in the Employment Tribunals Act 1996 s 18A(1) (requirement to contact ACAS before instituting proceedings: see PARA 152) in relation to the matter in respect of which the proceedings are brought, and Day B is the day on which the worker concerned receives or, if earlier, is treated as receiving (by virtue of regulations made under s 18A(11)) the certificate issued under s 18A(4): Employment Tribunals Extension of Jurisdiction (England and Wales) Order 1994, SI 1994/1623, art 8B(2) (as so added).

3   Ie under the Employment Tribunals Extension of Jurisdiction (England and Wales) Order 1994, SI 1994/1623, art 3: see PARA 1408. As to the meaning of 'employee' see PARA 2; and as to the meaning of 'contract claim' see PARA 1408 note 1.

4   Employment Tribunals Extension of Jurisdiction (England and Wales) Order 1994, SI 1994/1623, art 7 (amended by the Employment Rights (Dispute Resolution) Act 1998 s 1(2)(a); and by SI 2011/1133; SI 2014/431). As to time limits generally see PARA 1453; and as to the presentation of a complaint to an employment tribunal see PARA 1453 et seq.

5   As to the meaning of 'effective date of termination' see PARA 755 note 11. A tribunal may not consider a claim presented before the effective date of termination: *Capek v Lincolnshire County Council* [2000] ICR 878, [2000] IRLR 590, CA.

6   Employment Tribunals Extension of Jurisdiction (England and Wales) Order 1994, SI 1994/1623, art 7(a).

7   Employment Tribunals Extension of Jurisdiction (England and Wales) Order 1994, SI 1994/1623, art 7(b).

8   Ie extended by the Employment Act 2002 (Dispute Resolution) Regulations 2004, SI 2004/752, reg 15: see PARA 133. See also PARA 698.

9   Employment Tribunals Extension of Jurisdiction (England and Wales) Order 1994, SI 1994/1623, art 7(ba) (added by SI 2004/752).

10   Employment Tribunals Extension of Jurisdiction (England and Wales) Order 1994, SI 1994/1623, art 7(c). Where the tribunal has the power under art 7(c) to extend a period of limitation, the power is exercisable in relation to the period of limitation as extended by art 8A (see note 1): art 8A(13) (as added: see note 1). Where an employment tribunal has power under the 1994 Order to extend the time limit set by a relevant provision, the power is exercisable in relation to that time limit as extended by art 8B: art 8B(5) (as added: see note 2).

11   Ie subject to the Employment Tribunals Extension of Jurisdiction (England and Wales) Order 1994, SI 1994/1623, arts 8A, 8B: see notes 1–2, 10, 15.

12 Employment Tribunals Extension of Jurisdiction (England and Wales) Order 1994, SI 1994/1623, art 8 (amended by the Employment Rights (Dispute Resolution) Act 1998 s 1(2)(a); and by SI 2011/1133; SI 2014/431).

13 Employment Tribunals Extension of Jurisdiction (England and Wales) Order 1994, SI 1994/1623, art 8(a).

14 Employment Tribunals Extension of Jurisdiction (England and Wales) Order 1994, SI 1994/1623, art 8(b).

15 Employment Tribunals Extension of Jurisdiction (England and Wales) Order 1994, SI 1994/1623, art 8(c). Where (1) a time limit is set by art 8(c)(i) (see head (iii)(A) in the text in relation to the whole or part of a relevant dispute; (2) a mediation in relation to the relevant dispute starts before the time limit expires; and (3) if not extended by art 8A the time limit would expire before the mediation ends or less than two weeks after it ends, the time limit expires instead at the end of two weeks after the mediation ends (subject to art 8A(7)): art 8A(5), (6) (as added: see note 1). If a time limit mentioned in head (1) above has been extended by art 8A, art 8A(5), (6) applies to the extended time limit as it applies to a time limit mentioned in head (1) above: art 8A(7) (as so added).

Where the tribunal has the power under art 8(c)(ii) (see head (iii)(B) in the text) to extend a period of limitation, the power is exercisable in relation to the period of limitation as extended by art 8A: art 8A(13). See further note 1. Where an employment tribunal has power under the 1994 Order to extend the time limit set by a relevant provision, the power is exercisable in relation to that time limit as extended by art 8B (see note 2): art 8B(5) (as added: see note 2).

16 Employment Tribunals Extension of Jurisdiction (England and Wales) Order 1994, SI 1994/1623, art 9(1) (art 9 amended by the Employment Rights (Dispute Resolution) Act 1998 s 1(2)(a)).

17 Employment Tribunals Extension of Jurisdiction (England and Wales) Order 1994, SI 1994/1623, art 9(2) (as amended: see note 16).

C. POWERS TO MAKE REGULATIONS ETC IN RELATION TO EMPLOYMENT TRIBUNALS

1410. Power to make employment tribunal procedure regulations; in general.
The Secretary of State[1] may by regulations ('employment tribunal procedure regulations') make such provision as appears to him to be necessary or expedient with respect to proceedings before employment tribunals[2].

Employment tribunal procedure regulations may, in particular, include provision:

(1) for determining by which tribunal any proceedings are to be determined;

(2) for enabling an employment tribunal to hear and determine proceedings brought under the statutory provisions relating to awarding damages etc for breach of a contract of employment[3] concurrently with proceedings brought before the tribunal otherwise than by virtue of those provisions;

(3) for treating the Secretary of State, either generally or in such circumstances as may be prescribed by the regulations, as a party to any proceedings before an employment tribunal, where he would not otherwise be a party to them, and entitling him to appear and to be heard accordingly;

(4) for requiring persons to attend to give evidence and produce documents, and for authorising the administration of oaths to witnesses;

(5) for enabling an employment tribunal, on the application of any party to proceedings before it or of its own motion, to order, in England and Wales[4], such disclosure or inspection of documents, or the furnishing of such further particulars, as might be ordered by the County Court on an application by a party to proceedings before it[5];

(6) for prescribing the procedure to be followed in any proceedings before an employment tribunal, including provision for:

(a) postponing fixing a time and place for a hearing, or postponing a time fixed for a hearing, for such period as may be determined in accordance with the regulations for the purpose of giving an opportunity for the proceedings to be settled by way of conciliation and withdrawn; and

(b) enabling an employment tribunal to review its decisions, and revoke or vary its orders and awards, in such circumstances as may be determined in accordance with the regulations;

(7) for the appointment of one or more assessors for the purposes of any proceedings before an employment tribunal, where the proceedings are brought under an enactment which provides for one or more assessors to be appointed;

(8) for authorising an employment tribunal to require persons to furnish information and produce documents to a person required for certain the purposes of the Equality Act 2010[6] to prepare a report; and

(9) for the registration and proof of decisions, orders and awards of employment tribunals[7].

Employment tribunal procedure regulations may:

(i) authorise the Secretary of State to prescribe, or prescribe requirements in relation to, any form which is required by such regulations to be used for the purpose of instituting, or entering an appearance to, proceedings before employment tribunals[8];

(ii) authorise the Secretary of State to prescribe requirements in relation to documents to be supplied with any such form, including certificates from the conciliation officer that a settlement is not possible or has not been reached within the prescribed period[9];

(iii) make provision about the publication of anything prescribed under authority conferred by virtue of head (i) or head (ii) above[10];

(iv) authorise the determination of proceedings without any hearing in such circumstances as the regulations may prescribe[11];

(v) authorise the determination of proceedings without hearing anyone other than the person or persons by whom the proceedings are brought, or his or their representatives, where:

(A) the person (or, where more than one, each of the persons) against whom the proceedings are brought has done nothing to contest the case; or

(B) it appears from the application made by the person (or, where more than one, each of the persons) bringing the proceedings that he is not (or they are not) seeking any relief which an employment tribunal has power to give or that he is not (or they are not) entitled to such relief[12];

(vi) authorise the determination of proceedings without hearing anyone other than the person or persons by whom, and the person or persons against whom, the proceedings are brought, or his or their representatives, where:

(A) an employment tribunal is on undisputed facts bound by the decision of a court in another case to dismiss the case of the person or persons by whom, or of the person or persons against whom, the proceedings are brought; or

(B) the proceedings relate only to a preliminary issue which may be heard and determined in accordance with regulations[13] relating to pre-hearing reviews and preliminary matters[14].

Employment tribunal procedure regulations may[15] include provision authorising or requiring an employment tribunal, in circumstances specified in the regulations, to send notice or a copy of any document specified in the regulations which relates to any proceedings before the tribunal, or of any decision, order or award of the tribunal, to any government department or other person or body so specified[16].

A person who without reasonable excuse fails to comply with any requirement imposed by virtue of head (4) or head (8) above or any requirement with respect to the disclosure, recovery or inspection of documents imposed by virtue of head (5) above or any requirement imposed by virtue of employment tribunal procedure regulations to give written answers for the purpose of facilitating the determination of proceedings[17] is guilty of an offence and liable to a penalty[18].

1　As to the Secretary of State see PARA 5 note 21.

2　Employment Tribunals Act 1996 s 7(1) (amended by the Employment Rights (Dispute Resolution) Act 1998 s 1(2)(a), (b)); Employment Tribunals Act 1996 s 42(1) (definition amended by the Employment Rights (Dispute Resolution) Act 1998 s 1(2)(a)). 'Employment tribunal procedure regulations' must be construed in accordance with the Employment Tribunals Act 1996 s 7(1): s 42(1). As to the regulations made see the Employment Tribunals (Constitution and Rules of Procedure) Regulations 2013, SI 2013/1237; and PARAS 1400 et seq, 1421 et seq. As to the making of regulations under the Employment Tribunals Act 1996 generally see PARA 162.

3　Ie proceedings brought by virtue of the Employment Tribunals Act 1996 s 3: see PARA 1407. For these purposes, 'statutory provision' means a provision, whether of a general or a special nature, contained in, or in any document made or issued under, any Act, whether of a general or special nature: s 42(1). As to the meaning of 'contract of employment' see PARA 2.

4　As to the meanings of 'England' and 'Wales' see PARA 2 note 12.

5　As to the powers of the County Court to order disclosure and inspection see CPR Pt 31; and CIVIL PROCEDURE vol 11 (2009) PARA 538 et seq. As to further information (formerly known as further and better particulars) see CPR Pt 18; and CIVIL PROCEDURE vol 11 (2009) PARAS 611–612.

6　Ie for the purposes of the Equality Act 2010 s 131(2): see DISCRIMINATION vol 33 (2013) PARA 349.

7　Employment Tribunals Act 1996 s 7(3) (amended by the Employment Rights (Dispute Resolution) Act 1998 s 1(2)(a), (b), Sch 1 para 14(1), (2), Sch 2; the Employment Act 2002 s 24(1); the Equality Act 2010 Sch 26 Pt 1 paras 27, 29 (as added by SI 2010/2279); the Crime and Courts Act 2013 Sch 9 Pt 3 para 52(1)(b), (2)).

8　Employment Tribunals Act 1996 s 7(3ZA)(a) (s 7(3ZA) added by the Employment Act 2002 s 25). See PARA 1461.

9　See the Employment Tribunals Act 1996 s 7(3ZA)(b) (as added (see note 8); amended by the Enterprise and Regulatory Reform Act 2013 s 7(2), Sch 1, paras 2, 3). See PARA 1461. The certificate referred to in head (ii) in the text is a certificate under the Employment Tribunals Act 1996 s 18A(4): see PARA 152.

10　Employment Tribunals Act 1996 s 7(3ZA)(c) (as added: see note 8). See PARA 1461.

11　Employment Tribunals Act 1996 s 7(3A) (added by the Employment Rights (Dispute Resolution) Act 1998 s 2; substituted by the Employment Act 2002 s 26). See PARA 1466. Employment tribunal procedure regulations under the Employment Tribunals Act 1996 s 7(3A) may only authorise the determination of proceedings without any hearing in circumstances where (1) all the parties to the proceedings consent in writing to the determination without a hearing; or (2) the person (or, where more than one, each of the persons) against whom the proceedings are brought (a) has presented no response in the proceedings; or (b) does not contest the case: s 7(3AA) (s 7(3AA), (3AB) added by the Employment Act 2008 s 4). For the purposes of head (2) above, a person does not present a response in the proceedings if he presents a response but, in accordance with provision made by the regulations, it is not accepted: Employment Tribunals Act 1996 s 7(3AB) (as so added).

12　Employment Tribunals Act 1996 s 7(3B) (added by the Employment Rights (Dispute Resolution) Act 1998 s 2).

13　Ie regulations under the Employment Tribunals Act 1996 s 9(4): see PARA 1414.

14 Employment Tribunals Act 1996 s 7(3C) (added by the Employment Rights (Dispute Resolution) Act 1998 s 2).

15 Ie subject to any regulations under the Employment Tribunals Act 1996 s 11(1)(a): see PARA 1416 head (1).

16 Employment Tribunals Act 1996 s 7(5) (amended by the Employment Rights (Dispute Resolution) Act 1998 s 1(2)(a)).

17 Ie such proceedings as are mentioned in the Employment Tribunals Act 1996 s 7(3A), s 7(3B) or s 7(3C): see the text and notes 11–14.

18 Employment Tribunals Act 1996 s 7(4) (amended by the Employment Rights (Dispute Resolution) Act 1998 Sch 1 para 14(1), (3)). The penalty on summary conviction is a fine not exceeding level 3 on the standard scale: see the Employment Tribunals Act 1996 s 7(4) (as so amended). As to the standard scale see SENTENCING AND DISPOSITION OF OFFENDERS vol 92 (2010) PARA 142.

1411. Power to make order prescribing employment tribunal fees. The Lord Chancellor[1] may by order prescribe fees payable in respect of anything dealt with by an employment tribunal[2] or mediation conducted by tribunal staff[3].

1 As to the Lord Chancellor see CONSTITUTIONAL AND ADMINISTRATIVE LAW vol 20 (2014) PARA 255 et seq.

2 See the Tribunals, Courts and Enforcement Act 2007 s 42(1)(d), which refers to 'an added tribunal'. Employment tribunals are 'added tribunals' for these purposes: see the Added Tribunals (Employment Tribunals and Employment Appeal Tribunal) Order 2013, SI 2013/1892; and COURTS AND TRIBUNALS vol 24 (2010) PARA 871. See also the Employment Tribunals and the Employment Appeal Tribunal Fees Order 2013, SI 2013/1893, made in exercise of the powers conferred by the Tribunals, Courts and Enforcement Act 2007 ss 42(1)(d), (2), 49(3); and PARA 1457 et seq. The amendments made by the Courts and Tribunals Fees (Miscellaneous Amendments) Order 2014, SI 2014/590, to the Employment Tribunals and the Employment Appeal Tribunal Fees Order 2013, SI 2013/1893, Sch 2 Table 2 (employment tribunals: issue and hearing fee) have no effect in relation to the issue fee or the hearing fee payable in any claim where the claim form was presented before 6 April 2014: Courts and Tribunals Fees (Miscellaneous Amendments) Order 2014, SI 2014/590, art 7.

3 See the Tribunals, Courts and Enforcement Act 2007 s 42(1)(e), which refers to mediation by staff appointed under s 40(1); and COURTS AND TRIBUNALS vol 24 (2010) PARA 871. See also note 2.

1412. Practice directions about employment tribunal procedure. The Senior President of Tribunals may make directions about the procedure of employment tribunals[1]. This power[2] includes: (1) power to vary or revoke directions made in exercise of the power; and (2) power to make different provision for different purposes, including different provision for different areas[3].

Employment tribunal procedure regulations[4] may include provision:

(a) enabling the territorial President[5] to make directions about the procedure of employment tribunals[6], including directions about the exercise by tribunals of powers under such regulations[7];

(b) for securing compliance with directions; and

(c) about the publication of directions[8].

Employment tribunal procedure regulations may, instead of providing for any matter, refer to provision made or to be made about that matter by directions made under the relevant provisions[9].

The President[10] may make, vary or revoke practice directions about the procedure of the tribunals[11] in England and Wales, including:

(i) practice directions about the exercise by tribunals of powers under the Employment Tribunals (Constitution and Rules of Procedure) Regulations 2013[12]; and

(ii) practice directions about the provision by employment judges[13] of mediation, in relation to disputed matters in a case that is the subject of proceedings, and may permit an employment judge to act as mediator in a case even though he has been selected to decide matters in that case[14].

Practice directions may make different provision for different cases, different areas, or different types of proceedings[15]. Any practice direction made, varied or revoked must be published by the President in an appropriate manner to bring it to the attention of the persons to whom it is addressed[16].

1 Employment Tribunals Act 1996 s 7A(A1) (s 7A added by the Employment Act 2002 s 27; the Employment Tribunals Act 1996 s 7A(A1) added by the Tribunals, Courts and Enforcement Act 2007 Sch 8 paras 35, 41(1), (2)). As to the Senior President of Tribunals see COURTS AND TRIBUNALS vol 24 (2010) PARA 867. Directions under the Employment Tribunals Act 1996 s 7A(A1) may not be made without the approval of the Lord Chancellor: s 7A(2B) (s 7A(2A)–(2E) added by the Tribunals, Courts and Enforcement Act 2007 Sch 8 para 35, 41(1), (5)). As to the Lord Chancellor see CONSTITUTIONAL AND ADMINISTRATIVE LAW vol 20 (2014) PARA 255 et seq. The Lord Chancellor's functions under the Employment Tribunals Act 1996 s 7A are protected functions under the Constitutional Reform Act 2005: see Sch 7 para 4 Pt A (prospectively amended for these purposes by the Tribunals, Courts and Enforcement Act 2007 s 144(1), (8)). As to the protected functions of the Lord Chancellor see CONSTITUTIONAL AND ADMINISTRATIVE LAW vol 20 (2014) PARA 261.

   The Employment Tribunals Act 1996 s 7A(2B), (2C)(b) (see note 7 head (2)) does not apply to directions to the extent that they consist of guidance about any of the following: (1) the application or interpretation of the law; (2) the making of decisions by members of an employment tribunal: s 7A(2D) (as so added). Section 7A(2B), (2C)(b) also does not apply to directions to the extent that they consist of criteria for determining which members of employment tribunals may be selected to decide particular categories of matter; but the directions may, to that extent, be made only after consulting the Lord Chancellor: s 7A(2E) (as so added).

2 Ie the power under the Employment Tribunals Act 1996 s 7A(A1).

3 Employment Tribunals Act 1996 s 7A(2A) (as added: see note 1).

4 As to the meaning of 'employment tribunal procedure regulations' see PARA 1410.

5 For these purposes, references to the territorial President are references to a person appointed in accordance with regulations under the Employment Tribunals Act 1996 s 1(1) as President of the Employment Tribunals (England and Wales) (see PARAS 1399, 1402): s 7A(3) (as added (see note 1); amended by the Tribunals, Courts and Enforcement Act 2007 Sch 8 paras 35, 41(1), (6)).

6 As to the procedure of employment tribunals see PARA 1453 et seq.

7 Directions under the Employment Tribunals Act 1996 s 7A(1)(a) (see head (a) in the text) may not be made without the approval of: (1) the Senior President of Tribunals; and (2) the Lord Chancellor: s 7A(2C) (as added: see note 1). See note 1.

8 Employment Tribunals Act 1996 s 7A(1) (as added (see note 1); amended by the Tribunals, Courts and Enforcement Act 2007 Sch 8 paras 35, 41(1), (3)). The reference to directions in heads (b) and (c) in the text is to directions under the Employment Tribunals Act 1996 s 7A(A1) (see the text and note 1) or s 7A(1)(a) (see head (a) in the text).

9 Employment Tribunals Act 1996 s 7A(2) (as added (see note 1); amended by the Tribunals, Courts and Enforcement Act 2007 Sch 8 paras 35, 41(1), (4)). The reference to directions is to directions made under the Employment Tribunals Act 1996 s 7A(A1) (see the text and note 1) or s 7A(1)(a) (see head (a) in the text).

10 As to the meaning of 'President' see PARA 1399 note 7.

11 As to the meaning of 'tribunal' see PARA 1399 note 8.

12 Ie the Employment Tribunals (Constitution and Rules of Procedure) Regulations 2013, SI 2013/1237, including Schs 1–3.

13 As to the meaning of 'employment judge' see PARA 1401 note 3.

14 See the Employment Tribunals (Constitution and Rules of Procedure) Regulations 2013, SI 2013/1237, reg 11(1).

15 Employment Tribunals (Constitution and Rules of Procedure) Regulations 2013, SI 2013/1237, reg 11(2).

16 Employment Tribunals (Constitution and Rules of Procedure) Regulations 2013, SI 2013/1237, reg 11(3). Practice directions made by the President under reg 11 are published on the government's Justice website (whose address, at the date at which this volume states the law, is

to be found at: *http://www.justice.gov.uk*): see eg *Presidential Practice Direction—Presentation of Claims* (July 2013); *Presidential Practice Direction—Addresses for Serving documents in Special Cases* (December 2013).

1413. Power to make practice directions regarding mediation. Employment tribunal procedure regulations[1] may include provision enabling practice directions[2] to provide for members[3] to act as mediators[4] in relation to disputed matters in a case that is the subject of proceedings[5]. Before making a practice direction that makes provision in relation to mediation, the person making the direction must consult the Advisory, Conciliation and Arbitration Service ('ACAS')[6].

The provision that may thus[7] be included in employment tribunal procedure regulations includes provision for enabling practice directions to provide for a member to act as mediator in relation to disputed matters in a case even though the member has been selected to decide matters in the case[8]. Once a member has begun to act as mediator in relation to a disputed matter in a case that is the subject of proceedings, the member may decide matters in the case only with the consent of the parties[9].

1 As to the meaning of 'employment tribunal procedure regulations' see PARA 1410.
2 For these purposes, 'practice direction' means a direction under the Employment Tribunals Act 1996 s 7A (see PARA 1412): s 7B(6) (s 7B added by the Tribunals, Courts and Enforcement Act 2007 Sch 8 paras 35, 42).
3 For these purposes, 'member' means a member of a panel of members of employment tribunals, whether or not a panel of employment judges: Employment Tribunals Act 1996 s 7B(6) (as added (see note 2); definition amended by the Crime and Courts Act 2013 s 21(4), Sch 14 Pt 7 para 13(e)). As to the meaning of 'employment judge' see PARA 1401 note 3; and as to the meaning of 'panel of employment judges' see PARA 1401 head (1).
4 Staff appointed under the Tribunals, Courts and Enforcement Act 2007 s 40(1) (staff for employment and other tribunals) (see COURTS AND TRIBUNALS vol 24 (2010) PARA 869) may, subject to their terms of appointment, act as mediators in relation to disputed matters in a case that is the subject of proceedings: Employment Tribunals Act 1996 s 7B(4) (as added: see note 2).
5 Employment Tribunals Act 1996 s 7B(1) (as added: see note 2). For these purposes, 'proceedings' means proceedings before an employment tribunal: s 7B(6) (as so added).
6 Employment Tribunals Act 1996 s 7B(5) (as added (see note 2); amended by the Enterprise and Regulatory Reform Act 2013 s 7(2), Sch 1 paras 2, 4). As to the constitution and powers of ACAS see PARA 1213 et seq.
7 Ie by virtue of the Employment Tribunals Act 1996 s 7B(1): see the text and notes 1–5.
8 Employment Tribunals Act 1996 s 7B(2) (as added: see note 2).
9 Employment Tribunals Act 1996 s 7B(3) (as added: see note 2).

1414. Power to make provision for pre-hearing reviews and preliminary matters. Employment tribunal procedure regulations[1] may include provision:

(1) for authorising the carrying out by an employment tribunal of a preliminary consideration of proceedings before it (a 'pre-hearing review')[2];

(2) for enabling such powers to be exercised in connection with a pre-hearing review as may be prescribed by the regulations[3].

Such regulations may, in particular, include provision:

(a) for authorising any tribunal carrying out a pre-hearing review under the regulations to make, in circumstances specified in the regulations, an order requiring a party to the proceedings in question to pay a deposit[4] as a condition of continuing to participate in those proceedings, or pursuing any specified allegations or arguments; and

(b) for prescribing:

(i)   the manner in which the amount of any such deposit is to be determined in any particular case;

(ii)   the consequences of non-payment of any such deposit; and

(iii)   the circumstances in which any deposit, or any part of it, may be refunded to the party who paid it or be paid over to another party to the proceedings[5].

Employment tribunal procedure regulations may also include provision for authorising an employment tribunal to hear and determine separately any preliminary issue of a description prescribed by the regulations which is raised by any case[6].

1   As to the meaning of 'employment tribunal procedure regulations' see PARA 1410.

2   Employment Tribunals Act 1996 s 9(1)(a) (amended by the Employment Rights (Dispute Resolution) Act 1998 s 1(2)(a)). As from a day to be appointed, employment tribunal procedure regulations may include provision for authorising an employment tribunal to carry out a review of any proceedings before it at any time before a hearing held for the purpose of determining them (a 'pre-hearing review'): Employment Tribunals Act 1996 s 9(1)(a) (prospectively substituted by the Employment Act 2002 s 28(1), (2)). At the date at which this volume states the law, no such day had been appointed.

3   Employment Tribunals Act 1996 s 9(1)(b). Such regulations, so far as relating to striking out, may not provide for striking out on a ground which does not apply outside a pre-hearing review: s 9(2A) (added by the Employment Act 2002 s 28(1), (3)). As to striking out see PARA 1466. As to the making of regulations under the Employment Tribunals Act 1996 generally see PARA 162.

4   Ie of an amount not exceeding £1,000. The Secretary of State may from time to time by order substitute for the sum so specified (which was originally £500) such other sum as is specified in the order: Employment Tribunals Act 1996 s 9(3). As to the exercise of this power see note 5. As to the Secretary of State see PARA 5 note 21; and as to the making of orders under the Employment Tribunals Act 1996 generally see PARA 162.

5   Employment Tribunals Act 1996 s 9(2) (amended by the Enterprise and Regulatory Reform Act 2013 s 21(1), (2); and by SI 2012/149).

6   Employment Tribunals Act 1996 s 9(4) (amended by the Employment Rights (Dispute Resolution) Act 1998 s 1(2)(a), Sch 1 para 15).

1415. Power to make provision regarding confidential information. Employment tribunal procedure regulations[1] may enable an employment tribunal to sit in private for the purpose of hearing evidence from any person which, in the opinion of the tribunal is likely to consist of:

(1)   information which he could not disclose without contravening a prohibition imposed by or by virtue of any enactment;

(2)   information which has been communicated to him in confidence or which he has otherwise obtained in consequence of the confidence reposed in him by another person; or

(3)   information the disclosure of which would, for reasons other than its effect on negotiations with respect to any specified matters mentioned in the Trade Union and Labour Relations (Consolidation) Act 1992[2], cause substantial injury to any undertaking of his or in which he works[3].

1   As to the meaning of 'employment tribunal procedure regulations' see PARA 1410.

2   Ie any of the matters mentioned in the Trade Union and Labour Relations (Consolidation) Act 1992 s 178(2) (matters to which trade disputes relate): see PARA 1093.

3   Employment Tribunals Act 1996 s 10A(1) (s 10A added by the Employment Relations Act 1999 Sch 8 para 3). For these purposes, the reference to any undertaking of a person or in which he works is to be construed: (1) in relation to a person in Crown employment, as a reference to the national interest; (2) in relation to a person who is a relevant member of the House of Lords staff, as a reference to the national interest or, if the case so requires, the interests of the House of Lords; and (3) in relation to a person who is a relevant member of the House of Commons

staff, as a reference to the national interest or, if the case so requires, the interests of the House of Commons: Employment Tribunals Act 1996 s 10A(2) (as so added). As to the meaning of 'Crown employment' see PARA 163; as to the meaning of 'relevant member of the House of Lords staff' see PARA 164 note 3; and as to the meaning of 'relevant member of the House of Commons staff' see PARA 165 note 3. See further PARA 1466.

1416. Restriction of publicity in cases involving sexual misconduct.
Employment tribunal procedure regulations[1] may include provision:

(1) for cases involving allegations of the commission of sexual offences[2], for securing that the registration or other making available of documents or decisions is to be so effected as to prevent the identification of any person affected by or making the allegation;

(2) for cases involving allegations of sexual misconduct[3], enabling an employment tribunal, on the application of any party to proceedings before it or of its own motion, to make a restricted reporting order[4] having effect, if not revoked earlier, until the promulgation of the decision of the tribunal[5].

If any identifying matter is published or included in a relevant programme in contravention of a restricted reporting order:

(a) in the case of publication in a newspaper or periodical, any proprietor, any editor and any publisher of the newspaper or periodical;

(b) in the case of publication in any other form, the person publishing the matter; and

(c) in the case of matter included in a relevant programme any body corporate engaged in providing the service in which the programme is included, and any person having functions in relation to the programme corresponding to those of an editor of a newspaper,

is guilty of an offence and liable on summary conviction to a fine not exceeding level 5 on the standard scale[6]. Where a person is charged with such an offence it is, however, a defence to prove that at the time of the alleged offence he was not aware, and neither suspected nor had reason to suspect, that the publication or programme in question was of, or included, the matter in question[7].

Where such an offence committed by a body corporate is proved to have been committed with the consent or connivance of, or to be attributable to any neglect on the part of a director[8], manager, secretary or other similar officer of the body corporate, or a person purporting to act in any such capacity, he as well as the body corporate is guilty of the offence and liable to be proceeded against and punished accordingly[9].

1 As to the meaning of 'employment tribunal procedure regulations' see PARA 1410.
2 For these purposes, 'sexual offence' means any offence to which the Sexual Offences (Amendment) Act 1976 s 4 (repealed) or the Sexual Offences (Amendment) Act 1992 (see CRIMINAL LAW vol 25 (2010) PARA 270 et seq) applies: Employment Tribunals Act 1996 s 11(6).
3 For these purposes, 'sexual misconduct' means the commission of a sexual offence, sexual harassment or other adverse conduct, of whatever nature, related to sex; and conduct is related to sex whether the relationship with sex lies in the character of the conduct or in its having reference to the sex or sexual orientation of the person at whom the conduct is directed: Employment Tribunals Act 1996 s 11(6).
4 For these purposes, 'restricted reporting order' means an order: (1) made in the exercise of a power conferred by regulations made by virtue of the Employment Tribunals Act 1996 s 11; and (2) prohibiting the publication in Great Britain of identifying matter in a written publication available to the public or its inclusion in a relevant programme for reception in Great Britain: s 11(6). 'Identifying matter', in relation to any person, means any matter likely to lead members of the public to identify him as a person affected by, or as the person making, the allegation: s 11(6). 'Written publication' and 'relevant programme' have the same meanings as in the Sexual

Offences (Amendment) Act 1992 (see CRIMINAL LAW vol 25 (2010) PARA 271): Employment Tribunals Act 1996 s 11(6). As to the meaning of 'Great Britain' see PARA 2 note 12.

5 Employment Tribunals Act 1996 s 11(1) (amended by the Employment Rights (Dispute Resolution) Act 1998 s 1(2)(a)). As to the regulations made see the Employment Tribunals (Constitution and Rules of Procedure) Regulations 2013, SI 2013/1237, reg 13(1), Sch 1 r 50; and PARA 1472. As to the making of regulations under the Employment Tribunals Act 1996 generally see PARA 162.

6 Employment Tribunals Act 1996 s 11(2). As to the standard scale see SENTENCING AND DISPOSITION OF OFFENDERS vol 92 (2010) PARA 142.

7 Employment Tribunals Act 1996 s 11(3).

8 In relation to a body corporate whose affairs are managed by its members 'director', for these purposes, means a member of the body corporate: Employment Tribunals Act 1996 s 11(5).

9 Employment Tribunals Act 1996 s 11(4).

1417. Power to restrict publicity in disability cases. Employment tribunal procedure regulations[1] may include provision in relation to proceedings on a complaint under the Equality Act 2010[2] in which evidence of a personal nature[3] is likely to be heard by the employment tribunal hearing the complaint:

(1) enabling an employment tribunal, on the application of the complainant or of its own motion, to make a restricted reporting order[4] having effect, if not revoked earlier, until the promulgation[5] of the decision of the tribunal; and

(2) where a restricted reporting order is made in relation to a complaint which is being dealt with by the tribunal together with any other proceedings, enabling the tribunal to direct that the order is to apply also in relation to those other proceedings or such part of them as the tribunal may direct[6].

If any identifying matter is published or included in a relevant programme in contravention of a restricted reporting order:

(a) in the case of publication in a newspaper or periodical, any proprietor, any editor and any publisher of the newspaper or periodical;

(b) in the case of publication in any other form, the person publishing the matter, and

(c) in the case of matter included in a relevant programme, any body corporate engaged in providing the service in which the programme is included, and any person having functions in relation to the programme corresponding to those of an editor of a newspaper,

is guilty of an offence and liable on summary conviction to a fine not exceeding level 5 on the standard scale[7]. Where a person is charged with such an offence it is, however, a defence to prove that at the time of the alleged offence he was not aware, and neither suspected nor had reason to suspect, that the publication or programme in question was of, or included, the matter in question[8].

Where such an offence committed by a body corporate is proved to have been committed with the consent or connivance of, or to be attributable to any neglect on the part of a director[9], manager, secretary or other similar officer of the body corporate, or a person purporting to act in any such capacity, he as well as the body corporate is guilty of the offence and liable to be proceeded against and punished accordingly[10].

1 As to the meaning of 'employment tribunal procedure regulations' see PARA 1410.

2 Ie under the Equality Act 2010 s 120: see DISCRIMINATION vol 33 (2013) PARA 344.

3 For these purposes, 'evidence of a personal nature' means any evidence of a medical, or other intimate, nature which might reasonably be assumed to be likely to cause significant embarrassment to the complainant if reported: Employment Tribunals Act 1996 s 12(7).

4   For these purposes, 'restricted reporting order' means an order: (1) made in the exercise of a power conferred by regulations made by virtue of the Employment Tribunals Act 1996 s 12; and (2) prohibiting the publication in Great Britain of identifying matter in a written publication available to the public or its inclusion in a relevant programme for reception in Great Britain: s 12(7). 'Identifying matter' means any matter likely to lead members of the public to identify the complainant or such other persons, if any, as may be named in the order: s 12(7). 'Written publication' includes a film, a soundtrack and any other record in permanent form but does not include an indictment or other document prepared for use in particular legal proceedings: s 12(7). 'Relevant programme' means a programme included in a programme service, within the meaning of the Broadcasting Act 1990 (see BROADCASTING vol 4 (2011) PARA 507): Employment Tribunals Act 1996 s 12(7). As to the meaning of 'Great Britain' see PARA 2 note 12.

5   For these purposes, 'promulgation' has such meaning as may be prescribed by regulations made by virtue of the Employment Tribunals Act 1996 s 12: s 12(7). At the date at which this volume states the law, the Employment Tribunals (Constitution and Rules of Procedure) Regulations 2013, SI 2013/1237, do not define that term.

6   Employment Tribunals Act 1996 s 12(1), (2) (amended by the Employment Rights (Dispute Resolution) Act 1998 s 1(2)(a); the Equality Act 2010 Sch 26 Pt 1 paras 27, 30 (as added by SI 2010/2279)). As to the regulations made see the Employment Tribunals (Constitution and Rules of Procedure) Regulations 2013, SI 2013/1237, reg 13(1), Sch 1 r 50; and PARA 1472. As to the making of regulations under the Employment Tribunals Act 1996 generally see PARA 162.

7   Employment Tribunals Act 1996 s 12(3). As to the standard scale see SENTENCING AND DISPOSITION OF OFFENDERS vol 92 (2010) PARA 142.

8   Employment Tribunals Act 1996 s 12(4).

9   In relation to a body corporate whose affairs are managed by its members 'director', for these purposes, means a member of the body corporate: Employment Tribunals Act 1996 s 12(6).

10 Employment Tribunals Act 1996 s 12(5).

1418. Power to make provision for costs and expenses. Employment tribunal procedure regulations[1] may include provision:

(1)   for the award of costs or expenses[2];

(2)   for the award of any allowances payable to any persons[3] required for certain purposes of the Equality Act 2010 to prepare reports or to any other persons[4] as the Secretary of State may, with the consent of the Treasury, determine for the purposes of, or in connection with, their attendance at employment tribunals[5].

Such regulations may include provision:

(a)   authorising an employment tribunal to have regard to a person's ability to pay when considering the making of an award against him under such regulations[6];

(b)   for authorising an employment tribunal:

(i)   to disallow all or part of the costs or expenses of a representative of a party to proceedings before it by reason of that representative's conduct of the proceedings;

(ii)   to order a representative of a party to proceedings before it to meet all or part of the costs or expenses incurred by a party by reason of the representative's conduct of the proceedings;

(iii) to order a representative of a party to proceedings before it to meet all or part of any allowances payable by the Secretary of State[7] by reason of the representative's conduct of the proceedings[8];

(c)   for taxing or otherwise settling the costs or expenses referred to in heads (1) and (b)(ii) above and, in particular, for enabling the amount of such costs to be assessed by way of detailed assessment in the County Court[9].

In relation to proceedings on a complaint of unfair dismissal[10], where the employee[11] has expressed a wish to be reinstated or re-engaged which has been communicated to the employer[12] at least seven days before the hearing of the complaint, employment tribunal procedure regulations must include provision for requiring the employer to pay the costs or expenses of any postponement or adjournment of the hearing caused by his failure, without a special reason, to adduce reasonable evidence as to the availability of the job from which the complainant was dismissed, or of comparable or suitable employment[13].

1 As to the meaning of 'employment tribunal procedure regulations' see PARA 1410.
2 Employment Tribunals Act 1996 s 13(1)(a) (s 13(1) substituted, s 13(1A)–(1B) added by the Employment Act 2002 s 22(1)). See *Dionissiou-Moussaoui v Dean & Dean* (a firm) [2008] All ER (D) 36 (Nov), EAT (unsuccessful constructive unfair dismissal case not considered one in which powers to order costs should be exercised in favour of the employer). As to the regulations made see the Employment Tribunals (Constitution and Rules of Procedure) Regulations 2013, SI 2013/1237, reg 13(1), Sch 1 r 74 et seq; and PARA 1480.
3 Ie payable under the Employment Tribunals Act 1996 s 5(2)(c): see PARA 1405 head (c).
4 Ie payable under the Employment Tribunals Act 1996 s 5(3): see PARA 1405.
5 See the Employment Tribunals Act 1996 s 13(1)(b) (as substituted: see note 2). As to the regulations made see the Employment Tribunals (Constitution and Rules of Procedure) Regulations 2013, SI 2013/1237, reg 13(1), Sch 1 r 83; and PARA 1480. As to the making of regulations under the Employment Tribunals Act 1996 generally see PARA 162.
6 Employment Tribunals Act 1996 s 13(1A) (as added: see note 2). As to the regulations made see the Employment Tribunals (Constitution and Rules of Procedure) Regulations 2013, SI 2013/1237, reg 13(1), Sch 1 r 84; and PARA 1480.
7 Ie under the Employment Tribunals Act 1996 s 5(2)(c) or (3): see notes 3–4. As to the Secretary of State see PARA 5 note 21.
8 Employment Tribunals Act 1996 s 13(1B) (as added: see note 2). As to the regulations made see the Employment Tribunals (Constitution and Rules of Procedure) Regulations 2013, SI 2013/1237, reg 13(1), Sch 1 rr 80–83; and PARA 1480.
9 Employment Tribunals Act 1996 s 13(1C) (as added (see note 2); amended by the Crime and Courts Act 2013 s 17(5), Sch 9 Pt 3 para 52(1)(b), (2)). As to the regulations made see the Employment Tribunals (Constitution and Rules of Procedure) Regulations 2013, SI 2013/1237, reg 13(1), Sch 1 r 78; and PARA 1480. As to detailed assessment see CPR Pt 47; and CIVIL PROCEDURE vol 12 (2009) PARA 1779 et seq.
10 Ie proceedings under the Employment Rights Act 1996 s 111: see PARA 804.
11 As to the meaning of 'employee' see PARA 2.
12 As to the meaning of 'employer' see PARA 2.
13 Employment Tribunals Act 1996 s 13(2) (amended by the Employment Rights (Dispute Resolution) Act 1998 s 1(2)(a); the Employment Relations Act 1999 Sch 4 Pt III para 4(a)–(c), Sch 9). As to the regulations made see the Employment Tribunals (Constitution and Rules of Procedure) Regulations 2013, SI 2013/1237, reg 13(1), Sch 1 r 76(3); and PARA 1480.

1419. Power to make provision for payments in respect of preparation time.

Employment tribunal procedure regulations[1] may include provision for authorising an employment tribunal to order a party to proceedings before it to make a payment to any other party in respect of time spent in preparing that other party's case[2]; and if they include such provision as well as provision for the award of costs or expenses[3], they must also include provision to prevent an employment tribunal exercising its powers under both kinds of provision in favour of the same person in the same proceedings[4]; but this does not require the regulations to include provision to prevent an employment tribunal from making an order for payments in respect of preparation time[5] and an award of costs or expenses[6] that is limited to witnesses' expenses[7].

Regulations made in respect of payments for preparation time may include provision authorising an employment tribunal to have regard to a person's ability to pay when considering the making of an order against him under such regulations[8].

1 As to the meaning of 'employment tribunal procedure regulations' see PARA 1410.

2 Employment Tribunals Act 1996 s 13A(1) (s 13A added by the Employment Act 2002 s 22(2)). As to the regulations made see the Employment Tribunals (Constitution and Rules of Procedure) Regulations 2013, SI 2013/1237, reg 13(1), Sch 1 r 75 et seq ; and PARA 1480. As to the making of regulations under the Employment Tribunals Act 1996 generally see PARA 162.

3 Ie of the kind mentioned in the Employment Tribunals Act 1996 s 13(1)(a): see PARA 1418 head (1).

4 Employment Tribunals Act 1996 s 13A(3) (as added: see note 2). This is subject to s 13A(4) (see the text and notes 5–7): s 13A(3) (as so added: amended by the Enterprise and Regulatory Reform Act 2013 s 21(1), (3)(a)). As to the regulations made see the Employment Tribunals (Constitution and Rules of Procedure) Regulations 2013, SI 2013/1237, reg 13(1), Sch 1 r 75(3); and PARA 1480.

5 Ie an order of the kind mentioned in the Employment Tribunals Act 1996 s 13A(1): see the text and notes 1–2.

6 See note 3.

7 Employment Tribunals Act 1996 s 13A(4) (added by the Enterprise and Regulatory Reform Act 2013 s 21(1), (3)(b)).

8 Employment Tribunals Act 1996 s 13A(2) (as added: see note 2). As to the regulations made see the Employment Tribunals (Constitution and Rules of Procedure) Regulations 2013, SI 2013/1237, reg 13(1), Sch 1 r 84; and PARA 1480.

1420. Provision as to conciliation procedure. Employment tribunal procedure regulations[1] must include, in relation to employment tribunal proceedings in the case of which any enactment makes provision for conciliation:

(1) provisions requiring a copy of the application by which the proceedings are instituted, and a copy of any notice relating to it which is lodged by or on behalf of the person against whom the proceedings are brought, to be sent to a conciliation officer[2]; and

(2) provisions securing that the applicant and the person against whom the proceedings are brought are notified that the services of a conciliation officer are available to them[3].

If (a) a conciliation officer has taken action[4] in a case, and issues a certificate in writing stating that a settlement[5] has been reached in the case; and (b) all of the terms of the settlement are set out in a single relevant document[6], or in a combination of two or more relevant documents, the following applies[7]:

(i) any sum payable by a person under the terms of the settlement (a 'settlement sum') is[8] recoverable in England and Wales by execution issued from the County Court or otherwise as if the sum were payable under an order of that court[9];

(ii) a settlement sum is not recoverable under head (i) above if the person by whom it is payable applies for a declaration that the sum would not be recoverable from him under the general law of contract, and that declaration is made[10];

(iii) if rules of court so provide[11], a settlement sum is not recoverable under head (i) above during the period beginning with the issue of the certificate, and ending at such time as may be specified in, or determined under, rules of court[12];

(iv) if the terms of the settlement provide for the person to whom a settlement sum is payable to do anything in addition to discontinuing or not starting proceedings, that sum is recoverable by him under head (i) above in England and Wales only if the County Court so orders[13].

Once an application has been made for a declaration under head (ii) above in relation to a sum, no further reliance may be placed on head (i) above for the recovery of the sum while the application is pending[14]. An application for a declaration under head (ii) above may be made to an employment tribunal or the County Court[15].

Employment tribunal procedure regulations may, in particular, make provision as to the time within which an application to an employment tribunal for a declaration under head (ii) above is to be made[16]. Nothing in these provisions[17] is to be taken to prejudice any rights or remedies that a person otherwise has[18].

1 As to the meaning of 'employment tribunal procedure regulations' see PARA 1410.
2 For these purposes, 'conciliation officer' means an officer designated by the Advisory, Conciliation and Arbitration Service ('ACAS') under the Trade Union and Labour Relations (Consolidation) Act 1992 s 211 (see PARA 1214): Employment Tribunals Act 1996 s 42(1).
3 Employment Tribunals Act 1996 s 19(1) (amended by the Employment Rights (Dispute Resolution) Act 1998 s 1(2)(a); the Employment Act 2002 Sch 7 para 23(1), (3), Sch 8). As to the regulations made see the Employment Tribunals (Constitution and Rules of Procedure) Regulations 2013, SI 2013/1237, reg 13(1), Sch 1 r 93; and PARA 1468. As to the making of regulations under the Employment Tribunals Act 1996 generally see PARA 162.
4 Ie action under any of the Employment Tribunals Act 1996 ss 18A–18C: see PARAS 152, 153.
5 For these purposes, 'settlement' (except in the phrase 'settlement sum') means a settlement to avoid proceedings or bring proceedings to an end: Employment Tribunals Act 1996 s 19A(12) (s 19A added by the Tribunals, Courts and Enforcement Act 2007 s 142; the Employment Tribunals Act 1996 s 19A(12) amended by the Enterprise and Regulatory Reform Act 2013 s 23(2)(b)).
6 A document is a 'relevant document' for these purposes if (1) it is the certificate; or (2) it is a document that is referred to in the certificate or that is referred to in a document that is within this provision: Employment Tribunals Act 1996 s 19A(2) (as added: see note 5).
7 Employment Tribunals Act 1996 s 19A(1) (as added (see note 5); amended by the Enterprise and Regulatory Reform Act 2013 ss 7(2), 23(2)(a), Sch 1 paras 2, 7.)
8 Ie subject to the Employment Tribunals Act 1996 s 19A(4)–(7).
9 Employment Tribunals Act 1996 s 19A(3)(a) (as added (see note 5); amended by the Enterprise and Regulatory Reform Act 2013 s 23(2)(a); the Crime and Courts Act 2013 Sch 9 Pt 3 para 52(1)(b), (2)).
10 Employment Tribunals Act 1996 s 19A(4) (as added (see note 5); amended by the Enterprise and Regulatory Reform Act 2013 s 23(2)(a)).
11 Rules of court may make provision as to (1) the time within which an application to the County Court for a declaration under the Employment Tribunals Act 1996 s 19A(4) (see head (ii) in the text) is to be made; (2) when an application (whether made to the County Court or an employment tribunal) for a declaration under s 19A(4) is pending for the purposes of s 19A(7) (see the text and note 14): s 19A(10) (as added (see note 5); amended by the Crime and Courts Act 2013 s 17(5), Sch 9 Pt 3 para 52(1)(b), (2)).
12 Employment Tribunals Act 1996 s 19A(5) (as added (see note 5); amended by the Enterprise and Regulatory Reform Act 2013 s 23(2)(a)).
13 Employment Tribunals Act 1996 s 19A(6)(a) (as added (see note 5); amended by the Enterprise and Regulatory Reform Act 2013 s 23(2)(a); the Crime and Courts Act 2013 s 17(5), Sch 9 Pt 3 para 52(1)(b), (2)).
14 Employment Tribunals Act 1996 s 19A(7) (as added: see note 5).
15 See the Employment Tribunals Act 1996 s 19A(8) (as added (see note 5); amended by the Crime and Courts Act 2013 s 17(5), Sch 9 Pt 3 para 52(1)(b), (2)).
16 Employment Tribunals Act 1996 s 19A(9) (as added: see note 5).
17 Ie in the Employment Tribunals Act 1996 s 19A: see the text and notes 4–16.
18 See the Employment Tribunals Act 1996 s 19A(11) (as added: see note 5).

D. RULES OF PROCEDURE MADE IN RELATION TO EMPLOYMENT TRIBUNALS

1421. Rules of procedure in employment tribunals; in general. The rules set out in Schedule 1 to the Employment Tribunals (Constitution and Rules of Procedure) Regulations 2013[1] apply to all proceedings before a tribunal[2] except where separate rules of procedure made under the provisions of any enactment are applicable[3]. Those rules are, however, modified in relation to proceedings which are national security proceedings[4] or proceedings[5] which involve an equal value claim[6].

The overriding objective of those rules is to enable employment tribunals[7] to deal with cases fairly and justly. Dealing with a case fairly and justly includes, so far as practicable:

(1)   ensuring that the parties are on an equal footing;

(2)   dealing with cases in ways which are proportionate to the complexity and importance of the issues;

(3)   avoiding unnecessary formality and seeking flexibility in the proceedings;

(4)   avoiding delay, so far as compatible with proper consideration of the issues; and

(5)   saving expense.

A tribunal must seek to give effect to the overriding objective in interpreting, or exercising any power given to it by, those rules. The parties and their representatives must assist the tribunal to further the overriding objective and in particular must co-operate generally with each other and with the tribunal[8].

1   Ie the Employment Tribunals (Constitution and Rules of Procedure) Regulations 2013, SI 2013/1237, Sch 1: see PARAS 1430, 1448, 1450, 1457, 1459; the text and notes 7–8; and PARA 1460 et seq.

2   As to the meaning of 'tribunal' see PARA 1399 note 8.

3   Employment Tribunals (Constitution and Rules of Procedure) Regulations 2013, SI 2013/1237, reg 13(1).

4   As to the meaning of 'national security proceedings' see PARA 1447 note 1.

5   Ie proceedings which involve an equal value claim as defined in the Employment Tribunals (Constitution and Rules of Procedure) Regulations 2013, SI 2013/1237, Sch 3 r 1: see PARA 1491 note 3.

6   See the Employment Tribunals (Constitution and Rules of Procedure) Regulations 2013, SI 2013/1237, reg 13(2), Schs 2, 3: and PARAS 1450, 1466, 1472, 1476, 1491–1494.

7   As to the meaning of 'employment tribunal' for these purposes see PARA 1448 note 14.

8   Employment Tribunals (Constitution and Rules of Procedure) Regulations 2013, SI 2013/1237, Sch 1 r 2. In *Goldman Sachs Services Ltd v Montali* [2002] ICR 1251, EAT, the overriding objective in the previous rules was used in order to hold that tribunals (in relation to interim orders) will follow similar principles to those spelt out in the Civil Procedure Rules.

(ii) Employment Appeal Tribunal

A. CONSTITUTION OF THE APPEAL TRIBUNAL

1422. Constitution of the Employment Appeal Tribunal. The Employment Appeal Tribunal (the 'Appeal Tribunal')[1] consists of:

(1)   such number of judges as may be nominated from time to time by the Lord Chief Justice[2], after consulting the Lord Chancellor[3], from the judges of the High Court and the Court of Appeal and the other specified judges[4];

(2)   at least one judge of the Court of Session nominated from time to time by the Lord President of that Court[5]; and

(3)   such number of other members as may be appointed[5] from time to time by Her Majesty on the joint recommendation of the Lord Chancellor and the Secretary of State ('appointed members')[6].

No judge is, however, to be nominated a member of the Appeal Tribunal under head (2) above except with his consent[7].

The Lord Chief Justice must appoint one of the judges nominated under the above provisions to be President of the Appeal Tribunal[8]. However the Lord Chief Justice must not make such an appointment[9] unless he has consulted the Lord Chancellor, and the Lord President of the Court of Session agrees[10].

1　The Employment Appeal Tribunal established under the Employment Protection Act 1975 s 87 (repealed) continues in existence: Employment Tribunals Act 1996 s 20(1). For these purposes, 'Appeal Tribunal' means the Employment Appeal Tribunal: s 42(1). As to the use of the abbreviation 'EAT' see PARA 1435 note 2.

　　As to the training, guidance and welfare of judges and other members of the Appeal Tribunal, and oaths, see PARA 1425.

2　As to the Lord Chief Justice see COURTS AND TRIBUNALS vol 24 (2010) PARA 842. The Lord Chief Justice may nominate a judicial office holder (as defined in the Constitutional Reform Act 2005 s 109(4)) (see COURTS AND TRIBUNALS vol 24 (2010) PARA 961 note 7) to exercise his functions under the Employment Tribunals Act 1996 s 22: s 22(5) (s 22(5), (6) added by the Constitutional Reform Act 2005 Sch 4 Pt 1 paras 245, 246(1), (5)).

3　As to the Lord Chancellor see CONSTITUTIONAL AND ADMINISTRATIVE LAW vol 20 (2014) PARA 255 et seq.

4　Ie the judges within the Employment Tribunals Act 1996 s 22(2A). A person is a judge within s 22(2A) if the person (1) is the Senior President of Tribunals; (2) is a deputy judge of the High Court; (3) is the Judge Advocate General; (4) is a Circuit judge; (5) is a Chamber President, or a Deputy Chamber President, of a chamber of the Upper Tribunal or of a chamber of the First-tier Tribunal; (6) is a judge of the Upper Tribunal by virtue of appointment under the Tribunals, Courts and Enforcement Act 2007 Sch 3 para 1(1) (see COURTS AND TRIBUNALS vol 24 (2010) PARA 896); (7) is a transferred-in judge of the Upper Tribunal (see s 31(2); and COURTS AND TRIBUNALS vol 24 (2010) PARA 866); (8) is a deputy judge of the Upper Tribunal (whether under Sch 3 para 7 or s 31(2): see COURTS AND TRIBUNALS vol 24 (2010) PARAS 866, 899)); (9) is a district judge, which here does not include a deputy district judge; or (10) is a District Judge (Magistrates' Courts), which here does not include a Deputy District Judge (Magistrates' Courts): Employment Tribunals Act 1996 s 22(2A) (added by the Crime and Courts Act 2013 s 21(4), Sch 14 Pt 5, para 11(1), (3)).

4　The Lord President of the Court of Session may nominate a judge of the Court of Session who is a member of the First or Second Division of the Inner House of that Court to exercise his functions under the Employment Tribunals Act 1996 s 22(3A)(b) (see head (2) in the text): s 22(6) (as added: see note 2).

5　The members so appointed must be persons who appear to the Lord Chancellor and the Secretary of State to have special knowledge or experience of industrial relations, either as representatives of employers or as representatives of workers (within the meaning of the Trade Union and Labour Relations (Consolidation) Act 1992): Employment Tribunals Act 1996 s 22(2). The Lord Chancellor's functions under s 22(1)(c) (see head (3) in the text), s 22(2) are protected functions under the Constitutional Reform Act 2005: see Sch 7 para 4 Pt A. As to the protected functions of the Lord Chancellor see CONSTITUTIONAL AND ADMINISTRATIVE LAW vol 20 (2014) PARA 261. As to the tenure of office of such members see PARA 1423.

6　Employment Tribunals Act 1996 ss 22(1), 42(1) (s 22(1) amended by the Constitutional Reform Act 2005 Sch 4 Pt 1 paras 245, 246(1), (2), Sch 18 Pt 2; the Crime and Courts Act 2013 s 21(4), Sch 14 Pt 5 para 11(1), (2)). As to temporary membership of the tribunal see PARA 1424. As to the Secretary of State see PARA 5 note 21. The practice whereby part-time judges in the Employment Appeal Tribunal might appear as counsel before a tribunal, having previously sat with one or more lay members of the bench hearing the appeal, should be discontinued, as a fair-minded and informed observer, having considered the given facts, would conclude that there was a real possibility that the lay member might be subconsciously biased: *Lawal v Northern Spirit Ltd* [2003] UKHL 35, [2004] 1 All ER 187, [2003] ICR 856. See also PARA 1497.

　　Any recommendation for appointment to the office of member of the Employment Appeal Tribunal in exercise of the function under the Employment Tribunals Act 1996 s 22(1)(c) (see head (3) in the text) must be made, by virtue of the Constitutional Reform Act 2005 s 85, Sch 14 Pt 1, in accordance with ss 85–93, 96: see COURTS AND TRIBUNALS vol 24 (2010) PARAS 944–949.

7　Employment Tribunals Act 1996 s 22(4) (amended by the Crime and Courts Act 2013 s 21(4), Sch 14 Pt 5 para 11(1), (4)).

8　Employment Tribunals Act 1996 s 22(3) (amended by the Constitutional Reform Act 2005 Sch 4 Pt 1 paras 245, 246(1), (3)).

9　Ie under the Employment Tribunals Act 1996 s 22(3).

10　Employment Tribunals Act 1996 s 22(3A) (added by the Constitutional Reform Act 2005 Sch 4 Pt 1 paras 245, 246(1), (4)).

1423. Tenure of office of appointed members of the Appeal Tribunal. A
member of the Employment Appeal Tribunal (the 'Appeal Tribunal') appointed[1]

by Her Majesty on the joint recommendation of the Lord Chancellor[2] and the Secretary of State[3] (an 'appointed member') must hold and vacate office in accordance with the terms of his appointment[4].

An appointed member:

(1)   may at any time resign his membership by notice in writing addressed to the Lord Chancellor and the Secretary of State[5]; and

(2)   must vacate his office on the day on which he attains the age of 70[6].

If, after consultation with the Secretary of State, the Lord Chancellor is satisfied that an appointed member:

(a)   has been absent from sittings of the Appeal Tribunal for a period longer than six consecutive months without the permission of the President of the Appeal Tribunal[7]; or

(b)   has become bankrupt or had a debt relief order[8] made in respect of him or has made an arrangement with his creditors; or

(c)   is incapacitated by physical or mental illness; or

(d)   is otherwise unable or unfit to discharge the functions of a member,

the Lord Chancellor may declare his office as a member to be vacant and must notify the declaration in such manner as the Lord Chancellor thinks fit; and, when the Lord Chancellor does so, the office becomes vacant[9].

1   Ie a member appointed under the Employment Tribunals Act 1996 s 22(1)(c): see PARA 1422 head (3).

2   As to the Lord Chancellor see CONSTITUTIONAL AND ADMINISTRATIVE LAW vol 20 (2014) PARA 255 et seq.

3   As to the Secretary of State see PARA 5 note 21.

4   Employment Tribunals Act 1996 ss 25(1), 42(1). As to the training, guidance and welfare of judges and other members of the Appeal Tribunal, and oaths, see PARA 1425.

5   Employment Tribunals Act 1996 s 25(2)(a).

6   Employment Tribunals Act 1996 s 25(2)(b). Section 25(2)(b) is subject to the Judicial Pensions and Retirement Act 1993 s 26(4)–(6) (Lord Chancellor's power to authorise continuance of office up to the age of 75) (see COURTS AND TRIBUNALS vol 24 (2010) PARA 956): Employment Tribunals Act 1996 s 25(3).

7   As to the President of the Employment Tribunals (England and Wales) see PARA 1400.

8   Ie under the Insolvency Act 1986 Pt VIIA (ss 251A–251X): see BANKRUPTCY AND INDIVIDUAL INSOLVENCY vol 5 (2013) PARA 91 et seq.

9   Employment Tribunals Act 1996 s 25(4) (amended by SI 2012/2404). The Lord Chancellor may declare an appointed member's office vacant under the Employment Tribunals Act 1996 s 25(4) only with the concurrence of the appropriate senior judge: s 25(5) (s 25(5), (6) added by the Constitutional Reform Act 2005 Sch 4 para 249). The appropriate senior judge is the Lord Chief Justice of England and Wales, unless the member whose office is to be declared vacant exercises functions wholly or mainly in Scotland, in which case it is the Lord President of the Court of Session: Employment Tribunals Act 1996 s 25(6). As to the Lord Chief Justice see COURTS AND TRIBUNALS vol 24 (2010) PARA 842.

1424.   Temporary membership of Appeal Tribunal.   At any time when the office of President of the Employment Appeal Tribunal[1] (the 'Appeal Tribunal') is vacant, or the person holding that office is temporarily absent or otherwise unable to act as President of the Appeal Tribunal, the Lord Chief Justice[2] may nominate another judge[3] to act temporarily in his place[4].

At any time when a judge of the Appeal Tribunal nominated[5] is temporarily absent or otherwise unable to act as a member of the Appeal Tribunal, the Lord Chief Justice may nominate another judge who is qualified to be nominated[6] to act temporarily in his place[7]; and at any time when a judge of the Appeal Tribunal nominated[8] by the Lord President of the Court of Session is temporarily absent or otherwise unable to act as a member of the Appeal Tribunal, the Lord President may nominate another judge who is qualified to be nominated[9] to act temporarily in his place[10]. No judge is, however, to be nominated to act temporarily as a member of the Appeal Tribunal except with his consent[11].

At any time when an appointed member[12] of the Appeal Tribunal is temporarily absent or otherwise unable to act as a member of the Appeal Tribunal, the Lord Chancellor and the Secretary of State[13] may jointly appoint a person appearing to them to have the qualifications for appointment as an appointed member to act temporarily in his place[14].

Where (1) the Lord Chancellor thinks that it is expedient, after consulting the Lord Chief Justice, for a qualified person[15] to be appointed to be a temporary additional judge of the Appeal Tribunal in order to facilitate in England and Wales the disposal of business in the Appeal Tribunal; and (2) the Lord Chancellor requests the Lord Chief Justice to make such an appointment[16], the Lord Chief Justice may, after consulting the Lord Chancellor, appoint such a qualified person[17]. Such an appointment[18] is for such period, or on such occasions, as the Lord Chief Justice determines, after consulting the Lord Chancellor[19].

A person nominated or appointed to act temporarily in place of the President or any other member of the Appeal Tribunal has, when so acting, all the functions of the person in whose place he acts[20]; and a person appointed to be a temporary additional judge of the Appeal Tribunal has all the functions of a nominated[21] judge[22].

1   As to the President of the Employment Tribunals (England and Wales) see PARA 1400.
2   As to the Lord Chief Justice see COURTS AND TRIBUNALS vol 24 (2010) PARA 842. The functions conferred on the Lord Chief Justice by the Employment Tribunals Act 1996 s 23(1)–(5) (see the text and notes 3–11) may be exercised only after consulting the Lord Chancellor: s 23(6) (s 23(6)–(8) added by the Constitutional Reform Act 2005 Sch 4 Pt 1 paras 245, 247(1), (4)). The Lord Chief Justice may nominate a judicial office holder (as defined in the Constitutional Reform Act 2005 s 109(4)) (see COURTS AND TRIBUNALS vol 24 (2010) PARA 961 note 7) to exercise his functions under the Employment Tribunals Act 1996 s 23: s 23(8) (as so added). As to the Lord Chancellor see CONSTITUTIONAL AND ADMINISTRATIVE LAW vol 20 (2014) PARA 255 et seq.
3   Ie another judge nominated under the Employment Tribunals Act 1996 s 22(1)(a): see PARA 1422 head (1).
4   Employment Tribunals Act 1996 ss 23(1), 42(1) (s 23(1) amended by the Constitutional Reform Act 2005 Sch 4 Pt 1 paras 245, 247(1), (2)). As to the training, guidance and welfare of judges and other members of the Appeal Tribunal, and oaths, see PARA 1425.
5   Ie under the Employment Tribunals Act 1996 s 22(1)(a): see PARA 1422 head (1).
6   See note 5.
7   Employment Tribunals Act 1996 s 23(2)(a) (amended by the Constitutional Reform Act 2005 Sch 4 Pt 1 paras 245, 247(1), (3)).
8   Ie under the Employment Tribunals Act 1996 s 22(1)(b): see PARA 1422 head (2).
9   See note 8.
10 Employment Tribunals Act 1996 s 23(2)(b).
11 Employment Tribunals Act 1996 s 23(5).
12 As to the meaning of 'appointed member' see PARA 1422.
13 As to the Secretary of State see PARA 5 note 21.
14 Employment Tribunals Act 1996 s 23(3). The functions conferred on the Lord Chancellor by s 23(3) may be exercised only after consultation with the Lord Chief Justice: s 23(7) (as added: see note 2).
15 For the purposes of the Employment Tribunals Act 1996 s 24, 'qualified person' means a person who (1) is qualified for appointment as a judge of the High Court under the Senior Courts Act 1981 s 10 (see COURTS AND TRIBUNALS vol 24 (2010) PARA 842); or (2) has held office as a judge of the High Court or of the Court of Appeal: Employment Tribunals Act 1996 s 24(2) (amended by the Constitutional Reform Act 2005 Sch 4 Pt 1 paras 245, 248(1), (3), Sch 11 Pt 1 para 1(2)).

16 Employment Tribunals Act 1996 s 24(1) (s 24(1) substituted, s 24(1A), (1B) added by the Constitutional Reform Act 2005 Sch 4 Pt 1 paras 245, 248(1), (2)).

17 Employment Tribunals Act 1996 s 24(1A) (as added: see note 16). The Lord Chief Justice may nominate a judicial office holder (as defined in the Constitutional Reform Act 2005 s 109(4)) (see COURTS AND TRIBUNALS vol 24 (2010) PARA 961 note 7) to exercise his functions under the Employment Tribunals Act 1996 s 24: s 24(4) (added by the Constitutional Reform Act 2005 Sch 4 Pt 1 paras 245, 248(1), (4)).

18 Ie under the Employment Tribunals Act 1996 s 24.

19 Employment Tribunals Act 1996 s 24(1B) (as added: see note 16).

20 Employment Tribunals Act 1996 s 23(4).

21 See note 5.

22 Employment Tribunals Act 1996 s 24(3).

1425. Training, guidance and welfare of Appeal Tribunal members; oaths. The Senior President of Tribunals[1] is responsible, within the resources made available by the Lord Chancellor[2], for the maintenance of appropriate arrangements for the training, guidance and welfare of judges, and other members, of the Employment Appeal Tribunal, in their capacities as members of the Appeal Tribunal[3].

An appointee[4] must take the required oaths before (1) the Senior President of Tribunals; or (2) an eligible person[5] who is nominated by the Senior President of Tribunals for the purpose of taking the oaths from the appointee[6].

1 As to the Senior President of Tribunals see COURTS AND TRIBUNALS vol 24 (2010) PARA 867. As to the President of the Employment Tribunals (England and Wales) see PARA 1400.

2 As to the Lord Chancellor see CONSTITUTIONAL AND ADMINISTRATIVE LAW vol 20 (2014) PARA 255 et seq.

3 Employment Tribunals Act 1996 s 24A (added by the Tribunals, Courts and Enforcement Act 2007 Sch 8 paras 35, 44).

4 Ie a person (1) who is appointed under the Employment Tribunals Act 1996 s 22(1)(c) (see PARA 1422 head (3)) or s 23(3) (see PARA 1424 text and notes 12–14); or (2) who is appointed under s 24(1A) (see PARA 1424 text and note 17) and (a) falls when appointed within s 24(2)(a) (see PARA 1424 note 15 head (1)), but not s 24(2)(b) (see PARA 1424 note 15 head (2)); and (b) has not previously taken the required oaths after accepting another office: s 24B(1) (s 24B added by the Tribunals, Courts and Enforcement Act 2007 Sch 8 paras 35, 44). For these purposes, 'required oaths' means the oath of allegiance, and the judicial oath as set out in the Promissory Oaths Act 1868 (see CONSTITUTIONAL AND ADMINISTRATIVE LAW vol 20 (2014) PARAS 597–598): Employment Tribunals Act 1996 s 24B(5) (as so added).

5 A person is eligible for these purposes if one or more of the following applies to him: (1) he holds high judicial office as defined in the Constitutional Reform Act 2005 s 60(2) (see COURTS AND TRIBUNALS vol 24 (2010) PARA 645 note 2); (2) he holds judicial office as defined in s 109(4) (see COURTS AND TRIBUNALS vol 24 (2010) PARA 961 note 7); (3) he holds (in Scotland) the office of sheriff: Employment Tribunals Act 1996 s 24B(4) (as added: see note 4).

6 Employment Tribunals Act 1996 s 24B(2) (as added: see note 4). If the appointee is a member of the Appeal Tribunal appointed before the coming into force of s 24B, the requirement in s 24B(2) applies in relation to the appointee from the coming into force of s 24B: s 24B(3) (as so added).

1426. Organisation and sittings of the Appeal Tribunal. The Employment Appeal Tribunal (the 'Appeal Tribunal') is a superior court of record and has an official seal which must be judicially noticed[1].

The Appeal Tribunal must have a central office in London[2]. It may, however, sit at any time and in any place in Great Britain[3]; and it may sit, in accordance with directions given by the President of the Appeal Tribunal[4], either as a single tribunal or in two or more divisions concurrently[5].

The Lord Chancellor may by order provide for proceedings of a description specified in the order to be heard by a judge and either two or four appointed members[6]. A judge may direct that proceedings are to be heard by a judge and either two or four appointed members[7] or, with the consent of the parties, may direct that proceedings are to be heard by a judge and either one or three appointed members[8]. In proceedings heard by a judge and two or four appointed members, there must be an equal number of employer-representative members[9] and worker-representative members[10]. Otherwise, proceedings before the Appeal Tribunal are to be heard by a judge alone[11].

1 Employment Tribunals Act 1996 ss 20(3), 42(1).

2 Employment Tribunals Act 1996 s 20(2). Section 20(2) is subject to (1) the Transnational Information and Consultation of Employees Regulations 1999, SI 1999/3323, reg 34 (see PARA 1279); (2) the European Public Limited-Liability Company Regulations 2004, SI 2004/2326, reg 46(1) (revoked (conciliation)); (3) the Information and Consultation of Employees Regulations 2004, SI 2004/3426, reg 36(1) (see PARA 1315); (4) the European Cooperative Society (Involvement of Employees) Regulations 2006, SI 2006/2059, reg 37(1) (see PARA 1338); (5) the Companies (Cross-Border Mergers) Regulations 2007, SI 2007/2974, reg 58(1) (see COMPANIES vol 15 (2009) PARA 1451); and (6) the European Public Limited-Liability Company (Employee Involvement) (Great Britain) Regulations 2009, SI 2009/2401, reg 33(1) (sic) (amendment of the Employment Tribunals Act 1996 s 18 (conciliation: see PARA 152)): Employment Tribunals Act 1996 s 20(4) (added by SI 1999/3323; amended by SI 2004/3426; SI 2004/2326; SI 2006/2059; SI 2007/2974; SI 2009/2401); Interpretation Act 1978 s 17(2).

3 Employment Tribunals Act 1996 s 20(2). As to the meaning of 'Great Britain' see PARA 2 note 12.

4 As to the President of the Employment Tribunals (England and Wales) see PARA 1400.

5 Employment Tribunals Act 1996 s 28(1). Section 29A(6) (Senior President of Tribunals and the Lord Chancellor to approve directions: see PARA 1435 note 3) does not apply to directions under s 28(1): s 29A(10) (added by the Tribunals, Courts and Enforcement Act 2007 Sch 8 paras 35, 47).

6 Employment Tribunals Act 1996 s 28(5) (s 28(2)–(4) substituted, and s 28(5)–(7) added, by the Enterprise and Regulatory Reform Act 2013 s 12(1), (2)). No order may be so made unless a draft of the order has been laid before Parliament and approved by resolution of each House of Parliament: Employment Tribunals Act 1996 s 41(2) (amended by the Enterprise and Regulatory Reform Act 2013 s 12(1), (4)). At the date at which this volume states the law, no such order had been made. As to the meaning of 'appointed member' see PARA 1422 head (3). As to the Lord Chancellor see CONSTITUTIONAL AND ADMINISTRATIVE LAW vol 20 (2014) PARA 255 et seq.

7 Employment Tribunals Act 1996 s 28(3) (as substituted: see note 6).

8 Employment Tribunals Act 1996 s 28(4) (as substituted: see note 6). As to obtaining the parties' consent see *Practice Direction (Employment Appeal Tribunal—Procedure) 2013* [2014] IRLR 92 para 20.1. For a party to consent to a hearing by a judge and one appointed member, the party consenting must be made aware of whether the appointed member is representative of employers or employees: *de Haney v Brent MIND* [2003] EWCA Civ 1637, [2004] ICR 348.

9 'Employer-representative members' means appointed members whose knowledge or experience of industrial relations is as representatives of employers: Employment Tribunals Act 1996 s 28(7) (as added: see note 6).

10 Employment Tribunals Act 1996 s 28(6) (as added: see note 6). 'Worker-representative members' means appointed members whose knowledge or experience of industrial relations is as representatives of workers: s 28(7) (as so added).

11 See the Employment Tribunals Act 1996 s 28(2) (as substituted: see note 6). This is subject to s 28(3)–(6) (see the text and notes 6–10) and to any provision made by virtue of s 30(2)(f) or (2A) (see PARA 1431): s 28(2) (as so substituted).

1427. Remuneration and allowances etc for Appeal Tribunal members.

The Secretary of State[1] must pay:

(1) the appointed members[2] of the Employment Appeal Tribunal (the 'Appeal Tribunal'); and

(2) any person appointed to act temporarily in the place of an appointed member[3],

such remuneration and such travelling and other allowances as he may, with the approval of the Treasury[4], determine[5].

A person appointed to be a temporary additional judge of the Appeal Tribunal[6] must be paid such remuneration and allowances as the Lord Chancellor[7] may, with the approval of the Treasury, determine[8].

If the Secretary of State determines, with the approval of the Treasury, that this provision applies in the case of an appointed member, the Secretary of State must pay such pension, allowance or gratuity to or in respect of that person on his retirement or death, or make to the member such payments towards the provision of a pension, allowance or gratuity for his retirement or death as the Secretary of State may, with the approval of the Treasury, determine[9].

Where a person ceases to be an appointed member otherwise than on his retirement or death, and it appears to the Secretary of State that there are special circumstances which make it right for him to receive compensation, the Secretary of State may make to him a payment of such amount as the Secretary of State may, with the approval of the Treasury, determine[10].

1   As to the Secretary of State see PARA 5 note 21.
2   As to the meaning of 'appointed member' see PARA 1422.
3   As to the appointment of persons to act temporarily as appointed members see PARA 1424.
4   As to the Treasury see CONSTITUTIONAL AND ADMINISTRATIVE LAW vol 20 (2014) PARA 262 et seq.
5   See the Employment Tribunals Act 1996 ss 27(1), 42(1) (s 27(1) amended by the Tribunals, Courts and Enforcement Act 2007 Sch 8 paras 35, 45, Sch 23 Pt 1).
6   As to the appointment of temporary additional judges see PARA 1424.
7   As to the Lord Chancellor see CONSTITUTIONAL AND ADMINISTRATIVE LAW vol 20 (2014) PARA 255 et seq. The Lord Chancellor's functions under the Employment Tribunals Act 1996 s 27 are protected functions under the Constitutional Reform Act 2005: see Sch 7 para 4 Pt A. As to the protected functions of the Lord Chancellor see CONSTITUTIONAL AND ADMINISTRATIVE LAW vol 20 (2014) PARA 261.
8   Employment Tribunals Act 1996 s 27(2).
9   Employment Tribunals Act 1996 s 27(3).
10 Employment Tribunals Act 1996 s 27(4).

B.   JURISDICTION OF THE APPEAL TRIBUNAL

1428.   Jurisdiction of the Appeal Tribunal; in general.   An appeal lies to the Employment Appeal Tribunal[1] on any question of law[2] arising from any decision[3] of, or arising in any proceedings before, an employment tribunal under, or by virtue of:

(1)   the Trade Union and Labour Relations (Consolidation) Act 1992[4];
(2)   the Employment Rights Act 1996[5];
(3)   the Employment Tribunals Act 1996[6];
(4)   the National Minimum Wage Act 1998[7];
(5)   the Employment Relations Act 1999[8];
(6)   the Equality Act 2006[9];
(7)   the Pensions Act 2008[10];
(8)   the Equality Act 2010[11];
(9)   the Working Time Regulations 1998[12];
(10) the Transnational Information and Consultation of Employees Regulations 1999[13];
(11) the Part-time Workers (Prevention of Less Favourable Treatment) Regulations 2000[14];
(12) the Fixed-term Employees (Prevention of Less Favourable Treatment) Regulations 2002[15];
(13) the Merchant Shipping (Working Time: Inland Waterways) Regulations 2003[16];

(14) the European Public Limited-Liability Company Regulations 2004[17];

(15) the Fishing Vessels (Working Time: Sea-fishermen) Regulations 2004[18];

(16) the Information and Consultation of Employees Regulations 2004[19];

(17) the Schedule to the Occupational and Personal Pension Schemes (Consultation by Employers and Miscellaneous Amendment) Regulations 2006[20];

(18) the European Cooperative (Involvement of Employees) Regulations 2006[21];

(19) the Companies (Cross-Border Mergers) Regulations 2007[22];

(20) the Cross-border Railway Services (Working Time) Regulations 2008[23];

(21) the European Public Limited-Liability Company (Employee Involvement) (Great Britain) Regulations 2009[24];

(22) the Employment Relations Act 1999 (Blacklists) Regulations 2010[25];

(23) the Agency Workers Regulations 2010[26]; or

(24) the Merchant Shipping (Hours of Work) Regulations 2002[27].

In addition an appeal lies to the Appeal Tribunal from a determination or decision of the certification officer[28]:

(a) on a question of law relating to the exercise of his powers in relation to union registers of members[29], access to union accounts[30], exclusion of certain offenders from union office[31], union elections[32], political funds and ballots[33], trade union amalgamations[34] or breach of union rules[35];

(b) on a question of law or fact relating to the exercise of his powers in relation to the listing or certification as independent of trade unions[36], or the listing of employers' associations[37].

An appeal also lies to the Appeal Tribunal on a question of law from a declaration or order of the Central Arbitration Committee ('the CAC') under the provisions relating to European Works Councils[38].

The Employment Appeal Tribunal also has jurisdiction, in respect of matters other than appeals, which is conferred on it by or under the Trade Union and Labour Relations (Consolidation) Act 1992, the Employment Tribunals Act 1996 or any other Act[39].

An appeal may not be brought if there is in fact no real dispute between the parties, but where the parties are seeking instead to establish a point of principle[40], or challenge the tribunal's reasoning, the actual decision being accepted[41], or further a real dispute with some other body, such as the Revenue and Customs[42].

The tribunal may not substitute its own view of the facts on matters lying within the jurisdiction of an employment tribunal and must be prepared to uphold a tribunal decision, as being not incorrect in law, even if it would itself have come to a different conclusion on the facts[43].

Unusually, the Appeal Tribunal has original jurisdiction to grant penalty notices in relation to certain provisions relating to European Works Councils[44].

Public funding is available for advocacy in proceedings in the Employment Appeal Tribunal, but only to the extent that the proceedings concern contravention of the Equality Act 2010[45].

The parties must expect any decision of fact made by an employment tribunal, the certification officer or the Central Arbitration Committee to be decisive[46]. It is not an error of law for a tribunal, a judge, the certification officer or the CAC to reach a decision which one party to the case thinks should have been differently made. The appeal is not a rehearing of the case, and the Appeal Tribunal must be shown to have made an error of law[47]. If a party is in any doubt about whether a point is one of law or not, legal advice should be sought. The Appeal Tribunal cannot and does not give legal advice to any party[48].

1 As to the procedure for bringing appeals see PARA 1495 et seq.
2 As to points of law and fact before the Employment Appeal Tribunal see PARA 1429.
3 It is the actual decision which must be under appeal, not just the reasons (for an otherwise favourable decision): *Harrod v Ministry of Defence* [1981] ICR 8, EAT. Hypothetical appeals will not, however, be entertained: see the text and notes 40–43.
4 See PARA 891 et seq.
5 See PARA 1406.
6 See PARAS 152 et seq, 1399 et seq, 1430 et seq.
7 See PARA 169 et seq.
8 See PARA 717 et seq.
9 See DISCRIMINATION vol 33 (2013) PARA 334 et seq.
10 See PERSONAL AND OCCUPATIONAL PENSIONS vol 80 (2013) PARA 737 et seq.
11 See DISCRIMINATION vol 33 (2013) PARA 1 et seq.
12 See PARA 268 et seq.
13 Ie the Transnational Information and Consultation of Employees Regulations 1999, SI 1999/3323: see PARA 1236 et seq.
14 Ie the Part-time Workers (Prevention of Less Favourable Treatment) Regulations 2000, SI 2000/1551: see PARA 74 et seq.
15 Ie the Fixed-term Employees (Prevention of Less Favourable Treatment) Regulations 2002, SI 2002/2034: see PARA 85 et seq.
16 Ie the Merchant Shipping (Working Time: Inland Waterways) Regulations 2003, SI 2003/3049: see SHIPPING AND MARITIME LAW vol 94 (2008) PARA 625.
17 Ie the European Public Limited-Liability Company Regulations 2004, SI 2004/2326: see COMPANIES vol 15 (2009) PARA 1633 et seq.
18 Ie the Fishing Vessels (Working Time: Sea-fishermen) Regulations 2004, SI 2004/1713: see SHIPPING AND MARITIME LAW vol 94 (2008) PARA 625.
19 Ie the Information and Consultation of Employees Regulations 2004, SI 2004/3426: see PARA 1289 et seq.
20 Ie the Occupational and Personal Pension Schemes (Consultation by Employers and Miscellaneous Amendment) Regulations 2006, SI 2006/349, Schedule: see PERSONAL AND OCCUPATIONAL PENSIONS vol 80 (2013) PARA 486.
21 Ie the European Cooperative (Involvement of Employees) Regulations 2006, SI 2006/2059: see PARA 1338.
22 Ie the Companies (Cross-Border Mergers) Regulations 2007, SI 2007/2974: see COMPANIES vol 15 (2009) PARA 1451.
23 Ie the Cross-border Railway Services (Working Time) Regulations 2008, SI 2008/1660: see RAILWAYS AND TRAMWAYS vol 86 (2013) PARA 328.
24 Ie the European Public Limited-Liability Company (Employee Involvement) (Great Britain) Regulations 2009, SI 2009/2401: see PARA 1317 et seq.
25 Ie the Employment Relations Act 1999 (Blacklists) Regulations 2010, SI 2010/493: see PARA 1037 et seq.
26 Ie the Agency Workers Regulations 2010, SI 2010/93: see PARA 97 et seq.
27 Employment Tribunals Act 1996 s 21(1) (amended by the Employment Rights (Dispute Resolution) Act 1998 s 1(2)(a), Sch 1 para 17(1), (2), Sch 2; the National Minimum Wage Act 1998 Sch 3; the Tax Credits Act 1999 Sch 3 para 5, Sch 6; the Tax Credits Act 2002 Sch 6; the Employment Relations Act 2004 s 38; the Equality Act 2006 Sch 3 para 57; the Pensions Act 2008 s 59; the Equality Act 2010 Sch 26 Pt 1 paras 27, 32, Sch 27 Pt 1 (as amended by SI 2010/2279); and by SI 1998/1833; SI 1999/3323; SI 2000/1551; SI 2002/2034; SI 2003/1660; SI 2003/1661; SI 2003/3049; SI 2004/1713; SI 2004/2326; SI 2004/3426; SI 2006/349; SI 2006/1031; SI 2006/2059; SI 2007/2974; and SI 2008/1660; SI 2009/2401; SI 2010/93; SI 2010/493; SI 2014/308). As to the Merchant Shipping (Hours of Work) Regulations 2002, SI 2002/2125, see SHIPPING AND MARITIME LAW vol 94 (2008) PARA 625.
   The Employment Tribunals Act 1996 s 21(1) does not affect any provision contained in, or made under, any Act which provides for an appeal to lie to the Employment Appeal Tribunal, whether from an employment tribunal, the certification officer or any other person or body, otherwise than on a question to which s 21(1) applies: s 21(3) (amended by the Employment Rights (Dispute Resolution) Act 1998 s 1(2)(a)). No appeal lies except to the Employment Appeal Tribunal from any decision of an employment tribunal under or by virtue of the Acts

listed, or the regulations referred to, in the Employment Tribunals Act 1996 s 21(1): s 21(2) (amended by the Employment Rights (Dispute Resolution) Act 1998 s 1(2)(a); and by SI 1998/1833).

28 As to the certification officer see PARA 1443 et seq.
29 See the Trade Union and Labour Relations (Consolidation) Act 1992 ss 25, 45D; and PARA 938.
30 See the Trade Union and Labour Relations (Consolidation) Act 1992 ss 31, 45D; and PARA 942.
31 See the Trade Union and Labour Relations (Consolidation) Act 1992 s 45C; and PARA 958.
32 See the Trade Union and Labour Relations (Consolidation) Act 1992 s 56A; and PARA 972.
33 See the Trade Union and Labour Relations (Consolidation) Act 1992 s 95; and PARA 997.
34 See the Trade Union and Labour Relations (Consolidation) Act 1992 s 104; and PARA 1011.
35 See the Trade Union and Labour Relations (Consolidation) Act 1992 s 108C; and PARA 918.
36 See the Trade Union and Labour Relations (Consolidation) Act 1992 s 9; and PARAS 902–903, 905–906.
37 See the Trade Union and Labour Relations (Consolidation) Act 1992 s 126; and PARAS 1084–1085.
38 See the Transnational Information and Consultation of Employees Regulations 1999, SI 1999/3323, reg 38(8); and PARA 1280.
39 Employment Tribunals Act 1996 s 21(4) (added by the Employment Rights (Dispute Resolution) Act 1998 Sch 1 para 17(1), (3)).
40 *IMI Yorkshire Imperial Ltd v Olender* [1982] ICR 69, EAT.
41 *Harrod v Ministry of Defence* [1981] ICR 8, EAT.
42 *Baker v Superite Tools Ltd* [1986] ICR 189, EAT. Likewise, an appeal will not lie simply on the basis that the parties agree that there was an error of law: *J Sainsbury plc v Moger* [1994] ICR 800, EAT.
43 *Retarded Children's Aid Society Ltd v Day* [1978] 1 WLR 763, [1978] ICR 437, CA; *Martin v Glynwed Distribution Ltd* [1983] ICR 511, [1983] IRLR 198, CA; *O'Kelly v Trusthouse Forte plc* [1984] QB 90, [1983] ICR 728, CA; *Spook Erection v Thackray* [1984] IRLR 116, Ct of Sess; *Neale v Hereford and Worcester County Council* [1986] ICR 471, sub nom *Hereford and Worcester County Council v Neale* [1986] IRLR 168, CA; *British Telecommunications plc v Sheridan* [1990] IRLR 27, CA; *Wakefield v HM Land Registry* [2009] All ER (D) 205 (Jan), EAT.
44 See the Transnational Information and Consultation of Employees Regulations 1999, SI 1999/3323, reg 20(7)–(8) (failure to establish a council or alternative machinery); and PARA 1269; reg 21(6)–(7) (disputes about operation of a council or alternative machinery); and PARA 1270.
45 See the Legal Aid, Sentencing and Punishment of Offenders Act 2012 Sch 1 Pt 3 para 20. See further LEGAL AID.
46 *Practice Direction (Employment Appeal Tribunal—Procedure) 2013* [2014] IRLR 92 para 2.1.
47 *Practice Direction (Employment Appeal Tribunal—Procedure) 2013* [2014] IRLR 92 para 2.2.
48 *Practice Direction (Employment Appeal Tribunal—Procedure) 2013* [2014] IRLR 92 para 2.3.

1429. Points of law and fact before the Appeal Tribunal. The restriction of appeals to those on points of law[1] is part of a deliberate policy to stress the primacy of tribunals on all questions of fact; and thus the approach of the courts, particularly the Court of Appeal, has been to construe the expression 'a point of law' narrowly, and not to allow appellants to dress up points of fact as points of law[2].

In order to maintain an appeal, the appellant must be able to show either: (1) that the tribunal misdirected itself in law in some way; or (2) that the tribunal's decision on the facts was perverse, that is to say that the decision was one no reasonable tribunal could have reached[3].

The following are examples of questions of fact:

(a) whether a person is employed under a contract of employment[4];
(b) whether a particular activity constitutes 'industrial action' in unfair dismissal law[5];
(c) whether an employee was constructively dismissed[6];
(d) whether an employee resigned[7];
(e) whether it was reasonably practicable to present a claim in time[8];

(f)   whether a requirement that discriminates indirectly against women is justifiable[9];

(g)   what is reasonable time off work[10].

Similarly, the Employment Appeal Tribunal is slow to interfere with an employment tribunal's assessment of compensation[11] or contributory fault[12].

The like restricted approach applies to appeals on procedural matters[13].

1   See PARA 1428.
2   See *Retarded Children's Aid Society Ltd v Day* [1978] 1 WLR 763, [1978] ICR 437, CA; *Hollister v National Farmers' Union* [1979] ICR 542, [1979] IRLR 238, CA; *Thomas and Betts Manufacturing Co Ltd v Harding* [1980] IRLR 255, CA; *Methven and Musiolik v Cow Industrial Polymers Ltd* [1980] ICR 463, [1978] IRLR 289, CA; *Pedersen v Camden London Borough Council* [1981] ICR 674, [1981] IRLR 173, CA; *Woods v WM Car Services (Peterborough) Ltd* [1982] ICR 693, [1982] IRLR 413, CA; *Hollier v Plysu Ltd* [1983] IRLR 260, CA; *O'Kelly v Trusthouse Forte plc* [1984] QB 90, [1983] ICR 728, CA; *Nethermere (St Neots) Ltd v Gardiner* [1984] ICR 612, sub nom *Nethermere (St Neots) Ltd v Taverna and Gardiner* [1984] IRLR 240, CA; *Palmer v Southend-on-Sea Borough Council* [1984] 1 All ER 945, [1984] ICR 372, CA; *Wakefield v HM Land Registry* [2009] All ER (D) 205 (Jan), EAT. The Employment Appeal Tribunal has a limited discretion to introduce a new point of law for want of adequate facts when the point could not have been fairly disposed of in previous proceedings: *Gloystarne & Co Ltd v Martin* [2001] IRLR 15, EAT. See also *Woodman v Monitus Ltd* [2005] All ER (D) 351 (Dec), EAT (transfer of undertaking).
3   *British Telecommunications plc v Sheridan* [1990] IRLR 27, CA, disapproving *Watling v William Bird & Son (Contractors) Ltd* (1976) 11 ITR 70 to the extent that it suggested a third ground, namely where a tribunal misunderstood or misapplied the facts. Likewise, interference on the weight to be given to particular evidence will not normally be permissible: *Post Office v Lewis* (1997) 141 Sol Jo LB 105, [1997] 18 LS Gaz R 32, CA; *Wade v Chief Constable of West Yorkshire Police* (1998) Times, 9 September, CA. If there is no evidence to support a particular finding of fact, that constitutes an error of law: *British Telecommunications plc v Sheridan* [1990] IRLR 27 at 30, CA, per Lord Donaldson MR. 'Perversity' is now construed narrowly: see *Neale v Hereford and Worcester County Council* [1986] ICR 471, sub nom *Hereford and Worcester County Council v Neale* [1986] IRLR 168, CA (see, in particular, at 483 and at 174 per May LJ); *Melon v Hector Powe Ltd* [1981] 1 All ER 313, [1981] ICR 43, HL; *Royal Society for the Protection of Birds v Croucher* [1984] ICR 604, [1984] IRLR 425, EAT; *Piggott Bros & Co Ltd v Jackson* [1991] IRLR 309, CA; cf *East Berkshire Health Authority v Matadeen* [1992] ICR 723, [1992] IRLR 336, EAT. See also *Yeboah v Crofton* [2002] EWCA Civ 794, [2002] IRLR 634 (ground of appeal based on perversity should always be fully particularised and ought only to succeed where an overwhelming case is made out); *Elmbridge Housing Trust v O'Donoghue* [2004] EWCA Civ 939, (2004) Times, 24 June, sub nom *O'Donoghue v Elmbridge Housing Trust* [2004] All ER (D) 126 (Jun); *Anglian Home Improvements Ltd v Kelly* [2004] EWCA Civ 901, [2005] ICR 242, [2004] IRLR 793; *Stanley v Capital Law LLP* [2009] All ER (D) 52 (Apr), EAT; *Wakefield v HM Land Registry* [2009] All ER (D) 205 (Jan), EAT. A tribunal can substitute reasons raised in proceedings for an employee's dismissal for other substantial reasons provided the difference between the reasons does not go to the facts and substance of the case: *Jocic v Hammersmith & Fulham London Borough Council* [2007] All ER (D) 443 (Oct), EAT. See also *Salford Royal NHS Foundation Trust v Roldan* [2010] EWCA Civ 522, [2010] IRLR 721, [2010] ICR 1457 (parties had been told that issues of liability and remedy would be heard together and any submissions going to liability should have been advanced at the initial stage; in any event, absent a formal application for a review of the finding of unfair dismissal, there had been no jurisdiction for the tribunal to revisit its conclusion that the dismissal was fair).

An appellant may not state as a ground of appeal simply words to the effect that 'the judgment or order was contrary to the evidence', or that 'there was no evidence to support the judgment or order', or that 'the judgment or order was one which no reasonable tribunal could have reached and was perverse' unless the notice of appeal also sets out full particulars of the matters relied on in support of those general grounds: *Practice Direction (Employment Appeal Tribunal—Procedure) 2013* [2014] IRLR 92 para 3.8. As to the notice of appeal see further PARAS 1495, 1498.

4   *O'Kelly v Trusthouse Forte plc* [1984] QB 90, [1983] ICR 728, CA; *Nethermere (St Neots) Ltd v Gardiner* [1984] ICR 612, sub nom *Nethermere (St Neots) Ltd v Taverna and Gardiner* [1984] IRLR 240, CA; *Lee v Chung* [1990] ICR 409, [1990] IRLR 236, PC. If the employment status depends on the construction of a governing document, the position may be otherwise: see

Davies v Presbyterian Church of Wales [1986] 1 All ER 705, [1986] ICR 280, HL, as explained in *Hellyer Bros Ltd v McLeod* [1987] 1 WLR 728, [1987] ICR 526, CA. Normally the documentation will be only one of several factors and the overall question will remain one of fact: *Carmichael v National Power plc* [1999] ICR 1226, [2000] IRLR 43, HL (distinguished in *Haggerty v St Ives Plymouth Ltd* [2008] All ER (D) 317 (May), EAT, where *O'Kelly v Trusthouse Forte plc* [1984] QB 90, [1983] ICR 728, CA and *Nethermere (St Neots) Ltd v Taverna and Gardiner* [1984] ICR 612, sub nom *Nethermere (St Neots) Ltd v Taverna and Gardiner* [1984] IRLR 240, CA were applied).

5 *Coates v Modern Methods and Materials Ltd* [1982] ICR 763, [1982] IRLR 318, CA; *Naylor v Orton and Smith Ltd* [1983] ICR 665, [1983] IRLR 233, EAT; and see PARA 1340.

6 *Pedersen v Camden London Borough Council* [1981] ICR 674n, [1981] IRLR 173, CA; *Woods v WM Car Services (Peterborough) Ltd* [1982] ICR 693, [1982] IRLR 413, CA. Where, however, constructive dismissal depends on whether a term is to be implied into a contract, especially a mobility term, it would seem that question is one of law: *Courtaulds Northern Spinning Ltd v Sibson* [1988] ICR 451, [1988] IRLR 305, CA, applying *O'Brien v Associated Fire Alarms Ltd* [1969] 1 All ER 93, [1968] 1 WLR 1916, CA. As to constructive dismissal see PARA 763.

7 *Martin v Glynwed Distribution Ltd* [1983] ICR 511, [1983] IRLR 198, CA; and see PARAS 722, 763.

8 *Palmer v Southend-on-Sea Borough Council* [1984] 1 All ER 945, [1984] ICR 372, CA (cited in PARA 1453 note 6).

9 *Home Office v Holmes* [1984] 3 All ER 549, [1984] ICR 678, EAT; *Greater Glasgow Health Board v Carey* [1987] IRLR 484, EAT. As to indirect discrimination see DISCRIMINATION vol 33 (2013) PARA 72.

10 *Thomas Scott & Sons (Bakers) Ltd v Allen* [1983] IRLR 329, CA; and see PARA 325 et seq.

11 *Fougère v Phoenix Motor Co Ltd* [1977] 1 All ER 237, [1976] ICR 495, EAT.

12 *Hollier v Plysu Ltd* [1983] IRLR 260, EAT; and see PARA 821.

13 *Medallion Holidays Ltd v Birch* [1985] ICR 578, [1985] IRLR 406, EAT, disapproving *British Library v Palyza* [1984] ICR 504, [1984] IRLR 306, EAT (procedural decision fully reviewable on appeal); *Adams v West Sussex County Council* [1990] ICR 546, [1990] IRLR 215, EAT; *Dietmann v London Borough of Brent, Wahlstrom v London Borough of Brent* [1987] IRLR 146, CA. *Adams v West Sussex County Council* [1990] ICR 546, [1990] IRLR 215, EAT was applied in *Smith v Chelsea Football Club plc* [2008] All ER (D) 111 (Aug), EAT. However, the Employment Tribunals Act 1996 s 21(1) (see PARA 1428) is not confined to questions of law to be found in the substantive decision itself and does not exclude a right of appeal where, due to excessive delay, there is a real risk that the litigant had been denied or deprived of the benefit of the right to a fair trial under the Convention for the Protection of Human Rights and Fundamental Freedoms (Rome, 25 March 1957; TS 1 (1973); Cmnd 5179), art 6(1) (incorporated into domestic law by the Human Rights Act 1998 Sch 1 Pt I art 6(1): see RIGHTS AND FREEDOMS vol 88A (2013) PARA 243 et seq) and where it would be unfair or unjust to allow the delayed decision to stand: *Bangs v Connex South Eastern Ltd* [2005] EWCA Civ 14, [2005] 2 All ER 316, [2005] IRLR 389 (delay in promulgating decision had not created a real risk that the employer had been deprived of the benefit of a full and fair trial).

As to the equally restricted approach in the modern case law to the giving of guidelines by higher courts see PARA 1445.

1430. Restrictions of vexatious proceedings. An application may be made by the Attorney General or the Lord Advocate to the Employment Appeal Tribunal (the 'Appeal Tribunal') for a restriction of proceedings order; and every such application must be made in writing[1] in, or substantially in, accordance with the prescribed form[2], accompanied by an affidavit in support, and must be served on the Appeal Tribunal[3]. On receipt of such an application, the registrar[4] must seal it with the Appeal Tribunal's seal and must serve a sealed copy on the Attorney General or the Lord Advocate, as the case may be, on the secretary of the Employment Tribunals[5] and on the person named in the application[6]. A person named in such an application who wishes to resist the application must, within 14 days of receiving the sealed copy of the application, enter an appearance in, or substantially in, accordance with the prescribed form[7], accompanied by an affidavit in support[8]. On receipt of the notice of appearance, the registrar must serve a copy of it on the Attorney General or the Lord Advocate, as the case may be[9]. The registrar must, as soon as practicable, give notice to the parties to such an application of the arrangements made by the Appeal Tribunal for hearing the application[10]; and any such notice must state the date appointed by the Appeal Tribunal by which any interim application must be made[11].

If, on an application made by the Attorney General or the Lord Advocate, the Appeal Tribunal is satisfied that a person has habitually and persistently and without any reasonable ground:

(1)   instituted vexatious proceedings, whether before the certification officer[12], in an employment tribunal or before the Appeal Tribunal, and whether against the same person or against different persons; or

(2)   made vexatious applications in any proceedings, whether before the certification officer, in an employment tribunal or before the Appeal Tribunal,

the Appeal Tribunal may, after hearing the person or giving him an opportunity of being heard, make a restriction of proceedings order[13].

A 'restriction of proceedings order' is an order that:

(a)   no proceedings are without the leave of the Appeal Tribunal to be instituted before the certification officer, in any employment tribunal or before the Appeal Tribunal by the person against whom the order is made;

(b)   any proceedings instituted by him before the certification officer, in any employment tribunal or before the Appeal Tribunal before the making of the order are not to be continued by him without the leave of the Appeal Tribunal; and

(c)   no application, other than one for leave[14], is to be made by him in any proceedings before the certification officer, in any employment tribunal or before the Appeal Tribunal without the leave of the Appeal Tribunal[15].

A restriction of proceedings order may provide that it is to cease to have effect at the end of a specified period, but otherwise it remains in force indefinitely[16].

Leave for the institution or continuance of, or for the making of an application in, any proceedings before the certification officer, in an employment tribunal or before the Appeal Tribunal by a person who is the subject of a restriction of proceedings order must not be given unless the Appeal Tribunal is satisfied:

(i)   that the proceedings or application are not an abuse of the process of the tribunal in question; and

(ii)   that there are reasonable grounds for the proceedings or application[17].

A copy of a restriction of proceedings order must be published in the London Gazette and the Edinburgh Gazette[18].

An employment tribunal may provide any information or documents requested by the Attorney General or the Lord Advocate for the purpose of preparing an application or considering whether to make an application under the above provisions[19].

Where the Attorney General, or Lord Advocate, makes a request to search for, inspect and take a copy of any relevant documents within a case file (including documents held electronically) for the purpose of preparing a relevant application[19] or considering whether to make such an application, the secretary must send notice of or a copy of any relevant document which relates to any proceedings before the tribunal, or any decision, order or award of the tribunal[20].

1   For these purposes, 'writing' includes writing delivered by means of electronic communication; and 'electronic communication' has the meaning given to it by the Electronic Communications Act 2000 s 15(1) (see CIVIL PROCEDURE vol 11 (2009) PARA 947): Employment Appeal Tribunal Rules 1993, SI 1993/2854, r 2(1) (definitions added by SI 2004/2526).

2   As to the prescribed form of application see the Employment Appeal Tribunal Rules 1993, SI 1993/2854, r 13, Schedule, Form 6 (amended by SI 2001/1128).

3   Employment Appeal Tribunal Rules 1993, SI 1993/2854, r 13 (as amended: see note 2).

4   For these purposes, 'registrar' means the person appointed to be registrar of the Appeal Tribunal and includes any officer of the Appeal Tribunal authorised by the President to act on behalf of the registrar: Employment Appeal Tribunal Rules 1993, SI 1993/2854, r 2(1) (substituted by SI 2001/1128). As to the meaning of 'President' see PARA 1451 note 4.

5   For these purposes, 'secretary of Employment Tribunals' means the person acting for the time being as the secretary of the Central Office of the Employment Tribunals (England and Wales) or, as may be appropriate, of the Central Office of the Employment Tribunals (Scotland): Employment Appeal Tribunal Rules 1993, SI 1993/2854, r 2(1) (substituted by SI 2001/1128).

6   Employment Appeal Tribunal Rules 1993, SI 1993/2854, r 14 (amended by the Employment Rights (Dispute Resolution) Act 1998 s 1(2)(b)).

7   As to the prescribed form of notice of appearance see the Employment Appeal Tribunal Rules 1993, SI 1993/2854, r 15, Schedule, Form 7 (Form 7 amended by SI 2001/1128).

8   Employment Appeal Tribunal Rules 1993, SI 1993/2854, r 15.

9   Employment Appeal Tribunal Rules 1993, SI 1993/2854, r 16.

10 Employment Appeal Tribunal Rules 1993, SI 1993/2854, r 17(1) (amended by SI 2001/1128; SI 2004/2526; SI 2010/1088).

11 Employment Appeal Tribunal Rules 1993, SI 1993/2854, r 17(2) (amended by SI 2004/2526).

12 For these purposes, 'certification officer' must be construed in accordance with the Trade Union and Labour Relations (Consolidation) Act 1992 s 254 (see PARA 1443): Employment Tribunals Act 1996 s 42(1) (definition added by the Employment Relations Act 2004 s 49(8)).

13 Employment Tribunals Act 1996 s 33(1) (amended by the Employment Rights (Dispute Resolution) Act 1998 s 1(2)(a); the Employment Relations Act 2004 s 49(1), (2), (3)). This power may be exercised even though the person's past proceedings have been against different respondents, and even though the proceedings have always been withdrawn after an unfavourable pre-hearing review: *A-G v Wheen* [2000] IRLR 461, EAT; affd [2001] IRLR 91, CA.

14 Ie under the Employment Tribunals Act 1996 s 33.

15 Employment Tribunals Act 1996 s 33(2) (amended by the Employment Rights (Dispute Resolution) Act 1998 s 1(2)(a); the Employment Relations Act 2004 s 49(1), (4)–(6)). Where an application is made for leave to institute or continue relevant proceedings by a person who has been made the subject of a Restriction of Proceedings Order pursuant to the Employment Tribunals Act 1996 s 33, that application will be considered on paper by a judge, who may make an order granting, refusing or otherwise dealing with such application on paper: *Practice Direction (Employment Appeal Tribunal—Procedure) 2013* [2014] IRLR 92 para 3.11. As to procedure see further PARA 1435 et seq.

16 Employment Tribunals Act 1996 s 33(3).

17 Employment Tribunals Act 1996 s 33(4) (amended by the Employment Rights (Dispute Resolution) Act 1998 s 1(2)(a); the Employment Relations Act 2004 s 49(1), (7)).

18 Employment Tribunals Act 1996 s 33(5).

19 See the Employment Tribunals (Constitution and Rules of Procedure) Regulations 2013, SI 2013/1237, Sch 1 r 102.

C. POWER TO MAKE APPEAL TRIBUNAL PROCEDURE RULES ETC

1431.   Power to make Appeal Tribunal procedure rules; in general. After consultation with the Lord President of the Court of Session, the Lord Chancellor[1] must make rules ('Appeal Tribunal procedure rules') with respect to proceedings before the Employment Appeal Tribunal (the 'Appeal

Tribunal')[2]. Subject to Appeal Tribunal procedure rules, and to directions[3], the Appeal Tribunal has power to regulate its own procedure[4].

Appeal Tribunal procedure rules may, in particular, include provision:

(1)   with respect to the manner in which, and the time within which, an appeal may be brought;

(2)   with respect to the manner in which any application or complaint to the Appeal Tribunal may be made;

(3)   for requiring persons to attend to give evidence and produce documents, and for authorising the administration of oaths to witnesses;

(4)   for requiring or enabling the Appeal Tribunal to sit in private in circumstances in which an employment tribunal is required or empowered[5] to sit in private; and

(5)   for interim matters arising on any appeal or application to the Appeal Tribunal[6] to be dealt with by an officer of the Appeal Tribunal[7].

Appeal Tribunal procedure rules may include provision for the award of costs or expenses[8]; and such rules may include provision:

(a)   authorising the Appeal Tribunal to have regard to a person's ability to pay when considering the making of an award against him under such rules[9];

(b)   for authorising the Appeal Tribunal:

　　(i)   to disallow all or part of the costs or expenses of a representative of a party to proceedings before it by reason of that representative's conduct of the proceedings;

　　(ii)   to order a representative of a party to proceedings before it to meet all or part of the costs or expenses incurred by a party by reason of the representative's conduct of the proceedings[10];

(c)   for taxing or otherwise settling the award of costs or expenses by the party[11] or by a representative of a party[12] and, in particular, for enabling the amount of such costs to be assessed by way of detailed assessment in the High Court[13].

1   As to the Lord Chancellor see CONSTITUTIONAL AND ADMINISTRATIVE LAW vol 20 (2014) PARA 255 et seq. The Lord Chancellor's functions under the Employment Tribunals Act 1996 s 30 (see the text and notes 2–7) are protected functions under the Constitutional Reform Act 2005: see Sch 7 para 4 Pt A. As to the protected functions of the Lord Chancellor see CONSTITUTIONAL AND ADMINISTRATIVE LAW vol 20 (2014) PARA 261.

2   Employment Tribunals Act 1996 ss 30(1), 42(1). 'Appeal Tribunal procedure rules' must be construed in accordance with s 30(1): s 42(1). At the date at which this volume states the law no such rules had been made but, by virtue of s 44, Sch 2 para 2 (see PARA 162), the Employment Appeal Tribunal Rules 1993, SI 1993/2854 (see PARAS 1430, 1495 et seq) have effect as if so made. As to the making of rules under the Employment Tribunals Act 1996 generally see PARA 162.

3   Ie directions under the Employment Tribunals Act 1996 s 28(1) (see PARA 1426) or s 29A(1) (see PARA 1435).

4   Employment Tribunals Act 1996 s 30(3) (amended by the Tribunals, Courts and Enforcement Act 2007 Sch 8 paras 35, 48). The Appeal Tribunal has power under this provision to anonymise a judgment and delete from the public record any matter that is likely to lead members of the public to identify the employee: see *A v B* [2010] IRLR 844, [2010] ICR 849, EAT, cited in PARA 1432.

5   Ie by virtue of the Employment Tribunals Act 1996 s 10A: see PARA 1415.

6   Ie for interim proceedings to be dealt with otherwise than in accordance with the Employment Tribunals Act 1996 s 28(2)–(4): see PARA 1426.

7   Employment Tribunals Act 1996 s 30(2) (amended by the Employment Rights (Dispute Resolution) Act 1998 s 1(2)(a); the Employment Relations Act 1999 Sch 8 para 5(1), (2); the Employment Relations Act 2004 Sch 1 para 26, Sch 2; the Enterprise and Regulatory Reform Act 2013 s 12(1), (3); and by SI 1999/3323. Appeal Tribunal procedure rules may make

provision of a kind which may be made by employment tribunal procedure regulations under the Employment Tribunals Act 1996 s 10(2), (5), (6) or (7) (see PARA 1448): s 30(2A) (s 30(2A)–(2C) added by the Employment Relations Act 1999 Sch 8 para 5(1), (3)). For these purposes: (1) the reference in the Employment Tribunals Act 1996 s 10(2) to s 4 is to be treated as a reference to s 28 (see PARA 1426); and (2) the reference in s 10(4) to the President or regional employment judge is to be treated as a reference to a judge of the Appeal Tribunal: s 30(2B) (as so added; amended by the Crime and Courts Act 2013 s 21(4), Sch 14 Pt 7 para 13(3). The Employment Tribunals Act 1996 s 10B (see PARA 1449) has effect in relation to a direction to or determination of the Appeal Tribunal as it has effect in relation to a direction or determination of an employment tribunal: s 30(2C) (as so added).

8 Employment Tribunals Act 1996 s 34(1) (s 34 substituted by the Employment Act 2002 s 23). By virtue of the Employment Tribunals Act 1996 s 44, Sch 2 para 2 (see PARA 162), the Employment Appeal Tribunal Rules 1993, SI 1993/2854, r 34 et seq (see PARAS 1525–1527) have effect as if so made.

9 Employment Tribunals Act 1996 s 34(2) (as substituted: see note 8). By virtue of s 44, Sch 2 para 2 (see PARA 162), the Employment Appeal Tribunal Rules 1993, SI 1993/2854, r 34B(2) (see PARA 1525) has effect as if so made.

10 Employment Tribunals Act 1996 s 34(3) (as substituted: see note 8). By virtue of the Employment Tribunals Act 1996 s 44, Sch 2 para 2 (see PARA 162), the Employment Appeal Tribunal Rules 1993, SI 1993/2854, r 34C (see PARA 1526) has effect as if so made.

11 Ie those costs or expenses referred to in the Employment Tribunals Act 1996 s 34(1): see the text and note 8.

12 Ie those costs or expenses referred to in the Employment Tribunals Act 1996 s 34(3)(b): see head (b)(ii) in the text.

13 Employment Tribunals Act 1996 s 34(4) (as substituted: see note 8). By virtue of s 44, Sch 2 para 2 (see PARA 162), the Employment Appeal Tribunal Rules 1993, SI 1993/2854, r 34B (see PARA 1525) has effect as if so made. As to detailed assessment see CPR Pt 47; and CIVIL PROCEDURE vol 12 (2009) PARA 1779 et seq.

1432. Restriction of publicity in cases involving sexual misconduct. Appeal tribunal procedure rules[1] may, as respects:

(1) proceedings on an appeal against a decision of an employment tribunal to make, or not to make, a restricted reporting order[2]; or

(2) proceedings on an appeal against any interim decision of an employment tribunal in proceedings in which the employment tribunal has made a restricted reporting order which it has not revoked,

include provision:

(a) for cases involving allegations of the commission of sexual offences[3], for securing that the registration or other making available of documents or decisions is to be so effected as to prevent the identification of any person affected by or making the allegation; and

(b) for cases involving allegations of sexual misconduct[4], enabling the Employment Appeal Tribunal (the 'Appeal Tribunal'), on the application of any party to the proceedings before it or of its own motion, to make a restricted reporting order having effect, if not revoked earlier, until the promulgation of the decision of the Appeal Tribunal[5].

If any identifying matter is published or included in a relevant programme in contravention of a restricted reporting order:

(i) in the case of publication in a newspaper or periodical, any proprietor, any editor and any publisher of the newspaper or periodical;

(ii) in the case of publication in any other form, the person publishing the matter; and

(iii) in the case of matter included in a relevant programme, any body corporate engaged in providing the service in which the programme is included, and any person having functions in relation to the programme corresponding to those of an editor of a newspaper,

Is guilty of an offence and liable on summary conviction to a fine not exceeding level 5 on the standard scale[6]. Where a person is charged with such an offence it is, however, a defence to prove that at the time of the alleged offence he was not aware, and neither suspected nor had reason to suspect, that the publication or programme in question was of, or included, the matter in question[7].

Where such an offence committed by a body corporate is proved to have been committed with the consent or connivance of, or to be attributable to any neglect on the part of a director[8], manager, secretary or other similar officer of the body corporate, or a person purporting to act in any such capacity, he as well as the body corporate is guilty of the offence and liable to be proceeded against and punished accordingly[9].

The above provisions do not apply where the Appeal Tribunal is considering an appeal against the substantive order of an employment tribunal, as opposed to such an appeal as is described in heads (1) and (2) above. On the face of it, therefore, the Appeal Tribunal has no power to make a permanent anonymity order affecting its own record, even in circumstances where the tribunal had been required to do so. This has been judicially described as producing 'a remarkable anomaly and a wholly unfair situation'[10]. However, both the statutory provisions and the common law provision are to be construed in the light of the right to respect for private and family life under the European Convention on Human Rights[11]. The effect of the Convention is that the Appeal Tribunal, exercising its statutory powers to regulate its procedure[12], ought in an appropriate case to confirm the steps already taken to protect the employee's identity by anonymising its judgment and by deleting from the public record any matter that is likely to lead members of the public to identify him[13].

1   As to the meaning of 'Appeal Tribunal procedure rules' see PARA 1431 note 2.
2   For these purposes, 'restricted reporting order' means: (1) in the Employment Tribunals Act 1996 s 31(1) (see heads (a)–(b) in the text) and s 31(3) (see the text and note 6), an order made in exercise of a power conferred by rules made by virtue of s 31 and prohibiting the publication in Great Britain of identifying matter in a written publication available to the public or its inclusion in a relevant programme for reception in Great Britain; and (2) in s 31(2) (see heads (1)–(2) in the text), an order which is a restricted reporting order for the purposes of s 11 (see PARA 1416): s 31(7). 'Identifying matter', in relation to a person, means any matter likely to lead members of the public to identify him as a person affected by, or as the person making, the allegation: s 31(8). 'Written publication' and 'relevant programme' have the same meanings as in the Sexual Offences (Amendment) Act 1992 (see CRIMINAL LAW vol 25 (2010) PARA 271): Employment Tribunals Act 1996 s 31(8). As to the meaning of 'Great Britain' see PARA 2 note 12.
3   For these purposes, 'sexual offence' means any offence to which the Sexual Offences (Amendment) Act 1976 s 4 (repealed) or the Sexual Offences (Amendment) Act 1992 (see CRIMINAL LAW vol 25 (2010) PARA 270 et seq) applies: Employment Tribunals Act 1996 s 31(8).
4   For these purposes, 'sexual misconduct' means the commission of a sexual offence, sexual harassment or other adverse conduct, of whatever nature, related to sex; and conduct is related to sex whether the relationship with sex lies in the character of the conduct or in its having reference to the sex or sexual orientation of the person at whom the conduct is directed: Employment Tribunals Act 1996 s 31(8).
5   Employment Tribunals Act 1996 ss 31(1), (2), 42(1) (s 31(2) amended by the Employment Rights (Dispute Resolution) Act 1998 s 1(2)(a)).
6   Employment Tribunals Act 1996 s 31(3). As to the standard scale see SENTENCING AND DISPOSITION OF OFFENDERS vol 92 (2010) PARA 142.
7   Employment Tribunals Act 1996 s 31(4).
8   In relation to a body corporate whose affairs are managed by its members 'director', for these purposes, means a member of the body corporate: Employment Tribunals Act 1996 s 31(6).
9   Employment Tribunals Act 1996 s 31(5).

10 *A v B* [2010] ICR 849, [2010] IRLR 844, EAT.

11 See the Convention for the Protection of Human Rights and Fundamental Freedoms (Rome, 25 March 1957; TS 1 (1973); Cmnd 5179), art 8 (incorporated into domestic law by the Human Rights Act 1998 Sch 1 Pt I art 8); and RIGHTS AND FREEDOMS vol 88A (2013) PARA 317 et seq.

12 Ie under the Employment Tribunals Act 1996 s 30(3): see PARA 1431.

13 See *A v B* [2010] ICR 849, [2010] IRLR 844, EAT; applied in *F v G* [2012] ICR 246, [2011] All ER (D) 42 (Dec), EAT.

1433. Restriction of publicity in disability cases. Appeal Tribunal procedure rules[1] may, as respects:

    (1) proceedings on an appeal against a decision of an employment tribunal to make, or not to make, a restricted reporting order[2]; or

    (2) proceedings on an appeal against any interim decision of an employment tribunal in proceedings in which the employment tribunal has made a restricted reporting order which it has not revoked,

include provision:

    (a) for enabling the Employment Appeal Tribunal (the 'Appeal Tribunal'), on the application of the complainant[3] or of its own motion, to make a restricted reporting order having effect, if not revoked earlier, until the promulgation[4] of the decision of the Appeal Tribunal; and

    (b) for, where a restricted reporting order is made in relation to an appeal which is being dealt with by the Appeal Tribunal together with any other proceedings, enabling the Appeal Tribunal to direct that the order is to apply also in relation to those other proceedings or such part of them as the Appeal Tribunal may direct[5].

If any identifying matter is published or included in a relevant programme in contravention of a restricted reporting order:

    (i) in the case of publication in a newspaper or periodical, any proprietor, any editor and any publisher of the newspaper or periodical;

    (ii) in the case of publication in any other form, the person publishing the matter; and

    (iii) in the case of matter included in a relevant programme, any body corporate engaged in providing the service in which the programme is included, and any person having functions in relation to the programme corresponding to those of an editor of a newspaper,

is guilty of an offence and liable on summary conviction to a fine not exceeding level 5 on the standard scale[6]. Where a person is charged with such an offence it is, however, a defence to prove that at the time of the alleged offence he was not aware, and neither suspected nor had reason to suspect, that the publication or programme in question was of, or included, the matter in question[7].

Where such an offence committed by a body corporate is proved to have been committed with the consent or connivance of, or to be attributable to any neglect on the part of a director[8], manager, secretary or other similar officer of the body corporate, or a person purporting to act in any such capacity, he as well as the body corporate is guilty of the offence and liable to be proceeded against and punished accordingly[9].

1 As to the meaning of 'Appeal Tribunal procedure rules' see PARA 1431 note 2.

2 For these purposes, 'restricted reporting order' means: (1) in the Employment Tribunals Act 1996 s 32(1) (see heads (1)–(2) in the text), an order which is a restricted reporting order for the purposes of s 12 (see PARA 1417); and (2) in s 32(2) (see heads (a)–(b) in the text) and in s 32(3) (see the text and note 6), an order made in exercise of a power conferred by rules made by virtue of s 32 and prohibiting the publication in Great Britain of identifying matter in a

written publication available to the public or its inclusion in a relevant programme for reception in Great Britain: s 32(7). 'Identifying matter' means any matter likely to lead members of the public to identify the complainant or such other persons, if any, as may be named in the order: s 32(8). 'Written publication' includes a film, a soundtrack and any other record in permanent form but does not include an indictment or other document prepared for use in particular legal proceedings: s 32(7). 'Relevant programme' means a programme included in a programme service, within the meaning of the Broadcasting Act 1990 (see BROADCASTING vol 4 (2011) PARA 507): Employment Tribunals Act 1996 s 32(7). As to the meaning of 'Great Britain' see PARA 2 note 12.

3   For these purposes, 'complainant' means the person who made the complaint to which the proceedings before the Appeal Tribunal relate: Employment Tribunals Act 1996 s 32(8).

4   For these purposes, 'promulgation' has the same meaning as may be prescribed by rules made by virtue of the Employment Tribunals Act 1996 s 32: s 32(7). See the Employment Appeal Tribunal Rules 1993, SI 1993/2854, r 23(9); and PARA 1517.

5   Employment Tribunals Act 1996 ss 32(1), (2), 42(1) (s 32(1) amended by the Employment Rights (Dispute Resolution) Act 1998 s 1(2)(a)). See eg *Flattley v Cleveland Police Authority, Cleveland Police Authority v Flattley* (2013) UKEATPA/0986/12/LA, UKEATPA/1021/12/LA, UKEAT/0619/12/LA, UKEAT/0620/12/LA (no statutory basis for making restricted reporting order as former order made at some stage in employment tribunal proceedings had lapsed and not been renewed; no compelling case under the Human Rights Act 1998 Sch 1 Pt I art 8 for anonymity in order to preserve claimant's privacy).

6   Employment Tribunals Act 1996 s 32(3). As to the standard scale see SENTENCING AND DISPOSITION OF OFFENDERS vol 92 (2010) PARA 142.

7   Employment Tribunals Act 1996 s 32(4).

8   In relation to a body corporate whose affairs are managed by its members 'director', for these purposes, means a member of the body corporate: Employment Tribunals Act 1996 s 32(6).

9   Employment Tribunals Act 1996 s 32(5).

1434.   Power to make order prescribing Appeal Tribunal fees.   The Lord Chancellor[1] may by order prescribe fees payable in respect of anything dealt with by the Employment Appeal Tribunal[2] or mediation conducted by Appeal Tribunal staff[3].

1   As to the Lord Chancellor see CONSTITUTIONAL AND ADMINISTRATIVE LAW vol 20 (2014) PARA 255 et seq.

2   See the Tribunals, Courts and Enforcement Act 2007 s 42(1)(d), which refers to 'an added tribunal'. The Employment Appeal Tribunals is an 'added tribunal' for these purposes: see the Added Tribunals (Employment Tribunals and Employment Appeal Tribunal) Order 2013, SI 2013/1892; and COURTS AND TRIBUNALS vol 24 (2010) PARA 871. See also the Employment Tribunals and the Employment Appeal Tribunal Fees Order 2013, SI 2013/1893, made in exercise of the powers conferred by the Tribunals, Courts and Enforcement Act 2007 ss 42(1)(d), (2), 49(3); and PARA 1496.

3   See the Tribunals, Courts and Enforcement Act 2007 s 42(1)(e), which refers to mediation by staff appointed under s 40(1); and COURTS AND TRIBUNALS vol 24 (2010) PARA 871. See also note 2.

D.   RULES OF PROCEDURE MADE IN RELATION TO EMPLOYMENT APPEAL TRIBUNALS

1435.   Employment Appeal Tribunal rules of procedure; in general.   The provisions of the Employment Tribunals Act 1996 and the Employment Appeal Tribunal Rules 1993[1] (the 'Rules') apply to the way appeals are handled at the Employment Appeal Tribunal[2], whenever those appeals were begun[3]. However, a failure to comply with any requirements of the Rules does not invalidate any proceedings unless the Appeal Tribunal[4] otherwise directs[5]. Where the Rules do not otherwise provide, the procedure in the Appeal Tribunal's own Practice Direction[6] will apply to all appeals to that tribunal[7].

The Appeal Tribunal has power[8] to regulate its own procedure[9] and, in so doing, regards itself as subject in all its actions to the duties imposed by the overriding objective of the Rules[10]. It will seek to apply the overriding objective when it exercises any power given to it by the Rules or interprets any Rule[11]. The overriding objective of the Rules and of the Appeal Tribunal's own Practice Direction is to enable the Appeal Tribunal to deal with cases justly[12].

Dealing with a case justly includes, so far as practicable:

(1) ensuring that the parties are on an equal footing[13];

(2) dealing with the case in ways which are proportionate to the importance and complexity of the issues[14];

(3) ensuring that it is dealt with expeditiously and fairly[15]; and

(4) saving expense[16].

Dealing with a case justly also includes safeguarding the resources of the Appeal Tribunal so that each case gets its fair share of available time, but no more[17]. The parties must assist the Appeal Tribunal to further the overriding objective[18]. The Appeal Tribunal may, if it considers that to do so would lead to the more expeditious or economical disposal of any proceedings or would otherwise be desirable in the interests of justice, dispense with the taking of any step required or authorised by the Rules, or may direct that any such steps be taken in some manner other than that prescribed by the Rules[19].

When exercising its functions, the Appeal Tribunal must ensure that information is not disclosed contrary to the interests of national security[20].

Where it is appropriate to the Appeal Tribunal's jurisdiction, procedure, unrestricted rights of representation and restricted costs regime, it is guided by the Civil Procedure Rules[21].

1 Ie the Employment Appeal Tribunal Rules 1993, SI 1993/2854.

2 As to the Employment Appeal Tribunal see PARA 1422 et seq. In *Practice Direction (Employment Appeal Tribunal—Procedure) 2013* [2014] IRLR 92 that Tribunal is referred to as the 'EAT' but in this title that abbreviation is only used in the notes and not in the text.

3 *Practice Direction (Employment Appeal Tribunal—Procedure) 2013* [2014] IRLR 92 para 1.2.
   Directions about the procedure of the Appeal Tribunal may be given (1) by the Senior President of Tribunals; or (2) by the President of the Appeal Tribunal: Employment Tribunals Act 1996 s 29A(1) (s 29A added by the Tribunals, Courts and Enforcement Act 2007 Sch 8 paras 35, 47). A power under the Employment Tribunals Act 1996 s 29A(1) includes power to vary or revoke directions given in exercise of the power, and power to make different provision for different purposes: s 29A(2) (as so added). Directions under head (1) above may not be given without the approval of the Lord Chancellor: s 29A(3) (as so added). Directions under head (2) above may not be given without the approval of (a) the Senior President of Tribunals; and (b) the Lord Chancellor: s 29A(4) (as so added). As to the President of Tribunals see PARA 1400; and as to the President of the Appeal Tribunal see PARA 1451 note 4. As to the Senior President of Tribunals see COURTS AND TRIBUNALS vol 24 (2010) PARA 867. As to the Lord Chancellor see CONSTITUTIONAL AND ADMINISTRATIVE LAW vol 20 (2014) PARA 255 et seq.
   Section 29A(1) does not prejudice any power apart from that provision to give directions about the procedure of the Appeal Tribunal: s 29A(5) (as so added). Directions may not be given in exercise of any such power as is mentioned in s 29A(5) without the approval of (i) the Senior President of Tribunals; and (ii) the Lord Chancellor: s 29A(6) (as so added). The provisions of s 29A(3), (4)(b) (see head (b) above) and (6)(b) (see head (ii) above) do not apply to directions to the extent that they consist of guidance about any of the following: (A) the application or interpretation of the law; (B) the making of decisions by members of the Appeal Tribunal: s 29A(7) (as so added). The provisions of s 29A(3), (4)(b), (6)(b) also do not apply to directions to the extent that they consist of criteria for determining which members of the Appeal Tribunal may be chosen to decide particular categories of matter; but the directions may, to that extent, be given only after consulting the Lord Chancellor: s 29A(8) (as so added). The provisions of s 29A(4), (6) do not apply to directions given in a particular case for the purposes of that case only: s 29A(9) (as so added). Section 29A(6) does not apply to directions under s 28(1) (see PARA 1426): s 29A(10) (as so added).

4 As to the meaning of 'Appeal Tribunal' for the purposes of the Employment Appeal Tribunal Rules 1993, SI 1993/2854, see PARA 1451 note 4.

5 Employment Appeal Tribunal Rules 1993, SI 1993/2854, r 39(1).

6 Ie *Practice Direction (Employment Appeal Tribunal—Procedure) 2013* [2014] IRLR 92, which came into force on 29 July 2013: para 1.1.
  The provisions of the Practice Direction are subject to any specific directions which the EAT makes in any particular case. Otherwise, the directions set out in the Practice Direction must be complied with in all appeals from employment tribunals. In national security appeals, and appeals from the Certification Officer and the Central Arbitration Committee, the Rules set out the separate procedures to be followed and the EAT will normally give specific directions: para 1.9. As to the Employment Tribunals Act 1996 s 29A (practice directions) see note 3.

7 *Practice Direction (Employment Appeal Tribunal—Procedure) 2013* [2014] IRLR 92 para 1.3.

8 Ie by the Employment Tribunals Act 1996 s 30(3) (see PARA 1431) but subject to the Rules.

9 *Practice Direction (Employment Appeal Tribunal—Procedure) 2013* [2014] IRLR 92 para 1.4. See *A v B* [2010] IRLR 844, [2010] ICR 849, EAT (Appeal Tribunal had the power to make a permanent anonymity order by regulating its own procedures to protect the identity of an employee), cited in PARA 1432.

10 Ie the Employment Appeal Tribunal Rules 1993, SI 1993/2854, r 2A: see the text and notes 12–18.

11 *Practice Direction (Employment Appeal Tribunal—Procedure) 2013* [2014] IRLR 92 para 1.4.

12 Employment Appeal Tribunal Rules 1993, SI 1993/2854, r 2A(1) (r 2A added by SI 2004/2526); *Practice Direction (Employment Appeal Tribunal—Procedure) 2013* [2014] IRLR 92 para 1.5. The existence of the 'overriding objective' does not mean the overturning of other detailed procedural rules such as the time limit for appealing: *Jurkowska v Hlmad Ltd* [2008] EWCA Civ 231, [2008] ICR 841, [2008] IRLR 430.

13 Employment Appeal Tribunal Rules 1993, SI 1993/2854, r 2A(2)(a) (as added: see note 12); *Practice Direction (Employment Appeal Tribunal—Procedure) 2013* [2014] IRLR 92 para 1.5.1.

14 Employment Appeal Tribunal Rules 1993, SI 1993/2854, r 2A(2)(b) (as added: see note 12); *Practice Direction (Employment Appeal Tribunal—Procedure) 2013* [2014] IRLR 92 para 1.5.2.

15 Employment Appeal Tribunal Rules 1993, SI 1993/2854, r 2A(2)(c) (as added: see note 12); *Practice Direction (Employment Appeal Tribunal—Procedure) 2013* [2014] IRLR 92 para 1.5.3.

16 Employment Appeal Tribunal Rules 1993, SI 1993/2854, r 2A(2)(d) (as added: see note 12); *Practice Direction (Employment Appeal Tribunal—Procedure) 2013* [2014] IRLR 92 para 1.5.4.

17 *Practice Direction (Employment Appeal Tribunal—Procedure) 2013* [2014] IRLR 92 para 1.6.

18 Employment Appeal Tribunal Rules 1993, SI 1993/2854, r 2A(3) (as added: see note 12); and see *Practice Direction (Employment Appeal Tribunal—Procedure) 2013* [2014] IRLR 92 para 1.7.

19 Employment Appeal Tribunal Rules 1993, SI 1993/2854, r 39(2). By virtue of r 39(2), the Appeal Tribunal has a discretion to hear an appeal in the absence of full reasons: *William Hill Organisation Ltd v Gavas* [1990] IRLR 488, CA; *Wolesley Centers Ltd v Simmons* [1994] ICR 503, EAT.

20 Employment Appeal Tribunal Rules 1993, SI 1993/2854, r 30 (substituted by SI 2001/1128). See further PARAS 1451, 1452.

21 *Practice Direction (Employment Appeal Tribunal—Procedure) 2013* [2014] IRLR 92 para 1.8. As to the Civil Procedure Rules see CIVIL PROCEDURE vol 11 (2009) PARA 30 et seq. So, for example, for the purpose of serving a valid notice of appeal under *Practice Direction (Employment Appeal Tribunal—Procedure) 2013* [2014] IRLR 92 para 3 and the Employment Appeal Tribunal Rules 1993, SI 1993/2854, r 3 (see PARA 1495), when an employment tribunal decision is sent to parties on a Wednesday, that day does not count and the notice of appeal must arrive at the Employment Appeal Tribunal on or before the Wednesday six weeks (ie 42 days) later: *Practice Direction (Employment Appeal Tribunal—Procedure) 2013* [2014] IRLR 92 para 1.8.1.

(iii) Employment Jurisdiction of Civil Courts

A. EMPLOYMENT JURISDICTION OF CIVIL COURTS; IN GENERAL

1436. Jurisdiction of civil courts in employment cases. Employment tribunals were established to exercise jurisdiction given by statute only[1]. Consequently the civil courts still exercise their jurisdiction in respect of:

(1) claims for breach of the contract of employment, including claims for wrongful dismissal[2];

(2) claims for an injunction or damages arising out of industrial action[3];

(3) claims seeking public law remedies in respect of certain dismissals[4]; and

(4) claims for personal injury arising from industrial accidents or diseases[5].

In the rare cases where an appeal from an employment tribunal does not lie to the Employment Appeal Tribunal, appeal lies instead to the High Court on a point of law[6].

No appeal lies except to the Employment Appeal Tribunal from any decision of an employment tribunal under or by virtue of the specified[7] statutory provisions[8].

If, however, any party to other proceedings before an employment tribunal is dissatisfied in point of law with any other decision of an employment tribunal, he may, according as rules of court may provide[9], either appeal from the tribunal to the High Court or require the employment tribunal to state and sign a case for the opinion of the High Court[10].

There is no separate industrial court in England and Wales. This means that disputes which are not reserved exclusively for the separate jurisdiction of employment tribunals[11] must go to the ordinary civil courts[12]. Certain statutory claims under the Trade Union and Labour Relations (Consolidation) Act 1992 are specifically made triable by the civil courts[13]. More particularly, industrial dispute cases are inherently within the jurisdiction of the civil courts because they are based on allegations by employers of common law torts committed by workers or their trade unions[14]. Thus, ordinary court procedures for claims for damages will apply, and ultimately court orders will be enforceable through the ordinary law of contempt of court[15]. However, in such cases, there are the following restrictions:

(a) the amounts that may be awarded in damages against trade unions are controlled[16];

(b) there are categories of protected property of a trade union which may not be seized to satisfy an order for damages[17];

(c) there are restrictions on the granting of without notice and interim injunctions[18]; and

(d) no injunction may be made obliging an employee to work[19].

1   See PARA 1399 note 3. As to the extension of that jurisdiction, in relation to termination of employment only, into common law claims based on the contract of employment see the Employment Tribunals Extension of Jurisdiction (England and Wales) Order 1994, SI 1994/1623; and PARAS 1408–1409. Certain common law claims during employment may be brought before a tribunal where the complaint can be cast in terms of an unlawful deduction from wages under the Employment Rights Act 1996 Pt II (ss 13–27): see PARA 254 et seq.

2   See PARA 1399 note 3.

3   See PARA 1342 et seq.

4   See PARA 827.

5   See TORT vol 97 (2010) PARA 672 et seq.

6   See PARA 1531.

7   Ie the Acts listed, or the regulations referred to, in the Employment Tribunals Act 1996 s 21(1): see PARA 1428.

8   See the Employment Tribunals Act 1996 s 21(2); and PARA 1428.

9   See PARA 1531.

10 Tribunals and Inquiries Act 1992 s 11(1), Sch 1 para 16 (Sch 1 para 16 amended by the Employment Tribunals Act 1996 Sch 1 para 9(1), (3)(a); the Employment Rights (Dispute Resolution) Act 1998 s 1(2)). There are a number of amendments to the Tribunals and Inquiries Act 1992 s 11(1) which do not affect the text to note 9 and this note. Section 11(1) does not apply in relation to proceedings before employment tribunals which arise under or by virtue of

any of the enactments mentioned in the Employment Tribunals Act 1996 s 21(1): Tribunals and Inquiries Act 1992 s 11(2)(a) (amended by the Employment Rights Act 1996 Sch 1 para 57; the Employment Tribunals Act 1996 Sch 1 para 9(1), (2); the Employment Rights (Dispute Resolution) Act 1998 s 1(2); the Abolition of Feudal Tenure etc (Scotland) Act 2000 s 22).

11 See PARA 1406.

12 For the purposes of the Trade Union and Labour Relations (Consolidation) Act 1992 Pt I (ss 1–121) (see PARA 891 et seq), the 'court', except where it is expressed to be to the County Court, means the High Court: s 121.

13 See the Trade Union and Labour Relations (Consolidation) Act 1992 s 16 (remedy against trustees for unlawful use of union property) (see PARA 923), s 26 (remedy for failure to keep register of members) (see PARA 939), s 31 (remedy for failure to comply with request for access) (see PARA 942), s 56 (failure to comply with election requirements for union office) (see PARA 973), s 62 (right to ballot before industrial action) (see PARA 1025); and s 81 (complaint of failure to hold a regular political resolution ballot) (see PARA 984).

14 See PARA 1343.

15 See PARA 1442.

16 See the Trade Union and Labour Relations (Consolidation) Act 1992 s 22; and PARA 1390.

17 See the Trade Union and Labour Relations (Consolidation) Act 1992 s 23; and PARA 928.

18 See the Trade Union and Labour Relations (Consolidation) Act 1992 s 221; and PARAS 1438–1439.

19 See the Trade Union and Labour Relations (Consolidation) Act 1992 s 236; and PARA 1348.

B. INJUNCTIONS

1437. Injunctions and the contract of employment. An injunction will not normally be granted if it would have the effect of indirectly enforcing a contract of employment, primarily on the ground of the personal nature of such a contract, but also on the ground that in normal circumstances it would be difficult or impossible to secure compliance[1].

In addition, and of more relevance in industrial dispute cases, it is specifically provided that a court may not compel an employee to do any work or attend at any place for the doing of any work[2].

1 See PARA 826.
2 See the Trade Union and Labour Relations (Consolidation) Act 1992 s 236; and PARA 1348.

1438. Injunctions without notice in trade dispute cases. Where an application for an injunction is made to a court in the absence of a party against whom it is sought or any representative of his, and he claims, or in the opinion of the court would be likely to claim, that he acted in contemplation or furtherance of a trade dispute[1], the court must not grant the injunction unless satisfied that all steps which in the circumstances were reasonable have been taken with a view to securing that notice of the application and an opportunity of being heard with respect to the application have been given to him[2].

1 As to the meaning of 'trade dispute' see PARAS 1360–1361; and as to the meaning of 'in contemplation or furtherance' of such a dispute see PARA 1362.

2 Trade Union and Labour Relations (Consolidation) Act 1992 s 221(1). A party seeking an injunction without notice must bring the provisions of s 221(1) to the court's notice: *Patrick Stevedores Operation Pty Ltd v International Transport Workers' Federation* [1998] 2 Lloyd's Rep 523. The question is whether such a claim would be made in good faith, not whether it would be successful: see *Gouriet v Union of Post Office Workers* [1978] AC 435, [1977] 3 All ER 70, HL. As to the procedure for applications for injunctions without notice see CIVIL PROCEDURE vol 11 (2009) PARA 334; and as to the procedure for granting injunctions generally see CIVIL PROCEDURE vol 11 (2009) PARA 331 et seq.

1439. Interim injunctions. Where an application for an interim injunction[1] is made to a court pending the trial of an action, and the party against whom it is sought claims that he acted in contemplation or furtherance of a trade dispute[2], the court must, in exercising its discretion[3] whether or not to grant the injunction, have regard to the likelihood of that party successfully establishing a statutory defence[4] at the trial[5].

1   As to interim injunctions generally see CIVIL PROCEDURE vol 11 (2009) PARA 334.
2   As to the meaning of 'trade dispute' see PARAS 1360–1361; and as to the meaning of 'in contemplation or furtherance' of such a dispute see PARA 1362.
3   An appeal court will be reluctant to interfere with the decision of the court of first instance in the exercise of such a discretion: *Hadmor Productions Ltd v Hamilton* [1983] 1 AC 191, [1982] ICR 114, HL.
4   Ie establishing any matter which would afford a defence under the Trade Union and Labour Relations (Consolidation) Act 1992 s 219 (protection from certain tort liabilities) (see PARAS 1359–1364) or s 220 (peaceful picketing) (see PARA 1385).
5   Trade Union and Labour Relations (Consolidation) Act 1992 s 221(2). The aim of this provision is to try to ensure that interim injunctions are not granted in industrial dispute cases too readily, under the normal rules in *American Cyanamid Co v Ethicon Ltd* [1975] AC 396, [1975] 1 All ER 504, HL (ie: (1) is there a serious issue to be tried? (2) where lies the balance of convenience?), but instead that there is at least some consideration of the merits in relation to the possible 'trade dispute' defences: *NWL Ltd v Woods, NWL Ltd v Nelson* [1979] 3 All ER 614, [1979] ICR 867, HL. However, the practical effectiveness of this provision is doubtful, for several reasons: (a) it only requires the court to 'have regard' to the likelihood of a trade dispute, which falls far short of making it a predominant factor (*NWL Ltd v Woods, NWL Ltd v Nelson* [1979] 3 All ER 614, [1979] ICR 867, HL; (b) there are dicta that a court may still grant an injunction (in spite of the likelihood of a trade dispute defence) where the consequences of the industrial action would be extreme, for the claimant or the public (*NWL Ltd v Woods, NWL Ltd v Nelson*; [1979] 3 All ER 614, [1979] ICR 867, HL, *Duport Steels Ltd v Sirs* [1980] 1 All ER 529, [1980] ICR 161, HL; *Express Newspapers Ltd v McShane* [1980] AC 672, [1980] ICR 42, HL; *Associated British Ports v Transport and General Workers' Union* [1989] 3 All ER 796, [1989] ICR 557, CA (revsd on other grounds [1989] 3 All ER 822, [1989] ICR 557 at 590, HL)); (c) although *NWL Ltd v Woods, NWL Ltd v Nelson* [1979] 3 All ER 614, [1979] ICR 867, HL considered the operation of this provision against the 'practical realities' that full trial of the claim was unlikely to occur and the interim stage was likely to be final, those realities changed in 1982 when the unions' complete immunity was abolished, so that now there can be a more realistic chance of a full claim going ahead against the union itself for damages, which weakens the need to deal more fully with the trade dispute defences at the interim stage (*Dimbleby & Sons Ltd v National Union of Journalists* [1984] 1 All ER 751, [1984] ICR 386, HL); (d) under the current legislation there are now so many ways in which a union may lose its trade dispute immunity (see PARAS 1365–1382) that it may find it correspondingly difficult to show the necessary 'likelihood' of the immunity defence succeeding; (e) moreover, on all matters other than that defence, the ordinary principles in *American Cyanamid Co v Ethicon Ltd* [1975] AC 396, [1975] 1 All ER 504, HL ('Is there a serious issue to be tried?') continue to apply (*Dimbleby & Sons Ltd v National Union of Journalists* 1984] 1 All ER 751 at 755, [1984] ICR 386 at 406, HL, per Lord Diplock). See also eg *Landmark Brickwork Ltd v Sutcliffe* [2011] EWHC 1239 (QB), [2011] IRLR 976; *Metroline Travel Ltd v Unite* [2012] EWHC 1778 (QB), [2012] IRLR 749, [2012] All ER (D) 185 (Jun); *Serco Ltd (t/a Serco Docklands) v National Union of Rail, Maritime and Transport Workers, London and Birmingham Railway Ltd (t/a London Midland) v Associated Society of Locomotive Engineers and Firemen* [2011] EWCA Civ 226 at [13], [2011] 3 All ER 913 at [13], [2011] ICR 848 at [13]; *Balfour Beatty Engineering Services Ltd v Unite the Union* [2012] EWHC 267 (QB), [2012] ICR 822, [2012] IRLR 452.

1440.   Pre-emptive injunctions; mandatory injunctions.   Subject to certain specific limitations[1], the ordinary rules on the granting of injunctions apply in industrial cases[2]. Thus, in addition to an injunction to prevent continuation of unlawful action[3], there can also be an injunction on a quia timet basis to restrain threatened unlawful action[4], including in interim proceedings. Where, however, the proceedings relate to the operation of a domestic tribunal (such as a trade union's disciplinary committee which is about to hear a complaint against the individual member seeking the injunction), a court will not normally act in advance of that tribunal's decision by making an order preventing the hearing of the complaint, unless there is clear evidence of inevitable impropriety in that hearing[5].

With regard to mandatory injunctions, courts are in general wary of making such orders[6], but will be particularly so in industrial cases (especially in interim proceedings) because of the danger of such an order doing more harm than good, or giving one side to the dispute a greater bargaining position than it would otherwise have[7].

1   See PARAS 1348, 1437–1438.
2   See generally CIVIL PROCEDURE vol 11 (2009) PARA 331 et seq.
3   Where an act is deemed to be that of a trade union by virtue of the statutory vicarious liability rules in the Trade Union and Labour Relations (Consolidation) Act 1992 s 20 (see PARA 1388), it is specifically provided that the power of the court to grant an injunction includes power to require the union to take steps to prevent any further inducement of persons to take part in industrial action: see s 20(6); and PARA 1388 text and notes 16–17.
4   As to quia timet injunctions see CIVIL PROCEDURE vol 11 (2009) PARA 362.
5   *Longley v National Union of Journalists* [1987] IRLR 109, CA (distinguishing *Esterman v National and Local Government Officers' Association* [1974] ICR 625); *McKenzie v National Union of Public Employees* [1991] ICR 155. A similar approach was taken in refusing to restrain pending disciplinary proceedings by an employer in *Ali v Southwark London Borough Council* [1988] ICR 567, [1988] IRLR 100. The court's discretion in this matter is distinct from the rules on the exhaustion of internal remedies and the statutory right not to be denied access to the court: see the Trade Union and Labour Relations (Consolidation) Act 1992 s 63; and PARAS 914–915.
6   As to mandatory injunctions see CIVIL PROCEDURE vol 11 (2009) PARA 332.
7   *Jakeman v South West Thames Regional Health Authority and London Ambulance Service* [1990] IRLR 62 at 66 per Auld J, applying *Harold Stephen & Co Ltd v Post Office* [1978] 1 All ER 939, [1977] 1 WLR 1172, CA, and *Parker v Camden London Borough Council* [1986] Ch 162, [1985] 2 All ER 141, CA. 'In these cases the forensic battle is often a small, though visible, part of a larger campaign': *MacPherson v Lambeth London Borough Council* [1988] IRLR 470 at 477 per Vinelott J.

C. INDUSTRIAL ACTION AFFECTING SUPPLY OF GOODS AND SERVICES

1441.   Industrial action affecting the supply of goods and services to an individual.   Where an individual claims that:

(1)   any trade union[1] or other person has done, or is likely to do, an unlawful act[2] to induce any person to take part, or to continue to take part, in industrial action; and

(2)   an effect, or a likely effect, of the industrial action is or will be to prevent or delay the supply[3] of goods or services or reduce the quality of goods or services supplied, to the individual making the claim,

he may apply to the High Court for an order[4].

Where, on such an application, the court is satisfied that the claim is well-founded, it must make such order as it considers appropriate for requiring the person by whom the act of inducement has been, or is likely to be, done to take steps for ensuring that no, or no further, act is done by him to induce any person to take part, or to continue to take part, in the industrial action, and that no person engages in conduct after the making of the order by virtue of having been induced by him before the making of the order to take part, or continue to take part, in the industrial action[5].

1   As to the meaning of 'trade union' see PARA 891. For these purposes, an act of inducement is taken to be done by a trade union if it is authorised or indorsed by the union; and the provisions of the Trade Union and Labour Relations (Consolidation) Act 1992 s 20(2)–(4) (see PARA 1388) apply for the purposes of determining whether such an act is to be taken to be so authorised or

indorsed: s 235A(6) (s 235A added by the Trade Union Reform and Employment Rights Act 1993 s 22). Those provisions also apply in relation to proceedings for failure to comply with an order under the Trade Union and Labour Relations (Consolidation) Act 1992 s 235A as they apply in relation to the original proceedings: s 235A(6) (as so added).

2 For these purposes, an act to induce any person to take part, or to continue to take part, in industrial action is unlawful: (1) if it is actionable in tort by any one or more persons; or (2) where it is or would be the act of a trade union, if it could form the basis of an application by a member under the Trade Union and Labour Relations (Consolidation) Act 1992 s 62 (complaint by a member of failure by the union to hold a ballot before industrial action) (see PARA 1025): s 235A(2) (as added: see note 1). This provision enacts the key principle that the union's action, or that of another person, does not have to constitute a definable tort against the individual complainant himself; it would be enough, e g that it constitutes a non-immune tort against the employer in dispute (eg through lack of a ballot) or against some other employer (e g under the provisions on secondary action: see PARA 1367). The individual complainant could even rely on some illegality that at first sight is purely between the union and the employer in dispute, such as a failure to give that employer strike notice (see PARA 1382). As to the meaning of 'industrial action' see PARA 1370 note 5.

3 In determining whether an individual may make an application under these provisions, it is immaterial whether or not that individual is entitled to be supplied with the goods or services in question: Trade Union and Labour Relations (Consolidation) Act 1992 s 235A(3) (as added: see note 1).

4 Trade Union and Labour Relations (Consolidation) Act 1992 s 235A(1) (as added: see note 1). On such an application the court may grant such interim relief as it considers appropriate, without prejudice to any other power of the court: see s 235A(5) (as so added). The statutory wording is 'interlocutory relief'.

5 Trade Union and Labour Relations (Consolidation) Act 1992 s 235A(4) (as added: see note 1). There are no specific provisions governing the enforcement of such an order, which, therefore, remains enforceable through the general law relating to contempt of court in a case of failure to comply: see PARA 1442.

D. CONTEMPT OF COURT IN INDUSTRIAL RELATIONS CASES

1442. Contempt of court by individual or trade union. If a person disobeys or fails to comply with[1] the terms of an injunction or other court order, he may be in contempt of court and, on further complaint to the court, liable to a fine or imprisonment[2]. A trade union[3] or other organisation in contempt of court may be fined or subject to sequestration of its assets[4].

In deciding whether a trade union is liable for actions in contempt of a court order, the same rules as to authorisation or indorsement by a union[5] apply as apply to the liability of the union for the tortious conduct in the original proceedings[6]. However, a fine for contempt of court is not subject to the statutory limits on awards of damages in claims in tort against trade unions[7]; and the statutory rules on union property protected from enforcement of damages awards[8] do not apply to an order for sequestration, which may, therefore, apply to all the union's property[9].

1 A court will look to substance rather than form when deciding whether there is a failure to comply; thus, half-hearted or apparent compliance may still constitute contempt, especially if accompanied by acts inconsistent with compliance: *Express & Star Ltd v National Graphical Association (1982)* [1986] ICR 589, [1986] IRLR 222, CA; *Kent Free Press v National Graphical Association* [1987] IRLR 267. Cf, however, note 6.

2 See CONTEMPT OF COURT vol 22 (2012) PARA 65 et seq. Although the state of mind of the defendant is not normally relevant to whether an order has been complied with, the blameworthiness or otherwise of the defendant can be taken into account when deciding on the penalty: *Austin Rover Group Ltd v Amalgamated Union of Engineering Workers (Technical and Supervisory Section)* [1985] IRLR 162. A court may refuse to hear a party in contempt until that contempt is purged: *Clarke v Heathfield* [1985] ICR 203, CA.

3 As to the meaning of 'trade union' see PARA 891.

4 As to sequestration of assets see CIVIL PROCEDURE vol 12 (2009) PARAS 1269, 1380 et seq; CONTEMPT OF COURT vol 22 (2012) PARA 113. During the miners' strike of 1984–1985,

non-payment of a fine on the National Union of Mineworkers for contempt of court led to the union's assets being sequestrated; further actions by the union's trustees inconsistent with that sequestration led the court to order the removal of those trustees and their replacement with a receiver: see *Clarke v Heathfield (No 2)* [1985] ICR 606. The court did so in an exercise of its inherent jurisdiction; but there is now a special statutory right for a trade union member to seek an order from the court removing the union's trustees and appointing a receiver, where those trustees have caused or permitted the unlawful application of the union's property or have complied with unlawful directions given to them under the union's rules: see the Trade Union and Labour Relations (Consolidation) Act 1992 s 16; and PARA 923.

5   Ie the Trade Union and Labour Relations (Consolidation) Act 1992 s 20(2)–(4): see PARA 1388.
6   See the Trade Union and Labour Relations (Consolidation) Act 1992 s 20(6); and PARA 1388. This used not to be the case, and what constituted effective compliance with a court order remained a matter of fact and argument; in particular, a court might expect positive steps to be taken by a union to ensure that its officers and members did not act inconsistently with the order: *Richard Read (Transport) Ltd v National Union of Mineworkers (South Wales Area)* [1985] IRLR 67; *Heatons Transport (St Helens) Ltd v Transport and General Workers' Union* [1973] AC 15, [1972] ICR 308, HL. However, the Employment Act 1990 (repealed and consolidated in the Trade Union and Labour Relations (Consolidation) Act 1992) altered the position, applying the statutory test of vicarious liability of a trade union to proceedings for contempt, as well as the original tort claim (thus reversing *Express & Star Ltd v National Graphical Association (1982)* [1986] ICR 589, [1986] IRLR 222, CA on this point). Now, therefore, the question whether a union is in contempt for the actions of its members or officials is likely to be resolved not by reference to older case law but by reference to the provisions of the Trade Union and Labour Relations (Consolidation) Act 1992 s 20(2)–(4) and also (equally importantly) of s 21, which governs the repudiation by a union of acts omits members or officials (see PARA 1389).
7   These limits are contained in the Trade Union and Labour Relations (Consolidation) Act 1992 s 22: see PARA 1390.
8   Ie the Trade Union and Labour Relations (Consolidation) Act 1992 s 23: see PARA 928.
9   Care may, however, be needed in determining what in fact is the property of the trade union in contempt, especially in the case of a union with a decentralised constitution: see *News Group Newspapers Ltd v Society of Graphical and Allied Trades 1982* [1986] ICR 716, [1986] IRLR 227, CA. As to the position of a third party in relation to a sequestration order see *Messenger Newspapers Group Ltd v National Graphical Association* [1984] 1 All ER 293, [1984] ICR 345, CA.

(iv) The Certification Officer

1443. Office and functions of the certification officer. There continues to be an officer called the certification officer[1], who is to be appointed by the Secretary of State after consultation with the Advisory, Conciliation and Arbitration Service[2] ('ACAS') and may appoint one or more assistant certification officers[3]. He may delegate to an assistant certification officer such functions as he thinks appropriate; and references to the certification officer in enactments relating to his functions are to be construed accordingly[4].

Although the name of his office is taken specifically from one of his functions in certifying trade unions as independent[5], the certification officer in fact has considerably wider administrative functions covering the initial listing of trade unions[6], the keeping of registers of members[7], the making of annual returns by trade unions and the investigation of their financial affairs[8], the supervision of members' superannuation schemes[9], union amalgamations[10] and the approval of political ballot rules[11]. In addition, the certification officer has functions of a judicial nature[12], hearing complaints by union members that a trade union has failed to comply with the legal requirements relating to access to accounting records[13], has failed to exclude from office persons convicted of financial offences[14], has failed to comply with the statutory requirements for elections for union office[15], has failed to comply with the balloting requirements for union political funds[16], has broken the union's political fund rules[17], has failed to comply with the statutory rules on expending money on political objects[18] or has failed to comply with the legal requirements for ballots on union amalgamations[19]. The certification officer also has a general jurisdiction to hear complaints by a union member that there has been a breach or threatened breach of certain specified union rules[20].

ACAS must:

(1)   provide the requisite staff for the certification officer from among the officers and servants of ACAS[21] and must also provide him with the requisite accommodation, equipment and other facilities[22];

(2)   pay to the certification officer such sums as he may require for the performance of any of his functions[23];

(3)   pay to the certification officer and any assistant certification officer such remuneration and travelling and other allowances as may be determined by the Secretary of State with the approval of the Treasury[24].

The certification officer continues to have custody of the annual returns, accounts, copies of rules and other documents submitted for certain statutory purposes[25] of which he took custody[26] under earlier legislation[27]. He must keep available for public inspection, either free of charge or on payment of a reasonable charge, at all reasonable hours such of those documents as were available for public inspection in pursuance of those earlier provisions[28].

As soon as practicable after the end of each financial year[29], the certification officer must make a report of his activities during that year to ACAS and to the Secretary of State; and the Secretary of State must lay a copy of the report before each House of Parliament and arrange for it to be published[30].

1   Trade Union and Labour Relations (Consolidation) Act 1992 s 254(1). The office of certification officer was established by the Employment Protection Act 1975 s 7 (repealed), which conferred on him certain functions under the Trade Union Act 1913 (repealed), the Trade Union (Amalgamations, etc) Act 1964 (repealed) and the Trade Union and Labour Relations Act 1974 (repealed) previously performed by the Chief Registrar of Friendly Societies: see the Employment Protection Act 1975 s 7(2) (repealed). The office of certification officer is subject to investigation by the Parliamentary Commissioner for Administration: see the Parliamentary Commissioner Act 1967 s 4, Sch 2; and CONSTITUTIONAL AND ADMINISTRATIVE LAW vol 20 (2014) PARA 634.

2   Trade Union and Labour Relations (Consolidation) Act 1992 s 254(2). As to the Secretary of State see PARA 5 note 21. As to ACAS see PARA 1213 et seq.

3   Trade Union and Labour Relations (Consolidation) Act 1992 s 254(3). He must appoint an assistant certification officer for Scotland: s 254(3). The certification officer or any assistant certification officer is disqualified for membership of the House of Commons: see the House of Commons Disqualification Act 1975 s 1(1), Sch I Pt III; and PARLIAMENT vol 78 (2010) PARA 908.

4   Trade Union and Labour Relations (Consolidation) Act 1992 s 254(4).

5   See PARAS 904–908. This was a function of particular importance when the office was first established in 1975.

6   See PARAS 900–903.

7   See PARAS 930–939.

8   See PARAS 943–952.

9   See PARAS 953–955.

10   See PARAS 998–1016.

11   See PARA 978.

12   As to appeals from a decision of the certification officer to the Employment Appeal Tribunal see PARA 1428.

13   See PARA 942.

14   See PARA 958.

15   See PARA 971.

16   See PARA 982.

17   See PARA 985.

18   See PARA 976.

19 See PARA 1011.
20 See PARAS 916–917.
21 As to ACAS staff see PARA 1214.
22 Trade Union and Labour Relations (Consolidation) Act 1992 s 254(5).
23 Trade Union and Labour Relations (Consolidation) Act 1992 s 254(5A) (added by the Trade Union Reform and Employment Rights Act 1993 Sch 8 para 78). The Trade Union and Labour Relations (Consolidation) Act 1992 s 254(5A) is expressed to be subject to s 254(6), which provides that the Secretary of State must pay to the certification officer such sums as he may require for making payments under the scheme under s 115 (payments towards expenditure in connection with secret ballots). Section 115 was, however, repealed by the Trade Union Reform and Employment Rights Act 1993 ss 7(1), (4), 51, Sch 10.
24 Trade Union and Labour Relations (Consolidation) Act 1992 s 255(1), (4). The Secretary of State may pay, or make provision for payment, to or in respect of the certification officer and any assistant certification officer such pension, allowance or gratuity on death or retirement as he may determine with the approval of the Treasury: s 255(2), (4). Where a person ceases to be the certification officer or an assistant certification officer otherwise than on the expiry of his term of office and it appears to the Secretary of State that there are special circumstances which make it right for him to receive compensation, he may make him a payment of such amount as he may determine with the approval of the Treasury: s 255(3), (4).
25 Ie for the purposes of the Trade Union Acts 1871 to 1964, the Industrial Relations Act 1971 or the Trade Union and Labour Relations Act 1974 (all repealed).
26 Ie under the Employment Protection Act 1975 s 9 (repealed).
27 Trade Union and Labour Relations (Consolidation) Act 1992 s 257(1).
28 Trade Union and Labour Relations (Consolidation) Act 1992 s 257(2).
29 As to the meaning of 'financial year' see PARA 1216 note 1.
30 Trade Union and Labour Relations (Consolidation) Act 1992 s 258(1) (amended by the Employment Relations Act 1999 Sch 6 paras 1, 24). The accounts prepared by ACAS in respect of any financial year must show separately any sums disbursed to or on behalf of the certification officer: Trade Union and Labour Relations (Consolidation) Act 1992 s 258(2).

1444. Procedure before the certification officer. Except in relation to matters as to which express provision is made by or under an enactment, the certification officer[1] may regulate the procedure to be followed:

(1) on any application or complaint made to him;

(2) where his approval is sought with respect to any matter; or

(3) as from a day to be appointed[2], on determining whether to make

   (a) a declaration or enforcement order where a trade union has failed to comply with its duties etc relating to the register of members[3] or

   (b) an order[4] with regard to production of documents or investigations by inspectors[5].

He must, in particular, make provision about the disclosure, and restriction of the disclosure, of the identity of an individual who has made, or is proposing to make, any such application or complaint[6]. He may refuse to entertain any application or complaint made to him under certain provisions[7] by a vexatious litigant[8], giving reasons for such a refusal[9].

The Secretary of State[10] may, with the consent of the Treasury[11], make a scheme providing for the payment by the certification officer to persons of such sums as may be specified in or determined under the scheme in respect of expenses incurred by them for the purposes of, or in connection with, their attendance at hearings held by him in the course of carrying out his functions[12].

At any stage of proceedings on an application or complaint made to the certification officer, he may:

(i) order the application or complaint, or any response[13], to be struck out on the grounds that it is scandalous, vexatious, has no reasonable prospect of success or is otherwise misconceived;

(ii)   order anything in the application or complaint, or in any response, to be amended or struck out on those grounds; or

(iii)   order the application or complaint, or any response, to be struck out on the grounds that the manner in which the proceedings have been conducted by or on behalf of the applicant or complainant or, as the case may be, respondent has been scandalous, vexatious, or unreasonable[14].

The certification officer may also order an application or complaint made to him to be struck out for excessive delay in proceeding with it[15]. Such an order[16] may be made on the certification officer's own initiative and may also be made (A) if the order sought is to strike out an application or complaint, or to amend or strike out anything in an application or complaint, on an application by the respondent; or (B) if the order sought is to strike out any response, or to amend or strike out anything in any response, on an application by the person who made the application or complaint[17].

1   As to the certification officer see PARA 1443.
2   Ie as from a day to be appointed under the Transparency of Lobbying, Non-Party Campaigning and Trade Union Administration Act 2014 s 45(1)(c). At the date at which this volume states the law, no such day had been appointed.
3   Ie a declaration or enforcement order under the Trade Union and Labour Relations (Consolidation) Act 1992 s 24B: see PARA 935.
4   Ie an order under the Trade Union and Labour Relations (Consolidation) Act 1992 s 24C: see PARA 936.
5   Trade Union and Labour Relations (Consolidation) Act 1992 s 256(1) (prospectively amended, as from a day to be appointed (see note 2), by the Transparency of Lobbying, Non-Party Campaigning and Trade Union Administration Act 2014 s 43(1), (7); at the date at which this volume states the law, that amendment was not yet in force).
6   Trade Union and Labour Relations (Consolidation) Act 1992 s 256(2) (s 256(2) substituted, s 256(2A) added by the Employment Relations Act 1999 Sch 6 paras 1, 22). Provision under the Trade Union and Labour Relations (Consolidation) Act 1992 s 256(2) must be such that, if the application or complaint relates to a trade union: (1) the individual's identity is disclosed to the union unless the certification officer thinks the circumstances are such that it should not be so disclosed; and (2) the individual's identity is disclosed to such other persons, if any, as the certification officer thinks fit: s 256(2A) (as so added). As to the meaning of 'trade union' see PARA 891.
7   Ie the provisions of the Trade Union and Labour Relations (Consolidation) Act 1992 Pt I Chs III–VIIA (ss 24–108C) (see PARA 930 et seq), except in the case of a complaint under s 37E(1)(b) (see PARAS 949–950) or an application under s 41 (see PARAS 954–955).
8   For these purposes, a vexatious litigant is a person who is the subject of a civil proceedings order or an all proceedings order made under the Senior Courts Act 1981 s 42(1) (see CIVIL PROCEDURE vol 11 (2009) PARA 258) and which remains in force: Trade Union and Labour Relations (Consolidation) Act 1992 s 256A(4) (s 256A added by the Employment Relations Act 1999 Sch 6 paras 1, 23; the Trade Union and Labour Relations (Consolidation) Act 1992 s 256A(4) amended by the Employment Relations Act 2004 Sch 2; the Constitutional Reform Act 2005 Sch 11 Pt 1 para 1(2)). The Senior Courts Act 1981 was previously known as the Supreme Court Act 1981 and was renamed by the Constitutional Reform Act 2005 s 59(5), Sch 11 Pt 1 as from 1 October 2009: see the Constitutional Reform Act 2005 (Commencement No 11) Order 2009, SI 2009/1604: and COURTS AND TRIBUNALS vol 24 (2010) PARA 687.
9   Trade Union and Labour Relations (Consolidation) Act 1992 s 256A(1)–(3) (as added: see note 8). For the purposes of s 26(8) (see PARA 939), s 31(7) (see PARA 942), s 45C(5B) (see PARA 958), s 56(8) (see PARA 973), s 72A(10) (see PARA 976), s 81(8) (see PARA 984) and s 108A(13) (see PARA 916), an application to the certification officer is to be disregarded if: (1) it was made under a provision mentioned above; and (2) it was refused by the certification officer under s 256A(1): s 256B(1), (2) (s 256B added by the Employment Relations Act 1999 Sch 6 paras 1, 23).
10   As to the Secretary of State see PARA 5 note 21.
11   As to the Treasury see CONSTITUTIONAL AND ADMINISTRATIVE LAW vol 20 (2014) PARA 262 et seq.
12   Trade Union and Labour Relations (Consolidation) Act 1992 s 256(3).

13 For these purposes, 'response' means any response made by a trade union or other body in the exercise of a right to be heard, or to make representations, in response to the application or complaint, and 'respondent' means any trade union, or other body, that has such a right: Trade Union and Labour Relations (Consolidation) Act 1992 s 256ZA(8) (s 256ZA added by the Employment Relations Act 2004 s 48).

14 Trade Union and Labour Relations (Consolidation) Act 1992 s 256ZA(1) (as added: see note 13). Before making such an order, the certification officer must send notice to the party against whom it is proposed that the order should be made giving him an opportunity to show cause why the order should not be made: s 256ZA(4) (as so added). However, this does not require the certification officer to send a notice if the party against whom it is proposed that the order should be made has been given an opportunity to show cause orally why the order should not be made: s 256ZA(5) (as so added). Nothing in s 256ZA prevents the certification officer from making further provision under s 256(1) (see the text and notes 1–5) about the striking out of proceedings on any application or complaint made to him: s 256ZA(6) (as so added). An appeal lies to the Employment Appeal Tribunal on any question of law arising from a decision of the certification officer: s 256ZA(7) (as so added). As to the Employment Appeal Tribunal see PARA 1422 et seq.

15 Trade Union and Labour Relations (Consolidation) Act 1992 s 256ZA(2) (as added: see note 13). See note 14.

16 Ie an order under the Trade Union and Labour Relations (Consolidation) Act 1992 s 256ZA.

17 Trade Union and Labour Relations (Consolidation) Act 1992 s 256ZA(3) (as added: see note 13). See note 14.

(v) Guideline Decisions and Precedents

1445. Guideline decisions and precedents in tribunal proceedings. The Employment Appeal Tribunal[1] is bound by decisions of the House of Lords and the Court of Appeal, but not by decisions of the High Court, the former National Industrial Relations Court or its own previous decisions, although such decisions have persuasive authority[2].

The Employment Appeal Tribunal, and its predecessor the National Industrial Relations Court, have on occasions given guideline decisions[3] for employment tribunals to adopt in order to achieve a measure of consistency in their decisions[4]; but any such guidelines are not rules of law, failure to follow which amounts to error of law which can be the subject of an appeal[5].

1 As to the Employment Appeal Tribunal see PARA 1422 et seq.

2 See CIVIL PROCEDURE vol 11 (2009) PARAS 97–98. 'The Employment Appeal Tribunal is not bound by its previous decisions, although they will only be departed from in exceptional circumstances, or where there are previous inconsistent decisions': *Secretary of State for Trade and Industry v Cook* [1997] ICR 288 at 292, [1997] IRLR 150, at 151, EAT, per Morison P.

3 See eg *Norton Tool Co Ltd v Tewson* [1972] ICR 501, [1972] IRLR 86, NIRC (assessment of compensation for unfair dismissal); *East Lindsey District Council v Daubney* [1977] ICR 566, [1977] IRLR 181, EAT (dismissal for sickness); *British Home Stores Ltd v Burchell* [1980] ICR 303n, [1978] IRLR 379, EAT (suspected misconduct); *Rowan v Environment Agency* [2008] ICR 218 at [27], [2008] IRLR 20 at [27], EAT (employer's failure to make reasonable adjustments for disabled person); *Metropolitan Resources Ltd v Churchill Dulwich Ltd* [2009] ICR 1380, [2009] IRLR 700, EAT (meaning of 'service provision charge'); *AB v Ministry of Defence* [2010] ICR 54 at [19], [2009] All ER (D) 135 (Sep) at [19], EAT (approach to be adopted by tribunals in national security cases).

4 The Court of Appeal reacted strongly against guideline decisions as part of the desire to curb an over-legalistic approach in the tribunal system: see eg *Bailey v BP Oil (Kent Refinery) Ltd* [1980] ICR 642 at 648, [1980] IRLR 287 at 289, CA, per Lawton LJ ('Each case must depend on its own facts. In our judgment it is unwise for this court or the Employment Appeal Tribunal to set out guidelines, and wrong to make rules and establish presumptions for [employment] tribunals to follow or take into account ... '); *Thomas & Betts Manufacturing Co Ltd v Harding* [1980] IRLR 255 at 257, CA, per Eveleigh LJ ('I myself deprecate the attempts that are made in these industrial relations cases to spell out a point of law developed upon precedent to create rules that have to be applied by the [employment] tribunal ... '); *Varndell v Kearney & Trecker Marwin Ltd* [1983] ICR 683 at 695, sub nom *Kearney & Trecker Marwin Ltd v Varndell*

[1983] IRLR 335 at 340, CA, per Eveleigh LJ ('I regard the guidelines ... as being virtually a public relations exercise .... There is today too great a tendency to seize upon words in a judgment and use them as though they were laying down some new rule of law .... We must not strive to create a body of judge-made law supplementing the law as laid down in the Employment Protection (Consolidation) Act 1978 [now repealed]').

The extent to which such adverse reaction has been embraced has depended on the attitude of the various Presidents for the time being of the Employment Appeal Tribunal: see e g *Williams v Compair Maxam Ltd* [1982] ICR 156, [1982] IRLR 83, EAT; *Grundy (Teddington) Ltd v Plummer and Salt* [1983] ICR 367, [1983] IRLR 98, EAT (decisions of Browne-Wilkinson P, who considered that the Court of Appeal had gone too far, but that there was some scope for guidelines, albeit to be used more sparingly); *Siggs & Chapman (Contractors) Ltd v Knight* [1984] IRLR 83, EAT; *Anandarajah v Lord Chancellor's Department* [1984] IRLR 131, EAT; *Royal Society for the Protection of Birds v Croucher* [1984] ICR 604, [1984] IRLR 425, EAT (decisions of Waite P, who was prepared not only to decline to give further guidelines but also to call in question long accepted guidelines, an approach followed in turn by his successor, Popplewell P); *Aberdeen Steak Houses Group plc v Ibrahim* [1988] ICR 550, [1988] IRLR 420, EAT (procedure to be adopted by tribunals: see PARA 1472 note 3); *ILEA v Gravett* [1988] IRLR 497, EAT, reaffirming the guidelines in *British Home Stores Ltd v Burchell* [1980] ICR 303n, [1978] IRLR 379, EAT (see note 3); *Linfood Cash and Carry Ltd v Thomson* [1989] ICR 518, [1989] IRLR 235, EAT (dealing with anonymous informants: see PARA 703 note 1); *Dyke v Hereford and Worcester County Council* [1989] ICR 800, EAT (redundancy consultation: see PARA 782 note 4); *Parr v Whitbread & Co plc* [1990] ICR 427, sub nom *Parr v Whitbread plc (t/a Threshers Wine Merchants)* [1990] IRLR 39, EAT; *St Basil's Centre v McCrossan* [1992] ICR 140, [1991] IRLR 455, EAT (cited in PARA 1453 note 11) (decisions of Wood P, who was prepared to issue guidelines, though with considerable circumspection). Under the Presidencies of Mummery P, Morison P, Lindsay P, Burton P, Elias P, Underhill P, and Langstaff P, this process was continued, though without overstepping the bounds set out by the Court of Appeal, with increasing numbers of cases involving European law and discrimination law where guidance to tribunals is clearly desirable. In *Langston v Cranfield University* [1998] IRLR 172, EAT, Judge Peter Clark held that certain guidelines (in that case, on fairness in a redundancy dismissal, but also instancing *British Home Stores Ltd v Burchell* [1980] ICR 303n, [1978] IRLR 379, EAT on misconduct dismissals and *Norton Tool Co Ltd v Tewson* [1973] 1 All ER 183, [1972] ICR 501, NIRC on calculating compensation) are now so well accepted that a tribunal should consider them of its own motion, even if not raised by the parties (especially by a litigant in person).

5   *Jowett v Earl of Bradford (No 2)* [1978] ICR 431 at 436, sub nom *Earl of Bradford v Jowett* [1978] IRLR 16 at 18, EAT, per Bristow J.

(vi) National Security Issues in Employment Cases

1446.   Restrictions on disclosure of information on national security grounds. Where, in the opinion of any Minister of the Crown, the disclosure of any information would be contrary to the interests of national security, nothing in any of the specified statutory provisions[1] requires any person to disclose the information and no person is to disclose the information in proceedings in any court or tribunal relating to any of those provisions[2].

1   Ie: (1) the Employment Rights Act 1996 Pt I (ss 1–12) (see PARA 119 et seq) (so far as it relates to employment particulars); (2) s 43M (see PARA 613), s 44 (see PARA 614), s 45A (see PARA 616), s 47 (employee representatives) (see PARA 1208), s 47C (see PARA 620), and ss 48, 49 (see PARAS 625–626) (so far as they relate to s 44, s 45A, s 47 and s 47C); (3) s 55 (see PARA 333), s 56 (see PARA 333), s 57 (see PARA 334), s 57A (see PARA 347), s 57B (see PARA 348), ss 61–63 (employee representatives) (see PARA 1209); (4) s 66 (see PARA 598), s 67 (see PARA 600), s 68 (see PARA 598), and ss 69, 70 (see PARAS 604–606) (so far as relating to ss 66–68); (5) Pt VIII (ss 71–80E) (see PARA 355 et seq); (6) ss 92, 93 (see PARAS 755–756) (where they apply by virtue of s 92(4) (see PARA 755)); (7) Pt X (ss 94–134A) (see PARA 757 et seq (so far as relating to a dismissal which is treated as unfair: (a) by s 98B (see PARA 785), s 99 (see PARA 784), s 100 (see PARA 786), s 101A(1)(d) (see PARA 788) or s 103 (see PARA 791) or by s 104 (see PARA 793) in its application in relation to time off under s 57A (see PARA 347); or (b) by s 105(1) (see PARA 781) by reason of the application of s 105(2A), (3) or (6) (see PARA 781), or by reason of the application of s 105(4A) (see PARA 781) in so far as it applies where the reason (or, if more than

one, the principal reason) for which the employee was selected for dismissal was that specified in s 101A(d)); (8) Pt XIII (ss 191–209) (miscellaneous provisions), Pt XIV (ss 210–235) (interpretation) and Pt XV (ss 236–245) (general and supplementary provisions) (so far as relating to any of the provisions in heads (1)–(7) above): s 202(2) (amended by the Employment Relations Act 1999 Sch 4 Pt III paras 5, 36(a)–(c); the Employment Relations Act 2004 Sch 1 para 39(1)–(3); and by SI 1998/1833).

2	Employment Rights Act 1996 s 202(1).

1447. Membership of tribunals for the purpose of national security proceedings. National security proceedings[1] before an employment tribunal[2] must be heard[3] by the employment judge[4] and two other members[5] but may, with the consent of the parties, be heard and determined in the absence of any one of those members other than the employment judge[6].

The President[7] must select:

(1)	a panel of persons from the panel of employment judges[8];

(2)	a panel of persons from the panel of persons appointed by the Lord Chancellor after consultation with organisations or associations representative of employees[9]; and

(3)	a panel of persons from the panel of persons appointed by the Lord Chancellor after consultation with organisations or associations representative of employers[10],

who may act in national security proceedings[11]. Where proceedings become national security proceedings, the President or a regional employment judge[12] must select an employment judge from the panel referred to in head (1) above and may select himself[13]. Where the proceedings are to be determined by a tribunal comprising an employment judge and two other members, the President or an regional employment judge must select in addition one member from each of the panels referred to in heads (2) and (3) above[14].

1	For these purposes, 'national security proceedings' means proceedings in relation to which a direction is given under the Employment Tribunals (Constitution and Rules of Procedure) Regulations 2013, SI 2013/1237, Sch 1 r 94 (see PARA 1450): reg 3.

2	As to the establishment of tribunals see PARA 1399.

3	Ie subject to the provisions of the Employment Tribunals Act 1996 s 4(2)–(6C) (see PARAS 1402 note 3, 1403) and s 7(3A) (see PARA 1410).

4	As to the meaning of 'employment judge' see PARA 1401 note 3.

5	As to the selection of the other members of the tribunal see the text and notes 12–14.

6	See the Employment Tribunals Act 1996 s 4(1); and PARA 1402.

7	As to the meaning of 'President' see PARA 1399 note 7.

8	Ie the panel referred to in the Employment Tribunals (Constitution and Rules of Procedure) Regulations 2013, SI 2013/1237, reg 8(2)(a): see PARA 1401 head (1).

9	Ie the panel referred to in the Employment Tribunals (Constitution and Rules of Procedure) Regulations 2013, SI 2013/1237, reg 8(2)(b): see PARA 1401 head (2).

10	Ie the panel referred to in the Employment Tribunals (Constitution and Rules of Procedure) Regulations 2013, SI 2013/1237, reg 8(2)(c): see PARA 1401 head (3).

11	Employment Tribunals (Constitution and Rules of Procedure) Regulations 2013, SI 2013/1237, reg 10(1).

12	As to the meaning of 'regional employment judge' see PARA 1399 note 9.

13	Employment Tribunals (Constitution and Rules of Procedure) Regulations 2013, SI 2013/1237, reg 10(2)(a).

14	Employment Tribunals (Constitution and Rules of Procedure) Regulations 2013, SI 2013/1237, reg 10(2)(b).

1448. Procedure where proceedings involve national security; in general. If on a complaint under provisions of the Trade Union and Labour Relations (Consolidation) Act 1992 relating to inducements and detriments in respect of trade union membership[1], of the Employment Rights Act 1996 relating to unfair dismissal[2], or of the Employment Relations Act 1999 (Blacklists) Regulations 2010 relating to victimisation[3], it is shown that the action complained of was taken for the purpose of safeguarding national security, the employment tribunal must dismiss the complaint[4].

Employment tribunal procedure regulations[5] may make provision about the composition of the tribunal, including provision disapplying or modifying the provisions relating to the composition of tribunals[6], for the purposes of proceedings in relation to which a direction is given by a Minister of the Crown which relates to particular Crown employment proceedings[7] if the minister considers it expedient in the interests of national security or in relation to which an order is made by the President or a regional employment judge[8] in relation to particular proceedings if he considers it expedient in the interests of national security[9].

Employment tribunal procedure regulations may also make provision enabling a Minister of the Crown, if he considers it expedient in the interests of national security:

(1) to direct a tribunal to sit in private for all or part of particular Crown employment proceedings;

(2) to direct a tribunal to exclude the applicant from all or part of particular Crown employment proceedings;

(3) to direct a tribunal to exclude the applicant's representatives from all or part of particular Crown employment proceedings;

(4) to direct a tribunal to take steps to conceal the identity of a particular witness in particular Crown employment proceedings;

(5) to direct a tribunal to take steps to keep secret all or part of the reasons for its decision in particular Crown employment proceedings[10].

Employment tribunal procedure regulations may enable a tribunal, if it considers it expedient in the interests of national security, to do in relation to particular proceedings before it anything of a kind which, by virtue of heads (1) to (5) above, employment tribunal procedure regulations may enable a Minister of the Crown to direct a tribunal to do in relation to particular Crown employment proceedings[11].

In relation to cases where a person has been excluded[12], employment tribunal procedure regulations may make provision:

(a) for the appointment by the Attorney General of a person to represent the interests of the applicant;

(b) about the publication and registration of reasons for the tribunal's decision;

(c) permitting an excluded person to make a statement to the tribunal before the commencement of the proceedings, or the part of the proceedings, from which he is excluded[13].

The tribunal[14] must ensure that in exercising its functions, information is not disclosed contrary to the interests of national security[15].

1　Ie the Trade Union and Labour Relations (Consolidation) Act 1992 s 145A (see PARA 1051), s 145B (see PARA 1052) or s 146 (see PARA 1048).

2　Ie the Employment Rights Act 1996 s 111: see PARA 804.

3　Ie the Employment Relations Act 1999 (Blacklists) Regulations 2010, SI 2010/493, reg 9: see PARA 1040.

4　Employment Tribunals Act 1996 s 10(1) (s 10 substituted by the Employment Relations Act 1999 Sch 8 para 3; the Employment Tribunals Act 1996 s 10(1) amended by the Employment Relations Act 2004 Sch 1 para 24; and by SI 2010/493).

Under the Employment Tribunals Act 1996 s 10(1), employers do not need to prove the underlying facts but they must justify the unfair dismissal, not just the dismissal, and consequently the Employment Rights Act 1996 s 98(4) (see PARAS 765, 767) has to be addressed and shown to fall within the Employment Tribunals Act 1996 s 10(1): *B v BAA plc* [2005] ICR 1530, [2005] IRLR 927, EAT (tribunal wrongly felt itself precluded from considering whether the employer, faced with a refusal of security clearance, acted outside the range of reasonable responses, including any question of whether redeployment was possible, and if so whether such an act, being the action complained of, even if otherwise unreasonable, was itself for the purpose of safeguarding national security).

5 As to the meaning of 'employment tribunal procedure regulations' see PARA 1410.

6 Ie including provision disapplying or modifying the Employment Tribunals Act 1996 s 4: see PARAS 1402, 1403.

7 For these purposes, proceedings are Crown employment proceedings if the employment to which the complaint relates is Crown employment or is connected with the performance of functions on behalf of the Crown: Employment Tribunals Act 1996 s 10(8) (as substituted: see note 4). As to the meaning of 'Crown employment' see PARA 163.

8 For these purposes, the reference to the President or a regional employment judge is a reference to a person appointed in accordance with regulations under the Employment Tribunals Act 1996 s 1(1) (see PARA 1399) as the President of the Employment Tribunals (England and Wales) (see PARA 1400) or as a regional employment judge (see PARA 1401): s 10(9) (as substituted: see note 4); Interpretation Act 1978 s 17(2)(a).

9 See the Employment Tribunals Act 1996 s 10(2)–(4) (as substituted (see note 3); amended by the Crime and Courts Act 2013 Sch 14 Pt 7 para 13(3)).

10 Employment Tribunals Act 1996 s 10(5) (as substituted: see note 4). See further PARA 1449.

11 Employment Tribunals Act 1996 s 10(6) (substituted by the Employment Relations Act 2004 s 36). See further PARA 1449.

12 Ie by virtue of the Employment Tribunals Act 1996 s 10(5)(b) or (c) (see heads (2)–(3) in the text) or s 10(6) (see the text and note 7).

13 Employment Tribunals Act 1996 s 10(7) (as substituted: see note 4).

14 For these purposes, 'employment tribunal' or 'tribunal' means an employment tribunal established in accordance with the Employment Tribunals (Constitution and Rules of Procedure) Regulations 2013, SI 2013/1237, reg 4 (see PARA 1399), and in relation to any proceedings means the tribunal responsible for the proceedings in question, whether performing administrative or judicial functions: Sch 1 r 1(1). Any reference in the Employment Tribunals Rules of Procedure (set out in the Employment Tribunals (Constitution and Rules of Procedure) Regulations 2013, SI 2013/1237, Sch 1 to a tribunal applies to both a full tribunal (ie a tribunal constituted in accordance with the Employment Tribunals Act 1996 s 4(1): see PARA 1402) and to an employment judge acting alone in accordance with s 4(2) or (6) (see PARAS 1402, 1403): Sch 1 r 1(2).

15 Employment Tribunals (Constitution and Rules of Procedure) Regulations 2013, SI 2013/1237, Sch 1 r 94(10).

1449. Restrictions on publicity in national security cases. Where a tribunal has been directed[1] or has made a determination[2] in the interest of national security to take steps to conceal the identity of a particular witness or to take steps to keep secret all or part of the reasons for its decision, then if a person publishes[3] anything likely to lead to the identification of the witness or the reasons for the tribunal's decision or the part of its reasons which it is directed or has determined to keep secret, he is guilty of an offence and liable to a penalty[4].

Where a person is charged with such an offence, it is a defence to prove that at the time of the alleged offence he was not aware, and neither suspected nor had reason to suspect, that the publication in question was of, or included, the matter in question[5].

Where such an offence committed by a body corporate is proved to have been committed with the consent or connivance of, or to be attributable to any neglect on the part of, a director, manager[6], secretary or other similar officer of the body corporate or a person purporting to act in any such capacity, he, as well as the body corporate, is guilty of the offence and liable to be proceeded against and punished accordingly[7].

1 Ie under the Employment Tribunals Act 1996 s 10(5): see PARA 1448.
2 Ie under the Employment Tribunals Act 1996 s 10(6): see PARA 1448.
3 For these purposes, a reference to publication includes a reference to inclusion in a programme
   which is included in a programme service, within the meaning of the Broadcasting Act 1990 (see
   BROADCASTING vol 4 (2011) PARA 507): Employment Tribunals Act 1996 s 10B(6) (s 10B
   substituted by the Employment Relations Act 1999 Sch 8 para 3).
4 Employment Tribunals Act 1996 s 10B(1)–(3) (as substituted: see note 3). The penalty on
   summary conviction is a fine not exceeding level 5 on the standard scale: see s 10B(1)–(3) (as so
   substituted). As to the standard scale see SENTENCING AND DISPOSITION OF OFFENDERS vol 92
   (2010) PARA 142.
5 Employment Tribunals Act 1996 s 10B(4) (as substituted: see note 3).
6 As to the meaning of 'manager' see PARA 40 note 11.
7 Employment Tribunals Act 1996 s 10B(5) (as substituted: see note 3).

1450. Special advocate in employment tribunal proceedings. Where in
relation to particular Crown employment proceedings[1] a minister considers that
it would be expedient in the interests of national security, the minister may direct
a tribunal[2] to:

(1)   conduct all or part of the proceedings in private;
(2)   exclude a person from all or part of the proceedings;
(3)   take steps to conceal the identity of a witness in the proceedings[3].

Where the tribunal considers it expedient in the interests of national security,
it may order:

(a)   in relation to particular proceedings, including Crown employment
      proceedings, anything which can be required to be done under heads (1)
      to (3) above;
(b)   a person not to disclose any document, or the contents of any
      document, where provided for the purposes of the proceedings, to any
      other person, save for any specified person;

and any order made must be kept under review by the tribunal[4].

Where the tribunal considers that it may be necessary to make such an order
in relation to particular proceedings, including Crown employment proceedings,
the tribunal may consider any material provided by a party (or where a minister
is not a party, by a minister) without providing that material to any other person.
Such material must be used by the tribunal solely for the purposes of deciding
whether to make that order, unless that material is subsequently used as evidence
in the proceedings by a party[5].

Where a minister considers that it would be appropriate for the tribunal to
make such an order, the minister may make an application for such an order[6].
Where a minister has made such an application, the tribunal may order:

(i)   in relation to the part of the proceedings preceding the outcome of the
       application, anything which can be required to be done under heads (1)
       to (3) above;
(ii)   a person not to disclose any document, or the contents of any
       document, to any other person, save for any specified person, where
       provided for the purposes of the proceedings preceding the outcome of
       the application[7].

Where a minister has made such an application for an order to exclude any
person from all or part of the proceedings, the tribunal must not send a copy of
the response to that person, pending the decision on the application[8]. Where the
tribunal decides not to make an order under heads (a) and (b) above, the reasons
will not be entered on the register[9].

Where a direction is given, or order made, under the above provisions that
proceedings are to be conducted in private, the tribunal must inform the

Attorney General[10] if a party becomes an excluded person[11]. The Attorney General may appoint a special advocate[12] to represent the interests of a person in respect of those parts of the proceedings from which:

(i)   a person's representative is excluded;

(ii)   a person and his representative are excluded;

(iii) a person is excluded and is unrepresented[13].

An excluded person, where that person is a party, may make a statement to the tribunal before the commencement of the proceedings or the relevant part of the proceedings[14].

The special advocate may communicate, directly or indirectly, with an excluded person at any time before receiving material from a minister in relation to which the minister states an objection to disclosure to the excluded person ('closed material')[15]. After receiving closed material, the special advocate must not communicate with any person about any matter connected with the proceedings, except in accordance with the following provisions[16] or with an order of the tribunal[17]. The special advocate may communicate about the proceedings with:

(A)   the tribunal;

(B)   the minister, or his representative;

(C)   the Attorney General, or his representative;

(D)   any other person, except for an excluded person or his representative, with whom it is necessary for administrative purposes to communicate about matters not connected with the substance of the proceedings[18].

After the special advocate has received closed material, an excluded person may only communicate with the special advocate in writing[19] and the special advocate must not reply to the communication, except that the special advocate may send a written acknowledgment of receipt to the legal representative[20].

The special advocate may apply for an order from the tribunal to authorise communication with an excluded person or with any other person and if such an application is made the tribunal must notify the minister of the request[21]. The minister may, within a period specified by the tribunal, present to the tribunal and serve on the special advocate notice of any objection to the proposed communication[22].

1   As to the meaning of 'Crown employment proceedings' see PARA 1448 note 7.

2   As to the meaning of 'tribunal' for these purposes see PARA 1448 note 14.

3   Employment Tribunals (Constitution and Rules of Procedure) Regulations 2013, SI 2013/1237, Sch 1 r 94(1). If before the expiry of the time limit in Sch 1 r 16 (see PARA 1462) a minister makes a direction under Sch 1 r 94(1) or makes an application under Sch 1 r 94(4) (see the text and note 6), the minister may apply for an extension of that time limit: Sch 1 r 94(7). 'Minister' means a Minister of the Crown: Sch 1 r 1(1).

    A direction under Sch 1 r 94(1) or an application under Sch 1 r 94(4) may be made irrespective of whether or not the minister is a party: Sch 1 r 94(8).

4   Employment Tribunals (Constitution and Rules of Procedure) Regulations 2013, SI 2013/1237, Sch 1 r 94(2). Guidance as to the approach to be adopted by tribunals when considering an application for a private hearing in the interests of national security under what is now Sch 1 r 94(2) was given in *AB v Ministry of Defence* [2010] ICR 54 at [19], [2009] All ER (D) 135 (Sep) at [19], EAT per Underhill J ((1) as with any exception to the rule of open justice, an application for a private hearing under this rule has to be capable of cogent justification; (2) although the interests of national security are capable of justifying such an exception, the tribunal must make a judicial assessment as to whether they do so in the particular case by balancing (a) the seriousness of the prejudice to national security that is asserted, and the degree of risk that the prejudice may occur if the exception is not made, against (b) the extent of the infringement of the principle of open justice and the risk of prejudice to the public interest or the interests of the individual in the particular case; (3) where the interests of national security are genuinely engaged, real risks to the lives of members of the armed forces or the security services

or others must weigh heavily against the principle of open justice; (4) recognition of these limitations does not mean that the proportionality exercise is unnecessary or that it can only have one outcome; tribunals should not abdicate their responsibilities to make the necessary assessment whenever national security is invoked).

A holding that a closed material procedure is admissible even if it leads to a claimant not knowing in sufficient detail the allegations against him in order to instruct his legal team should only ever be permitted if the court is satisfied that it is essential in the particular case: *Home Office v Tariq* [2011] UKSC 35, [2012] 1 AC 452, [2012] 1 All ER 58, [2011] ICR 938, [2011] IRLR 843 (procedure not in essence unlawful). It is expedient in the interests of national security that a racial discrimination hearing dealing with an employee's service overseas be held in private as there is a real risk of prejudice to the operations carried out: *AB v Ministry of Defence* [2010] ICR 54, [2009] All ER (D) 135 (Sep), EAT.

5   Employment Tribunals (Constitution and Rules of Procedure) Regulations 2013, SI 2013/1237, Sch 1 r 94(3).

6   Employment Tribunals (Constitution and Rules of Procedure) Regulations 2013, SI 2013/1237, Sch 1 r 94(4). See also note 3.

7   Employment Tribunals (Constitution and Rules of Procedure) Regulations 2013, SI 2013/1237, Sch 1 r 94(5).

8   Employment Tribunals (Constitution and Rules of Procedure) Regulations 2013, SI 2013/1237, Sch 1 r 94(6).

9   See the Employment Tribunals (Constitution and Rules of Procedure) Regulations 2013, SI 2013/1237, Sch 1 r 94(9). Schedule 2 r 6 (see PARA 1476) otherwise applies to the reasons given by the tribunal under Sch 1 r 62 (see PARA 1476) for that decision: Sch 1 r 94(9).

10 Ie as the 'relevant Law Officer' in relation to England and Wales: see the Employment Tribunals (Constitution and Rules of Procedure) Regulations 2013, SI 2013/1237, Sch 2 r 4(1).

11 Employment Tribunals (Constitution and Rules of Procedure) Regulations 2013, SI 2013/1237, Sch 2 r 4(1). 'Excluded person' means, in relation to any proceedings, a person who has been excluded from all or part of the proceedings by virtue of a direction under Sch 1 r 94(1)(b) or an order under Sch 1 r 94(2)(a) (read with Sch 1 r 94(1)(b)): Sch 2 r 1(2), (3). The Tribunal must not send a copy of the response to any excluded person (see also the text and note 8): Sch 2 r 2.

12 A special advocate must be a person who has a right of audience in relation to any class of proceedings in any part of the Senior Courts or all proceedings in the County Court or magistrates' courts, or an advocate or a solicitor admitted in Scotland: Employment Tribunals (Constitution and Rules of Procedure) Regulations 2013, SI 2013/1237, Sch 2 r 4(3) (amended by virtue of the Crime and Courts Act 2013 Sch 9 para 11). References in the Employment Tribunals (Constitution and Rules of Procedure) Regulations 2013, SI 2013/1237, and Schs 1, 2 to a party include any special advocate appointed in particular proceedings, save that the references to 'party' or 'parties' in Sch 1 rr 3, 6(c), 22, 26, 34, 36(2), 36(3), the first reference in r 37, 38, 39, 40, 41, 45, 47, 64, 74–84, 86, 96 and 98(3) do not include the special advocate: Sch 2 r 4(10).

13 Employment Tribunals (Constitution and Rules of Procedure) Regulations 2013, SI 2013/1237, Sch 2 r 4(2).

14 Employment Tribunals (Constitution and Rules of Procedure) Regulations 2013, SI 2013/1237, Sch 2 r 4(4).

15 Employment Tribunals (Constitution and Rules of Procedure) Regulations 2013, SI 2013/1237, Sch 2 r 4(5).

16 Ie except in accordance with the Employment Tribunals (Constitution and Rules of Procedure) Regulations 2013, SI 2013/1237, Sch 2 r 4(7) or (9): see the text and notes 18–20.

17 Employment Tribunals (Constitution and Rules of Procedure) Regulations 2013, SI 2013/1237, Sch 2 r 4(6).

18 Employment Tribunals (Constitution and Rules of Procedure) Regulations 2013, SI 2013/1237, Sch 2 r 4(7).

19 'Writing' includes writing delivered by means of electronic communication: Employment Tribunals (Constitution and Rules of Procedure) Regulations 2013, SI 2013/1237, Sch 1 r 1(1). As to the meaning of 'electronic communications' see PARA 1430 note 1.

20 Employment Tribunals (Constitution and Rules of Procedure) Regulations 2013, SI 2013/1237, Sch 2 r 4(9).

21 Employment Tribunals (Constitution and Rules of Procedure) Regulations 2013, SI 2013/1237, Sch 2 r 4(8)(a).

22 Employment Tribunals (Constitution and Rules of Procedure) Regulations 2013, SI 2013/1237, Sch 2 r 4(8)(b).

1451. Procedure on appeals to the Appeal Tribunal in relation to national security proceedings; in general. In the case of an appeal from a judgment or order of the employment tribunal in relation to national security proceedings[1], the appellant must not set out the grounds of appeal in his notice of appeal and must not append to his notice of appeal the written reasons for the judgment of the tribunal[2]. In an appeal from the employment tribunal in relation to national security proceedings in relation to which the appellant was the respondent in the proceedings before the employment tribunal, the appellant must, within the prescribed period[3], provide to the Appeal Tribunal[4] a document[5] setting out the grounds on which the appeal is brought[6]. In an appeal from the employment tribunal in relation to national security proceedings in relation to which the appellant was the claimant in the proceedings before the employment tribunal[7]:

(1) the appellant may, within whichever prescribed period[8] is applicable, provide to the Appeal Tribunal a document setting out the grounds on which the appeal is brought; and

(2) a special advocate[9] appointed in respect of the appellant may, within whichever prescribed period[10] is applicable, or within 21 days of his appointment, whichever is later, provide to the Appeal Tribunal a document setting out the grounds on which the appeal is brought or providing supplementary grounds of appeal[11].

Where it appears to a judge or the registrar that a notice of appeal or a document so provided[12] discloses no reasonable grounds for bringing the appeal[13] or is an abuse of the Appeal Tribunal's process or is otherwise likely to obstruct the just disposal of proceedings[14], he must notify the appellant or special advocate accordingly informing him of the reasons for his opinion and no further action must be taken[15] on the notice of appeal or document so provided[16]. Where a judge or the registrar has taken such a decision, and also considers that the notice of appeal or document so provided[17] is totally without merit, the judge or registrar may order that the appellant or special advocate is not entitled to have the matter heard before a judge[18], with such order to be included as part of the notice issued[19] to the appellant or special advocate[20]. Subject to that, where notification has been given of the judge's or registrar's opinion[21] and within 28 days of the date the notification was sent, an appellant or special advocate expresses dissatisfaction in writing with the reasons given by the judge or registrar for his opinion, he is entitled to have the matter heard before a judge who must make a direction as to whether any further action should be taken on the notice of appeal or document[22].

While the relevant practice direction[23] is expressed to apply to all appeals to the Appeal Tribunal, that Tribunal will normally give specific directions in national security appeals[24].

1 'National security proceedings' has the meaning given to it in the Employment Tribunals (Constitution and Rules of Procedure) Regulations 2013, SI 2013/1237, reg 3 (see PARA 1447 note 1): Employment Appeal Tribunal Rules 1993, SI 1993/2854, r 2(1) (definition added by SI 2004/2526; amended by SI 2013/1693).

2 Employment Appeal Tribunal Rules 1993, SI 1993/2854, r 3(4) (r 3 substituted by SI 2001/1128; the Employment Appeal Tribunal Rules 1993, SI 1993/2854, r 3(4) amended by SI 2004/2526).

3 Ie the period described in the Employment Appeal Tribunal Rules 1993, SI 1993/2854, r 3(3)(a): see PARA 1495.

4 'The Appeal Tribunal' means the Employment Appeal Tribunal established under the Employment Protection Act 1975 s 87 (repealed) and continued in existence under the Employment Tribunals Act 1996 s 20 (see PARAS 1422, 1426) and includes the President, a judge, a member or the registrar acting on behalf of the Appeal Tribunal: see the Employment

Appeal Tribunal Rules 1993, SI 1993/2854, r 2(1) (r 2 substituted by SI 2001/1128). 'The President' means the judge appointed under the Employment Tribunals Act 1996 s 22(3) (see PARA 1422) to be President of the Appeal Tribunal and includes a judge nominated under s 23(1) (see PARA 1424) to act temporarily in his place; 'judge' means a judge of the Appeal Tribunal nominated under s 22(1)(a) or (b) (see PARA 1422 heads (1)–(2)) and includes a judge nominated under s 23(2) (see PARA 1424), or a judge appointed under s 24(1) (see PARA 1424), to be a temporary additional judge of the Appeal Tribunal; and 'member' means a member of the Appeal Tribunal appointed under s 22(1)(c) (see PARA 1422 head (3)) and includes a member appointed under s 23(3) (see PARA 1424) to act temporarily in the place of a member appointed under that provision: see the Employment Appeal Tribunal Rules 1993, SI 1993/2854, r 2(1) (as so substituted). As to the meaning of 'the registrar' see PARA 1430 note 4.

5 'Document' includes a document delivered by way of electronic communication: Employment Appeal Tribunal Rules 1993, SI 1993/2854, r 2(1) (definition added by SI 2004/2526). As to the meaning of 'electronic communication' see PARA 1430 note 1.

6 Employment Appeal Tribunal Rules 1993, SI 1993/2854, r 3(5) (amended by SI 2004/2526).

7 Any reference in the Employment Appeal Tribunal Rules 1993, SI 1993/2854, to a person who was the claimant or, as the case may be, the respondent in the proceedings before an employment tribunal includes, where those proceedings are still continuing, a reference to a person who is the claimant or, as the case may be, is the respondent in those proceedings: r 3(3) (amended by SI 2004/2526).

8 Ie the period described in the Employment Appeal Tribunal Rules 1993, SI 1993/2854, r 3(3)(3(a)(ii) or (iii) or r 3(3)(b): see PARA 1495.

9 'Special advocate' means a person appointed pursuant to the Employment Appeal Tribunal Rules 1993, SI 1993/2854, r 30A (see PARA 1452): r 2(1) (as substituted: see note 4).

10 See note 8.

11 Employment Appeal Tribunal Rules 1993, SI 1993/2854, r 3(6) (amended by SI 2004/2526).

12 Ie provided under the Employment Appeal Tribunal Rules 1993, SI 1993/2854, r 3(5) (see the text and notes 3–6) or r 3(6) (see the text and notes 7–12). In r 3(7), (7ZA), (10) (see the text and notes 13–22) reference to a notice of appeal or a document provided under r 3(5) or r 3(6) includes reference to part of a notice of appeal or document provided under r 3(5) or r 3(6): r 3(7A) (added by SI 2004/2526; amended by SI 2013/1693).

13 Employment Appeal Tribunal Rules 1993, SI 1993/2854, r 3(7)(a) (r 3(7) substituted by SI 2004/2526. It is important that the grounds of appeal are drafted with precision as additional grounds will only be permitted to be argued in limited circumstances: *Miriki v General Council of the Bar* [2001] EWCA Civ 1973, [2002] ICR 505; *Tran v Greenwich Vietnam Community Project* [2002] EWCA Civ 553 at [42], [2002] ICR 1101 at [42], [2002] IRLR 735 at [42] per Arden LJ. As to the need for particularisation in the case of 'perversity appeals' see *Yeboah v Crofton* [2002] EWCA Civ 794 at [92], [2002] IRLR 634 at [92] per Mummery LJ.

14 Employment Appeal Tribunal Rules 1993, SI 1993/2854, r 3(7)(b) (substituted by SI 2004/2526).

15 Ie subject to the Employment Appeal Tribunal Rules 1993, SI 1993/2854, r 3(10) (see the text and notes 21–22).

16 Employment Appeal Tribunal Rules 1993, SI 1993/2854, r 3(7) (substituted by SI 2004/2526; amended by SI 2013/1693).

17 See note 12.

18 Ie under the Employment Appeal Tribunal Rules 1993, SI 1993/2854, r 3(10): see the text and notes 21–22.

19 Ie under the Employment Appeal Tribunal Rules 1993, SI 1993/2854, r 3(7): see the text and notes 12–16.

20 See the Employment Appeal Tribunal Rules 1993, SI 1993/2854, r 3(7ZA) (added by SI 2013/1693).

21 See note 19.

22 Employment Appeal Tribunal Rules 1993, SI 1993/2854, r 3(10) (substituted by SI 2004/2526; amended by SI 2013/1693). For the application of the Employment Appeal Tribunal Rules 1993, SI 1993/2854, r 3(7), (8), (10) in the context of the judicial 'sift' (see PARA 1501), see *Haritaki v South East England Development Agency* [2008] IRLR 945, EAT. At such a hearing the judge may confirm the earlier decision or order that the appeal proceeds to a preliminary hearing (see PARA 1519) or a full hearing (see PARA 1520), giving appropriate directions: *Practice Direction (Employment Appeal Tribunal—Procedure) 2013* [2014] IRLR 92 para 11.6. These directions may permit an amendment to be made to the grounds of appeal. Such a proposed amendment should wherever practicable be made available in writing at the hearing or on the same day, and will not take effect unless the judge has approved it: para 11.6. A hearing under the Employment Appeal Tribunal Rules 1993, SI 1993/2854, r 3(10), including

judgment and any directions, will normally last not more than one hour including time for oral judgment to be given: *Practice Direction (Employment Appeal Tribunal—Procedure) 2013* [2014] IRLR 92 para 11.7.

23 Ie *Practice Direction (Employment Appeal Tribunal—Procedure) 2013* [2014] IRLR 92.

24 See *Practice Direction (Employment Appeal Tribunal—Procedure) 2013* [2014] IRLR 92 para 1.9.

1452. Special advocate before the Employment Appeal Tribunal. A Minister of the Crown (whether or not he is a party to the proceedings) may, if he considers it expedient in the interests of national security, direct the Appeal Tribunal[1] by notice to the registrar[2] to:

(1) sit in private for all or part of particular Crown employment proceedings[3];

(2) exclude any party who was the claimant[4] in the proceedings before the employment tribunal[5] from all or part of particular Crown employment proceedings[6];

(3) exclude the representatives of any party who was the claimant in the proceedings before the employment tribunal from all or part of particular Crown employment proceedings[7];

(4) take steps to conceal the identity of a particular witness in particular Crown employment proceedings[8].

The Appeal Tribunal may, if it considers it expedient in the interests of national security, by order:

(a) do in relation to particular proceedings before it anything of a kind which the Appeal Tribunal can be required to do in relation to particular Crown employment proceedings by direction under heads (1) to (4) above[9];

(b) direct any person to whom any document (including any decision or record of the proceedings) has been provided for the purposes of the proceedings not to disclose any such document or the content thereof[10]:

(i) to any excluded person[11];

(ii) in any case in which a direction has been given under head (1) above or an order has been made under head (a) above read with head (1) above, to any person excluded from all or part of the proceedings by virtue of such direction or order[12]; or

(iii) in any case in which a Minister of the Crown has informed the registrar[13] that he wishes to address the Appeal Tribunal with a view to the Appeal Tribunal making an order under head (a) above read with head (2) or head (3) above, to any person who may be excluded from all or part of the proceedings by virtue of such an order, if an order is made, at any time before the Appeal Tribunal decides whether or not to make such an order[14];

(c) take steps to keep secret all or part of the reasons for any order it makes[15],

but the Appeal Tribunal must keep under review any order it so makes[16].

In any proceedings in which a Minister of the Crown considers that it would be appropriate for the Appeal Tribunal to make an order as referred to in heads (a) to (c) above, he is (whether or not he is a party to the proceedings) entitled to appear before and to address the Appeal Tribunal thereon[17]. The minister must inform the registrar by notice that he wishes to address the Appeal Tribunal and the registrar must copy the notice to the parties[18].

In any proceedings in which there is an excluded person, the Appeal Tribunal must inform the Attorney General[19] of the proceedings before it with a view to the Attorney General, if he thinks it fit to do so, appointing a special advocate[20] to represent the interests of the person who was the claimant in the proceedings before the employment tribunal in respect of those parts of the proceedings from which any representative of his is excluded, from which both he and his representative are excluded, or from which he is excluded, where he does not have a representative[21].

Where the excluded person is a party to the proceedings, he must be permitted to make a statement to the Appeal Tribunal before the commencement of the proceedings, or the part of the proceedings, from which he is excluded[22].

The special advocate may not communicate directly or indirectly with any person, including an excluded person:

(A)   except in the case of the Appeal Tribunal or the party who was the respondent in the proceedings before the employment tribunal[23], on any matter contained in the documents disclosing the grounds[24] and/or the supplementary grounds[25] on which the appeal is brought, the grounds[26] and/or the supplementary grounds[27] for resisting the appeal or of any cross-appeal[28];

(B)   except in the case of a person who was present, on any matter discussed or referred to during any part of the proceedings in which the Appeal Tribunal sat in private pursuant to a direction of the minister under head (1) above or an order of the Appeal Tribunal under head (a) above read with head (1) above[29].

However, the special advocate may apply for directions from the Appeal Tribunal authorising him to seek instructions from, or otherwise to communicate with, an excluded person on any matter contained in the documents referred to in head (A) above, or on any matter discussed or referred to during any part of the proceedings in which the Appeal Tribunal sat in private as referred to in head (B) above[30]. Such an application must be made by presenting to the registrar a notice of application, which must state the title of the proceedings and set out the grounds of the application[31]. The registrar must notify the minister of such an application for directions and the minister is entitled to address the Appeal Tribunal on the application[32].

1   As to the meaning of 'Appeal Tribunal' see PARA 1451 note 4.

2   As to the meaning of 'registrar' see PARA 1430 note 4.

3   Employment Appeal Tribunal Rules 1993, SI 1993/2854, r 30A(1)(a) (r 30A added by SI 2001/1128). For these purposes, 'Crown employment proceedings' has the meaning given by the Employment Tribunals Act 1996 s 10(8) (see PARA 1448): Employment Appeal Tribunal Rules 1993, SI 1993/2854, r 2(1) (substituted by SI 2001/1128).

4   As to the claimant see PARA 1461.

5   As to proceedings before the employment tribunal see PARA 1453 et seq.

6   Employment Appeal Tribunal Rules 1993, SI 1993/2854, r 30A(1)(b) (as added (see note 3); amended by SI 2004/2526).

7   Employment Appeal Tribunal Rules 1993, SI 1993/2854, r 30A(1)(c) (as added (see note 3); amended by SI 2004/2526).

8   Employment Appeal Tribunal Rules 1993, SI 1993/2854, r 30A(1)(d) (as added: see note 3).

9   Employment Appeal Tribunal Rules 1993, SI 1993/2854, r 30A(2)(a) (as added (see note 3); amended by SI 2005/1871).

10   Employment Appeal Tribunal Rules 1993, SI 1993/2854, r 30A(2)(b) (as added: see note 3). As to the meaning of 'document' see PARA 1451 note 5.

11   Employment Appeal Tribunal Rules 1993, SI 1993/2854, r 30A(2)(b)(i) (as added: see note 3). For these purposes, 'excluded person' means, in relation to any proceedings, a person who has been excluded from all or part of the proceedings by virtue of: (1) a direction of a Minister of

the Crown under r 30A(1)(b) or (c) (see heads (2)–(3) in the text); or (2) an order of the tribunal under r 30A(2)(a) (see head (a) in the text) read with r 30A(1)(b) or (c): r 2(1) (as substituted: see note 3).

12 Employment Appeal Tribunal Rules 1993, SI 1993/2854, r 30A(2)(b)(ii) (as added: see note 3).

13 Ie in accordance with the Employment Appeal Tribunal Rules 1993, SI 1993/2854, r 30A(3): see the text and notes 17–18.

15 Employment Appeal Tribunal Rules 1993, SI 1993/2854, r 30A(2)(c) (as added: see note 3).

16 Employment Appeal Tribunal Rules 1993, SI 1993/2854, r 30A(2) (as added: see note 3).

17 Employment Appeal Tribunal Rules 1993, SI 1993/2854, r 30A(3) (as added: see note 3).

18 See note 17.

19 As to the Attorney General see CONSTITUTIONAL AND ADMINISTRATIVE LAW vol 20 (2014) PARA 273 et seq.

19 As to the meaning of 'special advocate' see PARA 1451 note 9. A special advocate must have a general qualification for the purposes of the Courts and Legal Services Act 1990 s 71 (see LEGAL PROFESSIONS vol 65 (2008) PARA 742: Employment Appeal Tribunal Rules 1993, SI 1993/2854, r 30A(5) (as added: see note 3). In the Employment Appeal Tribunal Rules 1993, SI 1993/2854, in any case in which a special advocate has been appointed in respect of a party, any reference to a 'party' or 'parties' includes the special advocate, except in the following cases: (1) r 5 (see PARA 1498 note 4); (2) r 18 (see PARA 1513); (3) the first and second references in r 27(1A) (see PARA 1514); (4) r 30A(1) (see the text and notes 1–8), r 30A(6) (see the text and note 22); (5) the first reference in r 30A(3) (see the text and notes 17–18); (6) r 34(1) (see PARA 1525); and (7) the references in r 3(1), Schedule, Form 1 item 4 and Form 1A item 4 (see PARA 1495 note 3): r 30A(11), (12) (as added: see note 3).

21 Employment Appeal Tribunal Rules 1993, SI 1993/2854, r 30A(4) (as added (see note 3); amended by SI 2004/2526).

22 Employment Appeal Tribunal Rules 1993, SI 1993/2854, r 30A(6) (as added: see note 3).

23 As to the meaning of 'respondent' see PARA 1498 note 4.

24 Ie the grounds contained in the document referred to in the Employment Appeal Tribunal Rules 1993, SI 1993/2854, r 3(5): see PARA 1451.

25 Ie the grounds and/or the supplementary grounds contained in the document referred to in the Employment Appeal Tribunal Rules 1993, SI 1993/2854, r 3(6): see PARA 1451.

26 Ie the grounds contained in the document referred to in the Employment Appeal Tribunal Rules 1993, SI 1993/2854, r 6(7): see PARA 1499.

27 Ie the grounds and/or the supplementary grounds contained in the document referred to in the Employment Appeal Tribunal Rules 1993, SI 1993/2854, r 6(8)(b): see PARA 1499.

28 Employment Appeal Tribunal Rules 1993, SI 1993/2854, r 30A(7)(a) (as added: see note 3).

29 Employment Appeal Tribunal Rules 1993, SI 1993/2854, r 30A(7)(b) (as added: see note 3).

30 Employment Appeal Tribunal Rules 1993, SI 1993/2854, r 30A(8) (as added: see note 3).

31 Employment Appeal Tribunal Rules 1993, SI 1993/2854, r 30A(9) (as added: see note 3).

32 Employment Appeal Tribunal Rules 1993, SI 1993/2854, r 30A(10) (as added: see note 3).

(2) PROCEEDINGS BEFORE EMPLOYMENT TRIBUNALS

(i) Time Limits in Employment Cases

1453. Time limits for presenting complaints to employment tribunals; in general. An employment tribunal may not in general entertain a complaint by an employee unless his complaint is presented[1] to the tribunal within a prescribed period[2] or within such further period as the tribunal considers reasonable in a case where it is satisfied that it was not reasonably practicable[3] for the complaint to be presented within the prescribed period[4].

Whether it was not reasonably practicable so to present a complaint is a question of fact for the tribunal whose decision will not normally be reversed on appeal[5]. Although previous decisions may suggest factors which a tribunal may consider relevant in reaching its decision, they do not establish rules of law[6]. The following factors may, however, be considered:

(1) mere ignorance of rights is not normally a good ground for an extension of time unless in all the circumstances it was reasonable[7];

(2) reliance on bad advice from an adviser is not normally a good ground, the applicant possibly being left with a civil remedy against the adviser[8];

(3) reliance on bad advice from an official source may, however, be a good ground[9];

(4) awaiting the outcome of other proceedings, including criminal proceedings, is not normally a good ground[10];

(5) postal delays may justify an extension of time, but regard should be had to the date, time and method of postage used and to the reasonable expectations of the parties[11];

(6) illness may justify an extension, even if only in the latter part of the time limitation period (but in effect preventing the employee from claiming when he had envisaged doing so)[12].

1 As to when an application is taken to be presented to an employment tribunal see PARA 1461 note 3.

2 See, in particular, the Employment Rights Act 1996 s 111(2); and PARA 804 (the three-month time limit for a claim for unfair dismissal, which has produced most of the case law). Time limits as expressed in the Employment Rights Act 1996 are jurisdictional, not merely procedural. Thus, unless the time limit is extended, a claim out of time deprives the tribunal of jurisdiction; and the failure to comply with the time limit cannot be waived by the respondent: *Westward Circuits Ltd v Read* [1973] 2 All ER 1013, [1973] ICR 301, NIRC; *Rogers v Bodfari (Transport) Ltd* [1973] ICR 325, [1973] IRLR 172, NIRC; *Dedman v British Building and Engineering Appliances Ltd* [1974] 1 All ER 520, [1974] ICR 53, CA. Cf *Grimes v Sutton London Borough Council* [1973] 2 All ER 448, [1973] ICR 240, NIRC where it was held that the time limit under what is now the Employment Rights Act 1996 s 11(4) (see PARA 125) was procedural; but this may be open to question. As to time limits in cases of discrimination on the grounds of sex, race or disability (which are differently drafted and work on different principles) see DISCRIMINATION vol 33 (2013) PARA 345.

 The time limit does not apply to adding a further respondent, provided that the original action was begun in good time: *Gillick v BP Chemicals Ltd* [1993] IRLR 437, EAT; *Drinkwater Sabey Ltd v Burnett* [1995] ICR 328, sub nom *Drinkwater Sabey Ltd v Burnett and Kent County Council* [1995] IRLR 238, EAT.

3 The burden of proof is on the claimant to show that it was not reasonably practicable to do so: *Porter v Bandridge Ltd* [1978] 1 WLR 1145, [1978] ICR 943, CA.

4 The expiration of a limitation period only extinguishes the right to present a claim form: *Prison Officers Association v Nottinghamshire Healthcare NHS Trust* [2003] ICR 1192, EAT (claim form presented to an employment tribunal without authority did not mean that it lacked legal authority at the time it had been presented). As to the special provisions which apply in the case of claims for redundancy payments see the Employment Rights Act 1996 s 164; and PARA 880. As to the calculation of time limits for doing actions prescribed by the employment tribunal procedure regulations themselves see PARA 1460.

5 *Wall's Meat Co Ltd v Khan* [1979] ICR 52, [1978] IRLR 499, CA; *Palmer v Southend-on-Sea Borough Council* [1984] 1 All ER 945, [1984] ICR 372, CA; *James W Cook & Co (Wivenhoe) Ltd v Tipper* [1990] ICR 716, [1990] IRLR 386, CA. There is no principle of law which dictates how generously or sparingly the power to extend time in employment tribunal proceedings is to be exercised: *Caston v Chief Constable of Lincolnshire Police* [2009] EWCA Civ 1298, [2010] IRLR 327, (2010) Times, 26 January (Employment Appeal Tribunal had been right to hold that it had been open to the employment tribunal to find that it was just and equitable to extend the employee's time).

6 A particularly useful summary of the correct approach and of relevant factors is contained in the judgment of May LJ in *Palmer v Southend-on-Sea Borough Council* [1984] 1 All ER 945 at 955, [1984] ICR 372 at 385, CA.

7 *Dedman v British Building and Engineering Appliances Ltd* [1974] 1 All ER 520, [1974] ICR 53, CA; *Wall's Meat Co Ltd v Khan* [1979] ICR 52, [1978] IRLR 499, CA; *Riley v Tesco Stores Ltd* [1980] ICR 323, [1980] IRLR 103, CA; *Porter v Bandridge Ltd* [1978] 1 WLR 1145, [1978] ICR 943, CA; *Avon County Council v Haywood-Hicks* [1978] ICR 646, [1978] IRLR 118, EAT; *Brown v Islington London Borough Council* [2008] All ER (D) 28 (Aug), EAT. Where, however, the employee was ignorant of a fact fundamental to the right to claim until close to or after the expiry of the time limit, that may be a good ground for extension: *Churchill v A Yeates & Sons Ltd* [1983] ICR 380, [1983] IRLR 187, EAT; *Machine Tool Industry*

Research Association v Simpson [1988] ICR 558, [1988] IRLR 212, CA; *Marley (UK) Ltd v Anderson* [1996] ICR 728, [1996] IRLR 163, CA (holding that this factor can be applied over a period of time if the employee gradually becomes aware of the facts; applied in *Heslip v Teva (UK) Ltd* [2009] All ER (D) 277 (Jul), EAT (judge had been entitled to find that it was not reasonably practicable for the claim to have been presented until the employee acquired knowledge that another employee had been doing work in her former area)); *Post Office v Sanhotra* [2000] ICR 866, EAT (employee unaware that he had not been given a good reference, a fact that was crucial to his submission that the employer had made a fraudulent misrepresentation to him and proof of which was crucial to his right to bring his complaint); *Shotton v Royal Mail Group plc* [2005] All ER (D) 235 (May), EAT (genuine error by management, not spotted by the union, to implement a national collective agreement; authority did not require a relationship to be established between the primary limitation period and the discretionary extension). See also *Crouchman v Cambridge and Peterborough Foundation NHS Trust* [2009] ICR 1306, [2009] All ER (D) 96 (May), EAT (where *Churchill v A Yeates & Sons Ltd*[1983] ICR 380, [1983] IRLR 187, EAT, *Machine Tool Industry Research Association v Simpson*[1988] ICR 558, [1988] IRLR 212, CA, and *Marley (UK) Ltd v Anderson* [1996] ICR 728, [1996] IRLR 163, CA were applied).

8   *Riley v Tesco Stores Ltd* [1980] ICR 323, [1980] IRLR 103, CA. See *Williams-Ryan v Marks & Spencer plc* [2004] All ER (D) 73 (Sep), EAT; affd sub nom *Marks & Spencer plc v Williams-Ryan* [2005] EWCA Civ 470, [2005] ICR 1293, [2005] IRLR 562 (extension allowed for employee who received mistaken advice that she should await the outcome of internal appeal procedure before making a complaint to the tribunal). The adviser may be a solicitor (*Dedman v British Building and Engineering Appliances Ltd* [1974] 1 All ER 520, [1974] ICR 53, CA; *Papparis v Charles Fulton & Co Ltd* [1981] IRLR 104, EAT; *Trevelyans (Birmingham) Ltd v Norton* [1991] ICR 488, EAT), the Free Representation Unit (*Croydon Health Authority v Jaufurally* [1986] ICR 4, EAT), a trade union official (*Times Newspapers Ltd v O'Regan* [1977] IRLR 101, EAT; *Syed v Ford Motor Co Ltd* [1979] IRLR 335, IT; but see also *Wright v Wolverhampton City Council* [2009] All ER (D) 179 (Feb), EAT), a professional body (*Hammond v Haigh Castle & Co Ltd* [1973] 2 All ER 289, [1973] ICR 148, NIRC) or a body such as the Citizens' Advice Bureau (*Riley v Tesco Stores Ltd* [1980] ICR 323, [1980] IRLR 103, CA). *Riley v Tesco Stores Ltd* [1980] ICR 323, [1980] IRLR 103, CA, and *Syed v Ford Motor Co Ltd* [1979] IRLR 335, IT, were applied in *Brown v Islington London Borough Council* [2008] All ER (D) 28 (Aug), EAT. Solicitors acting in criminal proceedings connected with allegations of conduct arising out of employment may be expected to advise on the time limit for claims of unfair dismissal: *Trevelyans (Birmingham) Ltd v Norton* [1991] ICR 488, EAT. There is, however, no absolute rule that consulting a solicitor renders it reasonably practicable to comply, and the facts must still be considered: *London International College Ltd v Sen* [1993] IRLR 333, CA. See *Northamptonshire County Council v Entwhistle* [2010] IRLR 740, [2010] All ER (D) 35 (Sep), EAT (no extension of time where employee's solicitor negligently failed to spot error by employer in setting out the time limit for presenting a claim).

9   *Harvey's Household Linens Ltd v Benson* [1974] ICR 306, NIRC (Department of Employment official; but it is otherwise if the advice was asked for in a misleading or incoherent way (*W Press & Son Ltd v Hall* [1974] ICR 21, NIRC; *Rybak v Jean Sorrelle Ltd* [1991] ICR 127, sub nom *Jean Sorelle Ltd v Rybak* [1991] IRLR 153, EAT (employment tribunal official)). See also *Wright v Wolverhampton City Council* [2009] All ER (D) 179 (Feb), EAT (where the advice was from a trade union representative, and the Appeal Tribunal found for the employee as the reasons for delay were the same as those accepted by the judge had the original claim form been successfully delivered).

10 *Norgett v Luton Industrial Co-operative Society Ltd* [1976] ICR 442, [1976] IRLR 306, EAT; *House of Clydesdale Ltd v Foy* [1976] IRLR 391, EAT; *Porter v Bandridge Ltd* [1978] 1 WLR 1145, [1978] ICR 943, CA; *Wall's Meat Co Ltd v Khan* [1979] ICR 52, [1978] IRLR 499, CA; *Riley v Tesco Stores Ltd* [1980] ICR 323, [1980] IRLR 103, CA; *Trevelyans (Birmingham) Ltd v Norton* [1991] ICR 488, EAT. See also *Bevan v Royal Bank of Scotland* [2008] ICR 682, [2007] All ER (D) 389 (Nov), EAT.

Delay ascribed to an employee exercising a right of internal appeal under the employer's disciplinary procedure will not usually be a good ground: see *Palmer v Southend-on-Sea Borough Council* [1984] 1 All ER 945, [1984] ICR 372, CA (approving on this point *Bodha v Hampshire Area Health Authority* [1982] ICR 200, EAT, and disapproving dicta to the contrary in *Crown Agents for Overseas Governments and Administration v Lawal* [1979] ICR 103, [1978] IRLR 542, EAT); *Croydon Health Authority v Jaufurally* [1986] ICR 4, EAT; *London Underground Ltd v Noel* [2000] ICR 109, [1999] IRLR 621, CA.

11 *Sturges v AE Farr Ltd* [1975] ICR 356, [1975] IRLR 312; *Burton v Field Sons & Co Ltd* [1977] ICR 106, EAT; *Beanstalk Shelving Ltd v Horn* [1980] ICR 273, EAT; *Birmingham Midshires*

Building Society v Horton [1991] ICR 648, EAT; *St Basil's Centre v McCrossan* [1992] ICR 140, [1991] IRLR 455, EAT; *Thompson v GEC Avionics Ltd* [1991] IRLR 488, EAT. It is open to an employment tribunal to examine the procedures in a solicitor's office to see whether it feels that they are reasonable in the circumstances: *Birmingham Midshires Building Society v Horton* [1991] ICR 648 at 652, EAT, per Wood P. Where an application is posted in good time but lost in the post, the relevant question may be whether all reasonable steps were taken to check safe delivery: *Capital Foods Retail Ltd v Corrigan* [1993] IRLR 430, EAT; *Camden and Islington Community Services NHS Trust v Kennedy* [1996] IRLR 381, EAT. For general guidance as to what is a reasonable expectation for delivery of post see *St Basil's Centre v McCrossan* [1992] ICR 140 at 145, [1991] IRLR 455 at 457, EAT, obiter per Wood P. See also note 1.

12 *Schultz v Esso Petroleum Ltd* [1999] 3 All ER 338, [1999] ICR 1202, CA.

1454.   Extension of time limits because of mediation in certain cross-border disputes.   Where a time limit is set by a provision of the Employment Rights Act 1996 in relation to the whole or part of a relevant dispute[1], and a mediation[2] in relation to the relevant dispute starts[3] before the time limit expires[4], then if the time limit, if not extended by the following provisions, would expire before the mediation ends[5] or less than four weeks after it ends[6], the time limit expires instead[7] at the end of four weeks after the mediation ends[8], if the 1996 Act provides for this to apply for the purposes of the above-mentioned provision setting the time limit[9].

Where a time limit is set on a claim for a redundancy payment[10] in relation to the whole or part of a relevant dispute[11], a mediation in relation to the relevant dispute starts before the time limit expires[12], and if not extended by these provisions, the time limit would expire before the mediation ends or less than eight weeks after it ends[13], the time limit expires instead[14] at the end of eight weeks after the mediation ends[15].

Where more than one time limit applies in relation to a relevant dispute, the extension by the above provisions[16] of one of those time limits does not affect the others[17].

1 See the Employment Rights Act 1996 s 207A(2)(b) (s 207A added by SI 2011/1133). For these purposes, 'relevant dispute' means a dispute to which European Parliament and Council Directive (EC) 2008/52 (OJ L136, 24.5.2008, p 3) art 8(1) applies (certain cross-border disputes): Employment Rights Act 1996 s 207A(1)(a), (d) (as so added).

2 For these purposes, 'mediation' means a structured process, however named or referred to, whereby two or more parties to a dispute attempt by themselves, on a voluntary basis, to reach an agreement on the settlement of their dispute with the assistance of a mediator. This process may be initiated by the parties or suggested or ordered by a court or prescribed by the law of a member state. It includes mediation conducted by a judge who is not responsible for any judicial proceedings concerning the dispute in question. It excludes attempts made by the court or the judge seised to settle a dispute in the course of judicial proceedings concerning the dispute in question: European Parliament and Council Directive (EC) 2008/52 (OJ L136, 24.5.2008, p 3) art 3(a) (definition applied by the Employment Rights Act 1996 s 207A(1)(a), (b) (as added: see note 1)). In the case of any relevant dispute, references in s 207A to a mediation are references to the mediation so far as it relates to that dispute, and references to a party are to be read accordingly: s 207A(12) (as so added).

3 For these purposes, a mediation starts on the date of the agreement to mediate that is entered into by the parties and the mediator: Employment Rights Act 1996 s 207A(9) (as added: see note 1).

4 See the Employment Rights Act 1996 s 207A(2)(c) (as added: see note 1).

5 For these purposes, a mediation ends on the date of the first of these to occur: (1) the parties reach an agreement in resolution of the relevant dispute; (2) a party completes the notification of the other parties that it has withdrawn from the mediation; (3) a party to whom a qualifying request is made fails to give a response reaching the other parties within 14 days of the request; (4) the parties, after being notified that the mediator's appointment has ended (by death, resignation or otherwise), fail to agree within 14 days to seek to appoint a replacement mediator; (5) the mediation otherwise comes to an end pursuant to the terms of the agreement

to mediate: Employment Rights Act 1996 s 207A(10) (as added: see note 1). A 'qualifying request' is a request by a party that another ('A') confirm to all parties that A is continuing with the mediation: s 207A(11) (as so added).

    For these purposes, 'mediator' means any third person who is asked to conduct a mediation in an effective, impartial and competent way, regardless of the denomination or profession of that third person in the member state concerned and of the way in which the third person has been appointed or requested to conduct the mediation: European Parliament and Council Directive (EC) 2008/52 (OJ L136, 24.5.2008, p 3) art 3(b) (definition applied by the Employment Rights Act 1996 s 207A(1)(a), (c) (as so added)).

6   See the Employment Rights Act 1996 s 207A(2)(d) (as added: see note 1).

7   Ie subject to the Employment Rights Act 1996 s 207A(4): see note 9.

8   Employment Rights Act 1996 s 207A(3) (as added: see note 1).

9   See the Employment Rights Act 1996 s 207A(2)(a) (as added: see note 1). If a time limit mentioned in s 207A(2)(b) (see the text and note 1) has been extended by s 207A, s 207A(2), (3) applies to the extended time limit as it applies to a time limit mentioned in s 207A(2)(b): s 207A(4) (as so added).

    Where an employment tribunal has power under the Employment Rights Act 1996 to extend a time limit to which s 207A(3) applies, the power is exercisable in relation to the time limit as extended by s 207A: s 207A(13) (as so added).

10 Ie a time limit is set by the Employment Rights Act 1996 s 164(1)(c) or (2): see PARA 880.

11 See the Employment Rights Act 1996 s 207A(5)(a) (as added: see note 1).

12 See the Employment Rights Act 1996 s 207A(5)(b) (as added: see note 1).

13 See the Employment Rights Act 1996 s 207A(5)(c) (as added: see note 1).

14 Ie subject to the Employment Rights Act 1996 s 207A(7): see note 15.

15 Employment Rights Act 1996 s 207A(6) (as added: see note 1). If a time limit mentioned in s 207A(5)(a) (see the text and notes 10–11) has been extended by s 207A, s 207A(5), (6) applies to the extended time limit as it applies to a time limit mentioned in s 207A(5)(a): s 207A(7) (as so added).

16 Ie by the Employment Rights Act 1996 s 207A(3) or (6): see the text and notes 7–8, 14–15.

17 Employment Rights Act 1996 s 207A(8) (as added: see note 1).

1455.   Extension of time limits to facilitate conciliation before the institution of proceedings. Where the Employment Rights Act 1996 or the Trade Union and Labour Relations (Consolidation) Act 1992 provides for the following provisions to apply for the purposes of a provision of the Act in question (a 'relevant provision')[1], then in working out when a time limit set by a relevant provision expires, the period:

(1)   beginning with the day after the day on which the complainant or applicant concerned complies with the statutory requirement[2] to contact the Advisory, Conciliation and Arbitration Service ('ACAS')[3] before instituting proceedings in relation to the matter in respect of which the proceedings are brought ('Day A')[4]; and

(2)   ending with the day on which the complainant or applicant concerned receives (or, if earlier, is treated as receiving[5]) the certificate issued by the conciliation officer[6] to the effect either that he has concluded that a settlement is not possible within the prescribed period or that the prescribed period has expired without a settlement having been reached ('Day B')[7],

is not to be counted[8].

If a time limit set by a relevant provision would, if not extended by this provision, expire during the period beginning with Day A and ending one month after Day B, the time limit expires instead at the end of that period[9].

Where an employment tribunal has power under the Employment Rights Act 1996 or the Trade Union and Labour Relations (Consolidation) Act 1992 to extend a time limit set by a relevant provision, the power is exercisable in relation to the time limit as extended by the above provisions[10].

A number of regulations make similar provision for extending time limits to facilitate conciliation before the institution of proceedings[11].

1 See the Employment Rights Act 1996 s 207B(1) (s 207B added by the Enterprise and Regulatory Reform Act 2013 Sch 2 paras 15, 35); the Trade Union and Labour Relations (Consolidation) Act 1992 s 292A(1) (s 292A added by the Enterprise and Regulatory Reform Act 2013 Sch 2 paras 1, 13).
  The Employment Rights Act 1996 s 207B it does not apply to a dispute that is (or so much of a dispute as is) a relevant dispute for the purposes of s 207A (see PARA 1454): s 207B(1) (as so added).
2 Ie the requirement in the Employment Tribunals Act 1996 s 18A(1): see PARA 152.
3 As to ACAS see PARA 1213 et seq.
4 See the Employment Rights Act 1996 s 207B(2)(a), (3) (as added: see note 1); the Trade Union and Labour Relations (Consolidation) Act 1992 s 292A(2)(a), (3) (as added: see note 1).
5 Ie by virtue of regulations made under the Employment Tribunals Act 1996 s 18A(11): see PARA 152.
6 Ie the certificate issued under the Employment Tribunals Act 1996 s 18A(4): see PARA 152.
7 See the Employment Rights Act 1996 s 207B(2)(b), (3) (as added: see note 1); the Trade Union and Labour Relations (Consolidation) Act 1992 s 292A(2)(b), (3) (as added: see note 1).
8 See the Employment Rights Act 1996 s 207B(3) (as added: see note 1); the Trade Union and Labour Relations (Consolidation) Act 1992 s 292A(3) (as added: see note 1).
9 Employment Rights Act 1996 s 207B(4) (as added: see note 1); Trade Union and Labour Relations (Consolidation) Act 1992 s 292A(4) (as added: see note 1).
10 Employment Rights Act 1996 s 207B(5) (as added: see note 1); Trade Union and Labour Relations (Consolidation) Act 1992 s 292A(5) (as added: see note 1).
11 See eg the Part-time Workers (Prevention of Less Favourable Treatment) Regulations 2000, SI 2000/1551, reg 8A; and PARA 80; the Fixed-term Employees (Prevention of Less Favourable Treatment) Regulations 2002, SI 2002/2034, reg 7A; and PARA 91; the Health and Safety (Consultation with Employees) Regulations 1996, SI 1996/1513, Sch 2 para 3A; and PARA 1210; the Information and Consultation of Employees Regulations 2004, SI 2004/3426, reg 29A; and PARA 1311.

(ii) Death of Employer or Employee

1456. Institution or continuance of tribunal proceedings after death of employer or employee. In the context of the Employment Rights Act 1996, where an employer[1] or employee[2] has died, any tribunal proceedings arising under any of the relevant provisions[3] may be defended by a personal representative of the deceased employer or, as the case may be, instituted or continued by a personal representative of the deceased employee[4].

If there is no personal representative of a deceased employee, any tribunal proceedings arising under any of the relevant provisions may be instituted or continued on behalf of the estate of the deceased employee by such other person as may be appointed by the employment tribunal being either:

(1) a person who is authorised by the employee before his death to act in connection with the proceedings; or

(2) the widow or widower, surviving civil partner, child, parent or brother or sister of the deceased employee[5];

and, in such a case, any award made by the employment tribunal must be made in such terms and is enforceable in such manner as the Secretary of State may by regulations provide[6].

In relation to an employer or employee who has died:

(a) any reference in the relevant provisions to the doing of anything by or in relation to an employer or employee includes a reference to the doing of the thing by or in relation to a personal representative of the deceased employer or employee[7]; and

(b) any reference in the relevant provisions to a thing required or authorised to be done by or in relation to an employer or employee includes a reference to a thing required or authorised to be done by or in relation to a personal representative of the deceased employer or employee[8]; and heads (a) and (b) above do not prevent a reference to a successor of an employer from including a personal representative of a deceased employer[9].

Any right arising under any of the relevant provisions which accrues after the death of an employee devolves as if it had accrued before his death[10].

Where a personal representative is liable[11] to pay any amount and the liability has not accrued before the death of the employer, it is to be treated as a liability of the deceased employer which had accrued immediately before his death[12].

In the context of the Trade Union and Labour Relations (Consolidation) Act 1992, where the employee[13] or worker[14] or employer[15] dies, tribunal proceedings in relation to the statutory right for time off work for trade union duties and activities[16] or the statutory procedure for handling redundancies[17] may be instituted or continued by a personal representative[18] of the deceased employee or worker or, as the case may be, defended by a personal representative of the deceased employer[19]. This provision[20] also has effect in relation to provisions on inducements and detriment[21].

Any right arising under any of the relevant statutory provisions[22] which so accrues after the death of the employee or worker in question devolves as if it had accrued before his death[23]; and any liability so arising which so accrues after the death of the employer in question is to be treated for all purposes as if it had accrued immediately before his death[24].

1　As to the meaning of 'employer' see PARA 2.
2　As to the meaning of 'employee' see PARA 2.
3　The Employment Rights Act 1996 ss 206, 207 (see the text and notes 4–12) apply to Pt I (ss 1–12) (see PARA 119 et seq), so far as it relates to itemised pay statements; Pt III (ss 28–35) (see PARA 261 et seq), Pt V (ss 43M–49A) (see PARA 612 et seq), Pt VI (ss 50–63C) (see PARA 350 et seq), apart from ss 58–60 (right to time off for employee representatives and right to remuneration) (see PARAS 352–353), Pt VII (ss 64–70A) (see PARA 596 et seq), Pt VIII (ss 71–80E) (see PARA 355 et seq), s 92 (see PARA 755), s 93 (see PARA 756), Pt X (ss 94–134A) (see PARA 757 et seq), Pt XI (ss 135–181) (see PARA 835 et seq) and Pt XII (ss 182–190) (see PARA 628 et seq): s 206(2).
4　Employment Rights Act 1996 s 206(1), (3).
5　Employment Rights Act 1996 s 206(4), (5) (s 206(4) amended by the Employment Rights (Dispute Resolution) Act 1996 s 1(2)(a); the Employment Rights Act 1996 s 206(5) amended by SI 2005/3129). In the Employment Rights Act 1996 Pt XI (ss 135–181) (see PARA 835 et seq), s 206(6)–(9) (see the text and notes 6–9) and s 207 (see the text and notes 10–12) references to a personal representative include a person appointed under s 206(4): s 206(5).
　　Where a claim is presented by a person who has not been appointed under s 206(4) the claim is a nullity and cannot be retrospectively validated; an appointment under s 206(4) must precede the issue of the proceedings: *Fox v British Airways plc* [2013] ICR 51, [2012] All ER (D) 21 (Sep), EAT; affd (but this point not in issue) [2009] EWCA Civ 1202, [2010] ICR 397, [2010] IRLR 47 (see PARA 818).
6　Employment Rights Act 1996 s 206(6) (amended by the Employment Rights (Dispute Resolution) Act 1996 s 1(2)(a)). At the date at which this volume states the law no such regulations had been made but, by virtue of the Employment Rights Act 1996 s 241, Sch 2 para 2(1) (see PARA 162), the Employment Tribunals Awards (Enforcement in case of Death) Regulations 1976, SI 1976/663 (see PARA 1485) have effect as if so made. As to the Secretary of State see PARA 5 note 21; and as to the making of regulations under the Employment Rights Act 1996 generally see PARA 162.
7　Employment Rights Act 1996 s 206(7).
8　Employment Rights Act 1996 s 206(8).
9　Employment Rights Act 1996 s 206(9).
10　Employment Rights Act 1996 s 207(1). Where, under any provision of Pt XI (ss 135–181) (see PARA 835 et seq), an employment tribunal determines that an employer is liable to pay to a personal representative of a deceased employee the whole of a redundancy payment to which he

would have been entitled, but for some provision of Pt XI (ss 135–181) or s 206 (see the text and notes 1–9), or such part of such a redundancy payment as the tribunal thinks fit, the reference in s 207(1) to a right includes any right to receive it: s 207(2) (amended by the Employment Rights (Dispute Resolution) Act 1996 s 1(2)(a)).

11 Ie by virtue of any of the provisions to which the Employment Rights Act 1996 s 207 applies: see note 3.

12 Employment Rights Act 1996 s 207(3).

13 As to the meaning of 'employee' see PARA 892.

14 As to the meaning of 'worker' see PARA 892.

15 As to the meaning of 'employer' see PARA 892.

16 Ie the Trade Union and Labour Relations (Consolidation) Act 1992 ss 168–173 (see PARA 1065 et seq) so far as those provisions confer rights on employees or make provision in connection therewith.

17 Ie the Trade Union and Labour Relations (Consolidation) Act 1992 ss 188–198 (see PARA 1185 et seq) so far as those provisions confer rights on employees or make provision in connection therewith.

18 If there is no personal representative of a deceased employee, tribunal proceedings or proceedings to enforce a tribunal award may be instituted or continued on behalf of his estate by such other such person as the employment tribunal may appoint, being either: (1) a person authorised by the employee or worker to act in connection with the proceedings before his death; or (2) the widower, widow, surviving civil partner, child, father, mother, brother or sister of the employee or worker; and, in such a case, any award made by the employment tribunal must be in such terms and enforceable in such manner as may be prescribed: Trade Union and Labour Relations (Consolidation) Act 1992 s 292(3) (amended by the Employment Rights (Dispute Resolution) Act 1998 s 1(2)(a); the Employment Relations Act 2004 Sch 1 para 20(1), (4); the Civil Partnership Act 2004 Sch 27 para 146). As to the Secretary of State's power to make regulations prescribing certain matters under the Trade Union and Labour Relations (Consolidation) Act 1992 see s 293; and PARA 902 note 8. At the date at which this volume states the law no regulations had been made prescribing any of the matters mentioned in s 292(3) but, by virtue of s 300(3), Sch 3 para 1(2) (see PARA 891 note 1) and the Interpretation Act 1978 s 17(2)(b), the Employment Tribunals Awards (Enforcement in case of Death) Regulations 1976, SI 1976/663, have effect as if so made: see PARA 1485.

19 Trade Union and Labour Relations (Consolidation) Act 1992 s 292(1), (2) (amended by the Employment Relations Act 2004 Sch 1 para 20(1), (2), (3), Sch 2).

20 Ie the Trade Union and Labour Relations (Consolidation) Act 1992 s 292.

21 Trade Union and Labour Relations (Consolidation) Act 1992 s 292(1A) (added by the Employment Relations Act 2004 Sch 1 para 20(1), (3)). The reference is to the Trade Union and Labour Relations (Consolidation) Act 1992 ss 145A–151 (see PARA 1048 et seq) so far as they confer rights on workers or make provision in connection therewith: see s 292(1A) (as so added).

22 Ie the provisions mentioned in the Trade Union and Labour Relations (Consolidation) Act 1992 s 292(1) or (1A): see the text and notes 13–21.

23 Trade Union and Labour Relations (Consolidation) Act 1992 s 292(4) (amended by the Employment Relations Act 2004 Sch 1 para 20(1), (4), (5)).

24 Trade Union and Labour Relations (Consolidation) Act 1992 s 292(5).

(iii) Fees for Claims made to Employment Tribunals

1457. Fees payable for claims made to employment tribunals; effect of non-payment. As from 29 July 2013[1], fees are payable in respect of any claim[2] presented to an employment tribunal, as provided for in the Employment Tribunals and the Employment Appeal Tribunal Fees Order 2013[3]. Where, however, by any convention, treaty or other instrument entered into by Her Majesty with any foreign power it is provided that no fee is required to be paid in respect of any proceedings, the fees specified in that Order are not payable in respect of those proceedings[4].

A fee is payable:

(1) by a single claimant or a fee group[5]:

    (a) when a claim form is presented to an employment tribunal ('the issue fee'); and;

    (b)   on a date specified in a notice accompanying the notification of the listing of a final hearing of the claim ('the hearing fee')[6];

(2)   by the party making a specified application[7] on a date specified by the Lord Chancellor in a notice following the making of the application[8];

(3)   by the respondent on a date specified in a notice accompanying a notification of listing for judicial mediation[9].

The amount of the fee depends upon the type of the claim and the number of claimants. Claims known as 'type A claims'[10] incur lower fees than claims known as 'type B claims'[11]; and separate provision is made for fees payable by fee groups[12]. Where, on the date on which a fee is payable in accordance with head (1) above, the claim form contains:

    (i)   one or more type A claim and one or more type B claim, the total amount of the fees payable in respect of all the claims is the fee specified in respect of a type B claim; or

    (ii)   more than one claim of the same type, then the total amount of the fees payable in respect of all the claims is the amount specified[13] for that type of claim[14].

Any fee payable by a fee group[15]:

    (A)   must not exceed an amount equal to the sum of the fees which the members of the fee group would have been liable to pay as single claimants; and

    (B)   where one or more members of the group is entitled to remission[16] must not exceed an amount equal to the sum of the fees which the members of the fee group would be liable to pay as single claimants, taking into account any remission which would have been granted to individual members of the group if they were single claimants[17].

Where a fee payable by a fee group remains unpaid after the date specified in accordance with head (1) above, a member of that fee group may, before the date on which the claim to which the fee relates is liable to be dismissed for non-payment, notify the Lord Chancellor of that member's decision no longer to be part of the group[18]. Where a notice is received by the Lord Chancellor before the date on which the claim is liable to be dismissed, the member of the fee group who has given the notification is to be treated as a single claimant for the purposes of the claim to which the notice relates[19].

Provision is made for the remission of fees in some circumstances[20].

The tribunal[21] must reject a claim[22] if it is not accompanied by a tribunal fee[23] or a remission application[24]. Where a claim is accompanied by a tribunal fee but the amount paid is lower than the amount payable for the presentation of that claim, the tribunal must send the claimant[25] a notice specifying a date for payment of the additional amount due and the claim, or part of it in respect of which the relevant tribunal fee has not been paid, must be rejected by the tribunal if the amount due is not paid by the date specified[26]. If a claim, or part of it, is rejected, the form must be returned to the claimant with a notice of rejection explaining why it has been rejected[27]. Subject to the above provisions[28], where a party has not paid a relevant tribunal fee or presented a remission application in respect of that fee the tribunal will send the party a notice specifying a date for payment of the tribunal fee or presentation of a remission application[29]. If at the date specified in a notice so sent the party has not paid the tribunal fee and no remission application in respect of that fee has been presented:

(*aa*) where the tribunal fee is payable in relation to a claim, the claim must be dismissed without further order;

(*bb*) where the tribunal fee is payable in relation to an employer's contract claim, the employer's contract claim must be dismissed without further order;

(*cc*) where the tribunal fee is payable in relation to an application, the application must be dismissed without further order;

(*dd*) where the tribunal fee is payable in relation to judicial mediation, the judicial mediation is not to take place[30].

Where a remission application is refused in part or in full, the tribunal must send the claimant a notice specifying a date for payment of the tribunal fee[31]. If at the date specified in a notice so sent the party has not paid the tribunal fee, the consequences are those referred to in heads (*aa*) to (*dd*) above[32]. In the event of a dismissal under these provisions[33] a party may apply for the claim or response, or part of it, which was dismissed to be reinstated and the tribunal may order a reinstatement. A reinstatement is effective only if the tribunal fee is paid, or a remission application is presented and accepted, by the date specified in the order[34].

The 2013 Order introducing fees for claims made to employment tribunals has been the subject of an unsuccessful application for judicial review[35]. In dismissing the application, the court commented that the proceedings were premature and that the evidence at that stage lacked the robustness that would be necessary to overturn the fees regime[36].

1   See the Employment Tribunals and the Employment Appeal Tribunal Fees Order 2013, SI 2013/1893, art 1.

2   'Claim' means any proceedings brought before an employment tribunal and includes an appeal, application, complaint, reference or question, and 'claimant' is to be construed accordingly: Employment Tribunals and the Employment Appeal Tribunal Fees Order 2013, SI 2013/1893, art 2.

3   Employment Tribunals and the Employment Appeal Tribunal Fees Order 2013, SI 2013/1893, art 3. No fee is payable in respect of a claim where the claim form was presented before 29 July 2013: see art 15. 'Claim form' means the form by means of which a person presents a claim: art 2.

   The 2013 Order was made by the Lord Chancellor in exercise of the powers conferred by the Tribunals, Courts and Enforcement Act 2007 ss 42(1)(d), (2), 49(3): see COURTS AND TRIBUNALS vol 24 (2010) PARA 871. As to the Lord Chancellor see CONSTITUTIONAL AND ADMINISTRATIVE LAW vol 20 (2014) PARA 255 et seq.

4   Employment Tribunals and the Employment Appeal Tribunal Fees Order 2013, SI 2013/1893, art 19.

5   'Single claimant' means a claimant who is the only claimant named in the claim form: Employment Tribunals and the Employment Appeal Tribunal Fees Order 2013, SI 2013/1893, art 2. 'Fee group' means (1) in relation to the payment of the issue fee, the group of persons named as claimants in the claim form at the time the claim was presented; (2) subject to art 12(2) (see the text and note 19), in relation to the payment of a hearing fee, the group of persons each of whom were named as claimants in the claim form at the time the claim was presented and are named as claimants in the notification of the listing of the final hearing: art 2. 'Final hearing' means the first hearing at which an employment tribunal will determine liability, remedy or costs: art 2.

6   Employment Tribunals and the Employment Appeal Tribunal Fees Order 2013, SI 2013/1893, art 4(1).

7   Ie an application listed in the Employment Tribunals and the Employment Appeal Tribunal Fees Order 2013, SI 2013/1893, Sch 1 col 1. Those applications are: (1) reconsideration of a default judgment; (2) reconsideration of a judgment following a final hearing; (3) dismissal following withdrawal; (4) an employer's contract claim made by way of application as part of the response to the employee's contract claim: Sch 1 col 1. 'Employer's contract claim' means a claim brought by an employer in accordance with the Employment Tribunals Extension of Jurisdiction (England and Wales) Order 1994, SI 1994/1623, arts 4, 8 (see PARAS 1408–1409): Employment

Tribunals and the Employment Appeal Tribunal Fees Order 2013, SI 2013/1893, art 2. An identical definition appears in Employment Tribunals (Constitution and Rules of Procedure) Regulations 2013, SI 2013/1237, Sch 1 r 1(1).

The fee payable in relation to an application listed in the Employment Tribunals and the Employment Appeal Tribunal Fees Order 2013, SI 2013/1893, Sch 1 col 1, irrespective of the number of claims or of claimants named in the application is the amount specified in the relevant part of Sch 1 col 2: art 11(1). Where such an application is made in respect of one or more type A claims and one or more type B claims, the amount of the fee payable in respect of the application is the amount specified in Sch 1 col 2 in respect of a type B claim: art 11(2).

8   Employment Tribunals and the Employment Appeal Tribunal Fees Order 2013, SI 2013/1893, art 4(2).

9   Employment Tribunals and the Employment Appeal Tribunal Fees Order 2013, SI 2013/1893, art 4(3). The fee in this case is £600: art 4(3).

10 The issue fee and hearing fee payable by a single claimant in respect of a claim listed in the Employment Tribunals and the Employment Appeal Tribunal Fees Order 2013, SI 2013/1893, Sch 2 Table 2 (substituted by SI 2014/590) ('a type A claim') is the amount specified in the Employment Tribunals and the Employment Appeal Tribunal Fees Order 2013, SI 2013/1893, Sch 2 Table 3 col 2: art 6.

11 The issue fee and hearing fee payable by a single claimant in respect of any claim other than one listed in the Employment Tribunals and the Employment Appeal Tribunal Fees Order 2013, SI 2013/1893, Sch 2 Table 2 (as substituted: see note 10) ('a type B claim') is the amount specified in Sch 2 Table 3 col 3: art 7.

12 Subject to the Employment Tribunals and the Employment Appeal Tribunal Fees Order 2013, SI 2013/1893, arts 9, 10 (see the text and notes 13–16), the issue fee and hearing fee payable by a fee group is the amount calculated by reference to Sch 2 Table 4: art 8.

13 Ie the amount specified in the Employment Tribunals and the Employment Appeal Tribunal Fees Order 2013, SI 2013/1893, Sch 2 Table 3 or, in the case of a fee group, Sch 2 Table 4.

14 Employment Tribunals and the Employment Appeal Tribunal Fees Order 2013, SI 2013/1893, art 9. This is subject to art 10: see the text and notes 15–16.

15 Ie under the Employment Tribunals and the Employment Appeal Tribunal Fees Order 2013, SI 2013/1893, art 8 or 9: see the text and notes 12–14.

16 Ie in accordance with the Employment Tribunals and the Employment Appeal Tribunal Fees Order 2013, SI 2013/1893, Sch 3: see PARA 1458.

17 Employment Tribunals and the Employment Appeal Tribunal Fees Order 2013, SI 2013/1893, art 10.

18 Employment Tribunals and the Employment Appeal Tribunal Fees Order 2013, SI 2013/1893, art 12(1) (amended by SI 2014/590).

19 Employment Tribunals and the Employment Appeal Tribunal Fees Order 2013, SI 2013/1893, art 12(2) (amended by SI 2014/590).

20 See PARA 1458.

21 As to the meaning of 'tribunal' see PARA 1448 note 14.

22 For these purposes, 'claim' means any proceedings before an employment tribunal making a complaint: Employment Tribunals (Constitution and Rules of Procedure) Regulations 2013, SI 2013/1237, Sch 1 r 1(1).

23 'Tribunal fee' means any fee which is payable by a party under any enactment in respect of a claim, employer's contract claim, application or judicial mediation in an employment tribunal: Employment Tribunals (Constitution and Rules of Procedure) Regulations 2013, SI 2013/1237, Sch 1 r 1(1).

24 Employment Tribunals (Constitution and Rules of Procedure) Regulations 2013, SI 2013/1237, Sch 1 r 11(1). 'Remission application' means any application which may be made under any enactment for remission or part remission of a tribunal fee: Sch 1 r 1(1).

25 For these purposes, 'claimant' means the person bringing the claim: Sch 1 r 1(1).

26 Employment Tribunals (Constitution and Rules of Procedure) Regulations 2013, SI 2013/1237, Sch 1 r 11(2).

27 Employment Tribunals (Constitution and Rules of Procedure) Regulations 2013, SI 2013/1237, Sch 1 r 11(4).

28 Ie subject to the Employment Tribunals (Constitution and Rules of Procedure) Regulations 2013, SI 2013/1237, Sch 1 r 11: see the text and notes 20–27.

29 Employment Tribunals (Constitution and Rules of Procedure) Regulations 2013, SI 2013/1237, Sch 1 r 40(1).

30 Employment Tribunals (Constitution and Rules of Procedure) Regulations 2013, SI 2013/1237, Sch 1 r 40(2).

31 Employment Tribunals (Constitution and Rules of Procedure) Regulations 2013, SI 2013/1237, Sch 1 r 40(3).
32 Employment Tribunals (Constitution and Rules of Procedure) Regulations 2013, SI 2013/1237, Sch 1 r 40(4).
33 Ie under the Employment Tribunals (Constitution and Rules of Procedure) Regulations 2013, SI 2013/1237, Sch 1 r 40(2) or Sch 1 r 40(4): see the text and notes 30, 32.
34 Employment Tribunals (Constitution and Rules of Procedure) Regulations 2013, SI 2013/1237, Sch 1 r 40(5).
35 See *R (on the application of Unison) v Lord Chancellor (Equality and Human Rights Commission intervening)* [2014] EWHC 218 (Admin), [2014] ICR 498, [2014] IRLR 266 (it was not possible to identify any test for judging when a fee regime was excessive; the jurisprudence suggested that the principle of effectiveness was not violated even if the imposition of fees caused difficulty and rendered the prospect of launching proceedings daunting, provided that they were not so high that the prospective litigant was clearly unable to pay them; the mere fact that fees imposed a burden on families with limited means and that they had to use hard earned savings was not enough).
36 See *R (on the application of Unison) v Lord Chancellor (Equality and Human Rights Commission intervening)* [2014] EWHC 218 (Admin) at [90], [2014] ICR 498 at [90], [2014] IRLR 266 at [90].

1458. Entitlement to remission of employment tribunal fees. Schedule 3 to the Employment Tribunals and the Employment Appeal Tribunal Fees Order 2013[1] applies for the purposes of determining whether a person is entitled to a remission or part remission of any fee otherwise payable under that Order[2]. Where an application for remission is made by a member of a fee group[3], that Schedule 3 has effect for the purposes of determining whether or not the member of the group would be entitled to remission, whether wholly or in part, if that person was a single claimant[4].

If a party[5] satisfies the disposable capital test[6], the amount of any fee remission[7] is calculated by applying the gross monthly income test[8]. The disposable capital and gross monthly income of a partner of a party is to be treated as disposable capital and gross monthly income of the party[9]. Where, however, the partner of a party has a contrary interest to the party in the matter to which the fee relates, the disposable capital and gross monthly income of that partner, if any, is not treated as the disposable capital and gross monthly income of the party[10].

A fee specified in the 2013 Order may be remitted where the Lord Chancellor is satisfied that there are exceptional circumstances which justify doing so[11].

No remissions or refunds are available in respect of the fee payable for copy or duplicate documents or searches[12].

A party is not entitled to a fee remission if, under Part 1 of the Legal Aid, Sentencing and Punishment of Offenders Act 2012[13], he is in receipt of the certain civil legal services[14].

Where a restraint order[15] is in force against a party and that party makes an application for permission to issue proceedings or take a step in proceedings as required by the restraint order, apply for amendment or discharge of the order, or appeal the order, the fee prescribed[16] for the application is payable in full[17]. If the party is granted permission, he is to be refunded the difference between the fee paid and the fee that would have been payable if Schedule 3 to the 2013 Order had been applied without reference to this provision[18].

1 Ie the Employment Tribunals and the Employment Appeal Tribunal Fees Order 2013, SI 2013/1893, Sch 3 (substituted by SI 2013/2302): see the text and notes 5–18; and PARA 1459.
2 Employment Tribunals and the Employment Appeal Tribunal Fees Order 2013, SI 2013/1893, art 17(1).
3 As to the meaning of 'fee group' see PARA 1457 note 5.

4 Employment Tribunals and the Employment Appeal Tribunal Fees Order 2013, SI 2013/1893, art 17(2). As to the meaning of 'single claimant' see PARA 1457 note 5.

5 'Party' means the individual who would, but for the Employment Tribunals and the Employment Appeal Tribunal Fees Order 2013, SI 2013/1893, Sch 3, be liable to pay a fee under that Order: Sch 3 para 1(1) (as substituted: see note 1).

6 Subject to the Employment Tribunals and the Employment Appeal Tribunal Fees Order 2013, SI 2013/1893, Sch 3 para 4, a party satisfies the disposable capital test if the fee payable by the party and for which an application for remission is made, falls within a fee band set out in Sch 3 para 3, Table col 1, and the party's disposable capital is less than the amount in the corresponding row of Sch 3 para 3, Table col 2: Sch 3 para 3 (as substituted: see note 1). Subject to Sch 3 para 14 (see the text and notes 9–10): (1) if a party or his partner is aged 61 or over, that party satisfies the disposable capital test if that party's disposable capital is less than £16,000; (2) disposable capital is the value of every resource of a capital nature belonging to the party on the date on which the application for remission is made, unless it is treated as income by the 2013 Order, or it is disregarded as excluded disposable capital: Sch 3 paras 4, 5 (as so substituted). 'Partner' means a person with whom the party lives as a couple and includes a person with whom the party is not currently living but from whom the party is not living separate and apart; and 'couple' has the meaning given in the Tax Credits Act 2002 s 3(5A) (s 3 prospectively repealed): Employment Tribunals and the Employment Appeal Tribunal Fees Order 2013, SI 2013/1893, Sch 3 para 1(1) (as so substituted).

The value of a resource of a capital nature that does not consist of money is calculated as the amount which that resource would realise if sold, less 10% of the sale value and the amount of any borrowing secured against that resource that would be repayable on sale: Sch 3 para 6 (as so substituted). Capital resources in a country outside the United Kingdom count towards disposable capital: Sch 3 para 7(1) (as so substituted). If there is no prohibition in that country against the transfer of a resource into the United Kingdom, the value of that resource is the amount which that resource would realise if sold in that country, in accordance with Sch 3 para 6: Sch 3 para 7(2) (as so substituted). If there is a prohibition in that country against the transfer of a resource into the United Kingdom, the value of that resource is the amount that resource would realise if sold to a buyer in the United Kingdom: Sch 3 para 7(3) (as so substituted). As to the meaning of 'United Kingdom' see PARA 2 note 12. Where disposable capital is held in currency other than sterling, the cost of any banking charge or commission that would be payable if that amount were converted into sterling, is deducted from its value: Sch 3 para 8 (as so substituted). Where any resource of a capital nature is owned jointly or in common, there is a presumption that the resource is owned in equal shares, unless evidence to the contrary is produced: Sch 3 para 9 (as so substituted).

The following things are excluded disposable capital (Sch 3 para 10 (as so substituted)), ie;

(a) a property which is the main or only dwelling occupied by the party;
(b) the household furniture and effects of the main or only dwelling occupied by the party;
(c) articles of personal clothing;
(d) any vehicle, the sale of which would leave the party, or their partner, without motor transport;
(e) tools and implements of trade, including vehicles used for business purposes;
(f) the capital value of the party's or their partner's business, where the party or their partner is self-employed;
(g) the capital value of any funds or other assets held in trust, where the party or their partner is a beneficiary without entitlement to advances of any trust capital;
(h) a jobseeker's back to work bonus;
(i) a payment made as a result of a determination of unfair dismissal by a court or tribunal, or by way of settlement of a claim for unfair dismissal;
(j) any compensation paid as a result of a determination of medical negligence or in respect of any personal injury by a court, or by way of settlement of a claim for medical negligence or personal injury;
(k) the capital held in any personal or occupational pension scheme;
(l) any cash value payable on surrender of a contract of insurance;
(m) any capital payment made out of the Independent Living Funds;
(n) any bereavement payment;
(o) any capital insurance or endowment lump sum payments that have been paid as a result of illness, disability or death;
(p) any student loan or student grant;
(q) any payments under the criminal injuries compensation scheme.

'Independent Living Funds' means the funds listed at the Criminal Legal Aid (Financial Resources) Regulations 2013, SI 2013/471, reg 20(2)(b): Employment Tribunals and the

Employment Appeal Tribunal Fees Order 2013, SI 2013/1893, Sch 3 para 1(1) (as substituted: see note 1). The Independent Living Funds are due to be closed on 30 June 2015; at the date at which this volume states the law, information about the closure was available on the government's website (whose address, at the date at which this volume states the law, is to be found at: *http://www.gov.uk*): see *ILF Closure Programme: Guide* (April 2014).

7 For these purposes, references to remission of a fee are to be read as including references to a part remission of a fee as appropriate and 'remit' and 'remitted' are to be construed accordingly: Employment Tribunals and the Employment Appeal Tribunal Fees Order 2013, SI 2013/1893, Sch 3 para 1(2) (as substituted: see note 1).

8 Employment Tribunals and the Employment Appeal Tribunal Fees Order 2013, SI 2013/1893, Sch 3 para 2 (as substituted: see note 1). Subject to Sch 3 para 14 (see the text and notes 9–10), gross monthly income means the total monthly income, for the month preceding that in which the application for remission is made, from all sources, other than receipt of any of the excluded benefits: Sch 3 para 13(1) (as so substituted). Income from a trade, business or gainful occupation other than an occupation at a wage or salary is calculated (1) as the profits which have accrued or will accrue to the party; and (2) the drawings of the party, in the month preceding that in which the application for remission is made: Sch 3 para 13(2) (as so substituted). In calculating profits under head (1) above, all sums necessarily expended to earn those profits are deducted: Sch 3 para 13(3) (as so substituted). As to the excluded benefits see Sch 3 para 1(1) (definition substituted by SI 2014/590).

Subject to the gross monthly income cap set out in the Employment Tribunals and the Employment Appeal Tribunal Fees Order 2013, SI 2013/1893, Sch 3 para 12, if a party satisfies the disposable capital test, no fee is payable under the Employment Tribunals and the Employment Appeal Tribunal Fees Order 2013, SI 2013/1893, if, at the time when the fee would otherwise be payable, the party or his partner has the number of children specified in Sch 3 para 11(1), Table 2 col 1 and (a) if the party is single, his gross monthly income does not exceed the amount set out in the appropriate row of Table 2 col 2; or (b) if the party is one of a couple, the gross monthly income of that couple does not exceed the amount set out in the appropriate row of Table 2 col 3: Sch 3 para 11(1), (4) (as substituted: see note 1). If a party or his partner has more than two children, the relevant amount of gross monthly income is the appropriate amount specified in Sch 3 para 11(1), Table 2 for two children, plus the sum of £245 for each additional child: Sch 3 para 11(2) (as so substituted). For every £10 of gross monthly income received above the appropriate amount in Sch 3 para 11(1), Table 2, including any additional amount added under Sch 3 para 11(2), the party must pay £5 towards the fee payable, up to the maximum amount of the fee payable: Sch 3 para 11(3) (as so substituted). For these purposes, 'child' means a person (i) whose main residence is with a party and who is aged either (a) under 16 years; or (b) 16 to 19 years and is not married or in a civil partnership and is enrolled or accepted in full-time education that is not advanced education, or approved training; or (ii) in respect of whom a party or his partner pays child support maintenance or periodic payments in accordance with a maintenance agreement; and 'full-time education', 'advanced education' and 'approved training' have the meaning given by the Child Benefit (General) Regulations 2006, SI 2006/223: Employment Tribunals and the Employment Appeal Tribunal Fees Order 2013, SI 2013/1893, Sch 3 para 1(1) (as so substituted). 'Child support maintenance' has the meaning given in the Child Support Act 1991 s 3(6); and 'maintenance agreement' has the meaning given in the Child Support Act 1991 s 9(1): Employment Tribunals and the Employment Appeal Tribunal Fees Order 2013, SI 2013/1893, Sch 3 para 1(1) (as so substituted).

No remission is available if a party or his partner has the number of children specified in Sch 3 para 12(1), Table 3 col 1 and if the party is single, his gross monthly income exceeds the amount set out in the appropriate row of Sch 3 para 12(1), Table 3 col 2 or, if the party is one of a couple, the gross monthly income of that couple exceeds the amount set out in the appropriate row of Sch 3 para 12(1), Table 3 col 3: Sch 3 para 12(1) (as so substituted). If a party or his partner has more than two children, the relevant amount of gross monthly income is the appropriate amount specified in Sch 3 para 12(1), Table 3 for two children, plus the sum of £245 for each additional child: Sch 3 para 12(2) (as so substituted).

Marriage of same sex couples is lawful in the law of England and Wales, and such marriages have the same effect as marriages of opposite sex couples: see the Marriage (Same Sex Couples) Act 2013 s 1(1), 11(1); and MATRIMONIAL AND CIVIL PARTNERSHIP LAW vol 72 (2009) PARA 1 et seq.

9 Employment Tribunals and the Employment Appeal Tribunal Fees Order 2013, SI 2013/1893, Sch 3 para 14(1) (as substituted: see note 1).

10 Employment Tribunals and the Employment Appeal Tribunal Fees Order 2013, SI 2013/1893, Sch 3 para 14(2) (as substituted: see note 1).

11 Employment Tribunals and the Employment Appeal Tribunal Fees Order 2013, SI 2013/1893, Sch 3 para 16 (as substituted: see note 1). As to the Lord Chancellor see CONSTITUTIONAL AND ADMINISTRATIVE LAW vol 20 (2014) PARA 255 et seq.

12 Employment Tribunals and the Employment Appeal Tribunal Fees Order 2013, SI 2013/1893, Sch 3 para 20 (as substituted: see note 1).

13 Ie the Legal Aid, Sentencing and Punishment of Offenders Act 2012 Pt 1 (ss 1–43): see LEGAL AID.

14 Employment Tribunals and the Employment Appeal Tribunal Fees Order 2013, SI 2013/1893, Sch 3 para 18 (as substituted: see note 1). The civil legal services mentioned in the text are (1) legal representation within the meaning of the Civil Legal Aid (Merits Criteria) Regulations 2013 reg 18(2); or (2) family help (higher) within the meaning of reg 15(3) or family help (lower) within the meaning of reg 15(2) in respect of applying for a consent order: Employment Tribunals and the Employment Appeal Tribunal Fees Order 2013, SI 2013/1893, Sch 3 paras 1(1), 18 (as substituted: see note 1).

15 For these purposes, 'restraint order' means (1) an order under the Senior Courts Act 1981 s 42(1A) (see CIVIL PROCEDURE vol 11 (2009) PARAS 244, 258; (2) an order under the Employment Tribunals Act 1996 s 33 (see PARA 1430); (3) a civil restraint order made under CPR 3.11 or a practice direction made under that rule; or (4) a civil restraint order under the Family Procedure Rules 2010, SI 2010/2955, r 4.8 or the practice direction referred to in that rule: Employment Tribunals and the Employment Appeal Tribunal Fees Order 2013, SI 2013/1893, Sch 3 para 1(1) (as substituted: see note 1).

16 Ie prescribed by the Employment Tribunals and the Employment Appeal Tribunal Fees Order 2013, SI 2013/1893: see PARA 1457.

17 Employment Tribunals and the Employment Appeal Tribunal Fees Order 2013, SI 2013/1893, Sch 3 para 19(1), (2) (as substituted: see note 1).

18 Employment Tribunals and the Employment Appeal Tribunal Fees Order 2013, SI 2013/1893, Sch 3 para 19(3) (as substituted: see note 1).

1459. Application for remission of employment tribunal fees. An application for remission[1] of a fee[2] must be made at the time when the fee would otherwise be payable[3]. Where an application for remission of a fee is made, the party[4] must:

(1) indicate the fee to which the application relates;

(2) declare the amount of his disposable capital[5]; and

(3) provide documentary evidence of his gross monthly income[6] and the number of children[7] relevant for the statutory purposes[8].

Where an application for remission of a fee is made on or before the date on which a fee is payable, the date for payment of the fee is disapplied[9].

Where an application for remission is refused, or if part remission of a fee is granted, the amount of the fee which remains unremitted must be paid within the period notified in writing to the party or the fee group[10] as the case may be[11].

The Lord Chancellor may disregard an application for remission by a member of a fee group if the amount of the fee payable by the fee group would not be altered in consequence of the application being granted[12].

If a remission application is refused in part or in full, the tribunal[13] must send the claimant[14] a notice specifying a date for payment of the tribunal fee[15] and the claim[16] must be rejected by the tribunal if the tribunal fee is not paid by the date specified[17]. If a claim, or part of it, is rejected, the form be returned to the claimant with a notice of rejection explaining why it has been rejected[18].

1 As to entitlement to remission of a fee see PARA 1458; and as to the meaning of 'remission' see PARA 1458 note 7.

2 Ie a fee prescribed by the Employment Tribunals and the Employment Appeal Tribunal Fees Order 2013, SI 2013/1893: see PARA 1457.

3 Employment Tribunals and the Employment Appeal Tribunal Fees Order 2013, SI 2013/1893, Sch 3 para 15(1) (Sch 3 substituted by SI 2013/2302).

4 As to the meaning of 'party' see PARA 1458 note 5.

5 As to the meaning of 'disposable capital' see PARA 1458 note 6.

6   As to the meaning of 'gross monthly income' see PARA 1458 note 8.

7   As to the meaning of 'child' for these purposes see PARA 1458 note 8.

8   Employment Tribunals and the Employment Appeal Tribunal Fees Order 2013, SI 2013/1893, Sch 3 para 15(2) (as substituted: see note 3). The statutory purposes referred to in the text are the purposes of Sch 3 paras 11, 12: see PARA 1458 note 8.

     Where a party pays a fee at a time when that party would have been entitled to a remission if they had provided the documentary evidence required by Sch 3 para 15, the fee, or the amount by which the fee would have been reduced as the case may be, must be refunded if documentary evidence relating to the time when the fee became payable is provided at a later date (Sch 3 para 17(1) (as so substituted)); and, where a fee has been paid at a time when the Lord Chancellor, if all the circumstances had been known, would have remitted the fee under Sch 3 para 15, the fee or the amount by which the fee would have been reduced, as the case may be, must be refunded to the party (Sch 3 para 17(2) (as so substituted)). No refund may be made in this way, however, unless the party who paid the fee applies within three months of the date on which the fee was paid: Sch 3 para 17(3) (as so substituted). The Lord Chancellor may extend the period of three months if considers that there is a good reason for a refund being made after the end of the period of three months: Sch 3 para 17(4) (as so substituted).

9   Employment Tribunals and the Employment Appeal Tribunal Fees Order 2013, SI 2013/1893, Sch 3 para 15(3) (as substituted: see note 3).

10   As to the meaning of 'fee group' see PARA 1457 note 5.

11   Employment Tribunals and the Employment Appeal Tribunal Fees Order 2013, SI 2013/1893, Sch 3 para 15(4) (as substituted (see note 3); amended by SI 2013/2302).

12   Employment Tribunals and the Employment Appeal Tribunal Fees Order 2013, SI 2013/1893, reg 18. As to the Lord Chancellor see CONSTITUTIONAL AND ADMINISTRATIVE LAW vol 20 (2014) PARA 255 et seq.

13   As to the meaning of 'tribunal' see PARA 1448 note 14.

14   As to the meaning of 'claimant' see PARA 1457 note 25.

15   As to the meaning of 'tribunal fee' see PARA 1457 note 23.

16   As to the meaning of 'claim' see PARA 1457 note 22.

17   Employment Tribunals and the Employment Tribunals (Constitution and Rules of Procedure) Regulations 2013, SI 2013/1237, Sch 1 r 11(3).

18   Employment Tribunals and the Employment Tribunals (Constitution and Rules of Procedure) Regulations 2013, SI 2013/1237, Sch 1 r 11(4).

(iv)   Preliminary Procedure in Employment Tribunals

1460.   Calculation of time limits under employment tribunal procedure rules.
Unless otherwise specified by the tribunal[1], an act required by the procedural rules[2], in a practice direction[3] or an order of a tribunal[4] to be done on or by a particular day may be done at any time before midnight on that day. If there is an issue as to whether the act has been done by that time, the party claiming to have done it must prove compliance[5].

     If the time specified by those rules, a practice direction or an order for doing any act ends on a day other than a working day[6], the act is done in time if it is done on the next working day[7].

     Where any act is required to be, or may be, done within a certain number of days of or from an event, the date of that event must not be included in the calculation[8].

     Where any act is required to be, or may be, done not less than a certain number of days before or after an event, the date of that event must not be included in the calculation[9].

     Where the tribunal imposes a time limit for doing any act, the last date for compliance must, wherever practicable, be expressed as a calendar date[10].

     Where time is specified by reference to the date when a document is sent to a person by the tribunal, the date when the document was sent must, unless the contrary is proved, be regarded as the date indorsed on the document as the date of sending or, if there is no such indorsement, the date shown on the letter accompanying the document[11].

The tribunal may, on its own initiative or on the application of a party, extend or shorten any time limit specified in the rules[12] or in any decision, whether or not, in the case of an extension, it has expired[13].

1   As to the meaning of 'the tribunal' see PARA 1448 note 14.
2   Ie the rules set out in the Employment Tribunals (Constitution and Rules of Procedure) Regulations 2013, SI 2013/1237, Sch 1.
3   As to practice directions see PARA 1412.
4   An order or other decision of the tribunal is either (1) a 'case management order', being an order or decision of any kind in relation to the conduct of proceedings, not including the determination of any issue which would be the subject of a judgment; or (2) a 'judgment', being a decision, made at any stage of the proceedings (but not including a decision under the Employment Tribunals (Constitution and Rules of Procedure) Regulations 2013, SI 2013/1237, Sch 1 r 13 or r 19 (see PARAS 1461, 1462), which finally determines (a) a claim, or part of a claim, as regards liability, remedy or costs (including preparation time and wasted costs); (b) any issue which is capable of finally disposing of any claim, or part of a claim, even if it does not necessarily do so (for example, an issue whether a claim should be struck out or a jurisdictional issue); (c) the imposition of a financial penalty under the Employment Tribunals Act 1996 s 12A (see PARA 1477): Employment Tribunals (Constitution and Rules of Procedure) Regulations 2013, SI 2013/1237, Sch 1 r 1(3) (amended by SI 2014/271).
5   Employment Tribunals (Constitution and Rules of Procedure) Regulations 2013, SI 2013/1237, Sch 1 r 4(1).
6   'Working day' means any day except a Saturday or Sunday, Christmas Day, Good Friday or a bank holiday under the Banking and Financial Dealings Act 1971 s 1: Employment Tribunals (Constitution and Rules of Procedure) Regulations 2013, SI 2013/1237, Sch 1 r 4(2). As to bank holidays see further TIME vol 97 (2010) PARA 321.
7   Employment Tribunals (Constitution and Rules of Procedure) Regulations 2013, SI 2013/1237, Sch 1 r 4(2).
8   Employment Tribunals (Constitution and Rules of Procedure) Regulations 2013, SI 2013/1237, Sch 1 r 4(3). For example, a response must be presented within 28 days of the date on which the respondent was sent a copy of the claim: if the claim was sent on 1 October the last day for presentation of the response is 29 October: Sch 1 r 4(3). 'Respondent' means the person or persons against whom the claim is made: Sch 1 r 1(1). As to the meaning of 'claim' see PARA 1457 note 22.
    Where a claim includes a complaint under the Equality Act 2010 s 146(1) relating to a term of a collective agreement, the following persons, whether or not identified in the claim, are to be regarded as the persons against whom a remedy is claimed and must be treated as respondents for the purposes of the Employment Tribunals (Constitution and Rules of Procedure) Regulations 2013, SI 2013/1237, Sch 1: (1) the claimant's employer (or prospective employer); and (2) every organisation of employers and organisation of workers, and every association of or representative of such organisations, which, if the terms were to be varied voluntarily, would be likely, in the opinion of an employment judge, to negotiate the variation. An organisation or association is not, however, to be treated as a respondent if the judge, having made such enquiries of the claimant and such other inquiries as the judge thinks fit, is of the opinion that it is not reasonably practicable to identify the organisation or association: Sch 1 r 97.
9   Employment Tribunals (Constitution and Rules of Procedure) Regulations 2013, SI 2013/1237, Sch 1 r 4(4). For example, if a party wishes to present representations in writing for consideration by a tribunal at a hearing, they must be presented not less than seven days before the hearing: if the hearing is fixed for 8 October, the representations must be presented no later than 1 October: Sch 1 r 4(4). As to the meaning of 'writing' see PARA 1450 note 19.
10 Employment Tribunals (Constitution and Rules of Procedure) Regulations 2013, SI 2013/1237, Sch 1 r 4(5).
11 Employment Tribunals (Constitution and Rules of Procedure) Regulations 2013, SI 2013/1237, Sch 1 r 4(6).
12 See note 2.
13 Employment Tribunals (Constitution and Rules of Procedure) Regulations 2013, SI 2013/1237, Sch 1 r 5.

1461.   Starting a claim in an employment tribunal.   A claim[1] must be started by presenting a completed claim form using a prescribed form[2] in accordance with any supplementary practice direction[3].

A claim may be presented in England and Wales[4] if:

(1)   the respondent, or one of the respondents, resides or carries on business in England and Wales[5];

(2)   one or more of the acts or omissions complained of took place in England and Wales[6];

(3)   the claim relates to a contract under which the work is or has been performed partly in England and Wales[7]; or

(4)   the tribunal has jurisdiction to determine the claim by virtue of a connection with Great Britain[8] and the connection in question is at least partly a connection with England and Wales[9].

Two or more claimants may make their claims on the same claim form if their claims are based on the same set of facts. Where two or more claimants wrongly include claims on the same claim form, this must be treated as an irregularity[10].

If a claim alleges that the claimant has made a protected disclosure[11], the tribunal may, with the consent of the claimant, send a copy of any accepted claim to a listed[12] regulator[13].

The tribunal must reject a claim if:

(a)   it is not made on a prescribed form[14];

(b)   it does not contain all of the following information:
    (i)   each claimant's name;
    (ii)   each claimant's address;
    (iii)   each respondent's name;
    (iv)   each respondent's address[15]; or

(c)   it does not contain one of the following:
    (i)   an early conciliation number[16];
    (ii)   confirmation that the claim does not institute any relevant proceedings[17]; or
    (iii)   confirmation that one of the early conciliation exemptions[18] applies[19].

The form must be returned to the claimant with a notice of rejection explaining why it has been rejected. The notice must contain information about how to apply for a reconsideration of the rejection[20].

The tribunal must also reject a claim if it is not accompanied by a tribunal fee[21] or a remission application[22].

The staff of the tribunal office must refer a claim form to an employment judge[23] if they consider that the claim, or part of it, may be:

(A)   one which the tribunal has no jurisdiction to consider;

(B)   in a form which cannot sensibly be responded to or is otherwise an abuse of the process;

(C)   one which institutes relevant proceedings and is made on a claim form that does not contain either an early conciliation number or confirmation that one of the early conciliation exemptions applies;

(D)   one which institutes relevant proceedings, is made on a claim form which contains confirmation that one of the early conciliation exemptions applies, and an early conciliation exemption does not apply;

(E)   one which institutes relevant proceedings and the name of the claimant on the claim form is not the same as the name of the prospective claimant on the early conciliation certificate to which the early conciliation number relates; or

(F)   one which institutes relevant proceedings and the name of the respondent on the claim form is not the same as the name of the prospective respondent on the early conciliation certificate to which the early conciliation number relates[24].

The claim, or part of it, must be rejected if the judge considers that the claim, or part of it, is of a kind described in head (A), head (B), head (C) or head (D) above[25]. The claim, or part of it, must also be rejected if the judge considers that the claim, or part of it, is of a kind described in head (E) or head (F) above unless the judge considers that the claimant made a minor error in relation to a name or address and it would not be in the interests of justice to reject the claim[26]. If the claim is rejected, the form must be returned to the claimant together with a notice of rejection giving the judge's reasons for rejecting the claim, or part of it. The notice must contain information about how to apply for a reconsideration of the rejection[27].

A claimant whose claim has been rejected on the grounds set out in heads (a) to (c) or (A) to (F) above[28], in whole or in part, may apply for a reconsideration on the basis that either the decision to reject was wrong or the notified defect can be rectified[29]. The application must be in writing and presented to the tribunal within 14 days[30] of the date that the notice of rejection was sent. It must explain why the decision is said to have been wrong or rectify the defect and if the claimant wishes to request a hearing this must be requested in the application[31]. If the claimant does not request a hearing, or an employment judge decides, on considering the application, that the claim must be accepted in full, the judge must determine the application without a hearing. Otherwise the application must be considered at a hearing attended only by the claimant[32]. If the judge decides that the original rejection was correct but that the defect has been rectified, the claim must be treated as presented on the date that the defect was rectified[34].

1   As to the meaning of 'claim' see PARA 1457 note 22.
2   'Prescribed form' means any appropriate form prescribed by the Secretary of State in accordance with the Employment Tribunals (Constitution and Rules of Procedure) Regulations 2013, SI 2013/1237, reg 12: Sch 1 r 1(1). The Secretary of State may prescribe (1) one or more versions of a form which must be used by claimants to start proceedings in a tribunal; (2) one or more versions of a form which must be used by respondents to respond to a claim before a tribunal; and (3) that the provision of certain information on the prescribed forms is mandatory: reg 12(1). It is not necessary to use a form prescribed under reg 12(1) if the proceedings are (a) referred to a Tribunal by a court; (b) proceedings in which a tribunal will be exercising its appellate jurisdiction; or (c) proceedings brought by an employer under the Employment Rights Act 1996 s 11 (see PARA 125): Employment Tribunals (Constitution and Rules of Procedure) Regulations 2013, SI 2013/1237, reg 12(2). The Secretary of State must publish the prescribed forms in an appropriate manner to bring them to the attention of prospective claimants, respondents and their advisers: reg 12(3). As to the meaning of 'claimant' see PARA 1457 note 25; and as to the meaning of 'respondent' see PARA 1460 note 8.
3   See the Employment Tribunals (Constitution and Rules of Procedure) Regulations 2013, SI 2013/1237, Sch 1 r 8(1). The practice direction referred to in the text is any practice direction made under reg 11 (see PARA 1412) which supplements Sch 1 r 8. 'Present' means deliver (by any means permitted under Sch 1 r 85 (see PARA 1467) to a tribunal office: Sch 1 r 1(1). A claim form may only be delivered in accordance with the practice direction made under reg 11 which supplements Sch 1 r 8: Sch 1 r 85(2). A completed claim form may be presented online, by post or in person: see *Presidential Practice Direction—Presentation of Claims* (July 2013) para 4. 'Tribunal office' means any office which has been established for any area in either England and Wales or Scotland and which carries out administrative functions in support of the tribunal, and in relation to particular proceedings it is the office notified to the parties as dealing with the proceedings: Employment Tribunals (Constitution and Rules of Procedure) Regulations 2013, SI 2013/1237, Sch 1 r 1(1).
    An application is presented to an employment tribunal when it is received at the office of the tribunal: *Hammond v Haigh Castle & Co Ltd* [1973] 2 All ER 289, [1973] ICR 148, NIRC;

House v Emerson Electric Industrial Controls [1980] ICR 795, EAT; *Dodd v British Telecommunications plc* [1988] ICR 116, [1988] IRLR 16, EAT. See also *Mossman v Bray Management Ltd* [2005] All ER (D) 06 (Apr), EAT (where the tribunal had no record of a claim which had been sent electronically, no claim had been presented and it was not right to extend time). There is, however, no requirement that the application be delivered personally into the hands of an official: *Post Office v Moore* [1981] ICR 623, EAT (employee's application presented before midnight on the last day of the limitation period; application held to have been presented in time and the employment tribunal had jurisdiction to hear the appeal). Applications should not be left until the last minute as it is probably no longer reasonable to expect that first-class post will arrive on the following day: *Birmingham Midshires Building Society v Horton* [1991] ICR 648, EAT. Moreover, lateness (even if short) due to a failure of electronic communication is unlikely to be looked on indulgently: *Beasley v National Grid* [2008] EWCA Civ 742. As to postal delays see also PARA 1453 head (5).

4 As to the meanings of 'England' and 'Wales' see PARA 2 note 12.
5 Employment Tribunals (Constitution and Rules of Procedure) Regulations 2013, SI 2013/1237, Sch 1 r 8(2)(a). See *Hasan v Shell International Shipping Services (PTE) Ltd* [2014] All ER (D) 15 (Feb), EAT (employee had not worked at an establishment in the UK or aboard a UK registered vessel with a port in Great Britain specified as the vessel's registered port of choice; on the facts, the test under the predecessor rule to the Employment Tribunals (Constitution and Rules of Procedure) Regulations 2013, SI 2013/1237, Sch 1 r 8(2)(a), that the employer carried on business in England and Wales, had not been made out).
6 Employment Tribunals (Constitution and Rules of Procedure) Regulations 2013, SI 2013/1237, Sch 1 r 8(2)(b).
7 Employment Tribunals (Constitution and Rules of Procedure) Regulations 2013, SI 2013/1237, Sch 1 r 8(2)(c). This provision was introduced to rectify the problem that arose in the context of the wording of the Employment Tribunals (Constitution and Rules of Procedure) Regulations 2004, SI 2004/1861, reg 19(1) (revoked) (which provided that a tribunal in England and Wales only had jurisdiction to deal with proceedings where, inter alia, the respondent resided or carried on business in England and Wales) in *Pervez v Macquarie Bank Ltd (London Branch)* [2011] IRLR 284, [2011] ICR 266, EAT (wording of reg 19(1) (now revoked) was capable of having effect of depriving an English tribunal of jurisdiction where the claimant worked in England (on secondment) but the respondent company, his employers, neither resided nor carried on business there, being a company based in Hong Kong; the unfairness resulting from this could only be overcome by giving a strained meaning to the phrase 'carries on business').
8 As to the meaning of 'Great Britain' see PARA 2 note 12.
9 Employment Tribunals (Constitution and Rules of Procedure) Regulations 2013, SI 2013/1237, Sch 1 r 8(2)(d).
10 Employment Tribunals (Constitution and Rules of Procedure) Regulations 2013, SI 2013/1237, Sch 1 r 9. The reference in the text to an irregularity is to an irregularity falling within Sch 1 r 6: see PARA 1465.
11 'Protected disclosure' has the meaning given to it by the Employment Rights Act 1996 s 43A (see PARA 69): Employment Tribunals (Constitution and Rules of Procedure) Regulations 2013, SI 2013/1237, Sch 1 r 14.
12 Ie a regulator listed in the Public Interest Disclosure (Prescribed Persons) Order 1999, SI 1999/1549, Schedule: see PARA 69.
13 Employment Tribunals (Constitution and Rules of Procedure) Regulations 2013, SI 2013/1237, Sch 1 r 14.
14 Employment Tribunals (Constitution and Rules of Procedure) Regulations 2013, SI 2013/1237, Sch 1 r 10(1)(a) (amended by SI 2014/271).
15 Employment Tribunals (Constitution and Rules of Procedure) Regulations 2013, SI 2013/1237, Sch 1 r 10(1)(b) (amended by SI 2014/271). It is not for an employment tribunal judge to prescribe how a claim is presented on the claim form: *Fairbank v Care Management Group* [2012] All ER (D) 198 (Jun), EAT.
16 'Early conciliation number' means the unique reference number which appears on an early conciliation certificate; and 'early conciliation certificate' means a certificate issued by ACAS in accordance with the Employment Tribunals (Early Conciliation: Exemptions and Rules of Procedure) Regulations 2014, SI 2014/254 (see PARA 152): Employment Tribunals (Constitution and Rules of Procedure) Regulations 2013, SI 2013/1237, Sch 1 r 1(1) (definitions added by SI 2014/271).
17 'Relevant proceedings' means those proceedings listed in the Employment Tribunals Act 1996 s 18(1) (see PARA 152): Employment Tribunals (Constitution and Rules of Procedure) Regulations 2013, SI 2013/1237, Sch 1 r 1(1) (definition added by SI 2014/271).

18 'Early conciliation exemption' means an exemption contained in the Employment Tribunals
     (Early Conciliation: Exemptions and Rules of Procedure) Regulations 2014, SI 2014/254,
     reg 3(1) (see PARA 152): Employment Tribunals (Constitution and Rules of Procedure)
     Regulations 2013, SI 2013/1237, Sch 1 r 1(1) (definition added by SI 2014/271).
19 Employment Tribunals (Constitution and Rules of Procedure) Regulations 2013, SI 2013/1237,
     Sch 1 r 10(1)(c) (added by SI 2014/271).
20 Employment Tribunals (Constitution and Rules of Procedure) Regulations 2013, SI 2013/1237,
     Sch 1 r 10(2).
21 As to the meaning of 'tribunal fee' see PARA 1457 note 23.
22 See the Employment Tribunals (Constitution and Rules of Procedure) Regulations 2013,
     SI 2013/1237, Sch 1 r 11(1); and PARA 1457. As to the meaning of 'remission application' see
     PARA 1457 note 24; and as to such applications see PARA 1459.
23 As to the meaning of 'employment judge' see PARA 1401 note 3.
24 Employment Tribunals (Constitution and Rules of Procedure) Regulations 2013, SI 2013/1237,
     Sch 1 r 12(1) (amended by SI 2014/271).
25 Employment Tribunals (Constitution and Rules of Procedure) Regulations 2013, SI 2013/1237,
     Sch 1 r 12(2) (amended by SI 2014/271).
26 Employment Tribunals (Constitution and Rules of Procedure) Regulations 2013, SI 2013/1237,
     Sch 1 r 12(2A) (added by SI 2014/271).
27 Employment Tribunals (Constitution and Rules of Procedure) Regulations 2013, SI 2013/1237,
     Sch 1 r 12(3).
28 Ie rejected under the Employment Tribunals (Constitution and Rules of Procedure)
     Regulations 2013, SI 2013/1237, Sch 1 r 10 or Sch 1 r 12: see the text and notes 14–20, 23–27.
29 Employment Tribunals (Constitution and Rules of Procedure) Regulations 2013, SI 2013/1237,
     Sch 1 r 13(1).
30 As to the calculation of time limits see PARA 1460.
31 Employment Tribunals (Constitution and Rules of Procedure) Regulations 2013, SI 2013/1237,
     Sch 1 r 13(2).
33 Employment Tribunals (Constitution and Rules of Procedure) Regulations 2013, SI 2013/1237,
     Sch 1 r 13(3).
34 Employment Tribunals (Constitution and Rules of Procedure) Regulations 2013, SI 2013/1237,
     Sch 1 r 13(4).

1462. Response to the claim. Unless the claim[1] is rejected[2], the tribunal[3] must
send a copy of the claim form, together with a prescribed response form[4], to each
respondent[5] with a notice which includes information on:

(1)   whether any part of the claim has been rejected; and
(2)   how to submit a response to the claim, the time limit[6] for doing so and
         what will happen if a response is not received by the tribunal within that
         time limit[7].

The response must be on a prescribed form and presented to the tribunal
office within 28 days of the date that the copy of the claim form was sent by the
tribunal[8]. A response form may include the response of more than one
respondent if they are responding to a single claim and either they all resist the
claim on the same grounds or they do not resist the claim[9]. It may include the
response to more than one claim if the claims are based on the same set of facts
and either the respondent resists all of the claims on the same grounds or the
respondent does not resist the claims[10].

The tribunal must reject a response if it is not made on a prescribed form or it
does not contain all of the following information:

(a)   the respondent's full name;
(b)   the respondent's address;
(c)   whether the respondent wishes to resist any part of the claim[11].

The form must be returned to the respondent with a notice of rejection
explaining why it has been rejected. The notice must explain what steps may be
taken by the respondent, including the need, if appropriate, to apply for an
extension of time, and how to apply for a reconsideration of the rejection[12].

A response must be rejected by the tribunal if it is received outside the time limit[13] or any extension of that limit granted within the original limit, unless an application for extension has already been made[14] or the response includes or is accompanied by such an application, in which case the response must not be rejected pending the outcome of the application[15]. The response must be returned to the respondent together with a notice of rejection explaining that the response has been presented late. The notice must explain how the respondent can apply for an extension of time and how to apply for a reconsideration[16].

A respondent whose response has been rejected[17] may apply for a reconsideration on the basis that the decision to reject was wrong or, in the case of a rejection because the response was defective[18], on the basis that the notified defect can be rectified[19]. The application must be in writing[20] and presented[21] to the tribunal within 14 days of the date that the notice of rejection was sent. It must explain why the decision is said to have been wrong or rectify the defect and it must state whether the respondent requests a hearing[22]. If the respondent does not request a hearing, or the employment judge[23] decides, on considering the application, that the response is to be accepted in full, the judge must determine the application without a hearing. Otherwise the application must be considered at a hearing attended only by the respondent[24]. If the judge decides that the original rejection was correct but that the defect has been rectified, the response is to be treated as presented on the date that the defect was rectified, but the judge may[25] extend time[26].

An application for an extension of time for presenting a response must be presented in writing and copied to the claimant[27]. It must set out the reason why the extension is sought and must, except where the time limit has not yet expired, be accompanied by a draft of the response which the respondent wishes to present or an explanation of why that is not possible and if the respondent wishes to request a hearing this must be requested in the application[28]. The claimant may within seven days of receipt of the application give reasons in writing explaining why the application is opposed[29]. An employment judge may determine the application without a hearing[30]. If the decision is to refuse an extension, any prior rejection of the response stands. If the decision is to allow an extension, any judgment issued under the following provision[31] must be set aside[32].

Where on the expiry of the time limit[33] no response has been presented, or any response received has been rejected and no application for a reconsideration is outstanding, or where the respondent has stated that no part of the claim is contested[34], an employment judge must decide whether on the available material, which may include further information which the parties are required by a judge to provide, a determination can properly be made of the claim, or part of it. To the extent that a determination can be made, the judge must issue a judgment accordingly. Otherwise, a hearing must be fixed before a judge alone[35]. The respondent is entitled to notice of any hearings and decisions of the tribunal but, unless and until an extension of time is granted, is only entitled to participate in any hearing to the extent permitted by the judge[36].

Where the tribunal accepts the response it must send a copy of it to all other parties[37]. In national security cases, however, the tribunal must not send a copy of the response to any excluded person[38].

1   As to the meaning of 'claim' see PARA 1457 note 22. As to starting a claim see PARA 1461.
2   As to rejection of a claim see PARA 1461.
3   As to the meaning of 'tribunal' for these purposes see PARA 1448 note 14.

4   As to the meaning of 'prescribed form' see PARA 1461 note 2.
5   As to the meaning of 'respondent' see PARA 1460 note 8.
6   As to the calculation of time limits see PARA 1460.
7   Employment Tribunals (Constitution and Rules of Procedure) Regulations 2013, SI 2013/1237, Sch 1 r 15.
8   Employment Tribunals (Constitution and Rules of Procedure) Regulations 2013, SI 2013/1237, Sch 1 r 16(1). The 28-day period will be strictly construed as running from the date when the document was actually sent by the tribunal; there is no scope for construing it as running from the date when it was received by the respondent: see *Bone v Fabcon Projects Ltd* [2007] 1 All ER 1071, [2006] ICR 1421, [2006] IRLR 908, EAT.
9   Employment Tribunals (Constitution and Rules of Procedure) Regulations 2013, SI 2013/1237, Sch 1 r 16(2).
10 Employment Tribunals (Constitution and Rules of Procedure) Regulations 2013, SI 2013/1237, Sch 1 r 16(3).
11 Employment Tribunals (Constitution and Rules of Procedure) Regulations 2013, SI 2013/1237, Sch 1 r 17(1).
12 Employment Tribunals (Constitution and Rules of Procedure) Regulations 2013, SI 2013/1237, Sch 1 r 17(2).
13 Ie the time limit in the Employment Tribunals (Constitution and Rules of Procedure) Regulations 2013, SI 2013/1237, Sch 1 r 16: see the text and note 8.
14 Ie under the Employment Tribunals (Constitution and Rules of Procedure) Regulations 2013, SI 2013/1237, Sch 1 r 20: see the text and notes 27–31.
15 Employment Tribunals (Constitution and Rules of Procedure) Regulations 2013, SI 2013/1237, Sch 1 r 18(1).
16 Employment Tribunals (Constitution and Rules of Procedure) Regulations 2013, SI 2013/1237, Sch 1 r 18(2).
17 Ie under the Employment Tribunals (Constitution and Rules of Procedure) Regulations 2013, SI 2013/1237, Sch 1 r 17 or Sch 1 r 18: see the text and notes 11–16.
18 Ie a rejection under the Employment Tribunals (Constitution and Rules of Procedure) Regulations 2013, SI 2013/1237, Sch 1 r 17: see the text and notes 11–12.
19 Employment Tribunals (Constitution and Rules of Procedure) Regulations 2013, SI 2013/1237, Sch 1 r 19(1).
20 As to the meaning of 'writing' see PARA 1450 note 19.
21 As to the meaning of 'present' see PARA 1461 note 3.
22 Employment Tribunals (Constitution and Rules of Procedure) Regulations 2013, SI 2013/1237, Sch 1 r 19(2).
23 As to the meaning of 'employment judge' see PARA 1401 note 3.
24 Employment Tribunals (Constitution and Rules of Procedure) Regulations 2013, SI 2013/1237, Sch 1 r 19(3).
25 Ie under the Employment Tribunals (Constitution and Rules of Procedure) Regulations 2013, SI 2013/1237, Sch 1 r 5: see PARA 1460.
26 Employment Tribunals (Constitution and Rules of Procedure) Regulations 2013, SI 2013/1237, Sch 1 r 19(4).
27 As to the meaning of 'claimant' see PARA 1457 note 25.
28 Employment Tribunals (Constitution and Rules of Procedure) Regulations 2013, SI 2013/1237, Sch 1 r 20(1).
29 Employment Tribunals (Constitution and Rules of Procedure) Regulations 2013, SI 2013/1237, Sch 1 r 20(2).
30 Employment Tribunals (Constitution and Rules of Procedure) Regulations 2013, SI 2013/1237, Sch 1 r 20(3).
31 Ie under the Employment Tribunals (Constitution and Rules of Procedure) Regulations 2013, SI 2013/1237, Sch 1 r 21: see the text and notes 33–36.
32 Employment Tribunals (Constitution and Rules of Procedure) Regulations 2013, SI 2013/1237, Sch 1 r 20(4). The principles to be applied when considering an application for an extension of time for presenting a response are those set out by Mummery J in *Kwik Save Stores Ltd v Swain* [1997] ICR 49, EAT (see *Moroak (t/a Blake Envelopes) v Cromie* [2005] ICR 1226 at [30], sub nom *Cromie v Moroak (t/a Blake Envelopes)* [2005] IRLR 535 at [30], EAT, per Burton J).
33 See note 13.
34 Employment Tribunals (Constitution and Rules of Procedure) Regulations 2013, SI 2013/1237, Sch 1 r 21(1).
35 Employment Tribunals (Constitution and Rules of Procedure) Regulations 2013, SI 2013/1237, Sch 1 r 21(2).

36   Employment Tribunals (Constitution and Rules of Procedure) Regulations 2013, SI 2013/1237, Sch 1 r 21(3). A respondent who has not entered a response to the employment tribunal may still appeal to the Employment Appeal Tribunal ('EAT'): see *Atos Origin IT Services UK Ltd v Haddock* [2005] ICR 277, [2005] IRLR 20, EAT (the entitlement to appeal is governed by the Employment Appeal Tribunal's own rules and practice direction, and there is nothing there which purports to restrict the right of respondents who have not presented a response in the employment tribunal to participate in an appeal).

37   Employment Tribunals (Constitution and Rules of Procedure) Regulations 2013, SI 2013/1237, Sch 1 r 22.

38   See the Employment Tribunals (Constitution and Rules of Procedure) Regulations 2013, SI 2013/1237, Sch 1 r 2. As to proceedings involving national security issues see PARA 1446 et seq; and as to the meaning of 'excluded person' see PARA 1450 note 11.

1463.   Employer's contract claim. Any employer's contract claim[1] must be made as part of the response, presented in accordance with the relevant rule[2], to a claim[3] which includes an employee's contract claim[4]. An employer's contract claim may be rejected on the same basis as a claimant's[5] claim may be rejected[6], in which case the employer may apply[7] for a reconsideration of the rejection[8].

When the tribunal[9] sends the response to the other parties[10] it must notify the claimant that the response includes an employer's contract claim and include information on how to submit a response to the claim, the time limit for doing so[11], and what will happen if a response is not received by the tribunal within that time limit[12].

A claimant's response to an employer's contract claim must be presented to the tribunal office[13] within 28 days of the date that the response was sent to the claimant[14].

1   As to the meaning of 'employer's contract claim' see PARA 1457 note 7.
2   Ie in accordance with the Employment Tribunals (Constitution and Rules of Procedure) Regulations 2013, SI 2013/1237, Sch 1 r 16: see PARA 1462. As to the meaning of 'present' see PARA 1461 note 3.
3   As to the meaning of 'claim' see PARA 1457 note 22.
4   Employment Tribunals (Constitution and Rules of Procedure) Regulations 2013, SI 2013/1237, Sch 1 r 23. 'Employee's contract claim' means a claim brought by an employee in accordance with the Employment Tribunals Extension of Jurisdiction (England and Wales) Order 1994, SI 1994/1623, arts 3, 7 (see PARAS 1408–1409): Employment Tribunals (Constitution and Rules of Procedure) Regulations 2013, SI 2013/1237, Sch 1 r 1(1).
5   As to the meaning of 'claimant' see PARA 1457 note 25.
6   Ie under the Employment Tribunals (Constitution and Rules of Procedure) Regulations 2013, SI 2013/1237, Sch 1 r 12: see PARA 1461.
7   Ie the Employment Tribunals (Constitution and Rules of Procedure) Regulations 2013, SI 2013/1237, Sch 1 r 13 (see PARA 1461) applies.
8   See the Employment Tribunals (Constitution and Rules of Procedure) Regulations 2013, SI 2013/1237, Sch 1 r 23.
9   As to the meaning of 'tribunal' for these purposes see PARA 1448 note 14.
10   Ie in accordance with the Employment Tribunals (Constitution and Rules of Procedure) Regulations 2013, SI 2013/1237, Sch 1 r 22: see PARA 1462.
11   As to the calculation of time limits see PARA 1460.
12   Employment Tribunals (Constitution and Rules of Procedure) Regulations 2013, SI 2013/1237, Sch 1 r 24.
13   As to the meaning of 'tribunal office' see PARA 1461 note 3.
14   Employment Tribunals (Constitution and Rules of Procedure) Regulations 2013, SI 2013/1237, Sch 1 r 25. If no response is presented within that time limit, Sch 1 rr 20, 21 (see PARA 1462) apply: Sch 1 r 25.

1464.   Initial consideration of claim form and response. As soon as possible after the acceptance of the response[1], the employment judge[2] must consider all of the documents held by the tribunal[3] in relation to the claim[4], to confirm whether there are arguable complaints[5] and defences within the jurisdiction of the tribunal, and for that purpose the judge may order a party to provide further information[6]. Except in a case where notice is given under either of the following provisions[7], the judge conducting the initial consideration must make a case management order[8], unless made already, which may deal with the listing of a preliminary or final hearing, and may propose judicial mediation or other forms of dispute resolution[9].

If the employment judge considers either that the tribunal has no jurisdiction to consider the claim, or part of it, or that the claim, or part of it, has no reasonable prospect of success, the tribunal must send a notice to the parties setting out the judge's view and the reasons for it, and ordering that the claim, or the part in question, is to be dismissed on such date as is specified in the notice unless before that date the claimant has presented written representations to the tribunal explaining why the claim, or part, should not be dismissed[10]. If no such representations are received, the claim must be dismissed from the date specified without further order, although the tribunal must write to the parties to confirm what has occurred[11]. If representations are received within the specified time they must be considered by an employment judge, who must either permit the claim, or part, to proceed or fix a hearing for the purpose of deciding whether it should be permitted to do so. The respondent[12] may, but need not, attend and participate in the hearing[13]. If any part of the claim is permitted to proceed the judge must make a case management order[14].

If the employment judge considers that the response to the claim, or part of it, has no reasonable prospect of success the tribunal must send a notice to the parties:

(1)   setting out the judge's view and the reasons for it;

(2)   ordering that the response, or the part in question, is to be dismissed on such date as is specified in the notice unless before that date the respondent has presented written representations to the tribunal explaining why the response, or part, should not be dismissed; and

(3)   specifying the consequences of the dismissal of the response[15].

If no such representations are received, the response must be dismissed from the date specified without further order, although the tribunal must write to the parties to confirm what has occurred[16]. If representations are received within the specified time they must be considered by an employment judge, who must either permit the response, or part, to stand or fix a hearing for the purpose of deciding whether it should be permitted to do so. The claimant[17] may, but need not, attend and participate in the hearing[18]. If any part of the response is permitted to stand the judge must make a case management order[19]. Where a response is dismissed, the effect is[20] as if no response had been presented[21].

1   As to the response see PARA 1462.
2   As to the meaning of 'employment judge' see PARA 1401 note 3.
3   As to the meaning of 'tribunal' for these purposes see PARA 1448 note 14.
4   As to the meaning of 'claim' see PARA 1457 note 22.
5   'Complaint' means anything that is referred to as a claim, complaint, reference, application or appeal in any enactment which confers jurisdiction on the tribunal: Employment Tribunals (Constitution and Rules of Procedure) Regulations 2013, SI 2013/1237, Sch 1 r 1(1).
6   Employment Tribunals (Constitution and Rules of Procedure) Regulations 2013, SI 2013/1237, Sch 1 r 26(1).
7   Ie under the Employment Tribunals (Constitution and Rules of Procedure) Regulations 2013, SI 2013/1237, Sch 1 r 27 or Sch 1 r 28: see the text and notes 10–21.
8   As to the meaning of 'case management order' see PARA 1460 note 4.
9   Employment Tribunals (Constitution and Rules of Procedure) Regulations 2013, SI 2013/1237, Sch 1 r 26(2).

10 Employment Tribunals (Constitution and Rules of Procedure) Regulations 2013, SI 2013/1237, Sch 1 r 27(1).
11 Employment Tribunals (Constitution and Rules of Procedure) Regulations 2013, SI 2013/1237, Sch 1 r 27(2).
12 As to the meaning of 'respondent' see PARA 1460 note 8.
13 Employment Tribunals (Constitution and Rules of Procedure) Regulations 2013, SI 2013/1237, Sch 1 r 27(3).
14 Employment Tribunals (Constitution and Rules of Procedure) Regulations 2013, SI 2013/1237, Sch 1 r 27(4).
15 Employment Tribunals (Constitution and Rules of Procedure) Regulations 2013, SI 2013/1237, Sch 1 r 28(1). As to the consequence of dismissal see Sch 1 r 28(5); and the text and notes 20–21.
16 Employment Tribunals (Constitution and Rules of Procedure) Regulations 2013, SI 2013/1237, Sch 1 r 28(2).
17 As to the meaning of 'claimant' see PARA 1457 note 25.
18 Employment Tribunals (Constitution and Rules of Procedure) Regulations 2013, SI 2013/1237, Sch 1 r 28(3).
19 Employment Tribunals (Constitution and Rules of Procedure) Regulations 2013, SI 2013/1237, Sch 1 r 28(4).
20 Ie as set out in the Employment Tribunals (Constitution and Rules of Procedure) Regulations 2013, SI 2013/1237, Sch 1 r 21: see PARA 1462.
21 Employment Tribunals (Constitution and Rules of Procedure) Regulations 2013, SI 2013/1237, Sch 1 r 28(5).

(v) Case Management in Employment Tribunals

1465. Compliance with rules, orders and practice directions. Subject to certain exceptions[1], a failure to comply with any provision of the procedural rules[2] or with any order of the tribunal[3] does not of itself render void the proceedings or any step taken in the proceedings[4]. In the case of such non-compliance, the tribunal may take such action as it considers just, which may include all or any of the following[5]:

(1) waiving or varying the requirement[6];
(2) striking out[7] the claim[8] or the response, in whole or in part[9];
(3) barring or restricting a party's participation in the proceedings[10];
(4) awarding costs in accordance with the relevant[11] rules[12].

The President[13] may publish guidance for England and Wales[14] as to matters of practice and as to how the powers conferred by those rules may be exercised. Any such guidance must be published by the President in an appropriate manner to bring it to the attention of claimants[15], respondents[16] and their advisers. Tribunals must have regard to any such guidance, but they are not bound by it[17].

1 The Employment Tribunals (Constitution and Rules of Procedure) Regulations 2013, SI 2013/1237, Sch 1 r 6 (see the text and notes 2–11) does not apply to a failure to comply with Sch 1 r 8(1) (see PARA 1461), Sch 1 r 16(1) (see PARA 1462), Sch 1 r 23 (see PARA 1463) or Sch 1 r 25 (see PARA 1463) or with an order under Sch 1 r 38 or Sch 1 r 39 (see PARA 1466): Sch 1 r 6.
2 Ie the rules set out in the Employment Tribunals (Constitution and Rules of Procedure) Regulations 2013, SI 2013/1237, Sch 1.
3 As to orders of the tribunal see PARA 1460 note 4; and as to the meaning of 'tribunal' for these purposes see PARA 1448 note 14. See also *Uyamnwa-Odu v Schools Offices Services Ltd* [2005] All ER (D) 377 (Nov), EAT (unless order under the predecessor to the Employment Tribunals (Constitution and Rules of Procedure) Regulations 2013, SI 2013/1237, Sch 1 r 38(2) amounted to a conditional judgment). See also *Lafferty v EPI Coaches Ltd* [2009] All ER (D) 81 (Apr), EAT.
4 Employment Tribunals (Constitution and Rules of Procedure) Regulations 2013, SI 2013/1237, Sch 1 r 6.
5 In determining what sanction to impose for a failure to obey directions, the overriding objective (see PARA 1421) is the guiding principle and requires the tribunal to consider all the

circumstances of the case: *Weir Valves and Controls (UK) Ltd v Armitage* [2004] ICR 371, EAT (tribunal should always consider whether striking out or a lesser remedy was an appropriate response where a party disobeyed an order).

6   Employment Tribunals (Constitution and Rules of Procedure) Regulations 2013, SI 2013/1237, Sch 1 r 6(a).

7   Ie in accordance with the Employment Tribunals (Constitution and Rules of Procedure) Regulations 2013, SI 2013/1237, Sch 1 r 37: see PARA 1466.

8   As to the meaning of 'claim' see PARA 1457 note 22.

9   Employment Tribunals (Constitution and Rules of Procedure) Regulations 2013, SI 2013/1237, Sch 1 r 6(b). An over-rigid approach is not required when an employment tribunal considers an application for relief from sanction, for example, a strike-out founded on breach of an unless order: *Neary v Governing Body of St Albans Girls' School* reversed [2009] EWCA Civ 1190, [2010] IRLR 124, [2010] ICR 473 (Parliament had deliberately not incorporated CPR 3.9(1) into employment tribunal practice when it chose to incorporate the overriding objective of the CPR, since it had always been the intention of Parliament that tribunal proceedings should be as short, simple and informal as possible). See also *Thind v Salvesen Logistics Ltd* [2010] All ER (D) 05 (Sep) (unless orders were an important part of the tribunal's procedural armoury, and they had to be taken very seriously but that is no more than one consideration and no one factor was necessarily determinative of the course that the tribunal should take), EAT; *Murray v Standard Life* [2014] All ER (D) 124 (Aug), EAT (information supplied by claimant was sufficient to give notice of her case and respondent had been prepared).

10 Employment Tribunals (Constitution and Rules of Procedure) Regulations 2013, SI 2013/1237, Sch 1 r 6(c).

11 Ie in accordance with the Employment Tribunals (Constitution and Rules of Procedure) Regulations 2013, SI 2013/1237, Sch 1 rr 74–84: see PARA 1480.

12 Employment Tribunals (Constitution and Rules of Procedure) Regulations 2013, SI 2013/1237, Sch 1 r 6(d).

13 As to the meaning of 'President' see PARA 1399 note 7.

14 As to the meanings of 'England' and 'Wales' see PARA 2 note 12.

15 As to the meaning of 'claimant' see PARA 1457 note 25.

16 As to the meaning of 'respondent' see PARA 1460 note 8.

17 Employment Tribunals (Constitution and Rules of Procedure) Regulations 2013, SI 2013/1237, Sch 1 r 7.

1466.   Case management orders and other powers. A tribunal[1] must wherever practicable and appropriate encourage the use by the parties of the services of the Advisory, Conciliation and Arbitration Service ('ACAS')[2], judicial or other mediation, or other means of resolving their disputes by agreement[3].

The tribunal may at any stage of the proceedings, on its own initiative or on application, make a case management order[4]. The particular powers identified in the rules set out below do not restrict that general power. A case management order may vary, suspend or set aside an earlier case management order where that is necessary in the interests of justice, and in particular where a party affected by the earlier order did not have a reasonable opportunity to make representations before it was made[5].

An application by a party for a particular case management order may be made either at a hearing or presented in writing[6] to the tribunal[7]. Where a party applies in writing, he must notify the other parties that any objections to the application should be sent to the tribunal as soon as possible[8]. The tribunal may deal with such an application in writing or order that it be dealt with at a preliminary or final hearing[9].

The tribunal may order any person in Great Britain[10] to disclose documents or information to a party, by providing copies or otherwise, or to allow a party to inspect such material as might be ordered by the County Court or, in Scotland, by a sheriff[11]. It may also order any person in Great Britain to attend a hearing to give evidence, produce documents, or produce information[12] and may use prescribed procedures[13] for obtaining evidence from other EU member states[14].

The tribunal may on its own initiative, or on the application of a party or any other person wishing to become a party, add any person as a party, by way of substitution or otherwise, if it appears that there are issues between that person and any of the existing parties falling within the jurisdiction of the tribunal which it is in the interests of justice to have determined in the proceedings; and it may remove any party apparently wrongly included[15]. It may permit any person to participate in proceedings, on such terms as may be specified, in respect of any matter in which that person has a legitimate interest[16].

Where a tribunal considers that two or more claims give rise to common or related issues of fact or law, the tribunal or the President[17] may make an order specifying one or more of those claims as a lead case and staying the other claims ('the related cases')[18]. When the tribunal makes a decision in respect of the common or related issues it must send a copy of that decision to each party in each of the related cases and that decision is binding[19] on each of those parties[20]. Within 28 days[21] after the date on which the tribunal sent a copy of the decision to a party under the above provision, however, that party may apply in writing for an order that the decision does not apply to, and is not binding on the parties to, a particular related case[22]. If a lead case is withdrawn before the tribunal makes a decision in respect of the common or related issues, it must make an order as to whether another claim is to be specified as a lead case and whether any order[23] affecting the related cases should be set aside or varied[24].

At any stage of the proceedings, either on its own initiative or on the application of a party, a tribunal may strike out all or part of a claim[25] or response on any of the following grounds[26]:

(1)   that it is scandalous or vexatious or has no reasonable prospect of success[27];

(2)   that the manner in which the proceedings have been conducted by or on behalf of the claimant[28] or the respondent[29], as the case may be, has been scandalous, unreasonable or vexatious[30];

(3)   for non-compliance with any of the procedural rules[31] or with an order of the tribunal[32];

(4)   that it has not been actively pursued[33];

(5)   that the tribunal considers that it is no longer possible to have a fair hearing in respect of the claim or response, or the part to be struck out[34].

A claim or response may not, however, be struck out unless the party in question has been given a reasonable opportunity to make representations, either in writing or, if requested by the party, at a hearing[35]. Where a response is struck out, the effect is[36] as if no response had been presented[37].

An order may specify that if it is not complied with by the date specified, the claim or response, or part of it, is to be dismissed without further order (known generally as an 'unless order'). If a claim or response, or part of it, is dismissed on this basis the tribunal must give written notice to the parties confirming what has occurred[38]. A party whose claim or response has been dismissed, in whole or in part, as a result of such an order may apply to the tribunal in writing, within 14 days of the date that the notice was sent, to have the order set aside on the basis that it is in the interests of justice to do so. Unless the application includes a request for a hearing, the tribunal may determine it on the basis of written representations[39]. Where a response is dismissed under this provision, the effect is[40] as if no response had been presented[41].

Where at a preliminary hearing[42] the tribunal considers that any specific allegation or argument in a claim or response has little reasonable prospect of success, it may make an order requiring a party ('the paying party') to pay a deposit not exceeding £1,000 as a condition of continuing to advance that allegation or argument[43]. The tribunal must make reasonable inquiries into the paying party's ability to pay the deposit and have regard to any such information when deciding the amount of the deposit[44]. The tribunal's reasons for making the deposit order must be provided with the order and the paying party must be notified about the potential consequences of the order[45]. If the paying party fails to pay the deposit by the date specified the specific allegation or argument to which the deposit order relates must be struck out. Where a response is struck out, the consequences are[46] as if no response had been presented[47]. If the tribunal at any stage following the making of a deposit order decides the specific allegation or argument against the paying party for substantially the reasons given in the deposit order:

(a)　　the paying party is to be treated as having acted unreasonably in pursuing that specific allegation or argument for the purpose of the rule about costs orders or preparation time orders[48], unless the contrary is shown; and

(b)　　the deposit must be paid to the other party or, if there is more than one, to such other party or parties as the tribunal orders[49].

Otherwise the deposit must be refunded[50].

If a deposit has been paid to a party under head (b) above and a costs or preparation time order has been made against the paying party in favour of the party who received the deposit, the amount of the deposit counts towards the settlement of that order[51].

The tribunal's powers where a tribunal fee has not been paid have already been discussed[52].

1　As to the meaning of 'tribunal' for these purposes see PARA 1448 note 14.
2　As to the Central Arbitration Committee see PARA 1226 et seq.
3　Employment Tribunals (Constitution and Rules of Procedure) Regulations 2013, SI 2013/1237, Sch 1 rr 1(1), 3.
4　As to the meaning of 'case management order' see PARA 1460 note 4.
5　Employment Tribunals (Constitution and Rules of Procedure) Regulations 2013, SI 2013/1237, Sch 1 r 29. Case management powers must not be used to contradict rules of substantive law (in this case, equal pay law): *Amey Services Ltd v Cardigan, City of Edinburgh Council v Marr* [2008] IRLR 279, EAT. The tribunal is to be wary of embarking down the road of trying to investigate a party's mental capacity: *Johnson v Edwardian International Hotels Ltd* [2008] All ER (D) 23 (May), EAT.
6　As to the meaning of 'writing' see PARA 1450 note 19.
7　Employment Tribunals (Constitution and Rules of Procedure) Regulations 2013, SI 2013/1237, Sch 1 r 30(1).
8　Employment Tribunals (Constitution and Rules of Procedure) Regulations 2013, SI 2013/1237, Sch 1 r 30(2).
9　Employment Tribunals (Constitution and Rules of Procedure) Regulations 2013, SI 2013/1237, Sch 1 r 30(3).
10　As to the meaning of 'Great Britain' see PARA 2 note 12.
11　Employment Tribunals (Constitution and Rules of Procedure) Regulations 2013, SI 2013/1237, Sch 1 r 31 (amended by virtue of the Crime and Courts Act 2013 Sch 9 Pt 2 para 11). Disclosure of statistical information on the number of white and non-white applicants for posts is probative, not merely going to credit: *West Midlands Passenger Transport Executive v Jaquant Singh* [1988] ICR 614, [1988] IRLR 186, CA, disapproving *Jalota v Imperial Metal Industry (Kynoch) Ltd* [1979] IRLR 313, EAT (where it was held that discovery would not be ordered if it goes merely to credit). Disclosure will not be ordered for the purpose of 'fishing': *Clwyd County Council v Leverton* [1985] IRLR 197, EAT. In a case of redundancy selection, this may mean that disclosure of other employees' results on a grading or 'points' exercise will not be

ordered unless there is some existing evidence of unfair selection: *British Aerospace plc v Green* [1995] ICR 1006, [1995] IRLR 433, CA; *FDR Ltd v Holloway* [1995] IRLR 400, EAT. Although cost is an important consideration when deciding whether to order the disclosure of documents, it must not be used as a means with which to deprive an claimant of his rights: *Knight v Department of Social Security* [2002] IRLR 249, EAT. If a party voluntarily discloses any documents, he must not be unfairly or misleadingly selective: *Birds Eye Walls Ltd v Harrison* [1985] ICR 278, [1985] IRLR 47, EAT.

Where disclosure is to be ordered in a reduced form or anonymously, the employer and the claimant's legal representatives should be allowed to make representations on the tribunal's proposals: *Asda Stores Ltd v Thompson (No 2)* [2004] IRLR 598, EAT. For a suggested procedure for the production of verified abstracts from confidential job applications see *Williams v Dyfed County Council* [1986] ICR 449 at 454–455, EAT, per Wood J. Restrictions on disclosure of medical reports may be ordered to protect the party seeking the order (*Department of Health and Social Security v Sloan* [1981] ICR 313, EAT); but, if disclosure of such reports is ordered, it must be done fully, in that disclosure of a doctor's conclusions alone may be insufficient (*Ford Motor Co Ltd v Nawaz* [1987] ICR 434, [1987] IRLR 163, EAT). The defence of public interest immunity may be raised in an application for disclosure: *Halford v Sharples* [1992] ICR 146, EAT (applying *Campbell v Tameside Metropolitan Borough Council* [1982] QB 1065, [1982] 2 All ER 791, CA); *Balfour v Foreign and Commonwealth Office* [1994] 2 All ER 588, [1994] ICR 277, CA. However, the success of such a defence may depend on the nature of the procedure to which the documents relate: *Metropolitan Police Comr v Locker* [1993] 3 All ER 584, [1993] ICR 440, EAT (internal police grievance procedure not akin to the police complaints procedure, so disclosure ordered; *Halford v Sharples* [1992] ICR 146, EAT distinguished).

Where a person or his representative has been excluded under the Employment Tribunals (Constitution and Rules of Procedure) Regulations 2013, SI 2013/1237, Sch 1 r 94 (national security proceedings: see PARA 1450) from all or part of the proceedings and a tribunal is considering whether to make an order under Sch 1 r 31 or Sch 1 r 32, a minister (whether or not he is a party to the proceedings) may make an application to the tribunal objecting to that order. If such an order has been made, the minister may make an application to vary or set aside the order: Sch 2 r 3(1). The tribunal must hear and determine the minister's application in private and the minister is entitled to address the tribunal: Sch 2 r 3(2).

12 Employment Tribunals (Constitution and Rules of Procedure) Regulations 2013, SI 2013/1237, Sch 1 r 32. See also Sch 2 r 3, cited in note 11. In deciding whether to make a witness order, the tribunal should consider: (1) the likely relevance of the witness's testimony to the issue in dispute; and (2) the necessity for an order to ensure the witness's attendance: *Eagle Star Insurance Co Ltd v Hayward* [1981] ICR 860, EAT; *Dada v Metal Box Co Ltd* [1974] ICR 559, [1974] IRLR 251, NIRC. See also *Wilcox v HGS* [1976] ICR 306, sub nom *HGS v Wilcox* [1976] IRLR 222, CA. The discretion to make a witness order is a matter for the tribunal, whose decision is to be overturned on appeal only if it shows an error of law, improper considerations or manifest unreasonableness: *Noorani v Merseyside TEC Ltd* [1999] IRLR 184, CA. See also *Canadian Imperial Bank of Commerce v Beck* [2009] EWCA Civ 619, [2009] IRLR 740.

13 Ie the procedures for obtaining evidence prescribed in Council Regulation (EC) 1206/2001 (OJ L174, 27.6.2001, p 1) of 28 May 2001 on co-operation between the courts of the member states in the taking of evidence in civil or commercial matters: see CIVIL PROCEDURE vol 11 (2009) PARA 1002.

14 See the Employment Tribunals (Constitution and Rules of Procedure) Regulations 2013, SI 2013/1237, Sch 1 r 33 (amended by SI 2014/271).

15 Employment Tribunals (Constitution and Rules of Procedure) Regulations 2013, SI 2013/1237, Sch 1 r 34. A tribunal has always had the power to add or substitute respondents as part of the general power to regulate its own procedure: see *Cocking v Sandhurst (Stationers) Ltd* [1974] ICR 650, NIRC; *Watts v Seven Kings Motor Co Ltd* [1983] ICR 135, EAT. See also *Ryan v Bennington Training Services Ltd* [2008] All ER (D) 251 (Dec), EAT where aspects of *Cocking v Sandhurst (Stationers) Ltd* [1974] ICR 650, NIRC were considered. A party can be added in exercise of the tribunal's discretion even after the expiry of what would have been the normal time limitation: *Gillick v BP Chemicals Ltd* [1993] IRLR 437, EAT; *Drinkwater Sabey Ltd v Burnett* [1995] ICR 328, sub nom *Drinkwater Sabey Ltd v Burnett and Kent County Council* [1995] IRLR 238, EAT.

16 Employment Tribunals (Constitution and Rules of Procedure) Regulations 2013, SI 2013/1237, Sch 1 r 35.

17 As to the meaning of 'President' see PARA 1399 note 7.

18 Employment Tribunals (Constitution and Rules of Procedure) Regulations 2013, SI 2013/1237, Sch 1 r 36(1).
19 Ie subject to the Employment Tribunals (Constitution and Rules of Procedure) Regulations 2013, SI 2013/1237, Sch 1 r 36(3): see the text and notes 21–22.
20 Employment Tribunals (Constitution and Rules of Procedure) Regulations 2013, SI 2013/1237, Sch 1 r 36(2).
21 As to the calculation of time limits see PARA 1460.
22 Employment Tribunals (Constitution and Rules of Procedure) Regulations 2013, SI 2013/1237, Sch 1 r 36(3).
23 As to orders of the tribunal see PARA 1460 note 4.
24 Employment Tribunals (Constitution and Rules of Procedure) Regulations 2013, SI 2013/1237, Sch 1 r 36(4).
25 As to the meaning of 'claim' see PARA 1457 note 22.
26 Employment Tribunals (Constitution and Rules of Procedure) Regulations 2013, SI 2013/1237, Sch 1 r 37(1).
27 Employment Tribunals (Constitution and Rules of Procedure) Regulations 2013, SI 2013/1237, Sch 1 r 37(1)(a). See *Tayside Public Transport Co Ltd (t/a Travel Dundee) v Reilly* [2012] CSIH 46, [2012] IRLR 755 (employment tribunal in error in striking out claim where factual disputes outstanding).
28 As to the meaning of 'claimant' see PARA 1457 note 25.
29 As to the meaning of 'respondent' see PARA 1460 note 8.
30 Employment Tribunals (Constitution and Rules of Procedure) Regulations 2013, SI 2013/1237, Sch 1 r 37(1)(b). See eg *De Keyser Ltd v Wilson* [2001] IRLR 324, EAT (employer's solicitor's letter of instruction to medical expert questioning extent of employee's illness and its cause not scandalous); *Bennett v Southwark London Borough Council* [2002] EWCA Civ 223, [2002] ICR 881, [2002] IRLR 407 (single outburst by lay representative accusing tribunal of bias did not entitle its members to strike out proceedings); *Bolch v Chipman* [2004] IRLR 140 (conduct outside the curtilage of the tribunal may be relevant but there must be a finding with appropriate reasons that the rule has been broken); *Lecerf-Kiener v Computer Associates International* [2005] All ER (D) 21 (Jan), EAT (claimant had ignored the specific warning of the chairman (now employment judge) to refrain from sending upsetting and distressing material to the respondent's employees and had refused to obey the rules of the tribunal); *James v Blockbuster Entertainment Ltd* [2006] EWCA Civ 684, [2006] IRLR 630 (two cardinal conditions for the exercise of the tribunal's power to intervene: either that the unreasonable conduct had taken the form of deliberate and persistent disregard of the required procedural steps, or that it had made a fair trial impossible; in the instant case it was right to intervene); *Force One Utilities Ltd v Hatfield* [2009] IRLR 45, [2008] All ER (D) 130 (May), EAT (striking out may be the only proportionate response to serious intimidation of one party by another); *Pik v Goldman Sachs Services Ltd* [2009] All ER (D) 110 (Jan), EAT (fair trial not possible where employee pursuing cause in an obsessive way, on the premise that all involved in the case including the tribunal were acting on behalf of the British Secret Service).
31 Ie the rules set out in the Employment Tribunals (Constitution and Rules of Procedure) Regulations 2013, SI 2013/1237, Sch 1.
32 Employment Tribunals (Constitution and Rules of Procedure) Regulations 2013, SI 2013/1237, Sch 1 r 37(1)(c).
33 Employment Tribunals (Constitution and Rules of Procedure) Regulations 2013, SI 2013/1237, Sch 1 r 37(1)(d). This may apply in two different cases: (1) intentional and contumelious default by the claimant and (2) inordinate and inexcusable delay meaning that a fair trial is not possible or that there would be serious prejudice to the respondent: *Rolls Royce plc v Riddle* [2008] IRLR 873, EAT. See also *Shah v Haden Building Management Ltd* (2005) Times, 2 November, [2005] All ER (D) 09 (Oct), EAT (striking out upheld as chairman (now employment judge) had exercised her discretion correctly). However a tribunal should not usually strike out at this stage if material facts are still in issue: *Ezsias v Glamorgan NHS Trust* [2007] EWCA Civ 330, [2007] 4 All ER 940, [2007] ICR 1126. See also *Abegaze v Shrewsbury College of Arts & Technology* [2009] EWCA Civ 96, [2010] IRLR 238 (no proper basis for strike-out order; it was severe step to deprive employee of any remedy when some injury to feelings compensation arose from act of direct discrimination).
34 Employment Tribunals (Constitution and Rules of Procedure) Regulations 2013, SI 2013/1237, Sch 1 r 37(1)(e). See *Riley v Crown Prosecution Service* [2013] EWCA Civ 951, [2013] IRLR 966 (strike out where fair trial not possible because claimant unfit to attend hearing for two years). See also *Ezsias v Glamorgan NHS Trust* [2007] EWCA Civ 330, [2007] 4 All ER 940, [2007] ICR 1126.

35 Employment Tribunals (Constitution and Rules of Procedure) Regulations 2013, SI 2013/1237, Sch 1 r 37(2).

36 Ie as set out in the Employment Tribunals (Constitution and Rules of Procedure) Regulations 2013, SI 2013/1237, Sch 1 r 21: see PARA 1462.

37 Employment Tribunals (Constitution and Rules of Procedure) Regulations 2013, SI 2013/1237, Sch 1 r 37(3).

38 Employment Tribunals (Constitution and Rules of Procedure) Regulations 2013, SI 2013/1237, Sch 1 r 38(1). An 'unless order' should make clear exactly what it requires and in the case of a litigant in person should avoid legal terms such as 'disclosure': *Mace v Ponders End International Ltd* [2014] IRLR 697, EAT.

39 Employment Tribunals (Constitution and Rules of Procedure) Regulations 2013, SI 2013/1237, Sch 1 r 38(2).

40 See note 36.

41 Employment Tribunals (Constitution and Rules of Procedure) Regulations 2013, SI 2013/1237, Sch 1 r 38(3).

42 Ie a preliminary hearing under the Employment Tribunals (Constitution and Rules of Procedure) Regulations 2013, SI 2013/1237, Sch 1 r 53: see PARA 1473.

43 Employment Tribunals (Constitution and Rules of Procedure) Regulations 2013, SI 2013/1237, Sch 1 r 39(1).

44 Employment Tribunals (Constitution and Rules of Procedure) Regulations 2013, SI 2013/1237, Sch 1 r 39(2).

45 Employment Tribunals (Constitution and Rules of Procedure) Regulations 2013, SI 2013/1237, Sch 1 r 39(3).

46 See note 36.

47 Employment Tribunals (Constitution and Rules of Procedure) Regulations 2013, SI 2013/1237, Sch 1 r 39(4).

48 Ie for the purposes of the Employment Tribunals (Constitution and Rules of Procedure) Regulations 2013, SI 2013/1237, Sch 1 r 76: see PARA 1480.

49 Employment Tribunals (Constitution and Rules of Procedure) Regulations 2013, SI 2013/1237, Sch 1 r 39(5)(a), (b).

50 Employment Tribunals (Constitution and Rules of Procedure) Regulations 2013, SI 2013/1237, Sch 1 r 39(5).

51 Employment Tribunals (Constitution and Rules of Procedure) Regulations 2013, SI 2013/1237, Sch 1 r 39(6).

52 See PARA 1457.

1467. Delivery of documents to and by employment tribunals. A claim form may only be delivered in accordance with the relevant practice direction[1]. Subject to that, documents may be delivered to the tribunal[2] by post[3], by direct delivery to the appropriate tribunal office[4], including delivery by a courier or messenger service[5], or by electronic communication[6]. The tribunal must notify the parties following the presentation of the claim[7] of the address of the tribunal office dealing with the case, including any fax or email or other electronic address, and all documents must be delivered to either the postal or the electronic address so notified. The tribunal may from time to time notify the parties of any change of address, or that a particular form of communication should or should not be used, and any documents must be delivered in accordance with that notification[8].

Documents may be delivered to a party, whether by the tribunal or by another party:

(1)   by post[9];

(2)   by direct delivery to that party's address, including delivery by a courier or messenger service[10];

(3)   by electronic communication[11]; or

(4)   by being handed personally to that party, if an individual and if no representative has been named in the claim form or response; or to any individual representative named in the claim form or response; or, on

the occasion of a hearing, to any person identified by the party as representing that party at that hearing[12].

Subject to certain special cases[13], documents must be sent to non-parties at any address for service which they may have notified and otherwise at any known address or place of business in the United Kingdom[14] or, if the party is a corporate body, at its registered or principal office in the United Kingdom or, if permitted by the President[15], at an address outside the United Kingdom[16].

Where no address for service in accordance with the above rules is known or it appears that service at any such address is unlikely to come to the attention of the addressee, the President or a regional employment judge[17] may order that there is to be substituted service in such manner as appears appropriate[18].

Where a document has been delivered in accordance with the relevant rule[19], it must, unless the contrary is proved, be taken to have been received by the addressee:

(a) if sent by post, on the day on which it would be delivered in the ordinary course of post;

(b) if sent by means of electronic communication, on the day of transmission;

(c) if delivered directly or personally, on the day of delivery[20].

A tribunal may treat any document as delivered to a person, notwithstanding any non-compliance with the above rules[21], if satisfied that the document in question, or its substance, has in fact come to the attention of that person[22].

Where a party sends a communication[23] to the tribunal it must send a copy to all other parties, and state that it has done so[24]. The tribunal may order a departure from this rule where it considers it in the interests of justice to do so[25].

1 See the Employment Tribunals (Constitution and Rules of Procedure) Regulations 2013, SI 2013/1237, Sch 1 r 85(2), cited in PARA 1461 note 3.

2 As to the meaning of 'tribunal' for these purposes see PARA 1448 note 14.

3 Employment Tribunals (Constitution and Rules of Procedure) Regulations 2013, SI 2013/1237, Sch 1 r 85(1)(a).

4 As to the meaning of 'tribunal office' see PARA 1461 note 3.

5 Employment Tribunals (Constitution and Rules of Procedure) Regulations 2013, SI 2013/1237, Sch 1 r 85(1)(b).

6 Employment Tribunals (Constitution and Rules of Procedure) Regulations 2013, SI 2013/1237, Sch 1 r 85(1)(c). As to the meaning of 'electronic communication' see PARA 1430 note 1.

7 As to the meaning of 'claim' see PARA 1457 note 22.

8 Employment Tribunals (Constitution and Rules of Procedure) Regulations 2013, SI 2013/1237, Sch 1 r 85(3).

9 Employment Tribunals (Constitution and Rules of Procedure) Regulations 2013, SI 2013/1237, Sch 1 r 86(1)(a). For the purposes of heads (1)–(3) in the text, the document must be delivered to the address given in the claim form or response (which must be the address of the party's representative, if one is named) or to a different address as notified in writing by the party in question: Sch 1 r 86(2). If a party has given both a postal address and one or more electronic addresses, any of them may be used unless the party has indicated in writing that a particular address should or should not be used: Sch 1 r 86(3). As to the meaning of 'writing' see PARA 1450 note 19.

10 Employment Tribunals (Constitution and Rules of Procedure) Regulations 2013, SI 2013/1237, Sch 1 r 86(1)(b). See also note 9.

11 Employment Tribunals (Constitution and Rules of Procedure) Regulations 2013, SI 2013/1237, Sch 1 r 86(1)(c). See also note 9.

12 Employment Tribunals (Constitution and Rules of Procedure) Regulations 2013, SI 2013/1237, Sch 1 r 86(1)(d).

13 Ie the special cases which are the subject of the Employment Tribunals (Constitution and Rules of Procedure) Regulations 2013, SI 2013/1237, Sch 1 r 88. Addresses for serving the Secretary of State, the law officers, and the Counsel General to the Welsh Assembly Government, in cases where they are not parties, must be issued by practice direction: Sch 1 r 88. As to the Secretary

of State see PARA 5 note 21; as to the law officers see CONSTITUTIONAL AND ADMINISTRATIVE LAW vol 20 (2014) PARA 273 et seq; and as to the Counsel General to the Welsh Assembly Government see CONSTITUTIONAL AND ADMINISTRATIVE LAW vol 20 (2014) PARA 376.

14 As to the meaning of 'United Kingdom' see PARA 2 note 12.

15 As to the meaning of 'President' see PARA 1399 note 7.

16 Employment Tribunals (Constitution and Rules of Procedure) Regulations 2013, SI 2013/1237, Sch 1 r 87. The reference to 'any other known address or place of business' includes a last known place of business and good service may be made at such an address, with documents sent there presumed to have been received: *Zietsman (t/a Berkshire Orthodontics) v Stubbington* [2002] ICR 249, EAT.

17 As to the meaning of 'regional employment judge' see PARA 1399 note 9.

18 Employment Tribunals (Constitution and Rules of Procedure) Regulations 2013, SI 2013/1237, Sch 1 r 89.

19 Ie in accordance with the Employment Tribunals (Constitution and Rules of Procedure) Regulations 2013, SI 2013/1237, Sch 1 r 85 or Sch 1 r 86: see the text and notes 1–12.

20 Employment Tribunals (Constitution and Rules of Procedure) Regulations 2013, SI 2013/1237, Sch 1 r 90. As to delivery by post see also the Interpretation Act 1978 s 7; and STATUTES AND LEGISLATIVE PROCESS vol 96 (2012) PARA 1219; *Migwain Ltd v Transport and General Workers' Union* [1979] ICR 597, EAT; *T and D Transport (Portsmouth) Ltd v Limburn* [1987] ICR 696, EAT.

21 Ie any non-compliance with the Employment Tribunals (Constitution and Rules of Procedure) Regulations 2013, SI 2013/1237, Sch 1 rr 86–88: see the text and notes 9–16.

22 Employment Tribunals (Constitution and Rules of Procedure) Regulations 2013, SI 2013/1237, Sch 1 r 91.

23 Ie except an application under the Employment Tribunals (Constitution and Rules of Procedure) Regulations 2013, SI 2013/1237, Sch 1 r 32: see PARA 1466.

24 This may be done by use of 'cc' or otherwise: see the Employment Tribunals (Constitution and Rules of Procedure) Regulations 2013, SI 2013/1237, Sch 1 r 92.

25 Employment Tribunals (Constitution and Rules of Procedure) Regulations 2013, SI 2013/1237, Sch 1 r 92.

1468. Provisions with regard to conciliation. Where proceedings concern an enactment which provides for conciliation, the tribunal[1] must send a copy of the claim form and the response to an ACAS conciliation officer[2] and inform the parties that the services of an ACAS conciliation officer are available to them[3]. A representative of the Advisory, Conciliation and Arbitration Service ('ACAS')[4] may[5] attend any preliminary hearing[6].

1 As to the meaning of 'tribunal' for these purposes see PARA 1448 note 14.

2 As to the meaning of 'conciliation officer' see PARA 1420 note 2.

3 Employment Tribunals (Constitution and Rules of Procedure) Regulations 2013, SI 2013/1237, Sch 1 r 93(1). This requirement does not go to the jurisdiction of the tribunal so that a failure to send the documents to a conciliation officer should not nullify the proceedings: see *Sheringham Development Co Ltd v Browne* [1977] ICR 20, EAT.

4 As to ACAS see PARA 1213 et seq.

5 This is subject to the Employment Tribunals (Constitution and Rules of Procedure) Regulations 2013, SI 2013/1237, Sch 1 r 50 (see PARA 1472) and Sch 1 para 94 (see PARA 1450): Sch 1 r 93(2).

6 Employment Tribunals (Constitution and Rules of Procedure) Regulations 2013, SI 2013/1237, Sch 1 r 93(2).

1469. Transfer of proceedings within the United Kingdom; transfer from a court. The President (England and Wales)[1] or a regional employment judge[2] may at any time, on his own initiative or on the application of a party, with the consent of the President (Scotland), transfer to a tribunal office[3] in Scotland any proceedings started in England and Wales which could[4] have been started in Scotland and which in that person's opinion would more conveniently be determined there[5]. Similarly, the President (Scotland) or the Vice President[6] may at any time, on his own initiative or on the application of a party, with the consent of the President (England and Wales), transfer to a tribunal office in England and Wales any proceedings started in Scotland which could[7] have been started in England and Wales and in that person's opinion would more conveniently be determined there[8].

Where proceedings are referred to a tribunal[9] by a court, the procedural rules[10] apply as if the proceedings had been presented[11] by the claimant[12].

1 As to the meaning of 'President' see PARA 1399 note 7. As to the meanings of 'England' and 'Wales' see PARA 2 note 12.

2 As to the meaning of 'regional employment judge' see PARA 1399 note 9.

3 As to the meaning of 'tribunal office' see PARA 1461 note 3.

4 Ie in accordance with the Employment Tribunals (Constitution and Rules of Procedure) Regulations 2013, SI 2013/1237, Sch 1 r 8(3) (claims presented in Scotland).

5 Employment Tribunals (Constitution and Rules of Procedure) Regulations 2013, SI 2013/1237, Sch 1 r 99(1).

6 'Vice President' means a person appointed or nominated in accordance with the Employment Tribunals (Constitution and Rules of Procedure) Regulations 2013, SI 2013/1237, reg 6(3) or (4) (see PARA 1401): Sch 1 r 1(1).

7 Ie in accordance with the Employment Tribunals (Constitution and Rules of Procedure) Regulations 2013, SI 2013/1237, Sch 1 r 8(2): see PARA 1461.

8 Employment Tribunals (Constitution and Rules of Procedure) Regulations 2013, SI 2013/1237, Sch 1 r 99(2).

9 As to the meaning of 'tribunal' for these purposes see PARA 1448 note 14.

10 Ie the rules set out in the Employment Tribunals (Constitution and Rules of Procedure) Regulations 2013, SI 2013/1237, Sch 1.

11 As to the meaning of 'present' see PARA 1461 note 3.

12 Employment Tribunals (Constitution and Rules of Procedure) Regulations 2013, SI 2013/1237, Sch 1 r 101.

1470. Devolution issues. Where a devolution issue[1] arises, the tribunal[2] must as soon as practicable send notice of that fact and a copy of the claim form and response to the Advocate General for Scotland and the Lord Advocate, where it is a Scottish devolution issue, or to the Attorney General[3] and the Counsel General to the Welsh Assembly Government[4], where it is a Welsh devolution issue, unless they are a party to the proceedings[5]. A person to whom notice is sent may be treated as a party to the proceedings, so far as the proceedings relate to the devolution issue, if that person sends notice to the tribunal within 14 days[6] of receiving such a notice[7].

Any notices sent under the above provisions must at the same time be sent to the parties[8].

1 'Devolution issue' has the meaning given to it in the Scotland Act 1998 Sch 6 para 1 (for the purposes of a Scottish devolution issue), and in the Government of Wales Act 2006 Sch 9 para 1 (see STATUTES AND LEGISLATIVE PROCESS vol 96 (2012) PARAS 988, 1041, 1042, 1044) (for the purposes of a Welsh devolution issue): Employment Tribunals (Constitution and Rules of Procedure) Regulations 2013, SI 2013/1237, Sch 1 r 98(4).

2 As to the meaning of 'tribunal' for these purposes see PARA 1448 note 14.

3 As to the Attorney General see CONSTITUTIONAL AND ADMINISTRATIVE LAW vol 20 (2014) PARA 273 et seq.

4 As to the Counsel General to the Welsh Assembly Government see CONSTITUTIONAL AND ADMINISTRATIVE LAW vol 20 (2014) PARA 376.

5 Employment Tribunals (Constitution and Rules of Procedure) Regulations 2013, SI 2013/1237, Sch 1 r 98(1).

6 As to the calculation of time limits see PARA 1460.

7 Employment Tribunals (Constitution and Rules of Procedure) Regulations 2013, SI 2013/1237, Sch 1 r 98(2).

8 Employment Tribunals (Constitution and Rules of Procedure) Regulations 2013, SI 2013/1237, Sch 1 r 98(3).

1471. Reference to the Court of Justice of the European Union. Where a tribunal[1] decides to refer a question to the Court of Justice of the European Union for a preliminary ruling[2] a copy of that decision must be sent to the registrar of that court[3].

1   As to the meaning of 'tribunal' for these purposes see PARA 1448 note 14.
2   Ie under the TFEU art 267. As to the TFEU see EUROPEAN UNION vol 47A (2014) PARA 6; and as to the making of references to the Court of Justice of the EU generally see CIVIL PROCEDURE vol 12 (2009) PARA 1720 et seq; EUROPEAN UNION vol 47A (2014) PARA 154 et seq.
3   Employment Tribunals (Constitution and Rules of Procedure) Regulations 2013, SI 2013/1237, Sch 1 r 100.

(vi) Hearings before Employment Tribunals

1472. Rules common to all kinds of hearing. The tribunal[1] may regulate its own procedure and must conduct the hearing in the manner it considers fair, having regard to the principles contained in the overriding objective[2]. The following rules do not restrict that general power. The tribunal must seek to avoid undue formality and may itself question the parties or any witnesses so far as appropriate in order to clarify the issues or elicit the evidence. The tribunal is not bound by any rule of law relating to the admissibility of evidence in proceedings before the courts[3].

The tribunal[4] must consider any written representations from a party, including a party who does not propose to attend the hearing, if they are delivered to the tribunal and to all other parties not less than seven days[4] before the hearing[5].

Where a witness is called to give oral evidence, any witness statement of that person ordered by the tribunal is to stand as that witness's evidence in chief unless the tribunal orders otherwise. Witnesses must be required to give their oral evidence on oath or affirmation. The tribunal may exclude from the hearing any person who is to appear as a witness in the proceedings until such time as that person gives evidence if it considers it in the interests of justice to do so[6]. Subject to certain restrictions[7], any witness statement which stands as evidence in chief must be available for inspection during the course of the hearing by members of the public attending the hearing unless the tribunal decides that all or any part of the statement is not to be admitted as evidence, in which case the statement or that part must not be available for inspection[8].

A tribunal may impose limits on the time that a party may take in presenting evidence, questioning witnesses or making submissions, and may prevent the party from proceeding beyond any time so allotted[9].

A hearing may be conducted, in whole or in part, by use of electronic communication[10], including by telephone, provided that the tribunal considers that it would be just and equitable to do so and provided that the parties and members of the public attending the hearing are able to hear what the tribunal hears and see any witness as seen by the tribunal[11].

If a party fails to attend or to be represented at the hearing, the tribunal may dismiss the claim or proceed with the hearing in the absence of that party. Before doing so, it must consider any information which is available to it, after any inquiries that may be practicable, about the reasons for the party's absence[12].

A tribunal conducting a preliminary hearing may order that it be treated as a final hearing, or vice versa, if the tribunal is properly constituted for the purpose and if it is satisfied that neither party will be materially prejudiced by the change[13].

Where a tribunal is composed of three persons any decision may be made by a majority and if it is composed of two persons the employment judge[14] has a second or casting vote[15].

A tribunal may at any stage of the proceedings, on its own initiative or on application, make an order[16] with a view to preventing or restricting the public disclosure of any aspect of those proceedings so far as it considers necessary in the interests of justice or in order to protect the Convention rights[17] of any person or in the circumstances identified[18] in the provision of the Employment Tribunals Act 1996 relating to confidential information[19]. In considering whether to make such an order, the tribunal must give full weight to the principle of open justice and to the Convention right to freedom of expression[20]. Such orders may include:

(1)   an order that a hearing that would otherwise be in public be conducted, in whole or in part, in private[21];

(2)   an order that the identities of specified parties, witnesses or other persons referred to in the proceedings should not be disclosed to the public, by the use of anonymisation or otherwise, whether in the course of any hearing or in its listing or in any documents entered on the register[22] or otherwise forming part of the public record[23];

(3)   an order for measures preventing witnesses at a public hearing being identifiable by members of the public[24];

(4)   a restricted reporting order[25].

Any party, or other person with a legitimate interest, who has not had a reasonable opportunity to make representations before such an order is made may apply to the tribunal in writing[26] for the order to be revoked or discharged, either on the basis of written representations or, if requested, at a hearing[27]. Where an order is made under head (4) above:

(a)   it must specify the person whose identity is protected and may specify particular matters of which publication is prohibited as likely to lead to that person's identification[28];

(b)   it must specify the duration of the order[29];

(c)   the tribunal must ensure that a notice of the fact that such an order has been made in relation to those proceedings is displayed on the notice board of the tribunal with any list of the proceedings taking place before the tribunal, and on the door of the room in which the proceedings affected by the order are taking place[30]; and

(d)   the tribunal may order that it applies also to any other proceedings being heard as part of the same hearing[31].

In national security proceedings[32], subject to any order under the above provisions preventing or restricting public disclosure[33] or any direction or order under the relevant rule relating to such proceedings[34], any hearing must take place in public, and any party may attend and participate in the hearing[35].

The Secretary of State[36] is entitled to appear and be heard at any hearing in relation to proceedings which may involve a payment out of the National Insurance Fund[37] and must treated as a party for the purposes of the procedural rules[38].

1   As to the meaning of 'tribunal' for these purposes see PARA 1448 note 14.
2   As to the overriding objective see PARA 1421.
3   Employment Tribunals (Constitution and Rules of Procedure) Regulations 2013, SI 2013/1237, Sch 1 r 41. The tribunals have always had a discretion in their procedures and admission of evidence which must be exercised judicially: see *Aberdeen Steak Houses Group plc v Ibrahim*

[1988] ICR 550 at 557–558, [1988] IRLR 420 at 423, EAT, per Wood P. Over the years a number of cases have given guidance on the appropriate procedures and on rules of evidence, examples of which are to be found as follows:

(1) decisions bearing upon the party who should present his case first (*Gill v Harold Andrews Sheepbridge Ltd* [1974] ICR 294, [1974] IRLR 109, NIRC; *Oxford v Department of Health and Social Security* [1977] ICR 884, [1977] IRLR 225, EAT);

(2) it is for the party and not the tribunal to decide the order in which he calls his witnesses (*Barnes v BPC (Business Forms) Ltd* [1976] 1 All ER 237, [1975] ICR 390);

(3) it is the duty of the parties to ensure that all relevant evidence is put before the tribunal and it is not for the tribunal itself to do this (*Craig v British Railways (Scottish Region)* (1973) 8 ITR 636, NIRC; *Derby City Council v Marshall* [1979] ICR 731, [1979] IRLR 261, EAT);

(4) a tribunal should not allow a party to be taken by surprise by an allegation of dishonesty made at the last minute, but should adjourn and give directions (*Hotson v Wisbech Conservative Club* [1984] ICR 859, [1984] IRLR 422, EAT);

(5) where a party specifically states that he will not be calling evidence, he will normally be bound by his statement (*Stokes v Hampstead Wine Co Ltd* [1979] IRLR 298, EAT);

(6) although on general principles evidence that is relevant is admissible, a tribunal has discretion to exclude such evidence if necessary to pursue the overriding objective, e g where it is repetitive or only of marginal relevance (*Digby v Cambridgeshire District Council* [2007] IRLR 585, EAT, disapproving a statement to the contrary in *Rosedale Mouldings Ltd v Sibley* [1980] ICR 816, [1980] IRLR 387, EAT (tribunals cannot refuse to admit evidence which is admissible and probative of one or more issues));

(7) where a third party proffers information or opinion about the merits of a case, or the parties in it, to a tribunal, without being invited to do so, the parties should be made aware of what has happened without delay (*Begraj v Heer Manak Solicitors* [2014] IRLR 689, EAT).

Tribunals on occasions can and should admit hearsay evidence, as is done sometimes in other courts: *Aberdeen Steak Houses Group plc v Ibrahim* [1988] ICR 550 at 557–558, [1988] IRLR 420 at 423, EAT, per Wood P. However, whilst recognising that tribunals have a wide discretion in these matters of procedure and evidence, it must be remembered that the rules of procedure and evidence have been built up over very many years in order to guide courts and tribunals in the fairest and simplest way of dealing with and deciding issues; it is possible for informality to go too far and it is important for parties appearing before any judicial body, and for their legal advisers in preparing for trial, to know the rules normally to be applied during that hearing; it is important that there should be consistency: see *Aberdeen Steak Houses Group plc v Ibrahim* [1988] ICR 550 at 557–558, [1988] IRLR 420 at 423, EAT, per Wood P. Under normal circumstances the party opening a case should call his evidence, and should then close his case; and when, in cross-examination, questions go to credit only, the party cross-examining should be bound by the answers of the witness: see *Aberdeen Steak Houses Group plc v Ibrahim* [1988] ICR 550 at 557–558, [1988] IRLR 420 at 423, EAT, per Wood P.

In conducting the hearing, the chairman (now the employment judge) should avoid the use of immoderate or intemperate language: *Kennedy v Metropolitan Police Comr* (1990) Times, 8 November, EAT. As to the exclusion of evidence see *Digby v East Cambridgeshire District Council* [2007] IRLR 585, [2007] All ER (D) 24 (Mar), EAT. The tribunal employment judge (formerly chairman) is under a judicial duty to make notes of evidence, production of which may be ordered by the Employment Appeal Tribunal for the purposes of an appeal (see PARA 1515): *Webb v Anglian Water Authority* [1981] ICR 811, [1981] IRLR 494, EAT; *Houston v Lightwater Farms Ltd* [1990] ICR 502, [1990] IRLR 469, EAT; and see *Piggott Bros & Co Ltd v Jackson* [1992] ICR 85, [1991] IRLR 309, CA (where an appeal is based on, or includes, an allegation that the tribunal's decision was perverse, notes of all the relevant evidence should be requested). There is no automatic right to such notes, and reasons for requesting them must be given: *Burnett v Value Travel Agency Ltd* [1989] ICR 79, EAT.

The exercise of the tribunal's discretion to admit evidence may only be successfully challenged if exercised in a manner that is contrary to legal principle or plainly wrong: *ALM Medical Services v Bladon* [2002] EWCA Civ 1085, [2002] ICR 1444, [2002] IRLR 807. See also *Coral Squash Clubs Ltd v Matthews* [1979] ICR 607, [1979] IRLR 390, EAT (discretion of tribunal to admit evidence of complaints made to employers concerning employees). Statements ruled inadmissible in criminal proceedings may be considered: *Dhaliwal v British Airways Board, British Airways Board v Day* [1985] ICR 513, EAT. For example, the rule excluding 'without prejudice' negotiations from later being used in evidence will have a particularly narrow application in tribunal proceedings: *BNP Paribas v Mezzotero* [2004] IRLR 508, EAT. Evidence which is admissible must, however, be accepted; a tribunal should normally adhere to generally recognised rules of procedure and evidence: see *Aberdeen Steak Houses Group plc v Ibrahim* [1988] ICR 550, [1988] IRLR 420, EAT. The tribunal should also apply the principle that a party has the right to examine any relevant material which his opponent is placing before a tribunal and should not reserve access to requested documents to itself: *Knight v Department of Social Security* [2002] IRLR 249, EAT (disclosure of confidential test papers). Secret recordings of disciplinary proceedings where the parties had agreed to allow the panel to deliberate in private are not admissible: *Dogherty v Chairman and Governors of Amwell View School* [2007] ICR 135, sub nom *Chairman and Governors of Amwell View School v Dogherty* [2007] IRLR 198, EAT.

A tribunal must not decide a case on a ground not raised by the parties without giving the latter a proper opportunity to make representations on that ground: *Laurie v Holloway* [1994] ICR 32, EAT. Likewise, a tribunal should not normally rely on case authorities arising from its own researches, without giving the parties an opportunity to consider these cases and address the tribunal on them (*Albion Hotel (Freshwater) Ltd v Maia e Silva* [2002] IRLR 200, EAT), at least where such authorities could have an effect on the outcome of the case, as opposed to being uncontroversial or merely illustrative (*Stanley Cole (Wainfleet) Ltd v Sheridan* [2003] EWCA Civ 1046, [2003] 4 All ER 1181, [2003] ICR 1449).

Regardless of the strength of a particular case, a tribunal should not normally conclude proceedings where there is still evidence or argument to hear: *Ellis v Ministry of Defence* [1985] ICR 257, EAT; *Hackney London Borough Council v Usher* [1997] ICR 705, EAT (submission of no case to answer halfway through case). Although there is no inflexible rule of law and practice that a tribunal always has to hear both sides, that should normally be done: *Logan v Customs and Excise Comrs* [2003] EWCA Civ 1068, [2004] ICR 1, [2004] IRLR 63 (only in exceptional or frivolous cases would it be right to halt proceedings at the end of the first party's case). It is not objectionable in principle for a tribunal to indicate its thinking before the hearing is concluded, but if it decides to do so it must make clear that any expression of view is only provisional and that it remains open to persuasion: *Jiminez v Southwark London Borough Council* [2003] EWCA Civ 502, [2003] ICR 1176, [2003] IRLR 477.

4   As to the calculation of time limits see PARA 1460.
5   Employment Tribunals (Constitution and Rules of Procedure) Regulations 2013, SI 2013/1237, Sch 1 r 42. Since written representations are not subject to cross-examination, they may be accorded less weight than oral evidence: *Oliver v RF Tilney & Son Ltd* (1966) 2 ITR 183; *Hardisty v Lowton Construction Group Ltd* (1973) 8 ITR 603, NIRC. The position may be particularly difficult where both parties submit written representations only and there are disputed questions of fact: *Tesco Stores Ltd v Patel* (1986) Times, 15 March, EAT.
6   Employment Tribunals (Constitution and Rules of Procedure) Regulations 2013, SI 2013/1237, Sch 1 r 43.
7   Ie subject to the Employment Tribunals (Constitution and Rules of Procedure) Regulations 2013, SI 2013/1237, Sch 1 r 50 (see the text and notes 16–31) and Sch 1 r 94 (see PARA 1450).
8   Employment Tribunals (Constitution and Rules of Procedure) Regulations 2013, SI 2013/1237, Sch 1 r 44.
9   Employment Tribunals (Constitution and Rules of Procedure) Regulations 2013, SI 2013/1237, Sch 1 r 45.
10 As to the meaning of 'electronic communication' see PARA 1430 note 1.
11 Employment Tribunals (Constitution and Rules of Procedure) Regulations 2013, SI 2013/1237, Sch 1 r 46.
12 Employment Tribunals (Constitution and Rules of Procedure) Regulations 2013, SI 2013/1237, Sch 1 r 47.

Where there is an unexplained failure to attend, before deciding whether to proceed with the hearing in a party's absence, the tribunal should consider telephoning the party to find out whether they intend to appear, and should make inquiries of any representative of the other side: *Cooke v Glenrose Fish Co* [2004] ICR 1188, [2004] IRLR 866, EAT.

Adjournment may be appropriate where there is a definite, temporary reason for absence: *Priddle v Fisher & Sons* [1968] 3 All ER 506, [1968] 1 WLR 1478 (bad weather); *Holland v Cyprane Ltd* [1977] ICR 355, EAT (ill health); *Masters of Beckenham Ltd v Green* [1977] ICR 535, EAT (internal difficulties due to a resignation).

There is no legal obligation on a tribunal to consider each and every allegation in a claim, even if it is not eventually relied on by the claimant: *Mensah v East Hertfordshire NHS Trust* [1998] IRLR 531, CA; applied in *Hyde-Walsh v Ashby* [2008] All ER (D) 225 (Feb), EAT. A tribunal's discretion to reject evidence applies to evidence of advice not to attend on medical grounds: *Teinaz v Wandsworth London Borough Council* [2002] EWCA Civ 1040, [2002] ICR 1471, [2002] IRLR 721.

See also *Duffy v George* [2013] EWCA Civ 908, [2013] IRLR 883, [2013] ICR 1229 (unusual situation had arisen as a result of the employee's decision not to give oral evidence but tribunal erred in failing to hold pre-trial review to consider options for conduct of fair hearing in light of employee's resolve not to attend or give oral evidence, particularly with regard to the need to test her evidence by way of cross examination; tribunal should have explored with the parties the following procedural points and possibilities: (1) whether the tribunal had been satisfied by evidence that the employee had grounds for and was fearful of attending the hearing to be cross examined by the defendant; (2) if so, whether the tribunal should have dispensed with such a hearing; (3) if so, whether the tribunal should have held separate hearings at which the parties each gave their evidence in the absence of the other; and (4) if so, whether the parties should have been invited to submit to the tribunal in advance questions to be put to the other party at the hearing; *McBride v British Railways Board* (1971) 7 ITR 84, NIRC applied); *Iqbal v Metropolitan Police Service* [2012] All ER (D) 302 (Nov), EAT (unfair for tribunal to proceed with hearing without allowing short adjournment for employee suffering depression and disabilities to acquire medical evidence).

13 Employment Tribunals (Constitution and Rules of Procedure) Regulations 2013, SI 2013/1237, Sch 1 r 48.

14 As to the meaning of 'employment judge' see PARA 1401 note 3.

15 Employment Tribunals (Constitution and Rules of Procedure) Regulations 2013, SI 2013/1237, Sch 1 r 49. In a case of unfair dismissal, it is most desirable for a tribunal to reach a unanimous verdict and the chairman (now employment judge) should reserve the decision where there is no unanimity: *Anglian Home Improvements Ltd v Kelly* [2004] EWCA Civ 901 at [12], [2005] ICR 242 at [12], [2004] IRLR 793 at [12] per Mummery LJ.

16 As to orders of the tribunal see PARA 1460 note 4.

17 For these purposes, 'Convention rights' has the meaning given to it in the Human Rights Act 1998 s 1 (see RIGHTS AND FREEDOMS vol 88A (2013) PARA 14): Employment Tribunals (Constitution and Rules of Procedure) Regulations 2013, SI 2013/1237, Sch 1 r 50(6).

18 Ie identified in the Employment Tribunals Act 1996 s 10A: see PARA 1415.

19 See the Employment Tribunals (Constitution and Rules of Procedure) Regulations 2013, SI 2013/1237, Sch 1 r 50(1).

20 Employment Tribunals (Constitution and Rules of Procedure) Regulations 2013, SI 2013/1237, Sch 1 r 50(2).

21 Employment Tribunals (Constitution and Rules of Procedure) Regulations 2013, SI 2013/1237, Sch 1 r 50(3)(a). The normal practice is to consider any application for a private hearing immediately before the hearing itself or, as appropriate, during the hearing. A party does not have the right to insist upon such an application being heard in advance of the hearing to enable him to appeal if the application is refused: *Milne and Lyall v Waldren* [1980] ICR 138, EAT. See also *Jones v Enham Industries* [1983] ICR 580n. What constitutes 'in private' is a question of fact and degree: *Fry v Foreign and Commonwealth Office* [1997] ICR 512, EAT (claimant allowed to be accompanied by her husband who was helping her with the case). See also *Eversheds LLP v Gray* [2012] All ER (D) 111 (Feb), EAT. As to the case where a minister directs or a tribunal orders that the hearing be held in private on grounds of national security see PARA 1450.

22 'Register' means the register of judgments and written reasons kept in accordance with the Employment Tribunals (Constitution and Rules of Procedure) Regulations 2013, SI 2013/1237, reg 14 (see PARA 1476): Sch 1 r 1(1).

23 Employment Tribunals (Constitution and Rules of Procedure) Regulations 2013, SI 2013/1237, Sch 1 r 50(3)(b).

24 Employment Tribunals (Constitution and Rules of Procedure) Regulations 2013, SI 2013/1237, Sch 1 r 50(3)(c).

25 Employment Tribunals (Constitution and Rules of Procedure) Regulations 2013, SI 2013/1237, Sch 1 r 50(3)(d). The reference in head (4) in the text to a restricted reporting order is to such an order within the terms of the Employment Tribunals Act 1996 s 11 or s 12 (see PARAS 1416–1417); see the Employment Tribunals (Constitution and Rules of Procedure) Regulations 2013, SI 2013/1237, Sch 1 r 50(3)(d). A restricted reporting order cannot be made in favour of a body corporate: *Leicester University v A* [1999] ICR 701, [1999] IRLR 352, EAT (disapproving *M v Vincent* [1998] ICR 73, EAT). As to restricted reporting orders see also *F v G* [2012] ICR 246, EAT.

26 As to the meaning of 'writing' see PARA 1450 note 19.

27 Employment Tribunals (Constitution and Rules of Procedure) Regulations 2013, SI 2013/1237, Sch 1 r 50(4).

28 Employment Tribunals (Constitution and Rules of Procedure) Regulations 2013, SI 2013/1237, Sch 1 r 50(5)(a).

29 Employment Tribunals (Constitution and Rules of Procedure) Regulations 2013, SI 2013/1237, Sch 1 r 50(5)(b).

30 Employment Tribunals (Constitution and Rules of Procedure) Regulations 2013, SI 2013/1237, Sch 1 r 50(5)(c).

31 Employment Tribunals (Constitution and Rules of Procedure) Regulations 2013, SI 2013/1237, Sch 1 r 50(5)(d).

32 Ie proceedings in relation to which a direction is given, or order is made, under the Employment Tribunals (Constitution and Rules of Procedure) Regulations 2013, SI 2013/1237, Sch 1 r 94 (see PARA 1450): see Sch 2 r 1(1).

33 Ie any order under the Employment Tribunals (Constitution and Rules of Procedure) Regulations 2013, SI 2013/1237, Sch 1 r 50: see the text and notes 16–31.

34 Ie under the Employment Tribunals (Constitution and Rules of Procedure) Regulations 2013, SI 2013/1237, Sch 1 r 94: see PARA 1450.

35 Employment Tribunals (Constitution and Rules of Procedure) Regulations 2013, SI 2013/1237, Sch 2 r 5(1). As the duty to sit in public is mandatory, subject to the exceptions allowed under Sch 1 rr 50, 94, a failure to have a public hearing will render a decision unlawful and liable to be set aside, the test being whether it was possible for a member of the public to attend, regardless of whether anyone was actually debarred: *Storer v British Gas plc* [2000] 2 All ER 440, [2000] ICR 603, CA.

36 As to the Secretary of State see PARA 5 note 21.

37 As to the National Insurance Fund see WELFARE BENEFITS AND STATE PENSIONS vol 104 (2014) PARA 15.

38 See the Employment Tribunals (Constitution and Rules of Procedure) Regulations 2013, SI 2013/1237, Sch 1 r 96.

1473. Preliminary hearings. A preliminary hearing is a hearing at which the tribunal[1] may do one or more of the following:

(1) conduct a preliminary consideration of the claim[2] with the parties and make a case management order[3], including an order relating to the conduct of the final hearing[4];

(2) determine any preliminary issue[5];

(3) consider whether a claim or response, or any part, should be struck out[6];

(4) make a deposit order[7];

(5) explore the possibility of settlement or alternative dispute resolution, including judicial mediation[8].

There may be more than one preliminary hearing in any case[9].

A preliminary hearing may be directed by the tribunal on its own initiative following its initial consideration[10] or at any time thereafter or as the result of an application by a party. The tribunal must give the parties reasonable notice of the date of the hearing and in the case of a hearing involving any preliminary issues at least 14 days notice[11] must be given and the notice must specify the preliminary issues that are to be, or may be, decided at the hearing[12].

Preliminary hearings are to be conducted by an employment judge[13] alone, except that where notice has been given that any preliminary issues are to be, or may be, decided at the hearing a party may request in writing[14] that the hearing be conducted by a full tribunal[15] in which case an employment judge must decide whether that would be desirable[16].

Preliminary hearings must be conducted in private, except that where the hearing involves a determination under head (2) or head (3) above, any part of the hearing relating to such a determination must, subject to certain exceptions[17], be in public, and the tribunal may direct that the entirety of the hearing be in public[18].

When a tribunal hears certain applications for interim relief or for its variation or revocation[19], the above provisions apply to the hearing and the tribunal is not to hear oral evidence unless it directs otherwise[20].

1 As to the meaning of 'tribunal' for these purposes see PARA 1448 note 14.
2 As to the meaning of 'claim' see PARA 1457 note 22.
3 As to the meaning of 'case management order' see PARA 1460 note 4.
4 Employment Tribunals (Constitution and Rules of Procedure) Regulations 2013, SI 2013/1237, Sch 1 r 53(1)(a).
5 Employment Tribunals (Constitution and Rules of Procedure) Regulations 2013, SI 2013/1237, Sch 1 r 53(1)(b). 'Preliminary issue' means, as regards any complaint, any substantive issue which may determine liability (for example, an issue as to jurisdiction or as to whether an employee was dismissed): Sch 1 r 53(3). As to the meaning of 'complaint' see PARA 1464 note 5.
6 Employment Tribunals (Constitution and Rules of Procedure) Regulations 2013, SI 2013/1237, Sch 1 r 53(1)(c). The reference in head (3) in the text to striking out is to striking out under Sch 1 r 37 (see PARA 1466): Sch 1 r 53(1)(c).
7 Employment Tribunals (Constitution and Rules of Procedure) Regulations 2013, SI 2013/1237, Sch 1 r 53(1)(d). The reference in head (4) in the text to a deposit order is to a deposit order under Sch 1 r 39 (see PARA 1466): Sch 1 r 53(1)(d).
8 Employment Tribunals (Constitution and Rules of Procedure) Regulations 2013, SI 2013/1237, Sch 1 r 53(1)(e).
9 Employment Tribunals (Constitution and Rules of Procedure) Regulations 2013, SI 2013/1237, Sch 1 r 53(2).
10 Ie under the Employment Tribunals (Constitution and Rules of Procedure) Regulations 2013, SI 2013/1237, Sch 1 r 26: see PARA 1464.
11 As to the calculation of time limits see PARA 1460; and as to the giving of notice see PARA 1467.
12 Employment Tribunals (Constitution and Rules of Procedure) Regulations 2013, SI 2013/1237, Sch 1 r 54.
13 As to the meaning of 'employment judge' see PARA 1401 note 3.
14 As to the meaning of 'writing' see PARA 1450 note 19.
15 As to the meaning of 'full tribunal' see PARA 1448 note 14.
16 Employment Tribunals (Constitution and Rules of Procedure) Regulations 2013, SI 2013/1237, Sch 1 r 55. Where the discretion to convene a full tribunal is exercised, the observations in *Sutcliffe v Big C's Marine Ltd* [1998] ICR 913 at 917–918, [1998] IRLR 428 at 430–431, EAT, per Morison J may still be relevant (many of the issues involve questions of mixed fact and law where the good sense and experience of lay members would be beneficial and of great assistance to [judges] in reaching a decision). See also *Geere v Worcester Citizens Advice Bureau* [2014] All ER (D) 122 (Aug), EAT (where Employment Judge had granted request that the pre-hearing review be so heard, it was a fundamental error to have the case decided by a tribunal other than one comprising three persons).
17 Ie subject to the Employment Tribunals (Constitution and Rules of Procedure) Regulations 2013, SI 2013/1237, Sch 1 r 50 (see PARA 1472) and Sch 1 r 94 (see PARA 1450).
18 Employment Tribunals (Constitution and Rules of Procedure) Regulations 2013, SI 2013/1237, Sch 1 r 56. As to the conduct of preliminary hearings see further PARA 1472.
19 Ie under the Trade Union and Labour Relations (Consolidation) Act 1992 s 161 (see PARA 1058) or s 165 (see PARA 1060) or under the Employment Rights Act 1996 s 128 (see PARA 805) or s 131 (see PARA 808).
20 Employment Tribunals (Constitution and Rules of Procedure) Regulations 2013, SI 2013/1237, Sch 1 r 95.

1474. Final hearing. A final hearing is a hearing at which the tribunal[1] determines the claim[2] or such parts as remain outstanding following the initial consideration[3] or any preliminary hearing[4]. There may be different final hearings for different issues, for example, liability, remedy or costs[5].

The tribunal must give the parties not less than 14 days' notice[6] of the date of a final hearing[7].

Subject to certain exceptions[8], any final hearing must be in public[9].

1 As to the meaning of 'tribunal' for these purposes see PARA 1448 note 14.
2 As to the meaning of 'claim' see PARA 1457 note 22.
3 Ie under the Employment Tribunals (Constitution and Rules of Procedure) Regulations 2013, SI 2013/1237, Sch 1 r 26: see PARA 1464.
4 Employment Tribunals (Constitution and Rules of Procedure) Regulations 2013, SI 2013/1237, Sch 1 r 57. As to preliminary hearings see PARA 1473.

5 Employment Tribunals (Constitution and Rules of Procedure) Regulations 2013, SI 2013/1237, Sch 1 r 57.
6 As to the calculation of time limits see PARA 1460; and as to the giving of notice see PARA 1467.
7 Employment Tribunals (Constitution and Rules of Procedure) Regulations 2013, SI 2013/1237, Sch 1 r 58.
8 Ie subject to the Employment Tribunals (Constitution and Rules of Procedure) Regulations 2013, SI 2013/1237, Sch 1 r 50 (see PARA 1472) and Sch 1 r 94 (see PARA 1450).
9 Employment Tribunals (Constitution and Rules of Procedure) Regulations 2013, SI 2013/1237, Sch 1 r 59. As to the conduct of the hearing see further PARA 1472.

1475. Withdrawal of claim. Where a claimant[1] informs the tribunal[2], either in writing[3] or in the course of a hearing, that a claim[4], or part of it, is withdrawn, the claim, or part, comes to an end, subject to any application that the respondent[5] may make for a costs, preparation time or wasted costs order[6].

Where a claim, or part of it, has been withdrawn under the above provision, the tribunal must issue a judgment dismissing it, which means that the claimant may not commence a further claim against the respondent raising the same, or substantially the same, complaint[7], unless:

(1) the claimant has expressed at the time of withdrawal a wish to reserve the right to bring such a further claim and the tribunal is satisfied that there would be legitimate reason for doing so[8]; or

(2) the tribunal believes that to issue such a judgment would not be in the interests of justice[9].

1 As to the meaning of 'claimant' see PARA 1457 note 25.
2 As to the meaning of 'tribunal' for these purposes see PARA 1448 note 14.
3 As to the meaning of 'writing' see PARA 1450 note 19.
4 As to the meaning of 'claim' see PARA 1457 note 22.
5 As to the meaning of 'respondent' see PARA 1460 note 8.
6 Employment Tribunals (Constitution and Rules of Procedure) Regulations 2013, SI 2013/1237, Sch 1 r 51. As to the orders mentioned in the text see PARA 1480. Employment tribunals do not have jurisdiction to set aside a notice of withdrawal of a claim which has been given: *Khan v Heywood and Middleton Primary Care Trust* [2006] EWCA Civ 1087, [2007] ICR 24, [2006] IRLR 345. Moreover, it will only be in rare cases that a tribunal should query the claimant's decision to withdraw (to ensure it is genuinely meant), whether the claimant is professionally represented (*Ako v Rothchild Asset Management* [2002] EWCA Civ 236, [2002] ICR 899, [2002] IRLR 348) or not (*Drydale v Department of Transport* [2014] EWCA Civ 1083).
7 Employment Tribunals (Constitution and Rules of Procedure) Regulations 2013, SI 2013/1237, Sch 1 r 52. See *Fox v Bassetlaw District Council* [2013] All ER (D) 240 (Jan), EAT (where an employee sought to terminate the first set of proceedings by withdrawal with a view to bringing a second set of proceedings raising the same or substantially the same cause of action or otherwise in circumstances amounting to an abuse of process in the sense identified in *Johnson v Gore Wood & Co (a firm)* [2002] 2 AC 1, [2001] 1 All ER 481, HL, the tribunal would be entitled to dismiss the first proceedings and bar the employee from bringing the second proceedings; dismissal of further claim on same cause of action as an abuse of process following dismissal of original claim). See also *Agbenowossi-Koffi v Donvand Ltd* [2014] EWCA Civ 855, [2014] All ER (D) 190 (Jun). As to the meaning of 'complaint' see PARA 1464 note 5.
8 Employment Tribunals (Constitution and Rules of Procedure) Regulations 2013, SI 2013/1237, Sch 1 r 52(a). Where the withdrawal of a claim is in substance a discontinuance of the proceedings, cause of action estoppel (see generally CIVIL PROCEDURE vol 12 (2009) PARA 1169 et seq), as applied in the ordinary court, does not apply: *Ako v Rothschild Asset Management Ltd* [2002] EWCA Civ 236, [2002] 2 All ER 693, [2002] IRLR 348. As to issue estoppel (see generally CIVIL PROCEDURE vol 12 (2009) PARA 1179 et seq) where dismissal followed a withdrawal without evidence or argument being heard see *Lennon v Birmingham City Council* [2001] EWCA Civ 435, [2001] IRLR 826. As to the difference between a mere withdrawal and a formal dismissal of proceedings (and the potential consequences) see also *Verdin v Harrods Ltd* [2006] ICR 396, [2006] IRLR 339, EAT; *Cokayne v British Association of Shooting and Conservation* [2008] ICR 185, [2007] All ER (D) 290 (Oct), EAT.
9 Employment Tribunals (Constitution and Rules of Procedure) Regulations 2013, SI 2013/1237, Sch 1 r 52(b).

(vii) Decisions and Reasons of Employment Tribunals

1476. Decisions and reasons; in general. Decisions made without a hearing must be communicated in writing[1] to the parties, identifying the employment judge[2] who has made the decision[3]. Where there is a hearing the tribunal[4] may either announce its decision in relation to any issue at the hearing or reserve it to be sent to the parties as soon as practicable in writing[5]. If the decision is announced at the hearing, a written record, in the form of a judgment[6] if appropriate, must be provided to the parties (and, where the proceedings were referred to the tribunal by a court, to that court) as soon as practicable. Decisions concerned only with the conduct of a hearing need not, however, be identified in the record of that hearing unless a party requests that a specific decision is so recorded[7]. The written record must be signed by the employment judge[8].

The tribunal must give reasons for its decision on any disputed issue, whether substantive or procedural, including any decision on an application for reconsideration or for orders for costs, preparation time or wasted costs[9]. In the case of a decision given in writing the reasons must also be given in writing. In the case of a decision announced at a hearing the reasons may be given orally at the hearing or reserved to be given in writing later, which may, but need not, be as part of the written record of the decision. Written reasons must be signed by the employment judge[10]. Where reasons have been given orally, the employment judge must announce that written reasons will not be provided unless they are asked for by any party at the hearing itself or by a written request presented[11] by any party within 14 days[12] of the sending of the written record of the decision. The written record of the decision must repeat that information. If no such request is received, the tribunal must provide written reasons only if requested to do so by the Employment Appeal Tribunal[13] or a court[14].

The reasons given for any decision must be proportionate to the significance of the issue and for decisions other than judgments may be very short[15]. In the case of a judgment the reasons must (1) identify the issues which the tribunal has determined; (2) state the findings of fact made in relation to those issues; (3) concisely identify the relevant law; and (4) state how that law has been applied to those findings in order to decide the issues. Where the judgment includes a financial award the reasons must identify, by means of a table or otherwise, how the amount to be paid has been calculated[16].

If the parties agree in writing or orally at a hearing upon the terms of any order[17] or judgment a tribunal may, if it thinks fit, make such order or judgment, in which case it must be identified as having been made by consent[18].

A judgment or order takes effect from the day when it is given or made, or on such later date as specified by the tribunal[19]. A party must comply with a judgment or order for the payment of an amount of money within 14 days of the date of the judgment or order, unless either the judgment, order, or any of the procedural rules[20] specifies a different date for compliance, or the tribunal has stayed the proceedings or judgment[21].

Where the proceedings were referred to the tribunal by a court a copy of any judgment and of any written reasons must be provided to that court[22].

An employment judge may at any time correct any clerical mistake or other accidental slip or omission in any order, judgment or other document produced by a tribunal. If such a correction is made, any published version of the document must also be corrected. If any document is so corrected, a copy of the corrected version, signed by the judge, must be sent to all the parties[23].

The Lord Chancellor[24] must maintain a register containing a copy of all judgments and written reasons issued by a tribunal[25] which are required[26] to be entered in the register[27]. A document purporting to be certified by a member of staff of a tribunal to be a true copy of an entry of a judgment in the register is, unless the contrary is proved, sufficient evidence of the document and its contents[28]. Subject to certain exceptions[29], a copy of any judgment and of any written reasons for a judgment must be entered in the register[30].

The above procedural rules are modified in relation to reasons in national security proceedings[31].

1   As to the meaning of 'writing' see PARA 1450 note 19.
2   As to the meaning of 'employment judge' see PARA 1401 note 3.
3   Employment Tribunals (Constitution and Rules of Procedure) Regulations 2013, SI 2013/1237, Sch 1 r 60.
4   As to the meaning of 'tribunal' for these purposes see PARA 1448 note 14.
5   Employment Tribunals (Constitution and Rules of Procedure) Regulations 2013, SI 2013/1237, Sch 1 r 61(1).
6   As to the meaning of 'judgment' see PARA 1460 note 4. See *Kudjodji v Lidl Ltd* [2011] ICR D23, [2011] All ER (D) 165 (Jul), EAT (cardinal principle that, once a final, as opposed to an interim, judgment or order, had been drawn up and perfected, it could not be altered except by appeal or, where there was a power to do so, on review; law demonstrated that a tribunal should think long and hard before coming to a determination in respect of a matter which had been considered by a previous tribunal but about which there had been no judgment or order).
7   Employment Tribunals (Constitution and Rules of Procedure) Regulations 2013, SI 2013/1237, Sch 1 r 61(2).
8   Employment Tribunals (Constitution and Rules of Procedure) Regulations 2013, SI 2013/1237, Sch 1 r 61(3). If it is impossible or not practicable for the written record to be signed by the employment judge as a result of death, incapacity or absence, it must be signed by the other member or members (in the case of a full tribunal) or by the President or a regional employment judge (in the case of a Judge sitting alone): Sch 1 r 63. As to the meaning of 'full tribunal' see PARA 1448 note 14; as to the meaning of 'President' see PARA 1399 note 7; and as to the meaning of 'regional employment judge' see PARA 1399 note 9.
9   Employment Tribunals (Constitution and Rules of Procedure) Regulations 2013, SI 2013/1237, Sch 1 r 62(1). As to applications for reconsideration see PARA 1479; and as to the costs etc orders mentioned in the text see PARA 1480.
    It necessarily follows from the Employment Tribunals Act 1996 s 4 (see PARA 1402), and from the Employment Tribunals (Constitution and Rules of Procedure) Regulations 2013, SI 2013/1237, reg 9 (see PARA 1402), that the decision of the Tribunal must be that of all the members sitting (or, where they cannot agree, that the view of the minority member is recorded); and the same must be true of the essential reasoning which leads to that decision: *Eyitene v Wirral Metropolitan Borough Council* [2014] EWCA Civ 1243, [2014] All ER (D) 99 (Oct). As to whether written reasons can be said to represent the reasons of all the members where the lay members have not seen and approved the form in which they are finally promulgated see *Eyitene v Wirral Metropolitan Borough Council* at [13]-[15] per Underhill LJ.
10 Employment Tribunals (Constitution and Rules of Procedure) Regulations 2013, SI 2013/1237, Sch 1 r 62(2). If it is impossible or not practicable for the written reasons to be signed by the employment judge as a result of death, incapacity or absence, they must be signed by the other member or members (in the case of a full tribunal) or by the President or a regional employment judge (in the case of a Judge sitting alone): Sch 1 r 63.
11 As to the meaning of 'present' see PARA 1461 note 3.
12 As to the calculation of time limits see PARA 1460.
13 As to the Employment Appeal Tribunal see PARA 1422 et seq.
14 Employment Tribunals (Constitution and Rules of Procedure) Regulations 2013, SI 2013/1237, Sch 1 r 62(3).
15 Employment Tribunals (Constitution and Rules of Procedure) Regulations 2013, SI 2013/1237, Sch 1 r 62(4).
16 Employment Tribunals (Constitution and Rules of Procedure) Regulations 2013, SI 2013/1237, Sch 1 r 62(5). If a tribunal arrives at a different finding of fact to that advanced by the parties

and the tribunal does not realise what the parties' arguments were likely to be in relation to it, it would usually be necessary to invite all the parties to make submissions, most likely in writing. However, that was not an invariable requirement, as is clear from the wide discretion as to procedural matters given to employment tribunals: *Judge v Crown Leisure Ltd* [2004] All ER (D) 293 (Nov), EAT; affd [2005] EWCA Civ 571, [2005] IRLR 823, [2005] All ER (D) 283 (Apr). *Judge v Crown Leisure Ltd* was applied in *Webster v Woodhouse School* [2009] EWCA Civ 91, [2009] All ER (D) 184 (Feb). See also *Fisher v Hoopoe Finance Ltd* [2005] All ER (D) 51 (Jun), EAT; *Burmis v Governing Body of Aylesford School* [2008] All ER (D) 28 (Oct), EAT. As to reasons see also PARA 821.

17 As to orders of the tribunal see PARA 1460 note 4.

18 Employment Tribunals (Constitution and Rules of Procedure) Regulations 2013, SI 2013/1237, Sch 1 r 64.

19 Employment Tribunals (Constitution and Rules of Procedure) Regulations 2013, SI 2013/1237, Sch 1 r 65.

20 Ie the rules set out in the Employment Tribunals (Constitution and Rules of Procedure) Regulations 2013, SI 2013/1237, Sch 1.

21 Employment Tribunals (Constitution and Rules of Procedure) Regulations 2013, SI 2013/1237, Sch 1 r 66.

22 Employment Tribunals (Constitution and Rules of Procedure) Regulations 2013, SI 2013/1237, Sch 1 r 68.

23 Employment Tribunals (Constitution and Rules of Procedure) Regulations 2013, SI 2013/1237, Sch 1 r 69. Whether, and if so to what extent, a tribunal has inherent power to alter a decision before it is entered in the register is unclear. On the one hand, it has been held or assumed that there is such a power, albeit to be exercised sparingly, since the decision is not perfected until entered in the register (*Hanks v Ace High Productions Ltd* [1978] ICR 1155, [1979] IRLR 32, EAT; *Lamont v Fry's Metals Ltd* [1985] ICR 566, [1985] IRLR 470, CA; *Arthur Guinness Son & Co (Great Britain) Ltd v Green* [1989] ICR 241, [1989] IRLR 288, EAT); but, on the other hand, it has been held that, once an oral decision has been communicated to the parties, it cannot be altered or the matter reopened, except by way of a review (*Jowett v Earl of Bradford* [1977] 2 All ER 33, [1977] ICR 342, EAT; *Spring Grove Services Group plc v Hickinbottom* [1990] ICR 111, EAT). More recently it has been said that what is now the Employment Tribunals (Constitution and Rules of Procedure) Regulations 2013, SI 2013/1237, Sch 1 r 69 can only be used for minor errors, and that it is not to be used to amend a judgment as such (eg where a substantive finding was omitted): *Bone v Newham London Borough Council* [2008] EWCA Civ 435, [2008] ICR 923, [2008] IRLR 546.

24 As to the Lord Chancellor see CONSTITUTIONAL AND ADMINISTRATIVE LAW vol 20 (2014) PARA 255 et seq.

25 As to the meaning of 'tribunal' for these purposes see PARA 1399 note 8.

26 Ie under the Employment Tribunals (Constitution and Rules of Procedure) Regulations 2013, SI 2013/1237, Schs 1–3.

27 Employment Tribunals (Constitution and Rules of Procedure) Regulations 2013, SI 2013/1237, reg 14(1).

28 Employment Tribunals (Constitution and Rules of Procedure) Regulations 2013, SI 2013/1237, reg 14(3).

29 Ie subject to the Employment Tribunals (Constitution and Rules of Procedure) Regulations 2013, SI 2013/1237, Sch 1 r 50 (see PARA 1472) and Sch 1 r 94 (see PARA 1450).

30 Employment Tribunals (Constitution and Rules of Procedure) Regulations 2013, SI 2013/1237, Sch 1 r 67.
    The tribunal must send to the Commission for Equality and Human Rights copies of all judgments and written reasons relating to complaints under the Equality Act 2010 s 120 (see DISCRIMINATION vol 33 (2013) PARA 344) s 127 (see DISCRIMINATION vol 33 (2013) PARA 347) or s 146 (see DISCRIMINATION vol 33 (2013) PARA 5). That obligation does not apply in any proceedings where a Minister of the Crown has given a direction, or a tribunal has made an order, under the Employment Tribunals (Constitution and Rules of Procedure) Regulations 2013, SI 2013/1237, Sch 1 r 94 (see PARA 1450) and either the Security Service, the Secret Intelligence Service or the Government Communications Headquarters is a party to the proceedings: Sch 1 r 103. As to the Commission for Equality and Human Rights see DISCRIMINATION vol 33 (2013) PARA 30 et seq.

31 The following provisions apply to proceedings in relation to which a direction is given, or order is made, under the Employment Tribunals (Constitution and Rules of Procedure) Regulations 2013, SI 2013/1237, Sch 1 r 94: Sch 2 r 1(1). The tribunal must send a copy of the written reasons given under Sch 1 r 62 to the minister and allow 42 days for the minister to make a direction under Sch 2 r 6(3) before sending them to any party or entering them onto the

register: Sch 2 r 6(1). If the tribunal considers it expedient in the interests of national security, it may by order take steps to keep secret all or part of the written reasons: Sch 2 r 6(2). If the minister considers it expedient in the interests of national security, he may direct that the written reasons (1) are not to be disclosed to specified persons and require the tribunal to prepare a further document which sets out the reasons for the decision, but omits specified information ('the edited reasons'); (2) are not to be disclosed to specified persons and that no further document setting out the reasons for the decision should be prepared: Sch 2 r 6(3). Where the minister has directed the tribunal to prepare edited reasons, the employment judge must initial each omission: Sch 2 r 6(4).

Where a direction has been made under head (1) above, the tribunal must: (a) send the edited reasons to the specified persons; (b) send the edited reasons and the written reasons to the relevant persons listed in Sch 2 r 6(7); and (c) where the written reasons relate to a judgment, enter the edited reasons on the register but not enter the written reasons on the register: Sch 2 r 6(5). Where a direction has been made under head (2) above, the tribunal must send the written reasons to the relevant persons listed in Sch 2 r 6(7), but not enter the written reasons on the register: Sch 2 r 6(6). The relevant persons are (i) the respondent or the respondent's representative, provided that they were not specified in the direction made under heads (1)–(2) above; (ii) the claimant or the claimant's representative, provided that they were not specified in the direction so made; (iii) any special advocate appointed in the proceedings; and (iv) where the proceedings were referred to the tribunal by a court, that court: Sch 2 r 6(7). As to the meaning of 'claimant' see PARA 1457 note 25; and as to the meaning of 'respondent' see PARA 1460 note 8.

Where written reasons or edited reasons are corrected under Sch 1 r 69, the tribunal must send a copy of the corrected reasons to the same persons who had been sent the reasons: Sch 2 r 6(8).

1477. Financial penalty payable to Secretary of State for aggravated breach of worker's rights. Where an employment tribunal[1] determining a claim[2] involving an employer[3] and a worker[4] concludes that the employer has breached any of the worker's rights to which the claim relates, and is of the opinion that the breach has one or more aggravating features, the tribunal may order the employer to pay a penalty to the Secretary of State[5], whether or not it also makes a financial award[6] against the employer on the claim[7]. The tribunal must have regard to an employer's ability to pay (1) in deciding whether to order the employer to pay such a penalty; (2) in deciding the amount of a penalty[8].

The amount of such a penalty must be at least £100 and no more than £5,000, subject to the following provisions[9]. Where an employment tribunal makes a financial award against an employer on a claim, and also orders the employer to pay a penalty under these provisions in respect of the claim[10], the amount of the penalty must be 50 per cent[11] of the amount of the award, except that:

(a)   if the amount of the financial award is less than £200, the amount of the penalty must be £100;

(b)   if the amount of the financial award is more than £10,000, the amount of the penalty must be £5,000[12].

Where, however, an employment tribunal considers together two or more claims involving different workers but the same employer, and orders the employer to pay a penalty under these provisions in respect of any of those claims[13]:

(i)   the amount of the penalties in total must be at least £100;

(ii)   the amount of a penalty in respect of a particular claim must be no more than £5,000, and, where the tribunal makes a financial award against the employer on the claim, no more than 50 per cent[14] of the amount of the award;

but where the tribunal makes a financial award on any of the claims and the amount awarded is less than £200 in total, the amount of the penalties in total must be £100 and heads (i) and (ii) above do not apply[15].

An employer's liability to pay a penalty under these provisions is discharged if 50 per cent[16] of the amount of the penalty is paid no later than 21 days after the day on which notice of the decision to impose the penalty is sent to the employer[17].

1 As to employment tribunals see PARA 1399 et seq.
2 For these purposes, 'claim' (1) means anything that is referred to in the relevant legislation as a claim, a complaint or a reference, other than a reference made by virtue of the Equality Act 2010 s 122(2) or 128(2) (reference by court of question about a non-discrimination or equality rule etc: see DISCRIMINATION vol 33 (2013) PARA 344, 347); and (2) also includes an application, under regulations made under the Employment Act 2002 s 45 (see PARA 85), for a declaration that a person is a permanent employee: Employment Tribunals Act 1996 s 12A(11) (s 12A added by the Enterprise and Regulatory Reform Act 2013 s 16(1)). Two or more claims in respect of the same act and the same worker are to be treated as a single claim for the purposes of the Employment Tribunals Act 1996 s 12A: s 12A(8) (as so added). The Secretary of State may by order amend s 12A so as to alter the meaning of 'claim': s 12A(12)(c) (as so added). As to the Secretary of State see PARA 5 note 21.
3 For these purposes, 'employer' has the same meaning as in the Employment Rights Act 1996 Pt IVA (ss 43A–43L) (see PARA 69), and also (1) in relation to an individual seeking to be employed by a person as a worker, includes that person; (2) in relation to a right conferred by the Employment Rights Act 1996 s 47A or s 63A (right to time off for young person for study or training: see PARA 331), includes the principal within the meaning of s 63A(3); (3) in relation to a right conferred by the Agency Workers Regulations 2010, SI 2010/93 (see PARA 97 et seq), includes the hirer within the meaning of those Regulations and (where the worker is not actually employed by the temporary work agency) the temporary work agency within that meaning: Employment Tribunals Act 1996 s 12A(11) (as added: see note 2).
4 For these purposes, 'worker' has the same meaning as in the Employment Rights Act 1996 Pt IVA (ss 43A–43L) (see PARA 69), and also includes an individual seeking to be employed by a person as a worker: Employment Tribunals Act 1996 s 12A(11) (as added: see note 2).
5 The Secretary of State must pay sums received under the Employment Tribunals Act 1996 s 12A into the Consolidated Fund: s 12A(13) (as added: see note 2). As to the Consolidated Fund see CONSTITUTIONAL AND ADMINISTRATIVE LAW vol 20 (2014) PARA 480 et seq; PARLIAMENT vol 78 (2010) PARA 1028 et seq.
6 'Financial award' means an award of a sum of money, but does not including anything payable by virtue of the Employment Tribunals Act 1996 s 13 (costs and expenses: see PARA 1418): Employment Tribunals Act 1996 s 12A(11) (as added: see note 2).
7 Employment Tribunals Act 1996 s 12A(1) (as added: see note 2).
8 Employment Tribunals Act 1996 s 12A(2) (as added: see note 2). Head (2) in the text is subject to s 12A(3)–(7) (see the text and notes 9–15): s 12A(2) (as so added).
9 Employment Tribunals Act 1996 s 12A(3) (as added: see note 2). The Secretary of State may by order amend s 12A(3), (5) or (7) by substituting a different amount: s 12A(12)(a) (as so added).
10 Employment Tribunals Act 1996 s 12A(4) (as added: see note 2).
11 The Secretary of State may by order amend the Employment Tribunals Act 1996 s 12A(5), (7) or (10) by substituting a different percentage: s 12A(12)(b) (as so added).
12 Employment Tribunals Act 1996 s 12A(5) (as added: see note 2). See also note 9. Section 12A(5) or (7) does not require or permit an order under s 12A(1) (or a failure to make such an order) to be reviewed where the tribunal subsequently awards compensation under (1) the Trade Union and Labour Relations (Consolidation) Act 1992 s 140(3) (failure to comply with tribunal's recommendation: see PARA 1045); (2) the Employment Rights Act 1996 s 117 (failure to reinstate etc: see PARA 813); (3) the Equality Act 2010 s 124(7) (failure to comply with tribunal's recommendation: see DISCRIMINATION vol 33 (2013) PARA 346); or (4) any other provision empowering the tribunal to award compensation, or further compensation, for a failure to comply (or to comply fully) with an order or recommendation of the tribunal: Employment Tribunals Act 1996 s 12A(9) (as added: see note 2).
13 Employment Tribunals Act 1996 s 12A(6) (as added: see note 2).
14 See note 11.
15 Employment Tribunals Act 1996 s 12A(7) (as added: see note 2). See also notes 9, 12.
16 See note 11.
17 Employment Tribunals Act 1996 s 12A(10) (as added: see note 2).

1478. Recoupment of allowances etc. No regard is to be had[1], in assessing the amount of a monetary award, to the amount of any jobseeker's allowance[2], income-related employment and support allowance[3], universal credit[4] or any income support[5] which may have been paid to or claimed by the employee for a period which coincides with any part of a period to which the prescribed element[6] is attributable[7].

Where the employment tribunal, in arriving at a monetary award, makes a reduction on account of the employee's contributory fault or on account of any limit imposed under the Employment Rights Act 1996, a proportionate reduction must be made in arriving at the amount of the prescribed element[8].

It is the duty of the employment tribunal[9] to set out in any decision which includes a monetary award the following particulars:

(1)   the monetary award;
(2)   the amount of the prescribed element, if any;
(3)   the dates of the period to which the prescribed element is attributable;
(4)   the amount, if any, by which the monetary award exceeds the prescribed element[10].

Where the employment tribunal at the hearing announces to the parties the effect of a decision which includes a monetary award, it must inform those parties at the same time of the amount of any prescribed element in the monetary award and must explain the effect of the statutory provisions relating to postponement of awards[11] and recoupment of benefit[12] in relation to the prescribed element[13]. Where the employment tribunal has made such an announcement, the Secretary of the Employment Tribunals[14] must forthwith notify the Secretary of State that the tribunal has decided to make a monetary award including a prescribed element and must notify him of the particulars set out in heads (1) to (4) above[15]. As soon as reasonably practicable after the Secretary has sent a copy of a decision containing the particulars set out in heads (1) to (4) above to the parties, he must send a copy of that decision to the Secretary of State[16].

1   Ie where the Employment Protection (Recoupment of Benefits) Regulations 1996, SI 1996/2349, apply. The Employment Protection (Recoupment of Benefits) Regulations 1996, SI 1996/2349, apply to (inter alia): (1) guarantee payments under the Employment Rights Act 1996 s 28 (see PARA 261), being a payment which is the subject of employment tribunal proceedings on a complaint under s 34 (see PARA 265), the prescribed element being so much of the relevant monetary award as is attributable to any amount found to be due to the employee and ordered to be paid under s 34(3) (see PARA 265) for a period before the conclusion of the tribunal proceedings; (2) payments under any collective agreement having regard to which the appropriate minister has made an exemption order under s 35 (see PARA 266), being a payment which is the subject of employment tribunal proceedings on a complaint under s 35(4) (see PARA 266), the prescribed element being so much of the relevant monetary award as is attributable to any amount found to be due to the employee and ordered to be paid under s 34(3) (see PARA 265), as applied by s 35(4), for a period before the conclusion of the tribunal proceedings; (3) payments of remuneration in respect of a period of suspension on medical grounds under s 64 (see PARA 596) and s 108(2) (see PARA 758), being a payment which is the subject of employment tribunal proceedings on a complaint under s 70 (see PARA 606), the prescribed element being so much of the relevant monetary award as is attributable to any amount found to be due to the employee and ordered to be paid under s 70(3) (see PARA 606) for a period before the conclusion of the tribunal proceedings; (4) payments of remuneration in respect of a period of suspension on maternity grounds under s 68 (see PARA 598), being a payment which is the subject of employment tribunal proceedings on a complaint under s 70 (see PARA 606), the prescribed element being so much of the relevant monetary award as is attributable to any amount found to be due to the employee and ordered to be paid under s 70(3) (see PARA 606) for a period before the conclusion of the tribunal proceedings; (5) payments under an order for reinstatement under s 114(1) (see PARA 811), being a payment which is the subject of employment tribunal proceedings on a complaint of unfair dismissal under s 111(1) (see PARA 804), the prescribed element being so much of the relevant monetary award as is attributable to any amount ordered to be paid under s 114(2)(a) (see PARA 811 head (1)) in respect of arrears of

pay for a period before the conclusion of the tribunal proceedings; (6) payments under an order for re-engagement under s 117(8) (see PARA 813 note 12), being a payment which is the subject of employment tribunal proceedings on a complaint of unfair dismissal under s 111(1) (see PARA 804), the prescribed element being so much of the relevant monetary award as is attributable to any amount ordered to be paid under s 115(2)(d) (see PARA 811 head (d)) in respect of arrears of pay for a period before the conclusion of the tribunal proceedings; (7) payments under an award of compensation for unfair dismissal in cases falling under s 112(4) (see PARA 810), being a payment which is the subject of employment tribunal proceedings on a complaint of unfair dismissal under s 111(1) (see PARA 804), the prescribed element being so much of the relevant monetary award as is attributable to any amount ordered to be paid and calculated under s 123 (see PARA 818) in respect of compensation for loss of wages for a period before the conclusion of the tribunal proceedings; (8) payments under an award of compensation for unfair dismissal under s 117(3) (see PARA 813) where a reinstatement order is not complied with, being a payment which is the subject of employment tribunal proceedings on proceedings in respect of non-compliance with such an order, the prescribed element being so much of the relevant monetary award as is attributable to any amount ordered to be paid and calculated under s 123 (see PARA 818) in respect of compensation for loss of wages for a period before the conclusion of the tribunal proceedings; (9) payments under an award of compensation for unfair dismissal under s 117(3) (see PARA 813) where a re-engagement order is not complied with, being a payment which is the subject of employment tribunal proceedings on proceedings in respect of non-compliance with such an order, the prescribed element being so much of the relevant monetary award as is attributable to any amount ordered to be paid and calculated under s 123 (see PARA 818) in respect of compensation for loss of wages for a period before the conclusion of the tribunal proceedings: Employment Protection (Recoupment of Benefits) Regulations 1996, SI 1996/2349, reg 3(1)(a), Schedule, Table relating to Monetary Awards, items 1–9 (reg 3(1)(a) amended by the Employment Rights (Dispute Resolution) Act 1998 s 1(2)(a); the 1996 Regulations retitled by SI 2013/630).

2   As to jobseeker's allowance see WELFARE BENEFITS AND STATE PENSIONS vol 104 (2014) PARA 262 et seq.

3   As to income-related employment and support allowance see WELFARE BENEFITS AND STATE PENSIONS vol 104 (2014) PARA 252 et seq.

4   As to universal credit see WELFARE BENEFITS AND STATE PENSIONS vol 104 (2014) PARA 45 et seq.

5   As to income support see WELFARE BENEFITS AND STATE PENSIONS vol 104 (2014) PARA 292 et seq.

6   For these purposes, 'prescribed element' has the meaning given by the Employment Protection (Recoupment of Benefits) Regulations 1996, SI 1996/2349, reg 3 (see note 1): reg 2(1) (retitled: see note 1).

7   Employment Protection (Recoupment of Benefits) Regulations 1996, SI 1996/2349, reg 4(1) (amended by SI 2010/2429; SI 2013/630). As to orders made in secondary proceedings see the Employment Protection (Recoupment of Benefits) Regulations 1996, SI 1996/2349, reg 9 (reg 9(1) amended by the Employment Rights (Dispute Resolution) Act 1998 s 1(2)(a); and retitled (see note 1)).

6   Employment Protection (Recoupment of Benefits) Regulations 1996, SI 1996/2349, reg 4(2) (amended by the Employment Rights (Dispute Resolution) Act 1998 s 1(2)(a); and retitled (see note 1)).

9   Ie subject to the Employment Protection (Recoupment of Benefits) Regulations 1996, SI 1996/2349, reg 4(4)–(8): see the text and notes 11–16.

10   Employment Protection (Recoupment of Benefits) Regulations 1996, SI 1996/2349, reg 4(3) (amended by the Employment Rights (Dispute Resolution) Act 1996 s 1(2)(a); and retitled (see note 1)). In addition to containing the particulars required under the Employment Protection (Recoupment of Benefits) Regulations 1996, SI 1996/2349, reg 4(3), any such decision as is mentioned in reg 4(3) must contain a statement explaining the effect of reg 7 (see note 11) and reg 8 (see note 12) in relation to the prescribed element: reg 4(7). The requirements of reg 4(3)–(7) do not apply where the tribunal is satisfied that, in respect of each day falling within the period to which the prescribed element relates, the employee has neither received nor claimed jobseeker's allowance, income-related employment and support allowance, universal credit or income support: reg 4(8) (amended by SI 2010/2429; SI 2013/630).

11   Ie the effect of the Employment Protection (Recoupment of Benefits) Regulations 1996, SI 1996/2349, reg 7 (reg 7(3) amended by the Employment Rights (Dispute Resolution) Act 1998 s 1(2)(a); and retitled (see note 1)). The Employment Protection (Recoupment of Benefits) Regulations 1996, SI 1996/2349, reg 7 has effect for the purpose of postponing relevant awards in order to enable the Secretary of State to initiate recoupment under reg 8 (see

note 12): reg 7(1). Accordingly, so much of the monetary award as consists of the prescribed element is to be treated as stayed as respects the relevant employee until the Secretary of State has served a recoupment notice on the employee or the Secretary of State has notified the employer in writing that he does not intend to serve a recoupment notice: reg 7(2). As to the Secretary of State see PARA 5 note 21.

12 Ie the effect of the Employment Protection (Recoupment of Benefits) Regulations 1996, SI 1996/2349, reg 8 (retitled: see note 1). Recoupment is to be initiated by the Secretary of State serving on the employer a recoupment notice claiming by way of total or partial recoupment of jobseeker's allowance, income-related employment and support allowance, universal credit or income support the appropriate amount, computed, as the case may require, in accordance with the relevant provisions: reg 8(1) (amended by SI 2010/2429; SI 2013/630). As to the method of calculation, as to the mode of serving a recoupment notice, and as to the effect of a recoupment notice, see the Employment Protection (Recoupment of Benefits) Regulations 1996, SI 1996/2349, reg 8(2)–(10), (12) (as so amended). The recoupable amount is recoverable by the Secretary of State from the employer as a debt: reg 8(11). As to the determination and review of benefit recouped see reg 10 (amended by the Employment Rights (Dispute Resolution) Act 1996 s 1(2)(a); and by SI 1999/3178; SI 2008/2683; SI 2010/2429; SI 2013/630).

13 Employment Protection (Recoupment of Benefits) Regulations 1996, SI 1996/2349, reg 4(4) (amended by the Employment Rights (Dispute Resolution) Act 1996 s 1(2)(a); and retitled (see note 1)). See also note 10.

12 For these purposes, 'Secretary of the Tribunals' means the Secretary of the Central Office of the Employment Tribunals (England and Wales): Employment Protection (Recoupment of Benefits) Regulations 1996, SI 1996/2349, reg 2(1) (definition amended by the Employment Rights (Dispute Resolution) Act 1996 s 1(2)(b)).

15 Employment Protection (Recoupment of Benefits) Regulations 1996, SI 1996/2349, reg 4(5) (amended by the Employment Rights (Dispute Resolution) Act 1998 s 1(2)(a); and retitled (see note 1)). See also note 10.

16 Employment Protection (Recoupment of Benefits) Regulations 1996, SI 1996/2349, reg 4(6) (retitled: see note 1). See also note 10.

1479. Reconsideration of judgments. A tribunal[1] may, either on its own initiative (which may reflect a request from the Employment Appeal Tribunal)[2] or on the application of a party, reconsider any judgment[3] where it is necessary in the interests of justice to do so. On reconsideration, the decision ('the original decision') may be confirmed, varied or revoked. If it is revoked it may be taken again[4].

Except where it is made in the course of a hearing, an application for reconsideration must be presented[5] in writing[6], and copied to all the other parties, within 14 days[7] of the date on which the written record, or other written communication, of the original decision was sent to the parties or within 14 days of the date that the written reasons were sent (if later) and must set out why reconsideration of the original decision is necessary[8]. An employment judge[9] must consider any such application[10]. If the judge considers that there is no reasonable prospect of the original decision being varied or revoked, including, unless there are special reasons, where substantially the same application has already been made and refused, the application must be refused and the tribunal must inform the parties of the refusal. Otherwise the tribunal must send a notice[11] to the parties setting a time limit for any response to the application by the other parties and seeking the views of the parties on whether the application can be determined without a hearing. The notice may set out the judge's provisional views on the application[12].

If the application has not been refused[13], the original decision must be reconsidered at a hearing unless the employment judge considers, having regard to any response to the notice provided under the above provision[14], that a hearing is not necessary in the interests of justice. If the reconsideration proceeds without a hearing the parties must be given a reasonable opportunity to make further written representations[15].

Where the tribunal proposes to reconsider a decision on its own initiative, it must inform the parties of the reasons why the decision is being reconsidered and the decision must be reconsidered[16] as if an application had been made and not refused[17].

1   As to the meaning of 'tribunal' for these purposes see PARA 1448 note 14.
2   As to the Employment Appeal Tribunal see PARA 1422 et seq.
3   As to the meaning of 'judgment' see PARA 1460 note 4.
4   Employment Tribunals (Constitution and Rules of Procedure) Regulations 2013, SI 2013/1237, Sch 1 r 70. See *Hutchinson 3G UK Ltd v Francois* [2009] EWCA Civ 405, [2009] ICR 1323, [2009] All ER (D) 127 (May) (in interest of justice to review claim which had been rejected because claimant failed to send supporting documents with claim form).
5   As to the meaning of 'present' see PARA 1461 note 3.
6   As to the meaning of 'writing' see PARA 1450 note 19.
7   As to the calculation of time limits see PARA 1460.
8   Employment Tribunals (Constitution and Rules of Procedure) Regulations 2013, SI 2013/1237, Sch 1 r 71.
9   As to the meaning of 'employment judge' see PARA 1401 note 3.
10 Employment Tribunals (Constitution and Rules of Procedure) Regulations 2013, SI 2013/1237, Sch 1 r 72(1). Where practicable, the consideration under Sch 1 r 72(1) must be by the employment judge who made the original decision or, as the case may be, chaired the full tribunal which made it; and any reconsideration under Sch 1 r 72(2) (see the text and notes 13–15) must be made by the judge or, as the case may be, the full tribunal which made the original decision. Where that is not practicable, the President or a regional employment judge must appoint another employment judge to deal with the application or, in the case of a decision of a full tribunal, must either direct that the reconsideration be by such members of the original tribunal as remain available or reconstitute the tribunal in whole or in part: Sch 1 r 72(3). As to the meaning of 'full tribunal' see PARA 1448 note 14; and as to the meaning of 'President' see PARA 1399 note 7.
11 As to the giving of notices see PARA 1467.
12 Employment Tribunals (Constitution and Rules of Procedure) Regulations 2013, SI 2013/1237, Sch 1 r 72(1).
13 Ie under the Employment Tribunals (Constitution and Rules of Procedure) Regulations 2013, SI 2013/1237, Sch 1 r 72(1): see the text and notes 9–12.
14 See note 13.
15 Employment Tribunals (Constitution and Rules of Procedure) Regulations 2013, SI 2013/1237, Sch 1 r 72(2). See also note 10.
16 Ie in accordance with the Employment Tribunals (Constitution and Rules of Procedure) Regulations 2013, SI 2013/1237, Sch 1 r 72(2): see the text and notes 13–15.
17 Employment Tribunals (Constitution and Rules of Procedure) Regulations 2013, SI 2013/1237, Sch 1 r 73. See *CK Heating Ltd v Doro* [2010] ICR 1449, EAT (Sc) (tribunal entitled of its own motion to recall a decision made orally until it was formally signed; process was not completed by tribunal announcing decision orally; it was obliged still to give reasons for the decision and, if it now doubted the correctness of that decision, was entitled of its own motion to recall that decision until it was formally signed).

(viii) Costs Orders etc in Employment Tribunals

1480. Costs orders, preparation time orders and wasted costs orders. A costs order is an order that a party ('the paying party') make a payment to:

(1)   another party ('the receiving party') in respect of the costs[1] that the receiving party has incurred while legally represented[2] or while represented by a lay representative[3];

(2)   the receiving party in respect of a tribunal fee[4] paid by the receiving party; or

(3)   another party or a witness in respect of expenses incurred, or to be incurred, for the purpose of, or in connection with, an individual's attendance as a witness at the tribunal[5].

A preparation time order is an order that a party ('the paying party') make a payment to another party ('the receiving party') in respect of the receiving party's preparation time[6] while not legally represented[7].

A costs order under head (1) above and a preparation time order may not both be made in favour of the same party in the same proceedings. A tribunal may, if it wishes, decide in the course of the proceedings that a party is entitled to one order or the other but defer until a later stage in the proceedings deciding which kind of order to make[8].

A tribunal may make a costs order or a preparation time order, and must consider whether to do so, where it considers that:

(a)   a party or that party's representative has acted vexatiously, abusively, disruptively or otherwise unreasonably in either the bringing of the proceedings, or part, or the way that the proceedings, or part, have been conducted[9]; or

(b)   any claim or response had no reasonable prospect of success[10].

A tribunal may also make such an order where a party has been in breach of any order[11] or practice direction or where a hearing has been postponed or adjourned on the application of a party[12].

Where in proceedings for unfair dismissal[13] a final hearing is postponed or adjourned, the tribunal must order the respondent[14] to pay the costs incurred as a result of the postponement or adjournment if the claimant[15] has expressed a wish to be reinstated or re-engaged which has been communicated to the respondent not less than seven days[16] before the hearing and the postponement or adjournment of that hearing has been caused by the respondent's failure, without a special reason, to adduce reasonable evidence as to the availability of the job from which the claimant was dismissed or of comparable or suitable employment[17].

A tribunal may make a costs order of the kind described in head (2) above where a party has paid a tribunal fee in respect of a claim[18], employer's contract claim[19] or application and that claim, counterclaim or application is decided in whole, or in part, in favour of that party[20].

A tribunal may make a costs order of the kind described in head (3) above on the application of a party or the witness in question, or on its own initiative, where a witness has attended or has been ordered to attend to give oral evidence at a hearing[21].

A party may apply for a costs order or a preparation time order at any stage up to 28 days after the date on which the judgment[22] finally determining the proceedings in respect of that party was sent to the parties. No such order may be made unless the paying party has had a reasonable opportunity to make representations, in writing[23] or at a hearing, as the tribunal may order, in response to the application[24].

A costs order may:

(i)   order the paying party to pay the receiving party a specified amount, not exceeding £20,000, in respect of the costs of the receiving party[25];

(ii)   order the paying party to pay the receiving party the whole or a specified part of the costs of the receiving party, with the amount to be paid being determined, in England and Wales, by way of detailed assessment carried out either by the County Court in accordance with the Civil Procedure Rules 1998[26], or by an employment judge[27] applying the same principles[28];

(iii) order the paying party to pay the receiving party a specified amount as reimbursement of all or part of a tribunal fee paid by the receiving party[29];

(iv) order the paying party to pay another party or a witness, as appropriate, a specified amount in respect of necessary and reasonably incurred expenses of the kind described in head (3) above[30]; or

(v) if the paying party and the receiving party agree as to the amount payable, be made in that amount[31].

The tribunal must decide the number of hours in respect of which a preparation time order should be made, on the basis of information provided by the receiving party on time spent in preparation time[32] and the tribunal's own assessment of what it considers to be a reasonable and proportionate amount of time to spend on such preparatory work, with reference to such matters as the complexity of the proceedings, the number of witnesses and documentation required[33]. The hourly rate is £33 and increases on 6 April each year by £1[34]. The amount of a preparation time order must be the product of the number of hours so assessed and the hourly rate[35].

A tribunal may make a wasted costs order against a representative[36] in favour of any party ('the receiving party') where that party has incurred costs:

(A) as a result of any improper, unreasonable or negligent act or omission on the part of the representative[37]; or

(B) which, in the light of any such act or omission occurring after they were incurred, the tribunal considers it unreasonable to expect the receiving party to pay[38].

Costs so incurred are described as 'wasted costs'[39]. A wasted costs order may be made in favour of a party whether or not that party is legally represented and may also be made in favour of a representative's own client. A wasted costs order may not, however, be made against a representative where that representative is representing a party in his or her capacity as an employee of that party[40].

A wasted costs order may order the representative to pay the whole or part of any wasted costs of the receiving party, or disallow any wasted costs otherwise payable to the representative, including an order that the representative repay to its client any costs which have already been paid. The amount to be paid, disallowed or repaid must in each case be specified in the order[41].

A wasted costs order may be made by the tribunal on its own initiative or on the application of any party. A party may apply for a wasted costs order at any stage up to 28 days after the date on which the judgment finally determining the proceedings as against that party was sent to the parties. No such order may, however, be made unless the representative has had a reasonable opportunity to make representations, in writing or at a hearing, as the tribunal may order, in response to the application or proposal. The tribunal must inform the representative's client in writing of any proceedings under this provision and of any order made against the representative[42].

In deciding whether to make a costs, preparation time, or wasted costs order, and if so in what amount, the tribunal may have regard to the paying party's (or, where a wasted costs order is made, the representative's) ability to pay[43].

Where the tribunal makes a costs, preparation time, or wasted costs order, it may also make an order that the paying party (or, where a wasted costs order is made, the representative) pay to the Secretary of State[44], in whole or in part, any allowances (other than allowances paid to members of the tribunal) paid by the Secretary of State[45] to any person for the purposes of, or in connection with, that person's attendance at the tribunal[46].

1 'Costs' means fees, charges, disbursements or expenses incurred by or on behalf of the receiving party, including expenses that witnesses incur for the purpose of, or in connection with, attendance at a tribunal hearing: Employment Tribunals (Constitution and Rules of Procedure) Regulations 2013, SI 2013/1237, Sch 1 r 74(1).

2 'Legally represented' means having the assistance of a person (including where that person is the receiving party's employee) who (1) has a right of audience in relation to any class of proceedings in any part of the Senior Courts of England and Wales, or all proceedings in the County Court or magistrates' courts; (2) is an advocate or solicitor in Scotland; or (30 is a member of the Bar of Northern Ireland or a solicitor of the Court of Judicature of Northern Ireland: Employment Tribunals (Constitution and Rules of Procedure) Regulations 2013, SI 2013/1237, Sch 1 r 74(2) amended by virtue of the Crime and Courts Act 2013 Sch 9 Pt 2 para 11).

3 'Represented by a lay representative' means having the assistance of a person who does not satisfy any of the criteria in the Employment Tribunals (Constitution and Rules of Procedure) Regulations 2013, SI 2013/1237, Sch 1 r 74(2) (see note 2) and who charges for representation in the proceedings: Sch 1 r 74(3).

4 As to the meaning of 'tribunal fee' see PARA 1457 note 23.

5 Employment Tribunals (Constitution and Rules of Procedure) Regulations 2013, SI 2013/1237, Sch 1 r 75(1).

6 'Preparation time' means time spent by the receiving party (including by any employees or advisers) in working on the case, except for time spent at any final hearing: Employment Tribunals (Constitution and Rules of Procedure) Regulations 2013, SI 2013/1237, Sch 1 r 75(2).

7 Employment Tribunals (Constitution and Rules of Procedure) Regulations 2013, SI 2013/1237, Sch 1 r 75(2). See eg *Ramsay v Bowercross Construction Ltd* [2008] All ER (D) 131 (Aug), EAT.

8 Employment Tribunals (Constitution and Rules of Procedure) Regulations 2013, SI 2013/1237, Sch 1 r 75(3). See *Agassi v Robinson (Inspector of Taxes) (Bar Council intervening)* [2005] EWCA Civ 1507, [2006] 1 All ER 900, [2006] 1 WLR 2126; *Ramsay v Bowercross Construction Ltd* [2008] All ER (D) 131 (Aug), EAT.

9 Employment Tribunals (Constitution and Rules of Procedure) Regulations 2013, SI 2013/1237, Sch 1 r 76(1)(a). The phrase 'vexatiously, abusively, disruptively or otherwise unreasonably' applies only to the way a party had brought or conducted proceedings and not to his conduct prior to proceedings or in relation to the dismissal itself; in spite of the wording, the aim remains compensation of the party who has incurred expense in winning his case, not punishment of the losing party: *Davidson v John Calder (Publishers) Ltd and Calder Educational Trust Ltd* [1985] ICR 143, [1985] IRLR 97, EAT; *Health Development Agency v Parrish* [2004] IRLR 550, EAT.

Parties should not be discouraged from making sensible decisions in the conduct of their litigation by tribunal practice on costs. In considering a party who has withdrawn a claim, the question is not whether the withdrawal itself was unreasonable but whether in all the circumstances of the case the applicant's conduct of the proceedings was unreasonable (*McPherson v BNP Paribas (London Branch)* [2004] EWCA Civ 569, [2004] 3 All ER 266, [2004] IRLR 558); and it is extremely unlikely that a tribunal will make a costs order against a party who proceeds with a claim simply because the claim fails, ie in the absence of the claim being misconceived or unreasonable (*Gee v Shell UK Ltd* [2002] EWCA Civ 1479, [2003] IRLR 82, CA). A tribunal should be careful in giving a party an informal warning as to possible costs if they proceed because costs remain exceptional and a tribunal must not put unfair pressure on a party, particularly a litigant in person: *Gee v Shell UK Ltd* [2002] EWCA Civ 1479, [2003] IRLR 82, CA. *McPherson v BNP Paribas (London Branch)* [2004] EWCA Civ 569, [2004] 3 All ER 266, [2004] IRLR 558 was applied in *Salinas v Bear Stearns International Holdings Inc* [2005] ICR 1117, [2004] All ER (D) 296 (Oct), EAT; *Ramsay v Bowercross Construction Ltd* [2008] All ER (D) 131 (Aug), EAT; *Unegbu v Newman Stone Ltd* [2008] All ER (D) 164 (Aug), EAT; *Davies v J & R Farragher (t/a Potens)* [2009] All ER (D) 103 (Jan), EAT. The principle of a 'Calderbank' offer (where a party has refused an offer, made without prejudice except as to costs, which was greater than any amount actually recovered) does not apply directly in a tribunal but the fact that a party has refused such an offer may be a relevant factor in the tribunal's assessment of a party's conduct: *Kopel v Safeway Stores plc* [2003] IRLR 753, [2003] All ER (D) 05 (Sep), EAT.

See also *Yerrakalva v Barnsley Metropolitan Borough Council* [2011] EWCA Civ 1255, [2012] 2 All ER 215, [2012] IRLR 78, [2012] ICR 420 (although the tribunal had had jurisdiction and broad discretion to make a costs order, it had erred in law in the exercise of its discretion. The employee's conduct and its effect on the costs should not have been considered in isolation from the rest of the case, including the employer's conduct and its likely effect on the length and costs of the pre-hearing review); *Raggett v John Lewis plc* [2012] IRLR 906, EAT; *Vaughan v Lewisham London Borough Council (No 2)* [2013] IRLR 713, EAT (costs order made even though receiving party had not been put on notice that she was at risk as to costs, the respondents had made an offer to settle (not undermined by subsequently contending that the claim was misconceived) and she had not had the financial means to satisfy the award (nothing wrong in principle in the tribunal setting the cap at a level which gave the respondents the benefit of any doubt, even to a generous extent)); *Sud v Ealing London Borough Council* [2013] EWCA Civ 949, (2013) Times, 23 October, [2013] ICR D39, [2013] All ER (D) 386 (Jul) (although an award of costs against a paying party in the employment tribunal was an exceptional event, if the tribunal concluded that the claimant's conduct of the proceedings had been unreasonable the tribunal should identify the particular unreasonable conduct, along with its effect, by a broad brush approach and award costs accordingly; tribunal's decision came well within the proper exercise of its discretion).

10   Employment Tribunals (Constitution and Rules of Procedure) Regulations 2013, SI 2013/1237, Sch 1 r 76(1)(b).

11   As to orders of the tribunal see PARA 1460 note 4.

12   Employment Tribunals (Constitution and Rules of Procedure) Regulations 2013, SI 2013/1237, Sch 1 r 76(2).

13   See *Agassi v Robinson (Inspector of Taxes) (Bar Council intervening)* [2005] EWCA Civ 1507, [2006] 1 All ER 900, [2006] 1 WLR 2126; *Ramsay v Bowercross Construction Ltd* [2008] All ER (D) 131 (Aug), EAT. As to unfair dismissal see PARA 762 et seq.

14   As to the meaning of 'respondent' see PARA 1460 note 8.

15   As to the meaning of 'claimant' see PARA 1457 note 25.

16   As to the calculation of time limits see PARA 1460.

17   Employment Tribunals (Constitution and Rules of Procedure) Regulations 2013, SI 2013/1237, Sch 1 r 76(3).

18   As to the meaning of 'claim' see PARA 1457 note 22.

19   As to the meaning of 'employer's contract claim' see PARA 1457 note 7.

20   Employment Tribunals (Constitution and Rules of Procedure) Regulations 2013, SI 2013/1237, Sch 1 r 76(4).

21   Employment Tribunals (Constitution and Rules of Procedure) Regulations 2013, SI 2013/1237, Sch 1 r 76(5).

22   As to the meaning of 'judgment' see PARA 1460 note 4.

23   As to the meaning of 'writing' see PARA 1450 note 19.

24   Employment Tribunals (Constitution and Rules of Procedure) Regulations 2013, SI 2013/1237, Sch 1 r 77.

25   Employment Tribunals (Constitution and Rules of Procedure) Regulations 2013, SI 2013/1237, Sch 1 r 78(1)(a). Where the costs order includes an amount in respect of fees charged by a lay representative, for the purposes of the calculation of the order, the hourly rate applicable for the fees of the lay representative must be no higher than the rate under Sch 1 r 79(2) (see the text and note 34): Sch 1 r 78(2).

26   As to detailed assessment see CPR Pt 47; and CIVIL PROCEDURE vol 12 (2009) PARA 1779 et seq.

27   As to the meaning of 'employment judge' see PARA 1401 note 3.

28   Employment Tribunals (Constitution and Rules of Procedure) Regulations 2013, SI 2013/1237, Sch 1 r 78(1)(b) (amended by virtue of the Crime and Courts Act 2013 Sch 9 Pt 2 para 11). For the avoidance of doubt, the amount of a costs order under the Employment Tribunals (Constitution and Rules of Procedure) Regulations 2013, SI 2013/1237, Sch 1 r 78(1)(b)–(e) (see heads (ii)–(v) in the text) may exceed £20,000: Sch 1 r 78(3). See also note 25.

29   Employment Tribunals (Constitution and Rules of Procedure) Regulations 2013, SI 2013/1237, Sch 1 r 78(1)(c). See also notes 25, 28.

30   Employment Tribunals (Constitution and Rules of Procedure) Regulations 2013, SI 2013/1237, Sch 1 r 78(1)(d). See also notes 25, 28.

31   Employment Tribunals (Constitution and Rules of Procedure) Regulations 2013, SI 2013/1237, Sch 1 r 78(1)(e). See also notes 25, 28.

32   Ie time spent falling within the Employment Tribunals (Constitution and Rules of Procedure) Regulations 2013, SI 2013/1237, Sch 1 r 75(2): see the text and notes 6–7.

33   Employment Tribunals (Constitution and Rules of Procedure) Regulations 2013, SI 2013/1237, Sch 1 r 79(1).

34 Employment Tribunals (Constitution and Rules of Procedure) Regulations 2013, SI 2013/1237, Sch 1 r 79(2).

35 Employment Tribunals (Constitution and Rules of Procedure) Regulations 2013, SI 2013/1237, Sch 1 r 79(3).

36 'Representative' means a party's legal or other representative or any employee of such representative, but it does not include a representative who is not acting in pursuit of profit with regard to the proceedings. A person acting on a contingency or conditional fee arrangement is considered to be acting in pursuit of profit: Employment Tribunals (Constitution and Rules of Procedure) Regulations 2013, SI 2013/1237, Sch 1 r 80(2). An award is unlikely if the client went ahead with a weak case, contrary to the representative's advice: *Ratcliffe Duce v Binns (t/a Parc Ferme)* UKEAT/0100/08/CEA.

37 Employment Tribunals (Constitution and Rules of Procedure) Regulations 2013, SI 2013/1237, Sch 1 r 80(1)(a).

38 Employment Tribunals (Constitution and Rules of Procedure) Regulations 2013, SI 2013/1237, Sch 1 r 80(1)(b).

39 Employment Tribunals (Constitution and Rules of Procedure) Regulations 2013, SI 2013/1237, Sch 1 r 80(1).

40 Employment Tribunals (Constitution and Rules of Procedure) Regulations 2013, SI 2013/1237, Sch 1 r 80(3).

41 Employment Tribunals (Constitution and Rules of Procedure) Regulations 2013, SI 2013/1237, Sch 1 r 81.

42 Employment Tribunals (Constitution and Rules of Procedure) Regulations 2013, SI 2013/1237, Sch 1 r 82.

43 Employment Tribunals (Constitution and Rules of Procedure) Regulations 2013, SI 2013/1237, Sch 1 r 84. If a tribunal decides not to take ability to pay into account, it has to say why: *Jilley v Birmingham and Solihull Mental Health NHS Trust* [2008] All ER (D) 35 (Feb), EAT. See also *Doyle v North West London Hospitals NHS Trust* [2012] ICR D21, [2012] All ER (D) 205 (Jun), EAT (it was established law that the tribunal was not obliged to take the employee's ability to pay into account in deciding the amount of any costs order, but, if the tribunal decided not to do so, it should say why. Further, it was open to a tribunal to place a cap on an award of costs, even where it ordered a detailed assessment).

44 As to the Secretary of State see PARA 5 note 21.

45 Ie under the Employment Tribunals Act 1996 s 5(2) or (3): see PARA 1405.

46 Employment Tribunals (Constitution and Rules of Procedure) Regulations 2013, SI 2013/1237, Sch 1 r 83.

1481. Interest on sums awarded. The Secretary of State[1] may by order[2] made with the approval of the Treasury[3] provide that sums payable in pursuance of decisions of employment tribunals[4] are to carry interest at such rate and between such times as may be prescribed by the order[5].

Any interest due by virtue of such an order is recoverable as a sum payable in pursuance of the decision[6].

The power so conferred includes power:

(1)   to specify cases or circumstances in which interest is not payable;

(2)   to provide that interest is payable only on sums exceeding a specified amount or falling between specified amounts;

(3)   to make provision for the manner in which, and the periods by reference to which, interest is to be calculated and paid;

(4)   to provide that any enactment does or does not apply in relation to interest payable by virtue of any such order or applies to it with such modifications as may be specified in the order;

(5)   to make provision for cases where sums are payable in pursuance of decisions or awards made on appeal from employment tribunals;

(6)   to make such incidental or supplemental provision as the Secretary of State considers necessary[7].

1 As to the Secretary of State see PARA 5 note 21.

2 As to the making of orders under the Employment Tribunals Act 1996 see PARA 162.

3   As to the Treasury see CONSTITUTIONAL AND ADMINISTRATIVE LAW vol 20 (2014) PARA 262 et seq.

4   As to employment tribunals see PARA 1399 et seq.

5   Employment Tribunals Act 1996 s 14(1) (amended by the Employment Rights (Dispute Resolution) Act 1998 s 1(2)(b)). In particular, an order under the Employment Tribunals Act 1996 s 14(1) may provide that the rate of interest is to be the rate specified in the Judgments Act 1838 s 17 (see CIVIL PROCEDURE vol 12 (2009) PARA 1149) as that enactment has effect from time to time: Employment Tribunals Act 1996 s 14(4). The Employment Tribunals (Interest) Order (Amendment) Order 2013, SI 2013/1671, has been made in the exercise of this power. Additionally, by virtue of the Employment Tribunals Act 1996 Sch 2 para 2 (see PARA 162), the Employment Tribunals (Interest) Order 1990, SI 1990/479 (see PARAS 1482–1483) has effect as if so made.

6   Employment Tribunals Act 1996 s 14(2).

7   Employment Tribunals Act 1996 s 14(3) (amended by the Employment Rights (Dispute Resolution) Act 1998 s 1(2)(b)).

1482. Computation of interest on sums awarded. Where the whole or any part of a sum of money payable by virtue of a relevant decision[1] of a tribunal[2] remains unpaid on the calculation day[3], the sum of money remaining unpaid on the calculation day carries interest[4] at the stipulated rate of interest[5] from the calculation day, including that day[6]. Notwithstanding this provision, however, no interest is payable if payment of the full amount of the award[7] is made within 14 days after the relevant decision day[8].

Where, after the calculation day, a party[9] pays to another party some, but not all, of such a sum of money remaining unpaid on the calculation day, then, beginning with the day on which the payment is made, interest continues to accrue only on that part of the sum of money which then remains unpaid[10].

For the purposes of the computation of such interest, there must be disregarded:

(1)   any part of a sum of money which has been claimed by the Secretary of State in a recoupment notice[11]; and

(2)   any part of a sum of money which the party required to pay the sum of money is required, by virtue of any provision contained in or having effect under any enactment, to deduct and pay over to a public authority in respect of income tax or contributions under the Social Security Contributions and Benefits Act 1992[12].

Where a decision of a tribunal is a relevant decision and a copy of a document recording that decision is sent to all parties entitled to receive that decision, it is the duty of the secretary of the Central Office of the Employment Tribunals (England and Wales) to cause a notice (containing prescribed matters, namely the decision day, the stipulated rate of interest and the calculation day in respect of the decision concerned) to accompany that document[13]. The failure to discharge that duty correctly or at all has, however, no effect on the liability of one party to pay to another party any sum of money which is payable by virtue of the above provisions[14].

1   For these purposes, 'relevant decision', in relation to a tribunal, means any award or other determination of the tribunal by virtue of which one party to proceedings before the tribunal is required to pay a sum of money, excluding a sum representing costs or expenses, to another party to those proceedings: Employment Tribunals (Interest) Order 1990, SI 1990/479, art 2(1). A sum of money is required to be paid by one party to proceedings to another such party if, and only if, an amount of money required to be so paid is: (1) specified in an award or other determination of a tribunal or, as the case may be, in an order or decision of an appellate court; or (2) otherwise ascertainable solely by reference to the terms of such an award or determination or, as the case may be, solely by reference to the terms of such an order or decision; but, where a tribunal or, as the case may be, appellate court has made a declaration as to entitlement under

a contract, nothing in the Employment Tribunals (Interest) Order 1990, SI 1990/479, is to be taken to provide for interest to be payable on any payment under that contract in respect of which no obligation to make the payment has arisen under that contract before the declaration was made: art 2(2). 'Appellate court' means the Employment Appeal Tribunal, the High Court, the Court of Appeal, the Court of Session or the Supreme Court, as the case may be: art 2(1) (amended by virtue of the Constitutional Reform Act 2005 s 40(3)). As to the meaning of 'tribunal' see note 2.

2   For these purposes, 'tribunal' means an employment tribunal (England and Wales) established in pursuance of the Employment Tribunals (Constitution and Rules of Procedure) Regulations 2013, SI 2013/1237 (see PARA 1399): Employment Tribunals (Interest) Order 1990, SI 1990/479, art 2(1) (definition amended by the Employment Rights (Dispute Resolution) Act 1998 s 1(2)(a)); Interpretation Act 1978 s 17(2).

3   For these purposes, 'calculation day', in relation to a relevant decision, means the day immediately following the relevant decision day: Employment Tribunals (Interest) Order 1990, SI 1990/479, art 2(1) (definition substituted by SI 2013/1671). As to the meanings of 'decision day' and 'relevant decision day' see PARA 1483.

4   For these purposes, 'interest' means simple interest which accrues from day to day: Employment Tribunals (Interest) Order 1990, SI 1990/479, art 2(1).

5   For these purposes, the stipulated rate of interest is the rate of interest specified in the Judgments Act 1838 s 17 (see CIVIL PROCEDURE vol 12 (2009) PARA 1149) on the relevant decision day: Employment Tribunals (Interest) Order 1990, SI 1990/479, arts 2(1), 4.

6   Employment Tribunals (Interest) Order 1990, SI 1990/479, art 3(1). Article 3(1) is subject to art 3(2), (3) (see the text and notes 9–12) and art 11 (see PARA 1483 note 5): art 3(1).

7   Ie including any interest under the Employment Tribunals (Interest on Awards in Discrimination Cases) Regulations 1996, SI 1996/2803, reg 2: see DISCRIMINATION vol 33 (2013) PARAS 346, 350.

8   Employment Tribunals (Interest) Order 1990, SI 1990/479, art 3(4) (added by SI 2013/1671).

9   For these purposes, 'party' includes the Secretary of State where he has elected to appear as if he were a party in accordance with a rule of procedure entitling him so to elect: Employment Tribunals (Interest) Order 1990, SI 1990/479, art 2(4). 'Rules of procedure' means rules having effect in relation to proceedings before a tribunal by virtue of any regulations or order made pursuant to an enactment: art 2(1). As to the Secretary of State see PARA 5 note 21.

10 Employment Tribunals (Interest) Order 1990, SI 1990/479, art 3(2).

11 Ie under the Employment Protection (Recoupment of Benefits) Regulations 1996, SI 1996/2349: see PARA 1478.

12 Employment Tribunals (Interest) Order 1990, SI 1990/479, art 3(3); Employment Tribunals Act 1996 Sch 2 para 2; Interpretation Act 1978 s 17(2).

13 Employment Tribunals (Interest) Order 1990, SI 1990/479, art 12(1), (2) (art 12(1) amended by the Employment Rights (Dispute Resolution) Act 1998 s 1(2)(b)).

14 Employment Tribunals (Interest) Order 1990, SI 1990/479, art 12(3).

1483.   Meanings of 'decision day' and 'relevant decision day'. Except in so far as the context otherwise requires, 'decision day' means the day signified by the date recording the sending of the document which is sent to the parties[1] recording an award or other determination of a tribunal[2]; and 'relevant decision day' means the day so signified in relation to a relevant decision[3].

Where a tribunal reviews its decision pursuant to the rules of procedure[4] and the effect of the review, or of any rehearing which takes place as a result of the review, is that a sum of money payable by one party to another party is confirmed or varied, the relevant decision day is the decision day of the decision which is the subject of the review[5].

Where an appellate court[6] remits a matter to a tribunal for reassessment of the sum of money which would have been payable by virtue of a previous relevant decision or by virtue of an order of another appellate court, the relevant decision day is the decision day of that previous relevant decision or the day on which the other appellate court promulgated its order, as the case may be[7].

Where, on an appeal from a relevant decision, or on a further appeal arising from a relevant decision, an appellate court makes an order which confirms or varies the sum of money which would have been payable by virtue of that relevant decision if there had been no appeal, the relevant decision day is the decision day of that relevant decision[8].

In relation to any order made by an appellate court on an appeal from a determination of any issue by a tribunal which is not a relevant decision, or on any further appeal arising from such a determination, where the effect of the order is that, for the first time in relation to that issue, one party to the proceedings is required to pay a sum of money, other than a sum representing costs or expenses, to another party to the proceedings[9], the provisions relating to the computation of interest[10] apply to the sum of money payable by virtue of the order as if it were a sum of money payable by virtue of a relevant decision and as if the day on which the appellate court promulgated the order were the relevant decision day[11]. Where, on an appeal from any such order[12] or on a further appeal arising from such an order, an appellate court makes an order which confirms or varies the sum of money which would have been payable by virtue of the order[13] if there had been no appeal, the day to be treated as the relevant decision day is the day on which the order was promulgated[14]. Where the Employment Appeal Tribunal reviews any such order[15], the day to be treated as the relevant decision day is the day on which the order reviewed was promulgated[16].

1   As to the meaning of 'party' see PARA 1482 note 9.
2   As to the meaning of 'tribunal' see PARA 1482 note 2.
3   Employment Tribunals (Interest) Order 1990, SI 1990/479, art 2(3). Article 2(3) is subject to arts 5–7 (see the text and notes 4–8): art 2(3). As to the meaning of 'relevant decision' see PARA 1482 note 1.
4   As to the meaning of 'rules of procedure' see PARA 1482 note 9.
5   Employment Tribunals (Interest) Order 1990, SI 1990/479, art 5. Where a sum of money payable by virtue of a relevant decision is varied under one of the procedures referred to in art 5 and arts 6, 7 (see the text and notes 6–8), or a sum of money treated as being so payable by virtue of art 8 (see the text and notes 9–11) is varied under one of the procedures referred to in arts 6, 9–10 (see the text and notes 6, 7, 12–16), the reference in art 3(1) (see PARA 1482) to a sum of money payable by virtue of a relevant decision is to be treated as if it were a reference to that sum as so varied: art 11.
6   As to the meaning of 'appellate court' see PARA 1482 note 1.
7   Employment Tribunals (Interest) Order 1990, SI 1990/479, art 6. See also note 5.
8   Employment Tribunals (Interest) Order 1990, SI 1990/479, art 7. See also note 5.
9   As to when a sum of money is required to be paid by one party to proceedings to another such party see PARA 1482 note 1.
10 Ie the Employment Tribunals (Interest) Order 1990, SI 1990/479, arts 3, 4: see PARA 1482.
11 Employment Tribunals (Interest) Order 1990, SI 1990/479, art 8(1), (2). See also note 5.
12 Ie an order in relation to which the Employment Tribunals (Interest) Order 1990, SI 1990/479, art 8 applies: see the text and notes 9–11.
13 See note 12.
14 Employment Tribunals (Interest) Order 1990, SI 1990/479, art 9. See also note 5.
15 See note 12. As to the Employment Appeal Tribunal see PARA 1422 et seq.
16 Employment Tribunals (Interest) Order 1990, SI 1990/479, art 10. See also note 5.

1484. Recovery of sums awarded. Any sum payable in pursuance of a decision of an employment tribunal[1] in England and Wales[2] which has been duly registered[3] is recoverable under the County Courts Act 1984[4] or otherwise as if it were payable under an order of the County Court[5].

1   For these purposes, a reference to a decision or order of an employment tribunal: (1) does not include a decision or order which, on being reviewed, has been revoked by the tribunal (see PARA 1479); and (2) in relation to a decision or order which, on being reviewed, has been varied by

the tribunal, is to be construed as a reference to the decision or order as so varied: Employment Tribunals Act 1996 s 15(3) (amended by the Employment Rights Act 1998 s 1(2)(a)). As to employment tribunals see PARA 1399 et seq.

2 As to the meanings of 'England' and 'Wales' see PARA 2 note 12.

3 Ie in accordance with employment tribunal procedure regulations. As to the meaning of 'employment tribunal procedure regulations' see PARA 1410.

4 Ie under the County Courts Act 1985 s 84: see CIVIL PROCEDURE vol 12 (2009) PARA 1283.

5 Employment Tribunals Act 1996 s 15(1) (amended by the Employment Rights Act 1998 s 1(2)(a); the Tribunals, Courts and Enforcement Act 2007 Sch 8 paras 35, 43, Sch 13 para 125; the Crime and Courts Act 2013 Sch 9 Pt 3 para 52(1)(b), (2)).

1485. Enforcement of awards in case of death. Where there is no personal representative of a deceased employee in proceedings arising under any of the relevant provisions in which an employment tribunal makes any award[1], the terms of the award and the manner of its award are governed by the following provisions[2].

Where, in proceedings before an employment tribunal arising under any of the relevant provisions, either:

(1) a person has been appointed[3] to institute or continue those proceedings on behalf of the estate[4]; or

(2) an employee who is a party to those proceedings dies before the tribunal's award is made,

any award of the tribunal must be made in favour of the estate[5].

Where any person is appointed[6] to enforce an award made by an employment tribunal in favour of the estate or, as the case may be, in favour of an employee who has since died, that person may enforce such award on behalf of the estate without the grant of letters of administration or probate of any will; and the receipt of that person is a sufficient discharge to the employer[7] for any sum payable to the estate under that award[8]. In any other case[9], any award made in favour of the estate or in favour of an employee who has since died is enforceable on behalf of the estate by the person to whom a grant of letters of administration or probate is made in respect of that estate[10].

1 For these purposes, 'relevant provisions' means the provisions of the Employment Rights Act 1996 conferring rights on employees, or connected therewith, relating to redundancy (see PARA 835 et seq) and unfair dismissal (see PARA 757 et seq): Employment Tribunals Awards (Enforcement in case of Death) Regulations 1976, SI 1976/663, reg 2(2); Employment Tribunals Act 1996 Sch 2 para 2.

2 Employment Tribunals Awards (Enforcement in case of Death) Regulations 1976, SI 1976/663, reg 3.

3 Ie under the Employment Rights Act 1996 s 206: see PARA 1456.

4 For these purposes, 'estate' means the estate of the deceased employee: Employment Tribunals Awards (Enforcement in case of Death) Regulations 1976, SI 1976/663, reg 2(2).

5 Employment Tribunals Awards (Enforcement in case of Death) Regulations 1976, SI 1976/663, reg 4; Employment Tribunals Act 1996 Sch 2 para 2.

6 See note 3.

7 For these purposes, 'employer' includes a successor of an employer or a personal representative of a deceased employer: Employment Tribunals Awards (Enforcement in case of Death) Regulations 1976, SI 1976/663, reg 2(2).

8 Employment Tribunals Awards (Enforcement in case of Death) Regulations 1976, SI 1976/663, reg 5.

9 Ie in any case where the Employment Tribunals Awards (Enforcement in case of Death) Regulations 1976, SI 1976/663, reg 5 (see the text and notes 6–8) does not apply.

10 Employment Tribunals Awards (Enforcement in case of Death) Regulations 1976, SI 1976/663, reg 6.

(3) PROCEDURE ON INDUSTRIAL TRAINING LEVY APPEALS

1486. Rules of procedure for levy appeals. The procedural rules for employment tribunals[1] apply to levy appeals[2], with references in them to a claim[3] or claimant[4] being read as references to a levy appeal or to an appellant in a levy appeal respectively[5].

1 Ie the rules set out in the Employment Tribunals (Constitution and Rules of Procedure) Regulations 2013, SI 2013/1237, Sch 1.
2 'Levy appeal' mean an appeal against an assessment to a levy imposed under the Industrial Training Act 1982 s 11 (see PARA 678): Employment Tribunals (Constitution and Rules of Procedure) Regulations 2013, SI 2013/1237, Sch 1 r 1(1).
3 As to the meaning of 'claim' see PARA 1457 note 22.
4 As to the meaning of 'claimant' see PARA 1457 note 25.
5 See the Employment Tribunals (Constitution and Rules of Procedure) Regulations 2013, SI 2013/1237, Sch 1 r 104.

1487. Notice of levy appeal. A person assessed to levy imposed under a levy order[1] or a revocation order[2] may appeal to an employment tribunal[3]; and the levy order or, as the case may be, revocation order must make provision as to the time within which such an appeal may be made[4].

1 As to the meaning of 'levy order' see PARA 678 note 7.
2 As to the meaning of 'revocation order' see PARA 677.
3 As to employment tribunals see PARA 1399 et seq.
4 Industrial Training Act 1982 ss 4(4), 12(4) (amended by the Employment Rights (Dispute Resolution) Act 1998 s 1(2)(a)).

1488. Determination of levy appeal by tribunal. On an appeal by a person assessed to levy imposed under a levy order[1] or, as the case may be, a revocation order[2]:

(1) if the appellant[3] satisfies the tribunal[4] that he ought not to have been assessed to the levy or ought to have been assessed in a smaller amount, the tribunal must rescind or, as the case may be, reduce the assessment but, subject to head (2) below, in any other case must confirm it[5]; and

(2) if it appears to the tribunal that the appellant ought to have been assessed to the levy in a larger amount, the tribunal may increase the assessment accordingly[6].

1 Ie an appeal under the Industrial Training Act 1982 s 12(4): see PARA 1487. As to the meaning of 'levy order' see PARA 678 note 7.
2 Ie an appeal under the Industrial Training Act 1982 s 4(4): see PARA 1487. As to the meaning of 'revocation order' see PARA 677.
3 As to the meaning of 'appellant' see PARA 1486.
4 As to employment tribunals see PARA 1399 et seq.
5 Industrial Training Act 1982 ss 4(5)(a), 12(5)(a).
6 Industrial Training Act 1982 ss 4(5)(b), 12(5)(b).

(4) PROCEDURE ON APPEALS AGAINST IMPROVEMENT AND PROHIBITION NOTICES

1489. Improvement and prohibition notices. A person ('the appellant') may appeal a health and safety improvement notice[1] or prohibition notice[2] by presenting[3] a claim[4] to a tribunal office[5]:

(1)   before the end of the period of 21 days[6] beginning with the date of the service on the appellant of the notice which is the subject of the appeal; or

(2)   within such further period as the tribunal[7] considers reasonable where it is satisfied that it was not reasonably practicable for an appeal to be presented within that time[8].

For the purposes of an appeal against an improvement notice or a prohibition notice, the procedural rules for employment tribunals[9] are to be treated as modified in the specified[10] ways[11].

A person ('the appellant') may appeal an Energy Act improvement notice (an 'Energy Act IN')[12] or prohibition notice (an 'Energy Act PN')[13] by presenting a claim to a tribunal office:

(a)   before the end of the period of 21 days beginning with the date on which the notice which is the subject of the appeal is given to the appellant; or

(b)   within such further period as the tribunal considers reasonable where it is satisfied that it was not reasonably practicable for an appeal to be presented within that period[14].

For the purposes of such an appeal the procedural rules for employment tribunals[15] are to be treated as modified in the specified[16] ways[17].

1   'Improvement notice' means a notice under the Health and Safety at Work etc Act 1974 s 21 (see HEALTH AND SAFETY AT WORK vol 52 (2014) PARA 340): Employment Tribunals (Constitution and Rules of Procedure) Regulations 2013, SI 2013/1237, Sch 1 r 1(1).

2   'Prohibition notice' means a notice under the Health and Safety at Work etc Act 1974 s 22 (see HEALTH AND SAFETY AT WORK vol 52 (2014) PARA 341): Employment Tribunals (Constitution and Rules of Procedure) Regulations 2013, SI 2013/1237, Sch 1 r 1(1).

3   As to the meaning of 'present' see PARA 1461 note 3.

4   As to the meaning of 'claim' see PARA 1457 note 22. See also, however, notes 10, 16.

5   As to the meaning of 'tribunal office' see PARA 1461 note 3.

6   As to the calculation of time limits see PARA 1460.

7   As to the meaning of 'tribunal' for these purposes see PARA 1448 note 14.

8   See the Employment Tribunals (Constitution and Rules of Procedure) Regulations 2013, SI 2013/1237, Sch 1 r 105(1).

9   Ie the rules set out in the Employment Tribunals (Constitution and Rules of Procedure) Regulations 2013, SI 2013/1237, Sch 1.

10   For these purposes, references to a claim or claimant are to be read as references to an appeal or to an appellant in an appeal respectively; and references to a respondent are to be read as references to the inspector appointed under the Health and Safety at Work etc Act 1974 s 19(1) (see HEALTH AND SAFETY AT WORK vol 52 (2014) PARA 338) who issued the notice which is the subject of the appeal: Employment Tribunals (Constitution and Rules of Procedure) Regulations 2013, SI 2013/1237, Sch 1 rr 1(1), 105(2)(a), (b).

11   See the Employment Tribunals (Constitution and Rules of Procedure) Regulations 2013, SI 2013/1237, Sch 1 r 105(2).

12   'Energy Act IN' means a notice given by an inspector under the Energy Act 2013 Sch 8 para 3 (see ENERGY AND CLIMATE CHANGE): Employment Tribunals (Constitution and Rules of Procedure) Regulations 2013, SI 2013/1237, Sch 1 r 1(1) (definition added by SI 2014/468).

13   'Energy Act PN' means a notice given by an inspector under the Energy Act 2013 Sch 8 para 4 (see ENERGY AND CLIMATE CHANGE): Employment Tribunals (Constitution and Rules of Procedure) Regulations 2013, SI 2013/1237, Sch 1 r 1(1) (definition added by SI 2014/468).

14   Employment Tribunals (Constitution and Rules of Procedure) Regulations 2013, SI 2013/1237, Sch 1 r 105A(1) (Sch 1 r 105A added by SI 2014/468).

15   See note 9.

16   For these purposes, references to a claim or claimant are to be read as references to an appeal or to an appellant in an appeal respectively; and references to a respondent are to be read as references to the inspector appointed under the Energy Act 2013 Sch 8 para 1 (see ENERGY AND CLIMATE CHANGE) who issued the notice which is the subject of the appeal: Employment Tribunals (Constitution and Rules of Procedure) Regulations 2013, SI 2013/1237, Sch 1 r 105A(2)(a), (b) (as added: see note 14).

17 See the Employment Tribunals (Constitution and Rules of Procedure) Regulations 2013, SI 2013/1237, Sch 1 r 105A(2) (as added: see note 14).

(5) PROCEDURE ON APPEALS AGAINST UNLAWFUL ACT NOTICES

1490. Unlawful act notices. For the purposes of an appeal against an unlawful act notice[1], the procedural rules for employment tribunals[2] are to be treated as modified in the following ways[3]:

(1) references in those rules to a claim[4] or claimant[5] are to be read as references to a notice of appeal or to an appellant in an appeal against an unlawful act notice respectively[6];

(2) references to a respondent[7] are to be read as references to the Commission for Equality and Human Rights[8].

1 'Unlawful act notice' means a notice under the Equality Act 2006 s 21 (see DISCRIMINATION vol 33 (2013) PARAS 334–335): Employment Tribunals (Constitution and Rules of Procedure) Regulations 2013, SI 2013/1237, Sch 1 r 1(1).
2 Ie the rules set out in the Employment Tribunals (Constitution and Rules of Procedure) Regulations 2013, SI 2013/1237, Sch 1.
3 Employment Tribunals (Constitution and Rules of Procedure) Regulations 2013, SI 2013/1237, Sch 1 r 106.
4 As to the meaning of 'claim' see PARA 1457 note 22.
5 As to the meaning of 'claimant' see PARA 1457 note 25.
6 Employment Tribunals (Constitution and Rules of Procedure) Regulations 2013, SI 2013/1237, Sch 1 r 106(a).
7 As to the meaning of 'respondent' see PARA 1460 note 8.
8 Employment Tribunals (Constitution and Rules of Procedure) Regulations 2013, SI 2013/1237, Sch 1 r 106(b). As to the Commission for Equality and Human Rights see DISCRIMINATION vol 33 (2013) PARA 30 et seq.

(6) PROCEDURE ON EQUAL VALUE CLAIMS

1491. Procedure on equal value claims; in general. The Equality Act 2010 makes provision as to the assessment of whether a person's work is of equal value to another's[1].

In any proceedings before a tribunal[2] involving an equal value claim[3], the procedural rules for employment tribunals[4] apply with specified modifications and additions[5].

The tribunal may[6] order:

(1) that no new facts are to be admitted in evidence by the tribunal unless they have been disclosed to all other parties in writing[7] before a date specified by the tribunal, unless it was not reasonably practicable for a party to have done so;

(2) the parties to send copies of documents or provide information to the independent expert[8];

(3) the respondent[9] to grant the independent expert access to the respondent's premises during a period specified in the order to allow the independent expert to conduct interviews with persons identified as relevant by the independent expert;

(4) when more than one expert is to give evidence in the proceedings, that those experts present[10] to the tribunal a joint statement of matters which are agreed between them and matters on which they disagree[11].

The tribunal must restrict expert evidence to that which it considers is reasonably required to resolve the proceedings[12]. An expert has a duty to assist the tribunal on matters within his expertise. This duty overrides any obligation to the person from whom the expert has received instructions or by whom the expert is paid[13]. No party may call an expert or put in evidence an expert's report without the permission of the tribunal. No expert report must be put in evidence unless it has been disclosed to all other parties and any independent expert at least 28 days[14] before the final hearing[15]. In proceedings in which an independent expert has been required to prepare a report on the question[16], the tribunal must not admit evidence of another expert on the question unless such evidence is based on the facts relating to the question[17]. Unless the tribunal considers it inappropriate to do so, any such expert report must be disclosed to all parties and to the tribunal on the same date on which the independent expert is required to send his report to the parties and to the tribunal[18]. If an expert (other than an independent expert) does not comply with the procedural rules or an order made by the tribunal, the tribunal may order that the evidence of that expert is not to be admitted[19]. Where two or more parties wish to submit expert evidence on a particular issue, the tribunal may order that the evidence on that issue is to be given by one joint expert only and if the parties wishing to instruct the joint expert cannot agree an expert, the tribunal may select an expert[20].

When an expert has prepared a report, a party or any other expert involved in the proceedings may put written questions about the report to the expert who has prepared the report[21]. Unless the tribunal agrees otherwise, such written questions:

(a)   may be put once only;
(b)   must be put within 28 days of the date on which the parties were sent the report;
(c)   must be for the purpose only of clarifying the factual basis of the report; and
(d)   must be copied to all other parties and experts involved in the proceedings at the same time as they are sent to the expert who prepared the report[22].

An expert must answer written questions within 28 days of receipt and the answers are to be treated as part of the expert's report[23]. Where a party has put a written question to an expert instructed by another party and the expert does not answer that question within 28 days, the tribunal may order that the party instructing that expert may not rely on the evidence of that expert[24].

1   See the Equality Act 2010 s 131; and DISCRIMINATION vol 33 (2013) PARA 349.
2   As to the meaning of 'tribunal' for these purposes see PARA 1448 note 14.
3   For these purposes, 'equal value claim' means a claim relating to a breach of a sex equality clause or rule within the meaning of the Equality Act 2010 in a case involving work within s 65(1)(c) (see DISCRIMINATION vol 33 (2013) PARA 131): Employment Tribunals (Constitution and Rules of Procedure) Regulations 2013, SI 2013/1237, Sch 3 r 1(2).
4   Ie the rules set out in the Employment Tribunals (Constitution and Rules of Procedure) Regulations 2013, SI 2013/1237, Sch 1.
5   See the Employment Tribunals (Constitution and Rules of Procedure) Regulations 2013, SI 2013/1237, reg 13(2)(b), Sch 2 r 1(1). The definitions set out in Sch 1 apply for these purposes: Sch 1 r 1(2).
       Any power conferred on an employment judge by Sch 1 may (subject to the provisions of Sch 3) in an equal value claim be carried out by a full tribunal or an employment judge: Sch 3 r 12(3). As to the meaning of 'full tribunal' see PARA 1448 note 14; and as to the meaning of 'employment judge' see PARA 1401 note 3.
6   Ie subject to the Employment Tribunals (Constitution and Rules of Procedure) Regulations 2013, SI 2013/1237, Sch 3 rr 3(1), 6(1): see PARAS 1492–1493.

7 As to the meaning of 'writing' see PARA 1450 note 19.
8 'Independent expert' means a member of the panel of independent experts mentioned in the Equality Act 2010 s 131(8) (see DISCRIMINATION vol 33 (2013) PARA 349): Employment Tribunals (Constitution and Rules of Procedure) Regulations 2013, SI 2013/1237, Sch 3 r 1(2).
9 As to the meaning of 'respondent' see PARA 1460 note 8.
10 As to the meaning of 'present' see PARA 1461 note 3.
11 Employment Tribunals (Constitution and Rules of Procedure) Regulations 2013, SI 2013/1237, Sch 3 r 2(1). In managing the proceedings, the tribunal must have regard to the indicative timetable in the Annex to Sch 3: Sch 3 r 2(2).
12 Employment Tribunals (Constitution and Rules of Procedure) Regulations 2013, SI 2013/1237, Sch 3 r 10(1).
13 Employment Tribunals (Constitution and Rules of Procedure) Regulations 2013, SI 2013/1237, Sch 3 r 10(2).
14 As to the calculation of time limits see PARA 1460.
15 Employment Tribunals (Constitution and Rules of Procedure) Regulations 2013, SI 2013/1237, Sch 3 r 10(3).
16 As to the meanings of 'the question' and 'report' see PARA 1492 notes 9, 11.
17 As to the meaning of 'the facts relating to the question' see PARA 1493 head (1).
18 Employment Tribunals (Constitution and Rules of Procedure) Regulations 2013, SI 2013/1237, Sch 3 r 10(4).
19 Employment Tribunals (Constitution and Rules of Procedure) Regulations 2013, SI 2013/1237, Sch 3 r 10(5).
20 Employment Tribunals (Constitution and Rules of Procedure) Regulations 2013, SI 2013/1237, Sch 3 r 10(6).
21 Employment Tribunals (Constitution and Rules of Procedure) Regulations 2013, SI 2013/1237, Sch 3 r 11(1).
22 Employment Tribunals (Constitution and Rules of Procedure) Regulations 2013, SI 2013/1237, Sch 3 r 11(2).
23 Employment Tribunals (Constitution and Rules of Procedure) Regulations 2013, SI 2013/1237, Sch 3 r 11(3).
24 Employment Tribunals (Constitution and Rules of Procedure) Regulations 2013, SI 2013/1237, Sch 3 r 11(4).

1492. Stage 1 hearing in equal value claim. Where there is a dispute as to whether one person's work is of equal value to another's[1] the tribunal[2] must conduct a hearing, referred to as a 'stage 1 equal value hearing'[3]. At that hearing the tribunal must:

(1) strike out the claim[4] (or the relevant part of it) if the tribunal must determine[5] that the work of the claimant[6] and the comparator[7] are not of equal value[8];

(2) determine the question[9] or require an independent expert[10] to prepare a report[11] on the question[12];

(3) if the tribunal has decided to require an independent expert to prepare a report on the question, fix a date for a further hearing, referred to as a 'stage 2 equal value hearing'[13]; and

(4) if the tribunal has not decided to require an independent expert to prepare a report on the question, fix a date for the final hearing[14].

The tribunal must give the parties reasonable notice of the date of the stage 1 equal value hearing and the notice must specify the matters that are to be, or may be, considered at the hearing and give notice of the standard orders[15].

At a stage 1 equal value hearing a tribunal must, unless it considers it inappropriate to do so, order that:

(a) before the end of the period of 14 days[16] the claimant is to:

(i) disclose in writing[17] to the respondent[18] the name of any comparator, or, if the claimant is not able to name the comparator, disclose information which enables the respondent to identify the comparator; and

(ii) identify to the respondent in writing the period in relation to which the claimant considers that the claimant's work and that of the comparator are to be compared[19];

(b) before the end of the period of 28 days:

    (i) where the claimant has not disclosed the name of the comparator to the respondent under head (a) above and the respondent has been provided with sufficient detail to be able to identify the comparator, the respondent is to disclose in writing the name of the comparator to the claimant;

    (ii) the parties are to provide each other with written job descriptions for the claimant and any comparator;

    (iii) the parties are to identify to each other in writing the facts which they consider to be relevant to the question[20];

(c) the respondent is to grant access to the respondent's premises during a period specified in the order to allow the claimant and his or her representative to interview any comparator[21];

(d) the parties are, before the end of the period of 56 days, to present[22] to the tribunal an agreed written statement specifying:

    (i) job descriptions for the claimant and any comparator;

    (ii) the facts which both parties consider are relevant to the question;

    (iii) the facts on which the parties disagree (as to the fact or as to the relevance to the question) and a summary of their reasons for disagreeing[23];

(e) the parties are, at least 56 days before the final hearing, to disclose to each other, to any independent or other expert and to the tribunal written statements of any facts on which they intend to rely in evidence at the final hearing[24]; and

(f) the parties are, at least 28 days before the final hearing, to present to the tribunal a statement of facts and issues on which the parties are in agreement, a statement of facts and issues on which the parties disagree and a summary of their reasons for disagreeing[25].

The tribunal may add to, vary or omit any of these standard orders[26].

There may be more than one stage 1 equal value hearing in any case[27].

1 Equal value is to be construed in accordance with the Equality Act 2010 s 65(6) (see DISCRIMINATION vol 33 (2013) PARA 131): Employment Tribunals (Constitution and Rules of Procedure) Regulations 2013, SI 2013/1237, Sch 3 r 3(1).
2 As to the meaning of 'tribunal' for these purposes see PARA 1448 note 14.
3 Employment Tribunals (Constitution and Rules of Procedure) Regulations 2013, SI 2013/1237, Sch 3 r 3(1).
4 As to the meaning of 'claim' see PARA 1457 note 22.
5 Ie in accordance with the Equality Act 2010 s 131(6): see DISCRIMINATION vol 33 (2013) PARA 349.
6 As to the meaning of 'claimant' see PARA 1457 note 25.
7 'Comparator' means the person of the opposite sex to the claimant in relation to whom the claimant alleges that his or her work is of equal value: Employment Tribunals (Constitution and Rules of Procedure) Regulations 2013, SI 2013/1237, Sch 3 r 1(2).
8 Employment Tribunals (Constitution and Rules of Procedure) Regulations 2013, SI 2013/1237, Sch 3 r 3(1)(a). Before a claim or part is struck out under Sch 3 r 3(1)(a), the tribunal must send notice to the claimant and allow the claimant to make representations to the tribunal as to whether the evaluation contained in the study in question falls within the Equality Act 2010 s 131(6)(a) or (b). The tribunal is not, however, required to send such a notice if the claimant has been given an opportunity to make such representations orally to the tribunal: Employment Tribunals (Constitution and Rules of Procedure) Regulations 2013, SI 2013/1237, Sch 3 r 3(2).

9 'The question' means whether the claimant's work is of equal value to that of the comparator: Employment Tribunals (Constitution and Rules of Procedure) Regulations 2013, SI 2013/1237, Sch 3 r 1(2).

10 As to the meaning of 'independent expert' see PARA 1491 note 8.

11 'Report' means a report required by a tribunal to be prepared in accordance with the Equality Act 2010 s 131(2) (see DISCRIMINATION vol 33 (2013) PARA 349): Employment Tribunals (Constitution and Rules of Procedure) Regulations 2013, SI 2013/1237, Sch 3 r 1(2).

12 Employment Tribunals (Constitution and Rules of Procedure) Regulations 2013, SI 2013/1237, Sch 3 r 3(1)(b). The tribunal may, on the application of a party, hear evidence and submissions on the issue contained in the Equality Act 2010 s 69 (defence of material factor: see DISCRIMINATION vol 33 (2013) PARA 136) before determining whether to require an independent expert to prepare a report under the Employment Tribunals (Constitution and Rules of Procedure) Regulations 2013, SI 2013/1237, Sch 3 r 3(1)(b): Sch 3 r 3(3).

Where the tribunal has decided to require an independent expert to prepare a report on the question, it may at any stage of the proceedings, on its own initiative or on the application of a party, order the independent expert to assist the tribunal in establishing the facts on which the independent expert may rely in preparing the report: Sch 3 r 5.

When a tribunal makes an order under Sch 3 r 3(1)(b) or under Sch 3 r 5, it must inform that independent expert of the duties and powers under Sch 3 r 9: Sch 3 r 9(1). The independent expert has a duty to the tribunal to (1) assist it in furthering the overriding objective set out in Sch 1 r 2 (see PARA 1421); (2) comply with the requirements of the procedural rules and any orders made by the tribunal; (3) keep the tribunal informed of any delay in complying with any order (with the exception of minor or insignificant delays in compliance); (4) comply with any timetable imposed by the tribunal in so far as this is reasonably practicable; (5) when requested, inform the tribunal of progress in the preparation of the report; (6) prepare a report on the question based on the facts relating to the question and (subject to Sch 3 r 13 (national security proceedings: see PARA 1493 note 12) send it to the tribunal and the parties; and (7) attend hearings: Sch 3 r 9(2). The independent expert may make an application for any order or for a hearing to be held as if he were a party to the proceedings: Sch 3 r 9(3). At any stage of the proceedings the tribunal may, after giving the independent expert the opportunity to make representations, withdraw the requirement on the independent expert to prepare a report. If it does so, the tribunal may itself determine the question, or it may require a different independent expert to prepare the report: Sch 3 r 9(4). When Sch 3 r 9(4) applies the independent expert who is no longer required to prepare the report must provide the tribunal with all documentation and work in progress relating to the proceedings by a specified date. Such documentation and work in progress must be in a form which the tribunal is able to use and may be used in relation to those proceedings by the tribunal or by another independent expert: Sch 3 r 9(5).

Where an independent expert has been required to prepare a report, the tribunal must send that expert notice of any hearing, application, order or judgment in the proceedings as if the independent expert were a party to those proceedings and when the procedural rules or an order requires a party to provide information to another party, such information must also be provided to the independent expert: Sch 3 r 12(1).

13 Employment Tribunals (Constitution and Rules of Procedure) Regulations 2013, SI 2013/1237, Sch 3 r 3(1)(c).

14 Employment Tribunals (Constitution and Rules of Procedure) Regulations 2013, SI 2013/1237, Sch 3 r 3(1)(d).

15 Employment Tribunals (Constitution and Rules of Procedure) Regulations 2013, SI 2013/1237, Sch 3 r 3(4). The standard orders are those in Sch 3 r 4: see the text and notes 16–25.

16 As to the calculation of time limits see PARA 1460.

17 As to the meaning of 'writing' see PARA 1450 note 19.

18 As to the meaning of 'respondent' see PARA 1460 note 8.

19 Employment Tribunals (Constitution and Rules of Procedure) Regulations 2013, SI 2013/1237, Sch 3 r 4(1)(a).

20 Employment Tribunals (Constitution and Rules of Procedure) Regulations 2013, SI 2013/1237, Sch 3 r 4(1)(b).

21 Employment Tribunals (Constitution and Rules of Procedure) Regulations 2013, SI 2013/1237, Sch 3 r 4(1)(c).

22 As to the meaning of 'present' see PARA 1461 note 3.

23 Employment Tribunals (Constitution and Rules of Procedure) Regulations 2013, SI 2013/1237, Sch 3 r 4(1)(d).

24 Employment Tribunals (Constitution and Rules of Procedure) Regulations 2013, SI 2013/1237, Sch 3 r 4(1)(e).

25 Employment Tribunals (Constitution and Rules of Procedure) Regulations 2013, SI 2013/1237, Sch 3 r 4(1)(f).
26 Employment Tribunals (Constitution and Rules of Procedure) Regulations 2013, SI 2013/1237, Sch 3 r 4(2).
27 Employment Tribunals (Constitution and Rules of Procedure) Regulations 2013, SI 2013/1237, Sch 3 r 12(2).

1493. Stage 2 hearing in equal value claim. Any stage 2 equal value hearing[1] must be conducted by a full tribunal[2] and at the hearing the tribunal[3] must:

(1) make a determination of facts on which the parties cannot agree which relate to the question[4] and must require the independent expert[5] to prepare the report[6] on the basis of facts which have, at any stage of the proceedings, either been agreed between the parties or determined by the tribunal ('the facts relating to the question')[7]; and

(2) fix a date for the final hearing[8].

At any stage of the proceedings the independent expert may make an application to the tribunal for some or all of the facts relating to the question to be amended, supplemented or omitted[9]. Subject to that, the facts relating to the question must, in relation to the question, be the only facts on which the tribunal is to rely at the final hearing[10].

The tribunal must give the parties reasonable notice of the date of the stage 2 equal value hearing and the notice must draw the attention of the parties to the above provisions and give notice of the standard orders[11].

At a stage 2 equal value hearing a tribunal must, unless it considers it inappropriate to do so, order that:

(a) by a specified date the independent expert is to prepare his report on the question and must[12] send copies of it to the parties and to the tribunal[13]; and

(b) the independent expert is to prepare his report on the question on the basis only of the facts relating to the question[14].

The tribunal may add to, vary or omit any of these standard orders[15].
There may be more than one stage 2 equal value hearing in any case[16].

1 As to the meaning of 'stage 2 equal value hearing' see PARA 1492 head (3).
2 As to the meaning of 'full tribunal' see PARA 1448 note 14.
3 As to the meaning of 'tribunal' for these purposes see PARA 1448 note 14.
4 As to the meaning of 'the question' see PARA 1492 note 9.
5 As to the meaning of 'independent expert' see PARA 1491 note 8; and as to his role see PARA 1492 note 12.
6 As to the meaning of 'report' see PARA 1492 note 11.
7 Employment Tribunals (Constitution and Rules of Procedure) Regulations 2013, SI 2013/1237, Sch 3 r 6(1)(a).
8 Employment Tribunals (Constitution and Rules of Procedure) Regulations 2013, SI 2013/1237, Sch 3 r 6(1)(b).
9 Employment Tribunals (Constitution and Rules of Procedure) Regulations 2013, SI 2013/1237, Sch 3 r 6(3).
10 Employment Tribunals (Constitution and Rules of Procedure) Regulations 2013, SI 2013/1237, Sch 3 r 6(2).
11 Employment Tribunals (Constitution and Rules of Procedure) Regulations 2013, SI 2013/1237, Sch 3 r 6(4). The standard orders referred to in the text are the standard orders in Sch 3 r 7: see the text and notes 12–15.
12 Ie subject to the Employment Tribunals (Constitution and Rules of Procedure) Regulations 2013, SI 2013/1237, Sch 3 r 13. Where in an equal value claim a direction is given, or order is made, under Sch 1 r 94 (national security proceedings: see PARA 1450), any independent expert appointed must send a copy of any report and any responses to written questions to the tribunal only, and before the tribunal sends the parties a copy of a report or answers which have been received from an independent expert, it must follow the procedure set

out in Sch 2 r 6 (see PARA 1476 note 31) as if that rule referred to the independent expert's report or answers (as the case may be) instead of written reasons, except that the independent expert's report or answers are not to be entered on the register: Sch 3 r 13. As to the meaning of 'register' see PARA 1472 note 22.

13 Employment Tribunals (Constitution and Rules of Procedure) Regulations 2013, SI 2013/1237, Sch 3 r 7(1)(a).
14 Employment Tribunals (Constitution and Rules of Procedure) Regulations 2013, SI 2013/1237, Sch 3 r 7(1)(b).
15 Employment Tribunals (Constitution and Rules of Procedure) Regulations 2013, SI 2013/1237, Sch 3 r 7(2).
16 Employment Tribunals (Constitution and Rules of Procedure) Regulations 2013, SI 2013/1237, Sch 3 r 12(2).

1494. Final hearing in equal value claim. Where an independent expert[1] has prepared a report[2], unless the tribunal[3] determines that the report is not based on the facts relating to the question[4], the report of the independent expert must be admitted in evidence[5].

If the tribunal does not admit the report of an independent expert in accordance with the above provision, it may determine the question itself or require another independent expert to prepare a report on the question[6].

The tribunal may refuse to admit evidence of facts or hear submissions on issues which have not been disclosed to the other party as required by the procedural rules or any order, unless it was not reasonably practicable for a party to have done so[7].

1 As to the meaning of 'independent expert' see PARA 1491 note 8; and as to his role see PARA 1492 note 12.
2 As to the meaning of 'report' see PARA 1492 note 11.
3 As to the meaning of 'tribunal' for these purposes see PARA 1448 note 14.
4 As to the meaning of 'the facts relating to the question' see PARA 1493 head (1); and as to the meaning of 'the question' see PARA 1492 note 9.
5 Employment Tribunals (Constitution and Rules of Procedure) Regulations 2013, SI 2013/1237, Sch 3 r 8(1).
6 Employment Tribunals (Constitution and Rules of Procedure) Regulations 2013, SI 2013/1237, Sch 3 r 8(2).
7 Employment Tribunals (Constitution and Rules of Procedure) Regulations 2013, SI 2013/1237, Sch 3 r 8().

(7) PROCEDURE ON APPEALS TO THE EMPLOYMENT APPEAL TRIBUNAL

(i) Employment Appeal Tribunal; Preliminary Matters

1495. Institution of appeal to Appeal Tribunal. Every appeal to the Appeal Tribunal[1] must be instituted by serving on the tribunal a notice of appeal[2] in, or substantially in accordance with, the prescribed form[3] and the following documents[4]:

(1) in the case of an appeal from a judgment of an employment tribunal[5]:
    (a) a copy of any claim[6] and response[7] in the proceedings before the employment tribunal or an explanation as to why either is not included[8]; and
    (b) a copy of the written record of the judgment of the employment tribunal which is subject to appeal and the written reasons for the judgment[9], or an explanation as to why written reasons are not included[10]; and

(2) in the case of an appeal from an order of an employment tribunal, a

copy of the written record of the order of the employment tribunal which is subject to appeal and (if available) the written reasons for the order[11]; and

(3)   in the case of an appeal from a declaration or order of the Central Arbitration Committee[12], a copy of that declaration or order[13]; and

(4)   in the case of an appeal from a decision or order of the certification officer[14], a copy of the decision or order of the certification officer which is subject to appeal and the written reasons for that decision or order[15].

In an appeal from a judgment or order of the employment tribunal in relation to national security proceedings[16] where the appellant was the claimant[17], the appellant is not required by virtue of head (1)(a) above to serve on the Appeal Tribunal a copy of the response if the response was not disclosed to the appellant[18]; and the appellant is not required by virtue of head (1)(b) or head (2) above to serve on the Appeal Tribunal a copy of the written reasons for the judgment or order if the written reasons were not sent to the appellant[19]. However, if a document containing edited reasons[20] was sent to the appellant, he must serve a copy of that document on the Appeal Tribunal[21].

The period within which an appeal to the Appeal Tribunal may be instituted[22] is:

(i)   in the case of an appeal from a judgment of the employment tribunal[23]:

(A)   where the written reasons for the judgment subject to appeal were requested orally at the hearing before the employment tribunal or in writing within 14 days of the date on which the written record of the judgment was sent to the parties[24], or were reserved and given in writing by the employment tribunal, 42 days from the date on which the written reasons were sent to the parties[25];

(B)   in an appeal from a judgment given in relation to national security proceedings, where there is a document containing edited reasons for the judgment subject to appeal, 42 days from the date on which that document was sent to the parties[27]; or

(C)   where the written reasons for the judgment subject to appeal were not requested orally at the hearing before the employment tribunal or in writing within 14 days of the date on which the written record of the judgment was sent to the parties and were not reserved and given in writing by the employment tribunal, 42 days from the date on which the written record of the judgment was sent to the parties[28];

(ii)   in the case of an appeal from an order of an employment tribunal, 42 days from the date of the order[29];

(iii)   in the case of an appeal from a decision of the certification officer, 42 days from the date on which the written record of that decision was sent to the appellant[30];

(iv)   in the case of an appeal from a declaration or order of the Central Arbitration Committee[31], 42 days from the date on which the written notification of that declaration or order was sent to the appellant[32].

These provisions are modified in relation to national security proceedings[33].

Where at any stage of any proceedings it appears to the Appeal Tribunal that there is a reasonable prospect of agreement being reached between the parties or of disposal of the appeal or a part of it by consensual means, the Appeal Tribunal may take such steps as it thinks fit to enable the parties to avail themselves of any opportunities for conciliation, whether by adjourning any proceedings or otherwise[34].

1   As to the meaning of the 'Appeal Tribunal' see PARA 1451 note 4. As to the use of the abbreviation 'EAT' see PARA 1435 note 2.

2   As to the mode of service see PARA 1504.

3   Employment Appeal Tribunal Rules 1993, SI 1993/2854, r 3(1)(a) (r 3 substituted by SI 2001/1128); *Practice Direction (Employment Appeal Tribunal—Procedure) 2013* [2014] IRLR 92 para 3.1. For the prescribed forms of notice of appeal see the Employment Appeal Tribunal Rules 1993, SI 1993/2854, r 3(1), Schedule, Form 1 (substituted by SI 2005/1871) (notice of appeal from decision of employment tribunal), the Employment Appeal Tribunal Rules 1993, SI 1993/2854, Schedule, Form 1A (notice of appeal from the Central Arbitration Committee (the 'CAC')), Schedule, Form 2 (notice of appeal from decision of certification officer). The printed form should be used in all but 'clearly exceptional cases'; and, where this form is not used, the document containing the notice should indicate 'the efforts made to acquire such a form; the names and addresses of each of the parties; the date and content of the decision; the identity of the tribunal; and sufficiently defined grounds of appeal': *Martin v British Railways Board* [1989] ICR 24 at 32, [1989] IRLR 198 at 202, EAT, per Wood J.

    The notice of appeal must identify the date of the judgment, decision or order being appealed (*Practice Direction (Employment Appeal Tribunal—Procedure) 2013* [2014] IRLR 92 para 3.1) and must clearly identify the point(s) of law which form(s) the ground(s) of appeal from the judgment, decision or order of the employment tribunal (para 3.5); it should also state the order which the appellant will ask the EAT to make at the hearing (para 3.5). A party cannot 'reserve a right' to amend, alter or add to, a notice of appeal or a respondent's answer. No party has the right to amend any notice of appeal or answer without the prior permission of the EAT. Any application for permission to amend must be made as soon as practicable and must be accompanied by a draft of the amended notice of appeal or amended answer which makes clear the precise amendments for which permission is sought: para 3.10. As to the meanings of 'order' and 'judgment' of an employment tribunal see PARA 1460 note 4. As to the use of the abbreviation 'EAT' see PARA 1435 note 2.

    A notice of appeal should be no longer than the making of a clear statement of the ground of appeal requires. This must be sufficient for a judge looking at the notice of appeal to know what the error of law is, or errors of law are, said to be, but except in the case of a perversity appeal or one which complains about the conduct and/or bias of the employment tribunal (see para 13; and PARA 1497) should be no longer: in any case, it should not set out detailed argument and citation from case law unless this is essential for understanding: para 3.6. If it appears to the judge or registrar that a notice of appeal or an application gives insufficient grounds of, or lacks clarity in identifying, a point of law, the judge or registrar may postpone any further consideration of the appeal pending the appellant's amplification or clarification of the notice of appeal or the receipt of further information from the employment tribunal: para 3.7.

4   As to the meaning of 'document' see PARA 1451 note 5. If the documentation specified in heads (1) to (4) in the text is not attached, the notice of appeal will not be validly presented: *Practice Direction (Employment Appeal Tribunal—Procedure) 2013* [2014] IRLR 92 para 3.1. If a document has started to be produced at the expiry of the deadline, it should be regarded as being in time so that, where the document had in fact been completed, had been in either electronic or readable form, and had been in the process of dispatch, and the dispatch had on the balance of probabilities started at the time of expiry of the deadline, that should count as good service or lodgment of the document: *Clark v Midland Packaging Ltd* [2005] 2 All ER 266, EAT (employer's notice of appeal which had been faxed on the final day of the time limit was deemed to be in time). The entire document, not merely the first part, must be delivered or transmitted before the deadline: *Woodward v Abbey National plc, JP Garrett Electrical Ltd v Cotton* [2005] 4 All ER 1346, [2005] ICR 1702, [2005] IRLR 782, EAT which disapproves *Clark v Midland Packaging Ltd* [2005] 2 All ER 266, EAT. An extension of time will not be granted to an appellant who lodges the notice of appeal within the time limit but who does not serve the additional required documents until after the time limit had expired: *Kanapathiar v London Borough of Harrow* [2003] IRLR 571, EAT. As to extension of time see PARA 1500.

5   As to proceedings before an employment tribunal see PARA 1453 et seq. If the appellant has made an application to the employment tribunal for a reconsideration of its judgment or decision, a copy of that application must accompany the notice of appeal together with the judgment and written reasons of the employment tribunal in respect of that reconsideration application, or a statement, if such be the case, that a judgment is awaited: *Practice Direction*

(Employment Appeal Tribunal—Procedure) 2013 [2014] IRLR 92 para 3.2. If any of these documents cannot be included, a written explanation must be given: para 3.3. The appellant must also attach (where they are relevant to the appeal) copies of any orders including case management orders made by the employment tribunal: para 3.3.

6   As to making a claim see PARA 1461 et seq.

7   As to making a response to a claim see PARA 1462. There is nothing in authorities or statute to prevent an Appeal Tribunal from considering an appeal by a respondent who had not made a response to a claim: *Atos Origin IT Services UK Ltd v Haddock* [2005] ICR 277, [2005] IRLR 20, EAT (employers not precluded from appealing against the decision of an employment tribunal in which they had not appeared). However, if the appellant in a case did not present a response to the employment tribunal and did not apply to the employment tribunal for an extension of time for doing so, or applied for such an extension and was refused, the notice of appeal must include particulars directed to the following issues, namely whether: (1) there is a good excuse for failing to present a response and (if that be the case) for failing to apply for such an extension of time; and (2) there is a reasonably arguable defence to the claim: *Practice Direction (Employment Appeal Tribunal—Procedure) 2013* [2014] IRLR 92 para 19.1. In order to satisfy the EAT on these issues, the appellant must present at the EAT, together with the notice of appeal, a witness statement explaining in detail the circumstances in which there has been a failure to serve a response in time or apply for such an extension of time, the reason for that failure and the facts and matters relied upon for contesting the claim on the merits. There must be exhibited to the witness statement all relevant documents and a completed draft response: para 19.2. As to an unsuccessful attempt to satisfy head (1) above see *Primmer v Koyunco* [2008] All ER (D) 57 (Oct), EAT.

8   Employment Appeal Tribunal Rules 1993, SI 1993/2854, r 3(1)(b) (substituted by SI 2004/2526); *Practice Direction (Employment Appeal Tribunal—Procedure) 2013* [2014] IRLR 92 para 3.1.

9   As to written judgments and reasons see PARA 1476.

10 Employment Appeal Tribunal Rules 1993, SI 1993/2854, r 3(1)(c) (substituted by SI 2004/2526); *Practice Direction (Employment Appeal Tribunal—Procedure) 2013* [2014] IRLR 92 para 3.1. Where written reasons of the employment tribunal are not attached to the notice of appeal, either (as set out in the written explanation) because a request for written reasons has been refused by the employment tribunal or for some other reason, an appellant must, when presenting the notice of appeal, apply in writing to the EAT to exercise its discretion to hear the appeal without written reasons or to exercise its power to request written reasons from the employment tribunal, setting out the full grounds of that application: *Practice Direction (Employment Appeal Tribunal—Procedure) 2013* [2014] IRLR 92 para 3.4.

11 Employment Appeal Tribunal Rules 1993, SI 1993/2854, r 3(1)(e) (added by SI 2004/2526). See also note 10.

12 Ie an appeal made pursuant to the Transnational Information and Consultation of Employees Regulations 1999, SI 1999/3323, reg 38(8) (see PARA 1280) or the European Public Limited-Liability Company Regulations 2004, SI 2004/2326, reg 47(6) (revoked; see now the European Public Limited-Liability Company (Employee Involvement) (Great Britain) Regulations 2009, SI 2009/2401, reg 34(6); and PARA 1335) and the Information and Consultation of Employees Regulations 2004, SI 2004/3426, reg 35(6) (see PARA 1314) or the Companies (Cross-Border) Regulations 2007, SI 2007/2974, reg 57(6) (see COMPANIES vol 15 (2009) PARA 1451). As to the Central Arbitration Committee see PARA 1226 et seq.

13 Employment Appeal Tribunal Rules 1993, SI 1993/2854, r 3(1)(d) (substituted by SI 2001/1128; amended by SI 2004/2526; SI 2004/3426; SI 2007/2974; Interpretation Act 1978 s 17(2).

14 For these purposes, 'certification officer' means the person appointed to be the certification officer under the Trade Union and Labour Relations (Consolidation) Act 1992 s 254(2) (see PARA 1443): Employment Appeal Tribunal Rules 1993, SI 1993/2854, r 2(1) (substituted by SI 2001/1128).

15 Employment Appeal Tribunal Rules 1993, SI 1993/2854, r 3(1)(f) (added by SI 2004/2526).

16 As to the meaning of 'national security proceedings' see PARA 1451 note 1.

17 Employment Appeal Tribunal Rules 1993, SI 1993/2854, r 3(2) (r 3(2) substituted by SI 2004/2526). As to the claimant see PARA 1461.

18 Employment Appeal Tribunal Rules 1993, SI 1993/2854, r 3(2)(i) (as substituted: see note 17).

19 Employment Appeal Tribunal Rules 1993, SI 1993/2854, r 3(2)(ii) (as substituted: see note 17). As to the withholding of written reasons in national security proceedings see PARA 1476.

20 As to the meaning of 'edited reasons' see PARA 1476 note 31.

21 Employment Appeal Tribunal Rules 1993, SI 1993/2854, r 3(2)(ii) (as substituted: see note 17).

22 The time within which an appeal must be instituted depends on whether the appeal is against a judgment (see head (i) in the text) or against an order (see head (ii) in the text), direction or

decision of the employment tribunal: *Practice Direction (Employment Appeal Tribunal—Procedure) 2013* [2014] IRLR 92 para 5.1. Guidance as to the calculation of time limits is given in the Practice Direction: see PARA 1435 note 21. The guidance is consistent with the developed case law which holds that the time for appealing runs from the date on which the document recording the decision or order of the employment tribunal was sent to the parties (albeit that that date is itself excluded from the computation), not from when it was reached or deemed to have been received in accordance with Interpretation Act 1978 s 7 (see STATUTES AND LEGISLATIVE PROCESS vol 96 (2012) PARA 1219): *Hammersmith and Fulham London Borough Council v Ladejobi* [1999] ICR 673, EAT; *Mock v IRC* [1999] IRLR 785, EAT (disapproving on this point *Immigration Advisory Service v Oommen* [1997] ICR 683, EAT; *Derrybaa Ltd v Castro-Blanco* [1986] ICR 546, sub nom *Derrybaa Ltd (t/a Le Mange Tout) v Castro-Blanco* [1986] IRLR 495, EAT); *Sian v Abbey National plc* [2004] ICR 55, [2004] IRLR 185, EAT. *Immigration Advisory Service v Oommen* [1997] ICR 683, EAT was followed in *Scotford v Smithkline Beecham* [2002] ICR 264, EAT, but was disapproved in *Chelminski v Gdynia America Shipping Lines (London) Ltd* [2004] EWCA Civ 871, [2004] 3 All ER 666, [2004] IRLR 725, which also disapproved *Scotford v Smithkline Beecham* [2002] ICR 264, EAT and reasserted the stronger line of authority by approving *Hammersmith and Fulham London Borough Council v Ladejobi* [1999] ICR 673, EAT and *Sian v Abbey National plc* [2004] ICR 55, [2004] IRLR 185, EAT. If a substitute judgment is made, even if only to effect a minor amendment, time runs from date of promulgation of the new judgment: see *Aziz-Mir v Sainsbury's Supermarket plc* [2007] All ER (D) 07 (Jan), EAT. As to other authority for the principle that extension of time should only be granted in rare and exceptional cases where an applicant had provided full, honest and acceptable explanation and excuse for the delay and where it was more than an administrative delay see *United Arab Emirates v Abdelghafar* [1995] ICR 65, [1995] IRLR 243, EAT; *Aziz v Bethnal Green City Challenge Co Ltd* [2000] IRLR 111, CA; *Jurkowska v Hlmad Ltd* [2008] EWCA Civ 231, [2008] ICR 841, [2008] IRLR 430; and *Slingsby v Griffith Smith Solicitors* [2009] All ER (D) 150 (Feb), EAT; and PARA 1500.

The time limit referred to in *Practice Direction (Employment Appeal Tribunal—Procedure) 2013* [2014] IRLR 92 paras 5.1–5.3 applies even though the question of remedy and assessment of compensation by the employment tribunal has been adjourned or has not been dealt with and even though an application has been made to the employment tribunal for a reconsideration: para 5.4. It is not usually a good reason for late presentation of a notice of appeal that (1) an application for litigation support from public funds has been made, but not yet determined or that support is being sought from, but has not yet been provided by, some other body, such as a trade union, employers' association or the Equality and Human Rights Commission; (2) that the appellant was waiting for the result of an application for reconsideration; (3) that negotiations between the parties were occurring: para 5.8. In any case of doubt or difficulty, a notice of appeal should be lodged in time, and an application made to the registrar for directions: para 5.9. Late appeals were not allowed in *Duke v Prospect Training Services Ltd* [1988] ICR 521, [1989] IRLR 196, EAT (one day late because of pressure of work on solicitors), not following dictum of Sir Samuel Cooke in *De Mars v Gurr Johns & Angier Bird Ltd* [1973] ICR 35 at 38, NIRC; *Martin v British Railways Board* [1989] ICR 24, [1989] IRLR 198, EAT (five days late because of delays in obtaining legal aid).

The powers of the Appeal Tribunal under the Employment Appeal Tribunal Rules 1993, SI 1993/2854, r 39(2) (see PARA 1435) extend to authorising the institution of an appeal notwithstanding that the period prescribed in r 3(3) may not have commenced: r 39(3). Although the Queen's printer's copy of the Employment Appeal Tribunal Rules 1993, SI 1993/2854, cites 'the period prescribed in rule 3(2)' it is submitted that a reference to r 3(3) is intended.

23 Employment Appeal Tribunal Rules 1993, SI 1993/2854, r 3(3)(a) (substituted by SI 2004/2526).

24 See PARA 1476. As to the meaning of 'writing' see PARA 1430 note 1.

25 Employment Appeal Tribunal Rules 1993, SI 1993/2854, r 3(3)(a)(i) (substituted by SI 2004/2526); *Practice Direction (Employment Appeal Tribunal—Procedure) 2013* [2014] IRLR 92 para 5.3. Time will not be extended where a request to the tribunal for written reasons is made out of time (whether or not such request is granted). The date of the written record of the judgment and of the written reasons for the judgment is the date when they are sent to the parties, which is normally recorded on or in the written record and the written reasons: para 5.3. See *Tasneem v Dudley Group of Hospitals NHS Trust* [2010] All ER (D) 112 (May), EAT (challenge to accuracy of sent date recorded on judgment)

27 Employment Appeal Tribunal Rules 1993, SI 1993/2854, r 3(3)(a)(ii) (substituted by SI 2004/2526).

28 Employment Appeal Tribunal Rules 1993, SI 1993/2854, r 3(3)(a)(iii) (substituted by SI 2004/2526); and see note 26.

29 Employment Appeal Tribunal Rules 1993, SI 1993/2854, r 3(3)(b) (substituted by SI 2004/2526); *Practice Direction (Employment Appeal Tribunal—Procedure) 2013* [2014] IRLR 92 para 5.2. The EAT will treat a tribunal's refusal to make an order or decision as itself constituting an order, direction or decision. The date of an order, direction or decision is the date when the order, direction or decision was sent to the parties, which is normally recorded on or in the order, direction or decision: para 5.2.

30 Employment Appeal Tribunal Rules 1993, SI 1993/2854, r 3(3)(c) (substituted by SI 2001/1128).

31 See note 12.

32 Employment Appeal Tribunal Rules 1993, SI 1993/2854, r 3(3)(d) (substituted by SI 2001/1128; amended by SI 2004/2526; SI 2004/3426; SI 2007/2974); Interpretation Act 1978 s 17(2).

33 See PARA 1451.

34 Employment Appeal Tribunal Rules 1993, SI 1993/2854, r 36 (amended by SI 2004/2526); and see *Practice Direction (Employment Appeal Tribunal—Procedure) 2013* [2014] IRLR 92 para 26.1. In all cases the parties should, and when so directed must, consider conciliation of their appeals. The registrar or a judge may at any stage make such a direction and require the parties to report on steps taken, but not the substance, to effect a conciliated settlement with the assistance of an ACAS officer notified by ACAS to the EAT: para 26.2. As to ACAS see PARA 1213 et seq; and as to the use of the abbreviation 'EAT' see PARA 1435 note 2.

1496. Fees in the Employment Appeal Tribunal. A fee of £400 is payable by an appellant[1] on the date specified in a notice issued by the Lord Chancellor[2], following the receipt by the Employment Appeal Tribunal[3] of a notice of appeal[4]. A fee is payable in respect of each separate decision appealed against. If in one judgment a tribunal[5] decides a number of separate heads of claim, or decides both issues of liability and of compensation, that will be treated as one decision for the purposes of fee payment. If separate heads of claim are decided on separate occasions, and separate judgments given, or if there are separate judgments or orders as to case management, or on preliminary issues, liability and compensation, they will be treated as separate decisions and a fee will be payable in respect of each in the event of an appeal[6].

The Appeal Tribunal ('EAT') does not handle fee payments; the fee must be paid to the appropriate office[7]. Provision is made for the remission of fees in prescribed circumstances[8].

The Registrar must strike out an appeal, and must notify each party that the appeal has been struck out: (1) where, upon receipt of a notice of appeal, or following a direction by the Appeal Tribunal that a matter proceed to an oral hearing, the Lord Chancellor has issued a notice to an appellant specifying that a fee is payable, and where the appellant has not paid the fee or presented a remission application on or before the date specified in that notice; or (2) after consideration of a remission application, the Lord Chancellor has issued a notice to an appellant specifying that a fee is payable, and where the appellant has not paid the fee on or before the date specified in that notice[9].

If an appeal is struck out for non-payment of the fee or failure to apply for remission, it is open to the intending appellant to seek reinstatement, provided the application is made promptly[10].

If an appeal is successful, the appellant has a right to ask the Appeal Tribunal to order that an amount no greater than the fees paid for bringing the appeal (and any fees paid for bringing the claim before the body or person against whose decision the appeal is made) should be paid by the losing party[11]. It should not, however, be assumed that a losing party will be ordered to pay an amount equal to the fees paid, or indeed any amount at all. A judge has a wide discretion and may wish to consider how far the appeal has succeeded and on how many grounds[12].

A fee of £1,200 is payable by an appellant on the date specified in a notice issued by the Lord Chancellor, following a direction by the Appeal Tribunal that a matter proceed to an oral hearing at which the appeal is to be finally disposed of[13]. Once a decision is made to permit an appeal to go forward to a full hearing, that further fee will become payable, or a further application for remission of fees must be made. Until it is paid, or remission granted, the appeal will not be listed for hearing, and non-payment of fees may result in the appeal being struck out[14].

If there is a cross-appeal, the cross-appellant must pay any fee which is due in respect of the cross-appeal or apply for remission[15].

The 2013 Order introducing fees for claims made to employment tribunals has been the subject of an unsuccessful application for judicial review[16].

1 'Appellant' means a person who appeals to the Employment Appeal tribunal against a decision of an employment tribunal: Employment Tribunals and the Employment Appeal Tribunal Fees Order 2013, SI 2013/1893, r 2.

2 As to the Lord Chancellor see CONSTITUTIONAL AND ADMINISTRATIVE LAW vol 20 (2014) PARA 255 et seq.

3 As to the Employment Appeal Tribunal see PARA 1422 et seq.

4 Employment Tribunals and the Employment Appeal Tribunal Fees Order 2013, SI 2013/1893, r 13. 'Notice of appeal' means the notice referred to in the Employment Appeal Tribunal Rules 1993, SI 1993/2854, r 3(1)(a) (see PARA 1495): Employment Tribunals and the Employment Appeal Tribunal Fees Order 2013, SI 2013/1893, r 2. No fee is, however, payable in respect of proceedings in the Appeal Tribunal where a notice of appeal was received by that tribunal before 29 July 2013: rr 1, 16.
  The Employment Tribunals and Employment Appeal Tribunal Fees Order 2013, SI 2013/1893, governs the payment of fees, and the Appeal Tribunal's own Practice Direction must be read as subject to that Order: *Practice Direction (Employment Appeal Tribunal—Procedure) 2013* [2014] IRLR 92 para 4.1. Unless an appellant is entitled to the remission of fees (see the text and note 9), a fee is payable on presentation of an appeal, (the appellant will be issued with a notice to pay) and a further fee if the appeal is allowed to proceed to a full hearing (see para 12; and the text and notes 14–15): para 4.2.

5 Ie an employment tribunal. As to employment tribunals see PARA 1399 et seq.

6 *Practice Direction (Employment Appeal Tribunal—Procedure) 2013* [2014] IRLR 92 para 4.3.

7 *Practice Direction (Employment Appeal Tribunal—Procedure) 2013* [2014] IRLR 92 para 4.4. In England and Wales the fee must be paid to Employment Appeal Tribunal (EAT) Fees, PO Box 10218, Leicester, LE1 8EG; in no circumstances may it be paid to the EAT: para 4.4. As to the use of the abbreviation 'EAT' see PARA 1435 note 2.

8 See the Employment Tribunals and the Employment Appeal Tribunal Fees Order 2013, SI 2013/1893, Sch 3; and PARAS 1458–1459.

9 Employment Appeal Tribunal Rules 1993, SI 1993/2854, r 17A (added by SI 2013/1693). If an appeal is struck out for failure to pay a fee by the date required by any relevant notice to pay it will not be open to the appellant to argue that the fee was tendered to the Appeal Tribunal itself within the time permitted: *Practice Direction (Employment Appeal Tribunal—Procedure) 2013* [2014] IRLR 92 para 4.4.

10 *Practice Direction (Employment Appeal Tribunal—Procedure) 2013* [2014] IRLR 92 para 4.5. Under the Employment Appeal Tribunal Rules 1993, SI 1993/2854, the appeal may be reinstated by the Registrar if the appellant applies to have the appeal reinstated and if the fee specified in the Lord Chancellor's notice has been paid (or a remission application has been presented and accepted, as the case may be): see r 17A (as added: see note 9). Any such application will be treated as an interim application under rr 19, 20 (see PARA 1511) and be considered by the registrar: see r 17A (as so added); and *Practice Direction (Employment Appeal Tribunal—Procedure) 2013* [2014] IRLR 92 para 4.5. The grant of relief is entirely discretionary, and applicants have no right to demand it. They are unlikely to succeed unless there is clear evidence that the fee has been paid beforehand, or that an application for remission has been made, together in either case with a good explanation why the fee was not paid within the time prescribed: para 4.5.

11 *Practice Direction (Employment Appeal Tribunal—Procedure) 2013* [2014] IRLR 92 para 4.6.

12 *Practice Direction (Employment Appeal Tribunal—Procedure) 2013* [2014] IRLR 92 para 4.6.1. In spite of this, the early EAT cases that have touched upon this provision suggest that, all things being equal, reimbursement of fees to the successful appellant should be the usual expectation: see e g *Portnykh v Nomura International plc* [2014] IRLR 251, EAT; and *Horizon Security Services Ltd v Nideze* [2014] All ER (D) 72 (Aug), EAT.

13 Employment Tribunals and the Employment Appeal Tribunal Fees Order 2013, SI 2013/1893, r 14. See also note 4.

14 *Practice Direction (Employment Appeal Tribunal—Procedure) 2013* [2014] IRLR 92 para 12.1. The appeal may be struck out in the same way as set out in paras 4.3–4.5 (see the text and notes 5–10): see para 12.1.

15 See *Practice Direction (Employment Appeal Tribunal—Procedure) 2013* [2014] IRLR 92 para 12.2.

16 *R (on the application of Unison) v Lord Chancellor (Equality and Human Rights Commission intervening)* [2014] EWHC 218 (Admin), [2014] ICR 498, [2014] IRLR 266 (cited in PARA 1457).

1497. Complaints about the conduct of the employment tribunal hearing. An appellant[1] who intends to complain about the conduct of the employment tribunal[2] (for example, bias, apparent bias or improper conduct by the employment judge[3] or lay members[4] or any procedural irregularity at the hearing) must include in the notice of appeal[5] full particulars of each complaint made[6].

An appeal which is wholly or in part based on such a complaint will be sifted[7] by a judge[8] or the registrar[9]. The judge or registrar may postpone a decision on the sift, and direct that the appellant or a representative provide an affidavit or statement setting out full particulars of all allegations of bias or misconduct relied upon, and/or may inquire of the party making the complaint whether it is intended to proceed with it[10].

If a decision is taken at the sift to proceed further with the appeal, the Employment Appeal Tribunal ('EAT')[11] may take the following steps prior to any hearing within a time-limit set out in the relevant order[12]:

(1) require the appellant or a representative to provide, if not already provided, an affidavit as set out[13] above[14];

(2) require any party to give an affidavit or to obtain a witness statement from any person who has represented any of the parties at the tribunal hearing, and any other person present at the tribunal hearing or a relevant part of it, giving their account of the events set out in the affidavit of the appellant or the appellant's representative[15];

(3) seek comments, upon all affidavits or witness statements received, from the employment judge of the employment tribunal from which the appeal is brought and may seek such comments from any lay members of the tribunal[16];

(4) on receipt supply to the parties copies of all affidavits, statements and comments received[17].

A respondent[18] who intends to make such a complaint must include the particulars set out[19] above[20]. A similar procedure will then be followed as in heads (1) to (4) above[21].

In every case which is permitted to go forward to a full hearing the Appeal Tribunal must give appropriate directions, ordinarily on the papers after notice to the appellant and respondent, as to the procedure to be adopted at, and material to be provided to, the full hearing; such directions may be given at any stage, but particularly at the sift stage or at a preliminary hearing[22].

The Appeal Tribunal will not permit complaints of the kind mentioned above to be raised or developed at the hearing of the appeal unless this procedure has been followed[23]. Unsuccessful pursuit of an allegation of bias or improper conduct, particularly in respect of case management decisions, may put the party raising it at risk of an order for costs against him[24].

1   As to making an appeal see PARA 1495.
2   As to proceedings before an employment tribunal see PARA 1453 et seq.
3   As to the meaning of 'employment judge' see PARA 1401 note 3.
4   As to membership of tribunals see PARA 1402.
5   As to the notice of appeal see PARA 1495.
6   *Practice Direction (Employment Appeal Tribunal—Procedure) 2013* [2014] IRLR 92 para 13.1. The Employment Appeal Tribunal recognises that employment judges and employment tribunals are themselves obliged to observe the overriding objective (see PARA 1421) and are given wide powers and duties of case management (see PARA 1466), so appeals in respect of their conduct of employment tribunals, which is in exercise of those powers and duties, are the less likely to succeed: para 13.6.2. See eg *Ezsias v Glamorgan NHS Trust* [2007] EWCA Civ 330, [2007] 4 All ER 940, [2007] ICR 1126 (apparent bias of chairman (now employment judge) at pre-trial hearing).
7   Ie as set out in *Practice Direction (Employment Appeal Tribunal—Procedure) 2013* [2014] IRLR 92 para 11.1: see PARA 1501.
8   As to the meaning of 'judge' for these purposes see PARA 1451 note 4.
9   *Practice Direction (Employment Appeal Tribunal—Procedure) 2013* [2014] IRLR 92 para 13.2. As to the meaning of 'registrar' see PARA 1430 note 4.
10   *Practice Direction (Employment Appeal Tribunal—Procedure) 2013* [2014] IRLR 92 para 13.2. The judge or registrar may also draw attention to para 13.6 (see note 6): para 13.2.
11   As to the Employment Appeal Tribunal see PARA 1422 et seq. As to the use of the abbreviation 'EAT' see PARA 1435 note 2.
12   *Practice Direction (Employment Appeal Tribunal—Procedure) 2013* [2014] IRLR 92 para 13.3.
13   Ie in *Practice Direction (Employment Appeal Tribunal—Procedure) 2013* [2014] IRLR 92 para 13.2: see the text and note 9.
14   *Practice Direction (Employment Appeal Tribunal—Procedure) 2013* [2014] IRLR 92 para 13.3.1.
15   *Practice Direction (Employment Appeal Tribunal—Procedure) 2013* [2014] IRLR 92 para 13.3.2. For this purpose, the EAT will provide copies of any affidavits received from or on behalf of the appellant to any other person from whom an account is sought: para 11.3.2. As to the appropriate procedure for the Employment Appeal Tribunal to follow on conflicts of facts, the resolution of which is material to the decision as to bias, see *Facey v Midas Retail Security* [2001] ICR 287, EAT, approved in *Stansbury v Datapulse plc* [2003] EWCA Civ 1951, [2004] ICR 523, [2004] IRLR 466. See also *Aziz-Mir v Sainsbury's Supermarkets plc* [2008] All ER (D) 102 (Dec), EAT.
16   *Practice Direction (Employment Appeal Tribunal—Procedure) 2013* [2014] IRLR 92 para 13.3.3. For this purpose, copies of all relevant documents will be provided by the EAT to the employment judge and, if appropriate, the lay members; such documents will include any affidavits and witness statements received, the notice of appeal and other relevant documents: para 13.3.3. See *Jiminez v Southwark London Borough Council* [2003] EWCA Civ 502, [2003] ICR 1176, [2003] IRLR 477 (Appeal Tribunal did not obtain the comments of the chairman (now employment judge) on allegations of apparent bias; the failure to do so constituted an error of law entitling the Court of Appeal to consider the issue of bias afresh).
17   *Practice Direction (Employment Appeal Tribunal—Procedure) 2013* [2014] IRLR 92 para 13.3.4.
18   As to the meaning of 'respondent' see PARA 1498 note 4.
19   Ie in *Practice Direction (Employment Appeal Tribunal—Procedure) 2013* [2014] IRLR 92 paras 13.1, 13.2: see the text and notes 1–10.
20   *Practice Direction (Employment Appeal Tribunal—Procedure) 2013* [2014] IRLR 92 para 13.4. The particulars mentioned in the text must be included (1) in the respondent's answer; or (2) in the cross-appeal referred to in para 11.5 (see PARA 1501); or (3) where a preliminary hearing is ordered in the absence of a cross-appeal, in written submissions, as referred to in para 11.9 (see PARA 1519): para 13.4.1–13.4.3.
21   *Practice Direction (Employment Appeal Tribunal—Procedure) 2013* [2014] IRLR 92 para 13.4.
22   *Practice Direction (Employment Appeal Tribunal—Procedure) 2013* [2014] IRLR 92 para 13.5.

23 *Practice Direction (Employment Appeal Tribunal—Procedure) 2013* [2014] IRLR 92 para 13.6.1.
24 *Practice Direction (Employment Appeal Tribunal—Procedure) 2013* [2014] IRLR 92 para 13.6.2.

1498. Service of notice of appeal. On receipt of notice of appeal[1], the registrar[2] must seal the notice with the Appeal Tribunal's[3] seal and must serve a sealed copy on the appellant and on:

(1) every person who is a respondent[4] to the appeal[5]; and

(2) the Secretary of Employment Tribunals[6] in the case of an appeal from an employment tribunal[7]; or

(3) the certification officer in the case of an appeal from any of his decisions[8]; or

(4) the Secretary of State[9] in the case of specified appeals[10] to which he is not a respondent[11];

(5) the chairman of the Central Arbitration Committee (the 'CAC') in the case of an appeal[12] from the CAC[13].

However, in an appeal from the employment tribunal in relation to national security proceedings[14] where the appellant was the respondent, on receipt of a document[15] setting out the grounds of appeal:

(a) the registrar must not send the document to a person in respect of whom a Minister of the Crown has informed the registrar that he wishes to address the Appeal Tribunal[16] with a view to the Appeal Tribunal making an order applicable to this stage of the proceedings excluding a party or his representative (an 'excluded person')[17], at any time before the Appeal Tribunal decides whether or not to make such an order[18]; but if it decides not to make such an order, the registrar must, subject to head (b) below, send the document to such a person 14 days after the Appeal Tribunal's decision not to make the order[19]; and

(b) the registrar must not send a copy of the document to an excluded person, but if a special advocate[20] is appointed in respect of such a person, the registrar must send a copy of the document to the special advocate[21].

In an appeal from the employment tribunal in relation to national security proceedings where the appellant was the claimant[22], on receipt of a document setting out the grounds on which the appeal is brought[23] or a document which might also provide supplementary grounds of appeal[24], the registrar must not send a copy of the document to an excluded person, but must send a copy of the document to the respondent[25].

1 Ie under the Employment Appeal Tribunal Rules 1993, SI 1993/2854, r 3: see PARA 1495.
2 As to the meaning of 'registrar' see PARA 1430 note 4.
3 As to the meaning of 'Appeal Tribunal' see PARA 1451 note 4.
4 For these purposes, the respondents to an appeal are: (1) in the case of an appeal from an employment tribunal or of an appeal made pursuant to the Trade Union and Labour Relations (Consolidation) Act 1992 s 45D (see PARAS 938, 942), s 56A (see PARA 972), s 95 (see PARA 997), s 104 (see PARA 1011) or s 108C (see PARA 918) from the decision of the certification officer, the parties (other than the appellant) to the proceedings before the employment tribunal or the certification officer; (2) in the case of an appeal made pursuant to s 9 (see PARA 901 et seq) or s 126 (see PARAS 1084, 1085) from the decision of the certification officer, that officer; (3) in the case of an appeal made pursuant to the Transnational Information and Consultation of Employees Regulations 1999, SI 1999/3323, reg 38(8) (see PARA 1280) or the European Public Limited-Liability Company Regulations 2004, SI 2004/2326, reg 47(6) (revoked: see now the European Public Limited-Liability Company (Employee Involvement) (Great Britain) Regulations 2009, SI 2009/2401, reg 34(6); and PARA 1335) or the Information and

Consultation of Employees Regulations 2004, SI 2004/3426, reg 35(6) (see PARA 1314) or the Companies (Cross-Border) Regulations 2007, SI 2007/2974, reg 57(6) (see COMPANIES vol 15 (2009) PARA 1451) from a declaration or order of the Central Arbitration Committee (the 'CAC'), the parties (other than the appellant) to the proceedings before the CAC: Employment Appeal Tribunal Rules 1993, SI 1993/2854, r 5(a)–(c) (amended by the Employment Rights (Dispute Resolution) Act 1998 s 1(2)(c); and by SI 2001/1128; SI 2004/2526; SI 2004/3426; SI 2007/2974); Interpretation Act 1978 s 17(2). As to the meaning of 'certification officer' see PARA 1495 note 14. As to the CAC see PARA 1226 et seq.

5 Employment Appeal Tribunal Rules 1993, SI 1993/2854, r 4(1)(a) (r 4(1) renumbered by SI 2001/1128).

6 As to the meaning of 'the Secretary of Employment Tribunals' see PARA 1430 note 5.

7 Employment Appeal Tribunal Rules 1993, SI 1993/2854, r 4(1)(b) (renumbered (see note 5); amended by the Employment Rights (Dispute Resolution) Act 1998 s 1(2)(a), (b)). As to proceedings before an employment tribunal see PARA 1453 et seq.

8 Employment Appeal Tribunal Rules 1993, SI 1993/2854, r 4(1)(c) (renumbered: see note 5).

9 As to the Secretary of State see PARA 5 note 21.

10 Ie in the case of an appeal under the Employment Rights Act 1996 Pt XI (ss 135–181) (see PARA 835 et seq) or the Trade Union and Labour Relations (Consolidation) Act 1992 Pt IV Ch II (ss 188–198B) (see PARA 1185 et seq) to which he is not a respondent.

11 Employment Appeal Tribunal Rules 1993, SI 1993/2854, r 4(1)(d) (renumbered (see note 5); amended by SI 2001/1128).

12 Ie under the provisions mentioned in note 4 head (3).

13 Employment Appeal Tribunal Rules 1993, SI 1993/2854, r 4(1)(e) (renumbered (see note 5); amended by SI 2001/1128; SI 2004/2526; SI 2004/3426; SI 2007/2974); Interpretation Act 1978 s 17(2).

14 As to the meaning of 'national security proceedings' see PARA 1451 note 1.

15 Ie provided under the Employment Appeal Tribunal Rules 1993, SI 1993/2854, r 3(5): see PARA 1451. As to the meaning of 'document' for these purposes see PARA 1451 note 5.

16 Ie in accordance with the Employment Appeal Tribunal Rules 1993, SI 1993/2854, r 30A(3): see PARA 1452.

17 Ie under the Employment Appeal Tribunal Rules 1993, SI 1993/2854, r 30A(2)(a) read with r 30A(1)(b) or (c): see PARA 1452. As to the meaning of 'excluded person' see PARA 1452 note 11.

18 Employment Appeal Tribunal Rules 1993, SI 1993/2854, r 4(2)(a) (r 4(2), (3) added by SI 2001/1128).

19 Employment Appeal Tribunal Rules 1993, SI 1993/2854, r 4(2)(a) (as added: see note 18).

20 As to the meaning of 'special advocate' see PARA 1451 note 9.

21 Employment Appeal Tribunal Rules 1993, SI 1993/2854, r 4(2)(b) (added by SI 2001/1128).

22 As to the claimant see PARA 1461.

23 Ie provided under the Employment Appeal Tribunal Rules 1993, SI 1993/2854, r 3(6)(a): see PARA 1451.

24 Ie provided under the Employment Appeal Tribunal Rules 1993, SI 1993/2854, r 3(6)(b): see PARA 1451.

25 Employment Appeal Tribunal Rules 1993, SI 1993/2854, r 4(3) (as added: see note 18).

1499. Respondent's answer and notice of cross-appeal. As soon as practicable, the registrar[1] must notify every respondent[2] of the date appointed by the Appeal Tribunal[3] by which any answer[4] must be delivered[5].

A respondent who wishes to resist an appeal must[6] deliver to the Appeal Tribunal an answer in writing in, or substantially in accordance with, the prescribed form[7] setting out the grounds on which he relies[8].

A respondent who wishes to cross-appeal may[9] do so by including in his answer a statement of the grounds of his cross-appeal; and in that event an appellant who wishes to resist the cross-appeal must, within a time to be appointed by the Appeal Tribunal, deliver to the Appeal Tribunal a reply in writing setting out the grounds on which he relies[10].

The registrar must serve a copy of every answer and reply to a cross-appeal on every party other than the party by whom it was delivered[11].

Where the respondent does not wish to resist an appeal, the parties may deliver to the Appeal Tribunal an agreed draft of an order allowing the appeal and the Appeal Tribunal may, if it thinks it right to do so, make an order allowing the appeal in the terms agreed[12].

However, in an appeal from the employment tribunal in relation to national security proceedings[13], the respondent must not set out the grounds on which he relies in his answer to an appeal, nor include in his answer a statement of the grounds of any cross-appeal[14].

In such an appeal in relation to which the respondent was not the claimant[15] in the proceedings before the employment tribunal, the respondent must, within the time appointed[16], provide to the registrar a document, setting out the grounds on which he intends to resist the appeal, and may include in that document a statement of the grounds of any cross-appeal[17].

In such an appeal in relation to which the respondent was the claimant in the proceedings before the employment tribunal[18]:

(1)   the respondent may, within the time appointed[19], provide to the registrar a document, setting out the grounds on which he intends to resist the appeal, and may include in that document a statement of the grounds of any cross-appeal[20]; and

(2)   a special advocate[21] appointed in respect of the respondent may, within the time appointed[22], or within 21 days of his appointment, whichever is the later, provide to the registrar a document, setting out the grounds, or the supplementary grounds, on which the respondent intends to resist the appeal, and may include in that document a statement of the grounds, or the supplementary grounds, of any cross-appeal[23].

In such an appeal, if the respondent, or any special advocate appointed in respect of a respondent, provides in the document containing grounds for resisting an appeal a statement of grounds of cross-appeal and the appellant wishes to resist the cross-appeal[24]:

(a)   where the appellant was not the claimant in the proceedings before the employment tribunal, the appellant must within a time to be appointed by the Appeal Tribunal deliver to the tribunal a reply in writing setting out the grounds on which he relies[25]; and

(b)   where the appellant was the claimant in the proceedings before the employment tribunal, the appellant, or any special advocate appointed in respect of him, may within a time to be appointed by the Appeal Tribunal deliver to the tribunal a reply in writing setting out the grounds on which the appellant relies[26].

Where it appears to a judge or the registrar that a statement of grounds of cross-appeal[27]:

(i)   discloses no reasonable grounds for bringing the cross-appeal[28]; or

(ii)   is an abuse of the Appeal Tribunal's process or is otherwise likely to obstruct the just disposal of proceedings[29],

he must notify the respondent or special advocate accordingly informing him of the reasons for his opinion and no further action must be taken[30] on the statement of grounds of cross-appeal[31]. Where a judge or the registrar has taken such a decision, and also considers that the statement of grounds of cross-appeal contained in the respondent's answer or document provided[32] is totally without merit, the judge or registrar may order that the respondent is not entitled to have the matter heard before a judge[33], with such order to be included as part of the notice issued[34] under the above provision[35]. Subject to that, where such notification has been given and within 28 days of the date the notification was sent, a respondent or special advocate expresses dissatisfaction in writing with the reasons given by the judge or registrar for his opinion, he is entitled to have the matter heard before a judge who must make a direction as to whether any further action should be taken on the statement of grounds of cross-appeal[36].

1 As to the meaning of 'registrar' see PARA 1430 note 4.

2 As to respondents to an appeal see PARA 1498 note 4.

3 As to the meaning of 'Appeal Tribunal' see PARA 1451 note 4.

4 Ie any answer under the Employment Appeal Tribunal Rules 1993, SI 1993/2854, r 6.

5 Employment Appeal Tribunal Rules 1993, SI 1993/2854, r 6(1). If a respondent to any proceedings fails to deliver an answer or, in the case of an application made under the Trade Union and Labour Relations (Consolidation) Act 1992 s 67 (see PARA 1032) or s 176 (see PARA 1028), the Employment Tribunals Act 1996 s 33 (see PARA 1430), the Transnational Information and Consultation of Employees Regulations 1999, SI 1999/3323, reg 20, reg 21 or reg 21A (see PARAS 1269–1271), the European Public Limited-Liability Company Regulations 2004, SI 2004/2326, reg 33 (revoked: see now the European Public Limited-Liability Company (Employee Involvement) (Great Britain) Regulations 2009, SI 2009/2401, reg 20; and PARA 1328) or the Information and Consultation of Employees Regulations 2004, SI 2004/3426, reg 22 (see PARA 1307) or the Companies (Cross-Border Mergers) Regulations 2007, SI 2007/2974, reg 53 (see COMPANIES vol 15 (2009) PARA 1451), a notice of appearance within the time appointed, or if any party fails to comply with an order or direction of the Appeal Tribunal, the Appeal Tribunal may order that he be debarred from taking any further part in the proceedings, or may make such other order as it thinks just: Employment Appeal Tribunal Rules 1993, SI 1993/2854, r 26(1) (numbered as such by SI 2013/1693; amended by SI 2001/1128; SI 2004/2526; SI 2004/3426; SI 2007/2974; SI 2010/1088); Interpretation Act 1978 s 17(2). An order made by the Appeal Tribunal under the Employment Appeal Tribunal Rules 1993, SI 1993/2854, r 26(1) may include, but is not limited to, an order that all or part of an appeal or answer is to be struck out: r 26(2) (r 26(2), (3) added by SI 2013/1693). An appeal or answer, or part of an appeal or answer, may not be struck out unless the party in question has been given a reasonable opportunity to make representations, either in writing, or if requested by the party, at a hearing: Employment Appeal Tribunal Rules 1993, SI 1993/2854, r 26(3) (as so added). As to the meaning of 'writing' see PARA 1430 note 1.

6 Ie within the time appointed by the Employment Appeal Tribunal Rules 1993, SI 1993/2854, r 6(1) (see the text and notes 1–5) and subject to r 6(6) (see the text and notes 13–14).

7 For the prescribed form of the respondent's answer see the Employment Appeal Tribunal Rules 1993, SI 1993/2854, r 6(2), Schedule, Form 3 (amended by SI 2005/1871).

8 Employment Appeal Tribunal Rules 1993, SI 1993/2854, r 6(2) (amended by SI 2001/1128). It is, however, sufficient for a respondent to an appeal referred to in the Employment Appeal Tribunal Rules 1993, SI 1993/2854, r 5(a) (see PARA 1498 note 4 head (1)) or r 5(c) (see PARA 1498 note 4 head (3)) who wishes to rely on any ground which is the same as a ground relied on by the employment tribunal, the certification officer or the Central Arbitration Committee (the 'CAC') for making the judgment, decision, declaration or order appealed from to state that fact in his answer: r 6(2) (amended by the Employment Rights (Dispute Resolution) Act 1998 s 1(2)(a); and by SI 2001/1128; SI 2004/2526). As to proceedings before an employment tribunal see PARA 1453 et seq. As to the meaning of 'certification officer' see PARA 1495 note 14; as to the meanings of 'judgment' and 'order' in relation to an employment tribunal see PARA 1460 note 4. As to the CAC see PARA 1226 et seq.

Once a fee has been paid, the EAT will send the notice of appeal, with any amendments which have been permitted, and any submissions or skeleton argument lodged by the appellant, to all parties who are respondents to the appeal. Within 14 days of the seal date of the order (unless otherwise directed), respondents must present to the EAT and serve on the other parties a respondent's answer. If it contains a cross-appeal, the cross-appellant must within 14 days of service (unless otherwise directed), pay any fee which is due in respect of the cross-appeal (or apply for remission). The appellant must present and serve a reply. The answer must show how the respondent would wish the EAT to deal with the appeal if the appellant succeeds (see *Practice Direction (Employment Appeal Tribunal—Procedure) 2013* [2014] IRLR 92 para 3.5): para 12.2. A respondent to the appeal who wishes to resist the appeal and/or to cross-appeal, but who has not delivered a respondent's answer as directed by the registrar, or otherwise ordered, may be barred from taking part in the appeal unless permission is granted to serve an answer out of time: para 12.3. Any reference in the Practice Direction to the date of an order means the date stamped upon the relevant order by the EAT ('the seal date'): para 1.10. As to being debarred see note 5; and as to extending time limits see PARA 1500.

A party cannot reserve a right to amend, alter or add, to a respondent's answer: see para 3.10, cited in PARA 1495 note 3.

If a respondent intends to contend at the full hearing that the appellant has raised a point which was not argued below, the respondent must say so: (1) if a preliminary hearing has been ordered, in writing to the EAT and all parties, within 14 days of receiving the notice of appeal; (2) if the case is listed for a full hearing without a preliminary hearing, in a respondent's answer. In the event of dispute the employment judge should be asked for his/her comments as to whether a particular legal argument was deployed: *Practice Direction (Employment Appeal Tribunal—Procedure) 2013* [2014] IRLR 92 para 10.6. As to the use of the abbreviation 'EAT' see PARA 1435 note 2.

9	Ie subject to the Employment Appeal Tribunal Rules 1993, SI 1993/2854, r 6(6) (see the text and notes 13–14).

10	Employment Appeal Tribunal Rules 1993, SI 1993/2854, r 6(3) (amended by SI 2001/1128).

11	Employment Appeal Tribunal Rules 1993, SI 1993/2854, r 6(4). After presentation and service of the respondent's answer and of any reply to a cross-appeal, the registrar may, where necessary, invite applications from the parties in writing, on notice to all other parties, for directions, and may give any appropriate directions on the papers or may fix a day when the parties should attend on an appointment for directions: *Practice Direction (Employment Appeal Tribunal—Procedure) 2013* [2014] IRLR 92 para 12.4. A judge may at any time, upon consideration of the papers or at a hearing, make an order requiring or recommending consideration by the parties or any of them of compromise, conciliation, mediation or, in particular, reference to ACAS: para 12.5. Because a cross-appeal can only arise out of the same order that is being appealed, if a respondent to an appeal wants to appeal a different order from that being appealed (even one relating to the same subject matter and involving the same parties) that will be an independent appeal and the time for appealing will run from the date of the original order: *Asda Stores Ltd v Thompson (No 2)* [2004] IRLR 598, EAT.

12	Employment Appeal Tribunal Rules 1993, SI 1993/2854, r 6(5). As to disposal of an appeal by consent see PARA 1503.

13	As to the meaning of 'national security proceedings' see PARA 1451 note 1.

14	Employment Appeal Tribunal Rules 1993, SI 1993/2854, r 6(6) (r 6(6)–(11) added by SI 2001/1128; amended by SI 2004/2526).

15	As to the claimant see PARA 1461.

16	Ie within the time appointed under the Employment Appeal Tribunal Rules 1993, SI 1993/2854, r 6(1): see the text and notes 1–5.

17	Employment Appeal Tribunal Rules 1993, SI 1993/2854, r 6(7) (as added and amended: see note 14). Any document provided under the Employment Appeal Tribunal Rules 1993, SI 1993/2854, r 6(7) or r 6(9)(a) (see head (a) in the text) must be treated by the registrar in accordance with r 4(2) (see PARA 1498), as though it were a document received under r 3(5) (see PARA 1451): r 6(10) (as so added). As to the meaning of 'document' see PARA 1451 note 5.

18	Employment Appeal Tribunal Rules 1993, SI 1993/2854, r 6(8) (as added and amended: see note 14).

19	See note 16.

20	Employment Appeal Tribunal Rules 1993, SI 1993/2854, r 6(8)(a) (as added: see note 4). Any document provided under r 6(8) or r 6(9)(b) (see head (b) in the text) must be treated by the registrar in accordance with r 4(3) (see PARA 1498), as though it were a document received under r 3(6)(a) or (b) (see PARA 1451): r 6(11) (as so added).

21	As to the special advocate see PARA 1450.

22	See note 16.

23	Employment Appeal Tribunal Rules 1993, SI 1993/2854, r 6(8)(b) (as added: see note 14).

24	Employment Appeal Tribunal Rules 1993, SI 1993/2854, r 6(9) (as added and amended: see note 14).

25	Employment Appeal Tribunal Rules 1993, SI 1993/2854, r 6(9)(a) (as added and amended: see note 14).

26	Employment Appeal Tribunal Rules 1993, SI 1993/2854, r 6(9)(b) (as added and amended: see note 14).

27	Ie contained in either the respondent's answer or the document provided under the Employment Appeal Tribunal Rules 1993, SI 1993/2854, r 6(7) (see the text and notes 15–17) or r 6(8) (see heads (1)–(2) in the text). For the purposes of r 6(12), (12A), (16) (see the text and notes 28–36), reference to a statement of grounds of cross-appeal includes reference to part of a statement of grounds of cross-appeal: r 6(13) (r 6(12), (13), (16) added by SI 2004/2526; the Employment Appeal Tribunal Rules 1993, SI 1993/2854, r 6(13) amended by SI 2013/1693).

28 Employment Appeal Tribunal Rules 1993, SI 1993/2854, r 6(12)(a) (as added: see note 27).

29 Employment Appeal Tribunal Rules 1993, SI 1993/2854, r 6(12)(b) (as added: see note 27).

30 Ie subject to the Employment Appeal Tribunal Rules 1993, SI 1993/2854, r 6(16): see the text and note 36.

31 Employment Appeal Tribunal Rules 1993, SI 1993/2854, r 6(12) (as added (see note 27); amended by SI 2013/1693).

32 See note 27.

33 Ie under the Employment Appeal Tribunal Rules 1993, SI 1993/2854, r 6(16): see the text and notes 36.

34 Ie under the Employment Appeal Tribunal Rules 1993, SI 1993/2854, r 6(12): see the text and notes 27–31.

35 Employment Appeal Tribunal Rules 1993, SI 1993/2854, r 6(12A) (added by SI 2013/1693).

36 Employment Appeal Tribunal Rules 1993, SI 1993/2854, r 6(16) (as added (see note 27); amended by SI 2013/1693).

1500. Time limits in the Employment Appeal Tribunal. The time prescribed[1] for doing any act[2] may be extended, whether it has already expired or not, or abridged, and the date appointed for any purpose may be altered, by order of the Appeal Tribunal[3]. Where the last day for the doing of any act falls on a day on which the appropriate office of the Appeal Tribunal is closed and, by reason of that, the act cannot be done on that day, it may be done on the next day on which that office is open[4]. An application for an extension of the time prescribed for the doing of an act, including the institution of an appeal[5], must be heard and determined[6] as an interim application[7].

1 Ie by the Employment Appeal Tribunal Rules 1993, SI 1993/2854 (see PARAS 1495 et seq, 1501 et seq) or by order of the Appeal Tribunal. As to the meaning of 'Appeal Tribunal' see PARA 1451 note 4.

2 Where an act is required to be done on or before a particular day it must be done by 4 pm on that day: Employment Appeal Tribunal Rules 1993, SI 1993/2854, r 37(1A) (added by SI 2004/2526).

3 Employment Appeal Tribunal Rules 1993, SI 1993/2854, r 37(1). The extension of time is a matter of judicial discretion to be exercised in a principled manner in accordance with reason and justice: *Peters v Sat Katar Co Ltd (in liquidation)* [2003] EWCA Civ 943, [2003] ICR 1574, [2003] IRLR 574 (employee, who had been acting in person, had been entitled to assume that her notice of appeal had been received). See also *Abedeji v Revenue & Customs Commissioners* [2008] All ER (D) 21 (Dec), EAT (the basic principles for exercising the discretion clearly set out; but it was also said that the time limits were not some tedious bureaucratic constraint but rather constituted a vital weapon against the danger of slippage in the consideration of cases and thus it should not become the norm for them to be ignored); *O'Cathail v Transport for London* [2012] EWCA Civ 1004, [2012] IRLR 1011, [2013] ICR D2 (Appeal Tribunal's general approach to applications to extend the generous time limit allowed for appealing from the employment tribunal is well settled on a principled basis and the Appeal Tribunal must be even-handed: it must consider judicially the conflicting positions of both parties and the public interest in good judicial administration, not just the plight and pleas of an applicant seeking an indulgence from the Appeal Tribunal: Appeal Tribunal had not erred in refusing to extend the time to appeal by one day, despite the applicant's disability).

4 Employment Appeal Tribunal Rules 1993, SI 1993/2854, r 37(2). The central office and any other office of the Appeal Tribunal must be open at such times as the President may direct (r 38(1)); and any proceedings before the Appeal Tribunal may be dealt with at the central office or at such other office as the President may direct (r 38(2)).

5 Ie under the Employment Appeal Tribunal Rules 1993, SI 1993/2854, r 3: see PARAS 1451, 1495. An application for an extension of the time prescribed for the institution of an appeal under r 3 must not be heard until the notice of appeal has been served on the Appeal Tribunal: r 37(4) (added by SI 2001/1128); and see *Practice Direction (Employment Appeal Tribunal—Procedure) 2013* [2014] IRLR 92 para 5.5. Any application for an extension of time for appealing must be made as an interim application to the registrar, who will normally determine the application after inviting and considering written representations from each side. An interim appeal lies from the registrar's decision to a judge. Such an appeal must be notified to the EAT within five working days of the date when the registrar's decision was sent to the

parties: this means that where, for example, the registrar's decision is sent to the parties on a Wednesday, any appeal against it must be received no later than 4pm on the following Wednesday: para 5.6. See further PARA 1511.

In determining whether to extend the time for appealing, particular attention will be paid to whether any good excuse for the delay has been shown and to the guidance contained in the decisions of the Employment Appeal Tribunal and the Court of Appeal, as summarised in cases such as *United Arab Emirates v Abdelghafar* [1995] ICR 65, [1995] IRLR 243, EAT; *Aziz v Bethnal Green City Challenge Co Ltd* [2000] IRLR 111, CA; and *Jurkowska v Hlmad Ltd* [2008] EWCA Civ 231, [2008] ICR 841, [2008] IRLR 430: *Practice Direction (Employment Appeal Tribunal—Procedure) 2013* [2014] IRLR 92 para 5.7. See also *Slingsby v Griffith Smith Solicitors* [2009] All ER (D) 150 (Feb), EAT where *United Arab Emirates v Abdelghafar* [1995] ICR 65, [1995] IRLR 243, EAT and *Jurkowska v Hlmad Ltd* [2008] EWCA Civ 231, [2008] ICR 841, [2008] IRLR 430 were applied. As to late service see also PARA 1495 note 22.

6   Ie under the Employment Appeal Tribunal Rules 1993, SI 1993/2854, r 20: see PARA 1511.
7   Employment Appeal Tribunal Rules 1993, SI 1993/2854, r 37(3) (amended by SI 2004/2526). See also note 5.

1501.   Case management in the Employment Appeal Tribunal. Consistent with the overriding objective[1], the Employment Appeal Tribunal[2] will seek to give directions for case management so that the case can be dealt with quickly, or better considered, and in the most effective and just way[3].

Applications and directions for case management will usually be dealt with on the papers (at the 'sift' stage) by a judge[4], or by the registrar[5] with an appeal to a judge[6]. Any party seeking directions must serve a copy on all parties[7]. Directions may be given at any stage, before or after the registration of a notice of appeal[8]. An order made will contain a time for compliance, which must be observed or be the subject of an application by any party to vary or discharge it, or to seek an extension of time[9]. Otherwise, failure to comply with an order in time or at all may result in the Appeal Tribunal exercising its power[10] to strike out the appeal, cross-appeal or respondent's answer[11] or debar the party from taking any further part in the proceedings or to make any other order it thinks fit, including an award of costs[12].

Any application to vary or discharge an order, or to seek an extension of time, must be lodged at the Appeal Tribunal and served on the other parties within the time fixed for compliance[13]. Such other parties must, if opposing the application and within 14 days (or such shorter period as may be ordered) of receiving it, submit their representations to the Appeal Tribunal and the other parties[14].

An application to amend a notice of appeal[15] or respondent's answer[16] must include the text of the original document with any changes clearly marked and identifiable[17].

Once a notice of appeal has been received, properly instituted, and any applicable fee has been paid or remission has been granted within time, it will be sifted by a judge or the registrar who will consider the notice of appeal and, if appropriate, obtain any additional information so as to determine:

(1)   whether it discloses any reasonable ground for bringing an appeal[18];

(2)   if so, whether the whole or only part of the grounds of appeal should be argued before a full hearing[19];

(3)   if not, whether the appeal is wholly without merit, in which case there is no right for the appellant to an oral hearing before a judge at the Appeal Tribunal, though this does not remove any right to appeal to the Court of Appeal[20].

The Appeal Tribunal will deal with applications in order, and parties must not expect their appeal to take precedence over any other unless there are truly exceptional circumstances[21].

If the notice of appeal does or might disclose a reasonable ground or grounds, the judge deciding the sift will determine the most effective case management of the appeal. This will be to allocate the relevant ground(s) of appeal for further consideration at a preliminary hearing[22], or for determination at a full hearing, and in either case to give appropriate directions[23]. The judge or registrar may also stay the appeal for a period, normally 21 days, pending the making or the conclusion of an application by the appellant to the employment tribunal for a reconsideration[24] (if necessary out of time) or pending the response by the employment tribunal to an invitation from the judge or registrar to clarify, supplement or give its written reasons[25]. Reasons must be sent and within 28 days the appellant may request an oral hearing (known as a 'Rule 3(10) hearing') before a judge unless the judge determining the sift has ruled that the appeal is wholly without merit[26].

1   As to the overriding objective see PARA 1435.
2   As to the Employment Appeal Tribunal see PARA 1422 et seq.
3   *Practice Direction (Employment Appeal Tribunal—Procedure) 2013* [2014] IRLR 92 para 14.1.
4   As to the meaning of 'judge' for these purposes see PARA 1451 note 4.
5   As to the meaning of 'registrar' see PARA 1430 note 4.
6   *Practice Direction (Employment Appeal Tribunal—Procedure) 2013* [2014] IRLR 92 para 14.2.
7   *Practice Direction (Employment Appeal Tribunal—Procedure) 2013* [2014] IRLR 92 para 14.3.
8   *Practice Direction (Employment Appeal Tribunal—Procedure) 2013* [2014] IRLR 92 para 14.4.
     As to the notice of appeal see PARA 1467, 1495–1498.
9   *Practice Direction (Employment Appeal Tribunal—Procedure) 2013* [2014] IRLR 92 para 14.4.
     As to extensions of time see PARA 1500.
10   Ie under the Employment Appeal Tribunal Rules 1993, SI 1993/2854, r 26: see PARA 1499 note 5.
11   As to the respondent's answer and notice of cross-appeal see PARA 1499. As to the meaning of 'respondent' see PARA 1498 note 4.
12   *Practice Direction (Employment Appeal Tribunal—Procedure) 2013* [2014] IRLR 92 para 14.4. The power to strike out an appeal, cross-appeal or answer to an appeal will not be exercised without the party subject to it being sent notification that the power may be exercised: but a notice stating that 'unless ... (a particular step is taken by a certain time) ... the appeal (or a specified part of it) will be struck out' is sufficient notification for this purpose, and if the step is not taken before the time specified has elapsed the consequential strike-out will occur automatically: para 14.4.
13   *Practice Direction (Employment Appeal Tribunal—Procedure) 2013* [2014] IRLR 92 para 14.5.
14   See note 13.
15   As to amendment see PARA 1495 note 3.
16   See PARA 1499 note 8.
17   *Practice Direction (Employment Appeal Tribunal—Procedure) 2013* [2014] IRLR 92 para 14.6. To make changes identifiable, for example, deletions might be struck through in red and the text of the amendment either written or underlined in red; and any subsequent amendments will be marked in a different identifiable colour. Where provided from a computer print-out, the deleted wording should be struck through, and new wording put in italics. Where re-amendment is made, the new wording must be in bold italics or a distinctive and easily readable font: para 14.6.
18   An appeal will not be treated as showing any reasonable ground for bringing the appeal in so far as it is an abuse of the process or otherwise likely to obstruct the just disposal of the matters in issue between the parties: *Practice Direction (Employment Appeal Tribunal—Procedure) 2013* [2014] IRLR 92 para 11.4.
19   As to the full hearing see PARA 1520.
20   *Practice Direction (Employment Appeal Tribunal—Procedure) 2013* [2014] IRLR 92 para 11.1. As to appeals to the Court of Appeal see PARA 1530.
21   *Practice Direction (Employment Appeal Tribunal—Procedure) 2013* [2014] IRLR 92 para 11.1.1.
22   As to preliminary hearings see PARA 1519.
23   *Practice Direction (Employment Appeal Tribunal—Procedure) 2013* [2014] IRLR 92 para 11.2.
24   As to applications for reconsideration see PARA 1479.
25   *Practice Direction (Employment Appeal Tribunal—Procedure) 2013* [2014] IRLR 92 para 11.3.

26 *Practice Direction (Employment Appeal Tribunal—Procedure) 2013* [2014] IRLR 92 para 11.5.
At a Rule 3(10) hearing, the judge may confirm the earlier decision or order that the appeal
proceeds in whole or in part to a preliminary hearing or full hearing, giving appropriate
directions: para 11.6. These directions may permit an amendment to be made to the grounds of
appeal, but any such proposed amendment should wherever practicable be made available in
writing at the hearing or on the same day, and will not take effect unless the judge has approved
it: para 11.6. A hearing under Rule 3(10), including judgment and any directions, will normally
last not more than one hour including time for oral judgment to be given: para 11.7.

1502.   Disposal of appeal.   As soon as practicable, the registrar[1] must give
notice of the arrangements made by the Appeal Tribunal[2] for hearing the appeal
to:

(1)   every party to the proceedings[3]; and

(2)   the Secretary of Employment Tribunals[4] in the case of an appeal from
an employment tribunal[5]; or

(3)   the certification officer[6] in the case of an appeal from one of his
decisions[7]; or

(4)   the Secretary of State[8] in the case of a specified appeal[9] to which he is
not a respondent[10]; or

(5)   the chairman of the Central Arbitration Committee (the 'CAC')[11] in the
case of an appeal[12] from a declaration or order of, or arising in any
proceedings before, the CAC[13].

Any such notice must state the date appointed by the Appeal Tribunal by
which any interim application must be made[14].

1   As to the meaning of 'registrar' see PARA 1430 note 4.
2   As to the listing of appeals see PARA 1509. As to the meaning of 'Appeal Tribunal' see PARA
1451 note 4.
3   Employment Appeal Tribunal Rules 1993, SI 1993/2854, r 7(1)(a).
4   As to the meaning of 'Secretary of Employment Tribunals' see PARA 1430 note 5.
5   Employment Appeal Tribunal Rules 1993, SI 1993/2854, r 7(1)(b) (amended by the
Employment Rights (Dispute Resolution) Act 1998 s 1(2)(a), (b)).
6   As to the meaning of 'certification officer' see PARA 1495 note 14.
7   Employment Appeal Tribunal Rules 1993, SI 1993/2854, r 7(1)(c).
8   As to the Secretary of State see PARA 5 note 21.
9   Ie in the case of an appeal under the Employment Rights Act 1996 Pt XI (ss 135–181) (see PARA
835 et seq) or the Trade Union and Labour Relations (Consolidation) Act 1992 Pt IV Ch II
(ss 188–198B) (see PARA 1185 et seq) to which he is not a respondent. As to the meaning of
'respondent' see PARA 1498 note 4.
10 Employment Appeal Tribunal Rules 1993, SI 1993/2854, r 7(1)(d) (amended by SI 2001/1128).
11 As to the CAC see PARA 1226 et seq.
12 Ie under the Transnational Information and Consultation of Employees Regulations 1999,
SI 1999/3323, reg 38(8) (see PARA 1280) or the European Public Limited-Liability Company
Regulations 2004, SI 2004/2326, reg 47(6) (revoked; see now the European Public
Limited-Liability Company (Employee Involvement) (Great Britain) Regulations 2009,
SI 2009/2401, reg 34(6); and PARA 1335) or the Information and Consultation of Employees
Regulations 2004, SI 2004/3426, reg 35(6) (see PARA 1314) or the Companies (Cross-Border)
Regulations 2007, SI 2007/2974, reg 57(6) (see COMPANIES vol 15 (2009) PARA 1451).
13 Employment Appeal Tribunal Rules 1993, SI 1993/2854, r 7(1)(e) (amended by SI 2001/1128;
SI 2004/2526; SI 2004/3426; SI 2007/2974); Interpretation Act 1978 s 17(2).
14 Employment Appeal Tribunal Rules 1993, SI 1993/2854, r 7(2) (amended by SI 2004/2526). As
to applications regarding interim matters see PARA 1511.

1503.   Disposal of appeals by consent.   An appellant who wishes to abandon
or withdraw an appeal[1] must notify the other parties and the Employment
Appeal Tribunal[2] immediately[3].

If a settlement is reached, the parties must inform the Appeal Tribunal as soon
as possible. The appellant must submit to the Appeal Tribunal a letter signed by

or on behalf of the appellant and signed also by or on behalf of the respondent[4], asking the Appeal Tribunal for permission to withdraw the appeal and to make a consent order in the form of an attached draft signed by or for both parties dismissing the appeal, together with any other agreed order sought[5].

If the other parties do not agree to the proposed order, the Appeal Tribunal must be informed. Written submissions must be lodged at the Appeal Tribunal and served on the parties. Any outstanding issue may be determined on the papers by the Appeal Tribunal, particularly if it relates to costs, but the Appeal Tribunal may fix an oral hearing to determine the outstanding matters in dispute between the parties[6].

If the parties reach an agreement that the appeal should be allowed by consent, and that an order made by the employment tribunal should be reversed or varied or the matter remitted to the employment tribunal on the ground that the decision contains an error of law, it is usually necessary for the matter to be heard by the Appeal Tribunal to determine whether there is a good reason for making the proposed order. On notification by the parties, the Appeal Tribunal will decide whether the appeal can be dealt with on the papers or by a hearing at which one or more parties or their representatives should attend to argue the case for allowing the appeal and making the order that the parties wish the Appeal Tribunal to make[7].

If the application for permission to withdraw an appeal is made close to the hearing date, the Appeal Tribunal may require the attendance of the appellant and/or a representative to explain the reasons for delay in making a decision not to pursue the appeal[8].

The terms of a settlement agreement are enforceable as a contract which the Appeal Tribunal has no power to set aside[9].

1 As to making an appeal see PARA 1495.
2 As to the Employment Appeal Tribunal see PARA 1422 et seq. As to the use of the abbreviation 'EAT' in the Employment Appeal Tribunal's own Practice Direction see PARA 1435 note 2.
3 *Practice Direction (Employment Appeal Tribunal—Procedure) 2013* [2014] IRLR 92 para 18.1.
4 As to the meaning of 'the respondent' see PARA 1498 note 4.
5 *Practice Direction (Employment Appeal Tribunal—Procedure) 2013* [2014] IRLR 92 para 18.1. Paragraph 18 formalises the procedure outlined in *J Sainsbury plc v Moger* [1994] ICR 800, EAT (the Appeal Tribunal will not reverse a decision of a tribunal on a point of law merely because the parties consent to an order to that effect). See also *Dozie v Addison Lee plc* UKEAT/0328/13 at [20].
6 *Practice Direction (Employment Appeal Tribunal—Procedure) 2013* [2014] IRLR 92 para 18.2.
7 *Practice Direction (Employment Appeal Tribunal—Procedure) 2013* [2014] IRLR 92 para 18.3.
8 *Practice Direction (Employment Appeal Tribunal—Procedure) 2013* [2014] IRLR 92 para 18.5. Note that the expected reference to para 18.4 in the *Practice Direction* appears to have been omitted.
9 *Eden v Humphries and Glasgow Ltd* [1981] ICR 183, EAT.

1504. Service of documents. Any notice or other document[1] required or authorised[2] to be served on, or delivered to, any person may be sent to him by post to his address for service or, where no address for service has been given, to his registered office, principal place of business, head or main office or last known address, as the case may be; and any notice or other document required or authorised to be served on, or delivered to, the Appeal Tribunal[3] may be sent by post or delivered to the registrar[4]:

(1) in the case of a notice instituting proceedings, at the central office or any other offices of the tribunal[5]; or

(2) in any other case, at the office of the Appeal Tribunal in which the proceedings in question are[6] being dealt with[7].

Any notice or other document required or authorised to be served on, or delivered to, an unincorporated body may be sent to its secretary, manager or other similar officer[8].

Every document served by post is assumed, in the absence of evidence to the contrary, to have been delivered in the normal course of post[9].

The Appeal Tribunal may: (a) inform itself in such manner as it thinks fit of the posting of any document by an officer of the Appeal Tribunal[10]; and (b) direct that service of any document be dispensed with or be effected otherwise than in the prescribed[11] manner[12].

1 As to the meaning of 'document' see PARA 1451 note 5.
2 Ie by the Employment Appeal Tribunal Rules 1993, SI 1993/2854: see PARAS 1451 et seq, 1495 et seq, 1511 et seq.
3 As to the meaning of 'Appeal Tribunal' see PARA 1451 note 4.
4 Employment Appeal Tribunal Rules 1993, SI 1993/2854, r 35(1). As to the meaning of 'registrar' see PARA 1430 note 4.
5 Employment Appeal Tribunal Rules 1993, SI 1993/2854, r 35(1)(a).
6 Ie in accordance with the Employment Appeal Tribunal Rules 1993, SI 1993/2854, r 38(2): see PARA 1500 note 4.
7 Employment Appeal Tribunal Rules 1993, SI 1993/2854, r 35(1)(b).
8 Employment Appeal Tribunal Rules 1993, SI 1993/2854, r 35(2).
9 Employment Appeal Tribunal Rules 1993, SI 1993/2854, r 35(3).
10 Employment Appeal Tribunal Rules 1993, SI 1993/2854, r 35(4).
11 Ie the manner prescribed by the Employment Appeal Tribunal Rules 1993, SI 1993/2854.
12 Employment Appeal Tribunal Rules 1993, SI 1993/2854, r 35(5).

1505. The right to inspect the register and certain documents and to take copies. Any document presented in the central office of the Employment Appeal Tribunal in London[1] in any proceedings before the Employment Appeal Tribunal must be sealed with the seal of the Employment Appeal Tribunal showing the date (and time, if received after 4 pm) on which the document was presented[2].

Particulars of the date of delivery at the central office of the Employment Appeal Tribunal of any document for filing or presentation together with the time (if received after 4 pm), the date of the document and the title of the appeal of which the document forms part of the record must be entered in the register of cases kept in London or in the file which forms part of the register of cases[3].

Any person is entitled during office hours[4] by appointment to inspect and request a copy of any of the following documents filed or presented to the London office, namely[5]:

(1) any notice of appeal[6] or respondent's answer[7] or any copy of them[8];
(2) any judgment or order given or made in court or any copy of such judgment or order[9]; and
(3) with the permission of the Appeal Tribunal, which may be granted on an application, any other document[10].

A copying charge per page is payable for those documents mentioned in heads (1) to (3) above[11].

Nothing in the Tribunal's Practice Direction[12] is to be taken as preventing any party to an appeal from inspecting and requesting a copy of any document filed or presented to the office in London before the commencement of the appeal, but made with a view to its commencement[13].

1 As to the requirement for the Employment Appeal Tribunal to have a central office in London see PARA 1426.
2 *Practice Direction (Employment Appeal Tribunal—Procedure) 2013* [2014] IRLR 92 para 7.1.
3 *Practice Direction (Employment Appeal Tribunal—Procedure) 2013* [2014] IRLR 92 para 7.2.

4 As to the opening times of the central office and of any other office of the Appeal Tribunal see PARA 1500 note 4.

5 *Practice Direction (Employment Appeal Tribunal—Procedure) 2013* [2014] IRLR 92 para 7.3.
6 As to the notice of appeal see PARA 1495.
7 As to the respondent's answer see PARA 1499. As to the meaning of 'respondent' see PARA 1498 note 4.

8 *Practice Direction (Employment Appeal Tribunal—Procedure) 2013* [2014] IRLR 92 para 7.3.1.

9 *Practice Direction (Employment Appeal Tribunal—Procedure) 2013* [2014] IRLR 92 para 7.3.2.

10 *Practice Direction (Employment Appeal Tribunal—Procedure) 2013* [2014] IRLR 92 para 7.4.

11 *Practice Direction (Employment Appeal Tribunal—Procedure) 2013* [2014] IRLR 92 para 7.5.

12 Ie *Practice Direction (Employment Appeal Tribunal—Procedure) 2013* [2014] IRLR 92.

13 *Practice Direction (Employment Appeal Tribunal—Procedure) 2013* [2014] IRLR 92 para 7.6.

1506.   Papers for use at the hearing.   It is the responsibility of the parties or their advisers to prepare a core bundle of papers for use at any hearing. Ultimate responsibility lies with the appellant, following consultation with other parties. The bundle must include only those exhibits and documents used before the employment tribunal which are considered to be necessary for the appeal. It is the duty of the parties or their advisers to ensure that only those documents are included which are (1) relevant to the point(s) of law raised in the appeal; and (2) likely to be referred to at the hearing. It is also the responsibility of parties to retain copies of all documents and correspondence, including hearing bundles, sent to the Employment Appeal Tribunal[1]. Bundles used at one Appeal Tribunal hearing will not be retained by the Appeal Tribunal for a subsequent hearing[2].

The documents in the core bundle must be numbered by item, then paginated continuously and indexed, in the order set out in the Appeal Tribunal's Practice Direction[3]. Other documents necessary for and relevant to the appeal, which were referred to at the employment tribunal, may follow[4] in the core or a supplementary bundle, subject to a page limit[5].

All documents must be legible and unmarked[6].

For preliminary hearing cases[7], appeals from registrar's orders[8], rule 3(10) hearings[9], or appointments for directions[10], the appellant must prepare and present two copies (four copies if the judge has directed a sitting with lay members) of the bundle as soon as possible after service of the notice of appeal and no later than 28 days prior to the date fixed for the hearing, unless otherwise directed[11].

For full hearing cases[12] the parties must co-operate in agreeing a bundle of papers for the hearing. By no later than 28 days prior to the date fixed for the hearing, unless otherwise directed, the appellant is responsible for ensuring that two copies (four copies if the judge has directed a sitting with lay members) of a bundle agreed by the parties is presented to the Appeal Tribunal[12]. For fast track full hearing cases the bundles must be presented as soon as possible and (unless the hearing date is within seven days) in any event within seven days after the parties have been notified that the case is expedited[13]. In the event of disagreement between the parties or difficulty in preparing the bundles, the registrar may give appropriate directions, whether on application in writing (on notice) by one or more of the parties or of his own initiative[14].

In no case other than those subject to the rule for proceedings in cases concerning national security[15] will the Appeal Tribunal accept documents or communications on the basis that they are to be confidential to the Appeal

Tribunal and are not to be disclosed to another party. All documents presented by one party are disclosable to the other(s), and the parties must expect that to be the case[16].

The parties can expect the Appeal Tribunal normally to have read the documents (or the documents indicated in any essential reading list if permission is granted[17] for an enlarged appeal bundle) in advance of any hearing[18].

1 *Practice Direction (Employment Appeal Tribunal—Procedure) 2013* [2014] IRLR 92 para 8.1. As to the Employment Appeal Tribunal see PARA 1422 et seq. As to the use of the abbreviation 'EAT' in the Employment Appeal Tribunal's own Practice Direction see PARA 1435 note 2.
2 *Practice Direction (Employment Appeal Tribunal—Procedure) 2013* [2014] IRLR 92 para 8.1.
3 See *Practice Direction (Employment Appeal Tribunal—Procedure) 2013* [2014] IRLR 92 para 8.2. That order is as follows (paras 8.2.1–8.2.10):
   (1) judgment, decision or order appealed from and written reasons;
   (2) sealed notice of appeal;
   (3) respondent's answer, if a full hearing; respondent's submissions if a preliminary hearing;
   (4) ET1 claim (and any additional Information or written answers);
   (5) ET3 response and any additional information or written answers);
   (6) questionnaire and replies, if any (discrimination and equal pay cases);
   (7) relevant orders, judgments and written reasons of the employment tribunal;
   (8) relevant orders and judgments of the EAT;
   (9) affidavits and employment tribunal comments (where ordered);
   (10) any documents agreed or ordered (subject to para 8.3: see the text and note 4).
4 Ie if the total pages additional to the documents set out in *Practice Direction (Employment Appeal Tribunal—Procedure) 2013* [2014] IRLR 92 paras 8.2–8.2.9 (see note 3 heads (1)–(9)) do not exceed 50.
5 See *Practice Direction (Employment Appeal Tribunal—Procedure) 2013* [2014] IRLR 92 para 8.3. No bundle containing more than 50 such additional pages should be agreed or lodged without the permission of the registrar or order of a judge which will not be granted without the provision of an essential reading list as soon as practicable thereafter. If permitted or ordered, further pages should follow, with consecutive pagination, in an additional bundle or bundles if appropriate: para 8.3.
6 *Practice Direction (Employment Appeal Tribunal—Procedure) 2013* [2014] IRLR 92 para 8.4.
7 As to preliminary hearings see PARA 1519.
8 See PARA 1511 note 12.
9 Ie hearings under the Employment Appeal Tribunal Rules 1993, SI 1993/2854, r 3(10) (certain oral hearings in national security proceedings): see PARA 1451.
10 See PARA 1512.
11 *Practice Direction (Employment Appeal Tribunal—Procedure) 2013* [2014] IRLR 92 para 8.5.
12 *Practice Direction (Employment Appeal Tribunal—Procedure) 2013* [2014] IRLR 92 para 8.6.
13 *Practice Direction (Employment Appeal Tribunal—Procedure) 2013* [2014] IRLR 92 para 8.7.
14 *Practice Direction (Employment Appeal Tribunal—Procedure) 2013* [2014] IRLR 92 para 8.8.
15 Ie cases subject to the Employment Appeal Tribunal Rules 1993, SI 1993/2854, r 30A: see PARA 1452.
16 *Practice Direction (Employment Appeal Tribunal—Procedure) 2013* [2014] IRLR 92 para 8.9.
17 Ie under *Practice Direction (Employment Appeal Tribunal—Procedure) 2013* [2014] IRLR 92 para 8.3: see the text and note 5.
18 *Practice Direction (Employment Appeal Tribunal—Procedure) 2013* [2014] IRLR 92 para 1.11.

1507. Skeleton arguments. Skeleton arguments must be provided by all parties in all hearings, unless either the Employment Appeal Tribunal[1] is notified by a party or representative in writing that the notice of appeal[2] or respondent's answer[3] or relevant application contains the full argument or it otherwise directs in a particular case. It is the practice of the Appeal Tribunal for all the members to read the papers in advance. A well-structured skeleton argument helps the members and the parties to focus on the point (or points) of law required to be decided and so makes the oral hearing more effective[4].

The skeleton argument should be concise and should identify and summarise the point (or points) of law, the steps in the legal argument and the statutory provisions and authorities to be relied on, identifying them by name, page and paragraph and stating the legal proposition sought to be derived from them[5]. It is not, however, the purpose of the skeleton argument to argue the case on paper in detail[6].

The skeleton argument should state the form of order[7] which the party will ask the Appeal Tribunal to make at the hearing[8].

The appellant's skeleton argument must, unless dispensed with by a direction of the registrar[9] or a judge[10], be accompanied by a chronology of events relevant to the appeal which, if possible, should be agreed by the parties. That will normally be taken as an uncontroversial document, unless corrected by another party or the Appeal Tribunal[11].

Unless impracticable, the skeleton argument should be prepared using the pagination in the index to the appeal bundle. In a case where a note of the evidence at the employment tribunal has been produced, the skeleton argument should identify the parts of the record to which that party wishes to refer[12].

Represented parties should give the instructions necessary for their representative to comply with this procedure within the time limits[13].

The fact that conciliation or settlement negotiations are in progress in relation to the appeal does not excuse delay in lodging and exchanging skeleton arguments[14].

A skeleton argument may be lodged by the appellant with the notice of appeal or by the respondent with the respondent's answer[15]. Skeleton arguments must, if not already so lodged:

(1) be lodged at the Appeal Tribunal not less than ten days (unless otherwise ordered) before the date fixed for the preliminary hearing[16], appeal against the registrar's order[17], rule 3(10) hearing[18] or appointment for directions[19]; or if the hearing is fixed at less than seven days' notice, as soon as possible after the hearing date has been notified, and unless otherwise directed by provided to the other party or parties[20];

(2) be lodged at the Appeal Tribunal, and exchanged between the parties, not less than 14 days before the full hearing[21];

(3) in the cases either fast-tracked or in the warned list[22], be lodged at the Appeal Tribunal and exchanged between the parties as soon as possible, and, unless the hearing date is less than seven days later, in any event within seven days after the parties have been notified that the case is expedited or in the warned list[23].

Failure to follow this procedure may lead to a postponement of an appeal or to dismissal for non-compliance with the Appeal Tribunal's Practice Direction[24], and to an award of costs. The party in default may also be required to attend before the Appeal Tribunal to explain his failure[25].

1   As to the Employment Appeal Tribunal see PARA 1422 et seq. As to the use of the abbreviation 'EAT' see PARA 1435 note 2.

2   As to the notice of appeal see PARA 1495.

3   As to the respondent's answer see PARA 1499. As to the meaning of 'respondent' see PARA 1498 note 4.

4   *Practice Direction (Employment Appeal Tribunal—Procedure) 2013* [2014] IRLR 92 para 16.2.

5   *Practice Direction (Employment Appeal Tribunal—Procedure) 2013* [2014] IRLR 92 para 16.3. The parties should be referred to by name or as they appeared at the employment tribunal, ie claimant (C) and respondent (R): para 16.4. As to proceedings before an employment tribunal see PARA 1453 et seq; and as to the claimant and as to the meaning of 'respondent' before such a tribunal see PARA 1460 note 8.

6 *Practice Direction (Employment Appeal Tribunal—Procedure) 2013* [2014] IRLR 92 para 16.3. A skeleton argument where possible should be in print, rather than hand-written, using A4 paper, 12 point typescript, arranged in consecutively numbered paragraphs each separated from the other by a double space, and in a standard readable font: para 16.3.

7 For example, in the case of an appellant, whether the EAT will be asked to remit the whole or part of the case to the same employment tribunal or to a different employment tribunal or whether the EAT will be asked to substitute a different decision for that of the employment tribunal: *Practice Direction (Employment Appeal Tribunal—Procedure) 2013* [2014] IRLR 92 para 16.5.

8 *Practice Direction (Employment Appeal Tribunal—Procedure) 2013* [2014] IRLR 92 para 16.5.

9 As to the meaning of 'the registrar' see PARA 1430 note 4.

10 As to the meaning of 'judge' see PARA 1451 note 4.

11 *Practice Direction (Employment Appeal Tribunal—Procedure) 2013* [2014] IRLR 92 para 16.6. It is good practice to give references to paragraphs in the employment tribunal judgment or pages in the EAT bundle: para 16.6.

12 *Practice Direction (Employment Appeal Tribunal—Procedure) 2013* [2014] IRLR 92 para 16.7.

13 *Practice Direction (Employment Appeal Tribunal—Procedure) 2013* [2014] IRLR 92 para 16.8.

14 *Practice Direction (Employment Appeal Tribunal—Procedure) 2013* [2014] IRLR 92 para 16.9.

15 *Practice Direction (Employment Appeal Tribunal—Procedure) 2013* [2014] IRLR 92 para 16.10.

16 As to preliminary hearings see PARA 1519.

17 See PARA 1511 note 12.

18 Ie hearing under the Employment Appeal Tribunal Rules 1993, SI 1993/2854, r 3(10) (certain oral hearings in national security proceedings): see PARA 1451.

19 See PARA 1512.

20 *Practice Direction (Employment Appeal Tribunal—Procedure) 2013* [2014] IRLR 92 para 16.11.1.

21 *Practice Direction (Employment Appeal Tribunal—Procedure) 2013* [2014] IRLR 92 para 16.11.2. As to the full hearing see PARA 1520.

22 As to listing of appeals see PARA 1509.

23 *Practice Direction (Employment Appeal Tribunal—Procedure) 2013* [2014] IRLR 92 para 16.11.3.

24 Ie pursuant the Employment Appeal Tribunal Rules 1993, SI 1993/2854, r 26: see PARA 1499 note 5.

25 *Practice Direction (Employment Appeal Tribunal—Procedure) 2013* [2014] IRLR 92 para 16.12. It will always mean that the defaulting party must immediately despatch any delayed skeleton argument to the EAT by hand or by fax or by email to londoneat@hmcts.gsi.gov.uk and (unless notified by the EAT to the contrary) bring to the hearing sufficient copies (a minimum of four, or six if the judge is sitting with lay members) of the skeleton argument and any authorities referred to unless they are contained in the 'familiar authorities' bundle details of which are given on the EAT website (whose address, at the date at which this volume states the law, is to be found at: *http://www.justice.gov.uk*). The EAT staff will not be responsible for supplying or copying other authorities on the morning of the hearing: para 16.12.

1508. Citation of authorities. It is undesirable for parties to an appeal before the Employment Appeal Tribunal[1] to cite the same case from different sets of reports. The parties should, if practicable, agree which report will be used at the hearing; and where the employment tribunal[2] has cited from a report it may be convenient to cite from the same report[3]. The parties must co-operate in agreeing a list of authorities[4].

It is the responsibility of a party wishing to cite any authority to provide photocopies for the use of each member of the Appeal Tribunal and photocopies or at least a list for the other parties. All authorities should be indexed and incorporated in an agreed bundle[5].

Some familiar authorities are so frequently cited to the Appeal Tribunal that sufficient copies of those authorities for any hearing will be maintained at the Appeal Tribunal in every court. This will avoid unnecessary work for the parties, and avoid overuse of paper and copying resources. A list of such cases will be maintained on the website of the Appeal Tribunal, and any case on the list should not be photocopied. It may be relied on if necessary in argument before the Appeal Tribunal (which may refer to the maintained copy), and if so it will be sufficient for the party relying upon it to identify the principle contended for, or said to be inapplicable, by reference to the paragraph number or numbers of the report[6].

Parties should note that in the Practice Direction in respect of civil appeals in England and Wales issued by the Lord Chief Justice and Heads of Division on 23 March 2012[7] (which parties should consider applicable to appeals to the Appeal Tribunal in England and Wales, subject only to necessary adaptations) it is directed that in the cases to which it relates reference should be made to no more than ten authorities unless the scale of the appeal warrants more extensive citation. Cases should set out legal principle, rather than be merely illustrative of an application of it. Parties must be prepared to justify more extensive citation of authority[8].

If it is thought necessary to cite any authority at a preliminary hearing[9], appeal against a registrar's order[10], rule 3(10) hearing[11] or appointment for directions[12], two copies should be provided for the Appeal Tribunal (four copies if a judge is sitting with members) no less than ten days before the hearing, unless otherwise ordered, and additional copies for any other parties notified. All authorities should be bundled, indexed and incorporated in one bundle as set out above[13].

The parties are reminded that the Appeal Tribunal will expect them to identify authorities which stand in opposition to their case on the question of law raised in the appeal, just as much as those which favour it[14].

1 As to the Employment Appeal Tribunal see PARA 1422 et seq. As to the use of the abbreviation 'EAT' see PARA 1435 note 2.
2 As to proceedings before an employment tribunal see PARA 1453 et seq.
3 *Practice Direction (Employment Appeal Tribunal—Procedure) 2013* [2014] IRLR 92 para 17.1.
4 *Practice Direction (Employment Appeal Tribunal—Procedure) 2013* [2014] IRLR 92 para 17.2.
5 *Practice Direction (Employment Appeal Tribunal—Procedure) 2013* [2014] IRLR 92 para 17.3.
      For those parties who are represented, best practice is to use photo or online copies of formal reports, such as the ICR's or IRLR's rather than those available from other on-line sources. These reports have head notes and are more useful to the court than other electronic copies of the same case. The reports should be presented in a bundle, in chronological order, because that assists the court in seeing how the law has developed. Relevant passages on which a party intends to rely should be sidelined and/or highlighted clearly. If ring binders are used, they should be properly tabulated: *Practice Direction (Employment Appeal Tribunal—Procedure) 2013* [2014] IRLR 92 para 17.4.
      If a party intends to refer to any extract from Hansard in support of any argument as permitted by the decisions in *Pepper (Inspector of Taxes) v Hart* [1993] AC 593, [1993] 1 All ER 42, HL and *Pickstone v Freemans plc* [1989] AC 66, [1988] 2 All ER 803, HL (see CIVIL PROCEDURE vol 11 (2009) PARA 106), he must serve on all other parties and the Employment Appeal Tribunal copies of any such extract together with a brief summary of the argument intended to be based on it not less than five clear working days before the first day of the hearing: see *Practice Note (Procedure: Reference to Hansard)* [1995] 1 All ER 234, [1995] 1 WLR 192. Where copies of authorities are lodged for the purpose of an appeal to an appeal tribunal, parties must ensure that copies of reported cases are included in the list of authorities in the bundle: *Sage (UK) Ltd v Bacco* (2007) Times, 11 October, [2007] All ER (D) 170 (Aug), EAT.
6 *Practice Direction (Employment Appeal Tribunal—Procedure) 2013* [2014] IRLR 92 para 17.5.
7 Ie *Practice Direction (Citation of Authorities 2012)* [2012] 2 All ER 255. See further CIVIL PROCEDURE vol 11 (2009) PARA 106.
8 *Practice Direction (Employment Appeal Tribunal—Procedure) 2013* [2014] IRLR 92 para 17.6.
9 As to a preliminary hearing see PARA 1519.
10 See PARA 1511 note 12.

11 Ie hearing under the Employment Appeal Tribunal Rules 1993, SI 1993/2854, r 3(10) (certain oral hearings in national security proceedings): see PARA 1451.
12 See PARA 1512.
13 *Practice Direction (Employment Appeal Tribunal—Procedure) 2013* [2014] IRLR 92 para 17.7.
14 *Practice Direction (Employment Appeal Tribunal—Procedure) 2013* [2014] IRLR 92 para 17.8.

1509. Listing of appeals. The Employment Appeal Tribunal[1] will normally consult the parties on dates, and will accommodate reasonable requests if practicable, but is not bound to do so. Once the date is fixed, the appeal will be set down in the list. A party finding that the date which has been fixed causes serious difficulties may apply to the listing officer for it to be changed, having first notified all other parties entitled to appear on the date, of his application and the reasons for it[2]. Parties receiving such an application must, as soon as possible and within seven days, notify the listing officer of their views[3].

In addition to this fixed date procedure, a list ('the warned list') may be drawn up. Cases will be placed in such warned list at the discretion of the listing officer or may be so placed by the direction of a judge or the registrar[4]. These will ordinarily be short cases, or cases where expedition has been ordered. Parties or their representatives will be notified that their case has been included in this list, and as much notice as possible will be given of the intention to list a case for hearing, when representations by way of objection from the parties will be considered by the listing officer and if necessary on appeal to the registrar or a judge. The parties may apply on notice to all other parties for a fixed date for hearing[5].

Other cases may be put in the list by the Appeal Tribunal with the consent of the parties at shorter notice: for example, where other cases have been settled or withdrawn or where it appears that they will take less time than originally estimated. Parties who wish their cases to be taken as soon as possible and at short notice should notify the listing officer. Representations by way of objection may be made by the parties to the listing officer and if necessary by appeal to a judge or the registrar[6].

Each week an up-to-date list for the following week will be prepared, including any changes which have been made, in particular specifying cases which by then have been given fixed dates. The list appears on the Appeal Tribunal website[7].

Cases which are permitted to go forward to a full hearing have a listing category assigned at the preliminary hearing[8].

1 As to the Employment Appeal Tribunal see PARA 1422 et seq. As to the use of the abbreviation 'EAT' see PARA 1435 note 2.
2 *Practice Direction (Employment Appeal Tribunal—Procedure) 2013* [2014] IRLR 92 para 15.5.
3 *Practice Direction (Employment Appeal Tribunal—Procedure) 2013* [2014] IRLR 92 para 15.6.
4 As to the meaning of 'judge' for these purposes see PARA 1451 note 4; and as to the meaning of 'the registrar' see PARA 1430 note 4.
5 *Practice Direction (Employment Appeal Tribunal—Procedure) 2013* [2014] IRLR 92 para 15.7.
6 *Practice Direction (Employment Appeal Tribunal—Procedure) 2013* [2014] IRLR 92 para 15.8.
7 *Practice Direction (Employment Appeal Tribunal—Procedure) 2013* [2014] IRLR 92 para 15.9. The address of the Appeal Tribunal website, at the date at which this volume states the law, is to be found at: *http://www.justice.gov.uk*.
8 See PARA 1519 text and notes 31–33.

1510. Estimate of length of hearing. All parties are required to ensure that the estimates of length of hearing, allowing for the fact that the parties can expect the Employment Appeal Tribunal[1] to have pre-read the papers[2] and for deliberation and the giving of a judgment[3], are accurate when first given. This is of particular importance in any case in which it is directed that lay members should sit. The lay members of the Appeal Tribunal are part-time members[4]. They attend when available on pre-arranged dates and do not sit for continuous periods. Consequently appeals which run beyond their estimated length invariably have to be adjourned part-heard, often with substantial delay, until a day on which the judge[5] and members are all available again[6].

Any change in the estimate, or disagreement with an estimate made by the Appeal Tribunal on a sift[7] or at a preliminary hearing[8], must be notified immediately to the listing officer[9].

If the Appeal Tribunal concludes that the hearing is likely to exceed the estimate, or if for other reasons the hearing may not be concluded within the time available, it may seek to avoid such adjournment by placing the parties under appropriate time limits in order to complete the presentation of the submissions within the estimated or available time[10].

A judge may at any time during any hearing, and with a view to achieving the overriding objective[11], require submissions to take place in whatever order he considers appropriate, and within whatever time limit seems fit. It will not be a legitimate objection that different time limits are prescribed for different parties: where this happens, it will be with a view to ensuring overall fairness[12].

1   As to the Employment Appeal Tribunal see PARA 1422 et seq. As to the use of the abbreviation 'EAT' see PARA 1435 note 2.
2   See PARAS 1506–1507.
3   The estimate should include time for judgment to be considered and delivered orally on the day of hearing: *Practice Direction (Employment Appeal Tribunal—Procedure) 2013* [2014] IRLR 92 para 15.2.
4   As to membership of the Employment Appeal Tribunal see PARA 1422.
5   As to the meaning of 'judge' for these purposes see PARA 1451 note 4.
6   *Practice Direction (Employment Appeal Tribunal—Procedure) 2013* [2014] IRLR 92 para 15.1.
7   As to the sift see PARA 1501.
8   As to the preliminary hearing see PARA 1519.
9   *Practice Direction (Employment Appeal Tribunal—Procedure) 2013* [2014] IRLR 92 para 15.1.
10   *Practice Direction (Employment Appeal Tribunal—Procedure) 2013* [2014] IRLR 92 para 15.3.
11   As to the overriding objective see PARA 1435.
12   *Practice Direction (Employment Appeal Tribunal—Procedure) 2013* [2014] IRLR 92 para 15.4.

(ii) Employment Appeal Tribunal; Interim Matters

1511. Interim matters in the Appeal Tribunal. An interim application may be made to the Appeal Tribunal[1] by giving notice in writing specifying the direction or order sought[2]. On receipt of such a notice, the registrar[3] must serve a copy on every other party to the proceedings who appears to him to be concerned in the matter to which the notice relates and must notify the applicant and every such party of the arrangements made by the Appeal Tribunal for disposing of the application[4].

Every interim application made to the Appeal Tribunal must be considered in the first place by the registrar who will have regard to the overriding objective[5] and, where applicable, to the provisions[6] relating to restricted reporting orders[7].

Every interim application must be disposed of[8] by the registrar except that any matter which he thinks should properly be decided by the President[9] or a judge[10] must be referred by him to the President or a judge, who may dispose of it himself or refer it in whole or in part to the Appeal Tribunal[11] or refer it back to the registrar with such directions as he thinks fit[12].

The Appeal Tribunal may[13] sit either in private or in public for the hearing of any interim application[14].

1   As to the meaning of 'Appeal Tribunal' see PARA 1451 note 4.
2   Employment Appeal Tribunal Rules 1993, SI 1993/2854, r 19(1) (amended by SI 2004/2526).
    As to the meaning of 'writing' see PARA 1430 note 1. Parties are encouraged to make any such
    applications at a preliminary hearing (see PARA 1519) or an appointment for directions if one is
    ordered (see PARA 1512); no particular form is required: *Practice Direction (Employment
    Appeal Tribunal—Procedure) 2013* [2014] IRLR 92 para 6.1.
3   As to the meaning of 'registrar' see PARA 1430 note 4.
4   Employment Appeal Tribunal Rules 1993, SI 1993/2854, r 19(2).
5   Ie the Employment Appeal Tribunal Rules 1993, SI 1993/2854, r 2A: see PARA 1435.
6   Ie the Employment Appeal Tribunal Rules 1993, SI 1993/2854, r 23(5): see PARA 1517.
7   Employment Appeal Tribunal Rules 1993, SI 1993/2854, r 20(1) (r 20 substituted by
    SI 2004/2526); and see *Practice Direction (Employment Appeal Tribunal—Procedure) 2013*
    [2014] IRLR 92 para 6.1. Unless otherwise ordered, any application for extension of time will
    be considered and determined as though it were an interim application to the registrar, who will
    normally determine the application after inviting and considering written representations from
    each side: para 6.2.
8   Ie subject to the Employment Appeal Tribunal Rules 1993, SI 1993/2854, r 20(3), (4): see note
    12.
9   As to the meaning of 'President' see PARA 1451 note 4.
10 As to the meaning of 'judge' for these purposes see PARA 1451 note 4.
11 Ie as required to be constituted by the Employment Tribunals Act 1996 s 28: see PARA 1426.
12 Employment Appeal Tribunal Rules 1993, SI 1993/2854, r 20(2) (as substituted: see note 7);
    and see *Practice Direction (Employment Appeal Tribunal—Procedure) 2013* [2014] IRLR 92
    para 6.1. Where an application is so disposed of by the registrar, any party aggrieved by the
    registrar's decision may appeal to a judge; and in that case the judge may determine the appeal
    himself or refer it in whole or in part to the Appeal Tribunal as required to be constituted by the
    Employment Tribunals Act 1996 s 28 (see PARA 1426): Employment Appeal Tribunal
    Rules 1993, SI 1993/2854, r 21(1) (amended by SI 2001/1128). Notice of any such appeal may
    be given to the Appeal Tribunal, either orally or in writing, within five days of the decision
    appealed from; and the registrar must notify every other party who appears to him to be
    concerned in the appeal and must inform every such party and the appellant of the arrangements
    made by the Appeal Tribunal for disposing of the appeal: Employment Appeal Tribunal
    Rules 1993, SI 1993/2854, r 21(2); and see *Practice Direction (Employment Appeal
    Tribunal—Procedure) 2013* [2014] IRLR 92 para 6.3.
        Every interim application for a restricted reporting order must be disposed of by the
    President or a judge or, if he so directs, the application is to be referred to the Appeal Tribunal,
    as required to be constituted by the Employment Tribunals Act 1996 s 28, which must dispose
    of it: Employment Appeal Tribunal Rules 1993, SI 1993/2854, r 20(3) (as substituted: see note
    7). Every interim application for permission to institute or continue or to make a claim or
    application in any proceedings before an employment tribunal or the Appeal Tribunal, pursuant
    to the Employment Tribunals Act 1996 s 33(4) (see PARA 1430), must be disposed of by the
    President or a judge, or, if he so directs, the application is to be referred to the Appeal Tribunal
    as required to be constituted by s 28, which must dispose of it: Employment Appeal Tribunal
    Rules 1993, SI 1993/2854, r 20(4) (as substituted: see note 7).
13 Ie subject to any direction of a Minister of the Crown under the Employment Appeal Tribunal
    Rules 1993, SI 1993/2854, r 30A(1) (see PARA 1452) or order of the Appeal Tribunal under
    r 30A(2)(a) (see PARA 1452) read with r 30A(1) and, where applicable, r 23(6) (see PARA 1517):
    r 22(1) (amended by SI 2001/1128; SI 2004/2526).
14 Employment Appeal Tribunal Rules 1993, SI 1993/2854, r 22(1) (as amended: see note 13).

1512.   Directions by the Appeal Tribunal.   Where it appears to the Appeal
Tribunal[1] that the future conduct of any proceedings would thereby be
facilitated, the Appeal Tribunal may, either of its own motion or on application,
at any stage in the proceedings appoint a date for a meeting for directions as to
their future conduct and thereupon the following provisions apply[2].

The registrar[3] must give to every party in the proceedings notice of the date so
appointed; and any party applying for directions must, if practicable, before that
date give to the Appeal Tribunal particulars of any direction for which he asks[4].

The registrar must take such steps as may be practicable to inform every party
of any directions applied for by any other party[5].

On the date so appointed, the Appeal Tribunal must consider every application for directions made by any party and any written[6] representations relating to the application submitted to the Appeal Tribunal and must give such directions as it thinks fit for the purpose of securing the just, expeditious and economical disposal of the proceedings, including, where appropriate, directions[7] for the purpose of ensuring that the parties are enabled to avail themselves of opportunities for conciliation[8].

The Appeal Tribunal may[9] give such directions as it thinks fit as to:

(1) the amendment of any notice, answer or other document[10];
(2) the admission of any facts or documents;
(3) the admission in evidence of any documents;
(4) the mode in which evidence is to be given at the hearing;
(5) the consolidation of the proceedings with any other proceedings pending before the Appeal Tribunal;
(6) the place and date of the hearing[11].

An application for further directions or for the variation of any directions already given may[12] be made[13].

The Appeal Tribunal may either of its own motion or on application, at any stage of the proceedings, give any party directions as to any steps to be taken by him in relation to the proceedings[14].

Facilities can exceptionally be arranged for the purpose of holding short appointments for directions by video or telephone link[15].

1 As to the meaning of 'Appeal Tribunal' see PARA 1451 note 4.
2 Employment Appeal Tribunal Rules 1993, SI 1993/2854, r 24(1). As to directions for case management see PARA 1501.
3 As to the meaning of 'registrar' see PARA 1430 note 4.
4 Employment Appeal Tribunal Rules 1993, SI 1993/2854, r 24(2).
5 Employment Appeal Tribunal Rules 1993, SI 1993/2854, r 24(3).
6 As to the meaning of 'writing' see PARA 1430 note 1.
7 Ie in pursuance of the Employment Appeal Tribunal Rules 1993, SI 1993/2854, r 36: see PARA 1495.
8 Employment Appeal Tribunal Rules 1993, SI 1993/2854, r 24(4). As to conciliation see PARA 1495.
9 Ie without prejudice to the generality of the Employment Appeal Tribunal Rules 1993, SI 1993/2854, r 24(4): see the text and notes 6–8.
10 As to the meaning of 'document' see PARA 1451 note 5.
11 Employment Appeal Tribunal Rules 1993, SI 1993/2854, r 24(5).
12 Ie may be made in accordance with the Employment Appeal Tribunal Rules 1993, SI 1993/2854, r 19: see PARA 1511.
13 Employment Appeal Tribunal Rules 1993, SI 1993/2854, r 24(6).
14 Employment Appeal Tribunal Rules 1993, SI 1993/2854, r 25.
15 See PARA 1522 text and notes 18–20.

1513. Joinder of parties. On the application of any person or of its own motion, the Appeal Tribunal[1] may direct that any person not already a party to the proceedings be added as a party, or that any party to proceedings is to cease to be a party, and in either case may give such consequential directions as it considers necessary[2].

1 As to the meaning of 'Appeal Tribunal' see PARA 1451 note 4.
2 Employment Appeal Tribunal Rules 1993, SI 1993/2854, r 18.

1514. Attendance of witnesses; production of documents. The Appeal Tribunal[1] may, on the application of any party, order any person to attend before the Appeal Tribunal as a witness or to produce any document[2]. However, where a minister has at any stage issued a direction[3] to exclude a party or his representative, or the Appeal Tribunal has at any stage made such an order[4], and the Appeal Tribunal is considering whether to impose or has imposed a requirement on any person either to attend as a witness or to produce documents, the minister (whether or not he is a party to the proceedings) may make an application to the Appeal Tribunal objecting to the imposition of the requirement or, where such a requirement has been imposed, an application to vary or set aside the requirement, as the case may be[5]. The Appeal Tribunal must hear and determine the minister's application in private and the minister is entitled to address the Appeal Tribunal thereon[6]. The application must be made by notice to the registrar[7] and the registrar must give notice of the application to each party[8].

No person to whom an order either to attend as a witness or to produce documents is directed is, however, to be treated as having failed to obey that order unless at the time at which the order was served on him there was tendered to him a sufficient sum of money to cover his costs of attending before the Appeal Tribunal[9].

In relation to the attendance and examination of witnesses, the production and inspection of documents and all other matters incidental to its jurisdiction, the Appeal Tribunal has the same powers, rights, privileges and authority in England and Wales[10] as the High Court[11].

1   As to the meaning of 'Appeal Tribunal' see PARA 1451 note 4.
2   Employment Appeal Tribunal Rules 1993, SI 1993/2854, r 27(1). As to the meaning of 'document' see PARA 1451 note 5.
3   Ie under the Employment Appeal Tribunal Rules 1993, SI 1993/2854, r 30A(1)(b) or (c): see PARA 1452.
4   Ie under the Employment Appeal Tribunal Rules 1993, SI 1993/2854, r 30A(2)(a) read with r 30A(1)(b) or (c): see PARA 1452.
5   Employment Appeal Tribunal Rules 1993, SI 1993/2854, r 27(1A) (r 27(1A) added by SI 2001/1128).
6   Employment Appeal Tribunal Rules 1993, SI 1993/2854, r 27(1A) (as added: see note 5).
7   As to the meaning of 'registrar' see PARA 1430 note 4.
8   Employment Appeal Tribunal Rules 1993, SI 1993/2854, r 27(1A) (as added: see note 5).
9   Employment Appeal Tribunal Rules 1993, SI 1993/2854, r 27(2).
10   As to the meanings of 'England' and 'Wales' see PARA 2 note 12.
11   Employment Tribunals Act 1996 s 29(2). As to the High Court's power to order the attendance and examination of witnesses see CIVIL PROCEDURE vol 11 (2009) PARA 1058 et seq; and as to the powers of the County Court to order disclosure and inspection see CPR Pt 31; and CIVIL PROCEDURE vol 11 (2009) PARA 538 et seq. As to the Appeal Tribunal's power to inspect documents which are the subject of public interest immunity see *Halford v Sharples* [1992] 3 All ER 624, [1992] ICR 583, CA.

1515.   Reference to evidence given before the employment tribunal. An appellant who considers that a point of law raised in the notice of appeal[1] cannot be argued without reference to evidence given (or not given) at the employment tribunal[2], the nature or substance of which does not, or does not sufficiently, appear from the written reasons, must ordinarily submit an application with the notice of appeal[3]. The application is for the nature of such evidence (or lack of it) to be admitted, or if necessary for the relevant parts of the employment judge's notes of evidence[4] to be produced[5]. If such application is not so made, then it should be made:

   (1)   if a preliminary hearing[6] is ordered, in the skeleton argument or written submissions[7] presented prior to such a preliminary hearing[8]; or

(2)   if the case is listed for full hearing[9] without a preliminary hearing, then within 14 days of the seal date[10] of the order so providing[11].

Any such application by a respondent[12] to an appeal, must, if not made earlier, accompany the respondent's answer[13].

The application must explain why such a matter is considered necessary in order to argue the point of law raised in the notice of appeal or respondent's answer[14]. The application must identify:

(a)   the issue (or issues) in the notice of appeal or respondent's answer to which the material is relevant[15];

(b)   the names of the witnesses whose evidence is considered relevant; alternatively the nature of the evidence the absence of which is considered relevant[16];

(c)   (if applicable) the part of the hearing when the evidence was given[17];

(d)   the gist of the evidence (or absence of evidence) alleged to be relevant[18]; and

(e)   (if the party has a record of the evidence), saying so and by whom and when it was made, or producing an extract from a witness statement given in writing at the hearing[19].

The application will be considered on the papers, or if appropriate at a preliminary hearing, by the registrar[20] or a judge[21]. The registrar or a judge may give directions for written representations (if they have not already been lodged), or may determine the application, but will ordinarily make an order requiring the party who seeks to raise such a matter to give notice to the other party (or parties) to the appeal or cross-appeal. The notice will require the other party (or parties) to co-operate in agreeing, within 21 days (unless a shorter period is ordered), a statement or note of the relevant evidence, alternatively a statement that there was no such evidence[22].

All parties are required to use their best endeavours to agree such a statement or note[23]. However, in the absence of such agreement within 21 days (or such shorter period as may be ordered) of the requirement, any party may make an application within seven days thereafter to the Employment Appeal Tribunal[24] for directions. The party must enclose all relevant correspondence and give notice to the other parties. The directions may include:

(i)   the resolution of the disagreement on the papers or at a hearing;

(ii)   the administration by one party to the others of, or a request to the employment judge to provide, information; or

(iii)   if the Appeal Tribunal is satisfied that such notes are necessary, a request that the employment judge produce his notes of evidence either in whole or in part[25].

If the Appeal Tribunal requests any documents from the employment judge, it will supply copies to the parties upon receipt[26].

In an appeal from an employment tribunal which ordered its proceedings to be tape recorded, the Appeal Tribunal will apply the principles above to any application for a transcript[27].

A note of evidence is not to be produced and supplied to the parties to enable the parties to embark on a 'fishing expedition' to establish grounds or additional grounds of appeal or because they have not kept their own notes of the evidence. If an application for such a note is found by the Appeal Tribunal to have been unreasonably made or if there is unreasonable lack of co-operation in agreeing a relevant note or statement, the party behaving unreasonably is at risk of being ordered to pay costs[28].

1 As to the notice of appeal see PARA 1495.
2 As to proceedings before an employment tribunal see PARA 1453 et seq. Normally, the appeal
   will be based on the tribunal's written reasons: see PARA 1476.
3 *Practice Direction (Employment Appeal Tribunal—Procedure) 2013* [2014] IRLR 92 para 9.1.
4 As to the employment judge's duty to make notes of evidence see PARA 1472 note 3; and as to
   the meaning of 'employment judge' see PARA 1401 note 3. In determining whether such notes
   should be so provided to the parties, the general principle is that they should not be provided
   unless the notice of appeal raises a permissible ground for attacking the finding of fact: *Webb v
   Anglian Water Authority* [1981] ICR 811, [1981] IRLR 494, EAT. As to challenges made to a
   tribunal chairman's (now employment judge's) notes on the grounds of accuracy or
   completeness see *Dexine Rubber Co Ltd v Alker* [1977] ICR 434 at 438–439, EAT, per
   Cumming-Bruce J; *Aberdeen Steak Houses Group plc v Ibrahim* [1988] ICR 550 at 556, [1988]
   IRLR 420 at 423, EAT, per Wood P.
5 *Practice Direction (Employment Appeal Tribunal—Procedure) 2013* [2014] IRLR 92 para 9.1.
6 As to a preliminary hearing see PARA 1519.
7 See PARA 1507.
8 *Practice Direction (Employment Appeal Tribunal—Procedure) 2013* [2014] IRLR 92
   para 9.1.1.
9 As to the full hearing see PARA 1520.
10 As to the seal date of an order see PARA 1499 note 8.
11 *Practice Direction (Employment Appeal Tribunal—Procedure) 2013* [2014] IRLR 92
   para 9.1.2.
12 As to the meaning of 'respondent' see PARA 1498 note 4.
13 *Practice Direction (Employment Appeal Tribunal—Procedure) 2013* [2014] IRLR 92
   para 9.1.3. As to the respondent's answer see PARA 1499.
14 *Practice Direction (Employment Appeal Tribunal—Procedure) 2013* [2014] IRLR 92 para 9.2.
15 *Practice Direction (Employment Appeal Tribunal—Procedure) 2013* [2014] IRLR 92
   para 9.2.1.
16 *Practice Direction (Employment Appeal Tribunal—Procedure) 2013* [2014] IRLR 92
   para 9.2.2.
17 *Practice Direction (Employment Appeal Tribunal—Procedure) 2013* [2014] IRLR 92
   para 9.2.3.
18 *Practice Direction (Employment Appeal Tribunal—Procedure) 2013* [2014] IRLR 92
   para 9.2.4.
19 *Practice Direction (Employment Appeal Tribunal—Procedure) 2013* [2014] IRLR 92
   para 9.2.5.
20 As to the meaning of 'registrar' see PARA 1430 note 4.
21 *Practice Direction (Employment Appeal Tribunal—Procedure) 2013* [2014] IRLR 92 para 9.3.
   As to the meaning of 'judge' for these purposes see PARA 1451 note 4.
22 *Practice Direction (Employment Appeal Tribunal—Procedure) 2013* [2014] IRLR 92 para 9.3.
23 *Practice Direction (Employment Appeal Tribunal—Procedure) 2013* [2014] IRLR 92 para 9.3.
24 As to the Employment Appeal Tribunal see PARA 1422 et seq. As to the use of the abbreviation
   'EAT' see PARA 1435 note 2.
25 *Practice Direction (Employment Appeal Tribunal—Procedure) 2013* [2014] IRLR 92 para 9.4.
26 *Practice Direction (Employment Appeal Tribunal—Procedure) 2013* [2014] IRLR 92 para 9.5.
27 *Practice Direction (Employment Appeal Tribunal—Procedure) 2013* [2014] IRLR 92 para 9.6.
28 *Practice Direction (Employment Appeal Tribunal—Procedure) 2013* [2014] IRLR 92 para 9.7.

1516.   Fresh evidence and new points of law before the Appeal Tribunal.
Usually the Employment Appeal Tribunal[1] will not consider evidence which was
not placed before the employment tribunal[2] unless and until an application has
first been made to the employment tribunal against whose judgment the appeal is
brought for that tribunal to reconsider its judgment[3]. Where such an application
has been made, it is likely that unless a judge[4] of the Appeal Tribunal dismisses
the appeal as having no reasonable prospect of success the judge will stay any
further action on that appeal until the result of the reconsideration is known.
The employment tribunal as the fact-finding body, which has heard relevant
witnesses, is the appropriate forum to consider 'fresh evidence' and in particular
the extent to which (if at all) it would or might have made a difference to its
conclusions. It remains open to an intending appellant to contend that there has

been an error of law if the employment tribunal is in error of law in refusing to reconsider its decision, and if so then to refer to evidence which was not placed before the employment tribunal at the time it made its initial decision but was placed before that tribunal for the purposes of seeking or hearing a reconsideration of its decision[5].

Subject to the principles set out above[6], where an application is made by a party to an appeal to put in, at the hearing of the appeal, any document which was not before the employment tribunal, and which has not been agreed in writing by the other parties, the application and a copy of the documents sought to be admitted should be presented to the Appeal Tribunal with the notice of appeal[7] or the respondent's answer[8], as appropriate[9]. The application and copy should be served on the other parties. The same principle applies to any oral evidence not given at the employment tribunal which is sought to be adduced on the appeal. The nature and substance of such evidence together with the date when the party first became aware of its existence must be disclosed in a document, where appropriate a witness statement from the relevant witness with signed statement of truth, which must be similarly presented to the Appeal Tribunal and served[10].

In exercising its discretion to admit any fresh evidence or new document, the Employment Appeal Tribunal will apply the following principles[11], having regard to the overriding objective[12]:

(1)   the evidence could not have been obtained with reasonable diligence for use at the employment tribunal hearing[13];

(2)   it is relevant and would probably have had an important influence on the hearing[14];

(3)   it is apparently credible[15].

Accordingly the evidence and representations in support of the application must address these principles[16].

A party wishing to resist the application must, within 14 days of its being sent, submit any representations in response to the Appeal Tribunal and other parties[17].

Such an application is considered by the registrar[18] or a judge on the papers (or, if appropriate, at a preliminary hearing[19]) who may stay the appeal[20], determine the issue or give directions for a hearing or may seek comments from the employment judge[21]. A copy of any comments received from the employment judge will be sent to all parties[22].

If a respondent intends to contend at the full hearing[23] that the appellant has raised a point which was not argued below, the respondent must say so: (a) if a preliminary hearing has been ordered, in writing to the Appeal Tribunal and all parties, within 14 days of receiving the notice of appeal; (b) if the case is listed for a full hearing without a preliminary hearing, in a respondent's answer. In the event of dispute the employment judge should be asked for his comments as to whether a particular legal argument was deployed[24].

The following principles may be taken from the relevant authorities in relation to the arguing of new points:

(i)   there is a discretion, tightly regulated by case law, to allow a new point of law to be argued in the Appeal Tribunal;

(ii)   the discretion covers new points and the re-opening of conceded points;

(iii)   the discretion is only exercised in exceptional circumstances;.

(iv)   it would be even more exceptional to exercise the discretion where fresh issues of fact would have to be investigated;

(v)   where the new point relates to jurisdiction, this is not a trump card requiring the point to be taken; it remains discretionary;

(vi)   the discretion may be exercised, for example, in any of the following circumstances:

    (A)   it would be unjust to allow the other party to get away with some deception or unfair conduct which meant that the point was not taken below;

    (B)   the point can be taken if the Appeal Tribunal is in possession of all the material necessary to dispose of the matter fairly without recourse to further hearing;

    (C)   the new point enables the Appeal Tribunal plainly to say from existing material that the employment tribunal hearing was a nullity; for that is a consideration of overwhelming strength; in such a case, it is the Appeal Tribunal's duty to put right the law on the facts available to it;

    (D)   the Appeal Tribunal can see a glaring injustice in refusing to allow an unrepresented party to rely on evidence which could have been adduced before the employment tribunal;

    (E)   the Appeal Tribunal can see an obvious knock-out point;

    (F)   the issue is a discrete one of pure law requiring no further factual inquiry; or

    (G)   it is of particular public importance for a legal point to be decided provided no further factual investigation and no further evaluation by the specialist tribunal is required;

(vii)   the discretion is not, however, to be exercised where, by way of example:

    (A)   what is relied upon is a chance of establishing lack of jurisdiction by calling fresh evidence;

    (B)   the issue arises as a result of lack of skill by a represented party, for that is not a sufficient reason;

    (C)   the point was not taken below as a result of a tactical decision by a representative or party;

    (D)   all the material is before the Appeal Tribunal but what is required is an evaluation and an assessment of this material and application of the law to it by the specialist first instance tribunal;

    (E)   a represented party has fought and lost a jurisdictional issue and now seeks a new hearing; that applies whether the jurisdictional issue is the same as that originally canvassed, or is a different way of establishing jurisdiction as that originally canvassed; or

    (F)   what is relied upon is the high value of the case[25].

1 As to the Employment Appeal Tribunal see PARA 1422 et seq. As to the use of the abbreviation 'EAT' see PARA 1435 note 2.

2 As to proceedings before an employment tribunal see PARA 1453 et seq.

3 *Practice Direction (Employment Appeal Tribunal—Procedure) 2013* [2014] IRLR 92 para 10.1. As to applications for reconsideration see PARA 1479.

4 As to the meaning of 'judge' for these purposes see PARA 1451 note 4.

5 *Practice Direction (Employment Appeal Tribunal—Procedure) 2013* [2014] IRLR 92 para 10.1.

6 Ie subject to *Practice Direction (Employment Appeal Tribunal—Procedure) 2013* [2014] IRLR 92 para 10.1: see the text and notes 1–5.

7 As to the notice of appeal see PARA 1495.

8 As to the respondent's answer see PARA 1499. As to the meaning of 'respondent' see PARA 1498 note 4.

9 *Practice Direction (Employment Appeal Tribunal—Procedure) 2013* [2014] IRLR 92 para 10.2.

10 *Practice Direction (Employment Appeal Tribunal—Procedure) 2013* [2014] IRLR 92 para 10.2.

11 Ie the principles set out in *Ladd v Marshall* [1954] 3 All ER 745 at 748, [1954] 1 WLR 1489 at 1491, CA, per Denning LJ; applied in *Wileman v Minilec Engineering Ltd* [1988] ICR 318, [1988] IRLR 144, EAT. On the continuing strength of the rule against new evidence and the public policy ('no second bite of the cherry'), even where the new evidence would be highly relevant see *Cutter v Todd (t/a Hygia Professional Training)* [2007] All ER (D) 194 (Oct), where *Ladd v Marshall* [1954] 3 All ER 745, [1954] 1 WLR 1489, CA, was again applied; and *Switalski v F & C Asset Management plc* [2009] All ER (D) 06 (Jan), EAT. See also *Andorful v Reliance Security Services Ltd* [2009] All ER (D) 84 (Aug), EAT (when fresh material was admitted pursuant to the test in *Ladd v Marshall*, the appeal tribunal had to consider whether that material gave rise to an error of law enabling it to interfere and consequently either take the course of a remission, on whatever terms, to the tribunal, or reverse the decision below and substitute its own, and, for these purposes, the tribunal had to scrutinise the material itself in order to decide whether the fact that the evidence had not been available at first instance could have had such a significant effect as to give rise to an error of law; whilst the new evidence could not be regarded as conclusive, it nevertheless might have had an important bearing on the outcome and it had not been available to the tribunal); *Korashi v Abertawe Bro Morgannwg University Local Health Board* [2012] IRLR 4, EAT (Practice Direction allows applications to be made to admit new evidence but these must be sparingly granted and the EAT will always look to see if an application has been made to the tribunal and its response, and will stay proceedings in the EAT until the outcome of any such application). See also the text and note 25.

12 *Practice Direction (Employment Appeal Tribunal—Procedure) 2013* [2014] IRLR 92 para 10.3. As to the overriding objective see PARA 1435.

13 *Practice Direction (Employment Appeal Tribunal—Procedure) 2013* [2014] IRLR 92 para 10.3.1. See also *Borden (UK) Ltd v Potter* [1986] ICR 647 at 650, EAT, per Popplewell J.

14 *Practice Direction (Employment Appeal Tribunal—Procedure) 2013* [2014] IRLR 92 para 10.3.2.

15 *Practice Direction (Employment Appeal Tribunal—Procedure) 2013* [2014] IRLR 92 para 10.3.3.

16 *Practice Direction (Employment Appeal Tribunal—Procedure) 2013* [2014] IRLR 92 para 10.3.

17 *Practice Direction (Employment Appeal Tribunal—Procedure) 2013* [2014] IRLR 92 para 10.4.

18 As to the meaning of 'registrar' see PARA 1430 note 4.

19 As to a preliminary hearing see PARA 1519.

20 Ie in accordance with *Practice Direction (Employment Appeal Tribunal—Procedure) 2013* [2014] IRLR 92 para 10.1: see the text and notes 1–5.

21 *Practice Direction (Employment Appeal Tribunal—Procedure) 2013* [2014] IRLR 92 para 10.5. As to the meaning of 'employment judge' see PARA 1401 note 3.

22 *Practice Direction (Employment Appeal Tribunal—Procedure) 2013* [2014] IRLR 92 para 10.5.

23 As to the full hearing see PARA 1520.

24 *Practice Direction (Employment Appeal Tribunal—Procedure) 2013* [2014] IRLR 92 para 10.6.

25 See *Rance v Secretary of State for Health* [2007] IRLR 665 at [50], [2007] All ER (D) 81 (May) at [50], EAT, where the relevant authorities are reviewed; approved in *Jafri v Lincoln College* [2014] EWCA Civ 449 at [30], [2014] IRLR 544 at [30], [2014] All ER (D) 146 (Apr) at [30].

1517. Restricted reporting orders in cases involving sexual misconduct. In any proceedings[1] where the appeal involves allegations of the commission of a sexual offence[2], the registrar[3] must omit from any register kept by the Appeal Tribunal[4], which is available to the public, or delete from any order, judgment or other document[5], which is available to the public, any identifying matter[6] which is likely to lead members of the public to identify any person affected by or making such an allegation[7].

In any proceedings[8] where the appeal involves allegations of sexual misconduct[9], the Appeal Tribunal may at any time before the promulgation of its decision[10], either on the application of a party or of its own motion, make a restricted reporting order[11] having effect, if not revoked earlier by the Appeal Tribunal, until the promulgation of its decision[12]. The Appeal Tribunal must not make such an order unless it has given each party to the proceedings an opportunity to advance oral argument at a hearing, if they so wish[13]. However, the Appeal Tribunal may make a temporary restricted reporting order without a hearing[14]; and where such an order has been made the registrar must inform the parties to the proceedings in writing as soon as possible of[15]:

(1) the fact that the order has been made[16]; and

(2) their right to apply to have the temporary restricted reporting order revoked or converted into a full restricted reporting order within 14 days of the temporary order being made[17].

If no application is made under head (2) above within the 14 days, the temporary restricted reporting order lapses and ceases to have any effect on the fifteenth day after it was made; but when such an application is made the temporary restricted reporting order must continue to have effect until the hearing at which the application is considered[18].

Any hearing in relation to restricted reporting orders in cases involving sexual misconduct must[19] be held in public[20]. A restricted reporting order must specify the persons who may not be identified[21]. The Appeal Tribunal may revoke a restricted reporting order at any time when it thinks fit[22].

Where the Appeal Tribunal makes a restricted reporting order, the registrar must ensure that a notice of that fact is displayed on the notice board of the Appeal Tribunal at the office in which the proceedings in question are being dealt with, on the door of the room in which those proceedings are taking place and with any list of the proceedings taking place before the Appeal Tribunal[23].

It is an offence to publish, or include in a relevant programme[24], identifying matter in contravention of a restricted reporting order[25].

1 Ie proceedings to which the Employment Tribunals Act 1996 s 31 applies: see PARA 1432.
2 As to the meaning of 'sexual offence' see PARA 1432 note 3.
3 As to the meaning of 'registrar' see PARA 1430 note 4.
4 As to the meaning of 'Appeal Tribunal' see PARA 1451 note 4.
5 As to the meaning of 'document' see PARA 1451 note 5.
6 As to the meaning of 'identifying matter' see PARA 1432 note 2.
7 Employment Appeal Tribunal Rules 1993, SI 1993/2854, r 23(1), (2) (r 23(1) amended by SI 2001/1476).
8 See note 1.
9 As to the meaning of 'sexual misconduct' see PARA 1432 note 4.
10 For these purposes, 'promulgation of its decision' means the date recorded as being the date on which the Appeal Tribunal order finally disposing of the appeal is sent to the parties: Employment Appeal Tribunal Rules 1993, SI 1993/2854, r 23(9).
11 As to the meaning of 'restricted reporting order' see PARA 1432 note 2.
12 Employment Appeal Tribunal Rules 1993, SI 1993/2854, r 23(3).
13 Employment Appeal Tribunal Rules 1993, SI 1993/2854, r 23(5) (substituted by SI 2004/2526).
14 Employment Appeal Tribunal Rules 1993, SI 1993/2854, r 23(5A) (r 23(5A)–(5C) added by SI 2004/2526).
15 Employment Appeal Tribunal Rules 1993, SI 1993/2854, r 23(5B) (as added: see note 14). As to the meaning of 'writing' see PARA 1430 note 1.
16 Employment Appeal Tribunal Rules 1993, SI 1993/2854, r 23(5B)(a) (as added: see note 14).
17 Employment Appeal Tribunal Rules 1993, SI 1993/2854, r 23(5B)(b) (as added: see note 14).
18 Employment Appeal Tribunal Rules 1993, SI 1993/2854, r 23(5C) (as added: see note 14).
19 Ie subject to any direction of a Minister of the Crown under the Employment Appeal Tribunal Rules 1993, SI 1993/2854, r 30A(1) or order of the Appeal Tribunal under r 30A(2)(a) read with r 30A(1) (see PARA 1452), or unless the Appeal Tribunal decides for any of the reasons mentioned in r 29(2) (see PARA 1522) to sit in private to hear evidence.
20 Employment Appeal Tribunal Rules 1993, SI 1993/2854, r 23(6) (amended by SI 2001/1128; SI 2004/2526).
21 Employment Appeal Tribunal Rules 1993, SI 1993/2854, r 23(4).
22 Employment Appeal Tribunal Rules 1993, SI 1993/2854, r 23(7).
23 Employment Appeal Tribunal Rules 1993, SI 1993/2854, r 23(8).
24 As to the meaning of 'relevant programme' see PARA 1432 note 2.
25 See the Employment Tribunals Act 1996 s 31(3); and PARA 1432.

1518. Restricted reporting orders in disability cases. In any proceedings in a disability case[1], the Appeal Tribunal[2] may, on the application of the complainant or of its own motion, make a restricted reporting order[3] having effect, if not revoked earlier by the Appeal Tribunal, until the promulgation of its decision[4].

Where the Appeal Tribunal so makes a restricted reporting order in relation to an appeal which is being dealt with by the Appeal Tribunal together with any other proceedings, the Appeal Tribunal may direct that the order is to apply also in relation to those other proceedings or such part of them as it may direct[5].

The Appeal Tribunal must not make such an order unless it has given each party to the proceedings an opportunity to advance oral argument at a hearing, if they so wish[6]. However, the Appeal Tribunal may make a temporary restricted reporting order without a hearing[7]; and where such an order has been made the registrar[8] must inform the parties to the proceedings in writing as soon as possible of[9]:

(1)	the fact that the order has been made[10]; and

(2)	their right to apply to have the temporary restricted reporting order revoked or converted into a full restricted reporting order within 14 days of the temporary order being made[11].

If no application is made under head (2) above within the 14 days, the temporary restricted reporting order lapses and ceases to have any effect on the fifteenth day after it was made; but when such an application is made the temporary restricted reporting order must continue to have effect until the hearing at which the application is considered[12].

Any hearing in relation to restricted reporting orders in disability cases must[13] be held in public[14]. The Appeal Tribunal may revoke a restricted reporting order at any time when it thinks fit[15].

Where the Appeal Tribunal makes a restricted reporting order, the registrar must ensure that a notice of that fact is displayed on the notice board of the Appeal Tribunal at the office in which the proceedings in question are being dealt with, on the door of the room in which those proceedings are taking place and with any list of the proceedings taking place before the Appeal Tribunal[16].

It is an offence to publish, or include in a relevant programme[17], identifying matter[18] in contravention of a restricted reporting order[19].

1	Ie proceedings to which the Employment Tribunals Act 1996 s 32(1) applies: see PARA 1433.

2	As to the meaning of 'Appeal Tribunal' see PARA 1451 note 4.

3	As to the meaning of 'restricted reporting order' see PARA 1433 note 2.

4	Employment Appeal Tribunal Rules 1993, SI 1993/2854, r 23A(1), (2) (added by SI 1996/3216; amended by the Employment Rights (Dispute Resolution) Act 1998 s 1(2)(c); and by SI 2001/1128). For these purposes, 'promulgation of its decision' means the date recorded as being the date on which the Appeal Tribunal order finally disposing of the appeal is sent to the parties: Employment Appeal Tribunal Rules 1993, SI 1993/2854, r 23(9) (r 23(5)–(9) applied by r 23A(4) (added by SI 1996/3216)).

5	Employment Appeal Tribunal Rules 1993, SI 1993/2854, r 23A(3) (added by SI 1996/3216).

6	Employment Appeal Tribunal Rules 1993, SI 1993/2854, r 23(5) (substituted by SI 2004/2526; and applied (see note 4)).

7	Employment Appeal Tribunal Rules 1993, SI 1993/2854, r 23(5A) (added by SI 2004/2526; and applied (see note 4)).

8	As to the meaning of 'registrar' see PARA 1430 note 4.

9	Employment Appeal Tribunal Rules 1993, SI 1993/2854, r 23(5B) (r 23(5B) added by SI 2004/2526; and applied (see note 4)). As to the meaning of 'writing' see PARA 1430 note 1.

10	Employment Appeal Tribunal Rules 1993, SI 1993/2854, r 23(5B)(a) (as added (see note 9); and applied (see note 6)).

11	Employment Appeal Tribunal Rules 1993, SI 1993/2854, r 23(5B)(b) (as added (see note 9); and applied (see note 4)).

12 Employment Appeal Tribunal Rules 1993, SI 1993/2854, r 23(5C) (added by SI 2004/2526; and applied (see note 4)).
13 Ie subject to any direction of a Minister of the Crown under the Employment Appeal Tribunal Rules 1993, SI 1993/2854, r 30A(1) or order of the Appeal Tribunal under r 30A(2)(a) read with r 30A(1) (see PARA 1452), or unless the Appeal Tribunal decides for any of the reasons mentioned in r 29(2) (see PARA 1522) to sit in private to hear evidence.
14 Employment Appeal Tribunal Rules 1993, SI 1993/2854, r 23(6) (amended by SI 2001/1128; SI 2004/2526; and applied (see note 4)).
15 Employment Appeal Tribunal Rules 1993, SI 1993/2854, r 23(7) (as applied: see note 4).
16 Employment Appeal Tribunal Rules 1993, SI 1993/2854, r 23(8) (as applied: see note 4).
24 As to the meaning of 'relevant programme' see PARA 1433 note 2.
25 As to the meaning of 'identifying matter' see PARA 1433 note 2.
26 See the Employment Tribunals Act 1996 s 32(3); and PARA 1433.

(iii) Preliminary Hearing before the Appeal Tribunal

1519. Preliminary hearing. The purpose of a preliminary hearing is to determine whether:

(1)　the grounds in the notice of appeal[1] raise a point of law which gives the appeal a reasonable prospect of success at a full hearing[2]; or

(2)　for some other compelling reason the appeal should be heard[3], or to argue that a decision binding on the Employment Appeal Tribunal[4] should be considered by a higher court[5].

Prior to the preliminary hearing there will be automatic directions[6]. These include sending the notice of appeal to the respondent (or respondents) to the appeal[7]. The direction may order or in any event will enable the respondent (or respondents) to present and serve, within 14 days of the seal date of the order[8], unless otherwise directed, concise written submissions in response to the notice of appeal, dedicated to showing that there is no reasonable prospect of success for all or any grounds of any appeal; and such submissions will be considered at the preliminary hearing[9].

If the respondent to the appeal intends to serve a cross-appeal[10] this must be accompanied by written notice to that effect which must be presented and served within 14 days of service of the notice of appeal[11]. The respondent to the appeal must make clear whether it is intended to advance the cross-appeal:

(a)　in any event ('an unconditional cross-appeal')[12]; or

(b)　only if the appellant succeeds (a 'conditional cross-appeal')[13].

In either case the respondent is entitled to attend the preliminary hearing, which will also amount to a preliminary hearing of the cross-appeal, and to make submissions[14].

All parties will be notified of the date fixed for the preliminary hearing. In the normal case, unless ordered otherwise, only the appellant and/or a representative should attend to make submissions to the Appeal Tribunal on the issue whether the notice of appeal raises any reasonable ground for bringing an appeal, though it is open to the respondent to observe the proceedings, and though a respondent will not normally be permitted to take part in them he may, with the permission of the court, do so if the judge[15] considers it desirable[16]. If the appellant does not attend, the appeal may nevertheless be dealt with as above on written submissions, and may be dismissed wholly or in part or allowed to proceed[17].

The preliminary hearing, including judgment and directions, will normally last no more than one hour[18].

The sift procedure[19] will be applied to cross-appeals as well as appeals. If satisfied that the appeal, and/or the cross-appeal, should be heard at a full hearing on all or some of the grounds of appeal[20], the Appeal Tribunal will give directions relating to, for example, a time estimate, any application for fresh evidence, a procedure in respect of matters of evidence before the employment tribunal[21] not sufficiently appearing from the written reasons, the exchange and lodging of skeleton arguments[22] and an appellant's chronology, and bundles of documents and authorities[23].

Permission to amend a notice of appeal (or cross-appeal) may be granted at a preliminary hearing[24]. If the proposed amendment is produced at the hearing, then, if such amendment has not previously been notified to the other parties, and the appeal (or cross-appeal) might not have been permitted to proceed but for the amendment, the opposing party or parties will have the opportunity to apply on notice to vary or discharge the permission to proceed, and for consequential directions as to the hearing or disposal of the appeal or cross-appeal[25]. A draft amendment should wherever practicable be made available at the preliminary hearing or on the same day unless otherwise directed[26].

If not satisfied that the appeal, or any particular ground of it, should go forward to a full hearing, the Appeal Tribunal at the preliminary hearing will dismiss the appeal, wholly or in part, and give a judgment setting out the reasons for doing so[27].

If an appeal is permitted to go forward to a full hearing on all grounds, a reasoned judgment will not normally be given[28].

Parties who become aware that a similar point is raised in other proceedings at an employment tribunal or the Appeal Tribunal are encouraged to co-operate in bringing this to the attention of the registrar[29] so that consideration can be given to the most expedient way of dealing with the cases, in particular to the possibility of having two or more appeals heard together[30].

If an appeal is permitted to go forward to a full hearing, a listing category will be assigned, namely:

(i)   P (recommended to be heard in the President's[31] list);

(ii) A (complex, and raising a point or points of law of public importance;

(iii) B (any other cases)[32].

The President reserves the discretion to alter any relevant category as circumstances require[33].

Facilities can exceptionally be arranged for the purpose of holding short preliminary hearings by video or telephone link[34].

1   As to the notice of appeal see PARA 1495.
2   As to the full hearing see PARA 1520.
3   Eg that the appellant seeks a declaration of incompatibility under the Human Rights Act 1998: see RIGHTS AND FREEDOMS vol 88A (2013) PARA 18.
4   As to the Employment Appeal Tribunal see PARA 1422 et seq. As to the use of the abbreviation 'EAT' see PARA 1435 note 2.
5   *Practice Direction (Employment Appeal Tribunal—Procedure) 2013* [2014] IRLR 92 paras 11.8–11.8.2.
6   *Practice Direction (Employment Appeal Tribunal—Procedure) 2013* [2014] IRLR 92 para 11.9.
7   As to the meaning of 'respondent' see PARA 1498 note 4.
8   As to the seal date of the order see PARA 1499 note 8.
9   *Practice Direction (Employment Appeal Tribunal—Procedure) 2013* [2014] IRLR 92 para 11.9.
10 As to the respondent's notice of cross-appeal see PARA 1499.
11 *Practice Direction (Employment Appeal Tribunal—Procedure) 2013* [2014] IRLR 92 para 11.10.
12 *Practice Direction (Employment Appeal Tribunal—Procedure) 2013* [2014] IRLR 92 para 11.10.1.
13 *Practice Direction (Employment Appeal Tribunal—Procedure) 2013* [2014] IRLR 92 para 11.10.2.

14 *Practice Direction (Employment Appeal Tribunal—Procedure) 2013* [2014] IRLR 92 para 11.10.
15 As to the meaning of 'judge' for these purposes see PARA 1451 note 4.
16 *Practice Direction (Employment Appeal Tribunal—Procedure) 2013* [2014] IRLR 92 para 11.11. Any written submissions as referred to in para 11.9 (see the text and note 6) will be considered at the preliminary hearing: para 11.11.
17 *Practice Direction (Employment Appeal Tribunal—Procedure) 2013* [2014] IRLR 92 para 11.12.
18 *Practice Direction (Employment Appeal Tribunal—Procedure) 2013* [2014] IRLR 92 para 11.13. Arguments should be carefully planned so that this time is not exceeded; if it is, the Appeal Tribunal may impose a guillotine on further argument, in order to ensure that the case does not take a share of the Appeal Tribunal's resources which is disproportionate to that taken by other appeals yet to be heard: para 11.13.
19 As to the sift procedure see PARA 1501.
20 The preliminary hearing procedure has its value in cases where it is appropriate to permit an appeal to proceed on limited grounds; however, where the entire compass of a case is narrow, an Appeal Tribunal has to be cautious in allowing a case to proceed on one ground of appeal and not on another: *Vincent v MJ Gallagher Contractors Ltd* [2003] EWCA Civ 640, [2003] ICR 1244.
21 As to proceedings before employment tribunals see PARA 1453 et seq.
22 As to skeleton arguments see PARA 1507.
23 *Practice Direction (Employment Appeal Tribunal—Procedure) 2013* [2014] IRLR 92 para 11.14. As to bundles of documents and authorities see PARAS 1506, 1508.
24 *Practice Direction (Employment Appeal Tribunal—Procedure) 2013* [2014] IRLR 92 para 11.15.
25 *Practice Direction (Employment Appeal Tribunal—Procedure) 2013* [2014] IRLR 92 para 11.15.1.
26 *Practice Direction (Employment Appeal Tribunal—Procedure) 2013* [2014] IRLR 92 para 11.15.2.
27 *Practice Direction (Employment Appeal Tribunal—Procedure) 2013* [2014] IRLR 92 para 11.16.
28 *Practice Direction (Employment Appeal Tribunal—Procedure) 2013* [2014] IRLR 92 para 11.17.
29 As to the meaning of 'the registrar' see PARA 1430 note 4.
30 *Practice Direction (Employment Appeal Tribunal—Procedure) 2013* [2014] IRLR 92 para 11.18.
31 As to the meaning of 'the President' see PARA 1451 note 4.
32 *Practice Direction (Employment Appeal Tribunal—Procedure) 2013* [2014] IRLR 92 para 11.19.
33 See note 32.
34 See PARA 1522 text and notes 18–20.

(iv) Hearings before the Appeal Tribunal; Judgments

1520. Full hearing. If a judge[1] or the registrar[2] decides to list the case for a full hearing he must consider appropriate directions[3], relating for example to amendment[4], further information, a procedure in respect of matters of evidence at the employment tribunal[5] not sufficiently appearing from the written reasons[6], allegations of bias, apparent bias or improper conduct[7], provisions for skeleton arguments[8], appellant's chronology and bundles of documents[9] and of authorities[10], time estimates[11] and listing category[12].

1 As to the meaning of 'judge' for these purposes see PARA 1451 note 4.
2 As to the meaning of 'registrar' see PARA 1430 note 4.
3 As to directions see PARA 1512.
4 As to amendment see PARA 1512.
5 As to proceedings before an employment tribunal see PARA 1453 et seq.
6 See PARA 1515.
7 See PARA 1497.
8 See PARA 1507.
9 See PARA 1506.

10 See PARA 1508.
11 See PARA 1510.
12 *Practice Direction (Employment Appeal Tribunal—Procedure) 2013* [2014] IRLR 92 para 11.20. As to the listing category see PARA 1519 text and notes 31–33.

1521. Fast-tracked full hearing cases. The Employment Appeal Tribunal[1] aims to hear full hearing cases[2] in the order in which they are received. However, there are times when it is expedient to hear an appeal as soon as it can be fitted into the list. Appeals thus fast-tracked, at the discretion of a judge[3] or the registrar[4], will normally fall into the following cases[5]:

(1) appeals where the parties have made a reasoned case on the merits for an expedited hearing[6];

(2) appeals against interim orders[7] or decisions of an employment tribunal[8], particularly those which involve the taking of a step in the proceedings within a specified period, for example adjournments, further information, amendments, disclosure, witness orders[9];

(3) appeals on the outcome of which other applications to the employment tribunal or the Appeal Tribunal or the civil courts depend[10];

(4) appeals in which a reference to the Court of Justice of the European Union[11], or a declaration of incompatibility under the Human Rights Act 1998[12], is sought[13];

(5) appeals involving reinstatement, re-engagement or interim relief[14].

Category B cases[15] estimated to take two hours or less may also be fast-tracked[16].

1 As to the Employment Appeal Tribunal see PARA 1422 et seq. As to the use of the abbreviation 'EAT' see PARA 1435 note 2.
2 As to full hearing cases see PARA 1520.
3 As to the meaning of 'judge' for these purposes see PARA 1451 note 4.
4 As to the meaning of 'registrar' see PARA 1430 note 4.
5 *Practice Direction (Employment Appeal Tribunal—Procedure) 2013* [2014] IRLR 92 para 11.21.
6 *Practice Direction (Employment Appeal Tribunal—Procedure) 2013* [2014] IRLR 92 para 11.21.1.
7 As to appeals against interim orders see PARA 1511.
8 As to appeals against decisions of an employment tribunal see PARA 1495 et seq.
9 *Practice Direction (Employment Appeal Tribunal—Procedure) 2013* [2014] IRLR 92 para 11.21.2.
10 *Practice Direction (Employment Appeal Tribunal—Procedure) 2013* [2014] IRLR 92 para 11.21.3.
11 As to the making of references to the Court of Justice of the European Union generally see CIVIL PROCEDURE vol 12 (2009) PARA 1720 et seq.
12 See RIGHTS AND FREEDOMS vol 88A (2013) PARA 18.
13 *Practice Direction (Employment Appeal Tribunal—Procedure) 2013* [2014] IRLR 92 para 11.21.4.
14 *Practice Direction (Employment Appeal Tribunal—Procedure) 2013* [2014] IRLR 92 para 11.21.5.
15 As to 'Category B' cases see PARA 1519 head (iii).
16 *Practice Direction (Employment Appeal Tribunal—Procedure) 2013* [2014] IRLR 92 para 11.22.

1522. The hearing. An oral hearing at which any proceedings before the Appeal Tribunal[1] are finally disposed of must[2] take place in public before, where applicable, such members of the Appeal Tribunal as[3] the President[4] may nominate for the purpose[5].

Notwithstanding this, the Appeal Tribunal may sit in private for the purpose of hearing evidence from any person which, in the opinion of the Appeal Tribunal, is likely to consist of[6]:

(1) information which he could not disclose without contravening a prohibition imposed by or under any enactment[7]; or

(2) information which has been communicated to him in confidence or which he has otherwise obtained in consequence of the confidence reposed in him by another person[8]; or

(3) information the disclosure of which would cause substantial injury to any undertaking of his or any undertaking in which he works for reasons other than its effects on any negotiations[9] in respect of collective bargaining[10].

When exercising its functions, the Appeal Tribunal must ensure that information is not disclosed contrary to the interests of national security[11].

The Appeal Tribunal may, either of its own motion or on application, require any evidence to be given on oath[12]. The Appeal Tribunal has a discretion to admit further evidence but this discretion will be exercised only in limited circumstances[13]. Similarly, the Appeal Tribunal will not normally allow a party to raise a new point of law that was not raised before the employment tribunal, especially if it would necessitate further findings of fact[14].

A person may appear before the Appeal Tribunal in person or be represented by counsel or a solicitor, a representative of a trade union[15] or an employers' association[16] or any other person whom he desires to represent him[17].

Facilities can exceptionally be arranged for the purpose of holding short preliminary hearings[18] or short appointments for directions[19] by video or telephone link, upon the application in writing of an appellant or respondent who, or whose representative, has a relevant disability, supported by appropriate medical evidence[20]. Such facilities will, however, only be made available for a hearing at which the party or, if more than one party will take part, both or all parties is or are legally represented. An application that a hearing should be so held will be determined by a judge[21] or the registrar[22], and must be made well in advance of the date intended for the hearing, so that arrangements may be made. So far as concerns video conferencing facilities, they may not always be available, dependent on the location of the parties; as for telephone hearings or, especially, telephone conferencing facilities, consideration may need to be given as to payment by a party or parties of any additional expenditure resulting[23].

Hearings will not normally be recorded, except for the giving of any judgment. Parties are reminded that they are not permitted to make any video or audio recording nor take any photograph of the proceedings except with the express prior consent of the judge at the hearing, for which good reason must be shown, and that it is a contempt of court to do so, the penalties for which include fines and imprisonment[24].

No person is to be punished for contempt of the Appeal Tribunal except by, or with the consent of, a judge[25].

1 As to the meaning of 'Appeal Tribunal' see PARA 1451 note 4.

2 Ie subject to any direction of a Minister of the Crown under the Employment Appeal Tribunal Rules 1993, SI 1993/2854, r 30A(1)(a) (see PARA 1452) or order of the Appeal Tribunal under r 30A(2)(a) (see PARA 1452) read with r 30A(1)(a).

3 Ie subject to the Employment Tribunals Act 1996 s 28: see PARA 1426.

4 As to the meaning of 'President' see PARA 1451 note 4.

5 Employment Appeal Tribunal Rules 1993, SI 1993/2854, r 29(1) (amended by SI 2001/1128).

6 Employment Appeal Tribunal Rules 1993, SI 1993/2854, r 29(2) (r 29(2) substituted by SI 2001/1128).
7 Employment Appeal Tribunal Rules 1993, SI 1993/2854, r 29(2)(a) (as substituted: see note 6).
8 Employment Appeal Tribunal Rules 1993, SI 1993/2854, r 29(2)(b) (as substituted: see note 6).
9 Ie negotiations with respect to any of the matters mentioned in the Trade Union and Labour Relations (Consolidation) Act 1992 s 178(2) (matters to which trade disputes relate): see PARA 1093.
10 Employment Appeal Tribunal Rules 1993, SI 1993/2854, r 29(2)(c) (as substituted: see note 6).
11 Employment Appeal Tribunal Rules 1993, SI 1993/2854, r 30 (substituted by SI 2001/1128).
12 Employment Appeal Tribunal Rules 1993, SI 1993/2854, r 28.
13 See PARA 1516.
14 See PARA 1516. As to proceedings before an employment tribunal see PARA 1453 et seq. See also *Kumchyk v Derby City Council* [1978] ICR 1116, EAT; *GKN (Cwmbran) Ltd v Lloyd* [1972] ICR 214, NIRC; *Jones v RM Douglas Construction Ltd* [1979] ICR 278, EAT; *Secretary of State for Employment v Newcastle upon Tyne City Council* [1980] ICR 407, EAT. The approach in *Kumchyk v Derby City Council* [1978] ICR 1116, EAT was approved by the Court of Appeal: *Jones v Governing Body of Burdett Coutts School* [1999] ICR 38, [1998] IRLR 521, CA; *Divine-Bortey v Brent London Borough Council* [1998] ICR 886, [1998] IRLR 525, CA; *Mensah v East Hertfordshire NHS Trust* [1998] IRLR 531, CA; *Glennie v Independent Magazines (UK) Ltd* [1999] IRLR 719, CA; *Gloystarne & Co Ltd v Martin* [2001] IRLR 15, EAT. See also *Truelove v Safeway Stores plc* [2005] ICR 589, [2005] All ER (D) 343 (Feb), EAT.

There is no general duty on the chairman (now employment judge) of an employment tribunal to raise points on behalf of a party which the party's representative did not raise: *Kumchyk v Derby City Council*[1978] ICR 1116, EAT; *Dimtsu v Westminster City Council* [1991] IRLR 450, EAT. There is no general exception permitting the raising of a new point before the Appeal Tribunal on the ground that it goes to the Appeal Tribunal's jurisdiction: *Russell v Elmdon Freight Terminal Ltd* [1989] ICR 629, EAT, not following on this point *House v Emerson Electric Industrial Controls* [1980] ICR 795, EAT. If an employment tribunal has wrongly accepted jurisdiction, the Appeal Tribunal may hear a new argument that it was wrong to do so, on the basis that the employment tribunal's decision is arguably a nullity (*Russell v Elmdon Freight Terminal Ltd* [1989] ICR 629 at 632, EAT, per Knox J), but normally the Appeal Tribunal has to decide on balance whether justice requires that the new point be taken (*Barber v Thames Television plc* [1991] ICR 253, [1991] IRLR 236, EAT). The narrow approach applies to attempts to raise new points of law by respondents as well as appellants: *Hellyer Bros Ltd v McLeod, Boston Deep Sea Fisheries Ltd v Wilson* [1987] 1 WLR 728, [1987] ICR 526, CA; *Barber v Thames Television plc* [1991] ICR 253, [1991] IRLR 236, EAT.

One possible exception is where a principle of employment law is so well established that the employment tribunal should have considered it on its own initiative, even if not raised by the parties: *Langston v Cranfield University* [1998] IRLR 172, EAT.

If the Appeal Tribunal does decide to allow a new point to be raised, it must give its reasons: *Jones v Governing Body of Burdett Coutts School* [1999] ICR 38, [1998] IRLR 521, CA. See *Truelove v Safeway Stores plc* [2005] ICR 589, [2005] All ER (D) 343 (Feb), EAT.

See also *Rance v Secretary of State for Health* [2007] IRLR 665 at [50], [2007] All ER (D) 81 (May) at [50], EAT, where the relevant authorities are reviewed; approved in *Jafri v Lincoln College* [2014] EWCA Civ 449 at [30], [2014] 3 All ER 709 at [30], [2014] ICR 920 at [30], [2014] IRLR 544 at [30].

15 As to the meaning of 'trade union' see PARA 150 note 9.
16 As to the meaning of 'employers' association' see PARA 150 note 9.
17 Employment Tribunals Act 1996 s 29(1). This is a complete right, which is not to be diminished in the Appeal Tribunal's discretion: *Bache v Essex County Council* [2000] 2 All ER 847, [2000] ICR 313, CA (a case on the equivalent provision applying to employment tribunals). As to directions as to the procedure of the Appeal Tribunal see the Employment Tribunals Act 1996 s 29A; and PARA 1435 note 3.
18 As to the preliminary hearing see PARA 1519.
19 As to appointments for directions see PARA 1512.
20 *Practice Direction (Employment Appeal Tribunal—Procedure) 2013* [2014] IRLR 92 para 20.2.
21 As to the meaning of 'judge' for these purposes see PARA 1451 note 4.
22 As to the meaning of 'registrar' see PARA 1430 note 4.
23 *Practice Direction (Employment Appeal Tribunal—Procedure) 2013* [2014] IRLR 92 para 20.2.
24 *Practice Direction (Employment Appeal Tribunal—Procedure) 2013* [2014] IRLR 92 para 20.3.
25 Employment Tribunals Act 1996 s 36(4).

1523. Reasons for and enforcement of orders. For the purpose of disposing of an appeal, the Appeal Tribunal[1] may exercise any of the powers of the body or officer from whom the appeal was brought or may remit the case to that body or officer[2]. If the Appeal Tribunal finds that the employment tribunal has misdirected itself in law, it will normally remit the case[3]; and it will uphold the tribunal's decision, notwithstanding the misdirection, only if convinced that it is plainly and unarguably right[4]. It should, however, substitute its own decision, instead of remitting the case, only if it is clear that any tribunal properly directed must have reached the same conclusion on the facts[5].

Every order of the Appeal Tribunal must be drawn up by the registrar[6] and a copy, sealed with the seal of the Appeal Tribunal, must be served by the registrar on every party to the proceedings to which it relates and:

(1)   in the case of an order disposing of an appeal from an employment tribunal[7] or an order relating to a vexatious litigant[8], on the Secretary of Employment Tribunals[9]; or

(2)   in the case of an order disposing of an appeal from the certification officer[10], on that officer[11];

(3)   in the case of an order imposing a penalty notice[12], on the Secretary of State[13]; or

(4)   in the case of an order disposing of an appeal from the Central Arbitration Committee (the 'CAC')[14], on the chairman of the CAC[15].

On the application of any party made within 14 days after the making of an order finally disposing of any proceedings, the Appeal Tribunal must give its reasons in writing for the order, unless it was made after the delivery of a reasoned judgment[16]. However, where a document sets out either the reasons for the Appeal Tribunal's order or any reasoned judgment of the Appeal Tribunal in any particular Crown employment proceedings in which a direction of a Minister of the Crown has been given[17] or an order of the Appeal Tribunal has been made[18], then, before the Appeal Tribunal gives its reasons in writing for any order or delivers any reasoned judgment, the registrar must send a copy of the reasons or judgment to the minister[19].

If the minister considers it expedient in the interests of national security, he may:

(a)   direct the Appeal Tribunal that the document containing its reasons for any order or its reasoned judgment must not be disclosed to any person who was excluded from all or part of the proceedings[20] and to prepare a further document setting out the reasons for its order, or a further reasoned judgment, but with the omission of such reasons as are specified in the direction[21]; or

(b)   direct the Appeal Tribunal that the document containing its reasons for any order or its reasoned judgment must not be disclosed to any person who was excluded from all or part of the proceedings, but that no further document setting out the Appeal Tribunal's reasons for its order or further reasoned judgment should be prepared[22].

Where the minister has directed the Appeal Tribunal in accordance with head (a) above, the document prepared pursuant to that direction must be marked in each place where an omission has been made[23]. The document may then be given by the registrar to the parties[24]. The registrar must send both the edited document and the full document (that is, without the omissions made pursuant to that direction):

(i) to whichever of the appellant and the respondent[25] was not the claimant[26] in the proceedings before the employment tribunal[27];

(ii) if he was not an excluded person[28], to the person who was the claimant in the proceedings before the employment tribunal and, if he was not an excluded person, to his representative[29];

(iii) if applicable, to the special advocate[30]; and

(iv) where there are proceedings before a superior court relating to the order in question, to that court[31].

Where the Appeal Tribunal intends to take steps[32] to keep secret all or part of the reasons for any order it makes, it must send the full reasons for its order to the persons listed in heads (i) to (iv) above, as appropriate[33].

Subject to any order made by the Court of Appeal and to any directions given by the Appeal Tribunal, an appeal from the Appeal Tribunal does not suspend the enforcement of any order made by it[34].

1   As to the meaning of 'Appeal Tribunal' see PARA 1422 note 1.
2   Employment Tribunals Act 1996 s 35(1). As to the enforcement of any decision or award of the Appeal Tribunal on an appeal see s 35(2); and PARA 1529.
3   The power to remit is a wide, general power (*Askew v Victoria Sporting Club Ltd* [1976] ICR 302, EAT; *Irvine v Prestcold Ltd* [1981] IRLR 281, CA); but it is wrong in principle for the Appeal Tribunal to remit a case to an employment tribunal to enable a party to call a witness on an issue which was clearly relevant at the first hearing and who had been available to give evidence at the hearing before the tribunal (*Kingston v British Railways Board* [1984] ICR 781, [1984] IRLR 146, CA). Where the Appeal Tribunal remits a case after a successful appeal, that remission is in relation to the original grounds of decision, not to allow novel points to be raised: *Church v West Lancashire NHS Trust (No 2)* [1999] ICR 586, [1998] IRLR 492, EAT. As to guidance when deciding whether to remit a case to the same or a differently constituted tribunal see *Sinclair Roche & Temperley v Heard* [2004] IRLR 763 at [46], EAT. *Sinclair Roche & Temperley v Heard* was applied in *Switalski v F & C Asset Management plc* [2009] All ER (D) 06 (Jan), EAT; and also in *Celebi v Compass Group UK and Ireland Ltd (t/a Scolarest)* [2009] All ER (D) 172 (Jan), EAT. Any attempt by the employment tribunal to go beyond the terms of the remission is void: *Aparau v Iceland Frozen Foods plc (No 2)* [2000] IRLR 196, CA. See also *Bascetta v Abbey National plc* [2009] All ER (D) 54 (Feb), EAT (here the judge had not been given the full facts in reaching a case management decision and had therefore, through no fault of his own, failed to take a relevant factor into account; thus there had been an error in law in the judge's exercise of discretion and accordingly under the Employment Tribunals Act 1996 s 35(1) the question of any postponement of the relevant remedy hearing had to be considered afresh).

Given that the Appeal Tribunal is not supposed to make any factual assessment for itself (and only to supplemented facts known to the tribunal if at all only by undisputed or indisputable facts), nor make any judgment of its own as to the merits of the case, the Appeal Tribunal's function was and was only to see that the tribunal's decisions were lawfully made so that if the Appeal Tribunal detected a legal error by the tribunal, it had to send the case back unless: (1) it concluded that the error could not have affected the result as, in that case, the error would have been immaterial and the result as lawful as if it had not been made; or (2) without the error, the result would have been different, but the EAT was able to conclude what it had to have been: *Jafri v Lincoln College* [2014] EWCA Civ 449, [2014] IRLR 544, [2014] All ER (D) 146 (Apr) (tribunal's errors could not have affected the result so the ground of appeal contending that the Appeal Tribunal had applied the wrong test upon the question whether the case should be remitted had to fail). *Jafri v Lincoln College* was applied in *Burrell v Micheldever Tyre Services Ltd* [2014] EWCA Civ 716, [2014] IRLR 630, where the Court of Appeal observed that the EAT, within the confines of the conventional approach to remittal that was reaffirmed in *Jafri v Lincoln College*, was yet able to contain its application in a number of ways (see at [20] per Maurice Kay LJ).

The practice of remitting a matter to the tribunal for further reasons, where these are inadequate or unclear, is permitted at any stage of the proceedings: *Burns v Royal Mail Group plc (formerly Consignia plc)* [2004] ICR 1103, sub nom *Burns v Consignia (No 2)* [2004] IRLR 425, EAT. The adoption of the procedure in that case is pursuant to the power given by the Employment Tribunals Act 1996 s 35(1) and is an example of the tribunal's discretionary power in the exercise of case management which should be left to the EAT to make: *Barke v SEETEC Business Technology Centre Ltd* [2005] EWCA Civ 578, [2005] ICR 1373, [2005] IRLR 633. Cf *Tran v Greenwich Vietnam Community Project* [2002] EWCA Civ 553, [2002] ICR 1101, [2002] IRLR 735; *Reuben v London Borough of Brent* [2000] ICR 102, [2000] IRLR 176, EAT. *Burns v Royal Mail Group plc (formerly Consignia plc)* [2004] ICR 1103, sub nom *Burns v Consignia (No 2)* [2004] IRLR 425, EAT and *Barke v SEETEC Business Technology Centre Ltd* [2005] EWCA Civ 578, [2005] ICR 1373, [2005] IRLR 633 were applied in *Bone v Newham London Borough Council* [2008] EWCA Civ 435, [2008] ICR 923, [2008] All ER (D) 414 (Apr). If this procedure is adopted, the employment judge should confine himself to answering the questions posed by the Appeal Tribunal and should not seek to give further justification for the tribunal's decision: *Webster v Woodhouse School* [2009] EWCA Civ 91, [2009] ICR 818, [2009] IRLR 568.

4   *Dobie v Burns International Security Services (UK) Ltd* [1984] 3 All ER 333, [1984] ICR 812, CA. See also *Bache v Essex County Council* [2000] 2 All ER 847, [2000] IRLR 251, CA (procedural error). *Dobie v Burns International Security Services (UK) Ltd* [1984] 3 All ER 333, [1984] ICR 812, CA was applied in *Cafagna v ISS Mediclean Ltd* [2009] All ER (D) 233 (Jan), EAT.

5   *O'Kelly v Trusthouse Forte plc* [1984] QB 90 at 126, [1983] ICR 728 at 764, CA, per Sir John Donaldson MR; *Hellyer Bros Ltd v McLeod, Boston Deep Sea Fisheries Ltd v Wilson* [1987] 1 WLR 728 at 753, [1987] ICR 526 at 547, CA, per Slade LJ; *McLaren v National Coal Board* [1988] ICR 370 at 378, [1988] IRLR 215 at 218, CA, per Sir John Donaldson MR; *Kapadia v London Borough of Lambeth* [2000] IRLR 699, CA. In an unfair dismissal case, where the employment tribunal has erred in law in finding that an employee was unfairly dismissed, the Appeal Tribunal must remit the case unless no employment tribunal, properly directing itself, could have come to the conclusion that the employee was not unfairly dismissed: *Morgan v Electrolux Ltd* [1991] IRLR 89 at 92, CA, per Balcombe LJ. See also *Wakefield v HM Land Registry* [2009] All ER (D) 205 (Jan), EAT (a disability discrimination case).

6   As to the meaning of 'registrar' see PARA 1430 note 4.

7   As to proceedings before the employment tribunal see PARA 1453 et seq.

8   Ie within the Employment Tribunals Act 1996 s 33: see PARA 1430.

9   Employment Appeal Tribunal Rules 1993, SI 1993/2854, r 31(1)(a) (amended by the Employment Rights (Dispute Resolution) Act 1998 s 1(2)(a), (b); and by SI 2001/1128). As to the meaning of 'Secretary of Employment Tribunals' see PARA 1430 note 5.

10 As to the meaning of 'certification officer' see PARA 1495 note 14.

11 Employment Appeal Tribunal Rules 1993, SI 1993/2854, r 31(1)(b).

12 Ie under the Transnational Information and Consultation of Employees Regulations 1999, SI 1999/3323, reg 20, reg 21 or reg 21A (see PARAS 1269–1271), the European Public Limited-Liability Company Regulations 2004, SI 2004/2326, reg 33 (revoked: see now the European Public Limited-Liability Company (Employee Involvement) (Great Britain) Regulations 2009, SI 2009/2401, reg 20; and PARA 1328), the Information and Consultation of Employees Regulations 2004, SI 2004/3426, reg 22 (see PARA 1307) or the Companies (Cross-Border Mergers) Regulations 2007, SI 2007/2974, reg 53 (see COMPANIES vol 15 (2009) PARA 1451); Interpretation Act 1978 s 17(2).

13 Employment Appeal Tribunal Rules 1993, SI 1993/2854, r 31(1)(c) (added by SI 2001/1128; amended by SI 2004/2526; SI 2004/3426; SI 2007/2974; SI 2010/1088). As to the Secretary of State see PARA 5 note 21.

14 Ie made under the Transnational Information and Consultation of Employees Regulations 1999, SI 1999/3323, reg 38(8): see PARA 1280. As to the CAC see PARA 1226 et seq.

15 Employment Appeal Tribunal Rules 1993, SI 1993/2854, r 31(1)(d) (added by SI 2001/1128).

16 Employment Appeal Tribunal Rules 1993, SI 1993/2854, r 31(2) (amended by SI 2001/1128). As to the meaning of 'writing' see PARA 2 note 8. As to the handing down of judgments see PARA 1524.

17 Ie under the Employment Appeal Tribunal Rules 1993, SI 1993/2854, r 30A(1)(a), (b) or (c): see PARA 1452. As to the meaning of 'Crown employment proceedings' see PARA 1452 note 3.

18 Ie under the Employment Appeal Tribunal Rules 1993, SI 1993/2854, r 30A(2)(a) read with r 30A(1)(a), (b) or (c): see PARA 1452.

19 Employment Appeal Tribunal Rules 1993, SI 1993/2854, r 31A(1), (2) (r 31A added by SI 2001/1128).

20 As to excluded persons see PARA 1452.

21 Employment Appeal Tribunal Rules 1993, SI 1993/2854, r 31A(3)(a) (as added: see note 19).

22 Employment Appeal Tribunal Rules 1993, SI 1993/2854, r 31A(3)(b) (as added: see note 19).

23 Employment Appeal Tribunal Rules 1993, SI 1993/2854, r 31A(4) (as added: see note 19).

24 Employment Appeal Tribunal Rules 1993, SI 1993/2854, r 31A(4) (as added: see note 19).

25 As to the meaning of 'respondent' see PARA 1498 note 4.

26 As to the claimant see PARA 1461.
27 Employment Appeal Tribunal Rules 1993, SI 1993/2854, r 31A(5)(a) (as added (see note 19); amended by SI 2004/2526).
28 As to the meaning of 'excluded person' see PARA 1452 note 11.
29 Employment Appeal Tribunal Rules 1993, SI 1993/2854, r 31A(5)(b) (as added (see note 19); amended by SI 2004/2526).
30 Employment Appeal Tribunal Rules 1993, SI 1993/2854, r 31A(5)(c) (as added: see note 19).
31 Employment Appeal Tribunal Rules 1993, SI 1993/2854, r 31A(5)(d) (as added: see note 19).
32 Ie under the Employment Appeal Tribunal Rules 1993, SI 1993/2854, r 30A(2)(c): see PARA 1452.
33 Employment Appeal Tribunal Rules 1993, SI 1993/2854, r 31A(6) (as added: see note 19).
34 Employment Appeal Tribunal Rules 1993, SI 1993/2854, r 31(3). See *Watt v Ahsan* [2007] UKHL 51, [2008] 1 AC 696, sub nom *Ahsan v Watt* [2008] 1 All ER 869.

1524.   Handing down of judgments.   When the Employment Appeal Tribunal[1] reserves judgment to a later date[2], the parties will be notified of the date when it is ready to be handed down. It is not necessary for a party or representative to attend[3].

Where judgment at either a preliminary hearing[4] or a full hearing[5] is reserved, and later handed down in writing, a copy is provided to all parties, and to recognised law reporters. It will at the discretion of the judge[6] be provided in advance on suitable undertakings as to confidentiality for the purpose of correcting any obvious errors of transcription or expression; the reasoning is not open to revision unless a review[7] is applied for and granted. The parties may apply in advance of the handing down in respect of costs, or permission to appeal, and unless it is otherwise directed that application will normally be dealt with on paper without an oral hearing[8].

The judgment will be pronounced without being read aloud, by the judge who presided or by another judge, on behalf of the Appeal Tribunal. The judge may deal with any application or may refer it to the judge and/or the Appeal Tribunal who heard the appeal, whether to deal with on the papers or at a further oral hearing on notice[9].

Transcripts of unreserved judgments at a preliminary hearing, appeals against registrar's orders[10], an appointment for directions[11] and rule 3(10) hearings[12] will not be produced and provided to the parties[13], except:

(1)   where an appeal, or any ground of appeal, is dismissed in the presence of the appellant, in which case no transcript of the judgment is produced unless, within 14 days of the seal date of the order[14], either party applies to the Appeal Tribunal for a transcript, or the Appeal Tribunal of its own initiative directs[15] that a judgment be transcribed[16];

(2)   where an appeal or any ground of appeal is dismissed in the absence of the appellant, in which case a transcript will be supplied to the appellant[17];

(3)   where an appeal is allowed to go forward to a preliminary hearing or a full hearing[18], in which case if a judgment is given orally it will be transcribed and a transcript provided to the parties unless the judge considers a written note of his reasons is sufficient[19].

Where an unreserved judgment is delivered at a full hearing, no transcript will be produced and provided to the parties unless[20]:

(a)   either party applies for it to the Appeal Tribunal within 14 days of that hearing[21]; or

(b)   the Appeal Tribunal of its own initiative directs that the judgment be transcribed, for example where it is considered that a point of general importance arises or that the matter is to be remitted to, or otherwise continued before, the employment tribunal[22]; or

(c)   a party is not present at the hearing of the appeal[23].

All full hearing judgments which are transcribed or handed down will be posted on the Appeal Tribunal website. Any other judgment may be posted on that website if so directed by the registrar or a judge[24].

1   As to the Employment Appeal Tribunal see PARA 1422 et seq. As to the use of the abbreviation 'EAT' see PARA 1435 note 2.
2   See PARA 1524.
3   *Practice Direction (Employment Appeal Tribunal—Procedure) 2013* [2014] IRLR 92 para 21.1.
4   As to a preliminary hearing see PARA 1519.
5   As to the full hearing see PARA 1520.
6   As to the meaning of 'judge' for these purposes see PARA 1451 note 4.
7   See the Employment Appeal Tribunal Rules 1993, SI 1993/2854, r 33; and PARA 1528.
8   *Practice Direction (Employment Appeal Tribunal—Procedure) 2013* [2014] IRLR 92 para 21.5.
9   *Practice Direction (Employment Appeal Tribunal—Procedure) 2013* [2014] IRLR 92 para 21.2. Applications for permission to appeal should be made pursuant to para 25 (see PARA 1530 note 5) and applications for costs should be made pursuant to para 22.2 (see PARA 1525): para 21.2.
10 See PARA 1511 note 12. As to the meaning of 'registrar' see PARA 1430 note 4.
11 See PARA 1512.
12 Ie hearings under the Employment Appeal Tribunal Rules 1993, SI 1993/2854, r 3(10) (certain oral hearings in national security proceedings): see PARA 1451.
13 *Practice Direction (Employment Appeal Tribunal—Procedure) 2013* [2014] IRLR 92 para 21.3.
14 As to the seal date of an order see PARA 1499 note 8.
15 Ie in circumstances such as those set out in *Practice Direction (Employment Appeal Tribunal—Procedure) 2013* [2014] IRLR 92 para 21.4: see the text and notes 20–23.
16 See *Practice Direction (Employment Appeal Tribunal—Procedure) 2013* [2014] IRLR 92 para 21.3.1.
17 See *Practice Direction (Employment Appeal Tribunal—Procedure) 2013* [2014] IRLR 92 para 21.3.2.
18 Reasons will be given, either in the form of a short judgment or in a note made by the judge of the reasons for permitting the appeal to go forward: *Practice Direction (Employment Appeal Tribunal—Procedure) 2013* [2014] IRLR 92 para 21.3.3.
19 See *Practice Direction (Employment Appeal Tribunal—Procedure) 2013* [2014] IRLR 92 para 21.3.3.
20 See *Practice Direction (Employment Appeal Tribunal—Procedure) 2013* [2014] IRLR 92 para 21.4.
21 *Practice Direction (Employment Appeal Tribunal—Procedure) 2013* [2014] IRLR 92 para 21.4.1.
22 *Practice Direction (Employment Appeal Tribunal—Procedure) 2013* [2014] IRLR 92 para 21.4.2. Where the Appeal Tribunal orally makes an order remitting the case or part of it to an employment tribunal for further or re-hearing, the parties must immediately raise any uncertainty they or any of them have as to the precise scope of the remission, for it is this which defines the jurisdiction of the tribunal on the remitted issues. The scope of the remission will be recorded in the order following the hearing. It is the obligation of each party to ensure that the scope as there set out corresponds with their understanding and to raise the question without delay if it appears not to do so: para 23.1. If at a later hearing before an employment tribunal an issue arises as to the scope of remission, the tribunal may invite the Appeal Tribunal to give whatever clarification is thought necessary, and if given this will be conclusive: para 23.2.
23 *Practice Direction (Employment Appeal Tribunal—Procedure) 2013* [2014] IRLR 92 para 21.4.3.
24 *Practice Direction (Employment Appeal Tribunal—Procedure) 2013* [2014] IRLR 92 para 21.7. The address of the Appeal Tribunal website, at the date at which this volume states the law, is to be found at: *http://www.justice.gov.uk*.

1525.   Costs or expenses orders. The Appeal Tribunal[1] may make an order (a 'costs order') that a party[2] or a special advocate[3] (the 'paying party') make a payment in respect of the costs[4] incurred by another party[5] or a special advocate (the 'receiving party')[6]:

(1) on general grounds, where it appears to the Appeal Tribunal that any proceedings brought by the paying party were unnecessary, improper, vexatious or misconceived or that there has been unreasonable delay[7] or other unreasonable conduct[8] in the bringing or conducting of proceedings by the paying party[9]; or

(2) in particular when:

   (a) the paying party has not complied with a direction of the Appeal Tribunal[10];

   (b) when the paying party has amended its notice of appeal[11]; or, in national security proceedings,[12] the document disclosing the grounds[13] and/or the supplementary grounds[14] on which the appeal is brought; or the respondent's answer[15] or statement of grounds of cross-appeal[16]; or, in national security proceedings, the document disclosing the grounds[17] and/or the supplementary grounds[18] for resisting the appeal or of any cross-appeal[19];

   (c) when the paying party has caused an adjournment of proceedings[20].

In all the cases mentioned in heads (1) and (2) above the costs order is made against the paying party[21].

If the Appeal Tribunal allows an appeal, in full or in part, it may make a costs order against the respondent specifying the respondent pay to the appellant an amount no greater than any fee paid by the appellant under a notice issued by the Lord Chancellor[22]. Nothing in this provision, or in head (2) above, restricts the Appeal Tribunal's discretion to award costs under head (1) above[23].

A costs order may be made against or in favour of a respondent who has not had an answer accepted in the proceedings in relation to the conduct of any part which he has taken in the proceedings[24].

A party or special advocate may apply to the Appeal Tribunal for a costs order to be made at any time during the proceedings, or at the end of a hearing[25], or in writing[26] to the registrar[27] within 14 days of the date[28] on which the order of the Appeal Tribunal finally disposing of the proceedings was sent to the parties[29].

No costs order is to be made unless the registrar has sent notice to the party or special advocate against whom the order may be made giving him the opportunity to give reasons why the order should not be made; but this is not to be taken to require the registrar to send notice to the party or special advocate if the party or special advocate has been given an opportunity to give reasons orally to the Appeal Tribunal as to why the order should not be made[30].

Where the Appeal Tribunal makes a costs order it must provide written reasons for doing so if a request for written reasons is made within 21 days of the date of the costs order; and the registrar must send a copy of the written reasons to all the parties to the proceedings[31].

The amount of a costs order against the paying party can be determined in the following ways:

   (i)   the Appeal Tribunal may specify the sum which the paying party must pay to the receiving party[32];

   (ii) the parties may agree on a sum to be paid by the paying party to the receiving party and if they do so the costs order is to be for the sum so agreed[33];

   (iii) the Appeal Tribunal may order the paying party to pay the receiving party the whole or a specified part of the costs of the receiving party with the amount to be paid being determined by way of detailed assessment in the High Court[34].

The Appeal Tribunal may have regard to the paying party's ability to pay when considering the amount of a costs order[35].

The costs of an assisted person[36] must be determined by detailed assessment in accordance with the Civil Procedure Rules[37].

1   As to the meaning of 'Appeal Tribunal' see PARA 1451 note 4.

2   Costs can be awarded only against a person who was a party on the record at the time when the costs were incurred: *Lowbey v Lindo* [1981] ICR 216n, EAT.

3   As to the special advocate see PARA 1452.

4   For these purposes, 'costs' includes fees, charges, disbursements and expenses incurred by or on behalf of a party or special advocate, in relation to the proceedings, including the reimbursement allowed to a litigant in person under the Employment Appeal Tribunal Rules 1993, SI 1993/2854, r 34D (see PARA 1527): r 34(2) (r 34 substituted by SI 2004/2526). Any such costs may relate to interim applications or hearings or to a preliminary hearing or a full hearing and also include legal costs and expenses and allowances paid by the Secretary of State and payment in respect of time spent in preparing a case: *Practice Direction (Employment Appeal Tribunal—Procedure) 2013* [2014] IRLR 92 para 22.1.

   As to applications on interim matters see PARA 1511; as to preliminary hearings see PARA 1519; as to a full hearing see PARA 1520; and as to hearings see PARA 1522.

5   Costs cannot be recovered where they are incurred by a body which backs the appeal but is not a party to it (*Walsall Metropolitan Borough Council v Sidhu* [1980] ICR 519, EAT); or where they are incurred by the tribunal, however unreasonably (*Wilson v Knowsley Metropolitan Borough Council* (1989) Times, 11 November, EAT).

6   Employment Appeal Tribunal Rules 1993, SI 1993/2854, r 34(1) (as substituted: see note 4). As to costs in proceedings that are pursued for a declaration on unfair dismissal proceedings where any award of compensation could be severely limited or eliminated see PARA 1466.

7   See *Dacres v Walls Meat Co Ltd* [1976] ICR 44, [1976] IRLR 20, EAT. Costs may be awarded where an appeal is withdrawn at an unnecessarily late stage: *TVR Engineering Ltd v Johnson* [1978] IRLR 555, EAT.

8   What constitutes unreasonable conduct is a question for the Appeal Tribunal, to which the fact that the appeal was brought on legal advice will be relevant, though not decisive: *Stannard & Co (1969) Ltd v Wilson* [1983] ICR 86, EAT. Lack of any substantial grounds or point of law may be relevant (*Maroof v JB Battye & Co Ltd* (1973) 8 ITR 489, NIRC; *J & H Smith v Smith* [1974] ICR 156, [1974] IRLR 59, NIRC; *Redland Roof Tiles Ltd v Eveleigh* [1979] IRLR 11, EAT), as may failure to attend the hearing (*Croydon v Greenham (Plant Hire) Ltd* [1978] ICR 415, EAT) or the appellant's treatment of the Appeal Tribunal in a 'cavalier' manner (*Nial v Baxters (Butchers) Ltd* (1985) Times, 9 February, EAT). Costs may be awarded where an appeal is rejected for lack of an arguable point of law under the preliminary hearing procedure (see PARA 1519): *Ravelin v Bournemouth Borough Council* (1986) Times, 19 July, EAT, disapproving statements to the contrary in *Rattan v British Airways* (1986) Times, 18 July, EAT. In considering whether an appeal has been brought unreasonably, the fact it has gone through a preliminary hearing will always be a factor, but there is no practice which says that where a case has gone through a sift costs will only be awarded in exceptional circumstances: *Iron and Steel Trades Confederation v ASW Ltd (in liquidation)* [2004] IRLR 926, EAT. See also *Dunn v Estée Lauder Cosmetics Ltd* [2014] All ER (D) 228 (Jan), EAT (it was appropriate to make the costs order sought by the employer where employee sent abusive and threatening correspondence before withdrawing appeal two weeks before hearing; employee's appeal had been misconceived, and would have had no prospect of success anyway).

9   Employment Appeal Tribunal Rules 1993, SI 1993/2854, r 34A(1) (r 34A added by SI 2004/2526).

10 Employment Appeal Tribunal Rules 1993, SI 1993/2854, r 34A(2)(a) (as added: see note 9).

11 As to the notice of appeal see PARA 1495.

12 As to the meaning of 'national security proceedings' see PARA 1451 note 1.

13 Ie the grounds contained in the document referred to in the Employment Appeal Tribunal Rules 1993, SI 1993/2854, r 3(5): see PARA 1451.

14 Ie the grounds and/or the supplementary grounds contained in the document referred to in the Employment Appeal Tribunal Rules 1993, SI 1993/2854, r 3(6): see PARA 1451.

15 As to the respondent's answer see PARA 1499. As to the meaning of 'respondent' see PARA 1498 note 4.

16 As to the notice of cross-appeal see PARA 1499.

17 Ie the grounds contained in the document referred to in the Employment Appeal Tribunal Rules 1993, SI 1993/2854, r 6(7): see PARA 1499.

18 Ie the grounds and/or the supplementary grounds contained in the document referred to in the Employment Appeal Tribunal Rules 1993, SI 1993/2854, r 6(8): see PARA 1499.

19 See the Employment Appeal Tribunal Rules 1993, SI 1993/2854, r 34A(2)(b) (as added: see note 9).

20 Employment Appeal Tribunal Rules 1993, SI 1993/2854, r 34A(2)(c) (as added: see note 9).

21 Employment Appeal Tribunal Rules 1993, SI 1993/2854, r 34A(1), (2) (as added: see note 9).

22 Employment Appeal Tribunal Rules 1993, SI 1993/2854, r 34A(2A) (added by SI 2013/1693). As to fees payable in the Appeal Tribunal see PARA 1496; and as to the Lord Chancellor see CONSTITUTIONAL AND ADMINISTRATIVE LAW vol 20 (2014) PARA 255 et seq.

23 Employment Appeal Tribunal Rules 1993, SI 1993/2854, r 34A(3) (as added (see note 9); amended by SI 2013/1693).

24 Employment Appeal Tribunal Rules 1993, SI 1993/2854, r 34(3) (as substituted: see note 4).

25 Employment Appeal Tribunal Rules 1993, SI 1993/2854, r 34(4) (as substituted: see note 4); *Practice Direction (Employment Appeal Tribunal—Procedure) 2013* [2014] IRLR 92 para 22.2. The party seeking the order must state the legal ground on which the application is based and the facts on which it is based and, by a schedule or otherwise, show how the costs have been incurred. If the application is made in respect of only part of the proceedings, particulars must be given showing how the costs have been incurred on that specific part: para 22.3.

An application for costs may be resolved by the EAT on the papers, provided that the opportunity has been given for representations in writing by all relevant parties, or the EAT may refer the matter for an oral hearing, and may assess the costs either on the papers or at an oral hearing, or refer the matter for detailed assessment: para 22.4. Where the EAT makes any costs order by decision on the papers it must provide written reasons for so doing. If such order is made at a hearing, then written reasons will be provided if a request is made at the hearing or within 21 days of the seal date of the costs order. The registrar must send a copy of the written reasons to all the parties to the proceedings: para 22.6.

26 As to the meaning of 'writing' see PARA 1430 note 1.

27 As to the meaning of 'registrar' see PARA 1430 note 4.

28 Ie the seal date of an order: see PARA 1499 note 8.

29 Employment Appeal Tribunal Rules 1993, SI 1993/2854, r 34(4) (as substituted: see note 4); *Practice Direction (Employment Appeal Tribunal—Procedure) 2013* [2014] IRLR 92 para 22.2. See also note 25.

30 Employment Appeal Tribunal Rules 1993, SI 1993/2854, r 34(5) (as substituted: see note 4). See also note 25.

31 Employment Appeal Tribunal Rules 1993, SI 1993/2854, r 34(6) (as substituted: see note 4); and see *Practice Direction (Employment Appeal Tribunal—Procedure) 2013* [2014] IRLR 92 para 22.6, cited in note 25.

32 Employment Appeal Tribunal Rules 1993, SI 1993/2854, r 34B(1)(a) (r 34B added by SI 2004/2526).

33 Employment Appeal Tribunal Rules 1993, SI 1993/2854, r 34B(1)(b) (as added: see note 32).

34 Employment Appeal Tribunal Rules 1993, SI 1993/2854, r 34B(1)(c) (as added: see note 32). A detailed assessment is conducted pursuant to CPR Pt 47: CIVIL PROCEDURE vol 12 (2009) PARA 1779 et seq.

35 Employment Appeal Tribunal Rules 1993, SI 1993/2854, r 34B(2) (as added: see note 32). If the party against whom the order is sought wishes the EAT to have regard to means and/or an alleged inability to pay, a witness statement giving particulars and exhibiting any documents must be served on the other party or parties and presented to the EAT. Further directions may need to be given by the EAT in such cases: *Practice Direction (Employment Appeal Tribunal—Procedure) 2013* [2014] IRLR 92 para 22.3.

36 'Assisted person' means an assisted person within the statutory provisions relating to legal aid: CPR 43.2(1)(h) (definition saved by the Legal Aid, Sentencing and Punishment of Offenders Act 2012 (Consequential, Transitional and Saving Provisions) Regulations 2013, SI 2013/534, reg 14(4)(a), despite the revocation of CPR Pt 43 by the Civil Procedure (Amendment) Rules 2013, SI 2013/262).

37 Employment Appeal Tribunal Rules 1993, SI 1993/2854, r 34B(3) (as added: see note 32). As to detailed assessment in accordance with the Civil Procedure Rules see CIVIL PROCEDURE vol 12 (2009) PARA 1779 et seq.

1526.   Wasted costs order against a party's representative.   The Appeal Tribunal[1] may make a wasted costs[2] order against a party's representative[3].

In a wasted costs order, the Appeal Tribunal may disallow or order the representative of a party to meet the whole or part of any wasted costs of any party, including an order that the representative repay to his client any costs which have already been paid[4].

Before making a wasted costs order, the Appeal Tribunal must give the representative a reasonable opportunity to make oral or written representations as to reasons why such an order should not be made[5]. The Appeal Tribunal may also have regard to the representative's ability to pay when considering whether it is to make a wasted costs order or how much that order should be[6].

When the Appeal Tribunal makes a wasted costs order, it must specify in the order the amount to be disallowed or paid[7].

The registrar[8] must inform the representative's client in writing:

(1)   of any such proceedings[9]; or

(2)   of any such order made against the party's representative[10].

Where the Appeal Tribunal makes a wasted costs order it must provide written reasons for doing so if a request is made for written reasons within 21 days of the date of the wasted costs order. The registrar must send a copy of the written reasons to all parties to the proceedings[11].

1   As to the meaning of 'Appeal Tribunal' see PARA 1451 note 4. As to the use of the abbreviation 'EAT' see PARA 1435 note 2.
2   For these purposes, 'wasted costs' means any costs incurred by a party (including the representative's own client and any party who does not have a legal representative): (1) as a result of any improper, unreasonable or negligent act or omission on the part of any representative; or (2) which, in the light of any such act or omission occurring after they were incurred, the Appeal Tribunal considers it reasonable to expect that party to pay: Employment Appeal Tribunal Rules 1993, SI 1993/2854, r 34C(3) (r 34C added by SI 2004/2526). 'Representative' means a party's legal or other representative or any employee of such representative: Employment Appeal Tribunal Rules 1993, SI 1993/2854, r 34C(4) (as so added; amended by SI 2013/1693). 'Legal representative' means a person, including a person who is a party's employee, who has a general qualification within the meaning of the Courts and Legal Services Act 1990 (see LEGAL PROFESSIONS vol 65 (2008) PARA 742); is an advocate or solicitor in Scotland; or is a member of the Bar of Northern Ireland or a solicitor of the Court of Judicature of Northern Ireland: Employment Appeal Tribunal Rules 1993, SI 1993/2854, r 2(1) (definition added by SI 2004/2526; amended by the Constitutional Reform Act 2005 Sch 11 Pt 3 para 5).
3   Employment Appeal Tribunal Rules 1993, SI 1993/2854, r 34C(1) (as added: see note 2). An application for a wasted costs order must be made in writing, setting out the nature of the case upon which the application is based and the best particulars of the costs sought to be recovered. Such application must be presented to the EAT and served upon the party or parties who will pay the costs/expenses if the application succeeds. Further directions may need to be given by the EAT in such cases: *Practice Direction (Employment Appeal Tribunal—Procedure) 2013* [2014] IRLR 92 para 22.5. As to service of documents see PARA 1504; and as to directions see PARA 1512. As to the meaning of 'writing' see PARA 1430 note 1.
4   Employment Appeal Tribunal Rules 1993, SI 1993/2854, r 34C(2) (as added: see note 2).
5   Employment Appeal Tribunal Rules 1993, SI 1993/2854, r 34C(5) (as added: see note 2).
6   Employment Appeal Tribunal Rules 1993, SI 1993/2854, r 34C(5) (as added: see note 2).
7   Employment Appeal Tribunal Rules 1993, SI 1993/2854, r 34C(6) (as added: see note 2).
8   As to the meaning of 'registrar' see PARA 1430 note 4.
9   Employment Appeal Tribunal Rules 1993, SI 1993/2854, r 34C(7)(a) (as added: see note 2).
10 Employment Appeal Tribunal Rules 1993, SI 1993/2854, r 34C(7)(b) (as added: see note 2).
11 Employment Appeal Tribunal Rules 1993, SI 1993/2854, r 34C(8) (as added: see note 2).

1527.   Costs orders in favour of litigants in person.   Where the Appeal Tribunal[1] makes a costs order[2] in favour of a party who is a litigant in person[3], the costs[4] allowed must not exceed, except in the case of a disbursement, two-thirds of the amount which would have been allowed if the litigant in person had been represented by a legal representative[5].

The litigant in person must be allowed:

(1) costs for the same categories of work and disbursements, which would have been allowed if the work had been done or the disbursements had been made by a legal representative on the litigant in person's behalf[6];

(2) the payments reasonably made by him for legal services relating to the conduct of the proceedings[7];

(3) the costs of obtaining expert assistance in assessing the costs claim[8]; and

(4) other expenses incurred by him in relation to the proceedings[9].

The amount of costs to be allowed to the litigant in person for any item of work claimed is:

(a) where the litigant in person can prove financial loss, the amount that he can prove he had lost for the time reasonably spent on doing the work[10]; or

(b) where the litigant in person cannot prove financial loss, an amount for the time which the Appeal Tribunal considers reasonably spent on doing the work at the prescribed rate[11].

A litigant in person who is allowed costs for attending at court to conduct his case is not entitled to a witness allowance in respect of such attendance in addition to those costs[12].

1   As to the meaning of 'Appeal Tribunal' see PARA 1451 note 4.
2   As to costs orders see PARA 1525.
3   For these purposes, a litigant in person includes: (1) a company or other corporation which is acting without a legal representative; and (2) a barrister, solicitor, solicitor's employee or other authorised litigator (as defined in the Courts and Legal Services Act 1990) (see s 119(1); and LEGAL PROFESSIONS vol 65 (2008) PARA 498), who is acting for himself: Employment Appeal Tribunal Rules 1993, SI 1993/2854, r 34D(7) (r 34D added by SI 2004/2526). As to the meaning of 'legal representative' see PARA 1526 note 2.
4   As to the meaning of 'costs' for these purposes see PARA 1525 note 4.
5   Employment Appeal Tribunal Rules 1993, SI 1993/2854, r 34D(1), (2) (as added: see note 3).
6   Employment Appeal Tribunal Rules 1993, SI 1993/2854, r 34D(3)(a) (as added: see note 3).
7   Employment Appeal Tribunal Rules 1993, SI 1993/2854, r 34D(3)(b) (as added: see note 3).
8   Employment Appeal Tribunal Rules 1993, SI 1993/2854, r 34D(3)(c) (as added: see note 3).
9   Employment Appeal Tribunal Rules 1993, SI 1993/2854, r 34D(3)(d) (as added: see note 3).
10 Employment Appeal Tribunal Rules 1993, SI 1993/2854, r 34D(4)(a) (as added: see note 3).
11 Employment Appeal Tribunal Rules 1993, SI 1993/2854, r 34D(4)(b) (as added: see note 3). For the year commencing on 6 April 2006, the original hourly rate of £25 was to be increased by the sum of £1.00 and for each subsequent year commencing on 6 April, the hourly rate for the previous year is also to be increased by the sum of £1.00: see r 34D(5) (as so added).
12 Employment Appeal Tribunal Rules 1993, SI 1993/2854, r 34D(6) (as added: see note 3).

1528. Review of decisions; correction of errors. The Appeal Tribunal[1] may, either of its own motion or on application, review any order made by it[2] and may, on such review, revoke or vary that order on the grounds that[3]:

(1) the order was wrongly made as the result of an error on the part of the Appeal Tribunal or its staff[4];

(2) a party did not receive proper notice of the proceedings leading to the order[5]; or

(3) the interests of justice require such review[6].

An application for review must be made within 14 days of the date of the order[7]; and the decision to grant or refuse such an application may be made by a judge[8].

A clerical mistake in any order arising from an accidental slip or omission may at any time be corrected by, or on the authority of, a judge or member[9].

1   As to the meaning of 'Appeal Tribunal' see PARA 1451 note 4.
2   However, 'the cases in which an application to review [the Appeal Tribunal's] decision is appropriate must be very few indeed .... In a case where it is said that [the Appeal Tribunal's] decision is wrong as a matter of law, the right place to put right that error is the Court of Appeal. It is not a correct practice to come back to [the Appeal] Tribunal to review its decision under [the Employment Appeal Tribunal Rules 1993, SI 1993/2854, r 33]': *Stannard & Co (1969) Ltd v Wilson* [1983] ICR 86 at 87, EAT, per Browne-Wilkinson P; affd in *Blockleys plc v Miller* [1992] ICR 749, EAT. See also *Asda Stores Ltd v Thompson (No 2)* [2004] IRLR 598, EAT (the aim of the Appeal Tribunal is to give speedy justice and this should not be put at risk by cases coming back and back to it, except on remission by a higher court).
3   Employment Appeal Tribunal Rules 1993, SI 1993/2854, r 33(1).
4   Employment Appeal Tribunal Rules 1993, SI 1993/2854, r 33(1)(a). This rule should be construed as covering the situation where some alteration was necessary to the form of the order made as a result of the judgment: *Blockleys plc v Miller* [1992] ICR 749 at 756, EAT, per Wood J.
5   Employment Appeal Tribunal Rules 1993, SI 1993/2854, r 33(1)(b).
6   Employment Appeal Tribunal Rules 1993, SI 1993/2854, r 33(1)(c). This rule should be construed as being of limited scope intended to repair an error of jurisdiction or a defect in the process of the appeal, or the technical correctness of the decision: *Blockleys plc v Miller* [1992] ICR 749 at 756, EAT, per Wood J. See, however, *Nikitas v Solihull Metropolitan Borough Council* [1986] ICR 291, EAT (employment tribunal's interim powers); *Jenkins v P & O European Ferries (Dover) Ltd* [1991] ICR 652, EAT (decision taken in ignorance of contemporaneous decision of another division of the Appeal Tribunal).
    See *Davies v Cornwall Council* [2014] All ER (D) 275 (Mar), EAT (in considering whether, on a review, to revoke its original decision on the basis of new evidence, the tribunal had to find that new evidence not only had to be relevant, but would probably have had enough weight to be an important influence on the result of the case), applying *Marsden v Council of the City of Newcastle Upon Tyne* [2010] ICR 743, [2010] All ER (D) 74 (Feb), EAT. Also, the tribunal when considering the review application were entitled to take into account as a factor in the balancing exercise which they had to carry out that the likelihood that the claimant would be found, if there were to be a rehearing, to have been very substantially or totally at fault (and hence the issue of the extent of potential recovery, if any, which the claimant could expect from a rehearing), and to weigh that against the other relevant factors but the tribunal's broad discretion should not be shackled by a requirement to ignore the narrow point of potential compensation in deciding the wider issue (see PARA 1466): *Davies v Cornwall Council* [2014] All ER (D) 275 (Mar), EAT.
7   Employment Appeal Tribunal Rules 1993, SI 1993/2854, r 33(2). The date of the order means the 'seal date' of an order: see PARA 1499 note 8.
8   Employment Appeal Tribunal Rules 1993, SI 1993/2854, r 33(4) (added by SI 2004/2526). As to the meaning of 'judge' see PARA 1451 note 4. Where an application is made for a review of a judgment or order of the EAT, it will normally be considered by the judge or judge and lay members who heard the appeal in respect of which the review is sought, who may exercise any power of case management as seems appropriate. If the original judgment or order was made by the judge together with lay members, then the judge may, pursuant to the Employment Appeal Tribunal Rules 1993, SI 1993/2854, r 33, consider and refuse such application for review on the papers. If the judge does not refuse the application, he may make any relevant further order, but will not grant the application without notice to the opposing party and reference to the lay members, for consideration with them, either on paper or in open court. A request to review a judgment or order of the EAT must be made within 14 days of the seal date of the order, or must include an application, for an extension of time, with reasons, copied to all parties: *Practice Direction (Employment Appeal Tribunal—Procedure) 2013* [2014] IRLR 92 para 24.1.
    A refusal to grant a review is not an order finally disposing of proceedings and so does not require written reasons to be given (see PARA 1523): *Persson v Matra Marconi Space UK Ltd* (1996) Times, 10 December, CA.
9   Employment Appeal Tribunal Rules 1993, SI 1993/2854, r 33(3). As to the meaning of 'member' see PARA 1451 note 4.

1529.   Recovery of sums awarded; enforcement of fines. Any decision or award of the Employment Appeal Tribunal (the 'Appeal Tribunal')[1] on an appeal has the same effect, and may be enforced in the same manner, as a decision or award of the body or officer from whom the appeal was brought[2].

A magistrates' court must not remit the whole or any part of a fine imposed by the Appeal Tribunal, unless it has the consent of a judge who is a member of the Appeal Tribunal[3].

1 As to the Employment Appeal Tribunal see PARA 1422 et seq.
2 Employment Tribunals Act 1996 s 35(2).
3 Employment Tribunals Act 1996 s 36(5).

(8) APPEALS FROM THE EMPLOYMENT APPEAL TRIBUNAL

1530. Appeal from decision of the Employment Appeal Tribunal. An appeal on any question of law[1] lies[2] from any decision or order of the Employment Appeal Tribunal[3] to the Court of Appeal[4] with the leave of either the Appeal Tribunal or the Court of Appeal[5]. However, no appeal lies from a decision of the Appeal Tribunal refusing leave for the institution or continuance of, or the making of an application in, proceedings by a person who is the subject[6] of a restriction of proceedings order[7].

On any such appeal the Court of Appeal's primary concern is with whether the decision of the employment tribunal, not the decision of the Employment Appeal Tribunal, was right[8]. However, this does not mean that, in any particular case, the decision and reasoning of the Appeal Tribunal are irrelevant or may not form part of the appeal[9].

1 As to points of law and fact before the Employment Appeal Tribunal see PARA 1429. See also *Gover v Propertycare Ltd* [2006] EWCA Civ 286, [2006] 4 All ER 69, [2006] ICR 1073 (the Court of Appeal is not constrained only to consider the correctness of the employment tribunal's decision when hearing an appeal from the Employment Appeal Tribunal; it was appropriate to consider the Appeal Tribunal's decision as well. The Court of Appeal's jurisdiction to hear the appeal, coming from a statutory tribunal, was only to be found in the Employment Tribunals Act 1996 s 37(1) which provided for an appeal from the Appeal Tribunal on a question of law only. It could not in any realistic sense be hearing an appeal from the Appeal Tribunal if it was only concerned with whether the employment tribunal was right.)
2 Ie without prejudice to the Administration of Justice Act 1960 s 13: see CONTEMPT OF COURT vol 22 (2012) PARA 118 et seq.
3 As to the Employment Appeal Tribunal see PARA 1422 et seq.
4 As to the procedure for making appeals to the Court of Appeal generally see CPR Pt 52; *Practice Direction—Appeals* (2001) PD 52; and CIVIL PROCEDURE vol 12 (2009) PARA 1657 et seq.
5 Employment Tribunals Act 1996 s 37(1), (2), (4). See *Gover v Propertycare Ltd* [2006] EWCA Civ 286, [2006] 4 All ER 69, [2006] ICR 1073; and note 1.
   An application to the EAT for permission to appeal to the Court of Appeal must be made (unless the EAT otherwise orders) at the hearing or when a reserved judgment is handed down or in writing within seven days thereafter as provided in *Practice Direction (Employment Appeal Tribunal—Procedure) 2013* [2014] IRLR 92 para 21.5 (see PARA 1524): para 25.1. If not made then, or if refused, or unless the EAT otherwise orders, any such applications must be made to the Court of Appeal within 21 days of the sealed order. An application for an extension of time for permission to appeal may be entertained by the EAT where a case is made out to the satisfaction of a judge or registrar that there is a need to delay until after a transcript is received (expedited if appropriate) or for other good reason. Applications for an extension of time for permission to appeal should however normally be made to the Court of Appeal: para 25.1. The party seeking permission must state the point of law to be advanced and the grounds: para 25.2.
6 Ie the Employment Tribunals Act 1996 s 33: see PARA 1430.
7 Employment Tribunals Act 1996 s 37(3).
8 *Hennessy v Craigmyle & Co Ltd* [1986] ICR 461 at 470, [1986] IRLR 300 at 305, CA, per Sir John Donaldson MR ('it is too often forgotten that, in the context of appeals from the Employment Appeal Tribunal, [the Court of Appeal] is a second-tier appellate court ....

Second-tier appellate courts are primarily concerned with the correctness of the trial court's decision'); *Campion v Hamworthy Engineering Ltd* [1987] ICR 966, CA; *Walls Meat Co Ltd v Selby* [1989] ICR 601, CA; *Mensah v East Hertfordshire NHS Trust* [1998] IRLR 531, CA. See also *Grady v HM Prison Service* [2003] EWCA Civ 527, [2003] ICR 753, [2003] IRLR 474 (EAT had dismissed an appeal on jurisdictional grounds which were overturned by the Court of Appeal). Where the appeal is brought on a new, procedural ground, the appeal should be remitted to a differently constituted Employment Appeal Tribunal for rehearing: *Sukul-Lennard v Croydon Primary Care Trust* (2003) Times, 14 August, [2003] All ER (D) 369 (Jul), CA.

9   *Gover v Propertycare Ltd* [2006] EWCA Civ 286, [2006] 4 All ER 69, [2006] ICR 1073; *Balfour Beatty Power Networks Ltd v Wilcox* [2006] EWCA Civ 1240, [2007] IRLR 63. As to the rule that appeals are against orders, not reasons for judgment, see *Lawson v Governing Body of Aylesford School* [2014] EWCA Civ 491, [2014] All ER (D) 246 (Mar) (substance of appeal was against the tribunal's decision and the tribunal's findings of fact made against the appellant; the EAT order challenged in the appeal had been revoked).

(9) APPEALS TO THE HIGH COURT

1531.   Appeals from an employment tribunal to the High court; in general. A person who was a party to specified proceedings[1] before an employment tribunal and who is dissatisfied in point of law with the decision of the tribunal may appeal to the High Court[2].

If any party to proceedings before the industrial training levy exemption referees[3] is dissatisfied in point of law with a decision of the referees, he may, according as rules of court may provide, either appeal there from to the High Court or require the referees to state and sign a case[4] for the opinion of the High Court[5].

1   Ie proceedings apart from those where appeal lies only to the Employment Appeal Tribunal: see PARA 1436.
2   See CPR 52.19(1); and CIVIL PROCEDURE vol 12 (2009) PARA 1685.
3   See PARA 683 et seq.
4   See CIVIL PROCEDURE vol 12 (2009) PARA 1691.
5   See the Tribunals and Inquiries Act 1992 Sch 1 para 24.

(10) CRIMINAL PROCEEDINGS

1532.   Criminal proceedings with regard to employment rights; in general. Certain of the statutory provisions relating to employment rights create criminal offences[1], a person guilty of such an offence being liable on summary conviction to a fine not exceeding the statutory maximum[2], the prescribed sum[3] or a specified level on the standard scale[4], as the case may be, or imprisonment, or to both[5], or on conviction on indictment to a fine[6] or to a fine or imprisonment, or to both[7].

1   As to criminal procedure generally see CRIMINAL PROCEDURE.
2   See eg the Working Time Regulations 1998, SI 1998/1833, reg 29(1), (3); and PARA 317); the Employment Rights Act 1996 s 169(3), (4); and PARA 885. As to the statutory maximum see SENTENCING AND DISPOSITION OF OFFENDERS vol 92 (2010) PARA 140.
3   See eg the Industrial Training Act 1982 s 6(6)(a)–(c), (7); and PARAS 669, 671). As to the prescribed sum see SENTENCING AND DISPOSITION OF OFFENDERS vol 92 (2010) PARA 141.
4   See eg:
    (1)   the Employers' Liability (Compulsory Insurance) Act 1969 s 4(3); and PARA 45; s 5; and PARA 40; s 5A(1); and PARA 41;
    (2)   the Employment and Training Act 1973 s 4(5); and PARA 635; s 10B(5), (7); and PARA 641;
    (3)   the Industrial Training Act 1982 s 6(5); and PARA 669;
    (4)   the Employment Rights Act 1996 s 72(5); and PARA 355; s 165(2), (4); and PARA 882; s 169(2); and PARA 885; s 190(3), (4); and PARA 631;

    (5)   the Employment Tribunals Act 1996 s 7(4); and PARA 1410; s 10B(2), (3); and PARA 1449; ss 11(2), 12(3); and PARAS 1416, 1417; ss 31(3), 32(3); and PARAS 1433, 1434;

    (6)   the National Minimum Wage Act 1998 s 31(1)–(6), (9); and PARA 251;

    (7)   the Working Time Regulations 1998, SI 1998/1833, reg 29(6); and PARA 317;

    (8)   the Employment Relations Act 1999 s 19(5); and PARA 74.

    As to the standard scale see SENTENCING AND DISPOSITION OF OFFENDERS vol 92 (2010) PARA 142.

5   See eg the Employment Rights Act 1996 s 169(3), (4); and PARA 885; the Industrial Training Act 1982 s 6(6)(a)–(c), (7); and PARAS 669, 671.

6   See eg the Working Time Regulations 1998, SI 1998/1833, reg 29(1), (3); and PARA 317.

7   See eg the Employment Rights Act 1996 s 169(3), (4), cited in PARA 885.

INDEX

Employment

APPRENTICESHIP AGREEMENT
breach by apprentice, 747
consent requirements, 128
covenants in, 129
employee under, person treated as, 494
form of, 128
injunction against breach, restriction on
    right to, 747
justification for quitting service, 748
non-performance, excuses for, 748
outside UK, whether apprentice obliged
    to serve outside, 748
parties to, 128
specific performance, no right to, 747
termination—
    at will, prohibition on, 128n[1]
    bankruptcy of master, on, 752
    change in composition of firm or
        business, on, 753
    death of master or apprentice, on,
        751
    minimum period of notice,
        apprentice's right to, 750
    minor's power to dissolve, 749
    misconduct by apprentice, on, 754
    mutual consent, by, 750
woman treated as employee, for
    maternity pay purposes, 406
writing, need for, 128

ARBITRATION
ACAS involvement. *See* ADVISORY,
    CONCILIATION AND ARBITRATION
    SERVICE

ARBITRATION CLAUSE
minor, binding on, 15

ARMED FORCES, MEMBER
agency worker regulations, and, 107
continuous employment, following
    reinstatement with former
    employer, 419, 461, 507
industrial action, statutory restriction
    on, 1391
national minimum wage, not qualifying
    for, 192
part-time workers regulations—
    application of, 82
    employment tribunal, complaint to,
        82n[11]
substitute labour, use as, 1398
working time protection—
    exclusion from provisions, 306
    generally, 275

ATTENDANCE ALLOWANCE
wages, as part of, 255n[2]

AUDIT
industrial training board accounts, of,
    672
BAILMENT
employment relationship distinguished,
    13
BANKRUPTCY
apprenticeship agreement, effect on,
    752
contract of employment, effect on, 727
BETTING WORKER
meaning, 321n[2]
betting transactions: meaning, 321n[2]
betting work: meaning, 321n[2]
protected: meaning, 321
Sunday work—
    detriment—
        date of the act: meaning, 615n[7]
        examples of no detriment suffered,
            615n[6]
        opted-out worker, 615n[8]
        right not to suffer, 615
    enforceability of employment
        contract, 322
    explanatory statements, requirement
        for, 324
    opting-in notice, effect, 321, 322
    opting-out notice, 323
    protected betting worker: meaning,
        321
    protected shop worker: meaning, 321
    statutory protection, 320
    unfair dismissal, 320, 787
BODY CORPORATE
national minimum wage offence by,
    252
CADET FORCE
national minimum wage, member not
    qualifying for, 190
CAREERS GUIDANCE
providers of, application of redundancy
    payments legislation, 843
CAREERS SERVICES
ancillary goods and services, provision
    of, 642
Her Majesty's Chief Inspector of
    Education, Children's Services and
    Skills, inspection by, 641
inspection, 641
local authority—
    meaning, 640n[4]
    ancillary goods and services, provision
        of, 642
    arrangements with, 640
    control by Secretary of State, 643
    directions to, 640

CERTIFICATION OFFICER—*continued*
  certificate of trade union
    independence—
    application for—
      dealing with, 905
      duty to keep records, 905
    conclusive effect of decision, 907
    refusal of, 905
    withdrawal or cancellation, 906
  complaint by union members—
    power to hear, 1443
    procedure during, 1444
    striking out, 1444
  decision-making meeting: meaning, 916n[6]
  disciplinary proceedings: meaning, 916n[3]
  disqualified persons, declaration as to non-compliance with provisions, 958
  documents etc, power to require production of—
    financial affairs, investigation of, 949
    register of members, as to, 933
  election, declaration on failure to comply with requirements, 972
  employers' association—
    list kept by, 1083
    power to make entry in list, 1084
    power to remove from list, 1085
  functions, 1443
  inspectors—
    power to appoint, 950
    report of, duty to publish, 952
  membership audit certificate, union's duty to provide, 931
  office of, 1443
  political ballot rules—
    approval, 994
    declaration as to non-compliance with rules, 983
  political fund rules—
    approval of, 985, 994
    complaint by member, 985
  political objects, declaration as to use of funds for, 976
  procedure before, 1444
  register of trade union members—
    confidentiality during ballots, 937
    documents, power to require production of, 933, 936
    enforcement of union's duties as to—
      application to officer, 938
      confidentiality of register during ballots, 937
      court, effect of application to, 938

CERTIFICATION OFFICER—*continued*
  register of trade union
    members—*continued*
    enforcement of union's duties as to—*continued*
      declaration, power to make, 935, 938
      enforcement order: meaning, 935
      generally, 935
      inspectors, power to appoint, 934
      investigations and reports, 934, 936
      production of register etc, as to, 933, 936
      relevant documents, inspection of, 934n[9]
    power to require production of, 933, 936
  remuneration etc, 1443
  report on union's financial affairs—
    admissibility in legal proceedings, 952
    publication, 952
  staff and other facilities, ACAS's duty to provide, 1443
  trade unions, list of—
    entry onto list, application for, 902
    keeping of, 900
    removal of union from, 903
  transfer of engagements—
    approval of instrument, 999, 1001
    complaint by union member, 1010, 1011
    registration of instrument, 1007

CHANGE OF NAME
  employers' association, 1092
  trade union, 1016

CHARACTER REFERENCE
  employer, from—
    negligently written, 724
    no obligation to give, 724

CHARITABLE COMMUNITY
  residential member of, not qualifying for national minimum wage, 189

CHIEF CONSTABLE
  redundancy payments legislation, application of, 845

CIVIL DEFENCE
  redundancy payments legislation, application of, 845

CIVIL PROTECTION SERVICES
  meaning, 298n[2]
  working time provisions, exclusion from, 298

CONFIDENTIAL
INFORMATION—*continued*
information and consultation
representative—*continued*
withholding of information by
employer, 1310
misuse by employee—
exceptions to duty, 68
implied term, 67, 71
intelligence and security services,
71n[6]
termination of employment,
following, 7
trade secret, 71
protected disclosure—
meaning, 69
detriment, employee's right not to
suffer, 619
forms of making, 69
generally, 68
qualifying disclosure for purposes of,
70
unfair dismissal for making, 792
void term precluding the making of,
69
whistleblowing—
generally, 68
protected disclosure, 68, 69

CONSTRUCTIVE DISMISSAL
meaning, 763
annual pay rise etc, failure to honour
contractual entitlement, 763n[16]
anticipatory repudiatory conduct, 763n[6]
breaches of contract supporting findings
of, 763
generally, 763
grievances not treated seriously, where,
49
illegal or dangerous orders, for refusing
to obey, 63
past waived breaches, effect, 763n[10]

CONTEMPT OF COURT
acts giving rise to, 1442
trade union, by, 1442

CONTINENTAL SHELF
foreign sector of: meaning, 155n[5],
156n[2], 184n[4]
operations on, persons employed in—
continental shelf operations:
meaning, 407n[10]
statutory adoption pay, 499
statutory maternity pay, 411
statutory paternity pay, 453
statutory sick pay, 568
United Kingdom sector of: meaning,
155n[5], 184n[3]

CONTINUITY OF EMPLOYMENT
change of employer, 135
continuous employment, computation of
period of—
absence, weeks counting in case of,
131
beginning of period, 130
determination of questions, 130
generally, 130
incapacity, weeks counting in case
of, 131
temporary cessations of work, 131n[5]
dismissed employee, reinstatement or
re-engagement, 133
industrial disputes, effect of, 134
lockout, in case of, 134
military service, reinstatement after, 132
redundancy payment, right to. *See under*
REDUNDANCY PAYMENT
statutory concept, as, 130n[10]
strike, in case of, 134
transfer of undertaking. *See* TRANSFER
OF UNDERTAKING

CONTRACT
unfair terms—
consumer: meaning, 17
contract of employment, in, 17
legislation, applicability of, 17

CONTRACT OF EMPLOYMENT
meaning. See under WORDS AND
PHRASES *post*
breach, employment tribunal's
jurisdiction to hear complaint,
1407
capacity, 15
certainty, need for, 16
clarity, need for, 16
collective agreement incorporated into,
1176
consideration, need for, 16
constructive termination of, 867
consumer, party to contract dealing as,
17n[3]
contracting out of rights, void provision
as to, 150
contrary to statute, effect, 18
covenant in restraint of trade, 19
Crown employment, 6
effective date of termination: meaning,
755n[11]
employee's obligations—
competing with employer, restriction
on, 67
confidential information. *See*
CONFIDENTIAL INFORMATION
(misuse by employee)

CONTRACT OF
  EMPLOYMENT—*continued*
  employee's obligations—*continued*
    disruption of business operation,
      avoiding, 66
    duty of care in the workplace, 65
    fidelity, duty surviving termination of
      employment, 71
    good faith during employment, 67
    intellectual property rights, as to, 72
    invention or discovery, as trustee of,
      72
    new methods and techniques,
      adaptation to, 64
    no duty to volunteer information
      about misdeeds, 67n[3]
    obedience to lawful orders, 63
    secret profits, avoiding, 67
  employer's liabilities—
    Equality Act 2010, under, 51
    third parties, to, on contracts made.
      See third parties, contractual
      liability to *below*
    vicarious liability for employees'
      acts, 52
  employer's obligations—
    duty of care—
      equal treatment, 21
      health and safety, as to. *See* health
        and safety, as to *below*
      indemnification, implied duty of,
        39
      personal data, as to processing of,
        21
      remuneration, as to. *See*
        remuneration under *below*
      work, provision of. *See* work under,
        provision of *below*
    duty to insure. *See* EMPLOYERS'
      LIABILITY INSURANCE
    employee's losses and liabilities,
      indemnification etc, 39
    grievances, implied term to treat
      seriously, 49
    health and safety, as to—
      common law duty, extent of, 33
      consultation with employees, 38
      employee with mischievous
        tendencies, removal of, 33n[3]
      implied duty of care, 32
      level of duty, 32
      plant and equipment, adequacy of,
        33n[4]
      safety committee, 37
      safety representatives, 36

CONTRACT OF
  EMPLOYMENT—*continued*
  employer's obligations—*continued*
    health and safety, as to—*continued*
      statement of general policy, duty to
        prepare, 35
      statutory duties, 34
    insurance against liabilities etc. *See*
      EMPLOYERS' LIABILITY INSURANCE
    suitable working environment,
      implied term to provide, 50
    trust and respect—
      breach of, examples, 48
      duty to maintain, 48
      implied duty of, 48
  employment tribunal's approach to
    determining existence of, 14
  form of, 14
  garden leave clause, 19
  illegality—
    burden of proof, 18n[6]
    effect, 18
    severance of illegal element, 18
  immoral, effect, 18
  implied termination of, 867
  importance, 1
  inference as to—
    conduct, from, 14
    rebuttal, 14
  injunction to enforce, not normally
    granted, 1437
  limited-term contract, 755n[5]
  limiting event in, 755n[5]
  mental disorder, employer suffering
    from, 15
  minor entering into, 15
  mutuality of obligation, 16n[4]
  non-solicitation of staff clause, 19n[4]
  remuneration under—
    accruing from day to day, 22
    additional, 24
    apportionable nature of, 22
    common law claim to recover, 25n[1]
    evidential value of contract, 22
    fees or commission only, 22
    fixed by agreement, where, 22
    illness, employee's temporary
      incapacity through, 27
    irregular payment, 22
    itemised pay statement, right to, 124
    lay-off, payment during, 28
    minimum rates of pay—
      introduction of, 26
      See further NATIONAL MINIMUM
        WAGE
    mode of payment, 25

CONTRACT OF
   EMPLOYMENT—*continued*
  remuneration under—*continued*
    'no work, no pay', reliance on, 29
    non-financial benefits after
      retirement, 25n[1]
    overpayment, 25
    partial performance by employee,
      where, 29
    payment of, 22
    performance of duty as condition
      precedent, 23
    private sick pay, 27
    recoverable debt, as, 23
    refusal to work, non-payment of
      wages for, 29
    short-time, payment during, 28
    statutory sick pay, right to, 27
    tips as part of, 144n[7]
    tips only, 22
    varying with amount of work done,
      144n[9]
    week's pay. *See* WEEK'S PAY
  selection of employees, statutory
    restrictions on discretion, 21
  servile incidents in, 20
  Sunday working clause, whether
    enforceable, 322
  terminology, use of, 1n[1]
  terms. *See* TERMS OF EMPLOYMENT
  third parties, contractual liability to—
    apparent scope of employee's
      authority, contract within—
      circumstances of employment,
        relevance, 58
      corporation, liability of, 61
      determination of authority, liability
        after notice, 60
      generally, 57
      nature of contract, 58
      nature of employee's business, 59
    excluded, where, 53
    express authority, employee making
      contract under, 53
    fiduciary authority, person in position
      of, 62
    implied authority to bind employer,
      54
    personal representative's liability, 62
    representation of authority to bind,
      conduct amounting to, 56
    severance, where contract capable of,
      53
    trustee's liability, 62
    unauthorised contract, subsequent
      ratification, 55

CONTRACT OF
   EMPLOYMENT—*continued*
  Unfair Contract Terms Act 1977,
    applicability of, 17
  unlawful or dangerous orders, 31
  unreasonable restrictions in, 20
  void provisions, 150
  who may enter into, 15
  work under, provision of—
    exceptions to general rule, 30
    general rule, 30
    unlawful or dangerous orders, 31
  written particulars. *See* WRITTEN
    PARTICULARS OF EMPLOYMENT
CONTRACT OF SERVICE
  use of term, 1n[1]
CORPORATION
  liability for contract made by
    employee, 61
COURT OF APPEAL
  Employment Appeal Tribunal, appeal
    from, 1530
COURT OF JUSTICE OF THE
   EUROPEAN UNION
  employment tribunal referring question
    to, 1471
CRIMINAL PROCEEDINGS
  employment rights, offences, 1532
CROWN EMPLOYMENT
  meaning. See under WORDS AND
    PHRASES *post*
  agency worker regulations, application
    of, 107
  employment protection legislation,
    application of, 163
  information and consultation provisions
    applying to, 1292
  national minimum wage, right to, 180
  part-time workers regulations,
    application of, 82
  redundancy procedure, exclusion, 1194
  statutory adoption pay, application of
    provisions, 500
  statutory maternity pay, application of
    provisions, 412
  statutory paternity pay, application of
    provisions, 454
  statutory shared parental pay,
    application of provisions, 541
  statutory sick pay, application of
    provisions, 569
  terminable without notice, 6
  trade unions and industrial relations,
    application of provisions, 893
  working time protection, 274
  wrongful dismissal, and, 6n[2]

EMPLOYER—*continued*
insolvency—
arrears of pay: meaning, 628n^{12}
debts referable to period of time, limit on, 628
employee's rights on, 628
employment tribunal, complaint to, 629
guaranteed debt, remedy of person applying for, 629
holiday pay: meaning, 628n^{16}
payment of dents on, 628
preferential debts, 627
priority of certain debts, 627
requirements for employer to be regarded as insolvent, 628n^5
Secretary of State—
information, power to obtain, 631
transfer of rights and remedies to, 630
statutory maternity payments, and, 403n^{11}
termination of employment on, 727
liabilities—
Equality Ac 2010, under, 51
third parties, to, on contracts made. *See* third parties, contractual liability to *below*
vicarious liability for employees' acts, 52
mental disorder, suffering from, 15
obligations—
duty of care—
equal treatment, 21
health and safety, as to. *See* health and safety, as to *below*
indemnification, implied duty of, 39
personal data, as to processing of, 21
remuneration, as to. *See* remuneration under *below*
work, provision of. *See* work under, provision of *below*
duty to insure. *See* EMPLOYERS' LIABILITY INSURANCE
employee's losses and liabilities, indemnification etc, 39
grievances, implied term to treat seriously, 49
health and safety, as to—
common law duty, extent of, 33
consultation with employees, 38
employee with mischievous tendencies, removal of, 33n^3
implied duty of care, 32

EMPLOYER—*continued*
obligations—*continued*
health and safety, as to—*continued*
level of duty, 32
plant and equipment, adequacy of, 33n^4
safety committee, 37
safety representatives, 36
statement of general policy, duty to prepare, 35
statutory duties, 34
insurance against liabilities etc. *See* EMPLOYERS' LIABILITY INSURANCE
suitable working environment, implied term to provide, 50
trust and respect—
breach of, examples, 48
duty to maintain, 48
implied duty of, 48
part-time workers regulations, liability under, 81
selection of employees, limits on exercise of discretion, 21
third parties, contractual liability to—
apparent scope of employee's authority, contract within—
circumstances of employment, relevance, 58
corporation, liability of, 61
determination of authority, liability after notice, 60
generally, 57
nature of contract, 58
nature of employee's business, 59
excluded, where, 53
express authority, employee making contract under, 53
fiduciary authority, person in position of, 62
implied authority to bind employer, 54
personal representative's liability, 62
representation of authority to bind, conduct amounting to, 56
severance, where contract capable of, 53
trustee's liability, 62
unauthorised contract, subsequent ratification, 55
tort, liability for employee's, 62

EMPLOYERS' ASSOCIATION
meaning, 1079
administrative provisions applying to, 1089
amalgamations, 1091

EMPLOYERS'
ASSOCIATION—*continued*
awards against, restriction on
    enforcement of, 1088
certification officer—
    list kept by, 1083
    power to make entry in list, 1084
    power to remove from list, 1085
discrimination by, prohibition on, 1082
federated: meaning, 1079
friendly societies, application of law
    relating to, 1087
legal status—
    corporate, 1080
    quasi-corporate, 1080
list—
    certification officer, kept by, 1083
    entry in, application for, 1084
    fee for entry, 1084n[7]
    generally, 1083
    removal from, 1085
name, change of, 1092
political objects, application of funds
    for, 1090
property—
    awards against, restriction on
        enforcement of, 1088
    vesting of, 1086
restraint of trade, exclusion of common
    law rules as to, 1081
transfer of engagements, 1091
trustees—
    death, effect, 1086
    instrument of appointment, 1086n[12]
    instrument of discharge, 1086n[13]
    property vesting in, 1086

EMPLOYERS' LIABILITY INSURANCE
approved policy: meaning, 40n[3]
certificate of insurance—
    duty to display, 46
    inspection, 47
    offence and penalty, 45
    offshore installation etc, employee on
        or from, 46
    power to issue, 45
    production, 47
    surrender, 45
employees covered by, 42
excluded employees, 42
exempted employers, 43
generally, 40
offence where not insured, 40
offshore installation, and, 41
prohibited conditions in, 44
regulations as to limits, 40

EMPLOYMENT
meaning, 2
civil courts' jurisdiction, 1436
continuity. *See* CONTINUITY OF
    EMPLOYMENT
discrimination, protection from—
    Equality Act 2010, under—
        equal pay audit. *See* EQUAL PAY
            AUDIT
        generally, 608
        prohibited conduct, 51
        protected characteristics, 51
        sheltered employment. *See* SHELTERED
            EMPLOYMENT
    sheltered employment. *See* SHELTERED
        EMPLOYMENT
'subject to satisfactory references',
    construction of meaning, 724
suspension. *See* SUSPENSION FROM WORK
terms of. *See* TERMS OF EMPLOYMENT
trial period: meaning, 865n[13]
tribunals. *See* EMPLOYMENT APPEAL
    TRIBUNAL; EMPLOYMENT TRIBUNAL

EMPLOYMENT AGENCY
meaning, 1038n[8]
conduct of, 11
employment by, 11
trade union membership, refusal of
    services on grounds of, 1038

EMPLOYMENT APPEAL TRIBUNAL
(EAT)
appeal from, 1530
appeal to—
    abandonment or withdrawal, 1503
    case management, 1501
    cross-appeal, notice of, 1499
    disposal of—
        consent, by, 1503
        notice of hearing, 1502
    documents. *See* document *below*
    employment tribunal hearing,
        complaint about conduct of,
        1497
    fee for making. *See* fees *below*
    institution of, 1495
    listing of appeals. *See* listing of
        appeals *below*
    national security proceedings—
        answer and cross-appeal, restriction
            as to contents, 1499
        notice, service of, 1498
    no merit in cross-appeal, where, 1499
    notice of—
        amendment or clarification—
            application to amend, 1501
            generally, 1495n[3]

EMPLOYMENT APPEAL TRIBUNAL
(EAT)—*continued*
restricted reporting order—*continued*
disability cases, in, 1433, 1518
sexual misconduct case, in, 1532,
1517
restriction of proceedings order, 1430
rules of procedure—
Civil Procedure Rules, and, 1435
failure to comply with, effect, 1435
generally, 1435
overriding objective, 1435
See also procedure rules *above*
seal, judicial notice of, 1426
sexual misconduct cases, restriction of
publicity, 1432, 1517
sittings, 1426
skeleton arguments, 1507
sums awarded, recovery, 1529
superior court of record, as, 1426
time limits—
appeal, for making, 1495
extension, application for, 1500
trade union matters—
certificate of trade union
independence, refusal to issue,
905
political fund provisions, from
certification officer's decision,
997
trade union list, removal from, 903
vexatious proceedings, restriction of,
1430
wasted costs order—
party's representative, against, 1526
wasted costs: meaning, $1526n^2$
witnesses, attendance of, 1514

EMPLOYMENT RIGHTS
annual leave. *See under* WORKING TIME
benefits, recoupment of, 161
compromise agreement, conditions
regulating, 151
contracting out, restrictions on—
employment tribunal proceedings—
ACAS intervention prior to. *See*
ADVISORY, CONCILIATION AND
ARBITRATION SERVICE
agreement to refrain from
instituting, 152
conciliation to promote settlement
after start of proceedings, 153
conciliation to promote settlement
prior to proceedings, 152
relevant proceedings: meaning,
$152n^1$

EMPLOYMENT RIGHTS—*continued*
contracting out, restrictions
on—*continued*
statutory restrictions—
generally, 150
settlement agreement, 151
criminal proceedings with regard to,
1532
Crown employment, application of
legislation to, 163
detriment, right not to suffer—
action short of dismissal, 612
disciplinary or grievance procedures,
720
employee representative, 1208
employee safety, representative of,
1210
employee shareholder, for refusal to
become, 624
employment tribunal, complaint to—
remedies available on, 626
right to make, 625
time for making, 625
European Company employee etc,
1334
European Works Council etc, member
of, 1278
flexible working cases, in, 622
generally, 612
health and safer cases, 614
information and consultation
representative, 1278, 1313, 1334
jury service, employee called for, 613
leave for family or domestic reasons,
employee taking, 620
occupational pension scheme trustee,
617
protected disclosure, as to making
of—
act or omission influenced by,
$619n^5$
generally, 619
safety committee, member of, 1076
safety representative, 1076
special negotiating body, member of,
1278, 1334
special protection from being
dismissed, 612
study or training, employee exercising
rights as to, 618, 623
Sunday working for shop and betting
workers, 615
tax credit rights, exercise of, 621
trade union membership, from—
generally, 1048

EMPLOYMENT RIGHTS—*continued*
detriment, right not to
suffer—*continued*
trade union membership,
from—*continued*
See also under TRADE UNION
RECOGNITION
working time cases, 616
employee shareholder. See EMPLOYEE
SHAREHOLDER
employment outside Great Britain, 166
employment protection legislation—
amendment powers, 158
Crown employment, application to,
163
employment outside Great Britain,
166
House of Commons staff, application
to, 165
House of Lords staff, application to,
164
mariners, disapplication of
provisions, 167
Northern Ireland, provision for, 157
offshore areas, extension to, 155, 156
orders, rules and regulations, 162
police officers, whether applicable
to, 168
power to extend, 155
excluded classes of employment—
mariners, 167
outside Great Britain, 166
police officers, 168
generally, 149
guarantee payments. See GUARANTEE
PAYMENT
House of Commons staff, of, 165
House of Lords staff, of, 164
independent adviser, 151n[15, 24]
individuals, power to confer rights on,
159
mariners, of, 167
monetary limits, review of, 160
Northern Ireland authority, reciprocal
arrangements with, 157
origin and nature of, 149
police officers, of, 168
settlement agreement, conditions
regulating, 151
shareholder. See employee shareholder
above
statutory payments for family leave—
development, 400
See also STATUTORY ADOPTION LEAVE;
STATUTORY MATERNITY LEAVE;
STATUTORY PATERNITY LEAVE

EMPLOYMENT RIGHTS—*continued*
Sunday working. See SUNDAY WORKING
time off work. See TIME OFF WORK
working time. See WORKING TIME

EMPLOYMENT TRIBUNAL
ACAS services, duty to encourage use
of, 1466
agency worker—
compensation, payment of, 105n[31]
complaint by, 105, 607
detriment, right not to suffer. See
under complaint to *below*
aggravated breach of worker's rights,
financial penalty, 1477
allowances for attendance at, 1405
assessor, remuneration etc paid to, 1405
award—
adjustment for failure to comply with
Code of Practice, 1234
allowances etc, no recoupment of,
1478
contributory fault, deduction for,
1478
death, enforcement in case of, 1485
interest on—
meaning, 1482n[4]
computation, 1482
order for, 1481
particulars to be included when
making, 1478
prescribed element, 1478
recovery, 1484
bankruptcy of either party before
proceedings completed, 1409
case management—
ACAS services, encouraging use of,
1466
compliance with rules, orders and
practice directions, tribunal's
response to, 1465
conciliation, provisions as to, 1468
Court of Justice of the European
Union, reference of question to,
1471
deposit, payment of, 1466
devolution issues, 1470
documents, delivery to and by
tribunal, 1467
more than one claim, where, 1466
order—
meaning, 1460n[4]
application for, 1466
power to make, 1466
response permitted to stand,
where, 1464
scope of, 1466

EMPLOYMENT TRIBUNAL—*continued*
  complaint to—*continued*
    insolvency of employer, on, 629
    national minimum wage—
      arrears, recovery of, 246
      burden of proof, 250
      detriment, right not to suffer, 249
      failure to allow access to records,
        228
    parental leave cases, in, 397
    part-time workers regulations, under.
      See part-time workers
      regulations, complaint under
      below
    pension scheme trustee, employee's
      right to time off for work as,
      353
    public duties, employee's right to time
      off for, 351
    redundancies—
      failure to consult etc, 1189
      protective award, as to failure to
        make payment under, 1190
    study or training, employee's right to
      time off for, 330
    suspension of work on medical or
      maternity grounds, 606
    time limits—
      extension—
        conciliation, to facilitate, 1455
        mediation in cross-border
          dispute, 1454
      failure to meet, matters for
        consideration, 1453
      further respondent, when adding,
        $1453n^2$
      generally, 1409, 1453
    time off work—
      European Company employee,
        1332
      European Works Council functions,
        as to, 1276
      information and consultation
        representative, 1311, 1332
      negotiating representative, 1311
      redundancy, to look for work etc
        after, 327
      representative body, member of,
        1332
      special negotiating body member,
        1332
    trade union matters—
      dismissal. *See* TRADE UNION
        MEMBERSHIP (dismissal for
        reasons of)
      exclusion or expulsion from, 1027

EMPLOYMENT TRIBUNAL—*continued*
  complaint to—*continued*
    trade union matters—*continued*
      generally, 1406
      inducements, 1051–1055
      member unjustifiably disciplined,
        1031
      political fund contributions,
        objection to, 990
      prohibited list, for use of—
        award against third party, 1041
        joining another party to
          proceedings, 1039
        right to make complaint, 1038
        victimisation, 1040
      recognition, detriment suffered due
        to, 1170
      refusal of employment or
        employment agency services,
        1042–1047
      training for workers in bargaining
        unit, failure to consult, 1173
      unauthorised subscriptions,
        deduction of, 1035
      victimisation, 1048–1050
    transfer of undertaking, in connection
      with, 140
    unfair dismissal, in case of. *See*
      UNFAIR DISMISSAL (employment
      tribunal, complaint to)
    withdrawal, binding nature of,
      following consent order, $150n^4$
    written statement of reasons, as to,
      756
  composition, 1402
  conciliation—
    ACAS involvement, 1468
    procedure, regulations as to, 1420
    provisions with regard to, 1468
    settlement after start of proceedings,
      to promote, 153
    settlement prior to proceedings, to
      promote, 152
  confidential information before, 1415
  costs order—
    meaning, 1480
    ability to pay, regard to, 1480
    allowances for attendance at tribunal,
      payment of, 1480
    application for, 1480
    costs: meaning, $1480n^1$
    interest on—
      meaning, $1482n^4$
      computation, 1482
      order for, 1481
    legally represented: meaning, $1480n^2$

References are to paragraph numbers; superior figures refer to notes

EUROPEAN COMPANY—*continued*
employee involvement—*continued*
agreement—*continued*
representative body—*continued*
time off work for member of,
1332
unfair dismissal of member,
1333
standard rules on employee
involvement—
meaning, 1325n[15]
whether applicable, 1325
writing, need for, 1325
Central Arbitration Committee,
application to—
confidential information
requirements, as to, 1330,
1331
jurisdiction as to proceedings under
regulations, 1335
special negotiating body, as to
establishment of, 1320
Central Arbitration Committee,
complaint to—
employee involvement agreement,
as to operation of, 1328
failure to provide information, as
to, 1319
jurisdiction as to proceedings under
regulations, 1335
special negotiating body—
ballot arrangements, as to, 1321
consultative committee, as to
appointment of members
by, 1323
decisions taken by, as to, 1326
standard rules, as to
non-compliance with, 1328
confidential information—
breach of duty with regard to,
1330
withholding of information, 1331
consultative committee—
meaning, 1323n[4]
appointment of members by, 1323,
1324
information and consultation
function, 1323n[4]
Council Directive, implementation,
1317
detriment, employee's right not to be
subjected to, 1334
employees' representatives: meaning,
1319n[5]
participating company—
meaning, 1317n[6]

EUROPEAN COMPANY—*continued*
employee involvement—*continued*
participating company—*continued*
concerned subsidiary or
establishment: meaning,
1317n[13]
Great Britain, registered office in,
1317
information—
duty to provide, 1319
withholding, 1331
proceedings, jurisdiction as to, 1335–
1337
regulations—
application, 1317
contracting out, restrictions on,
1318
misuse of procedures under, 1329
special negotiating body—
ballot for election of UK
members—
arrangements, 1321
complaint as to arrangements,
1321
conduct of, 1322
ineffective ballot report, 1322
specified requirements, 1321
supervisor, 1322
composition, 1320
consultative committee,
appointment of members by,
1323, 1324
decisions of, 1326
detriment, member's right not to be
subjected to, 1334
eligible member: meaning, 1320n[11]
employees, member as representee
of, 1324
expenses incurred by, payment of,
1326
experts, use of, 1326
function, 1320
merger, European Company
established by, 1320
ordinary members, 1320
reduction of participation rights:
meaning, 1326n[5]
time off work for member, 1332
unfair dismissal of member, 1333
voting by members—
absolute majority vote, 1326n[4]
generally, 1326
two thirds majority vote, 1326n[6]
whether properly established,
application to CAC, 1320

References are to paragraph numbers; superior figures refer to notes

EUROPEAN WORKS
  COUNCIL—*continued*
  EU-scale undertaking—
    meaning, 1237n[11]
    agreements between June 2009 and
      June 2011 . . . 1286
    article 3 agreement, 1284
    article 13 agreement, 1284
    calculating number of employees for
      purposes of, 1241
    information requirements. *See*
      information *below*
    significant change in structure,
      adaptation where, 1268, 1286
  exceptions to provisions—
    agreements between June 2009 and
      June 2011 . . . 1286
    article 3 agreements, 1284
    article 6 agreements, 1282
    article 7 European Works Council,
      1283
    article 13 agreement, 1284
    member of merchant navy, 1287
  information—
    failure to provide, remedy, 1243
    management's duty to provide, 1242
    right to, 1242
  information and consultation
    procedure—
    meaning, 1240n[3]
    agency workers, information as to,
      1268
    agreement on arrangements,
      reaching, 1252
    agreements between June 2009 and
      June 2011 . . . 1286
    central management—
      acting on own initiative, 1244
      special negotiating body, convening
        meeting with, 1251
      withholding information, remedy,
        1274
    confidential information—
      breach of duty not to disclose,
        1273
      withholding of information by
        central management, 1274
    consultation: meaning, 1240n[3]
    content and outcome, duty to infirm
      employees' etc, 1266
    contracting out, restrictions on, 1238
    disputes about operation of, 1270
    European Works Council, as
      alternative to, 1252
    EU-scale group of undertakings,
      where change to, 1268

EUROPEAN WORKS
  COUNCIL—*continued*
  information and consultation
    procedure—*continued*
    EU-scale undertaking, where change
      to, 1268
    failure to establish, 1269
    financial and material resources,
      provision of, 1261
    generally, 1251
    information and consultation
      representative—
      meaning, 1240n[3]
      member of merchant navy,
        exclusion of, 1287
      time off work, 1332
      unfair dismissal, 1277, 1333
    meetings—
      cost of organising etc, responsibility
        for, 1261
      exceptional, 1260
      frequency, 1259
      management, without presence of,
        1261
      matters covered by, 1259
      procedure, 1261
      right to have, 1259
    national employee representation
      body: meaning, 1252n[9]
    request to negotiate—
      making of, 1244
      relevant obligation applying,
        dispute as to whether, 1245
      requirements for valid request,
        1244
      validity of request, dispute as to,
        1245
    special negotiating body. *See* special
      negotiating body *below*
    subsidiary requirements—
      application of, 1253
      continuing application, 1262
    time off work, representative's right
      to, 1275, 1276
  members—
    central management's duty towards,
      1264
    detriment, right not to be subjected
      to, 1278
    time off work—
      employment tribunal, complaint
        to, 1276
      restrictions on, 1264n[6]
      right to, 1275
    training, right to, 1265
    UK. *See* UK members *below*

References are to paragraph numbers; superior figures refer to notes

EUROPEAN WORKS
  COUNCIL—*continued*
members—*continued*
  unfair dismissal, 1277
national employee representation
    body—
  meaning, 1252n[9]
  links with, 1267
number of employees, calculating, 1241
regulations on information and
    consultation, 1237
special negotiating body—
  meaning, 1244n[13]
  ballot—
    arrangements, 1248
    conduct, 1249
    costs of, 1249
    defective arrangements, right to
        present complaint, 1248
    independent ballot supervisor:
        meaning, 1248n[10]
    ineffective ballot report, 1249
    requirements, 1248
  composition, 1247
  consultative committee—
    meaning, 1250n[1]
    information and consultation
        function: meaning, 1250n[1]
    nomination of UK members, 1250
  co-operative spirit, duty of, 1252
  expenses incurred by, payment, 1251
  experts, assistance of, 1251
  functions, 1246
  majority vote, decision-taking by,
      1251
  membership where consultative
      committee exists, 1250
  merchant navy, exclusion of member
      of, 1287
  time off work, 1275, 1276
  training, right to, 1265
  UK members—
    ballot. *See* ballot *above*
    nomination, 1250
    unfair dismissal of member, 1277
  subsidiary requirements—
    application of, 1253
    continuing application, 1262
  training, member's right to, 1265
  Transnational Information and
      Consultation Directive—
    consultation: meaning, 1236n[3]
    contracting out of provisions,
        restrictions on, 1238
    implementation, 1237
    information: meaning, 1236n[2]

EUROPEAN WORKS
  COUNCIL—*continued*
  Transnational Information and
      Consultation Directive—*continued*
    merchant navy crews, exemption for,
        1236
    purpose, 1236
    regulations implementing, 1237
    requirements, 1236
  UK members—
    appointment or election, 1255
    ballot—
      arrangements, 1256
      conduct, 1257
      costs, 1257
      defective arrangements, remedy,
          1256
      ineffective ballot report, 1257
      requirements to be satisfied, 1256
      supervisor, 1257
    unfair dismissal, 1277
FILM
  ownership, where made by employee,
      72
FINE
  discharging by unpaid work, no
      national minimum wage for, 191
  enforcement, where levied by
      Employment Appeal Tribunal,
      1529
FIRE AND RESCUE AUTHORITY
  redundancy payments legislation,
      application of, 845
FIRE AUTHORITY
  redundancy payments legislation,
      application of, 845
FISHING VESSEL
  master or crew—
    redundancy procedure, exclusion,
        1194
    trade union rights, exclusion of
        master and crew from, 1071
FIXED-TERM EMPLOYEE
  meaning, 86n[2]
  comparable permanent employee, 86
  detriment, right not to be subjected to,
      90
  employee: meaning, 85n[3]
  employment tribunal, complaint to, 91
  fixed-term contract, 86n[2], 1194n[2]
  less favourable treatment under
      regulations—
    detriment, right not to be subjected
        to, 90
    Employment Rights Act 1996 rights,
        and, 87

References are to paragraph numbers; superior figures refer to notes

GRIEVANCE PROCEDURE—*continued*
  revised system—*continued*
    ACAS code of practice—*continued*
      helpline, 701
      issue, 701
      non-mandatory nature of, 701
    appropriate action, decision as to,
      713
    collective grievances, 716
    disciplinary process, grievance arising
      during, 715
    general principles, 702
    generally, 698
    hearing, right to be accompanied at.
      See hearing, right to be
      accompanied at *above*
    meeting—
      companion accompanying employee
        to, 712
      discussion of grievance, for, 711
      nature of grievance, informing
        employee of, 710
    overlap with disciplinary case, 715
    taking grievance further if not
      resolved, 714
    two or more employees raising
      grievances, 716

GUARANTEE PAYMENT
  meaning, 261
  arrears of remuneration, treatment as,
    $261n^{10}$
  calculation, 263
  complaint to employment tribunal, 265
  contractual remuneration, effect, 261
  day for purposes of: meaning, $261n^1$
  exemption order, power to make, 266
  industrial action, effect of, 1354
  limits on amount of, 264
  no normal working hours in the day,
    where, $261n^{10}$
  orders relating to, $266n^7$
  right to—
    exclusions from, 262
    generally, 261
    limits on, 264
  specified number of days, for, 264

HEALTH AND SAFETY AT WORK
  detriment, employee's right not to
    suffer, 613
  improvement notice—
    meaning, $1489n^1$
    appeal against, 1489
  prohibition notice—
    meaning, $1489n^2$
    appeal against, 1489

HEALTH AND SAFETY AT
  WORK—*continued*
  safety committee. *See* SAFETY
    COMMITTEE
  safety representative. *See* SAFETY
    REPRESENTATIVE
  unfair dismissal for reasons related to,
    784
  welfare at work: meaning, $1073n^{10}$
  workplace: meaning, $1073n^9$
HEALTH AND SAFETY EXECUTIVE
  working time regulations, responsibility
    for enforcing, 311
HIGH COURT
  employment tribunal, appeal from—
    generally, 1531
    point of law, on, 1436
  industrial training levy exemption
    referees, appeal from, 1531
  trade union matters—
    accounting records, member refused
      access to, 942
    disqualified persons, declaration as to
      non-compliance with provisions,
      958
    election, declaration on failure to
      comply with requirements, 973
    political ballot rules, declaration as to
      non-compliance with rules, 984
    register of members, application to
      enforce statutory requirements,
      939
HOME WORKER
  meaning, 179
  national minimum wage, right to, 179
  sub-postmaster not qualifying as, $179n^2$
HOMELESS WORKER
  excluded from national minimum wage,
    where, 197
HOUSE OF COMMONS STAFF
  agency worker regulations, application
    of, 107
  employment protection legislation,
    application of, 165
  national minimum wage, right to, 182
  part-time workers regulations,
    application of, 82
  redundancy procedure, exclusion, 1194
  trade unions and industrial relations,
    application of provisions, 895
  working time protection, 277
HOUSE OF LORDS STAFF
  agency worker regulations, application
    of, 107
  employment protection legislation,
    application of, 165

References are to paragraph numbers; superior figures refer to notes

MARINER—*continued*
  statutory maternity pay, treatment for, 410
  statutory paternity pay, treatment for, 452
  statutory sick pay, treatment for, 566
  working time provisions, exclusion, 297

MATERNITY LEAVE
  additional—
    meaning, 356n[2]
    commencement, 358
    contractual rights in relation to, 359
    duration, 358
    regulations as to, power to make, 355
    right to, 356
    right to return after, 362
    terms and conditions of employment during, application of, 360
  compulsory—
    meaning, 363
    regulations as to, power to make, 355
  detriment, employee's right not to suffer, 620
  development of statutory rights, 354
  Directive, 354
  expected week of childbirth: meaning, 356n[4]
  notices to be given by employee, 365
  ordinary—
    meaning, 356n[2]
    commencement, 357
    contractual rights in relation to, 359
    duration, 357
    regulations as to, power to make, 355
    right to, 356
    right to return after, 361
    terms and conditions of employment during, application of, 360
  redundancy during, 364
  regulations, power to make, 355
  unfair dismissal in connection with, 784
  week's pay, calculation, 367
  work during leave period, 366

MATERNITY PAY
  statutory. *See* STATUTORY MATERNITY PAY

MEDIATION
  meaning, 319n[25]
  working time dispute—
    end of, 319n[29]
    mediator: meaning, 319n[26]
    start of, 319n[26]

MENTAL DISORDER
  employer suffering from, 15

MERCHANT NAVY
  member of. *See* MERCHANT SEAMAN

MERCHANT SEAMAN
  employment as: meaning, 167n[12]
  industrial action by, offences, 1393
  long haul crew member—
    meaning, 1293n[1]
    European Works Council, excluded from being member of, 1287
    information and consultation representative, excluded from being, 1287, 1293
    special negotiating body, excluded from being member of, 1287, 129

MINOR
  apprenticeship agreement, power to dissolve, 749
  arbitration clause binding on, 15
  contract of employment, entry into, 15
  employee of, implied authority, 15

MOBILE WORKER
  meaning, 305n[1]
  working time provisions, exclusion, 305

MUSEUM
  redundancy payments legislation, application of, 848

NATIONAL CRIME AGENCY
  industrial action, inducing officer to take part in, 1392

NATIONAL HEALTH SERVICE
  employee—
    statutory maternity pay, application of provisions, 413
    statutory paternity pay, application of provisions, 455
  redundancy payments. *See* REDUNDANCY PAYMENT (National Health Service employment)

NATIONAL MINIMUM WAGE
  additional remuneration, worker's right to—
    burden of proof in proceedings, 250
    generally, 242
  agency workers, 178
  apprentice, 199
  burden of proof in proceedings, 250
  Crown employees, 180
  detriment, worker's right not to suffer—
    complaint to tribunal, right to present, 249
    generally, 169, 249
  employee: meaning, 170
  employer: meaning, 170

References are to paragraph numbers; superior figures refer to notes

NATIONAL MINIMUM
WAGE—*continued*
records—*continued*
offence in connection with, 251
remuneration counting towards—
deductions to be subtracted from total
of remuneration, 222
living accommodation, provision of—
adjusted deductions and payments
for, 225
amount to be taken into account
where, 224
payments made by or due from
worker, subtraction, 223
payments taken into account—
list of, 220
reductions from, 221
revenue officials, supply of information
obtained by, 241
right to, 169, 176
salaried hours work—
meaning, 204
absence from work, effect, 204
contract to do, 204
determining hours of—
basic hours: meaning, 214n[5],
215n[3]
basic hours exceeded, where, 215
calculation year: meaning, 215n[1]
employment terminating, where,
216
method, 214
excluded time, 209
extension of scope of, 209
performance bonus, 204n[4]
travelling incidental to duties, 209n[11]
time work—
meaning, 203
determining hours of, 213
excluded time, 208
extension of scope of, 208
time spent on training treated as, 212
travelling as part of, 208n[7]
travelling incidental to duties, 208n[8]
underpayment—
additional remuneration, right to,
242
arrears—
payment of, 243
recovery of, 246
notice of. *See* notice of underpayment
above
unfair dismissal for attempting to secure
right to etc, 169, 794
unmeasured work—
meaning, 206

NATIONAL MINIMUM
WAGE—*continued*
unmeasured work—*continued*
ascertained hours: meaning, 218n[10]
determining hours of, 218
extension of scope of, 211
work: meaning, 172
worker: meaning, 171
workers not qualifying for—
armed forces, member of, 192
Cadet Forces, member of, 192
EU programmes, participation in, 198
generally, 186
government training scheme,
participation in, 194
homeless workers provide with shelter
and other benefits, 197
persons discharging fines by unpaid
work, 191
prisoners, 190
religious and other communities,
resident workers in, 189
share fishermen, 187
temporary work scheme, participation
in, 194
traineeship in England, participation
in, 195
voluntary workers, 188
work experience—
course in, attendance at, 196
participation in, 194
work-based learning programme,
participation in, 193
workers qualifying for—
agency workers, 178
Crown employees, 180
generally, 177
home workers, 179
House of Commons staff, 182
House of Lords staff, 181
individuals who are not otherwise
workers, 185
mariners, 183
offshore employment, in, 184
working time, determining—
output work, extension of scope of,
210
salaried hours work, extension of
scope of, 209
time work—
extension of scope of, 208
time spent on training treated as,
212
unmeasured work, extension of scope
of, 211
written statement, right to, 207

NATIONAL MINIMUM
    WAGE—*continued*
young persons, 199
NATIONAL SECURITY
disclosure of information, restrictions
    on, 1446
proceedings—
    meaning, 1447n[1]
    Employment Appeal Tribunal, before.
        See under EMPLOYMENT APPEAL
        TRIBUNAL
    employment tribunal, before. *See*
        under EMPLOYMENT TRIBUNAL
NORTHERN IRELAND
employment rights, 157
trade union reciprocal arrangements,
    1078
OCCUPATIONAL PENSION SCHEME
contracted-out certificate, issue of—
    consultation prior to, 1205
    notice of intention prior to, 1205
detriment, trustee's right not to suffer,
    617
listed changes to, 1302
transfer of undertaking, effect, 141n[21]
trust and respect, implied term of,
    48n[24]
trustee—
    detriment, right not to suffer, 617
    information, duty to disclose, 1206
    time off work—
        employment tribunal, complaint
            to, 353
        right to, 352
        unfair dismissal, 790
    unfair dismissal, 790
OFFICE-HOLDER
categorisation as, 7
company director as, 8
determining, matters relevant to, 7n[1]
wrongful deprivation of, 7
OFFSHORE AREA
employment protection legislation,
    extension of, 155, 156
Frigg Gas Field, 156n[4]
OFFSHORE EMPLOYMENT
meaning, 155n[5], 184
employment protection legislation,
    extension of, 155, 156
national minimum wage, right to, 184
working time provisions, exclusion of,
    308
OFFSHORE INSTALLATION
meaning, 40n[8], 156n[8]
associated structure, 40n[8], 41n[4]

OFFSHORE INSTALLATION—*continued*
employers' liability insurance—
    certificate of insurance, production
        of, 46
    duty to insure, 41
Frigg Gas Field, 156n[4]
PARENTAL LEAVE
basic rights, 354
default provisions—
    generally, 392
    workforce agreements used to
        replace, 393
detriment, employee's right not to
    suffer, 620
development of statutory rights, 354
Directive, 354
employment tribunal, complaint to, 397
entitlement to, 391
evidence of entitlement, 392n[9]
maximum period, 392
minimum period of, 390n[5]
notification requirements, 392
postponement, 392
regulations as to, power to make, 390
responsibility for child: meaning, 391n[5]
restrictions on taking, 392
return after, right to, 395
shared. *See* SHARED PARENTAL LEAVE
terms and conditions of employment,
    application during leave, 394
unfair dismissal in connection with, 784
week's pay, calculation of, 396
PARTNER
change of, as wrongful dismissal, 726
death of, whether dissolving
    partnership, 726
employee or agent as, 13
former, as employee, 13
salaried, 13
PARTNERSHIP
dissolution, termination of employment
    on, 726
PART-TIME WORK
Framework Agreement—
    comparable full-time worker:
        meaning, 73n[4]
    generally, 73
    implementation, 73n[1]
    purpose, 73
regulations—
    power to make, 74
    types of worker to be considered
        under, 75
workers. *See* PART-TIME WORKER
PART-TIME WORKER
meaning, 75

PICKETING—_continued_
  potential liability for—_continued_
    tort, 1384
  public, whether causing distress,
      hardship etc to, 1386
  statutory immunity, 1385
  unlawful picketing, 1369
POLICE AND CRIME COMMISSIONER
  redundancy payments legislation,
      application of, 845
POLICE CADET
  employment, nature of, 82, 93, 107,
      278
  working time protection, 278
POLICE CONSTABLE
  employment, nature of, 82, 93, 107,
      278
  working time protection, 278
POLICE FORCE
  redundancy payments legislation,
      application of, 845
POLICE FORCE, MEMBER
  industrial action, restriction on, 1392
POLICE OFFICER
  dependants, no right to time off work to
      make arrangements for, 347n[3]
  employment protection legislation,
      application of, 168
POSTAL WORKER
  industrial action by, offences, 1394
PRISON OFFICER
  industrial action by, restriction on, 1392
PRISONER
  meaning, 190n[1]
  national minimum wage, not qualifying
      for, 190
PROFIT SHARING SCHEME
  employee participating in, effect on
      status, 11
PROHIBITION NOTICE
  Energy Act notice, appeal against, 1489
  health and safety notice, appeal
      against, 1489
  working time regulations, under. _See_
      under WORKING TIME
PUBLIC TRANSPORT
  redundancy payments legislation,
      application of, 840
RECEIVER
  termination of employment on
      appointment of, 727
REDUNDANCY
  meaning, 870
  adoption leave, during, 386
  'bumping', by, 870n[3]

REDUNDANCY—_continued_
  changes in work, question of fact for
      tribunal, 870n[9]
  consultation with employees'
      representatives—
    adaptation of statutory procedure,
        1195
    appropriate representatives, where no
        union involved, 1187
    complete closure, 1185n[8]
    duty to consult, 835, 1185
    employee representative: meaning,
        1187n[12]
    employment tribunal, complaint to—
      declaration, 1189
      failure to comply with
          requirements, on, 1189
      grounds for making, 1189
      protective award. _See_ protective
          award _below_
      time limit for making, 1189
    failure to consult. _See_ employment
        tribunal, complaint to _above_
    information to be given—
      manner of giving, 1185n[16]
      nature of, 1185
    nature of consultation, 1185n[8]
    pre-transfer consultation, 1186
    sovereign nature, decision of,
        1185n[10]
    special circumstances defence, 1188
    time limit for starting, 1185
    transfer of employees from another
        undertaking, 1186
    variation of statutory procedure,
        1195
  dismissal by reason of, whether fair. _See_
      UNFAIR DISMISSAL (redundancy, on
      grounds of)
  employee representative—
    consultation with. _See_ consultation
        with employee representatives
        above
    detriment, right not to suffer, 1208
    employment protection generally,
        1207
    time off work, 1209
  maternity leave, during, 364
  notification to Secretary of State—
    adaptation of statutory procedure,
        1195
    employer's duty, 1192
    failure to notify, offence and penalty,
        1193
    non-compliance, special
        circumstances, 1192

REDUNDANCY PAYMENT—*continued*
　legislation—*continued*
　　generally, 835
　　Isle of Man, 835n[1]
　local government employment—
　　provisions applying to, 839
　　relevant service, employment possibly
　　　constituting, 850
　　specified employers—
　　　careers guidance, providers of, 843
　　　educational establishments, 842
　　　local government, 840
　　　miscellaneous bodies, 849
　　　museums, 848
　　　planning and development, 841
　　　police, fire and civil defence, 845
　　　public transport, 844
　　　social services, 847
　　　sports councils, 846
　loss of right to—
　　employee's conduct, due to, 872
　　industrial action, employee taking,
　　　873
　　misconduct, for, 873
　　renewal or re-engagement, offer of,
　　　874
　National Health Service employment—
　　legislation, applicable, 851
　　relevant service, employment possibly
　　　constituting, 853
　　specified employers, 852
　notices, method of giving, 837
　pension rights, exclusion or reduction
　　on account of—
　　annual value of the pension:
　　　meaning, 860n[5]
　　claim for, 858
　　employee's right to apply to tribunal,
　　　858
　　extent of, 860
　　pension: meaning, 859
　　pensioned employee: meaning, 858n[2]
　questions about, determining. *See*
　　employment tribunal determining
　　questions *above*
　redundancy: meaning, 870
　relevant date: meaning, 871
　right to, 836
　scheme—
　　purpose, 835n[2]
　　set off of amounts received, 883
　Secretary of State, payment by—
　　calculation of amount, 884
　　employer's payment: meaning, 884n[3]
　　employment tribunal, reference to,
　　　887

REDUNDANCY PAYMENT—*continued*
　Secretary of State, payment
　　by—*continued*
　　information, right to demand, 885
　short time—
　　meaning, 875
　　death of employee or employer,
　　　effect, 876n[8]
　　determination of questions by
　　　tribunal, 886
　　employee's noticed terminating
　　　contract, effect, 877
　　exclusion of right to payment, 878
　　notice of intention to claim—
　　　counter-notice by employer, 879
　　　employee's right to give, 876
　statutory compensation—
　　meaning, 883n[7]
　　reduction where payment received,
　　　883
　written particulars, employer's duty to
　　provide, 882

REHABILITATION OF OFFENDERS
　spent conviction, concealing from
　　employer, 779

RELIGIOUS COMMUNITY
　residential member of, not qualifying for
　　national minimum wage, 189

REMUNERATION
　contract of employment, under. *See*
　　under CONTRACT OF EMPLOYMENT
　national minimum wage. *See* NATIONAL
　　MINIMUM WAGE

RESERVE FORCES
　part-time workers regulations,
　　application of, 82
　working time protection, 275

RESTRAINT OF TRADE
　covenant in restraint of trade,
　　enforceability, 19
　employer's association, validity of rules
　　as to, 1081
　trade union, exclusion of common law
　　rules, 898

SAFETY COMMITTEE
　detriment, right of member not to
　　suffer, 1076
　establishment, 37, 1075
　functions, 37, 1075
　generally, 1075
　unfair dismissal of member, 1077

SAFETY REPRESENTATIVE
　appointment, 36, 1073
　consultation with—
　　employer's duty, 36, 1201

References are to paragraph numbers; superior figures refer to notes

SAFETY REPRESENTATIVE—*continued*
consultation with—*continued*
no trade union recognised, where—
duty to consult, 1203
employment rights, 1210
detriment, right not to suffer, 1076
facilities and assistance, employer's duty
to provide, 1073
functions, 1073
generally, 36
information, employer's duty to
disclose—
generally, 1202
no trade union recognised, where,
1204
time off with pay, right to, 1074
unfair dismissal, 1077
workplace in relation to, $1073n^9$

SALARY
itemised pay statement, right to, 124

SECRETARY OF STATE
meaning, $5n^{21}$
amalgamation of trade unions, power to
make regulations, 1000
annual leave for workers, power to
prescribe amount of, 270
careers service. *See under* CAREERS
SERVICE
Codes of Practice, power to issue and
revise, 1231
employment training—
disabled persons, duties in connection
with, $634n^7$
functions and powers, 634
information, disclosure of, 635
payments to facility providers etc,
$634n^{12, 13}$
fixed-term work regulations, power to
make, 85
flexible working regulations, power to
make, 108
industrial relations—
Codes of Practice, power to issue,
1231
court of inquiry, power to appoint,
1233
industrial training boards, powers as to.
See under INDUSTRIAL TRAINING
BOARD
information and consultation
regulations, power to make, 1288
national minimum wage regulations,
power to make, 200
part-time workers regulations, power to
make, 74

SHARE FISHERMAN
dependants, no right to time off work to
make arrangements for, $347n^3$
national minimum wage, not qualifying
for, 187

SHARE OPTION SCHEME
employee participating in, effect on
status, 11

SHARED PARENTAL LEAVE
on adoption—
maximum amount of leave, $399n^{26}$
regulations, power to make, 399
on birth—
maximum amount of leave, $398n^{26}$
regulations, power to make, 398

SHAREHOLDER
majority, whether employee in
employing company, 9

SHELLFISH
meaning, $12n^4$
gathering of, 12

SHELTERED EMPLOYMENT
company to provide, formation by
Secretary of State, $610n^8$
discretion in selecting persons for, 610
expenses, contribution towards
defraying, 610
generally, 610
provision of—
generally, 610
local authority, by, 611
Secretary of State's powers, 610

SHIFT WORKER
working time. *See under* WORKING TIME

SHIP
foreign-going: meaning, $452n^7$, $566n^{16}$
managing owner: meaning, $566n^5$
owner: meaning, $566n^5$
radio officer: meaning, $566n^7$

SHOP WORKER
meaning, $321n^1$
cash shortages, deduction or payment in
respect of, 257–258
protected: meaning, 321
shop: meaning, $321n^1$
shop work: meaning, $321n^1$
Sunday work—
detriment—
date of the act: meaning, $615n^7$
examples of no detriment suffered,
$615n^6$
opted-out worker, $615n^8$
right not to suffer, 615
enforceability of employment
contract, 322

References are to paragraph numbers; superior figures refer to notes

STATUTORY ADOPTION
PAY—*continued*
overseas, adoption from—*continued*
child not entering Great Britain on
expected date, 531
placement, cases not involving, 530
regulations, application of—
Commissioners for Revenue and
Customs, regarding payments
made by, 532
general regulations, 531
generally, 530
mariners, as to, 533
modification of entitlement
conditions, 530
persons abroad, as to, 533
payment of—
apportionment between employers,
513
earnings: meaning, 515
excluded types of payment, 513
normal weekly earnings, calculation
of, 514
penalty procedure and appeals in
connection with, 525
person unable to act, to, 519
rates, 513
remuneration, payments treated as,
518
time limit—
Commissioners for Revenue and
Customs, 517
employer, by, 516
penalties—
appeal against, 525
breach of regulations, for, 520
commencement of proceedings for,
525
failure to produce information or
documents, for, 523
mitigation, 525
payment date for, 525
procedure for imposing, 525
period of—
meaning, 511
commencement, 511
work during, 492, 512
records—
failure to keep or produce, 520
inspection and production—
copies, right to take, 522
generally, 522
prescribed place, at, 522n^3
receipt for removal of document,
522

STATUTORY ADOPTION
PAY—*continued*
records—*continued*
inspection and production—*continued*
regulations as to, power to make,
523
maintenance by employer, 521
penalty for breach of regulations,
520, 523
regulations, power to make, 520
recovery of amounts paid—
deduction from Class 1 contributions,
treatment of, 529
employer's liability, funding. *See*
employer's liability, funding
above
regulations—
excluding liability to make
payments, 491
general power to make, 490
production of information or
documents, as to, 523
records and information, as to, 520
special classes of person, modification
of provisions, 495
special classes of person, modification of
provisions, 495
statutory provisions, modification of,
495
void agreements, 488

STATUTORY MATERNITY PAY
meaning, 401
absence from work, notice of—
exemption, 420
requirements, 420
special cases, in, 421
writing, in, 420
conditions for entitlement to. *See*
entitlement to, conditions for *below*
confinement—
meaning, 415n^6
evidence of expected week of, 422
working after, liability to make
payments, 426
contract of service—
termination to avoid payments, 405
two or more contracts treated as one,
where, 406
contractual maternity pay—
meaning, 442n^1
refund of Class 1 contributions, 442
contractual remuneration, no effect on
right to, 433
development of statutory rights, 400
earnings: meaning, 430

References are to paragraph numbers; superior figures refer to notes

References are to paragraph numbers; superior figures refer to notes

References are to paragraph numbers; superior figures refer to notes

References are to paragraph numbers; superior figures refer to notes

References are to paragraph numbers; superior figures refer to notes

References are to paragraph numbers; superior figures refer to notes

TRADE UNION
  RECOGNITION—*continued*
  bargaining unit—
    agreement of parties, 1105
    appropriate bargaining unit—
      agreement as to what constitutes,
        1110
      Central Arbitration Committee,
        application to, 1133
      no longer appropriate, belief that—
        application to CAC, 1133
        bargaining arrangements ceasing
          to apply, 1136
        parties agreeing new unit or
          units, 1134
        parties not agreeing new unit or
          units, 1135
    ballot. *See* ballot *above*
    ceasing to exist, employer believing—
      application for questions to be
        decided—
        acceptance, 1138
        admissibility of application, 1138
        nature of questions, 1138
        notice of receipt, 1138
        procedure following acceptance,
          1139
      notice as to, 1137
      parties agreeing different unit or
        units, 1140
      validation period: meaning, $1137n^8$
    changes affecting—
      admissibility of applications as to,
        1146
      application of provisions, 1132
      appropriateness of bargaining unit.
        See appropriate bargaining unit
        above
      new unit. *See* new unit *below*
      unit ceasing to exist. *See* ceasing to
        exist, employer believing *above*
      withdrawal of applications as to,
        1147
    demand to be recognised as, 1097
    method of bargaining, negotiations as
      to, 1123
    new unit—
      construction of references to
        collective bargaining, $1132n^5$
      decision as to—
        procedure generally, 1141
        relevant bargaining arrangements:
          meaning, $1142n^5$
        secret ballot, notice of, 1144
        statutory outside unit, at least
          one worker within, 1142

TRADE UNION
  RECOGNITION—*continued*
  bargaining unit—*continued*
    new unit—*continued*
      decision as to—*continued*
        voluntary or statutory outside
          unit, no worker within,
          1144
        voluntary outside unit, at least
          one worker within, 1143
      guidance from Secretary of State,
        $1144n^{17}$
      method of bargaining in relation to,
        effect, 1148
      parties agreeing, 1134
      residual workers, provisions as to,
        1145
      secret ballot as to, 1144
    residual workers, provisions as to,
      1145
    specific performance for breach of
      arrangements, 1148
    statutory outside bargaining unit:
      meaning, $1142n^4$
    training for workers within—
      consultation provisions—
        complaint to tribunal, 1173
        employer's failure to consult,
          1173
        generally, 1172
        meeting. *See* meeting to discuss
          below
      meeting to discuss—
        arrangements for, 1172
        date for, $1172n^7$
        subsequent meeting, employer
          wishing to convene, $1172n^9$
    voluntary outside bargaining unit:
      meaning, $1143n^4$
  Central Arbitration Committee—
    application, consideration of. *See*
      under application for *above*
    appropriate bargaining unit,
      determining—
      application to CAC, 1133
      bargaining arrangements ceasing to
        apply, 1136
      parties agreeing new unit or units,
        1134
      parties not agreeing new unit or
        units, 1135
    ballot, notice as to holding of, 1117,
      1118
    CAC case manager: meaning, $1102n^5$

References are to paragraph numbers; superior figures refer to notes

References are to paragraph numbers; superior figures refer to notes

References are to paragraph numbers; superior figures refer to notes

References are to paragraph numbers; superior figures refer to notes

Words and Phrases

Words in parentheses indicate the context in which the word or phrase is used

References are to paragraph numbers; superior figures refer to notes

References are to paragraph numbers; superior figures refer to notes

England, $2n^{12}$
enters Great Britain (overseas adoption), $376n^{15}$, $485n^6$
entitlement limit (statutory sick pay), 579
entity, $137n^6$
equal pay audit, 609
equal value claim, $1491n^3$
essential supplies, services and operations, $1386n^{12}$
European Works Council, $1236n^6$
EU-scale group of undertakings, $1237n^{11}$
EU-scale undertaking, $1237n^{12}$
evidence of a personal nature, $1417n^3$
excluded conduct (trade union member), $1026n^{10}$
executive (trade union), $943n^9$
executive committee (trade union), $916n^5$
exemption certificate (industrial training board levy), 681
expected week (childbirth), $356n^4$, $370n^5$
external qualification, $331n^2$
fact, question of (Employment Appeal Tribunal), 1429
failure (transnational information and consultation), $1270n^7$, $1271n^3$
federated employers' association, 1079
federated trade union, 891
film (political object), $975n^7$
final instalment of wages, $257n^{11}$
financial participation scheme, $98n^6$
fixed-term contract, $86n^2$, $1194n^2$
fixed-term employee, $86n^2$
fixed-term worker, $84n^2$
flexible working application, $108n^1$
foreign sector of the continental shelf, $155n^5$, $156n^2$, $184n^4$, $970n^5$
foreign-going ship, $452n^7$, $566n^{16}$
Framework Agreement, $73n^1$
Frigg Gas Field, $156n^4$
full-time worker, 75
further education course, $196n^3$
government arrangements (work-based learning programme), $193n^4$
Great Britain, $2n^{12}$, $407n^7$
grievance hearing, $717n^4$
grievances, $702n^3$
guarantee payment, 261
health and safety improvement notice, $1489n^1$
health and safety prohibition notice, $1489n^2$
higher education course, $94n^4$, $196n^2$
hirer (agency worker), $97n^3$
holiday pay (insolvent employer), $628n^{16}$
home worker, 179, $718n^4$
home-trade ship, $410n^2$, $452n^2$

identifying matter, $1416n^4$, $1417n^4$, $1432n^2$, $1433n^2$
implied term (employment contract), $115n^3$
improvement notice (working time regulations), 314
in contemplation or furtherance of a trade dispute, 1362
income tax month, $482n^{12}$, $594n^5$
income tax quarter, $440n^8$, $482n^{13}$
independent ballot supervisor (special negotiating body), $1248n^{10}$
independent contractor, $1n^1$
independent person (trade union election), $962n^{14}$
independent trade union, $150n^9$, 904
inducement (industrial action), $1025n^3$
industrial action, $916n^4$, $1025n^5$
industrial training board, $658n^7$
industrial training order, $658n^6$
ineffective ballot report, 1249, 1257, 1322
information—
  (European Company), $1317n^{10}$
  (European Works Council), $1236n^2$
information and consultation function (consultative committee), $1323n^4$
information and consultation procedure (European Works Council), $1240n^3$
information and consultation representative (European Works Council), $1240n^3$
insolvent employer—
  (redundancy payment), $884n^6$
  (statutory adoption pay), $489n^{15}$
  (statutory maternity payment), $403n^{11}$
  (statutory paternity payment), $444n^{15}$
  (statutory sick pay), $559n^{15}$
inspector (certificate of insurance), $47n^1$
instrument of appointment—
  (employers' association trustee), $1086n^{12}$
  (trade union trustee), $921n^1$
instrument of discharge—
  (employers' association trustee), $1086n^{13}$
  (trade union trustee), $921n^2$
job (maternity and parental leave regulations), $361n^9$
lawful picketing, $1367n^5$
lay-off, 875
legally represented, $1480n^2$
levy order, 680
levy proposals (industrial training board), 678

References are to paragraph numbers; superior figures refer to notes

References are to paragraph numbers; superior figures refer to notes

shift worker, $302n^1$
shop, $321n^1$
shop work, $321n^1$
shop worker, $321n^1$
short time, 875
sickness, $27n^1$
signature (doctor's statement), $577n^{18}$
small employer (statutory maternity
    payment), $439n^7$, $440n^4$
special register body, 899
spell of incapacity, $577n^{15}$
stage 1 equal value hearing, 1492
stage 2 equal value hearing, 1492
standard rules on employee involvement
    (European Company), $1325n^{15}$
statutory adoption leave, $388n^3$
statutory adoption leave period, $388n^3$
statutory adoption pay, 488
statutory body (national minimum
    wage), $188n^6$
statutory maternity leave, $366n^3$
statutory maternity leave period, $366n^3$
statutory maternity pay, 401
statutory outside bargaining unit, $1142n^4$
statutory paternity pay, 443
statutory shared parental pay, 534
statutory sick pay, 558
stock deficiency, $257n^6$
strike, $134n^4$, $1025n^5$, 1340
structure (offshore installation), $156n^8$
subscription deduction arrangements,
    1034
subscription deductions, $1034n^4$
subsistence (national minimum wage),
    $188n^{13}$
substance (health and safety duties), $34n^7$
successor (employer), $133n^{10}$
suitable information relating to the use of
    agency workers, $1197n^9$, $1295n^5$,
    $1325n^{17}$
tag-along rights, $154n^7$
temporary agency worker, $96n^2$
temporary work agency, $96n^2$, 97
terms and conditions of employment—
    (adoption leave), $377n^{9, 25}$
    (maternity leave), $355n^{8, 26}$
    (parental leave), $390n^9$
    (paternity leave), $368n^{10}$
    (shared parental leave), $398n^{32}$, $399n^{32}$
territorial waters, $156n^2$
time of dismissal (industrial action),
    $1350n^2$
time work, 203
trade dispute, 1212, 1360
trade union, 891, $927n^1$
trial period, $865n^{13}$

UK employee, $1317n^8$
UK members of the special negotiating
    board, $1317n^{10}$
undertaking—
    (information and consultation of
        employees), $1289n^2$
    (redundancy), $781n^5$
    (transfer), $137n^3$
unfair practices (secret recognition
    ballot), 1119
unilateral theory (wrongful dismissal),
    $826n^4$
United Kingdom, $2n^{12}$
United Kingdom sector of the continental
    shelf, $155n^5$, $184n^3$, $970n^5$
unjustifiably disciplined (trade union
    member), 1030
unlawful act notice, $1490n^1$
unmeasured work, 206
user undertaking, $96n^2$
validation period—
    (collective bargaining unit), $1137n^8$
    (trade union derecognition), $1150n^{14}$
voluntary organisation (national minimum
    wage), $188n^4$
voluntary outside bargaining unit, $1143n^4$
voting member of the executive (trade
    union), $958n^9$, $960n^8$
wages, 254
Wales, $2n^{12}$
warned list, 1509
wasted costs—
    (Employment Appeal Tribunal), $1526n^2$
    (employment tribunal), 1480
week—
    (adoption pay period), $511n^3$
    (paternity leave), $368n^8$, $376n^{19}$
    (statutory adoption pay), $491n^{4, 17}$,
        $513n^3$
    (statutory maternity pay), $424n^3$
    (statutory paternity pay), $445n^{14}$,
        $457n^{26}$
week's pay, $144n^7$
weekly hours, $76n^6$
welfare at work, $1073n^{10}$
Welsh Ministers, $5n^{21}$
wholesale trade, $321n^1$
work—
    (health and safety duties), $34n^3$
    (national minimum wage), 171
worker—
    (Agency Workers Regulations 2010),
        $98n^7$
    (detriment from protected disclosure),
        $619n^1$
    (disciplinary or grievance hearing), 718

References are to paragraph numbers; superior figures refer to notes